Microeconomic Data

These microeconomic data series show some of the trends in what, how, and for whom goods and services are produced — the central quesťי֊֊ ⸳ ⸳ ⸳⸳⸳ ⸳⸳⸳⸳ ⸳⸳⸳ I find these data in a spreadsheet that you can download

		1960	1961	1962	1963	1964	1965	1966	1967	1968	1969	1970
WHAT WE PRODUCE												
Percentage of gross domestic product												
1	Agriculture, forestry, fishing, and hunting	3.2	3.2	3.0	2.8	2.5	2.6	2.5	2.3	2.1	2.2	2.1
2	Mining	1.3	1.3	1.2	1.2	1.1	1.1	1.0	1.0	1.0	0.9	1.0
3	Construction	4.3	4.3	4.3	4.4	4.5	4.5	4.5	4.5	4.5	4.6	4.6
4	Durable goods	14.6	13.9	14.5	14.7	14.7	15.3	15.4	14.8	14.8	14.4	12.7
5	Nondurable goods	11.1	10.9	10.6	10.5	10.4	10.3	10.3	10.0	10.0	9.7	9.4
6	Utilities	4.1	4.1	4.1	4.1	4.1	4.0	3.9	3.9	3.9	3.9	4.0
7	Wholesale trade	6.7	6.7	6.6	6.6	6.6	6.5	6.5	6.5	6.5	6.5	6.6
8	Retail trade	9.1	9.0	8.9	8.9	9.1	9.0	8.8	8.9	9.1	9.1	9.2
9	Transportation and warehousing	3.8	3.7	3.6	3.5	3.5	3.5	3.4	3.3	3.2	3.2	3.2
10	Finance, insurance, real estate, rental, and leasing	11.7	12.0	11.9	11.9	11.8	11.7	11.4	11.6	11.6	11.7	11.9
11	Professional and business services	—	—	—	—	—	—	—	—	—	—	—
12	Information	—	—	—	—	—	—	—	—	—	—	—
13	Educational services, health care, and social assistance	—	—	—	—	—	—	—	—	—	—	—
14	Arts, entertainment, recreation, accommodation, and food services	—	—	—	—	—	—	—	—	—	—	—
15	Other services, except government	—	—	—	—	—	—	—	—	—	—	—
HOW WE PRODUCE												
16	Average weekly hours	39.7	39.8	40.4	40.5	38.5	38.6	38.5	37.9	37.7	37.5	37
	Employment (percentage of total)											
17	Agriculture	10.2	10.0	9.5	8.8	8.2	7.5	6.7	6.1	5.8	5.4	5.3
18	Mining	1.3	1.2	1.2	1.1	1.1	1.1	1.0	1.0	0.9	0.9	0.9
19	Construction	4.9	4.8	4.9	4.9	4.9	5.0	4.9	4.7	4.7	4.9	4.9
20	Manufacturing	25.5	25.0	25.2	25.1	25.0	25.2	25.8	25.5	25.2	24.9	23.8
21	Services	58.1	59.0	59.3	60.0	60.8	61.2	61.6	62.7	63.3	63.9	65.1
FOR WHOM WE PRODUCE												
23	Wage rate (dollars per hour)	2.26	2.32	2.39	2.46	2.5	2.63	2.73	2.85	3.02	3.22	3.40
24	Real wage rate (2000 dollars per hour)	10.74	10.90	11.08	11.29	11.43	11.67	11.78	11.93	12.12	12.31	12.35
25	Stock price index (Dow Jones)	618	692	640	715	834	911	874	879	906	877	753
26	Real stock price index (2000 dollars)	2,937	3,250	2,966	3,279	3,769	4,042	3,769	3,679	3,637	3,353	2,735
27	Interest rate Aaa (percent per year)	4.4	4.4	4.3	4.3	4.4	4.5	5.1	5.5	6.2	7.0	8.0
28	Real interest rate (percent per year)	3.0	3.2	3.0	3.2	2.9	2.7	2.3	2.4	1.9	2.1	2.7
GOVERNMENT IN THE ECONOMY												
29	Government receipts (billions of dollars)	137	142	153	165	170	184	207	222	256	288	292
30	Government expenditures (billions of dollars)	138	150	161	169	178	189	215	243	268	286	313
31	Government surplus(+)/deficit(−) (billions of dollars)	−1	−8	−8	−4	−8	−5	−8	−21	−12	2	−21
32	Government debt (billions of dollars)	237	238	248	254	257	261	264	267	290	278	283

1995	1996	1997	1998	1999	2000	2001	2002	2003	2004	2005	2006	2007
1.3	1.5	1.3	1.2	1.0	1.0	1.0	0.9	1.0	1.2	1.0	1.0	1.2
1.0	1.1	1.1	0.9	0.9	1.2	1.2	1.0	1.3	1.5	1.8	2.0	2.0
3.9	4.0	4.1	4.3	4.4	4.4	4.6	4.6	4.5	4.6	4.9	4.8	4.1
9.2	9.0	9.1	9.2	8.9	8.8	7.7	7.4	7.0	6.9	6.8	6.7	6.7
6.8	6.4	6.3	6.1	6.0	5.7	5.6	5.5	5.4	5.3	5.2	5.1	5.0
2.5	2.3	2.2	2.1	2.0	1.9	2.0	2.0	2.0	2.1	2.0	2.1	2.1
6.2	6.3	6.3	6.2	6.2	6.0	6.0	5.9	5.8	5.9	5.8	5.8	5.8
7.0	7.0	6.9	6.8	6.9	6.7	6.8	6.9	6.9	6.6	6.5	6.4	6.4
3.1	3.0	3.1	3.1	3.1	3.1	2.9	2.9	2.9	2.9	2.9	2.9	2.9
18.7	18.8	19.2	19.3	19.4	19.7	20.3	20.5	20.5	20.4	20.5	20.9	20.7
10.0	10.4	10.8	11.2	11.5	11.6	11.5	11.4	11.4	11.5	11.7	11.8	12.2
4.2	4.3	4.2	4.4	4.7	4.7	4.7	4.6	4.5	4.5	4.6	4.5	4.7
7.2	7.1	6.9	6.9	6.8	6.9	7.3	7.6	7.8	7.8	7.7	7.7	7.9
3.4	3.4	3.5	3.5	3.5	3.6	3.6	3.6	3.6	3.7	3.6	3.6	3.7
2.4	2.4	2.4	2.4	2.3	2.3	2.4	2.4	2.4	2.3	2.3	2.3	2.3
34.3	34.3	34.5	34.5	34.3	34.3	34.0	33.9	33.7	33.7	33.8	33.9	33.8
2.2	2.0	2.0	1.8	1.7	1.6	1.6	1.6	1.5	1.5	1.5	1.4	1.4
0.5	0.5	0.5	0.5	0.5	0.4	0.5	0.4	0.4	0.4	0.5	0.5	0.5
4.4	4.5	4.6	4.8	5.0	5.1	5.1	5.1	5.1	5.2	5.4	5.6	5.5
14.4	14.1	13.9	13.7	13.2	12.9	12.3	11.5	11.0	10.7	10.5	10.3	10.0
78.5	78.8	79.0	79.2	79.6	80.0	80.6	81.4	81.9	82.1	82.2	82.3	82.6
11.43	12.03	12.49	13.00	13.47	14.00	14.53	14.95	15.35	15.67	16.11	16.59	17.26
12.41	12.82	13.09	13.48	13.76	14.00	14.19	14.35	14.43	14.32	14.25	14.25	14.39
4,494	5,743	7,441	8,626	10,465	10,735	10,189	9,226	8,994	10,317	10,548	11,409	13,170
4,879	6,119	7,799	8,941	10,693	10,735	9,950	8,856	8,452	9,426	9,331	9,778	10,992
7.6	7.4	7.3	6.5	7.0	7.6	7.1	6.5	5.7	5.6	5.2	5.6	5.6
5.5	5.5	5.6	5.4	5.6	5.4	4.7	4.7	3.5	2.8	2.0	2.4	2.9
2,233	2,399	2,579	2,757	2,932	3,162	3,149	2,992	3,064	3,285	3,651	3,997	4,209
2,465	2,570	2,645	2,719	2,853	3,003	3,188	3,388	3,593	3,793	4,055	4,292	4,609
−232	−171	−66	38	79	159	−39	−397	−530	−509	−405	−295	−399
3,604	3,734	3,772	3,721	3,632	3,410	3,320	3,540	3,913	4,296	4,592	4,892	5,035

Microeconomic Data

These microeconomic data series show some of the trends in what, how, and for whom goods and services are produced — the central questions of microeconomics. You will find these data in a spreadsheet that you can download from your MyEconLab Web site.

		1984	1985	1986	1987	1988	1989	1990	1991	1992	1993	1994
WHAT WE PRODUCE												
Percentage of gross domestic product												
1	Agriculture, forestry, fishing, and hunting	1.6	1.5	1.4	1.7	1.6	1.7	1.7	1.5	1.6	1.4	1.5
2	Mining	1.8	1.5	1.0	1.5	1.4	1.4	1.5	1.3	1.1	1.1	1.0
3	Construction	3.9	4.1	4.4	4.6	4.6	4.5	4.3	3.8	3.7	3.7	3.9
4	Durable goods	10.3	9.8	9.5	10.2	10.2	9.9	9.4	9.0	8.9	8.9	9.2
5	Nondurable goods	7.4	7.2	6.6	6.9	7.0	7.0	7.0	6.9	6.8	6.7	6.7
6	Utilities	4.3	4.2	4.1	2.6	2.4	2.5	2.5	2.5	2.5	2.5	2.5
7	Wholesale trade	6.3	6.2	6.1	6.0	6.2	6.2	6.0	6.0	6.0	6.0	6.3
8	Retail trade	8.6	8.7	8.7	7.4	7.2	7.1	6.9	6.8	6.8	6.9	7.0
9	Transportation and warehousing	2.8	2.7	2.7	3.2	3.2	3.0	2.9	3.0	2.9	3.0	3.1
10	Finance, insurance, real estate, rental, and leasing	13.4	13.6	14.0	17.7	17.8	17.8	18.0	18.4	18.6	18.6	18.4
11	Professional and business services	—	—	—	8.7	9.1	9.4	9.8	9.7	9.9	9.9	9.9
12	Information	—	—	—	3.9	3.8	3.8	3.9	3.9	4.0	4.1	4.2
13	Educational services, health care, and social assistance	—	—	—	6.0	6.1	6.3	6.7	7.1	7.3	7.3	7.2
14	Arts, entertainment, recreation, accommodation, and food services	—	—	—	3.2	3.3	3.3	3.4	3.4	3.4	3.4	3.3
15	Other services, except government	—	—	—	2.4	2.4	2.4	2.5	2.4	2.4	2.5	2.4
HOW WE PRODUCE												
16	Average weekly hours	35.1	34.9	34.7	34.7	34.6	34.5	34.3	34.1	34.2	34.3	34.5
	Employment (percentage of total)											
17	Agriculture	3.0	2.7	2.6	2.6	2.5	2.4	2.3	2.3	2.3	2.1	2.2
18	Mining	1.0	1.0	0.8	0.7	0.7	0.7	0.7	0.7	0.6	0.6	0.6
19	Construction	4.6	4.8	4.8	4.9	4.8	4.8	4.7	4.3	4.1	4.2	4.4
20	Manufacturing	18.4	17.8	17.2	16.8	16.6	16.3	15.8	15.4	15.1	14.8	14.6
21	Services	72.9	73.8	74.6	75.0	75.4	75.9	76.6	77.3	77.9	78.3	78.3
FOR WHOM WE PRODUCE												
23	Wage rate (dollars per hour)	8.48	8.73	8.92	9.13	9.43	9.80	10.01	10.32	10.57	10.83	11.12
24	Real wage rate (2000 dollars per hour)	12.53	12.52	12.52	12.47	12.46	12.48	12.27	12.22	12.24	12.25	12.32
25	Stock price index (Dow Jones)	1,178	1,328	1,793	2,276	2,061	2,509	2,679	2,929	3,284	3,522	3,794
26	Real stock price index (2000 dollars)	1,742	1,905	2,516	3,109	2,723	3,194	3,283	3,469	3,802	3,985	4,203
27	Interest rate Aaa (percent per year)	12.7	11.4	9.0	9.4	9.7	9.3	9.3	8.8	8.1	7.2	8.0
28	Real interest rate (percent per year)	9.0	8.3	6.8	6.6	6.3	5.5	5.5	5.3	5.8	4.9	5.8
GOVERNMENT IN THE ECONOMY												
29	Government receipts (billions of dollars)	1,121	1,222	1,299	1,414	1,513	1,639	1,724	1,774	1,860	1,963	2,109
30	Government expenditures (billions of dollars)	1,308	1,434	1,534	1,617	1,695	1,816	1,970	2,069	2,225	2,292	2,361
31	Government surplus(+)/deficit(−) (billions of dollars)	−187	−212	−234	−203	−182	−177	−246	−295	−366	−329	−252
32	Government debt (billions of dollars)	1,307	1,507	1,741	1,890	2,052	2,191	2,412	2,689	3,000	3,248	3,433

1971	1972	1973	1974	1975	1976	1977	1978	1979	1980	1981	1982	1983
2.1	2.3	3.2	2.8	2.7	2.3	2.0	2.1	2.2	1.8	2.0	1.8	1.3
1.0	1.0	1.0	1.4	1.5	1.4	1.6	1.5	1.7	2.4	2.9	2.5	1.9
4.7	4.7	4.8	4.7	4.3	4.4	4.4	4.6	4.7	4.4	3.9	3.7	3.7
12.4	12.7	13.0	12.3	11.5	12.1	12.5	12.7	12.3	11.3	11.0	10.0	9.8
9.1	8.9	8.7	8.8	8.8	8.9	8.8	8.6	8.6	8.5	8.5	8.2	7.8
4.0	4.0	3.9	3.8	4.1	4.1	4.1	4.1	3.8	4.0	4.1	4.5	4.4
6.5	6.6	6.6	6.9	6.9	6.6	6.5	6.6	6.6	6.5	6.4	6.3	6.1
9.2	9.1	9.0	8.7	8.9	9.0	9.0	8.9	8.6	8.3	8.2	8.3	8.5
3.2	3.3	3.3	3.3	3.0	3.2	3.2	3.2	3.2	3.1	2.9	2.7	2.7
12.1	12.0	11.7	11.8	12.0	11.7	11.8	11.9	11.8	12.3	12.5	13.1	13.4
—	—	—	—	—	—	—	—	—	—	—	—	—
—	—	—	—	—	—	—	—	—	—	—	—	—
—	—	—	—	—	—	—	—	—	—	—	—	—
—	—	—	—	—	—	—	—	—	—	—	—	—
—	—	—	—	—	—	—	—	—	—	—	—	—
36.8	36.9	36.9	36.4	36.0	36.1	35.9	35.8	35.6	35.2	35.2	34.7	34.9
5.1	5.0	4.9	4.8	4.7	4.5	4.2	4.1	3.8	3.7	3.5	3.5	3.3
0.9	0.9	0.9	0.9	1.0	1.0	1.0	1.0	1.1	1.1	1.2	1.3	1.1
5.0	5.1	5.2	5.0	4.5	4.4	4.6	4.8	4.9	4.7	4.5	4.3	4.4
22.8	22.7	23.0	22.5	20.9	21.1	21.1	20.9	20.8	19.9	19.7	18.7	18.3
66.1	66.3	66.1	66.9	68.9	69.0	69.1	69.2	69.5	70.5	71.0	72.2	73.0
3.63	3.90	4.14	4.43	4.73	5.06	5.44	5.87	6.33	6.84	7.43	7.86	8.19
12.56	12.93	13.00	12.76	12.45	12.59	12.72	12.83	12.78	12.66	12.57	12.53	12.56
885	951	924	759	802	975	895	820	844	891	933	884	1,190
3,060	3,152	2,901	2,187	2,112	2,425	2,093	1,793	1,704	1,649	1,578	1,410	1,825
7.4	7.2	7.4	8.6	8.8	8.4	8.0	8.7	9.6	11.9	14.2	13.8	12.0
2.4	2.9	1.9	−0.5	−0.6	2.7	1.7	1.7	1.3	2.9	4.8	7.7	8.1
309	354	397	438	448	513	576	653	736	807	927	949	1,008
340	370	400	453	533	573	620	682	760	879	996	1,106	1,206
−31	−16	−3	−15	−85	−61	−44	−29	−24	−73	−70	−158	−198
303	322	341	344	395	477	549	607	640	712	789	925	1,137

Reading Between the Lines

At the end of each chapter, *Reading Between the Lines* uses economic tools to critically evaluate a news article about the chapter-opening issue.

News-based End-of-chapter Problems

New end-of-chapter problems based on current news stories are also available for practice in MyEconLab.

17. "Inexpensive broadband access has done far more for online video than enable the success of services like YouTube and iTunes. By unchaining video watchers from their TV sets, it has opened the floodgates to a generation of TV producers for whom the Internet is their native medium."
The New York Times, December 2, 2007

a. How has inexpensive broadband changed the production possibilities of video entertainment and other goods and services?
b. Sketch a *PPF* for video entertainment and other goods and services before broadband.
c. Show how the arrival of inexpensive broadband has changed the *PPF*.
d. Sketch a marginal benefit curve for video entertainment.
e. Show how opening the "floodgates to a generation of TV producers for whom the Internet is their native medium" might have changed the marginal benefit from video entertainment.
f. Explain how the quantity of video entertainment that achieves allocative efficiency has changed.

Economics in the News

To keep you informed about the latest economic news, Parkin uploads two relevant articles daily, one each covering microeconomic and macroeconomic topics. He also includes discussion questions, links to additional online resources, and references to related textbook chapters in the textbook.

1) Why did you take Economics 51/52? (Check all that apply.)

☐ I have a personal interest in the subject.
☐ I am considering a major in economics.
☐ The course is required for my major. My major is _____.
☐ I am using this to fulfill a social science requirement needed to graduate.

2) Did you purchase a book for this course? Yes No

☐ I bought a new book.
☐ I bought a used book.
☐ I bought access to the e-book online.
☐ N/A. I did not buy a book for this course.

3) Where did you buy your textbook? Give the name of the store, e-commerce site, etc.

4) If your text was available in a format that was full-color, 3-hole punch, and loose leaf – and was priced lower than the regular bound book – would you be likely to buy that instead? [Note that if you choose the loose-leaf version, you'd be saving up front but you may not be able to sell it back after the course.]

☐ I would be more likely to buy the lower-priced, loose-leaf, 3-hole punched version.
☐ I would be more likely to buy the bound book.

5) The following questions ask you about how you use the textbook for this course.

a) Did you read the book before or after your professor covered the topic in class? (Circle one)
Before   After

b) How often did you refer the textbook during the course? (Check <u>only one</u>.)

☐ I referred to the book 3-5 times per week throughout the semester.
☐ I referred to the book only once each week.
☐ I waited to open the book until I was studying for the first big exam.
☐ N/A – I never referred to the book during the semester.

c) When you opened the book, how did you use the chapter material? (Check <u>only one</u>.)

☐ I read the chapter, from start to finish.
☐ I did not read the full chapter. I only read sections of the chapter that I did not fully understand from the lecture.
☐ N/A. I did not refer to the book during the semester.

d) Consider how you answered parts (5a) through (5c). Was this textbook effectively designed for the way that you use the book during this course? Why or why not?

6) Complete the following table by indicating how helpful you found each of these chapter resources. (Check one box in each row.)

	Extremely helpful when trying to master the material.	Somewhat helpful when trying to master the material.	I read this feature, but it didn't really help me master the material.	N/A I did not read or refer to this feature.
Figures and tables, along with their captions				
News and policy boxed examples				
End of chapter summary and key terms				
Reading Between the Lines				
Interviews with famous economists				
Study Guide				
Other: _____				

7) How would you describe the writing style for this text?

8) How useful did you find the graphs in the book? Were they clear and easy to follow? Are there ways in which they could be improved?

9) Did the text help you to understand the concepts you needed to know for this course? Explain your answer, highlighting specific aspects of the book that you found particularly helpful or that could be improved in future editions.

10) MyEconLab is an online tutorial and homework system that comes automatically with a new copy of the textbook. **Please answer questions (a) through (e) <u>regardless</u> of whether you used MyEconLab for this course.**

   a) Did you log into the MyEconLab site during the semester? Why or why not?

   b) If you did not log in, how did you work practice problems to prepare for your exams? (Which problems did you work? How did you practice?)

   c) Regardless of whether you used MyEconLab: For each chapter, MyEconLab has a practice test and at the end of the test, the program generates a personalized Study Plan that tells you which specific topics you've mastered, and which sections of the book you need to review.

   ☐ I used MyEconLab's Study Plan feature when studying for this course.
   ☐ I did not use MyEconLab's Study Plan feature because I did not know this was available.
   ☐ I knew about MyEconLab's Study Plan feature, but I chose not to use it.
   ☐ I did not log into MyEconLab, but I think this sounds like a useful feature.
   ☐ I did not log into MyEconLab, and I do not think this sounds like a useful feature.

   d) For every chapter in the book, MyEconLab offers two practice tests and then additional Study Plan practice problems. The practice problems give you automated feedback and includes Draw-Graph questions.

   ☐ I used MyEconLab for additional practice when studying for this course.
   ☐ I did not use MyEconLab for additional practice because I did not know it was available.
   ☐ I knew about MyEconLab's additional practice, but I chose not to use it.

   e) Regardless of whether you used MyEconLab: Do you think it would be helpful to study for this course using additional practice and draw-graph problems? Why or why not?

   f) <u>If you used MyEconLab</u> when studying for this course, would you recommend the program to a friend who is taking this course next semester? Why or why not?

11) Do you have any other comments or suggestions for the text and/or MyEconLab?

Thank you for filling out this questionnaire. Your feedback helps us to develop the books and software for future editions.

MICROECONOMICS

Third Custom Edition for Temple University

Michael Parkin

Taken from:

Microeconomics, Ninth Edition
by Michael Parkin

Custom Publishing

New York Boston San Francisco
London Toronto Sydney Tokyo Singapore Madrid
Mexico City Munich Paris Cape Town Hong Kong Montreal

Cover Art: Courtesy of PhotoDisc, EyeWire/Getty Images, brandXpictures

Taken from:

Microeconomics, Ninth Edition
by Michael Parkin
Copyright © 2010 by Pearson Education, Inc.
Addison Wesley
Boston, Massachusetts 02116

This special edition published in cooperation with Pearson Custom Publishing.

Printed in the United States of America

10 9 8 7 6 5 4 3

2009400076

RG

Pearson
Custom Publishing
is a division of

PEARSON

www.pearsonhighered.com

ISBN 10: 0-558-34713-4
ISBN 13: 978-0-558-34713-0

TO

ROBIN

ABOUT
THE AUTHOR

Michael Parkin received his training as an economist at the Universities of Leicester and Essex in England. Currently in the Department of Economics at the University of Western Ontario, Canada, Professor Parkin has held faculty appointments at Brown University, the University of Manchester, the University of Essex, and Bond University. He is a past president of the Canadian Economics Association and has served on the editorial boards of the *American Economic Review* and the *Journal of Monetary Economics* and as managing editor of the *Canadian Journal of Economics*. Professor Parkin's research on macroeconomics, monetary economics, and international economics has resulted in over 160 publications in journals and edited volumes, including the *American Economic Review*, the *Journal of Political Economy*, the *Review of Economic Studies*, the *Journal of Monetary Economics*, and the *Journal of Money, Credit and Banking*. He became most visible to the public with his work on inflation that discredited the use of wage and price controls. Michael Parkin also spearheaded the movement toward European monetary union. Professor Parkin is an experienced and dedicated teacher of introductory economics.

BRIEF
CONTENTS

PREFACE

Historic is a big word. Yet it accurately describes the economic events and policy responses that followed the sub-prime mortgage crisis of August 2007. Economics moved from the business report to the front page as fear gripped producers, consumers, financial institutions, and governments. The unimaginable repeat of a Great Depression gradually became imaginable as house prices plunged, credit markets froze, financial institutions failed, governments (both in the United States and around the world) mounted massive bailouts and rescues, the Fed made loans and bought debts of a quality that central banks don't normally touch, and the prices of items from gasoline and food to stocks and currencies fluctuated wildly.

Even the *idea* that the market is an efficient mechanism for allocating scarce resources came into question as some political leaders trumpeted the end of capitalism and the dawn of a new economic order in which tighter regulation reigned in unfettered greed.

Rarely do teachers of economics have such a rich feast on which to draw. And rarely are the principles of economics more surely needed to provide the solid foundation on which to think about economic events and navigate the turbulence of economic life.

Although thinking like an economist can bring a clearer perspective to and deeper understanding of today's events, students don't find the economic way of thinking easy or natural. *Microeconomics* seeks to put clarity and understanding in the grasp of the student through its careful and vivid exploration of the tension between self interest and the social interest, the role and power of incentives—of opportunity cost and marginal benefit—and demonstrating the possibility that markets supplemented by other mechanisms, might allocate resources efficiently.

Parkin students begin to think about issues the way real economists do and learn how to explore difficult policy problems and make more informed decisions in their own economic lives.

The Ninth Edition Revision

The ninth edition of *Microeconomics* retains all of the improvements achieved from its predecessors, with its thorough and detailed presentation of the principles of economics, its emphasis on real-world examples and applications, its development of critical thinking skills, its diagrams renowned for pedagogy and precision, and its path-breaking technology.

This comprehensive revision also incorporates and responds to the suggestions for improvements made by reviewers and users, in both the broad architecture of the text and chapter-by-chapter.

Current issues organize each chapter. News stories about today's major economic events tie each chapter together, from new chapter-opening vignettes to end-of-chapter problems and online practice. Students learn to use economic tools to analyze their own daily decisions and recent real-world events and issues.

Each chapter includes a discussion of a critical issue of our time, to demonstrate how economic theory can be applied to explore a particular debate or question. Issues of central importance include:

- Gains and tensions from globalization, the rise of Asia, and the changing structure of the global economy in Chapters 2 and 7
- High and rising cost of food in Chapters 2 and 3
- Fluctuations in gas and oil prices and the effects of high gas prices on auto sales in Chapters 3, 4, and 18
- Changing patterns of consumption in the information age in Chapter 8
- Climate change in Chapter 16
- Efficient use of natural resources and today's tragedies of the commons in Chapter 17
- Real-world examples and applications appear in the body of each chapter and in the end-of-chapter problems and applications. Each chapter has approximately 10 new additional problems tied to current news and events. All of these problems have parallel questions in MyEconLab.

Questions that appear daily in MyEconLab in the *Economics in the News* are also available in MyEconLab for assignment as homework, quizzes, or tests.

Highlights of the Micro Revision

In addition to being thoroughly updated and revised to include the topics and features just described, the microeconomics chapters feature the following seven major changes:

1. ***Global Markets in Action*** (Chapter 7): This new chapter explains the sources and effects of international trade, its winners and losers, and the effects of trade protection (tariffs and import quotas) on economic welfare. The chapter applies the tools of demand and supply, consumer and producer surplus, and deadweight loss explained in two earlier chapters. Offshore outsourcing and the ongoing failure of the Doha negotiations feature in this chapter.

2. ***Utility and Demand*** (Chapter 8): Extensively revised and reorganized, this chapter provides a more intuitive and less graphical analysis of utility maximization. Changes in consumer choices in the market for recorded music, in which digital downloads have almost driven out CDs, illustrate the predictions of marginal utility theory. The chapter includes an explanation of behavioral economics and neuroeconomics. (Material on the budget line found in the previous edition is omitted from this chapter but can be found in the first part of Chapter 9, an alternative chapter on indifference curves.)

3. ***Monopoly*** (Chapter 13): The final section of this chapter now covers the regulation of natural monopoly, which was previously found in a separate chapter. This change enables monopoly regulation to be covered when the material on unregulated monopoly and its inefficiency is fresh in the student's mind.

4. ***Monopolistic Competition*** (Chapter 14): In the ninth edition, this market type has its own full-chapter treatment. High selling costs are illustrated with the breakdown of the price of a pair of running shoes between manufacturing and selling. An example focused on cell phones illustrates product differentiation.

5. ***Oligopoly*** (Chapter 15): This market type also has its own chapter and is expanded to include a section on antitrust law. As with the change in the monopoly chapter, this change enables antitrust law to be studied when the coverage of cartels and the temptation to fix prices is still in the student's mind.

6. ***Externalities*** (Chapter 16): This ninth edition chapter focuses on climate change and the economic debate it engenders, as we feature these topics at several points as the major example of a negative externality and the alternative ways of dealing with it.

7. ***Uncertainty and Information*** (Chapter 20): This chapter contains a heavily revised explanation of the "lemon" problem and trading risk in credit and insurance markets. The dramatic changes in the price of risk during the subprime crisis illustrate the working of the market for risky loans.

◗ Features to Enhance Teaching and Learning

Chapter Openers

Each chapter opens with a student-friendly vignette that raises questions to motivate the student and focus the chapter. This chapter-opening story is woven into the main body of the chapter and is explored in the *Reading Between the Lines* feature that ends each chapter.

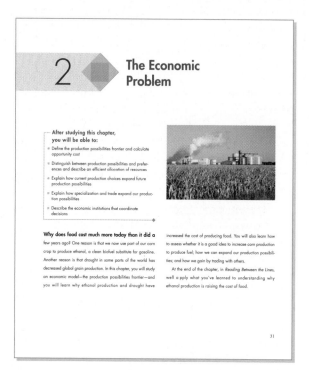

Chapter Objectives

A list of learning objectives enables students to see exactly where the chapter is going and to set their goals before they begin the chapter.

Key Terms

Highlighted terms simplify the student's task of learning the vocabulary of economics. Each highlighted term appears in an end-of-chapter list with page numbers, in an end-of-book glossary with page numbers, boldfaced in the index, in the Web glossary, and in the Web Flash Cards.

Diagrams That Show the Action

Through the past eight editions, this book has set new standards of clarity in its diagrams; the ninth edition continues to uphold this tradition. My goal has always been to show "where the economic action is." The diagrams in this book continue to generate an enormously positive response, which confirms my view that graphical analysis is the most powerful tool available for teaching and learning economics.

Because many students find graphs hard to work with, I have developed the entire art program with the study and review needs of the student in mind.

The diagrams feature:

- Original curves consistently shown in blue
- Shifted curves, equilibrium points, and other important features highlighted in red
- Color-blended arrows to suggest movement
- Graphs paired with data tables
- Diagrams labeled with boxed notes
- Extended captions that make each diagram and its caption a self-contained object for study and review.

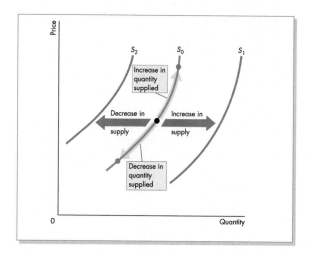

In-Text Review Quizzes

A review quiz at the end of most major sections enables students to determine whether a topic needs further study before moving on. This feature includes a reference to the appropriate MyEconLab study plan to help students further test their understanding.

Reading Between the Lines

In *Reading Between the Lines*, which appears at the end of each chapter, students apply the tools they have just learned by analyzing an article from a newspaper or news Web site. Each article sheds additional light on the questions first raised in the Chapter Opener.

Questions about the article also appear with the end-of-chapter problems and applications.

End-of-Chapter Study Material

Each chapter closes with a concise summary organized by major topics, lists of key terms, figures and tables (all with page references), problems and applications. These learning tools provide students with a summary for review and exam preparation.

News-Based End-of-Chapter Questions

Each chapter's problems and applications section now includes an additional set of news-based real-world problems that are new to the ninth edition. All of the problems and applications are also available for self-assessment or assignment as a homework, quiz, or test in MyEconLab.

Interviews with Economists

Each major part of the text closes with a summary feature that includes an interview with a leading economist whose research and expertise correlates to what the student has just learned. These interviews explore the background, education, and research these prominent economics have conducted, as well as advice for those who want to continue the study of economics. We would like to welcome Susan Athey, of Harvard University, to the ninth edition.

21. After you have studied *Reading Between the Lines* on pp. 46–47, answer the following questions:
    a. How has an Act of the United States Congress increased U.S. production of corn?
    b. Why would you expect an increase in the quantity of corn produced to raise the opportunity cost of corn?
    c. Why did the cost of producing corn increase in the rest of the world?
    d. Is it possible that the increased quantity of corn produced, despite the higher cost of production, moves the United States closer to allocative efficiency?

◆ For the Instructor

This book enables you to achieve three objectives in your principles course:

- Focus on the economic way of thinking
- Explain the issues and problems of our time
- Choose your own course structure

Focus on the Economic Way of Thinking

As an instructor, you know how hard it is to encourage a student to think like an economist. But that is your goal. Consistent with this goal, the text focuses on and repeatedly uses the central ideas: choice; tradeoff; opportunity cost; the margin; incentives; the gains from voluntary exchange; the forces of demand, supply, and equilibrium; the pursuit of economic rent; the tension between self-interest and the social interest; and the scope and limitations of government actions.

Explain the Issues of Our Global Economy

Students must *use* the central ideas and tools if they are to begin to *understand* them. There is no better way to motivate students than by using the tools of economics to explain the issues that confront today's world. Issues such as globalization and the emergence of China and India as major economic forces; the mortgage crisis, the recent bankruptcy, absorption or federally funded bailout of American banks, stock market fluctuations, the new economy with new near-monopolies such as eBay and Google; the widening income gap between rich and poor; the reallocation of resources toward counterterrorism; the disappearing tropical rain forests and the challenge that this tragedy of the commons creates; the challenge of managing the world's water resources; the looming debt that arises from our newly emerged federal budget deficit; our vast and rising international deficit and debt; and the tumbling value of the dollar on the foreign exchange market.

Flexible Structure

You have preferences for how you want to teach your course. I have organized this book to enable you to do so. The flexibility chart and alternative sequences table that appear on pages xxvii–xxviii demonstrate this book's flexibility. Whether you want to teach a traditional course that blends theory and policy or focuses on current policy issues, *Microeconomics* gives you the choice.

Supplemental Resources

Instructor's Manuals We have streamlined and reorganized the Instructor's Manual to reflect the focus and intuition of the ninth edition. The Instructor's Manual, written by Kelly Blanchard of Purdue University, integrates the teaching and learning package and serves as a guide to all the supplements.

Each chapter contains:

- A chapter overview.
- A list of what's new in the ninth edition.
- *Lecture Notes* Ready-to-use lecture notes from each chapter enable a new user of Parkin to walk into a classroom armed to deliver a polished lecture. The lecture notes provide an outline of the chapter; concise statements of key materials; alternate tables and figures, key concepts, and definitions; and boxes that suggest how to handle a difficult idea. Additional discussion questions and potential answers follow the lecture notes in each chapter. The chapter outline and teaching suggestions sections are keyed to the PowerPoint® lecture notes.
- *Worksheets* Another innovative feature, found online in the Instructor's Resource Center, is a set of Worksheets prepared by Patricia Kuzyk of Washington State University. These Worksheets ask students to contemplate real-world problems that illustrate economic principles. An example includes showing the effect of the catastrophic events of 9/11 using a marginal cost/marginal benefit diagram. Instructors can assign these as in-class group projects or as homework. There is a Worksheet for every chapter of the book.

Solutions Manual For ease of use and instructor reference, a comprehensive solutions manual provides instructors with solutions to the Review Quizzes and the end-of-chapter problems. The Solutions Manual is available in hard copy and electronically on the Instructor's Resource Center CD-ROM, in the instructor's resources section of MyEconLab, and on the Instructor's Resource Center.

Test Banks Three separate Test Banks provide multiple-choice, true-false, numerical, fill-in-the-blank, short-answer, and essay questions.

Mark Rush of the University of Florida reviewed and edited all existing questions to ensure their clarity and consistency with the ninth edition and incorporated new questions into the thousands of existing Test Bank questions. Written by Constantin Ogloblin of Georgia Southern University and Nora Underwood of the University of Central Florida, these problems follow the style and format of the end-of-chapter text problems and provide the instructor with a whole new set of testing opportunities and/or homework assignments. Additionally, end-of-part tests contain questions that cover all the chapters in the part and feature integrative questions that span more than one chapter.

New News-Based Problems The ninth edition includes a set of problems in each chapter that are based directly on current events, newspaper stories or magazine articles. Written by Karen Gebhardt of Colorado State University, these questions link the real world to concepts students have learned in class. With these news-based questions, instructors will be able to showcase how economics exists in the world outside the classroom.

The Test Banks are available in hard copy and electronically on the Instructor's Resource Center CD-ROM, in the instructor's resources section of MyEconLab, and on the Instructor's Resource Center.

PowerPoint® Resources Robin Bade and I have developed a full-color Microsoft® PowerPoint Lecture Presentation for each chapter that includes all the figures and tables from the text, animated graphs, and speaking notes. The lecture notes in the Instructor's Manual and the slide outlines are correlated, and the speaking notes are based on the Instructor's Manual teaching suggestions. A separate set of PowerPoint files containing large-scale versions of all the text's figures (most of them animated) and tables (some of which are animated) are also available. The presentations can be used electronically in the classroom or can be printed to create hard copy transparency masters. This item is available for Macintosh® and Windows®.

Clicker-Ready PowerPoint Resources This edition features the addition of clicker-ready PowerPoint slides for the Personal Response System you use. Each chapter of the text includes ten multiple-choice questions that test important concepts. Instructors can assign these as in-class assignments or review quizzes.

Instructor's Resource Center CD-ROM Fully compatible with Windows® and Macintosh®, this CD-ROM contains electronic files of every instructor supplement for the ninth edition. Files included are: Microsoft® Word and Adobe® PDF files of the Instructor's Manual, Test Bank and Solutions Manual; complete PowerPoint slides; and the Computerized TestGen® Test Bank. Add this useful resource to your exam copy bookbag, or locate your local Pearson Education sales representative at **www.pearsonhighered.educator** to request a copy.

Computerized Testbank Component Fully networkable, it is available for Windows and Macintosh. TestGen's graphical interface enables instructors to view, edit, and add questions; transfer questions to tests; and print different forms of tests. Tests can be formatted with varying fonts and styles, margins, and headers and footers, as in any word-processing document. Search and sort features let the instructor quickly locate questions and arrange them in a preferred order. QuizMaster, working with your school's computer network, automatically grades the exams, stores the results on disk, and allows the instructor to view or print a variety of reports.

Instructors can download supplements from a secure, instructor-only source via the Pearson Higher Education Instructor Resource Center Web page (www.pearsonhighered.com/irc).

Study Guide The ninth edition Study Guide by Mark Rush is carefully coordinated with the text, MyEconLab, and the Test Banks. Each chapter of the Study Guide contains:

- Key concepts
- Helpful hints
- True/false/uncertain questions
- Multiple-choice questions
- Short-answer questions
- Common questions or misconceptions that the student explains as if he or she were the teacher
- Each part allows students to test their cumulative understanding with questions that go across chapters and work a sample midterm examination.

MyEconLab MyEconLab creates a perfect pedagogical loop that provides not only text-specific assessment and practice problems, but also tutorial support to make sure students learn from their mistakes.

At the core of MyEconLab are the following features:

Auto-Graded Tests and Assignments MyEconLab comes with two preloaded Sample tests for each chapter so students can self-assess their understanding of the material. Instructors can assign these Sample Tests or create assignments using end-of-chapter problems and applications, Test Bank questions, or their own custom exercises.

Study Plan A Study Plan is generated from each student's results on Sample Tests and instructor assignments. Students can clearly see which topics they have mastered—and, more importantly, which they need to work on. The Study Plan consists of material from the in-text Review Quizzes and end-of-chapter Problems and Applications. The Study Plan links to additional practice problems and tutorial help on those topics.

Unlimited Practice Many Study Plan and instructor-assigned exercises contain algorithmically generated values to ensure that students get as much practice as they need. Every problem links students to learning resources that further reinforce concepts they need to master.

Learning Resources Each practice problem contains a link to the eText page that discusses the concept being applied. Students also have access to guided solutions, animated graphs, audio narrative, flashcards, and live tutoring.

Economics in the News Daily news updates during the school year are available in MyEconLab. Most days the author posts two links to relevant news articles from the day's headlines. One link directs students to a microeconomics article, and the other directs students to a macroeconomics article. Each article is accompanied by additional links, discussion questions, and a reference to relevant chapters in the textbook. An archive of *Economics in the News* articles and questions is also available.

New to the ninth edition are instructor-assignable *Economics in the News* questions in MyEconLab. These news analysis questions are updated routinely to ensure the latest news and news analysis problems are available for assignment.

Economics Videos and Assignable Questions Featuring abcNEWS

Economics videos featuring ABC news enliven your course with short news clips featuring real-world issues. These 10 videos, available in MyEconLab, feature news footage and commentary by economists. Questions and problems for each video clip are available for assignment in MyEconLab.

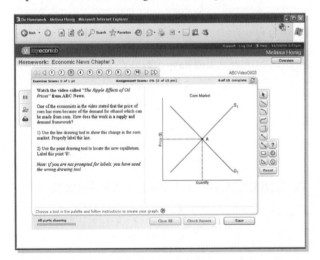

Pearson Tutoring Services powered by SMARTHINKING

A subscription to MyEconLab includes complimentary access to Pearson Tutor Services, powered by SMARTHINKING Inc. Highly qualified tutors use whiteboard technology and feedback tools to help students understand and master the major concepts of economics. Students can receive real-time, one-on-one instruction, submit questions for a response within 24 hours, and view archives of past sessions.

Special Editions

Economist.com Edition The premier online source of economic news analysis, Economist.com provides your students with insight and opinion on current economic events. Through an agreement between Addison-Wesley and *The Economist*, your students can receive a low-cost subscription to this premium Web site for 12 weeks, including the complete text of the current issue of *The Economist* and access to *The Economist's* searchable archives. Other features include Web-only weekly articles, news feeds with current world and business news, and stock market and currency data. Professors who adopt this special edition will receive a complimentary one-year subscription to Economist.com.

The Wall Street Journal Edition Addison-Wesley is also pleased to provide your students with access to *The Wall Street Journal*, the most respected and trusted daily source for information on business and economics. For a small additional charge, Addison-Wesley offers your students a subscription to *The Wall Street Journal* and WSJ.com. A 15-week subscription is available. Adopting professors will receive a complimentary one-year subscription to *The Wall Street Journal* as well as access to WSJ.com.

Financial Times Edition Featuring international news and analysis from FT journalists in more than 50 countries, the *Financial Times* will provide your students with insights and perspectives on economic developments around the world. The Financial Times Edition provides your students with a 15-week subscription to one of the world's leading business publications. Adopting professors will receive a complimentary one-year subscription to the *Financial Times* as well as access to FT.com.

Pearson Choices

With ever-increasing demand on time and resources, today's college faculty and students want greater value, innovation, and flexibility in products designed to meet teaching and learning goals. We've responded to that need by creating Pearson Choices, a unique program that allows faculty and students to choose from a range of text and media formats that match their teaching and learning styles and students' budgets.

Books à la Carte Plus Edition For the student who wants a more flexible portable text, there is a three-hole punched version of *Economics*. Students who use this version can take only what they need to class, incorporate their own notes, and save money. This version is packaged with a laminated study card and comes with access to MyEconLab.

CourseSmart CourseSmart's mission is to improve teaching and learning through the availability of a lower-cost alternative to the traditional textbook, in a reliable Web application. For additional information, log onto www.coursesmart.com

Standalone Access to MyEconLab and the Complete eText Students may purchase access to MyEconLab, which includes online access to the complete, searchable eText, online at www.myeconlab.com or through the campus bookstore.

MyEconLab Students may purchase access to MyEconLab's assessment and learning resources. Partial access to the eText is included, which links practice problems to relevant sections of the text. Go to www.myeconlab.com for more information.

Print Upgrade to the à la Carte Edition from within MyEconLab Students may purchase an upgrade to the à la carte edition of *Economics* at any point following their online purchase of MyEconLab.

Pearson Custom Business Resources The Pearson Custom Database offers instructors the option of building their own book by selecting just the chapters they want and ordering them to fit their syllabus. Professors can also select chapters of the accompanying Study Guide as well as readings from Miller/Benjamin/North's *The Economics of Public Issues* and Miller/Benjamin's *The Economics of Macro Issues*. For additional information contact your Pearson representative.

◆ Acknowledgments

I thank my current and former colleagues and friends at the University of Western Ontario who have taught me so much. They are Jim Davies, Jeremy Greenwood, Ig Horstmann, Peter Howitt, Greg Huffman, David Laidler, Phil Reny, Chris Robinson, John Whalley, and Ron Wonnacott. I also thank Doug McTaggart and Christopher Findlay, co-authors of the Australian edition, and Melanie Powell and Kent Matthews, co-authors of the European edition. Suggestions arising from their adaptations of earlier editions have been helpful to me in preparing this edition.

I thank the several thousand students whom I have been privileged to teach. The instant response that comes from the look of puzzlement or enlightenment has taught me how to teach economics.

It is a special joy to thank the many outstanding editors, media specialists, and others at Addison-Wesley who contributed to the concerted publishing effort that brought this edition to completion. Denise Clinton, Publisher, has played a major role in the evolution of this text since its third edition, and her insights and ideas can still be found in this new edition. Donna Battista, Editor-in-Chief for Economics and Finance, is hugely inspiring and has provided overall direction to the project. As ever, Adrienne D'Ambrosio, Senior Acquisitions Editor for Economics and my sponsoring editor, played a major role in shaping this revision and the many outstanding supplements that accompany it. Adrienne brings intelligence and insight to her work and is the unchallengeable pre-eminent economics editor. Deepa Chungi, Development Editor, brought a fresh eye to the development process, obtained outstanding reviews from equally outstanding reviewers, digested and summarized the reviews, and made many solid suggestions as she diligently worked through the drafts of this edition. Nancy Fenton, Managing Editor, managed the entire production and design effort with her usual skill, played a major role in envisioning and implementing the cover design, and coped fearlessly with a tight production schedule. Susan Schoenberg, Director of Media, directed the development of MyEconLab; Doug Ruby, Content Lead for MyEconLab, managed a complex and thorough reviewing process for the content of MyEconLab; and Melissa Honig, Senior Media Producer, ensured that all our media assets were correctly assembled. Roxanne McCarley, Executive Marketing Manager, provided inspired marketing strategy and direction. Catherine Baum provided a careful, consistent, and intelligent copy edit and accuracy check. Joyce Wells designed the cover and package and yet again surpassed the challenge of ensuring that we meet the highest design standards. Joe Vetere provided endless technical help with the text and art files. And Heather Johnson with the other members of an outstanding editorial and production team at Elm Street including Debbie Kubiak kept the project on track on an impossibly tight schedule. I thank all of these wonderful people. It has been inspiring to work with them and to share in creating what I believe is a truly outstanding educational tool.

I thank Luke Armstrong of Lee College for providing the news-based applications that appear at the end of each chapter. Luke has been using this type of material with his students and has now shared his talent with a wider audience.

I thank our talented ninth edition supplements authors—Kelly Blanchard, Pat Kuzyk, Nora Underwood, Constantin Ogloblin, and Karen Gebhardt.

I especially thank Mark Rush, who yet again played a crucial role in creating another edition of this text and package. Mark has been a constant source of good advice and good humor.

I thank the many exceptional reviewers who have shared their insights through the various editions of this book. Their contribution has been invaluable.

I thank the people who work directly with me. Jeannie Gillmore provided outstanding research assistance on many topics, including the *Reading Between the Lines* news articles. Richard Parkin created the electronic art files and offered many ideas that improved the figures in this book. And Laurel Davies managed an ever-growing and ever more complex MyEconLab database.

As with the previous editions, this one owes an enormous debt to Robin Bade. I dedicate this book to her and again thank her for her work. I could not have written this book without the tireless and unselfish help she has given me. My thanks to her are unbounded.

Classroom experience will test the value of this book. I would appreciate hearing from instructors and students about how I can continue to improve it in future editions.

Michael Parkin
London, Ontario, Canada
michael.parkin@uwo.ca

Reviewers

Eric Abrams, Hawaii Pacific University
Christopher Adams, Federal Trade Commission
Tajudeen Adenekan, Bronx Community College
Syed Ahmed, Cameron University
Frank Albritton, Seminole Community College
Milton Alderfer, Miami-Dade Community College
William Aldridge, Shelton State Community College
Donald L. Alexander, Western Michigan University
Terence Alexander, Iowa State University
Stuart Allen, University of North Carolina, Greensboro
Sam Allgood, University of Nebraska, Lincoln
Neil Alper, Northeastern University
Alan Anderson, Fordham University
Lisa R. Anderson, College of William and Mary
Jeff Ankrom, Wittenberg University
Fatma Antar, Manchester Community Technical College
Kofi Apraku, University of North Carolina, Asheville
Moshen Bahmani-Oskooee, University of Wisconsin, Milwaukee
Donald Balch, University of South Carolina
Mehmet Balcilar, Wayne State University
Paul Ballantyne, University of Colorado
Sue Bartlett, University of South Florida
Jose Juan Bautista, Xavier University of Louisiana
Valerie R. Bencivenga, University of Texas, Austin
Ben Bernanke, Chairman of Federal Reserve
Radha Bhattacharya, California State University, Fullerton
Margot Biery, Tarrant County College, South
John Bittorowitz, Ball State University
David Black, University of Toledo
Kelly Blanchard, Purdue University
S. Brock Blomberg, Claremont McKenna College
William T. Bogart, Case Western Reserve University
Giacomo Bonanno, University of California, Davis
Tan Khay Boon, Nanyard Technological University
Sunne Brandmeyer, University of South Florida
Audie Brewton, Northeastern Illinois University
Baird Brock, Central Missouri State University
Byron Brown, Michigan State University
Jeffrey Buser, Columbus State Community College
Alison Butler, Florida International University
Tania Carbiener, Southern Methodist University
Kevin Carey, American University
Kathleen A. Carroll, University of Maryland, Baltimore County
Michael Carter, University of Massachusetts, Lowell
Edward Castronova, California State University, Fullerton
Francis Chan, Fullerton College
Ming Chang, Dartmouth College

Subir Chakrabarti, Indiana University-Purdue University
Joni Charles, Texas State University
Adhip Chaudhuri, Georgetown University
Gopal Chengalath, Texas Tech University
Daniel Christiansen, Albion College
Kenneth Christianson, Binghamton University
John J. Clark, Community College of Allegheny County, Allegheny Campus
Cindy Clement, University of Maryland
Meredith Clement, Dartmouth College
Michael B. Cohn, U. S. Merchant Marine Academy
Robert Collinge, University of Texas, San Antonio
Carol Condon, Kean University
Doug Conway, Mesa Community College
Larry Cook, University of Toledo
Bobby Corcoran, retired, Middle Tennessee State University
Kevin Cotter, Wayne State University
James Peery Cover, University of Alabama, Tuscaloosa
Erik Craft, University of Richmond
Eleanor D. Craig, University of Delaware
Jim Craven, Clark College
Jeremy Cripps, American University of Kuwait
Elizabeth Crowell, University of Michigan, Dearborn
Stephen Cullenberg, University of California, Riverside
David Culp, Slippery Rock University
Norman V. Cure, Macomb Community College
Dan Dabney, University of Texas, Austin
Andrew Dane, Angelo State University
Joseph Daniels, Marquette University
Gregory DeFreitas, Hofstra University
David Denslow, University of Florida
Mark Dickie, University of Central Florida
James Dietz, California State University, Fullerton
Carol Dole, State University of West Georgia
Ronald Dorf, Inver Hills Community College
John Dorsey, University of Maryland, College Park
Eric Drabkin, Hawaii Pacific University
Amrik Singh Dua, Mt. San Antonio College
Thomas Duchesneau, University of Maine, Orono
Lucia Dunn, Ohio State University
Donald Dutkowsky, Syracuse University
John Edgren, Eastern Michigan University
David J. Eger, Alpena Community College
Harry Ellis, Jr., University of North Texas
Ibrahim Elsaify, Goldey-Beacom College
Kenneth G. Elzinga, University of Virginia
Patrick Emerson, Oregon State University
Tisha Emerson, Baylor University
Monica Escaleras, Florida Atlantic University
Antonina Espiritu, Hawaii Pacific University

Gwen Eudey, University of Pennsylvania
Barry Falk, Iowa State University
M. Fazeli, Hofstra University
Philip Fincher, Louisiana Tech University
F. Firoozi, University of Texas, San Antonio
Nancy Folbre, University of Massachusetts, Amherst
Kenneth Fong, Temasek Polytechnic (Singapore)
Steven Francis, Holy Cross College
David Franck, University of North Carolina, Charlotte
Mark Frank, Sam Houston State University
Roger Frantz, San Diego State University
Mark Frascatore, Clarkson University
Alwyn Fraser, Atlantic Union College
Marc Fusaro, East Carolina University
James Gale, Michigan Technological University
Susan Gale, New York University
Roy Gardner, Indiana University
Eugene Gentzel, Pensacola Junior College
Kirk Gifford, Brigham Young University, Idaho
Scott Gilbert, Southern Illinois University, Carbondale
Andrew Gill, California State University, Fullerton
Robert Giller, Virginia Polytechnic Institute and State University
Robert Gillette, University of Kentucky
James N. Giordano, Villanova University
Maria Giuili, Diablo College
Susan Glanz, St. John's University
Robert Gordon, San Diego State University
Richard Gosselin, Houston Community College
John Graham, Rutgers University
John Griffen, Worcester Polytechnic Institute
Wayne Grove, Syracuse University
Robert Guell, Indiana State University
Jamie Haag, Pacific University, Oregon
Gail Heyne Hafer, Lindenwood University
Rik W. Hafer, Southern Illinois University, Edwardsville
Daniel Hagen, Western Washington University
David R. Hakes, University of Northern Iowa
Craig Hakkio, Federal Reserve Bank, Kansas City
Bridget Gleeson Hanna, Rochester Institute of Technology
Ann Hansen, Westminster College
Seid Hassan, Murray State University
Jonathan Haughton, Suffolk University
Randall Haydon, Wichita State University
Denise Hazlett, Whitman College
Julia Heath, University of Memphis
Jac Heckelman, Wake Forest University
Jolien A. Helsel, Kent State University
James Henderson, Baylor University
Doug Herman, Georgetown University
Jill Boylston Herndon, University of Florida
Gus Herring, Brookhaven College

John Herrmann, Rutgers University
John M. Hill, Delgado Community College
Jonathan Hill, Florida International University
Lewis Hill, Texas Tech University
Steve Hoagland, University of Akron
Tom Hoerger, Fellow, Research Triangle Institute
Calvin Hoerneman, Delta College
George Hoffer, Virginia Commonwealth University
Dennis L. Hoffman, Arizona State University
Paul Hohenberg, Rensselaer Polytechnic Institute
Jim H. Holcomb, University of Texas, El Paso
Harry Holzer, Georgetown University
Linda Hooks, Washington and Lee University
Jim Horner, Cameron University
Djehane Hosni, University of Central Florida
Harold Hotelling, Jr., Lawrence Technical University
Calvin Hoy, County College of Morris
Ing-Wei Huang, Assumption University, Thailand
Julie Hunsaker, Wayne State University
Beth Ingram, University of Iowa
Jayvanth Ishwaran, Stephen F. Austin State University
Michael Jacobs, Lehman College
S. Hussain Ali Jafri, Tarleton State University
Dennis Jansen, Texas A&M University
Barbara John, University of Dayton
Barry Jones, Binghamton University
Garrett Jones, Southern Florida University
Frederick Jungman, Northwestern Oklahoma State University
Paul Junk, University of Minnesota, Duluth
Leo Kahane, California State University, Hayward
Veronica Kalich, Baldwin-Wallace College
John Kane, State University of New York, Oswego
Eungmin Kang, St. Cloud State University
Arthur Kartman, San Diego State University
Gurmit Kaur, Universiti Teknologi (Malaysia)
Louise Keely, University of Wisconsin, Madison
Manfred W. Keil, Claremont McKenna College
Elizabeth Sawyer Kelly, University of Wisconsin, Madison
Rose Kilburn, Modesto Junior College
Robert Kirk, Indiana University-Purdue University, Indianapolis
Norman Kleinberg, City University of New York, Baruch College
Robert Kleinhenz, California State University, Fullerton
John Krantz, University of Utah
Joseph Kreitzer, University of St. Thomas
Patricia Kuzyk, Washington State University
David Lages, Southwest Missouri State University
W. J. Lane, University of New Orleans
Leonard Lardaro, University of Rhode Island
Kathryn Larson, Elon College
Luther D. Lawson, University of North Carolina, Wilmington
Elroy M. Leach, Chicago State University

Jim Lee, Texas A & M, Corpus Christi
Sang Lee, Southeastern Louisiana University
Robert Lemke, Florida International University
Mary Lesser, Iona College
Jay Levin, Wayne State University
Arik Levinson, University of Wisconsin, Madison
Tony Lima, California State University, Hayward
William Lord, University of Maryland, Baltimore County
Nancy Lutz, Virginia Polytechnic Institute and State University
Brian Lynch, Lakeland Community College
Murugappa Madhavan, San Diego State University
K. T. Magnusson, Salt Lake Community College
Svitlana Maksymenko, University of Pittsburgh
Mark Maier, Glendale Community College
Jean Mangan, Staffordshire University Business School
Denton Marks, University of Wisconsin, Whitewater
Michael Marlow, California Polytechnic State University
Akbar Marvasti, University of Houston
Wolfgang Mayer, University of Cincinnati
John McArthur, Wofford College
Amy McCormick, Mary Baldwin College
Russel McCullough, Iowa State University
Gerald McDougall, Wichita State University
Stephen McGary, Brigham Young University-Idaho
Richard D. McGrath, Armstrong Atlantic State University
Richard McIntyre, University of Rhode Island
John McLeod, Georgia Institute of Technology
Mark McLeod, Virginia Polytechnic Institute and State University
B. Starr McMullen, Oregon State University
Mary Ruth McRae, Appalachian State University
Kimberly Merritt, Cameron University
Charles Meyer, Iowa State University
Peter Mieszkowski, Rice University
John Mijares, University of North Carolina, Asheville
Richard A. Miller, Wesleyan University
Judith W. Mills, Southern Connecticut State University
Glen Mitchell, Nassau Community College
Jeannette C. Mitchell, Rochester Institute of Technology
Khan Mohabbat, Northern Illinois University
Bagher Modjtahedi, University of California, Davis
W. Douglas Morgan, University of California, Santa Barbara
William Morgan, University of Wyoming
James Morley, Washington University in St. Louis
William Mosher, Clark University
Joanne Moss, San Francisco State University
Nivedita Mukherji, Oakland University
Francis Mummery, Fullerton College
Edward Murphy, Southwest Texas State University
Kevin J. Murphy, Oakland University
Kathryn Nantz, Fairfield University
William S. Neilson, Texas A&M University

Bart C. Nemmers, University of Nebraska, Lincoln
Melinda Nish, Orange Coast College
Anthony O'Brien, Lehigh University
Norman Obst, Michigan State University
Constantin Ogloblin, Georgia Southern University
Mary Olson, Tulane University
Terry Olson, Truman State University
James B. O'Neill, University of Delaware
Farley Ordovensky, University of the Pacific
Z. Edward O'Relley, North Dakota State University
Donald Oswald, California State University, Bakersfield
Jan Palmer, Ohio University
Michael Palumbo, Chief, Federal Reserve Board
Chris Papageorgiou, Louisiana State University
G. Hossein Parandvash, Western Oregon State College
Randall Parker, East Carolina University
Robert Parks, Washington University
David Pate, St. John Fisher College
James E. Payne, Illinois State University
Donald Pearson, Eastern Michigan University
Steven Peterson, University of Idaho
Mary Anne Pettit, Southern Illinois University, Edwardsville
William A. Phillips, University of Southern Maine
Dennis Placone, Clemson University
Charles Plot, California Institute of Technology, Pasadena
Mannie Poen, Houston Community College
Kathleen Possai, Wayne State University
Ulrika Praski-Stahlgren, University College in Gavle-Sandviken, Sweden
Edward Price, Oklahoma State University
Rula Qalyoubi, University of Wisconsin, Eau Claire
K. A. Quartey, Talladega College
Herman Quirmbach, Iowa State University
Jeffrey R. Racine, University of South Florida
Peter Rangazas, Indiana University-Purdue University, Indianapolis
Vaman Rao, Western Illinois University
Laura Razzolini, University of Mississippi
Rob Rebelein, University of Cincinnati
J. David Reed, Bowling Green State University
Robert H. Renshaw, Northern Illinois University
Javier Reyes, University of Arkansas
Jeff Reynolds, Northern Illinois University
Rupert Rhodd, Florida Atlantic University
W. Gregory Rhodus, Bentley College
Jennifer Rice, Indiana University, Bloomington
John Robertson, Paducah Community College
Malcolm Robinson, University of North Carolina, Greensboro
Richard Roehl, University of Michigan, Dearborn
Carol Rogers, Georgetown University
William Rogers, University of Northern Colorado

Thomas Romans, State University of New York, Buffalo

David R. Ross, Bryn Mawr College

Thomas Ross, Baldwin Wallace College

Robert J. Rossana, Wayne State University

Jeffrey Rous, University of North Texas

Rochelle Ruffer, Youngstown State University

Mark Rush, University of Florida

Allen R. Sanderson, University of Chicago

Gary Santoni, Ball State University

John Saussy, Harrisburg Area Community College

Don Schlagenhauf, Florida State University

David Schlow, Pennsylvania State University

Paul Schmitt, St. Clair County Community College

Jeremy Schwartz, Hampden-Sydney College

Martin Sefton, University of Nottingham

James Self, Indiana University

Esther-Mirjam Sent, University of Notre Dame

Rod Shadbegian, University of Massachusetts, Dartmouth

Gerald Shilling, Eastfield College

Dorothy R. Siden, Salem State College

Mark Siegler, California State University at Sacramento

Scott Simkins, North Carolina Agricultural and Technical State University

Chuck Skoro, Boise State University

Phil Smith, DeKalb College

William Doyle Smith, University of Texas, El Paso

Sarah Stafford, College of William and Mary

Rebecca Stein, University of Pennsylvania

Frank Steindl, Oklahoma State University

Jeffrey Stewart, New York University

Allan Stone, Southwest Missouri State University

Courtenay Stone, Ball State University

Paul Storer, Western Washington University

Richard W. Stratton, University of Akron

Mark Strazicich, Ohio State University, Newark

Michael Stroup, Stephen F. Austin State University

Robert Stuart, Rutgers University

Della Lee Sue, Marist College

Abdulhamid Sukar, Cameron University

Terry Sutton, Southeast Missouri State University

Gilbert Suzawa, University of Rhode Island

David Swaine, Andrews University

Jason Taylor, Central Michigan University

Mark Thoma, University of Oregon

Janet Thomas, Bentley College

Kiril Tochkov, SUNY at Binghamton

Kay Unger, University of Montana

Anthony Uremovic, Joliet Junior College

David Vaughn, City University, Washington

Don Waldman, Colgate University

Francis Wambalaba, Portland State University

Rob Wassmer, California State University, Sacramento

Paul A. Weinstein, University of Maryland, College Park

Lee Weissert, St. Vincent College

Robert Whaples, Wake Forest University

David Wharton, Washington College

Mark Wheeler, Western Michigan University

Charles H. Whiteman, University of Iowa

Sandra Williamson, University of Pittsburgh

Brenda Wilson, Brookhaven Community College

Larry Wimmer, Brigham Young University

Mark Witte, Northwestern University

Willard E. Witte, Indiana University

Mark Wohar, University of Nebraska, Omaha

Laura Wolff, Southern Illinois University, Edwardsville

Cheonsik Woo, Vice President, Korea Development Institute

Douglas Wooley, Radford University

Arthur G. Woolf, University of Vermont

John T. Young, Riverside Community College

Michael Youngblood, Rock Valley College

Peter Zaleski, Villanova University

Jason Zimmerman, South Dakota State University

David Zucker, Martha Stewart Living Omnimedia

Supplements Authors

Sue Bartlett, University of South Florida

Kelly Blanchard, Purdue University

James Cobbe, Florida State University

Carol Dole, Jacksonville University

Karen Gebhardt, Colorado State University

John Graham, Rutgers University

Jill Herndon, University of Florida

Patricia Kuzyk, Washington State University

Sang Lee, Southeastern Louisiana University

James Morley, Washington University in St. Louis

William Mosher, Clark University

Constantin Ogloblin, Georgia Southern University

Edward Price, Oklahoma State University

Mark Rush, University of Florida

Michael Stroup, Stephen F. Austin State University

Della Lee Sue, Marist College

Nora Underwood, University of Central Florida

FLEXIBILITY
BY CHAPTER

FOUR ALTERNATIVE
MICRO SEQUENCES

TABLE OF
CONTENTS

PART TWO
HOW MARKETS WORK 57

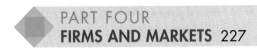

PART FOUR
FIRMS AND MARKETS 227

1

What Is Economics?

After studying this chapter, you will be able to:

- Define economics and distinguish between microeconomics and macroeconomics

- Explain the two big questions of economics

- Explain the key ideas that define the economic way of thinking

- Explain how economists go about their work as social scientists

You are studying economics at a time of extra-ordinary change. The United States is the world's most powerful nation, but China, India, Brazil, and Russia, nations with a combined population that dwarfs our own, are emerging to play ever greater roles in an expanding global economy. The technological change that is driving this expansion has brought us the laptops, wireless broadband, iPods, DVDs, cell phones, and video games that have transformed the way we work and play. But this expanding global economy has also brought us skyrocketing food and fuel prices and is contributing to global warming and climate change.

Your life will be shaped by the challenges you face and the opportunities that you create. But to face those challenges and seize the opportunities they present, you must understand the powerful forces at play. The economics that you're about to learn will become your most reliable guide. This chapter gets you started. It describes the questions that economists try to answer and the ways in which they search for the answers.

Definition of Economics

All economic questions arise because we want more than we can get. We want a peaceful and secure world. We want clean air, lakes, and rivers. We want long and healthy lives. We want good schools, colleges, and universities. We want spacious and comfortable homes. We want an enormous range of sports and recreational gear from running shoes to jet skis. We want the time to enjoy sports, games, novels, movies, music, travel, and hanging out with our friends.

What each one of us can get is limited by time, by the incomes we earn, and by the prices we must pay. Everyone ends up with some unsatisfied wants. What we can get as a society is limited by our productive resources. These resources include the gifts of nature, human labor and ingenuity, and tools and equipment that we have produced.

Our inability to satisfy all our wants is called **scarcity**. The poor and the rich alike face scarcity. A child wants a $1.00 can of soda and two 50¢ packs of gum but has only $1.00 in his pocket. He faces scarcity. A millionaire wants to spend the weekend playing golf *and* spend the same weekend attending a business strategy meeting. She faces scarcity. A society wants to provide improved health care, install a computer in every classroom, explore space, clean polluted lakes and rivers, and so on. Society faces scarcity. Even parrots face scarcity!

Faced with scarcity, we must *choose* among the available alternatives. The child must *choose* the soda

or the gum. The millionaire must *choose* the golf game *or* the meeting. As a society, we must *choose* among health care, national defense, and education.

The choices that we make depend on the incentives that we face. An **incentive** is a reward that encourages an action or a penalty that discourages one. If the price of soda falls, the child has an *incentive* to choose more soda. If a profit of $10 million is at stake, the millionaire has an *incentive* to skip the golf game. As computer prices tumble, school boards have an *incentive* to connect more classrooms to the Internet.

Economics is the social science that studies the *choices* that individuals, businesses, governments, and entire societies make as they cope with *scarcity* and the *incentives* that influence and reconcile those choices. The subject divides into two main parts:

- Microeconomics
- Macroeconomics

Microeconomics

Microeconomics is the study of the choices that individuals and businesses make, the way these choices interact in markets, and the influence of governments. Some examples of microeconomic questions are: Why are people buying more DVDs and fewer movie tickets? How would a tax on e-commerce affect eBay?

Macroeconomics

Macroeconomics is the study of the performance of the national economy and the global economy. Some examples of macroeconomic questions are: Why did income growth slow in the United States in 2008? Can the Federal Reserve keep our economy expanding by cutting interest rates?

Not only do I want a cracker—we all want a cracker!

Review Quiz

1 List some examples of scarcity in the United States today.
2 Use the headlines in today's news to provide some examples of scarcity around the world.
3 Use today's news to illustrate the distinction between microeconomics and macroeconomics.

 Work Study Plan 1.1 and get instant feedback.

Two Big Economic Questions

Two big questions summarize the scope of economics:

- How do choices end up determining *what, how,* and *for whom* goods and services are produced?
- How can choices made in the pursuit of *self-interest* also promote the *social interest*?

What, How, and For Whom?

Goods and services are the objects that people value and produce to satisfy human wants. *Goods* are physical objects such as cell phones and automobiles. *Services* are tasks performed for people such as cell-phone service and auto-repair service.

What? What we produce varies across countries and changes over time. In the United States today, agriculture accounts for less than 1 percent of total production, manufactured goods for 20 percent, and services (retail and wholesale trade, health care, and education are the biggest ones) for 80 percent. In contrast, in China today, agriculture accounts for more than 10 percent of total production, manufactured goods for 50 percent, and services for 40 percent. Figure 1.1 shows these numbers and also the percentages for Brazil, which fall between those for the United States and China.

What determines these patterns of production? How do choices end up determining the quantities of cell phones, automobiles, cell-phone service, auto-repair service, and the millions of other items that are produced in the United States and around the world?

How? Goods and services are produced by using productive resources that economists call **factors of production**. Factors of production are grouped into four categories:

- Land
- Labor
- Capital
- Entrepreneurship

Land The "gifts of nature" that we use to produce goods and services are called **land**. In economics, land is what in everyday language we call *natural*

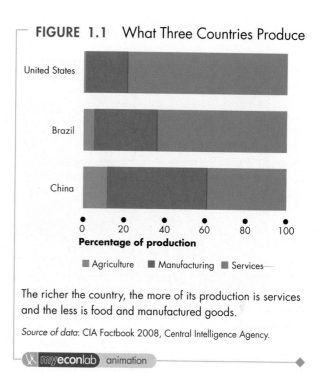

FIGURE 1.1   What Three Countries Produce

United States
Brazil
China

0   20   40   60   80   100
Percentage of production

■ Agriculture ■ Manufacturing ■ Services

The richer the country, the more of its production is services and the less is food and manufactured goods.

Source of data: CIA Factbook 2008, Central Intelligence Agency.

myeconlab   animation

resources. It includes land in the everyday sense together with minerals, oil, gas, coal, water, air, forests, and fish.

Our land surface and water resources are renewable and some of our mineral resources can be recycled. But the resources that we use to create energy are nonrenewable—they can be used only once.

Labor The work time and work effort that people devote to producing goods and services is called **labor**. Labor includes the physical and mental efforts of all the people who work on farms and construction sites and in factories, shops, and offices.

The *quality* of labor depends on **human capital**, which is the knowledge and skill that people obtain from education, on-the-job training, and work experience. You are building your own human capital right now as you work on your economics course, and your human capital will continue to grow as you gain work experience.

Human capital expands over time. Today, 86 percent of the population of the United States have completed high school and 28 percent have a college or university degree. Figure 1.2 shows these measures of the growth of human capital in the United States over the past century.

FIGURE 1.2   A Measure of Human Capital

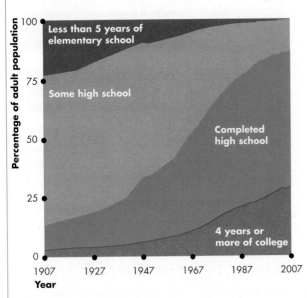

Today, 28 percent of the population have 4 years or more of college, up from 2 percent in 1905. A further 58 percent have completed high school, up from 10 percent in 1905.

Source of data: U.S. Census Bureau, *Statistical Abstract of the United States*.

myeconlab animation

Capital   The tools, instruments, machines, buildings, and other constructions that businesses use to produce goods and services are called **capital**.

In everyday language, we talk about money, stocks, and bonds as being "capital." These items are *financial* capital. Financial capital plays an important role in enabling businesses to borrow the funds that they use to buy physical capital. But because financial capital is not used to produce goods and services, it is not a productive resource.

Entrepreneurship   The human resource that organizes labor, land, and capital is called **entrepreneurship**. Entrepreneurs come up with new ideas about what and how to produce, make business decisions, and bear the risks that arise from these decisions.

What determines the quantities of factors of production that are used to produce goods and services?

For Whom?   Who consumes the goods and services that are produced depends on the incomes that people earn. A large income enables a person to buy large

quantities of goods and services. A small income leaves a person with few options and small quantities of goods and services.

People earn their incomes by selling the services of the factors of production they own:

- Land earns **rent**.
- Labor earns **wages**.
- Capital earns **interest**.
- Entrepreneurship earns **profit**.

Which factor of production earns the most income? The answer is labor. Wages and fringe benefits are around 70 percent of total income. Land, capital, and entrepreneurship share the rest. These percentages have been remarkably constant over time.

Knowing how income is shared among the factors of production doesn't tell us how it is shared among individuals. And the distribution of income among individuals is extremely unequal. You know of some people who earn very large incomes: Oprah Winfrey made $260 million in 2007; and Bill Gates' wealth increased by $2 billion in 2008.

You know of even more people who earn very small incomes. Servers at McDonald's average around $6.35 an hour; checkout clerks, cleaners, and textile and leather workers all earn less than $10 an hour.

You probably know about other persistent differences in incomes. Men, on the average, earn more than women; whites earn more than minorities; college graduates earn more than high-school graduates.

We can get a good sense of who consumes the goods and services produced by looking at the percentages of total income earned by different groups of people. The 20 percent of people with the lowest incomes earn about 5 percent of total income, while the richest 20 percent earn close to 50 percent of total income. So on average, people in the richest 20 percent earn more than 10 times the incomes of those in the poorest 20 percent.

Why is the distribution of income so unequal? Why do women and minorities earn less than white males?

Economics provides some answers to all these questions about what, how, and for whom goods and services are produced and much of the rest of this book will help you to understand those answers.

We're now going to look at the second big question of economics: When does the pursuit of self-interest promote the social interest? This question is a difficult one both to appreciate and to answer.

How Can the Pursuit of Self-Interest Promote the Social Interest?

Every day, you and 304 million other Americans, along with 6.7 billion people in the rest of the world, make economic choices that result in *what*, *how*, and *for whom* goods and services are produced.

Self-Interest A choice is in your **self-interest** if you think that choice is the best one available for you. You make most of your choices in your self-interest. You use your time and other resources in the ways that make the most sense to you, and you don't think too much about how your choices affect other people. You order a home delivery pizza because you're hungry and want to eat. You don't order it thinking that the delivery person needs an income.

When you act on your self-interested economic choices, you come into contact with thousands of other people who produce and deliver the goods and services that you decide to buy or who buy the things that you sell. These people have made their own choices—what to produce and how to produce it, whom to hire or to work for, and so on—in their self-interest. When the pizza delivery person shows up at your door, he's not doing you a favor. He's earning his income and hoping for a good tip.

Social Interest Self-interested choices promote the **social interest** if they lead to an outcome that is the best for society as a whole—an outcome that uses resources efficiently and distributes goods and services equitably (or fairly) among individuals.

Resources are used efficiently when goods and services are produced

1. At the lowest possible cost, and
2. In the quantities that give the greatest possible benefit.

The Big Question How can we organize our economic lives so that when each one of us makes choices that are in our self-interest, it turns out that these choices also promote the social interest? Does voluntary trading in free markets achieve the social interest? Do we need government action to guide our choices to achieve the social interest? Do we need international cooperation and treaties to achieve the global social interest?

Let's put flesh on these broad questions with some examples.

Self-Interest and the Social Interest

To get started thinking about the tension between self-interest and the social interest, we'll consider five topics that generate discussion in today's world. Here, we will briefly introduce the topics and identify some of the economic questions that they pose. We'll return to each one of them as you learn more of the economic ideas and tools that can be used to understand these issues. The topics are

- Globalization
- The information-age economy
- Global warming
- Natural resource depletion
- Economic instability

Globalization The term *globalization* means the expansion of international trade, borrowing and lending, and investment.

Whose self-interest does globalization serve? Is it only in the self-interest of the multinational firms that produce in low-cost regions and sell in high-price regions? Is globalization in the interest of consumers who buy lower-cost goods? Is globalization in the interest of the worker in Malaysia who sews your new running shoes? Is globalization in your self-interest and in the social interest? Or should we limit globalization and restrict imports of cheap foreign-produced goods and services?

Globalization Today
Life in a Small and Ever Shrinking World

Every day, 40,000 people travel by air between the United States and Asia and Europe. A phone call or a video-conference with people who live 10,000 miles apart is a common and easily affordable event.

When Nike produces sports shoes, people in China, Indonesia, or Malaysia get work. When Apple designs a new generation iPod, electronics factories in China, Japan, Korea, and Taiwan produce and assemble the parts. When Nintendo creates a new game for the Wii, programmers in India write the code. And when China Airlines buys new airplanes, Americans who work at Boeing build them.

While globalization brings expanded production and job opportunities for Asian workers, it destroys many American jobs. Workers across the manufacturing industries must learn new skills, or take lower-paid service jobs, or retire earlier than planned.

The Information-Age Economy The technological change of the 1990s and 2000s has been called the *Information Revolution*.

During the information revolution were scarce resources used in the best possible way? Who benefitted from Bill Gates' decision to quit Harvard and create Microsoft? Did Microsoft produce operating systems for the personal computer that served the social interest? Did it sell its programs for prices that served the social interest? Did Bill Gates have to be paid what has now grown to $55 billion to produce the successive generations of Windows, Microsoft Office, and other programs? Did Intel make the right quality of chips and sell them in the right quantities for the right prices? Or was the quality too low and the price too high? Would the social interest have been better served if Microsoft and Intel had faced competition from other firms?

The Source of the Information-Age
So Much from One Tiny Chip

The microprocessor or computer chip created the information age. Gordon Moore of Intel predicted in 1965 that the number of transistors that could be placed on one chip would double every 18 months (Moore's law). This prediction turned out to be remarkably accurate. In 1980, an Intel chip had 60,000 transistors. In 2008, Intel's Core 2 Duo processor that you might be using on your personal computer has 291 million transistors.

The spinoffs from faster and cheaper computing were widespread. Telecommunications became clearer and faster; music and movie recording became more realistic; routine tasks that previously required human decision and action were automated.

All the new products and processes, and the low-cost computing power that made them possible, were produced by people who made choices in their own self-interest. They did not result from any grand design or government economic plan.

When Gordon Moore set up Intel and started making chips, no one had told him to do so, and he wasn't thinking how much easier it would be for you to turn in your essay on time if you had a faster laptop. When Bill Gates quit Harvard to set up Microsoft, he wasn't thinking about making it easier to use a computer. Moore, Gates, and thousands of other entrepreneurs were in hot pursuit of the big prizes that many of them succeeded in winning.

Global Warming Global warming and its effect on climate change is a huge political issue today. Every serious political leader is acutely aware of the problem and of the popularity of having proposals that might lower carbon emissions.

Every day, when you make self-interested choices to use electricity and gasoline, you contribute to carbon emissions; you leave your carbon footprint. You can lessen your carbon footprint by walking, riding a bike, taking a cold shower, or planting a tree.

But can each one of us be relied upon to make decisions that affect the Earth's carbon-dioxide concentration in the social interest? Must governments change the incentives we face so that our self-interested choices advance the social interest? How can governments change incentives? How can we encourage the use of wind and solar power to replace the burning of fossil fuels that bring climate change?

A Hotter Planet
Melting Ice and the Changing Climate

Retreating polar icecaps are a vivid illustration of a warming planet. Over the past 100 years, the Earth's surface air temperature is estimated to have risen by about three quarters of a degree Celsius. Uncertainty surrounds the causes, likely future amount, and effects of this temperature increase.

The consensus is that the temperature is rising because the amount of carbon dioxide in the Earth's atmosphere is increasing, and that human economic activity is a source of the increased carbon concentration.

Forests convert carbon dioxide to oxygen and so act as carbon sinks, but they are shrinking.

Two thirds of the world's carbon emissions come from the United States, China, the European Union, Russia, and India. The fastest growing emissions are coming from India and China.

Burning fossil fuels—coal and oil—to generate electricity and to power airplanes, automobiles, and trucks pours a staggering 28 billions tons—4 tons per person—of carbon dioxide into the atmosphere each year.

The amount of future global warming and its effects are uncertain. If the temperature rise continues, the Earth's climate will change, ocean levels will rise, and low-lying coastal areas will need to be protected against the rising tides by expensive barriers.

Natural Resource Depletion Tropical rainforests and ocean fish stocks are disappearing quickly. No one owns these resources and everyone is free to take what they want. When Japanese, Spanish, and Russian trawlers scoop up fish in international waters, no one keeps track of the quantities of fish they catch and no one makes them pay. The fish are free.

Each one of us makes self-interested economic choices to buy products that destroy natural resources and kill wild fish stocks. When you buy soap or shampoo or eat fish and contribute to the depletion of natural resources, are your self-interested choices damaging the social interest? If they are, what can be done to change your choices so that they serve the social interest?

Economic Instability The past 20 years have been ones of remarkable economic stability, so much so that they've been called the *Great Moderation*. Even the economic shockwaves of 9/11 brought only a small dip in the strong pace of U.S. and global eco-

nomic expansion. But in August 2007, a period of financial stress began.

Banks' choices to lend and people's choices to borrow were made in self-interest. But did this lending and borrowing serve the social interest? Did the Fed's bail out of troubled banks serve the social interest? Or might the Fed's rescue action encourage banks to repeat their dangerous lending in the future?

Running Out of Natural Resources
Disappearing Forests and Fish

Tropical rainforests in South America, Africa, and Asia support the lives of 30 million species of plants, animals, and insects—approaching 50 percent of all the species on the planet. These rainforests provide us with the ingredients for many goods, including soaps, mouthwashes, shampoos, food preservatives, rubber, nuts, and fruits. The Amazon rainforest alone converts about 1 trillion pounds of carbon dioxide into oxygen each year.

Yet tropical rainforests cover less than 2 percent of the earth's surface and are heading for extinction. Logging, cattle ranching, mining, oil extraction, hydroelectric dams, and subsistence farming destroy an area the size of two football fields every second, or an area larger than New York City every day. At the current rate of destruction, almost all the tropical rainforest ecosystems will be gone by 2030.

What is happening to the tropical rainforests is also happening to ocean fish stocks. Overfishing has almost eliminated cod from the Atlantic Ocean and the southern bluefin tuna from the South Pacific Ocean. Many other species of fish are on the edge of extinction in the wild and are now available only from fish farms.

The End of the Great Moderation
A Credit Crunch

Flush with funds, and offering record low interest rates, banks went on a lending spree to home buyers. Rapidly rising home prices made home owners feel well off and they were happy to borrow and spend. Home loans were bundled into securities that were sold and resold to banks around the world.

In 2006, interest rates began to rise, the rate of rise in home prices slowed, and borrowers defaulted on their loans. What started as a trickle became a flood. By mid-2007, banks took losses that totaled billions of dollars as more people defaulted.

Global credit markets stopped working, and people began to fear a prolonged slowdown in economic activity. Some even feared the return of the economic trauma of the *Great Depression* of the 1930s when more than 20 percent of the U.S. labor force was unemployed. The Federal Reserve, determined to avoid a catastrophe, started lending on a very large scale to the troubled banks.

Review Quiz

1 Describe the broad facts about *what*, *how*, and *for whom* goods and services are produced.
2 Use headlines from the recent news to illustrate the potential for conflict between self-interest and the social interest.

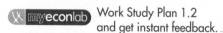 Work Study Plan 1.2 and get instant feedback.

We've looked at five topics that illustrate the big question: How can choices made in the pursuit of self-interest also promote the social interest? While working through this book, you will encounter the principles that help economists figure out when the social interest is being served, when it is not, and what might be done when the social interest is not being served?

◆ The Economic Way of Thinking

The questions that economics tries to answer tell us about the *scope of economics*. But they don't tell us how economists *think* about these questions and go about seeking answers to them.

You're now going to begin to see how economists approach economic questions. We'll look at the ideas that define the *economic way of thinking*. This way of thinking needs practice, but it is powerful, and as you become more familiar with it, you'll begin to see the world around you with a new and sharper focus.

Choices and Tradeoffs

Because we face scarcity, we must make choices. And when we make a choice, we select from the available alternatives. For example, you can spend Saturday night studying for your next economics test and having fun with your friends, but you can't do both of these activities at the same time. You must choose how much time to devote to each. Whatever choice you make, you could have chosen something else.

You can think about your choice as a tradeoff. A **tradeoff** is an exchange—giving up one thing to get something else. When you choose how to spend your Saturday night, you face a tradeoff between studying and hanging out with your friends.

Guns Versus Butter The classic tradeoff is between guns and butter. "Guns" and "butter" stand for any pair of goods. They might actually be guns and butter. Or they might be broader categories such as national defense and food. Or they might be any pair of specific goods or services such as cola and pizza, baseball bats and tennis rackets, colleges and hospitals, realtor services and career counseling.

Regardless of the specific objects that guns and butter represent, the guns-versus-butter tradeoff captures a hard fact of life: If we want more of one thing, we must give up something else to get it. To get more "guns" we must give up some "butter."

The idea of a tradeoff is central to economics. We'll look at some examples, beginning with the big questions: What, How, and For Whom goods and services are produced? We can view each of these questions in terms of tradeoffs.

What, How, and For Whom Tradeoffs

The questions what, how, and for whom goods and services are produced all involve tradeoffs that are similar to that between guns and butter.

What Tradeoffs What goods and services are produced depends on choices made by each one of us, by our government, and by the businesses that produce the things we buy. Each of these choices involves a tradeoff.

Each one of us faces a tradeoff when we choose how to spend our income. You go to the movies this week, but you forgo a few cups of coffee to buy the ticket. You trade off coffee for a movie.

The federal government faces a tradeoff when it chooses how to spend our tax dollars. Congress votes for more national defense but cuts back on educational programs. Congress trades off education for national defense.

Businesses face a tradeoff when they decide what to produce. Nike hires Tiger Woods and allocates resources to designing and marketing a new golf ball but cuts back on its development of a new running shoe. Nike trades off running shoes for golf balls.

How Tradeoffs How businesses produce the goods and services we buy depends on their choices. These choices involve tradeoffs. For example, when Krispy Kreme opens a new store with an automated production line and closes one with a traditional kitchen, it trades off labor for capital. When American Airlines replaces check-in agents with self check-in kiosks, it also trades off labor for capital.

For Whom Tradeoffs For whom goods and services are produced depends on the distribution of buying power. Buying power can be redistributed—transferred from one person to another—in three ways: by voluntary payments, by theft, or through taxes and benefits organized by government. Redistribution brings tradeoffs.

Each of us faces a tradeoff when we choose how much to contribute to the United Nations' famine relief fund. You donate $50 and cut your spending. You trade off your own spending for a small increase in economic equality. We also face a tradeoff when we vote to increase the resources for catching thieves and enforcing the law. We trade off goods and services for an increase in the security of our property.

We also face a *for whom* tradeoff when we vote for taxes and social programs that redistribute buying power from the rich to the poor. These redistribution programs confront society with what has been called the **big tradeoff**—the tradeoff between equality and efficiency. Taxing the rich and making transfers to the poor bring greater economic equality. But taxing productive activities such as running a business, working hard, and developing a more productive technology discourages these activities. So taxing productive activities means producing less. A more equal distribution means there is less to share.

Think of the problem of how to share a pie that everyone contributes to baking. If each person receives a share of the pie that is proportional to her or his effort, everyone will work hard and the pie will be as large as possible. But if the pie is shared equally, regardless of contribution, some talented bakers will slack off and the pie will shrink. The big tradeoff is one between the size of the pie and how equally it is shared. We trade off some pie for increased equality.

Choices Bring Change

What, how, and for whom goods and services are produced changes over time. The quantity and range of goods and services available today is much greater than it was a generation ago. But the quality of economic life (and its rate of improvement) doesn't depend purely on nature and on luck. It depends on many of the choices made by each one of us, by governments, and by businesses. These choices also involve tradeoffs.

One choice is that of how much of our income to consume and how much to save. Our saving can be channeled through the financial system to finance businesses and to pay for new capital that increases production. The more we save, the more financial capital is available for businesses to use to buy physical capital, so the more goods and services we can produce in the future. When you decide to save an extra $1,000 and forgo a vacation, you trade off the vacation for a higher future income. If everyone saves an extra $1,000 and businesses buy more equipment that increases production, future consumption per person rises. As a society, we trade off current consumption for economic growth and higher future consumption.

A second choice is how much effort to devote to education and training. By becoming better educated and more highly skilled, we become more productive and are able to produce more goods and services.

When you decide to remain in school for another two years to complete a professional degree and forgo a huge chunk of leisure time, you trade off leisure today for a higher future income. If everyone becomes better educated, production increases and income per person rises. As a society, we trade off current consumption and leisure time for economic growth and higher future consumption.

A third choice is how much effort to devote to research and the development of new products and production methods. Ford Motor Company can hire people either to design a new robotic assembly line or to operate the existing plant and produce cars. The robotic plant brings greater productivity in the future but means smaller current production—a tradeoff of current production for greater future production.

Seeing choices as tradeoffs emphasizes the idea that to get something, we must give up something. What we give up is the cost of what we get. Economists call this cost the *opportunity cost*.

Opportunity Cost

"There's no such thing as a free lunch" expresses the central idea of economics: Every choice has a cost. The **opportunity cost** of something is the highest-valued alternative that we must give up to get it.

For example, you face an opportunity cost of being in school. That opportunity cost is the highest-valued alternative that you would do if you were not in school. If you quit school and take a job at McDonald's, you earn enough to go to ball games and movies and spend lots of free time with your friends. If you remain in school, you can't afford these things. You will be able to buy these things when you graduate and get a job, and that is one of the payoffs from being in school. But for now, when you've bought your books, you have nothing left for games and movies. Working on assignments leaves even less time for hanging out with your friends. Giving up games, movies, and free time is part of the opportunity cost of being in school.

All the *what*, *how*, and *for whom* tradeoffs involve opportunity cost. The opportunity cost of some guns is the butter forgone; the opportunity cost of a movie ticket is the number of cups of coffee forgone.

And the choices that bring change also involve opportunity cost. The opportunity cost of more goods and services in the future is less consumption today.

Choosing at the Margin

You can allocate the next hour between studying and instant messaging your friends. But the choice is not all or nothing. You must decide how many minutes to allocate to each activity. To make this decision, you compare the benefit of a little bit more study time with its cost—you make your choice at the **margin**.

The benefit that arises from an increase in an activity is called **marginal benefit**. For example, suppose that you're spending four nights a week studying and your grade point average (GPA) is 3.0. You decide that you want a higher GPA and decide to study an extra night each week. Your GPA rises to 3.5. The marginal benefit from studying for one extra night a week is the 0.5 increase in your GPA. It is *not* the 3.5. You already have a 3.0 from studying for four nights a week, so we don't count this benefit as resulting from the decision you are now making.

The cost of an increase in an activity is called **marginal cost**. For you, the marginal cost of increasing your study time by one night a week is the cost of the additional night not spent with your friends (if that is your best alternative use of the time). It does not include the cost of the four nights you are already studying.

To make your decision, you compare the marginal benefit from an extra night of studying with its marginal cost. If the marginal benefit exceeds the marginal cost, you study the extra night. If the marginal cost exceeds the marginal benefit, you do not study the extra night.

By evaluating marginal benefits and marginal costs and choosing only those actions that bring greater benefit than cost, we use our scarce resources in the way that makes us as well off as possible.

Responding to Incentives

When we make choices we respond to incentives. A change in marginal cost or a change in marginal benefit changes the incentives that we face and leads us to change our choice.

For example, suppose your economics instructor gives you a set of problems and tells you that all the problems will be on the next test. The marginal benefit from working these problems is large, so you diligently work them all. In contrast, if your math instructor gives you a set of problems and tells you that none of the problems will be on the next test, the marginal benefit from working these problems is lower, so you skip most of them.

The central idea of economics is that we can predict how choices will change by looking at changes in incentives. More of an activity is undertaken when its marginal cost falls or its marginal benefit rises; less of an activity is undertaken when its marginal cost rises or its marginal benefit falls.

Incentives are also the key to reconciling self-interest and social interest. When our choices are *not* in the social interest, it is because of the incentives we face. One of the challenges for economists is to figure out the incentive systems that result in self-interested choices also being in the social interest.

Human Nature, Incentives, and Institutions

Economists take human nature as given and view people as acting in their self-interest. All people—consumers, producers, politicians, and public servants—pursue their self-interest.

Self-interested actions are not necessarily *selfish* actions. You might decide to use your resources in ways that bring pleasure to others as well as to yourself. But a self-interested act gets the most value for *you* based on *your* view about value.

If human nature is given and if people act in their self-interest, how can we take care of the social interest? Economists answer this question by emphasizing the crucial role that institutions play in influencing the incentives that people face as they pursue their self-interest.

A system of laws that protect private property and markets that enable voluntary exchange are the fundamental institutions. You will learn as you progress with your study of economics that where these institutions exist, self-interest can indeed promote the social interest.

Review Quiz

1 Provide three everyday examples of tradeoffs and describe the opportunity cost involved in each.
2 Provide three everyday examples to illustrate what we mean by choosing at the margin.
3 How do economists predict changes in choices?
4 What do economists say about the role of institutions in promoting the social interest?

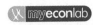 Work Study Plan 1.3 and get instant feedback.

Economics as Social Science and Policy Tool

Economics is both a science and a set of tools that can be used to make policy decisions.

Economics as Social Science

As social scientists, economists seek to discover how the economic world works. In pursuit of this goal, like all scientists, they distinguish between two types of statements: positive and normative.

Positive Statements *Positive* statements are about what is. They say what is currently believed about the way the world operates. A positive statement might be right or wrong, but we can test a positive statement by checking it against the facts. "Our planet is warming because of the amount of coal that we're burning" is a positive statement. "A rise in the minimum wage will bring more teenage unemployment" is another positive statement. Each statement might be right or wrong, and it can be tested.

A central task of economists is to test positive statements about how the economic world works and to weed out those that are wrong. Economics first got off the ground in the late 1700s, so economics is a young subject compared with, for example, math and physics, and much remains to be discovered.

Normative Statements *Normative* statements are statements about what ought to be. These statements depend on values and cannot be tested. The statement "We ought to cut back on our use of coal" is a normative statement. "The minimum wage should not be increased" is another normative statement. You may agree or disagree with either of these statements, but you can't test them. They express an opinion, but they don't assert a fact that can be checked. They are not economics.

Unscrambling Cause and Effect Economists are especially interested in positive statements about cause and effect. Are computers getting cheaper because people are buying them in greater quantities? Or are people buying computers in greater quantities because they are getting cheaper? Or is some third factor causing both the price of a computer to fall and the quantity of computers to increase?

To answer questions such as these, economists create and test economic models. An **economic model** is a description of some aspect of the economic world that includes only those features that are needed for the purpose at hand. For example, an economic model of a cell-phone network might include features such as the prices of calls, the number of cell-phone users, and the volume of calls. But the model would ignore such details as cell-phone colors and ringtones.

A model is tested by comparing its predictions with the facts. But testing an economic model is difficult because we observe the outcomes of the simultaneous operation of many factors. To cope with this problem, economists use natural experiments, statistical investigations, and economic experiments.

Natural Experiment A natural experiment is a situation that arises in the ordinary course of economic life in which the one factor of interest is different and other things are equal (or similar). For example, Canada has higher unemployment benefits than the United States, but the people in the two nations are similar. So to study the effect of unemployment benefits on the unemployment rate, economists might compare the United States with Canada.

Statistical Investigation A statistical investigation looks for correlation—a tendency for the values of two variables to move together (either in the same direction or in opposite directions) in a predictable and related way. For example, cigarette smoking and lung cancer are correlated. Sometimes a correlation shows a causal influence of one variable on the other. For example, smoking causes lung cancer. But sometimes the direction of causation is hard to determine.

Steven Levitt, the author of *Freakonomics*, whom you can meet on pp. 224–226, is a master in the use of a combination of the natural experiment and statistical investigation to unscramble cause and effect. He has used the tools of economics to investigate the effects of good parenting on education (not very strong), to explain why drug dealers live with their mothers (because they don't earn enough to live independently), and (controversially) the effects of abortion law on crime.

Economic Experiment An economic experiment puts people in a decision-making situation and varies the influence of one factor at a time to discover how they respond.

Economics as Policy Tool

Economics is useful. It is a toolkit for making decisions. And you don't need to be a fully-fledged economist to think like one and to use the insights of economics as a policy tool.

Economics provides a way of approaching problems in all aspects of our lives. Here, we'll focus on the three broad areas of:

- Personal economic policy
- Business economic policy
- Government economic policy

Personal Economic Policy Should you take out a student loan? Should you get a weekend job? Should you buy a used car or a new one? Should you rent an apartment or take out a loan and buy a condominium? Should you pay off your credit card balance or make just the minimum payment? How should you allocate your time between study, working for a wage, caring for family members, and having fun? How should you allocate your time between studying economics and your other subjects? Should you quit school after getting a bachelor's degree or should you go for a master's or a professional qualification?

All these questions involve a marginal benefit and a marginal cost. And although some of the numbers might be hard to pin down, you will make more solid decisions if you approach these questions with the tools of economics.

Business Economic Policy Should Sony make only flat panel televisions and stop making conventional ones? Should Texaco get more oil and gas from the Gulf of Mexico or from Alaska? Should Palm outsource its online customer services to India or run the operation from California? Should Marvel Studios produce Spider-Man 4, a sequel to Spider-Man 3? Can Microsoft compete with Google in the search engine business? Can eBay compete with the surge of new Internet auction services? Is Jason Giambi really worth $23,400,000 to the New York Yankees?

Like personal economic questions, these business questions involve the evaluation of a marginal benefit and a marginal cost. Some of the questions require a broader investigation of the interactions of individuals and firms. But again, by approaching these questions with the tools of economics and by hiring economists as advisers, businesses can make better decisions.

Government Economic Policy How can California balance its budget? Should the federal government cut taxes or raise them? How can the tax system be simplified? Should people be permitted to invest their Social Security money in stocks that they pick themselves? Should Medicaid and Medicare be extended to the entire population? Should there be a special tax to penalize corporations that send jobs overseas? Should cheap foreign imports of furniture and textiles be limited? Should the farms that grow tomatoes and sugar beets receive a subsidy? Should water be transported from Washington and Oregon to California?

These government policy questions call for decisions that involve the evaluation of a marginal benefit and a marginal cost and an investigation of the interactions of individuals and businesses. Yet again, by approaching these questions with the tools of economics, governments make better decisions.

Notice that all the policy questions we've just posed involve a blend of the positive and the normative. Economics can't help with the normative part—the objective. But for a given objective, economics provides a method of evaluating alternative solutions. That method is to evaluate the marginal benefits and marginal costs and to find the solution that brings the greatest available gain.

Review Quiz

1   What is the distinction between a positive statement and a normative statement? Provide an example (different from those in the chapter) of each type of statement.
2   What is a model? Can you think of a model that you might use (probably without thinking of it as a model) in your everyday life?
3   What are the three ways in which economists try to disentangle cause and effect?
4   How is economics used as a policy tool?
5   What is the role of marginal analysis in the use of economics as a policy tool?

 Work Study Plan 1.4 and get instant feedback.

SUMMARY

Key Points

Definition of Economics (p. 2)

- All economic questions arise from scarcity—from the fact that wants exceed the resources available to satisfy them.
- Economics is the social science that studies the choices that people make as they cope with scarcity.
- The subject divides into microeconomics and macroeconomics.

Two Big Economic Questions (pp. 3–7)

- Two big questions summarize the scope of economics:
  1. How do choices end up determining *what*, *how*, and *for whom* goods and services are produced?
  2. When do choices made in the pursuit of *self-interest* also promote the *social interest*?

The Economic Way of Thinking (pp. 8–10)

- Every choice is a tradeoff—exchanging more of something for less of something else.

- The classic guns-versus-butter tradeoff represents all tradeoffs.
- All economic questions involve tradeoffs.
- The big social tradeoff is that between equality and efficiency.
- The highest-valued alternative forgone is the opportunity cost of what is chosen.
- Choices are made at the margin and respond to incentives.

Economics as Social Science and Policy Tool (pp. 11–12)

- Economists distinguish between positive statements—what is—and normative statements—what ought to be.
- To explain the economic world, economists create and test economic models.
- Economics is used in personal, business, and government economic policy decisions.
- The main policy tool is the evaluation and comparison of marginal cost and marginal benefit.

Key Terms

Big tradeoff, 9
Capital, 4
Economic model, 11
Economics, 2
Entrepreneurship, 4
Factors of production, 3
Goods and services, 3
Human capital, 3
Incentive, 2

Interest, 4
Labor, 3
Land, 3
Macroeconomics, 2
Margin, 10
Marginal benefit, 10
Marginal cost, 10
Microeconomics, 2
Opportunity cost, 9

Profit, 4
Rent, 4
Scarcity, 2
Self-interest, 5
Social interest, 5
Tradeoff, 8
Wages, 4

PROBLEMS and APPLICATIONS

1. Apple Computer Inc. decides to make iTunes freely available in unlimited quantities.
   a. How does Apple's decision change the opportunity cost of a download?
   b. Does Apple's decision change the incentives that people face?
   c. Is Apple's decision an example of a microeconomic or a macroeconomic issue?

2. Which of the following pairs does not match:
   a. Labor and wages?
   b. Land and rent?
   c. Entrepreneurship and profit?
   d. Capital and profit?

3. Explain how the following news headlines concern self-interest and the social interest:
   a. Wal-Mart Expands in Europe
   b. McDonald's Moves into Salads
   c. Food Must Be Labeled with Nutrition Information

4. The night before an economics test, you decide to go to the movies instead of staying home and working your MyEconLab Study Plan. You get 50 percent on your test compared with the 70 percent that you normally score.
   a. Did you face a tradeoff?
   b. What was the opportunity cost of your evening at the movies?

5. Which of the following statements is positive, which is normative, and which can be tested?
   a. The U.S. government should cut its imports.
   b. China is the United States' largest trading partner.
   c. If the price of antiretroviral drugs increases, HIV/AIDS sufferers will decrease their consumption of the drugs.

6. As London prepares to host the 2012 Olympic Games, concern about the cost of the event increases. An example:
   Costs Soar for London Olympics
   The regeneration of East London is set to add extra £1.5 billion to taxpayers' bill.
   The Times, London, July 6, 2006
   Is the cost of regenerating East London an opportunity cost of hosting the 2012 Olympic Games? Explain why or why not.

7. Before starring as Tony Stark in *Iron Man*, Robert Downey Jr. had played in 45 movies that had average first-weekend box office revenues of a bit less than $5 million. *Iron Man* grossed $102 million on its opening weekend.
   a. How do you expect the success of *Iron Man* to influence the opportunity cost of hiring Robert Downey Jr.?
   b. How have the incentives for a movie producer to hire Robert Downey Jr. changed?

8. How would you classify a movie star as a factor of production?

9. How does the creation of a successful movie influence what, how, and for whom goods and services are produced?

10. How does the creation of a successful movie illustrate self-interested choices that are also in the social interest?

11. Look at today's *Wall Street Journal*.
    a. What is the top economic news story? With which of the big questions does it deal? (It must deal with at least one of them and might deal with more than one.)
    b. What tradeoffs does the news item discuss or imply?
    c. Write a brief summary of the news item using the economic vocabulary that you have learned in this chapter and as many as possible of the key terms listed on p. 13.

12. Use the link in MyEconLab (Textbook Resources, Chapter 1) to visit *Resources for Economists on the Internet*. This Web site is a good place from which to search for economic information on the Internet.
    Click on "Blogs, Commentaries, and Podcasts," and then click on the Becker-Posner Blog.
    a. Read the latest blog by these two outstanding economists.
    b. As you read this blog, think about what it is saying about the "what," "how," and "for whom" questions.
    c. As you read this blog, think about what it is saying about self-interest and the social interest.

APPENDIX

Graphs in Economics

**After studying this appendix,
you will be able to:**

- Make and interpret a time-series graph, a cross-section graph, and a scatter diagram

- Distinguish between linear and nonlinear relationships and between relationships that have a maximum and a minimum

- Define and calculate the slope of a line

- Graph relationships among more than two variables

Graphing Data

A graph represents a quantity as a distance on a line. In Fig. A1.1, a distance on the horizontal line represents temperature, measured in degrees Fahrenheit. A movement from left to right shows an increase in temperature. The point 0 represents zero degrees Fahrenheit. To the right of 0, the temperature is positive. To the left of 0 (as indicated by the minus sign), the temperature is negative. A distance on the vertical line represents height, measured in thousands of feet. The point 0 represents sea level. Points above 0 represent feet above sea level. Points below 0 (indicated by a minus sign) represent feet below sea level.

By setting two scales perpendicular to each other, as in Fig. A1.1, we can visualize the relationship between two variables. The scale lines are called *axes*. The vertical line is the *y*-axis, and the horizontal line is the *x*-axis. Each axis has a zero point, which is shared by the two axes and called the *origin*.

We need two bits of information to make a two-variable graph: the value of the *x* variable and the value of the *y* variable. For example, off the coast of Alaska, the temperature is 32 degrees—the value of *x*. A fishing boat is located at 0 feet above sea level—the value of *y*. These two bits of information appear as point *A* in Fig. A1.1. A climber at the top of Mount McKinley on a cold day is 20,320 feet above sea level in a zero-degree gale. These two pieces of information appear as point *B*. On a warmer day, a climber might

FIGURE A1.1   Making a Graph

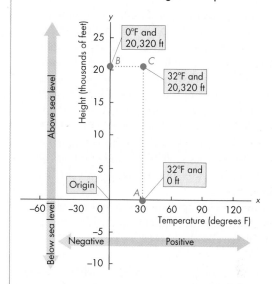

Graphs have axes that measure quantities as distances. Here, the horizontal axis (*x*-axis) measures temperature, and the vertical axis (*y*-axis) measures height. Point *A* represents a fishing boat at sea level (0 on the *y*-axis) on a day when the temperature is 32°F. Point *B* represents a climber at the top of Mt. McKinley, 20,320 feet above sea level at a temperature of 0°F. Point *C* represents a climber at the top of Mt. McKinley, 20,320 feet above sea level at a temperature of 32°F.

myeconlab   animation

be at the peak of Mt. McKinley when the temperature is 32 degrees, at point *C*.

We can draw two lines, called *coordinates*, from point *C*. One, called the *y*-coordinate, runs from *C* to the horizontal axis. Its length is the same as the value marked off on the *y*-axis. The other, called the *x*-coordinate, runs from *C* to the vertical axis. Its length is the same as the value marked off on the *x*-axis. We describe a point on a graph by the values of its *x*-coordinate and its *y*-coordinate.

Graphs like that in Fig. A1.1 can show any type of quantitative data on two variables. Economists use three types of graphs based on the principles in Fig. A1.1 to reveal and describe the relationships among variables. They are

- Time-series graphs
- Cross-section graphs
- Scatter diagrams

Time-Series Graphs

A **time-series graph** measures time (for example, months or years) on the *x*-axis and the variable or variables in which we are interested on the *y*-axis. Figure A1.2 is an example of a time-series graph. It provides some information about the price of gasoline. In this figure, we measure time in years starting in 1973. We measure the price of gasoline (the variable that we are interested in) on the *y*-axis.

The point of a time-series graph is to enable us to visualize how a variable has changed over time and how its value in one period relates to its value in another period.

A time-series graph conveys an enormous amount of information quickly and easily, as this example illustrates. It shows

- The *level* of the price of gasoline—when it is *high* and *low*. When the line is a long way from the *x*-axis, the price is high, as it was, for example, in 1981. When the line is close to the *x*-axis, the price is low, as it was, for example, in 1998.
- How the price *changes*—whether it *rises* or *falls*. When the line slopes upward, as in 1979, the price is rising. When the line slopes downward, as in 1986, the price is falling.
- The *speed* with which the price changes—whether it rises or falls *quickly* or *slowly*. If the line is very steep, then the price rises or falls quickly. If the line is not steep, the price rises or falls slowly. For example, the price rose quickly between 1978 and 1980 and slowly between 1994 and 1996. The price fell quickly between 1985 and 1986 and slowly between 1990 and 1994.

A time-series graph also reveals whether there is a **trend**—a general tendency for a variable to move in one direction. A trend might be upward or downward. In Fig. A1.2, the price of gasoline had a general tendency to fall during the 1980s and 1990s. That is, although the price rose and fell, the general tendency was for it to fall—the price had a downward trend. During the 2000s, the trend has been upward.

A time-series graph also helps us to detect fluctuations in a variable around its trend. You can see some peaks and troughs in the price of gasoline in Fig. A1.2.

Finally, a time-series graph also lets us quickly compare the variable in different periods. Figure A1.2 shows that the 1970s and 1980s were different from

FIGURE A1.2   A Time-Series Graph

A time-series graph plots the level of a variable on the *y*-axis against time (day, week, month, or year) on the *x*-axis. This graph shows the price of gasoline (in 2006 dollars per gallon) each year from 1973 to 2006. It shows us when the price of gasoline was *high* and when it was *low*, when the price *increased* and when it *decreased*, and when the price changed *quickly* and when it changed *slowly*.

myeconlab   animation

the 1990s. The price of gasoline fluctuated more during the 1970s and 1980s than it did in the 1990s.

You can see that a time-series graph conveys a wealth of information, and it does so in much less space than we have used to describe only some of its features. But you do have to "read" the graph to obtain all this information.

Cross-Section Graphs

A **cross-section graph** shows the values of an economic variable for different groups or categories at a point in time. Figure A1.3, called a *bar chart*, is an example of a cross-section graph.

The bar chart in Fig. A1.3 shows 10 leisure pursuits and the percentage of the U. S. population that participated in them during 2005. The length of each bar indicates the percentage of the population. This figure enables you to compare the popularity of these 10 activities. And you can do so much more quickly and clearly than by looking at a list of numbers.

FIGURE A1.3   A Cross-Section Graph

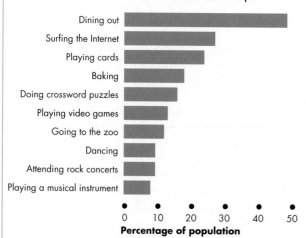

A cross-section graph shows the level of a variable across categories or groups. This bar chart shows 10 popular leisure activities and the percentage of the U.S. population that engages in each of them.

myeconlab   animation

Scatter Diagrams

A **scatter diagram** plots the value of one variable against the value of another variable. Such a graph reveals whether a relationship exists between two variables and describes their relationship. Figure A1.4(a) shows the relationship between expenditure and income. Each point shows expenditure per person and income per person in a given year from 1997 to 2007. The points are "scattered" within the graph. The point labeled A tells us that in 2000, income per person was $25,472 and expenditure per person was $23,862. The dots in this graph form a pattern, which reveals that as income increases, expenditure increases.

Figure A1.4(b) shows the relationship between the number of computers sold and the price of a computer. This graph shows that as the price of a computer falls, the number of computers sold increases.

Figure A1.4(c) shows a scatter diagram of inflation and unemployment in the United States. Here, the dots show no clear relationship between these two variables.

FIGURE A1.4   Scatter Diagrams

(a) Expenditure and income

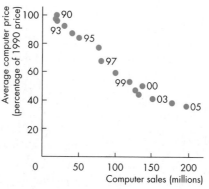

(b) Computer sales and prices

(c) Unemployment and inflation

A scatter diagram reveals the relationship between two variables. Part (a) shows the relationship between expenditure and income. Each point shows the values of the two variables in a specific year. For example, point A shows that in 2000, average income was $25,472 and average expenditure was $23,862. The pattern formed by the points shows that as income increases, expenditure increases.

Part (b) shows the relationship between the price of a computer and the number of computers sold from 1990 to 2005. This graph shows that as the price of a computer falls, the number of computers sold increases.

Part (c) shows a scatter diagram of the U.S. inflation rate and the unemployment rate from 1998 to 2008. This graph shows that inflation and unemployment are not closely related.

myeconlab   animation

Breaks in the Axes Two of the graphs you've just looked at, Fig. A1.4(a) and Fig. A1.4(c), have breaks in their axes, as shown by the small gaps. The breaks indicate that there are jumps from the origin, 0, to the first values recorded.

In Fig. A1.4(a), the breaks are used because the lowest value of expenditure exceeds $20,000 and the lowest value of income exceeds $20,000. With no breaks in the axes, there would be a lot of empty space, all the points would be crowded into the top right corner, and we would not be able to see whether a relationship exists between these two variables. By breaking the axes, we are able to bring the relationship into view.

Putting a break in one or both axes is like using a zoom lens to bring the relationship into the center of the graph and magnify it so that the relationship fills the graph.

Misleading Graphs Breaks can be used to highlight a relationship, but they can also be used to mislead—to make a graph that lies. The most common way of making a graph lie is to use axis breaks and to either stretch or compress a scale. For example, suppose that in Fig. A1.4(a), the y-axis that measures expenditure ran from zero to $35,000 while the x-axis was the same as the one shown. The graph would now create the impression that despite a huge increase in income, expenditure had barely changed.

To avoid being misled, it is a good idea to get into the habit of always looking closely at the values and the labels on the axes of a graph before you start to interpret it.

Correlation and Causation A scatter diagram that shows a clear relationship between two variables, such as Fig. A1.4(a) or Fig. A1.4(b), tells us that the two variables have a high correlation. When a high correlation is present, we can predict the value of one variable from the value of the other variable. But correlation does not imply causation.

Sometimes a high correlation is a coincidence, but sometimes it does arise from a causal relationship. It is likely, for example, that rising income causes rising expenditure (Fig. A1.4a) and that the falling price of a computer causes more computers to be sold (Fig. A1.4b).

You've now seen how we can use graphs in economics to show economic data and to reveal relationships. Next, we'll learn how economists use graphs to construct and display economic models.

◤ Graphs Used in Economic Models

The graphs used in economics are not always designed to show real-world data. Often they are used to show general relationships among the variables in an economic model.

An *economic model* is a stripped-down, simplified description of an economy or of a component of an economy such as a business or a household. It consists of statements about economic behavior that can be expressed as equations or as curves in a graph. Economists use models to explore the effects of different policies or other influences on the economy in ways that are similar to the use of model airplanes in wind tunnels and models of the climate.

You will encounter many different kinds of graphs in economic models, but there are some repeating patterns. Once you've learned to recognize these patterns, you will instantly understand the meaning of a graph. Here, we'll look at the different types of curves that are used in economic models, and we'll see some everyday examples of each type of curve. The patterns to look for in graphs are the four cases in which

- Variables move in the same direction.
- Variables move in opposite directions.
- Variables have a maximum or a minimum.
- Variables are unrelated.

Let's look at these four cases.

Variables That Move in the Same Direction

Figure A1.5 shows graphs of the relationships between two variables that move up and down together. A relationship between two variables that move in the same direction is called a **positive relationship** or a **direct relationship**. A line that slopes upward shows such a relationship.

Figure A1.5 shows three types of relationships, one that has a straight line and two that have curved lines. But all the lines in these three graphs are called curves. Any line on a graph—no matter whether it is straight or curved—is called a *curve*.

A relationship shown by a straight line is called a **linear relationship**. Figure A1.5(a) shows a linear relationship between the number of miles traveled in

FIGURE A1.5 Positive (Direct) Relationships

(a) Positive linear relationship   **(b) Positive, becoming steeper**   **(c) Positive, becoming less steep**

Each part of this figure shows a positive (direct) relationship between two variables. That is, as the value of the variable measured on the x-axis increases, so does the value of the variable measured on the y-axis. Part (a) shows a linear relationship—as the two variables increase together, we move along a straight line. Part (b) shows a positive relationship such that as the two variables increase together, we move along a curve that becomes steeper. Part (c) shows a positive relationship such that as the two variables increase together, we move along a curve that becomes flatter.

5 hours and speed. For example, point *A* shows that we will travel 200 miles in 5 hours if our speed is 40 miles an hour. If we double our speed to 80 miles an hour, we will travel 400 miles in 5 hours.

Figure A1.5(b) shows the relationship between distance sprinted and recovery time (the time it takes the heart rate to return to its normal resting rate). This relationship is an upward-sloping one that starts out quite flat but then becomes steeper as we move along the curve away from the origin. The reason this curve slopes upward and becomes steeper is because the additional recovery time needed from sprinting an additional 100 yards increases. It takes less than 5 minutes to recover from sprinting 100 yards but more than 10 minutes to recover from sprinting 200 yards.

Figure A1.5(c) shows the relationship between the number of problems worked by a student and the amount of study time. This relationship is an upward-sloping one that starts out quite steep and becomes flatter as we move along the curve away from the origin. Study time becomes less productive as the student spends more hours studying and becomes more tired.

Variables That Move in Opposite Directions

Figure A1.6 shows relationships between things that move in opposite directions. A relationship between variables that move in opposite directions is called a **negative relationship** or an **inverse relationship**.

Figure A1.6(a) shows the relationship between the hours spent playing squash and the hours spent playing tennis when the total number of hours available is 5. One extra hour spent playing tennis means one hour less playing squash and vice versa. This relationship is negative and linear.

Figure A1.6(b) shows the relationship between the cost per mile traveled and the length of a journey. The longer the journey, the lower is the cost per mile. But as the journey length increases, even though the cost per mile decreases, the fall in the cost is smaller the longer the journey. This feature of the relationship is shown by the fact that the curve slopes downward, starting out steep at a short journey length and then becoming flatter as the journey length increases. This relationship arises because some of the costs are fixed, such as auto insurance, and the fixed costs are spread over a longer journey.

FIGURE A1.6   Negative (Inverse) Relationships

(a) Negative linear relationship   **(b) Negative, becoming less steep**   **(c) Negative, becoming steeper**

Each part of this figure shows a negative (inverse) relationship between two variables. That is, as the value of the variable measured on the x-axis increases, the value of the variable measured on the y-axis decreases. Part (a) shows a linear relationship. The total time spent playing tennis and squash is 5 hours. As the time spent playing tennis increases, the time spent playing squash decreases, and we move along a straight line. Part (b) shows a negative relationship such that as the journey length increases, the travel cost decreases as we move along a curve that becomes less steep. Part (c) shows a negative relationship such that as leisure time increases, the number of problems worked decreases as we move along a curve that becomes steeper.

 animation

Figure A1.6(c) shows the relationship between the amount of leisure time and the number of problems worked by a student. Increasing leisure time produces an increasingly large reduction in the number of problems worked. This relationship is a negative one that starts out with a gentle slope at a small number of leisure hours and becomes steeper as the number of leisure hours increases. This relationship is a different view of the idea shown in Fig. A1.5(c).

Variables That Have a Maximum or a Minimum

Many relationships in economic models have a maximum or a minimum. For example, firms try to make the maximum possible profit and to produce at the lowest possible cost. Figure A1.7 shows relationships that have a maximum or a minimum.

Figure A1.7(a) shows the relationship between rainfall and wheat yield. When there is no rainfall, wheat will not grow, so the yield is zero. As the rainfall increases up to 10 days a month, the wheat yield increases. With 10 rainy days each month, the wheat yield reaches its maximum at 40 bushels an acre (point *A*). Rain in excess of 10 days a month starts to lower the yield of wheat. If every day is rainy, the wheat suffers from a lack of sunshine and the yield decreases to zero. This relationship is one that starts out sloping upward, reaches a maximum, and then slopes downward.

Figure A1.7(b) shows the reverse case—a relationship that begins sloping downward, falls to a minimum, and then slopes upward. Most economic costs are like this relationship. An example is the relationship between the cost per mile and speed for a car trip. At low speeds, the car is creeping in a traffic snarl-up. The number of miles per gallon is low, so the cost per mile is high. At high speeds, the car is traveling faster than its efficient speed, using a large quantity of gasoline, and again the number of miles per gallon is low and the cost per mile is high. At a speed of 55 miles an hour, the cost per mile is at its minimum (point *B*). This relationship is one that starts out sloping downward, reaches a minimum, and then slopes upward.

FIGURE A1.7   Maximum and Minimum Points

(a) Relationship with a maximum

(b) Relationship with a minimum

Part (a) shows a relationship that has a maximum point, *A*. The curve slopes upward as it rises to its maximum point, is flat at its maximum, and then slopes downward.

Part (b) shows a relationship with a minimum point, *B*. The curve slopes downward as it falls to its minimum, is flat at its minimum, and then slopes upward.

myeconlab animation

Variables That Are Unrelated

There are many situations in which no matter what happens to the value of one variable, the other variable remains constant. Sometimes we want to show the independence between two variables in a graph, and Fig. A1.8 shows two ways of achieving this.

In describing the graphs in Fig. A1.5 through A1.7, we have talked about curves that slope upward or slope downward, and curves that become less steep or steeper. Let's spend a little time discussing exactly what we mean by slope and how we measure the slope of a curve.

FIGURE A1.8   Variables That Are Unrelated

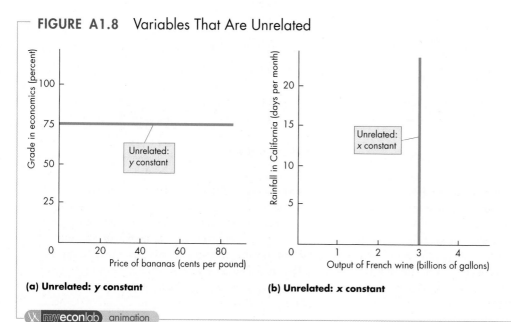

(a) Unrelated: *y* constant

(b) Unrelated: *x* constant

This figure shows how we can graph two variables that are unrelated. In part (a), a student's grade in economics is plotted at 75 percent on the *y*-axis regardless of the price of bananas on the *x*-axis. The curve is horizontal.

In part (b), the output of the vineyards of France on the *x*-axis does not vary with the rainfall in California on the *y*-axis. The curve is vertical.

myeconlab animation

◆ The Slope of a Relationship

We can measure the influence of one variable on another by the slope of the relationship. The **slope** of a relationship is the change in the value of the variable measured on the y-axis divided by the change in the value of the variable measured on the x-axis. We use the Greek letter Δ (*delta*) to represent "change in." Thus Δy means the change in the value of the variable measured on the y-axis, and Δx means the change in the value of the variable measured on the x-axis. Therefore the slope of the relationship is

$$\Delta y / \Delta x.$$

If a large change in the variable measured on the y-axis (Δy) is associated with a small change in the variable measured on the x-axis (Δx), the slope is large and the curve is steep. If a small change in the variable measured on the y-axis (Δy) is associated with a large change in the variable measured on the x-axis (Δx), the slope is small and the curve is flat.

We can make the idea of slope clearer by doing some calculations.

The Slope of a Straight Line

The slope of a straight line is the same regardless of where on the line you calculate it. The slope of a straight line is constant. Let's calculate the slopes of the lines in Fig. A1.9. In part (a), when x increases

FIGURE A1.9   The Slope of a Straight Line

(a) Positive slope

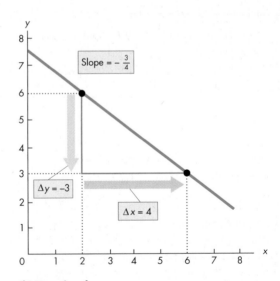

(b) Negative slope

To calculate the slope of a straight line, we divide the change in the value of the variable measured on the y-axis (Δy) by the change in the value of the variable measured on the x-axis (Δx) as we move along the curve.

Part (a) shows the calculation of a positive slope. When x increases from 2 to 6, Δx equals 4. That change in x

brings about an increase in y from 3 to 6, so Δy equals 3. The slope ($\Delta y / \Delta x$) equals 3/4.

Part (b) shows the calculation of a negative slope. When x increases from 2 to 6, Δx equals 4. That increase in x brings about a decrease in y from 6 to 3, so Δy equals –3. The slope ($\Delta y / \Delta x$) equals –3/4.

from 2 to 6, y increases from 3 to 6. The change in x is +4—that is, Δx is 4. The change in y is +3—that is, Δy is 3. The slope of that line is

$$\frac{\Delta y}{\Delta x} = \frac{3}{4}.$$

In part (b), when x increases from 2 to 6, y decreases from 6 to 3. The change in y is *minus* 3—that is, Δy is –3. The change in x is *plus* 4—that is, Δx is 4. The slope of the curve is

$$\frac{\Delta y}{\Delta x} = \frac{-3}{4}.$$

Notice that the two slopes have the same magnitude (3/4), but the slope of the line in part (a) is positive (+3/+4 = 3/4) while that in part (b) is negative (–3/+4 = –3/4). The slope of a positive relationship is positive; the slope of a negative relationship is negative.

The Slope of a Curved Line

The slope of a curved line is trickier. The slope of a curved line is not constant, so the slope depends on where on the curved line we calculate it. There are two ways to calculate the slope of a curved line: You can calculate the slope at a point, or you can calculate the slope across an arc of the curve. Let's look at the two alternatives.

Slope at a Point To calculate the slope at a point on a curve, you need to construct a straight line that has the same slope as the curve at the point in question. Figure A1.10 shows how this is done. Suppose you want to calculate the slope of the curve at point A. Place a ruler on the graph so that it touches point A and no other point on the curve, then draw a straight line along the edge of the ruler. The straight red line is this line, and it is the tangent to the curve at point A. If the ruler touches the curve only at point A, then the slope of the curve at point A must be the same as the slope of the edge of the ruler. If the curve and the ruler do not have the same slope, the line along the edge of the ruler will cut the curve instead of just touching it.

Now that you have found a straight line with the same slope as the curve at point A, you can calculate the slope of the curve at point A by calculating the slope of the straight line. Along the straight line, as x

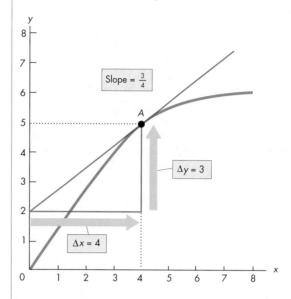

FIGURE A1.10   Slope at a Point

To calculate the slope of the curve at point A, draw the red line that just touches the curve at A—the tangent. The slope of this straight line is calculated by dividing the change in y by the change in x along the line. When x increases from 0 to 4, Δx equals 4. That change in x is associated with an increase in y from 2 to 5, so Δy equals 3. The slope of the red line is 3/4. So the slope of the curve at point A is 3/4.

myeconlab animation

increases from 0 to 4 ($\Delta x = 4$) y increases from 2 to 5 ($\Delta y = 3$). Therefore the slope of the straight line is

$$\frac{\Delta y}{\Delta x} = \frac{3}{4}.$$

So the slope of the curve at point A is 3/4.

Slope Across an Arc An arc of a curve is a piece of a curve. In Fig. A1.11, you are looking at the same curve as in Fig. A1.10. But instead of calculating the slope at point A, we are going to calculate the slope across the arc from B to C. You can see that the slope at B is greater than at C. When we calculate the slope across an arc, we are calculating the average slope between two points. As we move along the arc from B to C, x increases from 3 to 5 and y increases from 4 to 5.5. The change in x is 2 ($\Delta x = 2$), and the change

FIGURE A1.11   Slope Across an Arc

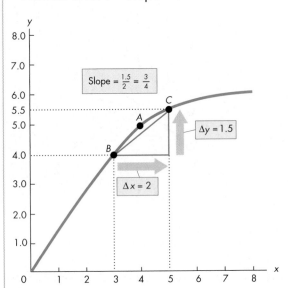

Slope = $\frac{1.5}{2}$ = $\frac{3}{4}$

$\Delta y = 1.5$

$\Delta x = 2$

To calculate the average slope of the curve along the arc
BC, draw a straight line from B to C. The slope of the line
BC is calculated by dividing the change in y by the change
in x. In moving from B to C, Δx equals 2 and Δy equals
1.5. The slope of the line BC is 1.5 divided by 2, or 3/4.
So the slope of the curve across the arc BC is 3/4.

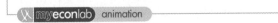

myeconlab   animation

in y is 1.5 (Δy = 1.5). Therefore the slope is

$$\frac{\Delta y}{\Delta x} = \frac{1.5}{2} = \frac{3}{4}.$$

So the slope of the curve across the arc *BC* is 3/4.

This calculation gives us the slope of the curve
between points *B* and *C*. The actual slope calculated
is the slope of the straight line from *B* to *C*. This
slope approximates the average slope of the curve
along the arc *BC*. In this particular example, the
slope across the arc *BC* is identical to the slope of the
curve at point *A*. But the calculation of the slope of a
curve does not always work out so neatly. You might
have fun constructing some more examples and a few
counterexamples.

You now know how to make and interpret a
graph. But so far, we've limited our attention to
graphs of two variables. We're now going to learn
how to graph more than two variables.

Graphing Relationships Among More Than Two Variables

We have seen that we can graph the relationship
between two variables as a point formed by the x-
and y-coordinates in a two-dimensional graph. You
might be thinking that although a two-dimensional
graph is informative, most of the things in which you
are likely to be interested involve relationships among
many variables, not just two. For example, the
amount of ice cream consumed depends on the price
of ice cream and the temperature. If ice cream is
expensive and the temperature is low, people eat
much less ice cream than when ice cream is inexpensive and the temperature is high. For any given price
of ice cream, the quantity consumed varies with the
temperature; and for any given temperature, the
quantity of ice cream consumed varies with its price.

Figure A1.12 shows a relationship among three
variables. The table shows the number of gallons of
ice cream consumed each day at various temperatures and ice cream prices. How can we graph these
numbers?

To graph a relationship that involves more than
two variables, we use the *ceteris paribus* assumption.

Ceteris Paribus   Ceteris paribus means "if all other relevant things remain the same." To isolate the relationship of interest in a laboratory experiment, we
hold other things constant. We use the same method
to graph a relationship with more than two variables.

Figure A1.12(a) shows an example. There, you
can see what happens to the quantity of ice cream
consumed when the price of ice cream varies and
the temperature is held constant. The line labeled
70°F shows the relationship between ice cream consumption and the price of ice cream if the temperature remains at 70°F. The numbers used to plot that
line are those in the third column of the table in
Fig. A1.12. For example, if the temperature is 70°F,
10 gallons are consumed when the price is 60¢ a
scoop, and 18 gallons are consumed when the price
is 30¢ a scoop. The curve labeled 90°F shows consumption as the price varies if the temperature
remains at 90°F.

We can also show the relationship between ice
cream consumption and temperature when the
price of ice cream remains constant, as shown in
Fig. A1.12(b). The curve labeled 60¢ shows how the
consumption of ice cream varies with the tempera-

FIGURE A1.12   Graphing a Relationship Among Three Variables

(a) Price and consumption at a given temperature

(b) Temperature and consumption at a given price

(c) Temperature and price at a given consumption

	Ice cream consumption (gallons per day)			
Price (cents per scoop)	30°F	50°F	70°F	90°F
15	12	18	25	50
30	10	12	18	37
45	7	10	13	27
60	5	7	**10**	20
75	3	5	7	14
90	2	3	5	10
105	1	2	3	6

Ice cream consumption depends on its price and the temperature. The table tell us how many gallons of ice cream are consumed each day at different prices and different temperatures. For example, if the price is 60¢ a scoop and the temperature is 70°F, 10 gallons of ice cream are consumed. This set of values is highlighted in the table and each part of the figure.

To graph a relationship among three variables, the value of one variable is held constant. Part (a) shows the relationship between price and consumption when temperature is held constant. One curve holds temperature at 90°F and the other holds it at 70°F. Part (b) shows the relationship between temperature and consumption when price is held constant. One curve holds the price at 60¢ a scoop and the other holds it at 15¢ a scoop. Part (c) shows the relationship between temperature and price when consumption is held constant. One curve holds consumption at 10 gallons and the other holds it at 7 gallons.

myeconlab animation

ture when the price of ice cream is 60¢ a scoop, and a second curve shows the relationship when the price is 15¢ a scoop. For example, at 60¢ a scoop, 10 gallons are consumed when the temperature is 70°F and 20 gallons are consumed when the temperature is 90°F.

Figure A1.12(c) shows the combinations of temperature and price that result in a constant consumption of ice cream. One curve shows the combinations that result in 10 gallons a day being consumed, and the other shows the combinations that result in 7 gallons a day being consumed. A high price and a

high temperature lead to the same consumption as a lower price and a lower temperature. For example, 10 gallons of ice cream are consumed at 70°F and 60¢ a scoop, at 90°F and 90¢ a scoop, and at 50°F and 45¢ a scoop.

With what you have learned about graphs, you can move forward with your study of economics. There are no graphs in this book that are more complicated than those that have been explained in this appendix.

MATHEMATICAL NOTE

Equations of Straight Lines

If a straight line in a graph describes the relationship between two variables, we call it a linear relationship. Figure 1 shows the *linear relationship* between a person's expenditure and income. This person spends $100 a week (by borrowing or spending previous savings) when income is zero. And out of each dollar earned, this person spends 50 cents (and saves 50 cents).

All linear relationships are described by the same general equation. We call the quantity that is measured on the horizontal axis (or x-axis) *x,* and we call the quantity that is measured on the vertical axis (or y-axis) *y.* In the case of Fig. 1, *x* is income and *y* is expenditure.

A Linear Equation

The equation that describes a straight-line relationship between *x* and *y* is

$$y = a + bx.$$

In this equation, *a* and *b* are fixed numbers and they are called constants. The values of *x* and *y* vary, so these numbers are called variables. Because the equation describes a straight line, the equation is called a *linear equation.*

The equation tells us that when the value of *x* is zero, the value of *y* is *a.* We call the constant *a* the *y*-axis intercept. The reason is that on the graph the straight line hits the *y*-axis at a value equal to *a.* Figure 1 illustrates the *y*-axis intercept.

For positive values of *x,* the value of *y* exceeds *a.* The constant *b* tells us by how much *y* increases above *a* as *x* increases. The constant *b* is the slope of the line.

Slope of Line

As we explain in the chapter, the *slope* of a relationship is the change in the value of *y* divided by the change in the value of *x.* We use the Greek letter Δ (delta) to represent "change in." So Δ*y* means the change in the value of the variable measured on the *y*-axis, and Δ*x* means the change in the value of the variable measured on the *x*-axis. Therefore the slope of the relationship is

$$\Delta y / \Delta x.$$

To see why the slope is *b,* suppose that initially the value of *x* is x_1, or $200 in Fig. 2. The corresponding value of *y* is y_1, also $200 in Fig. 2. The equation of the line tells us that

$$y_1 = a + bx_1. \tag{1}$$

Now the value of *x* increases by Δ*x* to $x_1 + \Delta x$ (or $400 in Fig. 2). And the value of *y* increases by Δ*y* to $y_1 + \Delta y$ (or $300 in Fig. 2).

The equation of the line now tells us that

$$y_1 + \Delta y = a + b(x_1 + \Delta x) \tag{2}$$

Figure 1 Linear relationship

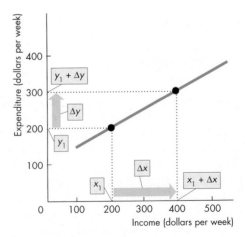

Figure 2 Calculating slope

To calculate the slope of the line, subtract equation (1) from equation (2) to obtain

$$\Delta y = b\Delta x \qquad (3)$$

and now divide equation (3) by Δx to obtain

$$\Delta y/\Delta x = b.$$

So the slope of the line is b.

Position of Line

The y-axis intercept determines the position of the line on the graph. Figure 3 illustrates the relationship between the y-axis intercept and the position of the line. In this graph, the y-axis measures saving and the x-axis measures income.

When the y-axis intercept, a, is positive, the line hits the y-axis at a positive value of y—as the blue line does. Its y-axis intercept is 100. When the y-axis intercept, a, is zero, the line hits the y-axis at the origin—as the purple line does. Its y-axis intercept is 0. When the y-axis intercept, a, is negative, the line hits the y-axis at a negative value of y—as the red line does. Its y-axis intercept is –100.

As the equations of the three lines show, the value of the y-axis intercept does not influence the slope of the line. All three lines have a slope equal to 0.5.

Positive Relationships

Figure 1 shows a positive relationship—the two variables x and y move in the same direction. All positive relationships have a slope that is positive. In the equation of the line, the constant b is positive. In this example, the y-axis intercept, a, is 100. The slope b equals $\Delta y/\Delta x$, which in Fig. 2 is 100/200 or 0.5. The equation of the line is

$$y = 100 + 0.5x.$$

Negative Relationships

Figure 4 shows a negative relationship—the two variables x and y move in the opposite direction. All negative relationships have a slope that is negative. In the equation of the line, the constant b is negative. In the example in Fig. 4, the y-axis intercept, a, is 30. The slope, b, equals $\Delta y/\Delta x$, which is –20/2 or –10. The equation of the line is

$$y = 30 + (-10)x$$

or

$$y = 30 - 10x.$$

Example

A straight line has a y-axis intercept of 50 and a slope of 2. What is the equation of this line?
The equation of a straight line is

$$y = a + bx$$

where a is the y-axis intercept and b is the slope. So the equation is

$$y = 50 + 2x.$$

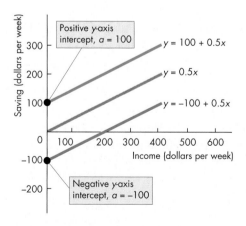

Figure 3 The y-axis intercept

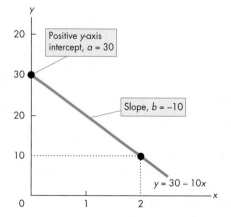

Figure 4 Negative relationship

Review Quiz

1 What are the three types of graphs used to show economic data?
2 Give an example of a time-series graph.
3 List three things that a time-series graph shows quickly and easily.
4 Give three examples, different from those in the chapter, of scatter diagrams that show a positive relationship, a negative relationship, and no relationship.
5 Draw some graphs to show the relationships between two variables
   a. That move in the same direction.
   b. That move in opposite directions.
   c. That have a maximum.
   d. That have a minimum.
6 Which of the relationships in question 5 is a positive relationship and which is a negative relationship?
7 What are the two ways of calculating the slope of a curved line?
8 How do we graph a relationship among more than two variables?

 Work Study Plan 1.A and get instant feedback.

SUMMARY

Key Points

Graphing Data (pp. 15–18)

- A time-series graph shows the trend and fluctuations in a variable over time.
- A cross-section graph shows how the value of a variable changes across the members of a population.
- A scatter diagram shows the relationship between two variables. It shows whether two variables are positively related, negatively related, or unrelated.

Graphs Used in Economic Models (pp. 18–21)

- Graphs are used to show relationships among variables in economic models.
- Relationships can be positive (an upward-sloping curve), negative (a downward-sloping curve), positive and then negative (have a maximum point), negative and then positive (have a minimum point), or unrelated (a horizontal or vertical curve).

The Slope of a Relationship (pp. 22–24)

- The slope of a relationship is calculated as the change in the value of the variable measured on the y-axis divided by the change in the value of the variable measured on the x-axis—that is, $\Delta y/\Delta x$.
- A straight line has a constant slope.
- A curved line has a varying slope. To calculate the slope of a curved line, we calculate the slope at a point or across an arc.

Graphing Relationships Among More Than Two Variables (pp. 24–25)

- To graph a relationship among more than two variables, we hold constant the values of all the variables except two.
- We then plot the value of one of the variables against the value of another.

Key Figures

Key Terms

PROBLEMS and APPLICATIONS

myeconlab Work problems 1–5 in Chapter 1A Study Plan and get instant feedback.
Work problems 6–10 as Homework, a Quiz, or a Test if assigned by your instructor.

1. The spreadsheet provides data on the U.S. economy: Column A is the year, column B is the inflation rate, column C is the interest rate, column D is the growth rate, and column E is the unemployment rate.

	A	B	C	D	E
1	1997	2.8	7.6	2.5	5.6
2	1998	2.9	7.4	3.7	5.4
3	1999	2.3	7.3	4.5	4.9
4	2000	1.6	6.5	4.2	4.5
5	2001	2.2	7.0	4.4	4.2
6	2002	3.4	7.6	3.7	4.0
7	2003	2.8	7.1	0.8	4.7
8	2004	1.6	6.5	3.6	5.8
9	2005	2.3	5.7	3.1	6.0
10	2006	2.5	5.6	2.9	4.6
11	2007	4.1	5.6	2.2	4.6

 a. Draw a time-series graph of the inflation rate.
 b. In which year(s) (i) was inflation highest, (ii) was inflation lowest, (iii) did it increase, (iv) did it decrease, (v) did it increase most, and (vi) did it decrease most?
 c. What was the main trend in inflation?
 d. Draw a scatter diagram of the inflation rate and the interest rate. Describe the relationship.
 e. Draw a scatter diagram of the growth rate and the unemployment rate. Describe the relationship.

2. **'Hulk' Tops Box Office With Sales of $54.5 Million:**

Movie	Theaters (number)	Revenue (dollars per theater)
Hulk	3,505	15,560
The Happening	2,986	10,214
Zohan	3,462	4,737
Crystal Skull	3,804	3,561

Bloomberg.com, June 15, 2008

 a. Draw a graph to show the relationship between the revenue per theater on the y-axis and the number of theaters on the x-axis. Describe the relationship.
 b. Calculate the slope of the relationship between 3,462 and 3,804 theaters.

3. Calculate the slope of the following relationship.

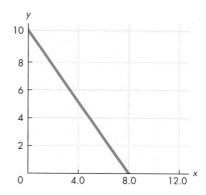

4. Calculate the slope of the following relationship:
 a. At point A and at point B.
 b. Across the arc AB.

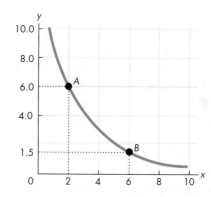

5. The table gives the price of a balloon ride, the temperature, and the number of rides a day.

Price (dollars per ride)	Balloon rides (number per day)		
	50°F	70°F	90°F
5	32	40	50
10	27	32	40
15	18	27	32

Draw graphs to show the relationship between
 a. The price and the number of rides, holding the temperature constant. Describe this relationship.
 b. The number of rides and temperature, holding the price constant.

6. The spreadsheet provides data on oil and gasoline: Column A is the year, column B is the price of oil (dollars per barrel), column C is the price of gasoline (cents per gallon), column D is U.S. oil production, and column E is the U.S. quantity of gasoline refined (both in millions of barrels per day).

	A	B	C	D	E
1	1997	16	117	2.35	8.3
2	1998	9	98	2.28	8.3
3	1999	24	131	2.15	8.3
4	2000	22	145	2.13	8.0
5	2001	18	111	2.12	8.3
6	2002	30	144	2.10	8.8
7	2003	28	153	2.07	8.7
8	2004	36	184	1.98	9.2
9	2005	52	224	1.89	8.9
10	2006	57	239	1.86	9.4
11	2007	90	303	1.86	9.1

a. Draw a time-series graph of the quantity of gasoline refined.
b. In which year(s) (i) was the quantity of gasoline refined highest, (ii) was it lowest, (iii) did it increase, (iv) did it decrease, (v) did it increase most, and (vi) did it decrease most?
c. What was the main trend in this quantity?
d. Draw a scatter diagram of the price of oil and the quantity of oil. Describe the relationship.
e. Draw a scatter diagram of the price of gasoline and the quantity of gasoline. Describe the relationship.

7. Draw a graph that shows the relationship between the two variables x and y:

x	0	1	2	3	4	5
y	25	24	22	18	12	0

a. Is the relationship positive or negative?
b. Does the slope of the relationship increase or decrease as the value of x increases?
c. Think of some economic relationships that might be similar to this one.
d. Calculate the slope of the relationship between x and y when x equals 3.
e. Calculate the slope of the relationship across the arc as x increases from 4 to 5.

8. Calculate the slope of the following relationship at point A.

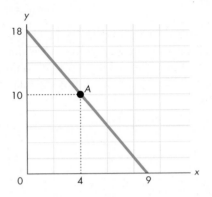

9. Calculate the slope of the following relationship:
a. At point A and at point B.
b. Across the arc AB.

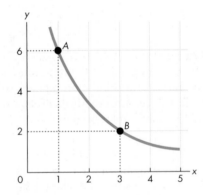

10. The table gives information about umbrellas: price, the number purchased, and rainfall.

Price (dollars per umbrella)	Umbrellas (number per day)		
	0	1	2
	(inches of rainfall)		
20	4	7	8
30	2	4	7
40	1	2	4

Draw graphs to show the relationship between
a. Price and the number of umbrellas purchased, holding the amount of rainfall constant. Describe this relationship.
b. The number of umbrellas purchased and the amount of rainfall, holding the price constant. Describe this relationship.

2

The Economic Problem

After studying this chapter, you will be able to:

- Define the production possibilities frontier and calculate opportunity cost

- Distinguish between production possibilities and preferences and describe an efficient allocation of resources

- Explain how current production choices expand future production possibilities

- Explain how specialization and trade expand our production possibilities

- Describe the economic institutions that coordinate decisions

Why does food cost much more today than it did a few years ago? One reason is that we now use part of our corn crop to produce ethanol, a clean biofuel substitute for gasoline. Another reason is that drought in some parts of the world has decreased global grain production. In this chapter, you will study an economic model—the production possibilities frontier—and you will learn why ethanol production and drought have increased the cost of producing food. You will also learn how to assess whether it is a good idea to increase corn production to produce fuel; how we can expand our production possibilities; and how we gain by trading with others.

At the end of the chapter, in *Reading Between the Lines*, we'll apply what you've learned to understanding why ethanol production is raising the cost of food.

Production Possibilities and Opportunity Cost

Every working day, in mines, factories, shops, and offices and on farms and construction sites across the United States, 138 million people produce a vast variety of goods and services valued at $50 billion. But the quantities of goods and services that we can produce are limited both by our available resources and by technology. And if we want to increase our production of one good, we must decrease our production of something else—we face a tradeoff. You are going to learn about the production possibilities frontier, which describes the limit to what we can produce and provides a neat way of thinking about and illustrating the idea of a tradeoff.

The **production possibilities frontier** (*PPF*) is the boundary between those combinations of goods and services that can be produced and those that cannot. To illustrate the *PPF*, we focus on two goods at a time and hold the quantities produced of all the other goods and services constant. That is, we look at a *model* economy in which everything remains the same except for the production of the two goods we are considering.

Let's look at the production possibilities frontier for cola and pizza, which stand for *any* pair of goods or services.

Production Possibilities Frontier

The *production possibilities frontier* for cola and pizza shows the limits to the production of these two goods, given the total resources and technology available to produce them. Figure 2.1 shows this production possibilities frontier. The table lists some combinations of the quantities of pizza and cola that can be produced in a month given the resources available. The figure graphs these combinations. The *x*-axis shows the quantity of pizzas produced, and the *y*-axis shows the quantity of cola produced.

The *PPF* illustrates *scarcity* because we cannot attain the points outside the frontier. These points describe wants that can't be satisfied. We can produce at any point *inside* the *PPF* or *on* the *PPF*. These points are attainable. Suppose that in a typical month, we produce 4 million pizzas and 5 million cans of cola. Figure 2.1 shows this combination as point *E* and as possibility *E* in the table. The figure

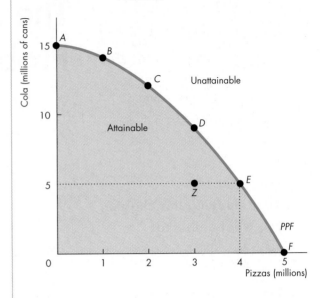

FIGURE 2.1   Production Possibilities Frontier

Possibility	Pizzas (millions)		Cola (millions of cans)
A	0	and	15
B	1	and	14
C	2	and	12
D	3	and	9
E	4	and	5
F	5	and	0

The table lists six production possibilities for cola and pizzas. Row *A* tells us that if we produce no pizza, the maximum quantity of cola we can produce is 15 million cans. Points *A, B, C, D, E,* and *F* in the figure represent the rows of the table. The curve passing through these points is the production possibilities frontier (*PPF*).

The *PPF* separates the attainable from the unattainable. Production is possible at any point *inside* the orange area or *on* the frontier. Points outside the frontier are unattainable. Points inside the frontier, such as point *Z*, are inefficient because resources are wasted or misallocated. At such points, it is possible to use the available resources to produce more of either or both goods.

myeconlab   animation

also shows other production possibilities. For example, we might stop producing pizza and move all the people who produce it into producing cola. Point *A* in the figure and possibility *A* in the table show this case. The quantity of cola produced increases to 15 million cans, and pizza production dries up. Alternatively, we might close the cola factories and switch all the resources into producing pizza. In this situation, we produce 5 million pizzas. Point *F* in the figure and possibility *F* in the table show this case.

Production Efficiency

We achieve **production efficiency** if we produce goods and services at the lowest possible cost. This outcome occurs at all the points *on* the *PPF*. At points *inside* the *PPF*, production is inefficient because we are giving up more than necessary of one good to produce a given quantity of the other good.

For example, at point *Z* in Fig. 2.1, we produce 3 million pizzas and 5 million cans of cola. But we could produce 3 million pizzas and 9 million cans of cola. Our pizzas cost more cola than necessary. We can get them for a lower cost. Only when we produce *on* the *PPF* do we incur the lowest possible cost of production.

Production is *inefficient* inside the *PPF* because resources are either *unused* or *misallocated* or both.

Resources are *unused* when they are idle but could be working. For example, we might leave some of the factories idle or some workers unemployed.

Resources are *misallocated* when they are assigned to tasks for which they are not the best match. For example, we might assign skilled pizza chefs to work in a cola factory and skilled cola producers to work in a pizza shop. We could get more pizzas *and* more cola from these same workers if we reassigned them to the tasks that more closely match their skills.

Tradeoff Along the *PPF*

Every choice *along* the *PPF* involves a *tradeoff*. On the *PPF* in Fig. 2.1, we trade off cola for pizzas.

Tradeoffs arise in every imaginable real-world situation, and you reviewed several of them in Chapter 1. At any given point in time, we have a fixed amount of labor, land, capital, and entrepreneurship. By using our available technologies, we can employ these resources to produce goods and services, but we are limited in what we can produce. This limit defines a

boundary between what we can attain and what we cannot attain. This boundary is the real-world's production possibilities frontier, and it defines the tradeoffs that we must make. On our real-world *PPF*, we can produce more of any one good or service only if we produce less of some other goods or services.

When doctors want to spend more on AIDS and cancer research, they face a tradeoff: more medical research for less of some other things. When Congress wants to spend more on education and health care, it faces a tradeoff: more education and health care for less national defense or less private spending (because of higher taxes). When an environmental group argues for less logging, it is suggesting a tradeoff: greater conservation of endangered wildlife for less paper. When you want to study more, you face a tradeoff: more study time for less leisure or sleep.

All tradeoffs involve a cost—an opportunity cost.

Opportunity Cost

The **opportunity cost** of an action is the highest-valued alternative forgone. The *PPF* makes this idea precise and enables us to calculate opportunity cost. Along the *PPF*, there are only two goods, so there is only one alternative forgone: some quantity of the other good. Given our current resources and technology, we can produce more pizzas only if we produce less cola. The opportunity cost of producing an additional pizza is the cola we *must* forgo. Similarly, the opportunity cost of producing an additional can of cola is the quantity of pizza we must forgo.

In Fig. 2.1, if we move from point *C* to point *D*, we get 1 million more pizzas but 3 million fewer cans of cola. The additional 1 million pizzas *cost* 3 million cans of cola. One pizza costs 3 cans of cola.

We can also work out the opportunity cost of moving in the opposite direction. In Fig. 2.1, if we move from point *D* to point *C*, the quantity of cola produced increases by 3 million cans and the quantity of pizzas produced decreases by 1 million. So if we choose point *C* over point *D*, the additional 3 million cans of cola *cost* 1 million pizzas. One can of cola costs 1/3 of a pizza.

Opportunity Cost Is a Ratio Opportunity cost is a ratio. It is the decrease in the quantity produced of one good divided by the increase in the quantity produced of another good as we move along the production possibilities frontier.

Because opportunity cost is a ratio, the opportunity cost of producing an additional can of cola is equal to the *inverse* of the opportunity cost of producing an additional pizza. Check this proposition by returning to the calculations we've just worked through. When we move along the *PPF* from *C* to *D*, the opportunity cost of a pizza is 3 cans of cola. The inverse of 3 is 1/3. If we decrease the production of pizza and increase the production of cola by moving from *D* to *C*, the opportunity cost of a can of cola must be 1/3 of a pizza. That is exactly the number that we calculated for the move from *D* to *C*.

Increasing Opportunity Cost The opportunity cost of a pizza increases as the quantity of pizzas produced increases. The outward-bowed shape of the *PPF* reflects increasing opportunity cost. When we produce a large quantity of cola and a small quantity of pizza—between points *A* and *B* in Fig. 2.1—the frontier has a gentle slope. An increase in the quantity of pizzas costs a small decrease in the quantity of cola—the opportunity cost of a pizza is a small quantity of cola.

When we produce a large quantity of pizza and a small quantity of cola—between points *E* and *F* in Fig. 2.1—the frontier is steep. A given increase in the quantity of pizzas *costs* a large decrease in the quantity of cola, so the opportunity cost of a pizza is a large quantity of cola.

The *PPF* is bowed outward because resources are not all equally productive in all activities. People with many years of experience working for PepsiCo are good at producing cola but not very good at making pizzas. So if we move some of these people from PepsiCo to Domino's, we get a small increase in the quantity of pizzas but a large decrease in the quantity of cola.

Similarly, people who have spent years working at Domino's are good at producing pizzas, but they have no idea how to produce cola. So if we move some of these people from Domino's to PepsiCo, we get a small increase in the quantity of cola but a large decrease in the quantity of pizzas. The more of either good we try to produce, the less productive are the additional resources we use to produce that good and the larger is the opportunity cost of a unit of that good.

Increasing Opportunity Cost
Opportunity Cost on the Farm

Sanders Wright, a homesick Mississippi native, is growing cotton in Iowa. But the growing season is short and commercial success unlikely. Cotton does not grow well in Iowa, but corn does. A farm with irrigation can produce 300 bushels of corn per acre—twice the U.S. average.

Ronnie Gerik, a Texas cotton farmer, has started to grow corn. But Ronnie doesn't have irrigation and instead relies on rainfall. That's not a problem for cotton, which just needs a few soakings a season. But it's a big problem for corn, which needs an inch of water a week. Also, corn can't take the heat like cotton, and if the temperature rises too much, Ronnie will be lucky to get 100 bushels an acre.

An Iowa corn farmer gives up almost no cotton to produce his 300 bushels of corn per acre—corn has a low opportunity cost. But Ronnie Gerick gives up a huge amount of cotton to produce his 100 bushels of corn per acre. By switching some land from cotton to corn, Ronnie has increased the production of corn, but the additional corn has a high opportunity cost.

"Deere worker makes 'cotton pickin' miracle happen," WCFCourier.com; and "Farmers stampede to corn," *USA Today*.

Review Quiz

1 How does the production possibilities frontier illustrate scarcity?
2 How does the production possibilities frontier illustrate production efficiency?
3 How does the production possibilities frontier show that every choice involves a tradeoff?
4 How does the production possibilities frontier illustrate opportunity cost?
5 Why is opportunity cost a ratio?
6 Why does the *PPF* for most goods bow outward so that opportunity cost increases as the quantity produced of a good increases?

 Work Study Plan 2.1 and get instant feedback.

We've seen that what we can produce is limited by the production possibilities frontier. We've also seen that production on the *PPF* is efficient. But we can produce many different quantities on the *PPF*. How do we choose among them? How do we know which point on the *PPF* is the best one?

◆ Using Resources Efficiently

We achieve *production efficiency* at every point on the *PPF*. But which point is best? The answer is the point on the *PPF* at which goods and services are produced in the quantities that provide the greatest possible benefit. When goods and services are produced at the lowest possible cost and in the quantities that provide the greatest possible benefit, we have achieved **allocative efficiency.**

The questions that we raised when we reviewed the five big issues in Chapter 1 are questions about allocative efficiency. To answer such questions, we must measure and compare costs and benefits.

The *PPF* and Marginal Cost

The **marginal cost** of a good is the opportunity cost of producing one more unit of it. We calculate marginal cost from the slope of the *PPF*. As the quantity of pizzas produced increases, the *PPF* gets steeper and the marginal cost of a pizza increases. Figure 2.2 illustrates the calculation of the marginal cost of a pizza.

Begin by finding the opportunity cost of pizza in blocks of 1 million pizzas. The cost of the first million pizzas is 1 million cans of cola; the cost of the second million pizzas is 2 million cans of cola; the cost of the third million pizzas is 3 million cans of cola, and so on. The bars in part (a) illustrate these calculations.

The bars in part (b) show the cost of an average pizza in each of the 1 million pizza blocks. Focus on the third million pizzas—the move from *C* to *D* in part (a). Over this range, because 1 million pizzas cost 3 million cans of cola, one of these pizzas, on average, costs 3 cans of cola—the height of the bar in part (b).

Next, find the opportunity cost of each additional pizza—the marginal cost of a pizza. The marginal cost of a pizza increases as the quantity of pizzas produced increases. The marginal cost at point *C* is less than it is at point *D*. On the average over the range from *C* to *D*, the marginal cost of a pizza is 3 cans of cola. But it exactly equals 3 cans of cola only in the middle of the range between *C* and *D*.

The red dot in part (b) indicates that the marginal cost of a pizza is 3 cans of cola when 2.5 million pizzas are produced. Each black dot in part (b) is interpreted in the same way. The red curve that passes through these dots, labeled *MC*, is the marginal cost curve. It shows the marginal cost of a pizza at each quantity of pizzas as we move along the *PPF*.

FIGURE 2.2   The *PPF* and Marginal Cost

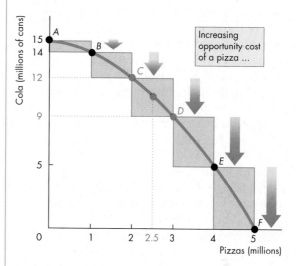

(a) PPF and opportunity cost

(b) Marginal cost

Marginal cost is calculated from the slope of the *PPF*. As the quantity of pizzas produced increases, the *PPF* gets steeper and the marginal cost of a pizza increases. The bars in part (a) show the opportunity cost of pizza in blocks of 1 million pizzas. The bars in part (b) show the cost of an average pizza in each of these 1 million blocks. The red curve, *MC*, shows the marginal cost of a pizza at each point along the *PPF*. This curve passes through the center of each of the bars in part (b).

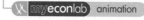

Preferences and Marginal Benefit

Look around your classroom and notice the wide variety of shirts, pants, and shoes that you and your fellow students are wearing today. Why is there such a huge variety? Why don't you all wear the same styles and colors? The answer lies in what economists call preferences. **Preferences** are a description of a person's likes and dislikes.

You've seen that we have a concrete way of describing the limits to production: the *PPF*. We need a similarly concrete way of describing preferences. To describe preferences, economists use the concept of marginal benefit. The **marginal benefit** from a good or service is the benefit received from consuming one more unit of it.

We measure the marginal benefit from a good or service by the most that people are *willing to pay* for an additional unit of it. The idea is that you are willing to pay less for a good than it is worth to you but you are not willing to pay more than it is worth. So the most you are willing to pay for something measures its marginal benefit.

Economists illustrate preferences using the **marginal benefit curve**, which is a curve that shows the relationship between the marginal benefit from a good and the quantity consumed of that good. It is a general principle that the more we have of any good or service, the smaller is its marginal benefit and the less we are willing to pay for an additional unit of it. This tendency is so widespread and strong that we call it a principle—the *principle of decreasing marginal benefit*.

The basic reason why marginal benefit from a good or service decreases as we consume more of it is that we like variety. The more we consume of any one good or service, the more we tire of it and would prefer to switch to something else.

Think about your willingness to pay for a pizza. If pizza is hard to come by and you can buy only a few slices a year, you might be willing to pay a high price to get an additional slice. But if pizza is all you've eaten for the past few days, you are willing to pay almost nothing for another slice.

You've learned to think about cost as opportunity cost, not as a dollar cost. You can think about marginal benefit and willingness to pay in the same way. The marginal benefit, measured by what you are willing to pay for something, is the quantity of other goods and services that you are willing to forgo. Let's continue with the example of cola and pizza and illustrate preferences this way.

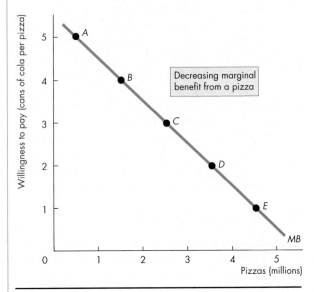

FIGURE 2.3 Preferences and the Marginal Benefit Curve

Decreasing marginal benefit from a pizza

Possibility	Pizzas (millions)	Willingness to pay (cans of cola per pizza)
A	0.5	5
B	1.5	4
C	2.5	3
D	3.5	2
E	4.5	1

The smaller the quantity of pizzas produced, the more cola people are willing to give up for an additional pizza. If pizza production is 0.5 million, people are willing to pay 5 cans of cola per pizza. But if pizza production is 4.5 million, people are willing to pay only 1 can of cola per pizza. Willingness to pay measures marginal benefit. A universal feature of people's preferences is that marginal benefit decreases.

myeconlab animation

Figure 2.3 illustrates preferences as the willingness to pay for pizza in terms of cola. In row *A*, pizza production is 0.5 million, and at that quantity, people are willing to pay 5 cans of cola per pizza. As the quantity of pizzas produced increases, the amount that people are willing to pay for a pizza falls. When pizza production is 4.5 million, people are willing to pay only 1 can of cola per pizza.

Let's now use the concepts of marginal cost and marginal benefit to describe allocative efficiency.

FIGURE 2.4   Efficient Use of Resources

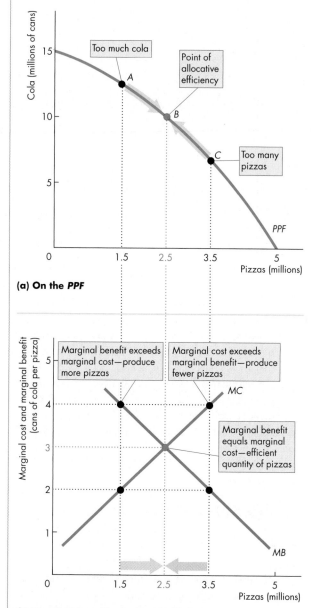

(a) On the PPF

(b) Marginal benefit equals marginal cost

The greater the quantity of pizzas produced, the smaller is the marginal benefit (*MB*) from pizza—the less cola people are willing to give up to get an additional pizza. But the greater the quantity of pizzas produced, the greater is the marginal cost (*MC*) of a pizza—the more cola people must give up to get an additional pizza. When marginal benefit equals marginal cost, resources are being used efficiently.

 animation

Allocative Efficiency

At *any* point on the *PPF*, we cannot produce more of one good without giving up some other good. At the *best* point on the *PPF*, we cannot produce more of one good without giving up some other good that provides greater benefit. We are producing at the point of allocative efficiency—the point on the *PPF* that we prefer above all other points.

Suppose in Fig. 2.4, we produce 1.5 million pizzas. The marginal cost of a pizza is 2 cans of cola, and the marginal benefit from a pizza is 4 cans of cola. Because someone values an additional pizza more highly than it costs to produce, we can get more value from our resources by moving some of them out of producing cola and into producing pizza.

Now suppose we produce 3.5 million pizzas. The marginal cost of a pizza is now 4 cans of cola, but the marginal benefit from a pizza is only 2 cans of cola. Because the additional pizza costs more to produce than anyone thinks it is worth, we can get more value from our resources by moving some of them away from producing pizza and into producing cola.

Suppose we produce 2.5 million pizzas. Marginal cost and marginal benefit are now equal at 3 cans of cola. This allocation of resources between pizza and cola is efficient. If more pizzas are produced, the forgone cola is worth more than the additional pizzas. If fewer pizzas are produced, the forgone pizzas are worth more than the additional cola.

Review Quiz

1   What is marginal cost? How is it measured?
2   What is marginal benefit? How is it measured?
3   How does the marginal benefit from a good change as the quantity produced of that good increases?
4   What is allocative efficiency and how does it relate to the production possibilities frontier?
5   What conditions must be satisfied if resources are used efficiently?

 Work Study Plan 2.2 and get instant feedback.

You now understand the limits to production and the conditions under which resources are used efficiently. Your next task is to study the expansion of production possibilities.

Economic Growth

During the past 30 years, production per person in the United States has doubled. Such an expansion of production is called **economic growth**. Economic growth increases our *standard of living*, but it doesn't overcome scarcity and avoid opportunity cost. To make our economy grow, we face a tradeoff—the faster we make production grow, the greater is the opportunity cost of economic growth.

The Cost of Economic Growth

Economic growth comes from technological change and capital accumulation. **Technological change** is the development of new goods and of better ways of producing goods and services. **Capital accumulation** is the growth of capital resources, including *human capital*.

Because of technological change and capital accumulation, we have an enormous quantity of cars that provide us with more transportation than was available when we had only horses and carriages; we have satellites that provide global communications on a much larger scale than that available with the earlier cable technology. But if we use our resources to develop new technologies and produce capital, we must decrease our production of consumption goods and services. New technologies and new capital have an opportunity cost. Let's look at this opportunity cost.

Instead of studying the *PPF* of pizza and cola, we'll hold the quantity of cola produced constant and examine the *PPF* for pizzas and pizza ovens. Figure 2.5 shows this *PPF* as the blue curve *ABC*. If we devote no resources to producing pizza ovens, we produce at point *A*. If we produce 3 million pizzas, we can produce 6 pizza ovens at point *B*. If we produce no pizza, we can produce 10 ovens at point *C*.

The amount by which our production possibilities expand depends on the resources we devote to technological change and capital accumulation. If we devote no resources to this activity (point *A*), our *PPF* remains at *ABC*—the blue curve in Fig. 2.5. If we cut the current production of pizza and produce 6 ovens (point *B*), then in the future, we'll have more capital and our *PPF* will rotate outward to the position shown by the red curve. The fewer resources we use for producing pizza and the more resources we use for producing ovens, the greater is the future expansion of our production possibilities.

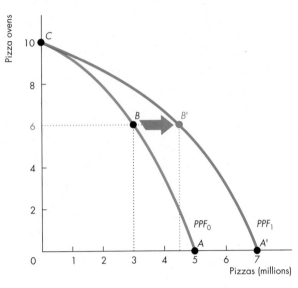

FIGURE 2.5   Economic Growth

PPF_0 shows the limits to the production of pizza and pizza ovens, with the production of all other goods and services remaining the same. If we devote no resources to producing pizza ovens and produce 5 million pizzas, our production possibilities will remain the same PPF_0. But if we decrease pizza production to 3 million and produce 6 ovens, at point *B*, our production possibilities expand. After one period, the *PPF* rotates outward to PPF_1 and we can produce at point *B'*, a point outside the original PPF_0. We can rotate the *PPF* outward, but we cannot avoid opportunity cost. The opportunity cost of producing more pizzas in the future is fewer pizzas today.

Economic growth is not free. To make it happen, we use more resources to produce new ovens and fewer resources to produce pizzas. In Fig. 2.5, we move from *A* to *B*. There is no free lunch. The opportunity cost of more pizzas in the future is fewer pizzas today. Also, economic growth is no magic formula for abolishing scarcity. On the new production possibilities frontier, we continue to face a tradeoff and opportunity cost.

The ideas about economic growth that we have explored in the setting of the pizza industry also apply to nations. Hong Kong and the United States provide an interesting case study.

Economic Growth
Hong Kong Catching Up to the United States

In 1968, the production possibilities per person in the United States were more than four times those in Hong Kong (see the figure). The United States devotes one fifth of its resources to accumulating capital and in 1968 was at point *A* on its *PPF*. Hong Kong devotes one third of its resources to accumulating capital and in 1968, Hong Kong was at point *A* on its *PPF*.

Since 1968, both countries have experienced economic growth, but because Hong Kong devotes a bigger fraction of its resources to accumulating capital, its production possibilities have expanded more quickly.

By 2008, production possibilities per person in Hong Kong had reached 94 percent of those in the United States. If Hong Kong continues to devote more resources to accumulating capital than we do (at point *B* on its 2008 *PPF*), it will continue to grow more rapidly. But if Hong Kong decreases capital accumulation (moving to point *D* on its 2008 *PPF*), then its rate of economic growth will slow.

Hong Kong is typical of the fast-growing Asian economies, which include Taiwan, Thailand, South Korea, and China. Production possibilities expand in these countries by between 5 and almost 10 percent a year.

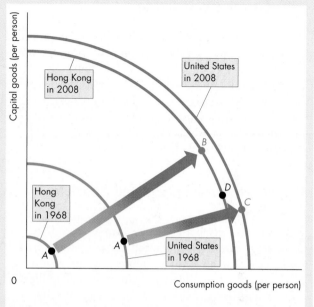

Economic Growth in the United States and Hong Kong

If such high economic growth rates are maintained, these other Asian countries will continue to close the gap between themselves and the United States, as Hong Kong is doing.

A Nation's Economic Growth

The experiences of the United States and Hong Kong make a striking example of the effects of our choices about consumption and capital goods on the rate of economic growth.

If a nation devotes all its factors of production to producing consumption goods and services and none to advancing technology and accumulating capital, its production possibilities in the future will be the same as they are today.

To expand production possibilities in the future, a nation must devote fewer resources to producing consumption goods and services and some resources to accumulating capital and developing new technologies. As production possibilities expand, consumption in the future can increase. The decrease in today's consumption is the opportunity cost of tomorrow's increase in consumption.

Review Quiz

1 What generates economic growth?
2 How does economic growth influence the production possibilities frontier?
3 What is the opportunity cost of economic growth?
4 Why has Hong Kong experienced faster economic growth than the United States?
5 Does economic growth overcome scarcity?

 Work Study Plan 2.3 and get instant feedback.

Next, we're going to study another way in which we expand our production possibilities—the amazing fact that *both* buyers and sellers gain from specialization and trade.

◗ Gains from Trade

People can produce for themselves all the goods and services that they consume, or they can produce one good or a few goods and trade with others. Producing only one good or a few goods is called *specialization*. We are going to learn how people gain by specializing in the production of the good in which they have a *comparative advantage* and trading with others.

Comparative Advantage and Absolute Advantage

A person has a **comparative advantage** in an activity if that person can perform the activity at a lower opportunity cost than anyone else. Differences in opportunity costs arise from differences in individual abilities and from differences in the characteristics of other resources.

No one excels at everything. One person is an outstanding pitcher but a poor catcher; another person is a brilliant lawyer but a poor teacher. In almost all human endeavors, what one person does easily, someone else finds difficult. The same applies to land and capital. One plot of land is fertile but has no mineral deposits; another plot of land has outstanding views but is infertile. One machine has great precision but is difficult to operate; another is fast but often breaks down.

Although no one excels at everything, some people excel and can outperform others in a large number of activities—perhaps even in all activities. A person who is more productive than others has an **absolute advantage**.

Absolute advantage involves comparing productivities—production per hour—whereas comparative advantage involves comparing opportunity costs.

Notice that a person who has an absolute advantage does not have a *comparative* advantage in every activity. John Grisham is a better lawyer and a better author of fast-paced thrillers than most people. He has an absolute advantage in these two activities. But compared to others, he is a better writer than lawyer, so his *comparative* advantage is in writing.

Because ability and resources vary from one person to another, people have different opportunity costs of producing various goods. These differences in opportunity cost are the source of comparative advantage.

Let's explore the idea of comparative advantage by looking at two smoothie bars: one operated by Liz and the other operated by Joe.

Liz's Smoothie Bar Liz produces smoothies and salads. In Liz's high-tech bar, she can turn out either a smoothie or a salad every 2 minutes—see Table 2.1. If Liz spends all her time making smoothies, she can produce 30 an hour. And if she spends all her time making salads, she can also produce 30 an hour. If she splits her time equally between the two, she can produce 15 smoothies and 15 salads an hour. For each additional smoothie Liz produces, she must decrease her production of salads by one, and for each additional salad she produces, she must decrease her production of smoothies by one. So

Liz's opportunity cost of producing 1 smoothie is 1 salad,

and

Liz's opportunity cost of producing 1 salad is 1 smoothie.

Liz's customers buy smoothies and salads in equal quantities, so she splits her time equally between the two items and produces 15 smoothies and 15 salads an hour.

Joe's Smoothie Bar Joe also produces smoothies and salads, but his bar is smaller than Liz's. Also, Joe has only one blender, and it's a slow, old machine. Even if Joe uses all his resources to produce smoothies, he can produce only 6 an hour—see Table 2.2. But Joe is good at making salads, so if he uses all his resources to make salads, he can produce 30 an hour.

Joe's ability to make smoothies and salads is the same regardless of how he splits an hour between the two tasks. He can make a salad in 2 minutes or a smoothie in 10 minutes. For each additional smoothie

TABLE 2.1 Liz's Production Possibilities

Item	Minutes to produce 1	Quantity per hour
Smoothies	2	30
Salads	2	30

TABLE 2.2   Joe's Production Possibilities

Item	Minutes to produce 1	Quantity per hour
Smoothies	10	6
Salads	2	30

Joe produces, he must decrease his production of salads by 5. And for each additional salad he produces, he must decrease his production of smoothies by 1/5 of a smoothie. So

> Joe's opportunity cost of producing 1 smoothie is 5 salads,

and

> Joe's opportunity cost of producing 1 salad is 1/5 of a smoothie.

Joe's customers, like Liz's, buy smoothies and salads in equal quantities. So Joe spends 50 minutes of each hour making smoothies and 10 minutes of each hour making salads. With this division of his time, Joe produces 5 smoothies and 5 salads an hour.

Liz's Absolute Advantage Table 2.3(a) summarizes the production of Liz and Joe. You can see that Liz is three times as productive as Joe—her 15 smoothies and salads an hour are three times Joe's 5. Liz has an absolute advantage over Joe in producing both smoothies and salads. But Liz has a comparative advantage in only one of the activities.

Liz's Comparative Advantage In which of the two activities does Liz have a comparative advantage? Recall that comparative advantage is a situation in which one person's opportunity cost of producing a good is lower than another person's opportunity cost of producing that same good. Liz has a comparative advantage in producing smoothies. Her opportunity cost of a smoothie is 1 salad, whereas Joe's opportunity cost of a smoothie is 5 salads.

Joe's Comparative Advantage If Liz has a comparative advantage in producing smoothies, Joe must have a comparative advantage in producing salads. Joe's opportunity cost of a salad is 1/5 of a smoothie, whereas Liz's opportunity cost of a salad is 1 smoothie.

Achieving the Gains from Trade

Liz and Joe run into each other one evening in a singles bar. After a few minutes of getting acquainted, Liz tells Joe about her amazing smoothie business. Her only problem, she tells Joe, is that she would like to produce more because potential customers leave when her lines get too long.

Joe isn't sure whether to risk spoiling his chances by telling Liz about his own struggling business. But he takes the risk. When he explains to Liz that he spends 50 minutes of every hour making 5 smoothies and 10 minutes making 5 salads, Liz's eyes pop. "Have I got a deal for you!" she exclaims.

Here's the deal that Liz sketches on a table napkin. Joe stops making smoothies and allocates all his time to producing salads. And Liz stops making salads and allocates all her time to producing smoothies. That is, they both specialize in producing the good in which they have a comparative advantage. Together they produce 30 smoothies and 30 salads—see Table 2.3(b).

TABLE 2.3   Liz and Joe Gain from Trade

(a) Before trade	Liz	Joe
Smoothies	15	5
Salads	15	5

(b) Specialization	Liz	Joe
Smoothies	30	0
Salads	0	30

(c) Trade	Liz	Joe
Smoothies	sell 10	buy 10
Salads	buy 20	sell 20

(d) After trade	Liz	Joe
Smoothies	20	10
Salads	20	10

(e) Gains from trade	Liz	Joe
Smoothies	+5	+5
Salads	+5	+5

They then trade. Liz sells Joe 10 smoothies and Joe sells Liz 20 salads—the price of a smoothie is 2 salads—see Table 2.3(c).

After the trade, Joe has 10 salads—the 30 he produces minus the 20 he sells to Liz. He also has the 10 smoothies that he buys from Liz. So Joe now has increased the quantities of smoothies and salads that he can sell—see Table 2.3(d).

Liz has 20 smoothies—the 30 she produces minus the 10 she sells to Joe. She also has the 20 salads that she buys from Joe. Liz has increased the quantities of smoothies and salads that she can sell—see Table 2.3(d). Liz and Joe both gain 5 smoothies and 5 salads an hour—see Table 2.3(e).

To illustrate her idea, Liz grabs a fresh napkin and draws the graphs in Fig. 2.6. The blue *PPF* in part (a) shows Joe's production possibilities. Before trade, he is producing 5 smoothies and 5 salads an hour at point *A*.

The blue *PPF* in part (b) shows Liz's production possibilities. Before trade, she is producing 15 smoothies and 15 salads an hour at point *A*.

Liz's proposal is that they each specialize in producing the good in which they have a comparative advantage. Joe produces 30 salads and no smoothies at point *B* on his *PPF*. Liz produces 30 smoothies and no salads at point *B* on her *PPF*.

Liz and Joe then trade smoothies and salads at a price of 2 salads per smoothie or 1/2 a smoothie per salad. Joe gets smoothies for 2 salads each, which is less than the 5 salads it costs him to produce a smoothie. Liz gets salads for 1/2 a smoothie each, which is less than the 1 smoothie that it costs her to produce a salad.

With trade, Joe has 10 smoothies and 10 salads at point *C*—a gain of 5 smoothies and 5 salads. Joe moves to a point *outside* his *PPF*.

FIGURE 2.6 The Gains from Trade

(a) Joe

(b) Liz

Joe initially produces at point *A* on his *PPF* in part (a), and Liz initially produces at point *A* on her *PPF* in part (b). Joe's opportunity cost of producing a salad is less than Liz's, so Joe has a comparative advantage in producing salads. Liz's opportunity cost of producing a smoothie is less than Joe's, so Liz has a comparative advantage in producing smoothies. If Joe specializes in making salads, he produces 30 salads and no smoothies at point *B* on his *PPF*. If Liz specializes in making smoothies, she produces 30 smoothies and no salads at point *B* on her *PPF*. They exchange salads for smoothies along the red "Trade line." Liz buys salads from Joe for less than her opportunity cost of producing them. Joe buys smoothies from Liz for less than his opportunity cost of producing them. Each goes to point *C*—a point outside his or her *PPF*. Both Joe and Liz increase production by 5 smoothies and 5 salads with no change in resources.

With trade, Liz has 20 smoothies and 20 salads at point *C*—a gain of 5 smoothies and 5 salads. Liz moves to a point *outside* her *PPF*.

Despite Liz's absolute advantage in producing smoothies and salads, both Liz and Joe gain from specializing—producing the good in which they have a comparative advantage—and trading.

The gains that we achieve from international trade are similar to those achieved by Joe and Liz in this example. When Americans buy T-shirts from China and when China buys Boeing aircraft from the United States, both countries gain. We get our shirts at a lower cost than that at which we can produce them, and China gets its aircraft at a lower cost than that at which it can produce them.

Dynamic Comparative Advantage

At any given point in time, the resources and technologies available determine the comparative advantages that individuals and nations have. But just by repeatedly producing a particular good or service, people become more productive in that activity, a phenomenon called **learning-by-doing**. Learning-by-doing is the basis of *dynamic* comparative advantage. **Dynamic comparative advantage** is a comparative advantage that a person (or country) has acquired by specializing in an activity and becoming the lowest-cost producer as a result of learning-by-doing.

Singapore, for example, pursued dynamic comparative advantage when it decided to begin a biotechnology industry in which it initially didn't have a comparative advantage.

Review Quiz

1 What gives a person a comparative advantage?
2 Distinguish between comparative advantage and absolute advantage.
3 Why do people specialize and trade?
4 What are the gains from specialization and trade?
5 What is the source of the gains from trade?
6 How does dynamic comparative advantage arise?

 Work Study Plan 2.4 and get instant feedback.

Economic Coordination

People gain by specializing in the production of those goods and services in which they have a comparative advantage and then trading with each other. Liz and Joe, whose production of salads and smoothies we studied earlier in this chapter, can get together and make a deal that enables them to enjoy the gains from specialization and trade. But for billions of individuals to specialize and produce millions of different goods and services, their choices must somehow be coordinated.

Two competing economic coordination systems have been used: central economic planning and decentralized markets.

Central economic planning might appear to be the best system because it can express national priorities. But when this system was tried, as it was for 60 years in Russia and for 30 years in China, it was a miserable failure. Today, these and most other previously planned economies are adopting a decentralized market system.

To make decentralized coordination work, four complementary social institutions that have evolved over many centuries are needed. They are

- Firms
- Markets
- Property rights
- Money

Firms

A **firm** is an economic unit that hires factors of production and organizes those factors to produce and sell goods and services. Examples of firms are your local gas station, Wal-Mart, and General Motors.

Firms coordinate a huge amount of economic activity. For example, Wal-Mart buys or rents large buildings, equips them with storage shelves and checkout lanes, and hires labor. Wal-Mart directs the labor and decides what goods to buy and sell.

But Wal-Mart doesn't produce the goods that it sells. It could do so. Wal-Mart could own and coordinate the production of all the things that it sells in its stores. It could also produce all the raw materials that are used to produce the things that it sells. But Sam Walton would not have become one of the wealthiest people in the world if he had followed that path. The reason is that if a firm gets too big, it can't keep track of all the information that is needed to coordinate its activities. It is more efficient for firms to specialize (just as Liz and Joe did) and trade with each other. This trade between firms takes place in markets.

Markets

In ordinary speech, the word *market* means a place where people buy and sell goods such as fish, meat, fruits, and vegetables. In economics, a *market* has a more general meaning. A **market** is any arrangement that enables buyers and sellers to get information and to do business with each other. An example is the market in which oil is bought and sold—the world oil market. The world oil market is not a place. It is the network of oil producers, oil users, wholesalers, and brokers who buy and sell oil. In the world oil market, decision makers do not meet physically. They make deals by telephone, fax, and direct computer link.

Markets have evolved because they facilitate trade. Without organized markets, we would miss out on a substantial part of the potential gains from trade. Enterprising individuals and firms, each pursuing their own self-interest, have profited from making markets—standing ready to buy or sell the items in which they specialize. But markets can work only when property rights exist.

Property Rights

The social arrangements that govern the ownership, use, and disposal of anything that people value are called **property rights**. *Real property* includes land and buildings—the things we call property in ordinary speech—and durable goods such as plant and equipment. *Financial property* includes stocks and bonds and money in the bank. *Intellectual property* is the intangible product of creative effort. This type of property includes books, music, computer programs, and inventions of all kinds and is protected by copyrights and patents.

Where property rights are enforced, people have the incentive to specialize and produce the goods in which they have a comparative advantage. Where people can steal the production of others, resources are devoted not to production but to protecting possessions. Without property rights, we would still be hunting and gathering like our Stone Age ancestors.

Money

Money is any commodity or token that is generally acceptable as a means of payment. Liz and Joe didn't use money in the example above. They exchanged salads and smoothies. In principle, trade in markets can exchange any item for any other item. But you can perhaps imagine how complicated life would be if we exchanged goods for other goods. The "invention" of money makes trading in markets much more efficient.

Circular Flows Through Markets

Figure 2.7 shows the flows that result from the choices that households and firms make. Households specialize and choose the quantities of labor, land, capital, and entrepreneurial services to sell or rent to firms. Firms choose the quantities of factors of production to hire. These (red) flows go through the *factor markets*. Households choose the quantities of goods and services to buy, and firms choose the quantities to produce. These (red) flows go through the *goods markets*. Households receive incomes and make expenditures on goods and services (the green flows).

How do markets coordinate all these decisions?

Coordinating Decisions

Markets coordinate decisions through price adjustments. To see how, think about your local market for hamburgers. Suppose that too few hamburgers are available and some people who want to buy hamburgers are not able to do so. To make buying and selling plans the same, either more hamburgers must be offered for sale or buyers must scale down their appetites (or both). A rise in the price of a hamburger produces this outcome. A higher price encourages producers to offer more hamburgers for sale. It also encourages some people to change their lunch plans. Fewer people buy hamburgers, and more buy hot dogs. More hamburgers (and more hot dogs) are offered for sale.

Alternatively, suppose that more hamburgers are available than people want to buy. In this case, to make the choices of buyers and sellers compatible, more hamburgers must be bought or fewer hamburgers must be offered for sale (or both). A fall in the price of a hamburger achieves this outcome. A lower price encourages firms to produce a smaller quantity of hamburgers. It also encourages people to buy more hamburgers.

FIGURE 2.7   Circular Flows in the Market Economy

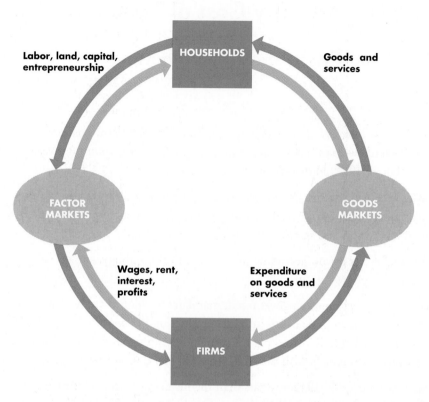

Households and firms make economic choices and markets coordinate these choices.

Households choose the quantities of labor, land, capital, and entrepreneurial services to sell or rent to firms in exchange for wages, rent, interest, and profit. Households also choose how to spend their incomes on the various types of goods and services available.

Firms choose the quantities of factors of production to hire and the quantities of goods and services to produce.

Goods markets and factor markets coordinate these choices of households and firms.

The counterclockwise red flows are real flows—the flow of factors of production from households to firms and the flow of goods and services from firms to households.

The clockwise green flows are the payments for the red flows. They are the flow of incomes from firms to households and the flow of expenditure on goods and services from households to firms.

myeconlab animation

Review Quiz

1 Why are social institutions such as firms, markets, property rights, and money necessary?
2 What are the main functions of markets?
3 What are the flows in the market economy that go from firms to households and the flows from households to firms?

myeconlab Work Study Plan 2.5 and get instant feedback.

◆ You have now begun to see how economists approach economic questions. Scarcity, choice, and divergent opportunity costs explain why we specialize and trade and why firms, markets, property rights, and money have developed. You can see all around you the lessons you've learned in this chapter. *Reading Between the Lines* on pp. 46–47 provides an opportunity to apply the *PPF* model to deepen your understanding of the reasons for the increase in the cost of food associated with the increase in corn production.

The Rising Opportunity Cost of Food

Fuel Choices, Food Crises, and Finger-Pointing

http://www.nytimes.com
April 15, 2008

The idea of turning farms into fuel plants seemed, for a time, like one of the answers to high global oil prices and supply worries. That strategy seemed to reach a high point last year when Congress mandated a fivefold increase in the use of biofuels.

But now a reaction is building against policies in the United States and Europe to promote ethanol and similar fuels, with political leaders from poor countries contending that these fuels are driving up food prices and starving poor people. …

In some countries, the higher prices are leading to riots, political instability, and growing worries about feeding the poorest people. …

Many specialists in food policy consider government mandates for biofuels to be ill advised, agreeing that the diversion of crops like corn into fuel production has contributed to the higher prices. But other factors have played big roles, including droughts that have limited output and rapid global economic growth that has created higher demand for food.

That growth, much faster over the last four years than the historical norm, is lifting millions of people out of destitution and giving them access to better diets. But farmers are having trouble keeping up with the surge in demand.

While there is agreement that the growth of biofuels has contributed to higher food prices, the amount is disputed. …

C. Ford Runge, an economist at the University of Minnesota, said it is "extremely difficult to disentangle" the effect of biofuels on food costs. Nevertheless, he said there was little that could be done to mitigate the effect of droughts and the growing appetite for protein in developing countries.

"Ethanol is the one thing we can do something about," he said. "It's about the only lever we have to pull, but none of the politicians have the courage to pull the lever." …

Essence of the Story

- In 2007, Congress mandated a fivefold increase in the use of biofuels.

- Political leaders in poor countries and specialists in food policy say the biofuel mandate is ill advised and the diversion of corn into fuel production has raised the cost of food.

- Drought that has limited corn production and global economic growth that has increased the demand for protein have also raised the cost of food.

- An economist at the University of Minnesota says that while it is difficult to determine the effect of biofuels on food costs, it is the only factor under our control.

Economic Analysis

- Ethanol is made from corn in the United States, so biofuel and food compete to use the same resources.

- To produce more ethanol and meet the Congress's mandate, farmers increased the number of acres devoted to corn production.

- In 2008, the amount of land devoted to corn production increased by 20 percent in the United States and by 2 percent in the rest of the world.

- Figure 1 shows the U.S. production possibilities frontier, *PPF*, for corn and other goods and services.

- The increase in the production of corn is illustrated by a movement along the *PPF* in Fig. 1 from point *A* in 2007 to point *B* in 2008.

- In moving from point *A* to point *B*, the United States incurs a higher opportunity cost of producing corn, indicated by the greater slope of the *PPF* at point *B*.

- In other regions of the world, despite the fact that more land was devoted to corn production, the amount of corn produced didn't change.

- The reason is that droughts in South America and Eastern Europe lowered the crop yield per acre in those regions.

- Figure 2 shows the rest of the world's *PPF* for corn and other goods and services in 2007 and 2008.

- The increase in the amount of land devoted to producing corn is illustrated by a movement along the PPF_{07}.

- With a decrease in the crop yield, production possibilities decreased and the *PPF* rotated inward.

- The rotation from PPF_{07} to PPF_{08} illustrates this decrease in production possibilities.

- The opportunity cost of producing corn in the rest of the world increased for two reasons: the movement along its *PPF* and the inward rotation of the *PPF*.

- With a higher opportunity cost of producing corn, the cost of both biofuel and food increases.

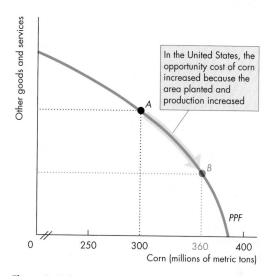

In the United States, the opportunity cost of corn increased because the area planted and production increased

Figure 1 U.S. *PPF*

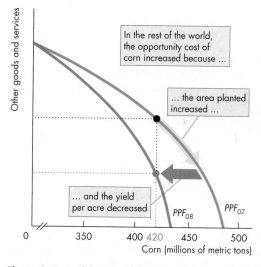

In the rest of the world, the opportunity cost of corn increased because ...

... the area planted increased ...

... and the yield per acre decreased

Figure 2 Rest of the World *PPF*

SUMMARY

Key Points

Production Possibilities and Opportunity Cost

(pp. 32–34)

- The production possibilities frontier, *PPF*, is the boundary between production levels that are attainable and those that are not attainable when all the available resources are used to their limit.
- Production efficiency occurs at points on the *PPF*.
- Along the *PPF*, the opportunity cost of producing more of one good is the amount of the other good that must be given up.
- The opportunity cost of all goods increases as the production of the good increases.

Using Resources Efficiently (pp. 35–37)

- Allocative efficiency occurs when goods and services are produced at the least possible cost and in the quantities that bring the greatest possible benefit.
- The marginal cost of a good is the opportunity cost of producing one more unit of it.
- The marginal benefit from a good is the benefit received from consuming one more unit of it, measured by the willingness to pay for it.
- The marginal benefit of a good decreases as the amount of the good available increases.
- Resources are used efficiently when the marginal cost of each good is equal to its marginal benefit.

Economic Growth (pp. 38–39)

- Economic growth, which is the expansion of production possibilities, results from capital accumulation and technological change.
- The opportunity cost of economic growth is forgone current consumption.

Gains from Trade (pp. 40–43)

- A person has a comparative advantage in producing a good if that person can produce the good at a lower opportunity cost than everyone else.
- People gain by specializing in the activity in which they have a comparative advantage and trading with others.
- Dynamic comparative advantage arises from learning-by-doing.

Economic Coordination (pp. 43–45)

- Firms coordinate a large amount of economic activity, but there is a limit to the efficient size of a firm.
- Markets coordinate the economic choices of people and firms.
- Markets can work efficiently only when property rights exist.
- Money makes trading in markets more efficient.

Key Figures

Key Terms

PROBLEMS and APPLICATIONS

1. Brazil produces ethanol from sugar, and the land used to grow sugar can be used to grow food crops. Suppose that Brazil's production possibilities for ethanol and food crops are as follows

Ethanol (barrels per day)		Food crops (tons per day)
70	and	0
64	and	1
54	and	2
40	and	3
22	and	4
0	and	5

   a. Draw a graph of Brazil's *PPF* and explain how your graph illustrates scarcity.
   b. If Brazil produces 40 barrels of ethanol a day, how much food must it produce if it achieves production efficiency?
   c. Why does Brazil face a tradeoff on its *PPF*?
   d. If Brazil increases its production of ethanol from 40 barrels per day to 54 barrels per day, what is the opportunity cost of the additional ethanol?
   e. If Brazil increases its production of food crops from 2 tons per day to 3 tons per day, what is the opportunity cost of the additional food?
   f. What is the relationship between your answers to d and e?
   g. Does Brazil face an increasing opportunity cost of ethanol? What feature of the *PPF* that you've drawn illustrates increasing opportunity cost?

2. Define marginal cost and use the information provided in the table in problem 1 to calculate the marginal cost of producing a ton of food when the quantity produced is 2.5 tons per day.

3. Define marginal benefit, explain how it is measured, and explain why the information provided in the table in problem 1 does not enable you to calculate the marginal benefit of food.

4. Distinguish between *production efficiency* and *allocative efficiency*. Explain why many production possibilities achieve production efficiency but only one achieves allocative efficiency.

5. Harry enjoys tennis but wants a high grade in his economics course. The figure shows the limits to what he can achieve: It is Harry's *PPF* for these two "goods."

The following figure shows Harry's *MB* curve for tennis.

   a. What is Harry's marginal cost of tennis if he plays for (i) 3 hours a week; (ii) 5 hours a week; and (iii) 7 hours a week?
   b. If Harry uses his time to achieve allocative efficiency, what is his economics grade and how many hours of tennis does he play?
   c. Explain why Harry would be worse off getting a grade higher than your answer to b.
   d. If Harry becomes a tennis superstar with big earnings from tennis, what happens to his *PPF*, *MB* curve, and efficient time allocation?

e. If Harry suddenly finds high grades in economics easier to attain, what happens to his *PPF*, *MB* curve, and efficient time allocation?

6. A farm grows wheat and produces pork. The marginal cost of producing each of these products increases as more of it is produced.
   a. Make a graph that illustrates the farm's *PPF*.
   b. The farm adopts a new technology that allows it to use fewer resources to fatten pigs. Use your graph to illustrate the impact of the new technology on the farm's *PPF*.
   c. With the farm using the new technology described in b, has the opportunity cost of producing a ton of wheat increased, decreased, or remained the same? Explain and illustrate your answer.
   d. Is the farm more efficient with the new technology than it was with the old one? Why?

7. In an hour, Sue can produce 40 caps or 4 jackets and Tessa can produce 80 caps or 4 jackets.
   a. Calculate Sue's opportunity cost of producing a cap.
   b. Calculate Tessa's opportunity cost of producing a cap.
   c. Who has a comparative advantage in producing caps?
   d. If Sue and Tessa specialize in producing the good in which each of them has a comparative advantage, and they trade 1 jacket for 15 caps, who gains from the specialization and trade?

8. Suppose that Tessa buys a new machine for making jackets that enables her to make 20 jackets an hour. (She can still make only 80 caps per hour.)
   a. Who now has a comparative advantage in producing jackets?
   b. Can Sue and Tessa still gain from trade?
   c. Would Sue and Tessa still be willing to trade 1 jacket for 15 caps? Explain your answer.

9. "America's baby-boomers are embracing tea for its health benefits," said *The Economist* (July 8, 2005, p. 65). The article went on to say: "Even though the climate is suitable, tea-growing [in the United States] is simply too costly, since the process is labor-intensive and resists automation." Using this information:
   a. Sketch a *PPF* for the production of tea and other goods and services in India.
   b. Sketch a *PPF* for the production of tea and other goods and services in the United States.
   c. Sketch a marginal cost curve for the production of tea in India.
   d. Sketch a marginal cost curve for the production of tea in the United States.
   e. Sketch the marginal benefit curve for tea in the United States before and after the baby-boomers began to appreciate the health benefits of tea.
   f. Explain why the United States does not produce tea and instead imports it from India.
   g. Explain how the quantity of tea that achieves allocative efficiency has changed.
   h. Does the change in preferences toward tea affect the opportunity cost of producing tea?

10. Brazil produces ethanol from sugar at a cost of 83 cents per gallon. The United States produces ethanol from corn at a cost of $1.14 per gallon. Sugar grown on one acre of land produces twice the quantity of ethanol as the corn grown on an acre. The United States imports 5 percent of its ethanol consumption and produces the rest itself. Since 2003, U.S. ethanol production has more than doubled and U.S. corn production has increased by 45 percent.
    a. Does Brazil or the United States have a comparative advantage in producing ethanol?
    b. Do you expect the opportunity cost of producing ethanol in the United States to have increased since 2003? Explain why.
    c. Sketch the *PPF* for ethanol and other goods and services for the United States.
    d. Sketch the *PPF* for ethanol and other goods and services for Brazil.
    e. Sketch a figure similar to Fig. 2.6 on p. 42 to show how both the United States and Brazil can gain from specialization and trade.
    f. Do you think the United States has achieved production efficiency in its manufacture of ethanol? Explain why or why not.
    g. Do you think the United States has achieved allocative efficiency in its manufacture of ethanol? Explain why or why not.

11. For 50 years, Cuba has had a centrally planned economy in which the government makes the big decisions on how resources will be allocated. Why would you expect Cuba's production possibilities (per person) to be smaller than those of the United States? What are the social institutions that help the U.S. economy achieve allocative efficiency that Cuba might lack?

12. Suppose that Yucatan's production possibilities are

Food (pounds per month)		Sunscreen (gallons per month)
300	and	0
200	and	50
100	and	100
0	and	150

a. Draw a graph of Yucatan's *PPF* and explain how your graph illustrates a tradeoff.

b. If Yucatan produces 150 pounds of food per month, how much sunscreen must it produce if it achieves production efficiency?

c. What is Yucatan's opportunity cost of producing 1 pound of food?

d. What is Yucatan's opportunity cost of producing 1 gallon of sunscreen?

e. What is the relationship between your answers to c and d?

f. Does Yucatan face an increasing opportunity cost of food? What feature of a *PPF* illustrates increasing opportunity cost and why does the *PPF* that you have drawn not have this feature?

13. What is the marginal cost of a pound of food in Yucatan in problem 12 when the quantity produced is 150 pounds per day? What is special about the marginal cost of food in Yucatan?

14. In Yucatan, which has the production possibilities shown in the table in problem 12, preferences are described by the following table.

Sunscreen (gallons per month)	Willingness to pay (pounds of food per gallon)
25	3
75	2
125	1

a. What is the marginal benefit from sunscreen and how it is measured?

b. What information provided in the table above and the table in problem 12 do we need to be able to calculate the marginal benefit from sunscreen in Yucatan?

c. Draw a graph of Yucatan's marginal benefit from sunscreen.

15. "Dr. Arata Kochi, the World Health Organization malaria chief, ... [says that] eradication is counterproductive. With enough money, he said, current tools like nets, medicines and DDT could drive down malaria cases 90 percent.

'But eliminating the last 10 percent is a tremendous task and very expensive,' Dr. Kochi said. 'Even places like South Africa should think twice before taking this path.'"

The New York Times, March 4, 2008

a. Is Dr. Kochi talking about *production efficiency* or *allocative efficiency* or both?

b. Make a graph with the percentage of malaria cases eliminated on the *x*-axis and the marginal cost and marginal benefit of driving down malaria cases on the *y*-axis. On your graph:
(i) Draw a marginal cost curve that is consistent with Dr. Kochi's opinion reported in the news article.
(ii) Draw a marginal benefit curve that is consistent with Dr. Kochi's opinion reported in the news article.
(iii) Identify the quantity of malaria eradicated that achieves allocative efficiency.

16. Capital accumulation and technological change bring economic growth, which means that the *PPF* keeps shifting outward: Production that was unattainable yesterday becomes attainable today; and production that is unattainable today will become attainable tomorrow. Why doesn't this process of economic growth mean that scarcity is being defeated and will one day be gone?

17. "Inexpensive broadband access has done far more for online video than enable the success of services like YouTube and iTunes. By unchaining video watchers from their TV sets, it has opened the floodgates to a generation of TV producers for whom the Internet is their native medium."

The New York Times, December 2, 2007

a. How has inexpensive broadband changed the production possibilities of video entertainment and other goods and services?

b. Sketch a *PPF* for video entertainment and other goods and services before broadband.

c. Show how the arrival of inexpensive broadband has changed the *PPF*.

d. Sketch a marginal benefit curve for video entertainment.

e. Show how opening the "floodgates to a generation of TV producers for whom the Internet is their native medium" might have changed the marginal benefit from video entertainment.

f. Explain how the quantity of video entertainment that achieves allocative efficiency has changed.

18. Kim can produce 40 pies an hour or 400 cookies an hour. Liam can produce 100 pies an hour or 200 cookies an hour.
    a. Calculate Kim's opportunity cost of producing a pie.
    b. Calculate Liam's opportunity cost of producing a pie.
    c. Who has a comparative advantage in producing pies?
    d. If Kim and Liam spend 30 minutes of each hour producing pies and 30 minutes producing cookies, how many pies and cookies does each of them produce?
    e. Suppose that Kim and Liam increase the time they spend producing the good in which they have a comparative advantage by 15 minutes. What will be the increase in the total number of pies and cookies they produce?
    f. What is the highest price of a pie at which Kim and Liam would agree to trade pies and cookies?
    g. If Kim and Liam specialize and trade, what are the gains from trade?

19. Before the Civil War, the South traded with the North and with England. The South sold cotton and bought manufactured goods and food. During the war, one of President Lincoln's first actions was to blockade the ports, which prevented this trade. The South had to increase its production of munitions and food.
    a. In what did the South have a comparative advantage?
    b. Draw a graph to illustrate production, consumption, and trade in the South before the Civil War.
    c. Was the South consuming inside, on, or outside its *PPF*? Explain your answer.
    d. Draw a graph to show the effects of the Civil War on consumption and production in the South.
    e. Did the Civil War change any opportunity costs in the South? Did the opportunity cost of everything rise? Did any items cost less?
    f. Illustrate your answer to e with appropriate graphs.

20. "A two-time N.B.A. All-Star, Barron Davis has quietly been moonlighting as a [movie] producer since 2005, when he and a high school buddy, Cash Warren, formed a production company called Verso Entertainment.

    In January, Verso's first feature-length effort, "Made in America," a gang-life documentary directed by Stacy Peralta, had its premiere to good reviews at Sundance Film Festival and is being courted by distributors."

    The New York Times, February 24, 2008
    a. Does Barron Davis have an *absolute* advantage in basketball and movie directing and is this the reason for his success in both activities?
    b. Does Barron Davis have a comparative advantage in basketball or movie directing or both and is this the reason for his success in both activities?
    c. Sketch a *PPF* between playing basketball and producing other goods and services for Barron Davis and for yourself.
    d. How do you (and people like you) and Barron Davis (and people like him) gain from specialization and trade?

21. After you have studied *Reading Between the Lines* on pp. 46–47, answer the following questions:
    a. How has an Act of the United States Congress increased U.S. production of corn?
    b. Why would you expect an increase in the quantity of corn produced to raise the opportunity cost of corn?
    c. Why did the cost of producing corn increase in the rest of the world?
    d. Is it possible that the increased quantity of corn produced, despite the higher cost of production, moves the United States closer to allocative efficiency?

22. Use the links on MyEconLab (Textbook Resources, Chapter 2, Weblinks) to obtain data on the tuition and other costs of enrolling in the MBA program at a school that interests you.

    a. Draw a *PPF* that shows the tradeoff that you would face if you decided to enroll in the MBA program.
    b. Do you think your marginal benefit of an MBA exceeds your marginal cost?
    c. Based on your answer to b, do you plan to enroll in an MBA program? Is your answer to this question consistent with using your time to achieve your self-interest?

UNDERSTANDING THE SCOPE OF ECONOMICS

Your Economic Revolution

Three periods in human history stand out as ones of economic revolution. The first, the *Agricultural Revolution,* occurred 10,000 years ago. In what is today Iraq, people learned to domesticate animals and plant crops. People stopped roaming in search of food and settled in villages, towns, and cities where they specialized in the activities in which they had a comparative advantage and developed markets in which to exchange their products. Wealth increased enormously.

You are studying economics at a time that future historians will call the *Information Revolution.* Over the entire world, people are embracing new information technologies and prospering on an unprecedented scale.

Economics was born during the *Industrial Revolution,* which began in England during the 1760s. For the first time, people began to apply science and create new technologies for the manufacture of textiles and iron, to create steam engines, and to boost the output of farms.

During all three economic revolutions, many have prospered but many have been left behind. It is the range of human progress that poses the greatest question for economics and the one that Adam Smith addressed in the first work of economic science: What causes the differences in wealth among nations?

Many people had written about economics before **Adam Smith,** *but he made economics a science. Born in 1723 in Kirkcaldy, a small fishing town near Edinburgh, Scotland, Smith was the only child of the town's customs officer. Lured from his professorship (he was a full professor at 28) by a wealthy Scottish duke who gave him a pension of £300 a year—ten times the average income at that time—Smith devoted ten years to writing his masterpiece:* An Inquiry into the Nature and Causes of the **Wealth of Nations,** *published in 1776.*

Why, Adam Smith asked , are some nations wealthy while others are poor? He was pondering these questions at the height of the Industrial Revolution, and he answered by emphasizing the role of the division of labor and free markets.

To illustrate his argument, Adam Smith described two pin factories. In the first, one person, using the hand tools available in the 1770s, could make 20 pins a day. In the other, by using those same hand tools but breaking the process into a number of individually small operations in which people specialize—by the division of labor—*ten people could make a staggering 48,000 pins a day. One*

> "It is not from the benevolence of the butcher, the brewer, or the baker that we expect our dinner, but from their regard to their own interest."
>
> **ADAM SMITH**
> *The Wealth of Nations*

draws out the wire, another straightens it, a third cuts it, a fourth points it, a fifth grinds it. Three specialists make the head, and a fourth attaches it. Finally, the pin is polished and packaged.

But a large market is needed to support the division of labor: One factory employing ten workers would need to sell more than 15 million pins a year to stay in business!

TALKING
WITH

Jagdish Bhagwati

Jagdish Bhagwati is University Professor at Columbia University. Born in India in 1934, he studied at Cambridge University in England, MIT, and Oxford University before returning to India. He returned to teach at MIT in 1968 and moved to Columbia in 1980. A prolific scholar, Professor Bhagwati also writes in leading newspapers and magazines throughout the world. He has been much honored for both his scientific work and his impact on public policy. His greatest contributions are in international trade but extend also to developmental problems and the study of political economy.

Michael Parkin talked with Jagdish Bhagwati about his work and the progress that economists have made in understanding the benefits of economic growth and international trade since the pioneering work of Adam Smith.

Professor Bhagwati, what attracted you to economics?

When you come from India, where poverty hits the eye, it is easy to be attracted to economics, which can be used to bring prosperity and create jobs to pull up the poor into gainful employment.

I learned later that there are two broad types of economist: those who treat the subject as an arid mathematical toy and those who see it as a serious social science.

If Cambridge, where I went as an undergraduate, had been interested in esoteric mathematical economics, I would have opted for something else. But the Cambridge economists from whom I learned—many among the greatest figures in the discipline—saw economics as a social science. I therefore saw the power of economics as a tool to address India's poverty and was immediately hooked.

Who had the greatest impact on you at Cambridge?

Most of all, it was Harry Johnson, a young Canadian of immense energy and profound analytical gifts. Quite unlike the shy and reserved British dons, Johnson was friendly, effusive, and supportive of students who flocked around him. He would later move to Chicago, where he became one of the most influential members of the market-oriented Chicago school. Another was Joan Robinson, arguably the world's most impressive female economist.

When I left Cambridge for MIT, going from one Cambridge to the other, I was lucky to transition from one phenomenal set of economists to another. At MIT, I learned much from future Nobel laureates Paul Samuelson and Robert Solow. Both would later become great friends and colleagues when I joined the MIT faculty in 1968.

After Cambridge and MIT, you went to Oxford and then back to India. What did you do in India?

I joined the Planning Commission in New Delhi, where my first big job was to find ways of raising the bottom 30 percent of India's population out of poverty to a "minimum income" level.

And what did you prescribe?

My main prescription was to "grow the pie." My research suggested that the share of the bottom 30 percent of the pie did not seem to vary dramatically with differences in economic and political systems. So growth in the pie seemed to be the principal (but not the only) component of an anti-poverty strategy. To supplement growth's good effects on the poor, the Indian planners were also dedicated to education, health, social reforms, and land reforms. Also, the access of the lowest-income and socially disadvantaged groups to the growth process and its benefits was to be improved in many ways, such as extension of credit without collateral.

Today, this strategy has no rivals. Much empirical work shows that where growth has occurred, poverty has lessened. It is nice to know that one's basic take on an issue of such central importance to humanity's well-being has been borne out by experience!

You left India in 1968 to come to the United States and an academic job at MIT. Why?

While the decision to emigrate often reflects personal factors—and they were present in my case—the offer of a professorship from MIT certainly helped me make up my mind. At the time, it was easily the world's most celebrated department. Serendipitously, the highest-ranked departments at MIT were not in engineering and the sciences but in linguistics (which had Noam Chomsky) and economics (which had Paul Samuelson). Joining the MIT faculty was a dramatic breakthrough: I felt stimulated each year by several fantastic students and by several of the world's most creative economists.

We hear a lot in the popular press about fair trade and level playing fields. What's the distinction between free trade and fair trade? How can the playing field be unlevel?

> My main prescription was to "grow the pie" … Today, this strategy has no rivals. Much empirical work shows that where growth has occurred, poverty has lessened.

> Fair trade … is almost always a sneaky way of objecting to free trade.

Free trade simply means allowing no trade barriers such as tariffs, subsidies, and quotas. Trade barriers make domestic prices different from world prices for traded goods. When this happens, resources are not being used efficiently. Basic economics from the time of Adam Smith tells us why free trade is good for us and why barriers to trade harm us, though our understanding of this doctrine today is far more nuanced and profound than it was at its creation.

Fair trade, on the other hand, is almost always a sneaky way of objecting to free trade. If your rivals are hard to compete with, you are not likely to get protection simply by saying that you cannot hack it. But if you say that your rival is an "unfair" trader, that is an easier sell! As international competition has grown fiercer, cries of "unfair trade" have therefore multiplied. The lesser rogues among the protectionists ask for "free and fair trade," whereas the worst ones ask for "fair, not free, trade."

At the end of World War II, the General Agreement of Tariffs and Trade (GATT) was established and there followed several rounds of multilateral trade negotiations and reductions in barriers to trade. How do you assess the contribution of GATT and its successor, the World Trade Organization (WTO)?

The GATT has made a huge contribution by overseeing massive trade liberalization in industrial goods among the developed countries. GATT rules, which "bind" tariffs to negotiated ceilings, prevent the raising of tariffs and have prevented tariff wars like those of the 1930s in which mutual and retaliatory tariff barriers were raised, to the detriment of everyone.

The GATT was folded into the WTO at the end of the Uruguay Round of trade negotiations, and the WTO is institutionally stronger. For instance, it has a binding dispute settlement mechanism, whereas the GATT had no such teeth. It is also more ambitious in its scope, extending to new areas such as the environment, intellectual property protection, and investment rules.

Running alongside the pursuit of multilateral free trade has been the emergence of bilateral trade agreements such as NAFTA and the European Union (EU). How do you view the bilateral free trade areas in today's world?

Unfortunately, there has been an explosion of bilateral free trade areas today. By some estimates, the ones in place and others being plotted approach 400! Each bilateral agreement gives preferential treatment to its trading partner over others. Because there are now so many bilateral agreements, such as those between the United States and Israel and between the United States and Jordan, the result is a chaotic pattern of different tariffs depending on where a product comes from. Also, "rules of origin" must be agreed upon to determine whether a product is, say, Jordanian or Taiwanese if Jordan qualifies for a preferential tariff but Taiwan does not and Taiwanese inputs enter the Jordanian manufacture of the product.

I have called the resulting crisscrossing of preferences and rules of origin the "spaghetti bowl" problem. The world trading system is choking under these proliferating bilateral deals. Contrast this complexity with the simplicity of a multilateral system with common tariffs for all WTO members.

We now have a world of uncoordinated and inefficient trade policies. The EU makes bilateral free trade agreements with different non-EU countries, so the United States follows with its own bilateral agreements; and with Europe and the United States doing it, the Asian countries, long wedded to multilateralism, have now succumbed to the mania.

Instead, if the United States had provided leadership by rewriting rules to make the signing of such bilateral agreements extremely difficult, this plague on the trading system today might well have been averted.

Despite the benefits that economics points to from multilateral free trade, the main organization that pursues

> We now have a world of uncoordinated and inefficient trade policies.

this goal, the WTO, is having a very hard time with the anti-globalization movement. What can we say about globalization that puts the WTO and its work in proper perspective?

The anti-globalization movement contains a diverse set of activists. Essentially, they all claim to be stakeholders in the globalization phenomenon. But there are those who want to drive a stake through the system, as in Dracula films, and there are those who want to exercise their stake in the system. The former want to be heard; the latter, to be listened to. For a while, the two disparate sets of critics were milling around together, seeking targets of opportunity at international conferences such as WTO's November 2000 meeting in Seattle, where the riots broke out. Now things have settled down, and the groups that want to work systematically and seriously at improving the global economy's functioning are much more in play.

But the WTO is also seen, inaccurately for the most part, as imposing trade sanctions that override concerns such as environmental protection. For example, U.S. legislation bans the importing of shrimp that is harvested without the use of turtle-excluding devices. India and others complained, but the WTO upheld the U.S. legislation. Ignorant of the facts, demonstrators took to the streets dressed as turtles protesting the WTO decision!

What advice do you have for a student who is just starting to study economics? Is economics a good subject in which to major?

I would say: enormously so. In particular, we economists bring three unique insights to good policy making.

First, economists look for second- and subsequent-round effects of actions.

Second, we correctly emphasize that a policy cannot be judged without using a counterfactual. It is a witticism that an economist, when asked how her husband was, said, "compared to what?"

Third, we uniquely and systematically bring the principle of social cost and social benefit to our policy analysis.

3 Demand and Supply

After studying this chapter,
you will be able to:

- Describe a competitive market and think about a price as an opportunity cost

- Explain the influences on demand

- Explain the influences on supply

- Explain how demand and supply determine prices and quantities bought and sold

- Use the demand and supply model to make predictions about changes in prices and quantities

What makes the prices of oil and gasoline double in just one year? Will these prices keep on rising? Are the oil companies taking advantage of people? This chapter enables you to answer these and similar questions about prices—prices that rise, prices that fall, and prices that fluctuate.

You already know that economics is about the choices people make to cope with scarcity and how those choices respond to incentives. Prices act as incentives. You're going to see how people respond to prices and how prices get determined by demand and supply. The demand and supply model that you study in this chapter is the main tool of economics. It

helps us to answer the big economic question: What, how, and for whom goods and services are produced?

At the end of the chapter, in *Reading Between the Lines,* we'll apply the model to market for gasoline and explain why the price increased so sharply in 2008.

◆ Markets and Prices

When you need a new pair of running shoes, want a bagel and a latte, plan to upgrade your cell phone, or need to fly home for Thanksgiving, you must find a place where people sell those items or offer those services. The place in which you find them is a *market*. You learned in Chapter 2 (p. 44) that a market is any arrangement that enables buyers and sellers to get information and to do business with each other.

A market has two sides: buyers and sellers. There are markets for *goods* such as apples and hiking boots, for *services* such as haircuts and tennis lessons, for *resources* such as computer programmers and earth-movers, and for other manufactured *inputs* such as memory chips and auto parts. There are also markets for money such as Japanese yen and for financial securities such as Yahoo! stock. Only our imagination limits what can be traded in markets.

Some markets are physical places where buyers and sellers meet and where an auctioneer or a broker helps to determine the prices. Examples of this type of market are the New York Stock Exchange and the wholesale fish, meat, and produce markets.

Some markets are groups of people spread around the world who never meet and know little about each other but are connected through the Internet or by telephone and fax. Examples are the e-commerce markets and the currency markets.

But most markets are unorganized collections of buyers and sellers. You do most of your trading in this type of market. An example is the market for basketball shoes. The buyers in this $3 billion-a-year market are the 45 million Americans who play basketball (or who want to make a fashion statement). The sellers are the tens of thousands of retail sports equipment and footwear stores. Each buyer can visit several different stores, and each seller knows that the buyer has a choice of stores.

Markets vary in the intensity of competition that buyers and sellers face. In this chapter, we're going to study a **competitive market**—a market that has many buyers and many sellers, so no single buyer or seller can influence the price.

Producers offer items for sale only if the price is high enough to cover their opportunity cost. And consumers respond to changing opportunity cost by seeking cheaper alternatives to expensive items.

We are going to study how people respond to *prices* and the forces that determine prices. But to pursue these tasks, we need to understand the relationship between a price and an opportunity cost.

In everyday life, the *price* of an object is the number of dollars that must be given up in exchange for it. Economists refer to this price as the **money price**.

The *opportunity cost* of an action is the highest-valued alternative forgone. If, when you buy a cup of coffee, the highest-valued thing you forgo is some gum, then the opportunity cost of the coffee is the *quantity* of gum forgone. We can calculate the quantity of gum forgone from the money prices of the coffee and the gum.

If the money price of coffee is $1 a cup and the money price of gum is 50¢ a pack, then the opportunity cost of one cup of coffee is two packs of gum. To calculate this opportunity cost, we divide the price of a cup of coffee by the price of a pack of gum and find the *ratio* of one price to the other. The ratio of one price to another is called a **relative price**, and a *relative price is an opportunity cost*.

We can express the relative price of coffee in terms of gum or any other good. The normal way of expressing a relative price is in terms of a "basket" of all goods and services. To calculate this relative price, we divide the money price of a good by the money price of a "basket" of all goods (called a *price index*). The resulting relative price tells us the opportunity cost of the good in terms of how much of the "basket" we must give up to buy it.

The demand and supply model that we are about to study determines *relative prices,* and the word "price" means *relative* price. When we predict that a price will fall, we do not mean that its *money* price will fall—although it might. We mean that its *relative* price will fall. That is, its price will fall *relative* to the average price of other goods and services.

Review Quiz ◆

1 What is the distinction between a money price and a relative price?
2 Explain why a relative price is an opportunity cost.
3 Think of examples of goods whose relative price has risen or fallen by a large amount.

 Work Study Plan 3.1 and get instant feedback.

Let's begin our study of demand and supply, starting with demand.

Demand

If you demand something, then you

1. Want it,
2. Can afford it, and
3. Plan to buy it.

Wants are the unlimited desires or wishes that people have for goods and services. How many times have you thought that you would like something "if only you could afford it" or "if it weren't so expensive"? Scarcity guarantees that many—perhaps most—of our wants will never be satisfied. Demand reflects a decision about which wants to satisfy.

The **quantity demanded** of a good or service is the amount that consumers plan to buy during a given time period at a particular price. The quantity demanded is not necessarily the same as the quantity actually bought. Sometimes the quantity demanded exceeds the amount of goods available, so the quantity bought is less than the quantity demanded.

The quantity demanded is measured as an amount per unit of time. For example, suppose that you buy one cup of coffee a day. The quantity of coffee that you demand can be expressed as 1 cup per day, 7 cups per week, or 365 cups per year.

Many factors influence buying plans, and one of them is the price. We look first at the relationship between the quantity demanded of a good and its price. To study this relationship, we keep all other influences on buying plans the same and we ask: How, other things remaining the same, does the quantity demanded of a good change as its price changes?

The law of demand provides the answer.

The Law of Demand

The **law of demand** states

> Other things remaining the same, the higher the price of a good, the smaller is the quantity demanded; and the lower the price of a good, the greater is the quantity demanded.

Why does a higher price reduce the quantity demanded? For two reasons:

- Substitution effect
- Income effect

Substitution Effect When the price of a good rises, other things remaining the same, its *relative* price— its opportunity cost—rises. Although each good is unique, it has *substitutes*—other goods that can be used in its place. As the opportunity cost of a good rises, the incentive to economize on its use and switch to a substitute becomes stronger.

Income Effect When a price rises, other things remaining the same, the price rises *relative* to income. Faced with a higher price and an unchanged income, people cannot afford to buy all the things they previously bought. They must decrease the quantities demanded of at least some goods and services. Normally, the good whose price has increased will be one of the goods that people buy less of.

To see the substitution effect and the income effect at work, think about the effects of a change in the price of an energy bar. Several different goods are substitutes for an energy bar. For example, an energy drink could be consumed instead of an energy bar.

Suppose that an energy bar initially sells for $3 and then its price falls to $1.50. People now substitute energy bars for energy drinks—the substitution effect. And with a budget that now has some slack from the lower price of an energy bar, people buy even more energy bars—the income effect. The quantity of energy bars demanded increases for these two reasons.

Now suppose that an energy bar initially sells for $3 and then the price doubles to $6. People now buy fewer energy bars and more energy drinks—the substitution effect. And faced with a tighter budget, people buy even fewer energy bars—the income effect. The quantity of energy bars demanded decreases for these two reasons.

Demand Curve and Demand Schedule

You are now about to study one of the two most used curves in economics: the demand curve. And you are going to encounter one of the most critical distinctions: the distinction between *demand* and *quantity demanded*.

The term **demand** refers to the entire relationship between the price of a good and the quantity demanded of that good. Demand is illustrated by the demand curve and the demand schedule. The term *quantity demanded* refers to a point on a demand curve—the quantity demanded at a particular price.

Figure 3.1 shows the demand curve for energy bars. A **demand curve** shows the relationship between the quantity demanded of a good and its price when all other influences on consumers' planned purchases remain the same.

The table in Fig. 3.1 is the demand schedule for energy bars. A *demand schedule* lists the quantities demanded at each price when all the other influences on consumers' planned purchases remain the same. For example, if the price of a bar is 50¢, the quantity demanded is 22 million a week. If the price is $2.50, the quantity demanded is 5 million a week. The other rows of the table show the quantities demanded at prices of $1.00, $1.50, and $2.00.

We graph the demand schedule as a demand curve with the quantity demanded on the *x*-axis and the price on the *y*-axis. The points on the demand curve labeled *A* through *E* correspond to the rows of the demand schedule. For example, point *A* on the graph shows a quantity demanded of 22 million energy bars a week at a price of 50¢ a bar.

Willingness and Ability to Pay Another way of looking at the demand curve is as a willingness-and-ability-to-pay curve. The willingness and ability to pay is a measure of *marginal benefit.*

If a small quantity is available, the highest price that someone is willing and able to pay for one more unit is high. But as the quantity available increases, the marginal benefit of each additional unit falls and the highest price that someone is willing and able to pay also falls along the demand curve.

In Fig. 3.1, if only 5 million energy bars are available each week, the highest price that someone is willing to pay for the 5 millionth bar is $2.50. But if 22 million energy bars are available each week, someone is willing to pay 50¢ for the last bar bought.

A Change in Demand

When any factor that influences buying plans other than the price of the good changes, there is a **change in demand**. Figure 3.2 illustrates an increase in demand. When demand increases, the demand curve shifts rightward and the quantity demanded at each price is greater. For example, at $2.50 a bar, the quantity demanded on the original (blue) demand curve is 5 million energy bars a week. On the new (red) demand curve, at $2.50 a bar, the quantity demanded is 15 million bars a week. Look closely at the numbers in the table and check that the quantity demanded at each price is greater.

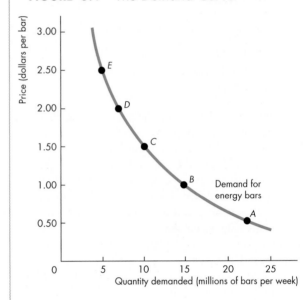

FIGURE 3.1 The Demand Curve

	Price (dollars per bar)	Quantity demanded (millions of bars per week)
A	0.50	22
B	1.00	15
C	1.50	10
D	2.00	7
E	2.50	5

The table shows a demand schedule for energy bars. At a price of 50¢ a bar, 22 million bars a week are demanded; at a price of $1.50 a bar, 10 million bars a week are demanded. The demand curve shows the relationship between quantity demanded and price, other things remaining the same. The demand curve slopes downward: As the price decreases, the quantity demanded increases.

The demand curve can be read in two ways. For a given price, the demand curve tells us the quantity that people plan to buy. For example, at a price of $1.50 a bar, people plan to buy 10 million bars a week. For a given quantity, the demand curve tells us the maximum price that consumers are willing and able to pay for the last bar available. For example, the maximum price that consumers will pay for the 15 millionth bar is $1.00.

myeconlab animation

FIGURE 3.2   An Increase in Demand

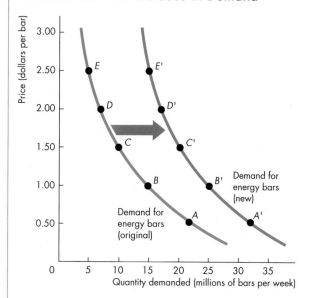

A change in any influence on buyers' plans other than the price of the good itself results in a new demand schedule and a shift of the demand curve. A change in income changes the demand for energy bars. At a price of $1.50 a bar, 10 million bars a week are demanded at the original income (row C of the table) and 20 million bars a week are demanded at the new higher income (row C'). A rise in income increases the demand for energy bars. The demand curve shifts *rightward*, as shown by the shift arrow and the resulting red curve.

Original demand schedule Original income		New demand schedule New higher income	
Price (dollars per bar)	Quantity demanded (millions of bars per week)	Price (dollars per bar)	Quantity demanded (millions of bars per week)
A 0.50	22	A' 0.50	32
B 1.00	15	B' 1.00	25
C 1.50	10	C' 1.50	20
D 2.00	7	D' 2.00	17
E 2.50	5	E' 2.50	15

myeconlab animation

Six main factors bring changes in demand. They are changes in

- The prices of related goods
- Expected future prices
- Income
- Expected future income and credit
- Population
- Preferences

Prices of Related Goods The quantity of energy bars that consumers plan to buy depends in part on the prices of substitutes for energy bars. A **substitute** is a good that can be used in place of another good. For example, a bus ride is a substitute for a train ride; a hamburger is a substitute for a hot dog; and an energy drink is a substitute for an energy bar. If the price of a substitute for an energy bar rises, people buy less of the substitute and more energy bars. For example, if the price of an energy drink rises, people buy fewer energy drinks and more energy bars. The demand for energy bars increases.

The quantity of energy bars that people plan to buy also depends on the prices of complements with energy bars. A **complement** is a good that is used in conjunction with another good. Hamburgers and fries are complements, and so are energy bars and exercise. If the price of an hour at the gym falls, people buy more gym time *and more* energy bars.

Expected Future Prices If the price of a good is expected to rise in the future and if the good can be stored, the opportunity cost of obtaining the good for future use is lower today than it will be when the price has increased. So people retime their purchases—they substitute over time. They buy more of the good now before its price is expected to rise (and less afterward), so the demand for the good today increases.

For example, suppose that a Florida frost damages the season's orange crop. You expect the price of orange juice to rise, so you fill your freezer with enough frozen juice to get you through the next six months. Your current demand for frozen orange juice has increased, and your future demand has decreased.

Similarly, if the price of a good is expected to fall in the future, the opportunity cost of buying the good today is high relative to what it is expected to be in the future. So again, people retime their purchases. They buy less of the good now before its price falls, so the demand for the good decreases today and increases in the future.

Computer prices are constantly falling, and this fact poses a dilemma. Will you buy a new computer now, in time for the start of the school year, or will you wait until the price has fallen some more? Because people expect computer prices to keep falling, the current demand for computers is less (and the future demand is greater) than it otherwise would be.

Income Consumers' income influences demand. When income increases, consumers buy more of most goods; and when income decreases, consumers buy less of most goods. Although an increase in income leads to an increase in the demand for *most* goods, it does not lead to an increase in the demand for *all* goods. A **normal good** is one for which demand increases as income increases. An **inferior good** is one for which demand decreases as income increases. As incomes increase, the demand for air travel (a normal good) increases and the demand for long-distance bus trips (an inferior good) decreases.

Expected Future Income and Credit When income is expected to increase in the future, or when credit is easy to obtain, demand might increase now. For example, a salesperson gets the news that she will receive a big bonus at the end of the year, so she goes into debt and buys a new car right now.

Population Demand also depends on the size and the age structure of the population. The larger the population, the greater is the demand for all goods and services; the smaller the population, the smaller is the demand for all goods and services.

For example, the demand for parking spaces or movies or just about anything that you can imagine is much greater in New York City (population 7.5 million) than it is in Boise, Idaho (population 150,000).

Also, the larger the proportion of the population in a given age group, the greater is the demand for the goods and services used by that age group.

For example, during the 1990s, a decrease in the college-age population decreased the demand for college places. During those same years, the number of Americans aged 85 years and over increased by more than 1 million. As a result, the demand for nursing home services increased.

TABLE 3.1   The Demand for Energy Bars

The Law of Demand

The quantity of energy bars demanded

Decreases if:	Increases if:
■ The price of an energy bar rises	■ The price of an energy bar falls

Changes in Demand

The demand for energy bars

Decreases if:	Increases if:
■ The price of a substitute falls	■ The price of a substitute rises
■ The price of a complement rises	■ The price of a complement falls
■ The price of an energy bar is expected to fall	■ The price of an energy bar is expected to rise
■ Income falls*	■ Income rises*
■ Expected future income falls or credit becomes harder to get	■ Expected future income rises or credit becomes easier to get
■ The population decreases	■ The population increases

*An energy bar is a normal good.

Preferences Demand depends on preferences. *Preferences* determine the value that people place on each good and service. Preferences depend on such things as the weather, information, and fashion. For example, greater health and fitness awareness has shifted preferences in favor of energy bars, so the demand for energy bars has increased.

Table 3.1 summarizes the influences on demand and the direction of those influences.

A Change in the Quantity Demanded Versus a Change in Demand

Changes in the influences on buyers' plans bring either a change in the quantity demanded or a change in demand. Equivalently, they bring either a movement along the demand curve or a shift of the demand curve. The distinction between a change in the quantity demanded and a change in demand is

Demand 63

the same as that between a movement along the demand curve and a shift of the demand curve.

A point on the demand curve shows the quantity demanded at a given price. So a movement along the demand curve shows a **change in the quantity demanded**. The entire demand curve shows demand. So a shift of the demand curve shows a *change in demand*. Figure 3.3 illustrates these distinctions.

Movement Along the Demand Curve If the price of the good changes but no other influence on buying plans changes, we illustrate the effect as a movement along the demand curve.

A fall in the price of a good increases the quantity demanded of it. In Fig. 3.3, we illustrate the effect of a fall in price as a movement down along the demand curve D_0.

A rise in the price of a good decreases the quantity demanded of it. In Fig. 3.3, we illustrate the effect of a rise in price as a movement up along the demand curve D_0.

A Shift of the Demand Curve If the price of a good remains constant but some other influence on buyers' plans changes, there is a change in demand for that good. We illustrate a change in demand as a shift of the demand curve. For example, if more people work out at the gym, consumers buy more energy bars regardless of the price of a bar. That is what a rightward shift of the demand curve shows—more energy bars are demanded at each price.

In Fig. 3.3, there is a *change in demand* and the demand curve shifts when any influence on buyers' plans changes, other than the price of the good. Demand *increases* and the demand curve *shifts rightward* (to the red demand curve D_1) if the price of a substitute rises, the price of a complement falls, the expected future price of the good rises, income increases (for a normal good), expected future income or credit increases, or the population increases. Demand *decreases* and the demand curve *shifts leftward* (to the red demand curve D_2) if the price of a substitute falls, the price of a complement rises, the expected future price of the good falls, income decreases (for a normal good), expected future income or credit decreases, or the population decreases. (For an inferior good, the effects of changes in income are in the opposite direction to those described above.)

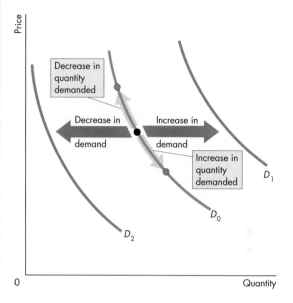

FIGURE 3.3 A Change in the Quantity Demanded Versus a Change in Demand

When the price of the good changes, there is a movement along the demand curve and *a change in the quantity demanded*, shown by the blue arrows on demand curve D_0. When any other influence on buyers' plans changes, there is a shift of the demand curve and a *change in demand*. An increase in demand shifts the demand curve rightward (from D_0 to D_1). A decrease in demand shifts the demand curve leftward (from D_0 to D_2).

myeconlab animation

Review Quiz

1 Define the quantity demanded of a good or service.
2 What is the law of demand and how do we illustrate it?
3 What does the demand curve tell us about the price that consumers are willing to pay?
4 List all the influences on buying plans that change demand, and for each influence, say whether it increases or decreases demand.
5 Why does demand not change when the price of a good changes with no change in the other influences on buying plans?

myeconlab Work Study Plan 3.2 and get instant feedback.

Supply

If a firm supplies a good or service, the firm

1. Has the resources and technology to produce it,
2. Can profit from producing it, and
3. Plans to produce it and sell it.

A supply is more than just having the *resources* and the *technology* to produce something. *Resources and technology* are the constraints that limit what is possible.

Many useful things can be produced, but they are not produced unless it is profitable to do so. Supply reflects a decision about which technologically feasible items to produce.

The **quantity supplied** of a good or service is the amount that producers plan to sell during a given time period at a particular price. The quantity supplied is not necessarily the same amount as the quantity actually sold. Sometimes the quantity supplied is greater than the quantity demanded, so the quantity sold is less than the quantity supplied.

Like the quantity demanded, the quantity supplied is measured as an amount per unit of time. For example, suppose that GM produces 1,000 cars a day. The quantity of cars supplied by GM can be expressed as 1,000 a day, 7,000 a week, or 365,000 a year. Without the time dimension, we cannot tell whether a particular quantity is large or small.

Many factors influence selling plans, and again one of them is the price of the good. We look first at the relationship between the quantity supplied of a good and its price. Just as we did when we studied demand, to isolate the relationship between the quantity supplied of a good and its price, we keep all other influences on selling plans the same and ask: How does the quantity supplied of a good change as its price changes when other things remain the same?

The law of supply provides the answer.

The Law of Supply

The **law of supply** states:

> Other things remaining the same, the higher the price of a good, the greater is the quantity supplied; and the lower the price of a good, the smaller is the quantity supplied.

Why does a higher price increase the quantity supplied? It is because *marginal cost increases.* As the quantity produced of any good increases, the marginal cost of producing the good increases. (You can refresh your memory of increasing marginal cost in Chapter 2, p. 35.)

It is never worth producing a good if the price received for the good does not at least cover the marginal cost of producing it. When the price of a good rises, other things remaining the same, producers are willing to incur a higher marginal cost, so they increase production. The higher price brings forth an increase in the quantity supplied.

Let's now illustrate the law of supply with a supply curve and a supply schedule.

Supply Curve and Supply Schedule

You are now going to study the second of the two most used curves in economics: the supply curve. And you're going to learn about the critical distinction between *supply* and *quantity supplied*.

The term **supply** refers to the entire relationship between the price of a good and the quantity supplied of it. Supply is illustrated by the supply curve and the supply schedule. The term *quantity supplied* refers to a point on a supply curve—the quantity supplied at a particular price.

Figure 3.4 shows the supply curve of energy bars. A **supply curve** shows the relationship between the quantity supplied of a good and its price when all other influences on producers' planned sales remain the same. The supply curve is a graph of a supply schedule.

The table in Fig. 3.4 sets out the supply schedule for energy bars. A *supply schedule* lists the quantities supplied at each price when all the other influences on producers' planned sales remain the same. For example, if the price of a bar is 50¢, the quantity supplied is zero—in row *A* of the table. If the price of a bar is $1.00, the quantity supplied is 6 million energy bars a week—in row *B*. The other rows of the table show the quantities supplied at prices of $1.50, $2.00, and $2.50.

To make a supply curve, we graph the quantity supplied on the *x*-axis and the price on the *y*-axis, just as in the case of the demand curve. The points on the supply curve labeled *A* through *E* correspond to the rows of the supply schedule. For example, point *A* on the graph shows a quantity supplied of zero at a price of 50¢ an energy bar.

FIGURE 3.4   The Supply Curve

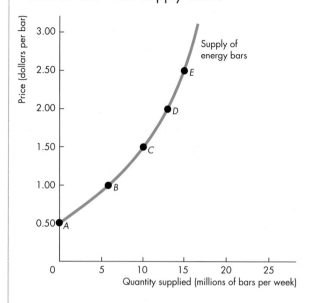

The table shows the supply schedule of energy bars. For example, at a price of $1.00, 6 million bars a week are supplied; at a price of $2.50, 15 million bars a week are supplied. The supply curve shows the relationship between the quantity supplied and the price, other things remaining the same. The supply curve slopes upward: As the price of a good increases, the quantity supplied increases.

A supply curve can be read in two ways. For a given price, the supply curve tells us the quantity that producers plan to sell at that price. For example, at a price of $1.50 a bar, producers are willing to sell 10 million bars a week. For a given quantity, the supply curve tells us the minimum price at which producers are willing to sell one more bar. For example, if 15 million bars are produced each week, the lowest price at which a producer is willing to sell the 15 millionth bar is $2.50.

Minimum Supply Price   The supply curve can be interpreted as a minimum-supply-price curve—a curve that shows the lowest price at which someone is willing to sell. This lowest price is the *marginal cost.*

If a small quantity is produced, the lowest price at which someone is willing to sell one more unit is low. But as the quantity produced increases, the marginal cost of each additional unit rises, so the lowest price at which someone is willing to sell rises along the supply curve.

In Fig. 3.4, if 15 million bars are produced each week, the lowest price at which someone is willing to sell the 15 millionth bar is $2.50. But if 10 million bars are produced each week, someone is willing to accept $1.50 for the last bar produced.

A Change in Supply

When any factor that influences selling plans other than the price of the good changes, there is a **change in supply**. Six main factors bring changes in supply. They are changes in

- The prices of factors of production
- The prices of related goods produced
- Expected future prices
- The number of suppliers
- Technology
- The state of nature

Prices of Factors of Production   The prices of the factors of production used to produce a good influence its supply. To see this influence, think about the supply curve as a minimum-supply-price curve. If the price of a factor of production rises, the lowest price that a producer is willing to accept for that good rises, so supply decreases. For example, during 2008, as the price of jet fuel increased, the supply of air travel decreased. Similarly, a rise in the minimum wage decreases the supply of hamburgers.

Prices of Related Goods Produced   The prices of related goods that firms produce influence supply. For example, if the price of energy gel rises, firms switch production from bars to gel. The supply of energy bars decreases. Energy bars and energy gel are *substitutes in production*—goods that can be produced by using the same resources. If the price of beef rises, the supply of cowhide increases. Beef and cowhide are *complements in production*—goods that must be produced together.

Expected Future Prices If the price of a good is expected to rise, the return from selling the good in the future is higher than it is today. So supply decreases today and increases in the future.

The Number of Suppliers The larger the number of firms that produce a good, the greater is the supply of the good. And as firms enter an industry, the supply in that industry increases. As firms leave an industry, the supply in that industry decreases.

Technology The term "technology" is used broadly to mean the way that factors of production are used to produce a good. A technology change occurs when a new method is discovered that lowers the cost of producing a good. For example, new methods used in the factories that produce computer chips have lowered the cost and increased the supply of chips.

The State of Nature The state of nature includes all the natural forces that influence production. It includes the state of the weather and, more broadly, the natural environment. Good weather can increase the supply of many agricultural products and bad weather can decrease their supply. Extreme natural events such as earthquakes, tornadoes, and hurricanes can also influence supply.

Figure 3.5 illustrates an increase in supply. When supply increases, the supply curve shifts rightward and the quantity supplied at each price is larger. For example, at $1.00 per bar, on the original (blue) supply curve, the quantity supplied is 6 million bars a week. On the new (red) supply curve, the quantity supplied is 15 million bars a week. Look closely at the numbers in the table in Fig. 3.5 and check that the quantity supplied is larger at each price.

Table 3.2 summarizes the influences on supply and the directions of those influences.

A Change in the Quantity Supplied Versus a Change in Supply

Changes in the influences on producers' planned sales bring either a change in the quantity supplied or a change in supply. Equivalently, they bring either a movement along the supply curve or a shift of the supply curve.

A point on the supply curve shows the quantity supplied at a given price. A movement along the supply curve shows a **change in the quantity supplied**. The entire supply curve shows supply. A shift of the supply curve shows a *change in supply*.

FIGURE 3.5 An Increase in Supply

Original supply schedule Old technology			New supply schedule New technology		
	Price (dollars per bar)	Quantity supplied (millions of bars per week)		Price (dollars per bar)	Quantity supplied (millions of bars per week)
A	0.50	0	A'	0.50	7
B	1.00	6	B'	1.00	15
C	1.50	10	C'	1.50	20
D	2.00	13	D'	2.00	25
E	2.50	15	E'	2.50	27

A change in any influence on sellers' plans other than the price of the good itself results in a new supply schedule and a shift of the supply curve. For example, a new, cost-saving technology for producing energy bars changes the supply of energy bars. At a price of $1.50 a bar, 10 million bars a week are supplied when producers use the old technology (row *C* of the table) and 20 million energy bars a week are supplied when producers use the new technology (row *C'*). An advance in technology *increases* the supply of energy bars. The supply curve shifts *rightward*, as shown by the shift arrow and the resulting red curve.

Figure 3.6 illustrates and summarizes these distinctions. If the price of the good falls and other things remain the same, the quantity supplied of that good decreases and there is a movement down along the supply curve S_0. If the price of the good rises and other things remain the same, the quantity supplied increases and there is a movement up along the supply curve S_0. When any other influence on selling plans changes, the supply curve shifts and there is a *change in supply*. If supply increases, the supply curve shifts rightward to S_1. If supply decreases, the supply curve shifts leftward to S_2.

TABLE 3.2   The Supply of Energy Bars

The Law of Supply

The quantity of energy bars supplied

Decreases if:	Increases if:
■ The price of an energy bar falls	■ The price of an energy bar rises

Changes in Supply

The supply of energy bars

Decreases if:	Increases if:
■ The price of a factor of production used to produce energy bars rises	■ The price of a factor of production used to produce energy bars falls
■ The price of a substitute in production rises	■ The price of a substitute in production falls
■ The price of a complement in production falls	■ The price of a complement in production rises
■ The price of an energy bar is expected to rise	■ The price of an energy bar is expected to fall
■ The number of suppliers of bars decreases	■ The number of suppliers of bars increases
■ A technology change decreases energy bar production	■ A technology change increases energy bar production
■ A natural event decreases energy bar production	■ A natural event increases energy bar production

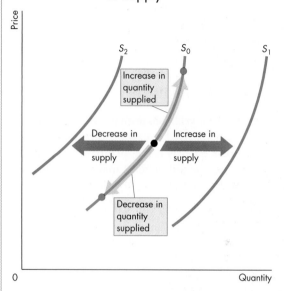

FIGURE 3.6   A Change in the Quantity Supplied Versus a Change in Supply

When the price of the good changes, there is a movement along the supply curve and *a change in the quantity supplied*, shown by the blue arrows on supply curve S_0. When any other influence on selling plans changes, there is a shift of the supply curve and a *change in supply*. An increase in supply shifts the supply curve rightward (from S_0 to S_1), and a decrease in supply shifts the supply curve leftward (from S_0 to S_2).

 animation

Review Quiz

1 Define the quantity supplied of a good or service.
2 What is the law of supply and how do we illustrate it?
3 What does the supply curve tell us about the producer's minimum supply price?
4 List all the influences on selling plans, and for each influence, say whether it changes supply.
5 What happens to the quantity of cell phones supplied and the supply of cell phones if the price of a cell phone falls?

myeconlab   Work Study Plan 3.3 and get instant feedback.

Now we're going to combine demand and supply and see how prices and quantities are determined.

Market Equilibrium

We have seen that when the price of a good rises, the quantity demanded *decreases* and the quantity supplied *increases*. We are now going to see how the price adjusts to coordinate the plans of buyers and sellers and achieve an equilibrium in the market.

An *equilibrium* is a situation in which opposing forces balance each other. Equilibrium in a market occurs when the price balances the plans of buyers and sellers. The **equilibrium price** is the price at which the quantity demanded equals the quantity supplied. The **equilibrium quantity** is the quantity bought and sold at the equilibrium price. A market moves toward its equilibrium because

- Price regulates buying and selling plans.
- Price adjusts when plans don't match.

Price as a Regulator

The price of a good regulates the quantities demanded and supplied. If the price is too high, the quantity supplied exceeds the quantity demanded. If the price is too low, the quantity demanded exceeds the quantity supplied. There is one price at which the quantity demanded equals the quantity supplied. Let's work out what that price is.

Figure 3.7 shows the market for energy bars. The table shows the demand schedule (from Fig. 3.1) and the supply schedule (from Fig. 3.4). If the price of a bar is 50¢, the quantity demanded is 22 million bars a week but no bars are supplied. There is a shortage of 22 million bars a week. This shortage is shown in the final column of the table. At a price of $1.00 a bar, there is still a shortage but only of 9 million bars a week. If the price of a bar is $2.50, the quantity supplied is 15 million bars a week but the quantity demanded is only 5 million. There is a surplus of 10 million bars a week. The one price at which there is neither a shortage nor a surplus is $1.50 a bar. At that price, the quantity demanded is equal to the quantity supplied: 10 million bars a week. The equilibrium price is $1.50 a bar, and the equilibrium quantity is 10 million bars a week.

Figure 3.7 shows that the demand curve and the supply curve intersect at the equilibrium price of $1.50 a bar. At each price *above* $1.50 a bar, there is a surplus of bars. For example, at $2.00 a bar, the surplus is 6

FIGURE 3.7   Equilibrium

Price (dollars per bar)	Quantity demanded	Quantity supplied	Shortage (–) or surplus (+)
	(millions of bars per week)		
0.50	22	0	–22
1.00	15	6	–9
1.50	10	10	0
2.00	7	13	+6
2.50	5	15	+10

The table lists the quantity demanded and the quantity supplied as well as the shortage or surplus of bars at each price. If the price is $1.00 a bar, 15 million bars a week are demanded and 6 million are supplied. There is a shortage of 9 million bars a week, and the price rises.

If the price is $2.00 a bar, 7 million bars a week are demanded and 13 million are supplied. There is a surplus of 6 million bars a week, and the price falls.

If the price is $1.50 a bar, 10 million bars a week are demanded and 10 million bars are supplied. There is neither a shortage nor a surplus. Neither buyers nor sellers have an incentive to change the price. The price at which the quantity demanded equals the quantity supplied is the equilibrium price. And 10 million bars a week is the equilibrium quantity.

million bars a week, as shown by the blue arrow. At each price *below* $1.50 a bar, there is a shortage of bars. For example, at $1.00 a bar, the shortage is 9 million bars a week, as shown by the red arrow.

Price Adjustments

You've seen that if the price is below equilibrium, there is a shortage and that if the price is above equilibrium, there is a surplus. But can we count on the price to change and eliminate a shortage or a surplus? We can, because such price changes are beneficial to both buyers and sellers. Let's see why the price changes when there is a shortage or a surplus.

A Shortage Forces the Price Up Suppose the price of an energy bar is $1. Consumers plan to buy 15 million bars a week, and producers plan to sell 6 million bars a week. Consumers can't force producers to sell more than they plan, so the quantity that is actually offered for sale is 6 million bars a week. In this situation, powerful forces operate to increase the price and move it toward the equilibrium price. Some producers, noticing lines of unsatisfied consumers, raise the price. Some producers increase their output. As producers push the price up, the price rises toward its equilibrium. The rising price reduces the shortage because it decreases the quantity demanded and increases the quantity supplied. When the price has increased to the point at which there is no longer a shortage, the forces moving the price stop operating and the price comes to rest at its equilibrium.

A Surplus Forces the Price Down Suppose the price of a bar is $2. Producers plan to sell 13 million bars a week, and consumers plan to buy 7 million bars a week. Producers cannot force consumers to buy more than they plan, so the quantity that is actually bought is 7 million bars a week. In this situation, powerful forces operate to lower the price and move it toward the equilibrium price. Some producers, unable to sell the quantities of energy bars they planned to sell, cut their prices. In addition, some producers scale back production. As producers cut the price, the price falls toward its equilibrium. The falling price decreases the surplus because it increases the quantity demanded and decreases the quantity supplied. When the price has fallen to the point at which there is no longer a surplus, the forces moving the price stop operating and the price comes to rest at its equilibrium.

The Best Deal Available for Buyers and Sellers

When the price is below equilibrium, it is forced upward. Why don't buyers resist the increase and refuse to buy at the higher price? Because they value the good more highly than the current price and they can't satisfy their demand at the current price. In some markets—for example, the markets that operate on eBay—the buyers might even be the ones who force the price up by offering to pay a higher price.

When the price is above equilibrium, it is bid downward. Why don't sellers resist this decrease and refuse to sell at the lower price? Because their minimum supply price is below the current price and they cannot sell all they would like to at the current price. Normally, it is the sellers who force the price down by offering lower prices to gain market share.

At the price at which the quantity demanded and the quantity supplied are equal, neither buyers nor sellers can do business at a better price. Buyers pay the highest price they are willing to pay for the last unit bought, and sellers receive the lowest price at which they are willing to supply the last unit sold.

When people freely make offers to buy and sell and when demanders try to buy at the lowest possible price and suppliers try to sell at the highest possible price, the price at which trade takes place is the equilibrium price—the price at which the quantity demanded equals the quantity supplied. The price coordinates the plans of buyers and sellers, and no one has an incentive to change it.

Review Quiz

1 What is the equilibrium price of a good or service?
2 Over what range of prices does a shortage arise?
3 Over what range of prices does a surplus arise?
4 What happens to the price when there is a shortage?
5 What happens to the price when there is a surplus?
6 Why is the price at which the quantity demanded equals the quantity supplied the equilibrium price?
7 Why is the equilibrium price the best deal available for both buyers and sellers?

 Work Study Plan 3.4 and get instant feedback.

Predicting Changes in Price and Quantity

The demand and supply model that we have just studied provides us with a powerful way of analyzing influences on prices and the quantities bought and sold. According to the model, a change in price stems from a change in demand, a change in supply, or a change in both demand and supply. Let's look first at the effects of a change in demand.

An Increase in Demand

When more and more people join health clubs, the demand for energy bars increases. The table in Fig. 3.8 shows the original and new demand schedules for energy bars (the same as those in Fig. 3.2) as well as the supply schedule of energy bars.

When demand increases, there is a shortage at the original equilibrium price of $1.50 a bar. To eliminate the shortage, the price must rise. The price that makes the quantity demanded and quantity supplied equal again is $2.50 a bar. At this price, 15 million bars are bought and sold each week. When demand increases, both the price and the quantity increase.

Figure 3.8 shows these changes. The figure shows the original demand for and supply of energy bars. The original equilibrium price is $1.50 an energy bar, and the quantity is 10 million energy bars a week. When demand increases, the demand curve shifts rightward. The equilibrium price rises to $2.50 an energy bar, and the quantity supplied increases to 15 million energy bars a week, as highlighted in the figure. There is an *increase in the quantity supplied* but *no change in supply*—a movement along, but no shift of, the supply curve.

A Decrease in Demand

We can reverse this change in demand. Start at a price of $2.50 a bar with 15 million energy bars a week being bought and sold, and then work out what happens if demand decreases to its original level. Such a decrease in demand might arise if people switch to energy gel (a substitute for energy bars). The decrease in demand shifts the demand curve leftward. The equilibrium price falls to $1.50 a bar, and the equilibrium quantity decreases to 10 million bars a week.

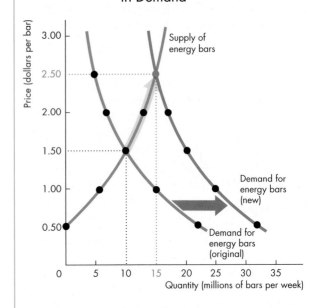

FIGURE 3.8   The Effects of a Change in Demand

Price (dollars per bar)	Quantity demanded (millions of bars per week)		Quantity supplied (millions of bars per week)
	Original	New	
0.50	22	32	0
1.00	15	25	6
1.50	**10**	20	**10**
2.00	7	17	13
2.50	5	15	15

Initially, the demand for energy bars is the blue demand curve. The equilibrium price is $1.50 a bar, and the equilibrium quantity is 10 million bars a week. When more health-conscious people do more exercise, the demand for energy bars increases and the demand curve shifts rightward to become the red curve.

At $1.50 a bar, there is now a shortage of 10 million bars a week. The price of a bar rises to a new equilibrium of $2.50. As the price rises to $2.50, the quantity supplied increases—shown by the blue arrow on the supply curve—to the new equilibrium quantity of 15 million bars a week. Following an increase in demand, the quantity supplied increases but supply does not change—the supply curve does not shift.

We can now make our first two predictions:

1. When demand increases, both the price and the quantity increase.
2. When demand decreases, both the price and the quantity decrease.

An Increase in Supply

When Nestlé (the producer of PowerBar) and other energy bar producers switch to a new cost-saving technology, the supply of energy bars increases. Figure 3.9 shows the new supply schedule (the same one that was shown in Fig. 3.5). What are the new equilibrium price and quantity? The price falls to $1.00 a bar, and the quantity increases to 15 million bars a week. You can see why by looking at the quantities demanded and supplied at the old price of $1.50 a bar. The quantity supplied at that price is 20 million bars a week, and there is a surplus of bars. The price falls. Only when the price is $1.00 a bar does the quantity supplied equal the quantity demanded.

Figure 3.9 illustrates the effect of an increase in supply. It shows the demand curve for energy bars and the original and new supply curves. The initial equilibrium price is $1.50 a bar, and the quantity is 10 million bars a week. When supply increases, the supply curve shifts rightward. The equilibrium price falls $1.00 a bar, and the quantity demanded increases to 15 million bars a week, highlighted in the figure. There is an *increase in the quantity demanded* but *no change in demand*—a movement along, but no shift of, the demand curve.

A Decrease in Supply

Start out at a price of $1.00 a bar with 15 million bars a week being bought and sold. Then suppose that the cost of labor or raw materials rises and the supply of energy bars decreases. The decrease in supply shifts the supply curve leftward. The equilibrium price rises to $1.50 a bar, and the equilibrium quantity decreases to 10 million bars a week.

We can now make two more predictions:

1. When supply increases, the quantity increases and the price falls.
2. When supply decreases, the quantity decreases and the price rises.

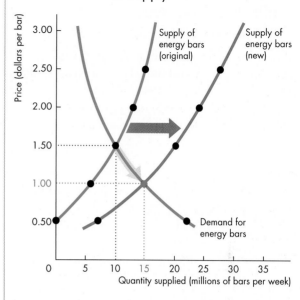

FIGURE 3.9 The Effects of a Change in Supply

Price (dollars per bar)	Quantity demanded (millions of bars per week)	Quantity supplied (millions of bars per week)	
		Original	New
0.50	22	0	7
1.00	15	6	15
1.50	10	10	20
2.00	7	13	25
2.50	5	15	27

Initially, the supply of energy bars is shown by the blue supply curve. The equilibrium price is $1.50 a bar, and the equilibrium quantity is 10 million bars a week. When the new cost-saving technology is adopted, the supply of energy bars increases and the supply curve shifts rightward to become the red curve.

At $1.50 a bar, there is now a surplus of 10 million bars a week. The price of an energy bar falls to a new equilibrium of $1.00 a bar. As the price falls to $1.00, the quantity demanded increases—shown by the blue arrow on the demand curve—to the new equilibrium quantity of 15 million bars a week. Following an increase in supply, the quantity demanded increases but demand does not change—the demand curve does not shift.

myeconlab animation

How Markets Interact to Reallocate Resources

Fuel, Food, and Fertilizer

The demand and supply model provides insights into all competitive markets. Here, we'll apply what you've learned to the markets for

- Crude oil
- Corn
- Fertilizers

Crude Oil

Crude oil is like the life-blood of the global economy. It is used to fuel our cars, airplanes, trains, and buses, to generate electricity, and to produce a wide range of plastics. When the price of crude oil rises, the cost of transportation, power, and materials all increase.

In 2006, the price of a barrel of oil was $50. In 2008, the price had reached $135. While the price of oil has been rising, the quantity of oil produced and consumed has barely changed. Since 2006, the world has produced a steady 85 million barrels of oil a day.

Who or what has been raising the price of oil? Is it the fault of greedy oil producers?

Oil producers might be greedy, and some of them might be big enough to withhold supply and raise the price, but it wouldn't be in their self-interest to do so. The higher price would bring forth a greater quantity supplied from other producers and the profit of the one limiting supply would fall.

Producers could try to cooperate and jointly withhold supply. The Organization of Petroleum Exporting Countries, OPEC, is such a group of suppliers. But OPEC doesn't control the world supply and its members self-interests are to produce the quantities that give them the maximum attainable profit.

So even though the global oil market has some big players, they don't fix the price. Instead, the actions of thousands of buyers and sellers and the forces of demand and supply determine the price of oil. So how have demand and supply changed?

Because the price has increased with an unchanged quantity, demand must have increased and supply must have decreased.

Demand has increased for two reasons. First, world production, particularly in China and India, is expanding at a rapid rate. The increased production of electricity, gasoline, plastics, and other oil-using goods has increased the demand for oil.

Second, the rapid expansion of production in China, India, and other developing economies is expected to continue. So the demand for oil is expected to keep increasing at a rapid rate. As the demand for oil keeps increasing, the price of oil will keep rising *and be expected* to keep rising.

A higher expected future price increases demand yet further. It also decreases supply because producers know they can get a greater return from their oil by leaving it in the ground and selling it in a later year.

So an *expected* rise in price brings both an increase in demand and a decrease in supply, which in turn brings an *actual* rise in price.

Because an expected price rise brings an actual price rise, it is possible for expectations to create a process called a **speculative bubble**. In a speculative bubble, the price rises purely because it is expected to rise and events reinforce the expectation. No one knows whether the world oil market was in a bubble in 2008, but bubbles always burst, so we will eventually know.

Figure 1 illustrates the events that we've just described and summarizes the forces at work on demand and supply in the world market for oil.

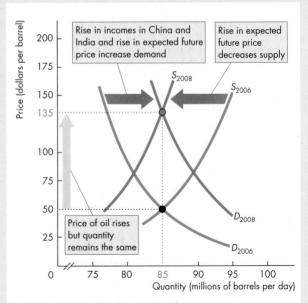

Figure 1 The Market for Crude Oil

Corn

Corn is used as food, animal feed, and a source of ethanol. Global corn production increased during the past few years, but the price also increased.

The story of the production and price of corn, like the story of the price of oil, begins in China and India. Greater production and higher incomes in these countries have increased the demand for corn.

Some of the increase in demand is for corn as food. But more of the increase is for corn as cattle feed, driven by an increased demand for beef—it takes 7 pounds of corn to produce 1 pound of beef.

In addition, mandated targets for ethanol production (see Chapter 2, pp. 34 and 46–47) have increased the demand for corn as a source of biofuel.

While the demand for corn has increased, the supply has decreased. Drought in several parts of the world cut production and decreased supply. Higher fertilizer prices increased the cost of growing corn, which also decreased supply.

So the demand for corn increased and the supply of corn decreased. This combination of changes in demand and supply raised the price of corn. Also, the increase in demand was greater than the decrease in supply, so the quantity of corn increased.

Figure 2 provides a summary of the events that we've just described in the market for corn.

Fertilizers

Nitrogen, potassium, and potash are not on your daily shopping list, but you consume them many times each day. They are the reason why our farms are so productive. And like the prices of oil and corn, the prices of fertilizers have gone skyward.

The increase in the global production of corn and other grains as food and sources of biofuels has increased the demand for fertilizers.

All fertilizers are costly to produce and use energy-intensive processes. Nitrogen is particularly energy intensive and uses natural gas. Potash is made from deposits of chloride and sodium chloride that are found 900 meters or deeper underground, and energy is required to bring the material to the surface and more energy is used to separate the chemicals and turn them into fertilizer.

All energy sources are substitutes, so the rise in the price of oil has increased the prices of all other energy sources. Consequently, the energy cost of producing fertilizers has risen. This higher cost of production has decreased the supply of fertilizers.

The increase in demand and the decrease in supply combine to raise the price. The increase in demand has been greater than the decrease in supply, so the quantity of fertilizer has increased. Figure 3 illustrates the market for fertilizers.

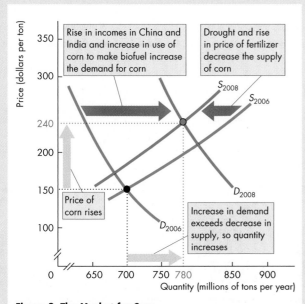

Figure 2 The Market for Corn

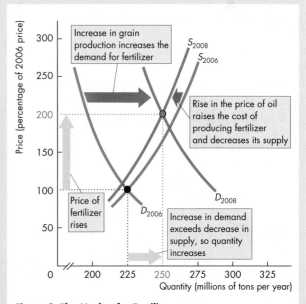

Figure 3 The Market for Fertilizer

FIGURE 3.10 The Effects of All the Possible Changes in Demand and Supply

(a) No change in demand or supply

(b) Increase in demand

(c) Decrease in demand

(d) Increase in supply

(e) Increase in both demand and supply

(f) Decrease in demand; increase in supply

(g) Decrease in supply

(h) Increase in demand; decrease in supply

(i) Decrease in both demand and supply

All the Possible Changes in Demand and Supply

Figure 3.10 brings together and summarizes the effects of all the possible changes in demand and supply. With what you've learned about the effects of a change in *either* demand or supply, you can predict what happens if *both* demand and supply change together. Let's begin by reviewing what you already know.

Change in Demand with No Change in Supply The first row of Fig. 3.10, parts (a), (b), and (c), summarizes the effects of a change in demand with no change in supply. In part (a), with no change in either demand or supply, neither the price nor the quantity changes. With an *increase* in demand and no change in supply in part (b), both the price and quantity increase. And with a *decrease* in demand and no change in supply in part (c), both the price and the quantity decrease.

Change in Supply with No Change in Demand The first column of Fig. 3.10, parts (a), (d), and (g), summarizes the effects of a change in supply with no change in demand. With an *increase* in supply and no change in demand in part (d), the price falls and quantity increases. And with a *decrease* in supply and no change in demand in part (g), the price rises and the quantity decreases.

Increase in Both Demand and Supply You've seen that an increase in demand raises the price and increases the quantity. And you've seen that an increase in supply lowers the price and increases the quantity. Fig. 3.10(e) combines these two changes. Because either an increase in demand or an increase in supply increases the quantity, the quantity also increases when both demand and supply increase. But the effect on the price is uncertain. An increase in demand raises the price and an increase in supply lowers the price, so we can't say whether the price will rise or fall when both demand and supply increase. We need to know the magnitudes of the changes in demand and supply to predict the effects on price. In the example in Fig. 3.10(e), the price does not change. But notice that if demand increases by slightly more than the amount shown in the figure, the price will rise. And if supply increases by slightly more than the amount shown in the figure, the price will fall.

Decrease in Both Demand and Supply Figure 3.10(i) shows the case in which demand and supply *both decrease*. For the same reasons as those we've just reviewed, when both demand and supply decrease, the quantity decreases, and again the direction of the price change is uncertain.

Decrease in Demand and Increase in Supply You've seen that a decrease in demand lowers the price and decreases the quantity. And you've seen that an increase in supply lowers the price and increases the quantity. Fig. 3.10(f) combines these two changes. Both the decrease in demand and the increase in supply lower the price, so the price falls. But a decrease in demand decreases the quantity and an increase in supply increases the quantity, so we can't predict the direction in which the quantity will change unless we know the magnitudes of the changes in demand and supply. In the example in Fig. 3.10(f), the quantity does not change. But notice that if demand decreases by slightly more than the amount shown in the figure, the quantity will decrease. And if supply increases by slightly more than the amount shown in the figure, the quantity will increase.

Increase in Demand and Decrease in Supply Figure 3.10(h) shows the case in which demand increases and supply decreases. Now, the price rises, and again the direction of the quantity change is uncertain.

Review Quiz

What is the effect on the price of an MP3 player (such as an iPod) and the quantity of MP3 players if

1 The price of a PC falls or the price of an MP3 download rises? (Draw the diagrams!)

2 More firms produce MP3 players or electronics workers' wages rise? (Draw the diagrams!)

3 Any two of the events in questions 1 and 2 occur together? (Draw the diagrams!)

myeconlab Work Study Plan 3.5 and get instant feedback.

◆ Now that you understand the demand and supply model and the predictions that it makes, try to get into the habit of using the model in your everyday life. To see how you might use the model, take a look at *Reading Between the Lines* on pp. 76–77, which uses the tools of demand and supply to explain the rising price of gasoline in 2008.

Demand and Supply: The Price of Gasoline

Record Gas Prices Squeeze Drivers

Americans feel the pinch as retail gasoline hits all-time high of $3.51 a gallon

CNN Money
April 22, 2008

NEW YORK (AP)—Cabbies here complain their take-home pay is thinner than it used to be. Trucking companies across the country are making drivers slow down to conserve fuel. Filling station owners plead that really, really, the skyrocketing prices aren't their fault. …

With gas prices now averaging $3.51 a gallon nationwide, … more and more Americans who have to drive are weighing the need for each and every trip. … Some would-be drivers are considering less energy-dependent alternatives simply for money's sake.

In Los Angeles, for example, fiction writer Brian Edwards sold his gas-guzzling Ford truck and now relies on his skateboard or the bus to get around. Sharon Cooper of Chicago, meanwhile, said she is planning to buy a bicycle to use on her 2 1/2-mile commute to work. …

"It's hell," said legal aide Zebib Yemane, … "When going downhill, I used to step on the gas. Now I don't." …

"Bottom line, we can't afford it no more, man. It's too much," Bak Zoumane said as he filled up his yellow cab at a BP station in midtown New York. The West African immigrant said his next car will likely be a hybrid so he won't have to pay so much at the pump.

Gasoline prices typically rise in the spring as stations switch over to pricier summer-grade fuel and demand picks up as more travelers take to the road.

But this year prices are rising even faster than normal, experts say, because of the massive jump in benchmark crude prices, which spiked to a record $117.76 a barrel Monday. …

Essence of the Story

- The retail price of gasoline hit a record high of $3.51 a gallon in April 2008.

- Gas station owners said the high prices weren't their fault.

- Drivers weighed the need for each trip and conserved energy by slowing down, easing off the gas when going down hill, or switching to hybrid vehicles.

- Some people found alternative means of transportation that include the bus, a bicycle, or even a skateboard.

- The switch to summer-grade fuel and a seasonal increase in travel normally raise the price of gasoline in the spring.

- In 2008, gas prices rose faster than normal because of a large rise in the price of crude oil, which reached $118 a barrel.

Economic Analysis

- In April 2007, the average price of gasoline was $2.75 a gallon and 9.3 million barrels of gasoline were consumed on average each day.

- Figure 1 shows the market for gasoline in April 2007. The demand curve is D, the supply curve is S_{2007}, and the market equilibrium is at 9.3 million barrels a day and $2.75 a gallon.

- Two main factors influenced the demand for gasoline in the year to April 2008.

- Slightly higher incomes increased demand and the gradual move toward hybrid vehicles and the increased use of ethanol decreased demand.

- The combined effects of these two factors left the demand for gasoline the same in 2008 as it had been in 2007.

- The price of crude oil was the biggest influence on the market for gasoline during 2007 and 2008.

- Between April 2007 and April 2008, the price of crude oil increased from $65 a barrel to $118 a barrel.

- The rise in the price of crude oil raised the cost of producing gasoline and decreased the supply of gasoline.

- Figure 2 shows what had happened in the market for gasoline by April 2008.

- Demand remained unchanged, but supply decreased from S_{2007} to S_{2008}.

- Because demand was unchanged and supply decreased, the price increased and the quantity decreased.

- The equilibrium price increased from $2.75 a gallon to $3.51 a gallon and the equilibrium quantity decreased from 9.3 million barrels a day to 9.2 million barrels a day.

- You can see the effects of drivers conserving gasoline, switching to hybrid vehicles, and finding alternative means of transportation that include the bus, a bicycle, or even a skateboard.

- This analysis of the market for gasoline emphasizes the distinction between a change in demand and a *change in the quantity demanded* and a change in supply and a *change in the quantity supplied.*

- In this example, there is a change in supply, no change in demand, and a change in the quantity demanded.

- Supply decreases—the supply curve shifts leftward.

- The demand curve does not shift, but as the price of gasoline rises, the quantity of gasoline demanded decreases in a movement along the demand curve D.

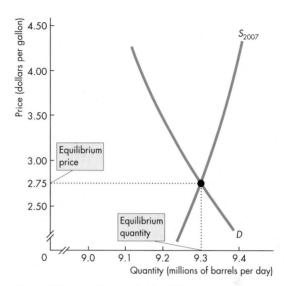

Figure 1 The gasoline market in 2007

Figure 2 The gasoline market in 2008

MATHEMATICAL NOTE

Demand, Supply, and Equilibrium

Demand Curve

The law of demand says that as the price of a good or service falls, the quantity demanded of that good or service increases. We can illustrate the law of demand by drawing a graph of the demand curve or writing down an equation. When the demand curve is a straight line, the following equation describes it:

$$P = a - bQ_D,$$

where P is the price and Q_D is the quantity demanded. The a and b are positive constants.

The demand equation tells us three things:

1. The price at which no one is willing to buy the good (Q_D is zero). That is, if the price is a, then the quantity demanded is zero. You can see the price a in Figure 1. It is the price at which the demand curve hits the y-axis—what we call the demand curve's "intercept on the y-axis."

2. As the price falls, the quantity demanded increases. If Q_D is a positive number, then the price P must be less than a. And as Q_D gets larger, the price P becomes smaller. That is, as the quantity increases, the maximum price that buyers are willing to pay for the last unit of the good falls.

3. The constant b tells us how fast the maximum price that someone is willing to pay for the good falls as the quantity increases. That is, the constant b tells us about the steepness of the demand curve. The equation tells us that the slope of the demand curve is $-b$.

Supply Curve

The law of supply says that as the price of a good or service rises, the quantity supplied of that good or service increases. We can illustrate the law of supply by drawing a graph of the supply curve or writing down an equation. When the supply curve is a straight line, the following equation describes it:

$$P = c + dQ_S,$$

where P is the price and Q_S is the quantity supplied. The c and d are positive constants.

The supply equation tells us three things:

1. The price at which sellers are not willing to supply the good (Q_S is zero). That is, if the price is c, then no one is willing to sell the good. You can see the price c in Figure 2. It is the price at which the supply curve hits the y-axis—what we call the supply curve's "intercept on the y-axis."

2. As the price rises, the quantity supplied increases. If Q_S is a positive number, then the price P must be greater than c. And as Q_S increases, the price P becomes larger. That is, as the quantity increases, the minimum price that sellers are willing to accept for the last unit rises.

3. The constant d tells us how fast the minimum price at which someone is willing to sell the good rises as the quantity increases. That is, the constant d tells us about the steepness of the supply curve. The equation tells us that the slope of the supply curve is d.

Figure 1 Demand curve

Figure 2 Supply curve

Market Equilibrium

Demand and supply determine market equilibrium. Figure 3 shows the equilibrium price (P^*) and equilibrium quantity (Q^*) at the intersection of the demand curve and the supply curve.

We can use the equations to find the equilibrium price and equilibrium quantity. The price of a good adjusts until the quantity demanded Q_D equals the quantity supplied Q_S. So at the equilibrium price (P^*) and equilibrium quantity (Q^*),

$$Q_D = Q_S = Q^*.$$

To find the equilibrium price and equilibrium quantity, substitute Q^* for Q_D in the demand equation and Q^* for Q_S in the supply equation. Then the price is the equilibrium price (P^*), which gives

$$P^* = a - bQ^*$$
$$P^* = c + dQ^*.$$

Notice that

$$a - bQ^* = c + dQ^*.$$

Now solve for Q^*:

$$a - c = bQ^* + dQ^*$$
$$a - c = (b + d)Q^*$$
$$Q^* = \frac{a - c}{b + d}.$$

To find the equilibrium price, (P^*), substitute for Q^* in either the demand equation or the supply equation.

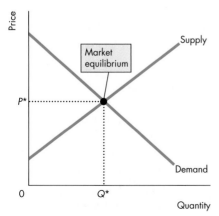

Price

Supply

Market equilibrium

P^*

Demand

0   Q^* Quantity

Figure 3 Market equilibrium

Using the demand equation, we have

$$P^* = a - b\left(\frac{a - c}{b + d}\right)$$
$$P^* = \frac{a(b + d) - b(a - c)}{b + d}$$
$$P^* = \frac{ad + bc}{b + d}.$$

Alternatively, using the supply equation, we have

$$P^* = c + d\left(\frac{a - c}{b + d}\right)$$
$$P^* = \frac{c(b + d) + d(a - c)}{b + d}$$
$$P^* = \frac{ad + bc}{b + d}.$$

An Example

The demand for ice-cream cones is

$$P = 800 - 2Q_D.$$

The supply of ice-cream cones is

$$P = 200 + 1Q_S.$$

The price of a cone is expressed in cents, and the quantities are expressed in cones per day.

To find the equilibrium price (P^*) and equilibrium quantity (Q^*), substitute Q^* for Q_D and Q_S and P^* for P. That is,

$$P^* = 800 - 2Q^*$$
$$P^* = 200 + 1Q^*.$$

Now solve for Q^*:

$$800 - 2Q^* = 200 + 1Q^*$$
$$600 = 3Q^*$$
$$Q^* = 200.$$

And

$$P^* = 800 - 2(200)$$
$$= 400.$$

The equilibrium price is $4 a cone, and the equilibrium quantity is 200 cones per day.

SUMMARY

Key Points

Markets and Prices (p. 58)

- A competitive market is one that has so many buyers and sellers that no single buyer or seller can influence the price.
- Opportunity cost is a relative price.
- Demand and supply determine relative prices.

Demand (pp. 59–63)

- Demand is the relationship between the quantity demanded of a good and its price when all other influences on buying plans remain the same.
- The higher the price of a good, other things remaining the same, the smaller is the quantity demanded—the law of demand.
- Demand depends on the prices of related goods (substitutes and complements), expected future prices, income, expected future income and credit, population, and preferences.

Supply (pp. 64–67)

- Supply is the relationship between the quantity supplied of a good and its price when all other influences on selling plans remain the same.
- The higher the price of a good, other things remaining the same, the greater is the quantity supplied—the law of supply.

- Supply depends on the prices of resources used to produce a good, the prices of related goods produced, expected future prices, the number of suppliers, technology, and the state of nature.

Market Equilibrium (pp. 68–69)

- At the equilibrium price, the quantity demanded equals the quantity supplied.
- At any price above equilibrium, there is a surplus and the price falls.
- At any price below equilibrium, there is a shortage and the price rises.

Predicting Changes in Price and Quantity (pp. 70–75)

- An increase in demand brings a rise in the price and an increase in the quantity supplied. A decrease in demand brings a fall in the price and a decrease in the quantity supplied.
- An increase in supply brings a fall in the price and an increase in the quantity demanded. A decrease in supply brings a rise in the price and a decrease in the quantity demanded.
- An increase in demand and an increase in supply bring an increased quantity but an uncertain price change. An increase in demand and a decrease in supply bring a higher price but an uncertain change in quantity.

Key Figures

Key Terms

PROBLEMS and APPLICATIONS ◆

 Work problems 1–13 in Chapter 3 Study Plan and get instant feedback.
Work problems 16–28 as Homework, a Quiz, or a Test if assigned by your instructor.

1. William Gregg owned a mill in South Carolina. In December 1862, he placed a notice in the *Edgehill Advertiser* announcing his willingness to exchange cloth for food and other items. Here is an extract:

   1 yard of cloth for 1 pound of bacon
   2 yards of cloth for 1 pound of butter
   4 yards of cloth for 1 pound of wool
   8 yards of cloth for 1 bushel of salt

   a. What is the relative price of butter in terms of wool?

   b. If the money price of bacon was 20¢ a pound, what do you predict was the money price of butter?

   c. If the money price of bacon was 20¢ a pound and the money price of salt was $2.00 a bushel, do you think anyone would accept Mr. Gregg's offer of cloth for salt?

2. The price of food increased during the past year.

   a. Explain why the law of demand applies to food just as it does to all other goods and services.

   b. Explain how the substitution effect influences food purchases and provide some examples of substitutions that people might make when the price of food rises and other things remain the same.

   c. Explain how the income effect influences food purchases and provide some examples of the income effect that might occur when the price of food rises and other things remain the same.

3. Place the following goods and services into pairs of likely substitutes and into pairs of likely complements. (You may use an item in more than one pair.) The goods and services are

   coal, oil, natural gas, wheat, corn, rye, pasta, pizza, sausage, skateboard, roller blades, video game, laptop, iPod, cell phone, text message, email, phone call, voice mail

4. During 2008, the average income in China increased by 10 percent. Compared to 2007, how do you expect the following would change:

   a. The demand for beef? Explain your answer.

   b. The demand for rice? Explain your answer.

5. In January 2007, the price of gasoline was $2.38 a gallon. By May 2008, the price had increased to $3.84 a gallon. Assume that there were no changes in average income, population, or any other influence on buying plans. How would you expect the rise in the price of gasoline to affect

   a. The demand for gasoline? Explain your answer.

   b. The quantity of gasoline demanded? Explain your answer.

6. In 2008, the price of corn increased by 35 percent and some cotton farmers in Texas stopped growing cotton and started to grow corn.

   a. Does this fact illustrate the law of demand or the law of supply? Explain your answer.

   b. Why would a cotton farmer grow corn?

7. **American to Cut Flights, Charge for Luggage**
   American Airlines announced yesterday that it will begin charging passengers $15 for their first piece of checked luggage, in addition to raising other fees and cutting domestic flights as it grapples with record-high fuel prices.
   Boston Herald, May 22, 2008

   a. How does this news clip illustrate a change in supply? Explain your answer.

   b What is the influence on supply identified in the news clip? Explain your answer.

   c. Explain how supply changes.

8. **Oil Soars to New Record Over $135**
   The price of oil hit a record high above $135 a barrel on Thursday—more than twice what it cost a year ago ... OPEC has so far blamed price rises on speculators and says there is no shortage of oil.
   BBC News, May 22, 2008

   a. Explain how the price of oil can rise even though there is no shortage of oil.

   b If a shortage of oil does occur, what does that imply about price adjustments and the role of price as a regulator in the market for oil?

   c If OPEC is correct, what factors might have

changed demand and/or supply and shifted the demand curve and/or the supply curve to cause the price to rise?

9. "As more people buy computers, the demand for Internet service increases and the price of Internet service decreases. The fall in the price of Internet service decreases the supply of Internet service." Is this statement true or false? Explain.

10. The following events occur one at a time:
    (i)   The price of crude oil rises.
    (ii) The price of a car rises.
    (iii) All speed limits on highways are abolished.
    (iv) Robots cut car production costs.

    Which of these events will increase or decrease (state which occurs)
    a. The demand for gasoline?
    b. The supply of gasoline?
    c. The quantity of gasoline demanded?
    d. The quantity of gasoline supplied?

11. The demand and supply schedules for gum are

Price (cents per pack)	Quantity demanded (millions of packs a week)	Quantity supplied (millions of packs a week)
20	180	60
40	140	100
60	100	140
80	60	180
100	20	220

    a. Draw a graph of the gum market, label the axes and the curves, and mark in the equilibrium price and quantity.
    b. Suppose that the price of gum is 70¢ a pack. Describe the situation in the gum market and explain how the price adjusts.
    c. Suppose that the price of gum is 30¢ a pack. Describe the situation in the gum market and explain how the price adjusts.
    d. A fire destroys some factories that produce gum and the quantity of gum supplied decreases by 40 million packs a week at each price. Explain what happens in the market for gum and illustrate the changes on your graph.
    e. If at the time the fire occurs in d, there is an increase in the teenage population, which increases the quantity of gum demanded by 40 million packs a week at each price, what are the new equilibrium price and quantity of gum? Illustrate these changes in your graph.

12. **Eurostar Boosted by Da Vinci Code**
    Eurostar, the train service linking London to Paris … , said on Wednesday first-half sales rose 6 per cent, boosted by devotees of the blockbuster Da Vinci movie.
    CNN, July 26, 2006
    a. Explain how Da Vinci Code fans helped to raise Eurostar's sales.
    b. CNN commented on the "fierce competition from budget airlines." Explain the effect of this competition on Eurostar's sales.
    c. What markets in Paris do you think these fans influenced? Explain the influence on three markets.

13. **Of Gambling, Grannies, and Good Sense**
    Nevada has the fastest growing elderly population of any state. … Las Vegas has … plenty of jobs for the over 50s.
    The Economist, July 26, 2006
    Explain how grannies have influenced the
    a. Demand side of some Las Vegas markets.
    b. Supply side of other Las Vegas markets.

14. Use the link on MyEconLab (Textbook Resources, Chapter 3, Web Links) to obtain data on the prices and quantities of bananas in 1985 and 2002.
    a. Make a graph to illustrate the market for bananas in 1985 and 2002.
    b. On the graph, show the changes in demand and supply and the changes in the quantity demanded and the quantity supplied that are consistent with the price and quantity data.
    c. Why do you think the demand for and supply of bananas changed?

15. Use the link on MyEconLab (Textbook Resources, Chapter 3, Web Links) to obtain data on the price of oil since 2000.
    a. Describe how the price of oil changed.
    b. Use a demand-supply graph to explain what happens to the price when supply increases or decreases and demand is unchanged.
    c. What do you predict would happen to the price of oil if a new drilling technology permitted deeper ocean sources to be used?
    d. What do you predict would happen to the price of oil if a clean and safe nuclear technology were developed?
    e. How does a higher price of oil influence the market for ethanol?
    f. How does an increase in the supply of ethanol influence the market for oil?

16. What features of the world market for crude oil make it a competitive market?

17. The money price of a textbook is $90 and the money price of the Wii game *Super Mario Galaxy* is $45.

   a. What is the opportunity cost of a textbook in terms of the Wii game?

   b. What is the relative price of the Wii game in terms of textbooks?

18. The price of gasoline has increased during the past year.

   a. Explain why the law of demand applies to gasoline just as it does to all other goods and services.

   b. Explain how the substitution effect influences gasoline purchases and provide some examples of substitutions that people might make when the price of gasoline rises and other things remain the same.

   c. Explain how the income effect influences gasoline purchases and provide some examples of the income effects that might occur when the price of gasoline rises and other things remain the same.

19. Classify the following pairs of goods and services as substitutes, complements, substitutes in production, or complements in production.

   a. Bottled water and health club memberships

   b. French fries and baked potatoes

   c. Leather purses and leather shoes

   d. SUVs and pickup trucks

   e. Diet coke and regular coke

   f. Low-fat milk and cream

20. Think about the demand for the three popular game consoles: XBox, PS3, and Wii. Explain the effect the following event on the demand for XBox games and the quantity of XBox games demanded, other things remaining the same.

   a. The price of an XBox falls.

   b. The prices of a PS3 and a Wii fall.

   c. The number of people writing and producing XBox games increases.

   d. Consumers' incomes increase.

   e. Programmers who write code for XBox games become more costly to hire.

   f. The price of an XBox game is expected to fall.

   g. A new game console comes onto the market, which is a close substitute for XBox.

21. In 2008, as the prices of homes fell across the United States, the number of homes offered for sale decreased.

   a. Does this fact illustrate the law of demand or the law of supply? Explain your answer.

   b. Why would home owners hold off trying to sell?

22. **G.M. Cuts Production for Quarter**

   General Motors cut its fourth-quarter production schedule by 10 percent on Tuesday as a tightening credit market caused sales at the Ford Motor Company, Chrysler and even Toyota to decline in August. ... Bob Carter, group vice president for Toyota Motor Sales USA, said ... dealerships were still seeing fewer potential customers browsing the lots.

   The New York Times, September 5, 2007

   Explain whether this news clip illustrates
   a. A change in supply
   b. A change in the quantity supplied
   c. A change in demand
   d. A change in the quantity demanded

23. The figure illustrates the market for pizza.

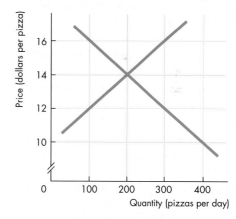

   a. Label the curves. Which curve shows the willingness to pay for a pizza?

   b. If the price of a pizza is $16, is there a shortage or a surplus and does the price rise or fall?

   c. Sellers want to receive the highest possible price, so why would they be willing to accept less than $16 a pizza?

   d. If the price of a pizza is $12, is there a shortage or a surplus and does the price rise or fall?

   e. Buyers want to pay the lowest possible price, so why would they be willing to pay more than $12 for a pizza?

24. **Plenty of "For Sale" Signs but Actual Sales Lagging**

Like spring flowers, the "For Sale" signs are sprouting in front yards all over the country. But anxious sellers are facing the most brutal environment in decades, with a slumping economy, falling home prices, and rising mortgage foreclosures.

The New York Times, May 26, 2008

a. Describe the changes in demand and supply in the market for homes in the United States.

b. Is there a surplus of homes?

c. What does the information in the news clip imply about price adjustments and the role of price as a regulator in the market for homes?

25. **'Popcorn Movie' Experience Gets Pricier**

… cinemas are raising … prices. … Demand for field corn, used for animal feed, … corn syrup and … ethanol, has caused its price to explode. That's caused some farmers to shift from popcorn to easier-to-grow field corn, cutting supply and pushing its price higher, too. …

USA Today, May 24, 2008

Explain and illustrate graphically the events described in the news clip in the markets for

a. Popcorn.

b. Viewing movies in the theater.

26. The table sets out the demand and supply schedules for potato chips.

Price (cents per bag)	Quantity demanded	Quantity supplied
	(millions of bags per week)	
50	160	130
60	150	140
70	140	150
80	130	160
90	120	170
100	110	180

a. Draw a graph of the potato chip market and mark in the equilibrium price and quantity.

b. If the price is 60¢ a bag, is there a shortage or a surplus, and how does the price adjust?

c. If a new dip increases the quantity of potato chips that people want to buy by 30 million bags per week at each price, how does the demand and/or supply of chips change?

d. If a new dip has the effect described in c, how does the price and quantity of chips change?

e. If a virus destroys potato crops and the quantity of potato chips produced decreases by 40 million bags a week at each price, how does the supply of chips change?

f. If the virus that destroys the potato crops in e hits just as the new dip in c comes onto the market, how does the price and quantity of chips change?

27. **Sony's Blu-Ray Wins High-Definition War**

Toshiba Corp. yesterday raised the white flag in the war over the next-generation home movie format, announcing the end of its HD DVD business in a victory for Sony Corp.'s Blu-ray technology. The move could finally jump-start a high-definition home DVD market that has been hamstrung as consumers waited on the sidelines for the battle to play out in a fight reminiscent of the VHS-Betamax videotape war of the 1980s.

The Washington Times, February 20, 2008

How would you expect the end of Toshiba's HD DVD format to influence

a. The price of a used Toshiba player on eBay? Would the outcome that you predict result from a change in demand or a change in supply or both, and in which directions?

b. The price of a Blu-ray player?

c. The demand for Blu-ray format movies?

d. The supply of Blu-ray format movies?

e. The price of Blu-ray format movies?

f. The quantity of Blu-ray format movies?

28. After you have studied *Reading Between the Lines* on pp. 76–77, answer the following questions:

a. How high did the retail price of gasoline go in April 2008?

b. What substitutions did drivers make to decrease the quantity of gasoline demanded?

c. Why would the switch to summer-grade fuel and the seasonal increase in travel normally raise the price of gasoline in the spring?

d. What were the two main factors that influenced the demand for gasoline in 2008 and how did they change demand?

e. What was the main influence on the supply of gasoline during 2007 and 2008 and how did supply change?

f. How did the combination of the factors you have noted in d and e influence the price and quantity of gasoline?

g. Was the change in quantity a change in the quantity demanded or a change in the quantity supplied?

4 Elasticity

After studying this chapter, you will be able to:

- Define, calculate, and explain the factors that influence the price elasticity of demand

- Define, calculate, and explain the factors that influence the cross elasticity of demand and the income elasticity of demand

- Define, calculate, and explain the factors that influence the elasticity of supply

What are the effects of a high gas price on buying

plans? You can see some of the biggest effects at car dealers' lots, where SUVs and other gas guzzlers remain unsold while sub-compacts and hybrids sell in greater quantities. But how big are these effects? When the price of gasoline doubles, as it has done over the past few years, by how much does the quantity of SUVs sold decrease, and by how much does the quantity of sub-compacts sold increase?

And what about gasoline purchases? Do we keep filling our tanks and spending more on gas? Or do we find substitutes on such a large scale that we end up cutting our expenditure on gas?

This chapter introduces you to elasticity: a tool that addresses these quantitative questions. At the end of the chapter, in *Reading Between the Lines*, we'll use the concept of elasticity to explain what was happening in the markets for gasoline and automobiles in 2008. But we'll explain and illustrate elasticity by studying another familiar market: the market for pizza.

◆ Price Elasticity of Demand

You know that when supply increases, the equilibrium price falls and the equilibrium quantity increases. But does the price fall by a large amount and the quantity increase by a little? Or does the price barely fall and the quantity increase by a large amount?

The answer depends on the responsiveness of the quantity demanded to a change in price. You can see why by studying Fig. 4.1, which shows two possible scenarios in a local pizza market. Figure 4.1(a) shows one scenario, and Fig. 4.1(b) shows the other.

In both cases, supply is initially S_0. In part (a), the demand for pizza is shown by the demand curve D_A. In part (b), the demand for pizza is shown by the demand curve D_B. Initially, in both cases, the price is $20 a pizza and the equilibrium quantity is 10 pizzas an hour.

Now a large pizza franchise opens up, and the supply of pizza increases. The supply curve shifts rightward to S_1. In case (a), the price falls by an enormous $15 to $5 a pizza, and the quantity increases by only 3 to 13 pizzas an hour. In contrast, in case (b), the price falls by only $5 to $15 a pizza and the quantity increases by 7 to 17 pizzas an hour.

The different outcomes arise from differing degrees of responsiveness of the quantity demanded to a change in price. But what do we mean by responsiveness? One possible answer is slope. The slope of demand curve D_A is steeper than the slope of demand curve D_B.

In this example, we can compare the slopes of the two demand curves, but we can't always make such a comparison. The reason is that the slope of a demand curve depends on the units in which we measure the price and quantity. And we often must compare the demand for different goods and services that are measured in unrelated units. For example, a pizza producer might want to compare the demand for pizza with the demand for soft drinks. Which quantity demanded is more responsive to a price change? This question can't be answered by comparing the slopes of two demand curves. The units of measurement of pizza and soft drinks are unrelated. The question can be answered with a measure of responsiveness that is independent of units of measurement. Elasticity is such a measure.

The **price elasticity of demand** is a units-free measure of the responsiveness of the quantity demanded of a good to a change in its price when all other influences on buying plans remain the same.

FIGURE 4.1 How a Change in Supply Changes Price and Quantity

(a) Large price change and small quantity change

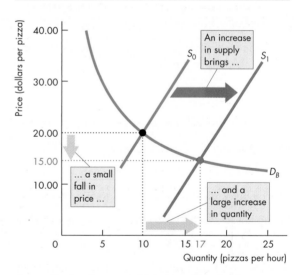

(b) Small price change and large quantity change

Initially, the price is $20 a pizza and the quantity sold is 10 pizzas an hour. Then supply increases from S_0 to S_1. In part (a), the price falls by $15 to $5 a pizza, and the quantity increases by 3 to 13 pizzas an hour. In part (b), the price falls by only $5 to $15 a pizza, and the quantity increases by 7 to 17 pizzas an hour. The price change is smaller and the quantity change is larger in case (b) than in case (a). The quantity demanded is more responsive to the change in the price in case (b) than in case (a).

 animation

Calculating Price Elasticity of Demand

We calculate the *price elasticity of demand* by using the formula:

$$\text{Price elasticity of demand} = \frac{\text{Percentage change in quantity demanded}}{\text{Percentage change in price}}.$$

To use this formula, we need to know the quantities demanded at different prices when all other influences on buying plans remain the same. Suppose we have the data on prices and quantities demanded of pizza and we calculate the price elasticity of demand for pizza.

Figure 4.2 zooms in on the demand curve for pizza and shows how the quantity demanded responds to a small change in price. Initially, the price is $20.50 a pizza and 9 pizzas an hour are sold—the original point in the figure. The price then falls to $19.50 a pizza, and the quantity demanded increases to 11 pizzas an hour—the new point in the figure. When the price falls by $1 a pizza, the quantity demanded increases by 2 pizzas an hour.

To calculate the price elasticity of demand, we express the changes in price and quantity demanded as percentages of the *average price* and the *average quantity*. By using the average price and average quantity, we calculate the elasticity at a point on the demand curve midway between the original point and the new point. The original price is $20.50 and the new price is $19.50, so the average price is $20. The $1 price decrease is 5 percent of the average price. That is,

$$\Delta P/P_{ave} = (\$1/\$20) \times 100 = 5\%.$$

The original quantity demanded is 9 pizzas and the new quantity demanded is 11 pizzas, so the average quantity demanded is 10 pizzas. The 2 pizza increase in the quantity demanded is 20 percent of the average quantity. That is,

$$\Delta Q/Q_{ave} = (2/10) \times 100 = 20\%.$$

So the price elasticity of demand, which is the percentage change in the quantity demanded (20 percent) divided by the percentage change in price (5 percent) is 4. That is,

$$\text{Price elasticity of demand} = \frac{\%\Delta Q}{\%\Delta P}$$
$$= \frac{20\%}{5\%} = 4.$$

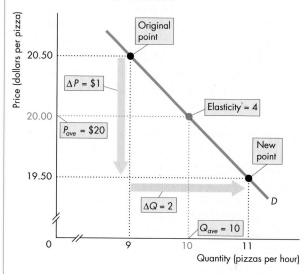

FIGURE 4.2   Calculating the Elasticity of Demand

The elasticity of demand is calculated by using the formula:*

$$\text{Price elasticity of demand} = \frac{\text{Percentage change in quantity demanded}}{\text{Percentage change in price}}$$
$$= \frac{\%\Delta Q}{\%\Delta P}$$
$$= \frac{\Delta Q/Q_{ave}}{\Delta P/P_{ave}}$$
$$= \frac{2/10}{1/20} = 4.$$

This calculation measures the elasticity at an average price of $20 a pizza and an average quantity of 10 pizzas an hour.

* In the formula, the Greek letter delta (Δ) stands for "change in" and %Δ stands for "percentage change in."

myeconlab animation

Average Price and Quantity Notice that we use the *average* price and *average* quantity. We do this because it gives the most precise measurement of elasticity—at the midpoint between the original price and the new price. If the price falls from $20.50 to $19.50, the $1 price change is 4.9 percent of $20.50. The 2 pizza change in quantity is 22.2 percent of 9 pizzas, the original quantity. So if we use these numbers, the price elasticity of demand is 22.2 divided by 4.9, which equals 4.5. If the price rises from $19.50 to $20.50, the $1 price change is 5.1 percent of $19.50. The 2 pizza change in quantity is 18.2 percent of 11 pizzas, the original quantity. So if we use these numbers, the price elasticity of demand is 18.2 divided by 5.1, which equals 3.6.

By using percentages of the *average* price and *average* quantity, we get the same value for the elasticity regardless of whether the price falls from $20.50 to $19.50 or rises from $19.50 to $20.50.

Percentages and Proportions Elasticity is the ratio of two percentage changes. So when we divide one percentage change by another, the 100s cancel. A percentage change is a *proportionate* change multiplied by 100. The proportionate change in price is $\Delta P/P_{ave}$, and the proportionate change in quantity demanded is $\Delta Q/Q_{ave}$. So if we divide $\Delta Q/Q_{ave}$ by $\Delta P/P_{ave}$ we get the same answer as we get by using percentage changes.

A Units-Free Measure Now that you've calculated a price elasticity of demand, you can see why it is a *units-free measure*. Elasticity is a units-free measure because the percentage change in each variable is independent of the units in which the variable is measured. And the ratio of the two percentages is a number without units.

Minus Sign and Elasticity When the price of a good *rises*, the quantity demanded *decreases*. Because a *positive* change in price brings a *negative* change in the quantity demanded, the price elasticity of demand is

a negative number. But it is the magnitude, or *absolute value*, of the price elasticity of demand that tells us how responsive the quantity demanded is. So to compare price elasticities of demand, we use the *magnitude* of the elasticity and ignore the minus sign.

Inelastic and Elastic Demand

Figure 4.3 shows three demand curves that cover the entire range of possible elasticities of demand. In Fig. 4.3(a), the quantity demanded is constant regardless of the price. If the quantity demanded remains constant when the price changes, then the price elasticity of demand is zero and the good is said to have a **perfectly inelastic demand**. One good that has a very low price elasticity of demand (perhaps zero over some price range) is insulin. Insulin is of such importance to some diabetics that if the price rises or falls, they do not change the quantity they buy.

If the percentage change in the quantity demanded equals the percentage change in the price, then the price elasticity equals 1 and the good is said to have a **unit elastic demand**. The demand in Fig. 4.3(b) is an example of a unit elastic demand.

Between the cases shown in Fig. 4.3(a) and Fig. 4.3(b) is the general case in which the percentage change in the quantity demanded is less than the percentage change in the price. In this case, the price elasticity of demand is between zero and 1 and the good is said to have an **inelastic demand**. Food and shelter are examples of goods with inelastic demand.

FIGURE 4.3 Inelastic and Elastic Demand

(a) Perfectly inelastic demand   **(b) Unit elastic demand**   **(c) Perfectly elastic demand**

Each demand illustrated here has a constant elasticity. The demand curve in part (a) illustrates the demand for a good that has a zero elasticity of demand. The demand curve in part (b) illustrates the demand for a good with a unit elasticity of demand. And the demand curve in part (c) illustrates the demand for a good with an infinite elasticity of demand.

myeconlab animation

If the quantity demanded changes by an infinitely large percentage in response to a tiny price change, then the price elasticity of demand is infinity and the good is said to have a **perfectly elastic demand**. Figure 4.3(c) shows a perfectly elastic demand. An example of a good that has a very high elasticity of demand (almost infinite) is a soft drink from two campus machines located side by side. If the two machines offer the same soft drinks for the same price, some people buy from one machine and some from the other. But if one machine's price is higher than the other's, by even a small amount, no one will buy from the machine with the higher price. Soft drinks from the two machines are perfect substitutes. The demand for a good that has a perfect substitute is perfectly elastic.

Between the cases in Fig. 4.3(b) and Fig. 4.3(c) is the general case in which the percentage change in the quantity demanded exceeds the percentage change in price. In this case, the price elasticity of demand is greater than 1 and the good is said to have an **elastic demand**. Automobiles and furniture are examples of goods that have elastic demand.

Elasticity Along a Straight-Line Demand Curve

Elasticity and slope are not the same, but they are related. To understand how they are related, let's look at elasticity along a straight-line demand curve—a demand curve that has a constant slope.

Figure 4.4 illustrates the calculation of elasticity along a straight-line demand curve. First, suppose the price falls from $25 to $15 a pizza. The quantity demanded increases from zero to 20 pizzas an hour. The average price is $20 a pizza, and the average quantity is 10 pizzas. So

$$\text{Price elasticity of demand} = \frac{\Delta Q / Q_{ave}}{\Delta P / P_{ave}}$$

$$= \frac{20/10}{10/20}$$

$$= 4.$$

That is, the price elasticity of demand at an average price of $20 a pizza is 4.

Next, suppose that the price falls from $15 to $10 a pizza. The quantity demanded increases from 20 to 30 pizzas an hour. The average price is now $12.50 a pizza, and the average quantity is 25 pizzas an hour. So

$$\text{Price elasticity of demand} = \frac{10/25}{5/12.50}$$

$$= 1.$$

That is, the price elasticity of demand at an average price of $12.50 a pizza is 1.

Finally, suppose that the price falls from $10 to zero. The quantity demanded increases from 30 to 50 pizzas an hour. The average price is now $5 a pizza, and the average quantity is 40 pizzas an hour. So

$$\text{Price elasticity of demand} = \frac{20/40}{10/5}$$

$$= 1/4.$$

That is, the price elasticity of demand at an average price of $5 a pizza is 1/4.

You've now seen how elasticity changes along a straight-line demand curve. At the midpoint of the curve, demand is unit elastic. Above the midpoint, demand is elastic. Below the midpoint, demand is inelastic.

FIGURE 4.4 Elasticity Along a Straight-Line Demand Curve

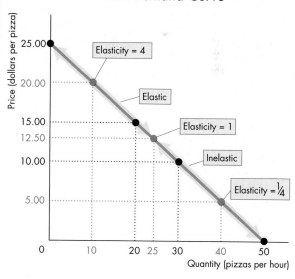

On a straight-line demand curve, elasticity decreases as the price falls and the quantity demanded increases. Demand is unit elastic at the midpoint of the demand curve (elasticity is 1). Above the midpoint, demand is elastic; below the midpoint, demand is inelastic.

myeconlab   animation

Total Revenue and Elasticity

The **total revenue** from the sale of a good equals the price of the good multiplied by the quantity sold. When a price changes, total revenue also changes. But a cut in the price does not always decrease total revenue. The change in total revenue depends on the elasticity of demand in the following way:

- If demand is elastic, a 1 percent price cut increases the quantity sold by more than 1 percent and total revenue increases.

- If demand is inelastic, a 1 percent price cut increases the quantity sold by less than 1 percent and total revenue decreases.

- If demand is unit elastic, a 1 percent price cut increases the quantity sold by 1 percent and total revenue does not change.

In Fig. 4.5(a), over the price range from $25 to $12.50, demand is elastic. Over the price range from $12.50 to zero, demand is inelastic. At a price of $12.50, demand is unit elastic.

Figure 4.5(b) shows total revenue. At a price of $25, the quantity sold is zero, so total revenue is zero. At a price of zero, the quantity demanded is 50 pizzas an hour and total revenue is again zero. A price cut in the elastic range brings an increase in total revenue—the percentage increase in the quantity demanded is greater than the percentage decrease in price. A price cut in the inelastic range brings a decrease in total revenue—the percentage increase in the quantity demanded is less than the percentage decrease in price. At unit elasticity, total revenue is at a maximum.

Figure 4.5 shows how we can use this relationship between elasticity and total revenue to estimate elasticity using the total revenue test. The **total revenue test** is a method of estimating the price elasticity of demand by observing the change in total revenue that results from a change in the price, when all other influences on the quantity sold remain the same.

- If a price cut increases total revenue, demand is elastic.

- If a price cut decreases total revenue, demand is inelastic.

- If a price cut leaves total revenue unchanged, demand is unit elastic.

FIGURE 4.5   Elasticity and Total Revenue

(a) Demand

(b) Total revenue

When demand is elastic, in the price range from $25 to $12.50, a decrease in price (part a) brings an increase in total revenue (part b). When demand is inelastic, in the price range from $12.50 to zero, a decrease in price (part a) brings a decrease in total revenue (part b). When demand is unit elastic, at a price of $12.50 (part a), total revenue is at a maximum (part b).

Your Expenditure and Your Elasticity

When a price changes, the change in your expenditure on the good depends on *your* elasticity of demand.

- If your demand is elastic, a 1 percent price cut increases the quantity you buy by more than 1 percent and your expenditure on the item increases.
- If your demand is inelastic, a 1 percent price cut increases the quantity you buy by less than 1 percent and your expenditure on the item decreases.
- If your demand is unit elastic, a 1 percent price cut increases the quantity you buy by 1 percent and your expenditure on the item does not change.

So if you spend more on an item when its price falls, your demand for that item is elastic; if you spend the same amount, your demand is unit elastic; and if you spend less, your demand is inelastic.

The Factors That Influence the Elasticity of Demand

What makes the demand for some goods elastic and the demand for others inelastic? The elasticity of demand for a good depends on

- The closeness of substitutes
- The proportion of income spent on the good
- The time elapsed since the price change

Closeness of Substitutes The closer the substitutes for a good or service, the more elastic is the demand for it. For example, oil from which we make gasoline has substitutes but none that are currently very close (imagine a steam-driven, coal-fueled car). So the demand for oil is inelastic. Plastics are close substitutes for metals, so the demand for metals is elastic.

The degree of substitutability between two goods also depends on how narrowly (or broadly) we define them. For example, a personal computer has no really close substitutes, but a Dell PC is a close substitute for a Hewlett-Packard PC. So the elasticity of demand for personal computers is lower than the elasticity of demand for a Dell or a Hewlett-Packard.

In everyday language we call goods such as food and shelter *necessities* and goods such as exotic vacations *luxuries*. A necessity is a good that has poor substitutes and that is crucial for our well-being. So generally, a necessity has an inelastic demand.

A luxury is a good that usually has many substitutes, one of which is not buying it. So a luxury generally has an elastic demand.

Some Real-World Elasticities of Demand

Elastic and Inelastic Demand

The real-world elasticities of demand in the table range from 1.52 for metals, the item with the most elastic demand in the table, to 0.05 for oil, the item with the most inelastic demand in the table.

Oil and food, which have poor substitutes and inelastic demand, might be classified as necessities. Furniture and motor vehicles, which have good substitutes and elastic demand, might be classified as luxuries.

Price Elasticities of Demand

Good or Service	Elasticity
Elastic Demand	
Metals	1.52
Electrical engineering products	1.39
Mechanical engineering products	1.30
Furniture	1.26
Motor vehicles	1.14
Instrument engineering products	1.10
Professional services	1.09
Transportation services	1.03
Inelastic Demand	
Gas, electricity, and water	0.92
Chemicals	0.89
Drinks (all types)	0.78
Clothing	0.64
Tobacco	0.61
Banking and insurance services	0.56
Housing services	0.55
Agricultural and fish products	0.42
Books, magazines, and newspapers	0.34
Food	0.12
Oil	0.05

Sources of data: Ahsan Mansur and John Whalley, "Numerical Specification of Applied General Equilibrium Models: Estimation, Calibration, and Data," in *Applied General Equilibrium Analysis*, eds. Herbert E. Scarf and John B. Shoven (New York: Cambridge University Press, 1984), 109, and Henri Theil, Ching-Fan Chung, and James L. Seale, Jr., *Advances in Econometrics, Supplement I, 1989, International Evidence on Consumption Patterns* (Greenwich, Conn.: JAI Press Inc., 1989), and Geoffrey Heal, Columbia University, Web site.

Proportion of Income Spent on the Good Other things remaining the same, the greater the proportion of income spent on a good, the more elastic is the demand for it.

Think about your own elasticity of demand for chewing gum and housing. If the price of chewing gum doubles, you consume almost as much gum as before. Your demand for gum is inelastic. If apartment rents double, you shriek and look for more students to share accommodation with you. Your demand for housing is not as inelastic as your demand for gum. Why the difference? Housing takes a large proportion of your budget, and gum takes only a tiny proportion. You don't like either price increase, but you hardly notice the higher price of gum, while the higher rent puts your budget under severe strain.

Time Elapsed Since Price Change The longer the time that has elapsed since a price change, the more elastic is demand. When the price of oil increased by 400 percent during the 1970s, people barely changed the quantity of oil and gasoline they bought. But gradually, as more efficient auto and airplane engines were developed, the quantity bought decreased. The demand for oil has become more elastic as more time has elapsed since the huge price hike. Similarly, when the price of a PC fell, the quantity of PCs demanded increased only slightly at first. But as more people have become better informed about the variety of ways of using a PC, the quantity of PCs bought has increased sharply. The demand for PCs has become more elastic.

Price Elasticities of Demand for Food

How Inelastic?

As the average income in a country increases and the proportion of income spent on food decreases, the demand for food becomes more inelastic.

The figure shows that the price elasticity of demand for food (green bars) is greatest in the poorest countries. The larger the proportion of income spent on food, the larger is the price elasticity of demand for food. In Tanzania, a nation where the average income is one-thirtieth that of the United States and where 62 percent of income is spent on food, the price elasticity of demand for food is 0.77. In contrast, in the United States, where 12 percent of income is spent on food, the price elasticity of demand for food is 0.12.

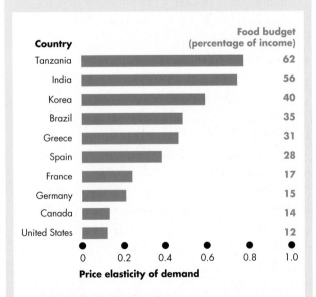

Price Elasticities in 10 Countries

Source of data: Henri Theil, Ching-Fan Chung, and James L. Seale, Jr., *Advances in Econometrics, Supplement 1, 1989, International Evidence on Consumption Patterns* (Greenwich, Conn.: JAI Press, Inc., 1989).

Review Quiz

1 Why do we need a units-free measure of the responsiveness of the quantity demanded of a good or service to a change in its price?
2 Define the price elasticity of demand and show how it is calculated.
3 Why, when we calculate the price elasticity of demand, do we express the change in price as a percentage of the *average* price and the change in quantity as a percentage of the *average* quantity?
4 What is the total revenue test? Explain how it works.
5 What are the main influences on the elasticity of demand that make the demand for some goods elastic and the demand for other goods inelastic?
6 Why is the demand for a luxury generally more elastic than the demand for a necessity?

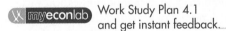 Work Study Plan 4.1 and get instant feedback.

You've now completed your study of the *price* elasticity of demand. Two other elasticity concepts tell us about the effects of other influences on demand. Let's look at these other elasticities of demand.

More Elasticities of Demand

Back at the pizzeria, you are trying to work out how a price rise by the burger shop next door will affect the demand for your pizza. You know that pizzas and burgers are substitutes. And you know that when the price of a substitute for pizza rises, the demand for pizza increases. But by how much?

You also know that pizza and soft drinks are complements. And you know that if the price of a complement of pizza rises, the demand for pizza decreases. So you wonder, by how much will a rise in the price of a soft drink decrease the demand for your pizza?

To answer these questions, you need to calculate the cross elasticity of demand. Let's examine this elasticity measure.

Cross Elasticity of Demand

We measure the influence of a change in the price of a substitute or complement by using the concept of the cross elasticity of demand. The **cross elasticity of demand** is a measure of the responsiveness of the demand for a good to a change in the price of a substitute or complement, other things remaining the same. We calculate the *cross elasticity of demand* by using the formula:

$$\text{Cross elasticity of demand} = \frac{\text{Percentage change in quantity demanded}}{\text{Percentage change in price of a substitute or complement}}.$$

The cross elasticity of demand can be positive or negative. It is *positive* for a *substitute* and *negative* for a *complement*.

Substitutes Suppose that the price of pizza is constant and people buy 9 pizzas an hour. Then the price of a burger rises from $1.50 to $2.50. No other influence on buying plans changes and the quantity of pizzas bought increases to 11 an hour.

The change in the quantity demanded is +2 pizzas—the new quantity, 11 pizzas, minus the original quantity, 9 pizzas. The average quantity is 10 pizzas. So the quantity of pizzas demanded increases by 20 percent. That is,

$$\Delta Q/Q_{ave} = (+2/10) \times 100 = +20\%.$$

The change in the price of a burger, a substitute for pizza, is +$1—the new price, $2.50, minus the original price, $1.50. The average price is $2 a burger. So the price of a burger rises by 50 percent. That is,

$$\Delta P/P_{ave} = (+1/2) \times 100 = +50\%.$$

So the cross elasticity of demand for pizza with respect to the price of a burger is

$$\frac{+20\%}{+50\%} = 0.4.$$

Figure 4.6 illustrates the cross elasticity of demand. Pizza and burgers are substitutes. Because they are substitutes, when the price of a burger rises, the demand for pizza increases. The demand curve for pizza shifts rightward from D_0 to D_1. Because a *rise* in the price of a burger brings an *increase* in the demand for pizza, the cross elasticity of demand for pizza with respect to the price of a burger is *positive*. Both the price and the quantity change in the same direction.

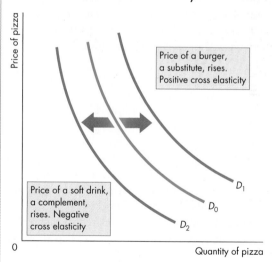

FIGURE 4.6   Cross Elasticity of Demand

A burger is a *substitute* for pizza. When the price of a burger rises, the demand for pizza increases and the demand curve for pizza shifts rightward from D_0 to D_1. The cross elasticity of demand is *positive*.

A soft drink is a *complement* of pizza. When the price of a soft drink rises, the demand for pizza decreases and the demand curve for pizza shifts leftward from D_0 to D_2. The cross elasticity of demand is *negative*.

Complements   Now suppose that the price of pizza is constant and 11 pizzas an hour are bought. Then the price of a soft drink rises from $1.50 to $2.50. No other influence on buying plans changes and the quantity of pizzas bought falls to 9 an hour.

The change in the quantity demanded is the opposite of what we've just calculated: The quantity of pizzas demanded decreases by 20 percent (–20%).

The change in the price of a soft drink, a complement of pizza, is the same as the percentage change in the price of a burger that we've just calculated. The price rises by 50 percent (+50%). So the cross elasticity of demand for pizza with respect to the price of a soft drink is

$$\frac{-20\%}{+50\%} = -0.4.$$

Because pizza and soft drinks are complements, when the price of a soft drink rises, the demand for pizza decreases. The demand curve for pizza shifts leftward from D_0 to D_2. Because a *rise* in the price of a soft drink brings a *decrease* in the demand for pizza, the cross elasticity of demand for pizza with respect to the price of a soft drink is *negative*. The price and quantity change in *opposite* directions.

The magnitude of the cross elasticity of demand determines how far the demand curve shifts. The larger the cross elasticity (absolute value), the greater is the change in demand and the larger is the shift in the demand curve.

If two items are close substitutes, such as two brands of spring water, the cross elasticity is large. If two items are close complements, such as movies and popcorn, the cross elasticity is large.

If two items are somewhat unrelated to each other, such as newspapers and orange juice, the cross elasticity is small—perhaps even zero.

Income Elasticity of Demand

Suppose the economy is expanding and people are enjoying rising incomes. This prosperity brings an increase in the demand for most types of goods and services. But by how much will the demand for pizza increase? The answer depends on the **income elasticity of demand**, which is a measure of the responsiveness of the demand for a good or service to a change in income, other things remaining the same.

The income elasticity of demand is calculated by using the formula:

$$\text{Income elasticity of demand} = \frac{\text{Percentage change in quantity demanded}}{\text{Percentage change in income}}.$$

Income elasticities of demand can be positive or negative and they fall into three interesting ranges:

- Greater than 1 (*normal* good, income elastic)
- Positive and less than 1 (*normal* good, income inelastic)
- Negative (*inferior* good)

Income Elastic Demand   Suppose that the price of pizza is constant and 9 pizzas an hour are bought. Then incomes rise from $975 to $1,025 a week. No other influence on buying plans changes and the quantity of pizzas sold increases to 11 an hour.

The change in the quantity demanded is +2 pizzas. The average quantity is 10 pizzas, so the quantity demanded increases by 20 percent. The change in income is +$50 and the average income is $1,000, so incomes increase by 5 percent. The income elasticity of demand for pizza is

$$\frac{20\%}{5\%} = 4.$$

The demand for pizza is income elastic. The percentage increase in the quantity of pizza demanded exceeds the percentage increase in income. *When the demand for a good is income elastic, the percentage of income spent on that good increases as income increases.*

Income Inelastic Demand   If the income elasticity of demand is positive but less than 1, demand is income inelastic. The percentage increase in the quantity demanded is positive but less than the percentage increase in income. *When the demand for a good is income inelastic, the percentage of income spent on that good decreases as income increases.*

Inferior Goods   If the income elasticity of demand is negative, the good is an *inferior* good. The quantity demanded of an inferior good and the amount spent on it *decrease* when income increases. Goods in this category include small motorcycles, potatoes, and rice. Low-income consumers buy most of these goods.

Income Elasticities of Demand
Necessities and Luxuries

The table shows estimates of some real-world income elasticities of demand. The demand for a necessity such as food or clothing is income inelastic, while the demand for a luxury such as transportation, which includes airline and foreign travel, is income elastic.

But what is a necessity and what is a luxury depends on the level of income. For people with a low income, food and clothing can be luxuries. So the level of income has a big effect on income elasticities of demand. The figure shows this effect on the income elasticity of demand for food in 10 countries. In countries with low incomes, such as Tanzania and India, the income elasticity of demand for food is high. In countries with high incomes, such as the United States, the income elasticity of

demand for food is low. That is as income increases, the income elasticity of demand for food decreases. Low-income consumers spend a larger percentage of any increase in income on food than do high-income consumers.

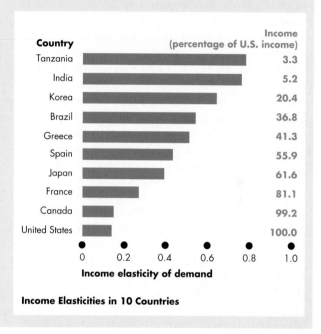

Income Elasticities in 10 Countries

Some Real-World Income Elasticities of Demand

Income Elastic Demand

Airline travel	5.82
Movies	3.41
Foreign travel	3.08
Electricity	1.94
Restaurant meals	1.61
Local buses and trains	1.38
Haircuts	1.36
Automobiles	1.07

Income Inelastic Demand

Tobacco	0.86
Alcoholic drinks	0.62
Furniture	0.53
Clothing	0.51
Newspapers and magazines	0.38
Telephone	0.32
Food	0.14

Sources of data: H.S. Houthakker and Lester D. Taylor, Consumer Demand in the United States (Cambridge, Mass.: Harvard University Press, 1970), and Henri Theil, Ching-Fan Chung, and James L. Seale, Jr., Advances in Econometrics, Supplement 1, 1989, International Evidence on Consumption Patterns (Greenwich, Conn.: JAI Press, Inc., 1989).

Review Quiz

1 What does the cross elasticity of demand measure?
2 What does the sign (positive versus negative) of the cross elasticity of demand tell us about the relationship between two goods?
3 What does the income elasticity of demand measure?
4 What does the sign (positive versus negative) of the income elasticity of demand tell us about a good?
5 Why does the level of income influence the magnitude of the income elasticity of demand?

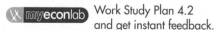 Work Study Plan 4.2 and get instant feedback.

You've now completed your study of the *cross elasticity* of demand and the *income elasticity* of demand. Let's look at the other side of the market and examine the elasticity of supply.

Elasticity of Supply

You know that when demand increases, the equilibrium price rises and the equilibrium quantity increases. But does the price rise by a large amount and the quantity increase by a little? Or does the price barely rise and the quantity increase by a large amount?

The answer depends on the responsiveness of the quantity supplied to a change in price. You can see why by studying Fig. 4.7, which shows two possible scenarios in a local pizza market. Figure 4.7(a) shows one scenario, and Fig. 4.7(b) shows the other.

In both cases, demand is initially D_0. In part (a), supply is shown by the supply curve S_A. In part (b), supply is shown by the supply curve S_B. Initially, in both cases, the price is $20 a pizza and the equilibrium quantity is 10 pizzas an hour.

Now increases in incomes and population increase the demand for pizza. The demand curve shifts rightward to D_1. In case (a), the price rises by $10 to $30 a pizza, and the quantity increases by only 3 to 13 pizzas an hour. In contrast, in case (b), the price rises by only $1 to $21 a pizza, and the quantity increases by 10 to 20 pizzas an hour.

The different outcomes arise from differing degrees of responsiveness of the quantity supplied to a change in price. We measure the degree of responsiveness by using the concept of the elasticity of supply.

Calculating the Elasticity of Supply

The **elasticity of supply** measures the responsiveness of the quantity supplied to a change in the price of a good when all other influences on selling plans remain the same. It is calculated by using the formula:

$$\text{Elasticity of supply} = \frac{\text{Percentage change in quantity supplied}}{\text{Percentage change in price}}.$$

We use the same method that you learned when you studied the elasticity of demand. (Refer back to p. 87 to check this method.) Let's calculate the elasticity of supply along the supply curves in Fig. 4.7.

In Fig. 4.7(a), when the price rises from $20 to $30, the price rise is $10 and the average price is $25, so the price rises by 40 percent of the average price. The quantity increases from 10 to 13 pizzas an hour,

---

FIGURE 4.7 How a Change in Demand Changes Price and Quantity

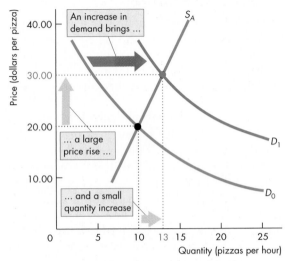

(a) Large price change and small quantity change

(b) Small price change and large quantity change

Initially, the price is $20 a pizza, and the quantity sold is 10 pizzas an hour. Then the demand for pizza increases. The demand curve shifts rightward to D_1. In part (a), the price rises by $10 to $30 a pizza, and the quantity increases by 3 to 13 pizzas an hour. In part (b), the price rises by only $1 to $21 a pizza, and the quantity increases by 10 to 20 pizzas an hour. The price change is smaller and the quantity change is larger in case (b) than in case (a). The quantity supplied is more responsive to a change in the price in case (b) than in case (a).

myeconlab animation

so the increase is 3 pizzas, the average quantity is 11.5 pizzas an hour, and the quantity increases by 26 percent. The elasticity of supply is equal to 26 percent divided by 40 percent, which equals 0.65.

In Fig. 4.7(b), when the price rises from $20 to $21, the price rise is $1 and the average price is $20.50, so the price rises by 4.9 percent of the average price. The quantity increases from 10 to 20 pizzas an hour, so the increase is 10 pizzas, the average quantity is 15 pizzas, and the quantity increases by 67 percent. The elasticity of supply is equal to 67 percent divided by 4.9 percent, which equals 13.67.

Figure 4.8 shows the range of elasticities of supply. If the quantity supplied is fixed regardless of the price, the supply curve is vertical and the elasticity of supply is zero. Supply is perfectly inelastic. This case is shown in Fig. 4.8(a). A special intermediate case occurs when the percentage change in price equals the percentage change in quantity. Supply is then unit elastic. This case is shown in Fig. 4.8(b). No matter how steep the supply curve is, if it is linear and passes through the origin, supply is unit elastic. If there is a price at which sellers are willing to offer any quantity for sale, the supply curve is horizontal and the elasticity of supply is infinite. Supply is perfectly elastic. This case is shown in Fig. 4.8(c).

The Factors That Influence the Elasticity of Supply

The elasticity of supply of a good depends on

- Resource substitution possibilities
- Time frame for the supply decision

Resource Substitution Possibilities Some goods and services can be produced only by using unique or rare productive resources. These items have a low, perhaps even a zero, elasticity of supply. Other goods and services can be produced by using commonly available resources that could be allocated to a wide variety of alternative tasks. Such items have a high elasticity of supply.

A Van Gogh painting is an example of a good with a vertical supply curve and a zero elasticity of supply. At the other extreme, wheat can be grown on land that is almost equally good for growing corn, so it is just as easy to grow wheat as corn. The opportunity cost of wheat in terms of forgone corn is almost constant. As a result, the supply curve of wheat is almost horizontal and its elasticity of supply is very large. Similarly, when a good is produced in many different countries (for example, sugar and beef), the supply of the good is highly elastic.

FIGURE 4.8   Inelastic and Elastic Supply

(a) Perfectly inelastic supply   **(b) Unit elastic supply**   **(c) Perfectly elastic supply**

Each supply illustrated here has a constant elasticity. The supply curve in part (a) illustrates the supply of a good that has a zero elasticity of supply. The supply curve in part (b) illustrates the supply of a good with a unit elasticity of supply. All linear supply curves that pass through the origin illustrate supplies that are unit elastic. The supply curve in part (c) illustrates the supply of a good with an infinite elasticity of supply.

myeconlab animation

The supply of most goods and services lies between these two extremes. The quantity produced can be increased but only by incurring a higher cost. If a higher price is offered, the quantity supplied increases. Such goods and services have an elasticity of supply between zero and infinity.

Time Frame for the Supply Decision To study the influence of the amount of time elapsed since a price change, we distinguish three time frames of supply:

1. Momentary supply
2. Long-run supply
3. Short-run supply

When the price of a good rises or falls, the *momentary supply curve* shows the response of the quantity supplied immediately following the price change.

Some goods, such as fruits and vegetables, have a perfectly inelastic momentary supply—a vertical supply curve. The quantities supplied depend on crop-planting decisions made earlier. In the case of oranges, for example, planting decisions have to be made many years in advance of the crop being available. The momentary supply curve is vertical because, on a given day, no matter what the price of oranges, producers cannot change their output. They have picked, packed, and shipped their crop to market, and the quantity available for that day is fixed.

In contrast, some goods have a perfectly elastic momentary supply. Long-distance phone calls are an example. When many people simultaneously make a call, there is a big surge in the demand for telephone cables, computer switching, and satellite time, and the quantity supplied increases. But the price remains constant. Long-distance carriers monitor fluctuations in demand and reroute calls to ensure that the quantity supplied equals the quantity demanded without changing the price.

The *long-run supply curve* shows the response of the quantity supplied to a price change after all the technologically possible ways of adjusting supply have been exploited. In the case of oranges, the long run is the time it takes new plantings to grow to full maturity—about 15 years. In some cases, the long-run adjustment occurs only after a completely new production plant has been built and workers have been trained to operate it—typically a process that might take several years.

The *short-run supply curve* shows how the quantity supplied responds to a price change when only *some*

of the technologically possible adjustments to production have been made. The short-run response to a price change is a sequence of adjustments. The first adjustment that is usually made is in the amount of labor employed. To increase output in the short run, firms work their labor force overtime and perhaps hire additional workers. To decrease their output in the short run, firms either lay off workers or reduce their hours of work. With the passage of time, firms can make additional adjustments, perhaps training additional workers or buying additional tools and other equipment.

The short-run supply curve slopes upward because producers can take actions quite quickly to change the quantity supplied in response to a price change. For example, if the price of oranges falls, growers can stop picking and leave oranges to rot on the trees. Or if the price rises, they can use more fertilizer and improved irrigation to increase the yields of their existing trees. In the long run, they can plant more trees and increase the quantity supplied even more in response to a given price rise.

Review Quiz

1 Why do we need a units-free measure of the responsiveness of the quantity supplied of a good or service to a change in its price?
2 Define the elasticity of supply and show how it is calculated.
3 What are the main influences on the elasticity of supply that make the supply of some goods elastic and the supply of other goods inelastic?
4 Provide examples of goods or services whose elasticities of supply are (a) zero, (b) greater than zero but less than infinity, and (c) infinity.
5 How does the time frame over which a supply decision is made influence the elasticity of supply? Explain your answer.

myeconlab Work Study Plan 4.3 and get instant feedback.

You have now learned about the elasticities of demand and supply. Table 4.1 summarizes all the elasticities that you've met in this chapter. In the next chapter, we study the efficiency of competitive markets. But first study *Reading Between the Lines* on pp. 100–101, which puts the elasticity of demand to work and looks at the markets for gasoline and automobiles.

TABLE 4.1   A Compact Glossary of Elasticities

Price Elasticities of Demand

A relationship is described as	When its magnitude is	Which means that
Perfectly elastic	Infinity	The smallest possible increase in price causes an infinitely large decrease in the quantity demanded*
Elastic	Less than infinity but greater than 1	The percentage decrease in the quantity demanded exceeds the percentage increase in price
Unit elastic	1	The percentage decrease in the quantity demanded equals the percentage increase in price
Inelastic	Greater than zero but less than 1	The percentage decrease in the quantity demanded is less than the percentage increase in price
Perfectly inelastic	Zero	The quantity demanded is the same at all prices

Cross Elasticities of Demand

A relationship is described as	When its value is	Which means that
Close substitutes	Large	The smallest possible increase in the price of one good causes an infinitely large increase in the quantity demanded of the other good
Substitutes	Positive	If the price of one good increases, the quantity demanded of the other good also increases
Unrelated goods	Zero	If the price of one good increases, the quantity demanded of the other good remains the same
Complements	Negative	If the price of one good increases, the quantity demanded of the other good decreases

Income Elasticities of Demand

A relationship is described as	When its value is	Which means that
Income elastic (normal good)	Greater than 1	The percentage increase in the quantity demanded is greater than the percentage increase in income
Income inelastic (normal good)	Less than 1 but greater than zero	The percentage increase in the quantity demanded is greater than zero less than the percentage increase in income
Negative (inferior good)	Less than zero	When income increases, quantity demanded decreases

Elasticities of Supply

A relationship is described as	When its magnitude is	Which means that
Perfectly elastic	Infinity	The smallest possible increase in price causes an infinitely large increase in the quantity supplied
Elastic	Less than infinity but greater than 1	The percentage increase in the quantity supplied exceeds the percentage increase in the price
Inelastic	Greater than zero but less than 1	The percentage increase in the quantity supplied is less than the percentage increase in the price
Perfectly inelastic	Zero	The quantity supplied is the same at all prices

*In each description, the directions of change may be reversed. For example, in this case, the smallest possible *decrease* in price causes an infinitely large *increase* in the quantity demanded.

The Elasticities of Demand for Gasoline, SUVs, and Subcompacts

As Gas Costs Soar, Buyers Are Flocking to Small Cars

Soaring gas prices have turned the steady migration by Americans to smaller cars into a stampede. ...

http://www.nytimes.com
May 2, 2008

Sales of Toyota's subcompact Yaris increased 46 percent, and Honda's tiny Fit had a record month. Ford's compact Focus model jumped 32 percent in April from a year earlier. All those models are rated at more than 30 miles per gallon for highway driving. ...

Sales of traditional SUV's are down more than 25 percent this year. In April, for example, sales of G.M.'s Chevrolet Tahoe fell 35 percent.

Full-size pickup sales have fallen more than 15 percent this year, with Ford's industry-leading F-Series pickup dropping 27 percent in April alone. Sales of pickups, though, are expected to strengthen with the economy, because of their use as commercial vehicles. ...

How the downsizing of America's vehicle fleet will affect fuel consumption is still largely unknown. When gas prices rise, as they are now, many drivers simply drive less to save money.

But there are some indications that the trend toward smaller vehicles will reduce the nation's fuel use. In California, motorists bought 4 percent less gasoline in January than they did the year before, a drop of more than 58 million gallons, according to the Oil Price Information Service.

"That is an incredible year-over-year drop," said Tom Kloza, the organization's chief oil analyst. "Some of it clearly has to do with changes in the vehicle fleet."...

Essence of the Story

- Faced with high gas prices, Americans are substituting smaller cars for SUVs.

- Toyota Yaris sales increased 46 percent and Ford Focus sales increased 32 percent in April 2008 from a year earlier.

- Sales of SUVs decreased by more than 25 percent in 2008 and Chevrolet Tahoe sales fell 35 percent.

- Full-size pickup sales decreased more than 15 percent in 2008 and Ford F-Series pickup sales decreased by 27 percent in April 2008.

- The effect of a downsized vehicle fleet on fuel consumption is unknown.

- In California, gasoline consumption decreased by 4 percent in January 2008 from a year earlier.

Economic Analysis

- Using data provided in this news article and by the Energy Information Administration, and assuming that no other influences on buying plans changed, we can estimate the price elasticity of demand for gasoline in California.

- Table 1 summarizes the gasoline price and quantity data and, using the midpoint method, calculates the price elasticity of demand.

Table 1 Price Elasticity of Demand for Gasoline in California

	Quantity (millions of gallons)	Price (dollars per gallon)
January-07	1450	2.29
January-08	1392	3.09
Change	−58	0.80
Average	1421	2.69
% change	−4.1	29.7
Elasticity	**0.14**	

- Figure 1 illustrates the changes in price and quantity and the elasticity calculation.

- The estimated price elasticity of demand for gasoline in California is 0.14, which means that the demand is inelastic. A large percentage change in price brings a small percentage change in the quantity of gasoline demanded.

- Table 2 shows the quantities sold of four vehicles and the price of gasoline in April 2007 and April 2008 and calculates some cross elasticities of demand.

Table 2 Cross Elasticities of Demand for Vehicles in the United States

Vehicle	Apr-07 Number	Apr-08 Number	% change	Cross elasticity of demand
Toyota Yaris	7,323	11,434	43.8	2.3
Ford Focus	16,626	23,850	35.7	1.8
Chevrolet Tahoe	10,980	8,139	−29.7	−1.5
Ford F-Series	56,692	44,813	−23.4	−1.2
Price of gasoline (dollars per gallon)	2.89	3.51	19.4	

- The cross elasticities of demand are calculated using the formula on p. 93.

- The cross elasticities of demand for the Yaris and Focus are positive and large. A rise in the price of gasoline increases the demand for these vehicles. A small car and gasoline are *substitutes*—a smaller car is used in place of a large gas bill. Figure 2 illustrates the cross elasticity of demand for small vehicles.

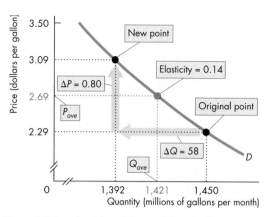

Figure 1 Price elasticity of demand for gasoline

Figure 2 Cross elasticity: Yaris and price of gasoline

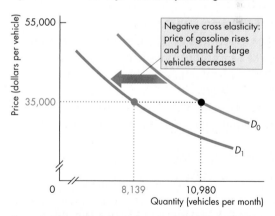

Figure 3 Cross elasticity: Tahoe and price of gasoline

- The cross elasticity of demand for the Tahoe and F-Series are negative and large. A rise in the price of gasoline decreases the demand for these vehicles. A large vehicle and gasoline are *complements*. Figure 3 illustrates the cross elasticity of demand for large vehicles.

SUMMARY

Key Points

Price Elasticity of Demand (pp. 86–92)

- Elasticity is a measure of the responsiveness of the quantity demanded of a good to a change in its price, other things remaining the same.
- Price elasticity of demand equals the percentage change in the quantity demanded divided by the percentage change in the price.
- The larger the magnitude of the price elasticity of demand, the greater is the responsiveness of the quantity demanded to a given price change.
- If demand is elastic, a cut in price leads to an increase in total revenue. If demand is unit elastic, a cut in price leaves total revenue unchanged. And if demand is inelastic, a cut in price leads to a decrease in total revenue.
- Price elasticity of demand depends on how easily one good serves as a substitute for another, the proportion of income spent on the good, and the length of time elapsed since the price change.

More Elasticities of Demand (pp. 93–95)

- Cross elasticity of demand measures the responsiveness of the demand for one good to a change in the price of a substitute or a complement, other things remaining the same.
- The cross elasticity of demand with respect to the price of a substitute is positive. The cross elasticity of demand with respect to the price of a complement is negative.
- Income elasticity of demand measures the responsiveness of demand to a change in income, other

things remaining the same. For a normal good, the income elasticity of demand is positive. For an inferior good, the income elasticity of demand is negative.

- When the income elasticity of demand is greater than 1 (income elastic), the percentage of income spent on the good increases as income increases.
- When the income elasticity of demand is less than 1 (income inelastic and inferior), the percentage of income spent on the good decreases as income increases.

Elasticity of Supply (pp. 96–98)

- Elasticity of supply measures the responsiveness of the quantity supplied of a good to a change in its price, other things remaining the same.
- The elasticity of supply is usually positive and ranges between zero (vertical supply curve) and infinity (horizontal supply curve).
- Supply decisions have three time frames: momentary, long run, and short run.
- Momentary supply refers to the response of the quantity supplied to a price change at the instant that the price changes.
- Long-run supply refers to the response of the quantity supplied to a price change when all the technologically feasible adjustments in production have been made.
- Short-run supply refers to the response of the quantity supplied to a price change after some of the technologically feasible adjustments in production have been made.

Key Figures and Table

Key Terms

PROBLEMS and APPLICATIONS

Work problems 1–12 in Chapter 4 Study Plan and get instant feedback.
Work problems 14–26 as Homework, a Quiz, or a Test if assigned by your instructor.

1. Rain spoils the strawberry crop. As a result, the price rises from $4 to $6 a box and the quantity demanded decreases from 1,000 to 600 boxes a week. Over this price range,
   a. What is the price elasticity of demand?
   b. Describe the demand for strawberries.

2. If the quantity of dental services demanded increases by 10 percent when the price of dental services falls by 10 percent, is the demand for dental services inelastic, elastic, or unit elastic?

3. The demand schedule for hotel rooms is

Price (dollars per night)	Quantity demanded (millions of rooms per night)
200	100
250	80
400	50
500	40
800	25
1,000	20

   a. What happens to total revenue if the price falls from $400 to $250 a night?
   b. What happens to total revenue if the price falls from $250 to $200 a night?
   c. At what price is total revenue at a maximum? Explain and interpret your answer.
   d. Is the demand for hotel rooms elastic, unit elastic, or inelastic?

4. **The Grip of Gas: Why You'll Pay Through the Nose to Keep Driving**

   Drivers in the United States consistently rank as the least sensitive to changes in gas prices. ... If prices rose from $3 per gallon to $4 per gallon and stayed there for a year ... purchases of gasoline in the United States would fall only about 5 percent.

   Slate, September 27, 2005

   a. Using the information provided, calculate the price elasticity of demand for gasoline.
   b. Does this measurement indicate that the demand for gasoline is elastic, unit elastic, or inelastic?
   c. If the price of gasoline rises, will total revenue from gasoline sales increase or decrease? Explain.

5. In 2003, when music downloading first took off, Universal Music slashed the price of a CD from an average of $21 to an average of $15. The company said that it expected the price cut to boost the quantity of CDs sold by 30 percent, other things remaining the same.
   a. What was Universal Music's estimate of the price elasticity of demand for CDs?
   b. Given your answer in a, if you were making the pricing decision at Universal Music, would you cut the price, raise the price, or not change the price? Explain your decision.

6. **Why the Tepid Response to Rising Gasoline Prices?**

   Estimates of the long-run response to past movements in [gasoline] prices imply that a 10 percent price rise causes 5 to 10 percent less consumption, other things being equal. ... The nationwide average price of gasoline surged 53 percent from 1998 to 2004, after adjusting for inflation. Yet consumption was up 10 percent in this period.

   Of course, many other things changed in this period. Perhaps most important, [incomes] grew by 19 percent. ... This would ordinarily be expected to push gasoline sales up about 20 percent ...

   The New York Times, October 13, 2005

   a. What does the above information tell us about the responsiveness of the quantity of gasoline demanded to a change in the price a long time after the price change occurs?
   b. Calculate the income elasticity of demand for gasoline implied by the above information.
   c. If other things remained the same except for the increase in income and the rise in price, what would the data for 1998 to 2004 imply about the price elasticity of demand for gasoline?
   d. List all the factors you can think of that might bias the estimate of the price elasticity of demand for gasoline, using just the data for 1998 to 2004.

7. If a 12 percent rise in the price of orange juice decreases the quantity of orange juice demanded by 22 percent and increases the quantity of apple juice demanded by 14 percent, calculate the

a. Price elasticity of demand for orange juice.

b. Cross elasticity of demand for apple juice with respect to the price of orange juice.

8. **Swelling Textbook Costs Have College Students Saying 'Pass'**

Textbook prices have been rising at double the rate of inflation for the past two decades … [and] nearly 60 percent of students nationwide choose not to buy all the course materials. … For students working to pay for school or for those whose parents sweat every increase in tuition, book prices can be a nasty surprise. … And plenty of students come up with their own strategies: Hunting down used copies and selling books back at the end of the semester; buying online, which is sometimes cheaper than the campus store; asking professors to put a copy in the library and waiting around till it's free. Or borrowing, copying, taking careful notes in class—and gambling that the exam questions don't come from the text. …

Washington Post, January 23, 2006

Explain what this news clip implies about

a. The price elasticity of demand for college textbooks.

b. The income elasticity of demand for college textbooks.

c. The cross elasticity of demand for college textbooks from the campus bookstore with respect to the online price of a textbook.

9. **Home Depot Earnings Hammered**

As home prices slump across the country, fewer people are spending money to renovate their homes, and the improvements that they are making are not as expensive. … People are spending on small ticket types of repairs, … not big ticket renovations. … With gas and food prices increasing … people have less extra income to spend on major home improvements.

CNN, May 20, 2008

a. What does this news clip imply about the income elasticity of demand for big-ticket home-improvement items?

b. Would the income elasticity of demand be greater or less than 1? Explain.

10. **Spam Sales Rise as Food Costs Soar**

Sales of Spam—that much maligned meat—are rising as consumers are turning more to lunch meats and other lower-cost foods to extend their already stretched food budgets. … Consumers are quick to realize that meats like Spam and other processed foods can be substituted for costlier cuts as a way of controlling costs.

AOL Money & Finance, May 28, 2008

a. Is Spam a normal good or inferior good? Explain.

b. Would the income elasticity of demand for Spam be negative or positive? Explain.

11. **Study Ranks Honolulu Third Highest for 'Unaffordable Housing'**

[Study ranks] Honolulu number 3 in the world for the most unaffordable housing market in urban locations. Honolulu is listed only behind Los Angeles and San Diego and is deemed "severely unaffordable." … Where there are significant constraints on the supply of land for residential development, housing inflation has occurred.

Hawaii Reporter, September 11, 2007

a. Would the supply of housing in Honolulu be elastic or inelastic?

b. Explain how the elasticity of supply plays an important role in influencing how rapidly housing prices in Honolulu rise.

12. The demand for illegal drugs is inelastic. Much of the expenditure on illegal drugs comes from crime. Assuming these statements to be correct,

a. How will a successful campaign that decreases the supply of drugs influence the price of illegal drugs and the amount spent on them?

b. What will happen to the amount of crime?

c. What is the most effective way of decreasing the quantity of illegal drugs bought and decreasing the amount of drug-related crime?

13. Use the links on MyEconLab (Textbook Resources, Chapter 4, Web links) to find the number of gallons in a barrel of oil and the prices of crude oil and gasoline in the summer of 2007 and 2008.

a. What are the other costs that make up the total cost of a gallon of gasoline?

b. If the price of crude oil falls by 10 percent, by what percentage do you expect the price of gasoline to change, other things remaining the same?

c. Which demand do you think is more elastic: that for crude oil or gasoline? Why?

d. Use the concepts of demand, supply, and elasticity to explain recent changes in the prices of crude oil and gasoline.

14. With higher fuel costs, airlines raise their fares. The average fare rises from 75¢ per passenger mile to $1.25 per passenger mile and the number of passenger miles decreases from 2.5 million a day to 1.5 million a day. Over this price range,
   a. What is the price elasticity of demand for air travel?
   b. Describe the demand for air travel.

15. The figure shows the demand for DVD rentals.

   a. Calculate the elasticity of demand when the price rises from $3 to $5 a DVD.
   b. At what price is the elasticity of demand for DVDs equal to 1?

16. The demand schedule for computer chips is

Price (dollars per chip)	Quantity demanded (millions of chips per year)
200	50
250	45
300	40
350	35
400	30

   a. What happens to total revenue if the price falls from $400 to $350 a chip?
   b. What happens to total revenue if the price falls from $350 to $300 a chip?
   c. At what price is total revenue at a maximum?
   d. At an average price of $350, is the demand for chips elastic, inelastic, or unit elastic? Use the total revenue test to answer this question.

17. In problem 16, at $250 a chip, is the demand for chips elastic or inelastic? Use the total revenue test to answer this question.

18. Your price elasticity of demand for bananas is 4. If the price of bananas rises by 5 percent, what is

   a. The percentage change in the quantity of bananas you buy?
   b. The change in your expenditure on bananas?

19. **Why Gasoline Follows Oil Up but Not Down**
   If it seems like gasoline prices are quick to sky-rocket when the price of oil goes up, but then take their sweet ol' time coming back down when crude prices sink, the answer is simple: They do. "There is a rocket and feather aspect."… The service stations are still selling the same amount of gasoline when wholesale prices fall … "so there's no reason to drop. … [Service stations] typically react [to a spike in oil prices] by pushing prices higher, even before they replace their inventories. …" Eventually, the free market steps in and prices begin going down when other nearby stations reduce their price.

   CNN, January 12, 2007

   a. Explain the link between the elasticity of supply of gasoline and gas price fluctuations.
   b. Explain the connection between the elasticity of demand for gasoline and the "rocket and feather" tendency of price fluctuations.

20. **As Gasoline Prices Soar, Americans Slowly Adapt**
   … in March, Americans drove 11 billion fewer miles than in March 2007. … "People have recognized that prices are not going down and are adapting to higher energy cost." … Americans spend 3.7 percent of their disposable income on transportation fuels. At its lowest point, that share was 1.9 percent in 1998, and at its highest it reached 4.5 percent in 1981. … "We actually have a lot of choices, based on what car we drive, where we live, how much time we choose to drive, and where we choose to go." For many people, higher energy costs mean fewer restaurant meals, deferred weekend outings with the kids, less air travel and more time closer to home. …

   International Herald Tribune, May 23, 2008

   a. List and explain the elasticities of demand that are implicitly referred to in the news clip.
   b. Explain the factors identified in the news clip that may make the demand for gasoline inelastic.

21. When Alex's income increased from $3,000 to $5,000, he increased his consumption of bagels from 4 to 8 a month and decreased his consumption of donuts from 12 to 6 a month. Calculate

Alex's income elasticity of demand for
a. Bagels.
b. Donuts.

22. **Wal-Mart's Recession-Time Pet Project**

Wal-Mart ... is "redefining" the pets business in its stores, including repositioning pet food and supplies right in front of its other fast-growing business, baby products. There lies the connection, according to retail industry experts, who point out that kids and pets tend to be fairly recession-resistant businesses. Even in a recession, dogs will be fed and kids will get their toys. ...

CNN, May 13, 2008

a. What does this news clip imply about the income elasticity of demand for pet food and baby products?
b. Would the income elasticity of demand be greater or less than 1? Explain.

23. **Netflix to Offer Online Movie Viewing**

Online movie rental service Netflix introduced a new feature Tuesday to allow customers to watch movies and television series on their personal computers. ... Netflix has been competing with video rental retailer Blockbuster, which has added an online rental service to the in-store rental service.

CNN, January 16, 2007

a. How will the offering of online movie viewing influence the price elasticity of demand for in-store movie rentals?
b. Would the cross elasticity of demand for online movies and in-store movie rentals be negative or positive? Explain.
c. Would the cross elasticity of demand for online movies with respect to high-speed Internet service be negative or positive? Explain.

24. **To Love, Honor, and Save Money**

Nearly half of caterers and event planners surveyed ... said they were seeing declines in wedding spending in response to the economic slowdown; 12% even reported wedding cancellations because of financial concerns.

Time, June 2, 2008

a. Based upon this news clip, are wedding events a normal good or inferior good? Explain.
b. Are wedding events more of a necessity or luxury? Explain.

c. Given your answer to b, would that make the income elasticity of demand greater than 1, less than 1, or equal to 1?

25. The table gives the supply schedule of long-distance phone calls.

Price (cents per minute)	Quantity supplied (millions of minutes per day)
10	200
20	400
30	600
40	800

Calculate the elasticity of supply when
a. The price falls from 40 cents to 30 cents a minute.
b. The average price is 20 cents a minute.

26. Study *Reading Between the Lines* on pp. 100–101 and then answer the following questions.
a. What factors other than the price of gasoline would you expect to influence California motorists' planned purchases of gasoline?
b. In which directions would the factors that you identified in a change the demand for gasoline in California?
c. How would the changes in the demand for gasoline have biased our estimate of the price elasticity of demand for gasoline?
d. Given the influence of the price of gasoline on the demand for small vehicles and large vehicles, how would you expect the prices of small vehicles and large vehicles to have changed in 2008?
e. What elasticities do you need to know to predict the magnitude of the changes in the prices of small vehicles and large vehicles?
f. If the prices of cars did change in 2008 in the directions that you have predicted in d, how would these changes impact our estimates of the cross elasticities of demand for small vehicles and large vehicles with respect to the price of gasoline?
g. How would you expect the demand for vehicles to change in the long run in response to a permanent rise in the price of gasoline?

5

Efficiency and Equity

**After studying this chapter,
you will be able to:**

- Describe the alternative methods of allocating scarce resources

- Explain the connection between demand and marginal benefit and define consumer surplus

- Explain the connection between supply and marginal cost and define producer surplus

- Explain the conditions under which markets are efficient and inefficient

- Explain the main ideas about fairness and evaluate claims that markets result in unfair outcomes

Every time you pour a glass of water or order a pizza, you express your view about how scarce resources should be used and you make choices in your *self-interest*. Markets coordinate your choices along with those of everyone else. But do markets do a good job? Do they allocate resources between water, pizza, and everything else efficiently?

The market economy generates huge income inequality. You can afford to buy a bottle of fresh spring water, while a student in India must make the best of dirty well water or expensive water from a tanker. Is this situation fair?

The *social interest* has the two dimensions that we've just discussed: efficiency and fairness (or equity). So our central question in this chapter is: Do markets operate in the social interest? At the end of the chapter, in *Reading Between the Lines*, we return to the issue of the use of the water resources. Do we use markets and other arrangements that allocate scarce water efficiently and fairly?

Resource Allocation Methods

The goal of this chapter is to evaluate the ability of markets to allocate resources efficiently and fairly. But to see whether the market does a good job, we must compare it with its alternatives. Resources are scarce, so they must be allocated somehow. And trading in markets is just one of several alternative methods.

Resources might be allocated by

- Market price
- Command
- Majority rule
- Contest
- First-come, first-served
- Lottery
- Personal characteristics
- Force

Let's briefly examine each method.

Market Price

When a market price allocates a scarce resource, the people who are willing and able to pay that price get the resource. Two kinds of people decide not to pay the market price: those who can afford to pay but choose not to buy and those who are too poor and simply can't afford to buy.

For many goods and services, distinguishing between those who choose not to buy and those who can't afford to buy doesn't matter. But for a few items, it does matter. For example, poor people can't afford to pay school fees and doctors' fees. Because poor people can't afford items that most people consider to be essential, these items are usually allocated by one of the other methods.

Command

A **command system** allocates resources by the order (command) of someone in authority. In the U.S. economy, the command system is used extensively inside firms and government departments. For example, if you have a job, most likely someone tells you what to do. Your labor is allocated to specific tasks by a command.

A command system works well in organizations in which the lines of authority and responsibility are clear and it is easy to monitor the activities being performed. But a command system works badly when the range of activities to be monitored is large and when it is easy for people to fool those in authority. The system works so badly in North Korea, where it is used extensively in place of markets, that it fails even to deliver an adequate supply of food.

Majority Rule

Majority rule allocates resources in the way that a majority of voters choose. Societies use majority rule to elect representative governments that make some of the biggest decisions. For example, majority rule decides the tax rates that end up allocating scarce resources between private use and public use. And majority rule decides how tax dollars are allocated among competing uses such as education and health care.

Majority rule works well when the decisions being made affect large numbers of people and self-interest must be suppressed to use resources most effectively.

Contest

A contest allocates resources to a winner (or a group of winners). Sporting events use this method. Tiger Woods competes with other golfers, and the winner gets the biggest payoff. But contests are more general than those in a sports arena, though we don't normally call them contests. For example, Bill Gates won a contest to provide the world's personal computer operating system.

Contests do a good job when the efforts of the "players" are hard to monitor and reward directly. When a manager offers everyone in the company the opportunity to win a big prize, people are motivated to work hard and try to become the winner. Only a few people end up with a big prize, but many people work harder in the process of trying to win. The total output produced by the workers is much greater than it would be without the contest.

First-Come, First-Served

A first-come, first-served method allocates resources to those who are first in line. Many casual restaurants won't accept reservations. They use first-come, first-served to allocate their scarce tables. Highway space is allocated in this way too: the first to arrive at the on-ramp gets the road space. If too many vehicles enter the highway, the speed slows and people wait in line for some space to become available.

First-come, first-served works best when, as in the above examples, a scarce resource can serve just one user at a time in a sequence. By serving the user who arrives first, this method minimizes the time spent waiting for the resource to become free.

Lottery

Lotteries allocate resources to those who pick the winning number, draw the lucky cards, or come up lucky on some other gaming system. State lotteries and casinos reallocate millions of dollars worth of goods and services every year.

But lotteries are more widespread than jackpots and roulette wheels in casinos. They are used to allocate landing slots to airlines at some airports and have been used to allocate fishing rights and the electromagnetic spectrum used by cell phones.

Lotteries work best when there is no effective way to distinguish among potential users of a scarce resource.

Personal Characteristics

When resources are allocated on the basis of personal characteristics, people with the "right" characteristics get the resources. Some of the resources that matter most to you are allocated in this way. For example, you will choose a marriage partner on the basis of personal characteristics. But this method is also used in unacceptable ways. Allocating the best jobs to white, Anglo-Saxon males and discriminating against visible minorities and women is an example.

Force

Force plays a crucial role, for both good and ill, in allocating scarce resources. Let's start with the ill.

War, the use of military force by one nation against another, has played an enormous role historically in allocating resources. The economic supremacy of European settlers in the Americas and Australia owes much to the use of this method.

Theft, the taking of the property of others without their consent, also plays a large role. Both large-scale organized crime and small-scale petty crime collectively allocate billions of dollars worth of resources annually.

But force plays a crucial positive role in allocating resources. It provides the state with an effective method of transferring wealth from the rich to the poor, and it provides the legal framework in which voluntary exchange in markets takes place.

A legal system is the foundation on which our market economy functions. Without courts to enforce contracts, it would not be possible to do business. But the courts could not enforce contracts without the ability to apply force if necessary. The state provides the ultimate force that enables the courts to do their work.

More broadly, the force of the state is essential to uphold the principle of the rule of law. This principle is the bedrock of civilized economic (and social and political) life. With the rule of law upheld, people can go about their daily economic lives with the assurance that their property will be protected—that they can sue for violations against their property (and be sued if they violate the property of others).

Free from the burden of protecting their property and confident in the knowledge that those with whom they trade will honor their agreements, people can get on with focusing on the activity at which they have a comparative advantage and trading for mutual gain.

Review Quiz

1 Why do we need methods of allocating scarce resources?
2 Describe the alternative methods of allocating scarce resources.
3 Provide an example of each allocation method that illustrates when it works well.
4 Provide an example of each allocation method that illustrates when it works badly.

 Work Study Plan 5.1 and get instant feedback.

In the next sections, we're going to see how a market can achieve an efficient use of resources, examine the obstacles to efficiency, and see how sometimes an alternative method might improve on the market. After looking at efficiency, we'll turn our attention to the more difficult issue of fairness.

◆ Demand and Marginal Benefit

Resources are allocated efficiently when they are used in the ways that people value most highly. This outcome occurs when marginal benefit equals marginal cost (Chapter 2, pp. 35–37). So to determine whether a competitive market is efficient, we need to see whether, at the market equilibrium quantity, marginal benefit equals marginal cost. We begin by seeing how market demand reflects marginal benefit.

Demand, Willingness to Pay, and Value

In everyday life, we talk about "getting value for money." When we use this expression, we are distinguishing between *value* and *price*. Value is what we get, and price is what we pay.

The value of one more unit of a good or service is its marginal benefit. And we measure marginal benefit by the maximum price that is willingly paid for another unit of the good or service. But willingness to pay determines demand. *A demand curve is a marginal benefit curve.*

In Fig. 5.1(a), Lisa is willing to pay $1 for the 30th slice of pizza and $1 is her marginal benefit from that slice. In Fig. 5.1(b), Nick is willing to pay $1 for the 10th slice of pizza and $1 is his marginal benefit from that slice. But at what quantity is the market willing to pay $1 for the marginal slice? The answer is provided by the *market demand curve*.

Individual Demand and Market Demand

The relationship between the price of a good and the quantity demanded by one person is called *individual demand*. And the relationship between the price of a good and the quantity demanded by all buyers is called *market demand*.

The market demand curve is the horizontal sum of the individual demand curves and is formed by adding the quantities demanded by all the individuals at each price.

Figure 5.1(c) illustrates the market demand for pizza if Lisa and Nick are the only people in the market. Lisa's demand curve in part (a) and Nick's demand curve in part (b) sum horizontally to the market demand curve in part (c).

FIGURE 5.1   Individual Demand, Market Demand, and Marginal Social Benefit

(a) Lisa's demand   **(b) Nick's demand**   **(c) Market demand**

At a price of $1 a slice, the quantity demanded by Lisa is 30 slices and the quantity demanded by Nick is 10 slices, so the quantity demanded by the market is 40 slices. Lisa's demand

curve in part (a) and Nick's demand curve in part (b) sum horizontally to the market demand curve in part (c). The market demand curve is the marginal social benefit (*MSB*) curve.

At a price of $1 a slice, Lisa demands 30 slices and Nick demands 10 slices, so the market quantity demanded at $1 a slice is 40 slices.

From the market demand curve, we see that the economy is willing to pay $1 for 40 slices a day. *The market demand curve is the marginal social benefit (MSB) curve.*

Although we're measuring the price in dollars, think of the price as telling us the number of *dollars' worth of other goods and services willingly forgone* to obtain one more slice of pizza.

Consumer Surplus

We don't always have to pay what we are willing to pay. We get a bargain. When people buy something for less than it is worth to them, they receive a consumer surplus. A **consumer surplus** is the value (or marginal benefit) of a good minus the price paid for it, summed over the quantity bought.

Figure 5.2(a) shows Lisa's consumer surplus from pizza when the price is $1 a slice. At this price, she buys 30 slices a month because the 30th slice is worth exactly $1 to her. But Lisa is willing to pay $2 for the 10th slice, so her marginal benefit from this slice is

$1 more than she pays for it—she receives a surplus of $1 on the 10th slice.

Lisa's consumer surplus is the sum of the surpluses on *all of the slices she buys*. This sum is the area of the green triangle—the area below the demand curve and above the market price line. The area of this triangle is equal to its base (30 slices) multiplied by its height ($1.50) divided by 2, which is $22.50. The area of the blue rectangle in Fig. 5.2(a) shows what Lisa pays for 30 slices of pizza.

Figure 5.2(b) shows Nick's consumer surplus, and part (c) shows the consumer surplus for the market. The consumer surplus for the market is the sum of the consumer surpluses of Lisa and Nick.

All goods and services, like pizza, have decreasing marginal benefit, so people receive more benefit from their consumption than the amount they pay.

Review Quiz

1 How do we measure the value or marginal benefit of a good or service?
2 What is consumer surplus? How is it measured?

 Work Study Plan 5.2 and get instant feedback.

FIGURE 5.2 Demand and Consumer Surplus

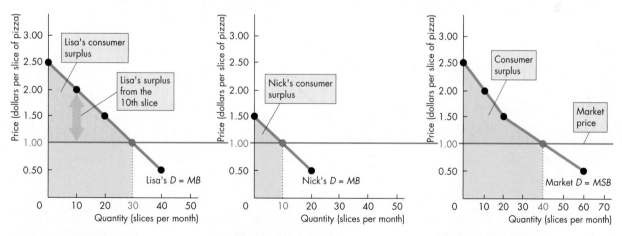

(a) Lisa's consumer surplus   **(b) Nick's consumer surplus**   **(c) Market consumer surplus**

Lisa is willing to pay $2.00 for her 10th slice of pizza in part (a). At a market price of $1 a slice, Lisa receives a surplus of $1 on the 10th slice. The green triangle shows her consumer surplus on the 30 slices she buys at $1 a slice.

The green triangle in part (b) shows Nick's consumer surplus on the 10 slices that he buys at $1 a slice. The green area in part (c) shows the consumer surplus for the market. The blue rectangles show the amounts spent on pizza.

 animation

Supply and Marginal Cost

We are now going to see how market supply reflects marginal cost. This section closely parallels the related ideas about market demand and marginal benefit that you've just studied. Firms are in business to make a profit. To do so, they must sell their output for a price that exceeds the cost of production. Let's investigate the relationship between cost and price.

Supply, Cost, and Minimum Supply-Price

Firms make a profit when they receive more from the sale of a good or service than the cost of producing it. Just as consumers distinguish between value and price, so producers distinguish between cost and price. Cost is what a producer gives up, and price is what a producer receives.

The cost of producing one more unit of a good or service is its marginal cost. Marginal cost is the minimum price that producers must receive to induce them to offer one more unit of a good or service for sale. But the minimum supply-price determines supply. *A supply curve is a marginal cost curve.*

In Fig. 5.3(a), Max is willing to produce the 100th pizza for $15, his marginal cost of that pizza. In Fig. 5.3(b), Mario is willing to produce the 50th pizza for $15, his marginal cost of that pizza. But what quantity is this market willing to produce for $15 a pizza? The answer is provided by the *market supply curve.*

Individual Supply and Market Supply

The relationship between the price of a good and the quantity supplied by one producer is called *individual supply*. And the relationship between the price of a good and the quantity supplied by all producers is called *market supply*.

> The market supply curve is the horizontal sum of the individual supply curves and is formed by adding the quantities supplied by all the producers at each price.

Figure 5.3(c) illustrates the market supply if Max and Mario are the only producers of pizzas. Max's supply curve in part (a) and Mario's supply curve in part (b) sum horizontally to the market supply curve in part (c).

FIGURE 5.3 Individual Supply, Market Supply, and Marginal Social Cost

(a) Max's supply

(b) Mario's supply

(c) Market supply

At a price of $15 a pizza, the quantity supplied by Max is 100 pizzas and the quantity supplied by Mario is 50 pizzas, so the quantity supplied by the market is 150 pizzas.

Max's supply curve in part (a) and Mario's supply curve in part (b) sum horizontally to the market supply curve in part (c). The market supply curve is the marginal social cost (MSC) curve.

At a price of $15 a pizza, Max supplies 100 pizzas and Mario supplies 50 pizzas, so the quantity supplied by the market at $15 a pizza is 150 pizzas.

So from the market supply curve, we see that the market is willing to supply 150 pizzas a month for $15 each. *The market supply curve is the marginal social cost (MSC) curve.*

Again, although we're measuring price in dollars, think of the price as telling us the number of *dollars' worth of other goods and services that must be forgone* to produce one more pizza.

Producer Surplus

When price exceeds marginal cost, the firm receives a producer surplus. A **producer surplus** is the price received for a good minus its minimum supply-price (or marginal cost), summed over the quantity sold.

Figure 5.4(a) shows Max's producer surplus from pizza when the price is $15 a pizza. At this price, he sells 100 pizzas a month because the 100th pizza costs him $15 to produce. But Max is willing to produce the 50th pizza for his marginal cost, which is $10, so he receives a surplus of $5 on this pizza.

Max's producer surplus is the sum of the surpluses on pizzas he sells. This sum is the area of the blue tri-angle—the area below the market price and above the supply curve. The area of this triangle is equal to its base (100) multiplied by its height ($10) divided by 2, which is $500.

The red area in Fig. 5.4(a) below the supply curve shows what it costs Max to produce 100 pizzas.

The area of the blue triangle in Fig. 5.4(b) shows Mario's producer surplus and the blue area in Fig. 5.4(c) shows the producer surplus for the market. The producer surplus for the market is the sum of the producer surpluses of Max and Mario.

Review Quiz

1 What is the relationship between the marginal cost, minimum supply-price, and supply?
2 What is producer surplus? How is it measured?

 Work Study Plan 5.3 and get instant feedback.

Consumer surplus and producer surplus can be used to measure the efficiency of a market. Let's see how we can use these concepts to study the efficiency of a competitive market.

FIGURE 5.4   Supply and Producer Surplus

(a) Max's producer surplus   **(b) Mario's producer surplus**   **(c) Market producer surplus**

Max is willing to produce the 50th pizza for $10 in part (a). At a market price of $15 a pizza, Max gets a surplus of $5 on the 50th pizza. The blue triangle shows his producer surplus on the 100 pizzas he sells at $15 each. The blue triangle in part (b) shows Mario's producer surplus on the 50 pizzas that he sells at $15 each. The blue area in part (c) shows producer surplus for the market. The red areas show the cost of producing the pizzas sold.

 animation

Is the Competitive Market Efficient?

Figure 5.5(a) shows the market for pizza. The market forces that you studied in Chapter 3 (pp. 68–69) pull the pizza market to its equilibrium price of $15 a pizza and equilibrium quantity of 10,000 pizzas a day. Buyers enjoy a consumer surplus (green area) and sellers enjoy a producer surplus (blue area), but is this competitive equilibrium efficient?

Efficiency of Competitive Equilibrium

You've seen that the demand curve tells us the marginal benefit from a pizza. If the only people who benefit from pizza are the people who buy it, then the demand curve for pizzas measures the marginal benefit to the entire society from pizza. We call the marginal benefit to the entire society, marginal *social* benefit, *MSB*. In this case, the demand curve is also the *MSB* curve.

You've also seen that the supply curve tells us the marginal cost of a pizza. If the only people who bear the cost of pizza are the people who produce it, then the supply curve of pizzas measures the marginal cost of a pizza to the entire society. We call the marginal cost to the entire society, marginal *social* cost, *MSC*. In this case, the supply curve is also the *MSC* curve.

So where the demand curve and the supply curve intersect in part (a), marginal social benefit equals marginal social cost in part (b). This condition delivers an efficient use of resources for the entire society.

If production is less than 10,000 pizzas a day, the marginal pizza is valued more highly than it costs to produce. If production exceeds 10,000 pizzas a day, the marginal pizza costs more to produce than the value that consumers place on it. Only when 10,000 pizzas a day are produced is the marginal pizza worth exactly what it costs.

The competitive market pushes the quantity of pizzas produced to its efficient level of 10,000 a day. If production is less than 10,000 pizzas a day, a shortage raises the price, which increases production. If production exceeds 10,000 pizzas a day, a surplus of pizzas lowers the price, which decreases production. So a competitive pizza market is efficient.

When the efficient quantity is produced, *total surplus* (the sum of consumer surplus and producer surplus) is maximized. Buyers and sellers acting in their self-interest end up promoting the social interest.

FIGURE 5.5   An Efficient Market for Pizza

(a) Equilibrium and surpluses

(b) Efficiency

Competitive equilibrium in part (a) occurs when the quantity demanded equals the quantity supplied. Consumer surplus is the area under the demand curve and above the market price (the green triangle). Producer surplus is the area above the supply curve and below the market price (the blue triangle). Resources are used efficiently in part (b) when marginal social benefit, *MSB*, equals marginal social cost, *MSC*.

The efficient quantity in part (b) is the same as the equilibrium quantity in part (a). The competitive pizza market produces the efficient quantity of pizzas.

myeconlab animation

Markets At Work
The Invisible Hand

Writing in his *Wealth of Nations* in 1776, Adam Smith was the first to suggest that competitive markets send resources to the uses in which they have the highest value (see p. 53). Smith believed that each participant in a competitive market is "led by an invisible hand to promote an end [the efficient use of resources] which was no part of his intention."

You can see the invisible hand at work in the cartoon and in the world today.

Umbrella for Sale The cold drinks vendor has cold drinks and shade and he has a marginal cost and a minimum supply-price of each. The reader on the park bench has a marginal benefit and willingness to pay for each. The reader's marginal benefit from shade exceeds the vendor's marginal cost; but the vendor's marginal cost of a cold drink exceeds the reader's marginal benefit. They trade the umbrella. The vendor gets a producer surplus from selling the shade for more than its marginal cost, and the reader gets a consumer surplus from buying the shade for less than its marginal benefit. Both are better off and the umbrella has moved to its highest-valued use.

The Invisible Hand at Work Today The market economy relentlessly performs the activity illustrated in the cartoon to achieve an efficient allocation of resources.

A Florida frost cuts the supply of oranges. With fewer oranges available, the marginal social benefit increases. A shortage of oranges raises their price, so the market allocates the smaller quantity available to the people who value them most highly.

A new technology cuts the cost of producing a computer. With a lower production cost, the supply of computers increases and the price of a computer falls. The lower price encourages an increase in the quantity demanded of this now less-costly tool. The marginal

social benefit from a computer is brought to equality with its marginal social cost.

In both the oranges and computer examples, market forces persistently bring marginal social cost and marginal social benefit to equality, allocate scarce resources efficiently, and maximize total surplus (consumer surplus plus producer surplus).

Underproduction and Overproduction

Inefficiency can occur because either too little of an item is produced (underproduction) or too much is produced (overproduction).

Underproduction In Fig. 5.6(a), the quantity of pizzas produced is 5,000 a day. At this quantity, consumers are willing to pay \$20 for a pizza that costs only \$10 to produce. By producing only 5,000 pizzas a day, total surplus is smaller than its maximum possible level. The quantity produced is inefficient—there is underproduction.

We measure the scale of inefficiency by **deadweight loss**, which is the decrease in total surplus that results

FIGURE 5.6   Underproduction and Overproduction

(a) Underproduction

(b) Overproduction

If pizza production is 5,000 a day in part (a), total surplus (shown by the green and blue areas) is smaller than its maximum level by the amount of the deadweight loss (shown by the gray triangle). At all production levels below 10,000 pizzas a day, the benefit from one more pizza exceeds its cost.

If pizza production is 15,000 a day in part (b), total surplus is also smaller than its maximum level by the amount of the deadweight loss. At all production levels in excess of 10,000 pizzas a day, the cost of one more pizza exceeds its benefit.

myeconlab   animation

from an inefficient level of production. The gray triangle in Fig. 5.6(a) shows the deadweight loss.

Overproduction In Fig. 5.6(b), the quantity of pizzas produced is 15,000 a day. At this quantity, consumers are willing to pay only $10 for a pizza that costs $20 to produce. By producing the 15,000th pizza, $10 of resources are wasted. Again, the gray triangle shows the deadweight loss, which reduces the total surplus to less than its maximum.

The deadweight loss is borne by the entire society: It is a social loss.

Obstacles to Efficiency

The obstacles to efficiency that bring underproduction or overproduction are

- Price and quantity regulations
- Taxes and subsidies
- Externalities
- Public goods and common resources
- Monopoly
- High transactions costs

Price and Quantity Regulations *Price regulations* that put a cap on the rent a landlord is permitted to charge and laws that require employers to pay a minimum wage sometimes block the price adjustments that balance the quantity demanded and the quantity supplied and lead to underproduction. *Quantity regulations* that limit the amount that a farm is permitted to produce also lead to underproduction.

Taxes and Subsidies *Taxes* increase the prices paid by buyers and lower the prices received by sellers. So taxes decrease the quantity produced and lead to underproduction. *Subsidies*, which are payments by the government to producers, decrease the prices paid by buyers and increase the prices received by sellers. So subsidies increase the quantity produced and lead to overproduction.

Externalities An *externality* is a cost or a benefit that affects someone other than the seller or the buyer. An *external cost* arises when an electric utility burns coal and emits carbon dioxide. The utility doesn't consider the cost of climate change when it decides how much power to produce. The result is overproduction. An *external benefit* arises when an apartment owner installs a smoke detector and decreases her neighbor's fire risk. She doesn't consider the benefit to her neighbor when she decides how many detectors to install. The result is underproduction.

Public Goods and Common Resources

A *public good* is a good or service that is consumed simultaneously by everyone even if they don't pay for it. National defense is an example. Competitive markets would underproduce national defense because it is in each person's interest to free ride on everyone else and avoid paying for her or his share of such a good.

A *common resource* is owned by no one but available to be used by everyone. Atlantic salmon is an example. It is in everyone's self-interest to ignore the costs they impose on others when they decide how much of a common resource to use. The result is that the resource is overused.

Monopoly

A *monopoly* is a firm that is the sole provider of a good or service. Local water supply and cable television are supplied by firms that are monopolies. The monopoly's self-interest is to maximize its profit. Because the monopoly has no competitors, it can set the price to achieve its self-interested goal. To achieve its goal, a monopoly produces too little and charges too high a price. It leads to underproduction.

High Transactions Costs

Stroll around a shopping mall and observe the retail markets in which you participate. You'll see that these markets employ enormous quantities of scarce labor and capital resources. It is costly to operate any market. Economists call the opportunity costs of making trades in a market **transactions costs**.

To use market price as the allocator of scarce resources, it must be worth bearing the opportunity cost of establishing a market. Some markets are just too costly to operate. For example, when you want to play tennis on your local "free" court, you don't pay a market price for your slot on the court. You hang around until the court becomes vacant, and you "pay" with your waiting time. When transactions costs are high, the market might underproduce.

You now know the conditions under which resource allocation is efficient. You've seen how a competitive market can be efficient, and you've seen some obstacles to efficiency. Can alternative allocation methods improve on the market?

Alternatives to the Market

When a market is inefficient, can one of the alternative nonmarket methods that we described at the beginning of this chapter do a better job? Sometimes it can.

Often, majority rule might be used in an attempt to improve the allocation of resources. But majority rule has its own shortcomings. A group that pursues the self-interest of its members can become the majority. For example, a price or quantity regulation that creates inefficiency is almost always the result of a self-interested group becoming the majority and imposing costs on the minority. Also, with majority rule, votes must be translated into actions by bureaucrats who have their own agendas based on their self-interest.

Managers in firms issue commands and avoid the transactions costs that they would incur if they went to a market every time they needed a job done.

First-come, first-served works best in some situations. Think about the scene at a busy ATM. Instead of waiting in line people might trade places at a "market" price. But someone would need to ensure that trades were honored. At a busy ATM, first-come, first-served is the most efficient arrangement.

There is no one efficient mechanism that allocates all resources efficiently. But markets, when supplemented by other mechanisms such as majority rule, command systems, and first-come, first-served, do an amazingly good job.

Review Quiz

1　Do competitive markets use resources efficiently? Explain why or why not.
2　What is deadweight loss and under what conditions does it occur?
3　What are the obstacles to achieving an efficient allocation of resources in the market economy?

 Work Study Plan 5.4 and get instant feedback.

Is an efficient allocation of resources also a fair allocation? Does the competitive market provide people with fair incomes for their work? Do people always pay a fair price for the things they buy? Don't we need the government to step into some competitive markets to prevent the price from rising too high or falling too low? Let's now study these questions.

Is the Competitive Market Fair?

When a natural disaster strikes, such as a severe winter storm or a hurricane, the prices of many essential items jump. The reason prices jump is that the demand and willingness to pay for these items has increased, but the supply has not changed. So the higher prices achieve an efficient allocation of scarce resources. News reports of these price hikes almost never talk about efficiency. Instead, they talk about equity or fairness. The claim that is often made is that it is unfair for profit-seeking dealers to cheat the victims of natural disaster.

Similarly, when low-skilled people work for a wage that is below what most would regard as a "living wage," the media and politicians talk of employers taking unfair advantage of their workers.

How do we decide whether something is fair or unfair? You know when you *think* something is unfair. But how do you *know?* What are the *principles* of fairness?

Philosophers have tried for centuries to answer this question. Economists have offered their answers too. But before we look at the proposed answers, you should know that there is no universally agreed upon answer.

Economists agree about efficiency. That is, they agree that it makes sense to make the economic pie as large as possible and to produce it at the lowest possible cost. But they do not agree about equity. That is, they do not agree about what are fair shares of the economic pie for all the people who make it. The reason is that ideas about fairness are not exclusively economic ideas. They touch on politics, ethics, and religion. Nevertheless, economists have thought about these issues and have a contribution to make. Let's examine the views of economists on this topic.

To think about fairness, think of economic life as a game—a serious game. All ideas about fairness can be divided into two broad groups. They are

- It's not fair if the *result* isn't fair.
- It's not fair if the *rules* aren't fair.

It's Not Fair If the *Result* Isn't Fair

The earliest efforts to establish a principle of fairness were based on the view that the result is what matters. The general idea was that it is unfair if people's incomes are too unequal. For example, it is

unfair that a bank president earns millions of dollars a year while a bank teller earns only thousands of dollars. It is unfair that a store owner makes a larger profit and her customers pay higher prices in the aftermath of a winter storm.

During the nineteenth century, economists thought they had made the incredible discovery: Efficiency requires equality of incomes. To make the economic pie as large as possible, it must be cut into equal pieces, one for each person. This idea turns out to be wrong. But there is a lesson in the reason that it is wrong, so this idea is worth a closer look.

Utilitarianism The nineteenth century idea that only equality brings efficiency is called *utilitarianism*. **Utilitarianism** is a principle that states that we should strive to achieve "the greatest happiness for the greatest number." The people who developed this idea were known as utilitarians. They included the most eminent thinkers, such as Jeremy Bentham and John Stuart Mill.

Utilitarians argued that to achieve "the greatest happiness for the greatest number," income must be transferred from the rich to the poor up to the point of complete equality—to the point at which there are no rich and no poor.

They reasoned in the following way: First, everyone has the same basic wants and a similar capacity to enjoy life. Second, the greater a person's income, the smaller is the marginal benefit of a dollar. The millionth dollar spent by a rich person brings a smaller marginal benefit to that person than the marginal benefit that the thousandth dollar spent brings to a poorer person. So by transferring a dollar from the millionaire to the poorer person, more is gained than is lost. The two people added together are better off.

Figure 5.7 illustrates this utilitarian idea. Tom and Jerry have the same marginal benefit curve, *MB*. (Marginal benefit is measured on the same scale of 1 to 3 for both Tom and Jerry.) Tom is at point *A*. He earns $5,000 a year, and his marginal benefit from a dollar is 3 units. Jerry is at point *B*. He earns $45,000 a year, and his marginal benefit from a dollar is 1 unit. If a dollar is transferred from Jerry to Tom, Jerry loses 1 unit of marginal benefit and Tom gains 3 units. So together, Tom and Jerry are better off—they are sharing the economic pie more efficiently. If a second dollar is transferred, the same thing happens: Tom gains more than Jerry loses. And the same is true for every dollar transferred until they both reach point *C*. At point *C*, Tom and Jerry have $25,000

FIGURE 5.7   Utilitarian Fairness

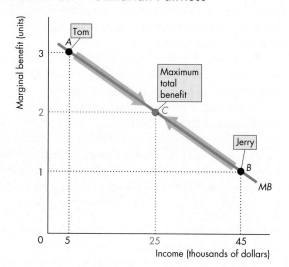

Tom earns $5,000 and has 3 units of marginal benefit at point A. Jerry earns $45,000 and has 1 unit of marginal benefit at point B. If income is transferred from Jerry to Tom, Jerry's loss is less than Tom's gain. Only when each of them has $25,000 and 2 units of marginal benefit (at point C) can the sum of their total benefit increase no further.

each and a marginal benefit of 2 units. Now they are sharing the economic pie in the most efficient way. It brings the greatest happiness to Tom and Jerry.

The Big Tradeoff   One big problem with the utilitarian ideal of complete equality is that it ignores the costs of making income transfers. Recognizing the costs of making income transfers leads to what is called the **big tradeoff**, which is a tradeoff between efficiency and fairness.

The big tradeoff is based on the following facts. Income can be transferred from people with high incomes to people with low incomes only by taxing the high incomes. Taxing people's income from employment makes them work less. It results in the quantity of labor being less than the efficient quantity. Taxing people's income from capital makes them save less. It results in the quantity of capital being less than the efficient quantity. With smaller quantities of both labor and capital, the quantity of goods and services produced is less than the efficient quantity. The economic pie shrinks.

The tradeoff is between the size of the economic pie and the degree of equality with which it is shared. The greater the amount of income redistribution through income taxes, the greater is the inefficiency—the smaller is the economic pie.

There is a second source of inefficiency. A dollar taken from a rich person does not end up as a dollar in the hands of a poorer person. Some of the dollar is spent on administration of the tax and transfer system. The cost of tax-collecting agencies, such as the IRS, and welfare-administering agencies, such as the Health Care Financing Administration, which administers Medicaid and Medicare, must be paid with some of the taxes collected. Also, taxpayers hire accountants, auditors, and lawyers to help them ensure that they pay the correct amount of taxes. These activities use skilled labor and capital resources that could otherwise be used to produce goods and services that people value.

When all these costs are taken into account, taking a dollar from a rich person does not give a dollar to a poor person. It is possible that with high taxes, people with low incomes might end up being worse off. Suppose, for example, that highly taxed entrepreneurs decide to work less hard and shut down some of their businesses. Low-income workers get fired and must seek other, perhaps even lower-paid, work.

Today, because of the big tradeoff, no one says that fairness requires equality of incomes.

Make the Poorest as Well Off as Possible   A new solution to the big tradeoff problem was proposed by philosopher John Rawls in a classic book entitled *A Theory of Justice*, published in 1971. Rawls says that, taking all the costs of income transfers into account, the fair distribution of the economic pie is the one that makes the poorest person as well off as possible. The incomes of rich people should be taxed, and after paying the costs of administering the tax and transfer system, what is left should be transferred to the poor. But the taxes must not be so high that they make the economic pie shrink to the point at which the poorest person ends up with a smaller piece. A bigger share of a smaller pie can be less than a smaller share of a bigger pie. The goal is to make the piece enjoyed by the poorest person as big as possible. Most likely, this piece will not be an equal share.

The "fair results" idea requires a change in the results after the game is over. Some economists say that these changes are themselves unfair and propose a different way of thinking about fairness.

It's Not Fair If the *Rules* Aren't Fair

The idea that it's not fair if the rules aren't fair is based on a fundamental principle that seems to be hardwired into the human brain: the symmetry principle. The **symmetry principle** is the requirement that people in similar situations be treated similarly. It is the moral principle that lies at the center of all the big religions and that says, in some form or other, "Behave toward other people in the way you expect them to behave toward you."

In economic life, this principle translates into *equality of opportunity*. But equality of opportunity to do what? This question is answered by the philosopher Robert Nozick in a book entitled *Anarchy, State, and Utopia*, published in 1974.

Nozick argues that the idea of fairness as an outcome or result cannot work and that fairness must be based on the fairness of the rules. He suggests that fairness obeys two rules:

1. The state must enforce laws that establish and protect private property.
2. Private property may be transferred from one person to another only by voluntary exchange.

The first rule says that everything that is valuable must be owned by individuals and that the state must ensure that theft is prevented. The second rule says that the only legitimate way a person can acquire property is to buy it in exchange for something else that the person owns. If these rules, which are the only fair rules, are followed, then the result is fair. It doesn't matter how unequally the economic pie is shared, provided that the pie is made by people, each one of whom voluntarily provides services in exchange for the share of the pie offered in compensation.

These rules satisfy the symmetry principle. If these rules are not followed, the symmetry principle is broken. You can see these facts by imagining a world in which the laws are not followed.

First, suppose that some resources or goods are not owned. They are common property. Then everyone is free to participate in a grab to use them. The strongest will prevail. But when the strongest prevails, the strongest effectively *owns* the resources or goods in question and prevents others from enjoying them.

Second, suppose that we do not insist on voluntary exchange for transferring ownership of resources from one person to another. The alternative is *involuntary* transfer. In simple language, the alternative is theft.

Both of these situations violate the symmetry principle. Only the strong acquire what they want. The weak end up with only the resources and goods that the strong don't want.

In a majority rule political system, the strong are those in the majority or those with enough resources to influence opinion and achieve a majority.

In contrast, if the two rules of fairness are followed, everyone, strong and weak, is treated in a similar way. Everyone is free to use their resources and human skills to create things that are valued by themselves and others and to exchange the fruits of their efforts with each other. This set of arrangements is the only one that obeys the symmetry principle.

Fairness and Efficiency If private property rights are enforced and if voluntary exchange takes place in a competitive market, resources will be allocated efficiently if there are no

1. Price and quantity regulations
2. Taxes and subsidies
3. Externalities
4. Public goods and common resources
5. Monopolies
6. High transactions costs

And according to the Nozick rules, the resulting distribution of income and wealth will be fair. Let's study an example to check the claim that if resources are allocated efficiently, they are also allocated fairly.

Case Study: A Water Shortage in a Natural Disaster

An earthquake has broken the pipes that deliver drinking water to a city. Bottled water is available, but there is no tap water. What is the fair way to allocate the bottled water?

Market Price Suppose that if the water is allocated by market price, the price jumps to $8 a bottle—five times its normal price. At this price, the people who own water can make a large profit by selling it. People who are willing and able to pay $8 a bottle get the water. And because most people can't afford the $8 price, they end up either without water or consuming just a few drops a day.

You can see that the water is being used efficiently. There is a fixed amount available, some people are willing to pay $8 to get a bottle, and the water goes to those people. The people who own and sell water receive a large producer surplus and total surplus is maximized.

In the rules view, the outcome is fair. No one is denied the water they are willing to pay for. In the results view, the outcome would most likely be regarded as unfair. The lucky owners of water make a killing, and the poorest end up the thirstiest.

Nonmarket Methods Suppose that by a majority vote, the citizens decide that the government will buy all the water, pay for it with a tax, and use one of the nonmarket methods to allocate the water to the citizens. The possibilities now are

Command Someone decides who is the most deserving and needy. Perhaps everyone is given an equal share. Or perhaps government officials and their families end up with most of the water.

Contest Bottles of water are prizes that go to those who are best at a particular contest.

First-come, first-served Water goes to the first off the mark or to those who place the lowest value on their time and can afford to wait in line.

Lottery Water goes to those in luck.

Personal characteristics Water goes to those with the "right" characteristics. Perhaps the old, the young, or pregnant women get the water.

Except by chance, none of these methods delivers an allocation of water that is either fair or efficient. It is unfair in the rules view because the tax involves involuntary transfers of resources among citizens. And it is unfair in the results view because the poorest don't end up being made as well off as possible.

The allocation is inefficient for two reasons. First, resources have been used to operate the allocation scheme. Second, some people are willing to pay for more water than the quantity they have been allocated and others have been allocated more water than they are willing to pay for.

The second source of inefficiency can be overcome if, after the nonmarket allocation, people are permitted to trade water at its market price. Those who value the water they have at less than the market price sell, and people who are willing to pay the market price to obtain more water buy. Those who value the water most highly are the ones who consume it.

Market Price with Taxes Another approach is to allocate the scarce water using the market price but then to alter the redistribution of buying power by taxing the sellers and providing benefits to the poor.

Suppose water owners are taxed on each bottle sold and the revenue from these taxes is given to the poorest people. People are then free, starting from this new distribution of buying power, to trade water at the market price.

Because the owners of water are taxed on what they sell, they have a weaker incentive to offer water for sale and the supply decreases. The equilibrium price rises to more than $8 a bottle. There is now a deadweight loss in the market for water—similar to the loss that arises from underproduction on pp. 115–116. (We study the effects of a tax and show its inefficiency in Chapter 6 on pp. 135–140.)

So the tax is inefficient. In the rules view, the tax is also unfair because it forces the owners of water to make a transfer to others. In the results view, the outcome might be regarded as being fair.

This brief case study illustrates the complexity of ideas about fairness. Economists have a clear criterion of efficiency but no comparably clear criterion of fairness. Most economists regard Nozick as being too extreme and want a fair tax system. But there is no consensus about what a fair tax system looks like.

Review Quiz

1 What are the two big approaches to thinking about fairness?
2 What is the utilitarian idea of fairness and what is wrong with it?
3 Explain the big tradeoff. What idea of fairness has been developed to deal with it?
4 What is the idea of fairness based on fair rules?

myeconlab Work Study Plan 5.5 and get instant feedback.

You've now studied the two biggest issues that run through the whole of economics: efficiency and equity, or fairness. In the next chapter, we study some sources of inefficiency and unfairness. At many points throughout this book—and in your life—you will return to and use the ideas about efficiency and fairness that you've learned in this chapter. *Reading Between the Lines* on pp. 122–123 looks at an example of an inefficiency in our economy today.

Is Water Use Efficient?

India Digs Deeper, but Wells Are Drying Up, and a Farming Crisis Looms

http://www.nytimes.com
September 30, 2006

… Across India, where most people still live off the land, the chief source of irrigation is groundwater, at least for those who can afford to pump it.

Indian law has virtually no restrictions on who can pump groundwater, how much and for what purpose. Anyone, it seems, can—and does—extract water as long as it is under his or her patch of land. That could apply to homeowner, farmer or industry. …

"We forgot that water is a costly item," lamented K. P. Singh, regional director of the Central Groundwater Board, in his office in the city of Jaipur. "Our feeling about proper, judicious use of water vanished."

… On a parched, hot morning … a train pulled into the railway station at a village called Peeplee Ka Bas. Here, the wells have run dry and the water table fallen so low that it is too salty even to irrigate the fields.

The train came bearing precious cargo: 15 tankers loaded with nearly 120,000 gallons of clean, sweet drinking water.

The water regularly travels more than 150 miles, taking nearly two days, by pipeline and then by rail, so that the residents of a small neighboring town can fill their buckets with water for 15 minutes every 48 hours.

It is a logistically complicated, absurdly expensive proposition. Bringing the water here costs the state about a penny a gallon; the state charges the consumer a monthly flat rate of 58 cents for about 5,300 gallons, absorbing the loss. …

Essence of the Story

- In India, groundwater is the chief source of irrigation.
- Indian law has few restrictions on who can pump groundwater.
- A regional director of the Central Groundwater Board laments that Indians are behaving as if water were a free resource.

- Where the wells have run dry, water is delivered by pipeline and then by train.
- Water is rationed by permitting residents to fill their buckets with water for 15 minutes every 48 hours.
- Transporting water costs 1 cent per gallon, but consumers pay about 11 cents per 1,000 gallons.

Economic Analysis

- Water is one of the world's most vital resources, and it is used inefficiently.

- Markets in water are not competitive. They are controlled by governments or private producers, and they do not work like the competitive markets that deliver an efficient use of resources.

- The major problem in achieving an efficient use of water is to get it from the places where it is most abundant to the places in which it has the most valuable uses.

- Some places have too little water, and some have too much.

- The news article tells us that the owners of land that has groundwater under it pump the water and sell it and pay little attention to the fact that they will pump the well dry.

- Figure 1 illustrates this situation. The curve D shows the demand for water and its marginal social benefit MSB. The curve S shows the supply of water and its marginal social cost MSC.

- Ignoring the high marginal social cost, land owners produce W_A gallons a day, which is greater than the efficient quantity. Farmers are willing to pay B, which is less than the marginal social cost C but enough to earn the land owner a profit.

- A deadweight loss arises from overproduction.

- Figure 2 shows the situation in places where the wells have run dry.

- A limited quantity of water, W_B, is transported in, and each consumer is restricted to the quantity that can be put into a bucket in 15 minutes every 48 hours.

- Consumers are willing to pay B per gallon, which is much more than the marginal social cost C.

- The green area shows the consumer surplus, and the red rectangle shows the cost of the water, which is paid by the government and borne by the taxpayers.

- A deadweight loss arises from underproduction.

- The situation in India is replicated in thousands of places around the world.

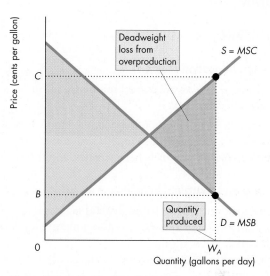

Figure 1 Overproduction where wells are not dry

Figure 2 Underproduction where wells run dry

SUMMARY

Key Points

Resource Allocation Methods (pp. 108–109)

- Because resources are scarce, some mechanism must allocate them.
- The alternative allocation methods are market price; command; majority rule; contest; first-come, first-served; lottery; personal characteristics; and force.

Demand and Marginal Benefit (pp. 110–111)

- The maximum price willingly paid is marginal benefit, so a demand curve is also a marginal benefit curve.
- The market demand curve is the horizontal sum of the individual demand curves and is the marginal social benefit curve.
- Value is what people are *willing to* pay; price is what people *must* pay.
- Consumer surplus equals value minus price, summed over the quantity bought.

Supply and Marginal Cost (pp. 112–113)

- The minimum supply-price is marginal cost, so a supply curve is also a marginal cost curve.
- The market supply curve is the horizontal sum of the individual supply curves and is the marginal social cost curve.

- Cost is what producers pay; price is what producers receive.
- Producer surplus equals price minus marginal cost, summed over the quantity sold.

Is the Competitive Market Efficient? (pp. 114–117)

- In a competitive equilibrium, marginal social benefit equals marginal social cost and resource allocation is efficient.
- Buyers and sellers acting in their self-interest end up promoting the social interest.
- The sum of consumer surplus and producer surplus is maximized.
- Producing less than or more than the efficient quantity creates deadweight loss.
- Price and quantity regulations; taxes and subsidies; externalities; public goods and common resources; monopoly; and high transactions costs can lead to underproduction or overproduction and create inefficiency.

Is the Competitive Market Fair? (pp. 118–121)

- Ideas about fairness can be divided into two groups: fair *results* and fair *rules*.
- Fair-results ideas require income transfers from the rich to the poor.
- Fair-rules ideas require property rights and voluntary exchange.

Key Figures

Key Terms

Big tradeoff, 119
Command system, 108
Consumer surplus, 111
Deadweight loss, 115
Producer surplus, 113
Symmetry principle, 120
Transactions costs, 117
Utilitarianism, 118

PROBLEMS and APPLICATIONS

 Work problems 1–9 in Chapter 5 Study Plan and get instant feedback.
Work problems 10–16 as Homework, a Quiz, or a Test if assigned by your instructor.

1. At Chez Panisse, the restaurant in Berkeley that is credited with having created California cuisine, reservations are essential. At Mandarin Dynasty, a restaurant near the University of California San Diego, reservations are recommended. At Eli Cannon's, a restaurant in Middletown, Connecticut, reservations are not accepted.
   a. Describe the method of allocating scarce table resources at these three restaurants.
   b. Why do you think restaurants have different reservations policies?
   c. Why might each restaurant be using an efficient allocation method?
   d. Why do you think restaurants don't use the market price to allocate their tables?
2. The table provides information on the demand schedules for train travel for Ann, Beth, and Cy, who are the only buyers in the market.

Price (dollars per mile)	Quantity demanded (miles)		
	Ann	Beth	Cy
3	30	25	20
4	25	20	15
5	20	15	10
6	15	10	5
7	10	5	0
8	5	0	0
9	0	0	0

   a. Construct the market demand schedule.
   b. What are the maximum prices that Ann, Beth, and Cy are willing to pay to travel 20 miles? Why?
   c. What is the marginal social benefit when the total distance travelled is 60 miles?
   d. What is the marginal private benefit for each person when they travel a total distance of 60 miles and how many miles does each of the people travel?
   e. What is each traveler's consumer surplus when the price is $4 a mile?
   f. What is the market consumer surplus when the price is $4 a mile?

3. **eBay Saves Billions for Bidders**
   If you think you would save money by bidding on eBay auctions, you would likely be right. … Two associate professors … calculate the difference between the actual purchase price paid for auction items and the top price bidders stated they were willing to pay … and the Maryland researchers found it averaged at least $4 per auction.
   Information Week, January 28, 2008
   a. What method is used to allocate goods on eBay?
   b. How do eBay auctions influence consumer surplus?
4. The table provides information on the supply schedules of hot air balloon rides by Xavier, Yasmin, and Zack, who are the only sellers in the market.

Price (dollars per ride)	Quantity supplied (rides per week)		
	Xavier	Yasmin	Zack
100	30	25	20
90	25	20	15
80	20	15	10
70	15	10	5
60	10	5	0
50	5	0	0
40	0	0	0

   a. Construct the market supply schedule.
   b. What are the minimum prices that Xavier, Yasmin, and Zack are willing to accept to supply 20 rides? Why?
   c. What is the marginal social cost when the total number of rides is 30?
   d. What is the marginal cost for each supplier when the total number of rides is 30 and how many rides does each of the firms supply?
   e. What is each firm's producer surplus when the price is $70 a ride?
   f. What is the market producer surplus when the price is $70 a ride?
5. Based on the information provided in the news clip in problem 3,

a. Can an eBay auction give the seller a surplus?

b. Draw a graph to illustrate an eBay auction and show the consumer surplus and producer surplus that it generates.

6. The figure illustrates the market for cell phones.

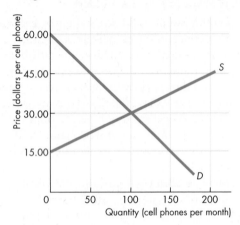

a. What are the equilibrium price and equilibrium quantity of cell phones?

b. Shade in and label the consumer surplus and the producer surplus.

c. Shade in and label the cost of producing the cell phones sold.

d. Calculate total surplus.

e. What is the efficient quantity of cell phones?

7. The table gives the demand and supply schedules for sunscreen.

Price (dollars per bottle)	Quantity demanded	Quantity supplied
	(bottles per day)	
0	400	0
5	300	100
10	200	200
15	100	300
20	0	400

Sunscreen factories are required to limit production to 100 bottles a day.

a. What is the maximum price that consumers are willing to pay for the 100th bottle?

b. What is the minimum price that producers are willing to accept for the 100th bottle?

c. Describe the situation in this market.

d. How can the 100 bottles be allocated to beachgoers? Which possible methods would be fair and which would be unfair?

8. **Wii Sells Out Across Japan**

... Japan finally came in for its share of Wii madness this weekend. ... However, given the large amount of interest in the console—which Nintendo has flogged with a TV-ad blitz for the past two months—demand is expected to be much higher than supply. ... Yodobashi Camera was selling Wii games on a first-come, first-served basis, so eager customers showed up early so as not to miss out on their favorite titles. [But] customers who tried to get in the ... line after 6 or 7 a.m. were turned away. ... [and] many could be spotted rushing off to the smaller Akihabara stores that were holding raffles to decide who got a Wii.

Gamespot News, December 1, 2006

a. Why was the quantity demanded of Wii expected to exceed the quantity supplied?

b. Did Nintendo produce the efficient quantity of Wii? Explain.

c. Can you think of reasons why Nintendo might want to underproduce and leave the market with fewer Wii than people want to buy?

d. What are the two methods of resource allocation described in the news clip?

e. Is either method of allocating Wii efficient?

f. What do you think some of the people who managed to buy a Wii did with it?

g. Explain which is the fairer method of allocating the Wii: the market price or the two methods described in the news clip.

9. **"Two Buck Chuck" Wine Cult**

It's the California wine with the cult following. "Charles Shaw is known in local circles as "Two Buck Chuck," ... the $1.99 nectar of the gods that is sinfully cheap and good. ... A full year after flooding the market largely on the West Coast, it's still being sold by the case to wine lovers who can't get enough. ... It's an over-abundance of grapes that's made Charles Shaw cheap to bottle—an estimated 5 million cases so far.

CBS, June 2, 2003

a. Explain how the Invisible Hand has worked in the market for this California wine.

b. How has "Two Buck Chuck" influenced consumer surplus from wine?

c. How has "Two Buck Chuck" influenced producer surplus for its producer and for the producers of other wines?

10. The table gives the supply schedules for jet-ski rides by three owners: Rick, Sam, and Tom, the only suppliers of jet-ski rides.

Price (dollars per ride)	Quantity supplied (rides per day)		
	Rick	Sam	Tom
10.00	0	0	0
12.50	5	0	0
15.00	10	5	0
17.50	15	10	5
20.00	20	15	10

a. What is each owner's minimum supply-price of 10 rides a day?

b. Which owner has the largest producer surplus when the price of a ride is $17.50? Explain.

c. What is the marginal social cost of producing 45 rides a day?

d. Construct the market supply schedule of jet-ski rides.

11. The table gives the demand and supply schedules for sandwiches.

Price (dollars per sandwich)	Quantity demanded	Quantity supplied
	(sandwiches per hour)	
0	300	0
1	250	50
2	200	100
3	150	150
4	100	200
5	50	250
6	0	300

a. What is the maximum price that consumers are willing to pay for the 200th sandwich?

b. What is the minimum price that producers are willing to accept for the 200th sandwich?

c. Are 200 sandwiches a day less than or greater than the efficient quantity?

d. If sandwich makers produce 200 a day, what is the deadweight loss?

e. If the sandwich market is efficient, what is the consumer surplus, what is the producer surplus, and what is the total surplus?

f. If the demand for sandwiches increases and sandwich makers produce the efficient quantity, what happens to producer surplus and deadweight loss?

12. **The Right Price for Digital Music: Why 99 cents per Song is Too Much, and Too Little**

Apple's 99-cents-for-everything model isn't perfect. Isn't 99 cents too much to pay for music that appeals to just a few people? What we need is a system that will continue to pack the corporate coffers yet be fair to music lovers. The solution: a real-time commodities market that combines aspects of Apple's iTunes, Nasdaq, the Chicago Mercantile Exchange, Priceline, and eBay. ... Songs would be priced strictly on demand. The more people who download [a particular song] ... the higher the price [of that song] will go. ... The fewer people who buy a [particular] song, the lower the price [of that song] goes. ... In essence, this is a pure free-market solution—the market alone would determine price.

Slate, December 5, 2005

Assume that the marginal social cost of downloading a song from the iTunes Store is zero. (This assumption means that the cost of operating the iTunes Store doesn't change if people download more songs.)

a. Draw a graph of the market for downloadable music with a price of 99 cents for everything. On your graph, show consumer surplus and producer surplus.

b. With a price of 99 cents for everything, is the market efficient or inefficient? If it is inefficient, show the deadweight loss on your graph.

c. If the pricing scheme described in the news clip were adopted, how would consumer surplus, producer surplus, and the deadweight loss change?

d. If the pricing scheme described in the news clip were adopted, would the market be efficient or inefficient? Explain.

e. Is the pricing scheme described in the news clip a "pure free-market solution"? Explain.

13. **Was Katie Holmes' Marathon Entrance Unfair?**

Runners in the recent New York Marathon have been asking why Katie Holmes was admitted to the race when 60,000 hopefuls were denied. ... Holmes was admitted to the race as a VIP. She was not given a spot through a lottery system, or for running in one of the 26 sanctioned New York Marathon charities ... or even for having a competitive running time. The minimum qualifying run time for a woman runner is 3 hours and 23 minutes. Katie completed the marathon in 5 hours, 29 minutes and 58 seconds.

MSNBC, November 9, 2007

a. By what allocation method did Holmes obtain entrance to the marathon?

b. Evaluate the "fairness" of Holmes being admitted to the marathon.

14. **MYTH: Price-Gouging Is Bad**

Mississippi Attorney General Jim Hood announced a crackdown on gougers after Hurricane Katrina. John Shepperson was one of the "gougers" authorities arrested. Shepperson and his family live in Kentucky. They watched news reports about Katrina and learned that people desperately needed things. Shepperson thought he could help and make some money, too, so he bought 19 generators. He and his family then rented a U-Haul and drove 600 miles to an area of Mississippi that was left without power in the wake of the hurricane. He offered to sell his generators for twice what he had paid for them, and people were eager to buy. Police confiscated his generators, though, and Shepperson was jailed for four days for price-gouging.

ABC News, May 12, 2006

a. Explain how the invisible hand (Shepperson) actually reduced deadweight loss in the market for generators following Katrina.

b. Evaluate the "fairness" of Shepperson's actions.

15. After you have studied *Reading Between the Lines* on pp. 122–123, answer the following questions:

a. What is the major problem in achieving an efficient use of the world's water?

b. If there were a global market in water, like there is in oil, how do you think the market would work?

c. Would a free world market in water achieve an efficient use of the world's water resources? Explain why or why not.

d. Would a free world market in water achieve a fair use of the world's water resources? Explain why or why not and be clear about the concept of fairness that you are using.

16. **Fight over Water Rates; Escondido Farmers Say Increase would Put Them out of Business**

The city is considering significant increases in water rates for agriculture, which historically has paid less than residential and business users. … [S]ince 1993, water rates have gone up more than 90 percent for residential customers while agricultural users … have seen increases of only about 50 percent, …

The San Diego Union-Tribune, June 14, 2006

a. Do you think that the allocation of water among San Diego agricultural and residential users is likely to be efficient? Explain your answer.

b. If agricultural users pay a higher price for water, will the allocation of resources become more efficient?

c. If agricultural users pay a higher price for water, what will happen to consumer surplus and producer surplus from water?

d. Is the difference in price paid by agricultural and residential users fair?

17. Use the link on MyEconLab (Chapter Resources, Chapter 5, Web links) to visit the Web site of Health Action International and read the article by Catrin Schulte-Hillen entitled "Study concerning the availability and price of AZT." Then answer the following questions and explain your answers using the concepts of marginal benefit, marginal cost, price, consumer surplus, and producer surplus.

a. What is the range of retail prices of AZT across the countries covered by the study?

b. What, if anything, do you think could be done to increase the quantity of AZT and decrease its price?

c. Canadian online pharmacies sell AZT to Americans for a price below the U.S. price. Does this practice increase or decrease consumer surplus, producer surplus, and deadweight loss from AZT in the United States?

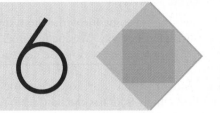

6

Government Actions in Markets

After studying this chapter, you will be able to:

- Explain how rent ceilings create housing shortages and inefficiency

- Explain how minimum wage laws create unemployment and inefficiency

- Explain the effects of a tax

- Explain the effects of production quotas and subsidies on production, costs, and prices

- Explain how markets for illegal goods work

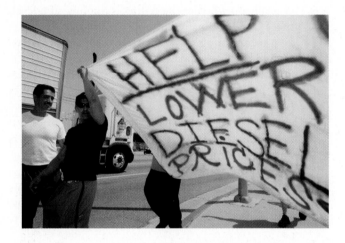

Even though house prices are falling, home renters in New York, San Francisco, and Boston saw their rents rise by an average of 10 percent in 2007. Can governments cap rents to help renters live in affordable housing? Or instead, can governments make housing more affordable by raising incomes with minimum wage laws?

Taxes put the hand of government in almost every pocket and market. We pay income taxes and Social Security taxes in the labor market and sales taxes in the markets for almost everything we buy. You probably think that you pay more than your fair share of taxes. But who actually pays and who benefits when a tax is cut: buyers or sellers?

In some markets, governments intervene with the opposite of a tax: a subsidy. For example, in the market for farm products, the U.S. government subsidizes producers to lower the price faced by consumers. Sometimes, governments limit the quantities that farms may produce. Do subsidies and production limits help to make markets efficient?

Price caps, tax cuts, and subsidies, three of the major topics that you study in this chapter, have been proposed as ways of dealing with the high price of gasoline. In *Reading Between the Lines* at the end of this chapter, we apply what you've learned to the market for gasoline to see how governments might try to influence the price and quantity in that market.

A Housing Market With a Rent Ceiling

We spend more of our income on housing than on any other good or service, so it isn't surprising that rents can be a political issue. When rents are high, or when they jump by a large amount, renters might lobby the government for limits on rents.

A government regulation that makes it illegal to charge a price higher than a specified level is called a **price ceiling** or **price cap**.

The effects of a price ceiling on a market depend crucially on whether the ceiling is imposed at a level that is above or below the equilibrium price.

A price ceiling set *above the equilibrium price* has no effect. The reason is that the price ceiling does not constrain the market forces. The force of the law and the market forces are not in conflict. But a price ceiling *below the equilibrium price* has powerful effects on a market. The reason is that the price ceiling attempts to prevent the price from regulating the quantities demanded and supplied. The force of the law and the market forces are in conflict.

When a price ceiling is applied to a housing market, it is called a **rent ceiling**. A rent ceiling set below the equilibrium rent creates

- A housing shortage
- Increased search activity
- A black market

A Housing Shortage

At the equilibrium price, the quantity demanded equals the quantity supplied. In a housing market, when the rent is at the equilibrium level, the quantity of housing supplied equals the quantity of housing demanded and there is neither a shortage nor a surplus of housing.

But at a rent set below the equilibrium rent, the quantity of housing demanded exceeds the quantity of housing supplied—there is a shortage. So if a rent ceiling is set below the equilibrium rent, there will be a shortage of housing.

When there is a shortage, the quantity available is the quantity supplied and somehow, this quantity must be allocated among the frustrated demanders. One way in which this allocation occurs is through increased search activity.

Increased Search Activity

The time spent looking for someone with whom to do business is called **search activity**. We spend some time in search activity almost every time we make a purchase. When you're shopping for the latest hot new cell phone, and you know four stores that stock it, how do you find which store has the best deal? You spend a few minutes on the internet, checking out the various prices. In some markets, such as the housing market, people spend a lot of time checking the alternatives available before making a choice.

When a price is regulated and there is a shortage, search activity increases. In the case of a rent-controlled housing market, frustrated would-be renters scan the newspapers, not only for housing ads but also for death notices! Any information about newly available housing is useful, and apartment seekers race to be first on the scene when news of a possible supplier breaks.

The *opportunity cost* of a good is equal not only to its price but also to the value of the search time spent finding the good. So the opportunity cost of housing is equal to the rent (a regulated price) plus the time and other resources spent searching for the restricted quantity available. Search activity is costly. It uses time and other resources, such as phone calls, automobiles, and gasoline that could have been used in other productive ways.

A rent ceiling controls only the rent portion of the cost of housing. The cost of increased search activity might end up making the full cost of housing *higher* than it would be without a rent ceiling.

A Black Market

A rent ceiling also encourages illegal trading in a **black market**, an illegal market in which the equilibrium price exceeds the price ceiling. Black markets occur in rent-controlled housing and many other markets. For example, scalpers run black markets in tickets for big sporting events and rock concerts.

When a rent ceiling is in force, frustrated renters and landlords constantly seek ways of increasing rents. One common way is for a new tenant to pay a high price for worthless fittings, such as charging $2,000 for threadbare drapes. Another is for the tenant to pay an exorbitant price for new locks and keys—called "key money."

The level of a black market rent depends on how tightly the rent ceiling is enforced. With loose enforcement, the black market rent is close to the unregulated rent. But with strict enforcement, the black market rent is equal to the maximum price that a renter is willing to pay.

Figure 6.1 illustrates the effects of a rent ceiling. The demand for housing is *D* and the supply is *S*. A rent ceiling is imposed at $800 a month. Rents that exceed $800 a month are in the gray-shaded illegal region in the figure. You can see that the equilibrium rent, where the demand and supply curves intersect, is in the illegal region.

At a rent of $800 a month, the quantity of housing supplied is 60,000 units and the quantity demanded is 100,000 units. So with a rent of $800 a month, there is a shortage of 40,000 units of housing.

To rent the 60,000th unit, someone is willing to pay $1,200 a month. They might pay this amount by incurring search costs that bring the total cost of housing to $1,200 a month, or they might pay a black market price of $1,200 a month. Either way, they end up incurring a cost that exceeds what the equilibrium rent would be in an unregulated market.

Inefficiency of a Rent Ceiling

A rent ceiling set below the equilibrium rent results in an inefficient underproduction of housing services. The *marginal social benefit* of housing exceeds its *marginal social cost* and a deadweight loss shrinks the producer surplus and consumer surplus (Chapter 5, pp. 115–116).

Figure 6.2 shows this inefficiency. The rent ceiling ($800 per month) is below the equilibrium rent ($1,000 per month) and the quantity of housing supplied (60,000 units) is less than the efficient quantity (80,000 units).

Because the quantity of housing supplied (the quantity available) is less than the efficient quantity, there is a deadweight loss, shown by the gray triangle. Producer surplus shrinks to the blue triangle and consumer surplus shrinks to the green triangle. The red rectangle represents the potential loss from increased search activity. This loss is borne by consumers and the full loss from the rent ceiling is the sum of the deadweight loss and the increased cost of search.

FIGURE 6.1   A Rent Ceiling

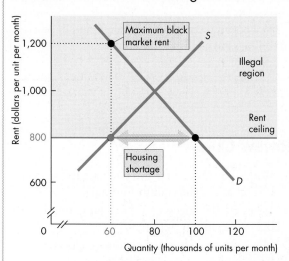

A rent above the rent ceiling of $800 a month is illegal (in the gray-shaded illegal region). At a rent of $800 a month, the quantity of housing supplied is 60,000 units. Frustrated renters spend time searching for housing and they make deals with landlords in a black market. Someone is willing to pay $1,200 a month for the 60,000th unit.

FIGURE 6.2   The Inefficiency of a Rent Ceiling

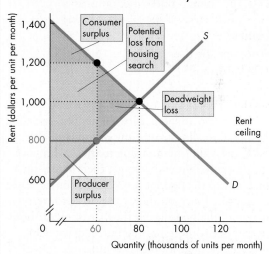

Without a rent ceiling, the market produces an efficient 80,000 units of housing at a rent of $1,000 a month. A rent ceiling of $800 a month decreases the quantity of housing supplied to 60,000 units. Producer surplus and consumer surplus shrink and a deadweight loss arises. The red rectangle represents the cost of resources used in increased search activity. The full loss from the rent ceiling equals the sum of the red rectangle and gray triangle.

Are Rent Ceilings Fair?

Rent ceilings might be inefficient, but don't they achieve a fairer allocation of scarce housing? Let's explore this question.

Chapter 5 (pp. 118–121) reviews two key ideas about fairness. According to the *fair rules* view, anything that blocks voluntary exchange is unfair, so rent ceilings are unfair. But according to the *fair result* view, a fair outcome is one that benefits the less well off. So according to this view, the fairest outcome is the one that allocates scarce housing to the poorest. To see whether rent ceilings help to achieve a fairer outcome in this sense, we need to consider how the market allocates scarce housing resources in the face of a rent ceiling.

Blocking rent adjustments doesn't eliminate scarcity. Rather, because it decreases the quantity of housing available, it creates an even bigger challenge for the housing market. Somehow, the market must ration a smaller quantity of housing and allocate that housing among the people who demand it.

When the rent is not permitted to allocate scarce housing, what other mechanisms are available, and are *they* fair? Some possible mechanisms are

- A lottery
- First-come, first-served
- Discrimination

A lottery allocates housing to those who are lucky, not to those who are poor. First-come, first-served (a method used to allocate housing in England after World War II) allocates housing to those who have the greatest foresight and who get their names on a list first, not to the poorest. Discrimination allocates scarce housing based on the views and self-interest of the owner of the housing. In the case of public housing, it is the self-interest of the bureaucracy that administers the allocation that counts.

In principle, self-interested owners and bureaucrats could allocate housing to satisfy some criterion of fairness, but they are not likely to do so. Discrimination based on friendship, family ties, and criteria such as race, ethnicity, or sex is more likely to enter the equation. We might make such discrimination illegal, but we cannot prevent it from occurring.

It is hard, then, to make a case for rent ceilings on the basis of fairness. When rent adjustments are blocked, other methods of allocating scarce housing resources operate that do not produce a fair outcome.

Rent Ceilings in Practice
The Rich and the Famous Win

New York, San Francisco, London, and Paris, four of the world's great cities, have rent ceilings in some part of their housing markets. Boston had rent ceilings for many years but abolished them in 1997. Many other U.S. cities do not have, and have never had, rent ceilings. Among them are Atlanta, Baltimore, Chicago, Dallas, Philadelphia, Phoenix, and Seattle.

To see the effects of rent ceilings in practice we can compare the housing markets in cities with ceilings with those without ceilings. We learn two main lessons from such a comparison.

First, rent ceilings definitely create a housing shortage. Second, they do lower the rents for some but raise them for others.

A survey[*] conducted in 1997 showed that the rents of housing units *actually available for rent* were 2.5 times the average of all rents in New York, but equal to the average rent in Philadelphia. The winners from rent ceilings are the families that have lived in a city for a long time. In New York, these families include some rich and famous ones. The voting power of the winners keeps the rent ceilings in place. Mobile newcomers are the losers in a city with rent ceilings.

The bottom line is that in principle and in practice, rent ceilings are inefficient and unfair.

---

[*] William Tucker, "How Rent Control Drives Out Affordable Housing."

Review Quiz

1 What is a rent ceiling and what are its effects if it is set above the equilibrium rent?

2 What are the effects of a rent ceiling that is set below the equilibrium rent?

3 How are scarce housing resources allocated when a rent ceiling is in place?

4 Why does a rent ceiling create an inefficient and unfair outcome in the housing market?

 Work Study Plan 6.1 and get instant feedback.

You now know how a price ceiling (rent ceiling) works. Next, we'll learn about the effects of a price floor by studying a minimum wage in a labor market.

A Labor Market With a Minimum Wage

For each one of us, the labor market is the market that influences the jobs we get and the wages we earn. Firms decide how much labor to demand, and the lower the wage rate, the greater is the quantity of labor demanded. Households decide how much labor to supply, and the higher the wage rate, the greater is the quantity of labor supplied. The wage rate adjusts to make the quantity of labor demanded equal to the quantity supplied.

When wage rates are low, or when they fail to keep up with rising prices, labor unions might turn to governments and lobby for a higher wage rate.

A government imposed regulation that makes it illegal to charge a price lower than a specified level is called a **price floor**.

The effects of a price floor on a market depend crucially on whether the floor is imposed at a level that is above or below the equilibrium price.

A price floor set *below the equilibrium price* has no effect. The reason is that the price floor does not constrain the market forces. The force of the law and the market forces are not in conflict. But a price floor *above the equilibrium price* has powerful effects on a market. The reason is that the price floor attempts to prevent the price from regulating the quantities demanded and supplied. The force of the law and the market forces are in conflict.

When a price floor is applied to a labor market, it is called a **minimum wage**. A minimum wage imposed at a level that is above the equilibrium wage creates unemployment. Let's look at the effects of a minimum wage.

Minimum Wage Brings Unemployment

At the equilibrium price, the quantity demanded equals the quantity supplied. In a labor market, when the wage rate is at the equilibrium level, the quantity of labor supplied equals the quantity of labor demanded: There is neither a shortage of labor nor a surplus of labor.

But at a wage rate above the equilibrium wage, the quantity of labor supplied exceeds the quantity of labor demanded—there is a surplus of labor. So when a minimum wage is set above the equilibrium wage, there is a surplus of labor. The demand for labor determines the level of employment, and the surplus of labor is unemployed.

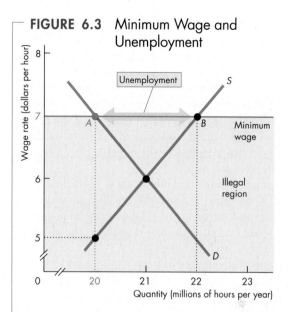

FIGURE 6.3   Minimum Wage and Unemployment

The minimum wage rate is set at $7 an hour. Any wage rate below $7 an hour is illegal (in the gray-shaded illegal region). At the minimum wage of $7 an hour, 20 million hours are hired but 22 million hours are available. Unemployment—AB—of 2 million hours a year is created. With only 20 million hours demanded, someone is willing to supply the 20 millionth hour for $5.

myeconlab   animation

Figure 6.3 illustrates the effect of the minimum wage on unemployment. The demand for labor is D and the supply of labor is S. The horizontal red line shows the minimum wage set at $7 an hour. A wage rate below this level is illegal, in the gray-shaded illegal region of the figure. At the minimum wage rate, 20 million hours of labor are demanded (point A) and 22 million hours of labor are supplied (point B), so 2 million hours of available labor are unemployed.

With only 20 million hours demanded, someone is willing to supply that 20 millionth hour for $5. Frustrated unemployed workers spend time and other resources searching for hard-to-find jobs.

Inefficiency of a Minimum Wage

In the labor market, the supply curve measures the marginal social cost of labor to workers. This cost is leisure forgone. The demand curve measures the marginal social benefit from labor. This benefit is the value of the goods and services produced. An unregulated labor market allocates the economy's scarce labor resources to the jobs in which they are valued most highly. The market is efficient.

The minimum wage frustrates the market mechanism and results in unemployment and increased job search. At the quantity of labor employed, the marginal social benefit of labor exceeds its marginal social cost and a deadweight loss shrinks the firms' surplus and the workers' surplus.

Figure 6.4 shows this inefficiency. The minimum wage ($7 an hour) is above the equilibrium wage ($6 an hour) and the quantity of labor demanded and employed (20 million hours) is less than the efficient quantity (21 million hours).

Because the quantity of labor employed is less than the efficient quantity, there is a deadweight loss, shown by the gray triangle. The firms' surplus shrinks to the blue triangle and the workers' surplus shrinks to the green triangle. The red rectangle shows the potential loss from increased job search, which is borne by workers. The full loss from the minimum wage is the sum of the deadweight loss and the increased cost of job search.

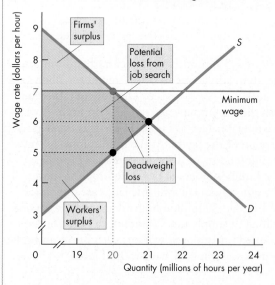

A minimum wage decreases employment. Firms' surplus (blue area) and workers' surplus (green area) shrink and a deadweight loss (gray area) arises. Job search increases and the red area shows the loss from this activity.

myeconlab animation

The Minimum Wage in Practice
Unscrambling Cause and Effect

In the United States, the federal government's Fair Labor Standards Act sets the minimum wage, which has fluctuated between 35 percent and 50 percent of the average wage, and in 2009 was $7.25 an hour. Most states have minimum wages that exceed the federal minimum.

Does the minimum wage result in unemployment, and if so, how much unemployment does it create? The consensus answer is that a 10 percent rise in the minimum wage decreases teenage employment by between 1 and 3 percent.

This consensus answer has been challenged by David Card of the University of California at Berkeley (see pp. 484–486) and Alan Krueger of Princeton University.

Card and Krueger say that increases in the minimum wage have *increased* teenage employment and *decreased* unemployment.

From their study of minimum wages in California, New Jersey, and Texas, Card and Krueger say that the employment rate of low-income workers increased following an increase in the minimum wage. They argue that a higher wage *increases* employment by making workers become more conscientious and productive

Is the Minimum Wage Fair?

The minimum wage is unfair on both views of fairness: It delivers an unfair *result* and imposes an unfair *rule*.

The *result* is unfair because only those people who have jobs and keep them benefit from the minimum wage. The unemployed end up worse off than they would be with no minimum wage. Some of those who search for jobs and find them end up worse off because of the increased cost of job search they incur. Also those who find jobs aren't always the least well off. When the wage rate doesn't allocate labor, other mechanisms determine who finds a job. One such mechanism is discrimination, which is yet another source of unfairness.

The minimum wage imposes an unfair *rule* because it blocks voluntary exchange. Firms are willing to hire more labor and people are willing to work more, but they are not permitted by the minimum wage law to do so.

and less likely to quit, which lowers unproductive labor turnover. They also argue that a higher wage rate makes managers seek ways to increase labor productivity.

Most economists are skeptical about Card and Krueger's argument. Why, economists ask, don't firms freely pay wage rates above the equilibrium wage to encourage more productive work habits? Also, they point to other explanations for the employment responses that Card and Krueger found.

According to Daniel Hamermesh of the University of Texas at Austin, Card and Krueger got the timing wrong. Hamermesh says that firms cut employment *before* the minimum wage is increased in anticipation of the increase. If he is correct, looking for the effects of an increase *after* it has occurred misses its main effects.

Finis Welch of Texas A&M University and Kevin Murphy of the University of Chicago say the employment effects that Card and Krueger found are caused by regional differences in economic growth, not by changes in the minimum wage.

One effect of the minimum wage is an increase in the quantity of labor supplied. If this effect occurs, it might show up as an increase in the number of people who quit school to look for work before completing high school. Some economists say that this response does occur.

Review Quiz

1 What is a minimum wage and what are its effects if it is set above the equilibrium wage?

2 What are the effects of a minimum wage set below the equilibrium wage?

3 Explain how scarce jobs are allocated when a minimum wage is in place.

4 Explain why a minimum wage creates an inefficient allocation of labor resources.

5 Explain why a minimum wage is unfair.

 myeconlab   Work Study Plan 6.2 and get instant feedback.

Next we're going to study a more widespread government action in markets: taxes. We'll see how taxes change prices and quantities. You will discover the surprising fact that while the government can impose a tax, it can't decide who will pay the tax! And you will see that a tax creates a deadweight loss.

Taxes

Everything you earn and almost everything you buy is taxed. Income taxes and Social Security taxes are deducted from your earnings and sales taxes are added to the bill when you buy something. Employers also pay a Social Security tax for their workers, and producers of tobacco products, alcoholic drinks, and gasoline pay a tax every time they sell something.

Who *really* pays these taxes? Because the income tax and Social Security tax are deducted from your pay, and the sales tax is added to the prices that you pay, isn't it obvious that *you* pay these taxes? And isn't it equally obvious that your employer pays the employer's contribution to the Social Security tax and that tobacco producers pay the tax on cigarettes?

You're going to discover that it isn't obvious who *really* pays a tax and that lawmakers don't make that decision. We begin with a definition of tax incidence.

Tax Incidence

Tax incidence is the division of the burden of a tax between buyers and sellers. When the government imposes a tax on the sale of a good*, the price paid by buyers might rise by the full amount of the tax, by a lesser amount, or not at all. If the price paid by buyers rises by the full amount of the tax, then the burden of the tax falls entirely on buyers—the buyers pay the tax. If the price paid by buyers rises by a lesser amount than the tax, then the burden of the tax falls partly on buyers and partly on sellers. And if the price paid by buyers doesn't change at all, then the burden of the tax falls entirely on sellers.

Tax incidence does not depend on the tax law. The law might impose a tax on sellers or on buyers, but the outcome is the same in either case. To see why, let's look at the tax on cigarettes in New York City.

A Tax on Sellers

On July 1, 2002, Mayor Bloomberg put a tax of $1.50 a pack on cigarettes sold in New York City. To work out the effects of this tax on the sellers of cigarettes, we begin by examining the effects on demand and supply in the market for cigarettes.

---

* These propositions also apply to services and factors of production (land, labor, capital).

In Fig. 6.5, the demand curve is D, and the supply curve is S. With no tax, the equilibrium price is $3 per pack and 350 million packs a year are bought and sold.

A tax on sellers is like an increase in cost, so it decreases supply. To determine the position of the new supply curve, we add the tax to the minimum price that sellers are willing to accept for each quantity sold. You can see that without the tax, sellers are willing to offer 350 million packs a year for $3 a pack. So with a $1.50 tax, they will offer 350 million packs a year only if the price is $4.50 a pack. The supply curve shifts to the red curve labeled S + *tax on sellers*.

Equilibrium occurs where the new supply curve intersects the demand curve at 325 million packs a year. The price paid by buyers rises by $1 to $4 a pack. And the price received by sellers falls by 50¢ to $2.50 a pack. So buyers pay $1 of the tax and sellers pay the other 50¢.

A Tax on Buyers

Suppose that instead of taxing sellers, New York City taxes cigarette buyers $1.50 a pack.

A tax on buyers lowers the amount they are willing to pay sellers, so it decreases demand and shifts the demand curve leftward. To determine the position of this new demand curve, we subtract the tax from the maximum price that buyers are willing to pay for each quantity bought. You can see, in Fig. 6.6, that without the tax, buyers are willing to buy 350 million packs a year for $3 a pack. So with a $1.50 tax, they are willing to buy 350 million packs a year only if the price including the tax is $3 a pack, which means that they're willing to pay sellers only $1.50 a pack. The demand curve shifts to become the red curve labeled D – *tax on buyers*.

Equilibrium occurs where the new demand curve intersects the supply curve at a quantity of 325 million packs a year. The price received by sellers is $2.50 a pack, and the price paid by buyers is $4.

Equivalence of Tax on Buyers and Sellers

You can see that the tax on buyers in Fig. 6.6 has the same effects as the tax on sellers in Fig. 6.5. In both cases, the equilibrium quantity decreases to 325 million packs a year, the price paid by buyers rises to $4 a pack, and the price received by sellers falls to $2.50 a pack. Buyers pay $1 of the $1.50 tax, and sellers pay the other 50¢ of the tax.

FIGURE 6.5   A Tax on Sellers

With no tax, 350 million packs a year are bought and sold at $3 a pack. A tax on sellers of $1.50 a pack shifts the supply curve leftward to *S + tax on sellers*. The equilibrium quantity decreases to 325 million packs a year, the price paid by buyers rises to $4 a pack, and the price received by sellers falls to $2.50 a pack. The tax raises the price paid by buyers by less than the tax and lowers the price received by sellers, so buyers and sellers share the burden of the tax.

myeconlab   animation

Can We Share the Burden Equally? Suppose that Mayor Bloomberg wants the burden of the cigarette tax to fall equally on buyers and sellers and declares that a 75¢ tax be imposed on each. Is the burden of the tax then shared equally?

You can see that it is not. The tax is still $1.50 a pack. And you've seen that the tax has the same effect regardless of whether it is imposed on sellers or buyers. So imposing half the tax on one and half on the other is like an average of the two cases you've examined. (Draw the demand-supply graph and work out what happens in this case. The demand curve shifts downward by 75¢ and the supply curve shifts upward by 75¢. The new equilibrium quantity is still 325 million packs a year. Buyers pay $4 a pack, of which 75¢ is tax. Sellers receive from buyers $3.25, but must pay a 75¢ tax, so sellers net $2.50 a pack.)

When a transaction is taxed, there are two prices: the price paid by buyers, which includes the tax; and the price received by sellers, which excludes the tax.

FIGURE 6.6   A Tax on Buyers

With no tax, 350 million packs a year are bought and sold at $3 a pack. A tax on buyers of $1.50 a pack shifts the demand curve leftward to *D – tax on buyers*. The equilibrium quantity decreases to 325 million packs a year, the price paid by buyers rises to $4 a pack, and the price received by sellers falls to $2.50 a pack. The tax raises the price paid by buyers by less than the tax and lowers the price received by sellers, so buyers and sellers share the burden of the tax.

myeconlab animation

Buyers respond to the price that *includes* the tax and sellers respond to the price that *excludes* the tax.

A tax is like a wedge between the price buyers pay and the price sellers receive. The size of the wedge determines the effects of the tax, not the side of the market on which the government imposes the tax.

The Social Security Tax   The Social Security tax is an example of a tax that Congress imposes equally on both buyers and sellers. But the principles you've just learned apply to this tax too. The market for labor, not Congress, decides how the burden of the Social Security tax is divided between firms and workers.

In the New York City cigarette tax example, buyers bear twice the burden of the tax borne by sellers. In special cases, either buyers or sellers bear the entire burden. The division of the burden of a tax between buyers and sellers depends on the elasticities of demand and supply, as you will now see.

Tax Incidence and Elasticity of Demand

The division of the tax between buyers and sellers depends in part on the elasticity of demand. There are two extreme cases:

- Perfectly inelastic demand—buyers pay.
- Perfectly elastic demand—sellers pay.

Perfectly Inelastic Demand   Figure 6.7 shows the market for insulin, a vital daily medication for those with diabetes. Demand is perfectly inelastic at 100,000 doses a day, regardless of the price, as shown by the vertical demand curve *D*. That is, a diabetic would sacrifice all other goods and services rather than not consume the insulin dose that provides good health. The supply curve of insulin is S. With no tax, the price is $2 a dose and the quantity is 100,000 doses a day.

If insulin is taxed at 20¢ a dose, we must add the tax to the minimum price at which drug companies are willing to sell insulin. The result is the new supply curve *S + tax*. The price rises to $2.20 a dose, but the quantity does not change. Buyers pay the entire tax of 20¢ a dose.

FIGURE 6.7   Tax with Perfectly Inelastic Demand

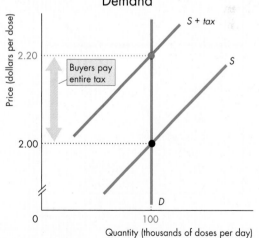

In this market for insulin, demand is perfectly inelastic. With no tax, the price is $2 a dose and the quantity is 100,000 doses a day. A tax of 20¢ a dose shifts the supply curve to *S + tax*. The price rises to $2.20 a dose, but the quantity bought does not change. Buyers pay the entire tax.

myeconlab animation

Perfectly Elastic Demand Figure 6.8 shows the market for pink marker pens. Demand is perfectly elastic at $1 a pen, as shown by the horizontal demand curve D. If pink pens are less expensive than the other colors, everyone uses pink. If pink pens are more expensive than other colors, no one uses pink. The supply curve is S. With no tax, the price of a pink pen is $1 and the quantity is 4,000 pens a week.

Suppose that the government imposes a tax of 10¢ a pen on pink marker pens but not on other colors. The new supply curve is S + tax. The price remains at $1 a pen, and the quantity decreases to 1,000 pink pens a week. The 10¢ tax leaves the price paid by buyers unchanged but lowers the amount received by sellers by the full amount of the tax. Sellers pay the entire tax of 10¢ a pink pen.

We've seen that when demand is perfectly inelastic, buyers pay the entire tax and when demand is perfectly elastic, sellers pay the entire tax. In the usual case, demand is neither perfectly inelastic nor perfectly elastic and the tax is split between buyers and sellers. But the division depends on the elasticity of demand: The more inelastic the demand, the larger is the amount of the tax paid by buyers.

FIGURE 6.8 Tax with Perfectly Elastic Demand

In this market for pink pens, demand is perfectly elastic. With no tax, the price of a pen is $1 and the quantity is 4,000 pens a week. A tax of 10¢ a pink pen shifts the supply curve to S + tax. The price remains at $1 a pen, and the quantity of pink pens sold decreases to 1,000 a week. Sellers pay the entire tax.

myeconlab animation

Tax Incidence and Elasticity of Supply

The division of the tax between buyers and sellers also depends, in part, on the elasticity of supply. Again, there are two extreme cases:

- Perfectly inelastic supply—sellers pay.
- Perfectly elastic supply—buyers pay.

Perfectly Inelastic Supply Figure 6.9(a) shows the market for water from a mineral spring that flows at a constant rate that can't be controlled. Supply is perfectly inelastic at 100,000 bottles a week, as shown by the supply curve S. The demand curve for the water from this spring is D. With no tax, the price is 50¢ and the quantity is 100,000 bottles.

Suppose this spring water is taxed at 5¢ a bottle. The supply curve does not change because the spring owners still produce 100,000 bottles a week, even though the price they receive falls. But buyers are willing to buy the 100,000 bottles only if the price is 50¢ a bottle, so the price remains at 50¢ a bottle. The tax reduces the price received by sellers to 45¢ a bottle, and sellers pay the entire tax.

Perfectly Elastic Supply Figure 6.9(b) shows the market for sand from which computer-chip makers extract silicon. Supply of this sand is perfectly elastic at a price of 10¢ a pound, as shown by the supply curve S. The demand curve for sand is D. With no tax, the price is 10¢ a pound and 5,000 pounds a week are bought.

If this sand is taxed at 1¢ a pound, we must add the tax to the minimum supply-price. Sellers are now willing to offer any quantity at 11¢ a pound along the curve S + tax. A new equilibrium is determined where the new supply curve intersects the demand curve: at a price of 11¢ a pound and a quantity of 3,000 pounds a week. The tax has increased the price buyers pay by the full amount of the tax—1¢ a pound—and has decreased the quantity sold. Buyers pay the entire tax.

We've seen that when supply is perfectly inelastic, sellers pay the entire tax, and when supply is perfectly elastic, buyers pay the entire tax. In the usual case, supply is neither perfectly inelastic nor perfectly elastic and the tax is split between buyers and sellers. But how the tax is split depends on the elasticity of supply: The more elastic the supply, the larger is the amount of the tax paid by buyers.

FIGURE 6.9 Tax and the Elasticity of Supply

(a) Perfectly inelastic supply

(b) Perfectly elastic supply

Part (a) shows the market for water from a mineral spring. Supply is perfectly inelastic. With no tax, the price is 50¢ a bottle. With a tax of 5¢ a bottle, the price remains at 50¢ a bottle. The number of bottles bought remains the same, but the price received by sellers decreases to 45¢ a bottle. Sellers pay the entire tax.

Part (b) shows the market for sand. Supply is perfectly elastic. With no tax, the price is 10¢ a pound. A tax of 1¢ a pound increases the minimum supply-price to 11¢ a pound. The supply curve shifts to *S + tax*. The price increases to 11¢ a pound. Buyers pay the entire tax.

myeconlab animation

Taxes and Efficiency

A tax drives a wedge between the buying price and the selling price and results in inefficient underproduction. The price buyers pay is also the buyers' willingness to pay, which measures *marginal social benefit*. The price sellers receive is also the sellers' minimum supply-price, which equals *marginal social cost*.

A tax makes marginal social benefit exceed marginal social cost, shrinks the producer surplus and consumer surplus, and creates a deadweight loss.

Figure 6.10 shows the inefficiency of a tax on MP3 players. The demand curve, *D*, shows marginal social benefit, and the supply curve, *S*, shows marginal social cost. Without a tax, the market produces the efficient quantity (5,000 players a week).

With a tax, the sellers' minimum supply-price rises by the amount of the tax and the supply curve shifts to *S + tax*. This supply curve does *not* show marginal social cost. The tax component isn't a *social* cost of

FIGURE 6.10 Taxes and Efficiency

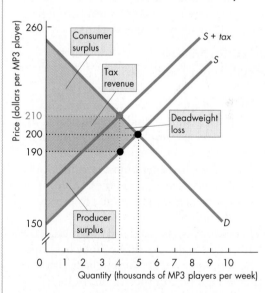

With no tax, 5,000 players a week are produced. With a $20 tax, the buyers' price rises to $210, the sellers' price falls to $190, and the quantity decreases to 4,000 players a week. Consumer surplus shrinks to the green area, and the producer surplus shrinks to the blue area. Part of the loss of consumer surplus and producer surplus goes to the government as tax revenue (the purple area) and part becomes a deadweight loss (the gray area).

myeconlab animation

production. It is a transfer of resources to the government. At the new equilibrium quantity (4,000 players a week), both consumer surplus and producer surplus shrink. Part of each surplus goes to the government in tax revenue—the purple area. And part becomes a deadweight loss—the gray area.

Only in the extreme cases of perfectly inelastic demand and perfectly inelastic supply does a tax not change the quantity bought and sold so that no deadweight loss arises.

Taxes and Fairness

We've examined the incidence and the efficiency of taxes. But when political leaders debate tax issues, it is fairness, not incidence and efficiency, that gets the most attention. Democrats complain that Republican tax cuts are unfair because they give the benefits of lower taxes to the rich. Republicans counter that it is fair that the rich get most of the tax cuts because they pay most of the taxes. No easy answers are available to the questions about the fairness of taxes.

Economists have proposed two conflicting principles of fairness to apply to a tax system:

- The benefits principle
- The ability-to-pay principle

The Benefits Principle The *benefits principle* is the proposition that people should pay taxes equal to the benefits they receive from the services provided by government. This arrangement is fair because it means that those who benefit most pay the most taxes. It makes tax payments and the consumption of government-provided services similar to private consumption expenditures.

The benefits principle can justify high fuel taxes to pay for freeways, high taxes on alcoholic beverages and tobacco products to pay for public health-care services, and high rates of income tax on high incomes to pay for the benefits from law and order and from living in a secure environment, from which the rich might benefit more than the poor.

The Ability-to-Pay Principle The *ability-to-pay principle* is the proposition that people should pay taxes according to how easily they can bear the burden of the tax. A rich person can more easily bear the burden than a poor person can, so the ability-to-pay principle can reinforce the benefits principle to justify high rates of income tax on high incomes.

Taxes in Practice
Workers and Consumers Pay the Most

Because the elasticity of the supply of labor is low and the elasticity of demand for labor is high, workers pay most of the personal income taxes and most of the Social Security taxes. Because the elasticities of demand for alcohol, tobacco, and gasoline are low and the elasticities of supply are high, the burden of these taxes (excise taxes) falls more heavily on buyers than on sellers.

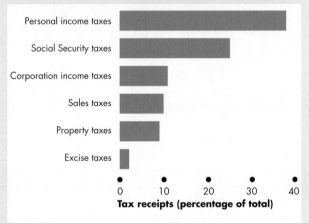

U.S. Taxes

Source of Data: Budget of the United States Government, Fiscal Year 2009, Historical Tables, Table 2.1

Review Quiz

1 How does the elasticity of demand influence the effect of a tax on the price buyers pay, the price sellers receive, the quantity bought, the tax revenue, and the deadweight loss?
2 How does the elasticity of supply influence the effect of a tax on the price buyers pay, the price sellers receive, the quantity bought, the tax revenue, and the deadweight loss?
3 Why is a tax inefficient?
4 When would a tax be efficient?
5 What are the two principles of fairness that are applied to tax systems?

 Work Study Plan 6.3 and get instant feedback.

Your next task is to study two other types of government actions in markets: production quotas and subsidies. These tools are often used to influence the markets for farm products.

Production Quotas and Subsidies

An early or late frost, a hot dry summer, and a wet spring present just a few of the challenges that fill the lives of farmers with uncertainty and sometimes with economic hardship. Fluctuations in the weather bring fluctuations in farm output and prices and sometimes leave farmers with low incomes. To help farmers avoid low prices and low incomes, governments intervene in the markets for farm products.

Price floors that work a bit like the minimum wage that you've already studied might be used. But as you've seen, this type of government action creates a surplus and is inefficient. These same conclusions apply to the effects of a price floor for farm products.

Governments often use two other methods of intervention in the markets for farm products:

- Production quotas
- Subsidies

Production Quotas

In the markets for sugarbeets, tobacco leaf, and cotton (among others), governments have, from time to time, imposed production quotas. A **production quota** is an upper limit to the quantity of a good that may be produced in a specified period. To discover the effects of a production quota, let's look at what a quota does to the market for sugarbeets.

Suppose that the growers of sugarbeets want to limit total production to get a higher price. They persuade the government to introduce a production quota on sugarbeets.

The effect of the production quota depends on whether it is set below or above the equilibrium quantity. If the government introduced a production quota above the equilibrium quantity, nothing would change because sugarbeets growers would already be producing less than the quota. But a production quota set *below the equilibrium quantity* has big effects, which are

- A decrease in supply
- A rise in price
- A decrease in marginal cost
- Inefficient underproduction
- An incentive to cheat and overproduce
  Figure 6.11 illustrates these effects.

FIGURE 6.11 The Effects of a Production Quota

With no quota, growers produce 60 million tons a year and the price is $30 a ton. A production quota of 40 million tons a year restricts total production to that amount. The quantity produced decreases to 40 million tons a year, the price rises to $50 a ton, and the farmers' marginal cost falls to $20 a ton. Because marginal cost (on the supply curve) is less than marginal benefit (on the demand curve), a deadweight loss arises from the underproduction.

myeconlab   animation

A Decrease in Supply A production quota on sugarbeets decreases the supply of sugarbeets. Each grower is assigned a production limit that is less than the amount that would be produced—and supplied—without the quota. The total of the growers' limits equals the quota, and any production in excess of the quota is illegal.

The quantity supplied becomes the amount permitted by the production quota, and this quantity is fixed. The supply of sugarbeets becomes perfectly inelastic at the quantity permitted under the quota.

In Fig. 6.11, with no quota, growers would produce 60 million tons of sugarbeets a year—the market equilibrium quantity. With a production quota set at 40 million tons a year, the gray-shaded area shows the illegal region. As in the case of price ceilings and price floors, market forces and political forces are in conflict in this illegal region.

The vertical red line labeled "Quota" becomes the supply curve of sugarbeets at prices above $20 a ton.

A Rise in Price The production quota raises the price of sugarbeets. When the government sets a production quota, it leaves market forces free to determine the price. Because the quota decreases the supply of sugarbeets, it raises the price. In Fig. 6.11, with no quota, the price is $30 a ton. With a quota of 40 million tons, the price rises to $50 a ton.

A Decrease in Marginal Cost The production quota lowers the marginal cost of growing sugarbeets. Marginal cost decreases because growers produce less and stop using the resources with the highest marginal cost. Sugarbeets growers slide down their supply (and marginal cost) curves. In Fig. 6.11, marginal cost decreases to $20 a ton.

Inefficiency The production quota results in inefficient underproduction. Marginal social benefit at the quantity produced is equal to the market price, which has increased. Marginal social cost at the quantity produced has decreased and is less than the market price. So marginal social benefit exceeds marginal social cost and a deadweight loss arises.

An Incentive to Cheat and Overproduce The production quota creates an incentive for growers to cheat and produce more than their individual production limit. With the quota, the price exceeds marginal cost, so the grower can get a larger profit by producing one more unit. Of course, if all growers produce more than their assigned limit, the production quota becomes ineffective, and the price falls to the equilibrium (no quota) price.

To make the production quota effective, growers must set up a monitoring system to ensure that no one cheats and overproduces. But it is costly to set up and operate a monitoring system and it is difficult to detect and punish producers who violate their quotas.

Because of the difficulty of operating a quota, producers often lobby governments to establish a quota and provide the monitoring and punishment systems that make it work.

Subsidies

In the United States, the producers of peanuts, sugarbeets, milk, wheat, and many other farm products receive subsidies. A **subsidy** is a payment made by the government to a producer. A large and controversial Farm Bill passed by Congress in 2008 renewed and extended a wide range of subsidies.

The effects of a subsidy are similar to the effects of a tax but they go in the opposite directions. These effects are

- An increase in supply
- A fall in price and increase in quantity produced
- An increase in marginal cost
- Payments by government to farmers
- Inefficient overproduction

Figure 6.12 illustrates the effects of a subsidy to peanut farmers.

An Increase in Supply In Fig. 6.12, with no subsidy, the demand curve D and the supply curve S determine the price of peanuts at $40 a ton and the quantity of peanuts at 40 million tons a year.

Suppose that the government introduces a subsidy of $20 a ton to peanut farmers. A subsidy is like a negative tax. A tax is equivalent to an increase in cost, so a subsidy is equivalent to a decrease in cost. The subsidy brings an increase in supply.

To determine the position of the new supply curve, we subtract the subsidy from the farmers' minimum supply-price. In Fig. 6.12, with no subsidy, farmers are willing to offer 40 million tons a year at a price of $40 a ton. With a subsidy of $20 a ton, they will offer 40 million tons a year if the price is as low as $20 a ton. The supply curve shifts to the red curve labeled $S - subsidy$.

A Fall in Price and Increase in Quantity Produced The subsidy lowers the price of peanuts and increases the quantity produced. In Fig. 6.12, equilibrium occurs where the new supply curve intersects the demand curve at a price of $30 a ton and a quantity of 60 million tons a year.

An Increase in Marginal Cost The subsidy lowers the price paid by consumers but increases the marginal cost of producing peanuts. Marginal cost increases because farmers grow more peanuts, which means that they must begin to use some resources that are less ideal for growing peanuts. Peanut farmers slide up their supply (and marginal cost) curves. In Fig. 6.12, marginal cost increases to $50 a ton.

Payments by Government to Farmers The government pays a subsidy to peanut farmers on each ton of peanuts produced. In this example, farmers increase production to 60 million tons a year and receive a

FIGURE 6.12   The Effects of a Subsidy

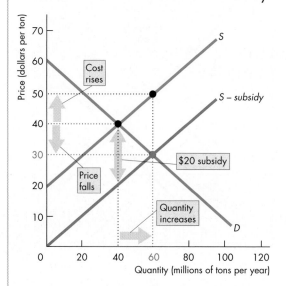

With no subsidy, farmers produce 40 million tons a year at $40 a ton. A subsidy of $20 a ton shifts the supply curve rightward to *S – subsidy*. The equilibrium quantity increases to 60 million tons a year, the price falls to $30 a ton, and the price plus the subsidy received by farmers rises to $50 a ton. In the new equilibrium, marginal cost (on the supply curve) exceeds marginal benefit (on the demand curve) and the subsidy results in inefficient overproduction.

myeconlab animation ◆

subsidy of $20 a ton. So peanut farmers receive payments from the government that total $1,200 million a year.

Inefficient Overproduction The subsidy results in inefficient overproduction. At the quantity produced with the subsidy, marginal social benefit is equal to the market price, which has fallen. Marginal social cost has increased and it exceeds the market price. Because marginal social cost exceeds marginal social benefit, the increased production brings inefficiency.

Subsidies spill over to the rest of the world. Because a subsidy lowers the domestic market price, subsidized farmers will offer some of their output for sale on the world market. The increase in supply on the world market lowers the price in the rest of the world. Faced with lower prices, farmers in other countries decrease production and receive smaller revenues.

Farm Subsidies Today
Rich High-Cost Farmers the Winners

Farm subsidies are a major obstacle to achieving an efficient use of resources in the global markets for farm products and are a source of tension between the United States, Europe, and developing nations.

The United States and the European Union are the world's two largest and richest economies. They also pay their farmers the biggest subsidies, which create inefficient overproduction of food in these rich economies.

At the same time, U.S. and European subsidies make it more difficult for farmers in the developing nations of Africa, Asia, and Central and South America to compete in global food markets. Farmers in these countries can often produce at a lower opportunity cost than the U.S. and European farmers.

Two rich countries, Australia and New Zealand, have stopped subsidizing farmers. The result has been an improvement in the efficiency of farming in these countries. New Zealand is so efficient at producing lamb and dairy products that it has been called the Saudi Arabia of milk (an analogy with Saudi Arabia's huge oil reserve and production.)

International opposition to U.S. and European farm subsidies is strong. Opposition to farm subsidies inside the United States and Europe is growing, but it isn't as strong as the pro-farm lobby, so don't expect an early end to these subsidies.

Review Quiz ◆

1 Summarize the effects of a production quota on the market price and the quantity produced.
2 Explain why a production quota is inefficient.
3 Explain why a voluntary production quota is difficult to operate.
4 Summarize the effects of a subsidy on the market price and the quantity produced.
5 Explain why a subsidy is inefficient.

  Work Study Plan 6.4 and get instant feedback.

Governments intervene in some markets by making it illegal to trade in a good. Let's now see how these markets work.

Markets for Illegal Goods

The markets for many goods and services are regulated, and buying and selling some goods is illegal. The best-known examples of such goods are drugs, such as marijuana, cocaine, ecstasy, and heroin.

Despite the fact that these drugs are illegal, trade in them is a multibillion-dollar business. This trade can be understood by using the same economic model and principles that explain trade in legal goods. To study the market for illegal goods, we're first going to examine the prices and quantities that would prevail if these goods were not illegal. Next, we'll see how prohibition works. Then we'll see how a tax might be used to limit the consumption of these goods.

A Free Market for a Drug

Figure 6.13 shows the market for a drug. The demand curve, D, shows that, other things remaining the same, the lower the price of the drug, the larger is the quantity of the drug demanded. The supply curve, S, shows that, other things remaining the same, the lower the price of the drug, the smaller is the quantity supplied. If the drug were not illegal, the quantity bought and sold would be Q_C and the price would be P_C.

A Market for an Illegal Drug

When a good is illegal, the cost of trading in the good increases. By how much the cost increases and who bears the cost depend on the penalties for violating the law and the degree to which the law is enforced. The larger the penalties and the better the policing, the higher are the costs. Penalties might be imposed on sellers, buyers, or both.

Penalties on Sellers Drug dealers in the United States face large penalties if their activities are detected. For example, a marijuana dealer could pay a $200,000 fine and serve a 15-year prison term. A heroin dealer could pay a $500,000 fine and serve a 20-year prison term. These penalties are part of the cost of supplying illegal drugs, and they bring a decrease in supply—a leftward shift in the supply curve. To determine the new supply curve, we add the cost of breaking the law to the minimum price that drug dealers are willing to accept. In Fig. 6.13, the cost of breaking the law by selling drugs (CBL) is added to the minimum price that

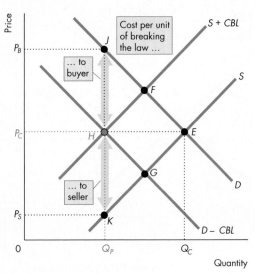

FIGURE 6.13   A Market for an Illegal Good

The demand curve for drugs is D, and the supply curve is S. If drugs are not illegal, the quantity bought and sold is Q_C at a price of P_C—point E. If selling drugs is illegal, the cost of breaking the law by selling drugs (CBL) is added to the minimum supply-price and supply decreases to $S + CBL$. The market moves to point F. If buying drugs is illegal, the cost of breaking the law is subtracted from the maximum price that buyers are willing to pay, and demand decreases to $D - CBL$. The market moves to point G. With both buying and selling illegal, the supply curve and the demand curve shift and the market moves to point H. The market price remains at P_C, but the market price plus the penalty for buying rises—point J—and the market price minus the penalty for selling falls—point K.

myeconlab   animation

dealers will accept and the supply curve shifts leftward to $S + CBL$. If penalties were imposed only on sellers, the market equilibrium would move from point E to point F.

Penalties on Buyers In the United States, it is illegal to *possess* drugs such as marijuana, cocaine, ecstasy, and heroin. Possession of marijuana can bring a prison term of 1 year, and possession of heroin can bring a prison term of 2 years. Penalties fall on buyers, and the cost of breaking the law must be subtracted from the value of the good to determine the maximum price buyers are willing to pay for the drugs. Demand decreases, and the demand curve shifts leftward. In Fig. 6.13, the demand curve shifts to $D - CBL$. If penalties were imposed only on buyers, the market equilibrium would move from point E to point G.

Penalties on Both Sellers and Buyers

If penalties are imposed on both sellers *and* buyers, both supply and demand decrease and both the supply curve and the demand curve shift. In Fig. 6.13, the costs of breaking the law are the same for both buyers and sellers, so both curves shift leftward by the same amount. The market equilibrium moves to point H. The market price remains at the competitive market price P_C, but the quantity bought decreases to Q_P. Buyers pay P_C plus the cost of breaking the law, which equals P_B. Sellers receive P_C minus the cost of breaking the law, which equals P_S.

The larger the penalties and the greater the degree of law enforcement, the larger is the decrease in demand and/or supply. If the penalties are heavier on sellers, the supply curve shifts farther than the demand curve and the market price rises above P_C. If the penalties are heavier on buyers, the demand curve shifts farther than the supply curve and the market price falls below P_C. In the United States, the penalties on sellers are larger than those on buyers, so the quantity of drugs traded decreases and the market price increases compared with a free market.

With high enough penalties and effective law enforcement, it is possible to decrease demand and/or supply to the point at which the quantity bought is zero. But in reality, such an outcome is unusual. It does not happen in the United States in the case of illegal drugs. The key reason is the high cost of law enforcement and insufficient resources for the police to achieve effective enforcement. Because of this situation, some people suggest that drugs (and other illegal goods) should be legalized and sold openly but also taxed at a high rate in the same way that legal drugs such as alcohol are taxed. How would such an arrangement work?

Legalizing and Taxing Drugs

From your study of the effects of taxes, it is easy to see that the quantity bought of a drug could be decreased if the drug was legalized and taxed. Imposing a sufficiently high tax could decrease the supply, raise the price, and achieve the same decrease in the quantity bought as does a prohibition on drugs. The government would collect a large tax revenue.

Illegal Trading to Evade the Tax It is likely that an extremely high tax rate would be needed to cut the quantity of drugs bought to the level prevailing with a prohibition. It is also likely that many drug dealers and consumers would try to cover up their activities to evade the tax. If they did act in this way, they would face the cost of breaking the law—the tax law. If the penalty for tax law violation is as severe and as effectively policed as drug-dealing laws, the analysis we've already conducted applies also to this case. The quantity of drugs bought would depend on the penalties for law breaking and on the way in which the penalties are assigned to buyers and sellers.

Taxes Versus Prohibition: Some Pros and Cons Which is more effective: prohibition or taxes? In favor of taxes and against prohibition is the fact that the tax revenue can be used to make law enforcement more effective. It can also be used to run a more effective education campaign against illegal drug use. In favor of prohibition and against taxes is the fact that prohibition sends a signal that might influence preferences, decreasing the demand for illegal drugs. Also, some people intensely dislike the idea of the government profiting from trade in harmful substances.

Review Quiz

1 How does the imposition of a penalty for selling an illegal drug influence demand, supply, price, and the quantity of the drug consumed?

2 How does the imposition of a penalty for possessing an illegal drug influence demand, supply, price, and the quantity of the drug consumed?

3 How does the imposition of a penalty for selling *or* possessing an illegal drug influence demand, supply, price, and the quantity of the drug consumed?

4 Is there any case for legalizing drugs?

 Work Study Plan 6.5 and get instant feedback.

You now know how to use the demand and supply model to predict prices, to study government actions in markets, and to study the sources and costs of inefficiency. In *Reading Between the Lines* on pp. 146–147, you will see how to apply what you've learned to the market for gasoline and see why it is difficult for the government to lower the price in that market.

Government Actions in Gasoline Markets

Drivers, Feeling the Pinch as Diesel Tops $4 a Gallon, Demand Congressional Action

The Washington Post, April 29, 2008

A caravan of horn-honking truck drivers rolled their rigs through Washington yesterday, protesting rising gasoline costs and demanding that Congress impose caps on prices at the pump. The truckers, who formed a long column, circled the Mall about noon and blared their horns. Some spectators waved while others covered their ears. "The high price for oil is hurting our economy," said Mark Kirsch, a trucker from Myerstown, Pa., who helped organize the rally. "It's hurting middle-class people." ...

Obama Assails Lifting of Gas Tax as "Gimmick"

The Boston Globe, April 30, 2008

Barack Obama didn't back down yesterday in his opposition to a so-called gas tax holiday this summer. ... He told voters in Winston-Salem, N.C., that suspending the 18.4-cents-a-gallon federal gas tax between Memorial Day and Labor Day would save them only about $25 to $30. Some economists, he said, believe the proposal could backfire and actually raise prices by increasing demand. "We don't know that the oil companies will actually pass on the savings," he added.

Citing Oil Prices, Asia Starts Reducing Fuel Subsidies

The New York Times, November 2, 2007

Consumers in Asia are feeling the heat of skyrocketing oil prices ... as governments start rolling back subsidies that have kept costs for gasoline and other fuel artificially low. ... Retail prices of petroleum-based products like gasoline, kerosene, and diesel are highly subsidized in many Asian countries, in part to make them affordable to citizens who earn lower wages than in the developed world. ...

Essence of the Story

- Truck drivers want Congress to impose a cap on the price of gasoline to stop high prices from hurting middle-class people.

- Barack Obama opposed a temporary suspension of the 18.4-cents-a-gallon federal gas tax because it would save only $25 to $30 and because the tax cut might not lower the price of gasoline.

- In some Asian countries, the government subsidizes gasoline and other petroleum-based products to make them affordable to low-wage citizens.

Economic Analysis

- With the price of gasoline passing $4 a gallon, there is no shortage of demands for government action to lower the price.

- Truck drivers want a price cap.

- But a price cap creates a shortage, which would mean lines at the pump, wasteful driving around to find a gas station with gas for sale, and possibly a black market in gasoline.

- Figure 1 illustrates these consequences of a $3 price cap in the market for gasoline. The figure shows a shortage, the possible black market price, and the deadweight loss created.

- Another proposal is to suspend the federal gas tax. A tax cut lowers the price paid by buyers, but it increases the quantity bought and raises the price received by sellers.

- Figure 2 illustrates these consequences of a tax holiday, and the effect is tiny.

- If supply is almost perfectly inelastic (not the case shown in the figure) the buyers' price doesn't fall at all and sellers get the entire benefit of the tax cut. This possibility was raised by Senator Obama in his opposition to the tax suspension.

- What about an outright subsidy to buyers? That's what happens in China, where until mid 2008 when the price began to rise sharply, a subsidy kept the price of gas at the equivalent of $1.50 a gallon.

- The problem with a subsidy is similar to that of a tax cut. It lowers the buyers' price but it increases the quantity bought and raises the sellers' price.

- Figure 3 illustrates these consequences of a subsidy. The figure is calibrated to the market for gasoline in China, where the price is $1.50 a gallon and quantity bought is a bit more than 1 million barrels per day.

- A subsidy of $1 a gallon lowers the price to $1.50 a gallon, but sellers receive $2.50 a gallon.

- Both a tax cut and a subsidy increase the quantity of gasoline bought. Because gasoline is produced from crude oil, these actions increase the demand for crude oil, which raises its price.

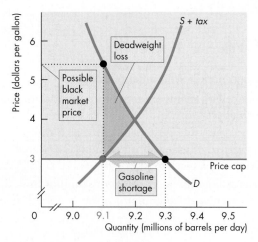

Figure 1 A price cap on gasoline

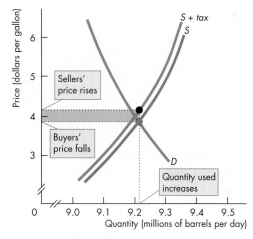

Figure 2 Summer suspension of the federal gas tax

Figure 3 Gasoline subsidy in China

147

SUMMARY

Key Points

A Housing Market With a Rent Ceiling (pp. 130–132)

- A rent ceiling that is set above the equilibrium rent has no effect.
- A rent ceiling that is set below the equilibrium rent creates a housing shortage, increased search activity, and a black market.
- A rent ceiling that is set below the equilibrium rent is inefficient and unfair.

A Labor Market With a Minimum Wage (pp. 133–135)

- A minimum wage set below the equilibrium wage rate has no effect.
- A minimum wage set above the equilibrium wage rate creates unemployment and increases the amount of time people spend searching for a job.
- A minimum wage set above the equilibrium wage rate is inefficient, unfair, and hits low-skilled young people hardest.

Taxes (pp. 135–140)

- A tax raises the price paid by buyers, but usually by less than the tax.
- The elasticity of demand and the elasticity of supply determine the share of a tax paid by buyers and sellers.

- The less elastic the demand or the more elastic the supply, the larger is the share of the tax paid by buyers.
- If demand is perfectly elastic or supply is perfectly inelastic, sellers pay the entire tax. And if demand is perfectly inelastic or supply is perfectly elastic, buyers pay the entire tax.

Production Quotas and Subsidies (pp. 141–143)

- A production quota leads to inefficient underproduction, which raises the price.
- A subsidy is like a negative tax. It lowers the price, increases the cost of production, and leads to inefficient overproduction.

Markets for Illegal Goods (pp. 144–145)

- Penalties on sellers increase the cost of selling the good and decrease the supply of the good.
- Penalties on buyers decrease their willingness to pay and decrease the demand for the good.
- Penalties on buyers and sellers decrease the quantity of the good, raise the price buyers pay, and lower the price sellers receive.
- Legalizing and taxing can achieve the same outcome as penalties on buyers and sellers.

Key Figures

Key Terms

PROBLEMS and APPLICATIONS

 Work problems 1–10 in Chapter 6 Study Plan and get instant feedback.
Work problems 11–19 as Homework, a Quiz, or a Test if assigned by your instructor.

1. The graph illustrates the market for rental housing in Townsville.

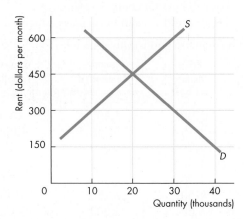

a. What are the equilibrium rent and equilibrium quantity of rental housing?

If a rent ceiling is set at $600 a month, what is
b. The quantity of housing rented?
c. The shortage of housing?

If a rent ceiling is set at $300 a month, what is
d. The quantity of housing rented?
e. The shortage of housing?
f. The maximum price that someone is willing to pay for the last unit of housing available?

2. **Capping Gasoline Prices**

The recent rise in gasoline prices has many people calling for price caps. … Price caps are a curse to consumers. … Capped prices … generate a distorted reflection of reality, causing buyers and suppliers to act in ways inconsistent with it. … By masking reality, price controls only make matters worse.

Pittsburgh Tribune-Review, September 12, 2005

If a price ceiling is set below the equilibrium price in the market for gasoline, what are its effects on
a. The quantity of gasoline supplied and the quantity demanded?
b. The quantity of gasoline sold and the shortage or surplus of gasoline?
c. The maximum price that someone is willing to pay for the last gallon of gasoline available on a black market?

d. Draw a demand and supply graph to illustrate the effects of a price ceiling set below the equilibrium price in the market for gasoline.

3. Explain the various ways in which a price ceiling on gasoline that is set below the equilibrium price would make buyers and sellers of gasoline better off or worse off. What would happen to total surplus and deadweight loss in this market?

4. The table gives the demand and supply schedules of teenage labor.

Wage rate (dollars per hour)	Quantity demanded	Quantity supplied
	(hours per month)	
4	3,000	1,000
5	2,500	1,500
6	2,000	2,000
7	1,500	2,500
8	1,000	3,000

a. What are the equilibrium wage rate and number of hours worked?
b. What is the quantity of unemployment?

If a minimum wage for teenagers is set at $5 an hour,
c. How many hours do they work?
d. How many hours of teenage labor are unemployed?

If a minimum wage for teenagers is set at $7 an hour,
e. How many hours do teenagers work and how many hours are unemployed?
f. Demand for teenage labor increases by 500 hours a month. What is the wage rate paid to teenagers and how many hours of teenage labor are unemployed?

5. **India Steps Up Pressure for Minimum Wage for Its Workers in the Gulf**

Oil-rich countries in the [Persian] Gulf, already confronted by strong labor protests, are facing renewed pressure from India to pay minimum wages for unskilled workers. The effort by India—the largest source of migrant workers in the region, with five million—is the strongest push yet by home countries to win better conditions for their citizens. …

International Herald Tribune, March 27, 2008

If the Persian Gulf countries paid a minimum wage above the equilibrium wage to Indian workers,

a. How would the market for labor be affected in the Gulf countries? Draw a supply and demand graph to illustrate your answer.

b. How would the market for labor be affected in India? Draw a supply and demand graph to illustrate your answer. [Be careful: the minimum wage is in the Gulf countries, not in India.]

c. Would migrant Indian workers be better off or worse off or unaffected by this minimum wage?

6. The table gives the demand and supply schedules for chocolate brownies.

Price (cents per brownie)	Quantity demanded (millions per day)	Quantity supplied (millions per day)
50	5	3
60	4	4
70	3	5
80	2	6
90	1	7

a. If brownies are not taxed, what is the price of a brownie and how many are bought?

b. If sellers are taxed 20¢ a brownie, what are the price and quantity bought? Who pays the tax?

c. If buyers are taxed 20¢ a brownie, what are the price and quantity bought? Who pays the tax?

7. **Luxury Tax Heavier Burden on Working Class, it would Seem**

The Omnibus Budget Reconciliation Act of 1990 … included … a stern tax on "luxury items." … In 1990 the Joint Committee on Taxation projected that the 1991 revenue yield from the luxury taxes would be $31 million. The actual yield was $16.6 million. Why? Because —surprise!—the taxation changed behavior.

The Topeka Capital-Journal, October 29, 1999

a. Would buyers or sellers of "luxury items" pay more of the luxury tax?

b. Explain why the luxury tax generated far less tax revenue than was originally anticipated.

8. **How to Take a Gas Holiday**

High fuel prices will probably keep Americans closer to home this summer, despite the gas-tax "holiday" supported by Hillary Clinton and John McCain that would shave 18 cents off every gallon of gas through Labor Day. …

Time, May 19, 2008

If the federal government removed the 18.4 cents per-gallon gas tax they currently impose,

a. Would the price of gasoline that consumers pay fall by 18.4 cents? Explain.

b. How would consumer surplus change?

9. The demand and supply schedules for rice are

Price (dollars per box)	Quantity demanded (boxes per week)	Quantity supplied (boxes per week)
1.00	3,500	500
1.10	3,250	1,000
1.20	3,000	1,500
1.30	2,750	2,000
1.40	2,500	2,500
1.50	2,250	3,000
1.60	2,000	3,500

What are the price, the marginal cost of producing rice, and the quantity produced if the government

a. Sets a production quota for rice of 2,000 boxes a week?

b. Introduces a subsidy to rice growers of $0.30 a box?

10. The figure illustrates the market for a banned substance.

What are the market price and the quantity consumed if a penalty of $20 a unit is imposed on

a. Sellers only?

b. Buyers only?

c. Both sellers and buyers?

11. **Coal Shortage at China Plants**

Chinese power plants have run short of coal, an unintended effect of government-mandated price controls—a throwback to communist central planning—to shield the public from rising global energy costs. ... Beijing has also frozen retail prices of gasoline and diesel. That helped farmers and the urban poor, but it has spurred sales of gas-guzzling luxury cars and propelled double-digit annual growth in fuel consumption.

Oil refiners say they are suffering heavy losses and some began cutting production last year, causing fuel shortages in parts of China's south.

CNN, May 20, 2008

a. Are China's price controls described in the news clip price floors or price ceilings?

b. Explain how China's price controls have created shortages or surpluses in the markets for coal, gasoline, and diesel.

c. Illustrate your answer to b graphically by using the supply and demand model.

d. Explain how China's price controls have changed consumer surplus, producer surplus, total surplus, and the deadweight loss in the markets for coal, gasoline, and diesel.

e. Illustrate your answer to d graphically by using the supply and demand model.

12. **Despite Protests, Rent Board Sets 7.25% Increase**

Rents for New York City's one million rent-stabilized apartments can increase by as much as 7.25 percent over the next two years, the city's Rent Guidelines Board voted last night. ... According to a report ... costs for the owners of rent-stabilized buildings rose by 7.8 percent in the last year. ... The rent-increase vote comes at a time of growing concern about the ability of the middle class to afford to live in New York City.

The New York Times, June 28, 2006

a. If rents for rent-stabilized apartments do not increase, how do you think the market for rental units in New York City will develop?

b. Are rent ceilings in New York City helpful to the middle class? Why or why not?

c. Explain the effect of the increase in the rent ceiling on the quantity of rent-stabilized apartments.

d. Why is rent stabilization a source of conflict between renters and owners of apartments?

13. **House Passes Increase in Minimum Wage to $7.25**

... first increase in the federal minimum wage in nearly a decade, boosting the wages of the lowest-paid American workers from $5.15 to $7.25 an hour. ... Republican leaders, backed by small-business lobbyists and restaurant groups, argued fiercely that raising the minimum wage would cripple the economy and must be accompanied by significant tax cuts for small businesses. ...

The Washington Post, January 11, 2007

a. Use a graph of the market for low-skilled labor to illustrate the effect of the increase in the minimum wage from $5.15 to $7.25 an hour on the quantity of labor employed.

b. Explain the effects of the higher minimum wage on the workers' surplus and the firms' surplus. Does the labor market become more efficient or less efficient? Explain.

c. Would a cut in the tax on the small business profits offset the effect of the higher minimum wage on employment? Explain.

d. Would a cut in the Social Security tax that small businesses pay offset the effect of the higher minimum wage on employment? Explain.

14. The demand and supply schedules for tulips are

Price (dollars per bunch)	Quantity demanded	Quantity supplied
	(bunches per week)	
10	100	40
12	90	60
14	80	80
16	70	100
18	60	120

a. If tulips are not taxed, what is the price and how many bunches are bought?

b. If tulips are taxed $6 a bunch, what are the price and quantity bought? Who pays the tax?

15. **Congress passes farm bill, defies Bush**

Congress sent the White House a huge election-year farm bill Thursday that includes a boost in farm subsidies. ... Bush has threatened to veto the $290 billion bill, saying it is fiscally irresponsible and too generous to wealthy corporate farmers in a time of record crop prices. ... $40 billion is for farm subsidies, while almost $30 billion would go to farmers to idle their land. ...

CNN, May 15, 2008

a. Why does the federal government subsidize farmers?

b. Explain how a subsidy paid to cotton farmers affects the price of cotton and the marginal cost of producing it.

c. Explain how a subsidy paid to cotton farmers affects the consumer surplus and the producer surplus from cotton. Does the subsidy make the cotton market more efficient or less efficient? Explain.

d. How would a payment to cotton farmers to idle their land influence the supply of cotton?

e. How would a payment to cotton farmers to idle their land affect the consumer surplus and the producer surplus from cotton? Explain.

16. **Cigarette Taxes, Black Markets, and Crime: Lessons from New York's 50-Year Losing Battle**

New York City now has the highest cigarette taxes in the country—a combined state and local tax rate of $3.00 per pack. Consumers have responded by turning to the city's bustling black market and other low-tax sources of cigarettes. During the four months following the recent tax hikes, sales of taxed cigarettes in the city fell by more than 50 percent. ... [H]igh taxes have created a thriving illegal market for cigarettes in the city. That market has diverted billions of dollars from legitimate businesses and governments to criminals. ...

Cato Institute, February 6, 2003

a. How has the market for cigarettes in New York City responded to the high cigarette taxes?

b. How does the emergence of a black market impact the elasticity of demand in a legal market?

c. Why might an increase in the tax rate actually cause a decrease in the tax revenue?

17. Study *Reading Between the Lines* (pp. 146–147) about the market for gasoline.

a. Explain to truck drivers why a cap on the price of gasoline would hurt middle class people more than the high price of gasoline hurts.

b. Explain why Barack Obama is right about the effects of a temporary suspension of the federal gas tax.

c. Explain why it is inefficient for Asian governments to subsidize gasoline.

18. On December 31, 1776, Rhode Island established wage controls to limit wages to 70¢ a day for carpenters and 42¢ a day for tailors.

a. Are these wage controls a price ceiling or a price floor? Why might they have been introduced?

b. If these wage controls are effective, would you expect to see a surplus or a shortage of carpenters and tailors?

19. The table gives the demand and supply schedules for an illegal drug.

Price (dollars per unit)	Quantity demanded	Quantity supplied
	(units per day)	
50	500	300
60	400	400
70	300	500
80	200	600
90	100	700

a. If there are no penalties on buying or selling the drug, what is the price and how many units are consumed?

b. If the penalty on sellers is $20 a unit, what are the price and quantity consumed?

c. If the penalty on buyers is $20 a unit, what are the price and quantity consumed?

20. Use the links in MyEconLab (Chapter Resources, Chapter 6, Web links) to get information about living wage campaigns and the Harvard Living Wage Campaign.

a. What is the campaign for a living wage?

b. How would you distinguish the minimum wage from a living wage?

c. If the Living Wage Campaign succeeds in raising the wage rate above the equilibrium wage rate, how would the living wage affect the quantity of labor employed and the amount of unemployment?

d. Would a living wage set above the equilibrium wage rate be efficient? Would it be fair?

21. Use the links in MyEconLab (Chapter Resources, Chapter 6, Web links) to get information about production quotas on sugar in Europe. Why do you think the European nations assign production quotas for sugar? If the European sugar quotas are less than the equilibrium quantities, who benefits from the quotas? Who loses from the production quotas?

7 ◆ Global Markets in Action

After studying this chapter, you will be able to:

- Explain how markets work with international trade
- Identify the gains from international trade and its winners and losers
- Explain the effects of international trade barriers
- Explain and evaluate arguments used to justify restricting international trade

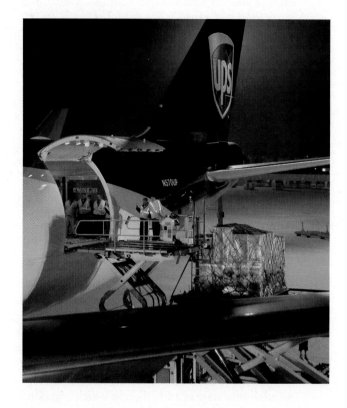

iPods, Wii games, and Nike shoes are just three of the items you might buy that are not produced in the United States. In fact, most of the goods that you buy are produced abroad, often in Asia, and transported here in container ships or cargo jets. And it's not just goods produced abroad that you buy—it is services too. When you make a technical support call, most likely you'll be talking with someone in India, or to a voice recognition system that was programmed in India. Satellites or fiber cables will carry your conversation along with huge amounts of other voice messages, video images, and data.

All these activities are part of the globalization process that is having a profound effect on our lives. Globalization is controversial and generates heated debate. Many Americans want to know how we can compete with people whose wages are a fraction of our own.

Why do we go to such lengths to trade and communicate with others in faraway places? You will find some answers in this chapter. And in *Reading Between the Lines* at the end of the chapter, you can apply what you've learned and examine the effects of a tariff on shoes—not designer shoes, but lower-priced and children's shoes.

153

How Global Markets Work

Because we trade with people in other countries, the goods and services that we can buy and consume are not limited by what we can produce. The goods and services that we buy from other countries are our **imports**; and the goods and services that we sell to people in other countries are our **exports**.

International Trade Today

Global trade today is enormous. In 2008, global exports and imports were $35 trillion, which is more than half of the value of global production. The United States is the world's largest international trader and accounts for 10 percent of world exports and 15 percent of world imports. Germany and China, which rank 2 and 3 behind the United States, lag by a large margin.

In 2008, total U.S. exports were $1.8 trillion, which is about 13 percent of the value of U.S. production. Total U.S. imports were $2.5 trillion, which is about 18 percent of total expenditure in the United States.

We trade both goods and services. In 2008, exports of services were about 30 percent of total exports and imports of services were about 16 percent of total imports.

What Drives International Trade?

Comparative advantage is the fundamental force that drives international trade. Comparative advantage (see Chapter 2, p. 40) is a situation in which a person can perform an activity or produce a good or service at a lower opportunity cost than anyone else. This same idea applies to nations. We can define *national comparative advantage* as a situation in which a nation can perform an activity or produce a good or service at a lower opportunity cost than any other nation.

The opportunity cost of producing a T-shirt is lower in China than in the United States, so China has a comparative advantage in producing T-shirts. The opportunity cost of producing an airplane is lower in the United States than in China, so the United States has a comparative advantage in producing airplanes.

You saw in Chapter 2 how Liz and Joe reap gains from trade by specializing in the production of the good at which they have a comparative advantage and trading. Both are better off.

Items Most Traded by the United States Trading Services for Oil

The figure shows the five largest exports and imports for the United States. Services top the list of exports and oil is the largest import by a large margin.

The services that we export are banking, insurance, business consulting, and other private services. Airplanes are the largest category of goods that we export.

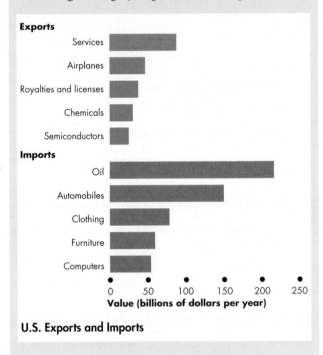

U.S. Exports and Imports

This same principle applies to trade among nations. Because China has a comparative advantage at producing T-shirts and the United States has a comparative advantage at producing airplanes, the people of both countries can gain from specialization and trade. China can buy airplanes from the United States at a lower opportunity cost than that at which Chinese firms can produce them. And Americans can buy T-shirts from China for a lower opportunity cost than that at which U.S. firms can produce them. Also, through international trade, Chinese producers can get higher prices for their T-shirts and Boeing can sell airplanes for a higher price. Both countries gain from international trade.

Let's now illustrate the gains from trade that we've just described by studying demand and supply in the global markets for T-shirts and airplanes.

Why the United States Imports T-Shirts

The United States imports T-shirts because the rest of the world has a comparative advantage in producing T-shirts. Figure 7.1 illustrates how this comparative advantage generates international trade and how trade affects the price of a T-shirt and the quantities produced and bought.

The demand curve D_{US} and the supply curve S_{US} show the demand and supply in the U.S. domestic market only. The demand curve tells us the quantity of T-shirts that Americans are willing to buy at various prices. The supply curve tells us the quantity of T-shirts that U.S. garment makers are willing to sell at various prices—that is, the quantity supplied at each price when all T-shirts sold in the United States are produced in the United States.

Figure 7.1(a) shows what the U.S. T-shirt market would be like with no international trade. The price

of a shirt would be $8 and 40 million shirts a year would be produced by U.S. garment makers and bought by U.S. consumers.

Figure 7.1(b) shows the market for T-shirts with international trade. Now the price of a T-shirt is determined in the world market, not the U.S. domestic market. The world price is less than $8 a T-shirt, which means that the rest of the world has a comparative advantage in producing T-shirts. The world price line shows the world price at $5 a shirt.

The U.S demand curve, D_{US}, tells us that at $5 a shirt, Americans buy 60 million shirts a year. The U.S. supply curve, S_{US}, tells us that at $5 a shirt, U.S. garment makers produce 20 million T-shirts a year. To buy 60 million T-shirts when only 20 million are produced in the United States, we must import T-shirts from the rest of the world. The quantity of T-shirts imported is 40 million a year.

FIGURE 7.1   A Market With Imports

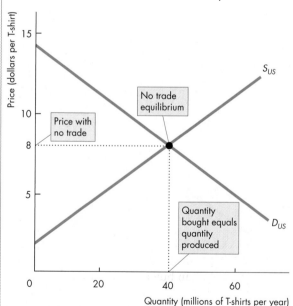

(a) Equilibrium with no international trade

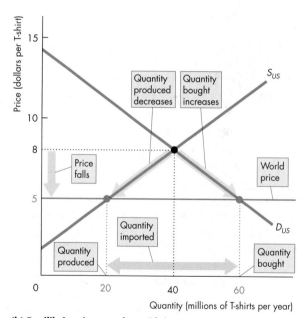

(b) Equilibrium in a market with imports

Part (a) shows the U.S. market for T-shirts with no international trade. The U.S. domestic demand curve D_{US} and U.S. domestic supply curve S_{US} determine the price of a T-shirt at $8 and the quantity of T-shirts produced and bought in the United States at 40 million a year.

Part (b) shows the U.S. market for T-shirts with interna-

tional trade. World demand and world supply determine the world price, which is $5 per T-shirt. The price in the U.S. market falls to $5 a shirt. U.S. purchases of T-shirts increases to 60 million a year, and U.S. production of T-shirts decreases to 20 million a year. The United States imports 40 million T-shirts a year.

Why the United States Exports Airplanes

Figure 7.2 illustrates international trade in airplanes. The demand curve D_{US} and the supply curve S_{US} show the demand and supply in the U.S. domestic market only. The demand curve tells us the quantity of airplanes that U.S. airlines are willing to buy at various prices. The supply curve tells us the quantity of airplanes that U.S. aircraft makers are willing to sell at various prices.

Figure 7.2(a) shows what the U.S. airplane market would be like with no international trade. The price of an airplane would be $100 million and 400 airplanes a year would be produced by U.S. aircraft makers and bought by U.S. airlines.

Figure 7.2(b) shows the U.S. airplane market with international trade. Now the price of an airplane is determined in the world market and the world price is higher than $100 million, which means that the United States has a comparative advantage in produc-

ing airplanes. The world price line shows the world price at $150 million.

The U.S. demand curve, D_{US}, tells us that at $150 million an airplane, U.S. airlines buy 200 airplanes a year. The U.S. supply curve, S_{US}, tells us that at $150 million an airplane, U.S. aircraft makers produce 700 airplanes a year. The quantity produced in the United States (700 a year) minus the quantity purchased by U.S. airlines (200 a year) is the quantity of airplanes exported, which is 500 airplanes a year.

Review Quiz

1 Describe the situation in the market for a good or service that the United States imports.
2 Describe the situation in the market for a good or service that the United States exports.

myeconlab Work Study Plan 7.1 and get instant feedback.

FIGURE 7.2 A Market With Exports

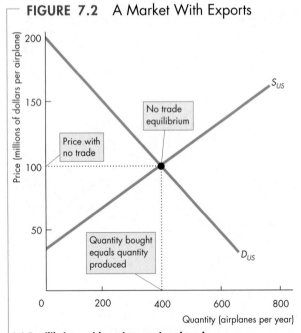

(a) Equilibrium without international trade

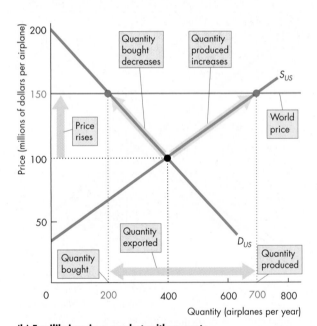

(b) Equilibrium in a market with exports

In part (a), the U.S. market with no international trade, the U.S. domestic demand curve D_{US} and the U.S. domestic supply curve S_{US} determine the price of an airplane at $100 million and 400 airplanes are produced and bought each year.

In part (b), the U.S. market with international trade,

world demand and world supply determine the world price, which is $150 million per airplane. The price in the U.S. market rises. U.S. airplane production increases to 700 a year, and U.S. purchases of airplanes decrease to 200 a year. The United States exports 500 airplanes a year.

myeconlab animation

Winners, Losers, and the Net Gain from Trade

International trade has winners but it also has losers. That's why you often hear people complaining about international competition. We're now going to see who wins and who loses from international trade. You will then be able to understand who complains about international competition and why. You will learn why we hear producers complaining about cheap foreign imports. You will also see why we never hear consumers of imported goods and services complaining and why we never hear exporters complaining except when they want greater access to foreign markets.

Gains and Losses from Imports

We measure the gains and losses from imports by examining their effect on consumer surplus, producer surplus, and total surplus. The winners are those whose surplus increases and the losers are those whose surplus decreases.

Figure 7.3(a) shows what consumer surplus and producer surplus would be with no international trade in T-shirts. U.S. domestic demand, D_{US}, and U.S. domestic supply, S_{US}, determine the price and quantity. The green area shows consumer surplus and the blue area shows producer surplus. Total surplus is the sum of consumer surplus and producer surplus.

Figure 7.3(b) shows how these surpluses change when the U.S. market opens to imports. The U.S. price falls to the world price. The quantity bought increases to the quantity demanded at the world price and consumer surplus expands from A to the larger green area $A + B + D$. The quantity produced in the United States decreases to the quantity supplied at the world price and producer surplus shrinks to the smaller blue area C.

Part of the gain in consumer surplus, the area B, is a loss of producer surplus—a redistribution of total surplus. But the other part of the increase in consumer

FIGURE 7.3   Gains and Losses in a Market With Imports

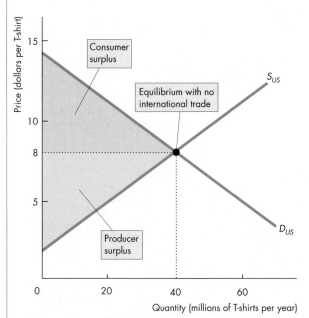

(a) Consumer surplus and producer surplus with no international trade

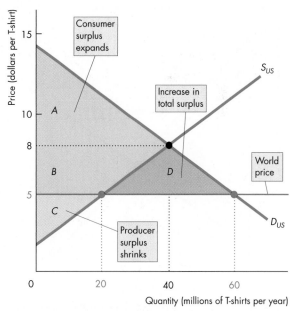

(b) Gains and losses from imports

In part (a), with no international trade, the green area shows the consumer surplus and the blue area shows the producer surplus.

In part (b), with international trade, the price falls to the world price of $5 a shirt. Consumer surplus expands to area $A + B + D$. Producer surplus shrinks to area C. Area B is a transfer of surplus from producers to consumers. Area D is an increase in total surplus—the gain from imports.

surplus, the area *D*, is a net gain. This increase in total surplus results from the lower price and increased purchases and is the gain from imports.

Gains and Losses from Exports

We measure the gains and losses from exports just like we measured those from imports, by their effect on consumer surplus, producer surplus, and total surplus.

Figure 7.4(a) shows what the consumer surplus and producer surplus would be with no international trade. Domestic demand, D_{US}, and domestic supply, S_{US}, determine the price and quantity. The green area shows consumer surplus and the blue area shows producer surplus. The two surpluses sum to total surplus.

Figure 7.4(b) shows how the consumer surplus and producer surplus change when the good is exported. The price rises to the world price. The quantity bought decreases to the quantity demanded at the world price and the consumer surplus shrinks to the green area *A*. The quantity produced increases

to the quantity supplied at the world price and the producer surplus expands from the blue area *C* to the larger blue area *B* + *C* + *D*.

Part of the gain of producer surplus, the area *B*, is a loss in consumer surplus—a redistribution of the total surplus. But the other part of the increase in producer surplus, the area *D*, is a net gain. This increase in total surplus results from the higher price and increased production and is the gain from exports.

Review Quiz

1 How is the gain from imports distributed between consumers and domestic producers?
2 How is the gain from exports distributed between consumers and domestic producers?
3 Why is the net gain from international trade positive?

myeconlab   Work Study Plan 7.2 and get instant feedback.

FIGURE 7.4   Gains and Losses in a Market With Exports

(a) **Consumer surplus and producer surplus with no international trade**

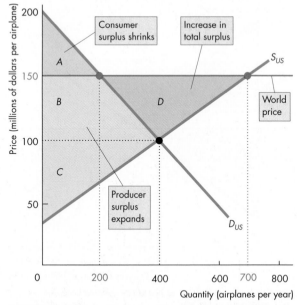

(b) **Gains and losses from exports**

In part (a), the U.S. market with no international trade, the green area shows the consumer surplus and the blue area shows the producer surplus. In part (b), the U.S. market with international trade, the price rises to the world price.

Consumer surplus shrinks to area *A*. Producer surplus expands to area *B* + *C* + *D*. Area *B* is a transfer of surplus from consumers to producers. Area *D* is an increase in total surplus—the gain from exports.

 myeconlab animation

◆ International Trade Restrictions

Governments use four sets of tools to influence international trade and protect domestic industries from foreign competition. They are

- Tariffs
- Import quotas
- Other import barriers
- Export subsidies

Tariffs

A **tariff** is a tax on a good that is imposed by the importing country when an imported good crosses its international boundary. For example, the government of India imposes a 100 percent tariff on wine imported from California. So when an Indian imports a $10 bottle of Californian wine, he pays the Indian government a $10 import duty.

The temptation for governments to impose tariffs is a strong one. First, they provide revenue to the government. Second, they enable the government to satisfy the self-interest of the people who earn their incomes in the import-competing industries. But as you will see, tariffs and other restrictions on free international trade decrease the gains from trade and are not in the social interest. Let's see why.

The Effects of a Tariff To see the effects of a tariff, let's return to the example in which the United States imports T-shirts. With free trade, the T-shirts are imported and sold at the world price. Then, under pressure from U.S. garment makers, the U.S. government imposes a tariff on imported T-shirts. Buyers of T-shirts must now pay the world price plus the tariff. Several consequences follow and Fig. 7.5 illustrates them.

Figure 7.5(a) shows the situation with free international trade. The United States produces 20 million

FIGURE 7.5 The Effects of a Tariff

(a) Free trade

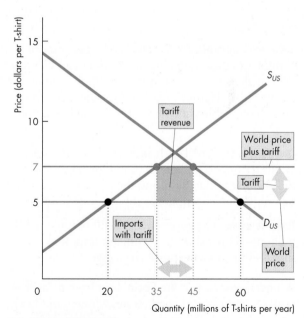

(b) Market with tariff

The world price of a T-shirt is $5. With free trade in part (a), Americans buy 60 million T-shirts a year. U.S. garment makers produce 20 million T-shirts a year and the United States imports 40 million a year.

With a tariff of $2 per T-shirt in part (b), the price in

the U.S. market rises to $7 a T-shirt. U.S. production increases, U.S. purchases decrease, and the quantity imported decreases. The U.S. government collects a tariff revenue of $2 on each T-shirt imported, which is shown by the purple rectangle.

T-shirts a year and imports 40 million a year at the world price of $5 a shirt. Figure 7.5(b) shows what happens with a tariff set at $2 per T-shirt. The following changes occur in the market for T-shirts:

- The price of a T-shirt in the United States rises by $2.
- The quantity of T-shirts bought in the United States decreases.
- The quantity of T-shirts produced in the United States increases.
- The quantity of T-shirts imported into the United States decreases.
- The U.S. government collects a tariff revenue.

Rise in Price of a T-Shirt To buy a T-shirt, Americans must pay the world price plus the tariff, so the price of a T-shirt rises by $2 to $7. Figure 7.5(b) shows the new domestic price line, which lies $2 above the world price line.

Decrease in Purchases The higher price of a T-shirt brings a decrease in the quantity demanded along the demand curve. Figure 7.5(b) shows the decrease from 60 million T-shirts a year at $5 a shirt to 45 million a year at $7 a shirt.

Increase in Domestic Production The higher price of a T-shirt stimulates domestic production, and U.S. garment makers increase the quantity supplied along the supply curve. Figure 7.5(b) shows the increase from 20 million T-shirts at $5 a shirt to 35 million a year at $7 a shirt.

Decrease in Imports T-shirt imports decrease by 30 million, from 40 million to 10 million a year. Both the decrease in purchases and the increase in domestic production contribute to this decrease in imports.

Tariff Revenue The government's tariff revenue is $20 million—$2 per shirt on 10 million imported shirts—shown by the purple rectangle.

Winners, Losers, and the Social Loss from a Tariff A tariff on an imported good creates winners and losers and a social loss. When the U.S. government imposes a tariff on an imported good,

- U.S. consumers of the good lose.
- U.S. producers of the good gain.
- U.S. consumers lose more than U.S. producers gain.
- Society loses: a deadweight loss arises.

U.S. Consumers of the Good Lose Because the price of a T-shirt in the United States rises, the quantity of T-shirts demanded decreases. The combination of a higher price and smaller quantity bought decreases consumer surplus—the loss to U.S. consumers that arises from a tariff.

U.S. Producers of the Good Gain Because the price of an imported T-shirt rises by the amount of the tariff, U.S. T-shirt producers are now able to sell their T-shirts for the world price plus the tariff. At the higher price, the quantity of T-shirts supplied by U.S. producers increases. The combination of a higher price and larger quantity produced increases producer surplus—the gain to U.S. producers from the tariff.

U.S. Consumers Lose More Than U.S. Producers Gain Consumer surplus decreases for four reasons: Some becomes producer surplus, some is lost in a higher cost of production (domestic producers have higher costs than foreign producers), some is lost because imports decrease, and some goes to the government as tariff revenue. Figure 7.6 shows these sources of lost consumer surplus.

Figure 7.6(a) shows the consumer surplus and producer surplus with free international trade in T-shirts. Figure 7.6(b) shows the consumer surplus and producer surplus with a $2 tariff on imported T-shirts. By comparing Fig. 7.6(b) with Fig. 7.6(a), you can see how a tariff changes these surpluses.

Consumer surplus—the green area—shrinks. The decrease in consumer surplus is made up of four parts. First, some of the consumer surplus is transferred to producers. The blue area *B* represents this loss (and gain of producer surplus). Second, part of the consumer surplus is lost in the higher cost of domestic production. The gray area *C* shows this loss. Third, some of the consumer surplus is transferred to the government. The purple area *D* shows this loss (and gain of government revenue). Fourth, some of the consumer surplus is lost because imports decrease. The gray area *E* shows this loss.

Society Loses: A Deadweight Loss Arises Some of the loss of consumer surplus is transferred to producers and some is transferred to the government and spent on government programs that people value. But the increase in production cost and the loss from decreased imports is transferred to no one: It is a social loss—a deadweight loss. The gray areas labeled *C* and *E* represent this deadweight loss. Total surplus decreases by the area *C* + *E*.

FIGURE 7.6 The Winners and Losers from a Tariff

(a) Free trade

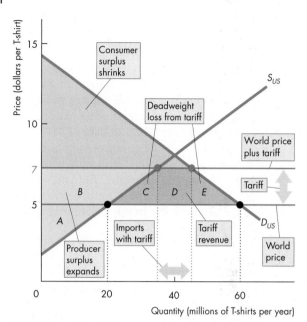

(b) Market with tariff

The world price of a T-shirt is $5. In part (a), with free trade, the United States imports 40 million T-shirts. Consumer surplus, producer surplus, and the gains from free trade are as large as possible.

In part (b), a tariff of $2 per T-shirt raises the U.S. price

of a T-shirt to $7. The quantity imported decreases. Consumer surplus shrinks by the areas *B*, *C*, *D*, and *E*. Producer surplus expands by area *B*. The government's tariff revenue is area *D*, and the tariff creates a deadweight loss equal to the area *C* + *E*.

myeconlab   animation

U.S. Tariffs
Almost Gone

The Smoot-Hawley Act, which was passed in 1930, took U.S. tariffs to a peak average rate of 20 percent in 1933. (One third of imports was subject to a 60 percent tariff.) The **General Agreement on Tariffs and Trade (GATT)**, was established in 1947. Since then tariffs have fallen in a series of negotiating rounds, the most significant of which are identified in the figure. Tariffs are now as low as they have ever been but import quotas and other trade barriers persist.

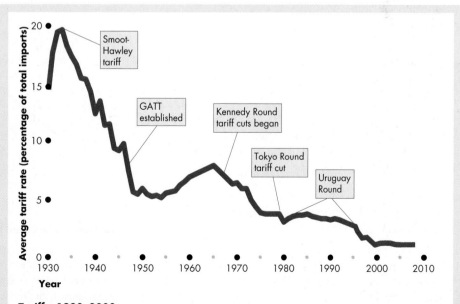

Tariffs: 1930–2008

Sources of data: U.S. Bureau of the Census, *Historical Statistics of the United States, Colonial Times to 1970*, Bicentennial Edition, Part 1 (Washington, D.C., 1975); Series U-212: updated from *Statistical Abstract of the United States*: various editions.

Import Quotas

We now look at the second tool for restricting trade: import quotas. An **import quota** is a restriction that limits the maximum quantity of a good that may be imported in a given period.

Most countries impose import quotas on a wide range of items. The United States imposes them on food products such as sugar and bananas and manufactured goods such as textiles and paper.

Import quotas enable the government to satisfy the self-interest of the people who earn their incomes in the import-competing industries. But you will discover that like a tariff, an import quota decreases the gains from trade and is not in the social interest.

The Effects of an Import Quota The effects of an import quota are similar to those of a tariff. The price rises, the quantity bought decreases, and the quantity produced in the United States increases. Figure 7.7 illustrates the effects.

Figure 7.7(a) shows the situation with free international trade. Figure 7.7(b) shows what happens with an import quota of 10 million T-shirts a year. The U.S. supply curve of T-shirts becomes the domestic supply curve, S_{US}, plus the quantity that the import quota permits. So the supply curve becomes S_{US} + *quota*. The price of a T-shirt rises to $7, the quantity of T-shirts bought in the United States decreases to 45 million a year, the quantity of T-shirts produced in the United States increases to 35 million a year, and the quantity of T-shirts imported into the United States decreases to the quota quantity of 10 million a year. All the effects of this quota are identical to the effects of a $2 per shirt tariff, as you can check in Fig. 7.6(b).

Winners, Losers, and the Social Loss from an Import Quota An import quota creates winners and losers that are similar to those of a tariff but with an interesting difference.

FIGURE 7.7   The Effects of an Import Quota

(a) Free trade

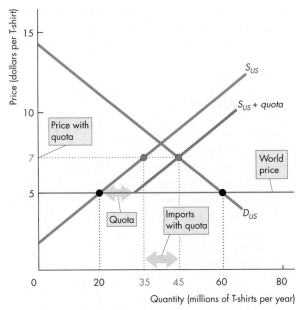

(b) Market with import quota

With free international trade, in part (a), Americans buy 60 million T-shirts at the world price. The United States produces 20 million T-shirts and imports 40 million a year. With an import quota of 10 million T-shirts a year, in part (b),

the supply of T-shirts in the United States is shown by the curve S_{US} + *quota*. The price in the United States rises to $7 a T-shirt. U.S. production increases, U.S. purchases decrease, and the quantity of T-shirts imported decreases.

When the government imposes an import quota,

- U.S. consumers of the good lose.
- U.S. producers of the good gain.
- Importers of the good gain.
- Society loses: a deadweight loss arises.

Figure 7.8 shows these gains and losses from a quota. By comparing Fig. 7.8(b) with a quota and Fig. 7.8(a) with free trade, you can see how an import quota of 10 million T-shirts a year changes the consumer and producer surpluses.

Consumer surplus—the green area—shrinks. This decrease is the loss to consumers from the import quota. The decrease in consumer surplus is made up of four parts. First, some of the consumer surplus is transferred to producers. The blue area *B* represents this loss of consumer surplus (and gain of producer surplus). Second, part of the consumer surplus is lost because the domestic cost of production is higher

than the world price. The gray area *C* represents this loss. Third, part of the consumer surplus is transferred to importers who buy T-shirts for $5 (the world price) and sell them for $7 (the U.S. domestic price). The two blue areas *D* represent this loss of consumer surplus and profit for importers. Fourth, part of the consumer surplus is lost because imports decrease. The gray area *E* represents this loss.

The losses of consumer surplus from the higher cost of production and the decrease in imports is a social loss—a deadweight loss. The gray areas labeled *C* and *E* represent this deadweight loss. Total surplus decreases by the area *C* + *E*.

You can now see the one difference between a quota and a tariff. A tariff brings in revenue for the government while a quota brings a profit for the importers. All the other effects are the same, provided the quota is set at the same quantity of imports that results from the tariff.

FIGURE 7.8   The Winners and Losers from an Import Quota

(a) Free trade

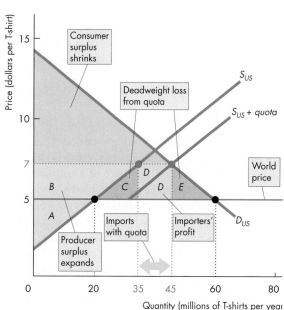

(b) Market with import quota

The world price of a T-shirt is $5. In part (a), with free trade, the United States produces 20 million T-shirts a year and imports 40 million T-shirts. Consumer surplus, producer surplus, and the gain from free international trade (darker green area) are as large as possible.

In part (b), the import quota raises the price of a T-shirt to $7. The quantity imported decreases. Consumer surplus shrinks by the areas *B*, *C*, *D*, and *E*. Producer surplus expands by area *B*. Importers' profit is the two areas *D*, and the quota creates a deadweight loss equal to *C* + *E*.

Other Import Barriers

Two sets of policies that influence imports are

- Health, safety, and regulation barriers
- Voluntary export restraints

Health, Safety, and Regulation Barriers   Thousands of detailed health, safety, and other regulations restrict international trade. For example, U.S. food imports are examined by the Food and Drug Administration to determine whether the food is "pure, wholesome, safe to eat, and produced under sanitary conditions." The discovery of BSE (mad cow disease) in just one U.S. cow in 2003 was enough to close down international trade in U.S. beef. The European Union bans imports of most genetically modified foods, such as U.S.-produced soybeans. Although regulations of the type we've just described are not designed to limit international trade, they have that effect.

Voluntary Export Restraints   A *voluntary export restraint* is like a quota allocated to a foreign exporter of a good. This type of trade barrier isn't common. It was initially used during the 1980s when Japan voluntarily limited its exports of car parts to the United States.

Export Subsidies

A *subsidy* is a payment by the government to a producer. You studied the effects of a subsidy on the quantity produced and the price of a subsidized farm product in Chapter 6, pp. 142–143.

An *export subsidy* is a payment by the government to the producer of an exported good. Export subsidies are illegal under a number of international agreements, including the North American Free Trade Agreement (NAFTA), and the rules of the World Trade Organization (WTO).

Although export subsidies are illegal, the subsidies that the U.S. and European Union governments pay to farmers end up increasing domestic production, some of which gets exported. These exports of subsidized farm products make it harder for producers in other countries, notably in Africa and Central and South America, to compete in global markets. Export subsidies bring gains to domestic producers, but they result in inefficient underproduction in the rest of the world and create a deadweight loss.

Failure in Doha
Self-Interest Beats the Social Interest

The **World Trade Organization (WTO)** is an international body established by the world's major trading nations for the purpose of supervising international trade and lowering the barriers to trade.

In 2001, at a meeting of trade ministers from all the WTO member-countries held in Doha, Qatar, an agreement was made to begin negotiations to lower tariff barriers and quotas that restrict international trade in farm products and services. These negotiations are called the **Doha Development Agenda** or the **Doha Round**.

In the period since 2001, thousands of hours of conferences in Cancún in 2003, Geneva in 2004, and Hong Kong in 2005, and ongoing meetings at WTO headquarters in Geneva, costing millions of taxpayers' dollars, have made disappointing progress.

Rich nations, led by the United States, the European Union, and Japan, want greater access to the markets of developing nations in exchange for allowing those nations greater access to the rich world's markets, especially for farm products.

Developing nations, led by Brazil, China, India, and South Africa, want access to the farm product markets of the rich world, but they also want to protect their infant industries.

With two incompatible positions, these negotiations are stalled and show no signs of a breakthrough. The self-interest of rich and developing nations is preventing the achievement of the social interest.

Review Quiz

1   What are the tools that a country can use to restrict international trade?
2   Explain the effects of a tariff on domestic production, the quantity bought, and the price.
3   Explain who gains and who loses from a tariff and why the losses exceed the gains.
4   Explain the effects of an import quota on domestic production, consumption, and price.
5   Explain who gains and who loses from an import quota and why the losses exceed the gains.

 Work Study Plan 7.3 and get instant feedback.

The Case Against Protection

For as long as nations and international trade have existed, people have debated whether a country is better off with free international trade or with protection from foreign competition. The debate continues, but for most economists, a verdict has been delivered and is the one you have just seen. Free trade promotes prosperity for all countries; protection is inefficient. We've seen the most powerful case for free trade—it brings gains for consumers that exceed any losses incurred by producers, so there is a net gain for society.

But there is a broader range of issues in the free trade versus protection debate. Let's review these issues.

Two classical arguments for restricting international trade are

- The infant-industry argument
- The dumping argument

The Infant-Industry Argument

The **infant-industry argument** for protection is that it is necessary to protect a new industry to enable it to grow into a mature industry that can compete in world markets. The argument is based on the idea of *dynamic comparative advantage*, which can arise from *learning-by-doing* (see Chapter 2, p. 43).

Learning-by-doing, a powerful engine of productivity growth, and on-the-job experience can change comparative advantage. But these facts do not justify protection.

First, the infant-industry argument is valid only if the benefits of learning-by-doing *not only* accrue to the owners and workers of the firms in the infant industry but also *spill over* to other industries and parts of the economy. For example, there are huge productivity gains from learning-by-doing in the manufacture of aircraft.

But almost all of these gains benefit the stockholders and workers of Boeing and other aircraft producers. Because the people making the decisions, bearing the risk, and doing the work are the ones who benefit, they take the dynamic gains into account when they decide on the scale of their activities. In this case, almost no benefits spill over to other parts of the economy, so there is no need for government assistance to achieve an efficient outcome.

Second, even if the case is made for protecting an infant industry, it is more efficient to do so by giving the firms in the industry a subsidy, which is financed out of taxes. Such a subsidy would encourage the industry to mature and to compete with efficient world producers and keep the price faced by consumers at the world price.

The Dumping Argument

Dumping occurs when a foreign firm sells its exports at a lower price than its cost of production. Dumping might be used by a firm that wants to gain a global monopoly. In this case, the foreign firm sells its output at a price below its cost to drive domestic firms out of business. When the domestic firms have gone, the foreign firm takes advantage of its monopoly position and charges a higher price for its product. Dumping is illegal under the rules of the WTO and is usually regarded as a justification for temporary tariffs, which are called *countervailing duties*.

But there are powerful reasons to resist the dumping argument for protection. First, it is virtually impossible to detect dumping because it is hard to determine a firm's costs. As a result, the test for dumping is whether a firm's export price is below its domestic price. But this test is a weak one because it can be rational for a firm to charge a low price in a market in which the quantity demanded is highly sensitive to price and a higher price in a market in which demand is less price-sensitive.

Second, it is hard to think of a good that is produced by a *global* monopoly. So even if all the domestic firms in some industry were driven out of business, it would always be possible to find alternative foreign sources of supply and to buy the good at a price determined in a competitive market.

Third, if a good or service were a truly global monopoly, the best way of dealing with it would be by regulation—just as in the case of domestic monopolies (see Chapter 13, pp. 313–315). Such regulation would require international cooperation.

The two arguments for protection that we've just examined have an element of credibility. The counterarguments are in general stronger, however, so these arguments do not make the case for protection. But they are not the only arguments that you might encounter. There are many other new arguments against globalization and for protection. The most common ones are that protection

- Saves jobs
- Allows us to compete with cheap foreign labor
- Penalizes lax environmental standards
- Prevents rich countries from exploiting developing countries

Saves Jobs

First, free trade does cost some jobs, but it also creates other jobs. It brings about a global rationalization of labor and allocates labor resources to their highest-valued activities. International trade in textiles has cost tens of thousands of jobs in the United States as textile mills and other factories closed. But tens of thousands of jobs have been created in other countries as textile mills opened. And tens of thousands of U.S. workers got better-paying jobs than as textile workers because U.S. export industries expanded and created new jobs. More jobs have been created than destroyed.

Although protection does save particular jobs, it does so at a high cost. For example, until 2005, U.S. textile jobs were protected by an international agreement called the Multifiber Arrangement. The U.S. International Trade Commission (ITC) has estimated that because of import quotas, 72,000 jobs existed in the textile industry that would otherwise have disappeared and that the annual clothing expenditure in the United States was $15.9 billion ($160 per family) higher than it would have been with free trade. Equivalently, the ITC estimated that each textile job saved cost $221,000 a year.

Imports don't only destroy jobs. They create jobs for retailers that sell imported goods and for firms that service those goods. Imports also create jobs by creating incomes in the rest of the world, some of which are spent on U.S.-made goods and services.

Allows Us to Compete with Cheap Foreign Labor

With the removal of tariffs on trade between the United States and Mexico, people said we would hear a "giant sucking sound" as jobs rushed to Mexico. Let's see what's wrong with this view.

The labor cost of a unit of output equals the wage rate divided by labor productivity. For example, if a U.S. autoworker earns $30 an hour and produces 15 units of output an hour, the average labor cost of a unit of output is $2. If a Mexican auto assembly worker earns $3 an hour and produces 1 unit of output an hour, the average labor cost of a unit of output is $3. Other things remaining the same, the higher a worker's productivity, the higher is the worker's wage rate. High-wage workers have high productivity; low-wage workers have low productivity.

Although high-wage U.S. workers are more productive, on average, than low-wage Mexican workers, there are differences across industries. U.S. labor is relatively more productive in some activities than in others. For example, the productivity of U.S. workers in producing movies, financial services, and customized computer chips is relatively higher than their productivity in the production of metals and some standardized machine parts. The activities in which U.S. workers are relatively more productive than their Mexican counterparts are those in which the United States has a *comparative advantage*. By engaging in free trade, increasing our production and exports of the goods and services in which we have a comparative advantage and decreasing our production and increasing our imports of the goods and services in which our trading partners have a comparative advantage, we can make ourselves and the citizens of other countries better off.

Penalizes Lax Environmental Standards

Another argument for protection is that many poorer countries, such as China and Mexico, do not have the same environmental policies that we have and, because they are willing to pollute and we are not, we cannot compete with them without tariffs. So if poorer countries want free trade with the richer and "greener" countries, they must raise their environmental standards.

This argument for protection is weak. First, a poor country cannot afford to be as concerned about its environmental standard as a rich country can. Today, some of the worst pollution of air and water is found in China, Mexico, and the former communist countries of Eastern Europe. But only a few decades ago, London and Los Angeles led the pollution league table. The best hope for cleaner air in Beijing and Mexico City is rapid income growth. And free trade contributes to that growth. As incomes in developing countries grow, they will have the *means* to match their desires to improve their environment. Second, a poor country may have a comparative advantage at doing "dirty" work, which helps it to raise its income and at the same time enables the global economy to achieve higher environmental standards than would otherwise be possible.

Prevents Rich Countries from Exploiting Developing Countries

Another argument for protection is that international trade must be restricted to prevent the people of the rich industrial world from exploiting the poorer people of the developing countries and forcing them to work for slave wages.

Child labor and near-slave labor are serious problems that are rightly condemned. But by trading with poor countries, we increase the demand for the goods that these countries produce and, more significantly, we increase the demand for their labor. When the demand for labor in developing countries increases, the wage rate also increases. So, rather than exploiting people in developing countries, trade can improve their opportunities and increase their incomes.

The arguments for protection that we've reviewed leave free-trade unscathed. But a new phenomenon is at work in our economy: *offshore outsourcing*. Surely we need protection from this new source of foreign competition. Let's investigate.

Offshore Outsourcing

Citibank, the Bank of America, Apple Computer, Nike, Wal-Mart: What do these U.S. icons have in common? They all send jobs that could be done in America to China, India, Thailand, or even Canada—they are offshoring. What exactly is offshoring?

What Is Offshoring? A firm in United States can obtain the things that it sells in any of four ways:

1. Hire American labor and produce in America.
2. Hire foreign labor and produce in other countries.
3. Buy finished goods, components, or services from other firms in the United States.
4. Buy finished goods, components, or services from other firms in other countries.

Activities 3 and 4 are **outsourcing**, and activities 2 and 4 are **offshoring**. Activity 4 is **offshore outsourcing**. Notice that offshoring includes activities that take place inside U.S. firms. If a U.S. firm opens its own facilities in another country, then it is offshoring.

Offshoring has been going on for hundreds of years,

but it expanded rapidly and became a source of concern during the 1990s as many U.S. firms moved information technology services and general office services such as finance, accounting, and human resources management overseas.

Why Did Offshoring of Services Boom During the 1990s? The gains from specialization and trade that you saw in the previous section must be large enough to make it worth incurring the costs of communication and transportation. If the cost of producing a T-shirt in China isn't lower than the cost of producing the T-shirt in the United States by more than the cost of transporting the shirt from China to America, then it is more efficient to produce shirts in the United States and avoid the transport costs.

The same considerations apply to trade in services. If services are to be produced offshore, then the cost of delivering those services must be low enough to leave the buyer with an overall lower cost. Before the 1990s, the cost of communicating across large distances was too high to make the offshoring of business services efficient. But during the 1990s, when satellites, fiber-optic cables, and computers cut the cost of a phone call between America and India to less than a dollar an hour, a huge base of offshore resources became competitive with similar resources in the United States.

What Are the Benefits of Offshoring? Offshoring brings gains from trade identical to those of any other type of trade. We could easily change the names of the items traded from T-shirts and airplanes (the examples in the previous sections of this chapter) to banking services and call center services (or any other pair of services). An American bank might export banking services to Indian firms, and Indians might provide call center services to U.S. firms. This type of trade would benefit both Americans and Indians provided the United States has a comparative advantage in banking services and India has a comparative advantage in call center services.

Comparative advantages like these emerged during the 1990s. India has the world's largest educated English-speaking population and is located in a time zone half a day ahead of the U.S. east coast and midway between Asia and Europe, which facilitates 24/7 operations. When the cost of communicating with a worker in India was several dollars a minute, as it was before the 1990s, tapping these vast resources was just too costly. But at today's cost of a long-distance telephone call or Internet connection, resources in India can be used to produce services in the United States at a lower cost than those services can be produced by using resources located in the United States. And with the incomes that Indians earn from exporting services, some of the services (and goods) that Indians buy are produced in the United States.

Why Is Offshoring a Concern? Despite the gain from specialization and trade that offshoring brings, many people believe that it also brings costs that eat up the gains. Why?

A major reason is that offshoring is taking jobs in services. The loss of manufacturing jobs to other countries has been going on for decades, but the U.S. service sector has always expanded by enough to create new jobs to replace the lost manufacturing jobs. Now that service jobs are also going overseas, the fear is that there will not be enough jobs for Americans. This fear is misplaced.

Some service jobs are going overseas, while others are expanding at home. The United States imports call center services, but it exports education, health care, legal, financial, and a host of other types of services. Jobs in these sectors are expanding and will continue to expand.

The exact number of jobs that have moved to lower-cost offshore locations is not known, and estimates vary. But even the highest estimate is a tiny number compared to the normal rate of job creation.

Winners and Losers Gains from trade do not bring gains for every single person. Americans, on average, gain from offshore outsourcing, but some people lose. The losers are those who have invested in the human capital to do a specific job that has now gone offshore.

Unemployment benefits provide short-term temporary relief for these displaced workers. But the long-term solution requires retraining and the acquisition of new skills.

Beyond providing short-term relief through unemployment benefits, there is a large role for government in the provision of education and training to enable the labor force of the twenty-first century to be capable of ongoing learning and rapid retooling to take on new jobs that today we can't foresee.

Schools, colleges, and universities will expand and get better at doing their jobs of producing a highly educated and flexible labor force.

Avoiding Trade Wars

We have reviewed the arguments commonly heard in favor of protection and the counterarguments against it. There is one counterargument to protection that is general and quite overwhelming: Protection invites retaliation and can trigger a trade war.

The best example of a trade war occurred during the Great Depression of the 1930s when the United States introduced the Smoot-Hawley tariff. Country after country retaliated with its own tariff, and in a short period, world trade had almost disappeared. The costs to all countries were large and led to a renewed international resolve to avoid such self-defeating moves in the future. The costs also led to the creation of GATT and are the impetus behind current attempts to liberalize trade.

Why Is International Trade Restricted?

Why, despite all the arguments against protection, is trade restricted? There are two key reasons:

- Tariff revenue
- Rent seeking

Tariff Revenue Government revenue is costly to collect. In developed countries such as the United States, a well-organized tax collection system is in place that can generate billions of dollars of income tax and sales tax revenues. This tax collection system is made possible by the fact that most economic transactions are done by firms that must keep properly audited financial records. Without such records, revenue collection agencies (the Internal Revenue Service in the United States) would be severely hampered in their work. Even with audited financial accounts, some potential tax revenue is lost. Nonetheless, for industrialized countries, the income tax and sales taxes are the major sources of revenue and tariffs play a very small role.

But governments in developing countries have a difficult time collecting taxes from their citizens. Much economic activity takes place in an informal economy with few financial records, so only a small amount of revenue is collected from income taxes and sales taxes. The one area in which economic transactions are well recorded and audited is international trade. So this activity is an attractive base for tax collection in these countries and is used much more extensively than it is in developed countries.

Rent Seeking Rent seeking is the major reason why international trade is restricted. **Rent seeking** is lobbying for special treatment by the government to create economic profit or to divert consumer surplus or producer surplus away from others. Free trade increases consumption possibilities *on average*, but not everyone shares in the gain and some people even lose. Free trade brings benefits to some and imposes costs on others, with total benefits exceeding total costs. The uneven distribution of costs and benefits is the principal obstacle to achieving more liberal international trade.

Returning to the example of trade in T-shirts and airplanes, the benefits from free trade accrue to all the producers of airplanes and to those producers of T-shirts that do not bear the costs of adjusting to a smaller garment industry. These costs are transition costs, not permanent costs. The costs of moving to free trade are borne by the garment producers and their employees who must become producers of other goods and services in which the United States has a comparative advantage.

The number of winners from free trade is large. But because the gains are spread thinly over a large number of people, the gain per person is small. The winners could organize and become a political force lobbying for free trade. But political activity is costly. It uses time and other scarce resources and the gains per person are too small to make the cost of political activity worth bearing.

In contrast, the number of losers from free trade is small, but the loss per person is large. Because the loss per person is large, the people who lose *are* willing to incur considerable expense to lobby against free trade.

Both the winners and losers weigh benefits and costs. Those who gain from free trade weigh the benefits it brings against the cost of achieving it. Those who lose from free trade and gain from protection weigh the benefit of protection against the cost of maintaining it. The protectionists undertake a larger quantity of political lobbying than the free traders.

Compensating Losers

If, in total, the gains from free international trade exceed the losses, why don't those who gain compensate those who lose so that everyone is in favor of free trade?

Some compensation does take place. When Congress approved the North American Free Trade

Agreement, (NAFTA), with Canada and Mexico, it set up a $56 million fund to support and retrain workers who lost their jobs as a result of the new trade agreement. During NAFTA's first six months, only 5,000 workers applied for benefits under this scheme. The losers from international trade are also compensated indirectly through the normal unemployment compensation arrangements. But only limited attempts are made to compensate those who lose.

The main reason why full compensation is not attempted is that the costs of identifying all the losers and estimating the value of their losses would be enormous. Also, it would never be clear whether a person who has fallen on hard times is suffering because of free trade or for other reasons that might be largely under her or his control. Furthermore, some people who look like losers at one point in time might, in fact, end up gaining. The young autoworker who loses his job in Michigan and becomes a computer assembly worker in Minneapolis resents the loss of work and the need to move. But a year later, looking back on events, he counts himself fortunate.

Because we do not, in general, compensate the losers from free international trade, protectionism is a popular and permanent feature of our national economic and political life.

Review Quiz

1 What are the infant industry and dumping arguments for protection? Are they correct?
2 Can protection save jobs and the environment and prevent workers in developing countries from being exploited?
3 What is offshore outsourcing? Who benefits from it and who loses?
4 What are the main reasons for imposing a tariff?
5 Why don't the winners from free trade win the political argument?

 Work Study Plan 7.4 and get instant feedback.

We end this chapter on global markets in action in *Reading Between the Lines* on pp. 170–171. It applies what you've learned by looking at the effects of a tariff on U.S. imports of children's shoes and who gains from passage of the Affordable Footwear Act.

A Worn-Out Tariff

Affordable Footwear Act Takes A Step Forward

just-style.com
20 June 2008

Legislation to eliminate import tariffs on about 60% of all shoes sold in the United States has reached another landmark on its way to final passage, a U.S. trade group said yesterday (19 June).

The Affordable Footwear Act (HR 3934/ S 2372) has now garnered support from one-third of the members of the US House of Representatives according, to the American Apparel & Footwear Association (AAFA).

The legislation aims to abolish old-fashioned import duties known collectively as the "shoe tax" on certain lower to moderately priced footwear and all children's shoes.

These types of shoes typically carry the highest rate of duty—up to 67.5%—despite being the lowest priced, with the shoe tax ultimately contributing to as much as 40% of the retail price.

"With 99% of all footwear sold in the United States imported, the shoe tax has worn out its purpose and remains as an unavoidable, harmful tax on something everyone must buy—shoes," said Kevin M. Burke, president and CEO of the American Apparel & Footwear Association (AAFA).

"The footwear industry unanimously agrees that this bill will not harm domestic footwear manufacturers, while granting significant tax relief to hard-working U.S. families at a time they need it most."

Essence of the Story

- Of the footwear sold in the United States, 99 percent is imported.

- Lower-priced shoes and children's shoes—60 percent of shoes sold—bear an import duty of up to 67.5 percent, which translates to 40 percent of the retail price.

- The Affordable Footwear Act seeks to abolish this tariff.

- The footwear industry agrees that it will not be harmed by removing the tariff.

Economic Analysis

- In the 1920s, most footwear sold in the United States was also produced in the United States.

- Lower-priced shoes produced in Mexico, Brazil, and Italy began to compete with U.S.-produced shoes and the shoemakers turned to Congress for protection.

- Congress met the shoemakers' demands by introducing a tariff on imported shoes.

- When the tariff was introduced, its effects were similar to those explained on pp. 159–161 and illustrated in Fig. 7.6 on p. 161.

- U.S. shoe producers enjoyed an increase in producer surplus, but the price of shoes increased, consumer surplus decreased, and a deadweight loss was incurred.

- During the 1990s, as the cost of producing shoes in Asia tumbled, even with the shoe tariff, U.S. shoe producers could not compete with foreign producers and the U.S. shoe industry all but disappeared.

- Today, no lower-priced or children's shoes are produced in the United States. They are all imported.

- With no domestic supply and no producer surplus, the only effects of the shoe tariff are to generate a small amount of revenue for the government, decrease consumer surplus, and bring deadweight loss.

- Figure 1 illustrates the situation in the market for lower-priced and children's shoes.

- The U.S. demand curve is D_{US}. There is no U.S. supply curve at the price shown in the figure. (There is a U.S. supply but at prices higher than those shown in the figure).

- The world price is $20 a pair and this price would be the U.S. price in the absence of the tariff.

- The tariff is $8 a pair and the U.S. price including the tariff is $28 a pair.

- The purple rectangle illustrates the tariff revenue, the green triangle is the consumer surplus, and the gray triangle is the deadweight loss.

- Figure 2 shows how consumer surplus expands with efficient free trade in shoes.

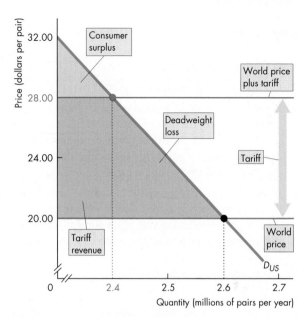

Figure 1 The shoe market with a tariff

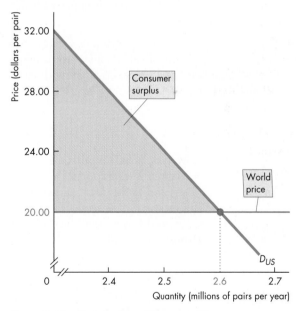

Figure 2 The shoe market without a tariff

171

SUMMARY ◆

Key Points

How Global Markets Work (pp. 154–156)

- Comparative advantage drives international trade.
- If the world price of a good is lower than the domestic price, the rest of the world has a comparative advantage in producing that good and the domestic country gains by producing less, consuming more, and importing the good.
- If the world price of a good is higher than the domestic price, the domestic country has a comparative advantage in producing that good and gains by producing more, consuming less, and exporting the good.

**Winners, Losers, and the Net Gain
from Trade** (pp. 157–158)

- Compared to a no-trade situation, in a market with imports, consumer surplus is larger, producer surplus is smaller, and total surplus is larger with free international trade.
- Compared to a no-trade situation, in a market with exports, consumer surplus is smaller, producer surplus is larger, and total surplus is larger with free international trade.

International Trade Restrictions (pp. 159–164)

- Countries restrict international trade by imposing tariffs, import quotas, and other import barriers.
- Trade restrictions raise the domestic price of imported goods, lower the quantity imported, decrease consumer surplus, increase producer surplus, and create a deadweight loss.

The Case Against Protection (pp. 165–169)

- Arguments that protection is necessary for infant industries and to prevent dumping are weak.
- Arguments that protection saves jobs, allows us to compete with cheap foreign labor, is needed to penalize lax environmental standards, and prevents exploitation of developing countries are flawed.
- Offshore outsourcing is just a new way of reaping gains from trade and does not justify protection.
- Trade restrictions are popular because protection brings a small loss per person to a large number of people and a large gain per person to a small number of people. Those who gain have a stronger political voice than those who lose and it is too costly to identify and compensate losers.

Key Figures

Key Terms

PROBLEMS and APPLICATIONS ◆

myeconlab   Work problems 1–10 in Chapter 7 Study Plan and get instant feedback.
Work problems 11–22 as Homework, a Quiz, or a Test if assigned by your instructor.

1. Wholesalers of roses (the firms that supply your local flower shop with roses for Valentine's Day) buy and sell roses in containers that hold 120 stems. The table provides information about the wholesale market for roses in the United States. The demand schedule is the wholesalers' demand and the supply schedule is the U.S. rose growers' supply.

Price (dollars per container)	Quantity demanded	Quantity supplied
	(millions of containers per year)	
100	15	0
125	12	2
150	9	4
175	6	6
200	3	8
225	0	10

Wholesalers can buy roses at auction in Aalsmeer, Holland, for $125 per container.

a. Without international trade, what would be the price of a container of roses and how many containers of roses a year would be bought and sold in the United States?

b. At the price in your answer to a, does the United States or the rest of the world have a comparative advantage in producing roses?

c. If U.S. wholesalers buy roses at the lowest possible price, how many do they buy from U.S. growers and how many do they import?

d. Draw a graph to illustrate the U.S. wholesale market for roses. Show the equilibrium in that market with no international trade and the equilibrium with free trade. Mark the quantity of roses produced in the United States, the quantity imported, and the total quantity bought.

2. **Underwater Oil Discovery to Transform Brazil into a Major Exporter**

A huge underwater oil field discovered late last year has the potential to transform South America's largest country into a sizable exporter. … Just a decade ago the notion that Brazil would become self-sufficient in energy, let alone emerge as an exporter, seemed far-fetched. … Petrobras was formed five decades ago largely as a trading company to import oil to support Brazil's growing economy. … Yet two years ago … Brazil reached its long-sought goal of energy self-sufficiency. …

International Herald Tribune, January 11, 2008

a. Describe Brazil's comparative advantage in producing oil and explain why its comparative advantage has changed.

b. Draw a graph to illustrate the Brazilian market for oil and explain why Brazil was an importer of oil until a few years ago.

c. Draw a graph to illustrate the Brazilian market for oil and explain why Brazil may become an exporter of oil in the near future.

3. Use the information on the U.S. wholesale market for roses in problem 1 to

a. Explain who gains and who loses from free international trade in roses compared to a situation in which Americans buy only roses grown in the United States.

b. Draw a graph to illustrate the gains and losses from free trade.

c. Calculate the gain from international trade.

4. **Postcard: Bangalore. Hearts Set on Joining the Global Economy, Indian IT Workers are Brushing up on Their Interpersonal Skills**

The huge number of Indian workers staffing the world's tech firms and call centers … possess cutting-edge technical knowledge, [but] their interpersonal and communication skills lag far behind. … Enter Bangalore's finishing schools.

Time, May 5, 2008

a. What comparative advantages does this news clip identify?

b. Using the information in this news clip, what services do you predict Bangalore (India) exports and what services do you predict it imports?

c. Who will gain and who will lose from the international trade that you described in your answer to b?

5. **Steel Tariffs Appear to Have Backfired on Bush**

President Bush set aside his free-trade principles last year and imposed heavy tariffs on imported steel to help out struggling mills in Pennsylvania and West Virginia, two states crucial for his reelection. ... Some economists say the tariffs may have cost more jobs than they saved, by driving up costs for automakers and other steel users. ...

The Washington Post, September 19, 2003

a. Explain how a high tariff on steel imports can help domestic steel producers.

b. Explain how a high tariff on steel imports can harm steel users.

c. Draw a graph of the U.S. market for steel to show how a high tariff on steel imports
  i. Helps U.S. steel producers.
  ii. Harms U.S. steel users.
  iii. Creates a deadweight loss.

6. Use the information on the U.S. wholesale market for roses in problem 1.

a. If the United States puts a tariff of $25 per container on imports of roses, what happens to the U.S. price of roses, the quantity of roses bought, the quantity produced in the United States, and the quantity imported?

b. Who gains and who loses from this tariff?

c. Draw a graph to illustrate the gains and losses from the tariff and on the graph identify the gains and losses, the tariff revenue, and the deadweight loss.

7. Use the information on the U.S. wholesale market for roses in problem 1.

a. If the United States puts an import quota on roses of 5 million containers, what happens to the U.S. price of roses, the quantity of roses bought, the quantity produced in the United States, and the quantity imported?

b. Who gains and who loses from this quota?

c. Draw a graph to illustrate the gains and losses from the import quota and on the graph identify the gains and losses, the importers' profit, and the deadweight loss.

8. **Car Sales Go Up as Prices Tumble**

Car affordability [in Australia] is now at its best in 20 years, fueling a surge in sales as prices tumble. ... [In 2000, Australia cut the tariff to 15 percent and] on January 1, 2005, the tariff on imported vehicles fell from 15 percent to 10 percent.

Courier Mail, February 26, 2005

a. Explain who gains and who loses from the lower tariff on imported cars.

b. Draw a graph to show how the price of a car, the quantity bought, the quantity produced in Australia, and imports of cars changed.

9. **Chinese Tire Maker Rejects U.S. Charge of Defects**

... regulators in the United States ordered the recall of more than 450,000 faulty tires . ... The Chinese company that produced the tires ... disputed the allegations Tuesday and hinted that the recall might be an effort by foreign competitors to hamper the company's exports to the United States. ... Mounting scrutiny of Chinese-made goods has become a source of new trade frictions between the United States and China and fueled worries among regulators, corporations, and consumers about the risks associated with many products imported from China. ...

International Herald Tribune, June 26, 2007

a. What does the information in the news clip imply about the comparative advantage of producing tires in the United States and China?

b. Could product quality be a valid argument against free trade?

c. How would the product-quality argument against free trade be open to abuse by domestic producers of the imported good?

10. **Why the World Can't Afford Food**

As [food] stocks dwindled, some countries placed export restrictions on food to protect their own supplies. This in turn drove up prices, punishing countries—especially poor ones—that depend on imports for much of their food.

Time, May 19, 2008

a. What are the benefits to a country from importing food?

b. What costs might arise from relying on imported food?

c. If a country restricts food exports, what effect does this restriction have in that country on
  i.   The price of food?
  ii. The quantity of food produced?
  iii. The quantity of food consumed?
  iv. The quantity of food exported?

d. Draw a graph of the market for food in a country that exports food. On the graph show how the price of food and the quantities of food consumed, produced, and exported change when food exports are restricted.

11. Suppose that the world price of sugar is 10 cents a pound, the United States does not trade internationally, and the equilibrium price of sugar in the United States is 20 cents a pound. The United States then begins to trade internationally.
    a. How does the price of sugar in the United States change?
    b. Do U.S. consumers buy more or less sugar?
    c. Do U.S. sugar growers produce more or less sugar?
    d. Does the United States export or import sugar and why?

12. Suppose that the world price of steel is $100 a ton, India does not trade internationally, and the equilibrium price of steel in India is $60 a ton. India then begins to trade internationally.
    a. How does the price of steel in India change?
    b. How does the quantity of steel produced in India change?
    c. How does the quantity of steel bought by India change?
    d. Does India export or import steel and why?

13. A semiconductor is a key component in your laptop, cell phone, and iPod. The table provides information about the market for semiconductors in the United States.

Price (dollars per unit)	Quantity demanded	Quantity supplied
	(billions of units per year)	
10	25	0
12	20	20
14	15	40
16	10	60
18	5	80
20	0	100

Producers of semiconductors can get $18 a unit on the world market.
    a. With no international trade, what would be the price of a semiconductor and how many semiconductors a year would be bought and sold in the United States?
    b. At the price in your answer to a, does the United States have a comparative advantage in producing semiconductors?
    c. If U.S. producers of semiconductors sell at the highest possible price, how many do they sell in the United States and how many do they export?

14. **South Korea to Resume U.S. Beef Imports**
    South Korea will open its market to most U.S. beef. … South Korea banned imports of U.S. beef in 2003 amid concerns over a case of mad cow disease in the United States. The ban closed what was then the third-largest market for U.S. beef exporters. …
    CNN, May 29, 2008
    a. Which country, South Korea or the United States, has a comparative advantage in producing beef? What fact in the news clip did you use to answer this question?
    b. Explain how South Korea's import ban on U.S. beef affected beef producers and consumers in South Korea.
    c. Draw a graph of the market for beef in South Korea to illustrate your answer to b. Identify the changes in consumer surplus, producer surplus, and deadweight loss.
    d. Assuming that South Korea is the only importer of U.S. beef, explain how South Korea's import ban on U.S. beef affected beef producers and consumers in the United States.
    e. Draw a graph of the market for beef in the United States to illustrate your answer to d. Identify the changes in consumer surplus, producer surplus, and deadweight loss.

15. **Act Now, Eat Later**
    … looming hunger crisis in poor countries … has its roots in … misguided policy in the U.S. and Europe of subsidizing the diversion of food crops to produce biofuels like corn-based ethanol … [That is,] doling out subsidies to put the world's dinner into the gas tank.
    Time, May 5, 2008
    a. What is the effect on the world price of corn of the increased use of corn to produce ethanol in the United States and Europe?
    b. How does the change in the world price of corn affect the quantity of corn produced in a poor developing country with a comparative advantage in producing corn, the quantity it consumes, and the quantity that it either exports or imports?
    c. Draw a graph of the market for corn in a poor developing country to illustrate your answer to b. Identify the changes in consumer surplus, producer surplus, and deadweight loss.

16. Before 1995, trade between the United States and Mexico was subject to tariffs. In 1995, Mexico joined NAFTA and all U.S. and Mexican tariffs are gradually being removed.

   a. Explain how the price that U.S. consumers pay for goods from Mexico and the quantity of U.S. imports from Mexico have changed. Who are the winners and who are the losers from this free trade?

   b. Explain how the quantity of U.S. exports to Mexico and the U.S. government's tariff revenue from trade with Mexico have changed.

   c. Suppose that in 2008, tomato growers in Florida lobby the U.S. government to impose an import quota on Mexican tomatoes. Explain who in the United States would gain and who would lose from such a quota.

17. Suppose that in response to huge job losses in the U.S. textile industry, Congress imposes a 100 percent tariff on imports of textiles from China.

   a. Explain how the tariff on textiles will change the price that U.S. buyers pay for textiles, the quantity of textiles imported, and the quantity of textiles produced in the United States.

   b. Explain how the U.S. and Chinese gains from trade will change. Who in the United States will lose and who will gain?

18. With free trade between Australia and the United States, Australia would export beef to the United States. But the United States imposes an import quota on Australian beef.

   a. Explain how this quota influences the price that U.S. consumers pay for beef, the quantity of beef produced in the United States, and the U.S. and the Australian gains from trade.

   b. Explain who in the United States gains from the quota on beef imports and who loses.

19. **Aid May Grow for Laid-Off Workers**

   … the expansion of the Trade Adjustment Assistance (TAA) program would begin to reweave the social safety net for the 21st century, as advances permit more industries to take advantage of cheap foreign labor—even for skilled, white-collar work. By providing special compensation to more of globalization's losers and retraining them for stable jobs at home, … an expanded program could begin to ease the resentment and insecurity arising from the new economy.

   The Washington Post, July 23, 2007

   a. Why does the United States engage in international trade if it causes U.S. workers to lose their jobs?

   b. Explain how an expansion of the Trade Adjustment Assistance will make it easier for the United States to move toward freer international trade.

20. Study *Reading Between the Lines* on pp. 170–171 and answer the following questions.

   a. Who will gain and who will lose if the tariff is abolished?

   b. If Congress imposed an import quota on shoes, who would gain and who would lose?

21. **Trading Up**

   … the cost of protecting jobs in uncompetitive sectors through tariffs is foolishly high. … The Federal Reserve Bank of Dallas reported in 2002 that saving a job in the sugar industry cost American consumers $826,000 in higher prices a year, saving a dairy industry job cost $685,000 per year, and saving a job in the manufacturing of women's handbags cost $263,000.

   The New York Times, June 26, 2006

   a. What are the arguments for saving the jobs mentioned in this news clip?

   b. Explain why these arguments are faulty.

   c. Is there any merit to saving these jobs?

22. **Vows of New Aid to the Poor Leave the Poor Unimpressed**

   … the United States, the European Union, and Japan [plan] to eliminate duties and [import] quotas on almost all goods from up to 50 of the world's poor nations. … The proposal for duty-free, quota-free treatment is so divisive among developing countries that even some negotiators … are saying that the plan must be broadened.

   The New York Times, December 15, 2005

   a. Why do the United States, the European Union, and Japan want to eliminate trade barriers on imports from only the poorest countries?

   b. Who will win from the elimination of these trade barriers? Who will lose?

   c. Why is the plan divisive among developing countries?

UNDERSTANDING HOW MARKETS WORK

The Amazing Market

The five chapters that you've just studied explain how markets work. The market is an amazing instrument. It enables people who have never met and who know nothing about each other to interact and do business. It also enables us to allocate our scarce resources to the uses that we value most highly. Markets can be very simple or highly organized. Markets are ancient and they are modern.

A simple and ancient market is one that the American historian Daniel J. Boorstin describes in *The Discoverers* (p. 161). In the late fourteenth century,

> *The Muslim caravans that went southward from Morocco across the Atlas Mountains arrived after twenty days at the shores of the Senegal River. There the Moroccan traders laid out separate piles of salt, of beads from Ceutan coral, and cheap manufactured goods. Then they retreated out of sight. The local tribesmen, who lived in the strip mines where they dug their gold, came to the shore and put a heap of gold beside each pile of Moroccan goods. Then they, in turn, went out of view, leaving the Moroccan traders either to take the gold offered for a particular pile or to reduce the pile of their merchandise to suit the offered price in gold. Once again the Moroccan traders withdrew, and the process went on. By this system of commercial etiquette, the Moroccans collected their gold.*

An organized and modern market is an auction at which the U.S. government sells rights to cell phone companies for the use of the airwaves.

Everything and anything that can be exchanged is traded in markets to the benefit of both buyers and sellers.

Alfred Marshall *(1842–1924) grew up in an England that was being transformed by the railroad and by the expansion of manufacturing. Mary Paley was one of Marshall's students at Cambridge, and when Alfred and Mary married, in 1877, celibacy rules barred Alfred from continuing to teach at Cambridge. By 1884, with more liberal rules, the Marshalls returned to Cambridge, where Alfred became Professor of Political Economy.*

Many economists had a hand in refining the demand and supply model, but the first thorough and complete statement of the model as we know it today was set out by Alfred Marshall, with the help of Mary Paley Marshall. Published in 1890, this monumental treatise, The Principles of Economics, *became the textbook on economics on both sides of the Atlantic for almost half a century.*

"The forces to be dealt with are . . . so numerous, that it is best to take a few at a time. . . . Thus we begin by isolating the primary relations of supply, demand, and price."

ALFRED MARSHALL
The Principles of Economics

TALKING
WITH

Susan Athey

Susan Athey is Professor of Economics at Harvard University. Born in 1970 in Boston and growing up in Rockville Maryland, she completed high school in three years, wrapped up three majors—in economics, mathematics, and computer science—at Duke University at 20, completed her Ph.D. at Stanford University at 24, and was voted tenure at MIT and Stanford at 29. After teaching at MIT for six years and Stanford for five years, she moved to Harvard in 2006. Among her many honors and awards, the most prestigious is the John Bates Clark Medal given to the best economist under 40. She is the first woman to receive this award.

Professor Athey's research is broad both in scope and style. A government that wants to auction natural resources will turn to her fundamental discoveries (and possibly consult with her) before deciding how to organize the auction. An economist who wants to test a theory using a large data set will use her work on statistics and econometrics.

Michael Parkin talked with Susan Athey about her research, the progress that economists have made in understanding and designing markets, and her advice to students.

What sparked your interest in economics?

I was studying mathematics and computer science, but I felt that the subjects were not as relevant as I would like.

I discovered economics through a research assistantship with a professor who was working on auctions. I had a summer job working for a firm that sold computers to the government through auctions. Eventually my professor, Bob Marshall, wrote two articles on the topic and testified before Congress to help reform the system for government procurement of computers. That really inspired me and showed me the power of economic ideas to change the world and to make things work more efficiently.

This original inspiration has remained and continues to drive much of your research. Can you explain how economists study auctions?

The study of the design of markets and auction-based marketplaces requires you to use all of the different tools that economics offers.

An auction is a well-defined game. You can write down the rules of the game and a formal theoretical model does a great job capturing the real problem that the players face. And theories do an excellent job predicting behavior.

Buyers have a valuation for an object that is private information. They do not know the valuations of other bidders, and sometimes they don't even know their own valuation. For example, if they're buying oil rights, there may be uncertainty about how much oil there is in the ground. In that case, information about the amount of oil available is dispersed among the bidders, because each bidder has done their own survey. The bidders face a strategic problem of bidding, and they face an informational problem of trying to draw inferences about how valuable the object will be if they win.

Bidders need to recognize that their bid only matters when they win the auction, and they only win when they bid the most. The knowledge that they were the most optimistic of all the competitors should cause them to revise their beliefs.

From the seller's perspective, there are choices about how an auction is designed—auctions can use sealed bidding, where the seller receives bids and then opens them at a pre-determined time, or alternatively bidding may be interactive, where each bidder has an opportunity to outbid the previous high bidder. There are also different ways to use bids received by the auctioneer to determine the price. The seller may consider revenue, though governments are often most concerned about efficient allocation.

Both revenue and efficiency are affected by auction design. One key question the seller must consider is how the design will affect the participation of bidders, as this will determine how competitive bidding will be as well as whether the object gets to the potential bidder who values the item the most.

What must the designer of an auction-based marketplace take into account?

An example of an auction-based market place is eBay, where the market designer sets the rules for buyers and sellers to interact.

When you design an auction-based market place, you have a whole new set of concerns. The buyers and sellers themselves are independent agents, each acting in their own interest. The design is a two step process: you need to design an auction that is going to achieve an efficient allocation; and you need design both the auction and the overall structure of the marketplace to attract participation.

In the case of eBay, the platform itself chooses the possible auction formats: auctions take place over time and bidders have the opportunity to outbid the standing high bidder during that time. The platform also allows sellers to use the "buy it now" option. The platform also makes certain tools and services available, such as the ability to search for items in various ways, track auctions, provide feedback, and monitor reputation. The sellers can select the level of the reserve price, whether they want to have a secret reserve price, how long the auction will last, whether to use "buy it now," what time of day the auction closes, how much information to provide, how many pictures they post.

These are all factors that impact participation of bidders and the revenue the seller will receive. The success of the platform hinges on both buyers and sellers choosing to participate.

> Sealed bid auctions can do a better job of deterring collusion ... and raise more revenue

Does auction theory enable us to predict the differences in the outcomes of an open ascending bid English auction and a sealed-bid auction?

Sure. In some of my research, I compared open ascending auctions and pay-your-bid, sealed-bid auctions. I showed how the choice of auction format can make a big difference when you have small bidders bidding against larger, stronger bidders who usually (but not always) have higher valuations.

In an open ascending auction, it is hard for a small weaker bidder to ever win, because a stronger bidder can see their bids, respond to them, and outbid them

But in a pay-your-bid, sealed-bid auction, bidders shade their bids—they bid less than their value, assuring themselves of some profit if they win—and a large bidder doesn't have the opportunity to see and respond to an unusually high bid from a weak bidder. Strong bidders realize that their competition is weak, and they shade their bids a lot—they bid a lot less than their value. That gives a small bidder the opportunity to be aggressive and outbid a larger bidder, even if it has a lower value. So what that does is encourage entry of small bidders. I found empirically that this entry effect was important and it helps sealed bid auctions generate larger revenue than open ascending-bid auctions.

Does a sealed bid auction always generate more revenue, other things equal, than an open ascending-bid auction?

Only if you have asymmetric bidders-strong large bidders and weaker small bidders-and even then the effect is ambiguous. It's an empirical question, but it tends to be true. We also showed that sealed bid auctions can do a better job of deterring collusion. There are theoretical reasons to suggest that sealed bid auctions are more difficult to collude at than open ascending auctions, since at open ascending auctions, bidders can detect an opponent who is bidding higher than an agreement specifies and then respond to that. We found empirically in U.S. Forest Service timber auctions that the gap between sealed bid auctions and ascending auctions was even greater than what a competitive model would predict, suggesting that some collusion may be at work.

What is the connection between auctions and the supply and demand model?

The basic laws of supply and demand can be seen in evidence in a market like eBay. The more sellers that are selling similar products, the lower the prices they can expect to achieve. Similarly the more buyers there are demanding those objects, the higher the prices the sellers can achieve.

An important thing for an auction marketplace is to attract a good balance of buyers and sellers so that both the buyers and the sellers find it more profitable to transact on that marketplace rather than using some other mechanism. From a seller's perspective, the more bidders there are on the platform, the greater the demand and the higher the prices. And from the buyer's perspective, the more sellers there are on the platform, the greater the supply and the lower the prices.

> The basic laws of supply and demand can be seen in evidence in a market like eBay.

Can we think of this thought experiment you just described as discovering demand and supply curves?

Exactly. When you study supply and demand curves, you wave your hands about how the prices actually get set. In different kinds of market settings, the actual mechanisms for setting prices are different. One way of setting prices is through auctions. But we tend to use auctions in settings where there are unique objects, so there isn't just one market price for the thing you are selling. If you were selling something that had lots of market substitutes, you can think of there being a market price in which this object can transact. An auction is a way to find a market price for something where there might not be a fixed market.

Can we think of an auction as a mechanism for finding the equilibrium price and quantity?

Exactly. We can think of the whole collection of auctions on eBay as being a mechanism to discover a market clearing price, and individual items might sell a little higher or a little lower but over all we believe that the prices on eBay auctions will represent market-clearing (equilibrium) prices.

Is economics a good subject in which to major? What subjects work well as complements with economics?

Of course I think economics is a fabulous major and I am passionate about it. I think it's a discipline that trains you to think rigorously. And if you apply yourself you'll finish an economics major with a more disciplined mind than when you started. Whether you go into the business world or academics, you'll be able to confront and think in a logical and structured way about whether a policy makes sense, a business model makes sense, or an industry structure is likely to be sustainable. You should look for that in an undergraduate major. You should not be looking to just absorb facts, but you should be looking to train your mind and to think in a way that you will be able to apply to the rest of your career. I think that economics combines well with statistics and mathematics or with more policy oriented disciplines.

Do you have anything special to say to women who might be making a career choice? Why is economics a good field for a woman?

On the academic side, economics is a fairly objective field, where the best ideas win, so it's a level playing field. Academics is not very family friendly before you get tenured and extremely family friendly after. Within academics or outside of it, there are a wide range of fairly high paying jobs that still allow some autonomy over your schedule and that have a deeper and more compelling meaning. For both and men and women, if you choose to have a family, you reevaluate your career choices and the tradeoff between time and money changes. And you're more likely to stick with and excel in a career if you find some meaning in it. So economics combines some of the advantages of having a strong job market and opportunities to have a large enough salary to pay for child care, and makes it economically worthwhile to stay in the work force, without sacrificing the sense of the greater good.

Utility and Demand

After studying this chapter, you will be able to:

- Describe preferences using the concept of utility, distinguish between total utility and marginal utility, and explain the marginal utility theory of consumer choice

- Use marginal utility theory to predict the effects of changes in prices and incomes and to explain the paradox of value

- Describe some new ways of explaining consumer choices

You want Coldplay's latest hit album, *Viva la Vida*, and you want the Justin Timberlake and Madonna single, *Four Minutes*. Will you download the album and the single? Or will you buy two CDs? Or will you buy the album on a CD and download the single? What determines our choices as buyers of recorded music? And how much better off are we because we can download a song for 99 cents?

You know that diamonds are expensive and water is cheap. Doesn't that seem odd? Why do we place a higher value on useless diamonds than on essential-to-life water? You can think of many other examples of this paradox. For example, paramedics who save people's lives get paid a tiny fraction of what a National Hockey League player earns. Do we really place less value on the people who take care of the injured and the sick than we place on those who provide us with entertaining hockey games? *Reading Between the Lines* answers this question.

The theory of consumer choice that you're going to study in this chapter answers questions like the ones we've just posed. The main purpose of this theory is to explain the law of demand and the influences on buying plans. To explain the theory, we will study the choices of Lisa, a student who loves movies and has a thirst for soda. But the theory explains all choices including your choices in the market for recorded music as well as the paradox that the prices of water and diamonds are so out of proportion with their benefits.

181

◈ Maximizing Utility

Your income and the prices that you face limit your consumption choices. You can buy only the things that you can afford. But you still have lots of choices. Of all the alternative combinations of goods and services that you can afford, what will you buy?

The economist's answer to this question is that you will buy the goods and services that maximize your utility. **Utility** is the benefit or satisfaction that a person gets from the consumption of goods and services. To understand how people's choices maximize utility, we distinguish between two concepts:

- Total utility
- Marginal utility

Total Utility

Total utility is the total benefit that a person gets from the consumption of all the different goods and services. Total utility depends on the level of consumption—more consumption generally gives more total utility.

To make the concept of total utility more concrete, think about the choices of Lisa, a student who spends all her income on two goods: movies and soda. We tell Lisa that we want to measure her utility from these two goods. We can use any scale that we wish to measure utility and give her two starting points: (1) we will call the total utility from no movies and no soda zero utility; and (2) we will call the total utility she gets from seeing 1 movie a month 50 units.

We then ask Lisa to tell us, using the same scale, how much she would like 2 movies, and more, up to 10 a month. We also ask her to tell us, on the same scale, how much she would like 1 case of soda a month, 2 cases, and more, up to 10 cases a month.

In Table 8.1, the columns headed "Total utility" show Lisa's answers. Looking at those numbers, you can say quite a lot about how much Lisa likes soda and movies. She says that 1 case of soda gives her 75 units of utility—50 percent more than the utility that she gets from seeing 1 movie.

But you can also see that her total utility from soda climbs more slowly than her total utility from movies. By the time she is buying 9 cases of soda and seeing 9 movies a month, she gets almost the same utility from each good. And at 10 of each, she gets

TABLE 8.1 Lisa's Utility from Movies and Soda

Movies			Soda		
Quantity (per month)	Total utility	Marginal utility	Cases (per month)	Total utility	Marginal utility
0	0		0	0	
		50			75
1	50		1	75	
		40			48
2	90		2	123	
		32			36
3	122		3	159	
		28			24
4	150		4	183	
		26			22
5	176		5	205	
		24			20
6	200		6	225	
		22			13
7	222		7	238	
		20			10
8	242		8	248	
		17			7
9	259		9	255	
		16			5
10	275		10	260	

more total utility from movies (275 units) than she gets from soda (260 units).

Marginal Utility

Marginal utility is the change in total utility that results from a one-unit increase in the quantity of a good consumed.

In Table 8.1, the columns headed "Marginal utility" show Lisa's marginal utility from movies and soda. You can see that if Lisa increases the soda she buys from 1 to 2 cases a month, her total utility from soda increases from 75 units to 123 units. For Lisa, the marginal utility from the second case each month is 48 units (123 – 75).

The marginal utility numbers appear midway between the quantities of soda because it is the *change* in the quantity she buys from 1 to 2 cases that produces the marginal utility of 48 units.

Marginal utility is *positive,* but it *diminishes* as the quantity consumed of a good increases.

Positive Marginal Utility All the things that people enjoy and want more of have a positive marginal utility. Some objects and activities can generate negative marginal utility—and lower total utility. Two examples are hard labor and polluted air. But the goods and services that people value and that we are thinking about here all have positive marginal utility: total utility increases as the quantity consumed increases.

Diminishing Marginal Utility As Lisa sees more movies, her total utility from movies increases but her marginal utility from movies decreases. Similarly, as she consumes more soda, her total utility from soda increases but her marginal utility from soda decreases.

The tendency for marginal utility to decrease as the consumption of a good increases is so general and universal that we give it the status of a *principle*—the principle of **diminishing marginal utility**.

You can see Lisa's diminishing marginal utility by calculating a few numbers. Her marginal utility from soda decreases from 75 units from the first case to 48 units from the second case and to 36 units from the third. Her marginal utility from movies decreases from 50 units for the first movie to 40 units for the second and 32 units for the third. Lisa's marginal utility diminishes as she buys more of each good.

You can confirm that the principle of diminishing marginal utility applies to your own utility by thinking about the following two situations: In one, you've been studying all through the day and evening, and you've been too busy finishing an assignment to go shopping. A friend drops by with a can of soda. The utility you get from that soda is the marginal utility from one can. In the second situation, you've been on a soda binge. You've been working on an assignment all day but you've guzzled ten cans of soda while doing so, and are now totally wired. You are happy enough to have one more can, but the thrill that you get from it is not very large. It is the marginal utility from the nineteenth can in a day.

Graphing Lisa's Utility Schedules

Figure 8.1(a) illustrates Lisa's total utility from soda. The more soda Lisa consumes in a month, the more total utility she gets. Her total utility curve slopes upward.

Figure 8.1(b) illustrates Lisa's marginal utility from soda. It is a graph of the marginal utility numbers in Table 8.1. This graph shows Lisa's diminishing marginal utility from soda. Her marginal utility curve slopes downward as she consumes more soda.

We've now described Lisa's preferences. Our next task is to see how she chooses what to consume to maximize her utility.

FIGURE 8.1   Total Utility and Marginal Utility

(a) Total utility

(b) Marginal utility

The figure graphs Lisa's total utility and marginal utility from soda based on the numbers for the first 5 cases of soda a month in Table 8.1. Part (a) shows that her total utility increases as her consumption of soda increases—increasing total utility. The bars along the total utility curve show the extra total utility from each additional case of soda—marginal utility. Part (b) shows that Lisa's marginal utility from soda diminishes as her consumption of soda increases—diminishing marginal utility. The bars that measure marginal utility get shorter as soda consumption increases.

 animation

The Utility-Maximizing Choice

Suppose that Lisa earns $40 a month and she spends it all on movies and soda. The prices that she faces are $8 for a movie and $4 for a case of soda.

Lisa's most direct way of finding the quantities of movies and soda that maximize her utility is to make a spreadsheet like Table 8.2.

The rows of the table show the combinations of movies and soda that Lisa can afford and that exhaust her $40 income. She can afford smaller quantities of movies and soda than those in the table, but smaller quantities don't maximize her utility. Why? Because her marginal utilities of movies and soda are positive, so the more of each that she buys, the more total utility she gets.

Table 8.2 shows the total utility that Lisa gets from the just-affordable quantities of movies and soda. The middle column adds the total utility from movies to the total utility from soda. This number, the total utility from movies *and* soda, is what Lisa wants to maximize.

In row *A*, Lisa watches no movies and buys 10 cases of soda. She gets no utility from movies and 260 units of utility from soda. Her total utility from movies and soda (the center column) is 260 units.

In row *C*, highlighted in the table, Lisa sees 2 movies and buys 6 cases of soda. She gets 90 units of utility from movies and 225 units of utility from soda. Her total utility from movies and soda is 315 units. This combination of movies and soda maximizes Lisa's total utility. This is the best Lisa can do, when she has only $40 to spend and given the prices of movies and cases. If Lisa buys 8 cases of soda, she can see only 1 movie. She gets 298 units of total utility, 17 less than the maximum attainable. If she sees 3 movies, she can buy only 4 cases of soda. She gets 305 units of total utility, 10 less than the maximum attainable.

We've just described Lisa's consumer equilibrium. A **consumer equilibrium** is a situation in which a consumer has allocated all of his or her available income in the way that maximizes his or her total utility, given the prices of goods and services. Lisa's consumer equilibrium is 2 movies and 6 cases of soda.

To find Lisa's consumer equilibrium, we measured her *total* utility from all the affordable combinations of movies and soda. But a simpler way of finding a consumer equilibrium uses the idea that choices are made at the margin—an idea that you first met in Chapter 1. Let's look at this approach.

TABLE 8.2   Lisa's Utility-Maximizing Combinations

	Movies $8		Total utility from movies and soda	Soda $4	
	Quantity (per month)	Total utility		Total utility	Cases (per month)
A	0	0	260	260	10
B	1	50	298	248	8
C	2	90	315	225	6
D	3	122	305	183	4
E	4	150	273	123	2
F	5	176	176	0	0

Choosing at the Margin

A consumer's total utility is maximized by following the rule:

- Spend all the available income
- Equalize the marginal utility per dollar for all goods

Spend All the Available Income Because more consumption brings more utility, only those choices that exhaust income can maximize utility. For Lisa, combinations of movies and soda that leave her with money to spend don't give her as much total utility as those that spend her entire income of $40 a month.

Equalize Marginal Utility per Dollar We've defined marginal utility as the increase in total utility from consuming *one more unit* of a good. **Marginal utility per dollar** is the marginal utility from a good obtained by spending *one more dollar* on that good.

The distinction between these two marginal concepts is clearest for a good that is infinitely divisible, such as gasoline. You can buy gasoline by the smallest fraction of a gallon and literally choose to spend one more or one less dollar at the pump. When you buy a movie ticket or a case of soda, you must spend your dollars in bigger lumps. But the principles that apply at the gas pump also apply at the movie house and the convenience store.

Let's see how this marginal approach works.

The Basic Idea The basic idea behind the utility maximizing rule is to move dollars from good *A* to good *B* if doing so increases the utility from good *A* by more than it decreases the utility from good *B*. Such a utility-increasing move is possible if the marginal utility per dollar from good *A* exceeds that from good *B*.

But buying more of good *A* decreases its marginal utility. And buying less of good *B* increases its marginal utility. So by moving dollars from good *A* to good *B*, total utility rises, but the gap between the marginal utilities per dollar gets smaller.

So long as a gap exists—so long as the marginal utility per dollar from good *A* exceeds that from good *B*, total utility can be increased by spending more on *A* and less on *B*. But when enough dollars have been moved from *B* to *A* to make the two marginal utilities per dollar equal, total utility cannot be increased further. Utility is maximized.

Lisa's Marginal Calculation Let's apply the basic idea to Lisa. To calculate Lisa's marginal utility per dollar, we divide her marginal utility numbers for each quantity of each good by the price of the good. Table 8.3 shows these calculations for Lisa. The rows of the table are affordable combinations of movies and soda.

Too Few Movies and Too Much Soda In row *B*, Lisa sees 1 movie a month and consumes 8 cases of soda a month. Her marginal utility from seeing 1 movie a month is 50 units. Because the price of a movie is $8, Lisa's marginal utility per dollar from movies is 50 units divided by $8, or 6.25 units of utility per dollar.

Lisa's marginal utility from soda when she consumes 8 cases of soda a month is 10 units. Because the price of soda is $4 a case, Lisa's marginal utility per dollar from soda is 10 units divided by $4, or 2.50 units of utility per dollar.

When Lisa consumes 1 movie and 8 cases of soda a month, her marginal utility per dollar from movies *exceeds* her marginal utility per dollar from soda. If Lisa spent an extra dollar on movies and a dollar less on soda, her total utility would increase. She would get 6.25 units from the extra dollar spent on movies and lose 2.50 units from the dollar less spent on soda. Her total utility would increase by 3.75 units (6.25 − 2.50).

But if Lisa sees more movies and consumes less soda, her marginal utility from movies falls and her marginal utility from soda rises.

TABLE 8.3 Equalizing Marginal Utilities per Dollar

	Movies ($8 each)			Soda ($4 per case)		
	Quantity	Marginal utility	Marginal utility per dollar	Cases	Marginal utility	Marginal utility per dollar
A	0	0		10	5	1.25
B	1	50	6.25	8	10	2.50
C	2	40	5.00	6	20	5.00
D	3	32	4.00	4	24	6.00
E	4	28	3.50	2	48	12.00
F	5	26	3.25	0	0	

Too Many Movies and Too Little Soda In row *D*, Lisa sees 3 movies a month and consumes 4 cases of soda. Her marginal utility from seeing the third movie a month is 32 units. At a price of $8 a movie, Lisa's marginal utility per dollar from movies is 32 units divided by $8, or 4 units of utility per dollar.

Lisa's marginal utility from soda when she buys 4 cases a month is 24 units. At a price of $4 a case, Lisa's marginal utility per dollar from soda is 24 units divided by $4, or 6 units of utility per dollar.

When Lisa sees 3 movies and consumes 4 cases of soda a month, her marginal utility from soda *exceeds* her marginal utility from movies. If Lisa spent an extra dollar on soda and a dollar less on movies, her total utility would increase. She would get 6 units from the extra dollar spent on soda and she lose 4 units from the dollar less spent on movies. Her total utility would increase by 2 units (6 − 4).

But if Lisa sees fewer movies and consumes more soda, her marginal utility from movies rises and her marginal utility from soda falls.

Utility-Maximizing Movies and Soda In Table 8.3, if Lisa moves from row *B* to row *C*, she increases the movies she sees from 1 to 2 a month and she decreases the soda she consumes from 8 to 6 cases a month. Her marginal utility per dollar from movies falls to 5 and her marginal utility per dollar from soda rises to 5.

Similarly, if Lisa moves from row *D* to row *C*, she

decreases the movies she sees from 3 to 2 a month and she increases the soda she consumes from 4 to 6 cases a month. Her marginal utility per dollar from movies rises to 5 and her marginal utility per dollar from soda falls to 5.

At this combination of movies and soda, Lisa is maximizing her utility. If she spent an extra dollar on movies and a dollar less on soda, or an extra dollar on soda and a dollar less on movies, her total utility would not change.

The Power of Marginal Analysis

The method we've just used to find Lisa's utility-maximizing choice of movies and soda is an example of the power of marginal analysis. Lisa doesn't need a computer and a spreadsheet program to maximize utility. She can achieve this goal by comparing the marginal gain from having more of one good with the marginal loss from having less of another good.

The rule that she follows is simple: If the marginal utility per dollar from movies exceeds the marginal utility per dollar from soda, see more movies and buy less soda; if the marginal utility per dollar from soda exceeds the marginal utility per dollar from movies, buy more soda and see fewer movies.

More generally, if the marginal gain from an action exceeds the marginal loss, take the action. You will meet this principle time and again in your study of economics, and you will find yourself using it when you make your own economic choices, especially when you must make big decisions.

Units of Utility In maximizing total utility by making the marginal utility per dollar equal for all goods, the units in which utility is measured do not matter. Any arbitrary units will work. In this respect, utility is like temperature. Predictions about the freezing point of water don't depend on the temperature scale; and predictions about a household's consumption choice don't depend on the units of utility.

When we introduced the idea of utility, we arbitrarily chose 50 units as Lisa's total utility from 1 movie. But we could have given her any number. And as you're now about to discover, we didn't even need to ask Lisa to tell us her preferences. We can figure out Lisa's preferences for ourselves by observing what she buys at various prices. To see how, we need to use a bit of math.

Call the marginal utility from movies MU_M and the price of a movie P_M. Then the marginal utility per dollar from movies is

$$MU_M/P_M.$$

Call the marginal utility from soda MU_S and the price of a case of soda P_S. Then the marginal utility per dollar from soda is

$$MU_S/P_S.$$

When Lisa maximizes utility,

$$MU_S/P_S = MU_M/P_M.$$

Multiply both sides of this equation by P_S to obtain

$$MU_S = MU_M \times P_S/P_M.$$

This equation says that the marginal utility from soda, MU_S, is equal to the marginal utility from movies, MU_M, multiplied by the ratio of the price of soda, P_S, to the price of a movie, P_M.

For Lisa, when $P_M = \$8$ and $P_S = \$4$ we observe that in a month she goes to the movies twice and buys 6 cases of soda. So we know that her MU_S from 6 cases of soda equals her MU_M from 2 movies multiplied by $\$4/\$8$ or 0.5. If we call MU_M from the second movie 40, then MU_S from the sixth case of soda is 20. If we observe enough prices and quantities, we can construct an entire utility schedule for an arbitrary starting value.

Review Quiz

1 What is utility and how do we use the concept of utility to describe a consumer's preferences?
2 What is the distinction between total utility and marginal utility?
3 What is the key assumption about marginal utility?
4 What two conditions are met when a consumer is maximizing utility?
5 Explain why equalizing the marginal utility per dollar from each good maximizes utility.

 Work Study Plan 8.1 and get instant feedback.

Predictions of Marginal Utility Theory

We're now going to use marginal utility theory to make some predictions. You will see that marginal utility theory predicts the law of demand. The theory also predicts that a fall in the price of a substitute of a good decreases the demand for the good and that for a normal good, a rise in income increases demand. All these effects, which in Chapter 3 we simply assumed, are predictions of marginal utility theory.

To derive these predictions, we will study the effects of three events:

- A fall in the price of a movie
- A rise in the price of soda
- A rise in income

A Fall in the Price of a Movie

With the price of a movie at $8 and the price of soda at $4, Lisa is maximizing utility by seeing 2 movies and buying 6 cases of soda each month. Then, with no change in her $40 income and no change in the price of soda, the price of a movie falls from $8 to $4. How does Lisa change her buying plans?

Finding the New Quantities of Movies and Soda

You can find the effect of a fall in the price of a movie on the quantities of movies and soda that Lisa buys in a three-step calculation.

1. Determine the just-affordable combinations of movies and soda at the new prices.

2. Calculate the new marginal utilities per dollar from the good whose price has changed.

3. Determine the quantities of movies and soda that make their marginal utilities per dollar equal.

Affordable Combinations The lower price of a movie means that Lisa can afford more movies or more soda. Table 8.4 shows her new affordable combinations. In row *A*, if she continues to see 2 movies a month, she can now afford 8 cases of soda and in row *B*, if she continues to buy 6 cases of soda, she can now afford 4 movies. Lisa can afford any of the combinations shown in the rows of Table 8.4.

The next step is to find her new marginal utilities per dollar from movies.

New Marginal Utilities per Dollar from Movies A person's preferences don't change just because a price has changed. With no change in her preferences, Lisa's marginal utilities in Table 8.4 are the same as those in Table 8.1. But because the price of a movie has changed, the marginal utility *per dollar* from movies changes. In fact, with a halving of the price from $8 to $4, the marginal utility per dollar from movies has doubled.

The numbers in Table 8.4 show Lisa's marginal utility per dollar from movies for each quantity of movies. The table also shows Lisa's marginal utility from soda for each quantity.

Equalizing the Marginal Utilities per Dollar You can see that if Lisa continues to see 2 movies a month (row *A*), her marginal utility per dollar from movies is 10 units and if Lisa continues to buy 6 cases of soda (row *B*), her marginal utility per dollar from soda is only 5 units. Lisa is buying too much soda and too few movies. If she spends a dollar more on movies and a dollar less on soda, her total utility increases by 5 units (10 − 5).

You can also see that if Lisa continues to buy 6 cases of soda and sees 4 movies (row *B*), her marginal

TABLE 8.4   How a Change in the Price of Movies Affects Lisa's Choices

	Movies ($4 each)			Soda ($4 per case)		
	Quantity	Marginal utility	Marginal utility per dollar	Cases	Marginal utility	Marginal utility per dollar
	0	0		10	5	1.25
	1	50	12.50	9	7	1.75
A	2	40	**10.00**	8	10	2.50
	3	32	8.00	7	13	3.25
B	4	28	7.00	**6**	20	**5.00**
	5	26	6.50	5	22	5.50
C	6	24	6.00	4	24	6.00
	7	22	5.50	3	36	9.00
	8	20	5.00	2	48	12.00
	9	17	4.25	1	75	18.75
	10	16	4.00	0	0	

utility per dollar from movies is 7 units and her marginal utility per dollar from soda is only 5 units. Lisa is still buying too much soda and seeing too few movies. If she spends a dollar more on movies and a dollar less on soda, her total utility increases by 2 units (7 – 5).

But if Lisa sees 6 movies and buys 4 cases of soda a month (row *C*), her marginal utility per dollar from movies (6 units) equals her marginal utility per dollar from soda. If Lisa moves from this allocation of her budget, her total utility decreases. She is maximizing utility.

Lisa's increased purchases of movies results from a substitution effect—she substitutes the now lower-priced movies for soda—and an income effect—she can afford more movies.

A Change in the Quantity Demanded Lisa's increase in the quantity of movies that she sees is a change in the quantity demanded. It is the change in the quantity of movies that she plans to see each month when the price of a movie changes and all other influences on buying plans remain the same. We illustrate a change in the quantity demanded by a movement along a demand curve.

Figure 8.2(a) shows Lisa's demand curve for movies. When the price of a movie is $8, Lisa sees 2 movies a month. And when the price of a movie falls to $4, she sees 6 movies a month. Lisa moves downward along her demand curve for movies.

The demand curve traces the quantities that maximize utility at each price, with all other influences remaining the same. You can also see that utility-maximizing choices generate a downward-sloping demand curve. Utility maximization with diminishing marginal utility implies the law of demand.

A Change in Demand Lisa's decrease in the quantity of soda that she buys is the change in the quantity of soda that she plans to buy each month at a given price of soda when the price of a movie changes. It is a change in her demand for soda. We illustrate a change in demand by a shift of a demand curve.

Figure 8.2(b) shows Lisa's demand for soda. The price of soda is fixed at $4 a case. When the price of a movie is $8, Lisa buys 6 cases of soda on demand curve D_0. When the price of a movie falls to $4, Lisa buys 4 cases of soda on demand curve D_1. The fall in the price of a movie decreases Lisa's demand for soda. Her demand curve for soda shifts leftward. For Lisa, soda and movies are substitutes.

FIGURE 8.2   A Fall in the Price of a Movie

(a) Demand for movies

(b) Demand for soda

When the price of a movie falls and the price of soda remains the same, the quantity of movies demanded by Lisa increases, and in part (a), Lisa moves along her demand curve for movies. Also, when the price of a movie falls, Lisa's demand for soda decreases, and in part (b), her demand curve for soda shifts leftward. For Lisa, soda and movies are substitutes.

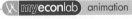

A Rise in the Price of Soda

Now suppose that with the price of a movie at $4, the price of soda rises from $4 to $8 a case. How does this price change influence Lisa's buying plans? We find the answer by repeating the three-step calculation with the new price of soda.

Table 8.5 shows Lisa's new affordable combinations. In row A, if she continues to buy 4 cases of soda a month she can afford to see only 2 movies; and in row B, if she continues to see 6 movies a month, she can afford only 2 cases of soda.

Table 8.5 show Lisa's marginal utility per dollar from soda for each quantity of soda when the price is $8 a case. The table also shows Lisa's marginal utility per dollar from movies for each quantity.

If Lisa continues to buy 4 cases of soda a month (row A), her marginal utility per dollar from soda is 3. But she must cut her movies to 2 a month, which gives her 12 units of utility per dollar from movies. Lisa is buying too much soda and too few movies. If she spends a dollar less on soda and a dollar more on movies, her utility increases by 9 units (12 – 3).

But if Lisa sees 6 movies a month and cuts her soda back to 2 cases (row B), her marginal utility per dollar from movies (6 units) equals her marginal utility per dollar from soda. She is maximizing utility.

Lisa's decreased purchases of soda results from an income effect—she can afford fewer cases and she buys fewer cases. But she continues to buy the same quantity of movies.

Lisa's Demand for Soda Now that we've calculated the effect of a change in the price of soda on Lisa's buying plans, we have found two points on her demand curve for soda: When the price of soda is $4 a case, Lisa buys 4 cases a month; and when the price rises to $8 a case, she buys 2 cases a month.

Figure 8.3 shows these points on Lisa's demand curve for soda. It also shows the change in the quantity of soda demanded when the price of soda rises and all other influences on Lisa's buying plans remain the same.

In this particular case, Lisa continues to buy the same quantity of movies. This outcome does not always occur. It is a consequence of Lisa's utility schedule. With different marginal utilities, she might have decreased or increased the quantity of movies that she sees when the price of soda changes.

You've seen that marginal utility theory predicts the law of demand—the way in which the quantity demanded of a good changes when its price changes. Next we'll see how marginal utility theory predicts the effect of a change in income on demand.

TABLE 8.5 How a Change in the Price of Soda Affects Lisa's Choices

	Quantity	Movies ($4 each) Marginal utility	Marginal utility per dollar	Cases	Soda ($8 per case) Marginal utility	Marginal utility per dollar
	0	0		5	22	2.75
A	2	40	12.00	4	24	3.00
	4	28	7.00	3	36	4.50
B	6	24	6.00	2	48	6.00
	8	20	5.00	1	75	9.38
	10	16	4.00	0	0	

FIGURE 8.3 A Rise in the Price of Soda

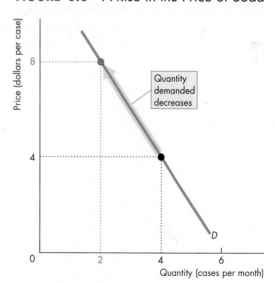

When the price of soda rises and the price of a movie and Lisa's income remain the same, the quantity of soda demanded by Lisa decreases. Lisa moves along her demand curve for soda.

myeconlab animation

A Rise in Income

Suppose that Lisa's income increases from $40 to $56 a month and that the price of a movie is $4 and the price of a case of soda is $4. With these prices and with an income of $40 a month, Lisa sees 6 movies and buys 4 cases of soda a month (Table 8.4). How does the increase in Lisa's income from $40 to $56 change her buying plans?

Table 8.6 shows the calculations needed to answer this question. If Lisa continues to see 6 movies a month, she can now afford to buy 8 cases of soda (row *A*); and if she continues to buy 4 cases of soda, she can now afford to see 10 movies (row *C*).

In row *A*, Lisa's marginal utility per dollar from movies is greater than her marginal utility per dollar from soda. She is buying too much soda and too few movies. In row *C*, Lisa's marginal utility per dollar from movies is less than her marginal utility per dollar from soda. She is buying too little soda and too many movies. But in row *B*, when Lisa sees 8 movies a month and buys 6 cases of soda, her marginal utility per dollar from movies equals that from soda. She is maximizing utility.

Figure 8.4 shows the effects of the rise in Lisa's income on her demand curves for movies and soda. The price of each good is $4. When Lisa's income

TABLE 8.6   Lisa's Choices with an Income of $56 a Month

	Movies ($4 each)			Soda ($4 per case)		
	Quantity	Marginal utility	Marginal utility per dollar	Cases	Marginal utility	Marginal utility per dollar
	4	28	7.00	10	5	1.25
	5	26	6.50	9	7	1.75
A	6	24	**6.00**	8	10	2.50
	7	22	5.50	7	13	3.25
B	8	20	5.00	6	20	5.00
	9	17	4.25	5	22	5.50
C	10	16	4.00	4	24	**6.00**

rises to $56 a month, she sees 2 more movies and buys 2 more cases of soda. Her demand curves for both movies and soda shift rightward—her demand for both movies and soda increases. With a larger income, the consumer always buys more of a *normal* good. For Lisa, movies and soda are normal goods.

FIGURE 8.4   The Effects of a Rise in Income

(a) Demand for movies

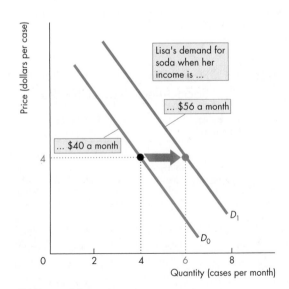

(b) Demand for soda

When Lisa's income increases, her demand for movies and her demand for soda increase. Lisa's demand curves for movies, in part (a), and for soda, in part (b), shift rightward. For Lisa, movies and soda are normal goods.

myeconlab animation

1

The Paradox of Value

The price of water is low and the price of a diamond is high, but water is essential to life while diamonds are used mostly just for decoration. How can valuable water be so cheap while a relatively useless diamond is so expensive? This so-called *paradox of value* has puzzled philosophers for centuries. Not until the theory of marginal utility had been developed could anyone give a satisfactory answer.

The Paradox Resolved The paradox is resolved by distinguishing between *total* utility and *marginal* utility. The total utility that we get from water is enormous. But remember, the more we consume of something, the smaller is its marginal utility.

We use so much water that its marginal utility—the benefit we get from one more glass of water or another 30 seconds in the shower—diminishes to a small value.

Diamonds, on the other hand, have a small total utility relative to water, but because we buy few diamonds, they have a high marginal utility.

When a household has maximized its total utility, it has allocated its income in the way that makes the marginal utility per dollar equal for all goods. That is, the marginal utility from a good divided by the price of the good is equal for all goods.

This equality of marginal utilities per dollar holds true for diamonds and water: Diamonds have a high price and a high marginal utility. Water has a low price and a low marginal utility. When the high marginal utility from diamonds is divided by the high price of a diamond, the result is a number that equals the low marginal utility from water divided by the low price of water. The marginal utility per dollar is the same for diamonds and water.

Value and Consumer Surplus Another way to think about the paradox of value and illustrate how it is resolved uses *consumer surplus*. Figure 8.5 explains the paradox of value by using this idea. The supply of water in part (a) is perfectly elastic at price P_W, so the quantity of water consumed is Q_W and the consumer surplus from water is the large green area. The supply of diamonds in part (b) is perfectly inelastic at the quantity Q_D, so the price of a diamond is P_D and the consumer surplus from diamonds is the small green area. Water is cheap but brings a large consumer surplus, while diamonds are expensive but bring a small consumer surplus.

FIGURE 8.5 The Paradox of Value

(a) Water

(b) Diamonds

Part (a) shows the demand for and supply of water. Supply is perfectly elastic at the price P_W. At this price, the quantity of water consumed is Q_W and consumer surplus is the large green triangle. Part (b) shows the demand for and supply of diamonds. Supply is perfectly inelastic at the quantity Q_D. At this quantity, the price of a diamond is P_D and consumer surplus is the small green triangle. Water is valuable—has a large consumer surplus—but cheap. Diamonds are less valuable than water—have a smaller consumer surplus—but are expensive.

myeconlab   animation

Temperature: An Analogy

Utility is similar to temperature. Both are abstract concepts, and both have units of measurement that are arbitrary. You can't *observe* temperature. You can observe water turning to steam if it is hot enough or turning to ice if it is cold enough. And you can construct an instrument—a thermometer—that can help you to predict when such changes will occur. We call the scale on the thermometer *temperature* and we call the units of temperature *degrees*. But these degree units are arbitrary. We can use Celsius units or Fahrenheit units or some other units.

The concept of utility helps us to make predictions about consumption choices in much the same way that the concept of temperature helps us to make predictions about physical phenomena.

Admittedly, marginal utility theory does not enable us to predict how buying plans change with the same precision that a thermometer enables us to predict when water will turn to ice or steam. But the theory provides important insights into buying plans and has some powerful implications. It helps us to understand why people buy more of a good or service when its price falls and why people buy more of most goods when their incomes increase. It also resolves the paradox of value.

We're going to end this chapter by looking at some new ways of studying individual economic choices and consumer behavior.

Review Quiz

1 When the price of a good falls and the prices of other goods and a consumer's income remain the same, what happens to the consumption of the good whose price has fallen and to the consumption of other goods?

2 Elaborate on your answer to the previous question by using demand curves. For which good does demand change and for which good does the quantity demanded change?

3 If a consumer's income increases and if all goods are normal goods, how does the quantity bought of each good change?

4 What is the paradox of value and how is the paradox resolved?

5 What are the similarities between utility and temperature?

myeconlab   Work Study Plan 8.2 and get instant feedback.

Maximizing Utility in Markets for Recorded Music

Downloads Versus Discs

In 2007, Americans spent $10 billion on recorded music, down from $14 billion in 2000. But the combined quantity of discs and downloads bought increased from 1 billion in 2000 to 1.8 billion in 2007 and the average price of a unit of recorded music fell from $14 to $5.50.

The average price fell because the mix of formats bought changed dramatically. In 2000, we bought 1 billion CDs; in 2007, we bought only 0.5 billion CDs and downloaded 1.3 billion music files.

Figure 1 shows the longer history of the changing formats of recorded music.

The music that we buy isn't just one good—it is several goods. Singles and albums are different goods; downloads and discs are different goods; and downloads to a computer and downloads to a cell phone are different goods. There are five major categories (excluding DVDs and cassettes) and the table shows the quantities of each that we bought in 2007.

Format	Singles	Albums
	(millions in 2007)	
Disc	3	500
Download	800	40
Mobile	400	–

Source of data: Recording Industry Association of America.

Most people buy all their music in digital form, but many still buy physical CDs and some people buy both downloads and CDs.

We get utility from the singles and albums that we buy, and the more songs and albums we have, the more utility we get. But our marginal utility from songs and albums decreases as the quantity that we own increases.

We also get utility from convenience. A song that we can buy with a mouse click and play with the spin of a wheel is more convenient both to buy and to use than a song on a CD. The convenience of songs downloaded over the Internet means that, song for song, we get more utility from songs in this format than we get from physical CDs.

But most albums are still played at home on a CD player. So for most people, a physical CD is a more convenient medium for delivering an album. Album

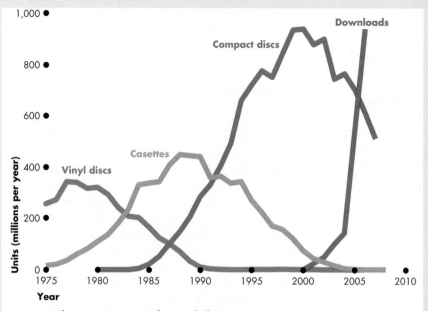

Figure 1 Changing Formats of Recorded Music

Source of data: www.swivel.com.

In the 1970s, recorded music came on vinyl discs. Cassettes gradually replaced vinyl, then compact discs gradually replaced cassettes, and today, digital files downloaded to computers and mobile devices are replacing physical CDs.

for album, people on average get more utility from a CD than from a download.

When we decide how many singles and albums to download and how many to buy on CD, we compare the marginal utility per dollar from each type of music in each format. We make the marginal utility per dollar from each type of music in each format equal, as the equations below show.

The market for single downloads has created an enormous consumer surplus. The table shows that the quantity of single downloads demanded at 99 cents each was 800 million in 2007, and the quantity of singles on a disc demanded at \$4.75 a disc was 3 million in 2007. If we assume that \$4.75 is the most that anyone would pay for a single download (probably an underestimate), the demand curve for single downloads is that shown in Fig. 2.

With the price of a single download at \$0.99, consumer surplus (the area of the green triangle) is \$1.5 billion.

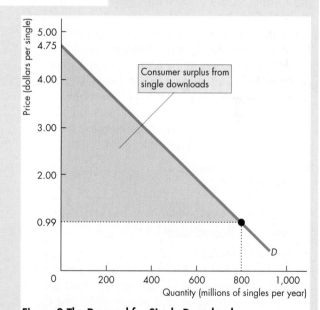

Figure 2 The Demand for Single Downloads

$$\frac{MU_{single\ downloads}}{P_{single\ downloads}} = \frac{MU_{album\ downloads}}{P_{album\ downloads}} = \frac{MU_{physical\ singles}}{P_{physical\ singles}} = \frac{MU_{physical\ albums}}{P_{physical\ albums}} = \frac{MU_{mobile}}{P_{mobile}}$$

$$\frac{MU_{single\ downloads}}{\$0.99} = \frac{MU_{album\ downloads}}{\$10} = \frac{MU_{physical\ singles}}{\$4.75} = \frac{MU_{physical\ albums}}{\$15} = \frac{MU_{mobile}}{\$2.50}$$

New Ways of Explaining Consumer Choices

When William Stanley Jevons developed marginal utility theory in the 1860s, he would have loved to look inside people's brains and "see" their utility. But he believed that the human brain was the ultimate black box that could never be observed directly. For Jevons, and for most economists today, the purpose of marginal utility theory is to explain our *actions*, not what goes on inside our brains.

Economics has developed over the past 150 years with little help from and paying little attention to advances being made in psychology. Both economics and psychology seek to explain human behavior, but they have developed different ways of attacking the challenge.

A few researchers *have* paid attention to the potential payoff from exploring economic problems by using the tools of psychology. These researchers, some economists and some psychologists, think that marginal utility theory is based on a view of how people make choices that attributes too much to reason and rationality. They propose an alternative approach based on the methods of psychology.

Other researchers, some economists and some neuroscientists, are using new tools to look inside the human brain and open up Jevons' "black box."

This section provides a very brief introduction to these new and exciting areas of economics. We'll explore the two related research agendas:

- Behavioral economics
- Neuroeconomics

Behavioral Economics

Behavioral economics studies the ways in which limits on the human brain's ability to compute and implement rational decisions influences economic behavior—both the decisions that people make and the consequences of those decisions for the way markets work.

Behavioral economics starts with observed behavior. It looks for anomalies—choices that do not seem to be rational. It then tries to account for the anomalies by using ideas developed by psychologists that emphasize features of the human brain that limit rational choice.

In behavioral economics, instead of being rational utility maximizers, people are assumed to have three impediments that prevent rational choice: bounded rationality, bounded willpower, and bounded self-interest.

Bounded Rationality Bounded rationality is rationality that is limited by the computing power of the human brain. We can't always work out the rational choice.

For Lisa, choosing between movies and soda, it seems unlikely that she would have much trouble figuring out what to buy. But toss Lisa some uncertainty and the task becomes harder. She's read the reviews of "Mamma Mia!" on Fandango, but does she really want to see that movie? How much marginal utility will it give her? Faced with uncertainty, people might use rules of thumb, listen to the views of others, and make decisions based on gut instinct rather than on rational calculation.

Bounded Willpower Bounded willpower is the less-than-perfect willpower that prevents us from making a decision that we know, at the time of implementing the decision, we will later regret.

Lisa might be feeling particularly thirsty when she passes a soda vending machine. Under Lisa's rational utility-maximizing plan, she buys her soda at the discount store, where she gets it for the lowest possible price. Lisa has already bought her soda for this month, but it is at home. Spending $1 on a can now means giving up a movie later this month.

Lisa's rational choice is to ignore the temporary thirst and stick to her plan. But she might not possess the will power to do so—sometimes she will and sometimes she won't.

Bounded Self-Interest Bounded self-interest is the limited self-interest that results in sometimes suppressing our own interests to help others.

A hurricane hits the Florida coast and Lisa, feeling sorry for the victims, donates $10 to a fund-raiser. She now has only $30 to spend on movies and soda this month. The quantities that she buys are not, according to her utility schedule, the ones that maximize her utility.

The main applications of behavioral economics are in two areas: finance, where uncertainty is a key factor in decision making, and savings, where the future is a key factor.

But one behavior observed by behavioral economists is more general and might affect your choices. It is called the endowment effect.

The Endowment Effect The endowment effect is the tendency for people to value something more highly simply because they own it. If you have allocated your income to maximize utility, the price you are willing to pay for a coffee mug should be the same as the price you would be willing to accept to give up an identical coffee mug that you own.

In experiments, students seem to display the endowment effect: The price they are willing to pay for a coffee mug is less than the price they would be willing to accept to give up an identical coffee mug that they own. Behavioral economists say that this behavior contradicts marginal utility theory.

Neuroeconomics

Neuroeconomics is the study of the activity of the human brain when a person makes an economic decision. The discipline uses the observational tools and ideas of neuroscience to better understand economic decisions.

Neuroeconomics is an experimental discipline. In an experiment, a person makes an economic decision and the electrical or chemical activity of the person's brain is observed and recorded using the same type of equipment that neurosurgeons use to diagnose brain disorders.

The observations provide information about which regions of the brain are active at different points in the process of making an economic decision.

It has been observed that some economic decisions generate activity in the area of the brain (called the prefrontal cortex) where we store memories, analyze data, and anticipate the consequences of our actions. If people make rational utility-maximizing decisions, it is in this region of the brain that the decision occurs.

But some economic decisions generate activity in the region of the brain (called the hippocampus) where we store memories of anxiety and fear. Decisions that are influenced by activity in this part of the brain might be non-rational and driven by fear or panic.

Neuroeconomists are also able to observe the amount of a brain hormone (called dopamine), the

quantity of which increases in response to pleasurable events and decreases in response to disappointing events. These observations might one day enable neuroeconomists to actually measure utility and shine a bright light inside what was once believed to be the ultimate black box.

Controversy

The new ways of studying consumer choice that we've briefly described here are being used more widely to study business decisions and decisions in financial markets, and this type of research is surely going to become more popular.

But behavioral economics and neuroeconomics generate controversy. Most economists hold the view of Jevons that the goal of economics is to explain the decisions that we observe people make, and not to explain what goes on inside people's heads.

Also, most economists would prefer to probe apparent anomalies more deeply and figure out why they are not anomalies after all.

Finally, economists point to the power of marginal utility theory and its ability to explain consumer choice and demand as well as resolve the paradox of value.

Review Quiz

1 Define behavioral economics.
2 What are the three limitations on human rationality that behavioral economics emphasizes?
3 Define neuroeconomics.
4 What do behavioral economics and neuroeconomics seek to achieve?

 Work Study Plan 8.3 and get instant feedback.

◆ You have now completed your study of the marginal utility theory and some new ideas about how people make economic choices. You can see marginal utility theory in action once again in *Reading Between the Lines* on pp. 196–197, where it is used to explain why paramedics who save people's lives earn so much less than hockey players who merely provide entertainment.

A Paradox of Value: Paramedics and Hockey Players

Salaries, Strong Recruitment Ease Area Paramedic Shortage

April 4, 2008

To curb a critical shortage, fire departments across the Washington region have pursued paramedics like star athletes in recent years, enticing them with signing bonuses, handsome salaries and the promise of fast-track career paths.

Montgomery County hired a marketing expert and launched a national recruiting drive, reaching out in particular to women and minorities. Fairfax County offered top starting salaries, now totaling about $57,000—as much as 50 percent higher than some other local jurisdictions, though Fairfax paramedics generally work longer hours. ...

Ducks Give Perry $26.6 Million Deal

July 2, 2008

The Ducks' first free-agent signing might also be their last, their biggest and their most expected.

Within the first hour of the NHL's free agency period, Corey Perry signed a five-year, $26.625 million contract that will keep the 23-year-old in Anaheim until 2013. Both parties had expressed an interest in completing the deal for several months but it wasn't possible until Tuesday, when the Ducks had enough room for long-term contracts under the salary cap.

"I really wanted to stay in Anaheim," Perry said. "It's home now and I didn't want to leave here. It's a great place to play hockey and it just shows how well the organization is run."

Including an $8 million signing bonus spread over its duration, the contract will pay Perry $4.5 million in 2008–09, then $6.5 million, $5.375 million, $5.375 million and $4.875 million, respectively, over the final four years. ...

Essence of the Stories

- In Washington, the starting salary for a paramedic is $57,000 per year.
- Corey Perry has a 5-year contract with the Anaheim Ducks that will earn him $26.6 million.

Economic Analysis

- If resources are used efficiently, the marginal utility per dollar from the services of a paramedic, MU_P/P_P, equals the marginal utility per dollar from the services of a hockey player, MU_H/P_H. That is,

$$\frac{MU_P}{P_P} = \frac{MU_H}{P_H}.$$

- A paramedic in Washington earns $57,000 a year, but the national average paramedic wage is $27,000 a year.

- Corey Perry earns $26.6 million over 5 years, or $5.32 million a year on average.

- If we put these numbers into the above formula, we get

$$\frac{MU_P}{\$27,000} = \frac{MU_H}{\$5,320,000}.$$

Equivalently,

$$\frac{MU_H}{MU_P} = 197.$$

- Is the marginal utility from Corey Perry's services really 197 times that from the paramedic's services?

- The answer is no. A paramedic might serve about 8 people a day, or perhaps 2,000 in a year; a hockey player like Corey Perry serves millions of people a year.

- If a paramedic serves 2,000 people a year, then the price of a paramedic's service per customer served is $27,000/2,000, which equals $13.50.

- If Corey Perry serves 1,000,000 people a year, then the price of Corey Perry's service per customer served is $5,320,000/1,000,000, which equals $5.32.

- Using these prices of the services per customer, a paramedic is worth 2.5 times as much as a hockey player—the marginal utility from the services of a paramedic is 2.5 times that from a hockey player.

- Figure 1 shows the market for paramedics. The equilibrium quantity is 200,000 workers, and the average wage rate is $27,000 a year.

- Figure 2 shows the market for professional hockey players. The equilibrium quantity is 500 players and the aver-

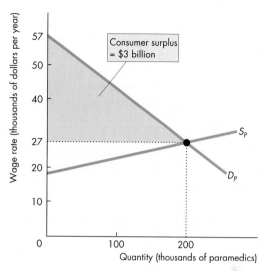

Figure 1 The value of paramedics

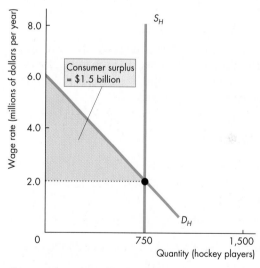

Figure 2 The value of hockey players

age wage rate is $4,000,000 a year. (Corey Perry earns more than the average player.)

- Not only is the marginal utility from a paramedic greater than that from a hockey player, but paramedics also create a greater consumer surplus.

SUMMARY

Key Points

Maximizing Utility (pp. 182–186)

- A household's preferences can be described by a utility schedule that lists the total utility and marginal utility derived from various quantities of goods and services consumed.
- The principle of diminishing marginal utility is that the marginal utility from a good or service decreases as consumption of the good or service increases.
- Total utility is maximized when all the available income is spent and when the marginal utility per dollar from all goods is equal.
- If the marginal utility per dollar for good A exceeds that for good B, total utility increases if the quantity purchased of good A increases and the quantity purchased of good B decreases.

Predictions of Marginal Utility Theory (pp. 187–193)

- Marginal utility theory predicts the law of demand. That is, other things remaining the same, the higher the price of a good, the smaller is the quantity demanded of that good.
- Marginal utility theory also predicts that, other things remaining the same, the larger the

consumer's income, the larger is the quantity demanded of a normal good.
- Marginal utility theory resolves the paradox of value.
- Total value is *total* utility or consumer surplus. But price is related to *marginal* utility.
- Water, which we consume in large amounts, has a high total utility and a large consumer surplus, but the price of water is low and the marginal utility from water is low.
- Diamonds, which we buy in small quantities, have a low total utility and a small consumer surplus, but the price of a diamond is high and the marginal utility from diamonds is high.

New Ways of Explaining Consumer Choices (pp. 194–195)

- Behavioral economics studies limits on the ability of the human brain to compute and implement rational decisions.
- Bounded rationality, bounded willpower, and bounded self-interest are believed to explain some choices.
- Neuroeconomics uses the ideas and tools of neuroscience to study the effects of economic events and choices inside the human brain.

Key Figures

Key Terms

PROBLEMS and APPLICATIONS

myeconlab Work problems 1–10 in Chapter 8 Study Plan and get instant feedback.
Work problems 11–21 as Homework, a Quiz, or a Test if assigned by your instructor.

1. Max enjoys windsurfing and snorkeling. The table shows the total utility he gets from each activity.

Hours per day	Total utility from windsurfing	Total utility from snorkeling
1	120	40
2	220	76
3	300	106
4	360	128
5	396	140
6	412	150
7	422	158

   a. Find Max's marginal utility from windsurfing at each number of hours per day.
   b. Find Max's marginal utility from snorkeling at each number of hours per day.
   c. Do Max's marginal utility from windsurfing and from snorkeling obey the principle of diminishing marginal utility?
   d. Which does Max enjoy more: his 6th hour of windsurfing or his 6th hour of snorkeling?

2. Max in problem 1 has $35 a day to spend, and he can spend as much time as he likes on his leisure pursuits. Windsurfing equipment rents for $10 an hour, and snorkeling equipment rents for $5 an hour.
   a. Make a table that shows the various combinations of hours spent windsurfing and snorkeling that Max can afford.
   b. In your table, add two columns and list Max's marginal utility per dollar from windsurfing and from snorkeling.
   c. How long does Max spend windsurfing and how long does he spend snorkeling to maximize his total utility?
   d. If compared to c, Max spent a dollar more on windsurfing and a dollar less on snorkeling, by how much would his total utility change?
   e. If compared to c, Max spent a dollar less on windsurfing and a dollar more on snorkeling, by how much would his total utility change?
   f. Explain why, if Max equalized the marginal utility per hour from windsurfing and from snorkeling, he would *not* maximize his utility.

3. Max in problems 1 and 2 is offered a special deal on windsurfing equipment: a rental rate of $5 an hour. His income remains at $35 a day and the rental price of snorkeling equipment remains at $5 an hour.
   a. Make a table that shows the new combinations of hours spent windsurfing and snorkeling that Max can afford.
   b. In your table, list Max's marginal utilities per dollar from windsurfing and snorkeling.
   c. How many hours does Max now spend windsurfing and how many hours does he spend snorkeling?

4. Given the information about Max in problems 1, 2, and 3,
   a. Find two points on Max's demand curve for rented windsurfing equipment.
   b. Draw Max's demand curve for rented windsurfing equipment.
   c. Is Max's demand for renting windsurfing equipment elastic or inelastic?

5. Max, with the utility schedules in problem 1, gets an increase in income from $35 to $55 a day. Windsurfing equipment rents for $10 an hour, and snorkeling equipment rents for $5 an hour. Show the effect of the increase in Max's income on Max's demand curve for
   a. Rented windsurfing equipment, and explain whether, for Max, windsurfing equipment is a normal good or an inferior good.
   b. Rented snorkeling equipment, and explain whether, for Max, snorkeling equipment is a normal good or an inferior good.

6. **Schools Get a Lesson in Lunch Line Economics**
   Sharp rises in the cost of milk, grain, and fresh fruits and vegetables are hitting cafeterias across the country, forcing cash-strapped schools to raise prices or pinch pennies by serving more economical dishes. ... Fairfax schools, for instance, serve oranges—14 cents each—instead of grapes, which are a quarter a serving.
   The Washington Post, April 14, 2008
   Assume that a Fairfax school has a $14 daily fruit budget.
   a. How many oranges a day can the school afford to serve if it serves no grapes?

b. How many servings of grapes can the school afford each day if it serves no oranges?

c. If the school provides 50 oranges a day and maximizes utility, how many servings of grapes does it provide?

d. If the marginal utility from an orange is 14 units of utility, what is the marginal utility from a serving of grapes?

7. **Can Money Buy Happiness?**

"Whoever said money can't buy happiness isn't spending it right."... You know that there must be some connection between money and happiness. If there weren't, you'd be less likely to stay late at work (or even come in at all). ... "Once you get basic human needs met, a lot more money doesn't make a lot more happiness." ... Going from earning less than $20,000 a year to making more than $50,000 makes you twice as likely to be happy, yet the payoff for then surpassing $90,000 is slight.

CNN, July 18, 2006

a. What does the fundamental assumption of marginal utility theory suggest about the connection between money and happiness?

b. Explain why this article is consistent with marginal utility theory.

8. **Eating Away the Innings in Baseball's Cheap Seats**

Baseball and gluttony, two of America's favorite pastimes, are merging in a controversial trend taking hold at Major League Baseball stadiums across the nation: all-you-can-eat seats. ... Some fans try to "set personal records" during their first game in the section. By their second or third time in such seats ... they eat like they normally would at a game.

USA Today, March 6, 2008

a. What conflict might exist between utility-maximization and setting "personal records" for eating?

b. What does the fact that fans eat less at subsequent games indicate about what happens to the marginal utility from ballpark food as the quantity consumed increases?

c. How can setting personal records for eating be reconciled with marginal utility theory?

d. Which ideas of behavioral economics are consistent with the information in the news clip?

9. **Compared to Other Liquids, Gasoline is Cheap**

Think a $4 gallon of gas is expensive? Consider the prices of these other fluids that people buy every day without complaint. ...

Gatorade, 20 oz @ $1.59   = $10.17 per gallon ...
Wite-Out, 7 oz @ $1.39   = $25.42 per gallon ...
HP Ink Cartridge, 16 ml @ $18 = $4,294.58 per gallon

The New York Times, May 27, 2008

a. What does marginal utility theory predict about the marginal utility per dollar from gasoline, Gatorade, Wite-Out, and printer ink?

b. What do the prices per gallon reported in this news clip tell you about the marginal utility from a gallon of gasoline, Gatorade, Wite-Out, and printer ink?

c. What do the prices per unit reported in this news clip tell you about the marginal utility from a gallon of gasoline, a 20 oz bottle of Gatorade, a 7 oz bottle of Wite-Out, and a cartridge of printer ink?

d. How can the paradox of value be used to explain why the fluids listed in the news clip might be less valuable than gasoline, yet far more expensive?

10. **Exclusive Status: It's in The Bag; $52,500 Purses. 24 Worldwide. 1 in Washington.**

Forget your Coach purse. Put away your Kate Spade. Even Hermes's famous Birkin bag seems positively discount.

The Louis Vuitton Tribute Patchwork is this summer's ultimate status bag, ringing in at $52,500. And it is arriving in Washington. ...

The company ... [is] offering only five for sale in North America and 24 worldwide. ...

The Washington Post, August 21, 2007

a. Use marginal utility theory to explain the facts reported in the news clip.

b. If Louis Vuitton offered 500 Tribute Patchwork bags in North America and 2,400 worldwide, what do you predict would happen to the price that buyers would be willing to pay and what would happen to the consumer surplus?

c. If the Tribute Patchwork bag is copied and thousands are sold illegally, what do you predict would happen to the price that buyers would be willing to pay for a genuine bag and what would happen to the consumer surplus?

11. Cindy enjoys golf and tennis. The table shows the marginal utility she gets from each activity.

Hours per month	Marginal utility from golf	Marginal utility from tennis
1	80	40
2	60	36
3	40	30
4	30	20
5	20	10
6	10	5
7	6	2

Cindy has $70 a month to spend, and she can spend as much time as she likes on her leisure pursuits. The price of an hour of golf is $10, and the price of an hour of tennis is $5.
   a. Make a table that shows the various combinations of hours spent playing golf and tennis that Cindy can afford.
   b. In your table, add two columns and list Cindy's marginal utility per dollar from golf and from tennis.
   c. How long does Cindy spend playing golf and how long does she spend playing tennis to maximize her utility?
   d. Compared to c, if Cindy spent a dollar more on golf and a dollar less on tennis, by how much would her total utility change?
   e. Compared to c, if Cindy spent a dollar less on golf and a dollar more on tennis, by how much would her total utility change?
   f. Explain why, if Cindy equalized the marginal utility per hour of golf and tennis, she would *not* maximize her utility.
12. Cindy's tennis club raises its price of an hour of tennis to $10. The price of golf and Cindy's income remain the same.
   a. Make a table that shows the combinations of hours spent playing golf and tennis that Cindy can now afford.
   b. In your table, list Cindy's marginal utility per dollar from golf and from tennis.
   c. How many hours does Cindy now spend playing golf and how many hours does she spend playing tennis?
13. Given the information in problems 11 and 12,
   a. Find two points on Cindy's demand curve for tennis.

   b. Draw Cindy's demand curve for tennis.
   c. Is Cindy's demand for tennis elastic or inelastic?
   d. Explain how Cindy's demand for golf changed when the price of an hour of tennis increased.
   e. What is Cindy's cross elasticity of demand for golf with respect to the price of tennis?
   f. Are tennis and golf substitutes or complements for Cindy?
14. Cindy, with the utility schedules in problem 11, loses her math tutoring job and her income falls to $35 a month. With golf at $10 an hour and tennis at $5 an hour, how does the decrease in Cindy's income change her demand for
   a. Golf, and explain whether, for Cindy, golf is a normal good or an inferior good.
   b. Tennis, and explain whether, for Cindy, tennis is a normal good or an inferior good.
15. Cindy in problem 11 takes a Club Med vacation, the cost of which includes unlimited sports activities. With no extra charge for golf and tennis, Cindy allocates a total of 4 hours a day to these activities.
   a. How many hours does Cindy play golf and how many hours does she play tennis?
   b. What is Cindy's marginal utility from golf and from tennis?
   c. Why does Cindy equalize the marginal utilities rather than the marginal utility per dollar from golf and from tennis?
16. Ben spends $50 a year on 2 bunches of flowers and $50 a year on 10,000 gallons of tap water. Ben is maximizing utility and his marginal utility from water is 0.5 unit per gallon.
   a. Are flowers or water more valuable to Ben?
   b. Explain how Ben's expenditure on flowers and water illustrates the paradox of value.
17. **Blu-Ray Format Expected to Dominate, but When?**
   Blu-ray stomped HD DVD to become the standard format for high-definition movie discs, but years may pass before it can claim victory over the good old DVD. … "The group that bought $2,000, 40-inch TVs are the ones that will lead the charge. … Everyone else will come along when the price comes down."… Blu-ray machine prices are starting to drop. Wal-Mart Stores Inc. began stocking a $298 Magnavox model. …

That's cheaper than most alternatives but a hefty price hike from a typical $50 DVD player.

CNN, June 2, 2008

a. What does marginal utility theory predict about the marginal utility from a Magnavox Blu-ray machine compared to the marginal utility from a typical DVD player?

b. What will have to happen to the marginal utility from a Blu-ray machine before it is able to "claim victory over the good old DVD"?

18. **Five Signs You Have Too Much Money**

Some people think bottled water is a fool's drink. I'm not among them, but when a bottle of water costs $38, it's hard not to see their point. The drink of choice these days among image-conscious status seekers and high-end tee-totalers in L.A. is Bling H2O… it's not the water that accounts for the cost. … Much of the $38 is due to the "limited edition" bottle decked out in Swarovski crystals.

CNN, January 17, 2006

a. Assuming that the price of a bottle of Bling H2O is $38 in all the major cities in the United States, what might its popularity in Los Angeles reveal about consumers' incomes or consumers' preferences in Los Angeles relative to other U.S. cities?

b. Why might the marginal utility from a bottle of Bling H2O decrease more rapidly than the marginal utility from ordinary bottled water?

19. **How To Buy Happiness. Cheap**

Sure, in any given country at any given point in time, the rich tend to be a bit happier than the poor. But across-the-board increases in living standards don't seem to make people any happier. Disposable income for the average American has grown about 80% since 1972, but the percentage describing themselves as "very happy" (roughly a third) has barely budged over the years. … As living standards increase, most of us respond by raising our own standards. Things that once seemed luxuries now seem necessities. … As a result, we're working harder than ever to buy stuff that satisfies us less and less.

CNN, October 1, 2004

a. According to this news clip, how do widespread increases in living standards influence total utility?

b. What does the news clip imply about how the total utility from consumption changes over time?

c. What does the news clip imply about how the marginal utility from consumption changes over time?

20. **Putting a Price on Human Life**

What's a healthy human life worth? According to Stanford and University of Pennsylvania Researchers, about $129,000. Using Medicare records on treatment costs for kidney dialysis as a benchmark, the authors tried to pinpoint the threshold beyond which ensuring another "quality" year of life was no longer financially worthwhile. The study comes amid debate over whether Medicare should start rationing health care on a cost-effectiveness basis. …

Time, June 9, 2008

a. Why might it be necessary for Medicare to ration health care according to treatment that is "financially worthwhile" as opposed to providing as much treatment as is needed by a patient, regardless of costs?

b. What conflict might exist between a person's valuation of his or her own life and the rest of society's valuation of that person's life?

c. How does the potential conflict between self-interest and the social interest complicate setting a financial threshold for Medicare treatments?

21. Study *Reading Between the Lines* (pp. 196–197).

a. If a wave of natural disasters put paramedics in the news and a large number of people decide to try to get jobs as paramedics, what happens to
 i. The marginal utility of the services of a paramedic?
 ii. Consumer surplus in the market for the services of paramedics?

b. If television advertising revenues during hockey games double, what happens to
 i. The marginal utility of the services of a hockey player?
 ii. Consumer surplus in the market for the services of hockey players?

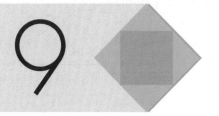

9 Possibilities, Preferences, and Choices

After studying this chapter, you will be able to:

- Describe a household's budget line and show how it changes when prices or income change

- Use indifference curves to map preferences and explain the principle of diminishing marginal rate of substitution

- Predict the effects of changes in prices and income on consumption choices

- Predict the effects of changes in wage rates on work-leisure choices

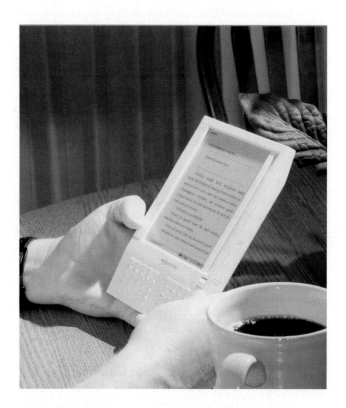

You buy your music online and play it on an iPod.
And as the prices of a music download and an iPod have tumbled, the volume of downloads and sales of iPods have skyrocketed. But a similar change hasn't occurred in the way we buy and read books. Sure, electronic textbooks—e-books—are widely available, and their prices have fallen. At the same time, the prices of old-tech, printed paper books have risen. Yet most students continue to buy printed textbooks. Why, when e-books are cheaper than printed books, have e-books not caught on and replaced printed books in the same way that the new music technologies have replaced physical discs?

Dramatic changes have occurred in the way we spend our time. The average workweek has fallen steadily from 70 hours a week in the nineteenth century to 35 hours a week today. While the average workweek is now much shorter than

it once was, far more people now have jobs. Why has the average workweek declined?

In this chapter, we're going to study a model of choice that predicts the effects of changes in prices and incomes on what people buy and the effects of changes in wage rates on how people allocate their time between leisure and work. At the end of the chapter, in *Reading Between the Lines*, we use the model to explain why e-books are having a hard time replacing printed books.

203

◆ Consumption Possibilities

Consumption choices are limited by income and by prices. A household has a given amount of income to spend and cannot influence the prices of the goods and services it buys. A household's **budget line** describes the limits to its consumption choices.

Let's look at Lisa's budget line.* Lisa has an income of $40 a month to spend. She buys two goods: movies and soda. The price of a movie is $6, and the price of soda is $4 a case.

Figure 9.1 shows alternative combinations of movies and soda that Lisa can afford. In row *A*, she sees no movies and buys 10 cases of soda. In row *F*, she sees 5 movies and buys no soda. Both of these combinations of movies and soda exhaust the $40 available. Check that the combination of movies and soda in each of the other rows also exhausts Lisa's $40 of income. The numbers in the table and the points *A* through *F* in the graph describe Lisa's consumption possibilities.

Divisible and Indivisible Goods Some goods— called divisible goods—can be bought in any quantity desired. Examples are gasoline and electricity. We can best understand household choice if we suppose that all goods and services are divisible. For example, Lisa can see half a movie a month on average by seeing one movie every two months. When we think of goods as being divisible, the consumption possibilities are not only the points *A* through *F* shown in Fig. 9.1, but also all the intermediate points that form the line running from *A* to *F*. This line is Lisa's budget line.

Affordable and Unaffordable Quantities Lisa's budget line is a constraint on her choices. It marks the boundary between what is affordable and what is unaffordable. She can afford any point on the line and inside it. She cannot afford any point outside the line. The constraint on her consumption depends on the prices and her income, and the constraint changes when the price of a good or her income changes. To see how, we use a budget equation.

---

* If you have studied Chapter 8 on marginal utility theory, you have already met Lisa. This tale of her thirst for soda and zeal for movies will sound familiar to you—up to a point. But in this chapter, we're going to use a different method for representing preferences—one that does not require the idea of utility.

FIGURE 9.1 The Budget Line

Consumption possibility	Movies (per month)	Soda (cases per month)
A	0	10
B	1	8
C	2	6
D	3	4
E	4	2
F	5	0

Lisa's budget line shows the boundary between what she can and cannot afford. The rows of the table list Lisa's affordable combinations of movies and soda when her income is $40, the price of soda is $4 a case, and the price of a movie is $8. For example, row *A* tells us that Lisa spends all of her $40 income when she buys 10 cases of soda and sees no movies. The figure graphs Lisa's budget line. Points *A* through *F* in the graph represent the rows of the table. For divisible goods, the budget line is the continuous line *AF*. To calculate the equation for Lisa's budget line, start with expenditure equal to income:

$$\$4Q_S + \$8Q_M = \$40.$$

Divide by $4 to obtain

$$Q_S + 2Q_M = 10.$$

Subtract $2Q_M$ from both sides to obtain

$$Q_S = 10 - 2Q_M.$$

Budget Equation

We can describe the budget line by using a *budget equation*. The budget equation starts with the fact that

$$\text{Expenditure} = \text{Income}.$$

Expenditure is equal to the sum of the price of each good multiplied by the quantity bought. For Lisa,

$$\text{Expenditure} = (\text{Price of soda} \times \text{Quantity of soda})$$
$$+ (\text{Price of movie} \times \text{Quantity of movies}).$$

Call the price of soda P_S, the quantity of soda Q_S, the price of a movie P_M, the quantity of movies Q_M, and income Y. We can now write Lisa's budget equation as

$$P_S Q_S + P_M Q_M = Y.$$

Or, using the prices Lisa faces, \$4 a case of soda and \$8 a movie, and Lisa's income, \$40, we get

$$\$4 Q_S + \$8 Q_M = \$40.$$

Lisa can choose any quantities of soda (Q_S) and movies (Q_M) that satisfy this equation. To find the relationship between these quantities, divide both sides of the equation by the price of soda (P_S) to get

$$Q_S + \frac{P_M}{P_S} \times Q_M = \frac{Y}{P_S}.$$

Now subtract the term $P_M/P_S \times Q_M$ from both sides of this equation to get

$$Q_S = \frac{Y}{P_S} - \frac{P_M}{P_S} \times Q_M.$$

For Lisa, income (Y) is \$40, the price of a movie (P_M) is \$8, and the price of soda (P_S) is \$4 a case. So Lisa must choose the quantities of movies and soda to satisfy the equation

$$Q_S = \frac{\$40}{\$4} - \frac{\$8}{\$4} \times Q_M,$$

or

$$Q_S = 10 - 2Q_M.$$

To interpret the equation, look at the budget line in Fig. 9.1 and check that the equation delivers that budget line. First, set Q_M equal to zero. The budget equation tells us that Q_S, the quantity of soda, is Y/P_S, which is 10 cases. This combination of Q_M and Q_S is the one shown in row A of the table in Fig. 9.1. Next set Q_M equal to 5. Q_S now equals zero (row F of the table). Check that you can derive the other rows.

The budget equation contains two variables chosen by the household (Q_M and Q_S) and two variables that the household takes as given (Y/P_S and P_M/P_S). Let's look more closely at these variables.

Real Income A household's **real income** is its income expressed as a quantity of goods that the household can afford to buy. Expressed in terms of soda, Lisa's real income is Y/P_S. This quantity is the maximum quantity of soda that she can buy. It is equal to her money income divided by the price of soda. Lisa's money income is \$40 and the price of soda is \$4 a case, so her real income in terms of soda is 10 cases, which is shown in Fig. 9.1 as the point at which the budget line intersects the y-axis.

Relative Price A **relative price** is the price of one good divided by the price of another good. In Lisa's budget equation, the variable P_M/P_S is the relative price of a movie in terms of soda. For Lisa, P_M is \$8 a movie and P_S is \$4 a case, so P_M/P_S is equal to 2 cases of soda per movie. That is, to see 1 movie, Lisa must give up 2 cases of soda.

You've just calculated Lisa's opportunity cost of seeing a movie. Recall that the opportunity cost of an action is the best alternative forgone. For Lisa to see 1 more movie a month, she must forgo 2 cases of soda. You've also calculated Lisa's opportunity cost of soda. For Lisa to buy 2 more cases of soda a month, she must forgo seeing 1 movie. So her opportunity cost of 2 cases of soda is 1 movie.

The relative price of a movie in terms of soda is the magnitude of the slope of Lisa's budget line. To calculate the slope of the budget line, recall the formula for slope (see the Chapter 1 Appendix): Slope equals the change in the variable measured on the y-axis divided by the change in the variable measured on the x-axis as we move along the line. In Lisa's case (Fig. 9.1), the variable measured on the y-axis is the quantity of soda and the variable measured on the x-axis is the quantity of movies. Along Lisa's budget line, as soda decreases from 10 to 0 cases, movies increase from 0 to 5. So the magnitude of the slope of the budget line is 10 cases divided by 5 movies, or 2 cases of soda per movie. The magnitude of this slope is exactly the same as the relative price we've just calculated. It is also the opportunity cost of a movie.

A Change in Prices When prices change, so does the budget line. The lower the price of the good measured on the x-axis, other things remaining the same, the flatter is the budget line. For example, if the price of a movie falls from \$8 to \$4, real income

FIGURE 9.2 Changes in Prices and Income

(a) A change in price

(b) A change in income

In part (a), the price of a movie changes. A fall in the price from $8 to $4 rotates the budget line outward and makes it flatter. A rise in the price from $8 to $16 rotates the budget line inward and makes it steeper.

In part (b), income falls from $40 to $20 while the prices of movies and soda remain the same. The budget line shifts leftward, but its slope does not change.

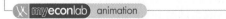 animation

in terms of soda does not change but the relative price of a movie falls. The budget line rotates outward and becomes flatter, as Fig. 9.2(a) illustrates. The higher the price of the good measured on the *x*-axis, other things remaining the same, the steeper is the budget line. For example, if the price of a movie rises from $8 to $16, the relative price of a movie increases. The budget line rotates inward and becomes steeper, as Fig. 9.2(a) illustrates.

A Change in Income A change in money income changes real income but does not change the relative price. The budget line shifts, but its slope does not change. An increase in money income increases real income and shifts the budget line rightward. A decrease in money income decreases real income and shifts the budget line leftward.

Figure 9.2(b) shows the effect of a change in money income on Lisa's budget line. The initial budget line when Lisa's income is $40 is the same as in Fig. 9.1. The new budget line shows how much Lisa can buy if her income falls to $20 a month. The two budget lines have the same slope because the relative price is the same. The new budget line is closer to the origin because Lisa's real income has decreased.

Review Quiz

1 What does a household's budget line show?
2 How does the relative price and a household's real income influence its budget line?
3 If a household has an income of $40 and buys only bus rides at $2 each and magazines at $4 each, what is the equation of the household's budget line?
4 If the price of one good changes, what happens to the relative price and the slope of the household's budget line?
5 If a household's money income changes and prices do not change, what happens to the household's real income and budget line?

  Work Study Plan 9.1 and get instant feedback.

We've studied the limits to what a household can consume. Let's now learn how we can describe preferences and make a map that contains a lot of information about a household's preferences.

Preferences and Indifference Curves

You are going to discover a very neat idea: that of drawing a map of a person's preferences. A preference map is based on the intuitively appealing idea that people can sort all the possible combinations of goods into three groups: preferred, not preferred, and indifferent. To make this idea more concrete, let's ask Lisa to tell us how she ranks various combinations of movies and soda.

Figure 9.3 shows part of Lisa's answer. She tells us that she currently sees 2 movies and buys 6 cases of soda a month at point C. She then lists all the combinations of movies and soda that she says are just as acceptable to her as her current situation. When we plot these combinations of movies and soda, we get the green curve in Fig. 9.3(a). This curve is the key element in a preference map and is called an indifference curve.

An **indifference curve** is a line that shows combinations of goods among which a consumer is *indifferent*. The indifference curve in Fig. 9.3(a) tells us that Lisa is just as happy to see 2 movies and buy 6 cases of soda a month at point C as she is to have the combination of movies and soda at point G or at any other point along the curve.

Lisa also says that she prefers all the combinations of movies and soda above the indifference curve in Fig. 9.3(a)—the yellow area—to those on the indifference curve. And she prefers any combination on the indifference curve to any combination in the gray area below the indifference curve.

The indifference curve in Fig. 9.3(a) is just one of a whole family of such curves. This indifference curve appears again in Fig. 9.3(b), labeled I_1. The curves labeled I_0 and I_2 are two other indifference curves. Lisa prefers any point on indifference curve I_2 to any point on indifference curve I_1, and she prefers any point on I_1 to any point on I_0. We refer to I_2 as being a higher indifference curve than I_1 and I_1 as being higher than I_0.

A preference map is a series of indifference curves that resemble the contour lines on a map. By looking at the shape of the contour lines on a map, we can draw conclusions about the terrain. Similarly, by looking at the shape of the indifference curves, we can draw conclusions about a person's preferences.

Let's learn how to "read" a preference map.

FIGURE 9.3   A Preference Map

(a) An indifference curve

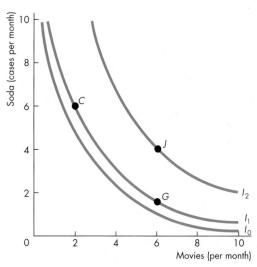

(b) Lisa's preference map

Part (a) shows one of Lisa's indifference curves. She is indifferent between point C (with 2 movies and 6 cases of soda) and all other points on the green indifference curve, such as G. She prefers points above the indifference curve (in the yellow area) to points on it, and she prefers points on the indifference curve to points below it (in the gray area).
Part (b) shows three of the indifference curves—I_0, I_1, and I_2—in Lisa's preference map. She prefers point J to point C or G, and she prefers all the points on I_2 to those on I_1.

myeconlab animation

Marginal Rate of Substitution

The **marginal rate of substitution** (*MRS*) is the rate at which a person will give up good *y* (the good measured on the *y*-axis) to get an additional unit of good *x* (the good measured on the *x*-axis) while remaining indifferent (remaining on the same indifference curve). The magnitude of the slope of an indifference curve measures the marginal rate of substitution.

- If the indifference curve is *steep*, the marginal rate of substitution is *high*. The person is willing to give up a large quantity of good *y* to get an additional unit of good *x* while remaining indifferent.
- If the indifference curve is *flat*, the marginal rate of substitution is *low*. The person is willing to give up a small amount of good *y* to get an additional unit of good *x* while remaining indifferent.

Figure 9.4 shows you how to calculate the marginal rate of substitution.

At point *C* on indifference curve *I*₁, Lisa buys 6 cases of soda and sees 2 movies. Her marginal rate of substitution is the magnitude of the slope of the indifference curve at point *C*. To measure this magnitude, place a straight line against, or tangent to, the indifference curve at point *C*. Along that line, as the quantity of soda decreases by 10 cases, the number of movies increases by 5—or 2 cases per movie. At point *C*, Lisa is willing to give up soda for movies at the rate of 2 cases per movie—a marginal rate of substitution of 2.

At point *G* on indifference curve *I*₁, Lisa buys 1.5 cases of soda and sees 6 movies. Her marginal rate of substitution is measured by the slope of the indifference curve at point *G*. That slope is the same as the slope of the tangent to the indifference curve at point *G*. Now, as the quantity of soda decreases by 4.5 cases, the number of movies increases by 9—or 1/2 case per movie. At point *G*, Lisa is willing to give up soda for movies at the rate of 1/2 case per movie—a marginal rate of substitution of 1/2.

As Lisa sees more movies and buys less soda, her marginal rate of substitution diminishes. Diminishing marginal rate of substitution is the key assumption about preferences. A **diminishing marginal rate of substitution** is a general tendency for a person to be willing to give up less of good *y* to get one more unit of good *x*, while at the same time remaining indifferent as the quantity of *x* increases. In Lisa's case, she is less willing to give up soda to see one more movie as the number of movies she sees increases.

FIGURE 9.4 The Marginal Rate of Substitution

The magnitude of the slope of an indifference curve is called the marginal rate of substitution (*MRS*). The red line at point *C* tells us that Lisa is willing to give up 10 cases of soda to see 5 movies. Her marginal rate of substitution at point *C* is 10 divided by 5, which equals 2. The red line at point *G* tells us that Lisa is willing to give up 4.5 cases of soda to see 9 movies. Her marginal rate of substitution at point *G* is 4.5 divided by 9, which equals 1/2.

myeconlab   animation

Your Own Diminishing Marginal Rate of Substitution Think about your own diminishing marginal rate of substitution. Imagine that in a week, you drink 10 cases of soda and see no movies. Most likely, you are willing to give up a lot of soda so that you can see just 1 movie. But now imagine that in a week, you buy 1 case of soda and see 6 movies. Most likely, you will now not be willing to give up much soda to see a seventh movie. As a general rule, the greater the number of movies you see, the smaller is the quantity of soda you are willing to give up to see one additional movie.

The shape of a person's indifference curves incorporates the principle of the diminishing marginal rate of substitution because the curves are bowed toward the origin. The tightness of the bend of an indifference curve tells us how willing a person is to substitute one good for another while remaining indifferent. Let's look at some examples that make this point clear.

Degree of Substitutability

Most of us would not regard movies and soda as being *close* substitutes, but they are substitutes. No matter how much you love soda, some increase in the number of movies you see will compensate you for being deprived of a can of soda. Similarly, no matter how much you love going to the movies, some number of cans of soda will compensate you for being deprived of seeing one movie. A person's indifference curves for movies and soda might look something like those for most ordinary goods and services shown in Fig. 9.5(a).

Close Substitutes Some goods substitute so easily for each other that most of us do not even notice which we are consuming. The different brands of marker pens and pencils are examples. Most people don't care which brand of these items they use or where they buy them. A marker pen from the campus bookstore is just as good as one from the local grocery store. You would be willing to forgo a pen from the campus store if you could get one more pen from

the local grocery store. When two goods are perfect substitutes, their indifference curves are straight lines that slope downward, as Fig. 9.5(b) illustrates. The marginal rate of substitution is constant.

Complements Some goods do not substitute for each other at all. Instead, they are complements. The complements in Fig. 9.5(c) are left and right running shoes. Indifference curves of perfect complements are L-shaped. One left running shoe and one right running shoe are as good as one left shoe and two right shoes. Having two of each is preferred to having one of each, but having two of one and one of the other is no better than having one of each.

The extreme cases of perfect substitutes and perfect complements shown here don't often happen in reality, but they do illustrate that the shape of the indifference curve shows the degree of substitutability between two goods. The closer the two goods are to perfect substitutes, the closer the marginal rate of substitution is to being constant (a straight line), rather than diminishing (a curved line). Indifference

FIGURE 9.5 The Degree of Substitutability

(a) Ordinary goods

(b) Perfect substitutes

(c) Perfect complements

The shape of the indifference curves reveals the degree of substitutability between two goods. Part (a) shows the indifference curves for two ordinary goods: movies and soda. To drink less soda and remain indifferent, one must see more movies. The number of movies that compensates for a reduction in soda increases as less soda is consumed. Part (b) shows the indifference curves for two perfect substitutes. For

the consumer to remain indifferent, one fewer marker pen from the local grocery store must be replaced by one extra marker pen from the campus bookstore. Part (c) shows two perfect complements—goods that cannot be substituted for each other at all. Having two left running shoes with one right running shoe is no better than having one of each. But having two of each is preferred to having one of each.

*"With the pork I'd recommend an Alsatian
white or a Coke."*

curves for poor substitutes are tightly curved and lie between the shapes of those shown in Figs. 9.5(a) and 9.5(c).

As you can see in the cartoon, according to the waiter's preferences, Coke and Alsatian white wine are perfect substitutes and each is a complement of pork. We hope the customers agree with him.

Review Quiz

1 What is an indifference curve and how does a preference map show preferences?

2 Why does an indifference curve slope downward and why is it bowed toward the origin?

3 What do we call the magnitude of the slope of an indifference curve?

4 What is the key assumption about a consumer's marginal rate of substitution?

myeconlab Work Study Plan 9.2
and get instant feedback.

The two components of the model of household choice are now in place: the budget line and the preference map. We will now use these components to work out a household's choice and to predict how choices change when prices and income change.

◆ Predicting Consumer Choices

We are now going to predict the quantities of movies and soda that Lisa chooses to buy. We're also going to see how these quantities change when a price changes or when Lisa's income changes. Finally, we're going to see how the *substitution effect* and the *income effect*, two ideas that you met in Chapter 3 (see p. 59), guarantee that for a normal good, the demand curve slopes downward.

Best Affordable Choice

When Lisa makes her best affordable choice of movies and soda, she spends all her income and is on her highest attainable indifference curve. Figure 9.6 illustrates this choice: The budget line is from Fig. 9.1 and the indifference curves are from Fig. 9.3(b). Lisa's best affordable choice is 2 movies and 6 cases of soda at point *C*—the *best affordable point*.

FIGURE 9.6   The Best Affordable Choice

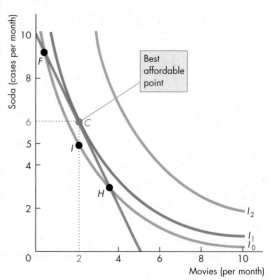

Lisa's best affordable choice is at point *C*, the point on her budget line and on her highest attainable indifference curve. At point *C*, Lisa's marginal rate of substitution between movies and soda (the magnitude of the slope of the indifference curve I_1) equals the relative price of movies and soda (the slope of the budget line).

myeconlab animation

On the Budget Line The best affordable point is on the budget line. For every point inside the budget line, such as point I, there are points on the budget line that Lisa prefers. For example, she prefers all the points on the budget line between F and H to point I, so she chooses a point on the budget line.

On the Highest Attainable Indifference Curve Every point on the budget line lies on an indifference curve. For example, points F and H lie on the indifference curve I_0. By moving along her budget line from either F or H toward C, Lisa reaches points on ever higher indifference curves that she prefers to points F or H. When Lisa gets to point C, she is on the highest attainable indifference curve.

Marginal Rate of Substitution Equals Relative Price At point C, Lisa's marginal rate of substitution between movies and soda (the magnitude of the slope of the indifference curve) is equal to the relative price of movies and soda (the magnitude of the slope of the budget line). Lisa's willingness to pay for a movie equals her opportunity cost of a movie.

Let's now see how Lisa's choices change when a price changes.

A Change in Price

The effect of a change in the price on the quantity of a good consumed is called the **price effect**. We will use Fig. 9.7(a) to work out the price effect of a fall in the price of a movie. We start with the price of a movie at $8, the price of soda at $4 a case, and Lisa's income at $40 a month. In this situation, she buys 6 cases of soda and sees 2 movies a month at point C.

Now suppose that the price of a movie falls to $4. With a lower price of a movie, the budget line rotates outward and becomes flatter. The new budget line is the darker orange one in Fig. 9.7(a). For a refresher on how a price change affects the budget line, check back to Fig. 9.2(a).

Lisa's best affordable point is now point J, where she sees 6 movies and drinks 4 cases of soda. Lisa drinks less soda and watches more movies now that movies are cheaper. She cuts her soda purchases from 6 to 4 cases and increases the number of movies she sees from 2 to 6 a month. When the price of a movie falls and the price of soda and her income remain constant, Lisa substitutes movies for soda.

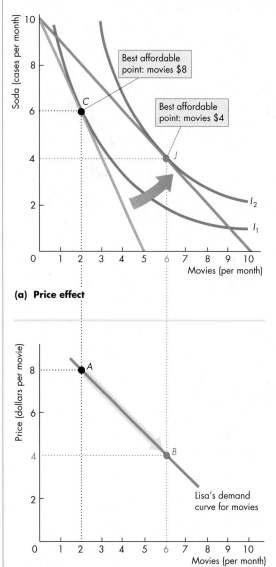

FIGURE 9.7   Price Effect and Demand Curve

(a) Price effect

(b) Demand curve

Initially, Lisa's best affordable point is C in part (a). If the price of a movie falls from $8 to $4, Lisa's best affordable point is J. The move from C to J is the price effect.

At a price of $8 a movie, Lisa sees 2 movies a month, at point A in part (b). At a price of $4 a movie, she sees 6 movies a month, at point B. Lisa's demand curve for movies traces out her best affordable quantity of movies as the price of a movie varies.

myeconlab   animation

The Demand Curve In Chapter 3, we asserted that the demand curve slopes downward. We can now derive a demand curve from a consumer's budget line and indifference curves. By doing so, we can see that the law of demand and the downward-sloping demand curve are consequences of a consumer's choosing her or his best affordable combination of goods.

To derive Lisa's demand curve for movies, lower the price of a movie and find her best affordable point at different prices. We've just done this for two movie prices in Fig. 9.7(a). Figure 9.7(b) highlights these two prices and two points that lie on Lisa's demand curve for movies. When the price of a movie is $8, Lisa sees 2 movies a month at point A. When the price falls to $4, she increases the number of movies she sees to 6 a month at point B. The demand curve is made up of these two points plus all the other points that tell us Lisa's best affordable quantity of movies at each movie price, with the price of soda and Lisa's income remaining the same. As you can see, Lisa's demand curve for movies slopes downward—the lower the price of a movie, the more movies she sees. This is the law of demand.

Next, let's see how Lisa changes her purchases of movies and soda when her income changes.

A Change in Income

The effect of a change in income on buying plans is called the **income effect**. Let's work out the income effect by examining how buying plans change when income changes and prices remain constant. Figure 9.8 shows the income effect when Lisa's income falls. With an income of $40, the price of a movie at $4, and the price of soda at $4 a case, Lisa's best affordable point is J—she buys 6 movies and 4 cases of soda. If her income falls to $28, her best affordable point is K—she sees 4 movies and buys 3 cases of soda. When Lisa's income falls, she buys less of both goods. Movies and soda are normal goods.

The Demand Curve and the Income Effect A change in income leads to a shift in the demand curve, as shown in Fig. 9.8(b). With an income of $40, Lisa's demand curve for movies is D_0, the same as in Fig. 9.7(b). But when her income falls to $28, she plans to see fewer movies at each price, so her demand curve shifts leftward to D_1.

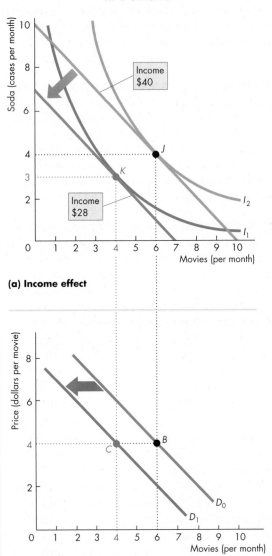

FIGURE 9.8   Income Effect and Change in Demand

(a) Income effect

(b) Demand curve for movies

A change in income shifts the budget line, changes the best affordable point, and changes demand.

In part (a), when Lisa's income decreases from $40 to $28, she sees fewer movies and buys less soda.

In part (b), when Lisa's income is $40, her demand curve for movies is D_0. When Lisa's income falls to $28, her demand curve for movies shifts leftward to D_1. For Lisa, going to the movies is a normal good. Her demand for movies decreases because she now sees fewer movies at each price.

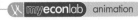

Substitution Effect and Income Effect

For a normal good, a fall in its price *always* increases the quantity bought. We can prove this assertion by dividing the price effect into two parts:

- Substitution effect
- Income effect

Figure 9.9(a) shows the price effect, and in Fig. 9.9(b) we separate the price effect into its two parts.

Substitution Effect The **substitution effect** is the effect of a change in price on the quantity bought when the consumer (hypothetically) remains indifferent between the original situation and the new one. To work out Lisa's substitution effect when the price of a movie falls, we cut her income by enough to keep her on the same indifference curve as before.

When the price of a movie falls from $8 to $4, suppose (hypothetically) that we cut Lisa's income to $28. What's special about $28? It is the income that is just enough, at the new price of a movie, to keep Lisa's best affordable point on the same indifference curve as her original point C. Lisa's budget line is now the light orange line in Fig. 9.9(b). With the lower price of a movie and a smaller income, Lisa's best affordable point is K on indifference curve I_1. The move from C to K along indifference curve I_1 is the substitution effect of the price change. The substitution effect of the fall in the price of a movie is an increase in the quantity of movies from 2 to 4. The direction of the substitution effect never varies: When the relative price of a good falls, the consumer substitutes more of that good for the other good.

Income Effect To calculate the substitution effect, we gave Lisa a $12 pay cut. To calculate the income effect, we give Lisa back her $12. The $12 increase in income shifts Lisa's budget line outward, as shown in Fig. 9.9(b). The slope of the budget line does not change because both prices remain the same. This change in Lisa's budget line is similar to the one illustrated in Fig. 9.8. As Lisa's budget line shifts outward, her consumption possibilities expand and her best affordable point becomes J on indifference curve I_2. The move from K to J is the income effect of the price change. In this example, as Lisa's income increases, she sees more movies. For Lisa, a movie is a normal good. For a normal good, the income effect reinforces the substitution effect.

FIGURE 9.9 Substitution Effect and Income Effect

(a) Price effect

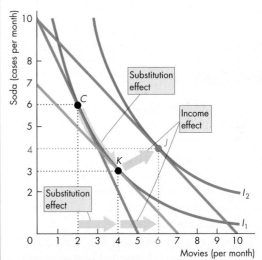

(b) Substitution effect and income effect

The price effect in part (a) is separated into a substitution effect and an income effect in part (b).

To isolate the substitution effect, we confront Lisa with the new price but keep her on her original indifference curve, I_1. The substitution effect is the move from C to K.

To isolate the income effect, we confront Lisa with the new price of movies but increase her income so that she can move from the original indifference curve, I_1, to the new one, I_2. The income effect is the move from K to J.

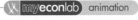

Inferior Goods The example that we have just studied is that of a change in the price of a normal good. The effect of a change in the price of an inferior good is different. Recall that an inferior good is one whose consumption decreases as income increases. For an inferior good, the income effect is negative and a lower price does not always lead to an increase in the quantity demanded. The lower price has a substitution effect that increases the quantity demanded, but a negative income effect that reduces the demand for the inferior good. The income effect works in the opposite direction to and offsets the substitution effect to some degree. If the negative income effect exceeded the positive substitution effect, the demand curve would slope upward. This case does not appear to occur in the real world.

Back to the Facts

We started this chapter by observing how the way we buy music has changed in recent years. The indifference curve model explains those changes. The best affordable choices determine spending patterns. Changes in prices and incomes change the best affordable choices and change consumption patterns.

Review Quiz

1 When a consumer chooses the combination of goods and services to buy, what is she or he trying to achieve?

2 Explain the conditions that are met when a consumer has found the best affordable combination of goods to buy. (Use the terms budget line, marginal rate of substitution, and relative price in your explanation.)

3 If the price of a normal good falls, what happens to the quantity demanded of that good?

4 Into what two effects can we divide the effect of a price change?

5 For a normal good, does the income effect reinforce the substitution effect or does it partly offset the substitution effect?

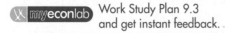 Work Study Plan 9.3 and get instant feedback.

The model of household choice can explain many other household choices. Let's look at one of them.

Work–Leisure Choices

People make many choices other than those about how to spend their income on the various goods and services available. Economists use the indifference curve model to understand many other choices, one of which is how to allocate time between working and leisure activities. This choice determines a person's supply of labor. Let's study this choice.

Labor Supply

Every week, we allocate our 168 hours between working—called *labor*—and all other activities—called *leisure*. How do we decide how to allocate our time between labor and leisure? We can answer this question by using the theory of household choice.

The more hours we spend on *leisure,* the smaller is our income. The relationship between leisure and income is described by an *income-time budget line*. Figure 9.10(a) shows Lisa's income-time budget line. If Lisa devotes the entire week to leisure—168 hours—she has no income and is at point Z. By supplying labor in exchange for a wage, she can convert hours into income along the income-time budget line. The slope of that line is determined by the hourly wage rate. If the wage rate is $5 an hour, Lisa faces the flattest budget line. If the wage rate is $10 an hour, she faces the middle budget line. And if the wage rate is $15 an hour, she faces the steepest budget line.

Lisa "buys" leisure by not supplying labor and by forgoing income. The opportunity cost of an hour of leisure is the hourly wage rate forgone.

Figure 9.10(a) also shows Lisa's indifference curves for income and leisure. Lisa chooses her best attainable point. This choice of income and time allocation is just like her choice of movies and soda. She gets onto the highest possible indifference curve by making her marginal rate of substitution between income and leisure equal to her wage rate.

Lisa's choice depends on the wage rate she can earn. At a wage rate of $5 an hour, Lisa chooses point A and works 20 hours a week (168 minus 148) for an income of $100 a week. At a wage rate of $10 an hour, she chooses point B and works 35 hours a week (168 minus 133) for an income of $350 a week. And at a wage rate of $15 an hour, she chooses point C and works 30 hours a week (168 minus 138) for an income of $450 a week.

FIGURE 9.10   The Supply of Labor

(a) Time allocation decision

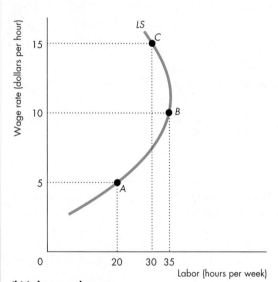

(b) Labor supply curve

In part (a), at a wage rate of $5 an hour, Lisa takes 148 hours of leisure and works 20 hours a week at point A. If the wage rate increases from $5 to $10 an hour, she decreases her leisure to 133 hours and increases her work to 35 hours a week at point B. But if the wage rate increases from $10 to $15 an hour, Lisa *increases* her leisure to 138 hours and *decreases* her work to 30 hours a week at point C. Part (b) shows Lisa's labor supply curve. Points A, B, and C on the supply curve correspond to Lisa's choices in part (a).

 animation

The Labor Supply Curve

Figure 9.10(b) shows Lisa's labor supply curve. This curve shows that as the wage rate increases from $5 an hour to $10 an hour, Lisa increases the quantity of labor supplied from 20 hours a week to 35 hours a week. But when the wage rate increases to $15 an hour, she decreases her quantity of labor supplied to 30 hours a week.

Lisa's supply of labor is similar to that described for the economy as a whole at the beginning of this chapter. As wage rates have increased, the workweek has shortened. At first, this pattern seems puzzling. We've seen that the wage rate is the opportunity cost of leisure, so a higher wage rate means a higher opportunity cost of leisure. This fact on its own leads to a decrease in leisure and an increase in work hours. But instead, we've cut our work hours. Why? Because our incomes have increased. As the wage rate increases, incomes increase, so people demand more of all normal goods. Leisure is a normal good, so as incomes increase, people demand more leisure.

The higher wage rate has both a *substitution effect* and an *income effect.* The higher wage rate increases the opportunity cost of leisure and so leads to a substitution effect away from leisure. The higher wage rate increases income and so leads to an income effect toward more leisure. This outcome of rational household choice explains why the average workweek has fallen steadily as wage rates have increased. With higher wage rates, people have decided to use their higher incomes in part to "buy" more leisure.

Review Quiz

1 What is the opportunity cost of leisure?
2 Why might a rise in the wage rate lead to an increase in leisure and a decrease in work hours?

myeconlab   Work Study Plan 9.4 and get instant feedback.

◆ *Reading Between the Lines* on pp. 216–217 shows you how the theory of household choice explains why e-books have not taken off, and why most people continue to buy their books in traditional paper format.

In the chapters that follow, we study the choices that firms make in their pursuit of profit and how those choices determine the supply of goods and services and the demand for productive resources.

Paper Books Versus e-Books

Are Books Passé?

http://www.iht.com
September 6, 2007

Technology evangelists have predicted the emergence of electronic books for as long as they have envisioned flying cars and video phones. It is an idea that has never caught on with mainstream book buyers. …

In October, the online retailer Amazon.com will unveil the Kindle, an electronic book reader that has been the subject of industry speculation for a year, according to several people who have tried the device and are familiar with Amazon's plans. The Kindle will be priced at $400 to $500 and will wirelessly connect to an e-book store on Amazon's site. …

Hopes for e-books began to revive last year with the introduction of the widely marketed Sony Reader. Sony's $300 gadget, the size of a trade paperback, has a six-inch screen, enough memory to hold 80 books and a battery that lasts for 7,500 page turns, according to the company. It uses screen display technology from E Ink, a company based in Cambridge, Mass., that emerged from the Media Lab at the Massachusetts Institute of Technology and creates power-efficient digital screens that uncannily mimic the appearance of paper. …

Essence of the Story

- Electronic books have not displaced paper books with mainstream book buyers.

- Amazon.com sells an electronic book reader called Kindle that wirelessly connects to Amazon's e-book store.

- Sony sells the Sony Reader, an electronic book reader the size of a paperback that mimics the appearance of paper, priced at $300.

Economic Analysis

- Print books and e-books are substitutes.

- For most people, though, e-books and print books are extremely poor substitutes.

- For a committed print-book lover, no quantity of e-books can compensate for a print book—the marginal rate of substitution between print books and e-books is zero.

- Beth is a print-book lover and Fig. 1 shows her indifference curves for print books and e-books.

- With print books on the x-axis, Beth's indifference curves are vertical. They tell us that Beth prefers more print books but gets no benefit from e-books.

- Beth's annual book budget is $500. The price of an e-book reader is $360 (the current price of the Kindle reader). The price of an e-book is $10 and the price of a print book is $20.

- We'll assume that an e-book reader has only a one-year life. (Buyers know they will want the next-generation, improved reader next year.)

- The orange line is Beth's budget line if she buys a reader. She can afford 14 e-books if she buys no print books ($360 + (14 × $10) = $500) and along this line, by forgoing 2 e-books she can buy 1 print book.

- If Beth doesn't buy an e-book reader, she buys no e-books and can afford 25 print books ($500 ÷ $20 = 25). The red dot shows this affordable point.

- The red dot is also the best affordable choice because this choice gets her onto her highest attainable indifference curve, I_2.

- Andy differs from Beth: He thinks that print books and e-books are perfect substitutes. But he also likes music and buys albums. Figure 2 shows Andy's indifference curves for books (all types) and albums.

- Andy's annual budget for albums and books is $720. The price of an album is $10 and the prices of an e-book reader, an e-book, and a print book are the same as those that Beth faces.

- Figure 2 shows Andy's two budget lines: one if he buys only e-books and albums and another if he buys only print books and albums.

- If Andy buys e-books, he must spend $360 on a reader, which leaves him with $360 for albums and e-books. If he buys 20 e-books, he can afford 16 albums. [(20 × $10) + (16 × $10) = $360].

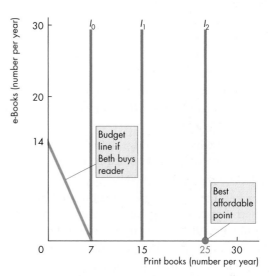

Figure 1 Print books versus e-books for a print-book lover

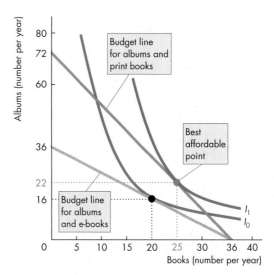

Figure 2 Books versus albums

- If Andy buys print books and albums, he can afford 25 print books and 22 albums [(25 × $20) + (22 × $10) = $720].

- Andy's best affordable choice is 25 print books and 22 albums.

- So even Andy, who thinks that e-books and print books are perfect substitutes, doesn't buy e-books. But he probably would if he had a larger budget.

217

SUMMARY

Key Points

Consumption Possibilities (pp. 204–206)

- The budget line is the boundary between what a household can and cannot afford, given its income and the prices of goods.

- The point at which the budget line intersects the *y*-axis is the household's real income in terms of the good measured on that axis.

- The magnitude of the slope of the budget line is the relative price of the good measured on the *x*-axis in terms of the good measured on the *y*-axis.

- A change in the price of one good changes the slope of the budget line. A change in income shifts the budget line but does not change its slope.

Preferences and Indifference Curves (pp. 207–210)

- A consumer's preferences can be represented by indifference curves. The consumer is indifferent among all the combinations of goods that lie on an indifference curve.

- A consumer prefers any point above an indifference curve to any point on it and prefers any point on an indifference curve to any point below it.

- The magnitude of the slope of an indifference curve is called the marginal rate of substitution.

- The marginal rate of substitution diminishes as consumption of the good measured on the *y*-axis decreases and consumption of the good measured on the *x*-axis increases.

Predicting Consumer Choices (pp. 210–214)

- A household consumes at its best affordable point. This point is on the budget line and on the highest attainable indifference curve and has a marginal rate of substitution equal to relative price.

- The effect of a price change (the price effect) can be divided into a substitution effect and an income effect.

- The substitution effect is the effect of a change in price on the quantity bought when the consumer (hypothetically) remains indifferent between the original choice and the new choice.

- The substitution effect always results in an increase in consumption of the good whose relative price has fallen.

- The income effect is the effect of a change in income on consumption.

- For a normal good, the income effect reinforces the substitution effect. For an inferior good, the income effect works in the opposite direction to the substitution effect.

Work–Leisure Choices (pp. 214–215)

- The indifference curve model of household choice enables us to understand how a household allocates its time between work and leisure.

- Work hours have decreased and leisure hours have increased because the income effect on the demand for leisure has been greater than the substitution effect.

Key Figures

Key Terms

PROBLEMS and APPLICATIONS ◆

1. Sara's income is $12 a week. The price of popcorn is $3 a bag, and the price of a smoothie is $3.
   a. What is Sara's real income in terms of smoothies?
   b. What is her real income in terms of popcorn?
   c. What is the relative price of smoothies in terms of popcorn?
   d. What is the opportunity cost of a smoothie?
   e. Calculate the equation for Sara's budget line (with bags of popcorn on the left side).
   f. Draw a graph of Sara's budget line with the quantity of smoothies on the x-axis.
   g. In f, what is the slope of Sara's budget line? What determines its value?

2. Sara's income falls from $12 to $9 a week, while the price of popcorn remains at $3 a bag and the price of a smoothie remains at $3.
   a. What is the effect of the fall in Sara's income on her real income in terms of smoothies?
   b. What is the effect of the fall in Sara's income on her real income in terms of popcorn?
   c. What is the effect of the fall in Sara's income on the relative price of a smoothie in terms of popcorn?
   d. What is the slope of Sara's new budget line if it is drawn with smoothies on the x-axis?

3. Sara's income is $12 a week. The price of popcorn rises from $3 to $6 a bag, and the price of a smoothie remains at $3.
   a. What is the effect of the rise in the price of popcorn on Sara's real income in terms of smoothies?
   b. What is the effect of the rise in the price of popcorn on Sara's real income in terms of popcorn?
   c. What is the effect of the rise in the price of popcorn on the relative price of a smoothie in terms of popcorn?
   d. What is the slope of Sara's new budget line if it is drawn with smoothies on the x-axis?

4. **The Year in Medicine**

   Sudafed, used to clear up those autumn sniffles, … contains as one of its active ingredients pseudoephedrine, widely used in backyard labs to make methamphetamine. … Now, allergy sufferers looking for relief have to ask a pharmacist or sales-clerk for their Sudafed, show photo ID, and sign a logbook. Unfortunately, the most common alternative, phenylephrine, isn't as effective.
   Time, December 4, 2006
   a. Draw an indifference curve for Sudafed and phenylephrine that is consistent with this news clip.
   b. On your graph in a, identify combinations that allergy sufferers prefer, do not prefer, and are indifferent among.
   c. Explain how the marginal rate of substitution changes along this indifference curve.

5. Draw figures that show your indifference curves for the following pairs of goods:
   ■ Right gloves and left gloves
   ■ Coca-Cola and Pepsi
   ■ Baseballs and baseball bats
   ■ Tylenol and acetaminophen (the generic form of Tylenol)
   ■ Eye glasses and contact lenses
   ■ Desktop computers and laptop computers
   ■ Skis and ski poles
   a. For each pair, state whether the goods are perfect substitutes, perfect complements, or neither.
   b. Discuss the shape of your indifference curve for each pair and explain the relationship between its shape and the marginal rate of substitution as the quantities of the two goods change.

6. Pam has chosen her best affordable combination of cookies and comic books. She has spent all of her income on 30 cookies at $1 each and 5 comic books at $2 each. Next month, the price of a cookie falls to 50¢ and the price of a comic book rises to $5.
   a. Will Pam be able to buy and want to buy 30 cookies and 5 comic books next month?
   b. Which situation does Pam prefer: cookies at $1 and comic books at $2 or cookies at 50¢ and comic books at $5?
   c. If Pam changes the quantities that she buys, will she buy more or fewer cookies and more or fewer comic books?

d. When the prices change next month, will there be an income effect and a substitution effect at work or just one of them?

7. **Boom Time For "Gently Used" Clothes**

Unlike most retailers who are blaming the economy for their poor sales, one store chain is boldly declaring that an economic downturn can actually be a boon for its business. … [It] sells used name-brand children's clothes, toys, and furniture. … Last year, the company took in $20 million in sales, up 5% from the previous year. "Our sales are already up 5% so far this year."

CNN, April 17, 2008

a. According to this article, is used clothing a normal good or an inferior good?

b. If the price of used clothing falls and income remains the same, explain how the quantity of used clothing bought changes.

c. If the price of used clothing falls and income remains the same, describe the substitution effect and the income effect that occur.

d. Draw a graph to illustrate a family's indifference curves for used clothing and other goods and services.

e. In your graph in d, draw two budget lines to show the effect of a fall in income on the quantity of used clothing purchased.

8. **Gas Prices to Stunt Memorial Day Travel**

12% have cancelled road trips altogether. … 11% of respondents will be vacationing closer to home this weekend. … That may save consumers some money, but it will also likely … hurt on a variety of businesses that serve the traveler. Service stations will suffer as they not only presumably sell less gas, but also fewer snacks, drinks and sundry items. … Hotel chains, especially those with a heavy roadside presence [suffer]. … Also under pressure are casual-dining chains that rely heavily on highway traffic. …

MarketWatch, May 22, 2008

a. Describe the degree of substitutability between gasoline and roadside hotels and draw a preference map that illustrates your description.

b. Draw a budget line for gasoline and roadside hotels and identify the best affordable point.

c. Show on your graph how the best affordable point changes when the price of gasoline rises.

9. **Does a Second Income Pay?**

When considering whether two paychecks are worth it, figure out how much of the lower earner's salary will be eaten [up] by expenses incurred if both parents work. Childcare is likely to be the biggest cost. … Also, take into account the costs of going to work. The commute, the clothes, the dry cleaning, the lunches. … And you may not have as much time or energy to do the housework or make dinner. So you may end up hiring a housekeeper or doing take-out more often. …

CNN, March 15, 2006

a. What is the opportunity cost of a parent staying home with her or his children?

b. What is the opportunity cost of a parent working instead of staying home?

c. Why does the opportunity cost of working increase as the number of children in a family increases?

d. How does the number of children in a family influence the marginal rate of substitution between leisure and goods and services?

10. **Floyd Mayweather Jr. Announces Retirement**

Unbeaten world champion boxer Floyd Mayweather Jr. backed out of negotiations for a September rematch against Oscar De La Hoya … announcing his retirement. …

In May 2007, Mayweather Jr. won a split-decision over De La Hoya in a bout that established new records for pay-per-view and total revenue. … [De La Hoya's business partner] didn't believe Mayweather is employing a tactic to earn more money in a De La Hoya fight. … "He has made enough money to live comfortably for the rest of his life, and if he wants to spend time with his babies, that's a good thing. …"

Los Angeles Times, June 6, 2008

a. Use the concepts of the substitution effect and the income effect to explain Mayweather's decision.

b. At the income he earns per fight, is Mayweather's labor supply curve upward-sloping or backward-bending?

c. Draw a graph of Mayweather's indifference curves and budget line between leisure time and income and illustrate his decision to fight or not to fight. Show how an increase in the income per fight changes his decision.

11. Gas Prices Straining Budgets

...many say they are staying in and scaling back spending to try to keep up, ... driving as little as possible, cutting back on shopping and eating out, and other discretionary spending.

CNN, February 29, 2008

a. Draw a budget line for a household that consumes only two goods: gasoline and eating out. Identify the combinations of gasoline and eating out that are affordable and those that are unaffordable.

b. Draw a second budget line to show how a rise in the price of gasoline changes the affordable and unaffordable combinations of gasoline and eating out. Describe how the household's consumption possibilities change.

c. How does a rise in the price of gasoline change the relative price of eating out?

d. How does a rise in the price of gasoline change real income in terms of eating out?

12. Rashid buys only books and albums and the figure shows his preferences.

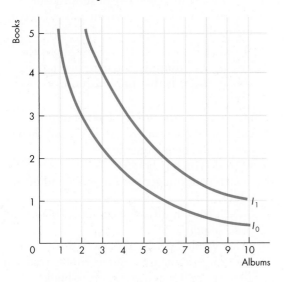

a. If Rashid chooses 3 books and 2 albums, what is his marginal rate of substitution?

b. If Rashid chooses 2 books and 6 albums, what is his marginal rate of substitution?

c. Do Rashid's indifference curves display diminishing marginal rate of substitution? Explain why or why not.

13. Sara's income is $12 a week. The price of popcorn is $3 a bag, and the price of cola is $1.50 a can.

The figure shows Sara's preference map for popcorn and cola.

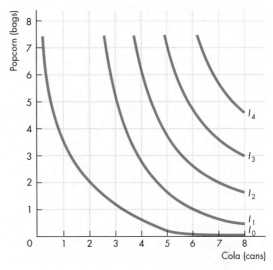

a. What quantities of popcorn and cola does Sara buy?

b. What is Sara's marginal rate of substitution at the point at which she consumes?

14. Now suppose that in problem 13, the price of cola rises to $3.00 a can and the price of popcorn and Sara's income remain the same.

a. What quantities of cola and popcorn does Sara now buy?

b. What are two points on Sara's demand curve for cola? Draw Sara's demand curve.

c. What is the substitution effect of this price change?

d. What is the income effect of the price change?

e. Is cola a normal good or an inferior good?

15. Jim has made his best affordable choice of muffins and coffee. He spends all of his income on 10 muffins at $1 each and 20 cups of coffee at $2 each. Now the price of a muffin rises to $1.50 and the price of coffee falls to $1.75 a cup.

a. Will Jim now be able and want to buy 10 muffins and 20 coffees?

b. Which situation does Jim prefer: muffins at $1 and coffee at $2 a cup or muffins at $1.50 and coffee at $1.75 a cup?

c. If Jim changes the quantities that he buys, will he buy more or fewer muffins and more or less coffee?

d. When the prices change, is there an income

effect and a substitution effect at work or just one of them?

16. **Rising Gas Costs Crimping Budgets**

    More Americans are substituting higher-priced goods with cheaper ones—choosing McDonald's coffee over Starbucks, for example, or hitting a bulk warehouse chain such as Costco or Sam's Club instead of a pricier grocery store.

    MSNBC, March 20, 2008

    a. If an increase in the price of gasoline results in consumers substituting McDonald's coffee for Starbucks coffee, what type of good is McDonald's coffee—normal or inferior? Explain.

    b. Draw a graph of an indifference curve and two budget lines to illustrate the effect of a rise in the price of gasoline on the quantity of coffee purchased from McDonald's and from Starbucks.

17. **Gas Prices Send Surge of Travelers to Mass Transit**

    With the price of gas approaching $4 a gallon, more commuters are abandoning their cars and taking the train or bus instead. … "It's very clear that a significant portion of the increase in transit use is directly caused by people who are looking for alternatives to paying $3.50 a gallon for gas." Some cities with long-established public transit systems, like New York and Boston, have seen increases in ridership of 5 percent or more so far this year. But the biggest surges — of 10 to 15 percent or more over last year — are occurring in many metropolitan areas in the South and West where the driving culture is strongest and bus and rail lines are more limited.

    The New York Times, May 10, 2008

    a. Draw a graph of a preference map and a budget line to illustrate the best affordable combination of gasoline and public transit.

    b. On your graph in a, show the effect of a rise in the price of gasoline on the quantities of gasoline and public transit services purchased.

    c. Assuming that the increase in the price of gasoline has been similar in all regions, compare the marginal rate of substitution in the Northeast to that in the South and West. Explain how you have inferred the different marginal rates of substitution from the information provided in the news clip.

18. **You May Be Paid More (or Less) Than You Think**

    It's so hard to put a price on happiness, isn't it? But if you've ever had to choose between a job you like and a better-paying one that you like less, you probably wished some economist would … tell you how much job satisfaction is worth. … Trust in management is by far the biggest component to consider. Say you get a new boss and your trust in management goes up a bit … (say, up one point on a 10-point scale). That's like getting a 36 percent pay raise. In other words, that increased level of trust will boost your level of overall satisfaction in life by about the same amount as a 36 percent raise would.

    CNN, March 29, 2006

    a. Measure trust in management on a 10–point scale, measure pay on the same 10–point scale, and think of them as two goods. Draw an indifference curve (with trust on the *x*-axis) that is consistent with the information in the news clip.

    b. What is the marginal rate of substitution between trust in management and pay according to this news clip?

    c. What does the news clip imply about the principle of diminishing marginal rate of substitution? Is that implication likely to be correct?

19. Study *Reading Between the Lines* about print books and e-books on pp. 216–217, and then answer the following questions.

    a. How do you buy books?

    b. Sketch your budget line for books and other goods.

    c. Sketch your indifference curves for books and other goods.

    d. What would happen to the way that you buy books if Amazon gave you its Kindle reader at a zero price if you buy just one e-book?

20. The sales tax is a tax on goods. Some people say that a consumption tax, a tax on both goods and services, would be better. Explain and illustrate with a graph what would happen if the sales tax were replaced with a consumption tax to

    a. The relative price of books and haircuts.

    b. The budget line showing the quantities of books and haircuts you can afford to buy.

    c. Your purchases of books and haircuts.

UNDERSTANDING HOUSEHOLDS' CHOICES

Making the Most of Life

The powerful forces of demand and supply shape the fortunes of families, businesses, nations, and empires in the same unrelenting way that the tides and winds shape rocks and coastlines. You saw in Chapters 3 through 7 how these forces raise and lower prices, increase and decrease quantities bought and sold, cause revenues to fluctuate, and send resources to their most valuable uses.

These powerful forces begin quietly and privately with the choices that each one of us makes. Chapters 8 and 9 probe these individual choices, offering two alternative approaches to explaining both consumption plans and the allocation of time. These explanations of consumption plans can also explain "non-economic" choices, such as whether to marry and how many children to have. In a sense, there are no non-economic choices. If there is scarcity, there must be choice, and economics studies all choices.

The earliest economists (Adam Smith and his contemporaries) did not have a very deep understanding of households' choices. It was not until the nineteenth century that progress was made in this area when Jeremy Bentham (below) introduced the concept of utility and applied it to the study of human choices. Today, Steven Levitt of the University of Chicago, whom you will meet on the following pages, is one of the most influential students of human behavior.

Jeremy Bentham *(1748–1832), who lived in London, was the son and grandson of a lawyer and was himself trained as a barrister. But Bentham rejected the opportunity to maintain the family tradition and, instead, spent his life as a writer, activist, and Member of Parliament in the pursuit of rational laws that would bring the greatest happiness to the greatest number of people.*

Bentham, whose embalmed body is preserved to this day in a glass cabinet in the University of London, was the first person to use the concept of utility to explain human choices. But in Bentham's day, the distinction between explaining and prescribing was not a sharp one, and Bentham was ready to use his ideas to tell people how they ought to behave. He was one of the first to propose pensions for the retired, guaranteed employment, minimum wages, and social benefits such as free education and free medical care.

"... It is the greatest happiness of the greatest number that is the measure of right and wrong."

JEREMY BENTHAM
Fragment on Government

TALKING
WITH

Steven D. Levitt

Steven D. Levitt is Alvin H. Baum Professor of Economics at the University of Chicago. Born in Minneapolis, he was an undergraduate at Harvard and a graduate student at MIT. Among his many honors, he was recently awarded the John Bates Clark Medal, given to the best economist under 40.

Professor Levitt has studied an astonishingly wide range of human choices and their outcomes. He has examined the effects of policing on crime, shown that real estate agents get a higher price when they sell their own homes than when they sell other people's, devised a test to detect cheating teachers, and studied the choices of drug dealers and gang members. Much of this research has been popularized in *Freakonomics* (Steven D. Levitt and Stephen J. Dubner, HarperCollins, 2005). What unifies this apparently diverse body of research is the use of natural experiments. Professor Levitt has an incredible ability to find just the right set of events and the data the events have generated to enable him to isolate the effect he's looking for.

Michael Parkin talked with Steven Levitt about his career and the progress that economists have made in understanding how people respond to incentives in all aspects of life.

Why did you become an economist?

As a freshman in college, I took introductory economics. All the ideas made perfect sense to me—it was the way I naturally thought. My friends were befuddled. I thought, "This is the field for me!"

The idea of rational choice made at the margin lies at the heart of economics. Would you say that your work generally supports that idea or challenges it? Can you provide some examples?

I don't like the word "rational" in this context. I think economists model agents as being rational just for convenience. What really matters is whether people respond to incentives. My work very much supports the idea that humans in all types of circumstances respond strongly to incentives. I've seen it with drug dealers, auto thieves, sumo wrestlers, real estate agents, and elementary school teachers, just to name a few examples.

Can you elaborate? What are the incentives to which drug dealers respond? And does an understanding of these responses tell us anything about how public policy might influence drug use?

The incentives people face differ depending on their particular circumstances. Drug dealers, for instance, want to make money, but they also want to avoid being arrested or even killed. In the data we have on drug sellers, we see that when the drug trade is more lucrative, dealers are willing to take greater risks of arrest to carve out a share of the market. On the other hand, they also do their best to minimize their risks. For example, crack sellers used to carry the crack with them. When laws were passed imposing stiff penalties on anyone caught with anything more than a minimal amount of crack, drug dealers responded by storing the crack somewhere else, and retrieving only the amount being sold to the current client. Sumo wrestlers, on the other hand, care mostly about their official ranking. Sometimes matches occur where one wrestler has more to lose or gain than the other wrestler. We find that sumo wrestlers make corrupt deals to make sure the wrestler who needs the win is the one who actually wins.

Why is an economist interested in crime and cheating?

I think of economics as being primarily about a way of looking at the world and a set of tools for thinking clearly. The topics you apply these tools to are unlimited. That is why I think economics has been so powerful. If you understand economics and use the tools wisely, you will be a better business person, doctor, public servant, parent.

What is the economic model of crime, and how does it help to design better ways of dealing with criminal activity? Can you illustrate by talking a bit about your work on the behavior of auto thieves?

The economic model of crime argues that people have a choice of either working for a wage in the legal sector or earning money from illegal activity. The model carefully lays out the set of costs associated with being a criminal (e.g., forgone wages and being punished) and benefits (e.g., the loot) associated with crime and analyzes how a maximizing individual will choose whether to commit crimes and how much crime to commit. One reason the model is useful is because it lays out the various ways in which public policy might influence crime rates. For instance, we can increase the probability of a criminal getting caught or make the prison sentence longer for those who are caught. The government might also try to intervene in the labor market to make legal work more attractive—for instance, with a minimum wage.

What is the problem in figuring out whether more police leads to less crime? How did you find the answer?

We think that when you add more police, crime will fall because the cost of being a criminal goes up because of increased detection. From a public policy perspective, understanding how much crime falls in response to police is an important question. In practice, it is hard to answer this question because we don't randomly hire police. Rather, where crime is bad, there is greater demand for police and thus more police. If you just look at different cities, the places with the most police also have the most crime, but it is not because police cause crime, it is because crime causes police to be hired.

To figure out a causal impact of police on crime, you would like to do a randomized experiment where you added a lot of police at random to some cities and took them away in other cities. That is something you cannot really do in real life. So instead, the economist has to look for "natural experiments" to answer the question.

I used the timing of mayoral elections. It turns out that mayors hire a lot of police before elections to "look tough on crime." If elections do not otherwise affect crime, then the election is kind of like a randomizing device that puts more police in some cities every once in a while. Indeed, I found that crime goes down in the year following elections once the police hired are up and running. It is indirect evidence, but it is an example of how economists use their toolbox to handle difficult questions.

Your work shows that legalized abortion leads to less crime. Can you explain how you reach that conclusion? Can you also explain its implications for the pro-life, pro-choice debate?

The theory is simple: Unwanted children have hard lives (including being much more likely to be criminals); after legalized abortion, there are fewer unwanted children. Therefore, there should be less crime (with a 15–20 year lag while the babies grow up and reach high-crime ages).

We looked at what happened to crime 15–20 years after *Roe v. Wade*, in states with high and low abortion rates and in states that legalized abortion a few years earlier than the rest of the country. We could even look at people born immediately before or after abortion became legal.

All the evidence pointed the same way: Crime fell a lot because abortion was legalized.

> I think of economics as being primarily about a way of looking at the world and a set of tools for thinking clearly.

> If you just look at different cities, the places with the most police also have the most crime, but it is not because police cause crime, it is because crime causes police to be hired.

Our results, however, don't have large implications for the abortion debate. If abortion is murder, as pro-life advocates argue, then the changes in crime we see are trivial in comparison. If a woman simply has the right to control her body, as pro-choice advocates argue, then our estimates about crime are likewise irrelevant.

Our results have more to say about unwantedness: There are big benefits to making sure that children who are brought into the world are wanted and well cared for, through either birth control, adoption, abortion, or parental education.

Terrorism is on everyone's minds these days. And presumably, terrorists respond to incentives. Have you thought about how we might be able to use the insights of economics to better understand and perhaps even combat terrorism?

Terrorism is an unusually difficult question to tackle through incentives. The religious terrorists we are most worried about are willing to give up their lives to carry out terrorist acts. So the only punishment we can really offer is preventing them from committing the act by catching them beforehand or maybe minimizing the damage they can do. Unlike typical criminals, the threat of punishing them after the fact will not help deter the crime. Luckily, even among extremists, there are not many people willing to give their lives for a cause.

Can a student learn how to use natural experiments or do you have a gift that is hard to teach?

I don't think I have such a gift. Most people who are good at something are good because they have worked hard and practiced. That is certainly true with me.

For a while, I just walked around and every time I observed anything in the world I asked myself, "Is that a natural experiment?" Every once in a while I stumbled onto one because I was on the lookout.

> . . . every time I observed anything in the world I asked myself, "Is that a natural experiment?"

What else can a student who wants to become a natural experimenting economist or broader social scientist do to better prepare for that career?

I would say that the best thing students can do is to try to really apply what they are learning to their lives, rather than just memorizing for an exam and quickly forgetting. If you are passionate about economics (or anything else for that matter), you are way ahead of others who are just trying to get by.

10 Organizing Production

After studying this chapter, you will be able to:

- Explain what a firm is and describe the economic problem that all firms face

- Distinguish between technological efficiency and economic efficiency

- Define and explain the principal–agent problem and describe how different types of business organizations cope with this problem

- Describe and distinguish between different types of markets in which firms operate

- Explain why markets coordinate some economic activities and why firms coordinate others

In the fall of 1990, a British scientist named Tim Berners-Lee invented the World Wide Web. This remarkable idea paved the way for the creation of thousands of profitable businesses. One of these businesses is Google, Inc. Built on the idea of two Stanford University graduate students, Larry Page and Sergey Brin, Google, Inc. opened its door for business—a garage door—in 1998. In just a few years, Google became the world's most used, most efficient, and most profitable search engine. How do Google and the other 20 million firms that operate in the United States make their business decisions?

Most of the firms that you can name don't *make* things; they *buy* and *sell* things. For example, Apple doesn't make the iPod.

Toshiba makes the iPod's hard drive and display module and a firm in Taiwan called Inventec assembles the components. Why doesn't Apple make its iPod? How do firms decide what to make themselves and what to buy from other firms?

In this chapter, you are going to learn about firms and the choices they make. In *Reading Between the Lines* at the end of the chapter, we'll apply some of what you've learned and look at some of the choices made by Google and Yahoo! in the search engine business.

227

◆ The Firm and Its Economic Problem

The 20 million firms in the United States differ in size and in the scope of what they do, but they all perform the same basic economic functions. Each **firm** is an institution that hires factors of production and organizes those factors to produce and sell goods and services. Our goal is to predict firms' behavior. To do so, we need to know a firm's goal and the constraints it faces. We start with the goal.

The Firm's Goal

When economists ask entrepreneurs what they are trying to achieve, they get many different answers. Some talk about making a high-quality product, others about business growth, others about market share, others about the job satisfaction of their work-force, and an increasing number today talk about social and environmental responsibility. All of these goals are pursued by firms, but they are not the fundamental goal: They are the means to that goal.

A firm's goal is to maximize profit. A firm that does not seek to maximize profit is either eliminated or taken over by a firm that does seek that goal.

What is the profit that a firm seeks to maximize? To answer this question, we'll look at Campus Sweaters, Inc., a small producer of knitted sweaters owned and operated by Cindy.

Accounting Profit

In 2008, Campus Sweaters received $400,000 for the sweaters it sold and paid out $80,000 for wool, $20,000 for utilities, $120,000 for wages, $5,000 for the lease of a computer, and $5,000 in interest on a bank loan. These expenses total $230,000, so the firm had a cash surplus of $170,000.

To measure the profit of Campus Sweaters, Cindy's accountant subtracted $20,000 for the depreciation of buildings and knitting machines from the $170,000 cash surplus. *Depreciation* is the fall in the value of a firm's capital. To calculate depreciation, accountants use Internal Revenue Service rules based on standards established by the Financial Accounting Standards Board. Using these rules, Cindy's accountant calculated that Campus Sweaters made a profit of $150,000 in 2008.

Economic Accounting

Accountants measure a firm's profit to ensure that the firm pays the correct amount of income tax and to show its investors how their funds are being used.

Economists measure a firm's profit to enable them to predict the firm's decisions, and the goal of these decisions is to maximize *economic profit*. **Economic profit** is equal to total revenue minus total cost, with total cost measured as the *opportunity cost of production*.

A Firm's Opportunity Cost of Production

The *opportunity cost* of any action is the highest-valued alternative forgone. The *opportunity cost of production* is the value of the best alternative use of the resources that a firm uses in production.

A firm's opportunity cost of production is the value of real alternatives forgone. We express opportunity cost in money units so that we can compare and add up the value of the alternatives forgone.

A firm's opportunity cost of production is the sum of the cost of using resources

- Bought in the market
- Owned by the firm
- Supplied by the firm's owner

Resources Bought in the Market A firm incurs an opportunity cost when it buys resources in the market. The amount spent on these resources is an opportunity cost of production because the firm could have bought different resources to produce some other good or service. For Campus Sweaters, the resources bought in the market are wool, utilities, labor, a leased computer, and a bank loan. The $230,000 spent on these items in 2008 could have been spent on something else, so it is an opportunity cost of producing sweaters.

Resources Owned by the Firm A firm incurs an opportunity cost when it uses its own capital. The cost of using capital owned by the firm is an opportunity cost of production because the firm could sell the capital that it owns and rent capital from another firm. When a firm uses its own capital, it implicitly rents it from itself. In this case, the firm's opportunity cost of using the capital it owns is called the **implicit rental rate** of capital. The implicit rental rate of capital has two components: economic depreciation and forgone interest.

Economic Depreciation Accountants measure *depreciation*, the fall in the value of a firm's capital, using formulas that are unrelated to the change in the market value of capital. **Economic depreciation** is the fall in the *market value* of a firm's capital over a given period. It equals the market price of the capital at the beginning of the period minus the market price of the capital at the end of the period.

Suppose that Campus Sweaters could have sold its buildings and knitting machines on January 1, 2008, for $400,000 and that it can sell the same capital on December 31, 2008, for $375,000. The firm's economic depreciation during 2008 is $25,000 ($400,000 − $375,000). This forgone $25,000 is an opportunity cost of production.

Forgone Interest The funds used to buy capital could have been used for some other purpose, and in their next best use, they would have earned interest. This forgone interest is an opportunity cost of production.

Suppose that Campus Sweaters used $300,000 of its own funds to buy capital. If the firm invested its $300,000 in bonds instead of a knitting factory (and rented the capital it needs to produce sweaters), it would have earned $15,000 a year in interest. This forgone interest is an opportunity cost of production.

Resources Supplied by the Firm's Owner A firm's owner might supply *both* entrepreneurship and labor.

Entrepreneurship The factor of production that organizes a firm and makes its decisions, entrepreneurship, might be supplied by the firm's owner or by a hired entrepreneur. The return to entrepreneurship is profit, and the profit that an entrepreneur earns *on the average* is called **normal profit**. Normal profit is the cost of entrepreneurship and is an opportunity cost of production.

If Cindy supplies entrepreneurial services herself, and if the normal profit she can earn on these services is $45,000 a year, this amount is an opportunity cost of production at Campus Sweaters.

Owner's Labor Services *In addition* to supplying entrepreneurship, the owner of a firm might supply labor but not take a wage. The opportunity cost of the owner's labor is the wage income forgone by not taking the best alternative job.

If Cindy supplies labor to Campus Sweaters, and if the wage she can earn on this labor at another firm is $55,000 a year, this amount of wages forgone is an opportunity cost of production at Campus Sweaters.

Economic Accounting: A Summary

Table 10.1 summarizes the economic accounting. Campus Sweaters' total revenue is $400,000; its opportunity cost of production is $370,000; and its economic profit is $30,000.

Cindy's personal income is the $30,000 of economic profit plus the $100,000 that she earns by supplying resources to Campus Sweaters.

Decisions

To achieve the objective of maximum economic profit, a firm must make five decisions:

1. What to produce and in what quantities
2. How to produce
3. How to organize and compensate its managers and workers
4. How to market and price its products
5. What to produce itself and buy from others

In all these decisions, a firm's actions are limited by the constraints that it faces. Your next task is to learn about these constraints.

TABLE 10.1   Economic Accounting

Item		Amount
Total Revenue		**$400,000**
Cost of Resources Bought in Market		
Wool	$80,000	
Utilities	20,000	
Wages	120,000	
Computer lease	5,000	
Bank interest	5,000	$230,000
Cost of Resources Owned by Firm		
Economic depreciation	$25,000	
Forgone interest	15,000	$40,000
Cost of Resources Supplied by Owner		
Cindy's normal profit	$45,000	
Cindy's forgone wages	55,000	$100,000
Opportunity Cost of Production		**$370,000**
Economic Profit		**$30,000**

The Firm's Constraints

Three features of a firm's environment limit the maximum economic profit it can make. They are

- Technology constraints
- Information constraints
- Market constraints

Technology Constraints Economists define technology broadly. A **technology** is any method of producing a good or service. Technology includes the detailed designs of machines and the layout of the workplace. It includes the organization of the firm. For example, the shopping mall is one technology for producing retail services. It is a different technology from the catalog store, which in turn is different from the downtown store.

It might seem surprising that a firm's profits are limited by technology because it seems that technological advances are constantly increasing profit opportunities. Almost every day, we learn about some new technological advance that amazes us. With computers that speak and recognize our own speech and cars that can find the address we need in a city we've never visited, we can accomplish more than ever.

Technology advances over time. But at each point in time, to produce more output and gain more revenue, a firm must hire more resources and incur greater costs. The increase in profit that a firm can achieve is limited by the technology available. For example, by using its current plant and workforce, Ford can produce some maximum number of cars per day. To produce more cars per day, Ford must hire more resources, which increases its costs and limits the increase in profit that it can make by selling the additional cars.

Information Constraints We never possess all the information we would like to have to make decisions. We lack information about both the future and the present. For example, suppose you plan to buy a new computer. When should you buy it? The answer depends on how the price is going to change in the future. Where should you buy it? The answer depends on the prices at hundreds of different computer shops. To get the best deal, you must compare the quality and prices in every shop. But the opportunity cost of this comparison exceeds the cost of the computer!

A firm is constrained by limited information about the quality and efforts of its workforce, the current and future buying plans of its customers, and the plans of its competitors. Workers might make too little effort, customers might switch to competing suppliers, and a competitor might enter the market and take some of the firm's business.

To address these problems, firms create incentives to boost workers' efforts even when no one is monitoring them; conduct market research to lower uncertainty about customers' buying plans, and "spy" on each other to anticipate competitive challenges. But these efforts don't eliminate incomplete information and uncertainty, which limit the economic profit that a firm can make.

Market Constraints The quantity each firm can sell and the price it can obtain are constrained by its customers' willingness to pay and by the prices and marketing efforts of other firms. Similarly, the resources that a firm can buy and the prices it must pay for them are limited by the willingness of people to work for and invest in the firm. Firms spend billions of dollars a year marketing and selling their products. Some of the most creative minds strive to find the right message that will produce a knockout television advertisement. Market constraints and the expenditures firms make to overcome them limit the profit a firm can make.

Review Quiz

1 What is a firm's fundamental goal and what happens if the firm doesn't pursue this goal?
2 Why do accountants and economists calculate a firm's cost and profit in different ways?
3 What are the items that make opportunity cost differ from the accountant's measure of cost?
4 Why is normal profit an opportunity cost?
5 What are the constraints that a firm faces? How does each constraint limit the firm's profit?

 Work Study Plan 10.1 and get instant feedback.

In the rest of this chapter and in Chapters 11 through 14, we study the choices that firms make. We're going to learn how we can predict a firm's decisions as the response to both the constraints that it faces and the changes in those constraints. We begin by taking a closer look at the technology constraints that firms face.

Technological and Economic Efficiency

Microsoft employs a large workforce, and most Microsoft workers possess a large amount of human capital. But the firm uses a small amount of physical capital. In contrast, a coal-mining company employs a huge amount of mining equipment (physical capital) and almost no labor. Why? The answer lies in the concept of efficiency. There are two concepts of production efficiency: technological efficiency and economic efficiency. **Technological efficiency** occurs when the firm produces a given output by using the least amount of inputs. **Economic efficiency** occurs when the firm produces a given output at the least cost. Let's explore the two concepts of efficiency by studying an example.

Suppose that there are four alternative techniques for making TVs:

A. *Robot production.* One person monitors the entire computer-driven process.
B. *Production line.* Workers specialize in a small part of the job as the emerging TV passes them on a production line.
C. *Hand-tool production.* A single worker uses a few hand tools to make a TV.
D. *Bench production.* Workers specialize in a small part of the job but walk from bench to bench to perform their tasks.

Table 10.2 sets out the amounts of labor and capital required by each of these four methods to make 10 TVs a day.

Which of these alternative methods are technologically efficient?

Technological Efficiency

Recall that *technological efficiency* occurs when the firm produces a given output by using the least amount of inputs. Look at the numbers in the table and notice that method A uses the most capital and the least labor. Method C uses the most labor and the least capital. Method B and method D lie between the two extremes. They use less capital and more labor than method A and less labor but more capital than method C.

Compare methods B and D. Method D requires 100 workers and 10 units of capital to produce 10

TABLE 10.2   Four Ways of Making 10 TVs a Day

| | Method | Quantities of inputs | |
		Labor	Capital
A	Robot production	1	1,000
B	Production line	10	10
C	Hand-tool production	1,000	1
D	Bench production	100	10

TVs. Those same 10 TVs can be produced by method B with 10 workers and the same 10 units of capital. Because method D uses the same amount of capital and more labor than method B, method D is not technologically efficient.

Are any of the other methods not technologically efficient? The answer is no. Each of the other methods is technologically efficient. Method A uses more capital but less labor than method B, and method C uses more labor but less capital than method B.

Which of the methods are economically efficient?

Economic Efficiency

Recall that *economic efficiency* occurs when the firm produces a given output at the least cost.

Method D, which is technologically inefficient, is also economically inefficient. It uses the same amount of capital as method B but 10 times as much labor, so it costs more. A technologically inefficient method is never economically efficient.

One of three technologically efficient methods is economically efficient. The other two are economically inefficient. But which method is economically efficient depends on factor prices.

In Table 10.3(a), the wage rate is $75 per day and the rental rate of capital is $250 per day. By studying Table 10.3(a), you can see that method B has the lowest cost and is the economically efficient method.

In Table 10.3(b), the wage rate is $150 a day and the rental rate of capital is $1 a day. Looking at Table 10.3(b), you can see that method A has the lowest cost and is the economically efficient method. In this case, capital is so cheap relative to labor that the

TABLE 10.3   The Costs of Different Ways of Making 10 TVs a Day

(a) Wage rate $75 a day; Capital rental rate $250 a day

Method	Inputs Labor	Inputs Capital	Labor cost ($75 per day)		Capital cost ($250 per day)		Total cost
A	1	1,000	$75	+	$250,000	=	$250,075
B	10	10	750	+	2,500	=	3,250
C	1,000	1	75,000	+	250	=	75,250

(b) Wage rate $150 a day; Capital rental rate $1 a day

Method	Inputs Labor	Inputs Capital	Labor cost ($150 per day)		Capital cost ($1 per day)		Total cost
A	1	1,000	$150	+	$1,000	=	$1,150
B	10	10	1,500	+	10	=	1,510
C	1,000	1	150,000	+	1	=	150,001

(c) Wage rate $1 a day; Capital rental rate $1,000 a day

Method	Inputs Labor	Inputs Capital	Labor cost ($1 per day)		Capital cost ($1,000 per day)		Total cost
A	1	1,000	$1	+	$1,000,000	=	$1,000,001
B	10	10	10	+	10,000	=	10,010
C	1,000	1	1,000	+	1,000	=	2,000

method that uses the most capital is the economically efficient method.

In Table 10.3(c), the wage rate is $1 a day and the rental rate of capital is $1,000 a day. You can see that method *C* has the lowest cost and is the economically efficient method. In this case, labor is so cheap relative to capital that the method that uses the most labor is the economically efficient method.

Economic efficiency depends on the relative costs of resources. The economically efficient method is the one that uses a smaller amount of the more expensive resource and a larger amount of the less expensive resource.

A firm that is not economically efficient does not maximize profit. Natural selection favors efficient firms and inefficient firms disappear. Inefficient firms go out of business or are taken over by firms that produce at lower costs.

Review Quiz

1 Is a firm technologically efficient if it uses the latest technology? Why or why not?
2 Is a firm economically inefficient if it can cut its costs by producing less? Why or why not?
3 Explain the key distinction between technological efficiency and economic efficiency.
4 Why do some firms use large amounts of capital and small amounts of labor while others use small amounts of capital and large amounts of labor?

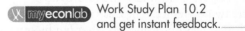 Work Study Plan 10.2 and get instant feedback.

Next we study the information constraints that firms face and the wide array of organization structures these constraints generate.

Information and Organization

Each firm organizes the production of goods and services by combining and coordinating the productive resources it hires. But there is variety across firms in how they organize production. Firms use a mixture of two systems:

- Command systems
- Incentive systems

Command Systems

A **command system** is a method of organizing production that uses a managerial hierarchy. Commands pass downward through the hierarchy, and information passes upward. Managers spend most of their time collecting and processing information about the performance of the people under their control and making decisions about what commands to issue and how best to get those commands implemented.

The military uses the purest form of command system. A commander-in-chief (in the United States, the President) makes the big decisions about strategic goals. Beneath this highest level, generals organize their military resources. Beneath the generals, successively lower ranks organize smaller and smaller units but pay attention to ever-increasing degrees of detail. At the bottom of the managerial hierarchy are the people who operate weapons systems.

Command systems in firms are not as rigid as those in the military, but they share some similar features. A chief executive officer (CEO) sits at the top of a firm's command system. Senior executives who report to and receive commands from the CEO specialize in managing production, marketing, finance, personnel, and perhaps other aspects of the firm's operations. Beneath these senior managers might be several tiers of middle management ranks that stretch downward to the managers who supervise the day-to-day operations of the business. Beneath these managers are the people who operate the firm's machines and who make and sell the firm's goods and services.

Small firms have one or two layers of managers, while large firms have several layers. As production processes have become ever more complex, management ranks have swollen. Today, more people have management jobs than ever before, even though the information revolution of the 1990s slowed the growth of management. In some industries, the information revolution reduced the number of layers of managers and brought a shakeout of middle managers.

Managers make enormous efforts to be well informed. They try hard to make good decisions and issue commands that end up using resources efficiently. But managers always have incomplete information about what is happening in the divisions of the firm for which they are responsible. For this reason, firms use incentive systems as well as command systems to organize production.

Incentive Systems

An **incentive system** is a method of organizing production that uses a market-like mechanism inside the firm. Instead of issuing commands, senior managers create compensation schemes to induce workers to perform in ways that maximize the firm's profit.

Selling organizations use incentive systems most extensively. Sales representatives who spend most of their working time alone and unsupervised are induced to work hard by being paid a small salary and a large performance-related bonus.

But incentive systems operate at all levels in a firm. The compensation plan of a CEO includes a share in the firm's profit, and factory floor workers sometimes receive compensation based on the quantity they produce.

Mixing the Systems

Firms use a mixture of commands and incentives, and they choose the mixture that maximizes profit. Firms use commands when it is easy to monitor performance or when a small deviation from an ideal performance is very costly. They use incentives when monitoring performance is either not possible or too costly to be worth doing.

For example, PepsiCo can easily monitor the performance of workers on a production line. If one person works too slowly, the entire line slows, so a production line is organized with a command system.

In contrast, it is costly to monitor a CEO. For example, what did Ken Lay (former CEO of Enron) contribute to the initial success and subsequent failure of Enron? This question can't be answered with certainty, yet Enron's stockholders had to put someone in charge of the business and provide that person with an incentive to maximize stockholders' returns.

The performance of Enron illustrates a general problem, known as the principal–agent problem.

The Principal–Agent Problem

The **principal–agent problem** is the problem of devising compensation rules that induce an *agent* to act in the best interest of a *principal*. For example, the stockholders of Texaco are *principals,* and the firm's managers are *agents.* The stockholders (the principals) must induce the managers (agents) to act in the stockholders' best interest. Similarly, Steve Jobs (a principal) must induce the designers who are working on the next generation iPhone (agents) to work efficiently.

Agents, whether they are managers or workers, pursue their own goals and often impose costs on a principal. For example, the goal of stockholders of Citicorp (principals) is to maximize the firm's profit—its true profit, not some fictitious paper profit. But the firm's profit depends on the actions of its managers (agents), and they have their own goals. Perhaps a manager takes a customer to a ball game on the pretense that she is building customer loyalty, when in fact she is simply enjoying on-the-job leisure. This same manager is also a principal, and her tellers are agents. The manager wants the tellers to work hard and attract new customers so that she can meet her operating targets. But the workers enjoy conversations with each other and take on-the-job leisure. Nonetheless, the firm constantly strives to find ways of improving performance and increasing profits.

Coping with the Principal–Agent Problem

Issuing commands does not address the principal-agent problem. In most firms, the shareholders can't monitor the managers and often the managers can't monitor the workers. Each principal must create incentives that induce each agent to work in the interests of the principal. Three ways of attempting to cope with the principal–agent problem are

- Ownership
- Incentive pay
- Long-term contracts

Ownership By assigning ownership (or part-ownership) of a business to managers or workers, it is sometimes possible to induce a job performance that increases a firm's profits. Part-ownership is quite common for senior managers but less com-

mon for workers. When United Airlines was running into problems a few years ago, it made most of its employees owners of the company.

Incentive Pay Incentive pay—pay related to performance—is very common. Incentives are based on a variety of performance criteria such as profits, production, or sales targets. Promoting an employee for good performance is another example of the use of incentive pay.

Long-Term Contracts Long-term contracts tie the long-term fortunes of managers and workers (agents) to the success of the principal(s)—the owner(s) of the firm. For example, a multiyear employment contract for a CEO encourages that person to take a long-term view and devise strategies that achieve maximum profit over a sustained period.

These three ways of coping with the principal–agent problem give rise to different types of business organization. Each type of business organization is a different response to the principal–agent problem. Each type uses a different combination of ownership, incentives, and long-term contracts. Let's look at the main types of business organization.

Types of Business Organization

The three main types of business organization are

- Proprietorship
- Partnership
- Corporation

Proprietorship A *proprietorship* is a firm with a single owner—a proprietor—who has unlimited liability. *Unlimited liability* is the legal responsibility for all the debts of a firm up to an amount equal to the entire wealth of the owner. If a proprietorship cannot pay its debts, those to whom the firm owes money can claim the personal property of the owner. Businesses of some farmers, computer programmers, and artists are examples of proprietorships.

The proprietor makes management decisions, receives the firm's profits, and is responsible for its losses. Profits from a proprietorship are taxed at the same rate as other sources of the proprietor's personal income.

Partnership A *partnership* is a firm with two or more owners who have unlimited liability. Partners must agree on an appropriate management structure and on how to divide the firm's profits among themselves. The profits of a partnership are taxed as the personal income of the owners, but each partner is legally liable for all the debts of the partnership (limited only by the wealth of that individual partner). Liability for the full debts of the partnership is called *joint unlimited liability*. Most law firms are partnerships.

Corporation A *corporation* is a firm owned by one or more limited liability stockholders. *Limited liability* means that the owners have legal liability only for the value of their initial investment. This limitation of liability means that if the corporation becomes bankrupt, its owners are not required to use their personal wealth to pay the corporation's debts.

Corporations' profits are taxed independently of stockholders' incomes. Stockholders pay a capital

gains tax on the profit they earn when they sell a stock for a higher price than they paid for it. Corporate stocks generate capital gains when a corporation retains some of its profit and reinvests it in profitable activities. So retained earnings are taxed twice because the capital gains they generate are taxed. Dividend payments are also taxed but at a lower rate than other sources of income.

Pros and Cons of Different Types of Firms

The different types of business organization arise from firms trying to cope with the principal–agent problem. Each type has advantages in particular situations and because of its special advantages, each type continues to exist. Each type of business organization also has disadvantages.

Table 10.4 summarizes these and other pros and cons of the different types of firms.

TABLE 10.4 The Pros and Cons of Different Types of Firms

Type of Firm	Pros	Cons
Proprietorship	■ Easy to set up ■ Simple decision making ■ Profits taxed only once as owner's income	■ Bad decisions not checked; no need for consensus ■ Owner's entire wealth at risk ■ Firm dies with owner ■ Cost of capital and labor is high relative to that of a corporation
Partnership	■ Easy to set up ■ Diversified decision making ■ Can survive withdrawal of partner ■ Profits taxed only once as owners' incomes	■ Achieving consensus may be slow and expensive ■ Owners' entire wealth at risk ■ Withdrawal of partner may create capital shortage ■ Cost of capital and labor is high relative to that of a corporation
Corporation	■ Owners have limited liability ■ Large-scale, low-cost capital available ■ Professional management not restricted by ability of owners ■ Perpetual life ■ Long-term labor contracts cut labor costs	■ Complex management structure can make decisions slow and expensive ■ Retained profits taxed twice: as company profit and as stockholders' capital gains

Types of Firms in the Economy
Corporations Dominate Mom and Pop

Proprietorships, partnerships, and corporations: These are the three types of firms that operate in the United States. Which type of firm dominates? Which produces most of the output of the U.S. economy?

Proprietorships Most Common Three quarters of the firms in the United States are proprietorships and they are mainly small businesses. Almost one fifth of the firms are corporations, and only a twentieth are partnerships (see Fig. 1).

Corporations Produce Most Corporations generate almost 90 percent of business revenue. Revenue is a measure of the value of production, so corporations produce most of the output in the U.S. economy.

Variety Across Industries In agriculture, forestry, and fishing, proprietorships generate about 40 percent of the total revenue. Proprietorships also generate a significant percentage of the revenue in services, construction, and retail trades. Partnerships account for a small percentage of revenue in all sectors and feature most in agriculture, forestry, and fishing, services, and mining. Corporations dominate all sectors and have the manufacturing industries almost to themselves.

Why do corporations dominate the business scene? Why do the other types of business survive? And why are proprietorships and partnerships more prominent in some sectors? The answers lie in the pros and cons of the different types of business organization. Corporations dominate where a large amount of capital is used; proprietorships dominate where flexibility in decision making is critical.

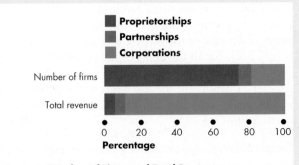

Figure 1 Number of Firms and Total Revenue

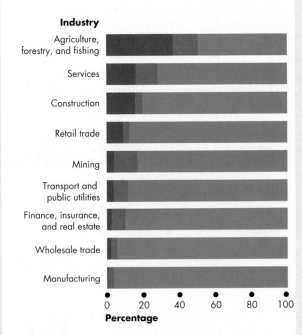

Figure 2 Total Revenue in Various Industries

Source of data: U.S. Bureau of the Census, *Statistical Abstract of the United States: 2001.*

Review Quiz

1 Explain the distinction between a command system and an incentive system.
2 What is the principal–agent problem? What are three ways in which firms try to cope with it?
3 What are the three types of firms? Explain the major advantages and disadvantages of each.
4 Why do all three types of firms survive and in which sectors is each type most prominent?

myeconlab Work Study Plan 10.3 and get instant feedback.

You've now seen how technology constraints and information constraints influence firms. You've seen why some firms operate with a large amount of labor and human capital and a small amount of physical capital. You've also seen how firms use a mixture of command and incentive systems and employ different types of business organization to cope with the principle–agent problem.

Your next task is to look at the variety of market situations in which firms operate and classify the different market environments in which firms do business.

Markets and the Competitive Environment

The markets in which firms operate vary a great deal. Some are highly competitive, and profits in these markets are hard to come by. Some appear to be almost free from competition, and firms in these markets earn large profits. Some markets are dominated by fierce advertising campaigns in which each firm seeks to persuade buyers that it has the best products. And some markets display the character of a strategic game.

Economists identify four market types:

1. Perfect competition
2. Monopolistic competition
3. Oligopoly
4. Monopoly

Perfect competition arises when there are many firms, each selling an identical product, many buyers, and no restrictions on the entry of new firms into the industry. The many firms and buyers are all well informed about the prices of the products of each firm in the industry. The worldwide markets for corn, rice, and other grain crops are examples of perfect competition.

Monopolistic competition is a market structure in which a large number of firms compete by making similar but slightly different products. Making a product slightly different from the product of a competing firm is called **product differentiation**. Product differentiation gives a firm in monopolistic competition an element of market power. The firm is the sole producer of the particular version of the good in question. For example, in the market for pizzas, hundreds of firms make their own version of the perfect pizza. Each of these firms is the sole producer of a particular brand. Differentiated products are not necessarily different products. What matters is that consumers perceive them to be different. For example, different brands of potato chips and ketchup might be almost identical but be perceived by consumers to be different.

Oligopoly is a market structure in which a small number of firms compete. Computer software, airplane manufacture, and international air transportation are examples of oligopolistic industries. Oligopolies might produce almost identical products, such as the colas produced by Coke and Pepsi. Or they might produce differentiated products such as Boeing and Airbus aircraft.

Monopoly arises when there is one firm, which produces a good or service that has no close substitutes and in which the firm is protected by a barrier preventing the entry of new firms. In some places, the phone, gas, electricity, cable television, and water suppliers are local monopolies—monopolies restricted to a given location. Microsoft Corporation, the software developer that created Windows and Vista, is an example of a global monopoly.

Perfect competition is the most extreme form of competition. Monopoly is the most extreme absence of competition. The other two market types fall between these extremes.

Many factors must be taken into account to determine which market structure describes a particular real-world market. One of these factors is the extent to which a small number of firms dominates the market. To measure this feature of markets, economists use indexes called measures of concentration. Let's look at these measures.

Measures of Concentration

Economists use two measures of concentration:

- The four-firm concentration ratio
- The Herfindahl-Hirschman Index

The Four-Firm Concentration Ratio The **four-firm concentration ratio** is the percentage of the value of sales accounted for by the four largest firms in an industry. The range of the concentration ratio is from almost zero for perfect competition to 100 percent for monopoly. This ratio is the main measure used to assess market structure.

Table 10.5 shows two calculations of the four-firm concentration ratio: one for tire makers and one for printers. In this example, 14 firms produce tires. The largest four have 80 percent of the sales, so the four-firm concentration ratio is 80 percent. In the printing industry, with 1,004 firms, the largest four firms have only 0.5 percent of the sales, so the four-firm concentration ratio is 0.5 percent.

A low concentration ratio indicates a high degree of competition, and a high concentration ratio indicates an absence of competition. A monopoly has a concentration ratio of 100 percent—the largest (and only) firm has 100 percent of the sales. A four-firm concentration ratio that exceeds 60 percent is regarded as an indication of a market that is highly concentrated and dominated by a few firms in an oligopoly. A ratio of less than 60 percent is regarded as an indication of a competitive market.

The Herfindahl-Hirschman Index The **Herfindahl-Hirschman Index**—also called the HHI—is the square of the percentage market share of each firm summed over the largest 50 firms (or summed over all the firms if there are fewer than 50) in a market. For example, if there are four firms in a market and the market shares of the firms are 50 percent, 25 percent, 15 percent, and 10 percent, the Herfindahl-Hirschman Index is

$$HHI = 50^2 + 25^2 + 15^2 + 10^2 = 3,450.$$

TABLE 10.5 Calculating the Four-Firm Concentration Ratio

Tire makers		Printers	
Firm	**Sales (millions of dollars)**	**Firm**	**Sales (millions of dollars)**
Top, Inc.	200	Fran's	2.5
ABC, Inc.	250	Ned's	2.0
Big, Inc.	150	Tom's	1.8
XYZ, Inc.	100	Jill's	1.7
Largest 4 firms	700	Largest 4 firms	8.0
Other 10 firms	175	Other 1,000 firms	1,592.0
Industry	875	Industry	1,600.0

Four-firm concentration ratios:

Tire makers: $\dfrac{700}{875} \times 100 = 80$ percent

Printers: $\dfrac{8}{1,600} \times 100 = 0.5$ percent

Concentration Measures in the U.S. Economy

Chewing Gum Monopoly

The U.S. Department of Commerce calculates and publishes data showing concentration ratios and the HHI for each industry in the United States. The bars in the figure show the four-firm concentration ratio and the number at the end of each bar is the HHI.

Chewing gum is one of the most concentrated industries. William Wrigley Jr. Company of Chicago employs 16,000 people and sells $5 billion worth of gum a year. It does have some competitors but they have a very small market share.

Household laundry equipment, light bulbs, breakfast cereal, and motor vehicles are highly concentrated industries. They are oligopolies.

Pet food, cookies and crackers, computers, and soft drinks are moderately concentrated industries. They are examples of monopolistic competition.

Ice cream, milk, clothing, concrete blocks and bricks, and commercial printing industries have low concentration measures and are highly competitive.

Concentration measures are useful indicators of the degree of competition in a market, but they must be supplemented by other information to determine the structure of the market.

Newspapers and automobiles are examples of how the concentration measures give a misleading reading of the degree of competition. Most newspapers are local. They serve a single city or even smaller area. So despite the low concentration measure, newspapers are concentrated in their own local areas. Automobiles are traded internationally and foreign cars are freely imported into the United States. Despite the high concentration measure, the automobile industry is competitive.

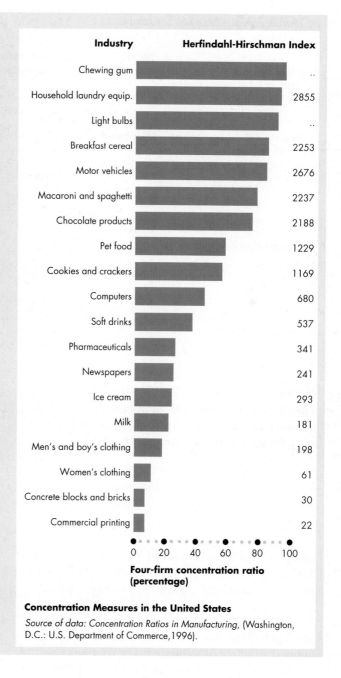

Concentration Measures in the United States

Source of data: Concentration Ratios in Manufacturing, (Washington, D.C.: U.S. Department of Commerce,1996).

In perfect competition, the HHI is small. For example, if each of the largest 50 firms in an industry has a market share of 0.1 percent, then the HHI is $0.1^2 \times 50 = 0.5$. In a monopoly, the HHI is 10,000. The firm has 100 percent of the market: $100^2 = 10,000$.

The HHI became a popular measure of the degree of competition during the 1980s, when the Justice Department used it to classify markets. A market in which the HHI is less than 1,000 is regarded as being competitive. A market in which the HHI lies between 1,000 and 1,800 is regarded as being moderately competitive. But a market in which the HHI exceeds 1,800 is regarded as being uncompetitive. The Justice Department scrutinizes any merger of firms in a market in which the HHI exceeds 1,000 and is likely to challenge a merger if the HHI exceeds 1,800.

TABLE 10.6   Market Structure

Characteristics	Perfect competition	Monopolistic competition	Oligopoly	Monopoly
Number of firms in industry	Many	Many	Few	One
Product	Identical	Differentiated	Either identical or differentiated	No close substitutes
Barriers to entry	None	None	Moderate	High
Firm's control over price	None	Some	Considerable	Considerable or regulated
Concentration ratio	0	Low	High	100
HHI (approx. ranges)	Less than 100	101 to 999	More than 1,000	10,000
Examples	Wheat, corn	Food, clothing	Automobiles, cereals	Local water supply

Limitations of a Concentration Measure

The three main limitations of using only concentration measures as determinants of market structure are their failure to take proper account of

- The geographical scope of the market
- Barriers to entry and firm turnover
- The correspondence between a market and an industry

Geographical Scope of Market Concentration measures take a national view of the market. Many goods are sold in a *national* market, but some are sold in a *regional* market and some in a *global* one. The concentration measures for newspapers are low, indicating competition, but in most cities the newspaper industry is highly concentrated. The concentration measures for automobiles is high, indicating little competition, but the biggest three U.S. car makers compete with foreign car makers in a highly competitive global market.

Barriers to Entry and Firm Turnover Some markets are highly concentrated but entry is easy and the turnover of firms is large. For example, small towns have few restaurants, but no restrictions hinder a new restaurant from opening and many attempt to do so.

Also, a market with only a few firms might be competitive because of *potential entry*. The few firms in a market face competition from the many potential firms that will enter the market if economic profit opportunities arise.

Market and Industry Correspondence To calculate concentration ratios, the Department of Commerce classifies each firm as being in a particular industry. But markets do not always correspond closely to industries for three reasons.

First, markets are often narrower than industries. For example, the pharmaceutical industry, which has a low concentration ratio, operates in many separate markets for individual products—for example, measles vaccine and AIDS-fighting drugs. These drugs do not compete with each other, so this industry, which looks competitive, includes firms that are monopolies (or near monopolies) in markets for individual drugs.

Second, most firms make several products. For example, Westinghouse makes electrical equipment and, among other things, gas-fired incinerators and plywood. So this one firm operates in at least three separate markets, but the Department of Commerce classifies Westinghouse as being in the electrical goods and equipment industry. The fact that Westinghouse competes with other producers of plywood does not

Market Structures in the U.S. Economy

A Highly Competitive Environment

How competitive are markets in the United States? Do most U.S. firms operate in competitive markets, in monopolistic competition, in oligopoly, or in monopoly markets?

The data needed to answer these questions are hard to get. The last attempt to answer the questions, in a study by William G. Shepherd, an economics professor at the University of Massachusetts at Amherst, covered the years from 1939 to 1980. The figure shows what he discovered.

In 1980, three quarters of the value of goods and services bought and sold in the United States was traded in markets that are essentially competitive—markets that have almost perfect competition or monopolistic competition. Monopoly and the dominance of a single firm accounted for about 5 percent of sales. Oligopoly, which is found mainly in manufacturing, accounted for about 18 percent of sales.

Over the period studied, the U.S. economy became increasingly competitive. The percentage of output sold by firms operating in competitive markets (blue bars) has expanded most, and has shrunk most in oligopoly markets (red bars).

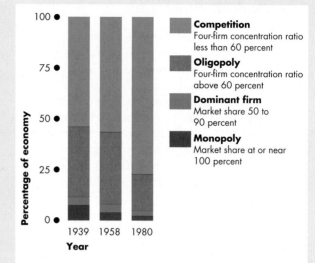

The Market Structure of the U.S. Economy

Source of data: William G. Shepherd, "Causes of Increased Competition in the U.S. Economy, 1939–1980," *Review of Economics and Statistics*, November 1982, pp. 613–626. © MIT Press Journals. Reprinted by permission.

But also during the past decades, the U.S. economy has become much more exposed to competition from the rest of the world. The data used by William G. Shepherd don't capture this international competition, so the data probably understate the degree of true competition in the U.S. economy.

show up in the concentration numbers for the plywood market.

Third, firms switch from one market to another depending on profit opportunities. For example, Motorola, which today produces cellular telephones and other communications products, has diversified from being a TV and computer chip maker. Motorola no longer produces TVs. Publishers of newspapers, magazines, and textbooks are today rapidly diversifying into Internet and multimedia products. These switches among markets show that there is much scope for entering and exiting a market, and so measures of concentration have limited usefulness.

Despite their limitations, concentration measures do provide a basis for determining the degree of competition in a market when they are combined with information about the geographical scope of the market, barriers to entry, and the extent to which large, multiproduct firms straddle a variety of markets.

Review Quiz

1 What are the four market types? Explain the distinguishing characteristics of each.
2 What are the two measures of concentration? Explain how each measure is calculated.
3 Under what conditions do the measures of concentration give a good indication of the degree of competition in a market?
4 Is our economy competitive? Is it becoming more competitive or less competitive?

 Work Study Plan 10.4 and get instant feedback.

You now know the variety of market types and how we identify them. Our final question in this chapter is: What determines the things that firms decide to buy from other firms rather than produce for themselves?

Markets and Firms

A firm is an institution that hires factors of production and organizes them to produce and sell goods and services. To organize production, firms coordinate the economic decisions and activities of many individuals. But firms are not the only coordinators of economic decisions. You learned in Chapter 3 that markets also coordinate decisions. They do so by adjusting prices and making the decisions of buyers and sellers consistent—making the quantity demanded equal to the quantity supplied for each good and service.

Market Coordination

Markets can coordinate production. For example, markets might coordinate the production of a rock concert. A promoter books a stadium, some stage equipment, audio and video recording engineers and technicians, some rock groups, a superstar, a publicity agent, and a ticket agent—all market transactions. The promoter sells tickets to thousands of rock fans, audio rights to a recording company, and video and broadcasting rights to a television network—another set of market transactions. Alternatively, if rock concerts were produced like cornflakes, the firm producing them would own all the capital used (stadiums, stage, sound and video equipment) and would employ all the labor needed (singers, engineers, and salespeople).

Outsourcing, buying parts or products from other firms, is another example of market coordination. Dell uses outsourcing for all the components of the computers it produces. The major automakers use outsourcing for windshields and windows, gearboxes, tires, and many other car parts.

What determines whether a firm or markets coordinate a particular set of activities? How do firms decide whether to buy from another firm or manufacture an item themselves? The answer is cost. Taking account of the opportunity cost of time as well as the costs of the other inputs, firms use the method that costs least. In other words, they use the economically efficient method.

Firms coordinate economic activity when they can perform a task more efficiently than markets can. In such a situation, it is profitable to set up a firm. If markets can perform a task more efficiently than a firm can, firms will use markets, and any attempt to set up a firm to replace such market coordination will be doomed to failure.

Why Firms?

Firms are often more efficient than markets as coordinators of economic activity because they can achieve

- Lower transactions costs
- Economies of scale
- Economies of scope
- Economies of team production

Transactions Costs The idea that firms exist because there are activities in which firms are more efficient than markets was first suggested by University of Chicago economist and Nobel Laureate Ronald Coase. Coase focused on the firm's ability to reduce or eliminate transactions costs. **Transactions costs** are the costs that arise from finding someone with whom to do business, of reaching an agreement about the price and other aspects of the exchange, and of ensuring that the terms of the agreement are fulfilled. Market transactions require buyers and sellers to get together and to negotiate the terms and conditions of their trading. Sometimes, lawyers have to be hired to draw up contracts. A broken contract leads to still more expense. A firm can lower such transactions costs by reducing the number of individual transactions undertaken.

Consider, for example, two ways of getting your rattling car fixed.

Firm coordination: You take the car to the garage. The garage owner coordinates parts and tools as well as the mechanic's time, and your car gets fixed. You pay one bill for the entire job.

Market coordination: You hire a mechanic, who diagnoses the problems and makes a list of the parts and tools needed to fix them. You buy the parts from the local wrecker's yard and rent the tools from ABC Rentals. You hire the mechanic again to fix the problems. You return the tools and pay your bills—wages to the mechanic, rental to ABC, and the cost of the parts used to the wrecker.

What determines the method that you use? The answer is cost. Taking account of the opportunity cost of your own time as well as the costs of the other inputs that you would have to buy, you will use the method that costs least. In other words, you will use the economically efficient method.

The first method requires that you undertake only one transaction with one firm. It's true that the firm has to undertake several transactions—hiring the labor and buying the parts and tools required to do the job. But the firm doesn't have to undertake those transactions simply to fix your car. One set of such transactions enables the firm to fix hundreds of cars. There is an enormous reduction in the number of individual transactions that take place if people get their cars fixed at the garage rather than going through an elaborate sequence of market transactions.

Economies of Scale When the cost of producing a unit of a good falls as its output rate increases, **economies of scale** exist. Automakers, for example, experience economies of scale because as the scale of production increases, the firm can use cost-saving equipment and highly specialized labor. An automaker that produces only a few cars a year must use hand-tool methods that are costly. Economies of scale arise from specialization and the division of labor that can be reaped more effectively by firm coordination rather than market coordination.

Economies of Scope A firm experiences **economies of scope** when it uses specialized (and often expensive) resources to produce a *range of goods and services*. For example, Toshiba uses its designers and specialized equipment to make the hard drive for the iPod. But it makes many different types of hard drives and other related products. As a result, Toshiba produces the iPod hard drive at a lower cost than a firm making only the iPod hard drive could achieve.

Economies of Team Production A production process in which the individuals in a group specialize in mutually supportive tasks is *team production*. Sports provide the best examples of team activity. In baseball, some team members specialize in pitching and others in fielding. In basketball, some team members specialize in defense and some in offense. The production of goods and services offers many examples of team activity. For example, production lines in automobile and TV manufacturing plants work most efficiently when individual activity is organized in teams, each specializing in a small task. You can also think of an entire firm as being a team. The team has buyers of raw material and other inputs, production workers, and salespeople. Each individual member of the team specializes, but the value of the output of the team and the profit that it earns depend on the coordinated activities of all the team's members. The

idea that firms arise as a consequence of the economies of team production was first suggested by Armen Alchian and Harold Demsetz of the University of California at Los Angeles.

Because firms can economize on transactions costs, reap economies of scale and economies of scope, and organize efficient team production, it is firms rather than markets that coordinate most of our economic activity. But there are limits to the economic efficiency of firms. If a firm becomes too big or too diversified, the cost of managing its activities, per unit of output, rises. When a firm is too big, it can become more efficient by trimming down and buying more inputs in the market from other firms.

IBM is an example of a firm that became too big to be efficient. In an attempt to restore efficient operations, IBM split up its large organization into a number of "Baby Blues," each of which specializes in a segment of the computer market.

Sometimes firms enter into long-term relationships that make it difficult to see where one firm ends and another begins. For example, GM has long-term relationships with suppliers of windows, tires, and other parts. Wal-Mart has long-term relationships with suppliers of the goods it sells. Such relationships make transactions costs lower than they would be if GM or Wal-Mart went shopping on the world market each time it wanted new supplies.

Review Quiz

1 What are the two ways in which economic activity can be coordinated?

2 What determines whether a firm or markets coordinate production?

3 What are the main reasons why firms can often coordinate production at a lower cost than markets can?

 Work Study Plan 10.5 and get instant feedback.

Reading Between the Lines on pp. 244–245 explores the Internet search business. We continue to study firms and their decisions in the next four chapters. In Chapter 11, we learn about the relationships between cost and output at different output levels. These relationships are common to all types of firms in all types of markets. We then turn to problems that are specific to firms in different types of markets.

Battling for Markets in Internet Search

Yawns for Yahoo, Ga-Ga for Google

Earnings from the two search leaders are coming and guess what?
Google's eating Yahoo's lunch.

http://money.cnn.com
October 13, 2006

… Google unveiled a deal to buy YouTube, for $1.6 billion, uniting the top search engine and No. 1 video site. Analysts were raving about Google's chances to get a big piece of the potentially lucrative online video advertising market. …

Yahoo is playing catch-up with Google in the hot market for paid search. According to the most recent numbers from Web tracking firm comScore Networks, Google widened its lead in search over Yahoo in August. …

And looking ahead to next year, Yahoo could face a much tougher challenge from Google in so-called display advertising, sales of video ads, banners and other ads not tied to search results, thanks to Google's pending deal for YouTube.

Yahoo has so far maintained an edge over Google in display advertising, which tends to be more attractive to big brand-name companies than search ads. But it is a big market opportunity for Google.

Essence of the Story

- Yahoo! lags behind Google in the market for advertising tied to keyword queries—known as paid search.

- Yahoo! leads Google in sales of video ads, banners, and other ads not tied to search results—known as display advertising.

- By buying YouTube (for $1.6 billion), Google has created a marriage of the top search engine and the top video sharing site.

- Google is expected to gain a large share of the profitable online video advertising market, which big brand-name companies use.

Economic Analysis

- Like all firms, Yahoo! and Google aim to maximize profit.

- Also, like all firms, Yahoo! and Google face constraints imposed by technology and the market.

- Both firms provide search engines to access information on the Internet.

- People who use a search engine demand information, and Yahoo! and Google (and other firms) supply information.

- The equilibrium price of search engine services to users is zero!

- To generate revenue and profit, search engine providers offer advertising services.

- Two types of advertising are offered: paid search and display.

- Google's focus is on paid search—see Figs. 1 and 2. Yahoo!'s focus is on display—see Fig. 3.

- To attract either type of advertising, a firm must be able to offer the advertiser access to a large potential customer base.

- To maximize the use of their search engines, Google and Yahoo! offer a variety of enticements to users.

- One enticement is the quality of the search engine itself. Most people think that Google has the better search technology, but Yahoo! is working on improved search.

- Another enticement is a variety of related attractions. Yahoo!'s photo-sharing service is an example.

- Search engines can also generate more revenue by enabling advertisers to more precisely target their potential customers. Again, the quality of the search technology is the key ingredient. And again, Google is seen by many to have the edge.

- Google hopes to attract even more users and to increase its ability to use video and other display technologies through its acquisition of YouTube.

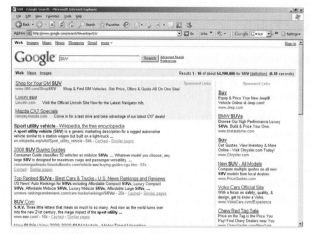

Figure 1 Paid search advertising

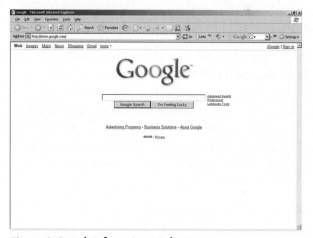

Figure 2 Google's focus is search

Figure 3 Yahoo! features display advertising

245

SUMMARY ►

Key Points

The Firm and Its Economic Problem (pp. 228–230)

- Firms hire and organize factors of production to produce and sell goods and services.
- A firm's goal is to maximize economic profit, which is total revenue minus total cost measured as the opportunity cost of production.
- A firm's opportunity cost of production is the sum of the cost of resources bought in the market, using the firm's own resources, and resources supplied by the firm's owner.
- Normal profit is the opportunity cost of entrepreneurship and is part of the firm's opportunity cost.
- Technology, information, and markets limit the economic profit that a firm can make.

Technological and Economic Efficiency (pp. 231–232)

- A method of production is technologically efficient when a firm uses the least amount of inputs to produce a given output.
- A method of production is economically efficient when the cost of producing a given output is as low as possible.

Information and Organization (pp. 233–236)

- Firms use a combination of command systems and incentive systems to organize production.

- Faced with incomplete information and uncertainty, firms induce managers and workers to perform in ways that are consistent with the firms' goals.
- Proprietorships, partnerships, and corporations use ownership, incentive pay, and long-term contracts to cope with the principal–agent problem.

Markets and the Competitive Environment (pp. 237–241)

- In perfect competition, many sellers offer an identical product to many buyers and entry is free.
- In monopolistic competition, many sellers offer slightly different products to many buyers and entry is free.
- In oligopoly, a small number of sellers compete and barriers to entry limit the number of firms.
- In monopoly, one firm produces an item that has no close substitutes and the firm is protected by a barrier to entry that prevents the entry of competitors.

Markets and Firms (pp. 242–243)

- Firms coordinate economic activities when they can perform a task more efficiently—at lower cost—than markets can.
- Firms economize on transactions costs and achieve the benefits of economies of scale, economies of scope, and economies of team production.

Key Tables

Table 10.4   The Pros and Cons of Different Types of Firms, 235

Table 10.5   Calculating the Four-Firm Concentration Ratio 238

Table 10.6   Market Structure, 240

Key Terms

Command system, 233
Economic depreciation, 229
Economic efficiency, 231
Economic profit, 228
Economies of scale, 243
Economies of scope, 243
Firm, 228

Four-firm concentration ratio, 238
Herfindahl-Hirschman Index, 238
Implicit rental rate, 228
Incentive system, 233
Monopolistic competition, 237
Monopoly, 237
Normal profit, 229

Oligopoly, 237
Perfect competition, 237
Principal–agent problem, 234
Product differentiation, 237
Technological efficiency, 231
Technology, 230
Transactions costs, 242

PROBLEMS and APPLICATIONS ◆

myeconlab Work problems 1–11 in Chapter 10 Study Plan and get instant feedback.
Work problems 12–23 as Homework, a Quiz, or a Test if assigned by your instructor.

1. One year ago, Jack and Jill set up a vinegar-bottling firm (called JJVB). Use the following information to calculate JJVB's opportunity cost of production during its first year of operation:
   ▪ Jack and Jill put $50,000 of their own money into the firm.
   ▪ They bought equipment for $30,000.
   ▪ They hired one employee to help them for an annual wage of $20,000.
   ▪ Jack gave up his previous job, at which he earned $30,000, and spent all his time working for JJVB.
   ▪ Jill kept her old job, which paid $30 an hour, but gave up 10 hours of leisure each week (for 50 weeks) to work for JJVB.
   ▪ JJVB bought $10,000 of goods and services from other firms.
   ▪ The market value of the equipment at the end of the year was $28,000.
   ▪ Jack and Jill have a $100,000 home loan on which they pay an interest rate of 6 percent a year.

2. Joe runs a shoeshine stand at the airport. With no skills and no job experience, Joe has no alternative employment. Other shoeshine stand operators that Joe knows earn $10,000 a year. Joe pays the airport $2,000 a year for the space he uses, and his total revenue from shining shoes is $15,000 a year. He spent $1,000 on a chair, polish, and brushes and paid for these items using his credit card. The interest on his credit card balance is 20 percent a year. At the end of the year, Joe was offered $500 for his business and all its equipment. Calculate Joe's opportunity cost of production and his economic profit.

3. Alternative ways of laundering 100 shirts are

Method	Labor (hours)	Capital (machines)
A	1	10
B	5	8
C	20	4
D	50	1

   a. Which methods are technologically efficient?
   b. Which method is economically efficient if the

hourly wage rate and implicit rental rate of capital are
   (i) Wage rate $1, rental rate $100?
   (ii) Wage rate $5, rental rate $50?
   (iii) Wage rate $50, rental rate $5?

4. Sales of the firms in the tattoo industry are

Firm	Sales (dollars per year)
Bright Spots	450
Freckles	325
Love Galore	250
Native Birds	200
Other 15 firms	800

   a. Calculate the four-firm concentration ratio.
   b. What is the structure of the tattoo industry?

5. In 2003 and 2004, Lego, the Danish toymaker that produces colored plastic bricks, incurred economic losses. The firm faced competition from low-cost copiers of its products and faced a fall in the number of 5- to 9-year-old boys (its main customers) in many rich countries. In 2004, Lego launched a plan to restore profits. It fired 3,500 of its 8,000 workers; closed factories in Switzerland and the United States; opened factories in Eastern Europe and Mexico; and introduced performance-based pay for its managers. Lego reported a return to profit in 2005.

   Based on **Picking Up the Pieces**,
   The Economist, October 28, 2006.
   a. Describe the problems that Lego faced in 2003 and 2004, using the concepts of the three types of constraints that all firms face.
   b. Which of the actions that Lego took to restore profits addressed an inefficiency? How did Lego seek to achieve economic efficiency?
   c. Which of the actions that Lego took to restore profits addressed an information and organization problem? How did Lego change the way in which it coped with the principal–agent problem?
   d. In what type of market does Lego operate?

6. **John Deere's Farm Team**
   Deere … opened up the Pune [India] center in 2001 as a way of entering the Indian market.

The move was unexpected: Deere is known for its heavy-duty farm equipment and big construction gear. Many of India's 300 million-plus farmers still use oxen-pulled plows. …

Fortune, April 14, 2008

a. Why do many Indian farmers still use oxen-pulled plows? Are they efficient or inefficient? Explain.

b. How might making John Deere farm equipment available to Indian farmers change the technology constraint they face?

c. How do you expect John Deere's move into the Indian farm equipment market to influence the firm's profit opportunities?

7. **Here It Is. Now, You Design It!**

The idea is that the most successful companies no longer invent new products and services on their own. They create them along with their customers, and they do it in a way that produces a unique experience for each customer. The important corollary is that no company owns enough resources—or can possibly own enough—to furnish unique experiences for each customer, so companies must organize a constantly shifting global web of suppliers and partners to do the job.

Fortune, May 26, 2008

a. Describe this method of organizing and coordinating production: Does it use a command system or incentive system?

b. How does this method of organizing and coordinating production help firms achieve lower costs?

8. **Rewarding Failure**

Over the past 25 years CEO pay has risen … faster than corporate profits, economic growth, or average workforce compensation. … A more sensible alternative to the current compensation system would require CEOs to own a lot of company stock. If the stock is given to the boss, his salary and bonus should be docked to reflect its value. As for bonuses, they should be based on improving a company's cash earnings relative to its cost of capital, not to more easily manipulated measures like earnings per share. … [Bonuses] should not be capped, but they should be unavailable to the CEO for some period of years.

Fortune, April 28, 2008

a. What is the economic problem that CEO compensation schemes are designed to solve?

b. How do the proposed changes to CEO compensation outlined in the news clip address the problem you described in a?

9. **GameStop Racks Up the Points**

No retailer has more cachet among gamers than GameStop, and only Wal-Mart has a larger share of the market—for now. … Wal-Mart had a 21.3% market share last year. GameStop's share was 21.1%, and may well overtake Wal-Mart this year … but [new women gamers] may prefer shopping at Target to GameStop. … A chance for Wal-Mart and Target to erode GameStop's market share. …

Fortune, June 9, 2008

a. According to the news clip, what is the structure of the U.S. retail video-game market?

b. Estimate a range for the four-firm concentration ratio and the HHI for the game market in the United States based on the information provided in this news clip.

10. **6 Steps to Creating a Super Startup**

But starting a business is a complicated, risky, all-consuming effort. Indeed, just two-thirds of new small businesses survive at least two years, and only 44 percent survive at least four years. … You have to be willing to take calculated risks. … Most entrepreneurs start their businesses by dipping into their savings, and hitting up friends and family. Perhaps half of all start-ups, in fact, are funded initially by the founder's credit cards. … Getting a bank loan is tough unless you have assets—and that often means using your home as collateral.

CNN, October 18, 2007

a. When starting a business, what are the risks and potential rewards associated with a proprietorship identified in the news clip?

b. How might a partnership help to overcome the risks identified in the news clip?

c. How might a corporation help to overcome the risks identified in the news clip?

11. Federal Express enters into contracts with independent truck operators who offer FedEx service and who are rewarded by the volume (cubic feet) of packages they carry.

a. Why doesn't FedEx buy more trucks and hire more drivers?

b. What incentive problems might arise from the arrangement that FedEx uses?

12. Lee is a computer programmer who earned $35,000 in 2007. But on January 1, 2008, Lee opened a body board manufacturing business. At the end of the first year of operation, he submitted the following information to his accountant:
    - He stopped renting out his cottage for $3,500 a year and used it as his factory. The market value of the cottage increased from $70,000 to $71,000.
    - He spent $50,000 on materials, phone, utilities, etc.
    - He leased machines for $10,000 a year.
    - He paid $15,000 in wages.
    - He used $10,000 from his savings account, which earns 5 percent a year interest.
    - He borrowed $40,000 at 10 percent a year from the bank.
    - He sold $160,000 worth of body boards.
    - Normal profit is $25,000 a year.
    a. Calculate Lee's opportunity cost of production and his economic profit.
    b. Lee's accountant recorded the depreciation on his cottage during 2008 as $7,000. According to the accountant, what profit did Lee make?

13. In 2007, Toni taught music and earned $20,000. She also earned $4,000 by renting out her basement. On January 1, 2008, she quit teaching, stopped renting out her basement, and began to use it as the office for her new Web site design business. She took $2,000 from her savings account to buy a computer. During 2008, she paid $1,500 for the lease of a Web server and $1,750 for high-speed Internet service. She received a total revenue from Web site designing of $45,000 and earned interest at 5 percent a year on her savings account balance. Normal profit is $55,000 a year. At the end of 2008, Toni could have sold her computer for $500. Calculate Toni's opportunity cost of production and her economic profit in 2008.

14. Four methods of completing a tax return and the time taken by each method are: with a PC, 1 hour; with a pocket calculator, 12 hours; with a pocket calculator and paper and pencil, 12 hours; and with a pencil and paper, 16 hours. The PC and its software cost $1,000, the pocket calculator costs $10, and the pencil and paper cost $1.
    a. Which, if any, of the methods is technologically efficient?

    b. Which method is economically efficient if the wage rate is
       (i) $5 an hour?
       (ii) $50 an hour?
       (iii) $500 an hour?

15. Wal-Mart has more than 3,700 stores, more than one million employees, and total revenues of close to a quarter of a trillion dollars in the United States alone. Sarah Frey-Talley runs the family-owned Frey Farms in Illinois and supplies Wal-Mart with pumpkins and other fresh produce.
    a. How do you think Wal-Mart coordinates its activities? Is it likely to use mainly a command system or also to use incentive systems? Why or why not?
    b. How do you think Sarah Frey-Talley coordinates the activities of Frey Farms? Is she likely to use mainly a command system or also to use incentive systems? Why?
    c. Describe, compare, and contrast the principal–agent problems faced by Wal-Mart and Frey Farms. How might these firms cope with their principal–agent problems?

16. Market shares of chocolate makers are

Firm	Market share (percent)
Mayfair, Inc.	15
Bond, Inc.	10
Magic, Inc.	20
All Natural, Inc.	15
Truffles, Inc.	25
Gold, Inc.	15

    a. Calculate the Herfindahl-Hirschman Index.
    b. What is the structure of the chocolate industry?

17. Two leading design firms, Astro Studios of San Francisco and Hers Experimental Design Laboratory, Inc. of Osaka, Japan, worked with Microsoft to design the Xbox 360 video game console. IBM, ATI, and SiS designed the Xbox 360's hardware. Three firms, Flextronics, Wistron, and Celestica, manufacture the Xbox 360 at their plants in China and Taiwan?
    a. Describe the roles of market coordination and coordination by firms in the design, manufacture, and marketing of the Xbox 360.
    b. Why do you think Microsoft works with a large number of other firms to bring the Xbox

to market, rather than performing all the required tasks at its headquarters in Seattle?

c. What are the roles of transactions costs, economies of scale, economies of scope, and economies of team production in the design, manufacture, and marketing of the Xbox?

d. Why do you think the Xbox is designed in the United States and Japan but built in China?

18. **The Colvin Interview: Chrysler**

The key driver of profitability will be that the focus of the company isn't on profitability. Our focus is on the customer. If we can find a way to give customers what they want better than anybody else, then what can stop us?

Fortune, April 14, 2008

a. In spite of what Chrysler's vice chairman and co-president claims, why is Chrysler's focus actually on profitability?

b. What would happen to Chrysler if they didn't focus on maximizing profits, but instead only focused their production and pricing decisions to "give customers what they want"?

19. **Must Watches**

Stocks too volatile? Bonds too boring? Then try an alternative investment—one you can wear on your wrist. ... [The] typical return on a watch over five to ten years is roughly 10%. [One could] do better in an index fund, but ... what other investment is so wearable?

Fortune, April 14, 2008

a. What is the cost of buying a watch?

b. What is the opportunity cost of owning a watch?

c. Does owning a watch create an economic profit opportunity?

20. **Where Does Google Go Next?**

He made full use of his "20% time," that famous one day a week that Google gives its engineers to work on whatever project they want. ... He and a couple of colleagues did what many of the young geniuses do at Google: They came up with a cool idea. ... At Google, what you often end up with instead of resource allocation is a laissez-faire mess. ...

Fortune, May 26, 2008

a. Describe Google's method of organizing production with their software engineers.

b. What are the potential gains and opportunity costs associated with this method?

21. **A Medical Sensation**

... hospitals continue to splurge on ... da Vinci surgical robots. ... Sitting comfortably at a da Vinci console, surgeons could use various robotic attachments to perform even the most complex procedures. ...

Fortune, April 28, 2008

a. Assume that performing a surgery with a surgical robot requires fewer surgeons and nurses. Is using the surgical robot technologically efficient?

b. What additional information would you need to be able to say that switching to surgical robots is economically efficient for a hospital?

22. **Long Reviled, Merit Pay Gains Among Teachers**

... school districts in dozens of states experiment with plans that compensate teachers partly based on classroom performance ... rather than their years on the job and coursework completed. ... Work with mentors to improve their instruction and get bonuses for raising student achievement ... encourages efforts to raise teaching quality

The New York Times, June 18, 2007

How does "merit pay" attempt to cope with the principal-agent problem in public education?

23. Study *Reading Between the Lines* about Google and Yahoo! on pp. 244–245, and then answer the following questions:

a. What are the products that Google and Yahoo! sell?

b. How do Internet search engine providers generate revenue and earn a profit?

c. What is the distinction between paid search advertising and display advertising? What types of firms use the latter?

d. Why do you think Google bought YouTube? How will this purchase enable Google to increase its revenue and profit?

e. What technological changes might increase the profitability of Internet search engines?

11 ◆ Output and Costs

After studying this chapter,
you will be able to:

- Distinguish between the short run and the long run

- Explain the relationship between a firm's output and labor employed in the short run

- Explain the relationship between a firm's output and costs in the short run and derive a firm's short-run cost curves

- Explain the relationship between a firm's output and costs in the long run and derive a firm's long-run average cost curve

What do the nation's largest automaker, General Motors, a big electricity supplier in Pennsylvania, PennPower, and a small (fictional) producer of knitwear, Campus Sweaters, have in common? Like every firm, they must decide how much to produce, how many people to employ, and how much and what type of capital equipment to use. How do firms make these decisions?

GM and the other automakers in the United States could produce more cars than they can sell. Why do automakers have expensive equipment lying around that isn't fully used?

PennPower and the other electric utilities in the United States use technologies that contribute to climate change and

global warming. Why don't they make more use of clean solar and wind technologies?

We are going to answer these questions in this chapter.

To explain the basic ideas as clearly as possible, we are going to focus on the economic decisions of Campus Sweaters, Inc. Studying the way Cindy copes with her firm's economic problems will give us a clear view of the problems faced by all firms. We'll then apply what we learn in this chapter to the real-world costs of producing cars and electricity. In *Reading Between the Lines*, we'll look at the effects of changing technologies that aim to lower the cost of clean electricity.

Decision Time Frames

People who operate firms make many decisions, and all of their decisions are aimed at achieving one overriding goal: maximum attainable profit. But not all decisions are equally critical. Some decisions are big ones. Once made, they are costly (or impossible) to reverse. If such a decision turns out to be incorrect, it might lead to the failure of the firm. Other decisions are small. They are easily changed. If one of these decisions turns out to be incorrect, the firm can change its actions and survive.

The biggest decision that an entrepreneur makes is in what industry to establish a firm. For most entrepreneurs, their background knowledge and interests drive this decision. But the decision also depends on profit prospects—on the expectation that total revenue will exceed total cost.

Cindy has already decided to set up Campus Sweaters. She has also decided the most effective method of organizing the firm. But she has not decided the quantity to produce, the factors of production to hire, or the price to charge for sweaters.

Decisions about the quantity to produce and the price to charge depend on the type of market in which the firm operates. Perfect competition, monopolistic competition, oligopoly, and monopoly all confront the firm with their own special problems. But decisions about *how* to produce a given output do not depend on the type of market in which the firm operates. *All* types of firms in *all* types of markets make similar decisions about how to produce.

The actions that a firm can take to influence the relationship between output and cost depend on how soon the firm wants to act. A firm that plans to change its output rate tomorrow has fewer options than one that plans to change its output rate six months or six years from now.

To study the relationship between a firm's output decision and its costs, we distinguish between two decision time frames:

- The short run
- The long run

The Short Run

The **short run** is a time frame in which the quantity of at least one factor of production is fixed. For most firms, capital, land, and entrepreneurship are fixed factors of production and labor is the variable factor of production. We call the fixed factors of production the firm's *plant*: In the short run, a firm's plant is fixed.

For Campus Sweaters, the fixed plant is its factory building and its knitting machines. For an electric power utility, the fixed plant is its buildings, generators, computers, and control systems.

To increase output in the short run, a firm must increase the quantity of a variable factor of production, which is usually labor. So to produce more output, Campus Sweaters must hire more labor and operate its knitting machines for more hours a day. Similarly, an electric power utility must hire more labor and operate its generators for more hours a day.

Short-run decisions are easily reversed. The firm can increase or decrease its output in the short run by increasing or decreasing the amount of labor it hires.

The Long Run

The **long run** is a time frame in which the quantities of *all* factors of production can be varied. That is, the long run is a period in which the firm can change its *plant*.

To increase output in the long run, a firm can change its plant as well as the quantity of labor it hires. Campus Sweaters can decide whether to install more knitting machines, use a new type of machine, reorganize its management, or hire more labor. Long-run decisions are *not* easily reversed. Once a plant decision is made, the firm usually must live with it for some time. To emphasize this fact, we call the past expenditure on a plant that has no resale value a **sunk cost**. A sunk cost is irrelevant to the firm's current decisions. The only costs that influence its current decisions are the short-run cost of changing its labor inputs and the long-run cost of changing its plant.

Review Quiz

1 Distinguish between the short run and the long run.
2 Why is a sunk cost irrelevant to a firm's current decisions?

 Work Study Plan 11.1 and get instant feedback.

We're going to study costs in the short run and the long run. We begin with the short run and describe a firm's technology constraint.

Short-Run Technology Constraint

To increase output in the short run, a firm must increase the quantity of labor employed. We describe the relationship between output and the quantity of labor employed by using three related concepts:

1. Total product
2. Marginal product
3. Average product

These product concepts can be illustrated either by product schedules or by product curves. Let's look first at the product schedules.

Product Schedules

Table 11.1 shows some data that describe Campus Sweaters' total product, marginal product, and average product. The numbers tell us how the quantity of sweaters increases as Campus Sweaters employs more workers. The numbers also tell us about the productivity of the labor that Campus Sweaters employs.

Focus first on the columns headed "Labor" and "Total product." **Total product** is the maximum output that a given quantity of labor can produce. You can see from the numbers in these columns that as Campus Sweaters employs more labor, total product increases. For example, when 1 worker is employed, total product is 4 sweaters a day, and when 2 workers are employed, total product is 10 sweaters a day. Each increase in employment increases total product.

The **marginal product** of labor is the increase in total product that results from a one-unit increase in the quantity of labor employed, with all other inputs remaining the same. For example, in Table 11.1, when Campus Sweaters increases employment from 2 to 3 workers and does not change its capital, the marginal product of the third worker is 3 sweaters—total product increases from 10 to 13 sweaters.

Average product tells how productive workers are on average. The **average product** of labor is equal to total product divided by the quantity of labor employed. For example, in Table 11.1, the average product of 3 workers is 4.33 sweaters per worker— 13 sweaters a day divided by 3 workers.

If you look closely at the numbers in Table 11.1, you can see some patterns. As Campus Sweaters hires more labor, marginal product increases initially, and then begins to decrease. For example, marginal product increases from 4 sweaters a day for the first worker to 6 sweaters a day for the second worker and then decreases to 3 sweaters a day for the third worker. Average product also increases at first and then decreases. You can see the relationships between the quantity of labor hired and the three product concepts more clearly by looking at the product curves.

Product Curves

The product curves are graphs of the relationships between employment and the three product concepts you've just studied. They show how total product, marginal product, and average product change as employment changes. They also show the relationships among the three concepts. Let's look at the product curves.

TABLE 11.1 Total Product, Marginal Product, and Average Product

	Labor (workers per day)	Total product (sweaters per day)	Marginal product (sweaters per additional worker)	Average product (sweaters per worker)
A	0	0		
			4	
B	1	4		4.00
			6	
C	2	10		5.00
			3	
D	3	13		4.33
			2	
E	4	15		3.75
			1	
F	5	16		3.20

Total product is the total amount produced. Marginal product is the change in total product that results from a one-unit increase in labor. For example, when labor increases from 2 to 3 workers a day (row C to row D), total product increases from 10 to 13 sweaters a day. The marginal product of going from 2 to 3 workers is 3 sweaters. Average product is total product divided by the quantity of labor employed. For example, the average product of 3 workers is 4.33 sweaters per worker (13 sweaters a day divided by 3 workers).

Total Product Curve

Figure 11.1 shows Campus Sweaters' total product curve, *TP*, which is a graph of the total product schedule. Points *A* through *F* correspond to rows *A* through *F* in Table 11.1. To graph the entire total product curve, we vary labor by hours rather than whole days.

Notice the shape of the total product curve. As employment increases from zero to 1 worker a day, the curve becomes steeper. Then, as employment increases to 3, 4, and 5 workers a day, the curve becomes less steep.

The total product curve is similar to the *production possibilities frontier* (explained in Chapter 2). It separates the attainable output levels from those that are unattainable. All the points that lie above the curve are unattainable. Points that lie below the curve, in the orange area, are attainable, but they are inefficient—they use more labor than is necessary to produce a given output. Only the points *on* the total product curve are technologically efficient.

FIGURE 11.1   Total Product Curve

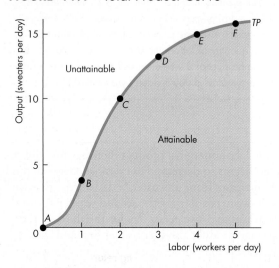

The total product curve, *TP*, is based on the data in Table 11.1. The total product curve shows how the quantity of sweaters produced changes as the quantity of labor employed changes. For example, 2 workers can produce 10 sweaters a day (point *C*). Points *A* through *F* on the curve correspond to the rows of Table 11.1. The total product curve separates attainable outputs from unattainable outputs. Points below the *TP* curve are inefficient.

Marginal Product Curve

Figure 11.2 shows Campus Sweaters' marginal product of labor. Part (a) reproduces the total product curve from Fig. 11.1 and part (b) shows the marginal product curve, *MP*.

In part (a), the orange bars illustrate the marginal product of labor. The height of a bar measures marginal product. Marginal product is also measured by the slope of the total product curve. Recall that the slope of a curve is the change in the value of the variable measured on the *y*-axis—output—divided by the change in the variable measured on the *x*-axis—labor—as we move along the curve. A one-unit increase in labor, from 2 to 3 workers, increases output from 10 to 13 sweaters, so the slope from point *C* to point *D* is 3 sweaters per additional worker, the same as the marginal product we've just calculated.

Again varying the amount of labor in the smallest units possible, we can draw the marginal product curve shown in Fig. 11.2(b). The *height* of this curve measures the *slope* of the total product curve at a point. Part (a) shows that an increase in employment from 2 to 3 workers increases output from 10 to 13 sweaters (an increase of 3). The increase in output of 3 sweaters appears on the *y*-axis of part (b) as the marginal product of going from 2 to 3 workers. We plot that marginal product at the midpoint between 2 and 3 workers. Notice that the marginal product shown in Fig. 11.2(b) reaches a peak at 1.5 workers, and at that point, marginal product is 6 sweaters per additional worker. The peak occurs at 1.5 workers because the total product curve is steepest when employment increases from 1 worker to 2 workers.

The total product and marginal product curves differ across firms and types of goods. GM's product curves are different from those of PennPower, whose curves in turn are different from those of Campus Sweaters. But the shapes of the product curves are similar because almost every production process has two features:

- Increasing marginal returns initially
- Diminishing marginal returns eventually

Increasing Marginal Returns   Increasing marginal returns occur when the marginal product of an additional worker exceeds the marginal product of the previous worker. Increasing marginal returns arise from increased specialization and division of labor in the production process.

FIGURE 11.2 Total Product and Marginal Product

(a) Total product

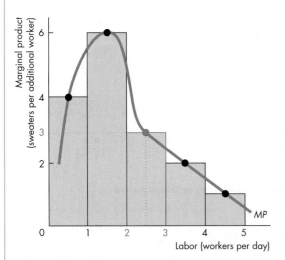

(b) Marginal product

Marginal product is illustrated by the orange bars. For example, when labor increases from 2 to 3 workers a day, marginal product is the orange bar whose height is 3 sweaters. (Marginal product is shown midway between the quantities of labor to emphasize that marginal product results from *changing* the quantity of labor.) The steeper the slope of the total product curve (*TP*) in part (a), the larger is marginal product (*MP*) in part (b). Marginal product increases to a maximum (in this example when 1.5 workers a day are employed) and then declines—diminishing marginal product.

(X myeconlab) animation

For example, if Campus Sweaters employs one worker, that person must learn all the aspects of sweater production: running the knitting machines, fixing breakdowns, packaging and mailing sweaters, buying and checking the type and color of the wool. All these tasks must be performed by that one person.

If Campus Sweaters hires a second person, the two workers can specialize in different parts of the production process and can produce more than twice as much as one worker. The marginal product of the second worker is greater than the marginal product of the first worker. Marginal returns are increasing.

Diminishing Marginal Returns Most production processes experience increasing marginal returns initially, but all production processes eventually reach a point of *diminishing* marginal returns. **Diminishing marginal returns** occur when the marginal product of an additional worker is less than the marginal product of the previous worker.

Diminishing marginal returns arise from the fact that more and more workers are using the same capital and working in the same space. As more workers are added, there is less and less for the additional workers to do that is productive. For example, if Campus Sweaters hires a third worker, output increases but not by as much as it did when it hired the second worker. In this case, after two workers are hired, all the gains from specialization and the division of labor have been exhausted. By hiring a third worker, the factory produces more sweaters, but the equipment is being operated closer to its limits. There are even times when the third worker has nothing to do because the machines are running without the need for further attention. Hiring more and more workers continues to increase output but by successively smaller amounts. Marginal returns are diminishing. This phenomenon is such a pervasive one that it is called a "law"—the law of diminishing returns. The **law of diminishing returns** states that

As a firm uses more of a variable factor of production, with a given quantity of the fixed factor of production, the marginal product of the variable factor eventually diminishes.

You are going to return to the law of diminishing returns when we study a firm's costs. But before we do that, let's look at the average product of labor and the average product curve.

Average Product Curve

Figure 11.3 illustrates Campus Sweaters' average product of labor and shows the relationship between average product and marginal product. Points *B* through *F* on the average product curve *AP* correspond to those same rows in Table 11.1. Average product increases from 1 to 2 workers (its maximum value at point *C*) but then decreases as yet more workers are employed. Notice also that average product is largest when average product and marginal product are equal. That is, the marginal product curve cuts the average product curve at the point of maximum average product. For the number of workers at which marginal product exceeds average product, average product is *increasing*. For the number of workers at which marginal product is less than average product, average product is *decreasing*.

The relationship between the average product and marginal product is a general feature of the relationship between the average and marginal values of any variable—even your grades.

FIGURE 11.3   Average Product

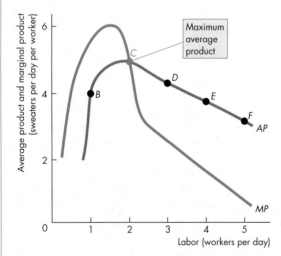

The figure shows the average product of labor and the connection between average product and marginal product. With 1 worker, marginal product exceeds average product, so average product is increasing. With 2 workers, marginal product equals average product, so average product is at its maximum. With more than 2 workers, marginal product is less than average product, so average product is decreasing.

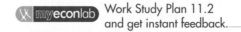 animation

Marginal Grades and Average Grades
How to Pull Up Your Average

Do you want to pull up your average grade? Then make sure that your next test is better than your current average! Your next test is your marginal test. If your marginal grade exceeds your average grade (like Economics in the graph), your average will rise. If your marginal grade equals your average grade (like English in the graph), your average won't change. If your marginal grade is below your average grade (like History in the figure), your average will fall.

The relationship between your marginal and average grades is exactly the same as that between marginal product and average product.

Marginal and Average Grade Curves

Review Quiz

1 Explain how the marginal product of labor and the average product of labor change as the quantity of labor employed increases (a) initially and (b) eventually.
2 What is the law of diminishing returns? Why does marginal product eventually diminish?
3 Explain the relationship between marginal product and average product.

myeconlab Work Study Plan 11.2 and get instant feedback.

Campus Sweaters' product curves influence its costs, as you are now going to see.

Short-Run Cost

To produce more output in the short run, a firm must employ more labor, which means that it must increase its costs. We describe the relationship between output and cost by using three cost concepts:

- Total cost
- Marginal cost
- Average cost

Total Cost

A firm's **total cost** (*TC*) is the cost of *all* the factors of production it uses. We separate total cost into total *fixed* cost and total *variable* cost.

Total fixed cost (*TFC*) is the cost of the firm's fixed factors. For Campus Sweaters, total fixed cost includes the cost of renting knitting machines and *normal profit*, which is the opportunity cost of Cindy's entrepreneurship (see Chapter 10, p. 229). The quantities of fixed factors don't change as output changes, so total fixed cost is the same at all outputs.

Total variable cost (*TVC*) is the cost of the firm's variable factors. For Campus Sweaters, labor is the variable factor, so this component of cost is its wage bill. Total variable cost changes as output changes.

Total cost is the sum of total fixed cost and total variable cost. That is,

$$TC = TFC + TVC.$$

The table in Fig. 11.4 shows total costs. Campus Sweaters rents one knitting machine for $25 a day, so its *TFC* is $25. To produce sweaters, the firm hires labor, which costs $25 a day. *TVC* is the number of workers multiplied by $25. For example, to produce 13 sweaters a day, in row *D*, the firm hires 3 workers and *TVC* is $75. *TC* is the sum of *TFC* and *TVC*, so to produce 13 sweaters a day, *TC* is $100. Check the calculations in the other rows of the table.

Figure 11.4 shows Campus Sweaters' total cost curves, which graph total cost against output. The green *TFC* curve is horizontal because total fixed cost ($25 a day) does not change when output changes. The purple *TVC* curve and the blue *TC* curve both slope upward because to increase output, more labor must be employed, which increases total variable cost. Total fixed cost equals the vertical distance between the *TVC* and *TC* curves.

Let's now look at a firm's marginal cost.

FIGURE 11.4 Total Cost Curves

$TC = TFC + TVC$

Labor (workers per day)	Output (sweaters per day)	Total fixed cost (*TFC*)	Total variable cost (*TVC*)	Total cost (*TC*)
		(dollars per day)		
A 0	0	25	0	25
B 1	4	25	25	50
C 2	10	25	50	75
D 3	**13**	**25**	**75**	**100**
E 4	15	25	100	125
F 5	16	25	125	150

Campus Sweaters rents a knitting machine for $25 a day, so this cost is the firm's total fixed cost. The firm hires workers at a wage rate of $25 a day, and this cost is its total variable cost. For example, in row *D*, Campus Sweaters employs 3 workers and its total variable cost is 3 × $25, which equals $75. Total cost is the sum of total fixed cost and total variable cost. For example, when Campus Sweaters employs 3 workers, total cost is $100—total fixed cost of $25 plus total variable cost of $75.

The graph shows Campus Sweaters' total cost curves. Total fixed cost is constant—the *TFC* curve is a horizontal line. Total variable cost increases as output increases, so the *TVC* curve and the *TC* curve increase as output increases. The vertical distance between the *TC* curve and the *TVC* curve equals total fixed cost, as illustrated by the two arrows.

Marginal Cost

Figure 11.4 shows that total variable cost and total cost increase at a decreasing rate at small outputs but eventually, as output increases, total variable cost and total cost increase at an increasing rate. To understand this pattern in the change in total cost as output increases, we need to use the concept of *marginal cost*.

A firm's **marginal cost** is the increase in total cost that results from a one-unit increase in output. We calculate marginal cost as the increase in total cost divided by the increase in output. The table in Fig. 11.5 shows this calculation. When, for example, output increases from 10 sweaters to 13 sweaters, total cost increases from $75 to $100. The change in output is 3 sweaters, and the change in total cost is $25. The marginal cost of one of those 3 sweaters is ($25 ÷ 3), which equals $8.33.

Figure 11.5 graphs the marginal cost data in the table as the red marginal cost curve, *MC*. This curve is U-shaped because when Campus Sweaters hires a second worker, marginal cost decreases, but when it hires a third, a fourth, and a fifth worker, marginal cost successively increases.

At small outputs, marginal cost decreases as output increases because of greater specialization and the division of labor, but as output increases further, marginal cost eventually increases because of the *law of diminishing returns*. The law of diminishing returns means that the output produced by each additional worker is successively smaller. To produce an additional unit of output, ever more workers are required, and the cost of producing the additional unit of output—marginal cost—must eventually increase.

Marginal cost tells us how total cost changes as output increases. The final cost concept tells us what it costs, on average, to produce a unit of output. Let's now look at Campus Sweaters' average costs.

Average Cost

Three average costs of production are

1. Average fixed cost
2. Average variable cost
3. Average total cost

Average fixed cost (*AFC*) is total fixed cost per unit of output. **Average variable cost** (*AVC*) is total variable cost per unit of output. **Average total cost** (*ATC*) is total cost per unit of output. The average cost con-

cepts are calculated from the total cost concepts as follows:

$$TC = TFV + TVC.$$

Divide each total cost term by the quantity produced, Q, to get

$$\frac{TC}{Q} = \frac{TFC}{Q} + \frac{TVC}{Q},$$

or

$$ATC = AFC + AVC.$$

The table in Fig. 11.5 shows the calculation of average total cost. For example, in row C, output is 10 sweaters. Average fixed cost is ($25 ÷ 10), which equals $2.50, average variable cost is ($50 ÷ 10), which equals $5.00, and average total cost is ($75 ÷ 10), which equals $7.50. Note that average total cost is equal to average fixed cost ($2.50) plus average variable cost ($5.00).

Figure 11.5 shows the average cost curves. The green average fixed cost curve (*AFC*) slopes downward. As output increases, the same constant total fixed cost is spread over a larger output. The blue average total cost curve (*ATC*) and the purple average variable cost curve (*AVC*) are U-shaped. The vertical distance between the average total cost and average variable cost curves is equal to average fixed cost—as indicated by the two arrows. That distance shrinks as output increases because average fixed cost declines with increasing output.

Marginal Cost and Average Cost

The marginal cost curve (*MC*) intersects the average variable cost curve and the average total cost curve *at their minimum points*. When marginal cost is less than average cost, average cost is decreasing, and when marginal cost exceeds average cost, average cost is increasing. This relationship holds for both the *ATC* curve and the *AVC* curve. It is another example of the relationship you saw in Fig. 11.3 for average product and marginal product and in your average and marginal grades.

Why the Average Total Cost Curve Is U-Shaped

Average total cost is the sum of average fixed cost and average variable cost, so the shape of the *ATC* curve

FIGURE 11.5 Marginal Cost and Average Costs

ATC = AFC + AVC

Marginal cost is calculated as the change in total cost divided by the change in output. When output increases from 4 to 10 sweaters, an increase of 6 sweaters, total cost increases by $25. Marginal cost is $25 ÷ 6, which is $4.17.

Each average cost concept is calculated by dividing the related total cost by output. When 10 sweaters are produced, AFC is $2.50 ($25 ÷ 10), AVC is $5 ($50 ÷ 10), and ATC is $7.50 ($75 ÷ 10).

The graph shows that the MC curve is U-shaped and intersects the AVC curve and the ATC curve at their minimum points. Average fixed cost curve (AFC) is downward sloping. The ATC curve and AVC curve are U-shaped. The vertical distance between the ATC curve and the AVC curve is equal to average fixed cost, as illustrated by the two arrows.

	Labor (workers per day)	Output (sweaters per day)	Total fixed cost (TFC)	Total variable cost (TVC)	Total cost (TC)	Marginal cost (MC) (dollars per additional sweater)	Average fixed cost (AFC)	Average variable cost (AVC)	Average total cost (ATC)
			(dollars per day)				(dollars per sweater)		
A	0	0	25	0	25		—	—	—
						.... 6.25			
B	1	4	25	25	50		6.25	6.25	12.50
						.... 4.17			
C	2	10	25	50	75		2.50	5.00	7.50
						.... 8.33			
D	3	13	25	75	100		1.92	5.77	7.69
						.......12.50			
E	4	15	25	100	125		1.67	6.67	8.33
						.......25.00			
F	5	16	25	125	150		1.56	7.81	9.38

myeconlab animation

combines the shapes of the *AFC* and *AVC* curves. The U shape of the *ATC* curve arises from the influence of two opposing forces:

1. Spreading total fixed cost over a larger output
2. Eventually diminishing returns

When output increases, the firm spreads its total fixed cost over a larger output and so its average fixed cost decreases—its *AFC* curve slopes downward.

Diminishing returns means that as output increases, ever-larger amounts of labor are needed to produce an additional unit of output. So as output increases, average variable cost decreases initially but

eventually increases, and the *AVC* curve slopes upward. The *AVC* curve is U shaped.

The shape of the *ATC* curve combines these two effects. Initially, as output increases, both average fixed cost and average variable cost decrease, so average total cost decreases. The *ATC* curve slopes downward.

But as output increases further and diminishing returns set in, average variable cost starts to increase. With average fixed cost decreasing more quickly than average variable cost is increasing, the *ATC* curve continues to slope downward. Eventually, average variable cost starts to increase more quickly than average fixed cost decreases, so average total cost starts to increase. The *ATC* curve slopes upward.

Cost Curves and Product Curves

The technology that a firm uses determines its costs. Figure 11.6 shows the links between the firm's product curves and its cost curves. The upper graph shows the average product curve, *AP*, and the marginal product curve, *MP*—like those in Fig. 11.3. The lower graph shows the average variable cost curve, *AVC*, and the marginal cost curve, *MC*—like those in Fig. 11.5.

As labor increases up to 1.5 workers a day (upper graph), output increases to 6.5 sweaters a day (lower graph). Marginal product and average product rise and marginal cost and average variable cost fall. At the point of maximum marginal product, marginal cost is at a minimum.

As labor increases to 2 workers a day, (upper graph) output increases to 10 sweaters a day (lower graph). Marginal product falls and marginal cost rises, but average product continues to rise and average variable cost continues to fall. At the point of maximum average product, average variable cost is at a minimum. As labor increases further, output increases. Average product diminishes and average variable cost increases.

Shifts in the Cost Curves

The position of a firm's short-run cost curves depends on two factors:

- Technology
- Prices of factors of production

Technology   A technological change that increases productivity increases the marginal product and average product of labor. With a better technology, the same factors of production can produce more output, so the technological advance lowers the costs of production and shifts the cost curves downward.

For example, advances in robot production techniques have increased productivity in the automobile industry. As a result, the product curves of Chrysler, Ford, and GM have shifted upward and their cost curves have shifted downward. But the relationships between their product curves and cost curves have not changed. The curves are still linked in the way shown in Fig. 11.6.

Often, as in the case of robots producing cars, a technological advance results in a firm using more capital, a fixed factor, and less labor, a variable factor.

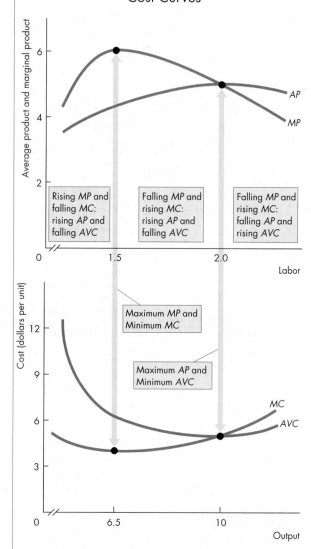

FIGURE 11.6   Product Curves and Cost Curves

A firm's *MP* curve is linked to its *MC* curve. If, as the firm increases its labor from 0 to 1.5 workers a day, the firm's marginal product rises, its marginal cost falls. If marginal product is at a maximum, marginal cost is at a minimum. If, as the firm hires more labor, its marginal product diminishes, its marginal cost rises.

A firm's *AP* curve is linked to its *AVC* curve. If, as the firm increases its labor to 2 workers a day, its average product rises, its average variable cost falls. If average product is at a maximum, average variable cost is at a minimum. If, as the firm hires more labor, its average product diminishes, its average variable cost rises.

TABLE 11.2   A Compact Glossary of Costs

Term	Symbol	Definition	Equation
Fixed cost		Cost that is independent of the output level; cost of a fixed factor of production	
Variable cost		Cost that varies with the output level; cost of a variable factor of production	
Total fixed cost	TFC	Cost of the fixed factors of production	
Total variable cost	TVC	Cost of the variable factors of production	
Total cost	TC	Cost of all factors of production	$TC = TFC + TVC$
Output (total product)	TP	Total quantity produced (output Q)	
Marginal cost	MC	Change in total cost resulting from a one-unit increase in total product	$MC = \Delta TC \div \Delta Q$
Average fixed cost	AFC	Total fixed cost per unit of output	$AFC = TFC \div Q$
Average variable cost	AVC	Total variable cost per unit of output	$AVC = TVC \div Q$
Average total cost	ATC	Total cost per unit of output	$ATC = AFC + AVC$

Another example is the use of ATMs by banks to dispense cash. ATMs, which are fixed capital, have replaced tellers, which are variable labor. Such a technological change decreases total cost but increases fixed costs and decreases variable cost. This change in the mix of fixed cost and variable cost means that at small outputs, average total cost might increase, while at large outputs, average total cost decreases.

Prices of Factors of Production An increase in the price of a factor of production increases the firm's costs and shifts its cost curves. But how the curves shift depends on which factor price changes.

An increase in rent or some other component of *fixed* cost shifts the *TFC* and *AFC* curves upward and shifts the *TC curve* upward but leaves the *AVC* and *TVC* curves and the *MC* curve unchanged. For example, if the interest expense paid by a trucking company increases, the fixed cost of transportation services increases.

An increase in wages, gasoline, or another component of *variable* cost shifts the *TVC* and *AVC* curves upward and shifts the *MC* curve upward but leaves the *AFC* and *TFC* curves unchanged. For example, if

truck drivers' wages or the price of gasoline increases, the variable cost and marginal cost of transportation services increase.

You've now completed your study of short-run costs. All the concepts that you've met are summarized in a compact glossary in Table 11.2.

Review Quiz

1 What relationships do a firm's short-run cost curves show?

2 How does marginal cost change as output increases (a) initially and (b) eventually?

3 What does the law of diminishing returns imply for the shape of the marginal cost curve?

4 What is the shape of the *AFC* curve and why does it have this shape?

5 What are the shapes of the *AVC* curve and the *ATC* curve and why do they have these shapes?

 Work Study Plan 11.3 and get instant feedback.

Long-Run Cost

We are now going to study the firm's long-run costs. In the long run, a firm can vary both the quantity of labor and the quantity of capital, so in the long run, all the firm's costs are variable.

The behavior of long-run cost depends on the firm's *production function*, which is the relationship between the maximum output attainable and the quantities of both labor and capital.

The Production Function

Table 11.3 shows Campus Sweaters' production function. The table lists total product schedules for four different quantities of capital. The quantity of capital identifies the plant size. The numbers for plant 1 are for a factory with 1 knitting machine—the case we've just studied. The other three plants have 2, 3, and 4 machines. If Campus Sweaters uses plant 2 with 2 knitting machines, the various amounts of labor can produce the outputs shown in the second column of the table. The other two columns show the outputs of yet larger quantities of capital. Each column of the table could be graphed as a total product curve for each plant.

Diminishing Returns Diminishing returns occur with each of the four plant sizes as the quantity of labor increases. You can check that fact by calculating the marginal product of labor in each of the plants with 2, 3, and 4 machines. With each plant size, as the firm increases the quantity of labor employed, the marginal product of labor (eventually) diminishes.

Diminishing Marginal Product of Capital
Diminishing returns also occur with each quantity of labor as the quantity of capital increases. You can check that fact by calculating the marginal product of capital at a given quantity of labor. The *marginal product of capital* is the change in total product divided by the change in capital when the quantity of labor is constant—equivalently, the change in output resulting from a one-unit increase in the quantity of capital. For example, if Campus Sweaters has 3 workers and increases its capital from 1 machine to 2 machines, output increases from 13 to 18 sweaters a day. The marginal product of the second machine is 5 sweaters a day. If the firm increases the number of

TABLE 11.3 The Production Function

Labor (workers per day)	Output (sweaters per day)			
	Plant 1	Plant 2	Plant 3	Plant 4
1	4	10	13	15
2	10	15	18	20
3	13	18	22	24
4	15	20	24	26
5	16	21	25	27
Knitting machines (number)	1	2	3	4

The table shows the total product data for four quantities of capital (plant sizes). The greater the plant size, the larger is the output produced by any given quantity of labor. But for a given plant size, the marginal product of labor diminishes as more labor is employed. For a given quantity of labor, the marginal product of capital diminishes as the quantity of capital used increases.

machines from 2 to 3, output increases from 18 to 22 sweaters a day. The marginal product of the third machine is 4 sweaters a day, down from 5 sweaters a day for the second machine.

Let's now see what the production function implies for long-run costs.

Short-Run Cost and Long-Run Cost

As before, Campus Sweaters can hire workers for $25 a day and rent knitting machines for $25 a day. Using these factor prices and the data in Table 11.3, we can calculate the average total cost and graph the ATC curves for factories with 1, 2, 3, and 4 knitting machines. We've already studied the costs of a factory with 1 machine in Figs. 11.4 and 11.5. In Fig. 11.7, the average total cost curve for that case is ATC_1. Figure 11.7 also shows the average total cost curve for a factory with 2 machines, ATC_2, with 3 machines, ATC_3, and with 4 machines, ATC_4.

You can see, in Fig. 11.7, that the plant size has a big effect on the firm's average total cost. Two things stand out:

FIGURE 11.7   Short-Run Costs of Four Different Plants

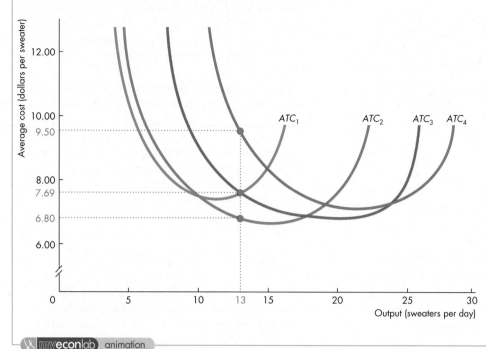

The figure shows short-run average total cost curves for four different quantities of capital at Campus Sweaters. The firm can produce 13 sweaters a day with 1 knitting machine on ATC_1 or with 3 knitting machines on ATC_3 for an average cost of $7.69 a sweater. The firm can produce 13 sweaters a day by using 2 machines on ATC_2 for $6.80 a sweater or by using 4 machines on ATC_4 for $9.50 a sweater.

If the firm produces 13 sweaters a day, the least-cost method of production, *the long-run method*, is with 2 machines on ATC_2.

1. Each short-run *ATC* curve is U-shaped.
2. For each short-run *ATC* curve, the larger the plant, the greater is the output at which average total cost is at a minimum.

Each short-run *ATC* curve is U-shaped because, as the quantity of labor increases, its marginal product initially increases and then diminishes. This pattern in the marginal product of labor, which we examined in some detail for the plant with 1 knitting machine on pp. 254–255, occurs at all plant sizes.

The minimum average total cost for a larger plant occurs at a greater output than it does for a smaller plant because the larger plant has a higher total fixed cost and therefore, for any given output, a higher average fixed cost.

Which short-run *ATC* curve a firm operates on depends on the plant it has. But in the long run, the firm can choose its plant and the plant it chooses is the one that enables it to produce its planned output at the lowest average total cost.

To see why, suppose that Campus Sweaters plans to produce 13 sweaters a day. In Fig. 11.7, with 1 machine, the average total cost curve is ATC_1 and the

average total cost of 13 sweaters a day is $7.69 a sweater. With 2 machines, on ATC_2, average total cost is $6.80 a sweater. With 3 machines, on ATC_3, average total cost is $7.69 a sweater, the same as with 1 machine. Finally, with 4 machines, on ATC_4, average total cost is $9.50 a sweater.

The economically efficient plant for producing a given output is the one that has the lowest average total cost. For Campus Sweaters, the economically efficient plant to use to produce 13 sweaters a day is the one with 2 machines.

In the long run, Cindy chooses the plant that minimizes average total cost. When a firm is producing a given output at the least possible cost, it is operating on its *long-run average cost curve*.

The **long-run average cost curve** is the relationship between the lowest attainable average total cost and output when the firm can change both the plant it uses and the quantity of labor it employs.

The long-run average cost curve is a planning curve. It tells the firm the plant and the quantity of labor to use at each output to minimize average cost. Once the firm chooses a plant, the firm operates on the short-run cost curves that apply to that plant.

The Long-Run Average Cost Curve

Figure 11.8 shows how a long-run average cost curve is derived. The long-run average cost curve *LRAC* consists of pieces of the four short-run *ATC* curves. For outputs up to 10 sweaters a day, average total cost is the lowest on ATC_1. For outputs between 10 and 18 sweaters a day, average total cost is the lowest on ATC_2. For outputs between 18 and 24 sweaters a day, average total cost is the lowest on ATC_3. And for outputs in excess of 24 sweaters a day, average total cost is the lowest on ATC_4. The piece of each *ATC* curve with the lowest average total cost is highlighted in dark blue in Fig. 11.8. This dark blue scallop-shaped curve made up of the pieces of the four *ATC* curves is the *LRAC* curve.

Economies and Diseconomies of Scale

Economies of scale are features of a firm's technology that make average total cost *fall* as output increases. When economies of scale are present, the *LRAC* curve slopes downward. In Fig. 11.8, Campus Sweaters has economies of scale for outputs up to 15 sweaters a day.

Greater specialization of both labor and capital is the main source of economies of scale. For example, if GM produces 100 cars a week, each worker must perform many different tasks and the capital must be general-purpose machines and tools. But if GM produces 10,000 cars a week, each worker specializes in a small number of tasks, uses task-specific tools, and becomes highly proficient.

Diseconomies of scale are features of a firm's technology that make average total cost *rise* as output increases. When diseconomies of scale are present, the *LRAC* curve slopes upward. In Fig. 11.8, Campus Sweaters experiences diseconomies of scale at outputs greater than 15 sweaters a day.

The challenge of managing a large enterprise is the main source of diseconomies of scale.

Constant returns to scale are features of a firm's technology that keep average total cost constant as output increases. When constant returns to scale are present, the *LRAC* curve is horizontal.

Economies of Scale at Campus Sweaters The economies of scale and diseconomies of scale at Campus Sweaters arise from the firm's production function in Table 11.3. With 1 machine and 1 worker, the firm produces 4 sweaters a day. With 2 machines and 2 workers, total cost doubles but out-

FIGURE 11.8   Long-Run Average Cost Curve

The long-run average cost curve traces the lowest attainable *ATC* when both labor and capital change. The green arrows highlight the output range over which each plant achieves the lowest *ATC*. Within each range, to change the quantity produced, the firm changes the quantity of labor it employs.

Along the *LRAC* curve, economies of scale occur if average cost falls as output increases; diseconomies of scale occur if average cost rises as output increases. Minimum efficient scale is the output at which average cost is lowest, 15 sweaters a day.

Economies of Scale at an Auto Plant
Produce More to Cut Cost

Why do GM, Ford, and the other automakers have expensive equipment lying around that isn't fully used? You can answer this question with what you've learned in this chapter.

The basic answer is that auto production enjoys economies of scale. A larger output rate brings a lower long-run average cost—the firm's *LRAC* curve slopes downward.

An auto producer's average total cost curves look like those in the figure. To produce 20 vehicles an hour, the firm installs the plant with the short-run average total cost curve ATC_1. The average cost of producing a vehicle is $20,000.

Producing 20 vehicles an hour doesn't use the plant at its lowest possible average total cost. If the firm could sell enough cars for it to produce 40 vehicles an hour, the firm could use its current plant and produce at an average cost of $15,000 a vehicle.

But if the firm planned to produce 40 vehicles an hour, it would not stick with its current plant. The firm would install a bigger plant with the short-run average total cost curve ATC_2, and produce 40 vehicles an hour for $10,000 a car.

Automobile Plant Average Cost Curves

put more than doubles to 15 sweaters a day, so average cost decreases and Campus Sweaters experiences economies of scale. With 4 machines and 4 workers, total cost doubles again but output less than doubles to 26 sweaters a day, so average cost increases and the firm experiences diseconomies of scale.

Minimum Efficient Scale A firm's **minimum efficient scale** is the smallest output at which long-run average cost reaches its lowest level. At Campus Sweaters, the minimum efficient scale is 15 sweaters a day.

The minimum efficient scale plays a role in determining market structure. In a market in which the minimum efficient scale is small relative to market demand, the market has room for many firms, and the market is competitive. In a market in which the minimum efficient scale is large relative to market demand, only a small number of firms, and possibly only one firm, can make a profit and the market is either an oligopoly or monopoly. We will return to this idea in the next three chapters.

Review Quiz

1 What does a firm's production function show and how is it related to a total product curve?

2 Does the law of diminishing returns apply to capital as well as labor? Explain why or why not.

3 What does a firm's long-run average cost curve show? How is it related to the firm's short-run average cost curves?

4 What are economies of scale and diseconomies of scale? How do they arise? What do they imply for the shape of the long-run average cost curve?

5 What is a firm's minimum efficient scale?

 Work Study Plan 11.4 and get instant feedback.

Reading Between the Lines on pp. 266–267 applies what you've learned about a firm's cost curves. It looks at the cost curves for generating electricity using a variety of technologies and compares the total cost and marginal cost of traditional and new technologies.

Cutting the Cost of Clean Electricity

Start-Up: Affordable Solar Power Possible in a Year

http://www.usatoday.com
April 29, 2008

A Silicon Valley start-up says it has developed technology that can deliver solar power in about a year at prices competitive with coal-fired electricity. …

SUNRGI's "concentrated photovoltaic" system relies on lenses to magnify sunlight 2,000 times, letting it produce as much electricity as standard panels with a far smaller system. Craig Goodman, head of the National Energy Marketers Association, is expected to announce the breakthrough today. …

Executives of the year-old company say they'll start producing solar panels by mid-2009 that will generate electricity for about 7 cents a kilowatt hour, including installation. That's roughly the price of cheap coal-fired electricity. …

Solar power is acclaimed as free of greenhouse gas emissions and able to supply electricity midday when demand is highest. But its cost—20 cents to 30 cents a kilowatt hour—has inhibited broad adoption. Solar makes up less than 1% of U.S. power generation.

An armada of solar technology makers aim to drive solar's price to 10 to 18 cents a kilowatt hour by 2010, and 5 to 10 cents by 2015, at or below utility costs. …

Essence of the Story

- A new Silicon Valley firm, SUNRGI, says it has developed technology that can deliver solar power for 7 cents a kilowatt hour.

- 7 cents a kilowatt hour is roughly the price of electricity produced by coal.

- Solar power on current technology costs 20 cents to 30 cents a kilowatt hour.

- A large number of solar technology makers aim to bring costs down to 10 to 18 cents a kilowatt hour by 2010 and to 5 to 10 cents by 2015.

Economic Analysis

- Figure 1 shows the average total cost (*ATC*) of producing electricity using seven alternative technologies.

- The cost differences come from differences in fuel and capital costs. Hydro, wind, and solar have zero fuel costs.

- Today's solar technology has the highest average total cost at 15 cents per kilowatt hour.

- The new SUNRGI technology slashes the average total cost of solar power, but the cost doesn't get it down to a level that competes with the other technologies.

- The news article says that SUNRGI's average total cost of 7 cents a kilowatt hour is "roughly the price of cheap coal-fired electricity."

- Figure 1 shows the average total cost of coal-generated electricity at 4 cents per kilowatt hour. Based on this (correct) cost, it appears that SUNRGI cannot compete with coal (if we ignore the emission costs of coal).

- Remember, though, that average total cost varies with the output rate. The costs in Fig. 1 are those for operating plants at their most efficient level—80 percent of maximum capacity. (The closer a plant operates to its theoretical maximum output, the higher are the maintenance costs and so the higher is the average total cost.)

- Figures 2 and 3 compare the *ATC* curves and *MC* curves for producing electricity by using coal and solar technologies.

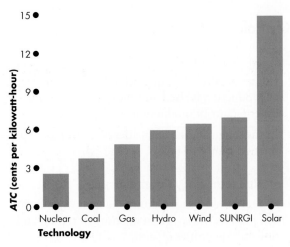

Figure 1 Average total costs compared

- In Fig. 2, the average total cost of electricity generated by coal has a minimum at 4 cents per kilowatt hour at 80 percent plant capacity.

- In Fig. 3, the average total cost of electricity generated by solar technology decreases as the plant is operated closer to capacity.

- The marginal cost of producing electricity by using coal eventually rises (Fig. 2), but the marginal cost of solar electricity is zero (Fig.3). All the costs for solar power are fixed costs.

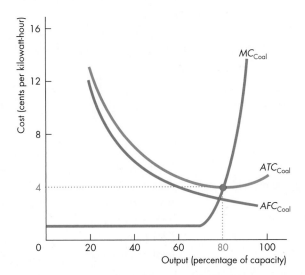

Figure 2 Cost curves for coal-generated electricity

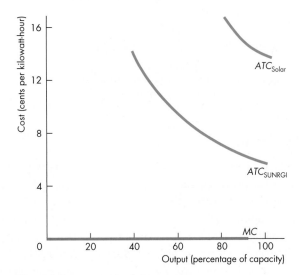

Figure 3 Cost curves for solar power

SUMMARY

Key Points

Decision Time Frames (p. 252)

- In the short run, the quantity of at least one factor of production is fixed and the quantities of the other factors of production can be varied.
- In the long run, the quantities of all factors of production can be varied.

Short-Run Technology Constraint (pp. 253–256)

- A total product curve shows the quantity a firm can produce with a given quantity of capital and different quantities of labor.
- Initially, the marginal product of labor increases as the quantity of labor increases, because of increased specialization and the division of labor.
- Eventually, marginal product diminishes because an increasing quantity of labor must share a fixed quantity of capital—the law of diminishing returns.
- Initially, average product increases as the quantity of labor increases, but eventually average product diminishes.

Short-Run Cost (pp. 257–261)

- As output increases, total fixed cost is constant, and total variable cost and total cost increase.
- As output increases, average fixed cost decreases and average variable cost, average total cost, and marginal cost decrease at low outputs and increase at high outputs. These cost curves are U-shaped.

Long-Run Cost (pp. 262–265)

- A firm has a set of short-run cost curves for each different plant. For each output, the firm has one least-cost plant. The larger the output, the larger is the plant that will minimize average total cost.
- The long-run average cost curve traces out the lowest attainable average total cost at each output when both capital and labor inputs can be varied.
- With economies of scale, the long-run average cost curve slopes downward. With diseconomies of scale, the long-run average cost curve slopes upward.

Key Figures and Table

Key Terms

PROBLEMS and APPLICATIONS

Work problems 1–11 in Chapter 11 Study Plan and get instant feedback.
Work problems 12–22 as Homework, a Quiz, or a Test if assigned by your instructor.

1. Which of the following news items involves a short-run decision and which involves a long-run decision? Explain.
   January 31, 2008: Starbucks will open 75 more stores abroad than originally predicted, for a total of 975.
   February 25, 2008: For three hours on Tuesday, Starbucks will shut down every single one of its 7,100 stores so that baristas can receive a refresher course.
   June 2, 2008: Starbucks replaces baristas with vending machines.
   July 18, 2008: Starbucks is closing 616 stores by the end of March.

2. The table sets out Sue's Surfboards' total product schedule.

Labor (workers per week)	Output (surfboards per week)
1	30
2	70
3	120
4	160
5	190
6	210
7	220

   a. Draw the total product curve.
   b. Calculate the average product of labor and draw the average product curve.
   c. Calculate the marginal product of labor and draw the marginal product curve.
   d. Over what output range does the firm enjoy the benefits of increased specialization and division of labor?
   e. Over what output range does the firm experience diminishing marginal product of labor?
   f. Over what output range does this firm experience an increasing average product of labor but a diminishing marginal product of labor?
   g. Explain how it is possible for a firm to experience simultaneously an increasing *average* product but a diminishing *marginal* product.

3. Sue's Surfboards, in problem 2, hires workers at $500 a week and its total fixed cost is $1,000 a week.

   a. Calculate total cost, total variable cost, and total fixed cost of each output in the table. Plot these points and sketch the short-run total cost curves passing through them.
   b. Calculate average total cost, average fixed cost, average variable cost, and marginal cost of each output in the table. Plot these points and sketch the short-run average and marginal cost curves passing through them.
   c. Illustrate the connection between Sue's *AP*, *MP*, *AVC*, and *MC* curves in graphs like those in Fig. 11.6.

4. Sue's Surfboards, in problems 2 and 3, rents a factory building and the rent is increased by $200 a week. If other things remain the same, how do Sue's Surfboards' short-run average cost curves and marginal cost curve change.

5. Workers at Sue's Surfboards, in problems 2 and 3, negotiate a wage increase of $100 a week for each worker. If other things remain the same, explain how Sue's Surfboards' short-run average cost curves and marginal cost curve change.

6. Sue's Surfboards, in problem 2, buys a second plant and the output produced by each worker increases by 50 percent. The total fixed cost of operating each plant is $1,000 a week. Each worker is paid $500 a week.

   a. Calculate the average total cost of producing 180 and 240 surfboards a week when Sue's Surfboards operates two plants. Graph these points and sketch the *ATC* curve.
   b. To produce 180 surfboards a week, is it efficient to operate one or two plants?
   c. To produce 160 surfboards a week, is it efficient for Sue's to operate one or two plants?

7. **Airlines Seek Out New Ways to Save on Fuel as Costs Soar**

   The financial pain of higher fuel prices is particularly acute for airlines because it is their single biggest expense. … [Airlines] pump about 7,000 gallons into a Boeing 737 and as much as 60,000 gallons into the bigger 747 jet. … Each generation of aircraft is more efficient. At Northwest, the Airbus A330 long-range jets use 38 percent less fuel than the DC-10s they replaced, while the Airbus A319 medium-range planes are 27 percent more efficient than DC-9s. ...

The New York Times, June 11, 2008

a. Is the price of fuel a fixed cost or a variable cost for an airline?

b. Explain how an increase in the price of fuel changes an airline's total costs, average costs, and marginal cost.

c. Draw a graph to show the effects of an increase in the price of fuel on an airline's *TFC*, *TVC*, *AFC*, *AVC*, and *MC* curves.

d. Explain how a technological advance that makes an airplane engine more fuel efficient changes an airline's total product, marginal product, and average product.

e. Draw a graph to illustrate the effects of a more fuel-efficient aircraft on an airline's *TP*, *MP*, and *AP* curves.

f. Explain how a technological advance that makes an airplane engine more fuel-efficient changes an airline's average variable cost, marginal cost, and average total cost.

g. Draw a graph to illustrate how a technological advance that makes an airplane engine more fuel efficient changes an airline's *AVC*, *MC*, and *ATC* curves.

8. The table shows the production function of Jackie's Canoe Rides.

Labor (workers per day)	Output (rides per day)			
	Plant 1	Plant 2	Plant 3	Plant 4
10	20	40	55	65
20	40	60	75	85
30	65	75	90	100
40	75	85	100	110
Canoes	10	20	30	40

Jackie's pays $100 a day for each canoe it rents and $50 a day for each canoe operator it hires.

a. Graph the *ATC* curves for Plant 1 and Plant 2.

b. On your graph in a, plot the *ATC* curves for Plant 3 and Plant 4.

c. On Jackie's *LRAC* curve, what is the average cost of producing 40, 75, and 85 rides a week?

d. What is Jackie's minimum efficient scale?

e. Explain how Jackie's uses its *LRAC* curve to decide how many canoes to rent.

f. Does Jackie's production function feature economies of scale or diseconomies of scale?

9. **Business Boot Camp**

At a footwear company called Caboots, sales rose from $160,000 in 2000 to $2.3 million in 2006. But in 2007 sales dipped to $1.5 million. Joey and Priscilla Sanchez, who run Caboots, blame the decline partly on a flood that damaged the firm's office and sapped morale.

Based on a *Fortune* article, *CNN*, April 23, 2008

If the Sanchezes are correct in their assumptions and the prices of footwear didn't change

a. Explain the effect of the flood on the total product curve and marginal product curve at Caboots.

b. Draw a graph to show the effect of the flood on the total product curve and marginal product curve at Caboots.

10. **No Need for Economies of Scale**

Illinois Tool Works Inc. might not seem like an incubator for innovation. The 93-year-old company manufactures a hodgepodge of mundane products, from automotive components and industrial fasteners to zip-strip closures for plastic bags ... and dedicates production lines and resources to high-volume products. A line will run only those three or four products. ... Runs are much longer and more efficient. By physically linking machines ... they are able to eliminate work in process and storage areas. ... All the material handling and indirect costs are reduced.

BusinessWeek, October 31, 2005

a. How would you expect "physically linking machines" to affect the firm's short-run product curves and short-run average cost curves?

b. Draw a graph to show your predicted effects of "physically linking machines" on the firm's short-run product curves and cost curves.

c. Explain how concentrating "production lines and resources to high-volume products" can influence long-run average cost as the output rate increases.

11. **Grain Prices Go the Way of the Oil Price**

Every morning millions of Americans confront the latest trend in commodities markets at their kitchen table. ... Rising prices for crops ... have begun to drive up the cost of breakfast.

The Economist, July 21, 2007

Explain how the rising price of crops affects the average total cost and marginal cost of producing breakfast cereals.

12. **Coffee King Starbucks Raises Its Prices**

    Blame the sour news at Starbucks this week on soaring milk costs. … The wholesale price [of] milk is up nearly 70% in the 12 months. …"There's a lot of milk in those [Starbucks] lattes," notes John Glass, CIBC World Markets restaurant analyst.

    USA Today, July 24, 2007

    a. Is milk a fixed factor of production or a variable factor of production?

    b. Describe how the increase in the price of milk changes Starbucks' short-run cost curves.

13. Bill's Bakery has a fire and Bill loses some of his cost data. The bits of paper that he recovers after the fire provide the information in the following table (all the cost numbers are dollars).

TP	AFC	AVC	ATC	MC
10	120	100	220	
				80
20	*A*	*B*	150	
				90
30	40	90	130	
				130
40	30	*C*	*D*	
				E
50	24	108	132	

    Bill asks you to come to his rescue and provide the missing data in the five spaces identified as *A*, *B*, *C*, *D*, and *E*.

14. ProPainters hires students at $250 a week to paint houses. It leases equipment at $500 a week. The table sets out its total product schedule.

Labor (students)	Output (houses painted per week)
1	2
2	5
3	9
4	12
5	14
6	15

    a. If ProPainters paints 12 houses a week, calculate its total cost, average total cost, and marginal cost

    b. At what output is average total cost a minimum?

c. Explain why the gap between total cost and total variable cost is the same at all outputs.

15. ProPainters hires students at $250 a week to paint houses. It leases equipment at $500 a week. Suppose that ProPainters doubles the number of students it hires and doubles the amount of equipment it leases. ProPainters experiences diseconomies of scale.

    a. Explain how the *ATC* curve with one unit of equipment differs from that when ProPainters uses double the amount of equipment.

    b. Explain what might be the source of the diseconomies of scale that ProPainters experiences.

16. The table shows the production function of Bonnie's Balloon Rides.

Labor (workers per day)	Output (rides per day)			
	Plant 1	Plant 2	Plant 3	Plant 4
10	4	10	13	15
20	10	15	18	20
30	13	18	22	24
40	15	20	24	26
50	16	21	25	27
Balloons (number)	1	2	3	4

    Bonnie's pays $500 a day for each balloon it rents and $25 a day for each balloon operator it hires.

    a. Graph the *ATC* curves for Plant 1 and Plant 2.

    b. On your graph in a, plot the *ATC* curves for Plant 3 and Plant 4.

    c. On Bonnie's *LRAC* curve, what is the average cost of producing 18 rides and 15 rides a day?

    d. Explain how Bonnie's uses its long-run average cost curve to decide how many balloons to rent.

17. A firm is producing at minimum average total cost with its current plant. Sketch the firm's short-run average total cost curve and long-run average cost curve for each of the following situations and explain, using the concepts of economies of scale and diseconomies of scale, the circumstances in which the firm

    a. Can lower its average total cost by increasing its plant.

    b. Can lower its average total cost by decreasing its plant.

    c. Cannot lower its average total cost.

18. **Starbucks Unit Brews Up Self-Serve Espresso Bars**

    … automated, self-serve espresso kiosks are in grocery stores. … The machines, which grind their own beans, crank out lattes, … and drip coffees … take credit and debit cards, [and] cash. … Concordia Coffee, a small Bellevue coffee equipment maker, builds the self-serve kiosks and sells them to Coinstar for just under $40,000 per unit. Coinstar installs them … and provides maintenance. The kiosks use [Starbucks'] Seattle's Best Coffee. … The self-serve kiosks remove the labor costs of having a barista. … Store personnel handle refills of coffee beans and milk. …

    MSNBC, June 1, 2008

    a. What is Coinstar's total fixed cost of operating one self-serve kiosk?
    b. What are Coinstar's variable costs of providing coffee at a self-serve kiosk?
    c. Assume that a coffee machine operated by a barista costs less than $40,000. Explain how the fixed costs, variable costs, and total costs of barista-served and self-served coffee differ.
    d. Sketch the marginal cost and average cost curves implied by your answer to c.

19. **A Bakery on the Rise**

    Some 500 customers a day line up to buy Avalon's breads, scones, muffins, and coffee. … Staffing and management are worries. Avalon now employs 35 … [and] it will hire 15 more. … Payroll will climb by 30% to 40%. … As new CEO, Victor has quickly executed an ambitious agenda that includes the move to a larger space. … Avalon's costs will soar. … Its monthly rent, for example, will leap to $10,000, from $3,500.

    CNN, March 24, 2008

    a. Which of Avalon's decisions described in the news clip is a short-run decision and which is a long-run decision?
    b. Why is Avalon's long-run decision riskier than its short-run decision?
    c. By how much will Avalon's short-run decision increase its total variable cost?
    d. By how much will Avalon's long-run decision increase its monthly total fixed cost?
    e. Draw a graph to illustrate Avalon's short-run *ATC* curve before and after the events described in the news clip.

20. **Gap Will Focus on Smaller Scale Stores**

    Gap has too many stores that are 12,500 square feet … deemed too large. … "Stores are larger than we need." … The target size of stores should be 6,000 square feet to 10,000 square feet. In addition, the company plans to combine previously separate concept stores. Some Gap body, adult, maternity, baby and kids stores will be combined in one, rather than in separate spaces as they have been previously.

    CNN, June 10, 2008

    a. Thinking of a Gap store as a production plant, explain why Gap is making a decision to reduce the size of its stores.
    b. Is Gap's decision a long-run decision or a short-run decision? Explain.
    c. How might combining Gap's concept stores into one store help better take advantage of economies of scale?

21. **The Sunk-Cost Fallacy**

    You have good tickets to a basketball game an hour's drive away. There's a blizzard raging outside, and the game is being televised. You can sit warm and safe at home by a roaring fire and watch it on TV, or you can bundle up, dig out your car, and go to the game. What do you do?

    Slate, September 9, 2005

    a. What type of cost is your expenditure on tickets?
    b. Why is the cost of the ticket irrelevant to your current decision about whether to stay at home or go to the game?

22. Study *Reading Between the Lines* on pp. 266-267 and then answer the following questions.
    a. Sketch the *AFC*, *AVC*, and *ATC* curves for electricity production using seven technologies: (i) nuclear, (ii) coal, (iii) gas, (iv) hydro (v) wind, (vi) SUNRGI's new solar system, and (vii) today's solar technology.
    b. Sketch the marginal cost curves for electricity production using seven technologies: (i) nuclear, (ii) coal, (iii) gas, (iv) hydro, (v) wind, (vi) SUNRGI's new solar system, and (vii) today's solar technology.
    c. Given the cost differences among the different methods of generating electricity, why do you think we use more than one method? If we could use only one method, which would it be?

12 ◆ Perfect Competition

After studying this chapter, you will be able to:

■ Define perfect competition

■ Explain how a firm makes its output decision and why it sometimes shuts down temporarily and lays off its workers

■ Explain how price and output are determined in a perfectly competitive market

■ Explain why firms enter and leave a competitive market and the consequences of entry and exit

■ Predict the effects of a change in demand and of a technological advance

◆ Explain why perfect competition is efficient

Airlines and producers of trucks, cars, and motor bikes are facing tough times: prices are being slashed to drive sales and profits are turning into losses. Airlines are cutting back on flights, charging to check bags, drink a soda, or use a blanket, and some are even going out of business. Vehicle production has been scaled back and workers have either been laid off temporarily or let go permanently.

Taking a longer view, astonishing transformations have occurred over the past decade. Today, at $600 for a powerful laptop, almost every student owns one. Fifteen years ago, at $6,000 for a heavy, slow portable computer, these machines were a rare sight on campus.

What forces are responsible for this diversity of performance of production, prices, and profits? What are the causes and consequences of firms entering or leaving a market? Why do firms sometimes stop producing and temporarily lay off their workers?

To study competitive markets, we are going to build a model of a market in which competition is as fierce and extreme as possible—more extreme than in the examples we've just considered. We call this situation "perfect competition." In *Reading Between the Lines* at the end of the chapter, we'll apply the model to the market for air transportation services and see how the effects of high fuel prices and a fall in demand are playing out in that market.

◆ What Is Perfect Competition?

The firms that you study in this chapter face the force of raw competition. We call this extreme form of competition perfect competition. **Perfect competition** is a market in which

- Many firms sell identical products to many buyers.
- There are no restrictions on entry into the market.
- Established firms have no advantage over new ones.
- Sellers and buyers are well informed about prices.

Farming, fishing, wood pulping and paper milling, the manufacture of paper cups and shopping bags, grocery retailing, photo finishing, lawn services, plumbing, painting, dry cleaning, and laundry services are all examples of highly competitive industries.

How Perfect Competition Arises

Perfect competition arises if the minimum efficient scale of a single producer is small relative to the market demand for the good or service. In this situation, there is room in the market for many firms. A firm's *minimum efficient scale* is the smallest output at which long-run average cost reaches its lowest level. (See Chapter 11, p. 265.)

In perfect competition, each firm produces a good that has no unique characteristics, so consumers don't care which firm's good they buy.

Price Takers

Firms in perfect competition are price takers. A **price taker** is a firm that cannot influence the market price because its production is an insignificant part of the total market.

Imagine that you are a wheat farmer in Kansas. You have a thousand acres planted—which sounds like a lot. But compared to the millions of acres in Colorado, Oklahoma, Texas, Nebraska, and the Dakotas, as well as the millions more in Canada, Argentina, Australia, and Ukraine, your thousand acres are a drop in the ocean. Nothing makes your wheat any better than any other farmer's, and all the buyers of wheat know the price at which they can do business.

If the market price of wheat is $4 a bushel, then that is the highest price you can get for your wheat. Ask for $4.10 and no one will buy from you. Offer it for $3.90 and you'll be sold out in a flash and have given away 10¢ a bushel. You take the market price.

Economic Profit and Revenue

A firm's goal is to maximize *economic profit*, which is equal to total revenue minus total cost. Total cost is the *opportunity cost* of production, which includes *normal profit*. (See Chapter 10, p. 228.)

A firm's **total revenue** equals the price of its output multiplied by the number of units of output sold (price × quantity). **Marginal revenue** is the change in total revenue that results from a one-unit increase in the quantity sold. Marginal revenue is calculated by dividing the change in total revenue by the change in the quantity sold.

Figure 12.1 illustrates these revenue concepts. In part (a), the market demand curve, *D*, and market supply curve, *S*, determine the market price. The market price is $25 a sweater. Campus Sweaters is one of the many producers of sweaters. So the best it can do is to sell its sweaters for $25 each.

Total Revenue Total revenue is equal to the price multiplied by the quantity sold. In the table in Fig. 12.1, if Campus Sweaters sells 9 sweaters, its total revenue is $225 (9 × $25).

Figure 12.1(b) shows the firm's total revenue curve (*TR*), which graphs the relationship between total revenue and the quantity sold. At point *A* on the *TR* curve, the firm sells 9 sweaters and has a total revenue of $225. Because each additional sweater sold brings in a constant amount—$25—the total revenue curve is an upward-sloping straight line.

Marginal Revenue Marginal revenue is the change in total revenue that results from a one-unit increase in quantity sold. In the table in Fig. 12.1, when the quantity sold increases from 8 to 9 sweaters, total revenue increases from $200 to $225, so marginal revenue is $25 a sweater.

Because the firm in perfect competition is a price taker, the change in total revenue that results from a one-unit increase in the quantity sold equals the market price. *In perfect competition, the firm's marginal revenue equals the market price.* Figure 12.1(c) shows the firm's marginal revenue curve (*MR*) as the horizontal line at the market price.

Demand for the Firm's Product The firm can sell any quantity it chooses at the market price. So the demand curve for the firm's product is a horizontal line at the market price, the same as the firm's marginal revenue curve.

FIGURE 12.1   Demand, Price, and Revenue in Perfect Competition

(a) Sweater market

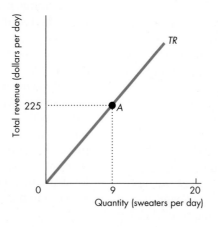

(b) Campus Sweaters total revenue

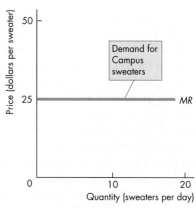

(c) Campus Sweaters marginal revenue

Quantity sold (Q) (sweaters per day)	Price (P) (dollars per sweater)	Total revenue (TR = P × Q) (dollars)	Marginal revenue (MR = ΔTR/ΔQ) (dollars per additional sweater)
8	25	200	
			 25
9	25	225	
			 25
10	25	250	

In part (a), market demand and market supply determine the market price (and quantity). Part (b) shows the firm's total revenue curve (*TR*). Point *A* corresponds to the second row of the table—Campus Sweaters sells 9 sweaters at $25 a sweater, so total revenue is $225. Part (c) shows the firm's marginal revenue curve (*MR*). This curve is also the demand curve for the firm's sweaters. The demand for sweaters from Campus Sweaters is perfectly elastic at the market price of $25 a sweater.

myeconlab   animation

A horizontal demand curve illustrates a perfectly elastic demand, so the demand for the firm's product is perfectly elastic. A sweater from Campus Sweaters is a *perfect substitute* for a sweater from any other factory. But the *market* demand for sweaters is *not* perfectly elastic: Its elasticity depends on the substitutability of sweaters for other goods and services.

The Firm's Decisions

The goal of the competitive firm is to maximize economic profit, given the constraints it faces. To achieve its goal, a firm must decide

1. How to produce at minimum cost
2. What quantity to produce
3. Whether to enter or exit a market

You've already seen how a firm makes the first decision. It does so by operating with the plant that minimizes long-run average cost—by being on its long-run average cost curve. We'll now see how the firm makes the other two decisions. We start by looking at the firm's output decision.

Review Quiz

1 Why is a firm in perfect competition a price taker?
2 In perfect competition, what is the relationship between the demand for the firm's output and the market demand?
3 In perfect competition, why is a firm's marginal revenue curve also the demand curve for the firm's output?
4 What decisions must a firm make to maximize profit?

myeconlab   Work Study Plan 12.1 and get instant feedback.

The Firm's Output Decision

A firm's cost curves (total cost, average cost, and marginal cost) describe the relationship between its output and costs (see pp. 257–261). A firm's revenue curves (total revenue and marginal revenue) describe the relationship between its output and revenue (p. 275). From the firm's cost curves and revenue curves, we can find the output that maximizes the firm's economic profit.

Figure 12.2 shows how to do this for Campus Sweaters. The table lists the firm's total revenue and total cost at different outputs, and part (a) of the figure shows the firm's total revenue curve, *TR*, and total cost curve, *TC*. These curves are graphs of the numbers in the first three columns of the table.

Economic profit equals total revenue minus total cost. The fourth column of the table in Fig. 12.2 shows the economic profit made by Campus Sweaters, and part (b) of the figure graphs these numbers as its economic profit curve, *EP*.

Economic profit is maximized at an output of 9 sweaters a day. At this output, total revenue is $225 a day, total cost is $183 a day, and economic profit is $42 a day. No other output rate achieves a larger profit. At outputs of less than 4 sweaters and more than 12 sweaters a day, the firm incurs an economic loss. At either 4 or 12 sweaters a day, the firm makes zero economic profit, called a *break-even* point.

FIGURE 12.2   Total Revenue, Total Cost, and Economic Profit

(a) Revenue and cost

(b) Economic profit and loss

Quantity (Q) (sweaters per day)	Total revenue (TR) (dollars)	Total cost (TC) (dollars)	Economic profit (TR – TC) (dollars)
0	0	22	–22
1	25	45	–20
2	50	66	–16
3	75	85	–10
4	100	100	0
5	125	114	11
6	150	126	24
7	175	141	34
8	200	160	40
9	225	183	42
10	250	210	40
11	275	245	30
12	300	300	0
13	325	360	–35

The table lists the total revenue, total cost, and economic profit of Campus Sweaters. Part (a) graphs the total revenue and total cost curves and part (b) graphs economic profit. Campus Sweaters makes maximum economic profit, $42 a day ($225 – $183), when it produces 9 sweaters a day. At outputs of 4 sweaters and 12 sweaters a day, Campus Sweaters makes zero economic profit—these are break-even points. At outputs less than 4 sweaters and greater than 12 sweaters a day, Campus Sweaters incurs an economic loss.

myeconlab   animation

Marginal Analysis and the Supply Decision

Another way to find the profit-maximizing output is to use *marginal analysis*, which compares marginal revenue, *MR*, with marginal cost, *MC*. As output increases, marginal revenue is constant but marginal cost eventually increases.

If marginal revenue exceeds the firm's marginal cost ($MR > MC$), then the revenue from selling one more unit exceeds the cost of producing that unit and an increase in output will increase economic profit. If marginal revenue is less than marginal cost ($MR < MC$), then the revenue from selling one more unit is less than the cost of producing that unit and a decrease in output will increase economic profit. If marginal revenue equals marginal cost ($MR = MC$), then the revenue from selling one more unit equals the cost incurred to produce that unit. Economic profit is maximized and either an increase or a decrease in output decreases economic profit.

Figure 12.3 illustrates these propositions. If Campus Sweaters increases its output from 8 sweaters to 9 sweaters a day, marginal revenue ($25) exceeds marginal cost ($23), so by producing the 9th sweater economic profit increases by $2 from $40 to $42 a day. The blue area in the figure shows the increase in economic profit when the firm increases production from 8 to 9 sweaters per day.

If Campus Sweaters increases its output from 9 sweaters to 10 sweaters a day, marginal revenue ($25) is less than marginal cost ($27), so by producing the 10th sweater, economic profit decreases. The last column of the table shows that economic profit decreases from $42 to $40 a day. The red area in the figure shows the economic loss that arises from increasing production from 9 to 10 sweaters a day.

Campus Sweaters maximizes economic profit by producing 9 sweaters a day, the quantity at which marginal revenue equals marginal cost.

A firm's profit-maximizing output is its quantity supplied at the market price. The quantity supplied at a price of $25 a sweater is 9 sweaters a day. If the price were higher than $25 a sweater, the firm would increase production. If the price were lower than $25 a sweater, the firm would decrease production. These profit-maximizing responses to different market prices are the foundation of the law of supply:

Other things remaining the same, the higher the market price of a good, the greater is the quantity supplied of that good.

FIGURE 12.3   Profit-Maximizing Output

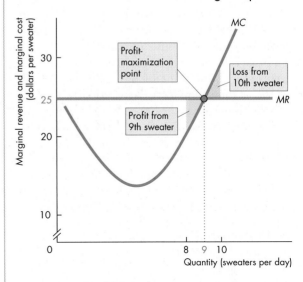

Quantity (Q) (sweaters per day)	Total revenue (TR) (dollars)	Marginal revenue (MR) (dollars per additional sweater)	Total cost (TC) (dollars)	Marginal cost (MC) (dollars per additional sweater)	Economic profit (TR − TC) (dollars)
7	175		141		34
		25		19	
8	200		160		40
		25		23	
9	225		183		42
		25		27	
10	250		210		40
		25		35	
11	275		245		30

The firm maximizes profit by producing the output at which marginal revenue equals marginal cost and marginal cost is increasing. The table and figure show that marginal cost equals marginal revenue and economic profit is maximized when Campus Sweaters produces 9 sweaters a day.

The table shows that if Campus Sweaters increases output from 8 to 9 sweaters, marginal cost is $23, which is less than the marginal revenue of $25. If output increases from 9 to 10 sweaters, marginal cost is $27, which exceeds the marginal revenue of $25. If marginal revenue exceeds marginal cost, an increase in output increases economic profit. If marginal revenue is less than marginal cost, an increase in output decreases economic profit. If marginal revenue equals marginal cost, economic profit is maximized.

Temporary Shutdown Decision

You've seen that a firm maximizes profit by producing the quantity at which marginal revenue (price) equals marginal cost. But suppose that at this quantity, price is less than average total cost. In this case, the firm incurs an economic loss. Maximum profit is a loss (a minimum loss). What does the firm do?

If the firm expects the loss to be permanent, it goes out of business. But if it expects the loss to be temporary, the firm must decide whether to shut down temporarily and produce no output, or to keep producing. To make this decision, the firm compares the loss from shutting down with the loss from producing and takes the action that minimizes its loss.

Loss Comparisons A firm's economic loss equals total fixed cost, *TFC*, plus total variable cost minus total revenue. Total variable cost equals average variable cost, *AVC* multiplied by the quantity produced, *Q*, and total revenue equals price, *P*, multiplied by the quantity *Q*. So

$$\text{Economic loss} = TFC + (AVC - P) \times Q.$$

If the firm shuts down, it produces no output (*Q* = 0). The firm has no variable costs and no revenue but it must pay its fixed costs, so its economic loss equals total fixed cost.

If the firm produces, then in addition to its fixed costs, it incurs variable costs. But it also receives revenue. Its economic loss equals total fixed cost—the loss when shut down—plus total variable cost minus total revenue. If total variable cost exceeds total revenue, this loss exceeds total fixed cost and the firm shuts down. Equivalently, if average variable cost exceeds price, this loss exceeds total fixed cost and the firm shuts down.

The Shutdown Point A firm's **shutdown point** is the price and quantity at which it is indifferent between producing and shutting down. The shutdown point occurs at the price and the quantity at which average variable cost is a minimum. At the shutdown point, the firm is minimizing its loss and its loss equals total fixed cost. If the price falls below minimum average variable cost, the firm shuts down temporarily and continues to incur a loss equal to total fixed cost. At prices above minimum average variable cost but below average total cost, the firm produces the loss minimizing output and incurs a loss, but a loss that is less than total fixed cost.

Figure 12.4 illustrates the firm's shutdown decision and the shutdown point that we've just described for Campus Sweaters.

The firm's average variable cost curve is *AVC* and the marginal cost curve is *MC*. Average variable cost has a minimum of $17 a sweater when output is 7 sweaters a day. The *MC* curve intersects the *AVC* curve at its minimum. (We explained this relationship between a marginal and average cost in Chapter 11; see pp. 258–259.)

The figure shows the marginal revenue curve *MR* when the price is $17 a sweater, a price equal to minimum average variable cost.

Marginal revenue equals marginal cost at 7 sweaters a day, so this quantity maximizes economic profit (minimizes economic loss). The *ATC* curve shows that the firm's average total cost of producing 7 sweaters a day is $20.14 a sweater. The firm incurs a loss equal to $3.14 a sweater on 7 sweaters a day, so its loss is $22 a day, which equals total fixed cost.

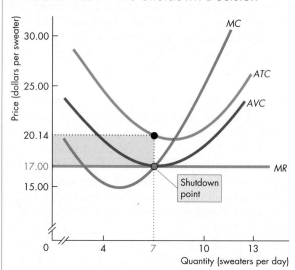

FIGURE 12.4   The Shutdown Decision

The shutdown point is at minimum average variable cost. At a price below minimum average variable cost, the firm shuts down and produces no output. At a price equal to minimum average variable cost, the firm is indifferent between shutting down and producing no output or producing the output at minimum average variable cost. Either way, the firm minimizes its economic loss and incurs a loss equal to total fixed cost.

myeconlab animation

The Firm's Supply Curve

A perfectly competitive firm's supply curve shows how its profit-maximizing output varies as the market price varies, other things remaining the same. The supply curve is derived from the firm's marginal cost curve and average variable cost curves. Figure 12.5 illustrates the derivation of the supply curve.

When the price *exceeds* minimum average variable cost (more than $17), the firm maximizes profit by producing the output at which marginal cost equals price. If the price rises, the firm increases its output—it moves up along its marginal cost curve.

When the price is *less than* minimum average variable cost (less than $17 a sweater), the firm maximizes profit by temporarily shutting down and producing no output. The firm produces zero output at all prices below minimum average variable cost.

When the price *equals* minimum average variable cost, the firm maximizes profit *either* by temporarily shutting down and producing no output *or* by producing the output at which average variable cost is a minimum—the shutdown point, T. The firm never produces a quantity between zero and the quantity at the shutdown point T (a quantity greater than zero and less than 7 sweaters a day).

The firm's supply curve in Fig. 12.5(b) runs along the y-axis from a price of zero to a price equal to minimum average variable cost, jumps to point T, and then, as the price rises above minimum average variable cost, follows the marginal cost curve.

Review Quiz

1 Why does a firm in perfect competition produce the quantity at which marginal cost equals price?
2 What is the lowest price at which a firm produces an output? Explain why.
3 What is the relationship between a firm's supply curve, its marginal cost curve, and its average variable cost curve?

myeconlab   Work Study Plan 12.2 and get instant feedback.

So far, we have studied a single firm in isolation. We have seen that the firm's profit-maximizing decisions depend on the market price, which the firm takes as given. But how is the market price determined? Let's find out.

FIGURE 12.5   A Firm's Supply Curve

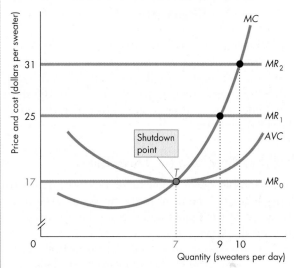

(a) Marginal cost and average variable cost

(b) Campus Sweaters short-run supply curve

Part (a) shows the firm's profit-maximizing output at various market prices. At $25 a sweater, it produces 9 sweaters, and at $17 a sweater, it produces 7 sweaters. At all prices below $17 a sweater, Campus Sweaters produces nothing. Its shutdown point is T. Part (b) shows the firm's supply curve—the quantity of sweaters it produces at each price. Its supply curve is made up of the marginal cost curve at all prices above minimum average variable cost and the vertical axis at all prices below minimum average variable cost.

 myeconlab   animation

◆ Output, Price, and Profit in the Short Run

To determine the price and quantity in a perfectly competitive market, we need to know how market demand and market supply interact. We start by studying a perfectly competitive market in the short run. The short run is a situation in which the number of firms is fixed.

Market Supply in the Short Run

The **short-run market supply curve** shows the quantity supplied by all the firms in the market at each price when each firm's plant and the number of firms remain the same.

You've seen how an individual firm's supply curve is determined. The market supply curve is derived from the individual supply curves. The quantity supplied by the market at a given price is the sum of the quantities supplied by all the firms in the market at that price.

Figure 12.6 shows the supply curve for the competitive sweater market. In this example, the market consists of 1,000 firms exactly like Campus Sweaters. At each price, the quantity supplied by the market is 1,000 times the quantity supplied by a single firm.

The table in Fig. 12.6 shows the firm's and the market's supply schedules and how the market supply curve is constructed. At prices below $17 a sweater, every firm in the market shuts down; the quantity supplied by the market is zero. At $17 a sweater, each firm is indifferent between shutting down and producing nothing or operating and producing 7 sweaters a day. Some firms will shut down, and others will supply 7 sweaters a day. The quantity supplied by each firm is *either* 0 or 7 sweaters, and the quantity supplied by the market is *between* 0 (all firms shut down) and 7,000 (all firms produce 7 sweaters a day each).

The market supply curve is a graph of the market supply schedules and the points on the supply curve *A* through *D* represent the rows of the table.

To construct the market supply curve, we sum the quantities supplied by all the firms at each price. Each of the 1,000 firms in the market has a supply schedule like Campus Sweaters. At prices below $17 a sweater, the market supply curve runs along the *y*-axis. At $17 a sweater, the market supply curve is horizontal—supply is perfectly elastic. As the price

FIGURE 12.6   Short-Run Market Supply Curve

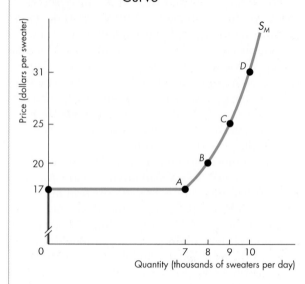

	Price (dollars per sweater)	Quantity supplied by Campus Sweaters (sweaters per day)	Quantity supplied by market (sweaters per day)
A	17	0 or 7	0 to 7,000
B	20	8	8,000
C	25	9	9,000
D	31	10	10,000

The market supply schedule is the sum of the supply schedules of all the individual firms. A market that consists of 1,000 identical firms has a supply schedule similar to that of one firm, but the quantity supplied by the market is 1,000 times as large as that of the one firm (see the table). The market supply curve is S_M. Points *A*, *B*, *C*, and *D* correspond to the rows of the table. At the shutdown price of $17 a sweater, each firm produces either 0 or 7 sweaters a day and the quantity supplied by the market is between 0 and 7,000 sweaters a day. The market supply is perfectly elastic at the shutdown price.

rises above $17 a sweater, each firm increases its quantity supplied and the quantity supplied by the market increases by 1,000 times that of one firm.

Short-Run Equilibrium

Market demand and short-run market supply determine the market price and market output. Figure 12.7(a) shows a short-run equilibrium. The short-run supply curve, S, is the same as S_M in Fig. 12.6. If the market demand curve is D_1, the market price is $20 a sweater. Each firm takes this price as given and produces its profit-maximizing output, which is 8 sweaters a day. Because the market has 1,000 identical firms, the market output is 8,000 sweaters a day.

A Change in Demand

Changes in demand bring changes to short-run market equilibrium. Figure 12.7 shows these changes.

If demand increases and the demand curve shifts rightward to D_2, the market price rises to $25 a sweater. At this price, each firm maximizes profit by increasing its output to 9 sweaters a day. The market output increases to 9,000 sweaters a day.

If demand decreases and the demand curve shifts leftward to D_3, the market price falls to $17. At this price, each firm maximizes profit by decreasing its output. If each firm produces 7 sweaters a day, the market output decreases to 7,000 sweaters a day.

If the demand curve shifts farther leftward than D_3, the market price remains at $17 a sweater because the market supply curve is horizontal at that price. Some firms continue to produce 7 sweaters a day, and others temporarily shut down. Firms are indifferent between these two activities, and whichever they choose, they incur an economic loss equal to total fixed cost. The number of firms continuing to produce is just enough to satisfy the market demand at a price of $17 a sweater.

Profits and Losses in the Short Run

In short-run equilibrium, although the firm produces the profit-maximizing output, it does not necessarily end up making an economic profit. It might do so, but it might alternatively break even or incur an economic loss. Economic profit (or loss) per sweater is price, P, minus average total cost, ATC. So economic profit (or loss) is $(P - ATC) \times Q$. If price

FIGURE 12.7   Short-Run Equilibrium

(a) Equilibrium

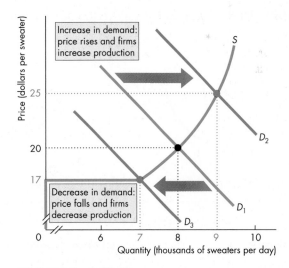

(b) Change in equilibrium

In part (a), the market supply curve is S and the market demand curve is D_1. The market price is $20 a sweater. At this price, each firm produces 8 sweaters a day and the market produces 8,000 sweaters a day.

In part (b), if the market demand increases to D_2, the price rises to $25 a sweater. Each firm produces 9 sweaters a day and market output is 9,000 sweaters. If market demand decreases to D_3, the price falls to $17 a sweater and each firm decreases its output. If each firm produces 7 sweaters a day, the market output is 7,000 sweaters a day.

equals average total cost, a firm breaks even—the entrepreneur makes normal profit. If price exceeds average total cost, a firm makes an economic profit. If price is less than average total cost, a firm incurs an economic loss. Figure 12.8 shows these three possible short-run profit outcomes for Campus Sweaters that correspond to the three different levels of market demand that we've just examined.

Three Possible Short-Run Outcomes

Figure 12.8(a) corresponds to the situation in Fig. 12.7(a) where the market demand is D_1. The equilibrium price of a sweater is $20 and the firm produces 8 sweaters a day. Average total cost is $20 a sweater. Price equals average total cost (ATC), so the firm breaks even (makes zero economic profit).

Figure 12.8(b) corresponds to the situation in Fig. 12.7(b) where the market demand is D_2. The equilibrium price of a sweater is $25 and the firm produces 9 sweaters a day. Here, price exceeds average total cost, so the firm makes an economic profit. Its economic profit is $42 a day, which equals $4.67 per sweater ($25.00 – $20.33) multiplied by 9, the

profit-maximizing number of sweaters produced. The blue rectangle shows this economic profit. The height of that rectangle is profit per sweater, $4.67, and the length is the quantity of sweaters produced, 9 a day. So the area of the rectangle is economic profit of $42 a day.

Figure 12.8(c) corresponds to the situation in Fig. 12.7(b) where the market demand is D_3. The equilibrium price of a sweater is $17. Here, the price is less than average total cost, so the firm incurs an economic loss. Price and marginal revenue are $17 a sweater, and the profit-maximizing (in this case, loss-minimizing) output is 7 sweaters a day. Total revenue is $119 a day (7 × $17). Average total cost is $20.14 a sweater, so the economic loss is $3.14 per sweater ($20.14 – $17.00). This loss per sweater multiplied by the number of sweaters is $22. The red rectangle shows this economic loss. The height of that rectangle is economic loss per sweater, $3.14, and the length is the quantity of sweaters produced, 7 a day. So the area of the rectangle is the firm's economic loss of $22 a day. If the price dips below $17 a sweater, the firm temporarily shuts down and incurs an economic loss equal to total fixed cost.

FIGURE 12.8   Three Short-Run Outcomes for the Firm

(a) Break even

(b) Economic profit

(c) Economic loss

In the short run, the firm might break even (make zero economic profit), make an economic profit, or incur an economic loss. In part (a), the price equals minimum average total cost. At the profit-maximizing output, the firm breaks even and makes zero economic profit. In part (b), the market price is $25 a sweater. At the profit-maximizing output,

the price exceeds average total cost and the firm makes an economic profit equal to the area of the blue rectangle. In part (c), the market price is $17 a sweater. At the profit-maximizing output, the price is below minimum average total cost and the firm incurs an economic loss equal to the area of the red rectangle.

Production Cutback and Temporary Shutdown
Drop in Demand for Bikes at Harley-Davidson

The high price of gasoline and anxiety about unemployment and future incomes brought a decrease in the demand for luxury goods including high-end motorcycles such as Harley-Davidsons.

Harley-Davidson's profit-maximizing response to the decrease in demand was to cut production and lay off workers. Some of the production cuts and lay-offs were temporary and some were permanent.

Harley-Davidson's bike production plant in York County, Pennsylvania, was temporarily shut down in the summer of 2008 because total revenue was insufficient to cover total variable cost.

The firm also permanently cut its workforce by 300 people. This permanent cut was like that at Campus Sweaters when the market demand for sweaters decreased from D_1 to D_3 in Fig. 12.7(b).

Review Quiz

1 How do we derive the short-run market supply curve in perfect competition?

2 In perfect competition, when market demand increases, explain how the price of the good and the output and profit of each firm changes in the short run.

3 In perfect competition, when market demand decreases, explain how the price of the good and the output and profit of each firm changes in the short run.

myeconlab Work Study Plan 12.3 and get instant feedback.

Output, Price, and Profit in the Long Run

In short-run equilibrium, a firm might make an economic profit, incur an economic loss, or break even. Although each of these three situations is a short-run equilibrium, only one of them is a long-run equilibrium. The reason is that in the long run, firms can enter or exit the market.

Entry and Exit

Entry occurs in a market when new firms come into the market and the number of firms increases. Exit occurs when existing firms leave a market and the number of firms decreases.

Firms respond to economic profit and economic loss by either entering or exiting a market. New firms enter a market in which existing firms are making an economic profit. Firms exit a market in which they are incurring an economic loss. Temporary economic profit and temporary economic loss don't trigger entry and exit. It's the prospect of persistent economic profit or loss that triggers entry and exit.

Entry and exit change the market supply, which influences the market price, the quantity produced by each firm, and its economic profit (or loss).

If firms enter a market, supply increases and the market supply curve shifts rightward. The increase in supply lowers the market price and eventually eliminates economic profit. When economic profit reaches zero, entry stops.

If firms exit a market, supply decreases and the market supply curve shifts leftward. The market price rises and economic loss decreases. Eventually, economic loss is eliminated and exit stops.

To summarize:

- New firms enter a market in which existing firms are making an economic profit.
- As new firms enter a market, the market price falls and the economic profit of each firm decreases.
- Firms exit a market in which they are incurring an economic loss.
- As firms leave a market, the market price rises and the economic loss incurred by the remaining firms decreases.
- Entry and exit stop when firms make zero economic profit.

A Closer Look at Entry

The sweater market has 800 firms with cost curves like those in Fig. 12.9(a). The market demand curve is D, the market supply curve is S_1, and the price is $25 a sweater in Fig. 12.9(b). Each firm produces 9 sweaters a day and makes an economic profit.

This economic profit is a signal for new firms to enter the market. As entry takes place, supply increases and the market supply curve shifts rightward toward S^*. As supply increases with no change in demand, the market price gradually falls from $25 to $20 a sweater. At this lower price, each firm makes zero economic profit and entry stops.

Entry results in an increase in market output, but each firm's output *decreases*. Because the price falls, each firm moves down its supply curve and produces less. Because the number of firms increases, the market produces more.

A Closer Look at Exit

Now, the sweater market has 1,200 firms with cost curves like those in Fig. 12.9(a). The market demand curve is D, the market supply curve is S_2, and the price is $17 a sweater in Fig. 12.9(b). Each firm produces 7 sweaters a day and incurs an economic loss.

This economic loss is a signal for firms to exit the market. As exit takes place, supply decreases and the market supply curve shifts leftward toward S^*. As supply decreases with no change in demand, the market price gradually rises from $17 to $20 a sweater. At this higher price, losses are eliminated, each firm makes zero economic profit, and exit stops.

Exit results in a decrease in market output, but each firm's output *increases*. Because the price rises, each firm moves up its supply curve and produces more. Because the number of firms decreases, the market produces less.

FIGURE 12.9 Entry, Exit, and Long-Run Equilibrium

(a) Campus Sweaters

(b) The sweater market

Each firm has cost curves like those of Campus Sweaters in part (a). The market demand curve is D in part (b). When the market supply in part (b) is S_1, the price is $25 a sweater. In part (a), each firm produces 9 sweaters a day and makes an economic profit. Profit triggers the entry of new firms and as new firms enter, the market supply curve shifts rightward, from S_1 toward S^*. The price falls from $25 to $20 a sweater, and the quantity produced increases from 7,200 to 8,000 sweaters. Each firm's output decreases to 8

sweaters a day and economic profit is zero. When the market supply is S_2, the price is $17 a sweater. In part (a), each firm produces 7 sweaters a day and incurs an economic loss. Loss triggers exit and as firms exit, the market supply curve shifts leftward, from S_2 toward S^*. The price rises from $17 to $20 a sweater, and the quantity produced decreases from 8,400 to 8,000 sweaters. Each firm's output increases from 7 to 8 sweaters a day and economic profit is zero.

Entry and Exit in Action
Personal Computers and Farm Machines

An example of entry and falling prices occurred during the 1980s and 1990s in the personal computer market. When IBM introduced its first PC in 1981, IBM had little competition. The price was $7,000 (about $16,850 in today's money) and IBM made a large economic profit selling the new machine.

Observing IBM's huge success, new firms such as Gateway, NEC, Dell, and a host of others entered the market with machines that were technologically identical to IBM's. In fact, they were so similar that they came to be called "clones." The massive wave of entry into the personal computer market increased the market supply and lowered the price. The economic profit for all firms decreased.

Today, a $400 computer is vastly more powerful than its 1981 ancestor that cost 42 times as much.

The same PC market that saw entry during the 1980s and 1990s has seen some exit more recently. In 2001, IBM, the firm that first launched the PC, announced that it was exiting the market. The intense competition from Gateway, NEC, Dell, and others that entered the market following IBM's lead has lowered the price and eliminated the economic profit. So IBM now concentrates on servers and other parts of the computer market.

IBM exited the PC market because it was incurring economic losses. Its exit decreased market supply and made it possible for the remaining firms in the market to make zero economic profit.

International Harvester, a manufacturer of farm equipment, provides another example of exit. For decades, people associated the name "International Harvester" with tractors, combines, and other farm machines. But International Harvester wasn't the only maker of farm equipment. The market became intensely competitive, and the firm began to incur economic losses. Now the firm has a new name, Navistar International, and it doesn't make tractors any more. After years of economic losses and shrinking revenues, it got out of the farm-machine business in 1985 and started to make trucks.

International Harvester exited because it was incurring an economic loss. Its exit decreased supply and made it possible for the remaining firms in the market to break even.

Long-Run Equilibrium

You've now seen how economic profit induces entry, which in turn eliminates the profit. You've also seen how economic loss induces exit, which in turn eliminates the loss.

When economic profit and economic loss have been eliminated and entry and exit have stopped, a competitive market is in *long-run equilibrium.*

You've seen how a competitive market adjusts toward its long-run equilibrium. But a competitive market is rarely *in* a state of long-run equilibrium. Instead, it is constantly and restlessly evolving toward long-run equilibrium. The reason is that the market is constantly bombarded with events that change the constraints that firms face.

Markets are constantly adjusting to keep up with changes in tastes, which change demand, and changes in technology, which change costs.

In the next sections, we're going to see how a competitive market reacts to changing tastes and technology and how it guides resources to their highest-valued use.

Review Quiz

1 What triggers entry in a competitive market? Describe the process that ends further entry.
2 What triggers exit in a competitive market? Describe the process that ends further exit.

 Work Study Plan 12.4 and get instant feedback.

◆ Changing Tastes and Advancing Technology

Increased awareness of the health hazards of smoking has decreased the demand for tobacco products. The development of inexpensive automobile and air transportation during the 1990s decreased the demand for long-distance trains and buses. Solid-state electronics has decreased the demand for TV and radio repair. The development of good-quality inexpensive clothing has decreased the demand for sewing machines. What happens in a competitive market when there is a permanent decrease in the demand for its product?

Microwave food preparation has increased the demand for paper, glass, and plastic cooking utensils and for plastic wrap. The Internet has increased the demand for a personal computer and the widespread use of the computer has increased the demand for high-speed connections and music downloads. What happens in a competitive market when the demand for its output increases?

Advances in technology are constantly lowering the costs of production. New biotechnologies have dramatically lowered the costs of producing many food and pharmaceutical products. New electronic technologies have lowered the cost of producing just about every good and service. What happens in a competitive market for a good when technological change lowers its production costs?

Let's use the theory of perfect competition to answer these questions.

A Permanent Change in Demand

Figure 12.10(a) shows a competitive market that initially is in long-run equilibrium. The demand curve is D_0, the supply curve is S_0, the market price is P_0, and market output is Q_0. Figure 12.10(b) shows a single firm in this initial long-run equilibrium. The firm produces q_0 and makes zero economic profit.

Now suppose that demand decreases and the demand curve shifts leftward to D_1, as shown in Fig. 12.10(a). The market price falls to P_1, and the quantity supplied by the market decreases from Q_0 to Q_1 as the market moves down along its short-run supply curve S_0. Figure 12.10(b) shows the situation facing a firm. The market price is now below the firm's minimum average total cost, so the firm incurs an eco-

nomic loss. But to minimize its loss, the firm adjusts its output to keep marginal cost equal to price. At a price of P_1, each firm produces an output of q_1.

The market is now in short-run equilibrium but not long-run equilibrium. It is in short-run equilibrium because each firm is maximizing profit; it is not in long-run equilibrium because each firm is incurring an economic loss—its average total cost exceeds the price.

The economic loss is a signal for some firms to exit the market. As they do so, short-run market supply decreases and the market supply curve gradually shifts leftward. As market supply decreases, the price rises. At each higher price, a firm's profit-maximizing output is greater, so the firms remaining in the market increase their output as the price rises. Each firm moves up along its marginal cost or supply curve in Fig. 12.10(b). That is, as some firms exit the market, market output decreases but the output of the firms that remain in the market increases.

Eventually, enough firms have exited the market for the market supply curve to have shifted to S_1 in Fig. 12.10(a). The market price has returned to its original level, P_0. At this price, the firms remaining in the market produce q_0, the same quantity that they produced before the decrease in demand. Because firms are now making zero economic profit, no firm has an incentive to enter or exit the market. The market supply curve remains at S_1, and market output is Q_2. The market is again in long-run equilibrium.

The difference between the initial long-run equilibrium and the final long-run equilibrium is the number of firms in the market. A permanent decrease in demand has decreased the number of firms. Each firm remaining in the market produces the same output in the new long-run equilibrium as it did initially and makes zero economic profit. In the process of moving from the initial equilibrium to the new one, firms incur economic losses.

We've just worked out how a competitive market responds to a permanent *decrease* in demand. A permanent increase in demand triggers a similar response, except in the opposite direction. The increase in demand brings a higher price, economic profit, and entry. Entry increases market supply and eventually lowers the price to its original level and economic profit to zero.

The demand for Internet service increased permanently during the 1990s and huge profit opportunities arose in this market. The result was a massive rate

FIGURE 12.10   A Decrease in Demand

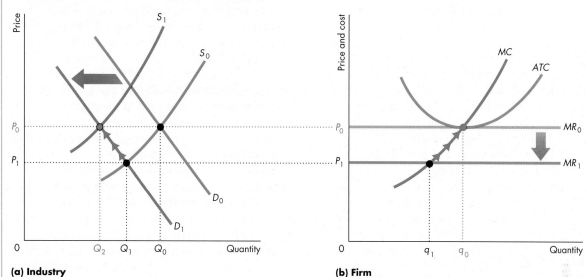

(a) Industry

(b) Firm

A market starts out in long-run competitive equilibrium. Part (a) shows the market demand curve D_0, the market supply curve S_0, the market price P_0, and the equilibrium quantity Q_0. Each firm sells its output at the price P_0, so its marginal revenue curve is MR_0 in part (b). Each firm produces q_0 and makes zero economic profit.

Market demand decreases permanently from D_0 to D_1 in part (a) and the market price falls to P_1. Each firm decreases its output to q_1 in part (b), and market output

decreases to Q_1 in part (a).

Firms now incur economic losses and some firms exit the market. As they do so, the market supply curve gradually shifts leftward, from S_0 toward S_1. This shift gradually raises the market price from P_1 back to P_0. While the price is below P_0, firms incur economic losses and some firms exit the market. Once the price has returned to P_0, each firm makes zero economic profit and has no incentive to exit. Each firm produces q_0, and market output is Q_2.

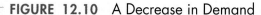 animation

of entry of Internet service providers. The process of competition and change in the Internet service market is similar to what we have just studied but with an increase in demand rather than a decrease in demand.

We've now studied the effects of a permanent change in demand for a good. In doing so, we began and ended in a long-run equilibrium and examined the process that takes a market from one equilibrium to another. It is this process, not the equilibrium points, that describes the real world.

One feature of the predictions that we have just generated seems odd: In the long run, regardless of whether demand increases or decreases, the market price returns to its original level. Is this outcome inevitable? In fact, it is not. It is possible for the equilibrium market price in the long run to remain the same, rise, or fall.

External Economies and Diseconomies

The change in the long-run equilibrium price depends on external economies and external diseconomies. **External economies** are factors beyond the control of an individual firm that lower the firm's costs as the *market* output increases. **External diseconomies** are factors outside the control of a firm that raise the firm's costs as the *market* output increases. With no external economies or external diseconomies, a firm's costs remain constant as the market output changes.

Figure 12.11 illustrates these three cases and introduces a new supply concept: the long-run market supply curve.

A **long-run market supply curve** shows how the quantity supplied in a market varies as the market price varies after all the possible adjustments have been made, including changes in each firm's plant and the number of firms in the market.

Figure 12.11(a) shows the case we have just studied—no external economies or diseconomies. The long-run market supply curve (LS_A) is perfectly elastic. In this case, a permanent increase in demand from D_0 to D_1 has no effect on the price in the long run. The increase in demand brings a temporary increase in price to P_S and in the short run the quantity increases from Q_0 to Q_S. Entry increases short-run supply from S_0 to S_1, which lowers the price from P_S back to P_0 and increases the quantity to Q_1.

Figure 12.11(b) shows the case of external diseconomies. The long-run market supply curve (LS_B) slopes upward. A permanent increase in demand from D_0 to D_1 increases the price in both the short run and the long run. The increase in demand brings a temporary increase in price to P_S and in the short run the quantity increases from Q_0 to Q_S. Entry increases short-run supply from S_0 to S_2, which lowers the price from P_S to P_2 and increases the quantity to Q_2.

One source of external diseconomies is congestion. The airline market provides a good example. With bigger airline market output, congestion at both airports and in the air increases, resulting in longer delays and extra waiting time for passengers and airplanes. These external diseconomies mean that as the output of air transportation services increases (in the absence of technological advances), average cost increases. As a result, the long-run market supply curve is upward sloping. A permanent increase in demand brings an increase in quantity and a rise in the price. (Markets with external diseconomies might nonetheless have a falling price because technological advances shift the long-run supply curve downward.)

Figure 12.11(c) shows the case of external economies. The long-run market supply curve (LS_C) slopes downward. A permanent increase in demand from D_0 to D_1 increases the price in the short run and lowers it in the long run. Again, the increase in demand brings a temporary increase in price to P_S and in the short run the quantity increases from Q_0 to Q_S. Entry increases short-run supply from S_0 to S_3, which lowers the price to P_3 and increases the quantity to Q_3.

An example of external economies is the growth of specialist support services for a market as it expands.

FIGURE 12.11   Long-Run Changes in Price and Quantity

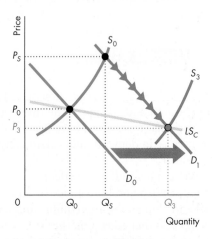

(a) Constant-cost industry

(b) Increasing-cost industry

(c) Decreasing-cost industry

Three possible changes in price and quantity occur in the long run. When demand increases from D_0 to D_1, entry occurs and the market supply curve shifts rightward from S_0 to S_1. In part (a), the long-run market supply curve, LS_A, is horizontal. The quantity increases from Q_0 to Q_1, and the price remains constant at P_0.

In part (b), the long-run market supply curve is LS_B; the price rises to P_2, and the quantity increases to Q_2. This case occurs in industries with external diseconomies. In part (c), the long-run market supply curve is LS_C; the price falls to P_3, and the quantity increases to Q_3. This case occurs in a market with external economies.

As farm output increased in the nineteenth and early twentieth centuries, the services available to farmers expanded. New firms specialized in the development and marketing of farm machinery and fertilizers. As a result, average farm costs decreased. Farms enjoyed the benefits of external economies. As a consequence, as the demand for farm products increased, the output increased but the price fell.

Over the long term, the prices of many goods and services have fallen, not because of external economies but because of technological change. Let's now study this influence on a competitive market.

Technological Change

Industries are constantly discovering lower-cost techniques of production. Most cost-saving production techniques cannot be implemented, however, without investing in new plant and equipment. As a consequence, it takes time for a technological advance to spread through a market. Some firms whose plants are on the verge of being replaced will be quick to adopt the new technology, while other firms whose plants have recently been replaced will continue to operate with an old technology until they can no longer cover their average variable cost. Once average variable cost cannot be covered, a firm will scrap even a relatively new plant (embodying an old technology) in favor of a plant with a new technology.

New technology allows firms to produce at a lower cost. As a result, as firms adopt a new technology, their cost curves shift downward. With lower costs, firms are willing to supply a given quantity at a lower price or, equivalently, they are willing to supply a larger quantity at a given price. In other words, market supply increases, and the market supply curve shifts rightward. With a given demand, the quantity produced increases and the price falls.

Two forces are at work in a market undergoing technological change. Firms that adopt the new technology make an economic profit, so there is entry by new-technology firms. Firms that stick with the old technology incur economic losses. They either exit the market or switch to the new technology.

As old-technology firms disappear and new-technology firms enter, the price falls and the quantity produced increases. Eventually, the market arrives at a long-run equilibrium in which all the firms use the new technology and make a zero economic profit. Because in the long run competition eliminates economic profit, technological change brings only temporary gains to producers. But the lower prices and better products that technological advances bring are permanent gains for consumers.

The process that we've just described is one in which some firms experience economic profits and others experience economic losses. It is a period of dynamic change in a market. Some firms do well, and others do badly. Often, the process has a geographical dimension—the expanding new-technology firms bring prosperity to what was once the boondocks, and traditional industrial regions decline. Sometimes, the new-technology firms are in a foreign country, while the old-technology firms are in the domestic economy. The information revolution of the 1990s produced many examples of changes like these. Commercial banking, which was traditionally concentrated in New York, San Francisco, and other large cities now flourishes in Charlotte, North Carolina, which has become the nation's number three commercial banking city. Television shows and movies, traditionally made in Los Angeles and New York, are now made in large numbers in Orlando.

Technological advances are not confined to the information and entertainment industries. Even food production is undergoing a major technological change because of genetic engineering.

Review Quiz

1   Describe the course of events in a competitive market following a permanent decrease in demand. What happens to output, price, and economic profit in the short run and in the long run?

2   Describe the course of events in a competitive market following a permanent increase in demand. What happens to output, price, and economic profit in the short run and in the long run?

3   Describe the course of events in a competitive market following the adoption of a new technology. What happens to output, price, and economic profit in the short run and in the long run?

 Work Study Plan 12.5 and get instant feedback.

We've seen how a competitive market operates in the short run and the long run, but is a competitive market efficient?

Competition and Efficiency

A competitive market can achieve an efficient use of resources. You first studied efficiency in Chapter 2. Then in Chapter 5, using only the concepts of demand, supply, consumer surplus, and producer surplus, you saw how a competitive market achieves efficiency. Now that you have learned what lies behind the demand and supply curves of a competitive market, you can gain a deeper understanding of the efficiency of a competitive market.

Efficient Use of Resources

Recall that resource use is efficient when we produce the goods and services that people value most highly (see Chapter 2, p. 37 and Chapter 5, p. 110). If someone can become better off without anyone else becoming worse off, resources are *not* being used efficiently. For example, suppose we produce a computer that no one wants and no one will ever use and, at the same time, some people are clamoring for more video games. If we produce fewer computers and reallocate the unused resources to produce more video games, some people will become better off and no one will be worse off. So the initial resource allocation was inefficient.

In the more technical language that you have learned, resource use is efficient when marginal social benefit equals marginal social cost. In the computer and video games example, the marginal social benefit of a video game exceeds its marginal social cost; the marginal social cost of a computer exceeds its marginal social benefit. So by producing fewer computers and more video games, we move resources toward a higher-valued use.

Choices, Equilibrium, and Efficiency

We can use what you have learned about the decisions made by consumers and competitive firms and market equilibrium to describe an efficient use of resources.

Choices Consumers allocate their budgets to get the most value possible out of them. We derive a consumer's demand curve by finding how the best budget allocation changes as the price of a good changes. So consumers get the most value out of their resources at all points along their demand curves. If the people who consume a good or service are the only ones who benefit from it, then the market demand curve measures the benefit to the entire society and is the marginal social benefit curve.

Competitive firms produce the quantity that maximizes profit. We derive the firm's supply curve by finding the profit-maximizing quantity at each price. So firms get the most value out of their resources at all points along their supply curves. If the firms that produce a good or service bear all the costs of producing it, then the market supply curve measures the marginal cost to the entire society and the market supply curve is the marginal social cost curve.

Equilibrium and Efficiency Resources are used efficiently when marginal social benefit equals marginal social cost. Competitive equilibrium achieves this efficient outcome because for consumers, price equals marginal social benefit, and for producers, price equals marginal social cost.

The gains from trade are the sum of consumer surplus and producer surplus. The gains from trade for consumers are measured by *consumer surplus*, which is the area below the demand curve and above the price paid. (See Chapter 5, p. 111.) The gains from trade for producers are measured by *producer surplus*, which is the area above the supply curve and below the price received. (See Chapter 5, p. 113.) The total gains from trade are the sum of consumer surplus and producer surplus. When the market for a good or service is in equilibrium, the gains from trade are maximized.

Illustrating an Efficient Allocation Figure 12.12 illustrates the efficiency of perfect competition in long-run equilibrium. Part (a) shows the individual firm, and part (b) shows the market. The equilibrium market price is P^*. At that price, each firm makes zero economic profit and each firm has the plant that enables it to produce at the lowest possible average total cost. Consumers are as well off as possible because the good cannot be produced at a lower cost and the price equals that least possible cost.

In part (b), consumers get the most out of their resources at all points on the market demand curve, $D = MSB$. Consumer surplus is the green area. Producers get the most out of their resources at all points on the market supply curve, $S = MSC$. Producer surplus is the blue area. Resources are used efficiently at the quantity Q^* and price P^*. At this point, marginal social benefit equals marginal social

FIGURE 12.12 Efficiency of Perfect Competition

(a) A single firm

(b) A market

In part (a), a firm in perfect competition produces at the lowest possible long-run average total cost at q^*. In part (b), consumers have made the best available choices and are on the market demand curve and firms are producing at least cost and are on the market supply curve. With no external benefits or external costs, resources are used efficiently at the quantity Q^* and the price P^*. Perfect competition achieves an efficient use of resources.

myeconlab   animation

cost, and total surplus (the sum of producer surplus and consumer surplus) is maximized.

When firms in perfect competition are away from long-run equilibrium, either entry or exit is taking place and the market is moving toward the situation depicted in Figure 12.12. But the market is still efficient. As long as marginal social benefit (on the market demand curve) equals marginal social cost (on the market supply curve), the market is efficient. But it is only in long-run equilibrium that consumers pay the lowest possible price.

You've now completed your study of perfect competition. *Reading Between the Lines* on pp. 292–293 gives you an opportunity to use what you have learned to understand the recent exit of small airlines from the U.S. airline market.

Although many markets approximate the model of perfect competition, many do not. In Chapter 13, we study markets at the opposite extreme of market power: monopoly. Then we'll study markets that lie between perfect competition and monopoly. In Chapter 14, we study monopolistic competition and in Chapter 15 we study oligopoly. When you have completed this study, you'll have a tool kit that will enable you to understand the variety of real-world markets.

Review Quiz

1 State the conditions that must be met for resources to be allocated efficiently.
2 Describe the choices that consumers make and explain why consumers are efficient on the market demand curve.
3 Describe the choices that producers make and explain why producers are efficient on the market supply curve.
4 Explain why resources are used efficiently in a competitive market.

myeconlab   Work Study Plan 12.6 and get instant feedback.

Airlines Exit

Fuel Costs, Economy Down 3 Airlines

http://www.washingtontimes.com
April 9, 2008

The loss of three airlines in little more than a week is prompting warnings from financial analysts that the worst is not over for the industry or its passengers.

Rising fuel prices and a slow economy mean higher expenses but fewer passengers. ATA Airlines, Aloha Airlines and Skybus Airlines all succumbed recently to that fatal combination.

The next airline expected to go belly up is Champion Air, a Bloomington, Minn., charter service that operates 14 Boeing 727 aircraft.

"Unfortunately, our business model is no longer viable in a world of $110 oil, a struggling economy and rapidly changing demand for our services," Chief Executive Officer Lee Steele said in announcing the airline's planned May 31 closure. …

Airlines already are starting to raise prices to cover their higher fuel costs—a risky business move that could reduce demand for tickets.

High fuel costs leave them few choices, analysts said. …

Major carriers, like Northwest Airlines and Delta Air Lines, are stepping in to absorb some of the defunct airlines' routes. …

In a bankruptcy filing Monday in U.S. Bankruptcy Court for the District of Delaware, Skybus Chief Financial Officer Barry Barnard said his airline failed largely because of high fuel prices and a "recession" that reduced demand for flights.

Essence of the Story

- High fuel prices and lower demand have put three airlines (ATA Airlines, Aloha Airlines and Skybus Airlines) out of business.

- Champion Air, a Bloomington, Minn., airline is also expected to go out of business.

- Airlines are raising prices to cover their higher fuel costs.

- Higher prices will decrease the quantity of tickets sold.

- Major carriers (Northwest Airlines and Delta Air Lines) are filling the gaps left by the exit of the three airlines.

Economic Analysis

- The market for air travel is not *perfectly* competitive but it is highly competitive and the perfect competition model provides insights into that market.

- In 2008, airlines were being squeezed by rising costs and falling demand.

- Figure 1 shows an airline's cost and revenue curves.

- Initially an airline's average total cost curve is ATC_0 and its marginal cost curve is MC_0.

- Figure 2 shows the market for air transportation services.

- Initially the demand curve is D_0 and the supply curve is S_0. The equilibrium price is $100 a trip.

- Airlines face a marginal revenue curve, MR, in Fig. 1 and maximize profit by producing 50 trips per day. Economic profit is zero. The market is in long-run equilibrium.

- Two events disturb this long-run equilibrium: (1) In what the news article calls a "slow economy," incomes stop growing and people decide to cut back on their air travel plans; and (2) fuel costs rocket upward.

- The "slow economy" decreases the demand for air travel and the demand curve shifts leftward to D_1.

- The rise in fuel prices increases the airline's costs.

- The airline's average total cost shifts upward to ATC_1 and the marginal cost curve shifts upward to MC_1.

- The increase in marginal cost decreases supply and the market supply curve shifts leftward to S_1.

- The market comes to a new equilibrium. The quantity decreases but (in this example) the price doesn't change.

- The combination of no change in price and a rise in costs results in the airlines incurring an economic loss.

- As the loss persists, some airlines exit.

- When airlines exit (not shown in the figures), market supply decreases, the price rises, and the airlines remaining in the industry (like Northwest and Delta in the news article) increase production.

- Eventually, exit stops and the market returns to long-run equilibrium but at a higher price.

Figure 1 An airline's cost and revenue curves

Figure 2 The market for air travel

293

SUMMARY

Key Points

What Is Perfect Competition? (pp. 274–275)

- In perfect competition, many firms sell identical products to many buyers; there are no restrictions on entry; and sellers and buyers are well informed about prices.
- A perfectly competitive firm is a price taker.
- A perfectly competitive firm's marginal revenue always equals the market price.

The Firm's Output Decision (pp. 276–279)

- The firm produces the output at which marginal revenue (price) equals marginal cost.
- In short-run equilibrium, a firm can make an economic profit, incur an economic loss, or break even.
- If price is less than minimum average variable cost, the firm temporarily shuts down.
- At prices below minimum average variable cost, a firm's supply curve runs along the y-axis; at prices above minimum average variable cost, a firm's supply curve is its marginal cost curve.

Output, Price, and Profit in the Short Run

(pp. 280–283)

- The market supply curve shows the sum of the quantities supplied by each firm at each price.
- Market demand and market supply determine price.
- A firm might make a positive economic profit, a zero economic profit, or incur an economic loss.

Output, Price, and Profit in the Long Run

(pp. 283–285)

- Economic profit induces entry and economic loss induces exit.
- Entry increases supply and lowers price and profit. Exit decreases supply and raises price and profit.
- In long-run equilibrium, economic profit is zero. There is no entry or exit.

Changing Tastes and Advancing Technology

(pp. 286–289)

- A permanent decrease in demand leads to a smaller market output and a smaller number of firms. A permanent increase in demand leads to a larger market output and a larger number of firms.
- The long-run effect of a change in demand on price depends on whether there are external economies (the price falls) or external diseconomies (the price rises) or neither (the price remains constant).
- New technologies increase supply and in the long run lower the price and increase the quantity.

Competition and Efficiency (pp. 290–291)

- Resources are used efficiently when we produce goods and services in the quantities that people value most highly.
- When there are no external benefits and external costs, perfect competition achieves an efficient allocation. In long-run equilibrium, consumers pay the lowest possible price and marginal social benefit equals marginal social cost.

Key Figures

Key Terms

PROBLEMS and APPLICATIONS ◆

myeconlab Work problems 1–10 in Chapter 12 Study Plan and get instant feedback.
Work problems 11–18 as Homework, a Quiz, or a Test if assigned by your instructor.

1. Lin's fortune cookies are identical to the fortune cookies made by dozens of other firms, and there is free entry in the fortune cookie market. Buyers and sellers are well informed about prices.
   a. In what type of market does Lin's operate?
   b. What determines the price of fortune cookies?
   c. What determines Lin's marginal revenue of fortune cookies?
   d. If fortune cookies sell for $10 a box and Lin offers his cookies for sale at $10.50 a box, how many boxes does he sell?
   e. If fortune cookies sell for $10 a box and Lin offers his cookies for sale at $9.50 a box, how many boxes does he sell?
   f. What is the elasticity of demand for Lin's fortune cookies and how does it differ from the elasticity of the market demand for fortune cookies?

2. Pat's Pizza Kitchen is a price taker. Its costs are

Output (pizzas per hour)	Total cost (dollars per hour)
0	10
1	21
2	30
3	41
4	54
5	69

   a. Calculate Pat's profit-maximizing output and economic profit if the market price is
      (i) $14 a pizza.
      (ii) $12 a pizza.
      (iii) $10 a pizza.
   b. What is Pat's shutdown point and what is Pat's economic profit if it shuts down temporarily?
   c. Derive Pat's supply curve.
   d. At what price will firms with costs identical to Pat's exit the pizza market in the long run?
   e. At what price will firms with costs identical to Pat's enter the pizza market in the long run?

3. The market is perfectly competitive and there are 1,000 firms that produce paper. The table sets out the market demand schedule for paper.

Price (dollars per box)	Quantity demanded (thousands of boxes per week)
3.65	500
5.20	450
6.80	400
8.40	350
10.00	300
11.60	250
13.20	200

Each producer of paper has the following costs when it uses its least-cost plant:

Output (boxes per week)	Marginal cost (dollars per additional box)	Average variable cost (dollars per box)	Average total cost (dollars per box)
200	6.40	7.80	12.80
250	7.00	7.00	11.00
300	7.65	7.10	10.43
350	8.40	7.20	10.06
400	10.00	7.50	10.00
450	12.40	8.00	10.22
500	20.70	9.00	11.00

   a. What is the market price of paper?
   b. What is the market's output?
   c. What is the output produced by each firm?
   d. What is the economic profit made or economic loss incurred by each firm?
   e. Do firms have an incentive to enter or exit the paper market in the long run?
   f. What is the number of firms in the long run?
   g. What is the market price in the long run?
   h. What is the equilibrium quantity of paper produced in the long run?

4. **Never Pay Retail Again**
   Not only has scouring the Web for the best possible price become standard protocol before buying a big-ticket item, but more consumers are employing creative strategies for scoring hot deals. ... Comparison shopping, haggling and swapping discount codes are all becoming mainstream marks of savvy shoppers ... online shoppers can check a comparison service like Price Grabber before making a purchase. ...
   CNN, May 30, 2008

a. Explain the effect of the Internet on the degree of competition in the market.

b. Explain how the Internet influences market efficiency.

5. As the quality of computer monitors improves, more people are reading documents online rather than printing them out. The demand for paper permanently decreases and the demand schedule becomes

Price (dollars per box)	Quantity demanded (thousands of boxes per week)
2.95	500
4.13	450
5.30	400
6.48	350
7.65	300
8.83	250
10.00	200
11.18	150

If each firm producing paper has the costs set out in problem 3,

a. What is the market price, market output, and economic profit or loss of each firm?

b. What is the long-run equilibrium price, market output, and economic profit or loss of each firm?

c. Does this market experience external economies, external diseconomies, or constant cost? Illustrate by drawing the long-run supply curve.

6. **Fuel Prices Could Squeeze Cheap Flights**

Continental has eliminated service to airports big and small all across the nation. … The money-losing airline market is scrapping its least-fuel efficient flights in step with the dramatic increases in energy costs. … Airlines are having difficulty keeping prices low for flights … especially as fuel prices keep rising. … Airlines have continually raised—or tried to raise—fares this year to make up for the fuel costs. … American Airlines increased its fuel surcharge by $20 a roundtrip. American had raised fares just days earlier—an increase that was matched by Delta Air Lines Inc. and UAL Corp.'s United Airlines and Continental—but retracted the increase. … United said it would start charging $15 for the first checked bag. … This follows an earlier announcement from American, which plans to begin charging $15 for the first checked bag. …

CNN, June 12, 2008

a. Explain how an increase in fuel prices might cause an airline to change its output (number of flights) in the short run.

b. Draw a graph to show the increase in fuel prices on an airline's output in the short run.

c. Explain why an airline might incur an economic loss in the short run as fuel prices rise.

d. If some airlines decide to exit the market, explain how the economic profit or loss of the remaining airlines will change.

7. **Coors Brewing Expanding Plant**

Coors Brewing Co. of Golden will expand its Virginia packaging plant at a cost of $24 million. The addition will accommodate a new production line that will bottle mostly Coors Light. … It also will bottle beer faster. … Coors Brewing employs roughly 470 people at its Virginia plant. The expanded packaging line will add another eight jobs.

Denver Business Journal, January 6, 2006

a. How will Coors' expansion of a plant change the firm's marginal cost curve and short-run supply curve?

b. What does this expansion decision imply about the point on Coors' *LRAC* curve at which the firm was before the expansion?

c. If other breweries follow the lead of Coors, what will happen to the market price of beer?

d. How will the adjustment that you have described in c influence the economic profit of Coors and other beer producers?

8. In a perfectly competitive market in long-run equilibrium can

a. Consumer surplus be increased?

b. Producer surplus be increased?

c. A consumer become better off by making a substitution away from this market?

d. The average total cost be reduced?

9. Explain and illustrate graphically how the growing world population is influencing the world market for wheat and a representative individual wheat farmer.

10. Explain and illustrate graphically how the diaper service market has been affected by the decrease in the North American birth rate and the development of disposable diapers.

11. The market demand schedule for smoothies is

Price (dollars per smoothie)	Quantity demanded (smoothies per hour)
1.90	1,000
2.00	950
2.20	800
2.91	700
4.25	550
5.25	400
5.50	300

The market is perfectly competitive, and each firm has the following costs when it uses its least-cost plant:

Output (smoothies per hour)	Marginal cost (dollars per additional smoothie)	Average variable cost (dollars per smoothie)	Average total cost (dollars per smoothie)
3	2.50	4.00	7.33
4	2.20	3.53	6.03
5	1.90	3.24	5.24
6	2.00	3.00	4.67
7	2.91	2.91	4.34
8	4.25	3.00	4.25
9	8.00	3.33	4.44

There are 100 smoothie sellers in the market.
a. What is the market price of a smoothie?
b. What is the market quantity of smoothies?
c. How many smoothies does each firm sell?
d. What is the economic profit made or economic loss incurred by each firm?
e. Do firms enter or exit the market in the long run?
f. What is the market price and the equilibrium quantity in the long run?

12. **Money in the Tank**

In Marietta, where the road hugs the Susquehanna River, a Rutter's Farm Store gas station stands on one side, a Sheetz gas station on the other. Kelly Bosley, who manages Rutter's, doesn't even have to look across the highway to know when Sheetz changes its price for a gallon of gas. When Sheetz raises prices, her own pumps are busy. When Sheetz lowers prices, she has not a car in sight. ... You think you feel helpless at the pump? Bosley makes a living selling gas—and even she has little control over what it costs.

The Mining Journal, May 24, 2008

a. Describe the elasticity of demand that each of these gas stations faces.

b. Why does each of these gas stations have so little control over the price of the gasoline they sell?
c. How do these gas stations decide how much gasoline to make available for sale?

13. Quick Copy is one of many copy shops near campus. The figure shows Quick Copy's costs.

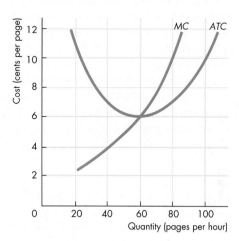

If the market price of copying a page is 10 cents, calculate Quick Copy's
a. Marginal revenue.
b. Profit-maximizing output.
c. Economic profit.

14. **Cadillac Plant Shuts Down Temporarily, Future Uncertain**

Delta Truss in Cadillac [Michigan] is shutting down in what [its] parent company, Pro-Build, calls "temporarily discontinuing truss production." Workers fear this temporary shut down will become permanent. About 60 people work at Delta Truss when it's in peak season. Right now, about 20 people work there. ... A corporate letter ... says "we are anticipating resuming production at these plants when the spring business begins."

9&10 News, February 18, 2008

a. Explain how the shutdown decision will affect Delta Truss' *TFC*, *TVC*, and *TC*.
b. Under what conditions would this shutdown decision maximize Delta Truss' economic profit (or minimize its loss)?
c. Under what conditions will Delta Truss start producing again?
d. Under what conditions will Delta Truss make the shutdown permanent and exit the market?

15. **Exxon Mobil Selling All Its Gas Stations to Distributors**

Exxon Mobil Corp. said Thursday it's getting out of the retail gasoline business, following other major oil companies. ... "As the highly competitive fuels marketing business in the U.S. continues to evolve, we believe this transition is the best way for Exxon Mobil to compete and grow in the future," said Ben Soraci, the director of Exxon Mobil's U.S. retail sales. Exxon Mobil is not alone among Big Oil exiting the retail gas business, a market where profits have gotten tougher as crude oil prices have risen. ... Station owners say they're struggling to turn a profit on gas because while wholesale gasoline prices have risen sharply, ... they've been unable to raise pump prices fast enough to keep pace.

Houston Chronicle, June 12, 2008

a. Is Exxon Mobil making a shutdown or exit decision in the retail gasoline market?
b. Under what conditions will this decision maximize Exxon Mobil's economic profit?
c. How might this decision by Exxon Mobil affect the economic profit made by other firms that sell retail gasoline?

16. **Another DVD Format, but This One Says It's Cheaper**

No sooner has the battle for the next-generation high definition DVD format ended, with Blu-ray triumphing over HD DVD, than a new contender has emerged. A new system ... called HD VMD ... is trying to find a niche. New Medium Enterprises, the London company behind HD VMD, says its system's quality is equal to Blu-ray's but it costs less. ... While Blu-ray players typically cost more than $300, an HD VMD unit is priced at $199. ... New Medium's price strategy will fail, said Andy Parsons, chairman of the Blu-ray Disc Association, ... because it relies on a false assumption: Blu-ray technology will always be more expensive. "When you mass produce blue lasers in large quantities, hardware costs will absolutely come down," Mr. Parsons said. "I'm sure we'll eventually be able to charge $90 for a Blu-ray player."

The New York Times, March 10, 2008

a. Explain how technological change in Blu-ray production might support Mr. Parson's predictions of lower prices in the long-run and illustrate your explanation with a graph.

b. Even if Blu-ray prices do drop to $90 in the long run, why might the red-laser HD VMD still end up being less expensive at that time?

17. **Cell Phone Sales Hit 1 Billion Mark**

More than 1.15 billion mobile phones were sold worldwide in 2007, a 16 percent increase from the 990.9 million phones sold in 2006. ... "Emerging markets, especially China and India, provided much of the growth as many people bought their first phone," Carolina Milanesi, research director for mobile devices at Gartner, said in a statement. "In mature markets, such as Japan and Western Europe, consumers' appetite for feature-laden phones was met with new models packed with TV tuners, global positioning satellite (GPS) functions, touch screens and high-resolution cameras."

CNET News, February 27, 2008

a. Explain the effects of the global increase in demand for cell phones on the market for cell phones and individual cell-phone producers in the short run.
b. Draw a graph to illustrate your explanation in a.
c. Explain the effects of the global increase in demand for cell phones on the market for cell phones in the long run.
d. What factors will determine whether the price of cell phones will rise, fall, or stay the same in the new long-run equilibrium?

18. Study *Reading Between the Lines* about the U.S. market for air travel on pp. 292–293, and then answer the following questions.

a. What are the features of the market for air travel that make it highly competitive?
b. If the fuel price increase had occurred with no decrease in demand, how would the outcome differ from that on p. 293?
c. Is the news article correct in its remark that it is risky for the airlines to raise prices because that move could reduce the demand for tickets? Explain your answer.
d. Explain how the market for air travel gets back to a long-run equilibrium.
e. Draw a graph to illustrate the market in the new long-run equilibrium.
f. Draw a graph of the cost and revenue curves of an airline to illustrate the situation in the new long-run equilibrium.

13 ◆ Monopoly

After studying this chapter, you will be able to:

- ▪ Explain how monopoly arises and distinguish between single-price monopoly and price-discriminating monopoly

- ▪ Explain how a single-price monopoly determines its output and price

- ▪ Compare the performance and efficiency of single-price monopoly and competition

- ▪ Explain how price discrimination increases profit

- ▪ Explain how monopoly regulation influences output, price, economic profit, and efficiency

Microsoft, Google, and eBay are dominant players in the markets they serve. Because most PCs use Windows, programmers write most applications for this operating system, which attracts more users. Because most Web searchers use Google, most advertisers use it too, which attracts more searchers. Because most online auction buyers use eBay, most online sellers do too, which attracts more buyers. Each of these firms benefits from a phenomenon called a network externality, which makes it hard for other firms to break into their markets.

Microsoft, Google, and eBay are obviously not like firms in perfect competition. How does their behavior compare with perfectly competitive firms? Do they charge prices that are too high and that damage the interests of consumers? What benefits do they bring?

In this chapter, we study markets in which the firm can influence the price. We also compare the performance of the firm in such a market with that in a competitive market and examine whether monopoly is as efficient as competition. In *Reading Between the Lines* at the end of the chapter, we'll take a look at what a European court thinks about some of Microsoft's profit-seeking practices.

Monopoly and How It Arises

A **monopoly** is a market with a single firm that produces a good or service for which no close substitute exists and that is protected by a barrier that prevents other firms from selling that good or service.

How Monopoly Arises

Monopoly arises for two key reasons:

- No close substitute
- Barrier to entry

No Close Substitute If a good has a close substitute, even though only one firm produces it, that firm effectively faces competition from the producers of the substitute. A monopoly sells a good or service that has no good substitute. Tap water and bottled water are close substitutes for drinking, but tap water has no effective substitute for showering or washing a car and a local public utility that supplies tap water is a monopoly.

Barrier to Entry A constraint that protects a firm from potential competitors is called a **barrier to entry**. The three types of barrier to entry are

- Natural
- Ownership
- Legal

Natural Barrier to Entry A natural barrier to entry creates a **natural monopoly**: an industry in which economies of scale enable one firm to supply the entire market at the lowest possible cost. The firms that deliver gas, water, and electricity to our homes are examples of natural monopoly.

In Fig. 13.1 the market demand curve for electric power is *D*, and the long-run average cost curve is *LRAC*. Economies of scale prevail over the entire length of the *LRAC* curve.

One firm can produce 4 million kilowatt-hours at 5 cents a kilowatt-hour. At this price, the quantity demanded is 4 million kilowatt-hours. So if the price was 5 cents, one firm could supply the entire market.

If two firms shared the market equally, it would cost each of them 10 cents a kilowatt-hour to produce a total of 4 million kilowatt-hours.

In conditions like those shown in Fig. 13.1, one firm can supply the entire market at a lower cost than

FIGURE 13.1   Natural Monopoly

The market demand curve for electric power is *D*, and the long-run average cost curve is *LRAC*. Economies of scale exist over the entire *LRAC* curve. One firm can distribute 4 million kilowatt-hours at a cost of 5 cents a kilowatt-hour. This same total output costs 10 cents a kilowatt-hour with two firms. One firm can meet the market demand at a lower cost than two or more firms can. The market is a natural monopoly.

myeconlab   animation

two or more firms can. The market is a natural monopoly.

Ownership Barrier to Entry An ownership barrier to entry occurs if one firm owns a significant portion of a key resource. An example of this type of monopoly occurred during the last century when De Beers controlled up to 90 percent of the world's supply of diamonds. (Today, its share is only 65 percent.)

Legal Barrier to Entry A legal barrier to entry creates a **legal monopoly**: a market in which competition and entry are restricted by the granting of a public franchise, government license, patent, or copyright.

A *public franchise* is an exclusive right granted to a firm to supply a good or service. An example is the U.S. Postal Service, which has the exclusive right to carry first-class mail. A *government license* controls entry into particular occupations, professions, and industries. Examples of this type of barrier to entry occur in medicine, law, dentistry, schoolteaching, architecture, and many other professional services. Licensing does not always create a monopoly, but it does restrict competition.

A *patent* is an exclusive right granted to the inventor of a product or service. A *copyright* is an exclusive right granted to the author or composer of a literary, musical, dramatic, or artistic work. Patents and copyrights are valid for a limited time period that varies from country to country. In the United States, a patent is valid for 20 years. Patents encourage the *invention* of new products and production methods. They also stimulate *innovation*—the use of new inventions—by encouraging inventors to publicize their discoveries and offer them for use under license. Patents have stimulated innovations in areas as diverse as soybean seeds, pharmaceuticals, memory chips, and video games.

Natural Monopoly Today
Information-Age Monopolies

Information-age technologies have created four big natural monopolies. These firms have large plant costs but almost zero marginal cost, so they experience economies of scale.

Microsoft has captured 90 percent of the personal computer operating system market with Windows and 73 percent of the Web browser market with Internet Explorer. eBay has captured 85 percent of the consumer-to-consumer Internet auction market and Google has 78 percent of the search engine market.

New technologies also destroy monopoly. FedEx, UPS, the fax machine, and e-mail have weakened the monopoly of the U.S. Postal Service; and the satellite dish has weakened the monopoly of cable television companies.

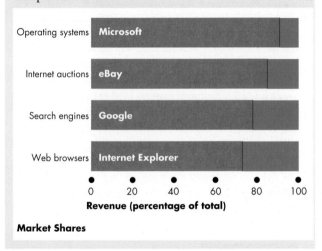

Market Shares

Monopoly Price-Setting Strategies

A major difference between monopoly and competition is that a monopoly sets its own price. In doing so, the monopoly faces a market constraint: To sell a larger quantity, the monopoly must set a lower price. There are two monopoly situations that create two pricing strategies;

- Single price
- Price discrimination

Single Price A **single-price monopoly** is a firm that must sell each unit of its output for the same price to all its customers. De Beers sells diamonds (of a given size and quality) for the same price to all its customers. If it tried to sell at a low price to some customers and at a higher price to others, only the low-price customers would buy from De Beers. Others would buy from De Beers' low-price customers. De Beers is a *single-price* monopoly.

Price Discrimination When a firm practices **price discrimination**, it sells different units of a good or service for different prices. Many firms price discriminate. Microsoft sells its Windows and Office software at different prices to different buyers. Computer manufacturers who install the software on new machines, students and teachers, governments, and businesses all pay different prices. Pizza producers offer a second pizza for a lower price than the first one. These are examples of *price discrimination*.

When a firm price discriminates, it looks as though it is doing its customers a favor. In fact, it is charging the highest possible price for each unit sold and making the largest possible profit.

Review Quiz

1 How does monopoly arise?
2 How does a natural monopoly differ from a legal monopoly?
3 Distinguish between a price-discriminating monopoly and a single-price monopoly.

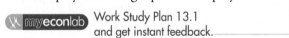 Work Study Plan 13.1 and get instant feedback.

We start with a single-price monopoly and see how it makes its decisions about the quantity to produce and the price to charge to maximize its profit.

A Single-Price Monopoly's Output and Price Decision

To understand how a single-price monopoly makes its output and price decision, we must first study the link between price and marginal revenue.

Price and Marginal Revenue

Because in a monopoly there is only one firm, the demand curve facing the firm is the market demand curve. Let's look at Bobbie's Barbershop, the sole supplier of haircuts in Cairo, Nebraska. The table in Fig. 13.2 shows the market demand schedule. At a price of $20, Bobbie sells no haircuts. The lower the price, the more haircuts per hour she can sell. For example, at $12, consumers demand 4 haircuts per hour (row E).

Total revenue (*TR*) is the price (*P*) multiplied by the quantity sold (*Q*). For example, in row *D*, Bobbie sells 3 haircuts at $14 each, so total revenue is $42. *Marginal revenue* (*MR*) is the change in total revenue (ΔTR) resulting from a one-unit increase in the quantity sold. For example, if the price falls from $16 (row *C*) to $14 (row *D*), the quantity sold increases from 2 to 3 haircuts. Total revenue increases from $32 to $42, so the change in total revenue is $10. Because the quantity sold increases by 1 haircut, marginal revenue equals the change in total revenue and is $10. Marginal revenue is placed between the two rows to emphasize that marginal revenue relates to the *change* in the quantity sold.

Figure 13.2 shows the market demand curve and marginal revenue curve (*MR*) and also illustrates the calculation we've just made. Notice that at each level of output, marginal revenue is less than price—the marginal revenue curve lies below the demand curve. Why is marginal revenue *less* than price? It is because when the price is lowered to sell one more unit, two opposing forces affect total revenue. The lower price results in a revenue loss, and the increased quantity sold results in a revenue gain. For example, at a price of $16, Bobbie sells 2 haircuts (point *C*). If she lowers the price to $14, she sells 3 haircuts and has a revenue gain of $14 on the third haircut. But she now receives only $14 on the first two—$2 less than before. As a result, she loses $4 of revenue on the first 2 haircuts. To calculate marginal revenue, she must deduct this amount from the revenue gain of $14. So her marginal revenue is $10, which is less than the price.

FIGURE 13.2   Demand and Marginal Revenue

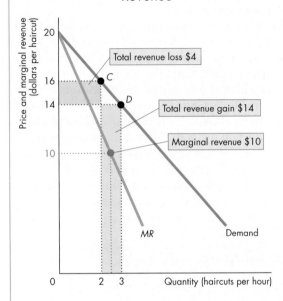

	Price (P) (dollars per haircut)	Quantity demanded (Q) (haircuts per hour)	Total revenue (TR = P × Q) (dollars)	Marginal revenue (MR = ΔTR/ΔQ) (dollars per haircut)
A	20	0	0	
				18
B	18	1	18	
				14
C	16	2	32	
				10
D	14	3	42	
				6
E	12	4	48	
				2
F	10	5	50	

The table shows the demand schedule. Total revenue (*TR*) is price multiplied by quantity sold. For example, in row *C*, the price is $16 a haircut, Bobbie sells 2 haircuts, and total revenue is $32. Marginal revenue (*MR*) is the change in total revenue that results from a one-unit increase in the quantity sold. For example, when the price falls from $16 to $14 a haircut, the quantity sold increases by 1 haircut and total revenue increases by $10. Marginal revenue is $10. The demand curve and the marginal revenue curve, *MR*, are based on the numbers in the table and illustrate the calculation of marginal revenue when the price falls from $16 to $14 a haircut.

Marginal Revenue and Elasticity

A single-price monopoly's marginal revenue is related to the *elasticity of demand* for its good. The demand for a good can be *elastic* (the elasticity is greater than 1), *inelastic* (the elasticity is less than 1), or *unit elastic* (the elasticity is equal to 1). Demand is *elastic* if a 1 percent fall in price brings a greater than 1 percent increase in the quantity demanded. Demand is *inelastic* if a 1 percent fall in price brings a less than 1 percent increase in the quantity demanded. Demand is *unit elastic* if a 1 percent fall in price brings a 1 percent increase in the quantity demanded. (See Chapter 4, pp. 86–87.)

If demand is elastic, a fall in price brings an increase in total revenue—the revenue gain from the increase in quantity sold outweighs the revenue loss from the lower price—and marginal revenue is *positive*. If demand is inelastic, a fall in price brings a decrease in total revenue—the revenue gain from the increase in quantity sold is outweighed by the revenue loss from the lower price—and marginal revenue is *negative*. If demand is unit elastic, total revenue does not change—the revenue gain from the increase in the quantity sold offsets the revenue loss from the lower price—and marginal revenue is *zero*. (See Chapter 4, p. 90.)

Figure 13.3 illustrates the relationship between marginal revenue, total revenue, and elasticity. As the price gradually falls from $20 to $10 a haircut, the quantity demanded increases from 0 to 5 haircuts an hour. Over this output range, marginal revenue is positive in part (a), total revenue increases in part (b), and the demand for haircuts is elastic. As the price falls from $10 to $0 a haircut, the quantity of haircuts demanded increases from 5 to 10 an hour. Over this output range, marginal revenue is negative in part (a), total revenue decreases in part (b), and the demand for haircuts is inelastic. When the price is $10 a haircut, marginal revenue is zero in part (a), total revenue is at a maximum in part (b), and the demand for haircuts is unit elastic.

In Monopoly, Demand Is Always Elastic

The relationship between marginal revenue and elasticity of demand that you've just discovered implies that a profit-maximizing monopoly never produces an output in the inelastic range of the market demand curve. If it did so, it could charge a higher price, produce a smaller quantity, and increase its profit. Let's now look at a monopoly's price and output decision.

FIGURE 13.3   Marginal Revenue and Elasticity

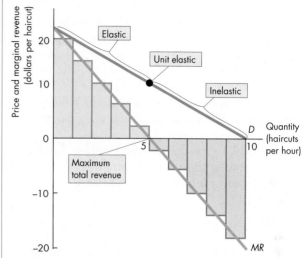

(a) Demand and marginal revenue curves

(b) Total revenue curve

In part (a), the demand curve is *D* and the marginal revenue curve is *MR*. In part (b), the total revenue curve is *TR*. Over the range 0 to 5 haircuts an hour, a price cut increases total revenue, so marginal revenue is positive—as shown by the blue bars. Demand is elastic. Over the range 5 to 10 haircuts an hour, a price cut decreases total revenue, so marginal revenue is negative—as shown by the red bars. Demand is inelastic. At 5 haircuts an hour, total revenue is maximized and marginal revenue is zero. Demand is unit elastic.

myeconlab animation

Price and Output Decision

A monopoly sets its price and output at the levels that maximize economic profit. To determine this price and output level, we need to study the behavior of both cost and revenue as output varies. A monopoly faces the same types of technology and cost constraints as a competitive firm, so its costs (total cost, average cost, and marginal cost) behave just like those of a firm in perfect competition. And a monopoly's revenues (total revenue, price, and marginal revenue) behave in the way we've just described.

Table 13.1 provides information about Bobbie's costs, revenues, and economic profit, and Fig. 13.4 shows the same information graphically.

Maximizing Economic Profit You can see in Table 13.1 and Fig. 13.4(a) that total cost (*TC*) and total revenue (*TR*) both rise as output increases, but *TC* rises at an increasing rate and *TR* rises at a decreasing rate. Economic profit, which equals *TR* minus *TC*, increases at small output levels, reaches a maximum, and then decreases. The maximum profit ($12) occurs when Bobbie sells 3 haircuts for $14 each. If she sells 2 haircuts for $16 each or 4 haircuts for $12 each, her economic profit will be only $8.

Marginal Revenue Equals Marginal Cost You can see Bobbie's marginal revenue (*MR*) and marginal cost (*MC*) in Table 13.1 and Fig. 13.4(b).

When Bobbie increases output from 2 to 3 haircuts, *MR* is $10 and *MC* is $6. *MR* exceeds *MC* by $4 and Bobbie's profit increases by that amount. If Bobbie increases output yet further, from 3 to 4 haircuts, *MR* is $6 and *MC* is $10. In this case, *MC* exceeds *MR* by $4, so profit decreases by that amount. When *MR* exceeds *MC*, profit increases if output increases. When *MC* exceeds *MR*, profit increases if output *decreases*. When *MC* equals *MR*, profit is maximized.

Figure 13.4(b) shows the maximum profit as price (on the demand curve *D*) minus average total cost (on the *ATC* curve) multiplied by the quantity produced—the blue rectangle.

Maximum Price the Market Will Bear Unlike a firm in perfect competition, a monopoly influences the price of what it sells. But a monopoly doesn't set the price at the maximum *possible* price. At the maximum possible price, the firm would be able to sell only one unit of output, which in general is less than the profit-maximizing quantity. Rather, a monopoly produces the profit-maximizing quantity and sells that quantity for the highest price it can get.

TABLE 13.1   A Monopoly's Output and Price Decision

Price (P) (dollars per haircut)	Quantity demanded (Q) (haircuts per hour)	Total revenue (TR = P × Q) (dollars)	Marginal revenue (MR = ΔTR/ΔQ) (dollars per haircut)	Total cost (TC) (dollars)	Marginal cost (MC = ΔTC/ΔQ) (dollars per haircut)	Profit (TR − TC) (dollars)
20	0	0		20		−20
			18		1	
18	1	18		21		−3
			14		3	
16	2	32		24		+8
			10		6	
14	3	42		30		+12
			6		10	
12	4	48		40		+8
			2		15	
10	5	50		55		−5

This table gives the information needed to find the profit-maximizing output and price. Total revenue (*TR*) equals price multiplied by the quantity sold. Profit equals total revenue minus total cost (*TC*). Profit is maximized when 3 haircuts are sold at a price of $14 each. Total revenue is $42, total cost is $30, and economic profit is $12 ($42 − $30).

FIGURE 13.4 A Monopoly's Output and Price

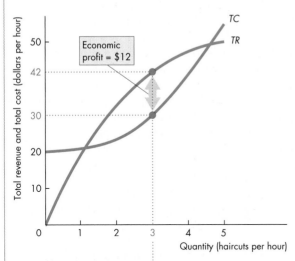

(a) Total revenue and total cost curves

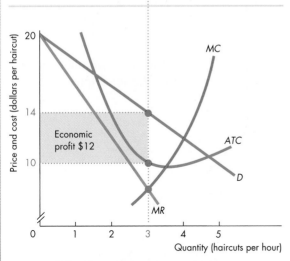

(b) Demand and marginal revenue and cost curves

In part (a), economic profit is the vertical distance equal to total revenue (*TR*) minus total cost (*TC*) and it is maximized at 3 haircuts an hour. In part (b), economic profit is maximized when marginal cost (*MC*) equals marginal revenue (*MR*). The profit-maximizing output is 3 haircuts an hour. The price is determined by the demand curve (*D*) and is $14 a haircut. The average total cost of a haircut is $10, so economic profit, the blue rectangle, is $12—the profit per haircut ($4) multiplied by 3 haircuts.

 animation

All firms maximize profit by producing the output at which marginal revenue equals marginal cost. For a competitive firm, price equals marginal revenue, so price also equals marginal cost. For a monopoly, price exceeds marginal revenue, so price also exceeds marginal cost.

A monopoly charges a price that exceeds marginal cost, but does it always make an economic profit? In Fig. 13.4(b), Bobbie produces 3 haircuts an hour. Her average total cost is $10 (on the *ATC* curve) and her price is $14 (on the *D* curve), so her profit per haircut is $4 ($14 minus $10). Bobbie's economic profit is shown by the area of the blue rectangle, which equals the profit per haircut ($4) multiplied by the number of haircuts (3), for a total of $12.

If firms in a perfectly competitive industry make a positive economic profit, new firms enter. That does *not* happen in monopoly. Barriers to entry prevent new firms from entering the market, so a monopoly can make a positive economic profit and might continue to do so indefinitely. Sometimes that economic profit is large, as in the international diamond business.

Bobbie makes a positive economic profit. But suppose that Bobbie's landlord increases the rent on her salon. If Bobbie pays an additional $12 an hour for rent, her fixed cost increases by $12 an hour. Her marginal cost and marginal revenue don't change, so her profit-maximizing output remains at 3 haircuts an hour. Her profit decreases by $12 an hour to zero. If Bobbie's salon rent increases by more than $12 an hour, she incurs an economic loss. If this situation were permanent, Bobbie would go out of business.

Review Quiz

1 What is the relationship between marginal cost and marginal revenue when a single-price monopoly maximizes profit?
2 How does a single-price monopoly determine the price it will charge its customers?
3 What is the relationship between price, marginal revenue, and marginal cost when a single-price monopoly is maximizing profit?
4 Why can a monopoly make a positive economic profit even in the long run?

myeconlab Work Study Plan 13.2 and get instant feedback.

Single-Price Monopoly and Competition Compared

Imagine an industry that is made up of many small firms operating in perfect competition. Then imagine that a single firm buys out all these small firms and creates a monopoly.

What will happen in this industry? Will the price rise or fall? Will the quantity produced increase or decrease? Will economic profit increase or decrease? Will either the original competitive situation or the new monopoly situation be efficient?

These are the questions we're now going to answer. First, we look at the effects of monopoly on the price and quantity produced. Then we turn to the questions about efficiency.

Comparing Price and Output

Figure 13.5 shows the market we'll study. The market demand curve is D. The demand curve is the same regardless of how the industry is organized. But the supply side and the equilibrium are different in monopoly and competition. First, let's look at the case of perfect competition.

Perfect Competition Initially, with many small perfectly competitive firms in the market, the market supply curve is S. This supply curve is obtained by summing the supply curves of all the individual firms in the market.

In perfect competition, equilibrium occurs where the supply curve and the demand curve intersect. The price is P_C, and the quantity produced by the industry is Q_C. Each firm takes the price P_C and maximizes its profit by producing the output at which its own marginal cost equals the price. Because each firm is a small part of the total industry, there is no incentive for any firm to try to manipulate the price by varying its output.

Monopoly Now suppose that this industry is taken over by a single firm. Consumers do not change, so the market demand curve remains the same as in the case of perfect competition. But now the monopoly recognizes this demand curve as a constraint on the price at which it can sell its output. The monopoly's marginal revenue curve is MR.

The monopoly maximizes profit by producing the quantity at which marginal revenue equals marginal cost. To find the monopoly's marginal cost curve, first

recall that in perfect competition, the industry supply curve is the sum of the supply curves of the firms in the industry. Also recall that each firm's supply curve is its marginal cost curve (see Chapter 12, p. 279). So when the industry is taken over by a single firm, the competitive industry's supply curve becomes the monopoly's marginal cost curve. To remind you of this fact, the supply curve is also labeled MC.

The output at which marginal revenue equals marginal cost is Q_M. This output is smaller than the competitive output Q_C. And the monopoly charges the price P_M, which is higher than P_C. We have established that

> Compared to a perfectly competitive industry, a single-price monopoly produces a smaller output and charges a higher price.

We've seen how the output and price of a monopoly compare with those in a competitive industry. Let's now compare the efficiency of the two types of market.

FIGURE 13.5   Monopoly's Smaller Output and Higher Price

A competitive industry produces the quantity Q_C at price P_C. A single-price monopoly produces the quantity Q_M at which marginal revenue equals marginal cost and sells that quantity for the price P_M. Compared to perfect competition, a single-price monopoly produces a smaller output and charges a higher price.

Efficiency Comparison

Perfect competition (with no external costs and benefits) is efficient. Figure 13.6(a) illustrates the efficiency of perfect competition and serves as a benchmark against which to measure the inefficiency of monopoly. Along the demand curve and marginal social benefit curve ($D = MSB$), consumers are efficient. Along the supply curve and marginal social cost curve ($S = MSC$), producers are efficient. In competitive equilibrium, the price is P_C, the quantity is Q_C, and marginal social benefit equals marginal social cost.

Consumer surplus is the green triangle under the demand curve and above the equilibrium price (see Chapter 5, p. 111). *Producer surplus* is the blue area above the supply curve and below the equilibrium price (see Chapter 5, p. 113). The sum of the consumer surplus and producer surplus is maximized.

Also, in long-run competitive equilibrium, entry and exit ensure that each firm produces its output at the minimum possible long-run average cost.

To summarize: At the competitive equilibrium, marginal social benefit equals marginal social cost; the sum of consumer surplus and producer surplus is maximized; firms produce at the lowest possible long-run average cost; and resource use is efficient.

Figure 13.6(b) illustrates the inefficiency of monopoly and the sources of that inefficiency. A monopoly produces Q_M and sells its output for P_M. The smaller output and higher price drive a wedge between marginal social benefit and marginal social cost and create a *deadweight loss*. The gray triangle shows the deadweight loss and its magnitude is a measure of the inefficiency of monopoly.

Consumer surplus shrinks for two reasons. First, consumers lose by having to pay more for the good. This loss to consumers is a gain for monopoly and increases the producer surplus. Second, consumers lose by getting less of the good, and this loss is part of the deadweight loss.

Although the monopoly gains from a higher price, it loses some producer surplus because it produces a smaller output. That loss is another part of the deadweight loss.

A monopoly produces a smaller output than perfect competition and faces no competition, so it does not produce at the minimum possible long-run average cost. As a result, monopoly damages the consumer interest in three ways: A monopoly produces less, increases the cost of production, and raises the price by more than the increased cost of production.

FIGURE 13.6   Inefficiency of Monopoly

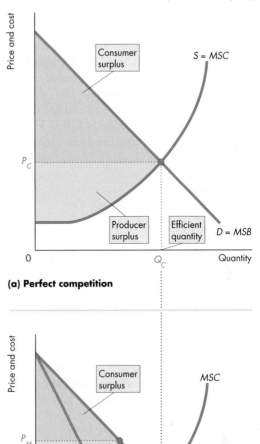

(a) Perfect competition

(b) Monopoly

In perfect competition in part (a), output is Q_C and the price is P_C. Marginal social benefit (*MSB*) equals marginal social cost (*MSC*); consumer surplus (the green triangle) plus producer surplus (the blue area) is maximized; and in the long run, firms produce at the lowest possible average cost. Monopoly in part (b) produces Q_M and raises the price to P_M. Consumer surplus shrinks, the monopoly gains, and a deadweight loss (the gray triangle) arises.

Redistribution of Surpluses

You've seen that monopoly is inefficient because marginal social benefit exceeds marginal social cost and there is deadweight loss—a social loss. But monopoly also brings a *redistribution* of surpluses.

Some of the lost consumer surplus goes to the monopoly. In Fig. 13.6, the monopoly takes the difference between the higher price, P_M, and the competitive price, P_C, on the quantity sold, Q_M. So the monopoly takes the part of the consumer surplus. This portion of the loss of consumer surplus is not a loss to society. It is redistribution from consumers to the monopoly producer.

Rent Seeking

You've seen that monopoly creates a deadweight loss and is inefficient. But the social cost of monopoly can exceed the deadweight loss because of an activity called rent seeking. Any surplus—consumer surplus, producer surplus, or economic profit—is called **economic rent**. And **rent seeking** is the pursuit of wealth by capturing economic rent.

You've seen that a monopoly makes its economic profit by diverting part of consumer surplus to itself—by converting consumer surplus into economic profit. So the pursuit of economic profit by a monopoly is rent seeking. It is the attempt to capture consumer surplus.

Rent seekers pursue their goals in two main ways. They might

- Buy a monopoly
- Create a monopoly

Buy a Monopoly To rent seek by buying a monopoly, a person searches for a monopoly that is for sale at a lower price than the monopoly's economic profit. Trading of taxicab licenses is an example of this type of rent seeking. In some cities, taxicabs are regulated. The city restricts both the fares and the number of taxis that can operate so that operating a taxi results in economic profit. A person who wants to operate a taxi must buy a license from someone who already has one. People rationally devote time and effort to seeking out profitable monopoly businesses to buy. In the process, they use up scarce resources that could otherwise have been used to produce goods and services. The value of this lost production is part of the social cost of monopoly. The amount paid for a

monopoly is not a social cost because the payment is just a transfer of an existing producer surplus from the buyer to the seller.

Create a Monopoly Rent seeking by creating a monopoly is mainly a political activity. It takes the form of lobbying and trying to influence the political process. Such influence might be sought by making campaign contributions in exchange for legislative support or by indirectly seeking to influence political outcomes through publicity in the media or more direct contacts with politicians and bureaucrats. An example of a monopoly created in this way is the government-imposed restrictions on the quantities of textiles that may be imported into the United States. Another is a regulation that limits the number of oranges that may be sold in the United States. These are regulations that restrict output and increase price.

This type of rent seeking is a costly activity that uses up scarce resources. Taken together, firms spend billions of dollars lobbying Congress, state legislators, and local officials in the pursuit of licenses and laws that create barriers to entry and establish a monopoly.

Rent-Seeking Equilibrium

Barriers to entry create monopoly. But there is no barrier to entry into rent seeking. Rent seeking is like perfect competition. If an economic profit is available, a new rent seeker will try to get some of it. And competition among rent seekers pushes up the price that must be paid for a monopoly, to the point at which the rent seeker makes zero economic profit by operating the monopoly. For example, competition for the right to operate a taxi in New York City leads to a price of more than $100,000 for a taxi license, which is sufficiently high to eliminate the economic profit made by a taxi operator.

Figure 13.7 shows a rent-seeking equilibrium. The cost of rent seeking is a fixed cost that must be added to a monopoly's other costs. Rent seeking and rent-seeking costs increase to the point at which no economic profit is made. The average total cost curve, which includes the fixed cost of rent seeking, shifts upward until it just touches the demand curve. Economic profit is zero. It has been lost in rent seeking.

Consumer surplus is unaffected, but the deadweight loss from monopoly is larger. The deadweight loss now includes the original deadweight loss triangle plus the lost producer surplus, shown by the enlarged gray area in Fig. 13.7.

FIGURE 13.7   Rent-Seeking Equilibrium

With competitive rent seeking, a monopoly uses all its economic profit to maintain its monopoly. The firm's rent-seeking costs are fixed costs. They add to total fixed cost and to average total cost. The ATC curve shifts upward until, at the profit-maximizing price, the firm breaks even.

X myeconlab   animation

Review Quiz

1 Why does a single-price monopoly produce a smaller output and charge more than the price that would prevail if the industry were perfectly competitive?

2 How does a monopoly transfer consumer surplus to itself?

3 Why is a single-price monopoly inefficient?

4 What is rent seeking and how does it influence the inefficiency of monopoly?

X myeconlab   Work Study Plan 13.3 and get instant feedback.

So far, we've considered only a single-price monopoly. But many monopolies do not operate with a single price. Instead, they price discriminate. Let's now see how a price-discriminating monopoly works.

Price Discrimination

You encounter *price discrimination*—selling a good or service at a number of different prices—when you travel, go to the movies, get your hair cut, buy pizza, or visit an art museum or theme park. Many of the firms that price discriminate are not monopolies, but monopolies price discriminate when they can do so.

To be able to price discriminate, a firm must be able to identify and separate different buyer types and sell a product that cannot be resold.

Not all price *differences* are price *discrimination*. Some goods that are similar have different prices because they have different costs of production. For example, the price per ounce of cereal is lower if you buy your cereal in a big box than if you buy individual serving size boxes. This price difference reflects a cost difference and is not price discrimination.

At first sight, price discrimination appears to be inconsistent with profit maximization. Why would a movie theater allow children to see movies at a discount? Why would a hairdresser charge students and senior citizens less? Aren't these firms losing profit by being nice to their customers?

Capturing Consumer Surplus

Price discrimination captures consumer surplus and converts it into economic profit. It does so by getting buyers to pay a price as close as possible to the maximum willingness to pay.

Firms price discriminate in two broad ways. They discriminate:

■ Among groups of buyers
■ Among units of a good

Discriminating Among Groups of Buyers People differ in the values they place on a good—their marginal benefit and willingness to pay. Some of these differences are correlated with features such as age, employment status, and other easily distinguished characteristics. When such a correlation is present, firms can profit by price discriminating among the different groups of buyers.

For example, a face-to-face sales meeting with a customer might bring a large and profitable order. So for salespeople and other business travelers, the marginal benefit from a trip is large and the price that such a traveler is willing to pay for a trip is high. In contrast, for a vacation traveler, any of several different trips and even no vacation trip are options. So for vacation travelers, the marginal benefit of a trip is small and the price that such a traveler is willing to pay for a trip is low. Because business travelers are willing to pay more than vacation travelers are, it is possible for an airline to profit by price discriminating between these two groups.

Discriminating Among Units of a Good Everyone experiences diminishing marginal benefit and has a downward-sloping demand curve. For this reason, if all the units of the good are sold for a single price, buyers end up with a consumer surplus equal to the value they get from each unit of the good minus the price paid for it.

A firm that price discriminates by charging a buyer one price for a single item and a lower price for a second or third item can capture some of the consumer surplus. Buy one pizza and get a second one free (or for a low price) is an example of this type of price discrimination.

(Note that some discounts for bulk arise from lower costs of production for greater bulk. In these cases, such discounts are not price discrimination.)

Let's see how price discriminating increases economic profit.

Profiting by Price Discriminating

Global Airlines has a monopoly on an exotic route. Figure 13.8 shows the market demand curve (*D*) for travel on this route. It also shows Global Airline's marginal revenue curve (*MR*), marginal cost curve (*MC*), and average total cost curve (*ATC*).

As a single-price monopoly, Global maximizes profit by producing the quantity at which *MR* equals *MC*, which is 8,000 trips a year, and charging $1,200 per trip. At this quantity, average total cost is $600 per trip, economic profit is $600 a trip, and Global's economic profit is $4.8 million a year, shown by the blue rectangle. Global's customers enjoy a consumer surplus shown by the green triangle.

Global is struck by the fact that many of its customers are business travelers, and it suspects they are willing to pay more than $1,200 a trip. Global does some market research, which reveals that some business travelers are willing to pay as much as $1,800 a trip. Also, these customers frequently change their travel plans at the last minute. Another group of business travelers is willing to pay $1,600. These cus-

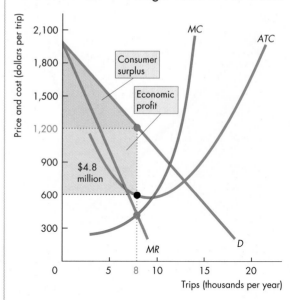

FIGURE 13.8 A Single Price of Air Travel

Global Airlines has a monopoly on an air route. The market demand curve is *D*. Global Airline's marginal revenue curve is *MR*, its marginal cost curve is *MC*, and its average total cost curve is *ATC*. As a single-price monopoly, Global maximizes profit by selling 8,000 trips a year at $1,200 a trip. Its profit is $4.8 million a year—the blue rectangle. Global's customers enjoy a consumer surplus—the green triangle.

myeconlab animation

tomers know a week ahead when they will travel, and they never want to stay over a weekend. Yet another group would pay up to $1,400. These travelers know two weeks ahead when they will travel and also don't want to stay away over a weekend.

Global announces a new fare schedule: no restrictions, $1,800; 7-day advance purchase, nonrefundable, $1,600; 14-day advance purchase, nonrefundable, $1,400; 14-day advance purchase, must stay over a weekend, $1,200.

Figure 13.9 shows the outcome with this new fare structure and also shows why Global is pleased with its new fares. It sells 2,000 seats at each of its four prices. Global's economic profit increases by the dark blue steps. Its economic profit is now its original $4.8 million a year plus an additional $2.4 million from its new higher fares. Consumer surplus shrinks to the sum of the smaller green areas.

FIGURE 13.9   Price Discrimination

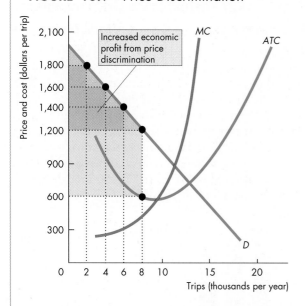

Global revises its fare structure: no restrictions at $1,800, 7-day advance purchase at $1,600, 14-day advance purchase at $1,400, and must stay over a weekend at $1,200. Global sells 2,000 trips at each of its four new fares. Its economic profit increases by $2.4 million a year to $7.2 million a year, which is shown by the original blue rectangle plus the dark blue steps. Global's customers' consumer surplus shrinks.

myeconlab animation

Perfect Price Discrimination

Perfect price discrimination occurs if a firm is able to sell each unit of output for the highest price anyone is willing to pay for it. In such a case, the entire consumer surplus is eliminated and captured by the producer. To practice perfect price discrimination, a firm must be creative and come up with a host of prices and special conditions, each one of which appeals to a tiny segment of the market.

With perfect price discrimination, something special happens to marginal revenue—the market demand curve becomes the marginal revenue curve. The reason is that when the price is cut to sell a larger quantity, the firm sells only the marginal unit at the lower price. All the other units continue to be sold for the highest price that each buyer is willing to pay. So for the perfect price discriminator, marginal revenue *equals* price and the demand curve becomes the marginal revenue curve.

With marginal revenue equal to price, Global can obtain even greater profit by increasing output up to the point at which price (and marginal revenue) is equal to marginal cost.

So Global seeks new travelers who will not pay as much as $1,200 a trip but who will pay more than marginal cost. Global offers a variety of vacation specials at different low fares that appeal only to new travelers. Existing customers continue to pay the higher fares. With all these fares and specials, Global increases sales, extracts the entire consumer surplus, and maximizes economic profit.

Figure 13.10 shows the outcome with perfect price discrimination. The fares paid by the original travelers extract the entire consumer surplus from this group. The new fares between $900 and $1,200 attract 3,000 additional travelers and take their entire consumer surplus also. Global now makes an economic profit of more than $9 million.

FIGURE 13.10   Perfect Price Discrimination

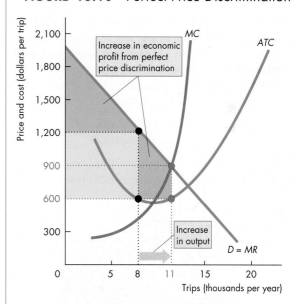

Dozens of fares discriminate among many different types of business traveler, and many new low fares with restrictions appeal to vacation travelers. With perfect price discrimination, the market demand curve becomes Global's marginal revenue curve. Economic profit is maximized when the lowest price equals marginal cost. Global sells 11,000 trips and makes an economic profit of $9.35 million a year.

myeconlab animation

Efficiency and Rent Seeking with Price Discrimination

With perfect price discrimination, output increases to the point at which price equals marginal cost—where the marginal cost curve intersects the demand curve (see Fig. 13.10). This output is identical to that of perfect competition. Perfect price discrimination pushes consumer surplus to zero but increases the monopoly's producer surplus to equal the sum of consumer surplus and producer surplus in perfect competition. With perfect price discrimination, deadweight loss is zero. So perfect price discrimination achieves efficiency.

> The more perfectly the monopoly can price discriminate, the closer its output is to the competitive output and the more efficient is the outcome.

But there are two differences between perfect competition and perfect price discrimination. First, the distribution of the total surplus is different. It is shared by consumers and producers in perfect competition, while the producer gets it all with perfect price discrimination. Second, because the producer grabs all the surplus, rent seeking becomes profitable.

People use resources in pursuit of economic rent, and the bigger the rents, the more resources get used in pursuing them. With free entry into rent seeking, the long-run equilibrium outcome is that rent seekers use up the entire producer surplus.

Real-world airlines are as creative as Global Airlines, as you can see in the cartoon!

You've seen that monopoly is profitable for the monopoly but costly for consumers. It results in inef-

Would it bother you to hear how little I paid for this flight?

From William Hamilton, "Voodoo Economics," © 1992 by The Chronicle Publishing Company, p.3. Reprinted with permission of Chronicle Books.

Attempting Perfect Price Discrimination
How Many Days at Disney World?

If you want to spend a day at Disney World in Orlando, it will cost you $75.62. You can spend a second (consecutive) day for an extra $72.42. A third day will cost you $68.17. But for a fourth day, you'll pay only $9.59 and for a fifth day, $3.20. For more days all the way up to 10, you'll pay only $2.12 a day.

The Disney Corporation hopes that it has read your willingness to pay correctly and not left you with too much consumer surplus. Disney figures though that after three days, your marginal benefit is crashing.

Disney's Ticket Prices

Review Quiz

1 What is price discrimination and how is it used to increase a monopoly's profit?
2 Explain how consumer surplus changes when a monopoly price discriminates.
3 Explain how consumer surplus, economic profit, and output change when a monopoly perfectly price discriminates.
4 What are some of the ways that real-world airlines price discriminate?

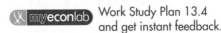 Work Study Plan 13.4 and get instant feedback.

ficiency. Because of these features of monopoly, it is subject to policy debate and regulation. We'll now study the key monopoly policy issues.

Monopoly Regulation

Natural monopoly presents a dilemma. With economies of scale, it produces at the lowest possible cost. But with market power, it has an incentive to raise the price above the competitive price and produce too little—to operate in the self-interest of the monopolist and not in the social interest.

Regulation—rules administered by a government agency to influence prices, quantities, entry, and other aspects of economic activity in a firm or industry—is a possible solution to this dilemma.

To implement regulation, the government establishes agencies to oversee and enforce the rules. For example, the Surface Transportation Board regulates prices on interstate railroads, some trucking and bus lines, and water and oil pipelines. By the 1970s, almost a quarter of the nation's output was produced by regulated industries (far more than just natural monopolies) and a process of deregulation began.

Deregulation is the process of removing regulation of prices, quantities, entry, and other aspects of economic activity in a firm or industry. During the past 30 years, deregulation has occurred in domestic air transportation, telephone service, interstate trucking, and banking and financial services. Cable TV was deregulated in 1984, re-regulated in 1992, and deregulated again in 1996.

Regulation is a possible solution to the dilemma presented by natural monopoly but not a guaranteed solution. There are two theories about how regulation actually works: *the social interest theory* and the *capture theory*.

The **social interest theory** is that the political and regulatory process relentlessly seeks out inefficiency and introduces regulation that eliminates deadweight loss and allocates resources efficiently.

The **capture theory** is that regulation serves the self-interest of the producer, who captures the regulator and maximizes economic profit. Regulation that benefits the producer but creates a deadweight loss gets adopted because the producer's gain is large and visible while each individual consumer's is small and invisible. No individual consumer has an incentive to oppose the regulation but the producer has a big incentive to lobby for it.

We're going to examine efficient regulation that serves the social interest and see why it is not a simple matter to design and implement such regulation.

Efficient Regulation of a Natural Monopoly

A cable TV company is a *natural monopoly*—it can supply the entire market at a lower price than two or more competing firms can. Cox Communications, based in Atlanta, provides cable TV to households in 20 states. The firm has invested heavily in satellite receiving dishes, cables, and control equipment and so has large fixed costs. These fixed costs are part of the firm's average total cost. Its average total cost decreases as the number of households served increases because the fixed cost is spread over a larger number of households.

Unregulated, Cox produces the quantity that maximizes profit. Like all single-price monopolies, the profit-maximizing quantity is less than the efficient quantity, and underproduction results in a deadweight loss.

How can Cox be regulated to produce the efficient quantity of cable TV service? The answer is by being regulated to set its price equal to marginal cost, known as the **marginal cost pricing rule**. The quantity demanded at a price equal to marginal cost is the efficient quantity—the quantity at which marginal benefit equals marginal cost.

Figure 13.11 illustrates the marginal cost pricing rule. The demand curve for cable TV is *D*. Cox's marginal cost curve is *MC*. That marginal cost curve is (assumed to be) horizontal at $10 per household per month—that is, the cost of providing each additional household with a month of cable programming is $10. The efficient outcome occurs if the price is regulated at $10 per household per month with 10 million households served.

But there is a problem: At the efficient output, average total cost exceeds marginal cost, so a firm that uses marginal cost pricing incurs an economic loss. A cable TV company that is required to use a marginal cost pricing rule will not stay in business for long. How can the firm cover its costs and, at the same time, obey a marginal cost pricing rule?

There are two possible ways of enabling the firm to cover its costs: price discrimination and a two-part price (called a *two-part tariff*).

For example, local telephone companies charge consumers a monthly fee for being connected to the telephone system and then charge a price equal to marginal cost (zero) for each local call. A cable TV operator can charge a one-time connection fee that covers its fixed cost and then charge a monthly fee equal to marginal cost.

FIGURE 13.11   Regulating a Natural Monopoly

A natural monopoly cable TV supplier faces the demand curve *D*. The firm's marginal cost is constant at $10 per household per month, as shown by the curve labeled *MC*. The long-run average cost curve is *LRAC*.

Unregulated, as a profit-maximizer, the firm serves 5 million households at a price of $60 a month. An efficient marginal cost pricing rule sets the price at $10 a month. The monopoly serves 10 million households and incurs an economic loss. A second-best average cost pricing rule sets the price at $30 a month. The monopoly serves 8 million households and earns zero economic profit.

 animation

Second-Best Regulation of a Natural Monopoly

A natural monopoly cannot always be regulated to achieve an efficient outcome. Two possible ways of enabling a regulated monopoly to avoid an economic loss are

- Average cost pricing
- Government subsidy

Average Cost Pricing The **average cost pricing rule** sets price equal to average total cost. With this rule the firm produces the quantity at which the average

total cost curve cuts the demand curve. This rule results in the firm making zero economic profit—breaking even. But because for a natural monopoly average total cost exceeds marginal cost, the quantity produced is less than the efficient quantity and a deadweight loss arises.

Figure 13.11 illustrates the average cost pricing rule. The price is $30 a month and 8 million households get cable TV.

Government Subsidy A government subsidy is a direct payment to the firm equal to its economic loss. To pay a subsidy, the government must raise the revenue by taxing some other activity. You saw in Chapter 6 that taxes themselves generate deadweight loss.

And the Second-Best Is ... Which is the better option, average cost pricing or marginal cost pricing with a government subsidy? The answer depends on the relative magnitudes of the two deadweight losses. Average cost pricing generates a deadweight loss in the market served by the natural monopoly. A subsidy generates deadweight losses in the markets for the items that are taxed to pay for the subsidy. The smaller deadweight loss is the second-best solution to regulating a natural monopoly. Making this calculation in practice is too difficult and average cost pricing is generally preferred to a subsidy.

Implementing average cost pricing presents the regulator with a challenge because it is not possible to be sure what a firm's costs are. So regulators use one of two practical rules:

- Rate of return regulation
- Price cap regulation

Rate of Return Regulation Under **rate of return regulation**, a firm must justify its price by showing that its return on capital doesn't exceed a specified target rate. This type of regulation can end up serving the self-interest of the firm rather than the social interest. The firm's managers have an incentive to inflate costs by spending on items such as private jets, free baseball tickets (disguised as public relations expenses), and lavish entertainment. Managers also have an incentive to use more capital than the efficient amount. The rate of return on capital is regulated but not the total return on capital, and the greater the amount of capital, the greater is the total return.

Price Cap Regulation For the reason that we've just examined, rate of return regulation is increasingly being replaced by price cap regulation. A **price cap regulation** is a price ceiling—a rule that specifies the highest price the firm is permitted to set. This type of regulation gives a firm an incentive to operate efficiently and keep costs under control. Price cap regulation has become common for the electricity and telecommunications industries and is replacing rate of return regulation.

To see how a price cap works, let's suppose that the cable TV operator is subject to this type of regulation. Figure 13.12 shows that without regulation, the firm maximizes profit by serving 5 million households and charging a price of $60 a month. If a price cap is set at $30 a month, the firm is permitted to sell

any quantity it chooses at that price or at a lower price. At 5 million households, the firm now incurs an economic loss. It can decrease the loss by increasing output to 8 million households. To increase output above 8 million households, the firm would have to lower the price and again it would incur a loss. So the profit-maximizing quantity is 8 million households—the same as with average cost pricing.

Notice that a price cap lowers the price and increases output. This outcome is in sharp contrast to the effect of a price ceiling in a competitive market that you studied in Chapter 6 (pp. 130–132). The reason is that in a monopoly, the unregulated equilibrium output is less than the competitive equilibrium output, and the price cap regulation replicates the conditions of a competitive market.

In Fig. 13.12, the price cap delivers average cost pricing. In practice, the regulator might set the cap too high. For this reason, price cap regulation is often combined with *earnings sharing regulation*—a regulation that requires firms to make refunds to customers when profits rise above a target level.

FIGURE 13.12 Price Cap Regulation

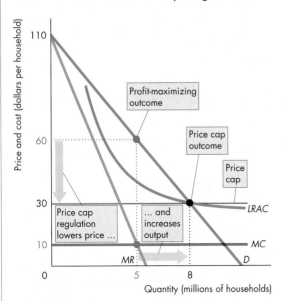

A natural monopoly cable TV supplier faces the demand curve D. The firm's marginal cost is constant at $10 per household per month, as shown by the curve labeled MC. The long-run average cost curve is LRAC.

Unregulated, the firm serves 5 million households at a price of $60 a month. A price cap sets the maximum price at $30 a month. The firm has an incentive to minimize cost and serve the quantity of households that demand service at the price cap. The price cap regulation lowers the price and increases the quantity.

 animation

Review Quiz

1 What is the pricing rule that achieves an efficient outcome for a regulated monopoly? What is the problem with this rule?
2 What is the average cost pricing rule? Why is it not an efficient way of regulating monopoly?
3 What is a price cap? Why might it be a more effective way of regulating monopoly than rate of return regulation?
4 Compare the consumer surplus, producer surplus, and deadweight loss that arise from average cost pricing with those that arise from profit-maximization pricing and marginal cost pricing.

myeconlab Work Study Plan 13.5 and get instant feedback.

◆ You've now completed your study of monopoly. *Reading Between the Lines* on pp. 316–317 looks at Microsoft's near monopoly in PC operating systems and a court challenge the firm faced in Europe. In the next chapter, we study markets that lie between the extremes of perfect competition and monopoly and that blend elements of the two.

European View of Microsoft

European Court Faults Microsoft On Competition

http://www.nytimes.com
September 18, 2007

Europe's second-highest court delivered a stinging rebuke to Microsoft Monday, ... [for] adding a digital media player to Windows, undercutting the early leader, Real Networks.

It also ordered Microsoft to ... share confidential computer code with competitors. The court also upheld the record fine levied against the company, 497.2 million euros ($689.4 million).

But the court decision comes as the center of gravity in computing is shifting away from the software for personal computers, Microsoft's stronghold. Increasingly, the e-mailing or word-processing functions of a computer can be performed with software delivered on a Web browser. Other devices like cell phones are now used as alternates to personal computers.

The real challenge to Microsoft, after more than a decade of dominating the technology industry, is coming not from the government, but from the marketplace. ...

[T]he Justice Department issued a statement expressing its concerns with the European decision, saying that tough restraints on powerful companies can be harmful. Thomas O. Barnett, assistant attorney general for the department's antitrust division, said that the effect "rather than helping consumers, may have the unfortunate consequence of harming consumers by chilling innovation and discouraging competition."

Consumer welfare, not protecting competitors, should be the guiding standard in antitrust, Mr. Barnett said. ...

In the United States, the Justice Department chose to settle the Microsoft antitrust case in 2001 without challenging the company's freedom to put whatever it wants in its operating system. ...

Essence of the Story

- A European court fined Microsoft $689 million for competing with Real Networks by adding a digital media player to Windows, and the court ordered Microsoft to share its code with competitors.

- The market, not government, is Microsoft's main challenge because the emphasis is shifting from PC software to software delivered on a Web browser, and to cell phone software.

- The U.S. Justice Department did not challenge Microsoft's right to put whatever it wants in Windows and says that consumer welfare, not protecting competitors, should be the guide.

Economic Analysis

- Microsoft's operating system, Windows, enables the hardware of a PC to accept and execute instructions from word processors, spreadsheets, Web browsers, media players, and a host of other applications.

- In addition to creating the operating system for a PC, Microsoft develops and sells applications, the most famous of which are contained in its Office package (Word, Excel, Outlook, and PowerPoint).

- Other applications created by Microsoft are the Web browser, Internet Explorer, and a digital media player, Windows Media Player (the subject of the European court's decision).

- In the market for PC operating systems, Microsoft has a near monopoly.

- In the markets for applications, Microsoft faces stiff competition from other producers. The stiffest competition comes from the Internet.

- In 1994, a firm called Mosaic Communications launched the first easy-to-use Web browser, Netscape.

- A year later, RealNetworks, Inc., launched its Real video and audio players.

- These two developments led to a rapid growth of Internet activity and left Microsoft behind the curve.

- PC users now needed Microsoft Windows, the Netscape browser, and the RealPlayer to enjoy the full scope of the Internet.

- Microsoft could have stood still and marketed Windows in its 1995 stripped-down form.

- If Microsoft had followed this strategy, it would have faced the market described in Fig. 1.

- As a profit-maximizing firm, Microsoft would have produced 20 million copies of Windows a year and sold them for $115 a copy.

- Instead, Microsoft improved Windows and added its own Web browser and media player.

- With a higher-value package, Microsoft faced the market shown in Fig. 2.

- Microsoft maximized profit by producing 20 million copies of Windows a year and selling them for $230 a copy.

- Microsoft's profit increased, but so did the consumer surplus of Windows users.

- As the U.S. Justice Department noted, limiting the actions of a monopoly doesn't always help the consumer.

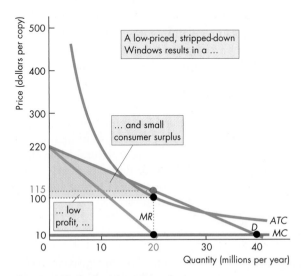

Figure 1 Windows stripped down

Figure 2 Windows with bells and whistles

317

SUMMARY

Key Points

Monopoly and How It Arises (pp. 300–301)

- A monopoly is an industry with a single supplier of a good or service that has no close substitutes and in which barriers to entry prevent competition.
- Barriers to entry may be legal (public franchise, license, patent, copyright, firm owns control of a resource) or natural (created by economies of scale).
- A monopoly might be able to price discriminate when there is no resale possibility.
- Where resale is possible, a firm charges one price.

A Single-Price Monopoly's Output and Price Decision (pp. 302–305)

- A monopoly's demand curve is the market demand curve and a single-price monopoly's marginal revenue is less than price.
- A monopoly maximizes profit by producing the output at which marginal revenue equals marginal cost and by charging the maximum price that consumers are willing to pay for that output.

Single-Price Monopoly and Competition Compared (pp. 306–309)

- A single-price monopoly charges a higher price and produces a smaller quantity than a perfectly competitive industry.

- A single-price monopoly restricts output and creates a deadweight loss.
- The total loss that arises from monopoly equals the deadweight loss plus the cost of the resources devoted to rent seeking.

Price Discrimination (pp. 309–312)

- Price discrimination converts consumer surplus into economic profit.
- Perfect price discrimination extracts the entire consumer surplus; each unit is sold for the maximum price that each consumer is willing to pay; the quantity produced is the efficient quantity.
- Rent seeking with perfect price discrimination might eliminate the entire consumer surplus and producer surplus.

Monopoly Regulation (pp. 313–315)

- Monopoly regulation might serve the social interest or the interest of the monopoly (the regulator being captured).
- Price equal to marginal cost achieves efficiency but results in economic loss.
- Price equal to average cost enables the firm to cover its cost but is inefficient.
- Rate of return regulation creates incentives for inefficient production and inflated cost.
- Price cap regulation with earnings share regulation can achieve a more efficient outcome than rate of return regulation.

Key Figures and Table

Key Terms

Average cost pricing rule, 314
Barriers to entry, 300
Capture theory, 313
Deregulation, 313
Economic rent, 308
Legal monopoly, 300

Marginal cost pricing rule, 313
Monopoly, 300
Natural monopoly, 300
Perfect price discrimination, 311
Price cap regulation, 315
Price discrimination, 301

Rate of return regulation, 314
Regulation, 313
Rent seeking, 308
Single-price monopoly, 301
Social interest theory, 313

PROBLEMS and APPLICATIONS

 Work problems 1–9 in Chapter 13 Study Plan and get instant feedback.
Work problems 10–17 as Homework, a Quiz, or a Test if assigned by your instructor.

1. The United States Postal Service has a monopoly on non-urgent First Class Mail and the exclusive right to put mail in private mailboxes. Pfizer Inc. makes LIPITOR, a prescription drug that lowers cholesterol. Cox Communications is the sole provider of cable television service in some parts of San Diego.
   a. What are the substitutes, if any, for the goods and services described above?
   b. What are the barriers to entry, if any, that protect these three firms from competition?
   c. Which of these three firms, if any, is a natural monopoly? Explain your answer and illustrate it by drawing an appropriate figure.
   d. Which of these three firms, if any, is a legal monopoly? Explain your answer.
   e. Which of these three firms are most likely to be able to profit from price discrimination and which are most likely to sell their good or service for a single price?

2. **Barbie's Revenge: Brawl over Doll is Heading to Trial**

   Four years ago, Mattel Inc. exhorted its executives to help save Barbie from a new doll clique called the Bratz. ... Market share was dropping at a "chilling rate," the presentation said. Barbie needed to be more "aggressive, revolutionary, and ruthless." That call to arms has led to a federal courthouse. ... Mattel accuses ... the maker of Bratz, of ... stealing the idea for the pouty-lipped dolls with the big heads. Mattel is trying to seize ownership of the Bratz line, ...
   The Wall Street Journal, May 23, 2008
   a. Before Bratz entered the market, what type of monopoly did Mattel Inc. possess in the market for "the pouty-lipped dolls with the big heads"?
   b. What is the barrier to entry that Mattel might argue should protect it from competition in the market for Barbie dolls?
   c. Explain how the entry of Bratz dolls might be expected to change the demand for Barbie dolls.

3. **Antitrust Inquiry Launched into Intel**

   The Federal Trade Commission has opened a formal probe into whether Intel, the world's largest chipmaker, has used its dominance to illegally stifle its few competitors. The move follows years of complaints from smaller chip rival Advanced Micro Devices. ... Intel is many times larger, holding 80 percent of the microprocessor market. ... In a sign that suggests the chip market remains competitive, Intel said, prices for microprocessors declined by 42.4 percent between 2000 and 2007... "evidence that this industry is fiercely competitive. ..." Intel said.
   The Washington Post, June 7, 2008
   a. Is Intel a monopoly in the chip market?
   b. Evaluate the argument made by Intel that the significant decline in prices is "evidence that this industry is fiercely competitive."

4. Minnie's Mineral Springs, a single-price monopoly, faces the market demand schedule:

Price (dollars per bottle)	Quantity demanded (bottles per hour)
10	0
8	1
6	2
4	3
2	4
0	5

   a. Calculate Minnie's total revenue schedule.
   b. Calculate its marginal revenue schedule.
   c. Draw a graph of the market demand curve and Minnie's marginal revenue curve.
   d. Why is Minnie's marginal revenue less than the price?
   e. At what price is Minnie's total revenue maximized?
   f. Over what range of prices is the demand for water from Minnie's Mineral Springs elastic?
   g. Why will Minnie not produce a quantity at which the market demand for water is inelastic?

5. Minnie's Mineral Springs faces the demand schedule in problem 4 and has the following total cost schedule:

Quantity produced (bottles per hour)	Total cost (dollars)
0	1
1	3
2	7
3	13
4	21
5	31

a. Calculate the marginal cost of producing each output listed in the table.
b. Calculate Minnie's profit-maximizing output and price.
c. Calculate the economic profit.

6. La Bella Pizza can produce a pizza for a marginal cost of $2. Its standard price is $15 a pizza. It offers a second pizza for $5. It also distributes coupons that give a $5 rebate on a standard-price pizza.
a. How can La Bella Pizza make a larger economic profit with this range of prices than it could if it sold every pizza for $15?
b. Draw a graph to illustrate your answer to a.
c. Can you think of a way of increasing La Bella Pizza's economic profit even more?
d. Is La Bella Pizza more efficient than it would be if it charged just one price?

7. **The Saturday-Night Stay Requirement Is on Its Final Approach**
The Saturday-night stay—that pesky and expensive requirement that airlines instituted to ensure that the business traveler pays outrageous airfares if he or she wants to go home to the family for the weekend—has gone the way of the dodo bird. …
Many low-fare carriers, such as Southwest, JetBlue and AirTran, never had the Saturday-night rule. Some of the so-called legacy airlines, including America West and Alaska, have eliminated the restriction. United and American did away with it in response to competition but only on some routes. Still others, including Continental, Delta, US Airways and Northwest, mostly continue to enforce the rule, especially in the markets they dominate. …

Experts and industry spokesmen agree that low-fare carriers are the primary reason legacy airlines are adopting more consumer-friendly fare structures, which include the elimination of the Saturday-night stay, the introduction of one-way and walk-up fares and the general restructuring of its fares. …
Los Angeles Times, August 15, 2004
a. Explain why the opportunity for price discrimination exists for air travel.
b. How does an airline profit from price discrimination?
c. Describe the change in price discrimination in the market for air travel when discount airlines entered the market.
d. Explain the effect of the change in price discrimination when discount airlines entered the market on the price and the quantity of air travel.

8. The figure shows a situation similar to that of Calypso U.S. Pipeline, a firm that operates a natural gas distribution system in the United States. Calypso is a natural monopoly that cannot price discriminate.

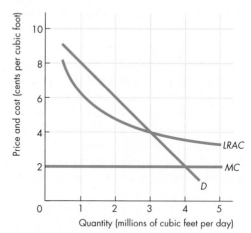

What quantity will Calypso produce and what is the price of natural gas if Calypso is
a. An unregulated profit-maximizing firm?
b. Regulated to make zero economic profit?
c. Regulated to be efficient?

9. In problem 8, what is the producer surplus, consumer surplus, and deadweight loss if Calypso is
a. An unregulated profit-maximizing firm?
b. Regulated to make zero economic profit?
c. Regulated to be efficient?

10. The following list gives some information about seven firms.
   - Coca-Cola cuts its price below that of Pepsi-Cola in an attempt to increase its market share.
   - A single firm, protected by a barrier to entry, produces a personal service that has no close substitutes.
   - A barrier to entry exists, but the good has some close substitutes.
   - A firm offers discounts to students and seniors.
   - A firm can sell any quantity it chooses at the going price.
   - The government issues Nike an exclusive license to produce golf balls.
   - A firm experiences economies of scale even when it produces the quantity that meets the entire market demand.
   a. In which of the seven cases might monopoly arise?
   b. Which of the seven cases are natural monopolies and which are legal monopolies?
   c. Which can price discriminate, which cannot, and why?

11. Hot Air Balloon Rides, a single-price monopoly, has the demand schedule shown in columns 1 and 2 of the table and the total cost schedule shown in columns 2 and 3 of the table:

Price (dollars per ride)	Quantity demanded (rides per month)	Total cost (dollars per month)
220	0	80
200	1	160
180	2	260
160	3	380
140	4	520
120	5	680

   a. Construct Hot Air's total revenue and marginal revenue schedules.
   b. Draw a graph of the demand curve and Hot Air's marginal revenue curve.
   c. Find Hot Air's profit-maximizing output and price and calculate the firm's economic profit.
   d. If the government imposes a tax on Hot Air's profit, how does its output and price change?
   e. If instead of taxing Hot Air's profit, the gov-

ernment imposes a sales tax on balloon rides of $30 a ride, what are the new profit-maximizing quantity, price, and economic profit?

12. The figure illustrates the situation facing the publisher of the only newspaper containing local

news in an isolated community.
   a. On the graph, mark the profit-maximizing quantity and price.
   b. On the graph, show the publisher's total revenue per day.
   c. At the price charged, is the demand for this newspaper elastic or inelastic? Why?
   d. What are consumer surplus and deadweight loss? Mark each on your graph.
   e. Explain why this market might encourage rent seeking.
   f. If this market were perfectly competitive, what would be the quantity, price, consumer surplus, and producer surplus? Mark each on your graph.

13. **Telecoms Look to Grow by Acquisition**
   A multibillion-dollar telecommunications merger announced Thursday … shows how global cellular powerhouses are scouting for growth in emerging economies while consolidating in their own, crowded backyards.
   France Télécom offered Thursday to buy TeliaSonera, a Swedish-Finnish telecommunications operator. … Within hours, TeliaSonera rejected the offer as too low, but analysts said higher bids—either from France Télécom or others—could persuade [TeliaSonera] to accept a deal.

Meanwhile, in the United States, Verizon Wireless, … agreed to buy Alltel for $28.1 billion, a deal that would make the company the biggest mobile phone operator in the country.

A combination of France Télécom and TeliaSonera would create the world's fourth-largest mobile operator … smaller only than China Mobile, Vodafone and Telefónica of Spain.

International Herald Tribune, June 5, 2008

a. Explain the rent seeking behavior of global telecommunications companies.
b. Explain how mergers may affect the efficiency of the telecommunications market.

14. **Zoloft Faces Patent Expiration**

… Pfizer's antidepressant Zoloft, with $3.3 billion in 2005 sales, loses patent protection on June 30. …

When a brand name drug loses its patent, both the price of the drug and the dollar value of its sales each tend to drop about 80 percent over the next year, as competition opens to a host of generic drugmakers. … Some of those lost revenue will go to generic drugmakers. … But the real winners are the patients and the insurers, who pay much lower prices. The Food and Drug Administration insists that generics work identically to brand-names.

CNN, June 15, 2006

a. Assume that Zoloft is the only antidepressant on the market and that price discrimination is not an option. Draw a graph to illustrate the market price and quantity of Zoloft sold.
b. On your graph, identify consumer surplus, producer surplus, and deadweight loss.
c. How might you justify protecting Pfizer from competition with a legal barrier to entry?
d. Explain how the market for an antidepressant drug changes when a patent expires.
e. Draw a graph to illustrate how the expiration of the Zoloft patent will change the price and quantity in the market for antidepressants.
f. Explain how consumer surplus, producer surplus, and deadweight loss change with the expiration of the Zoloft patent.

15. **iSurrender**

… Getting your hands on a new iPhone … [means] signing … a two-year AT&T contract.

… Some markets, because of the sheer costs of being a player, tend toward either a single firm or a small number of firms. … Everyone hoped and thought the wireless market would be different. … A telephone monopoly has been the norm for most of American telecommunication history, except for what may turn out to have been a brief experimental period from 1984 through 2012 or so. … [I]t may be that telephone monopolies in America are a national tradition.

Slate, June 10, 2008

a. How does AT&T being the exclusive provider of wireless service for the iPhone influence the wireless telecommunication market?
b. Explain why the wireless market may "tend toward either a single firm or a small number of firms." Why might this justify allowing a regulated monopoly to exist in this market?

16. **F.C.C. Planning Rules to Open Cable Market**

The Federal Communications Commission is preparing to impose significant new regulations to open the cable television market to independent programmers and rival video services. … The agency is also preparing to adopt a rule this month that would make it easier for independent programmers, which are often small operations, to lease access to cable channels … [and] set a cap on the size of the nation's largest cable companies so that no company could control more than 30 percent of the market. …

The New York Times, November 10, 2007

a. What barriers to entry exist in the cable television market?
b. Are high cable prices evidence of monopoly power?
c. Draw a graph to illustrate the effects of the F.C.C.'s new regulations on the price, quantity, consumer surplus, producer surplus, and deadweight loss.

17. Study *Reading Between the Lines* on pp. 316–317 and then answer the following questions:
a. What does the news article mean when it says that Microsoft's main challenge comes from the marketplace rather than government?
b. How does Microsoft try to raise barriers to the entry of competitors?
c. Compare and contrast the anti-monopoly regulation in Europe with that in the United States.

14 ◆ Monopolistic Competition

After studying this chapter, you will be able to:

- Define and identify monopolistic competition

- Explain how a firm in monopolistic competition determines its price and output in the short run and the long run

- Explain why advertising costs are high and why firms use brand names in a monopolistically competitive industry

Fifty years ago, Wichita, like most places in America, had no pizza restaurants. When Dan Carney opened his first Pizza Hut in a former beer shop, he was a local monopolist. Dan's business grew to become one of the world's largest pizza producers. But the pizza market is highly competitive. Today in Wichita, 185 pizza parlors compete for business. Pizza Hut is still there, but so are Old Chicago, Papa John's, Dmarios, Papa Murphys Take n Bake, Godfathers, Dominos, Cici's, Perfect Pizza, Villa Pizza, Knollas Pizza, Z Pizza, Bellinis Pizzeria, Il Vicino Wood Oven Pizza, Back Alley, and many others.

As you well know, a pizza is not just a pizza. People care about where they buy their pizza. They care about the crust, the sauce, the toppings, the style, and whether it's cooked in a wood-fired oven. The varieties are almost endless.

Because there are many different types of pizza, the market for pizza isn't perfectly competitive. Pizza producers compete, but each has a monopoly on its own special kind of pizza.

Most of the things that you buy are like pizza—they come in many different types. Running shoes and cell phones are two more striking examples.

The model of monopolistic competition that is explained in this chapter helps us to understand the competition that we see every day in the markets for pizza, shoes, cell phones, and for most other consumer goods and services.

Reading Between the Lines, at the end of this chapter, applies the model of monopolistic competition to the market for 3G cell phones and the flurry of activity in that market following the launch of the new iPhone in 2008.

◆ What Is Monopolistic Competition?

You have studied perfect competition, in which a large number of firms produce at the lowest possible cost, make zero economic profit, and are efficient. You've also studied monopoly, in which a single firm restricts output, produces at a higher cost and price than in perfect competition, and is inefficient.

Most real-world markets are competitive but not perfectly competitive, because firms in these markets have some power to set their prices, as monopolies do. We call this type of market *monopolistic competition*.

Monopolistic competition is a market structure in which

- A large number of firms compete.
- Each firm produces a differentiated product.
- Firms compete on product quality, price, and marketing.
- Firms are free to enter and exit the industry.

Large Number of Firms

In monopolistic competition, as in perfect competition, the industry consists of a large number of firms. The presence of a large number of firms has three implications for the firms in the industry.

Small Market Share In monopolistic competition, each firm supplies a small part of the total industry output. Consequently, each firm has only limited power to influence the price of its product. Each firm's price can deviate from the average price of other firms by only a relatively small amount.

Ignore Other Firms A firm in monopolistic competition must be sensitive to the average market price of the product, but the firm does not pay attention to any one individual competitor. Because all the firms are relatively small, no one firm can dictate market conditions, and so no one firm's actions directly affect the actions of the other firms.

Collusion Impossible Firms in monopolistic competition would like to be able to conspire to fix a higher price—called *collusion*. But because the number of firms in monopolistic competition is large, coordination is difficult and collusion is not possible.

Product Differentiation

A firm practices **product differentiation** if it makes a product that is slightly different from the products of competing firms. A differentiated product is one that is a close substitute but not a perfect substitute for the products of the other firms. Some people are willing to pay more for one variety of the product, so when its price rises, the quantity demanded of that variety decreases, but it does not (necessarily) decrease to zero. For example, Adidas, Asics, Diadora, Etonic, Fila, New Balance, Nike, Puma, and Reebok all make differentiated running shoes. If the price of Adidas running shoes rises and the prices of the other shoes remain constant, Adidas sells fewer shoes and the other producers sell more. But Adidas shoes don't disappear unless the price rises by a large enough amount.

Competing on Quality, Price, and Marketing

Product differentiation enables a firm to compete with other firms in three areas: product quality, price, and marketing.

Quality The quality of a product is the physical attributes that make it different from the products of other firms. Quality includes design, reliability, the service provided to the buyer, and the buyer's ease of access to the product. Quality lies on a spectrum that runs from high to low. Some firms—such as Dell Computer Corp.—offer high-quality products. They are well designed and reliable, and the customer receives quick and efficient service. Other firms offer a lower-quality product that is less well designed, that might not work perfectly, and that the buyer must travel some distance to obtain.

Price Because of product differentiation, a firm in monopolistic competition faces a downward-sloping demand curve. So, like a monopoly, the firm can set both its price and its output. But there is a tradeoff between the product's quality and price. A firm that makes a high-quality product can charge a higher price than a firm that makes a low-quality product.

Marketing Because of product differentiation, a firm in monopolistic competition must market its product. Marketing takes two main forms: advertising and packaging. A firm that produces a high-quality product wants to sell it for a suitably high price. To be able to do so, it must advertise and package its product in a way that convinces buyers that they are getting the higher quality for which they are paying a higher price. For example, pharmaceutical companies advertise and package their brand-name drugs to persuade buyers that these items are superior to the lower-priced generic alternatives. Similarly, a low-quality producer uses advertising and packaging to persuade buyers that although the quality is low, the low price more than compensates for this fact.

Entry and Exit

Monopolistic competition has no barriers to prevent new firms from entering the industry in the long run. Consequently, a firm in monopolistic competition cannot make an economic profit in the long run. When existing firms make an economic profit, new firms enter the industry. This entry lowers prices and eventually eliminates economic profit. When firms incur economic losses, some firms leave the industry in the long run. This exit increases prices and eventually eliminates the economic loss.

In long-run equilibrium, firms neither enter nor leave the industry and the firms in the industry make zero economic profit.

Examples of Monopolistic Competition

The box below shows 10 industries that are good examples of monopolistic competition. These industries have a large number of firms (shown in parentheses after the name of the industry). In the most concentrated of these industries, audio and video equipment, the largest 4 firms produce only 30 percent of the industry's total sales and the largest 20 firms produce 75 percent of total sales. The number on the right is the Herfindahl-Hirschman Index. Producers of clothing, jewelry, computers, and sporting goods operate in monopolistic competition.

Review Quiz

1   What are the distinguishing characteristics of monopolistic competition?
2   How do firms in monopolistic competition compete?
3   Provide some examples of industries near your school that operate in monopolistic competition (excluding those in the figure below).

 Work Study Plan 14.1 and get instant feedback.

Monopolistic Competition Today
Almost Everything You Buy

These ten industries operate in monopolistic competition. The number of firms in the industry is shown in parentheses after the name of the industry. The red bars show the percentage of industry sales by the largest 4 firms. The green bars show the percentage of industry sales by the next 4 largest firms, and the blue bars show the percentage of industry sales by the next 12 largest firms. So the entire length of the combined red, green, and blue bars shows the percentage of industry sales by the largest 20 firms. The Herfindahl-Hirschman Index is shown on the right.

Source of data: U.S. Census Bureau.

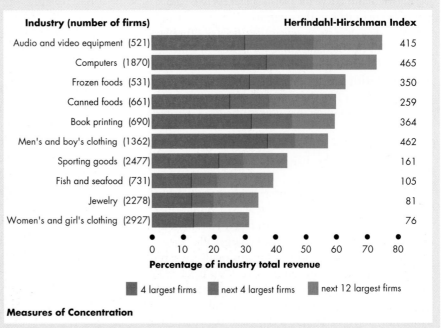

Measures of Concentration

◆ Price and Output in Monopolistic Competition

Suppose you've been hired by VF Corporation, the firm that owns Nautica Clothing Corporation, to manage the production and marketing of Nautica jackets. Think about the decisions that you must make at Nautica. First, you must decide on the design and quality of jackets and on your marketing program. Second, you must decide on the quantity of jackets to produce and the price at which to sell them.

We'll suppose that Nautica has already made its decisions about design, quality, and marketing and now we'll concentrate on the output and pricing decision. We'll study quality and marketing decisions in the next section.

For a given quality of jackets and marketing activity, Nautica faces given costs and market conditions. Given its costs and the demand for its jackets, how does Nautica decide the quantity of jackets to produce and the price at which to sell them?

The Firm's Short-Run Output and Price Decision

In the short run, a firm in monopolistic competition makes its output and price decision just like a monopoly firm does. Figure 14.1 illustrates this decision for Nautica jackets.

The demand curve for Nautica jackets is *D*. This demand curve tells us the quantity of Nautica jackets demanded at each price, given the prices of other jackets. It is not the demand curve for jackets in general.

The *MR* curve shows the marginal revenue curve associated with the demand curve for Nautica jackets. It is derived just like the marginal revenue curve of a single-price monopoly that you studied in Chapter 13.

The *ATC* curve and the *MC* curve show the average total cost and the marginal cost of producing Nautica jackets.

Nautica's goal is to maximize its economic profit. To do so, it produces the output at which marginal revenue equals marginal cost. In Fig. 14.1, this output is 125 jackets a day. Nautica charges the price that buyers are willing to pay for this quantity, which is determined by the demand curve. This price is $75 per jacket. When Nautica produces 125 jackets a day, its average total cost is $25 per jacket and it makes an economic profit of $6,250 a day ($50 per jacket mul-

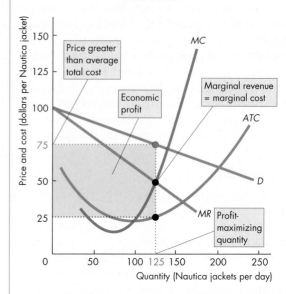

FIGURE 14.1 Economic Profit in the Short Run

Nautica maximizes profit by producing the quantity at which marginal revenue equals marginal cost, 125 jackets a day, and charging the price of $75 a jacket. This price exceeds the average total cost of $25 a jacket, so the firm makes an economic profit of $50 a jacket. The blue rectangle illustrates economic profit, which equals $6,250 a day ($50 a jacket multiplied by 125 jackets a day).

tiplied by 125 jackets a day). The blue rectangle shows Nautica's economic profit.

Profit Maximizing Might Be Loss Minimizing

Figure 14.1 shows that Nautica is earning a large economic profit. But such an outcome is not inevitable. A firm might face a level of demand for its product that is too low for it to make an economic profit.

Excite@Home was such a firm. Offering high-speed Internet service over the same cable that provides television, Excite@Home hoped to capture a large share of the Internet portal market in competition with AOL, MSN, and a host of other providers.

Figure 14.2 illustrates the situation facing Excite@Home in 2001. The demand curve for its portal service is *D*, the marginal revenue curve is *MR*, the average total cost curve is *ATC*, and the marginal cost curve is *MC*. Excite@Home maximized profit—

FIGURE 14.2   Economic Loss in the Short Run

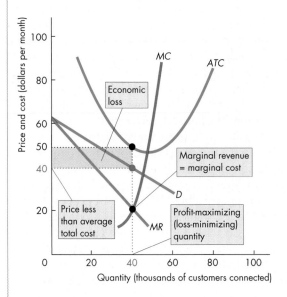

Profit is maximized where marginal revenue equals marginal cost. The loss-minimizing quantity is 40,000 customers. The price of $40 a month is less than the average total cost of $50 a month, so the firm incurs an economic loss of $10 a customer. The red rectangle illustrates economic loss, which equals $400,000 a month ($10 a customer multiplied by 40,000 customers).

equivalently, it minimized its loss—by producing the output at which marginal revenue equals marginal cost. In Fig. 14.2, this output is 40,000 customers. Excite@Home charged the price that buyers were willing to pay for this quantity, which was determined by the demand curve and which was $40 a month. With 40,000 customers, Excite@Home's average total cost was $50 per customer, so it incurred an economic loss of $400,000 a month ($10 a customer multiplied by 40,000 customers). The red rectangle shows Excite@Home's economic loss.

So far, the firm in monopolistic competition looks like a single-price monopoly. It produces the quantity at which marginal revenue equals marginal cost and then charges the price that buyers are willing to pay for that quantity, as determined by the demand curve. The key difference between monopoly and monopolistic competition lies in what happens next when firms either make an economic profit or incur an economic loss.

Long Run: Zero Economic Profit

A firm like Excite@Home is not going to incur an economic loss for long. Eventually, it goes out of business. Also, there is no restriction on entry into monopolistic competition, so if firms in an industry are making economic profit, other firms have an incentive to enter that industry.

As the Gap and other firms start to make jackets similar to those made by Nautica, the demand for Nautica jackets decreases. The demand curve for Nautica jackets and the marginal revenue curve shift leftward. As these curves shift leftward, the profit-maximizing quantity and price fall.

Figure 14.3 shows the long-run equilibrium. The demand curve for Nautica jackets and the marginal revenue curve have shifted leftward. The firm produces 75 jackets a day and sells them for $25 each. At this output level, average total cost is also $25 per jacket.

FIGURE 14.3   Output and Price in the Long Run

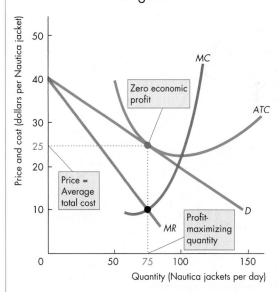

Economic profit encourages entry, which decreases the demand for each firm's product. When the demand curve touches the ATC curve at the quantity at which MR equals MC, the market is in long-run equilibrium. The output that maximizes profit is 75 jackets a day, and the price is $25 per jacket. Average total cost is also $25 per jacket, so economic profit is zero.

myeconlab animation

So Nautica is making zero economic profit on its jackets. When all the firms in the industry are making zero economic profit, there is no incentive for new firms to enter.

If demand is so low relative to costs that firms incur economic losses, exit will occur. As firms leave an industry, the demand for the products of the remaining firms increases and their demand curves shift rightward. The exit process ends when all the firms in the industry are making zero economic profit.

Monopolistic Competition and Perfect Competition

Figure 14.4 compares monopolistic competition and perfect competition and highlights two key differences between them:

- Excess capacity
- Markup

Excess Capacity A firm has **excess capacity** if it produces below its **efficient scale**, which is the quantity at which average total cost is a minimum—the quantity at the bottom of the U-shaped *ATC* curve. In Fig. 14.4, the efficient scale is 100 jackets a day. Nautica (part a) produces 75 Nautica jackets a day and has *excess capacity* of 25 jackets a day. But if all jackets are alike and are produced by firms in perfect competition (part b) each firm produces 100 jackets a day, which is the efficient scale. Average total cost is the lowest possible only in *perfect* competition.

You can see the excess capacity in monopolistic competition all around you. Family restaurants (except for the truly outstanding ones) almost always have some empty tables. You can always get a pizza delivered in less than 30 minutes. It is rare that every pump at a gas station is in use with customers waiting in line. There are always many real estate agents ready to help find or sell a home. These industries are examples of monopolistic competition. The firms

FIGURE 14.4   Excess Capacity and Markup

(a) Monopolistic competition

(b) Perfect competition

The efficient scale is 100 jackets a day. In monopolistic competition in the long run, because the firm faces a downward-sloping demand curve for its product, the quantity produced is less than the efficient scale and the firm has excess capacity. Price exceeds marginal cost by the amount of the markup.

In contrast, because in perfect competition the demand for each firm's product is perfectly elastic, the quantity produced equals the efficient scale and price equals marginal cost. The firm produces at the least possible cost and there is no markup.

myeconlab   animation

have excess capacity. They could sell more by cutting their prices, but they would then incur losses.

Markup A firm's **markup** is the amount by which price exceeds marginal cost. Figure 14.4(a) shows Nautica's markup. In perfect competition, price always equals marginal cost and there is no markup. Figure 14.4(b) shows this case. In monopolistic competition, buyers pay a higher price than in perfect competition and also pay more than marginal cost.

Is Monopolistic Competition Efficient?

Resources are used efficiently when marginal social benefit equals marginal social cost. Price equals marginal social benefit and the firm's marginal cost equals marginal social cost (assuming there are no external benefits or costs). So if the price of a Nautica jacket exceeds the marginal cost of producing it, the quantity of Nautica jackets produced is less than the efficient quantity. And you've just seen that in long-run equilibrium in monopolistic competition, price *does* exceed marginal cost. So is the quantity produced in monopolistic competition less than the efficient quantity?

Making the Relevant Comparison Two economists meet in the street, and one asks the other, "How is your husband?" The quick reply is "Compared to what?" This bit of economic wit illustrates a key point: Before we can conclude that something needs fixing, we must check out the available alternatives.

The markup that drives a gap between price and marginal cost in monopolistic competition arises from product differentiation. It is because Nautica jackets are not quite the same as jackets from Banana Republic, CK, Diesel, DKNY, Earl Jackets, Gap, Levi, Ralph Lauren, or any of the other dozens of producers of jackets that the demand for Nautica jackets is not perfectly elastic. The only way in which the demand for jackets from Nautica might be perfectly elastic is if there is only one kind of jacket and all firms make it. In this situation, Nautica jackets are indistinguishable from all other jackets. They don't even have identifying labels.

If there was only one kind of jacket, the total benefit of jackets would almost certainly be less than it is with variety. People value variety—not only because it enables each person to select what he or she likes best but also because it provides an external benefit. Most of us enjoy seeing variety in the choices of oth-

ers. Contrast a scene from the China of the 1960s, when everyone wore a Mao tunic, with the China of today, where everyone wears the clothes of their own choosing. Or contrast a scene from the Germany of the 1930s, when almost everyone who could afford a car owned a first-generation Volkswagen Beetle, with the world of today with its enormous variety of styles and types of automobiles.

If people value variety, why don't we see infinite variety? The answer is that variety is costly. Each different variety of any product must be designed, and then customers must be informed about it. These initial costs of design and marketing—called setup costs—mean that some varieties that are too close to others already available are just not worth creating.

The Bottom Line Product variety is both valued and costly. The efficient degree of product variety is the one for which the marginal social benefit of product variety equals its marginal social cost. The loss that arises because the quantity produced is less than the efficient quantity is offset by the gain that arises from having a greater degree of product variety. So compared to the alternative—product uniformity—monopolistic competition might be efficient.

Review Quiz

1 How does a firm in monopolistic competition decide how much to produce and at what price to offer its product for sale?
2 Why can a firm in monopolistic competition make an economic profit only in the short run?
3 Why do firms in monopolistic competition operate with excess capacity?
4 Why is there a price markup over marginal cost in monopolistic competition?
5 Is monopolistic competition efficient?

 Work Study Plan 14.2 and get instant feedback.

You've seen how the firm in monopolistic competition determines its output and price in both the short run and the long run when it produces a given product and undertakes a *given* marketing effort. But how does the firm choose its product quality and marketing effort? We'll now study these decisions.

◆ Product Development and Marketing

When Nautica made its price and output decision that we've just studied, it had already made its product quality and marketing decisions. We're now going to look at these decisions and see how they influence the firm's output, price, and economic profit.

Innovation and Product Development

The prospect of new firms entering the industry keeps firms in monopolistic competition on their toes! To enjoy economic profits, they must continually seek ways of keeping one step ahead of imitators—other firms who imitate the success of profitable firms.

One major way of trying to maintain economic profit is for a firm to seek out new products that will provide it with a competitive edge, even if only temporarily. A firm that introduces a new and differentiated product faces a demand that is less elastic and is able to increase its price and make an economic profit. Eventually, imitators will make close substitutes for the innovative product and compete away the economic profit arising from an initial advantage. So to restore economic profit, the firm must again innovate.

Profit-Maximizing Product Innovation The decision to innovate and develop a new or improved product is based on the same type of profit-maximizing calculation that you've already studied.

Innovation and product development are costly activities, but they also bring in additional revenues. The firm must balance the cost and revenue at the margin.

The marginal dollar spent on developing a new or improved product is the marginal cost of product development. The marginal dollar that the new or improved product earns for the firm is the marginal revenue of product development. At a low level of product development, the marginal revenue from a better product exceeds the marginal cost. At a high level of product development, the marginal cost of a better product exceeds the marginal revenue.

When the marginal cost and marginal revenue of product development are equal, the firm is undertaking the profit-maximizing amount of product development.

Efficiency and Product Innovation Is the profit-maximizing amount of product innovation also the efficient amount? Efficiency is achieved if the marginal social benefit of a new and improved product equals its marginal social cost.

The marginal social benefit of an innovation is the increase in price that consumers are willing to pay for it. The marginal social cost is the amount that the firm must pay to make the innovation. Profit is maximized when marginal *revenue* equals marginal cost. But in monopolistic competition, marginal revenue is less than price, so product innovation is probably not pushed to its efficient level.

Monopolistic competition brings many product innovations that cost little to implement and are purely cosmetic, such as new and improved packaging or a new scent in laundry powder. And even when there is a genuine improved product, it is never as good as what the consumer is willing to pay for. For example, "The Legend of Zelda: Twilight Princess" is regarded as an almost perfect and very cool game, but users complain that it isn't quite perfect. It is a game whose features generate a marginal revenue equal to the marginal cost of creating them.

Advertising

A firm with a differentiated product needs to ensure that its customers know how its product is different from the competition. A firm also might attempt to create a consumer perception that its product is different from its competitors, even when that difference is small. Firms use advertising and packaging to achieve this goal.

Advertising Expenditures Firms in monopolistic competition incur huge costs to ensure that buyers appreciate and value the differences between their own products and those of their competitors. So a large proportion of the price that we pay for a good covers the cost of selling it, and this proportion is increasing. Advertising in newspapers and magazines and on radio, television, and the Internet is the main selling cost. But it is not the only one. Selling costs include the cost of shopping malls that look like movie sets, glossy catalogs and brochures, and the salaries, airfares, and hotel bills of salespeople.

Advertising expenditures affect the profits of firms in two ways: They increase costs, and they change demand. Let's look at these effects.

Selling Costs in the United States
The Cost of Selling a Pair of Shoes

When you buy a pair of running shoes that cost you $70, you're paying $9 for the materials from which the shoes are made, $2.75 for the services of the Malaysian worker who made the shoes, and $5.25 for the production and transportation services of a manufacturing firm in Asia and a shipping company. These numbers total $17. You pay $3 to the U.S. government in import duty. So we've now accounted for a total of $20. Where did the other $50 go? It is the cost of advertising, retailing, and other sales and distribution services.

The selling costs associated with running shoes are not unusual. Almost everything that you buy includes a selling cost component that exceeds one half of the total cost. Your clothing, food, electronic items, DVDs, magazines, and even your textbooks cost more to sell than they cost to manufacture.

Advertising costs are only a part and often a small part of total selling costs. For example, Nike spends about $4 on advertising per pair of running shoes sold.

For the U.S. economy as a whole, there are some 20,000 advertising agencies, which employ more than 200,000 people and have sales of $45 billion. These numbers are only part of the total cost of advertising because firms have their own internal advertising departments, the costs of which we can only guess.

But the biggest part of selling costs is not the cost of advertising. It is the cost of retailing services. The retailer's selling costs (and economic profit) are often as much as 50 percent of the price you pay.

Selling Costs and Total Cost Selling costs are fixed costs and they increase the firm's total cost. So like fixed costs of producing the good, advertising costs per unit decrease as the quantity produced increases.

Figure 14.5 shows how selling costs change a firm's average total cost. The blue curve shows the average total cost of production. The red curve shows the firm's average total cost of production plus advertising. The height of the red area between the two curves shows the average fixed cost of advertising. The *total* cost of advertising is fixed. But the *average* cost of advertising decreases as output increases.

Figure 14.5 shows that if advertising increases the quantity sold by a large enough amount, it can lower average total cost. For example, if the quantity sold increases from 25 jackets a day with no advertising to 100 jackets a day with advertising, average total cost falls from $60 to $40 a jacket. The reason is that although the *total* fixed cost has increased, the greater fixed cost is spread over a greater output, so average total cost decreases.

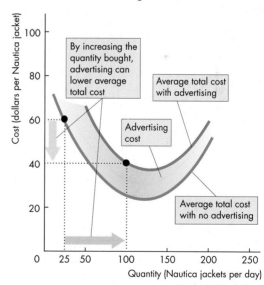

FIGURE 14.5 Selling Costs and Total Cost

Selling costs such as the cost of advertising are fixed costs. When added to the average total cost of production, selling costs increase average total cost by a greater amount at small outputs than at large outputs. If advertising enables sales to increase from 25 jackets a day to 100 jackets a day, average total cost *falls* from $60 to $40 a jacket.

Raw materials $9   Production costs $8   Import duty $3   Selling costs $50

Selling Costs and Demand Advertising and other selling efforts change the demand for a firm's product. But how? Does demand increase or does it decrease? The most natural answer is that advertising increases demand. By informing people about the quality of its products or by persuading people to switch from the products of other firms, a firm might expect to increase the demand for its own products.

But all firms in monopolistic competition advertise, and all seek to persuade customers that they have the best deal. If advertising enables a firm to survive, the number of firms in the market might increase. And to the extent that the number of firms does increase, advertising *decreases* the demand faced by any one firm. It also makes the demand for any one firm's product more elastic. So advertising can end up not only lowering average total cost but also lowering the markup and the price.

Figure 14.6 illustrates this possible effect of advertising. In part (a), with no advertising, the demand for Nautica jackets is not very elastic. Profit is maxi-

mized at 75 jackets per day, and the markup is large. In part (b), advertising, which is a fixed cost, increases average total cost from ATC_0 to ATC_1 but leaves marginal cost unchanged at MC. Demand becomes much more elastic, the profit-maximizing quantity increases, and the markup shrinks.

Using Advertising to Signal Quality

Some advertising, like the Maria Sharapova Canon camera ads on television and in glossy magazines or the huge number of dollars that Coke and Pepsi spend, seems hard to understand. There doesn't seem to be any concrete information about a camera in the glistening smile of a tennis player. And surely everyone knows about Coke and Pepsi. What is the gain from pouring millions of dollars a month into advertising these well-known colas?

One answer is that advertising is a signal to the consumer of a high-quality product. A **signal** is an action taken by an informed person (or firm) to send a mes-

---

FIGURE 14.6   Advertising and the Markup

(a) No firms advertise

(b) All firms advertise

If no firms advertise, demand for each firm's product is low and not very elastic. The profit-maximizing output is small, the markup is large, and the price is high.

Advertising increases average total cost and shifts the *ATC* curve upward from ATC_0 to ATC_1. If all firms advertise, the demand for each firm's product becomes more elastic. Output increases, the price falls, and the markup shrinks.

sage to uninformed people. Think about two colas: Coke and Oke. Oke knows that its cola is not very good and that its taste varies a lot depending on which cheap batch of unsold cola it happens to buy each week. So Oke knows that while it could get a lot of people to try Oke by advertising, they would all quickly discover what a poor product it is and switch back to the cola they bought before. Coke, in contrast, knows that its product has a high-quality consistent taste and that once consumers have tried it, there is a good chance they'll never drink anything else. On the basis of this reasoning, Oke doesn't advertise but Coke does. And Coke spends a lot of money to make a big splash.

Cola drinkers who see Coke's splashy ads know that the firm would not spend so much money advertising if its product were not truly good. So consumers reason that Coke is indeed a really good product. The flashy expensive ad has signaled that Coke is really good without saying anything about Coke.

Notice that if advertising is a signal, it doesn't need any specific product information. It just needs to be expensive and hard to miss. That's what a lot of advertising looks like. So the signaling theory of advertising predicts much of the advertising that we see.

Brand Names

Many firms create and spend a lot of money promoting a brand name. Why? What benefit does a brand name bring to justify the sometimes high cost of establishing it?

The basic answer is that a brand name provides information to consumers about the quality of a product, and is an incentive to the producer to achieve a high and consistent quality standard.

To see how a brand name helps the consumer, think about how you use brand names to get information about quality. You're on a road trip, and it is time to find a place to spend the night. You see roadside advertisements for Holiday Inn, Joe's Motel, and Annie's Driver's Stop. You know about Holiday Inn because you've stayed in it before. You've also seen their advertisements and know what to expect from them. You have no information at all about Joe's and Annie's. They might be better than the lodgings you do know about, but without that knowledge, you're not going to try them. You use the brand name as information and stay at Holiday Inn.

This same story explains why a brand name provides an incentive to achieve high and consistent quality. Because no one would know whether Joe's and

Annie's were offering a high standard of service, they have no incentive to do so. But equally, because everyone expects a given standard of service from Holiday Inn, a failure to meet a customer's expectation would almost surely lose that customer to a competitor. So Holiday Inn has a strong incentive to deliver what it promises in the advertising that creates its brand name.

Efficiency of Advertising and Brand Names

To the extent that advertising and brand names provide consumers with information about the precise nature of product differences and about product quality, they benefit the consumer and enable a better product choice to be made. But the opportunity cost of the additional information must be weighed against the gain to the consumer.

The final verdict on the efficiency of monopolistic competition is ambiguous. In some cases, the gains from extra product variety unquestionably offset the selling costs and the extra cost arising from excess capacity. The tremendous varieties of books and magazines, clothing, food, and drinks are examples of such gains. It is less easy to see the gains from being able to buy a brand-name drug that has a chemical composition identical to that of a generic alternative, but many people do willingly pay more for the brand-name alternative.

Review Quiz

1. How, other than by adjusting price, do firms in monopolistic competition compete?
2. Why might product innovation and development be efficient and why might it be inefficient?
3. How do selling costs influence a firm's cost curves and its average total cost?
4. How does advertising influence demand?
5. Are advertising and brand names efficient?

 Work Study Plan 14.3 and get instant feedback.

◆ Monopolistic competition is one of the most common market structures that you encounter in your daily life. *Reading Between the Lines* on pp. 334–335 applies the model of monopolistic competition to the market for 3G cell phones and shows you why you can expect continual innovation and the introduction of new phones from Apple and other producers.

Product Differentiation in the 3G Cell Phone Market

Watch Your Back Apple, These 10 iPhone Killers Are On the Prowl

http://www.crn.com
July 17, 2008

It's been a week since the Apple iPhone 3G launched in earnest, to throngs of Mac-faithful Appleheads looking to get their hands on the second-generation of the device. It took just a weekend for Apple to sell one million 3G iPhones, so says Apple.

But as the lines at the Apple Store vanish, the dust starts to clear and iPhone-mania wanes, smart phone makers are lining up to try and take a bite out of Apple iPhone's success. Some take elements from the iPhone and put a new spin on them though they're not necessarily iPhone clones.

Others take mobile computing in a different direction. Regardless, there is a crop of device makers lurking around the corner, peeler in hand, hoping to skin the iPhone, or at least give Apple a flesh wound.

Here we take a look at 10 iPhone killers, devices that have the potential to cut the core right out of Apple. Anyone else smell apple pie?

[The ten iPhone killers are the BlackBerry Bold 9000, Palm Treo 800w, Palm Centro, Samsung Instinct, Samsung Omnia, Nokia E90 Communicator, Nokia E71, Nokia E66, HTC Touch Diamond, and OpenMoko Neo FreeRunner.]

Essence of the Story

- On July 11, 2008, Apple launched its new 3G iPhone.

- World-wide interest in the new phone was high and Apple sold 1 million 3G iPhones in the first week.

- Anticipating Apple's success, other phone makers entered the market with 3G phones.

- Some of the new phones have features similar to those of the iPhone, but each phone is slightly different from the iPhone and from the other phones.

Economic Analysis

- On July 11, 2008, Apple launched its new 3G iPhone.

- By creating a substantially differentiated product, Apple was able to generate a great deal of interest in the new phone throughout the world.

- In the first weekend, Apple sold one million of the new phones.

- But within a month of the launch of the 3G iPhone, many competing but differentiated devices were on the market.

- The monopolistic competition model explains what is happening in the 3G cell phone market.

- Figure 1 shows the market for Apple's 3G iPhone in its first month. (The numbers are assumptions.)

- Because the Apple phone is different from its competitors and has features that users value, the demand curve, *D*, and marginal revenue curve, *MR*, provide a large short-run profit opportunity.

- The marginal cost curve is *MC* and the average total cost curve is *ATC*. Apple maximizes its economic profit by producing the quantity at which marginal revenue equals marginal cost, which in this example is 3 million iPhones a month.

- This quantity of phones can be sold for $200 each.

- The blue rectangle shows Apple's economic profit.

- Because this market is profitable, entry takes place.

- Within a month of the launch of the 3G iPhone, many competitors had entered the market.

- Figure 2 shows the the consequences of entry.

- The demand for the iPhone decreased as the market was shared with the other phones.

- Apple's profit-maximizing price decreased, and in the long run, economic profit is eliminated.

- With zero economic profit, Apple now has an incentive to develop an even better differentiated phone and start the cycle described here again, making an economic profit in a new phone in the short run.

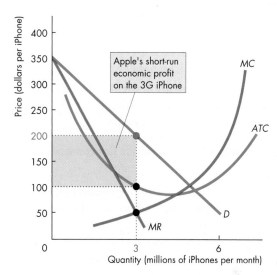

Figure 1 Economic profit in the short run

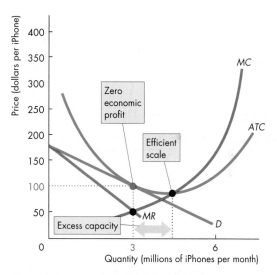

Figure 2 Zero economic profit in the long run

SUMMARY

Key Points

What Is Monopolistic Competition? (pp. 324–325)

- Monopolistic competition occurs when a large number of firms compete with each other on product quality, price, and marketing.

Price and Output in Monopolistic Competition
(pp. 326–329)

- Each firm in monopolistic competition faces a downward-sloping demand curve and produces the profit-maximizing quantity.
- Entry and exit result in zero economic profit and excess capacity in long-run equilibrium.

Product Development and Marketing (pp. 330–333)

- Firms in monopolistic competition innovate and develop new products.
- Advertising expenditures increase total cost, but average total cost might fall if the quantity sold increases by enough.
- Advertising expenditures might increase demand, but demand might decrease if competition increases.
- Whether monopolistic competition is inefficient depends on the value we place on product variety.

Key Figures

Key Terms

PROBLEMS and APPLICATIONS

 Work problems 1–12 in Chapter 14 Study Plan and get instant feedback.
Work problems 13–22 as Homework, a Quiz, or a Test if assigned by your instructor.

1. Sara is a dot.com entrepreneur who has established a Web site at which people can design and buy a sweatshirt. Sara pays $1,000 a week for her Web server and Internet connection. The sweatshirts that her customers design are made to order by another firm, and Sara pays this firm $20 a sweatshirt. Sara has no other costs. The table sets out the demand schedule for Sara's sweatshirts.

Price (dollars per sweatshirt)	Quantity demanded (sweatshirts per week)
0	100
20	80
40	60
60	40
80	20
100	0

   a. Calculate Sara's profit-maximizing output, price, and economic profit.
   b. Do you expect other firms to enter the Web sweatshirt business and compete with Sara?
   c. What happens to the demand for Sara's sweatshirts in the long run? What happens to Sara's economic profit in the long run?

2. The figure shows the situation facing Lite and Kool Inc., a producer of running shoes.

   a. What quantity does Lite and Kool produce?
   b. What is the price of a pair of Lite and Kool shoes?

   c. What is Lite and Kool's economic profit or economic loss?

3. In the market for running shoes, all the firms face a similar demand curve and have similar cost curves to those of Lite and Kool in problem 2.
   a. What happens to the number of firms producing running shoes in the long run?
   b. What happens to the price of running shoes in the long run?
   c. What happens to the quantity of running shoes produced by Lite and Kool in the long run?
   d. What happens to the quantity of running shoes in the entire market in the long run?
   e. Does Lite and Kool have excess capacity in the long run?
   f. Why, if Lite and Kool has excess capacity in the long run, doesn't the firm decrease its capacity?
   g. What is the relationship between Lite and Kool's price and marginal cost?

4. Is the market for running shoes described in problem 3 efficient or inefficient? Explain your answer.

5. Suppose that Tommy Hilfiger's marginal cost of a jacket is $100 (a constant marginal cost) and at one of the firm's shops, total fixed cost is $2,000 a day. The profit-maximizing number of jackets sold in this shop is 20 a day. Then the shops nearby start to advertise their jackets. The Tommy Hilfiger shop now spends $2,000 a day advertising its jackets, and its profit-maximizing number of jackets sold jumps to 50 a day.
   a. What is this shop's average total cost of a jacket sold before the advertising begins?
   b. What is this shop's average total cost of a jacket sold after the advertising begins?
   c. Can you say what happens to the price of a Tommy Hilfiger jacket? Why or why not?
   d. Can you say what happens to Tommy's markup? Why or why not?
   e. Can you say what happens to Tommy's economic profit? Why or why not?

6. How might Tommy Hilfiger in problem 5 use advertising as a signal? How is a signal sent and how does it work?

7. How does having a brand name help Tommy Hilfiger in problem 5 to increase its economic profit?

8. **Wake Up and Sell the Coffee**

Traffic at [Starbucks] U.S. stores dropped for the first time in its history … [amidst] … mounting complaints … that in its pursuit of growth, the company has strayed too far from its roots. … Starbucks will once again grind beans in its stores for drip coffee. It will give free drip refills … and provide two hours of wi-fi. …
Soon the company will roll out its new armor: a sleek, low-rise espresso machine that makes baristas more visible. …
Of course, every change that Starbucks has made over the past few years—automated espresso machines, preground coffee, drive-throughs, fewer soft chairs and less carpeting—was made for a reason: to smooth operations or boost sales. … Those may have been the right choices at the time … but together they ultimately diluted the coffee-centric experience.

Time, April 7, 2008

a. Explain how Starbucks' past attempts to maximize profits ended up eroding product differentiation.

b. Explain how Starbucks' new plan intends to increase economic profit.

9. **The Shoe That Won't Quit**

I finally decided to take the plunge this past winter and buy a pair of Uggs. … But when I got around to shopping for my Uggs in late January, the style that I wanted was sold out. … The scarcity factor was not a glitch in the supply chain, but rather a carefully calibrated strategy by Ugg parent Deckers Outdoor that is one of the big reasons behind the brand's success.
Deckers tightly controls distribution to ensure that supply does not outstrip demand. … If Deckers ever opened up the supply of Uggs to meet demand, sales would shoot up like a rocket, but they'd come back down just as fast.

Fortune, June 5, 2008

a. Explain why Deckers intentionally restricts the quantity of Uggs that the firm sells.

b. Draw a graph to illustrate how Deckers maximizes the economic profit from Uggs.

10. **My Life Without TV**

Should you go TV-free? YouTube is what first made this question worth asking. … NBC Universal and News Corp. announced last year that they were jointly starting their own YouTube knockoff. … Hulu … is a gorgeous piece of interface design laid over a technically sweet video player. … Hulu has reportedly already sold its entire advertising inventory. … There are plenty of other services waiting in the wings—such as Joost and Miro. …

Time, April 28, 2008

a. Draw a graph of the cost curves and revenue curves of YouTube if the firm is able to earn an economic profit in the short run.

b. What do you expect to happen to YouTube's economic profit in the long-run, given the information in the news clip?

c. Draw a graph to illustrate your answer to b.

11. **Food's Next Billion-Dollar Brand?**

While it's not the biggest brand in margarine, Smart Balance has an edge on its rivals in that it's made with a patented blend of vegetable and fruit oils that has been shown to raise levels of HDL, or "good" cholesterol, which can help improve consumers' cholesterol levels. … Smart Balance … sales have skyrocketed since its launch in 1997 while sales for the margarine category overall have stagnated. … Still, it remains to be seen whether Smart Balance's heart-healthy message (and higher prices) will resonate with mainstream consumers.

Fortune, June 4, 2008

a. How do you expect advertising and the Smart Balance brand name will affect Smart Balance's ability to earn an economic profit?

b. Are long-run economic profits a possibility for Smart Balance?

c. Does Smart Balance have either excess capacity or a markup in long-run equilibrium?

12. **Smith & Wesson Earnings Plummet 37%**

Smith & Wesson Holding Corp.'s fiscal fourth-quarter earnings dropped 37%, as higher marketing costs failed to boost sales, the gun maker said. …

CNN, June 12, 2008

Explain why Smith & Wesson's increased marketing actually decreased profits.

13. Lorie teaches singing. Her fixed costs are $1,000 a month, and it costs her $50 of labor to give one class. The table shows the demand schedule for Lorie's singing lessons.

Price (dollars per lesson)	Quantity demanded (lessons per month)
0	250
50	200
100	150
150	100
200	50
250	0

a. Calculate Lorie's profit-maximizing output, price, and economic profit.
b. Do you expect other firms to enter the singing lesson business and compete with Lorie?
c. What happens to the demand for Lorie's lessons in the long run? What happens to Lorie's economic profit in the long run?

14. The figure shows the situation facing Mike's Bikes Inc., a producer of mountain bikes.

a. What quantity does Mike's Bikes produce and what is its price?
b. Calculate Mike's Bikes' economic profit or economic loss.

15. In the market for mountain bikes, the demand for each firm's bikes and the firm's its cost curves are similar to those of Mike's Bikes in problem 14.
a. What happens to the number of firms producing mountain bikes?
b. What happens to the price of mountain bikes in the long run?
c. What happens to the quantity of bikes pro-

duced by Mike's Bikes in the long run?
d. What happens to the quantity of mountain bikes in the entire market in the long run?
e. Is there any way for Mike's Bikes to avoid having excess capacity in the long run?

16. Do you expect that the market for mountain bikes described in problem 15 is efficient or inefficient? Explain your answer.

17. Bianca bakes delicious cookies. Her total fixed cost is $40 a day, and her average variable cost is $1 a bag. Few people know about Bianca's Cookies, and she is maximizing her profit by selling 10 bags a day for $5 a bag. Bianca thinks that if she spends $50 a day on advertising, she can increase her market share and sell 25 bags a day for $5 a bag.
a. If Bianca's belief about the effect of advertising is correct, can she increase her economic profit by advertising?
b. If Bianca advertises, will her average total cost increase or decrease at the quantity produced?
c. If Bianca advertises, will she continue to sell her cookies for $5 a bag or will she raise her price or lower her price?

18. **Groceries for the Gourmet Palate**
No food, it seems, is safe these days from being repackaged in a shiny platinum case as an upscale product. ... Samuel Adams' $120 Utopias, in a ridiculous copper-covered 24-oz. (710 mL) bottle meant to resemble an old-fashioned brew kettle, ... [is] barely beer. It's not carbonated like a Bud but aged in oak barrels like scotch, and it has a vintage year, like a Bordeaux... light, complex and free of any alcohol sting, despite having six times as much alcohol content as a regular can of brew.

Time, April 14, 2008

a. Explain how Samuel Adams has differentiated its Utopias to compete with other beer brands in terms of quality, price, and marketing.
b. Predict whether Samuel Adams produces at, above, or below the efficient scale in the short run.
c. Predict whether the $120 price tag on the Utopias is at, above, or below marginal cost:
   i. In the short run.
   ii. In the long run.
d. Do you think that Samuel Adams Utopias makes the market for beer inefficient ?

19. **Swinging for Female Golfers**

One of the hottest areas of innovation is in clubs for women, who now make up nearly a quarter of the 24 million golfers in the U.S. ... Callaway and Nike, two of the leading golf-equipment manufacturers, recently released new clubs designed specifically for women. ...

Time, April 21, 2008

a. How are Callaway and Nike attempting to maintain economic profit?

b. Draw a graph to illustrate the cost curves and revenue curves of Callaway or Nike in the market for golf clubs for women.

c. Show on your graph (in b) the short-run economic profit.

d. Explain why the economic profit that Callaway and Nike make on golf clubs for women is likely to be temporary.

e. Draw a graph to illustrate the cost curves and revenue curves of Callaway or Nike in the market for golf clubs for women in the long run. Mark the firm's excess capacity.

20. **A Thirst for More Champagne**

Champagne exports have tripled in the past 20 years. That poses a problem for northern France, where the bubbly hails from—not enough grapes. So French authorities have unveiled a plan to extend the official Champagne grape-growing zone to cover 40 new villages. It's the first revision of the official appellation map since 1927, and—inevitably—it has provoked debate. Each plot must be tested for suitability, so the change will take several years to become effective. In the meantime the vineyard owners whose land values will jump markedly if the changes are finalized certainly have reason to raise a glass.

Fortune, May 12, 2008

a. Why is France so strict about designating the vineyards that can label their product Champagne?

b. Explain who would most likely oppose this plan.

c. Assuming that vineyards in these 40 villages are producing the same quality of grapes with or without this plan, why will their land values "jump markedly" if this plan is approved?

21. **Under Armour's Big Step Up**

Under Armour, the red-hot athletic-apparel brand, has joined Nike, Adidas, and New Balance as a major player on the market. ...

[Under Armour CEO] Plank prepares to move the Under Armour brand out of its comfort zone into the cutthroat, $18.3 billion athletic-footwear market. ... Under Armour announced it would try to revive the long-dead cross-training category. ... Under Armour tested the footwear landscape about two years ago, when it started making American-football cleats. Selling soccer shoes against Adidas and Nike would have been suicidal. Football is a small, specialized market. ... "Our No. 1 goal was authenticating ourselves as a footwear brand," says Plank. "Does the consumer accept putting the Under Armour logo on a shoe?" ... But will young athletes really spend $100 for a [cross training] shoe to lift weights in? "They're spending $40 on a T shirt," quips Plank, nodding to the premium price that consumers are paying for Under Armour's sweat-sopping gear.

Time, May 26, 2008

a. Explain how brand names initially prevented Under Armour from competing in the athletic shoe market.

b. What factors influence Under Armour's ability to earn an economic profit?

c. Will Under Armour be able to make a profit in the cross-training shoe market?

22. Study *Reading Between the Lines* on pp. 334–335 and then answer the following questions.

a. How did the creation of the 3G iPhone influence the demand and marginal revenue curves faced by Apple in the market for 3G phones?

b. How do you think the creation of the 3G iPhone influenced the demand for older generation cell phones?

c. Explain the effect on Nokia in the market for 3G cell phones of the introduction of the new iPhone.

d. Draw a graph to illustrate the effect on Nokia in the market for 3G cell phones of the introduction of the new iPhone.

e. Explain the effect on Apple of the decisions by BlackBerry, Palm, Samsung, Nokia, HTC, and OpenMoko to bring "iPhone killers" to market.

f. Draw a graph to illustrate the effect on Apple of the decisions by BlackBerry, Palm, Samsung, Nokia, HTC, and OpenMoko to bring "iPhone killers" to market.

g. Do you think the cell phone market is efficient? Explain your answer.

15 ◆ Oligopoly

An intense price war in the market for PCs has driven the price of a laptop below $1,000 and the price of a desktop below $500. A handful of firms—Dell, Hewlett-Packard, Lenovo, Acer, and Toshiba—account for more than one half of the global market. Each of these firms must pay close attention to what the other firms are doing

In some markets, there are only two firms. Computer chips are an example. The chips that drive most PCs are made by Intel and Advanced Micro Devices. How does competition between just two chip makers work?

When a small number of firms compete in a market, do they operate in the social interest, like firms in perfect competition?

Or do they restrict output to increase profit, like a monopoly?

The theories of perfect competition and monopoly don't predict the behavior of the firms we've just described. To understand how markets work when only a handful of firms compete, we need the richer models that are explained in this chapter. In *Reading Between the Lines* at the end of this chapter, we'll return to the market for personal computers and see how Dell and Hewlett-Packard slugged it out for dominance in that market.

What Is Oligopoly?

Oligopoly, like monopolistic competition, lies between perfect competition and monopoly. The firms in oligopoly might produce an identical product and compete only on price, or they might produce a differentiated product and compete on price, product quality, and marketing. **Oligopoly** is a market structure in which

- Natural or legal barriers prevent the entry of new firms.
- A small number of firms compete.

Barriers to Entry

Natural or legal barriers to entry can create oligopoly. You saw in Chapter 13 how economies of scale and demand form a natural barrier to entry that can create a *natural monopoly*. These same factors can create a *natural oligopoly*.

Figure 15.1 illustrates two natural oligopolies. The demand curve, *D* (in both parts of the figure), shows the demand for taxi rides in a town. If the average

total cost curve of a taxi company is ATC_1 in part (a), the market is a natural **duopoly**—an oligopoly market with two firms. You can probably see some examples of duopoly where you live. Some cities have only two taxi companies, two car rental firms, two copy centers, or two college bookstores.

The lowest price at which the firm would remain in business is $10 a ride. At that price, the quantity of rides demanded is 60 a day, the quantity that can be provided by just two firms. There is no room in this market for three firms. But if there were only one firm, it would make an economic profit and a second firm would enter to take some of the business and economic profit.

If the average total cost curve of a taxi company is ATC_2 in part (b), the efficient scale of one firm is 20 rides a day. This market is large enough for three firms.

A legal oligopoly arises when a legal barrier to entry protects the small number of firms in a market. A city might license two taxi firms or two bus companies, for example, even though the combination of demand and economies of scale leaves room for more than two firms.

FIGURE 15.1   Natural Oligopoly

(a) Natural duopoly

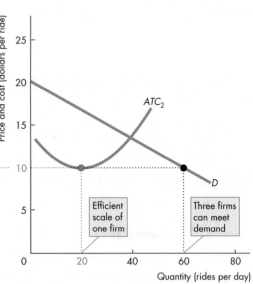

(b) Natural oligopoly with three firms

The lowest possible price is $10 a ride, which is the minimum average total cost. When a firm produces 30 rides a day, the efficient scale, two firms can satisfy the market demand. This natural oligopoly has two firms—a natural duopoly.

When the efficient scale of one firm is 20 rides per day, three firms can satisfy the market demand at the lowest possible price. This natural oligopoly has three firms.

Small Number of Firms

Because barriers to entry exist, oligopoly consists of a small number of firms, each of which has a large share of the market. Such firms are interdependent, and they face a temptation to cooperate to increase their joint economic profit.

Interdependence With a small number of firms in a market, each firm's actions influence the profits of all the other firms. When Penny Stafford opened her coffee shop in Bellevue, Washington, a nearby Starbucks coffee shop took a hit. Within days, Starbucks began to attract Penny's customers with enticing offers and lower prices. Starbucks survived but Penny eventually went out of business. Penny Stafford and Starbucks were interdependent.

Temptation to Cooperate When a small number of firms share a market, they can increase their profits by forming a cartel and acting like a monopoly. A **cartel** is a group of firms acting together—colluding—to limit output, raise price, and increase economic profit. Cartels are illegal, but they do operate in some markets. But for reasons that you'll discover in this chapter, cartels tend to break down.

Examples of Oligopoly

The box below shows some examples of oligopoly. The dividing line between oligopoly and monopolistic competition is hard to pin down. As a practical matter, we identify oligopoly by looking at concentration ratios, the Herfindahl-Hirschman Index, and information about the geographical scope of the market and barriers to entry. The HHI that divides oligopoly from monopolistic competition is generally taken to be 1,000. An HHI below 1,000 is usually an example of monopolistic competition, and a market in which the HHI exceeds 1,000 is usually an example of oligopoly.

Review Quiz

1 What are the two distinguishing characteristics of oligopoly?
2 Why are firms in oligopoly interdependent?
3 Why do firms in oligopoly face a temptation to collude?
4 Can you think of some examples of oligopolies that you buy from?

 Work Study Plan 15.1 and get instant feedback.

Oligopoly Today
Near Duopoly in Batteries

These markets are oligopolies. Although in some of them, the number of firms (in parentheses) is large, the share of the market held by the 4 largest firms (the red bars) is close to 100 percent.

The most concentrated markets—cigarettes, glass bottles and jars, washing machines and dryers, and batteries, are dominated by just one or two firms.

If you want to buy an AAA battery for your TV remote or toothbrush, you'll find it hard to avoid buying a Duracell or an Energizer.

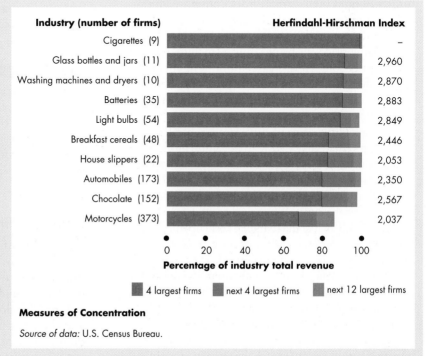

Measures of Concentration

Source of data: U.S. Census Bureau.

Two Traditional Oligopoly Models

Suppose you run one of three gas stations in a small town. You're trying to decide whether to cut your price. To make your decision, you must predict how the other firms will react and calculate the effects of those reactions on your profit. If you cut your price and your competitors don't cut theirs, you sell more and the other two firms sell less. But won't the other firms cut their prices too and make your profits fall? What will you do?

Several models have been developed to explain the prices and quantities in oligopoly markets. The models fall into two broad groups: traditional models and game theory models. We'll look at examples of both types, starting with two traditional models.

The Kinked Demand Curve Model

The kinked demand curve model of oligopoly is based on the assumption that each firm believes that if it raises its price, others will not follow, but if it cuts its price, other firms will cut theirs.

Figure 15.2 shows the demand curve (D) that a firm believes it faces. The demand curve has a kink at the current price, P, and quantity, Q. At prices above P, a small price rise brings a big decrease in the quantity sold. If one firm raises its price, other firms will hold their current price constant. The firm that raised its price will have the highest price and it will lose market share. At prices below P, even a large price cut brings only a small increase in the quantity sold. In this case, if one firm cuts its price, other firms will match the price cut. The firm that cuts its price will get no price advantage over its competitors.

The kink in the demand curve creates a break in the marginal revenue curve (MR). To maximize profit, the firm produces the quantity at which marginal cost equals marginal revenue. That quantity, Q, is where the marginal cost curve passes through the gap AB in the marginal revenue curve. If marginal cost fluctuates between A and B, like the marginal cost curves MC_0 and MC_1, the firm does not change its price or its output. Only if marginal cost fluctuates outside the range AB does the firm change its price and output. So the kinked demand curve model predicts that price and quantity are insensitive to small cost changes.

But this model has a problem. If marginal cost increases by enough to cause the firm to increase its price and if all firms experience the same increase in

FIGURE 15.2   The Kinked Demand Curve Model

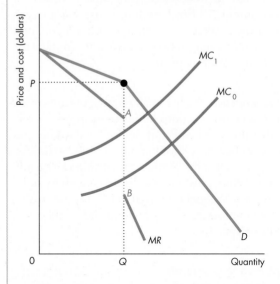

The price in an oligopoly market is P. Each firm believes it faces the demand curve D. At prices above P, a small price rise brings a big decrease in the quantity sold because other firms do not raise their prices. At prices below P, even a big price cut brings only a small increase in the quantity sold because other firms also cut their prices. Because the demand curve is kinked, the marginal revenue curve, MR, has a break AB. Profit is maximized by producing Q. The marginal cost curve passes through the break in the marginal revenue curve. Changes in marginal cost inside the range AB leave the price and quantity unchanged.

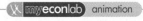 myeconlab animation

marginal cost, they all increase their prices together. The firm's belief that others will not join it in a price rise is incorrect. A firm that bases its actions on beliefs that are wrong does not maximize profit and might even end up incurring an economic loss.

Dominant Firm Oligopoly

A second traditional model explains a dominant firm oligopoly, which arises when one firm—the dominant firm—has a big cost advantage over the other firms and produces a large part of the industry output. The dominant firm sets the market price and the other firms are price takers. Examples of dominant firm oligopoly are a large gasoline retailer or a big box store that dominates its local market.

FIGURE 15.3   A Dominant Firm Oligopoly

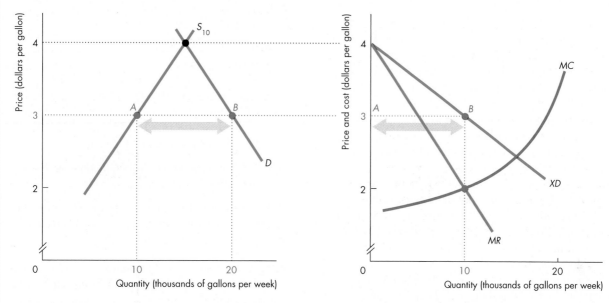

(a) Ten small firms and market demand

(b) Big-G's price and output decision

The demand curve for gas in a city is *D* in part (a). There are 10 small competitive firms that together have a supply curve of S_{10}. In addition, there is 1 large firm, Big-G, shown in part (b). Big-G faces the demand curve *XD*, determined as the market demand *D* minus the supply of the 10 small firms S_{10} —the demand that is not satisfied by the small firms. Big-G's mar-

ginal revenue curve is *MR* and its marginal cost curve is *MC*. Big-G sets its output to maximize profit by equating marginal cost and marginal revenue. This output is 10,000 gallons per week. The price at which Big-G can sell this quantity is $3 a gallon. The 10 small firms take this price, and each firm sells 1,000 gallons per week, point *A* in part (a).

To see how a dominant firm oligopoly works, suppose that 11 firms operate gas stations in a city. Big-G is the dominant firm. Figure 15.3 shows the market for gas in this city. In part (a), the demand curve *D* tells us the total quantity of gas demanded in the city at each price. The supply curve S_{10} is the supply curve of the 10 small firms. Part (b) shows the situation facing Big-G. Its marginal cost curve is *MC*. Big-G faces the demand curve *XD*, and its marginal revenue curve is *MR*. The demand curve *XD* shows the excess demand not met by the 10 small firms. For example, at a price of $3 a gallon, the quantity demanded is 20,000 gallons, the quantity supplied by the 10 small firms is 10,000 gallons, and the excess quantity demanded is 10,000 gallons, measured by the distance *AB* in both parts of the figure.

To maximize profit, Big-G operates like a monopoly. It sells 10,000 gallons a week, where its marginal revenue equals its marginal cost, for a price of $3 a gallon. The 10 small firms take the price of $3 a gal-

lon. They behave just like firms in perfect competition. The quantity of gas demanded in the entire city at $3 a gallon is 20,000 gallons, as shown in part (a). Of this amount, Big-G sells 10,000 gallons and the 10 small firms each sell 1,000 gallons.

Review Quiz

1   What does the kinked demand curve model predict and why must it sometimes make a prediction that contradicts its basic assumption?

2   Do you think a market with a dominant firm is in long-run equilibrium? Explain why or why not.

Work Study Plan 15.2 and get instant feedback.

The traditional models don't enable us to understand all oligopoly markets and we're now going to study some newer models based on game theory.

Oligopoly Games

Economists think about oligopoly as a game, and to study oligopoly markets they use a set of tools called game theory. **Game theory** is a tool for studying *strategic behavior*—behavior that takes into account the expected behavior of others and the recognition of mutual interdependence. Game theory was invented by John von Neumann in 1937 and extended by von Neumann and Oskar Morgenstern in 1944 (p. 369). Today, it is one of the major research fields in economics.

Game theory seeks to understand oligopoly as well as other forms of economic, political, social, and even biological rivalries by using a method of analysis specifically designed to understand games of all types, including the familiar games of everyday life (see Talking with Drew Fudenberg on pp. 370–372). We will begin our study of game theory and its application to the behavior of firms by thinking about familiar games.

What Is a Game?

What is a game? At first thought, the question seems silly. After all, there are many different games. There are ball games and parlor games, games of chance and games of skill. But what is it about all these different activities that make them games? What do all these games have in common? We're going to answer these questions by looking at a game called "the prisoners' dilemma." This game captures the essential features of many games, including oligopoly, and it gives a good illustration of how game theory works and how it generates predictions.

The Prisoners' Dilemma

Art and Bob have been caught red-handed stealing a car. Facing airtight cases, they will receive a sentence of two years each for their crime. During his interviews with the two prisoners, the district attorney begins to suspect that he has stumbled on the two people who were responsible for a multimillion-dollar bank robbery some months earlier. But this is just a suspicion. He has no evidence on which he can convict them of the greater crime unless he can get them to confess. But how can he extract a confession? The answer is by making the prisoners play a game. The district attorney makes the prisoners play the following game.

All games share four common features:

- Rules
- Strategies
- Payoffs
- Outcome

Rules Each prisoner (player) is placed in a separate room and cannot communicate with the other prisoner. Each is told that he is suspected of having carried out the bank robbery and that

> If both of them confess to the larger crime, each will receive a sentence of 3 years for both crimes.

> If he alone confesses and his accomplice does not, he will receive only a 1-year sentence while his accomplice will receive a 10-year sentence.

Strategies In game theory, **strategies** are all the possible actions of each player. Art and Bob each have two possible actions:

1. Confess to the bank robbery.
2. Deny having committed the bank robbery.

Because there are two players, each with two strategies, there are four possible outcomes:

1. Both confess.
2. Both deny.
3. Art confesses and Bob denies.
4. Bob confesses and Art denies.

Payoffs Each prisoner can work out his *payoff* in each of these situations, and we can tabulate the four possible payoffs for each of the prisoners in what is called a payoff matrix for the game. A **payoff matrix** is a table that shows the payoffs for every possible action by each player for every possible action by each other player.

Table 15.1 shows a payoff matrix for Art and Bob. The squares show the payoffs for each prisoner—the red triangle in each square shows Art's and the blue triangle shows Bob's. If both prisoners confess (top left), each gets a prison term of 3 years. If Bob confesses but Art denies (top right), Art gets a 10-year sentence and Bob gets a 1-year sentence. If Art confesses and Bob denies (bottom left), Art gets a 1-year sentence and Bob gets a 10-year sentence. Finally, if both of them deny (bottom right), neither can be convicted of the bank robbery charge but both are sentenced for the car theft—a 2-year sentence.

Outcome The choices of both players determine the outcome of the game. To predict that outcome, we use an equilibrium idea proposed by John Nash of Princeton University (who received the Nobel Prize for Economic Science in 1994 and was the subject of the 2001 movie *A Beautiful Mind*). In **Nash equilibrium**, player *A* takes the best possible action given the action of player *B* and player *B* takes the best possible action given the action of player *A*.

In the case of the prisoners' dilemma, the Nash equilibrium occurs when Art makes his best choice given Bob's choice and when Bob makes his best choice given Art's choice.

To find the Nash equilibrium, we compare all the possible outcomes associated with each choice and eliminate those that are dominated—that are not as good as some other choice. Let's find the Nash equilibrium for the prisoners' dilemma game.

Finding the Nash Equilibrium Look at the situation from Art's point of view. If Bob confesses (top row), Art's best action is to confess because in that case, he is sentenced to 3 years rather than 10 years. If Bob denies (bottom row), Art's best action is still to confess because in that case he receives 1 year rather than 2 years. So Art's best action is to confess.

Now look at the situation from Bob's point of view. If Art confesses (left column), Bob's best action is to confess because in that case, he is sentenced to 3 years rather than 10 years. If Art denies (right column), Bob's best action is still to confess because in that case, he receives 1 year rather than 2 years. So Bob's best action is to confess.

Because each player's best action is to confess, each does confess, each goes to jail for 3 years, and the district attorney has solved the bank robbery. This is the Nash equilibrium of the game.

The Dilemma Now that you have found the outcome to the prisoners' dilemma, you can better see the dilemma. The dilemma arises as each prisoner contemplates the consequences of denying. Each prisoner knows that if both of them deny, they will receive only a 2-year sentence for stealing the car. But neither has any way of knowing that his accomplice will deny. Each poses the following questions: Should I deny and rely on my accomplice to deny so that we will both get only 2 years? Or should I confess in the hope of getting just 1 year (provided that my accomplice denies) knowing that if my accomplice does confess,

TABLE 15.1 Prisoners' Dilemma Payoff Matrix

Each square shows the payoffs for the two players, Art and Bob, for each possible pair of actions. In each square, the red triangle shows Art's payoff and the blue triangle shows Bob's. For example, if both confess, the payoffs are in the top left square. The equilibrium of the game is for both players to confess and each gets a 3-year sentence.

we will both get 3 years in prison? The dilemma leads to the equilibrium of the game.

A Bad Outcome For the prisoners, the equilibrium of the game, with each confessing, is not the best outcome. If neither of them confesses, each gets only 2 years for the lesser crime. Isn't there some way in which this better outcome can be achieved? It seems that there is not, because the players cannot communicate with each other. Each player can put himself in the other player's place, and so each player can figure out that there is a best strategy for each of them. The prisoners are indeed in a dilemma. Each knows that he can serve 2 years only if he can trust the other to deny. But each prisoner also knows that it is not in the best interest of the other to deny. So each prisoner knows that he must confess, thereby delivering a bad outcome for both.

The firms in an oligopoly are in a similar situation to Art and Bob in the prisoners' dilemma game. Let's see how we can use this game to understand oligopoly.

An Oligopoly Price-Fixing Game

We can use game theory and a game like the prisoners' dilemma to understand price fixing, price wars, and other aspects of the behavior of firms in oligopoly. We'll begin with a price-fixing game.

To understand price fixing, we're going to study the special case of duopoly—an oligopoly with two firms. Duopoly is easier to study than oligopoly with three or more firms, and it captures the essence of all oligopoly situations. Somehow, the two firms must share the market. And how they share it depends on the actions of each. We're going to describe the costs of the two firms and the market demand for the item they produce. We're then going to see how game theory helps us to predict the prices charged and the quantities produced by the two firms in a duopoly.

Cost and Demand Conditions Two firms, Trick and Gear, produce switchgears. They have identical costs. Figure 15.4(a) shows their average total cost curve (*ATC*) and marginal cost curve (*MC*). Figure 15.4(b) shows the market demand curve for switchgears (*D*). The two firms produce identical switchgears, so one firm's switchgear is a perfect substitute for the other's, and the market price of each firm's product is identical. The quantity demanded depends on that price—the higher the price, the smaller is the quantity demanded.

This industry is a natural duopoly. Two firms can produce this good at a lower cost than either one firm or three firms can. For each firm, average total cost is at its minimum when production is 3,000 units a week. When price equals minimum average total cost, the total quantity demanded is 6,000 units a week, and two firms can just produce that quantity.

Collusion We'll suppose that Trick and Gear enter into a collusive agreement. A **collusive agreement** is an agreement between two (or more) producers to form a cartel to restrict output, raise the price, and increase profits. Such an agreement is illegal in the United States and is undertaken in secret. The strategies that firms in a cartel can pursue are to

- Comply
- Cheat

A firm that complies carries out the agreement. A firm that cheats breaks the agreement to its own benefit and to the cost of the other firm.

Because each firm has two strategies, there are four possible combinations of actions for the firms:

1. Both firms comply.
2. Both firms cheat.
3. Trick complies and Gear cheats.
4. Gear complies and Trick cheats.

FIGURE 15.4   Costs and Demand

(a) Individual firm

(b) Industry

The average total cost curve for each firm is *ATC*, and the marginal cost curve is *MC* (part a). Minimum average total cost is $6,000 a unit, and it occurs at a production of 3,000 units a week.

Part (b) shows the market demand curve. At a price of $6,000, the quantity demanded is 6,000 units per week. The two firms can produce this output at the lowest possible average cost. If the market had one firm, it would be profitable for another to enter. If the market had three firms, one would exit. There is room for only two firms in this industry. It is a natural duopoly.

Colluding to Maximize Profits Let's work out the payoffs to the two firms if they collude to make the maximum profit for the cartel by acting like a monopoly. The calculations that the two firms perform are the same calculations that a monopoly performs. (You can refresh your memory of these calculations by looking at Chapter 13, pp. 304–305.) The only thing that the firms in duopoly must do beyond what a monopoly does is to agree on how much of the total output each of them will produce.

Figure 15.5 shows the price and quantity that maximize industry profit for the duopoly. Part (a) shows the situation for each firm, and part (b) shows the situation for the industry as a whole. The curve labeled *MR* is the industry marginal revenue curve. This marginal revenue curve is like that of a single-price monopoly (Chapter 13, p. 302).The curve labeled MC_I is the industry marginal cost curve if each firm produces the same quantity of output. This curve is constructed by adding together the outputs of the two firms at each level of marginal cost. Because the two firms are the same size, at each level of marginal cost, the industry output is twice the output of one firm. The curve MC_I in part (b) is twice as far to the right as the curve *MC* in part (a).

To maximize industry profit, the firms in the duopoly agree to restrict output to the rate that makes the industry marginal cost and marginal revenue equal. That output rate, as shown in part (b), is 4,000 units a week. The demand curve shows that the highest price for which the 4,000 switchgears can be sold is $9,000 each. Trick and Gear agree to charge this price.

To hold the price at $9,000 a unit, production must be 4,000 units a week. So Trick and Gear must agree on output rates for each of them that total 4,000 units a week. Let's suppose that they agree to split the market equally so that each firm produces 2,000 switchgears a week. Because the firms are identical, this division is the most likely.

The average total cost (*ATC*) of producing 2,000 switchgears a week is $8,000, so the profit per unit is $1,000 and economic profit is $2 million (2,000 units × $1,000 per unit). The economic profit of each firm is represented by the blue rectangle in Fig. 15.5(a).

We have just described one possible outcome for a duopoly game: The two firms collude to produce the monopoly profit-maximizing output and divide that output equally between themselves. From the industry point of view, this solution is identical to a monopoly. A duopoly that operates in this way is indistinguishable from a monopoly. The economic profit that is made by a monopoly is the maximum total profit that can be made by the duopoly when the firms collude.

But with price greater than marginal cost, either firm might think of trying to increase profit by cheating on the agreement and producing more than the agreed amount. Let's see what happens if one of the firms does cheat in this way.

FIGURE 15.5   Colluding to Make Monopoly Profits

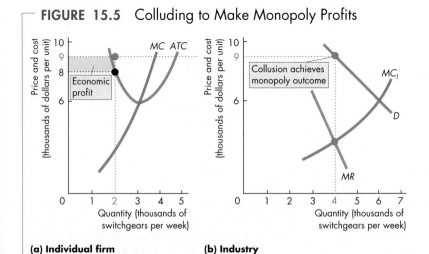

(a) Individual firm

(b) Industry

The industry marginal cost curve, MC_I in part (b), is the horizontal sum of the two firms' marginal cost curves, *MC* in part (a). The industry marginal revenue curve is *MR*. To maximize profit, the firms produce 4,000 units a week (the quantity at which marginal revenue equals marginal cost). They sell that output for $9,000 a unit. Each firm produces 2,000 units a week. Average total cost is $8,000 a unit, so each firm makes an economic profit of $2 million (blue rectangle)—2,000 units multiplied by $1,000 profit a unit.

One Firm Cheats on a Collusive Agreement To set the stage for cheating on their agreement, Trick convinces Gear that demand has decreased and that it cannot sell 2,000 units a week. Trick tells Gear that it plans to cut its price so that it can sell the agreed 2,000 units each week. Because the two firms produce an identical product, Gear matches Trick's price cut but still produces only 2,000 units a week.

In fact, there has been no decrease in demand. Trick plans to increase output, which it knows will lower the price, and Trick wants to ensure that Gear's output remains at the agreed level.

Figure 15.6 illustrates the consequences of Trick's cheating. Part (a) shows Gear (the complier); part (b) shows Trick (the cheat); and part (c) shows the industry as a whole. Suppose that Trick increases output to 3,000 units a week. If Gear sticks to the agreement to produce only 2,000 units a week, total output is now 5,000 a week, and given demand in part (c), the price falls to $7,500 a unit.

Gear continues to produce 2,000 units a week at a cost of $8,000 a unit and incurs a loss of $500 a unit, or $1 million a week. This economic loss is shown by the red rectangle in part (a). Trick produces 3,000 units a week at an average total cost of $6,000 each. With a price of $7,500, Trick makes a profit of

$1,500 a unit and therefore an economic profit of $4.5 million. This economic profit is the blue rectangle in part (b).

We've now described a second possible outcome for the duopoly game: One of the firms cheats on the collusive agreement. In this case, the industry output is larger than the monopoly output and the industry price is lower than the monopoly price. The total economic profit made by the industry is also smaller than the monopoly's economic profit. Trick (the cheat) makes an economic profit of $4.5 million, and Gear (the complier) incurs an economic loss of $1 million. The industry makes an economic profit of $3.5 million. This industry profit is $0.5 million less than the economic profit that a monopoly would make. But the profit is distributed unevenly. Trick makes a bigger economic profit than it would under the collusive agreement, while Gear incurs an economic loss.

A similar outcome would arise if Gear cheated and Trick complied with the agreement. The industry profit and price would be the same, but in this case, Gear (the cheat) would make an economic profit of $4.5 million and Trick (the complier) would incur an economic loss of $1 million.

Let's next see what happens if both firms cheat.

FIGURE 15.6   One Firm Cheats

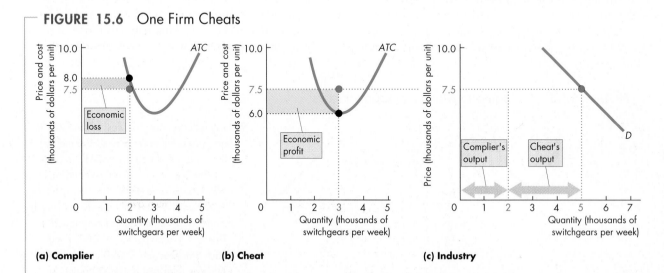

(a) Complier   **(b) Cheat**   **(c) Industry**

One firm, shown in part (a), complies with the agreement and produces 2,000 units. The other firm, shown in part (b), cheats on the agreement and increases its output to 3,000 units a week. Given the market demand curve, shown in part (c), and with a total production of 5,000 units a week,

the price falls to $7,500 a unit. At this price, the complier in part (a) incurs an economic loss of $1 million ($500 per unit × 2,000 units), shown by the red rectangle. In part (b), the cheat makes an economic profit of $4.5 million ($1,500 per unit × 3,000 units), shown by the blue rectangle.

Both Firms Cheat Suppose that both firms cheat and that each firm behaves like the cheating firm that we have just analyzed. Each tells the other that it is unable to sell its output at the going price and that it plans to cut its price. But because both firms cheat, each will propose a successively lower price. As long as price exceeds marginal cost, each firm has an incentive to increase its production—to cheat. Only when price equals marginal cost is there no further incentive to cheat. This situation arises when the price has reached $6,000. At this price, marginal cost equals price. Also, price equals minimum average total cost. At a price less than $6,000, each firm incurs an economic loss. At a price of $6,000, each firm covers all its costs and makes zero economic profit. Also, at a price of $6,000, each firm wants to produce 3,000 units a week, so the industry output is 6,000 units a week. Given the demand conditions, 6,000 units can be sold at a price of $6,000 each.

Figure 15.7 illustrates the situation just described. Each firm, in part (a), produces 3,000 units a week, and its average total cost is a minimum ($6,000 per unit). The market as a whole, in part (b), operates at the point at which the market demand curve (D) intersects the industry marginal cost curve (MC_I). Each firm has lowered its price and increased its output to try to gain an advantage over the other firm. Each has pushed this process as far as it can without incurring an economic loss.

We have now described a third possible outcome of this duopoly game: Both firms cheat. If both firms cheat on the collusive agreement, the output of each firm is 3,000 units a week and the price is $6,000 a unit. Each firm makes zero economic profit.

The Payoff Matrix Now that we have described the strategies and payoffs in the duopoly game, we can summarize the strategies and the payoffs in the form of the game's payoff matrix. Then we can find the Nash equilibrium.

Table 15.2 sets out the payoff matrix for this game. It is constructed in the same way as the payoff matrix for the prisoners' dilemma in Table 15.1. The squares show the payoffs for the two firms—Gear and Trick. In this case, the payoffs are profits. (For the prisoners' dilemma, the payoffs were losses.)

The table shows that if both firms cheat (top left), they achieve the perfectly competitive outcome—each firm makes zero economic profit. If both firms comply (bottom right), the industry makes the monopoly profit and each firm makes an economic profit of $2 million. The top right and bottom left squares show the payoff if one firm cheats while the other complies. The firm that cheats makes an economic profit of $4.5 million, and the one that complies incurs a loss of $1 million.

Nash Equilibrium in the Duopolists' Dilemma The duopolists have a dilemma like the prisoners' dilemma. Do they comply or cheat? To answer this question, we must find the Nash equilibrium.

FIGURE 15.7 Both Firms Cheat

(a) Individual firm   (b) Industry

If both firms cheat by increasing production, the collusive agreement collapses. The limit to the collapse is the competitive equilibrium. Neither firm will cut its price below $6,000 (minimum average total cost) because to do so will result in losses. In part (a), each firm produces 3,000 units a week at an average total cost of $6,000. In part (b), with a total production of 6,000 units, the price falls to $6,000. Each firm now makes zero economic profit. This output and price are the ones that would prevail in a competitive industry.

myeconlab   animation

TABLE 15.2   Duopoly Payoff Matrix

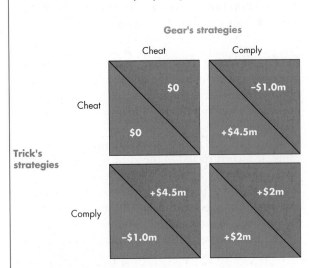

Each square shows the payoffs from a pair of actions. For example, if both firms comply with the collusive agreement, the payoffs are recorded in the bottom right square. The red triangle shows Gear's payoff, and the blue triangle shows Trick's. In Nash equilibrium, both firms cheat.

Look at things from Gear's point of view. Gear reasons as follows: Suppose that Trick cheats. If I comply, I will incur an economic loss of $1 million. If I also cheat, I will make zero economic profit. Zero is better than *minus* $1 million, so I'm better off if I cheat. Now suppose Trick complies. If I cheat, I will make an economic profit of $4.5 million, and if I comply, I will make an economic profit of $2 million. A $4.5 million profit is better than a $2 million profit, so I'm better off if I cheat. So regardless of whether Trick cheats or complies, it pays Gear to cheat. Cheating is Gear's best strategy.

Trick comes to the same conclusion as Gear because the two firms face an identical situation. So both firms cheat. The Nash equilibrium of the duopoly game is that both firms cheat. And although the industry has only two firms, they charge the same price and produce the same quantity as those in a competitive industry. Also, as in perfect competition, each firm makes zero economic profit.

This conclusion is not general and will not always arise. We'll see why not by looking first at some other games that are like the prisoners' dilemma. Then we'll broaden the types of games we consider.

Other Oligopoly Games

Firms in oligopoly must decide whether to mount expensive advertising campaigns; whether to modify their product; whether to make their product more reliable and more durable; whether to price discriminate and, if so, among which groups of customers and to what degree; whether to undertake a large research and development (R&D) effort aimed at lowering production costs; and whether to enter or leave an industry.

All of these choices can be analyzed as games that are similar to the one that we've just studied. Let's look at one example: an R&D game.

An R&D Game
Procter & Gamble Versus Kimberly-Clark

Disposable diapers have been around for a bit more than 40 years. Procter & Gamble (which has a 40 percent market share with Pampers) and Kimberly-Clark (which has a 33 percent market share with Huggies) have always been the market leaders.

When the disposable diaper was first introduced, it had to be cost-effective in competition with reusable, laundered diapers. A costly research and development effort resulted in the development of machines that could make disposable diapers at a low enough cost to achieve that initial competitive edge. But new firms tried to get into the business and take market share away from the two industry leaders, and the industry leaders themselves battled each other to maintain or increase their own market shares.

During the early 1990s, Kimberly-Clark was the first to introduce Velcro closures. And in 1996, Procter & Gamble was the first to introduce "breathable" diapers.

The key to success in this industry (as in any other) is to design a product that people value highly relative to the cost of producing it. The firm that creates the most highly valued product and also develops the least-cost technology for producing it gains a competitive edge, undercutting the rest of the market, increasing its market share, and increasing its profit.

But the R&D that must be undertaken to improve product quality and cut cost is itself costly. So the cost of R&D must be deducted from the profit resulting from the increased market share that lower costs achieve. If no firm does R&D, every firm can be better off, but if one firm initiates the R&D activity, all must follow.

Table 15.3 illustrates the dilemma (with hypothetical numbers) for the R&D game that Kimberly-Clark and Procter & Gamble play. Each firm has two strategies: Spend $25 million a year on R&D or spend nothing on R&D. If neither firm spends on R&D, they make a joint profit of $100 million: $30 million for Kimberly-Clark and $70 million for Procter & Gamble (bottom right of the payoff matrix). If each firm conducts R&D, market shares are maintained but each firm's profit is lower by the amount spent on R&D (top left square of the payoff matrix). If Kimberly-Clark pays for R&D but Procter & Gamble does not, Kimberly-Clark gains a large part of Procter & Gamble's market. Kimberly-Clark profits, and Procter & Gamble loses (top right square of the payoff matrix). Finally, if Procter & Gamble conducts R&D and Kimberly-Clark does not, Procter & Gamble gains market share from Kimberly-Clark, increasing its profit, while Kimberly-Clark incurs a loss (bottom left square).

TABLE 15.3   Pampers Versus Huggies: An R&D Game

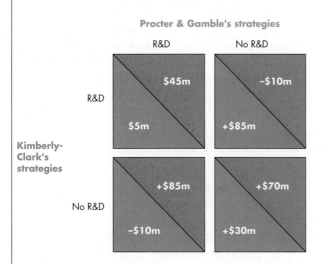

Procter & Gamble's strategies

	R&D	No R&D
R&D	$45m / $5m	–$10m / +$85m
No R&D	+$85m / –$10m	+$70m / +$30m

Kimberly-Clark's strategies

If both firms undertake R&D, their payoffs are those shown in the top left square. If neither firm undertakes R&D, their payoffs are in the bottom right square. When one firm undertakes R&D and the other one does not, their payoffs are in the top right and bottom left squares. The red triangle shows Procter & Gamble's payoff, and the blue triangle shows Kimberly-Clark's. The Nash equilibrium for this game is for both firms to undertake R&D. The structure of this game is the same as that of the prisoners' dilemma.

Confronted with the payoff matrix in Table 15.3, the two firms calculate their best strategies. Kimberly-Clark reasons as follows: If Procter & Gamble does not undertake R&D, we will make $85 million if we do and $30 million if we do not; so it pays us to conduct R&D. If Procter & Gamble conducts R&D, we will lose $10 million if we don't and make $5 million if we do. Again, R&D pays off. So conducting R&D is the best strategy for Kimberly-Clark. It pays, regardless of Procter & Gamble's decision.

Procter & Gamble reasons similarly: If Kimberly-Clark does not undertake R&D, we will make $70 million if we follow suit and $85 million if we conduct R&D. It therefore pays to conduct R&D. If Kimberly-Clark does undertake R&D, we will make $45 million by doing the same and lose $10 million by not doing R&D. Again, it pays us to conduct R&D. So for Procter & Gamble, R&D is also the best strategy.

Because R&D is the best strategy for both players, it is the Nash equilibrium. The outcome of this game is that both firms conduct R&D. They make less profit than they would if they could collude to achieve the cooperative outcome of no R&D.

The real-world situation has more players than Kimberly-Clark and Procter & Gamble. A large number of other firms share a small portion of the market, all of them ready to eat into the market share of Procter & Gamble and Kimberly-Clark. So the R&D efforts by these two firms not only serve the purpose of maintaining shares in their own battle but also help to keep barriers to entry high enough to preserve their joint market share.

The Disappearing Invisible Hand

All the games that we've studied are versions of the prisoners' dilemma. The essence of that game lies in the structure of its payoffs. The worst possible outcome for each player arises from cooperating when the other player cheats. The best possible outcome, for each player to cooperate, is not a Nash equilibrium because it is in neither player's *self-interest* to cooperate if the other one cooperates. It is this failure to achieve the best outcome for both players—the best social outcome if the two players are the entire economy—that led John Nash to claim (as he was portrayed as doing in the movie *A Beautiful Mind*) that he had challenged Adam Smith's idea that we are always guided, as if by an invisible hand, to promote the social interest when we are pursuing our self-interest.

A Game of Chicken

The Nash equilibrium for the prisoners' dilemma is called a **dominant strategy equilibrium**, which is an equilibrium in which the best strategy of each player is to cheat (confess) *regardless of the strategy of the other player*. Not all games have such an equilibrium, and one that doesn't is a game called "chicken."

In a graphic, if disturbing, version of this game, two cars race toward each other. The first driver to swerve and avoid a crash is "chicken." The payoffs are a big loss for both if no one "chickens," zero for the chicken, and a gain for the player who stays the course. If player 1 chickens, player 2's best strategy is to stay the course. And if player 1 stays the course, player 2's best strategy is to chicken.

For an economic form of this game, suppose the R&D that creates a new diaper technology results in information that cannot be kept secret or patented, so both firms benefit from the R&D of either firm. The chicken in this case is the firm that does the R&D.

Table 15.4 illustrates a payoff matrix for an R&D game of chicken between Kimberly-Clark and Procter & Gamble. Each firm has two strategies: Do the R&D (and "chicken") or do not do the R&D (and stand firm).

If neither "chickens," there is no R&D and each firm makes zero additional profit. If each firm conducts R&D—each "chickens"—each firm makes $5 million (the profit from the new technology minus the cost of the research). If one of the firms does the R&D, the payoffs are $1 million for the chicken and $10 million for the one who stands firm.

Confronted with the payoff matrix in Table 15.4, the two firms calculate their best strategies. Kimberly-Clark is better off doing R&D if Procter & Gamble does not undertake it. Procter & Gamble is better off doing R&D if Kimberly-Clark doesn't do it. There are two equilibrium outcomes: One firm does the R&D, but we can't predict which firm it will be.

You can see that it isn't a Nash equilibrium if no firm does the R&D because one firm would then be better off doing it. And you can see that it isn't a Nash equilibrium if both firms do the R&D because then one firm would be better off not doing it.

The firms could toss a coin or use some other random device to make a decision in this game. In some circumstances, such a strategy—called a mixed strategy—is actually better for both firms than choosing any of the strategies we've considered.

TABLE 15.4   An R&D Game of Chicken

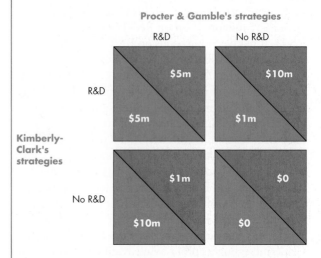

If both firms undertake R&D, their payoffs are those shown in the top left square. If neither firm undertakes R&D, their payoffs are in the bottom right square. When one firm undertakes R&D and the other one does not, their payoffs are in the top right and bottom left squares. The red triangle shows Procter & Gamble's payoff, and the blue triangle shows Kimberly-Clark's. The equilibrium for this R&D game of chicken is for only one firm to undertake R&D. We cannot tell which firm will do the R&D and which will not.

Review Quiz

1 What are the common features of all games?
2 Describe the prisoners' dilemma game and explain why the Nash equilibrium delivers a bad outcome for both players.
3 Why does a collusive agreement to restrict output and raise price create a game like the prisoners' dilemma?
4 What creates an incentive for firms in a collusive agreement to cheat and increase production?
5 What is the equilibrium strategy for each firm in a duopolists' dilemma and why do the firms not succeed in colluding to raise the price and profits?
6 Describe two structures of payoffs for an R&D game and contrast the prisoners' dilemma and the chicken game.

myeconlab   Work Study Plan 15.3
and get instant feedback.

Repeated Games and Sequential Games

The games that we've studied are played just once. In contrast, many real-world games are played repeatedly. This feature of games turns out to enable real-world duopolists to cooperate, collude, and make a monopoly profit.

Another feature of the games that we've studied is that the players move simultaneously. But in many real-world situations, one player moves first and then the other moves—the play is sequential rather than simultaneous. This feature of real-world games creates a large number of possible outcomes.

We're now going to examine these two aspects of strategic decision-making.

A Repeated Duopoly Game

If two firms play a game repeatedly, one firm has the opportunity to penalize the other for previous "bad" behavior. If Gear cheats this week, perhaps Trick will cheat next week. Before Gear cheats this week, won't it consider the possibility that Trick will cheat next week? What is the equilibrium of this game?

Actually, there is more than one possibility. One is the Nash equilibrium that we have just analyzed. Both players cheat, and each makes zero economic profit forever. In such a situation, it will never pay one of the players to start complying unilaterally because to do so would result in a loss for that player and a profit for the other. But a **cooperative equilibrium** in which the players make and share the monopoly profit is possible.

A cooperative equilibrium might occur if cheating is punished. There are two extremes of punishment. The smallest penalty is called "tit for tat." A *tit-for-tat strategy* is one in which a player cooperates in the current period if the other player cooperated in the previous period, but cheats in the current period if the other player cheated in the previous period. The most severe form of punishment is called a trigger strategy. A *trigger strategy* is one in which a player cooperates if the other player cooperates but plays the Nash equilibrium strategy forever thereafter if the other player cheats.

In the duopoly game between Gear and Trick, a tit-for-tat strategy keeps both players cooperating and making monopoly profits. Let's see why with an example.

Table 15.5 shows the economic profit that Trick and Gear will make over a number of periods under two alternative sequences of events: colluding and cheating with a tit-for-tat response by the other firm.

If both firms stick to the collusive agreement in period 1, each makes an economic profit of $2 million. Suppose that Trick contemplates cheating in period 1. The cheating produces a quick $4.5 million economic profit and inflicts a $1 million economic loss on Gear. But a cheat in period 1 produces a response from Gear in period 2. If Trick wants to get back into a profit-making situation, it must return to the agreement in period 2 even though it knows that Gear will punish it for cheating in period 1. So in period 2, Gear punishes Trick and Trick cooperates. Gear now makes an economic profit of $4.5 million, and Trick incurs an economic loss of $1 million. Adding up the profits over two periods of play, Trick would have made more profit by cooperating—$4 million compared with $3.5 million.

What is true for Trick is also true for Gear. Because each firm makes a larger profit by sticking with the collusive agreement, both firms do so and the monopoly price, quantity, and profit prevail.

In reality, whether a cartel works like a one-play game or a repeated game depends primarily on the

TABLE 15.5 Cheating with Punishment

Period of play	Collude		Cheat with tit-for-tat	
	Trick's profit	Gear's profit	Trick's profit	Gear's profit
	(millions of dollars)		(millions of dollars)	
1	2	2	4.5	–1.0
2	2	2	–1.0	4.5
3	2	2	2.0	2.0
4	.	.	.	.

If duopolists repeatedly collude, each makes a profit of $2 million per period of play. If one player cheats in period 1, the other player plays a tit-for-tat strategy and cheats in period 2. The profit from cheating can be made for only one period and must be paid for in the next period by incurring a loss. Over two periods of play, the best that a duopolist can achieve by cheating is a profit of $3.5 million, compared to an economic profit of $4 million by colluding.

number of players and the ease of detecting and punishing cheating. The larger the number of players, the harder it is to maintain a cartel.

Games and Price Wars

A repeated duopoly game can help us understand real-world behavior and, in particular, price wars. Some price wars can be interpreted as the implementation of a tit-for-tat strategy. But the game is a bit more complicated than the one we've looked at because the players are uncertain about the demand for the product.

Playing a tit-for-tat strategy, firms have an incentive to stick to the monopoly price. But fluctuations in demand lead to fluctuations in the monopoly price, and sometimes, when the price changes, it might seem to one of the firms that the price has fallen because the other has cheated. In this case, a price war will break out. The price war will end only when each firm is satisfied that the other is ready to cooperate again. There will be cycles of price wars and the restoration of collusive agreements. Fluctuations in the world price of oil might be interpreted in this way.

Some price wars arise from the entry of a small number of firms into an industry that had previously been a monopoly. Although the industry has a small number of firms, the firms are in a prisoners' dilemma and they cannot impose effective penalties for price cutting. The behavior of prices and outputs in the computer chip industry during 1995 and 1996 can be explained in this way. Until 1995, the market for Pentium chips for IBM-compatible computers was dominated by one firm, Intel Corporation, which was able to make maximum economic profit by producing the quantity of chips at which marginal cost equaled marginal revenue. The price of Intel's chips was set to ensure that the quantity demanded equaled the quantity produced. Then in 1995 and 1996, with the entry of a small number of new firms, the industry became an oligopoly. If the firms had maintained Intel's price and shared the market, together they could have made economic profits equal to Intel's profit. But the firms were in a prisoners' dilemma, so prices fell toward the competitive level.

Let's now study a sequential game. There are many such games, and the one we'll examine is among the simplest. It has an interesting implication and it will give you the flavor of this type of game. The sequential game that we'll study is an entry game in a contestable market.

A Sequential Entry Game in a Contestable Market

If two firms play a sequential game, one firm makes a decision at the first stage of the game and the other makes a decision at the second stage.

We're going to study a sequential game in a **contestable market**—a market in which firms can enter and leave so easily that firms in the market face competition from *potential* entrants. Examples of contestable markets are routes served by airlines and by barge companies that operate on the major waterways. These markets are contestable because firms could enter if an opportunity for economic profit arose and could exit with no penalty if the opportunity for economic profit disappeared.

If the Herfindahl-Hirschman Index (p. 238) is used to determine the degree of competition, a contestable market appears to be uncompetitive. But a contestable market can behave as if it were perfectly competitive. To see why, let's look at an entry game for a contestable air route.

A Contestable Air Route

Agile Air is the only firm operating on a particular route. Demand and cost conditions are such that there is room for only one airline to operate. Wanabe Inc. is another airline that could offer services on the route.

We describe the structure of a sequential game by using a *game tree* like that in Fig. 15.8. At the first stage, Agile Air must set a price. Once the price is set and advertised, Agile can't change it. That is, once set, Agile's price is fixed and Agile can't react to Wanabe's entry decision. Agile can set its price at either the monopoly level or the competitive level.

At the second stage, Wanabe must decide whether to enter or to stay out. Customers have no loyalty (there are no frequent-flyer programs) and they buy from the lowest-price firm. So if Wanabe enters, it sets a price just below Agile's and takes all the business.

Figure 15.8 shows the payoffs from the various decisions (Agile's in the red triangles and Wanabe's in the blue triangles).

To decide on its price, Agile's CEO reasons as follows: Suppose that Agile sets the monopoly price. If Wanabe enters, it earns 90 (think of all payoff numbers as thousands of dollars). If Wanabe stays out, it earns nothing. So Wanabe will enter. In this case Agile will lose 50.

FIGURE 15.8 Agile Versus Wanabe: A Sequential Entry Game in a Contestable Market

If Agile sets the monopoly price, Wanabe makes 90 (thousand dollars) by entering and earns nothing by staying out. So if Agile sets the monopoly price, Wanabe enters.

If Agile sets the competitive price, Wanabe earns nothing if it stays out and incurs a loss if it enters. So if Agile sets the competitive price, Wanabe stays out.

myeconlab animation

Now suppose that Agile sets the competitive price. If Wanabe stays out, it earns nothing, and if it enters, it loses 10, so Wanabe will stay out. In this case, Agile will make zero economic profit.

Agile's best strategy is to set its price at the competitive level and make zero economic profit. The option of earning 100 by setting the monopoly price with Wanabe staying out is not available to Agile. If Agile sets the monopoly price, Wanabe enters, undercuts Agile, and takes all the business.

In this example, Agile sets its price at the competitive level and makes zero economic profit. A less costly strategy, called **limit pricing**, sets the price at the highest level that inflicts a loss on the entrant. Any loss is big enough to deter entry, so it is not always necessary to set the price as low as the competitive price. In the example of Agile and Wanabe, at the competitive price, Wanabe incurs a loss of 10 if it enters. A smaller loss would still keep Wanabe out.

This game is interesting because it points to the possibility of a monopoly behaving like a competitive industry and serving the social interest without regulation. But the result is not general and depends on one crucial feature of the setup of the game: At the second stage, Agile is locked in to the price set at the first stage.

If Agile could change its price in the second stage, it would want to set the monopoly price if Wanabe stayed out—100 with the monopoly price beats zero with the competitive price. But Wanabe can figure out

what Agile would do, so the price set at the first stage has no effect on Wanabe. Agile sets the monopoly price and Wanabe might either stay out or enter.

We've looked at two of the many possible repeated and sequential games, and you've seen how these types of games can provide insights into the complex forces that determine prices and profits.

Review Quiz

1 If a prisoners' dilemma game is played repeatedly, what punishment strategies might the players employ and how does playing the game repeatedly change the equilibrium?

2 If a market is contestable, how does the equilibrium differ from that of a monopoly?

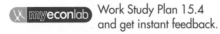 Work Study Plan 15.4 and get instant feedback.

So far, we've studied oligopoly with unregulated market power. Firms like Trick and Gear are free to collude to maximize their profit with no concern for the consumer or the law.

But when firms collude to achieve the monopoly outcome, they also have the same effects on efficiency and the social interest as monopoly. Profit is made at the expense of consumer surplus and a deadweight loss arises. Your next task is to see how U.S. antitrust law limits market power.

Antitrust Law

Antitrust law is the law that regulates oligopolies and prevents them from becoming monopolies or behaving like monopolies. Two government agencies cooperate to enforce the antitrust laws: the Federal Trade Commission and the Antitrust Division of the U.S. Department of Justice.

The Antitrust Laws

The two main antitrust laws are

- The Sherman Act, 1890
- The Clayton Act, 1914.

The Sherman Act The Sherman Act made it a felony to create or attempt to create a monopoly or a cartel.

During the 1880s, lawmakers and the general public were outraged and disgusted by the practices of some of the big-name leaders of American business. The actions of J.P. Morgan, John D. Rockefeller, and W.H. Vanderbilt led to them being called the "robber barons." It turns out that the most lurid stories of the actions of these great American capitalists were not of their creation of monopoly power to exploit consumers but of their actions to damage each other.

Nevertheless, monopolies that damaged the consumer interest did emerge. For example, John D. Rockefeller had a virtual monopoly in the market for oil.

Table 15.6 summarizes the two main provisions of the Sherman Act. Section 1 of the act is precise:

TABLE 15.6   The Sherman Act of 1890

Section 1:

Every contract, combination in the form of trust or otherwise, or conspiracy, in restraint of trade or commerce among the several States, or with foreign nations, is hereby declared to be illegal.

Section 2:

Every person who shall monopolize, or attempt to monopolize, or combine or conspire with any other person or persons, to monopolize any part of the trade or commerce among the several States, or with foreign nations, shall be deemed guilty of a felony.

Conspiring with others to restrict competition is illegal. But Section 2 is general and imprecise. Just what is an "attempt to monopolize"?

The Clayton Act The Clayton Act, which was passed in response to a wave of mergers that occurred at the beginning of the twentieth century, provided the answer to the question left dangling by the Sherman Act: It defined the "attempt to monopolize." The Clayton Act supplemented the Sherman Act and strengthened and clarified the antitrust law.

When Congress passed the Clayton Act, it also established the Federal Trade Commission, the federal agency charged with the task of preventing monopoly practices that damage the consumer interest.

Two amendments to the Clayton Act, the Robinson-Patman Act of 1936 and the Celler-Kefauver Act of 1950, outlaw specific practices and provided even greater precision to the antitrust law. Table 15.7 describes these practices and summarizes the main provisions of these three acts.

TABLE 15.7   The Clayton Act and Its Amendments

Clayton Act	**1914**
Robinson-Patman Act	**1936**
Celler-Kefauver Act	**1950**

These acts prohibit the following practices *only if* they substantially lessen competition or create monopoly:

1. Price discrimination

2. Contracts that require other goods to be bought from the same firm (called *tying arrangements*)

3. Contracts that require a firm to buy all its requirements of a particular item from a single firm (called *requirements contracts*)

4. Contracts that prevent a firm from selling competing items (called *exclusive dealing*)

5. Contracts that prevent a buyer from reselling a product outside a specified area (called *territorial confinement*)

6. Acquiring a competitor's shares or assets

7. Becoming a director of a competing firm

Price Fixing Always Illegal

Colluding to fix the price is *always* a violation of the antitrust law. If the Justice Department can prove the existence of a price fixing cartel, defendants can offer no acceptable excuse.

The predictions of the effects of price fixing that you saw in the previous sections of this chapter provide the reasons for the unqualified attitude toward price fixing. A duopoly cartel can maximize profit and behave like a monopoly. To achieve the monopoly outcome, the cartel restricts production and fixes the price at the monopoly level. The consumer suffers because consumer surplus shrinks. And the outcome is inefficient because a deadweight loss arises.

It is for these reasons that the law declares that all price fixing is illegal. No excuse can justify the practice.

Other antitrust practices are more controversial and generate debate among lawyers and economists. We'll examine three of these practices.

Three Antitrust Policy Debates

The three practices that we'll examine are

- Resale price maintenance
- Tying arrangements
- Predatory pricing

Resale Price Maintenance Most manufacturers sell their products to the final consumer indirectly through a wholesale and retail distribution system. **Resale price maintenance** occurs when a manufacturer agrees with a distributor on the price at which the product will be resold.

Resale price maintenance (also called vertical price fixing) *agreements* are illegal under the Sherman Act. But it isn't illegal for a manufacturer to refuse to supply a retailer who doesn't accept guidance on what the price should be.

Nor is it illegal to set a *minimum* retail price provided it is not anticompetitive. In 2007, the Supreme Court ruled that a handbag manufacturer could impose a minimum retail price on a Dallas store, Kay's Kloset. Since that ruling, many manufacturers have imposed minimum retail prices. The practice is judged on a case-by-case basis.

Does resale price maintenance create an inefficient or efficient use of resources? Economists can be found on both sides of this question.

Inefficient Resale Price Maintenance Resale price maintenance is inefficient if it enables dealers to charge the monopoly price. By setting and enforcing the resale price, the manufacturer might be able to achieve the monopoly price.

Efficient Resale Price Maintenance Resale price maintenance might be efficient if it enables a manufacturer to induce dealers to provide the efficient standard of service. Suppose that SilkySkin wants shops to demonstrate the use of its new unbelievable moisturizing cream in an inviting space. With resale price maintenance, SilkySkin can offer all the retailers the same incentive and compensation. Without resale price maintenance, a cut-price drug store might offer SilkySkin products at a low price. Buyers would then have an incentive to visit a high-price shop and get the product demonstrated and then buy from the low-price shop. The low-price shop would be a free rider (like the consumer of a public good in Chapter 17, p. xxx), and an inefficient level of service would be provided.

SilkySkin could pay a fee to retailers that provide good service and leave the resale price to be determined by the competitive forces of supply and demand. But it might be too costly for SilkySkin to monitor shops and ensure that they provided the desired level of service.

Tying Arrangements A **tying arrangement** is an agreement to sell one product only if the buyer agrees to buy another, different product. With tying, the only way the buyer can get the one product is to also buy the other product. Microsoft has been accused of tying Internet Explorer and Windows. Textbook publishers sometimes tie a Web site and a textbook and force students to buy both. (You can't buy the book you're now reading, new, without the Web site. But you can buy the Web site access without the book, so these products are not tied.)

Could textbook publishers make more money by tying a book and access to a Web site? The answer is sometimes but not always. Suppose that you and other students are willing to pay $80 for a book and $20 for access to a Web site. The publisher can sell these items separately for these prices or bundled for $100. The publisher does not gain from bundling.

But now suppose that you and only half of the students are willing to pay $80 for a book and $20 for a Web site and the other half of the students are willing to pay $80 for a Web site and $20 for a book. Now if the two items are sold separately, the publisher can charge $80 for the book and $80 for the Web site. Half the students buy the book but not the Web site, and the other half buy the Web site but not the book. But if the book and Web site are bundled for $100, everyone buys the bundle and the publisher makes an extra $20 per student. In this case, bundling has enabled the publisher to price discriminate.

There is no simple, clear-cut test of whether a firm is engaging in tying or whether, by doing so, it has increased its market power and profit and created inefficiency.

Predatory Pricing **Predatory pricing** is setting a low price to drive competitors out of business with the intention of setting a monopoly price when the com-petition has gone. John D. Rockefeller's Standard Oil Company was the first to be accused of this practice in the 1890s, and it has been claimed often in antitrust cases since then. Predatory pricing is an attempt to create a monopoly and as such it is illegal under Section 2 of the Sherman Act.

It is easy to see that predatory pricing is an idea, not a reality. Economists are skeptical that predatory pricing occurs. They point out that a firm that cuts its price below the profit-maximizing level loses during the low-price period. Even if it succeeds in driving its competitors out of business, new competitors will enter as soon as the price is increased, so any potential gain from a monopoly position is temporary. A high and certain loss is a poor exchange for a temporary and uncertain gain. No case of predatory pricing has been definitively found.

An Antitrust Showcase
The United States Versus Microsoft

In 1998, the Antitrust Division of the U.S. Department of Justice along with the Departments of Justice of a number of states charged Microsoft, the world's largest producer of software for personal computers, with violations of both sections of the Sherman Act.

A 78-day trial followed that pitched two prominent MIT economics professors against each other, Franklin Fisher for the government and Richard Schmalensee for Microsoft.

The Case Against Microsoft The claims against Microsoft were that it

- Possessed monopoly power
- Used predatory pricing and tying arrangements
- Used other anticompetitive practices

It was claimed that with 80 percent of the market for PC operating systems, Microsoft had excessive monopoly power. This monopoly power arose from two barriers to entry: economies of scale and network economies. Microsoft's average total cost falls as production increases (economies of scale) because the fixed cost of developing an operating system such as Windows is large while the marginal cost of producing one copy of Windows is small. Further, as the number of Windows users increases, the range of Windows applications expands (network economies), so a potential competitor would need to produce not only a competing operating system but also an entire range of supporting applications as well.

When Microsoft entered the Web browser market with its Internet Explorer, it offered the browser for a zero price. This price was viewed as predatory pricing. Microsoft integrated Internet Explorer with Windows so that anyone who uses this operating system would not need a separate browser such as Netscape Navigator. Microsoft's competitors claimed that this practice was an illegal tying arrangement.

Microsoft's Response Microsoft challenged all these claims. It said that Windows was vulnerable to competition from other operating systems such as Linux and Apple's Mac OS and that there was a permanent threat of competition from new entrants.

Microsoft claimed that integrating Internet Explorer with Windows provided a single, unified product of greater consumer value like a refrigerator with a chilled water dispenser or an automobile with a CD player.

The Outcome The court agreed that Microsoft was in violation of the Sherman Act and ordered that it be broken into two firms: an operating systems producer and an applications producer. Microsoft successfully appealed this order. In the final judgment, though, Microsoft was ordered to disclose to other software developers details of how its operating system works, so that they could compete effectively against Microsoft. In the summer of 2002, Microsoft began to comply with this order.

Mergers and Acquisitions

Mergers, which occur when two or more firms agree to combine to create one larger firm, and *acquisitions*, which occur when one firm buys another firm, are common events. Mergers occurred when Chrysler and the German auto producer Daimler-Benz combined to form DaimlerChrysler and when the Belgian beer producer InBev bought the U.S. brewing giant Anheuser-Busch and created a new combined company, Anheuser-Busch InBev. An acquisition occurred when Rupert Murdoch's News Corp bought Myspace.

The mergers and acquisitions that occur don't create a monopoly. But two (or more) firms might be tempted to try to merge so that they can gain market power and operate like a monopoly. If such a situation arises, the Federal Trade Commission (FTC) takes an interest in the move and stands ready to block the merger.

To determine which mergers it will examine and possibly block, the FTC uses guidelines, one of which is the Herfindahl-Hirschman Index (HHI) (see Chapter 10, pp. 238–239).

A market in which the HHI is less than 1,000 is regarded as competitive. An index between 1,000 and 1,800 indicates a moderately concentrated market,

and a merger in this market that would increase the index by 100 points is challenged by the FTC. An index above 1,800 indicates a concentrated market, and a merger in this market that would increase the index by 50 points is challenged. You can see an application of these guidelines in the box below.

Review Quiz

1 What are the two main antitrust laws and when were they enacted?
2 When is price fixing not a violation of the antitrust laws?
3 What is an attempt to monopolize an industry?
4 What are resale price maintenance, tying arrangements, and predatory pricing?
5 Under what circumstances is a merger unlikely to be approved?

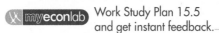 Work Study Plan 15.5 and get instant feedback.

Oligopoly is a market structure that you often encounter in your daily life. *Reading Between the Lines* on pp. 362–363 looks at a game played by Dell and HP in the market for personal computers.

Merger Guidelines
FTC Takes the Fizz out of Soda Mergers

The FTC used its HHI guidelines to block proposed mergers in the market for soft drinks. PepsiCo wanted to buy 7-Up and Coca-Cola wanted to buy Dr Pepper. The market for carbonated soft drinks is highly concentrated. Coca-Cola had a 39 percent share, PepsiCo had 28 percent, Dr Pepper was next with 7 percent, followed by 7-Up with 6 percent. One other producer, RJR, had a 5 percent market share. So the five largest firms in this market had an 85 percent market share.

The PepsiCo and 7-Up merger would have increased the HHI by more than 300 points. The Coca-Cola and Dr Pepper merger would have increased it by more than 500 points, and both mergers together would have increased the index by almost 800 points.

The FTC decided that increases in the HHI of these magnitudes were not in the social interest and blocked the mergers. The figure summarizes the HHI guideline and HHIs in the soft drinks market.

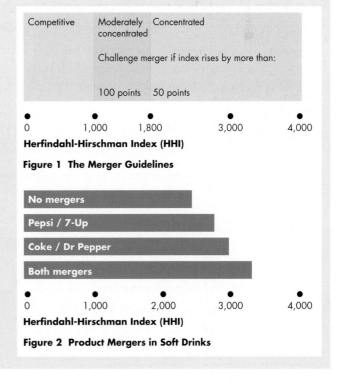

Figure 1 The Merger Guidelines

Figure 2 Product Mergers in Soft Drinks

Dell and HP in a Market Share Game

The Old Price-War Tactic May Not Faze Rivals Now

http://www.nytimes.com
May 13, 2006

Dell is sharply reducing prices on its computers.

The tactic is classic, straight out of the playbook that made the company the world's largest computer maker. As overall demand for personal computers slows, lower your prices. Profit margins will take a temporary hit, but the move would hurt competitors worse as you take market share and enjoy revenue growth for years to come.

Dell did it in 2000 and it worked beautifully. But after Dell rolled out the plan last month, knocking as much as $700 off a $1,200 Inspiron and $500 off a $1,079 Dimension desktop, many of the securities analysts who follow the company, based in Round Rock, Tex., said that this time around it could be folly. …

What changed? … More than anything else, Dell's competitors have changed. In particular, Hewlett-Packard is no longer the bloated and slow-moving company it was six years ago. …

The most telling evidence of the new landscape for PCs was seen in statistics on worldwide shipments. While the industry grew 12.9 percent in the first three months of the year, … Dell's shipments grew 10.2 percent. It was the first time since analysts began tracking Dell that its shipments grew more slowly than the industry's. Hewlett's shipments, meanwhile, grew 22.2 percent. …

Inside Hewlett, however, there is a feeling that it can beat Dell without resorting to price wars. … The company has started an ambitious marketing campaign to make that point with ads that proclaim, "the computer is personal again." …

The campaign … will feature celebrities and how they individualize their computers … [HP] has added technology like QuickPlay, which lets a user view a DVD or listen to a CD without waiting for the laptop's operating system to boot up. The ads will say, "Don't boot. Play." …

Essence of the Story

- Dell cut its prices in 2000 and increased its market share and revenue in the years that followed.

- In April 2006, Dell slashed its prices.

- Experts say the price cut will not work as well today.

- Hewlett-Packard (HP) is much stronger than it was six years ago.

- Total PC shipments increased by 12.9 percent in the first quarter of 2006: Dell's shipments increased by 10.2 percent, and HP's increased by 22.2 percent.

♦ HP says that it can beat Dell without a price cut. Instead it will launch a campaign to market PCs with new and improved features, such as one that plays DVDs and CDs without booting the operating system.

Economic Analysis

- The global PC market has many firms, but two firms dominate the market: Dell and Hewlett-Packard (HP).

- Figure 1 shows the shares in the global PC market. You can see that Dell and HP are the two biggest players but almost 50 percent of the market is served by small firms, each with less than 4 percent of the market.

- Table 1 shows the payoff matrix (millions of dollars of profit) for the game played by Dell and HP in 2000. (The numbers are hypothetical.)

- This game has a dominant strategy equilibrium similar to that for the duopoly game on p. 353.

- If HP cuts its price, Dell makes a larger profit by cutting its price (+$20m versus –$10m), and if HP holds its price constant, Dell again makes a larger profit by cutting its price (+$40m versus zero).

- So Dell's best strategy is to cut its price.

- If Dell cuts its price, HP makes a larger profit by cutting its price (+$5m versus –$20m), and if Dell holds its price constant, HP again makes a larger profit by cutting its price (+$10m versus zero).

- So HP's best strategy is to cut its price.

- Table 2 shows the payoffs from the game between Dell and HP in 2006.

- This game, too, has a dominant strategy equilibrium.

- If HP cuts its price, Dell makes a larger profit by cutting its price (+$10m versus –$10m), and if HP improves its marketing and design, Dell again makes a larger profit by cutting its price (+$5m versus –$20m).

- So Dell's best strategy is to cut its price.

- If Dell cuts its price, HP makes a larger profit by improving its marketing and design (+$20m versus +$10m), and if Dell holds its price constant, HP again makes a larger profit by improving its marketing and design (+$40m versus +$20m).

- So HP's best strategy is to improve its marketing and design.

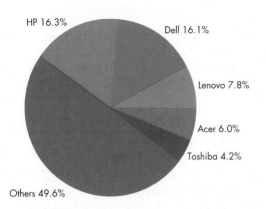

Figure 1 Market shares in the PC market in 2006

Table 1 The strategies and equilibrium in 2000

Table 2 The strategies and equilibrium in 2006

SUMMARY ◆

Key Points

What Is Oligopoly? (pp. 342–343)

- Oligopoly is a market in which a small number of firms compete.

Two Traditional Oligopoly Models (pp. 344–345)

- If rivals match price cuts but do not match price hikes, each firm faces a kinked demand curve.
- If one firm dominates a market, it acts like a monopoly and the small firms act as price takers.

Oligopoly Games (pp. 346–354)

- Oligopoly is studied by using game theory, which is a method of analyzing strategic behavior.
- In a prisoners' dilemma game, two prisoners acting in their own self-interest harm their joint interest.
- An oligopoly (duopoly) price-fixing game is a prisoners' dilemma in which the firms might collude or cheat.
- In Nash equilibrium, both firms cheat and output and price are the same as in perfect competition.
- Firms' decisions about advertising and R&D can be studied by using game theory.

Repeated Games and Sequential Games (pp. 355–357)

- In a repeated game, a punishment strategy can produce a cooperative equilibrium in which price and output are the same as in a monopoly.

- In a sequential contestable market game, a small number of firms can behave like firms in perfect competition.

Antitrust Law (pp. 358–361)

- The first antitrust law, the Sherman Act, was passed in 1890, and the law was strengthened in 1914 when the Clayton Act was passed and the Federal Trade Commission was created.
- All price-fixing agreements are violations of the Sherman Act, and no acceptable excuse exists.
- Resale price maintenance might be efficient if it enables a producer to ensure the efficient level of service by distributors.
- Tying arrangements can enable a monopoly to price discriminate and increase profit, but in many cases, tying would not increase profit.
- Predatory pricing is unlikely to occur because it brings losses and only temporary potential gains.
- The Federal Trade Commission uses guidelines such as the Herfindahl-Hirschman Index to determine which mergers to investigate and possibly block.

Key Figures and Tables

Key Terms

PROBLEMS and APPLICATIONS ◆

 Work problems 1–11 in Chapter 15 Study Plan and get instant feedback.
Work problems 12–19 as Homework, a Quiz, or a Test if assigned by your instructor.

1. Two firms make most of the chips that power a PC: Intel and Advanced Micro Devices. What makes the market for PC chips a duopoly? Sketch the market demand curve and cost curves that describe the situation in this market and that prevent other firms from entering.

2. The price at which Wal-Mart can buy flat-panel TVs has fallen, and it is making a decision about whether to cut its selling price. Wal-Mart believes that if it cuts its price, all its competitors will cut their prices, but if it raises its price, none of its competitors will raise theirs.
   a. Draw a figure to illustrate the situation that Wal-Mart believes it faces in the market for flat-panel TVs.
   b. Do you predict that Wal-Mart will lower its price of a flat-panel TV? Explain and illustrate your answer.

3. Big Joe's Trucking has lower costs than the other 20 small truckers in the market. The market operates like a dominant firm oligopoly and is initially in equilibrium. Then the demand for trucking services increases. Explain the effects of the increase in demand on the price, output, and economic profit of
   a. Big Joe's.
   b. A typical small firm.

4. Consider a game with two players, who cannot communicate, and in which each player is asked a question. The players can answer the question honestly or lie. If both answer honestly, each receives $100. If one answers honestly and the other lies, the liar receives $500 and the honest player gets nothing. If both lie, then each receives $50.
   a. Describe the strategies and payoffs of this game.
   b. Construct the payoff matrix.
   c. What is the equilibrium of this game?
   d. Compare this game to the prisoners' dilemma. Are the two games similar or different? Explain.

5. Soapy Inc. and Suddies Inc. are the only producers of soap powder. They collude and agree to share the market equally. If neither firm cheats

on the agreement, each makes $1 million profit. If either firm cheats, the cheat makes a profit of $1.5 million, while the complier incurs a loss of $0.5 million. If both cheat, they break even. Neither firm can monitor the other's actions.
   a. What are the strategies in this game?
   b. Construct the payoff matrix for this game.
   c. What is the equilibrium of this game if it is played only once?
   d. Is the equilibrium a dominant strategy equilibrium? Explain.

6. If Soapy Inc. and Suddies Inc. repeatedly play the duopoly game that has the payoffs described in problem 5 on each round of play,
   a. What now are the strategies that each firm might adopt?
   b. Can the firms adopt a strategy that gives the game a cooperative equilibrium?
   c. Would one firm still be tempted to cheat in a cooperative equilibrium? Explain your answer.

7. **Oil City**
   In the late '90s, Reliance spent $6 billion and employed 75,000 workers to build a world-class oil refinery at Jamnagar, India. … Now Reliance is more than doubling the size of the facility, which … will claim the title of the world's biggest … with an output of 1.2 million gallons of gasoline per day, or about 5% of global capacity. … Reliance plans to aim Jamnagar's spigots westward, at the U.S. and Europe, where it's too expensive and politically difficult to build new refineries. …The bulked-up Jamnagar will be able to move markets: Singapore traders expect a drop in fuel prices as soon as it's going full tilt.
   Fortune, April 28, 2008
   a. Explain this news clip's claims that the global market for gasoline is not perfectly competitive.
   b. What barriers to entry might limit competition in this market and give a firm such as Reliance power to influence the market price?

8. **Congress Examines Giant Airline Merger**
   Congress Wednesday examined a proposed $3.1 billion merger that would create the world's

largest carrier as critics of the deal warned it could drive up the price of air travel. … [Committee Chairman James Oberstar] said the Delta-Northwest merger would discourage competition at major hubs, reduce service to customers and result in higher fares. Delta Chief Executive Officer Richard Anderson said that the merger would not limit competition because the carriers primarily serve different geographic regions. … About a dozen witnesses scheduled to testify before the House Subcommittee on Transportation and Infrastructure were likely to focus on whether a merger between Delta Air Lines and Northwest Airlines would benefit consumers by lowering prices through cost savings, or harm them by reducing competition.

CNN, May 14, 2008

a. Explain how this airline merger might increase air travel prices.
b. Explain how this airline merger might lower air travel production costs.
c. Explain how cost savings might get passed on to travelers and might boost producers profits. Which do you predict will happen from this airline merger and why?
d. Explain the guidelines that the Federal Trade Commission uses to evaluate mergers and why it might permit or block this merger.

9. **U.K. Price Cuts Seen for Apple's New iPhone**

AT&T is planning to sell the new iPhone this summer for around $200. … The new iPhone would be available later this month in the U.S. through Apple and AT&T. AT&T pricing strategy calls for a $200 subsidy for customers who sign two-year service contracts. …

The lower-priced phones in the U.S. … would help juice the iPhone's sales volume and give the telcos an attractive weapon to win new subscribers.

In the United States, AT&T says it pulls in an average of $95 a month from each iPhone customer, nearly twice the average monthly bill of its conventional cell phone user. AT&T has a revenue-sharing agreement with Apple that requires it to give Apple as much as 25% of its iPhone customers' monthly payments.

Subsidies are a widespread pricing practice in the United States and overseas. In exchange for a cheaper phone, customers are locked in to a car-

rier for a year or two. It's a small investment by the telcos for a large return. … After giving Apple its cut of the revenue, the remaining take for AT&T is between $70 and $75 a month per iPhone user, totaling more than $1,700 over the life of the two-year contract. …

Fortune, June 2, 2008

a. How does this arrangement between AT&T and Apple regarding the iPhone affect competition in the market for cell phone service?
b. Does this arrangement between AT&T and Apple regarding the iPhone violate U.S. antitrust laws? Explain.

10. **Starbucks Sued for Trying to Sink Competition**

An independent coffee shop owner filed a lawsuit against Starbucks Corp. Monday, charging the coffee house giant with using anti-competitive tactics to rid itself of competition. The suit … was filed … by Penny Stafford, owner of the Seattle-based Belvi Coffee and Tea Exchange Inc. The lawsuit contends that Starbucks exploited its monopoly power in the specialty retail coffee market through such predatory practices as offering to pay leases that exceeded market value if the building owner would refuse to allow competitors from occupying the same building. Stafford says Starbucks also used methods such as having employees offer free drink samples in front of her store to lure away customers, which she says ultimately forced her to close her store. … The suit contends the world's largest specialty coffee retailer also used other predatory tactics nationwide including offering to buy out competitors at below-market prices and threatening to open nearby stores if the offer is rejected.

CNN, September 26, 2006

a. Explain how Starbucks is alleged to have violated U.S. antitrust laws in Seattle.
b. Explain why it is unlikely that Starbucks might use predatory pricing to permanently drive out competition.
c. What information would you need that is not provided in the news clip to decide whether Starbucks had practiced predatory pricing?
d. Draw a graph of the situation facing Belvi Coffee and Tea Exchange Inc. when Penny Stafford closed the firm.

11. **Oil Trading Probe May Uncover Manipulation**

    Amid soaring oil prices … the government Thursday announced a wide ranging probe into oil price manipulation. … The CFTC [Commodity Futures Trade Commission] is looking into … manipulation of the physical oil market … by commercial players who might literally withhold oil from the market in an attempt to drive prices higher.

    The CFTC has found evidence of this in the past. … Haigh [a former economist at CFTC] thinks it's likely CFTC will find evidence of this again given that the agency has been investigating for six months and has now chosen to make it public. But he stressed that a single player acting alone would in all likelihood not have a huge influence on prices. "It's difficult to imagine a price run-up of $90 to $135 being done by one entity," he said.

    CNN, May 30, 2008

    a. What type of market does former CFTC economist Haigh imply best describes the U.S. oil market?

    b. Is economist Haigh's comment consistent with the predictions of the kinked demand curve model of oligopoly? Explain.

    c. Is economist Haigh's comment consistent with the predictions of the dominant firm oligopoly model? Explain.

    d. Is economist Haigh's comment consistent with the predictions of any model of oligopoly? Explain.

12. Bud and Wise are the only two producers of aniseed beer, a New Age product designed to displace root beer. Bud and Wise are trying to figure out how much of this new beer to produce. They know that if they both limit production to 10,000 gallons a day, they will make the maximum attainable joint profit of $200,000 a day—$100,000 a day each. They also know that if either of them produces 20,000 gallons a day while the other produces 10,000 a day, the one that produces 20,000 gallons will make an economic profit of $150,000 and the one that sticks with 10,000 gallons will incur an economic loss of $50,000. Each also knows that if they both increase production to 20,000 gallons a day, they will both make zero economic profit.

    a. Construct a payoff matrix for the game that Bud and Wise must play.

    b. Find the Nash equilibrium of the game that Bud and Wise play.

    c. What is the equilibrium of the game if Bud and Wise play it repeatedly?

13. **Gadgets for Sale … or Not**

    How come some gadgets, like the iPod, cost the same no matter where you shop? … No, the answer isn't that Apple illegally manages prices. In reality, Steve Jobs and Co. use an accepted, if controversial, tactic, a retail strategy called minimum advertised price, to discourage resellers from discounting.

    The minimum advertised price, or MAP, is the absolute lowest price retailers are allowed to advertise a product for. MAP is usually enforced through marketing subsidies offered by a manufacturer to its resellers. If a retailer keeps prices at or above the minimum advertised price, then a manufacturer like Apple will give them money to help advertise. If a store's price dips too low, on the other hand, the manufacturer can withdraw these advertising subsidies. …

    Stable prices are important to the company, because it's a manufacturer and a retailer (both online and through its chain of Apple Stores). If Apple resellers dropped prices on iPods and iMacs—selling at or below cost to get customers in the door, or as a way to cross-sell stuff like software or iPod skins—they could squeeze the Apple Stores out of their own markets.

    There is a downside to all that stability, however. By limiting how low sellers can go, MAP keeps prices artificially high (or at least higher than they might otherwise be with unfettered price competition).

    Slate, December 22, 2006

    a. Describe the practice of resale price maintenance that violates the Sherman Act.

    b. Describe the MAP strategy used by iPod and explain how it differs from a resale price maintenance agreement that would violate the Sherman Act.

    c. Why might the MAP strategy be against the consumer interest?

    d. Why might the MAP strategy benefit the consumer?

    e. What is the bottom line on the MAP strategy: does it benefit the consumer or only the producer?

14. **Asian Rice Exporters to Discuss Cartel**

Rice-exporting nations planned to discuss a proposed cartel to control the price of the staple food. … Rice exporters Thailand, Cambodia, Laos and Myanmar planned to meet Tuesday to discuss a proposal by Thailand, the world's largest rice exporter, that they form a cartel. Ahead of the meeting … the countries sought to assuage concerns that they might force up prices by limiting supplies.

Unlike the Organization of Petroleum Exporting Countries, the purpose of the rice cartel would be "to contribute to ensuring food stability, not just in an individual country but also to address food shortages in the region and the world," Cambodian Prime Minister Hun Sen said Monday.

"We shall not hoard (rice) and raise prices when there are shortages," Hun Sen said. The Philippines wasn't convinced.

"It is a bad idea. … It will create an oligopoly and it's against humanity," Edgardo Angara, chairman of the Philippine Senate's Committee on Agriculture, said Friday, adding that the cartel could price the grain out of reach for "millions and millions of people."

CNN, May 6, 2008

a. Assuming the rice-exporting nations become a profit-maximizing colluding oligopoly, explain how they would influence the global market for rice and the world price of rice.

b. Assuming the rice-exporting nations become a profit-maximizing colluding oligopoly, draw a graph to illustrate their influence on the global market for rice.

c. Even in the absence of international antitrust laws, why might it be difficult for this cartel to successfully collude? Use the ideas of game theory to explain.

15. **An Energy Drink with a Monster of a Stock**

The $5.7 billion energy-drink category, in which Monster holds the No. 2 position behind industry leader Red Bull, has slowed down as copycat brands jostle for shelf space—and the attention of teen consumers. … Over the past five years Red Bull's market share in dollar terms has gone from 91 percent to well under 50 percent … and much of that loss has been Monster's gain.

Fortune, December 25, 2006

a. Describe the structure of the energy-drink market. How has that structure changed over the past few years?

b. Explain the various difficulties Monster and Red Bull would have if they attempted to collude and charge monopoly prices for energy drinks.

16. Suppose that Firefox and Microsoft each develop their own versions of an amazing new Web browser that allows advertisers to target consumers with great precision. Also, the new browser is easier and more fun to use than existing browsers. Each firm is trying to decide whether to sell the browser or to give it away. What are the likely benefits from each action? Which action is likely to occur?

17. Why do Coca-Cola and PepsiCo spend huge amounts on advertising? Do they benefit? Does the consumer benefit? Explain your answer by constructing a game to illustrate the choices Coca-Cola and PepsiCo make.

18. Microsoft with Xbox 360, Nintendo with Wii, and Sony with PlayStation 3 are slugging it out in the market for the latest generation of video games consoles. Xbox 360 was the first to market; Wii has the lowest price; PS3 uses the most advanced technology and has the highest price.

a. Thinking of the competition among these firms in the market for consoles as a game, describe the firms' strategies concerning design, marketing, and price.

b. What, based on the information provided, turned out to be the equilibrium of the game?

c. Can you think of reasons why the three consoles are so different?

19. Study *Reading Between the Lines* on pp. 362–363 and then answer the following questions.

a. What were the strategies of Dell and HP in 2000 and in 2006?

b. Why, according to the news article, was Dell having a harder time in 2006 than it had in 2000?

c. Why wouldn't HP launch its new product and marketing campaign *and* cut its price?

d. What do you think Dell must do to restore its place as market leader?

e. How would you describe the global market for PCs? Is it an example of oligopoly or monopolistic competition?

UNDERSTANDING FIRMS AND MARKETS

Managing Change and Limiting Market Power

Our economy is constantly changing. Every year, new goods appear and old ones disappear. New firms are born, and old ones die. This process of change is initiated and managed by firms operating in markets.

When a new product appears, just one or two firms sell it: Apple and IBM were the only producers of personal computers; Microsoft was (and almost still is) the only producer of the PC operating system; Intel was the only producer of the PC chip. These firms had enormous power to determine the quantity to produce and the price of their products.

In many markets, entry eventually brings competition. Even with just two rivals, the industry changes its face in a dramatic way. *Strategic interdependence* is capable of leading to an outcome like perfect competition.

With the continued arrival of new firms in an industry, the market becomes competitive. But in most markets, the competition isn't perfect: it becomes *monopolistic competition* with each firm selling its own differentiated product.

Often, an industry that is competitive becomes less so as the bigger and more successful firms in the industry begin to swallow up the smaller firms, either by driving them out of business or by acquiring their assets. Through this process, an industry might return to oligopoly or even monopoly. You can see such a movement in the auto and banking industries today.

By studying firms and markets, we gain a deeper understanding of the forces that allocate resources and begin to see the invisible hand at work.

John von Neumann *was one of the great minds of the twentieth century. Born in Budapest, Hungary, in 1903, Johnny, as he was known, showed early mathematical brilliance. He was 25 when he published the article that changed the social sciences and began a flood of research on* **game theory**—*a flood that has not subsided. In that article, von Neumann proved that in a zero-sum game (such as sharing a pie), there exists a best strategy for each player.*

Von Neumann did more than invent game theory: He also invented and built the first practical computer, and he worked on the Manhattan Project, which developed the atomic bomb during World War II.

Von Neumann believed that the social sciences would progress only if they used their own mathematical tools, not those of the physical sciences.

"Real life consists of bluffing, of little tactics of deception, of asking yourself what is the other man going to think I mean to do."

JOHN VON NEUMANN, told to Jacob Bronowski (in a London taxi) and reported in *The Ascent of Man*

TALKING
WITH

Drew Fudenberg

Drew Fudenberg is the Frederic E. Abbe Professor of Economics at Harvard University. Born in New York City in 1957, he studied applied mathematics at Harvard and economics at M.I.T., where he was awarded a Ph.D. in 1981. He began his research and teaching career at the University of California, Berkeley, and moved to M.I.T. in 1987 and to Harvard in 1993.

Professor Fudenberg is a leading game theorist and has worked on an incredibly wide range of problems that arise in games when players don't have enough information to play in the way they play the games that we describe in Chapter 15. This work has resulted in more than 60 articles and two major books: with Jean Tirole, *Game Theory* (MIT Press, 1991) and with David K. Levine, *The Theory of Learning in Games* (MIT Press, 1998).

Michael Parkin talked with Drew Fudenberg about his career, the promise held by game theory, and some of the results of his research.

Professor Fudenberg, was math a better undergraduate major than economics for a career in economics?

Math is a good preparation for graduate study in economics, particularly for economic theory, in part because some of the results are useful but mostly because it provides good training in abstract thinking and rigorous arguments.

That said, I didn't major in math but in "applied math," which at Harvard is a fairly flexible program that includes physics, computer science, and an area of application of the student's choice in addition to math and applied math classes. As an undergraduate, I actually took as many economics classes as math and applied math classes combined. Looking back, given how my research interests have developed, I probably should have taken more math and probability classes than I did. But I did leave college with what is probably the most important math skill for an economist: the willingness to pick up a textbook to learn new tools as they are needed.

Why did you become an economist?

I really enjoyed my economics classes in college, and by taking some graduate classes as an undergraduate, I found that I'd be able to hold my own in graduate school. I was lucky to have inspirational teachers such as Ken Arrow, Howard Raiffa, and Michael Spence, and to have an advisor (Steven Shavell) who encouraged me to think about graduate study and to start reading journals as an undergraduate. By senior year, I had narrowed things down to either economics or law, and I chose economics that spring.

Principles of economics texts (including this one) introduce game theory as a tool for understanding the strategic behavior of oligopolies. Can you provide some examples of the wider use of game theory?

Game theory is used in many areas of economics. It helps us to study the credibility of a central bank in its pursuit of anti-inflationary monetary policy, the dilemma faced by a government about whether to tax capital or renege on its debt, the negotiations between labor unions and management, the decisions of developing economies to nationalize foreign-owned assets, pretrial negotiations by lawyers, and lobbying by interest groups.

Game theory is also used outside economics. Political scientists use it to gain insights into arms races and other strategic decisions, and biologists use it to study the dynamics of the evolution and survival of species.

> ... the only alternative to a game theoretic analysis seems to be no analysis at all.

Some economists think that game theory is the only game worth playing. Others think that it has no empirical content. How would you explain the achievements and the promise of game theory to a beginning student?

The current state of game theory is far from perfect, but it does help us understand and make predictions about a very large and important set of situations. Everything in economics can be viewed as a game. There is no real gain from doing so in the case of single-agent decisions (where there are no other agents) or in the case of a perfectly competitive economy (where each agent cares only about the market price and his own decisions). But in all other cases, the only alternative to a game theoretic analysis seems to be no analysis at all.

Game theory has proved to be a useful way to think about qualitative issues like "how does repeated interaction help support cooperation" and "how might a dominant firm in a market with network externalities exploit its position," and it has long been used to motivate and explain the outcomes of games played in economics laboratory experiments.

It is more difficult to use game theory in econometric studies of field data, but there has been a lot of progress in this area in recent years, in part due to my colleagues Ariel Pakes and Susan Athey (You can read about Susan Athey on p. 178.).

The germs of truth behind the "no empirical content" criticism are that (a) seemingly small changes in the specification of a game can sometimes lead to large changes in its set of equilibria and (b) even when we are pretty sure we know the game being played, the predictions can be less accurate than we'd like. Of course, these same complaints can be made about many fields, but I have to admit that both academic and real-world life would be simpler if these complaints weren't true.

In the games that you study, players have limited knowledge. How is it possible for economists to study games in which the players don't know the payoffs and can't predict the actions of the other players?

The standard Nash equilibrium solution concept says that each player's strategy is a best response to the strategies being used by the others. The concept itself says nothing about the players' knowledge of the game being played nor about when and how a play might come to resemble an equilibrium. In some games, careful reasoning by sophisticated players will lead them to play the equilibrium the very first time they are in the game.

But in game theory experiments it is more typical for play to start away from the equilibrium and then move toward it as the players acquire more experience with the game. This adjustment can be the result of learning by human subjects who know they are in a game, but that's not necessary: Nash equilibrium can also arise when the players are genetically programmed agents who don't think at all, as in the games played by genes that evolutionary biologists study.

So the fact that the agents don't know the game doesn't make game theory irrelevant. However, these adaptive processes take time, and in many settings, it is not clear whether one should expect observed play to approximate an equilibrium.

It is fairly easy to distinguish equilibrium and nonequilibrium play in the lab, where the experimenter controls the payoff, and more difficult to do so in field data where the payoffs are part of what is being estimated.

The empirical application of game theory has advanced a lot in recent years but has mostly maintained equilibrium as an assumption. Devising empirical tests for equilibrium is one of the leading open problems in applied game theory.

How does someone get a reputation and how does that help to get a better outcome? Does reputation always improve the outcome?

To get a reputation for "doing x," you simply have to do x every chance you get! This may have some short-run costs, but if you will be playing this game very often and are patient, it can be worth incurring the costs to build the reputation you want.

Conversely, a short-run player or an impatient player isn't willing to invest in a reputation. The simplest case is of a single long-run player facing one short-run player after another in sequence, with the two sides choosing their actions simultaneously each round and the actions being observed by all subsequent players. Here, the opportunity to build a reputation can't hurt the long-run player, and it typically helps. Things get more complicated if there are two or more long-run players each trying to build their own reputation or if the actions played in a round are sequential instead of simultaneous.

For example, it's hard to build the reputation of "doing *x* after your opponent does *y*," if your opponent never plays *y*!

> To get a reputation for "doing *x*," you simply have to do *x* every chance you get!

One of your earliest papers has the intriguing title "The Fat-Cat Effect, the Puppy-Dog Ploy, and the Lean and Hungry Look." What did you study in this paper and what did you discover?

Earlier papers by Michael Spence and Avinash Dixit had shown how an incumbent firm might want to "overinvest" in capital to induce a subsequent ("second period") entrant to enter on a smaller scale. The logic of those papers was that by investing more in capital, the firm would lower its second-period cost of production, which would lead it to have higher second-period output, and that in turn would lead the entrant to produce less, which is to the incumbent's advantage.

Jean Tirole and I provided a systematic analysis and taxonomy of the way that an incumbent can alter its investment decisions to influence the behavior of a potential entrant. We identified four possible strategies and then spent several weeks looking for good names for each of them.

Here is the list: The "top dog" strategy is the one studied by Spence and Dixit, namely the incumbent does extra investment to make itself big and tough.

With product competition, this strategy both induces the entrant to produce less and makes it more likely to stay out, so it is a good strategy for both entry accommodation and entry deterrence.

The "fat cat" strategy is to do extra investment to make oneself fat and nonaggressive. This strategy is a good way to accommodate if nonaggressive play induces a favorable response from the entrant, but it is never a good way to deter entry.

The "puppy dog ploy" is more or less the reverse: underinvestment to be small and nonthreatening.

Finally, the "lean and hungry look" is staying lean and mean to intimidate rivals. This strategy turns out to apply when the first-period investment is in advertising as opposed to physical capital.

What advice do you have for someone who is just beginning to study economics? What other subjects do you think work well alongside economics? Do you have some reading suggestions?

I read Heilbronner's *The Worldly Philosophers* as part of my first economics class, and I still like it for an overview of the field. I also recommend the economic history of Douglas North, notably his *Structure and Change in Economic History*, and David S. Landes's *The Unbound Prometheus: Technological Change and Industrial Development in Western Europe from 1750 to the Present*.

I advise my students to regularly skim periodicals such as the *Economist*, the *Financial Times*, and the *Wall Street Journal* for interesting articles. As the students become more advanced, they should make an effort to regularly look at economics journals to see what current research looks like and whether any of the topics interest them.

In terms of coursework in other subjects, I advise students who are interested in graduate study in economics to learn math through an introduction to real analysis and to take one class each in probability and statistics. Some familiarity with computer programming is useful and can be acquired in or out of class. Beyond that, it comes down to the student's interests.

16

Externalities

After studying this chapter,
you will be able to:

- Explain how externalities arise

- Explain why negative externalities lead to inefficient over-production and how property rights, emission charges, marketable permits, and taxes can be used to achieve a more efficient outcome

- Explain why positive externalities lead to inefficient under-production and how public provision, subsidies, vouchers, and patents can increase economic efficiency

We burn huge quantities of fossil fuels—coal, natural gas, and oil—that cause acid rain and global warming. We dump toxic waste into rivers, lakes, and oceans. These environmental issues are simultaneously everybody's problem and nobody's problem. How can we take account of the damage that we cause others every time we turn on our heating or air-conditioning systems?

Almost every day, we hear about a new discovery—in medicine, engineering, chemistry, physics, or even economics. The advance of knowledge seems boundless. Ever more people are learning more and more of what is already known. The stock of knowledge is increasing, apparently without limit. But are we spending enough on research and education? Do enough people remain in school for long enough?

In this chapter, we study the problems that arise because many of our actions affect other people, for good or ill, in ways that we do not take into account when we make our own economic choices. We will focus on two big areas—pollution and knowledge. In *Reading Between the Lines* at the end of the chapter, we look at the effects of a carbon tax designed to lower carbon emissions and address global warming.

Externalities in Our Lives

An **externality** is a *cost* or a *benefit* that arises from *production* and falls on someone other than the producer, or a *cost* or *benefit* that arises from *consumption* and falls on someone other than the consumer. We call an externality that imposes a cost a **negative externality**; and we call an externality that provides a benefit a **positive externality**.

We identify externalities as four types:

- Negative production externalities
- Negative consumption externalities
- Positive production externalities
- Positive consumption externalities

Negative Production Externalities

Congestion, pollution, and carbon emission are the sources of the most costly and widespread negative production externalities.

Congestion The Lincoln Tunnel, which connects New Jersey to Manhattan under the Hudson River, is 1.5 miles long. Yet it can take 2 hours to get through the tunnel in the worst traffic.

The costs of congestion are time costs and fuel costs. Drivers and their passengers spend extra hours sitting in stalled traffic, burning additional fuel. Each rush-hour user of the Lincoln Tunnel imposes a cost on the other users. This cost is a negative production externality.

The economic analysis of externalities looks at alternative ways of dealing with problems such as the cost of congestion in the Lincoln Tunnel.

Pollution and Carbon Emission When you run your air-conditioning, use hot water, drive a car, take a trip by airplane, or even ride a bus or train, your action contributes to pollution and increases your carbon footprint.

Economic activity pollutes air, water, and land, and these individual areas of pollution interact through the *ecosystem*.

Air Pollution Sixty percent of our air pollution comes from road transportation and industrial processes. Only 20 percent arises from electric power generation. See the trends in U.S. air pollution since 1980 below.

A common belief is that air pollution is getting worse. In many developing countries, air pollution *is* getting worse. The rapid economic development of China has created a serious air quality problem for Beijing. During the 2008 Olympics, construction activity was halted and factories closed in an attempt

U.S. Air Pollution Trends
Cleaner and Safer

The figure shows the trends in the concentrations of six air pollutants. Lead has been almost eliminated from our air. Sulfur dioxide, carbon monoxide, and suspended particulates have been reduced to around a half of their 1980 levels. And even the more stubborn ozone and nitrogen dioxide have been reduced to around 70 percent of their 1980 levels.

These reductions in air pollution levels are even more impressive when they are seen against the trends in economic activity. Between 1980 and 2007, total production in the United States increased by 123 percent. During this same period, vehicle miles traveled increased by 90 percent, energy consumption increased by 82 percent, and the population increased by 35 percent. While all this economic activity was on the increase, air pollution from all sources *decreased* by more than 30 percent.

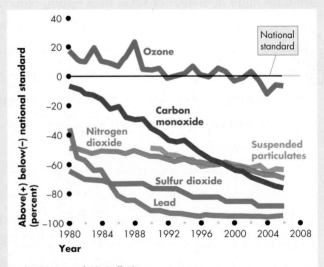

Six Sources of Air Pollution

Source of data: Latest Findings on National Air Quality: Status and Trends through 2006, United States Environmental Protection Agency, http://www.epa.gov/air/airtrends/2007/

to provide temporary relief from air that would endanger the health of athletes.

But air pollution in the world's richest countries is getting less severe for most substances. Air pollution in the United States has been on a downward trend for more than 30 years.

In contrast to the trends in air pollution, carbon emissions and emissions of other global warming gases such as methane are on the increase, and consequently the carbon dioxide concentration in the Earth's atmosphere is increasing at an unprecedented pace.

The costs of air pollution and carbon emission are high and widespread. Sulfur dioxide and nitrogen oxide emissions from coal-fired and oil-fired generators of electric utilities cause *acid rain*, which damages trees

and crops. Airborne substances such as lead from leaded gasoline are believed to cause cancer and other life-threatening conditions. Depletion of the *ozone layer* exposes us to higher doses of cancer-causing ultraviolet rays from the sun. And most costly of all, the increased carbon concentration is bringing global warming and potentially extremely costly climate change.

Some technological changes to cut costs, lessen air pollution, and slow the carbon buildup are possible either now or with further research and development.

Road vehicles can be made "greener" with new fuels including ethanol, alcohol, natural gas, propane and butane, and hydrogen. Vehicles can also be powered by electricity or batteries. But whether this

Global Temperature and CO_2 Trends
The Greatest Market Failure?

British economist Nicholas Stern prepared a major report on global warming and climate change for the United Kingdom government and his report, the *Stern Review on the Economics of Climate Change* has attracted a great deal of attention. Stern calls climate change "the greatest market failure the world has ever seen." To avoid the risk of catastrophic damage from climate change, he says that greenhouse gas levels must be held at not more than 550 parts per million (ppm) of CO_2 (and its equivalent in other greenhouse gases). The level in 2007 was 430ppm but it is rising at more than 2ppm a year, so the world will reach the critical level by about 2070.

Global temperature and CO_2 trends are starkly opposite to those of U.S. air pollution, as the figure shows. Scientists debate the contribution of human economic activity to these trends but most say it is the major source. Although ice-core estimates show long swings in CO_2, there has never been a time when its concentration increased so rapidly.

To hold greenhouse gas levels at 550ppm, emissions need to be cut to 75 percent or less of their current levels by 2050 and eventually, cut to 20 percent of their current levels.

The cost of achieving these cuts is high. Stern's estimate is 1 percent of the value of global production. If this cost were to be met by the people who live in the rich countries, and realistically they are the only ones who could afford to pay, it would cost about $750 per person every year.

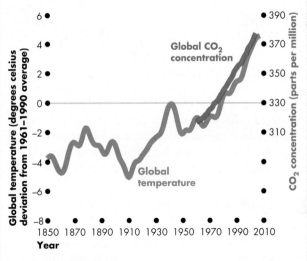

Global Warming Trends

Sources of data: Met Office Hadley Centre and Scripps Institution of Oceanography.

Some economists question Stern's assumptions and conclusions and argue that the cost of reducing emissions will be much lower if we go a bit more slowly and take advantage of future technological advances that will lower the cost of renewable energy sources—the sun, tide, and wind.

All economists agree that solving the global warming problem will require changes in the incentives that people face. The cost of carbon-emitting activities must rise and the cost of the search for new energy technologies must fall.

change lessens air pollution and carbon emissions depends on how electricity is produced.

Pollution-free electricity can be generated by harnessing wind power, solar power, tidal power, or geothermal power. Another alternative is nuclear power. This method is good for air pollution but creates a potential long-term problem for land and water pollution because there is no known entirely safe method of disposing of spent nuclear fuel.

Water Pollution The dumping of industrial waste and untreated sewage and the runoff from fertilizers pollute oceans, lakes, and rivers.

There are two main alternatives to polluting the waterways and oceans. One is the chemical processing of waste to render it inert or biodegradable. The other, in wide use for nuclear waste, is to use land sites for storage in secure containers.

Land Pollution Land pollution arises from dumping toxic waste products. Ordinary household garbage does not pose a pollution problem unless contaminants from dumped garbage seep into the water supply. Recycling is an apparently attractive alternative, but it requires an investment in new technologies to be effective. Incineration is a high-cost alternative to landfill, and it produces air pollution. Furthermore, these alternatives are not free, and they become efficient only when the cost of using landfill is high.

Negative Consumption Externalities

Negative consumption externalities are a source of irritation for most of us. Smoking tobacco in a confined space creates fumes that many people find unpleasant and that pose a health risk. Smoking creates a negative consumption externality. To deal with this externality, in many places and in almost all public places, smoking is banned. But banning smoking imposes a negative consumption externality on smokers! The majority imposes a cost on the minority—the smokers who would prefer to consume tobacco while dining or taking a plane trip.

Noisy parties and outdoor rock concerts are other examples of negative consumption externalities. They are also examples of the fact that a simple ban on an activity is not a solution. Banning noisy parties avoids the external cost on sleep-seeking neighbors, but it results in the sleepers imposing an external cost on the fun-seeking partygoers.

Permitting dandelions to grow in lawns, not picking up leaves in the fall, and allowing a dog to bark loudly or to foul a neighbor's lawn are other sources of negative consumption externalities.

Positive Production Externalities

If a honey farmer places beehives beside an orange grower's orchard, two positive production externalities arise. The honey farmer gets a positive production externality from the orange grower because the bees collect pollen and nectar from orange blossoms. And the orange grower gets a positive production externality because the bees pollinate the blossoms.

Positive Consumption Externalities

When you get a flu vaccination, you lower your risk of getting infected this winter. But if you avoid the flu, your neighbor who didn't get vaccinated has a better chance of avoiding it too. Flu vaccination generates positive consumption externalities.

When the owner of a historic building restores it, everyone who sees the building gets pleasure from it. Similarly, when someone erects a spectacular house—such as those built by Frank Lloyd Wright during the 1920s and 1930s—or another exciting building—such as the Chrysler Building and the Empire State Building in New York or the Wrigley Building in Chicago—an external consumption benefit flows to everyone who has an opportunity to view it. Education, which we examine in this chapter, is another example of this type of externality.

Review Quiz

1 What are the four types of externality?
2 Give an example of each type of externality that is different from the ones described above.
3 How are the externalities that you've described addressed, either by the market or by public policy?

 Work Study Plan 16.1 and get instant feedback.

We've described the four types of externalities and provided some examples of each. Pollution is the most important of the negative externalities and it is this example that we use to study the economics of external costs.

◆ Negative Externalities: Pollution

To study the economics of the negative externalities that arise from pollution, we distinguish between the private cost and the social cost of production.

Private Costs and Social Costs

A *private cost* of production is a cost that is borne by the producer of a good or service. *Marginal cost* is the cost of producing an *additional unit* of a good or service. So **marginal private cost** (*MC*) is the cost of producing an additional unit of a good or service that is borne by the producer of that good or service.

An *external cost* is a cost of producing a good or service that is *not* borne by the producer but borne by other people. A **marginal external cost** is the cost of producing an additional unit of a good or service that falls on people other than the producer.

Marginal social cost (*MSC*) is the marginal cost incurred by the producer and by everyone else on whom the cost falls—by society. It is the sum of marginal private cost and marginal external cost. That is,

$$MSC = MC + \text{Marginal external cost.}$$

We express costs in dollars, but we must always remember that a cost is an opportunity cost—something real, such as a clean river or clean air, is given up to get something.

Valuing an External Cost Economists use market prices to put a dollar value on the cost of pollution. For example, suppose that there are two similar rivers, one polluted and the other clean. Five hundred identical homes are built along the side of each river. The homes on the clean river rent for $2,500 a month, and those on the polluted river rent for $1,500 a month. If the pollution is the only detectable difference between the two rivers and the two locations, the rent decrease of $1,000 per month is the cost of the pollution. For the 500 homes on the polluted river, the external cost is $500,000 a month.

External Cost and Output Figure 16.1 shows an example of the relationship between output and cost in a chemical industry that pollutes. The marginal cost curve, *MC*, describes the marginal private cost borne by the firms that produce the chemical. Marginal cost increases as the quantity of chemical produced increases. If the firms dump waste into a

river, they impose an external cost that increases with the amount of the chemical produced. The marginal social cost curve, *MSC*, is the sum of marginal private cost and marginal external cost. For example, when output is 4,000 tons of chemical a month, marginal private cost is $100 a ton, marginal external cost is $125 a ton, and marginal social cost is $225 a ton.

In Fig. 16.1, when the quantity of chemical produced increases, the amount of pollution increases and the external cost of pollution increases.

Figure 16.1 shows the relationship between the quantity of chemical produced and the cost of the pollution it creates, but it doesn't tell us how much pollution gets created. That quantity depends on how the market for the chemical operates. First, we'll see what happens when the industry is free to pollute.

FIGURE 16.1   An External Cost

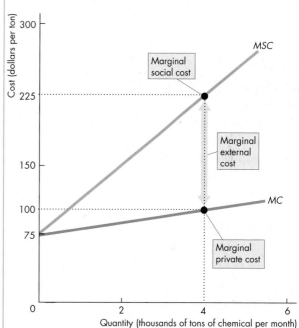

The *MC* curve shows the marginal private cost borne by the factories that produce a chemical. The *MSC* curve shows the sum of marginal private cost and marginal external cost. When output is 4,000 tons of chemical a month, marginal private cost is $100 a ton, marginal external cost is $125 a ton, and marginal social cost is $225 a ton.

 animation ◆

Production and Pollution: How Much?

When an industry is unregulated, the amount of pollution it creates depends on the market equilibrium price and quantity of the good produced. In Fig. 16.2, the demand curve for a pollution-creating chemical is *D*. This curve also measures the marginal social benefit, *MSB*, of the chemical. The supply curve is *S*. This curve also measures the producers' marginal private cost, *MC*. The supply curve is the marginal private cost curve because when firms make their production and supply decisions, they consider only the costs that they will bear. Market equilibrium occurs at a price of $100 a ton and 4,000 tons of chemical a month.

This equilibrium is inefficient. You learned in Chapter 5 that the allocation of resources is efficient when marginal social benefit equals marginal social cost. But we must count all the costs—private and external—when we compare marginal social benefit and marginal social cost. So with an external cost, the allocation is efficient when marginal social benefit equals marginal *social* cost. This outcome occurs when the quantity of chemical produced is 2,000 tons a month. The unregulated market overproduces by 2,000 tons of chemical a month and creates a deadweight loss shown by the gray triangle.

How can the people who live by the polluted river get the chemical factories to decrease their output of chemical and create less pollution? If some method can be found to achieve this outcome, everyone—the owners of the chemical factories and the residents of the riverside homes—can gain. Let's explore some solutions.

Property Rights

Sometimes it is possible to reduce the inefficiency arising from an externality by establishing a property right where one does not currently exist. **Property rights** are legally established titles to the ownership, use, and disposal of factors of production and goods and services that are enforceable in the courts.

Suppose that the chemical factories own the river and the 500 homes alongside it. The rent that people are willing to pay depends on the amount of pollution. Using the earlier example, people are willing to pay $2,500 a month to live alongside a pollution-free river but only $1,500 a month to live with the pollution created by 4,000 tons of chemical a month. If the factories produce this quantity, they lose $1,000 a month for each home for a total of $500,000 a month.

FIGURE 16.2 Inefficiency with an External Cost

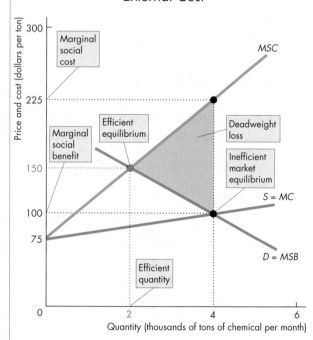

The supply curve is the marginal private cost curve, *S* = *MC*. The demand curve is the marginal social benefit curve, *D* = *MSB*. Market equilibrium at a price of $100 a ton and 4,000 tons a month is inefficient because marginal social cost exceeds marginal social benefit. The efficient quantity is 2,000 tons a month. The gray triangle shows the deadweight loss created by the pollution externality.

myeconlab animation

The chemical factories are now confronted with the cost of their pollution—forgone rent from the people who live by the river.

Figure 16.3 illustrates the outcome by using the same example as in Fig. 16.2. With property rights in place, the *MC* curve no longer measures all the costs that the factories face in producing the chemical. It excludes the pollution costs that they must now bear. The *MSC* curve now becomes the marginal private cost curve *MC*. All the costs fall on the factories, so the market supply curve is based on all the marginal costs and is the curve labeled *S* = *MC* = *MSC*.

Market equilibrium now occurs at a price of $150 a ton and 2,000 tons of chemical a month. This outcome is efficient. The factories still produce some pollution, but it is the efficient quantity.

FIGURE 16.3 Property Rights Achieve an Efficient Outcome

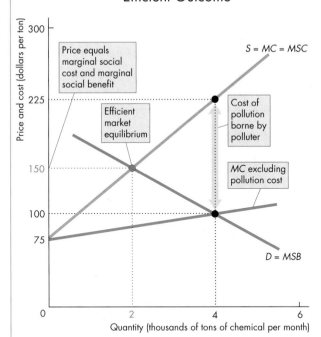

With property rights, the marginal cost curve that excludes pollution costs shows only part of the producers' marginal cost. The marginal private cost curve includes the cost of pollution, so the supply curve is $S = MC = MSC$. Market equilibrium is at a price of $150 a ton and 2,000 tons of chemical a month and is efficient because marginal social cost equals marginal social benefit. The efficient quantity of pollution is not zero.

(myeconlab) animation ◆

The Coase Theorem

Does it matter how property rights are assigned? Does it matter whether the polluter or the victim of the pollution owns the resource that might be polluted? Until 1960, everyone thought that it did matter. But in 1960, Ronald Coase (see p. 413) had a remarkable insight, now called the Coase theorem.

The **Coase theorem** is the proposition that if property rights exist, if only a small number of parties are involved, and if transactions costs are low, then private transactions are efficient. There are no externalities because the transacting parties take all the costs and benefits into account. Furthermore, it doesn't matter who has the property rights.

Application of the Coase Theorem In the example that we've just studied, the factories own the river and the homes. Suppose that instead, the residents own their homes and the river. Now the factories must pay a fee to the homeowners for the right to dump their waste. The greater the quantity of waste dumped into the river, the more the factories must pay. So again, the factories face the opportunity cost of the pollution they create. The quantity of chemical produced and the amount of waste dumped are the same whoever owns the homes and the river. If the factories own them, they bear the cost of pollution because they receive a lower income from home rents. And if the residents own the homes and the river, the factories bear the cost of pollution because they must pay a fee to the homeowners. In both cases, the factories bear the cost of their pollution and dump the efficient amount of waste into the river.

The Coase solution works only when transactions costs are low. **Transactions costs** are the opportunity costs of conducting a transaction. For example, when you buy a house, you incur a series of transactions costs. You might pay a real estate agent to help you find the best place and a lawyer to run checks that assure you that the seller owns the property and that after you've paid for it, the ownership has been properly transferred to you.

In the example of the homes alongside a river, the transactions costs that are incurred by a small number of chemical factories and a few homeowners might be low enough to enable them to negotiate the deals that produce an efficient outcome. But in many situations, transactions costs are so high that it would be inefficient to incur them. In these situations, the Coase solution is not available.

Suppose, for example, that everyone owns the airspace above their homes up to, say, 10 miles. If someone pollutes your airspace, you can charge a fee. But to collect the fee, you must identify who is polluting your airspace and persuade them to pay you. Imagine the costs of negotiating and enforcing agreements with the 50 million people who live in your part of the United States (and perhaps in Canada or Mexico) and the several thousand factories that emit sulfur dioxide and create acid rain that falls on your property! In this situation, we use public choices to cope with externalities. But the transactions costs that block a market solution are real costs, so attempts by the government to deal with externalities offer no easy solution. Let's look at some of these attempts.

Government Actions in the Face of External Costs

The three main methods that governments use to cope with externalities are

- Taxes
- Emission charges
- Marketable permits

Taxes The government can use taxes as an incentive for producers to cut back on pollution. Taxes used in this way are called **Pigovian taxes**, in honor of Arthur Cecil Pigou, the British economist who first worked out this method of dealing with externalities during the 1920s.

By setting the tax equal to the marginal external cost, firms can be made to behave in the same way as they would if they bore the cost of the externality directly. To see how government actions can change market outcomes in the face of externalities, let's return to the example of the chemical factories and the river.

Assume that the government has assessed the marginal external cost accurately and imposes a tax on the factories that exactly equals this cost. Figure 16.4 illustrates the effects of this tax.

The demand curve and marginal social benefit curve, $D = MSB$, and the firms' marginal cost curve, MC, are the same as in Fig. 16.2. The pollution tax equals the marginal external cost of the pollution. We add this tax to the marginal private cost to find the market supply curve. This curve is the one labeled $S = MC + tax = MSC$. This curve is the market supply curve because it tells us the quantity supplied at each price given the firms' marginal cost and the tax they must pay. This curve is also the marginal social cost curve because the pollution tax has been set equal to the marginal external cost.

Demand and supply now determine the market equilibrium price at $150 a ton and a quantity of 2,000 tons of chemical a month. At this quantity of chemical production, the marginal social cost is $150 and the marginal social benefit is $150, so the outcome is efficient. The firms incur a marginal cost of $88 a ton and pay a tax of $62 a ton. The government collects tax revenue of $124,000 a month.

Emission Charges Emission charges are an alternative to a tax for confronting a polluter with the external cost of pollution. The government sets a price per unit of pollution. The more pollution a firm creates, the more it

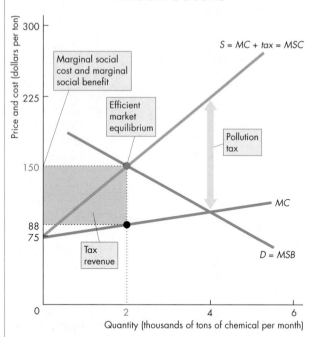

FIGURE 16.4 A Pollution Tax to Achieve an Efficient Outcome

A pollution tax is imposed equal to the marginal external cost of pollution. The supply curve becomes the marginal private cost curve, MC, plus the tax—$S = MC + tax$. Market equilibrium is at a price of $150 a ton and 2,000 tons of chemical a month and is efficient because marginal social cost equals marginal social benefit. The government collects a tax revenue shown by the purple rectangle.

myeconlab animation

pays in emission charges. This method of dealing with pollution externalities has been used only modestly in the United States but is common in Europe where, for example, France, Germany, and the Netherlands make water polluters pay a waste disposal charge.

To work out the emission charge that achieves efficiency, the government needs a lot of information about the polluting industry that, in practice, is rarely available.

Marketable Permits Instead of taxing or imposing emission charges on polluters, each potential polluter might be assigned a permitted pollution limit. Each firm knows its own costs and benefits of pollution, and making pollution limits marketable is a clever way of using this private information that is unknown to the government. The government issues each firm a permit to emit a certain amount of pollution, and firms can buy and sell these permits. Firms that have a low marginal cost of reducing pollution sell their permits, and firms that have a high marginal cost of reducing pollution buy permits. The market in permits determines the price at which firms trade permits. Each firm buys or sells permits until its marginal cost of pollution equals the market price of a permit.

This method of dealing with pollution provides an even stronger incentive than emission charges to find lower-polluting technologies because the price of a permit to pollute rises as the demand for permits increases.

The Market for Emission Permits in the United States Trading in lead pollution permits became common during the 1980s, and this marketable permit program has been rated a success. It enabled lead to be virtually eliminated from the atmosphere of the United States (see p. 374). But this success might not easily translate to other situations because lead pollution has some special features. First, most lead pollution came from a single source: leaded gasoline. Second, lead in gasoline is easily monitored. Third, the objective of the program was clear: to eliminate lead in gasoline.

The Environmental Protection Agency is now considering using marketable permits to promote efficiency in the control of chlorofluorocarbons, the gases that are believed to damage the ozone layer.

Review Quiz

1 What is the distinction between private cost and social cost?
2 How does a negative externality prevent a competitive market from allocating resources efficiently?
3 How can a negative externality be eliminated by assigning property rights? How does this method of coping with an externality work?
4 How do taxes help us to cope with negative externalities? At what level must a pollution tax be set if it is to induce firms to produce the efficient quantity of pollution?
5 How do emission charges and marketable pollution permits work?

 Work Study Plan 16.2 and get instant feedback.

◆ Positive Externalities: Knowledge

Knowledge comes from education and research. To study the economics of knowledge, we distinguish between private benefits and social benefits.

Private Benefits and Social Benefits

A *private benefit* is a benefit that the consumer of a good or service receives. *Marginal benefit* is the benefit from an *additional unit* of a good or service. So a **marginal private benefit** (*MB*) is the benefit from an additional unit of a good or service that the consumer of that good or service receives.

The *external benefit* from a good or service is the benefit that someone other than the consumer receives. A **marginal external benefit** is the benefit from an additional unit of a good or service that people other than the consumer enjoy.

Marginal social benefit (*MSB*) is the marginal benefit enjoyed by society—by the consumer of a good or service (marginal private benefit) plus the marginal benefit enjoyed by others (the marginal external benefit). That is,

$$MSB = MB + \text{Marginal external benefit.}$$

Figure 16.5 shows an example of the relationship between marginal private benefit, marginal external benefit, and marginal social benefit. The marginal benefit curve, *MB*, describes the marginal private benefit—such as expanded job opportunities and higher incomes—enjoyed by college graduates. Marginal private benefit decreases as the quantity of education increases.

But college graduates generate external benefits. On the average, they tend to be better citizens. Their crime rates are lower, and they are more tolerant of the views of others. A society with a large number of college graduates can support activities such as high-quality newspapers and television channels, music, theater, and other organized social activities.

In the example in Fig. 16.5, the marginal external benefit is $15,000 per student per year when 15 million students enroll in college. The marginal social benefit curve, *MSB*, is the sum of marginal private benefit and marginal external benefit. For example, when 15 million students a year enroll in college, the marginal private benefit is $10,000 per student and

FIGURE 16.5 An External Benefit

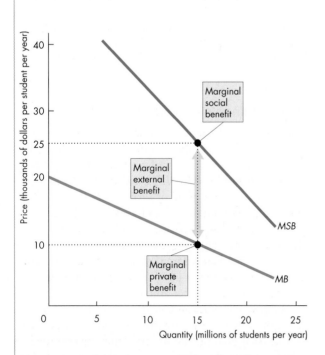

The *MB* curve shows the marginal private benefit enjoyed by the people who receive a college education. The *MSB* curve shows the sum of marginal private benefit and marginal external benefit. When 15 million students attend college, marginal private benefit is $10,000 per student, marginal external benefit is $15,000 per student, and marginal social benefit is $25,000 per student.

myeconlab animation

FIGURE 16.6 Inefficiency with an External Benefit

The market demand curve is the marginal private benefit curve, *D = MB*. The supply curve is the marginal social cost curve, *S = MSC*. Market equilibrium at a tuition of $15,000 a year and 7.5 million students is inefficient because marginal social benefit exceeds marginal social cost. The efficient quantity is 15 million students. A deadweight loss arises (gray triangle) because too few students enroll in college.

myeconlab animation

the marginal external benefit is $15,000 per student, so the marginal social benefit is $25,000 per student.

When people make schooling decisions, they ignore its external benefits and consider only its private benefits. So if education were provided by private schools that charged full-cost tuition, we would produce too few college graduates.

Figure 16.6 illustrates the underproduction that would exist if the government left education to the private market. The supply curve is the marginal social cost curve, *S = MSC*. The demand curve is the marginal private benefit curve, *D = MB*. Market equilibrium occurs at a tuition of $15,000 per student per year and 7.5 million students per year. At this equilibrium, marginal social benefit is $38,000 per student, which exceeds marginal social cost by $23,000. There are too few students in college. The efficient number is 15 million per year, where mar-

ginal social benefit equals marginal social cost. The gray triangle shows the deadweight loss.

Underproduction similar to that in Fig. 16.6 would occur in grade school and high school if public education was left to an unregulated market. When children learn basic reading, writing, and number skills, they receive the private benefit of increased earning power. But even these basic skills bring the external benefit of developing better citizens.

External benefits also arise from the discovery of new knowledge. When Isaac Newton worked out the formulas for calculating the rate of response of one variable to another—calculus—everyone was free to use his method. When a spreadsheet program called VisiCalc was invented, Lotus Corporation and Microsoft were free to copy the basic idea and create 1-2-3 and Excel. When the first shopping mall was built and found to be a successful way of arranging retailing, everyone was free to copy the idea, and malls sprouted like mushrooms.

Once someone has discovered a basic idea others can copy it. Because they do have to work to copy an idea, they face an opportunity cost, but they do not usually have to pay a fee for the idea. When people make decisions, they ignore the external benefits and consider only the private benefits.

When people make decisions about the amount of education or research to undertake, they balance the marginal private cost against the marginal private benefit. They ignore the external benefit. As a result, if we left education and research to unregulated market forces, we would get too little of these activities.

To get closer to producing the efficient quantity of a good or service that generates an external benefit, we make public choices, through governments, to modify the market outcome.

Government Actions in the Face of External Benefits

Four devices that governments can use to achieve a more efficient allocation of resources in the presence of external benefits are

- Public provision
- Private subsidies
- Vouchers
- Patents and copyrights

Public Provision Under **public provision**, a public authority that receives its revenue from the government produces the good or service. The education services produced by the public universities, colleges, and schools are examples of public provision.

Figure 16.7(a) shows how public provision might overcome the underproduction that arises in Fig. 16.6.

FIGURE 16.7 Public Provision or Private Subsidy to Achieve an Efficient Outcome

(a) Public provision

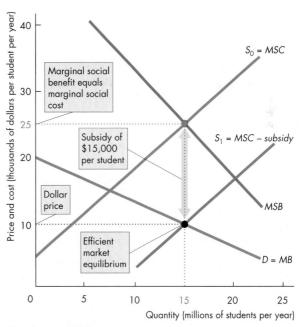

(b) Private subsidy

In part (a), marginal social benefit equals marginal social cost with 15 million students per year, the efficient quantity. Tuition is set at $10,000 per student equal to marginal private benefit. Taxpayers cover the other $15,000 of cost per student.

In part (b), with a subsidy of $15,000 per student, the supply curve is $S_1 = MSC - subsidy$. The equilibrium price is $10,000, and the market equilibrium is efficient with 15 million students per year. Marginal social benefit equals marginal social cost.

myeconlab animation

Public provision cannot lower the cost of production, so marginal social cost is the same as before. Marginal private benefit and marginal external benefit are also the same as before.

The efficient quantity occurs where marginal social benefit equals marginal social cost. In Fig. 16.7(a), this quantity is 15 million students. Tuition is set to ensure that the efficient number of students enrolls. That is, tuition is set equal to the marginal private benefit at the efficient quantity. In Fig. 16.7(a), tuition is $10,000 a year. The rest of the cost of the public university is borne by the taxpayers and, in this example, is $15,000 per student per year.

Private Subsidies A **subsidy** is a payment that the government makes to private producers. By making the subsidy depend on the level of output, the government can induce private decision makers to consider external benefits when they make their choices.

Figure 16.7(b) shows how a subsidy to private colleges works. In the absence of a subsidy, the market supply curve is $S_0 = MSC$. The demand curve is the marginal private benefit curve, $D = MB$. If the government provides a subsidy to colleges of $15,000 per student per year, we must subtract the subsidy from the colleges' marginal cost to find the new market supply curve. That curve is $S_1 = MSC - subsidy$. The market equilibrium is tuition of $10,000 a year and 15 million students a year. The marginal social cost of educating 15 million students is $25,000 and the marginal social benefit is $25,000. So with marginal social cost equal to marginal social benefit, the subsidy has achieved an efficient outcome. The tuition and the subsidy just cover the colleges' marginal cost.

Vouchers A **voucher** is a token that the government provides to households, which they can use to buy specified goods or services. Food stamps are examples of vouchers. The vouchers (stamps) can be spent only on food and are designed to improve the diet and health of extremely poor families.

School vouchers have been advocated as a means of improving the quality of education and are used in Washington D.C..

A school voucher allows parents to choose the school their children will attend and to use the voucher to pay part of the cost. The school cashes the vouchers to pay its bills. A voucher could be provided to a college student in a similar way, and although technically not a voucher, a federal Pell Grant has a similar effect.

FIGURE 16.8 Vouchers Achieve an Efficient Outcome

With vouchers, buyers are willing to pay MB plus the value of the voucher, so the demand curve becomes the marginal social benefit curve, $D = MSB$. Market equilibrium is efficient with 15 million students enrolled in college because price, marginal social benefit, and marginal social cost are equal. The tuition consists of the dollar price of $10,000 and a voucher valued at $15,000.

 animation

Because vouchers can be spent only on a specified item, they increase the willingness to pay for that item and so increase the demand for it. Figure 16.8 shows how a voucher system works. The government provides a voucher per student equal to the marginal external benefit. Parents (or students) use these vouchers to supplement the dollars they pay for education. The marginal social benefit curve becomes the demand for college education, $D = MSB$. The market equilibrium occurs at a price of $25,000 per student per year, and 15 million students attend college. Each student pays $10,000 tuition, and schools collect an additional $15,000 per student from the voucher.

If the government estimates the value of the external benefit correctly and makes the value of the voucher equal the marginal external benefit, the outcome from the voucher scheme is efficient.

Marginal social cost equals marginal social benefit, and the deadweight loss is eliminated.

Vouchers are similar to subsidies, but their advocates say that they are more efficient than subsidies because the consumer can monitor school performance more effectively than the government can.

Patents and Copyrights Knowledge might be an exception to the principle of diminishing marginal benefit. Additional knowledge (about the right things) makes people more productive. And there seems to be no tendency for the additional productivity from additional knowledge to diminish.

For example, in just 15 years, advances in knowledge about microprocessors have given us a sequence of processor chips that has made our personal computers increasingly powerful. Each advance in knowledge about how to design and manufacture a processor chip has brought apparently ever larger increments in performance and productivity. Similarly, each advance in knowledge about how to design and build an airplane has brought apparently ever larger increments in performance: Orville and Wilbur Wright's 1903 Flyer was a one-seat plane that could hop a farmer's field. The Lockheed Constellation, designed in 1949, was an airplane that could fly 120 passengers from New York to London, but with two refueling stops in Newfoundland and Ireland. The latest version of the Boeing 747 can carry 400 people nonstop from Los Angeles to Sydney, Australia, or New York to Tokyo (flights of 7,500 miles that take 13 hours). Similar examples can be found in agriculture, biogenetics, communications, engineering, entertainment, and medicine.

One reason why the stock of knowledge increases without diminishing returns is the sheer number of different techniques that can in principle be tried. Paul Romer, an economist at Stanford University, explains this fact. "Suppose that to make a finished good, 20 different parts have to be attached to a frame, one at a time. A worker could proceed in numerical order, attaching part one first, then part two. ... Or the worker could proceed in some other order, starting with part 10, then adding part seven. ...With 20 parts, ... there are [more] different sequences ... than the total number of seconds that have elapsed since the big bang created the universe, so we can be confident that in all activities, only a very small fraction of the possible sequences have ever been tried."[1]

---
[1] Paul Romer, "Ideas and Things," in *The Future Surveyed*, supplement to *The Economist*, September 11, 1993, pp. 71–72.

Think about all the processes, all the products, and all the different bits and pieces that go into each, and you can see that we have only begun to scratch the surface of what is possible.

Because knowledge is productive and generates external benefits, it is necessary to use public policies to ensure that those who develop new ideas have incentives to encourage an efficient level of effort. The main way of providing the right incentives uses the central idea of the Coase theorem and assigns property rights—called **intellectual property rights**—to creators. The legal device for establishing intellectual property rights is the patent or copyright. A **patent** or **copyright** is a government-sanctioned exclusive right granted to the inventor of a good, service, or productive process to produce, use, and sell the invention for a given number of years. A patent enables the developer of a new idea to prevent others from benefiting freely from an invention for a limited number of years.

Although patents encourage invention and innovation, they do so at an economic cost. While a patent is in place, its holder has a monopoly. And monopoly is another source of inefficiency (which is explained in Chapter 13). But without a patent, the effort to develop new goods, services, or processes is diminished and the flow of new inventions is slowed. So the efficient outcome is a compromise that balances the benefits of more inventions against the cost of temporary monopoly in newly invented activities.

Review Quiz

1 What is special about knowledge that creates external benefits?

2 How might governments use public provision, private subsidies, and vouchers to achieve an efficient amount of education?

3 How might governments use public provision, private subsidies, vouchers, and patents and copyrights to achieve an efficient amount of research and development?

 Work Study Plan 16.3 and get instant feedback.

Reading Between the Lines on pp. 386–387 looks at the effects of a carbon tax and solar subsidy to reduce greenhouse gas emissions.

Fighting Carbon Emissions with a Carbon Tax and Solar Subsidy

On Carbon, Tax and Don't Spend

http://www.nytimes.com
March 25, 2008

… a carbon tax isn't a new idea. Denmark, Finland, Norway and Sweden have had carbon taxes in place since the 1990s, but the tax has not led to large declines in emissions in most of these countries—in the case of Norway, emissions have actually increased by 43 percent per capita. …

The one country in which carbon taxes have led to a large decrease in emissions is Denmark, … What did Denmark do right? …

Denmark avoids the temptation to maximize the tax revenue by giving the proceeds back to industry, earmarking much of it to subsidize environmental innovation. Danish firms are pushed away from carbon and pulled into environmental innovation, and the country's economy isn't put at a competitive disadvantage. So this is lesson No. 1 from Denmark.

The second lesson is that the carbon tax worked in Denmark because it was easy for Danish firms to switch to cleaner fuels. Danish policy makers made huge investments in renewable energy and subsidized environmental innovation. Denmark back then was more reliant on coal than the other three countries were (but not more so than the United States is today), so when the tax gave companies a reason to leave coal and the investments in renewable energy gave them an easy way to do so, they switched. The key was providing easy substitutes. …

An increase in gasoline taxes … would … be the wrong policy. … Higher gas taxes would raise revenue but do little to curb pollution.

Instead, if we want to reduce carbon emissions, then we should follow Denmark's example: tax the industrial emission of carbon and return the revenue to industry through subsidies for research and investment in alternative energy sources, cleaner-burning fuel, carbon-capture technologies and other environmental innovations.

Essence of the Story

- Denmark, Finland, Norway and Sweden have had carbon taxes since the 1990s.
- Emissions increased in Norway, changed little in Finland and Sweden, and decreased in Denmark.
- Denmark used the carbon tax revenues to make it easy for power utilities to switch from coal.
- A gas tax increase in the United States would raise revenue but not curb pollution.
- The United States should follow Denmark's example.

Economic Analysis

- Figure 1 illustrates why, as the article states, a carbon tax on gasoline would do little to curb pollution.

- The demand for gasoline in the short run, D_{SR}, is inelastic. If the U.S. gas price was raised (by a carbon tax) to the European level, gasoline consumption would decrease by very little.

- The demand for gasoline in the long run, D_{LR}, is elastic, so consumption might fall to the European level eventually, but it would take many years.

- Figure 2 illustrates why a carbon tax that is spent on subsidies to clean fuel cuts pollution, as the article states.

- Figure 2(a) shows the costs of producing electricity using coal, which has an external cost: MSC exceeds MC. Figure 2(b) shows the cost using solar power, which has no external cost: $MC = MSC$.

- Assume that the marginal social cost of producing electricity equals the marginal benefit of electricity at 30 cents per kilowatt hour (kWh) and that the market price of electricity is also 30 cents per kWh.

- In part (a), a carbon tax equal to the marginal external cost raises the producer's marginal cost to equal the marginal social cost.

- With no subsidy for solar, a coal-fired power station continues to operate and produces 5 MWh.

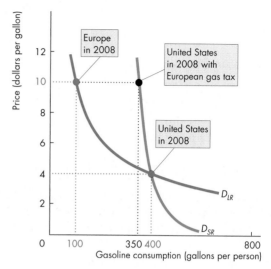

Figure 1 A carbon tax on gasoline

- But with a carbon tax and a solar subsidy, the marginal coal-fired power station shuts down and switches to solar power. As the article says, the subsidy makes fuel substitution easy for the producer.

- The combination of the tax and subsidy is *inefficient*. Electricity is now being produced by solar power at a marginal social cost of 50 cents per kWh instead of the efficient 30 cents per kWh using coal.

(a) Coal generation

(b) Solar generation

Figure 2 Using carbon tax to subsidize alternative fuels

SUMMARY ◆

Key Points

Externalities in Our Lives (p. 374–376)

- An externality can arise from either a production activity or a consumption activity.
- A negative externality imposes an external cost.
- A positive externality provides an external benefit.

Negative Externalities: Pollution (pp. 377–381)

- External costs are costs of production that fall on people other than the producer of a good or service. Marginal social cost equals marginal private cost plus marginal external cost.
- Producers take account only of marginal private cost and produce more than the efficient quantity when there is a marginal external cost.
- Sometimes it is possible to overcome a negative externality by assigning a property right.
- When property rights cannot be assigned, governments might overcome externalities by using taxes, emission charges, or marketable permits.

Positive Externalities: Knowledge (pp. 381–385)

- External benefits are benefits that are received by people other than the consumer of a good or service. Marginal social benefit equals marginal private benefit plus marginal external benefit.
- External benefits from education arise because better-educated people tend to be better citizens, commit fewer crimes, and support social activities.
- External benefits from research arise because once someone has worked out a basic idea, others can copy it.
- Vouchers or subsidies to schools or the provision of public education below cost can achieve a more efficient provision of education.
- Patents and copyrights create intellectual property rights and an incentive to innovate. But they do so by creating a temporary monopoly, the cost of which must be balanced against the benefit of more inventive activity.

Key Figures

Key Terms

PROBLEMS and APPLICATIONS

 Work problems 1–9 in Chapter 16 Study Plan and get instant feedback.
Work problems 10–18 as Homework, a Quiz, or a Test if assigned by your instructor.

1. Consider each of the following activities or events and say for each one whether it is an externality. If so, say whether it is a positive or negative production or consumption externality.
   - Airplanes take off from LaGuardia Airport during the U.S. Open tennis tournament, which is taking place nearby.
   - A sunset over the Pacific Ocean
   - An increase in the number of people who are studying for graduate degrees
   - A person wears strong perfume while attending an orchestra concert.
   - A homeowner plants an attractive garden in front of his house.
   - A person drives talking on a cell phone.
   - A bakery bakes bread.

2. The table provides information about costs and benefits that arise from the pesticide production that pollutes a lake used by a trout farmer.

Output of pesticide (tons per week)	Marginal cost	Marginal external cost	Marginal social benefit
		(dollars per ton)	
0	0	0	250
1	5	33	205
2	15	67	165
3	30	100	130
4	50	133	100
5	75	167	75
6	105	200	55
7	140	233	40

   a. If no one owns the lake and if there is no regulation of pollution, what is the quantity of pesticide produced and what is the marginal cost of pollution borne by the trout farmer?
   b. If the trout farm owns the lake, how much pesticide is produced and what does the pesticide producer pay the farmer per ton?
   c. If the pesticide producer owns the lake, and if a pollution-free lake rents for $1,000 a week, how much pesticide is produced and how much rent does the farmer pay the factory for the use of the lake?

   d. Compare the quantities of pesticide produced in b and c, and explain the relationship between these quantities.

3. Back at the pesticide plant and trout farm described in problem 2, suppose that no one owns the lake and that the government introduces a pollution tax.
   a. What is the tax per ton of pesticide produced that achieves an efficient outcome?
   b. Explain the connection between your answer to a and the answer to problem 2a.

4. Using the information provided in problem 2, suppose that no one owns the lake and that the government issues three marketable pollution permits, two to the farmer and one to the factory. Each permit allows the same amount of pollution of the lake, and the total amount of pollution is the efficient amount.
   a. What is the quantity of pesticide produced?
   b. What is the market price of a pollution permit? Who buys and who sells a permit?
   c. What is the connection between your answer and the answers to problems 2a and 3a?

5. The marginal cost of educating a student is $4,000 a year and is constant. The figure shows the marginal private benefit curve.

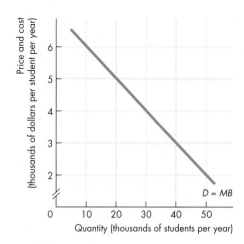

   a. With no government involvement and if the schools are competitive, how many students are enrolled and what is the tuition?

b. The external benefit from education is $2,000 per student per year and is constant. If the government provides the efficient amount of education, how many students will be accepted and what is the tuition?

6. **Bag Revolution**

[T]raditional plastic bags … aren't biodegradable and often end up in the ocean. … Americans consume roughly 110 billion bags annually. … 28 cities in the U.S. have proposed laws restricting the use of plastic bags. … But San Francisco now requires all retailers with revenue over $2 million to offer only compostable or reusable bags, and Seattle has proposed a 25-cent per-bag tax.

Fortune, May 12, 2008

a. Describe the externality that arises from plastic bags.
b. Draw a graph to illustrate how plastic bags create deadweight loss.
c. Explain the effects of Seattle's policy on the use of plastic bags.
d. Draw a graph to illustrate Seattle's policy and show the change in the deadweight loss that arises from this policy.
e. Explain why a complete ban on plastic bags might be inefficient.

7. **The Year in Medicine: Cell Phones**

Think you're safer because you talk on a hands-free cell phone while driving? Think again. Using either type of phone while trying to drive a car is roughly equivalent to driving with a blood-alcohol concentration … high enough to get you arrested … for driving under the influence. Folks who use hands-free cell phones in simulation trials also exhibited slower reaction times and took longer to hit the brakes than drivers who weren't otherwise distracted. Data from real-life driving tests show that cell-phone use rivals drowsy driving as a major cause of accidents.

Time, December 4, 2006

a. What negative externalities arise from using a cell phone while driving?
b. Explain why the market for cell-phone service creates a deadweight loss.
c. Draw a graph to illustrate how a deadweight loss arises from the use of cell phones.
d. Explain how government intervention might improve the efficiency of cell-phone use.

8. **D.C. Handgun Ban**

But it is not just D.C. that has experienced increases in murder and violent crime after guns are banned. Chicago also experienced an increase after its ban in 1982. Island nations supposedly present ideal environments for gun control because it is relatively easy for them to control their borders, but countries such as Great Britain, Ireland, and Jamaica have experienced large increases in murder and violent crime after gun bans. For example, after handguns were banned in 1997, the number of deaths and injuries from gun crime in England and Wales increased 340 percent in the seven years from 1998 to 2005. Passing a gun ban simply doesn't mean that we are going to get guns away from criminals. The real problem is that if it is the law-abiding good citizens who obey these laws and not the criminals, criminals have less to fear and crime can go up.

FOXNews, September 14, 2007

a. What external costs do handguns impose?
b. What external benefits do handguns bring?
c. If both negative and positive externalities arise from handguns, how can we determine whether gun ownership should be discouraged or encouraged or neither?

9. **My Child, My Choice**

Fully vaccinating all U.S. children born in a given year from birth to adolescence saves 33,000 lives, prevents 14 million infections and saves $10 billion in medical costs. Part of the reason is that vaccinations protect not only the kids that receive the shots but also those who can't receive them—such as newborns and cancer patients with suppressed immune systems. … The higher the immunization rate in any population, the less likely that a pathogen will penetrate the group and find a susceptible person inside.

Time, June 2, 2008

a. Describe the private benefits and external benefits of vaccinations and explain why a private market for vaccinations would produce an inefficient outcome.
b. Draw a graph to illustrate a private market for vaccinations and show the deadweight loss.
c. Explain how government intervention could achieve an efficient quantity of vaccinations and draw a graph to illustrate this outcome.

10. The figure illustrates the unregulated market for a pesticide. When factories produce pesticide, they also create waste, which they dump into a lake on the outskirts of the town. The marginal external cost of the dumped waste is equal to the marginal private cost of producing the pesticide (that is, the marginal social cost of producing the pesticide is double the marginal private cost).

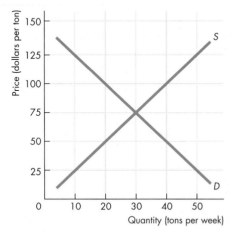

a. What is the quantity of pesticide produced if no one owns the lake and what is the efficient quantity of pesticide?
b. If the residents of the town own the lake, what is the quantity of pesticide produced and how much do residents of the town charge the factories to dump waste?
c. If the pesticide factories own the lake, how much pesticide is produced?
d. If no one owns the lake and the government levies a pollution tax, what is the tax that achieves the efficient outcome?

11. Betty and Anna work at the same office in Philadelphia. They both must attend a meeting in Pittsburgh, so they decide to drive to the meeting together. Betty is a cigarette smoker and her marginal benefit from smoking a package of cigarettes a day is $40. Cigarettes are $6 a pack. Anna dislikes cigarette smoke, and her marginal benefit from a smoke-free environment is $50 a day. What is the outcome if
a. Betty drives her car with Anna as a passenger?
b. Anna drives her car with Betty as a passenger?

12. The first two columns of the table show the demand schedule for electricity from a coal burning utility; the second and third columns show the utility's cost of producing electricity. The

Price (cents per kilowatt)	Quantity (kilowatts per day)	Marginal cost (cents per kilowatt)
4	500	10
8	400	8
12	300	6
16	200	4
20	100	2

marginal external cost of the pollution created is equal to the marginal cost.
a. With no pollution control, what is the quantity of electricity produced, the price of electricity, and the marginal external cost of the pollution generated?
b. With no pollution control, what is the marginal social cost of the electricity generated and the deadweight loss?
c. Suppose that the government levies a pollution tax, such that the utility produces the efficient quantity. What are the price of electricity, the tax, and the tax revenue per day?

13. Most nurses in the United States receive their education in community colleges. Mainly because of differences in class size, the cost of educating a nurse is about four times that of an average community college student. Community college budgets depend on the number of students and not on the subjects taught.
a. Explain why this funding arrangement might be expected to lead to an inefficiency in the number of nurses trained.
b. Suggest a better arrangement and explain how it would work.

14. **China Vows to Clean Up Polluted Lake**
… Officials in Jiangsu Province [announced] plans to spend 108.5 billion yuan, or $14.4 billion, for a cleanup of Lake Tai, the country's third-largest freshwater lake. The campaign would focus initially on eradicating the toxic algal bloom that choked the lake this spring and left more than two million people without drinking water. …
Lake Tai, known as China's ancient "land of rice and fish," is a legendary setting, once famous for its bounty of white shrimp, whitebait, and whitefish. But over time, an industrial buildup transformed the region. More than 2,800 chemical factories arose around the lake, and industrial dumping became a severe problem and, eventually, a crisis. …

"The pollution of Lake Tai has sounded the alarm for us," Mr. Wen [Prime Minister] said, "The problem has never been tackled at its root."

New York Times, October 27, 2007

a. What are the externalities included in this news clip?

b. What are the external costs associated with the pollution of Lake Tai?

c. What was the "alarm" that the pollution of Lake Tai sounded and why has the problem "never been tackled at its root"?

15. **Fast-Food Trash Be Gone!**

Some Oakland, Calif., residents are sick and tired of tripping over burger wrappers and soda cans, and the city is ready to do something about it. The Oakland City Council is proposing a tax on fast-food restaurants, gas station markets, liquor stores and convenience stores that serve take-out food or beverages. Councilwoman Jane Brunner, who wrote the legislation, estimates that the tax will raise approximately $237,000 a year, which would cover the cost of a clean-up crew and the initial purchase of trucks and equipment to keep the streets and sidewalks surrounding the city's schools litter-free. "Having a clean city affects everything," Brunner said.

CNN, February 6, 2006

a. What is the external cost associated with take-out food and beverages?

b. Draw a graph to illustrate and explain why the market for take-out food and beverages creates a deadweight loss.

c. Draw a graph to illustrate and explain how Oakland's policy might improve efficiency.

16. On April 7, 2008, MSNBC reported that:

Compact fluorescent light bulbs—the squiggly, coiled bulbs that generate light by heating gases in a glass tube—are generally considered to use more than 50 percent less energy and to last several times longer than incandescent bulbs. …

There is no disputing that overall, fluorescent bulbs save energy and reduce pollution in general. An average incandescent bulb lasts about 800 to 1,500 hours; a spiral fluorescent bulb can last as long as 10,000 hours. In just more than a year—since the beginning of 2007—9 million fluorescent bulbs have been purchased in California, preventing the release of 1.5 billion pounds of carbon dioxide compared with

traditional bulbs, according to the U.S. Environmental Protection Agency.

a. Relative to a traditional bulb, what is the external benefit associated with fluorescent bulbs?

b. Draw a graph to illustrate and explain why the market for fluorescent bulbs is inefficient.

c. Draw a graph to illustrate and explain how government actions might achieve an efficient outcome in the market for bulbs.

17. **Clean Green Flying Machine?**

… Aviation generates 2–3 percent of man-made emissions of carbon dioxide, the main greenhouse gas. … Most environmentalists think that the only solution is to make air travel more expensive, say through hefty fuel taxes. … But the airline industry [says it] produces far more benefits than ills—[contributing] 8 percent to global [output] by transporting tourists, business travelers, and cargo around the globe.

Economist.com, August 14, 2007

a. What are the externalities created by the airline industry?

b. Why will hefty fuel taxes encourage airlines to operate in the social interest?

18. After you have studied *Reading Between the Lines* on pp. 386–387, answer the following questions:

a. How does a carbon tax change the costs faced by the operator of a coal-fired power plant?

b. How does a solar subsidy change the costs faced by a solar power station?

c. Why might the operator of a coal-fired power station be influenced by a solar subsidy?

d. Why might the combination of a carbon tax and social subsidy lead to producing electricity at too high a marginal social cost?

e. Would it ever make sense to impose a carbon tax *and* pay a solar subsidy?

19. Use the link on MyEconlab (Textbook Resources, Chapter 16) and read the article about wind farms.

a. What types of externalities arise in the production of electricity using wind technologies?

b. Comparing the externalities from wind technologies with those from burning coal and oil, which are more costly?

c. How do you think the external costs of using wind technologies should be dealt with? Compare the alternative range of solutions considered in this chapter.

17 ◆ Public Goods and Common Resources

**After studying this chapter,
you will be able to:**

- Distinguish among private goods, public goods, and common resources

- Explain how the free-rider problem arises and how the quantity of public goods is determined

- Explain the tragedy of the commons and its possible solutions

What's the difference between the Los Angeles Police

Department and Brinks Security, between fish in the Pacific Ocean and fish produced by a Seattle fish farm, and between a live U2 concert and a show on network television?

Why does government provide some goods and services such as the enforcement of law and order and national defense? Why don't we let private firms produce these items and let people buy the quantities that they demand in the marketplace? Is the scale of provision of these government-provided services correct? Or do governments produce either too much or too little of these items?

More and more people with ever-increasing incomes demand ever greater quantities of most goods and services. One of these items is fish grown wild in the ocean. The fish stocks of the world's oceans are not owned by anyone. They are common resources, and everyone is free to use them. Are our fish stocks being overused? Are we in danger of bringing extinction to some

species? Must the price of fish inevitably keep rising? What can be done to conserve the world's fish stocks?

These are the questions that we study in this chapter. We begin by classifying goods and resources. We then explain what determines the scale of government provision of public services. Finally, we study the tragedy of the commons. In *Reading Between the Lines* at the end of the chapter, we look at a pressing tragedy of the commons in the world today: the problem of overuse of the tropical rainforests.

Classifying Goods and Resources

Goods, services, and resources differ in the extent to which people can be *excluded* from consuming them and in the extent to which one person's consumption *rivals* the consumption of others.

Excludable

A good is **excludable** if it is possible to prevent someone from enjoying its benefits. Brinks's security services, East Point Seafood's fish, and a U2 concert are examples. People must pay to consume them.

A good is **nonexcludable** if it is impossible (or extremely costly) to prevent anyone from benefiting from it. The services of the LAPD, fish in the Pacific Ocean, and a concert on network television are examples. When an LAPD cruiser enforces the speed limit, everyone on the highway benefits; anyone with a boat can fish in the ocean; and anyone with a TV can watch a network broadcast.

Rival

A good is **rival** if one person's use of it decreases the quantity available for someone else. A Brinks's truck can't deliver cash to two banks at the same time. A fish can be consumed only once.

A good is **nonrival** if one person's use of it does not decrease the quantity available for someone else. The services of the LAPD and a concert on network television are nonrival. One person's benefit doesn't lower the benefit of others.

A Fourfold Classification

Figure 17.1 classifies goods, services, and resources into four types.

Private Goods A **private good** is both rival and excludable. A can of Coke and a fish on East Point Seafood's farm are examples of private goods.

Public Goods A **public good** is both nonrival and nonexcludable. A public good can be consumed simultaneously by everyone, and no one can be excluded from enjoying its benefits. National defense is the best example of a public good.

Common Resources A **common resource** is rival and nonexcludable. A unit of a common resource can be used only once, but no one can be prevented from

FIGURE 17.1 Fourfold Classification of Goods

	Excludable	Nonexcludable
Rival	**Private goods** Food and drink Car House	**Common resources** Fish in ocean Atmosphere National parks
Nonrival	**Natural monopolies** Internet Cable television Bridge or tunnel	**Public goods** National defense The law Air traffic control

A private good is one for which consumption is rival and from which consumers can be excluded. A public good is one for which consumption is nonrival and from which it is impossible to exclude a consumer. A common resource is one that is rival but nonexcludable. A good that is nonrival but excludable is produced by a natural monopoly.

 animation

using what is available. Ocean fish are a common resource. They are rival because a fish taken by one person isn't available for anyone else, and they are nonexcludable because it is difficult to prevent people from catching them.

Natural Monopolies In a natural monopoly, economies of scale exist over the entire range of output for which there is a demand (see p. 300). A special case of natural monopoly arises when the good or service can be produced at zero marginal cost. Such a good is nonrival. If it is also excludable, it is produced by a natural monopoly. The Internet and cable television are examples.

Review Quiz

1 Distinguish among public goods, private goods, common resources, and natural monopolies.
2 Provide examples of goods (or services or resources) in each of the four categories that differ from the examples in this section.

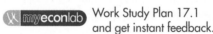 Work Study Plan 17.1 and get instant feedback.

Public Goods

Why does the U.S. government provide our national defense? Why don't we buy our national defense from North Pole Protection, Inc., a private firm that competes for our dollars in the marketplace in the same way that McDonald's does? The answer is that national defense is a public good—nonexcludable and nonrival—and it has a free-rider problem.

The Free-Rider Problem

A *free rider* enjoys the benefits of a good or service without paying for it. Because a public good is provided for everyone to use and no one can be excluded from its benefits, no one has an incentive to pay his or her share of the cost. Everyone has an incentive to free ride. The **free-rider problem** is that the market would provide an inefficiently small quantity of a public good. Marginal social benefit from the public good would exceed its marginal social cost and a deadweight loss would arise.

Let's look at the marginal social benefit and marginal social cost of a public good.

Marginal Social Benefit of a Public Good

Lisa and Max (the only people in an imagined society) value national defense. Figures 17.2(a) and 17.2(b) graph their marginal benefits from a defense satellite system as MB_L for Lisa and MB_M for Max. A person's marginal benefit from a public good, like that from a private good, diminishes as the quantity of the good increases—the marginal benefit curves slope downward.

Figure 17.2(c) shows the marginal *social* benefit curve, *MSB*. Because everyone gets the same quantity of a public good, its marginal social benefit curve is the sum of the marginal benefits of all individuals at each *quantity*—it is the *vertical* sum of the individual marginal benefit curves. So the curve *MSB* in part (c) is the marginal social benefit curve for the economy made up of Lisa and Max. For each satellite, Lisa's marginal benefit is added to Max's marginal benefit.

Contrast the marginal social benefit curve for a public good with that of a private good. To obtain the marginal social benefit curve for a private good, we *sum the quantities demanded* by all individuals at each *price*—we sum the individual marginal benefit curves *horizontally* (see Chapter 5, p. 110).

FIGURE 17.2 Benefits of a Public Good

(a) Lisa's marginal benefit

(b) Max's marginal benefit

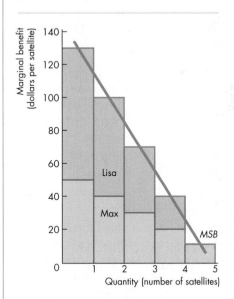

(c) Economy's marginal social benefit

The marginal social benefit at each quantity of the public good is the sum of the marginal benefits of all individuals. The marginal benefit curves are MB_L for Lisa and MB_M for Max. The economy's marginal social benefit curve is *MSB*.

myeconlab animation

Marginal Social Cost of a Public Good

The marginal social cost of a public good is determined in exactly the same way as that of a private good—see p. 112. The principle of increasing marginal cost applies to the marginal cost of a public good and the marginal social cost curve of a public good slopes upward.

Efficient Quantity of a Public Good

To determine the efficient quantity of a public good, we use the same principles that you learned in Chapter 5 and have used repeatedly: Find the quantity at which marginal social benefit equals marginal social cost.

Figure 17.3 shows the marginal social benefit curve, *MSB*, and the marginal social cost curve, *MSC*, for defense satellites. (We'll now think of society as consisting of Lisa and Max and 300 million others.)

If marginal social benefit exceeds marginal social cost, as it does when fewer than 2 satellites are provided, resources can be used more efficiently by increasing the quantity. The extra benefit exceeds the extra cost. If marginal social cost exceeds marginal social benefit, as it does when more than 2 satellites are provided, resources can be used more efficiently by decreasing the quantity. The saving in cost exceeds the loss of benefit.

If marginal social benefit equals marginal social cost, as it does when exactly 2 satellites are provided, resources cannot be used more efficiently. To provide more than 2 satellites would cost more than the additional coverage is worth, and to provide fewer satellites lowers the benefit by more than its cost saving. Resources are allocated efficiently.

Inefficient Private Provision

Could a private firm—North Pole Protection, Inc.—deliver the efficient quantity of satellites? Most likely, it couldn't because no one would have an incentive to buy his or her share of the satellite system. Everyone would reason as follows: "The number of satellites provided by North Pole Protection, Inc., is not affected by my decision to pay my share or not. But my own private consumption will be greater if I free ride and do not pay my share of the cost of the satellite system. If I don't pay, I enjoy the same level of security and I can buy more private goods. I will spend my money on private goods and free ride on the public good." Such reasoning is the free-rider problem. If everyone rea-

FIGURE 17.3 The Efficient Quantity of a Public Good

With fewer than 2 satellites, marginal social benefit, *MSB*, exceeds marginal social cost, *MSC*. With more than 2 satellites, *MSC* exceeds *MSB*. Only with 2 satellites is *MSC* equal to *MSB* and the quantity is efficient.

myeconlab animation

sons the same way, North Pole Protection, Inc., has no revenue and so provides no satellites. Because the efficient level is two satellites, private provision is inefficient.

Efficient Public Provision

The political process might be efficient or inefficient. We look first at an efficient outcome. There are two political parties: Hawks and Doves. They agree on all issues except for the number of defense satellites. The Hawks want three satellites, and the Doves want one satellite. But both parties want to get elected, so they run a voter survey and discover the marginal social benefit curve of Fig. 17.4. They also consult with satellite producers to establish the marginal cost schedule. The parties then do a "what-if" analysis. If the Hawks propose three satellites and the Doves propose one, the voters will be equally unhappy with both parties. Compared to the efficient quantity, the Doves want an underprovision of one satellite and the Hawks want an overprovision of one satellite. The deadweight losses are equal. So the election would be too close to call.

FIGURE 17.4   An Efficient Political Outcome

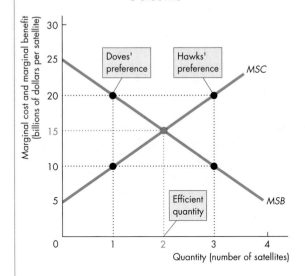

The Doves would like to provide one satellite and the Hawks would like to provide three satellites. The political outcome is two satellites because unless each party proposes two satellites, the other party beats it in an election.

Contemplating this outcome, the Hawks realize that they are too hawkish to get elected. They figure that if they scale back to two satellites, they will win the election if the Doves propose one satellite. The Doves reason in a similar way and figure that if they increase the number of satellites to two, they can win the election if the Hawks propose three.

So they both propose two satellites. The voters are indifferent between the parties, and each party receives 50 percent of the vote.

Regardless of which party wins the election, two satellites are provided and this quantity is efficient. Competition in the political marketplace results in the efficient provision of a public good.

The Principle of Minimum Differentiation The tendency for competitors to make themselves similar to appeal to the maximum number of clients or voters is called the **principle of minimum differentiation**. This principle describes the behavior of political parties. It also explains why fast-food restaurants cluster in the same block and even why new auto models have similar features. If McDonald's opens a new restaurant, it is likely that Wendy's will open near to

McDonald's rather than a mile down the road. If Chrysler designs a new van with a sliding door on the driver's side, most likely Ford will too.

For the political process to deliver the efficient outcome that you've just seen, voters must be well informed, evaluate the alternatives, and vote in the election. Political parties must be well informed about voter preferences. As the next section shows, we can't expect to achieve this outcome.

Inefficient Public Overprovision

If competition between two political parties is to deliver the efficient quantity of a public good, bureaucrats must cooperate and help to achieve this outcome. In the case of defense satellites, the Defense Department—the Pentagon—must cooperate.

Objective of Bureaucrats Bureaucrats want to maximize their department's budget because a bigger budget brings greater status and more power. So the Pentagon's objective is to maximize the defense budget.

Figure 17.5 shows the outcome if the Pentagon is successful in the pursuit of its goal. The Pentagon

FIGURE 17.5   Bureaucratic Overprovision

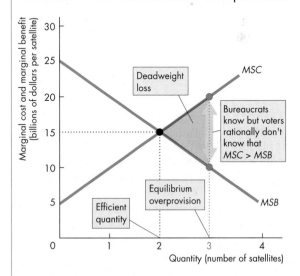

Well informed bureaucrats want to maximize their budget and rationally ignorant voters enable the bureaucrats to go some way toward achieving their goal. A public good might be inefficiently over-provided with a deadweight loss.

might try to persuade the politicians that two satellites cost more than the originally budgeted amount; or the Pentagon might press its position more strongly and argue for more than two satellites. In Fig. 17.5, the Pentagon persuades the politicians to go for three satellites.

Why don't the politicians block the Pentagon? Won't overproducing satellites cost future votes? It will if voters are well informed and know what is best for them. But voters might not be well informed. And well-informed interest groups might enable the Pentagon to achieve its objective and overcome the objections of the politicians.

Rational Ignorance A principle of the economic analysis of public choices is that it is rational for a voter to be ignorant about an issue unless that issue has a perceptible effect on the voter's economic welfare. **Rational ignorance** is the decision not to acquire information because the cost of doing so exceeds the expected benefit.

For example, each voter knows that he or she can make virtually no difference to the defense policy of the U.S. government. Each voter also knows that it would take an enormous amount of time and effort to become even moderately well informed about alternative defense technologies. So voters remain relatively uninformed about the technicalities of defense issues. Although we are using defense policy as an example, the same reasoning applies to all aspects of government economic activity.

All voters are consumers of national defense. But not all voters are producers of national defense. Only a small number are in this latter category. Voters who own or work for firms that produce satellites have a direct personal interest in defense because it affects their incomes. These voters have an incentive to become well informed about defense issues and to operate a political lobby aimed at furthering their own self-interests.

In collaboration with the defense bureaucracy, informed voters who produce public goods exert a larger influence than do the relatively uninformed voters who only use public goods.

When the rationality of the uninformed voter and special interest groups are taken into account, the political equilibrium provides public goods in excess of the efficient quantity. So in the satellite example, three or more satellites might be installed rather than the efficient quantity of two satellites.

Increase in Defense Spending
Efficient Response to 9/11 or Overprovision?

National defense spending fluctuates as global events change the risks that we face. The most recent increase in the defense budget occurred following the attacks of September 11, 2001.

The defense budget might increase as an efficient response to increased risk, which in turn increases the marginal social benefit of national defense. Or the defense budget might increase because bureaucrats take advantage of an increase in risk to increase their budget and inefficiently overprovide defense. It is also possible for both factors to be at work.

Figure 1 Defense Budget

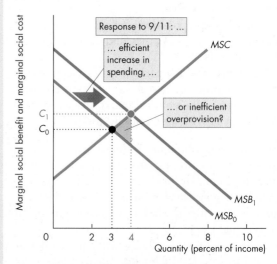

Figure 2 Marginal Social Benefit and Marginal Social Cost of Defense

Two Types of Political Equilibrium

We've seen that two types of political equilibrium are possible: efficient and inefficient. These two types of political equilibrium correspond to two theories of government:

- Social interest theory
- Public choice theory

Social Interest Theory Social interest theory predicts that governments make choices that achieve an efficient provision of public goods. This outcome occurs in a perfect political system in which voters are fully informed about the effects of policies and refuse to vote for outcomes that can be improved upon.

Public Choice Theory Public choice theory predicts that governments make choices that result in inefficient overprovision of public goods. This outcome occurs in political markets in which voters are rationally ignorant and base their votes only on issues that they know affect their own net benefit. Voters pay more attention to their self-interests as producers than their self-interests as consumers, and public officials also act in their own self-interest. The result is *government failure* that parallels market failure.

Why Government Is Large and Growing

Now that we know how the quantity of public goods is determined, we can explain part of the reason for the growth of government. Government grows in part because the demand for some public goods increases at a faster rate than the demand for private goods. There are two possible reasons for this growth:

- Voter preferences
- Inefficient overprovision

Voter Preferences The growth of government can be explained by voter preferences in the following way. As voters' incomes increase (as they do in most years), the demand for many public goods increases more quickly than income. (Technically, the *income elasticity of demand* for many public goods is greater than 1—see Chapter 4, pp. 94–95.) These goods include public health, education, national defense, highways, airports, and air-traffic control systems. If politicians did not support increases in expenditures on these items, they would not get elected.

Inefficient Overprovision Inefficient overprovision might explain the *size* of government but not its *growth rate*. It (possibly) explains why government is *larger* than its efficient scale, but it does not explain why governments use an increasing proportion of total resources.

Voters Strike Back

If government grows too large relative to the value that voters place on public goods, there might be a voter backlash against government programs and a large bureaucracy. Electoral success during the 1990s at the state and federal levels required politicians of all parties to embrace smaller, leaner, and more efficient government. The September 11 attacks have led to a greater willingness to pay for security but have probably not lessened the desire for lean government.

Another way in which voters—and politicians—can try to counter the tendency of bureaucrats to expand their budgets is to privatize the production of public goods. Government *provision* of a public good does not automatically imply that a government-operated bureau must *produce* the good. Garbage collection (a public good) is often done by a private firm, and experiments are being conducted with private fire departments and even private prisons.

Review Quiz

1 What is the free-rider problem and why does it make the private provision of a public good inefficient?
2 Under what conditions will competition among politicians for votes result in an efficient quantity of a public good?
3 How do rationally ignorant voters and budget-maximizing bureaucrats prevent competition in the political marketplace from producing the efficient quantity of a public good? Do they result in too much or too little public provision of public goods?

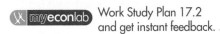 Work Study Plan 17.2 and get instant feedback.

You've seen how public goods create a free-rider problem that would result in the underprovision of such goods. We're now going to learn about common resources and see why they result in the opposite problem—the overuse of such resources.

Common Resources

Atlantic Ocean cod stocks have been declining since the 1950s, and some marine biologists fear that this species is in danger of becoming extinct in some regions. The whale population of the South Pacific has been declining also, and some groups are lobbying to establish a whale sanctuary in the waters around Australia and New Zealand to regenerate the population.

Logging, cattle-ranching, mining, oil extraction, and damming rivers are destroying the tropical rainforests of Southeast Asia, Africa, and Central and South America at an alarming rate. At the present rate of destruction, most will be gone by 2030.

These situations involve common property, and the problem that we have identified is called the *tragedy of the commons.*

The Tragedy of the Commons

The **tragedy of the commons** is the absence of incentives to prevent the overuse and depletion of a commonly owned resource. If no one owns a resource, no one considers the effects of her or his use of the resource on others.

The Original Tragedy of the Commons The term "tragedy of the commons" comes from fourteenth century England, where areas of rough grassland surrounded villages. The commons were open to all and used for grazing cows and sheep owned by the villagers.

Because the commons were open to all, no one had an incentive to ensure that the land was not over grazed. The result was a severe overgrazing situation. Because the commons were overgrazed, the quantity of cows and sheep that they could feed kept falling.

During the sixteenth century, the price of wool increased and England became a wool exporter to the world. Sheep farming became profitable, and sheep owners wanted to gain more effective control of the land they used. So the commons were gradually privatized and enclosed. Overgrazing ended, and land use became more efficient.

A Tragedy of the Commons Today One of today's pressing tragedies of the commons is overfishing. To study the tragedy of the commons, let's look at what has been happening to Atlantic Cod—just one species of fish that has been seriously overfished.

Sustainable Production

Sustainable production is the rate of production that can be maintained indefinitely. In the case of ocean fish, the sustainable production is the quantity of fish (of a given species) that can be caught each year into the indefinite future without wiping out the species.

This production rate depends on the existing stock of fish and the number of boats that go fishing. For a given stock of fish, sending more boats to sea increases the quantity of fish caught. But sending too many boats to sea depletes the stock.

So as the number of boats increases, the quantity of fish caught increases as long as the stock is maintained. But above some crucial level, as more boats go fishing, the stock of fish decreases and the number of fish caught also decreases.

Table 17.1 provides some numbers that illustrate the relationship between the number of boats that go fishing and the quantity of fish caught. The numbers in this example are hypothetical.

TABLE 17.1 Sustainable Production: Total, Average, and Marginal Catch

	Boats (thousands)	Total catch (thousands of tons per month)	Average catch (tons per boat)	Marginal catch (tons per boat)
A	0	0		
				90
B	1	90	90	
				70
C	2	160	80	
				50
D	3	210	70	
				30
E	4	240	60	
				10
F	5	250	50	
				−10
G	6	240	40	
				−30
H	7	210	30	
				−50
I	8	160	20	
				−70
J	9	90	10	
				−90
K	10	0	0	

As the number of fishing boats increases, the quantity of fish caught increases up to the maximum sustainable catch and then decreases. The average catch and marginal catch decrease as the number of boats increases.

Total Catch The total catch is the sustainable rate of production. The numbers in the first two columns of Table 17.1 show the relationship between the number of fishing boats and the total catch, and Fig. 17.6 illustrates this relationship.

You can see that as the number of boats increases from zero to 5,000, the sustainable catch increases to a maximum of 250,000 tons a month. As the number of boats increases above 5,000, the sustainable catch begins to decrease. By the time 10,000 boats are fishing, the fish stock is depleted to the point at which no fish can be caught.

With more than 5,000 boats, there is overfishing. Overfishing arises if the number of boats increases to the point at which the fish stock begins to fall and the remaining fish are harder to find and catch.

Average Catch The average catch is the catch per boat and equals the total catch divided by the number of boats. The numbers in the third column of Table 17.1 show the average catch.

With 1,000 boats, the total catch is 90,000 tons and the catch per boat is 90 tons. With 2,000 boats,

FIGURE 17.6 Sustainable Production of Fish

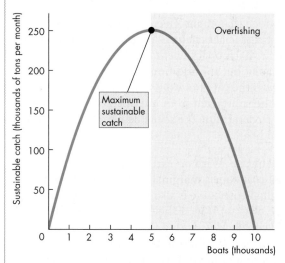

As the number of boats increases, the sustainable catch increases up to a maximum. Beyond that number, more boats will diminish the fish stock and the sustainable catch decreases. Overfishing occurs when the maximum sustainable catch decreases.

myeconlab animation

the total catch is 160,000 tons, and the catch per boat is 80 tons. As more boats take to the ocean, the catch per boat decreases. By the time 8,000 boats are fishing, each boat is catching just 20 tons a month.

The decreasing average catch is an example of the principle of diminishing returns.

Marginal Catch The marginal catch is the change in the total catch that occurs when one more boat joins the existing number. It is calculated as the change in the total catch divided by the increase in the number of boats. The numbers in the fourth column of Table 17.1 show the marginal catch.

For example, in rows C and D of the table, when the number of boats increases by 1,000, the catch increases by 50,000 tons, so the increase in the catch per boat equals 50 tons. In the table, we place this amount midway between the two rows because it is the marginal catch at 2,500 boats, midway between the two levels that we used to calculate it.

Notice that the marginal catch, like the average catch, decreases as the number of boats increases. Also notice that the marginal catch is always less than the average catch.

When the number of boats reaches that at which the sustainable catch is a maximum, the marginal catch is zero. At a larger number of boats, the marginal catch becomes negative—more boats decrease the total catch.

An Overfishing Equilibrium

The tragedy of the commons is that common resources are overused. Why might the fish stock be overused? Why might overfishing occur? Why isn't the maximum number of boats that take to the sea the number that maximizes the sustainable catch—5,000 in this example?

To answer this question, we need to look at the marginal cost and marginal private benefit to an individual fisher.

Suppose that the marginal cost of a fishing boat is the equivalent of 20 tons of fish a month. That is, to cover the opportunity cost of maintaining and operating a boat, the boat must catch 20 tons of fish a month. This quantity of fish also provides the boat owner with normal profit (part of the cost of operating the boat), so the boat owner is willing to go fishing.

The marginal private benefit of operating a boat is the quantity of fish the boat can catch. This quantity is the average catch that we've just calculated.

The average catch is the marginal private benefit because that is the quantity of fish that the boat owner gets by taking the boat to sea.

The boat owner will go fishing as long as the average catch (marginal private benefit) exceeds the marginal cost. And the boat owner will maximize profit when marginal private benefit equals marginal cost.

Figure 17.7 shows the marginal cost curve, MC, and the marginal private benefit curve, MB. The MB curve is based on the numbers for the average catch in Table 17.1.

You can see in Fig. 17.7 that with fewer than 8,000 boats, each boat catches more fish than it costs to catch them. Because boat owners can gain from fishing, the number of boats is 8,000 and there is an overfishing equilibrium.

If one boat owner stopped fishing, the overfishing would be less severe. But that boat owner would be giving up an opportunity to earn an economic profit.

The self-interest of the boat owner is to fish, but the social interest is to limit fishing. The quantity of

fish caught by each boat decreases as additional boats go fishing. But when individual boat owners are deciding whether to fish, they ignore this decrease. They consider only the marginal *private* benefit. The result is an *inefficient* overuse of the resource.

The Efficient Use of the Commons

What is the efficient use of a common resource? It is the use of the resource that makes the marginal cost of using the resource equal to the marginal *social* benefit from its use.

Marginal Social Benefit The marginal *social* benefit of a boat is the boat's marginal catch—the increase in the total catch that results from an additional boat. The reason is that when an additional boat puts to sea, it catches the average catch but it decreases the average catch for itself and for every other boat. The *marginal social benefit* is the *increase* in the quantity of fish caught per boat, not the average number of fish caught.

We calculated the marginal catch in Table 17.1 and we repeat part of that table for convenience in Fig. 17.8. The figure also shows the marginal private benefit curve, MB, and the marginal social benefit curve, MSB.

Notice that at any given number of boats, marginal social benefit is less than marginal private benefit. Each boat benefits privately from the average catch, but the addition of one more boat *decreases* the catch of every boat, and this decrease must be subtracted from the catch of the additional boat to determine the social benefit from the additional boat.

Efficient Use With no external costs, the marginal social cost equals marginal cost. In Fig. 17.8, the marginal cost curve is also the marginal social cost curve, MC = MSC. Efficiency is achieved when MSB equals MSC with 4,000 boats, each catching 60 tons of fish a month. You can see in the table that when the number of boats increases from 3,000 to 4,000 (with 3,500 being the midpoint), marginal social benefit is 30 tons, which exceeds marginal social cost. When the number of boats increases from 4,000 to 5,000 (with 4,500 being the midpoint), marginal social benefit is 10 tons, which is less than marginal social cost. At 4,000 boats, marginal social benefit is 20 tons, which equals marginal social cost.

FIGURE 17.7 Why Overfishing Occurs

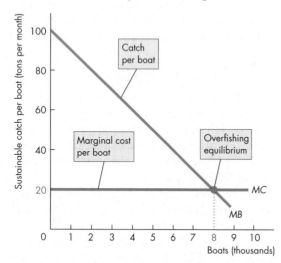

The average catch decreases as the number of boats increases. The average catch per boat is the marginal private benefit, MB, of a boat. The marginal cost of a boat is equivalent to 20 tons of fish, shown by the curve MC. The equilibrium number of boats is 8,000—an overfishing equilibrium.

FIGURE 17.8 Efficient Use of a Common Resource

Boats (thousands)	Total catch (thousands of tons per month)	Marginal private benefit	Marginal social benefit
		(tons per boat)	
A 0	0		
			90
B 1	90	90	
			70
C 2	160	80	
			50
D 3	210	70	
			30
E 4	240	60	
			10
F 5	250	50	

The marginal social benefit of a fishing boat is the change in total benefit that results from an additional boat. The table shows that when the number of boats increases from 2,000 to 3,000 (from row C to row D), the total catch increases from 160,000 to 210,000 tons a month and marginal catch and marginal social benefit is 50 tons.

The figure graphs the marginal social benefit curve, *MSB*, and the marginal private benefit curve, *MB*. Marginal social benefit is less than marginal private benefit and decreases as the number of boats increases. The efficient number of boats is 4,000—the number at which marginal social benefit equals marginal social cost of 20 tons per month. The common resource is used efficiently.

Achieving an Efficient Outcome

Defining the conditions under which a common resource is used efficiently is easier than generating those conditions. To use a common resource efficiently, it is necessary to design an incentive mechanism that confronts the users of the resource with the marginal social consequences of their actions. The same principles apply to common resources as those that you met when you studied externalities in Chapter 16.

Three main methods might be used to achieve the efficient use of a common resource. They are

- Property rights
- Production quotas
- Individual transferable quotas (ITQs)

Property Rights A common resource that no one owns and that anyone is free to use contrasts with *private property*, which is a resource that *someone* owns and has an incentive to use in the way that maximizes its value. One way of overcoming the tragedy of the commons is to remove the commons and make the resource private property. By assigning private property rights, each owner faces the same conditions as society faces. The *MSB* curve of Fig. 17.8 becomes the marginal *private* benefit curve, and the use of the resource is efficient.

The private property solution to the tragedy of the commons *is* available in some cases. It was the solution to the original tragedy of the commons in England's Middle Ages. It is also a solution that has been used to prevent overuse of the airwaves that carry our cell phone service. The right to use this space—called the frequency spectrum—has been auctioned by governments to the highest bidders, and the owner of a particular part of the spectrum is the only one permitted to use it (or to license someone else to use it).

But assigning private property rights is not always feasible. It would be difficult, for example, to assign private property rights to the oceans. It would not be impossible, but the cost of enforcing private property rights over thousands of square miles of ocean would be high. And it would be even more difficult to assign and protect private property rights to the atmosphere.

In some cases, there is an emotional objection to assigning private property rights. When private property rights are too costly to assign and enforce, some form of government intervention is used, and production quotas are the simplest.

Production Quotas You studied the effects of a production quota in Chapter 6 (pp. 141–142) and learned that a quota can drive a wedge between marginal social benefit and marginal social cost and create deadweight loss. In that earlier example, the market was efficient without a quota. But in the case of the use of a common resource, the market is inefficient. It is overproducing, so a quota that limits production can bring a move toward a more efficient outcome.

A quota might be placed either on the number of boats or on the catch. In our example, the catch is determined by the number of boats, so placing a quota on the number of boats is equivalent to placing a quota on the catch. We'll define the quota in terms of the number of boats permitted to fish.

Figure 17.9 shows a quota that achieves an efficient outcome. The quota limits the number of boats to 4,000, the number that catches the efficient quantity at which marginal social benefit, *MSB*, equals marginal social cost, *MSC*. If the boats allocated the

FIGURE 17.9 A Production Quota to Use a Common Resource Efficiently

A quota on the number of boats permitted to fish is set at 4,000, the number that catches the quantity of fish at which marginal social benefit, *MSB*, equals marginal social cost, *MSC*. If the quota is successfully enforced, the outcome is efficient.

right to fish are the only ones to do so, the outcome is efficient.

Implementing a production quota has two problems. First, it is in every boat owner's self-interest to cheat and send out more boats than the number permitted. The reason is that marginal private benefit exceeds marginal cost, so by using more boats, each boat owner gets a higher income. If enough boat owners break the quota, overfishing returns and the tragedy of the commons remains.

Second, marginal cost is not, in general, the same for all producers—as we're assuming here. Some producers have a comparative advantage in using a resource. Efficiency requires that the quota be allocated to the producers with the lowest marginal cost. But the government department that allocates quotas does not have information about the marginal cost of individual producers. Even if the government tried to get this information, producers would have an incentive to lie about their costs so as to get a bigger quota.

So a production quota can work, but only if the activities of every producer can be monitored and all producers have the same marginal cost. Where producers are difficult or very costly to monitor or where marginal costs vary across producers, a production quota cannot achieve an efficient outcome.

Individual Transferable Quotas Where producers are difficult to monitor or where marginal costs differ across producers, a more sophisticated quota system can be effective. It is an **individual transferable quota (ITQ)**, which is a production limit that is assigned to an individual who is then free to transfer (sell) the quota to someone else. A market in ITQs emerges and ITQs are traded at their market price.

The market price of an ITQ is the highest price that someone is willing to pay for one. That price is marginal benefit minus marginal cost. The price of an ITQ will rise to this level because the boat owners who don't have a quota would be willing to pay this amount to get one.

A boat owner with an ITQ could sell it for the market price, so by not selling the ITQ the boat owner incurs an opportunity cost. The marginal cost of fishing, which now includes the opportunity cost of the ITQ, equals the marginal social benefit of the efficient quantity.

Figure 17.10 illustrates how ITQs work. Each boat has a marginal cost equivalent to 20 tons per month. The efficient outcome is achieved with 4,000 boats, each catching 60 tons per month. The market price of

FIGURE 17.10 ITQs to Use a Common Resource Efficiently

ITQs are issued on a scale that keeps output at the efficient level. The market price of an ITQ equals the marginal private benefit minus marginal cost. Because each user of the common resource faces the opportunity cost of using the resource, self-interest achieves the social interest.

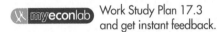

an ITQ equals the equivalent of 40 tons of fish per month. The marginal cost of fishing rises from MC_0 to MC_0 + *price of ITQ*, 4,000 boats go fishing, and each boat catches 60 tons of fish. The outcome is efficient.

Individual differences in marginal cost do not prevent an ITQ system from delivering the efficient outcome. Boat owners with a low marginal cost are willing and able to pay more for a quota than are boat owners with a high marginal cost. The market price of an ITQ will equal 60 tons minus the marginal cost of the marginal producer. Boat owners with higher marginal costs will not go fishing.

Public Choice and the Political Equilibrium

When we studied the provision of public goods, we saw that a political equilibrium might be inefficient—government failure might arise. Such a political outcome might arise with the use of a common resource. Defining an efficient allocation of resources and designing an ITQ system to achieve that allocation is not sufficient to ensure that the political process will deliver the efficient outcome. In the case of the ocean

fish stock, some countries have achieved an efficient political equilibrium, but not all have done so.

Economists agree that ITQs offer an effective tool for achieving an efficient use of the stock of ocean fish. So a political commitment to ITQs is an efficient outcome, and an unwillingness to use ITQs is an inefficient political outcome.

Australia and New Zealand have introduced ITQs to conserve fish stocks in the South Pacific and Southern Oceans. The evidence from these countries suggests that ITQs work well. Fishing boat operators have an incentive to catch more than the assigned quota, but such cheating seems to be relatively rare. Also, boats with an ITQ have an incentive to monitor and report cheating by others without an ITQ.

ITQs help maintain fish stocks, but they also reduce the size of the fishing industry. This consequence of ITQs puts them against the self-interest of fishing boat owners. In all countries, the fishing industry opposes restrictions on its activities, but in Australia and New Zealand, the opposition is not strong enough to block ITQs. In contrast, in the United States the opposition is so strong that the fishing industry persuaded Congress to outlaw ITQs. In 1996, Congress passed the Sustainable Fishing Act that put a moratorium on ITQs. Earlier attempts to introduce ITQs in the Gulf of Mexico and the Northern Pacific were abandoned.

Review Quiz

1 What is the tragedy of the commons? Give two examples, including one from your state.

2 Describe the conditions under which a common resource is used efficiently.

3 Review three methods that might achieve the efficient use of a common resource and explain the obstacles to efficiency.

myeconlab Work Study Plan 17.3 and get instant feedback.

◆ *Reading Between the Lines* on pp. 406–407 looks at the overuse of tropical rainforests.

The next chapter begins a new part of your study of microeconomics and examines the third big question of economics: For whom are goods and services produced? We examine the markets for factors of production and discover how wage rates and other incomes are determined.

Rainforests: A Tragedy of the Commons

Puerto Rico Rainforest on Edge

http://www.latimes.com
April 23, 2006

The scent of flowering tropical plants fills the moist air amid a chorus of whistling birds and singing frogs. The only other sound for a mile in any direction is the roar of a 100-foot waterfall.

Despite 28,000 acres of such lovely scenes, the tropical rainforest that Puerto Rico's prehistoric Taino Indians called El Yunque, or "Land of the White Clouds," is in grave danger. Thousands of acres of forests and green lands … are being cleared at a torrid pace. …

There are consequences to clearing these lands, beyond harm to hundreds of rare plants and wildlife in El Yunque. The rainforest … provides one-third of the island's fresh drinking water. …

Tropical forests such as El Yunque constitute about 6% of Earth's surface and account for 50% to 80% of the world's plant species. Rainforests once covered 14% of the planet's land surface, but have shrunk due to development and deforestation. …

"I'd like to think we live in harmony with El Yunque," said Martha Herrera, 69, who bought a two-story house next to the rainforest a decade ago.

"Some people say I'm hurting El Yunque. But how am I hurting anything?" she asked as her three dogs and flock of chickens roamed in and out of the park one recent morning.

About a quarter-mile away, construction crews were pouring concrete as they rushed to finish a 20-acre condominium complex.

"People who buy these units want the views of the rainforest," said Hecter Ramirez, 35, a construction worker at the site. "I have a job. That's important to my family and me. People tell me this isn't going to damage anything."

El Yunque is home to 240 native tree species—more than any other national forest. Federally listed endangered plants grow in the forest too, such as the miniature orchid and palo de jazmin. …

Essence of the Story

- Puerto Rico's El Yunque tropical rainforest has 240 native tree species—more than any other national forest.
- Tropical forests, which have shrunk from 14 percent to 6 percent of Earth's surface, account for 50 to 80 percent of the world's plant species.
- The rainforest near San Juan provides one third of the island's fresh drinking water.
- Puerto Rico's tropical rainforest is being cleared at a torrid pace.
- Condominium construction is taking place close to the rainforest.
- Construction workers and people who buy condominiums say they aren't doing any damage.

Economic Analysis

- The tropical rainforests of Puerto Rico grow on land that some people want to build on.

- These forests are home to many rare species of tree, a source of drinking water, and a carbon-dioxide sink that helps to maintain Earth's atmosphere.

- The forests are common property.

- The private incentive to exploit these forest resources is strong.

- Because no one owns the forests, there is no incentive to conserve the resources and use them on a sustainable basis.

- The result is overuse, just like the overuse of the commons of England in the Middle Ages.

- The figures illustrate the tragedy of the commons in a tropical rainforest.

- Figure 1 shows the relationship between the sustainable production of wood from a rainforest and the number of lumber producers working the forest.

- Figure 2 shows the marginal private benefit and marginal private cost of a producer and the marginal social benefit and marginal social cost of wood.

- The producer's marginal cost of felling a tree is assumed to be zero.

- For a common resource, the marginal private benefit received by a producer is MB and LD lumber producers acting in their self-interest deplete the resource. Sustainable production decreases to zero.

- For a privately owned resource, the marginal social benefit curve, MSB, becomes the marginal private benefit curve. Self-interest results in LP lumber producers who maximize the sustainable output of the rainforest.

- If the only benefit from the rainforest were its timber, maximum sustainable timber output would be efficient.

- But external benefits arise from the diversity of the wildlife supported by the forest, so marginal social cost exceeds the zero marginal private cost.

- Production in the social interest—the efficient level of production—is achieved with LS lumber producers and is less than the maximum sustainable production.

Figure 1 Rainforest timber production

Figure 2 Marginal benefits and marginal costs

407

SUMMARY

Key Points

Classifying Goods and Resources (p. 394)

- A private good is a good or service that is rival and excludable.
- A public good is a good or service that is nonrival and nonexcludable.
- A common resource is a resource that is rival but nonexcludable.

Public Goods (pp. 395–399)

- Because a public good is a good or service that is *nonrival* and *nonexcludable*, it creates a *free-rider* problem: No one has an incentive to pay their share of the cost of providing a public good.
- The efficient level of provision of a public good is that at which marginal social benefit equals marginal social cost.
- Competition between political parties, each of which tries to appeal to the maximum number of voters, can lead to the efficient scale of provision of a public good and to both parties proposing the same policies—the principle of minimum differentiation.
- Bureaucrats try to maximize their budgets, and if voters are rationally ignorant, public goods might be provided in quantities that exceed those that are efficient.

Common Resources (pp. 400–405)

- Common resources create a problem that is called the tragedy of the commons—no one has a private incentive to conserve the resources and use them at an efficient rate.
- A common resource is used to the point at which the marginal private benefit equals the marginal cost.
- A common resource might be used efficiently by creating a private property right, setting a quota, or issuing individual transferable quotas.

Key Figures

Key Terms

PROBLEMS and APPLICATIONS ◆

 Work problems 1–7 in Chapter 17 Study Plan and get instant feedback.
Work problems 8–16 as Homework, a Quiz, or a Test if assigned by your instructor.

1. Classify each of the following items as excludable, nonexcludable, rival, nonrival, a public good, a private good, or a common resource.
   - Gettysburg National Military Park
   - A Big Mac
   - Brooklyn Bridge
   - The Statue of Liberty
   - Air
   - Police protection
   - Sidewalks
   - U.S. Postal Service
   - FedEx courier service
   - The MyEconLab Web site

2. For each of the following goods, explain whether there is a free-rider problem. If there is no such problem, how is it avoided?
   - July 4th fireworks display
   - Interstate 81 in Virginia
   - Wireless Internet access in hotels
   - Sharing downloaded music
   - The public library in your city

3. The figure provides information about a sewage disposal system that a city of 1 million people is considering installing.

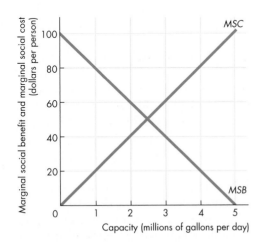

Capacity (millions of gallons per day)

   a. What is the capacity that achieves an efficient outcome?
   b. How much will each person have to pay in taxes to pay for the efficient capacity level?
   c. What is the political equilibrium if voters are well informed?

d. What is the political equilibrium if voters are rationally ignorant and bureaucrats achieve the highest attainable budget?

4. The table shows the value of cod caught in the North Atlantic Ocean by American, Canadian, and European fishing boats. The marginal cost of operating a boat is $80,000 a month.

Number of boats	Value of cod caught (thousands of dollars per month)
0	0
10	2,000
20	3,400
30	4,200
40	4,400
50	4,000
60	3,000
70	1,400

   a. What is the marginal private benefit of a fishing boat at each quantity of boats?
   b. What is the marginal social benefit of a fishing boat at each quantity of boats?
   c. With no regulation of cod fishing, what is the equilibrium number of boats and the value of cod caught?
   d. Is the equilibrium in c an overfishing equilibrium?
   e. What is the efficient number of boats?
   f. What is the efficient value of the cod catch?
   g. Do you think that the consumers of fish and the fishing industry will agree about how much cod should be caught?
   h. If the United States, Canada, and the European Union imposed a production quota to limit the catch to the efficient quantity, what would the total value of the catch be under the quota?
   i. If the United States, Canada, and the European Union issued ITQs to fishing boats to limit the catch to the efficient quantity, at what price would ITQs be traded?

5. "Free Riders" Must be Part of Health Debate

[Barack] Obama insists that "the reason people don't have health insurance isn't because they don't want it, it's because they can't afford it. ..." A free rider is someone who can afford a health insurance policy but won't buy any. Obama wants to give Americans the freedom to not buy insurance but the right to get government-subsidized coverage when they get sick.

The inevitable result is that a lot of healthy people will avoid contributing to the insurance pool. ... Why should they buy insurance at any price if they can glom on to a government program should disaster strike? There are 47 million uninsured people in the United States, and 16 percent have a family income above $75,000. Another 15 percent make between $50,000 and $75,000. ... About 16 percent of the patients who received "free" medical care in 2004 came from families making at least four times the federal poverty level. ... They racked up $5.8 billion in uncompensated care, which others had to pay for.

Los Angeles Times, March 4, 2008

a. Explain why government-subsidized coverage can create a free-rider problem in the health-care market.
b. Explain the evidence this article presents to contradict the argument that "the reason people don't have health insurance isn't because they don't want it, it's because they can't afford it."

6. The Wonder Fish

Our oceans are being drained of food. Doctors tell us to eat more fish. ... To meet this growing appetite, commercial fishermen are scooping up everything that's edible (and a lot of what's not). Couple that trend with the effects of global warming, and the situation has become so dire that some scientists think seafood stocks will totally collapse by 2048. ... A former fisheries researcher in the Cook Islands, [Kona Blue cofounder Neil] Sims was disgusted by how locals ravaged marine life there. But the scene also inspired his idea for a new (patents pending) style of deepwater fish farming. ... So just what is Kona Kampachi? Think of it as a more versa-

tile cousin of hamachi. It's not genetically engineered in any way, just well bred. ... Sims fastidiously controls every variable in the life of a fish. Kona Blue houses 150 brood stock on shore a few miles north of Kona. These breeders are continually refreshed with deep-ocean water and left to do nothing but eat, swim, and procreate. Every few days a female lays as many as 300,000 eggs, which are harvested and transferred to a nursery. ... When the fish reach an inch in length, they head to the ocean. In the wild the survival of two eggs would ensure sustainability for the species. Kona Blue does far better. "We get survival rates of 5% to 10%," says Sims.

Fortune, April 21, 2008

a. Why is the fish stock being overused?
b. How does Kona Blue help prevent overfishing, while at the same time allowing a greater amount of fish to be caught?
c. Use a model of the sustainable production of fish to illustrate your explanation.
d. Draw a graph to illustrate your answers to b and c.

7. A Bridge Too Far Gone

The gas taxes that paid for much of America's post-war freeway system have been eaten away by inflation and higher fuel efficiency. The federal tax has not been raised since 1993. California's 18-cent tax has remained unchanged since 1994. Motorists now pay about one-third in gas taxes to drive a mile as they did in the early 1960s. Yet raising such taxes is politically tricky. This would matter less if private cash was flooding into infrastructure, or if new ways were being found to control demand. Neither is happening. ... A new toll road in Texas, which is being built by a Spanish company, raised howls of outrage.

The Economist, August 9, 2007

a. Why is it "politically tricky" to raise gas taxes to finance infrastructure?
b. What in this news clip points to a distinction between public *production* of a public good and public *provision*? Give examples of three public goods that are *produced* by private firms but *provided* by government and paid for with taxes.

8. For each of the following goods, explain whether there is a free-rider problem. If there is no such problem, how is it avoided?
   - Fire protection
   - New Year's Eve celebrations in Times Square, New York
   - Interstate 80 in rural Wyoming
   - The Grand Canyon
   - Street lighting in urban areas
   - Flood control in the Mississippi watershed
   - The beach at Santa Monica

9. The table provides information about a mosquito control program.

Quantity sprayed (square miles per day)	Marginal social cost	Marginal social benefit
	(dollars per day)	
0	0	0
1	1,000	5,000
2	2,000	4,000
3	3,000	3,000
4	4,000	2,000
5	5,000	1,000

   a. What quantity of spraying would a private mosquito control program provide?
   b. What is the efficient quantity of spraying?
   c. Two political parties, the Conservers and the Eradicators, fight an election in which the only issue is the quantity of spraying to undertake. The Conservers want no spraying and the Eradicators want to spray 5 square miles per day. The voters are well-informed about the benefits and costs of mosquito control programs. What is the outcome of the election?
   d. Draw a graph to illustrate the outcome of the election.

10. In problem 9, the government sets up a Mosquito Control Unit and appoints a bureaucrat to run the department.
   a. Would the mosquito spraying most likely be underprovided, overprovided, or provided at the efficient quantity?
   b. How do rational voters behave and why do they enable bureaucrats to behave in the way you described in a?
   c. Draw a graph to illustrate the outcome when bureaucrats achieve their objective.

11. An oil reserve runs under plots of land owned by seven people. Each person has the right to sink a well on her or his land and take oil from the reserve. The amount of oil that is produced depends on the number of wells sunk and is shown in the table. The marginal private cost of a well is the equivalent of 4 gallons a day.

Number of wells	Oil output (gallons per day)
0	0
2	12
4	22
6	30
8	36
10	40
12	42
14	42

   a. What is the marginal private benefit at each quantity of wells?
   b. What are the equilibrium number of wells and quantity of oil produced?
   c. What is the marginal social benefit at each quantity of wells?
   d. What are the efficient number of wells and quantity of oil to produce?
   e. If the common reserve were owned by only one person, how many wells would be sunk and how much oil would be produced?
   f. How much would someone offer the seven owners to rent the rights to all the oil in the common reserve? (Use gallons of oil as the unit.)

12. If hikers and others were required to pay a fee to use the Appalachian Trail,
   a. Would the use of this common resource be more efficient?
   b. Would it be even more efficient if the most popular spots had the highest prices?
   c. Why do you think we don't see more market solutions to the tragedy of the commons?

13. **Who's Hiding under Our Umbrella?**

   Students of the Cold War learn that, to deter possible Soviet aggression, the United States placed a "strategic umbrella" over NATO Europe and Japan, declaring it would fight if their independence was threatened by the Soviet Union. ... European and Japanese allies have been taking economic advantage of the fact that the United States was providing for most of their own national security.

Under President Ronald Reagan, approximately 6 percent of the GDP of the United States was spent on defense, whereas the Europeans tended to spend only 2 to 3 percent and the Japanese a miserly 1 percent, although all faced a common enemy. Thus the American taxpayer bore a disproportionate burden for the overall defense spending, whereas those sheltering under its umbrella spent more on social or consumer goods, or saved while the U.S. went further into debt. …

Today, the United States, like Rome and Britain in their time, is the provider of international public goods. …

International Herald Tribune, January 30, 2008

a. Explain the free-rider problem described in this news clip.
b. Does the free-rider problem in international defense mean that the world has too little defense against aggression?
c. How do nations try to overcome the free-rider problem among nations?

14. **Commuting More than Pain at Pump**

… [T]he daily drive causes a large number of commuters everything from increased stress and anger to sleep deprivation and loss of productivity at work. … Nearly half (45 percent) of the 4,091 respondents polled in 10 major metropolitan areas said that traffic congestion increased their stress levels. Another 28 percent said it heightened their feelings of anger. Almost one in five said commuting problems cut down on their productivity at work and in school and a full 12 percent said they were sleep deprived. … The two biggest culprits: start-and-stop traffic and rude drivers.

Because traffic delays are typically random, commuters have to budget a larger amount of time to get from here to there. … [IBM's Institute for Electronic Government] has been devising ways to help cities deal with increased traffic congestion, and has helped deploy automated tolling, congestion pricing plans and real-time traffic modeling in cities such as Brisbane, London, Singapore and Stockholm. …

To help alleviate traffic problems, drivers said they wanted more options to work from home, improved public transportation, and better road condition information.

CNN, May 30, 2008

a. Are congested public roadways excludable or nonexcludable and rival or nonrival? Explain.
b. As a result of this classification, explain the problem associated with congested public roadways that results in an inefficient usage.
c. Draw a graph to illustrate the inefficient equilibrium.
d. How could government policies be used to achieve an efficient usage of roadways?

15. **Where the Tuna Roam**

… to the first settlers, the Great Plains posed the same problem as the oceans today: It was a vast, open area where there seemed to be no way to protect animals against relentless human predators. … But animals thrived in the West once the settlers divvied up the land and ingeniously devised new ways to protect their livestock. … Today the ocean is still pretty much an open range, and the fish are suffering the consequences. … Fishermen have a personal incentive to make as much as they can this year, even if they're destroying their own profession in the process. They figure any fish they don't take for themselves will just be taken by someone else. …

The New York Times, November 4, 2006

a. What are the similarities between the problems faced by the earliest settlers in the West and today's fishers?
b. Can the tragedy of the commons in the oceans be eliminated in the same manner used by the early settlers on the plains?
c. How can ITQs change the short-term outlook of fishers to a long-term outlook?

16. After you have studied *Reading Between the Lines* on pp. 406–407, answer the following questions:
a. What is happening in Puerto Rico that is causing the depletion of the country's tropical rainforests?
b. How would the creation of private property rights in Puerto Rico's rainforests change the way in which the forest resources are used?
c. Would private ownership solve all the problems of resource overuse? If not, why not?

UNDERSTANDING MARKET FAILURE AND GOVERNMENT

We, the People, …

Thomas Jefferson knew that creating a government of the people, by the people, and for the people was a huge enterprise and one that could easily go wrong. Creating a constitution that made despotic and tyrannical rule impossible was relatively easy. The founding fathers did their best to practice sound economics. They designed a sophisticated system of incentives—of carrots and sticks—to make the government responsive to public opinion and to limit the ability of individual self-interests to gain at the expense of the majority. But they were not able to create a constitution that effectively blocks the ability of special interest groups to capture the consumer and producer surpluses that result from specialization and exchange.

We have created a system of government to deal with four market failures: (1) monopoly; (2) externalities; (3) public goods; and (4) common resources.

Government might help cope with these market failures. But as the founding fathers knew well, government does not eliminate the pursuit of self-interest. Voters, politicians, and bureaucrats pursue their self-interest, sometimes at the expense of the social interest, and instead of market failure, we get government failure.

Many economists have thought long and hard about the problems discussed in this part. But none has had as profound an effect on our ideas in this area as Ronald Coase.

Ronald Coase *(1910–), was born in England and educated at the London School of Economics, where he was deeply influenced by his teacher, Arnold Plant, and by the issues of his youth: communist central planning versus free markets.*

Professor Coase has lived in the United States since 1951. He first visited America as a 20-year-old on a traveling scholarship during the depths of the Great Depression. It was on this visit, and before he had completed his bachelor's degree, that he conceived the ideas that 60 years later were to earn him the 1991 Nobel Prize for Economic Science.

Ronald Coase discovered and clarified the significance of transactions costs and property rights for the functioning of the economy. He has revolutionized the way we think about property rights and externalities and has opened up the growing field of law and economics.

"The question to be decided is: is the value of fish lost greater or less than the value of the product which contamination of the stream makes possible?"

RONALD H. COASE
The Problem of Social Cost

TALKING
WITH

Caroline M. Hoxby

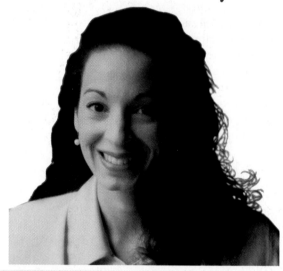

Caroline M. Hoxby is the Allie S. Freed Professor of Economics at Harvard University. Born in Cleveland, Ohio, she was an undergraduate at Harvard and a graduate student at Oxford and MIT.

Professor Hoxby is a leading student of the economics of education. She has written many articles on this topic and has published books entitled *The Economics of School Choice* and *College Choices* (both University of Chicago Press, 2003 and 2004, respectively). She is Program Director of the Economics of Education Program at the National Bureau of Economic Research, serves on several other national boards that study education issues, and has advised or provided testimony to several state legislatures and the United States Congress.

Michael Parkin talked with Caroline Hoxby about her work and the progress that economists have made in understanding how the financing and provision of education influence the quality of education and the equality of access to it.

Why did you decide to become an economist?

I've wanted to be an economist from about the age of 13. That was when I took my first class in economics (an interesting story in itself) and discovered that all of the thoughts swimming around in my head belonged to a "science" and there was an entire body of people who understood this science—a lot better than I did, anyway. I can still recall reading *The Wealth of Nations* for the first time; it was a revelation.

What drew you to study the economics of education?

We all care about education, perhaps because it is the key means by which opportunity is (or should be) extended to all in the United States. Also, nearly everyone now acknowledges that highly developed countries like the United States rely increasingly on education as the engine of economic growth. Thus, one reason I was drawn to education is its importance. However, what primarily drew me was that education issues were so clearly begging for economic analysis and that there was so little of it. I try hard to understand educational institutions and problems, but I insist on bringing economic logic to bear on educational issues.

Why is education different from fast food? Why don't we just let people buy it from private firms that are regulated to maintain quality standards analogous to the safety standards that the FDA imposes on fast-food producers?

The thing that makes education different from fast food is not that we cannot buy it from private institutions that are regulated to maintain quality standards. We do this all the time—think of private schools and colleges. What makes education different is that it is (a) an investment, not consumption, and (b) the capital markets for financing the investments work poorly when left on their own. Essentially, our country has an interest in every person investing optimally in his or her education. To make investments, however, people need funds that allow them to attend good schools and take time away from work. Children don't have these funds and cannot arrange for loans that they may or may not pay off decades later. Therefore, children depend on their families for funds, and families do not necessarily have the funds to invest optimally or the right incentives to do so. Society has a role in filling the gaps in the capital market; it fills this role by public funding of elementary and secondary education, government guaranteed loans, college savings programs, and so on. There is no particular reason, however, why government needs to actually run schools; it can provide the funding without actually providing schooling.

In one of your papers, you posed the question: Does competition among public schools benefit students or taxpayers? What are the issues, what was your answer, and how did you arrive at it?

We are all familiar with the fact that families choose public schools when they choose where to live. This traditional form is by far the most pervasive form of school choice in the United States, and few parents who exercise it would be willing to give it up. Yet, until quite recently, we did not know whether having such traditional school choice was good for students (high achievement) or taxpayers (more efficient schools). It is important to know because some people in the United States, especially poor people who live in central cities, are unable to exercise this form of school choice. Economists hypothesized that this lack of choice might be a reason why many children from poor, central city families receive such a deficient education, especially considering the dollars spent in their schools (which spend significantly more than the median school).

To investigate this hypothesis, I examined all of the metropolitan areas in the United States. They vary a great deal in the degree of traditional choice available to parents. On one extreme, there is a group of metropolitan areas with hundreds of school districts. On the other extreme, there is a group of metropolitan areas with only one school district. Most are somewhere in between. A family in a metropolitan area with one district may have no easy way of "escaping" a badly run district administration. A family in a metropolitan area with hundreds of districts can choose among several districts that match well with its job location, housing preferences, and so on.

Looking across metropolitan areas with many districts (lots of potential competition from traditional school choice) and few districts (little potential competition), I found that areas with greater competition had substantially higher student achievement for any given level of school spending. This suggests that schools are more efficient producers of achievement when they face competition.

What do we know about the relative productivity of public and private schools?

It is somewhat difficult to say whether achievement is higher at public or private schools in the United States. The best studies use randomly assigned private school scholarships, follow the same children over time, or use "natural experiments" in which some areas accidentally end up with more private schools than others. These studies tend to find that, for the same student, private schools produce achievement that is up to 10 percent higher. However, for understanding which type of school is more productive, we actually do not need private schools to have higher achievement. For the sake of argument, let's "call it a draw" on the achievement question.

In recent studies comparing achievement in public and private schools, the public schools spent an average of $9,662 per student and the private schools spent an average of $2,427 per student. These spending numbers, combined with achievement that we will call equal, suggest that the private schools were 298 percent more productive. I would not claim that this number is precisely correct; we could think of some minor adjustments. But it is difficult not to conclude that the private schools are significantly more productive. They produce equal achievement for a fraction of the cost.

What can economists say about the alternative methods of financing education? Is there a voucher solution that could work?

There is definitely a voucher solution that could work because vouchers are inherently an extremely flexible policy. People often see the word "voucher" and think of, say, a $2000 voucher being given to a small share of children. But this need not be so. Anything that we can do with public school financing we can do better with a voucher because vouchers can be specific to a student, whereas the government can never ensure that funds get to an individual student by giving those funds to his or her district.

Any well-designed voucher system will give schools an incentive to compete. However, when designing vouchers, we can also build in remedies for a variety of educational problems. Vouchers can be used to ensure that disabled children get the funding they need and the program choices they need. Compared to current school finance programs, vouchers can do a better job of ensuring that low-income families have sufficient funds to invest in the child's education. Well-designed vouchers can encourage schools to make their student bodies socio-economically diverse. Economists should say to policy makers: "Tell me your goals; I'll design you a voucher."

> Economists should say to policy makers: "Tell me your goals; I'll design you a voucher."

Is there a conflict between efficiency and equity in the provision of quality education?

To raise the public funds that allow all families to invest optimally in their children's education, we have to have taxes. Taxes always create some deadweight loss, so we always create some inefficiency when we raise the funds we need to provide equitable educational opportunities. However, if the funds are used successfully and actually induce people to make optimal investments in their education, we have eliminated much more inefficiency than the taxes created. Thus, in an ideal world, there need not be a conflict between efficiency and equity.

In the real world, public funds are often raised with taxes (creating deadweight loss) and then are not successfully used. If we spend twice as much on public schools and do not have higher achievement to show for it, then there are no efficiency gains to overwhelm the efficiency losses from taxation. In other words, to avoid a conflict between equity and efficiency, we must learn how to use public funds productively in education. This is what the economics of education is all about.

What advice do you have for a student who is just starting to study economics? Is economics a good subject in which to major? What other subjects go well alongside it? And do you have anything special to say to women who are making a career choice? What must we do to get more women involved in our subject?

Students who are just starting to study economics should do two things. First, learn the tools even if they seem abstruse. Once you have mastered the tools, you will be able to "see the forest for the trees." As long as you don't master the tools, you will be in the trees and will find it hard to think about economic problems. Second, think about economic problems! The real world is a great moving textbook of economics, once you have the tools to analyze it.

Economics is a great subject in which to major because it trains you for life, for many careers, and for the thinking that you would need in a leadership position. I think that it is the best training for a future career in business, the law, or policy making. Don't forget nonprofits: every year, nonprofit organizations try to hire people with economics skills who are also interested in charitable schemes.

Math and statistics courses are complementary to economics because they make it easier for a student to master the tools quickly. Economics goes well with many studies in the arts and sciences, too. It all depends on what you want to use economics for. If you want to do health policy making, take economics along with premedical courses. If you want to be a policy maker in the performing arts, take economics along with music.

I wish that there were more women in economics. Our field loses far too many talented minds. Also, women who need to understand economics for their careers are sometimes without it. To aspiring women economists, I can only say to hang in there. Mastering economics is empowering. You will never have to worry about your opinion not being taken seriously if you are a good economist.

18 ◆ Markets for Factors of Production

After studying this chapter, you will be able to:

- Describe the anatomy of factor markets
- Explain how the value of marginal product determines the demand for a factor of production
- Explain how wage rates and employment are determined and how labor unions influence the labor market
- Explain how capital and land rental rates and natural resource prices are determined

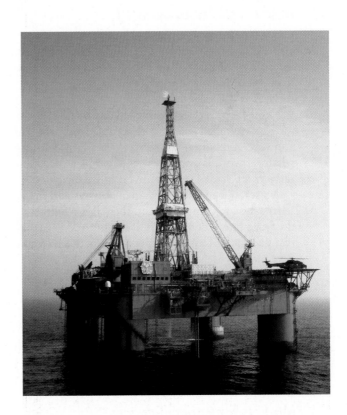

You know that wage rates vary a lot. A server at McDonald's earns $8 an hour. Demetrio Luna, who spends his days in a small container suspended from the top of Houston's high-rise buildings cleaning windows, makes $12 an hour. Richard Seymour, who plays for the New England Patriots, collects a cool $25 million a year. Some differences in earnings might seem surprising. For example, your college football coach earns much more than your economics professor. What determines the wages that people earn?

The price of oil became a big issue in 2008 as new record highs were set. What determines the prices of the natural resources that we use to produce goods and services? Why do these prices fluctuate and sometimes seem to lose connection with the fundamentals of supply and value?

In this chapter, we study the markets for labor, capital, and natural resources and learn how their prices are determined. *In Reading Between the Lines* at the end of the chapter, we focus on the market for oil and look at the debate over whether it would be a good idea to try to increase the supply of oil by exploring the undersea resources off the U.S. coast.

The Anatomy of Factor Markets

The four factors of production are

- Labor
- Capital
- Land (natural resources)
- Entrepreneurship

Let's take a brief look at the anatomy of the markets in which these factors of production are traded.

Markets for Labor Services

Labor services are the physical and mental work effort that people supply to produce goods and services. A labor market is a collection of people and firms who trade labor services. The price of labor services is the wage rate.

Some labor services are traded day by day. These services are called *casual labor*. People who pick fruit and vegetables often just show up at a farm and take whatever work is available that day. But most labor services are traded on a contract, called a **job**.

Most labor markets have many buyers and many sellers and are competitive. In these labor markets, the wage rate is determined by supply and demand, just like the price is determined in any other competitive market.

In some labor markets, a labor union organizes labor, which introduces an element of monopoly on the supply-side of the labor market. In this type of labor market, a bargaining process between the union and the employer determines the wage rate.

We'll study both competitive labor markets and labor unions in this chapter.

Markets for Capital Services

Capital consists of the tools, instruments, machines, buildings, and other constructions that have been produced in the past and that businesses now use to produce goods and services. These physical objects are themselves goods—capital goods. Capital goods are traded in goods markets, just as bottled water and toothpaste are. The price of a dump truck, a capital good, is determined by supply and demand in the market for dump trucks. This market is not a market for capital services.

A market for *capital services* is a *rental market*—a market in which the services of capital are hired.

An example of a market for capital services is the vehicle rental market in which Avis, Budget, Hertz, U-Haul, and many other firms offer automobiles and trucks for hire. The price in a capital services market is a *rental rate*.

Most capital services are not traded in a market. Instead, a firm buys capital and uses it itself. The services of the capital that a firm owns and operates have an implicit price that arises from depreciation and interest costs (see Chapter 10, pp. 228–229). You can think of this price as the implicit rental rate of capital. Firms that buy capital and use it themselves are *implicitly* renting the capital to themselves.

Markets for Land Services and Natural Resources

Land consists of all the gifts of nature—natural resources. The market for land as a factor of production is the market for the *services of land*—the use of land. The price of the services of land is a rental rate.

Most natural resources, such as farm land, can be used repeatedly. But a few natural resources are nonrenewable. **Nonrenewable natural resources** are resources that can be used only once. Examples are oil, natural gas, and coal. The prices of nonrenewable natural resources are determined in global *commodity markets* and are called *commodity prices*.

Entrepreneurship

Entrepreneurial services are not traded in markets. Entrepreneurs receive the profit or bear the loss that results from their business decisions.

Review Quiz

1 What are the factors of production and their prices?
2 What is the distinction between capital and the services of capital?
3 What is the distinction between the price of capital equipment and the rental rate of capital?

 Work Study Plan 18.1 and get instant feedback.

The rest of this chapter explores the influences on the demand and supply of factors of production. We begin by studying the demand for a factor of production.

The Demand for a Factor of Production

The demand for a factor of production is a **derived demand**—it is derived from the demand for the goods and services that it is used to produce. You've seen, in Chapters 10 through 15, how a firm determines its profit-maximizing output. The quantities of factors of production demanded are a consequence of firms' output decisions. A firm hires the quantities of factors of production that maximize its profit.

To decide the quantity of a factor of production to hire, a firm compares the cost of hiring an additional unit of the factor with its value to the firm. The cost of hiring an additional unit of a factor of production is the *factor price*. The value to the firm of hiring one more unit of a factor of production is called the factor's value of marginal product. The **value of marginal product** equals the price of a unit of output multiplied by the marginal product of the factor of production.

To study the demand for a factor of production, we'll use labor as the example. But what you learn here about the demand for labor applies to the demand for all factors of production.

Value of Marginal Product

Table 18.1 shows you how to calculate the value of the marginal product of labor at Angelo's Bakery.

The first two columns show Angelo's total product schedule—the number of loaves per hour that each quantity of labor can produce. The third column shows the marginal product of labor—the change in total product that results from a one-unit increase in the quantity of labor employed. (See Chapter 11, pp. 253–256 for a refresher on product schedules.)

Angelo can sell bread at the going market price of $2 a loaf. Given this information, we can calculate the value of marginal product (fourth column). It equals price multiplied by marginal product. For example, the marginal product of hiring the second worker is 6 loaves an hour. Each loaf sold brings in $2, so the value of the marginal product of the second worker is $12 (6 loaves at $2 each).

A Firm's Demand for Labor

The value of the marginal product of labor tells us what an additional worker is worth to a firm. It tells us the revenue that the firm earns by hiring one more worker. The wage rate tells us what an additional worker costs a firm.

The value of the marginal product of labor and the wage rate together determine the quantity of labor demanded by a firm. Because the value of marginal product decreases as the quantity of labor employed increases, there is a simple rule for maximizing profit: Hire the quantity of labor at which the value of marginal product equals the wage rate.

If the value of marginal product of labor exceeds the wage rate, a firm can increase its profit by hiring

---

TABLE 18.1   Value of Marginal Product at Angelo's Bakery

	Quantity of labor (L) (workers)	Total product (TP) (loaves per hour)	Marginal product (MP = ΔTP/ΔL) (loaves per worker)	Value of marginal product (VMP = MP × P) (dollars per worker)
A	0	0		
			7	14
B	1	7		
			6	**12**
C	**2**	13		
			5	10
D	3	18		
			4	8
E	4	22		
			3	6
F	5	25		

The value of the marginal product of labor equals the price of the product multiplied by marginal product of labor. If Angelo's hires 2 workers, the marginal product of the second worker is 6 loaves an hour (in the third column). The price of a loaf is $2, so the value of the marginal product of the second worker is $2 a loaf multiplied by 6 loaves an hour, which is $12 an hour (in fourth column).

one more worker. If the wage rate exceeds the value of marginal product of labor, a firm can increase its profit by firing one worker. But if the wage rate equals the value of the marginal product of labor, the firm cannot increase its profit by changing the number of workers it employs. The firm is making the maximum possible profit.

So the quantity of labor demanded by a firm is the quantity at which the value of the marginal product of labor equals the wage rate.

A Firm's Demand for Labor Curve

A firm's demand for labor curve is derived from its value of marginal product curve. Figure 18.1 shows these two curves. Figure 18.1(a) shows the value of marginal product curve at Angelo's Bakery. The blue bars graph the numbers in Table 18.1. The curve labeled *VMP* is Angelo's value of marginal product curve.

If the wage rate falls and other things remain the same, a firm hires more workers. Figure 18.1(b) shows Angelo's demand for labor curve.

Suppose the wage rate is $10 an hour. You can see in Fig.18.1(a) that if Angelo hires 2 workers, the value of the marginal product of labor is $12 an hour. At a wage rate of $10 an hour, Angelo makes a profit of $2 an hour on the second worker. If Angelo hires a third worker, the value of the marginal product of the that worker is $10 an hour. So on this third worker, Angelo breaks even.

If Angelo hired 4 workers, his profit would fall. The fourth worker generates a value of marginal product of only $8 an hour but costs $10 an hour, so Angelo does not hire 4 workers. When the wage rate is $10 an hour, the quantity of labor demanded by Angelo is 3 workers, which is a point on Angelo's demand for labor curve, *D*, in Fig. 18.2(b).

If the wage rate increased to $12 an hour, Angelo would decrease the quantity of labor demanded to 2 workers. If the wage rate decreased to $8 an hour, Angelo would increase the quantity of labor demanded to 4 workers.

A change in the wage rate brings a change in the quantity of labor demanded and a movement along the demand for labor curve.

A change in any other influence on a firm's labor-hiring plans changes the demand for labor and shifts the demand for labor curve.

FIGURE 18.1   The Demand for Labor at Angelo's Bakery

(a) Value of marginal product

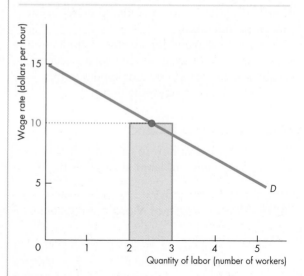

(b) Demand for labor

Angelo's Bakery can sell any quantity of bread at $2 a loaf. The blue bars in part (a) represent the firm's value of marginal product of labor (based on Table 18.1). The orange line is the firm's value of marginal product curve. Part (b) shows Angelo's demand for labor curve. Angelo hires the quantity of labor that makes the value of marginal product equal to the wage rate. The demand for labor curve slopes downward because the value of marginal product diminishes as the quantity of labor employed increases.

Changes in a Firm's Demand for Labor

A firm's demand for labor depends on

- The price of the firm's output
- The prices of other factors of production
- Technology

The Price of the Firm's Output The higher the price of a firm's output, the greater is the firm's demand for labor. The price of output affects the demand for labor through its influence on the value of marginal product of labor. A higher price for the firm's output increases the value of the marginal product of labor. A change in the price of a firm's output leads to a shift in the firm's demand for labor curve. If the price of the firm's output increases, the demand for labor increases and the demand for labor curve shifts rightward.

For example, if the price of bread increased to $3 a loaf, the value of the marginal product of Angelo's fourth worker would increase from $8 an hour to $12 an hour. At a wage rate of $10 an hour, Angelo would now hire 4 workers instead of 3.

The Prices of Other Factors of Production If the price of using capital decreases relative to the wage rate, a firm substitutes capital for labor and increases the quantity of capital it uses. Usually, the demand for labor will decrease when the price of using capital falls. For example, if the price of a bread-making machine falls, Angelo might decide to install one machine and lay off a worker. But the demand for labor could increase if the lower price of capital led to a sufficiently large increase in the scale of production. For example, with cheaper machines available, Angelo might install a machine and hire more labor to operate it. This type of factor substitution occurs in the long run when the firm can change the size of its plant.

Technology New technologies decrease the demand for some types of labor and increase the demand for other types. For example, if a new automated bread-making machine becomes available, Angelo might install one of these machines and fire most of his workforce—a decrease in the demand for bakery workers. But the firms that manufacture and service automated bread-making machines hire more labor, so there is an increase in the demand for this type of labor. An example occurred during the 1990s when electronic telephone exchanges decreased the demand for telephone operators and increased the demand for computer programmers and electronics engineers.

Table 18.2 summarizes the influences on a firm's demand for labor.

TABLE 18.2   A Firm's Demand for Labor

The Law of Demand
(Movements along the demand curve for labor)
The quantity of labor demanded by a firm

Decreases if:	Increases if:
■ The wage rate increases	■ The wage rate decreases

Changes in Demand
(Shifts in the demand curve for labor)
A firm's demand for labor

Decreases if:	Increases if:
■ The price of the firm's output decreases	■ The price of the firm's output increases
■ The price of a substitute for labor falls.	■ The price of a substitute for labor rises.
■ The price of a complement of labor rises.	■ The price of a complement of labor falls.
■ A new technology or new capital decreases the marginal product of labor	■ A new technology or new capital increases the marginal product of labor

Review Quiz

1 What is the value of marginal product of labor?
2 What is the relationship between the value of marginal product of labor and the marginal product of labor?
3 How is the demand for labor derived from the value of marginal product of labor?
4 What are the influences on the demand for labor?

myeconlab Work Study Plan 18.2 and get instant feedback.

Labor Markets

Labor services are traded in many different labor markets. Examples are markets for bakery workers, van drivers, crane operators, computer support specialists, air traffic controllers, surgeons, and economists. Some of these markets, such as the market for bakery workers, are local. They operate in a given urban area. Some labor markets, such as the market for air traffic controllers, are national. Firms and workers search across the nation for the right match of worker and job. And some labor markets are global, such as the market for super star hockey, basketball, and soccer players.

We'll look at a local market for bakery workers as an example. First, we'll look at a *competitive* labor market. Then, we'll see how monopoly elements can influence a labor market.

A Competitive Labor Market

A competitive labor market is one in which many firms demand labor and many households supply labor.

Market Demand for Labor Earlier in the chapter, you saw how an individual firm decides how much labor to hire. The market demand for labor is derived from the demand for labor by individual firms. We determine the market demand for labor by adding together the quantities of labor demanded by all the firms in the market at each wage rate. (The market demand for a good or service is derived in a similar way—see p. 110.)

Because each firm's demand for labor curve slopes downward, the market demand for labor curve also slopes downward.

The Market Supply of Labor The market supply of labor is derived from the supply of labor decisions made by individual households.

Individual's Labor Supply Decision People can allocate their time to two broad activities: labor supply and leisure. (Leisure is a catch-all term. It includes all activities other than supplying labor.) For most people, leisure is more fun than work so to induced them to work they must be offered a wage.

Think about the labor supply decision of Jill, one of the workers at Angelo's Bakery. Let's see how the wage rate influences the quantity of labor she is willing to supply.

Reservation Wage Rate Jill enjoys her leisure time, and she would be pleased if she didn't have to spend her time working at Angelo's Bakery. But Jill wants to earn an income, and as long as she can earn a wage rate of at least $5 an hour, she's willing to work. This wage is called her *reservation wage*. At any wage rate above her reservation wage, Jill supplies some labor.

The wage rate at Angelo's is $10 an hour, and at that wage rate, Jill chooses to work 30 hours a week. At a wage rate of $10 an hour, Jill regards this use of her time as the best available. Figure18.2 illustrates.

Backward-Bending Labor Supply Curve If Jill were offered a wage rate between $5 and $10 an hour, she would want to work fewer hours. If she were offered a wage rate above $10 an hour, she would want to work more hours, but only up to a point. If Jill could

FIGURE 18.2 Jill's Labor Supply Curve

Jill's labor supply curve is S. Jill supplies no labor at wage rates below her reservation wage of $5 an hour. As the wage rate rises above $5 an hour, the quantity of labor that Jill supplies increases to a maximum of 40 hours a week at a wage rate of $25 an hour. As the wage rate rises above $25 an hour, Jill supplies a decreasing quantity of labor: her labor supply curve bends backward. The income effect on the demand for leisure dominates the substitution effect.

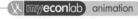

earn $25 an hour, she would be willing to work 40 hours a week (and earn $1,000 a week). But at a wage rate above $25 an hour, with the goods and services that Jill can buy for $1,000, her priority would be a bit more leisure time. So if the wage rate increased above $25 an hour, Jill would cut back on her work hours and take more leisure. Jill's labor supply curve eventually bends backward.

Jill's labor supply decisions are influenced by a substitution effect and an income effect.

Substitution Effect At wage rates below $25 an hour, the higher the wage rate Jill is offered, the greater is the quantity of labor that she supplies. Jill's wage rate is her *opportunity cost of leisure*. If she quits work an hour early to catch a movie, the cost of that extra hour of leisure is the wage rate that Jill forgoes. The higher the wage rate, the less willing Jill is to forgo the income and take the extra leisure time. This tendency for a higher wage rate to induce Jill to work longer hours is a *substitution effect*.

Income Effect The higher Jill's wage rate, the higher is her income. A higher income, other things remaining the same, induces Jill to increase her demand for most goods and services. Leisure is one of those goods. Because an increase in income creates an increase in the demand for leisure, it also creates a decrease in the quantity of labor supplied.

Market Supply Curve Jill's supply curve shows the quantity of labor supplied by Jill as her wage rate changes. Most people behave like Jill and have a backward bending labor supply curve, but they have different reservation wage rates and wage rates at which their labor supply curves bend backward.

A market supply curve shows the quantity of labor supplied by all households in a particular job market. It is found by adding together the quantities of labor supplied by all households to a given job market at each wage rate.

Also, along a supply curve in a particular job market, the wage rates available in other job markets remain the same. For example, along the supply curve of car-wash workers, the wage rates of car salespeople, mechanics, and all other labor are constant.

Despite the fact that an individual's labor supply curve eventually bends backward, the market supply curve of labor slopes upward. The higher the wage rate for car-wash workers, the greater is the quantity of labor supplied in that labor market.

Let's now look at labor market equilibrium.

Competitive Labor Market Equilibrium Labor market equilibrium determines the wage rate and employment. In Fig. 18.3, the market demand curve for bakery workers is D and the market supply curve of bakery workers is S. The equilibrium wage rate is $10 an hour, and the equilibrium quantity is 300 bakery workers. If the wage rate exceeded $10 an hour, there would be a surplus of bakery workers. More people would be looking for jobs in bakeries than firms were willing to hire. In such a situation, the wage rate would fall as firms found it easy to hire people at a lower wage rate. If the wage rate were less than $10 an hour, there would be a shortage of bakery workers. Firms would not be able to fill all the positions they had available. In this situation, the wage rate would rise as firms found it necessary to offer higher wages to attract labor. Only at a wage rate of $10 an hour are there no forces operating to change the wage rate.

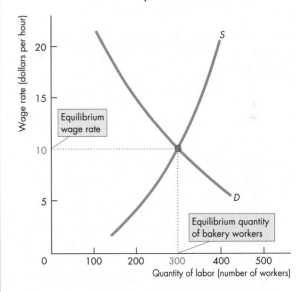

FIGURE 18.3 The Market for Bakery Workers

A competitive labor market coordinates firms' and households' plans. The market is in equilibrium—the quantity of labor demanded equals the quantity supplied at a wage rate of $10 an hour when 300 workers are employed. If the wage rate exceeds $10 an hour, the quantity supplied exceeds the quantity demanded and the wage rate will fall. If the wage rate is below $10 an hour, the quantity demanded exceeds the quantity supplied and the wage rate will rise.

 animation

A Labor Market with a Union

A **labor union** is an organized group of workers that aims to increase the wage rate and influence other job conditions. Let's see what happens when a union enters a competitive labor market.

Influences on Labor Supply One way of raising the wage rate is to decrease the supply of labor. In some labor markets, a union can restrict supply by controlling entry into apprenticeship programs or by influencing job qualification standards. Markets for skilled workers, doctors, dentists, and lawyers are the easiest ones to control in this way.

If there is an abundant supply of nonunion labor, a union can't decrease supply. For example, in the market for farm labor in southern California, the flow of nonunion labor from Mexico makes it difficult for a union to control the supply.

On the demand-side of the labor market, the union faces a tradeoff: The demand for labor curve slopes downward, so restricting supply to raise the wage rate costs jobs. For this reason, unions also try to influence the demand for union labor.

Influences on Labor Demand A union tries to increase the demand for the labor of its members in four main ways:

1. Increasing the value of marginal product of its members by organizing and sponsoring training schemes and apprenticeship programs, and by professional certification.
2. Lobbying for imports restrictions and encouraging people to buy goods made by unionized workers.
3. Supporting minimum wage laws, which increase the cost of employing low-skilled labor and lead firms to substitute high-skilled union labor for low-skilled nonunion labor.
4. Lobbying for restrictive immigration laws to decrease the supply of foreign workers.

Labor Market Equilibrium with a Union Figure 18.4 illustrates what happens to the wage rate and employment when a union successfully enters a competitive labor market. With no union, the demand curve is D_C, the supply curve is S_C, the wage rate is $10 an hour, and 300 workers have jobs.

Now a union enters this labor market. First, look at what happens if the union has sufficient control

FIGURE 18.4 A Union Enters a Competitive Labor Market

In a competitive labor market, the demand curve is D_C and the supply curve is S_C. The wage rate is $10 an hour and 300 workers are employed. If a union decreases the supply of labor and the supply of labor shifts to S_U, the wage rate rises to $15 an hour and employment decreases to 200 workers. If the union can also increase the demand for labor and shift the demand curve to D_U, the wage rate rises to $20 an hour and 250 workers are employed.

over the supply of labor to be able to restrict supply below its competitive level—to S_U. If that is all the union is able to do, employment falls to 200 workers and the wage rate rises to $15 an hour.

Suppose now that the union is also able to increase the demand for labor to D_U. The union can get an even bigger increase in the wage rate and with a smaller fall in employment. By maintaining the restricted labor supply at S_U, the union increases the wage rate to $20 an hour and achieves an employment level of 250 workers.

Because a union restricts the supply of labor in the market in which it operates, the union's actions spill over into nonunion markets. Workers who can't get union jobs must look elsewhere for work. This action increases the supply of labor in nonunion markets and lowers the wage rate in those markets. This spillover effect further widens the gap between union and nonunion wages.

Monopsony in the Labor Market Not all labor markets in which unions operate are competitive. Rather, they are labor markets in which the employer possesses market power and the union enters to try to counteract that power.

A market in which there is a single buyer is called a **monopsony**. A monopsony labor market has one employer. In some parts of the country, managed health-care organizations are the major employer of health-care professionals. In some communities, Wal-Mart is the main employer of sales clerks. These firms have monopsony power.

A monopsony acts on the buying side of a market in a similar way to a monopoly on the selling side. The firm maximizes profit by hiring the quantity of labor that makes the marginal cost of labor equal to the value of marginal product of labor and by paying the lowest wage rate at which it can attract this quantity of labor.

Figure 18.5 illustrates a monopsony labor market. Like all firms, a monopsony faces a downward-sloping value of marginal product curve, *VMP*, which is its demand for labor curve, *D*—the curve *VMP* = *D* in the figure.

What is special about monopsony is the marginal cost of labor. For a firm in a competitive labor market, the marginal cost of labor is the wage rate. For a monopsony, the marginal cost of labor exceeds the wage rate. The reason is that being the only buyer in the market, the firm faces an upward-sloping labor supply curve—the curve *S* in the figure.

To attract one more worker, the monopsony must offer a higher wage rate. But it must pay this higher wage rate to all its workers, so the marginal cost of a worker is the wage rate plus the increased wage bill that arises from paying all the workers the higher wage rate.

The supply curve is now the average cost of labor curve and the relationship between the supply curve and the marginal cost of labor curve, *MCL,* is similar to that between a monopoly's demand curve and marginal revenue curve (see p. 302). The relationship between the supply curve and the *MCL* curve is also similar to that between a firm's average cost curve and marginal cost curve (see pp. 258–259).

To find the profit-maximizing quantity of labor to hire, the monopsony sets the marginal cost of labor equal to the value of marginal product of labor. In Fig. 18.5, this outcome occurs when the firm employs 100 workers.

To hire 100 workers, the firm must pay $10 an hour (on the supply of labor curve). Each worker is paid $10 an hour, but the value of marginal product of labor is $20 an hour, so the firm makes an economic profit of $10 an hour on the marginal worker.

If the labor market in Fig. 18.5 were competitive, equilibrium wage rate and employment would be determined by the demand and supply curves. The wage rate would be $15 an hour, and 150 workers would be employed. So compared with a competitive labor market, a monopsony pays a lower wage rate and employs fewer workers.

A Union and a Monopsony A union is like a monopoly. If the union (monopoly seller) faces a monopsony buyer, the situation is called **bilateral monopoly**. The Writers Guild of America that represents film, television, and radio writers, and an alliance that represents CBS, MGM, NBC, and other entertainment

FIGURE 18.5 A Monopsony Labor Market

A monopsony is a market structure in which there is a single buyer. A monopsony in the labor market has a value of marginal product curve *VMP* and faces a labor supply curve *S*. The marginal cost of labor curve is *MCL*. Making the marginal cost of labor equal to value of marginal product maximizes profit. The monopsony hires 100 hours of labor and pays the lowest wage rate for which that quantity of labor will work, which is $10 an hour.

companies is an example of bilateral monopoly. Every three years, the Writers Guild and the alliance negotiate a pay deal.

The outcome of bargaining depends on the costs that each party can inflict on the other. The firm can shut down the plant and lock out its workers, and the workers can shut down the plant by striking. Each party estimates the other's strength and what it will lose if it does not agree to the other's demands.

Usually, an agreement is reached without a strike or a lockout. The threat is usually enough to bring the bargaining parties to an agreement. When a strike or lockout does occur, it is because one party has misjudged the costs each party can inflict on the other. Such an event occurred in November 2007 when the writers and entertainment producers failed to agree on a compensation deal. A 100-day strike followed that ended up costing the entertainment industry an estimated $2 billion.

In the example in Fig. 18.5, if the union and employer are equally strong, and each party knows the strength of the other, they will agree to split the gap between $10 (the wage rate on the supply curve) and $20 (the wage rate on the demand curve) and agree to a wage rate of $15 an hour.

You've now seen that in a monopsony, a union can bargain for a higher wage rate without sacrificing jobs. A similar outcome can arise in a monopsony labor market when a minimum wage law is enforced. Let's look at the effect of a minimum wage.

Monopsony and the Minimum Wage In a competitive labor market, a minimum wage that exceeds the equilibrium wage decreases employment (see pp. 133–134). In a monopsony labor market, a minimum wage can increase both the wage rate and employment. Let's see how.

Figure 18.6 shows a monopsony labor market without a union. The wage rate is $10 an hour and 100 workers are employed.

A minimum wage law is passed that requires employers to pay at least $15 an hour. The monopsony now faces a perfectly elastic supply of labor at $15 an hour up to 150 workers (along the minimum wage line). To hire more than 150 workers, a wage rate above $15 an hour must be paid (along the supply curve). Because the wage rate is $15 an hour up to 150 workers, so is the marginal cost of labor $15 an hour up to 150 workers. To maximize profit, the monopsony sets the marginal cost of labor equal to the value of marginal product of

FIGURE 18.6 Minimum Wage Law in Monopsony

In a monopsony labor market, the wage rate is $10 an hour and 100 workers are hired. If a minimum wage law increases the wage rate to $15 an hour, the wage rate rises to this level and employment increases to 150 workers.

labor (on the demand curve). That is, the monopsony hires 150 workers and pays $15 an hour. The minimum wage law has succeeded in raising the wage rate and increasing the amount of labor employed.

The Scale of the Union–Nonunion Wage Gap

You've seen how a union can influence the wage rate, but how much of a difference to wage rates do unions actually make? This question is difficult to answer. To measure the difference in wages attributable to unions, economists have looked at the wages of unionized and nonunionized workers who do similar work and have similar skills.

The evidence based on these comparisons is that the union–nonunion wage gap lies between 10 and 25 percent of the wage. For example, unionized airline pilots earn about 25 percent more than nonunion pilots with the same level of skill. In markets that have only a union wage rate, we might presume that the wage rate is 10 to 25 percent higher than it would be in the absence of a union.

Wage Rates in the United States
How School Pays

In 2007, the average wage rate in the United States was a bit less than $20 an hour. The figure shows the *average hourly wage rates* for twenty jobs selected from the more than 700 jobs for which the Bureau of Labor Statistics reports wage rate data.

You can see that a surgeon, on average, earns more than 11 times as much per hour as a fast-food worker and more than twice as much as an economist. Remember that these numbers are averages. Individual surgeons earn much more or much less than the average surgeon.

Many more occupations earn a wage rate below the national average than above it. And most of the occupations that earn more than the national average require a college degree and postgraduate training.

Earning differences are explained by differences in the value of the marginal product of the skills in the various occupations and in market power.

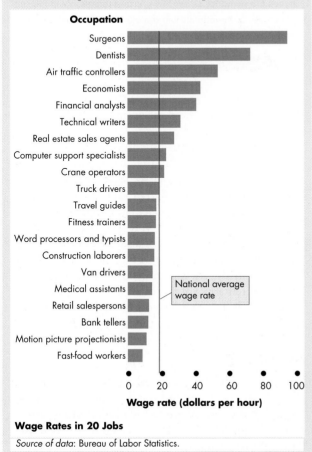

Wage Rates in 20 Jobs

Source of data: Bureau of Labor Statistics.

Trends and Differences in Wage Rates

You can use what you've learned about labor markets to explain the trends and differences in wage rates.

Wage rates increase over time—trend upward. The reason is that the value of marginal product of labor trends upward. Technological change and the new types of capital that it brings make workers more productive. With greater labor productivity, the demand for labor increases and so does the average wage rate. Even jobs in which productivity doesn't increase experience an increase in the *value* of marginal product. Child care is an example. A child-care worker can't care for an increasing number of children, but an increasing number of parents who earn high wages are willing to hire child-care workers. The *value* of marginal product of these workers increases.

Wage rates are unequal, and in recent years, they have become increasingly unequal. High wage rates have increased rapidly while low wage rates have stagnated or even fallen. The reasons are complex and not fully understood.

One reason is that the new technologies of the 1990s and 2000s made skilled workers more productive and destroyed some low-skilled jobs. An example is the ATM, which took the jobs and lowered the wage rate of bank tellers and created the jobs and increased the wage rates of computer programmers and electronic engineers. Another reason is that globalization has brought increased competition for low-skilled workers and opened global markets for high-skilled workers.

Review Quiz

1 What determines the amount of labor that households plan to supply?

2 How is the wage rate and employment determined in a competitive labor market?

3 How do labor unions influence wage rates?

4 What is a monopsony and why is a monopsony able to pay a lower wage rate than a firm in a competitive labor market?

5 How is the wage rate determined when a union faces a monopsony?

6 What is the effect of a minimum wage law in a monopsony labor market?

 Work Study Plan 18.3 and get instant feedback.

◆ Capital and Natural Resource Markets

The markets for capital and land can be understood by using the same basic ideas that you've seen when studying a competitive labor market. But markets for nonrenewable natural resources are different. We'll now examine three groups of factor markets:

- Capital rental markets
- Land rental markets
- Nonrenewable natural resource markets

Capital Rental Markets

The demand for capital is derived from the *value of marginal product of capital*. Profit-maximizing firms hire the quantity of capital services that makes the value of marginal product of capital equal to the *rental rate of capital*. The *lower* the rental rate of capital, other things remaining the same, the *greater* is the quantity of capital demanded. The supply of capital responds in the opposite way to the rental rate. The *higher* the rental rate, other things remaining the same, the *greater* is the quantity of capital supplied. The equilibrium rental rate makes the quantity of capital demanded equal to the quantity supplied.

Figure 18.7 illustrates the rental market for tower cranes—capital used to construct high-rise buildings. The value of marginal product and the demand curve is *VMP = D*. The supply curve is *S*. The equilibrium rental rate is $1,000 per day and 100 tower cranes are rented.

Rent-Versus-Buy Decision Some capital services are obtained in a rental market like the market for tower cranes. And like tower cranes, many of the world's large airlines rent their airplanes. But not all capital services are obtained in a rental market. Instead, firms buy the capital equipment that they use. You saw in Chapter 10 (pp. 228–229) that the cost of the services of the capital that a firm owns and operates itself is an implicit rental rate that arises from depreciation and interest costs. Firms that buy capital *implicitly* rent the capital to themselves.

The decision to obtain capital services in a rental market rather than buy capital and rent it implicitly is made to minimize cost. The firm compares the cost of explicitly renting the capital and the cost of buying and implicitly renting it. This decision is the same as

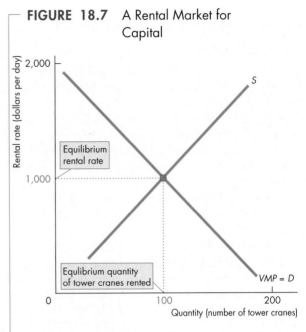

FIGURE 18.7 A Rental Market for Capital

The value of marginal product of tower cranes, *VMP*, determines the demand, *D*, for tower crane rentals. With the supply curve, *S*, the equilibrium rental rate is $1,000 a day and 100 cranes are rented.

myeconlab animation

the one that a household makes in deciding whether to rent or buy a home.

To make a rent-versus-buy decision, a firm must compare a cost incurred in the *present* with a stream of rental costs incurred over some *future* period. The Mathematical Note (pp. 434–435) explains how to make this comparison by calculating the *present value* of a future amount of money. If the *present value* of the future rental payments of an item of capital equipment exceeds the cost of buying the capital, the firm will buy the equipment. If the *present value* of the future rental payments of an item of capital equipment is less than the cost of buying the capital, the firm will rent (or lease) the equipment.

Land Rental Markets

The demand for land is based on the same factors as the demand for labor and the demand for capital—the *value of marginal product of land*. Profit-maximizing firms rent the quantity of land at which the value of marginal product of land is equal to the *rental rate of land*. The *lower* the rental rate, other things remaining the same, the *greater* is the quantity of land demanded.

But the supply of land is special: Its quantity is fixed, so the quantity supplied cannot be changed by people's decisions. The supply of each particular block of land is perfectly inelastic.

The equilibrium rental rate makes the quantity of land demanded equal to the quantity available. Figure 18.8 illustrates the market for a 10-acre block of land on 42nd Street in New York City. The quantity supplied is fixed and the supply curve is *S*. The value of marginal product and the demand curve is *VMP* = *D*. The equilibrium rental rate is $1,000 an acre per day.

The rental rate of land is high in New York because the willingness to pay for the services produced by that land is high, which makes the *VMP* of land high. A Big Mac costs more at McDonald's on 42nd Street, New York, than at McDonald's on Jefferson Avenue, St. Louis, but not because the rental rate of land is higher in New York. The rental rate of land is higher in New York because of the greater willingness to pay for a Big Mac (and other goods and services) in New York.

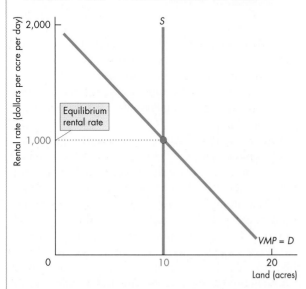

FIGURE 18.8 A Rental Market for Land

The value of marginal product of a 10-acre block, *VMP*, determines the rental demand, *D*, for this land. With the supply curve, *S*, the block rents for $10,000 a day.

🅧 myeconlab animation

Nonrenewable Natural Resource Markets

The nonrenewable natural resources are oil, gas, and coal. Burning one of these fuels converts it to energy and other by-products, and the used resource cannot be re-used. The natural resources that we use to make metals are also nonrenewable, but they can be used again, at some cost, by recycling them.

Oil, gas, and coal are traded in global commodity markets. The price of a given grade of crude oil is the same in New York, London, and Singapore. Traders, linked by telephone and the Internet, operate these markets around the clock every day of the year.

Demand and supply determine the prices and the quantities traded in these commodity markets. We'll look at the influences on demand and supply by considering the global market for crude oil.

The Demand for Oil The two key influences on the demand for oil are

1. The *value of marginal product* of oil
2. The expected future price of oil

The value of marginal product of oil is the *fundamental* influence on demand. It works in exactly the same way for a nonrenewable resource as it does for any other factor of production. The greater the quantity of oil used, the smaller is the value of marginal product of oil. Diminishing value of marginal product makes the demand curve slope downward. The lower the price, the greater is the quantity demanded.

The higher the expected future price of oil, the greater is the present demand for oil. The expected future price is a *speculative* influence on demand. Oil in the ground and oil in storage tanks are inventories that can be held or sold. A trader might plan to buy oil to hold now and to sell it later for a profit. Instead of buying oil to hold and sell later, the trader could buy a bond and earn interest. The forgone interest is the opportunity cost of holding the oil. If the price of oil is expected to rise by a bigger percentage than the interest rate, a trader will hold oil and incur the opportunity cost. In this case, the return from holding oil exceeds the return from holding bonds.

The Supply of Oil The three key influences on the supply of oil are

1. The known oil reserves
2. The scale of current oil production facilities
3. The expected future price of oil

Known oil reserves are the oil that has been discovered and can be extracted with today's technology. This quantity increases over time because advances in technology enable ever less accessible sources to be discovered. The greater the size of known reserves, the greater is the supply of oil. But this influence on supply is small and indirect. It operates by changing the expected distant future price of oil. Even a major new discovery of oil would have a negligible effect on current supply.

The scale of current oil production facilities is the *fundamental* influence on supply. Producing oil is like any production activity: it is subject to increasing marginal cost. The increasing marginal cost of extracting oil means that the supply curve of oil slopes upward. The higher the price of oil, the greater is the quantity supplied. When new oil wells are sunk or when new faster pumps are installed, the supply of oil increases. When existing wells run dry, the supply of oil decreases. Over time, the factors that increase supply are more powerful than those that decrease supply, so changes in the fundamental influence increase the supply of oil.

Speculative forces based on expectations about the future price also influence the supply of oil. The *higher* the expected future price of oil, the *smaller* is the present supply of oil. A trader with an oil inventory might plan to sell now or to hold and sell later. You've seen that forgone interest is the opportunity cost of holding the oil. If the price of oil is expected to rise by a bigger percentage than the interest rate, it is profitable to incur the opportunity cost of holding oil rather than selling it immediately.

The Equilibrium Price of Oil

The demand for oil and the supply of oil determine the equilibrium price and quantity traded. Figure 18.9 illustrates the market equilibrium.

The value of marginal product of oil, *VMP*, is the *fundamental determinant of demand*, and the marginal cost of extraction, *MC*, is the *fundamental determinant of supply*. Together, they determine the *market fundamentals price*.

If expectations about the future price are also based on fundamentals, the equilibrium price is the market fundamentals price. But if expectations about the future price of oil depart from what the market fundamentals imply, *speculation* can drive a wedge between the equilibrium price and the market fundamentals price.

FIGURE 18.9   A Nonrenewable Natural Resource Market

The value of marginal product of a natural resource, *VMP*, and the marginal cost of extraction, *MC*, determine the *market fundamentals* price. Demand, *D*, and supply, *S*, which determine the equilibrium price, are influenced by the expected future price. Speculation can bring a gap between the market fundamentals price and the equilibrium price.

The Hotelling Principle Harold Hotelling, an economist at Columbia University, had an incredible idea: Traders expect the price of a nonrenewable natural resource to rise at a rate equal to the interest rate. We call this idea the **Hotelling Principle.** Let's see why it is correct.

You've seen that the interest rate is the opportunity cost of holding an oil inventory. If the price of oil is expected to rise at a rate that exceeds the interest rate, it is profitable to hold a bigger inventory. Demand increases, supply decreases, and the price rises. If the interest rate exceeds the rate at which the price of oil is expected to rise, it is not profitable to hold an oil inventory. Demand decreases, supply increases, and the price falls. But if the price of oil is expected to rise at a rate equal to the interest rate, holding an inventory of oil is just as good as holding bonds. Demand and supply don't change and the price does not change. Only when the price of oil is expected to rise at a rate equal to the interest rate is the price at its equilibrium.

The World and U.S. Markets for Oil
Diverse Sources and Wild Prices

The world produced about 31 billion barrels of oil in 2008 and the price shot upward from $85 in January to $135 in June. The high price of oil and dependence on foreign supplies became major political issues.

Although the United States imports almost three quarters of its oil from other countries, much of it comes from close to home. Figure 1 provides the details: Only 14 percent of the U.S. oil supply comes from the Middle East and more than one third comes from Canada, Mexico, and other Western Hemisphere nations.

Even if the United States produced all its own oil, it would still face a fluctuating global price. U.S. producers would not willingly sell to U.S. buyers for a price below the world price. So energy independence doesn't mean an independent oil price.

The Hotelling Principle tells us that we must expect the price of oil to rise at a rate equal to the interest rate. But expecting the price to rise at a rate equal to the interest rate doesn't mean that the price will rise at this rate. As you can see in Fig. 2, the price of oil over the past 50 or so years has not followed the path predicted by the Hotelling Principle.

The future is unpredictable and expectations about future prices keep changing. The forces that influence expectations are not well understood. The expected future price of oil depends on its expected future rate of use and the rate of discovery of new sources of supply. One person's expectation about a future price also depends on guesses about other

Figure 2 The Price of Oil and Its Hotelling Path

people's expectations. These guesses can change abruptly and become self-reinforcing. When the expected future price of oil changes for whatever reason, demand and supply change, and so does the price. Prices in speculative markets are always volatile.

Review Quiz

1 What determines demand and supply in rental markets for capital and land?
2 What determines the demand for a nonrenewable natural resource?
3 What determines the supply of a nonrenewable natural resource?
4 What is the market fundamentals price and how might it differ from the equilibrium price?
5 Explain the Hotelling Principle.

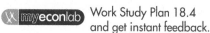 Work Study Plan 18.4 and get instant feedback.

◆ *Reading Between the Lines* on pp. 432–433 focuses on the market for oil and the political debate about increasing U.S. domestic production.

The next chapter looks at how the market economy distributes income and explains the trends in the distribution of income. The chapter also looks at the efforts by governments to redistribute income and modify the market outcome.

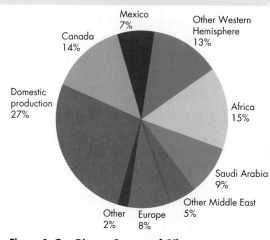

Figure 1 Our Diverse Sources of Oil

The Oil Market in Action

Offshore Drilling Backed as Remedy for Oil Prices

http://www.washingtonpost.com
July 14, 2008

… Polls show that Americans, pressed by high gasoline prices, may be open to offshore drilling. In a May Gallup poll, 57 percent of people surveyed were willing to allow drilling in coastal and wilderness areas currently off limits, if it had the potential to reduce high gas prices. …

The debate over offshore drilling has been muddied by a variety of claims about how much oil and gas might lie under the sea, what it would take to get hold of it and what the impact would be.

… [T]he U.S. Geological Survey estimates that there are "undiscovered conventionally recoverable resources" of 17.8 billion barrels. That's not the same thing as "reserves." In the oil business, "reserves" refers to oil that has been found and "proven," whereas "resources" refers to promising geological structures where the presence of oil remains uncertain.

In the eastern Gulf of Mexico, those "resources" are likely to represent actual oil because the geology is an extension of the western Gulf of Mexico, where oil has been drilled for years. There is less certainty about what may lie off the Atlantic coast.

If, in fact, there are 17.8 billion barrels of oil offshore, that would equal half the reserves of Nigeria or about 60 percent of proven U.S. reserves. It could substantially reduce U.S. imports for a decade or two or sustain U.S. production when other fields decline.

But developing those resources would take time. A report last year by the Energy Department's Energy Information Administration said that "access to the Pacific, Atlantic, and eastern Gulf regions would not have a significant impact on domestic crude oil and natural gas production or prices before 2030. Leasing would begin no sooner than 2012, and production would not be expected to start before 2017." It added, "Because oil prices are determined on the international market, however, any impact on average wellhead prices is expected to be insignificant." …

Essence of the Story

- 57 percent of respondents in a Gallup poll want to allow drilling for oil and gas in U.S. coastal waters and wilderness if it would lower the price of gasoline.

- The U.S. Geological Survey estimates "undiscovered conventionally recoverable resources" of 17.8 billion barrels.

- Proven reserves will likely equal half the 17.8 billion barrels of offshore oil—equivalent to half the reserves of Nigeria or 60 percent of proven U.S. reserves.

- The first oil and gas would flow in 2017.

- Full-scale production and an impact on price would become significant only after 2030.

Economic Analysis

- The market for oil is a global market, and demand and supply in the global oil market determine the price.

- Both demand and supply depend on expectations of the future price of oil.

- An expected future increase in production increases the expected future supply and lowers the expected future price. A lower expected future price immediately decreases demand, increases supply, and lowers the current price.

- The amount by which the current price falls depends on (1) the number of years in the future when the change in supply is expected to occur, (2) the expected increase in supply, and (3) the elasticity of demand.

- Using the ideas just reviewed, we can work out the likely effect of a decision by Congress to authorize offshore oil production in the United States.

- Based on the information provided in the news article, production would be expected to increase somewhat in 2017 and be in full operation by 2030.

- The quantity of oil likely to be found is guessed at 50 percent of the quantity in Nigeria. If we assume that production will also be 50 percent of Nigerian production, then U.S. oil production and global oil production, other things remaining the same, will increase by 1 million barrels per day.

- The demand for oil is inelastic, and we will assume that the elasticity is 0.1.

- An elasticity of demand equal to 0.1 means that a 10 percent rise in price brings a 1 percent decrease in the quantity demanded, other things remaining the same.

- It also means that a 1 percent increase in the quantity brings a 10 percent decrease in price, other things remaining the same.

- World oil production in 2009 was approximately 85 million barrels a day. So an increase of 1 million barrels is an increase of a bit more than 1 percent (1.18 percent).

- This percentage increase in the quantity would lower the price by 11.8 percent (10 times the percentage change in the quantity).

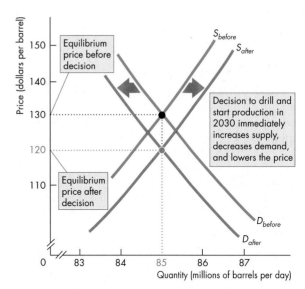

Figure 1 The global market for crude oil

- This percentage fall in the price is expected to occur when production is in full operation in 2030.

- To translate the price fall to its effects in 2009, we use the Hotelling Principle and the concept of present value (see Mathematical Note).

- The Hotelling Principle tells us that the price is expected to rise at a rate equal to the interest rate.

- Assume an interest rate of 2 percent a year. Then the price in 2030 is expected to be just over 50 percent higher than the price in 2009. ($1.02^{21} = 1.52$)

- Because the price in 2030 is expected to fall by 11.8 percent, the price today will fall by 11.8/1.52, or 7.8 percent.

- The figure illustrates what happens in 2009 if a decision is made to produce offshore oil. Demand decreases and supply increases immediately to reflect the lower expected future price and the price falls immediately.

- In the figure, the price in 2009 is assumed to be $130 a barrel. So a 7.8 percent fall in the price means the price will fall by $10 to $120 (rounding to the nearest dollar).

433

MATHEMATICAL NOTE

Present Value and Discounting

Rent-Versus-Buy Decision

To decide whether to rent an item of capital equipment or to buy the capital and implicitly rent it, a firm must compare the present expenditure on the capital with the future rental cost of the capital.

Comparing Current and Future Dollars

To compare a present expenditure with a future expenditure, we convert the future expenditure to its "present value."

The **present value** of a future amount of money is the amount that, if invested today, will grow to be as large as that future amount when the interest that it will earn is taken into account.

So the present value of a future amount of money is smaller than the future amount. The calculation that we use to convert a future amount of money to its present value is called **discounting**.

The easiest way to understand discounting and present value is to first consider its opposite: How a present value grows to a future amount of money because of *compound interest*.

Compound Interest

Compound interest is the interest on an initial investment plus the interest on the interest that the investment has previously earned. Because of compound interest, a present amount of money (a present value) grows into a larger future amount. The future amount is equal to the present amount (present value) plus the interest it will earn in the future. That is,

Future amount = Present value + Interest income.

The interest in the first year is equal to the present value multiplied by the interest rate, r, so

Amount after 1 year = Present value +
$\qquad\qquad\qquad$ ($r \times$ Present value).

or

Amount after 1 year = Present value $\times (1 + r)$.

If you invest $100 today and the interest rate is 10 percent a year ($r = 0.1$), one year from today you will have $110—the original $100 plus $10 interest.

Check that the above formula delivers that answer: $100 \times 1.1 = \$110$.

If you leave this $110 invested to earn 10 percent during a second year, at the end of that year you will have

Amount after 2 years = Present value $\times (1 + r)^2$.

With the numbers of the previous example, you invest $100 today at an interest rate of 10 percent a year ($r = 0.1$). After one year you will have $110—the original $100 plus $10 interest. And after the second year, you will have $121. In the second year, you earned $10 on your initial $100 plus $1 on the $10 interest that you earned in the first year.

Check that the above formula delivers that answer: $100 \times (1.1)^2 = \$100 \times 1.21 = \$121$.

If you leave your $100 invested for n years, it will grow to

Amount after n years = Present value $\times (1 + r)^n$.

With an interest rate of 10 percent a year, your $100 will grow to $195 after 7 years ($n = 7$)—almost double the present value of $100.

Discounting a Future Amount

We have just calculated future amounts one year, two years, and n years in the future, knowing the present value and the interest rate. To calculate the present value of these future amounts, we just work backward.

To find the present value of an amount one year in the future, we divide the future amount by $(1 + r)$. That is,

$$\text{Present value} = \frac{\text{Amount of money one year in future}}{(1 + r)}.$$

Let's check that we can use the present value formula by calculating the present value of $110 one year from now when the interest rate is 10 percent a year. You'll be able to guess that the answer is $100 because we just calculated that $100 invested today at 10 percent a year becomes $110 in one year. So the present value of $110 one year from today is $100. But let's use the formula. Putting the numbers into the above formula, we have

$$\text{Present value} = \frac{\$110}{(1 + 0.1)}$$

$$= \frac{\$110}{1.1} = \$100.$$

To calculate the present value of an amount of money two years in the future, we use the formula:

$$\text{Present value} = \frac{\text{Amount of money two years in future}}{(1 + r)^2}.$$

Use this formula to calculate the present value of $121 two years from now at an interest rate of 10 percent a year. With these numbers, the formula gives

$$\text{Present value} = \frac{\$121}{(1 + 0.1)^2}$$

$$= \frac{\$121}{(1.1)^2}$$

$$= \frac{\$121}{1.21}$$

$$= \$100$$

We can calculate the present value of an amount of money n years in the future by using the general formula

$$\text{Present value} = \frac{\text{Amount of money } n \text{ years in future}}{(1 + r)^n}.$$

For example, if the interest rate is 10 percent a year, $100 to be received 10 years from now has a present value of $38.55. That is, if $38.55 is invested today at 10 percent a year it will accumulate to $100 in 10 years.

Present Value of a Sequence of Future Amounts

You've seen how to calculate the present value of an amount of money one year, two years, and n years in the future. Most practical applications of present value calculate the present value of a sequence of future amounts of money that are spread over several years. An airline's payment of rent for the lease of airplanes is an example.

To calculate the present value of a sequence of amounts over several years, we use the formula you have learned and apply it to each year. We then sum the present values for all the years to find the present value of the sequence of amounts.

For example, suppose that a firm expects to pay $100 a year for each of the next five years and the interest rate is 10 percent a year ($r = 0.1$). The present value (PV) of these five payments of $100 each is calculated by using the following formula:

$$PV = \frac{\$100}{1.1} + \frac{\$100}{1.1^2} + \frac{\$100}{1.1^3} + \frac{\$100}{1.1^4} + \frac{\$100}{1.1^5},$$

which equals

$$PV = \$90.91 + \$82.64 + \$75.13 + \$68.30 + \$62.09$$
$$= \$379.07.$$

You can see that the firm pays $500 over five years. But because the money is paid in the future, it is not worth $500 today. Its present value is only $379.07. And the farther in the future the money is paid, the smaller is its present value. The $100 paid one year in the future is worth $90.91 today, but the $100 paid five years in the future is worth only $62.09 today.

The Decision

If this firm could lease a machine for five years at $100 a year or buy the machine for $500, it would jump at leasing. Only if the firm could buy the machine for less than $379.07 would it want to buy.

Many personal and business decisions turn on calculations like the one you've just made. A decision to buy or rent an apartment, to lease or rent a car, to pay off a student loan or let the loan run another year can all be made using the above calculation.

SUMMARY

Key Points

The Anatomy of Factor Markets (p. 418)

- The factor markets are: job markets for labor; rental markets (often implicit rental markets) for capital and land; and global commodity markets for nonrenewable natural resources.
- The services of entrepreneurs are not traded on a factor market.

The Demand for a Factor of Production (pp. 419–421)

- The value of marginal product determines the demand for a factor of production.
- The value of marginal product decreases as the quantity of the factor employed increases.
- The firm employs the quantity of each factor of production that makes the value of marginal product equal to the factor price.

Labor Markets (pp. 422–427)

- The value of marginal product of labor determines the demand for labor. A rise in the wage rate brings a decrease in the quantity demanded.
- The quantity of labor supplied depends on the wage rate. At low wage rates, a rise in the wage rate increases the quantity supplied. Beyond a high enough wage rate, a rise in the wage rate decreases the quantity supplied—the supply curve eventually bends backward.

- Demand and supply determine the wage rate in a competitive labor market.
- A labor union can raise the wage rate by restricting the supply or increasing the demand for labor.
- A monopsony can lower the wage rate below the competitive level.
- A union or a minimum wage in monopsony labor market can raise the wage rate without a fall in employment.

Capital and Natural Resource Markets (pp. 428–431)

- The value of marginal product of capital (and land) determines the demand for capital (and land).
- Firms make a rent-versus-buy decision by choosing the option that minimizes cost.
- The supply of land is inelastic and the demand for land determines the rental rate.
- The demand for a nonrenewable natural resource depends on the value of marginal product and on the expected future price.
- The supply of a nonrenewable natural resource depends on the known reserves, the cost of extraction, and the expected future price.
- The price of nonrenewable natural resources can differ from the market fundamentals price because of speculation based on expectations about the future price.
- The price of a nonrenewable natural resource is expected to rise at a rate equal to the interest rate.

Key Figures and Tables

Key Terms

PROBLEMS and APPLICATIONS

1. Wanda owns a fish shop. She employs students to sort and pack the fish. Students can pack the following amounts of fish in an hour:

Number of students	Quantity of fish (pounds)
1	20
2	50
3	90
4	120
5	145
6	165
7	180
8	190

The fish market is competitive and Wanda can sell her fish for 50¢ a pound. The market for packers is competitive and their market wage rate is $7.50 an hour.
a. Calculate the marginal product of the students and draw the marginal product curve.
b. Calculate the value of marginal product of labor and draw the value of marginal product curve.
c. Find Wanda's demand for labor curve.
d. How many students does Wanda employ?

2. Back at Wanda's fish shop described in problem 1, the market price of fish falls to 33.33¢ a pound but the wage rate of fish packers remains at $7.50 an hour.
a. How does the students' marginal product change?
b. How does the value of marginal product of labor change?
c. How does Wanda's demand for labor change?
d. What happens to the number of students that Wanda employs?

3. Back at Wanda's fish shop described in problem 1, packers' wages increase to $10 an hour but the price of fish remains at 50¢ a pound.
a. What happens to the value of marginal product of labor?
b. What happens to Wanda's demand for labor curve?
c. How many students does Wanda employ?

4. **In Modern Rarity, Workers Form Union at Small Chain**
Among the thousands of stores in New York's low-income neighborhoods, labor unions have virtually no presence, except in a few supermarkets. But in a remarkable culmination to a yearlong struggle, 95 workers at a chain of 10 sneaker stores have formed a union. ... On Jan. 18, after three months of negotiations, the two sides signed a contract. The three-year accord sets wages at $7.25 an hour, rising to $7.50 on July 1.
The New York Times, February 5, 2006
a. Why are labor unions scarce in New York's low-income neighborhoods?
b. Who wins from this new union contract? Who loses?
c. How can this union try to change the demand for labor?

5. Which of the following items are nonrenewable natural resources, which are renewable natural resources, and which are not natural resources? Explain your answers.
a. Trump Tower
b. Lake Michigan
c. Coal in a West Virginia coal mine
d. The Internet
e. Yosemite National Park
f. Power generated by wind turbines

6. **Trump Group Selling Parcel For $1.8 Billion**
A consortium of Hong Kong investors and Donald J. Trump are selling a stretch of riverfront land and three buildings on the Upper West Side for about $1.8 billion in the largest residential sale in city history. ... If it is completed, ... the deal should be a windfall for the investors and Mr. Trump, who acquired the land for less than $100 million a decade ago during a real estate recession. ...
The New York Times, June 1, 2005
a. Why has the price of land on the Upper West Side of New York City increased over the last decade? Include in your answer a discussion of the demand for land and the supply of land.
b. Use a graph to show why the price of land on

the Upper West Side of New York City increased over the last decade.
  c. Is the supply of land on the Upper West Side perfectly inelastic?
7. Keshia operates a bookkeeping service. She is considering buying or leasing some new laptop computers. The purchase price of a laptop is $1,500 and after three years it is worthless. The annual lease rate is $550 per laptop. The value of marginal product of one laptop is $700 a year. The value of marginal product of a second laptop is $625 a year. The value of marginal product of a third laptop is $575 a year. And the value of marginal product of a fourth laptop is $500 a year.
  a. How many laptops will Keshia lease or buy?
  b. If the interest rate is 4 percent a year, will Keshia lease or buy her laptops?
  c. If the interest rate is 6 percent a year, will Keshia lease or buy her laptops?
8. **British Construction Activity Falls**

Construction activity in Britain declined in June at the fastest rate in 11 years … and a major home builder said it had been unable to raise more capital—both signs of worsening conditions in the battered housing industry. … Construction employment declined in June after 23 months of growth. … The housing market has been hit by falling prices. … Average house prices in the United Kingdom fell 0.9 percent in June, the eighth consecutive month of declines, leaving the average 6.3 percent below June 2007.

Forbes, July 2, 2008
  a. Explain how a fall in house prices influences the market for construction labor.
  b. Draw a graph to illustrate the effect of a fall in house prices in the market for construction labor.
  c. Explain how a fall in house prices influences the market for construction equipment leases.
  d. Draw a graph to illustrate the effect of a fall in house prices in the market for construction equipment leases.
9. **Fixing Farming**

Backyard vegetable gardens are fine. So are organics, slow food and locavores—people who eat produce grown nearby. But solutions to the global food crisis will come from big business, genetically engineered crops and large-scale

farms. … The problem they face has made headlines lately. Demand for farm products—food, fiber and fuel—will keep growing, as the population grows and as hundreds of millions of people move into the middle class and consume more meat and dairy. Global per capita meat consumption has increased by 60 percent in the last 40 years—that's 60 percent per person. Meanwhile, the supply of farmland is limited. Agriculture already uses 55 percent of the habitable land on the planet … . The answer is for farmers to become more productive—generating more output from fewer inputs.

Fortune, May 22, 2008
  a. Is farmland a renewable or nonrenewable resource?
  b. Explain how the growing demand for farm products will affect the market for land.
  c. Draw a graph to illustrate how the growing demand for farm products will affect the market for land.
  d. How might farmers meet the growing demand for farm products without having to use a greater quantity of farmland?
10. **Copter Crisis**

Helicopters are in short supply these days. You could blame a rise in military spending, a jump in disaster relief, even crowded airports pushing executives into private travel. But the fastest growth is coming from the offshore oil-and-gas industry, where helicopters—affectionately known as "the pickups of the Gulf Coast"—are the only way to ferry crews to and from rigs and platforms. … Hundred-dollar oil has pushed producers to work existing fields harder than ever and open new frontiers like the coasts of Brazil, India, and Alaska. That has led the number of rigs and platforms to grow by 800, or 13%, over the past decade. … [Oil] companies are [facing] … a two-year backlog in orders for the Sikorsky S92, a favorite of the oil industry, and a 40% rise in prices for used models.

Fortune, May 12, 2008
  a. Explain how high oil prices influence the market for helicopter leases and services (such as the Sikorsky S92).
  b. What happens to the value of marginal product of helicopters as a firm leases or buys additional helicopters?

11. Kaiser's Ice Cream Parlor hires workers to produce smoothies. The market for smoothies is perfectly competitive, and the price of a smoothie is $4. The labor market is competitive, and the wage rate is $40 a day. The table shows the workers' total product schedule.

Number of workers	Quantity produced (smoothies per day)
1	7
2	21
3	33
4	43
5	51
6	55

a. Calculate the marginal product of hiring the fourth worker and the value of the marginal product of the fourth worker.
b. How many workers will Kaiser's hire to maximize its profit and how many smoothies a day will Kaiser's produce?
c. If the price rises to $5 a smoothie, how many workers will Kaiser's hire?

12. Kaiser's installs a new soda fountain that increases the productivity of workers by 50 percent. If the price of a smoothie remains at $4 and the wage rises to $48 a day, how many workers does Kaiser's hire?

13. **Detroit Oil Refinery Expansion Approved**
Marathon Oil Saturday started work on a $1.9 billion expansion of its gasoline refinery in Detroit. ... Marathon said the company will employ 800 construction workers and add 135 permanent jobs to the existing 480 workers at the refinery.

United Press International, June 21, 2008
a. Explain how rising gasoline prices influence the market for refinery labor.
b. Draw a graph to illustrate the effects of rising gasoline prices on the market for refinery labor.
c. How do rising gasoline prices affect a firm's demand for refineries and how does the implicit rental rate of refineries change?

14. **You May be Paid More (or Less) than You Think**
It's so hard to put a price on happiness, isn't it? But if you've ever had to choose between a job you like and a better-paying one that you like less, you probably wished some economist would get on the stick and tell you how much job satisfaction is worth. ...
Economists John Helliwell and Haifang Huang at the University of British Columbia have done just that. Their estimates are based on an analysis of life satisfaction surveys that consider four key factors of job satisfaction. Trust in management is ... like getting a 36 percent pay raise. ... Having a job that offers a lot of variety in projects ... is the equivalent of a 21 percent hike in pay. Having a position that requires a high level of skill is the equivalent of a 19 percent raise. And having enough time to finish your work is the equivalent of an 11 percent boost in pay. ...

CNN, March 29, 2006
a. How might the job characteristics described here affect the supply of labor for different types of jobs?
b. How might this influence on supply result in different wage rates that reflect the attractiveness of a job's characteristics?

15. **The New War over Wal-Mart**
Today, Wal-Mart employs more people—1.7 million—than any other private employer, and by this measure is not just the largest company in the world but the largest company in the history of the world. With size comes power. ... The Wal-Mart effect drives down consumer prices ... and, some argue, it also drives down wages and benefits. ...
One of the major forces opposing Wal-Mart is organized labor. The United Food and Commercial Workers International Union has long wanted to organize Wal-Mart's stores. Last year, it succeeded at a Canadian Wal-Mart, which the company immediately shut down. ... What the war against Wal-Mart tends to gloss over is that it's not at all clear that the company behaves any worse than its competitors. When it comes to payroll and benefits, Wal-Mart's median hourly wage pretty much tracks the national median wage for general merchandise retail jobs. And its health-care benefits are a good deal more accessible ... than those of many of its competitors.

The Atlantic, June 2006
a. Assuming that Wal-Mart has market power in a labor market, explain how the firm could use that market power in setting wages.

b. Draw a graph to illustrate how Wal-Mart might use labor market power to set wages.

c. Explain how a union of Wal-Mart's employees would attempt to counteract Wal-Mart's wage offers (a bilateral monopoly).

d. Explain the response by the Canadian Wal-Mart to the unionization of employees.

e. Based upon evidence presented in this article, does Wal-Mart function as a monopsony in labor markets, or is the market for retail labor more competitive? Explain.

f. If the market for retail labor is competitive, explain the potential effect of a union on the wage rates.

g. Draw a graph to illustrate the potential effect of a union on the wage rates in a competitive labor market.

16. **Gas Prices Create Land Rush**

There is a land rush going on across Pennsylvania, but buyers aren't interested in the land itself. Buyers are interested in what lies beneath the earth's surface—mineral rights to natural gas deposits. Record high crude oil and natural gas prices have already pushed up drilling activity in northwestern Pennsylvania and other areas of the state. But now that already heightened interest is spreading. The reason is the Marcellus Formation—a hardly tapped formation of deep gas-bearing shale that drilling companies have only recently found a way to exploit. Development companies, drilling companies and speculators have been crisscrossing the state, trying to lease mineral rights from landowners. ... Horizontal drilling techniques developed in Texas and Oklahoma might conservatively recover about 10 percent of those reserves, and that would ring up at a value of $1 trillion. ...

Erie Times-News, June 15, 2008

a. Is natural gas a renewable or nonrenewable resource? Explain.

b. Explain why the demand for land in Pennsylvania has increased.

c. If companies are responding to the higher prices for natural gas by drilling right now wherever they can, what does that imply about their assumptions about the future price of natural gas in relation to current interest rates?

d. What could cause the price of natural gas to fall in the future?

17. New technology has allowed oil to be pumped from much deeper offshore oil fields than before. For example, 28 deep ocean rigs operate in the deep waters of the Gulf of Mexico.

a. What effect do you think deep ocean sources have had on the world oil price?

b. Who will benefit from drilling for oil in the Gulf of Mexico? Explain your answer.

18. Water is a natural resource that is plentiful in Canada but not plentiful in Arizona and southern California.

a. If Canadians start to export bulk water to Arizona and southern California, what do you predict will be the effect on the price of bulk water?

b. Will Canada eventually run out of water?

c. Do you think the Hotelling Principle applies to Canada's water? Explain why or why not.

19. Study *Reading Between the Lines* on pp. 432–433 and answer the following questions:

a. What determines the demand for oil? In your answer, distinguish between the market fundamentals and speculative influences on demand.

b. What determines the supply of oil? In your answer, distinguish between the market fundamentals and speculative influences on supply.

c. What is the Hotelling Principle and why is it correct?

d. How does the Hotelling Principle tell us that a change in oil production in 2030 will change the price of oil today?

e. Suppose that the elasticity of demand for oil turns out to be close to 1 rather than approximately 0.1. Will the fall in today's price of oil resulting from an increase in oil production in 2030 exceed $10 a barrel? Explain your answer.

f. If the interest rate is 4 percent a year rather than the 2 percent a year assumed in the analysis on p. 433, does that make the effect on today's price of a change in production in 2030 greater or smaller? Explain your answer with reference to the Hotelling Principle.

19

Economic Inequality

After studying this chapter, you will be able to:

- Describe the inequality in income and wealth in the United States in 2007 and the trends in inequality

- Explain the features of the labor market that contribute to economic inequality

- Describe the scale of income redistribution by governments

Six percent of adults in Los Angeles County, some 375,000 people, experienced homelessness during the past five years. In this same part of the nation is Beverly Hills, with its mansions that are home to some fabulously wealthy movie stars. Los Angeles is not unusual. In New York City, where Donald Trump has built a luxury apartment tower with a penthouse priced at $13 million, more than 20,000 people, 9,000 of whom are children, seek a bed every night in a shelter for the homeless. Extreme poverty and extreme wealth exist side by side in every major city in the United States and in most parts of the world.

How many rich and poor people are there in the United

States? How are income and wealth distributed? Are the rich getting richer and the poor getting poorer?

What causes inequality in the distribution of economic well-being? How much redistribution does the government do to limit extreme poverty?

In this chapter, we study economic inequality—its extent, its sources, and the things governments do to make it less extreme. We begin by looking at some facts about economic inequality in the United States. We end, in *Reading Between the Lines*, by looking at the changing gap between the highest and lowest incomes over the past twenty years.

Measuring Economic Inequality

The most commonly used measure of economic inequality is the distribution of annual income. The Census Bureau defines income as **money income**, which equals *market income* plus cash payments to households by government. **Market income** equals wages, interest, rent, and profit earned in factor markets, before paying income taxes.

The Distribution of Income

Figure 19.1 shows the distribution of annual income across the 113 million households in the United States in 2007. Note that the *x*-axis measures household income and the *y*-axis is percentage of households.

The most common household income, called the *mode* income, was received by the 6.4 percent of the households whose incomes fell between $10,000 and $15,000. The value of $13,000 marked on the figure is an estimate.

The middle level of household income in 2007, called the *median* income, was $46,326. Fifty percent of households have an income that exceeds the median and fifty percent have an income below the median.

The average household money income in 2007, called the *mean* income, was $63,344. This number equals total household income, about $7.16 trillion, divided by the 113 million households.

You can see in Fig. 19.1 that the mode income is less than the median income and that the median income is less than the mean income. This feature of the distribution of income tells us that there are more households with low incomes than with high incomes. It also tells us that some of the high incomes are very high.

The income distribution in Fig. 19.1 is called a *positively skewed* distribution, which means that it has a long tail of high values. This distribution shape contrasts with a *bell-shaped* distribution such as the distribution of people's heights. In a bell-shaped distribution, the mean, median, and mode are all equal.

Another way of looking at the distribution of income is to measure the percentage of total income received by each given percentage of households. Data are reported for five groups—called *quintiles* or fifth shares—each consisting of 20 percent of households.

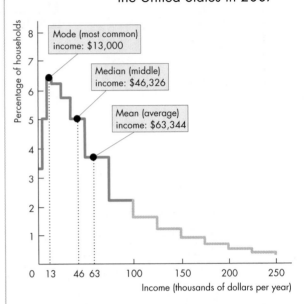

FIGURE 19.1 The Distribution of Income in the United States in 2007

Mode (most common) income: $13,000

Median (middle) income: $46,326

Mean (average) income: $63,344

The distribution of income is positively skewed. The mode (most common) income is less than the median (middle) income, which in turn is less than the mean (average) income. The shape of the distribution above $100,000 is an indication rather than a precise measure, and the distribution goes up to several million dollars a year.

Source of data: U.S. Bureau of the Census, "Income, Poverty, and Health Insurance Coverage in the United States: 2007," *Current Population Reports*, P-60-231 (Washington, DC: U.S. Government Printing Office, 2006).

myeconlab animation

Figure 19.2 shows the distribution based on these shares in 2007. The poorest 20 percent of households received 3.4 percent of total income; the second poorest 20 percent received 8.6 percent of total income; the middle 20 percent received 14.6 percent of total income; the next highest 20 percent received 23.0 percent of total income; and the highest 20 percent received 50.4 percent of total income.

The distribution of income in Fig. 19.1 and the quintile shares in Fig. 19.2 tell us that income is distributed unequally. But we need a way of comparing the distribution of income in different periods and using different measures. A clever graphical tool called the *Lorenz curve* enables us to make such comparisons.

FIGURE 19.2   U.S. Quintile Shares in 2007

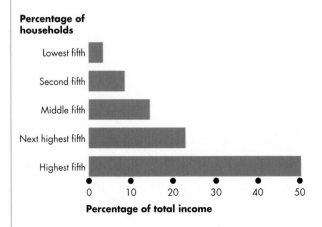

Households (percentage)	Income (percentage of total income)
Lowest 20	3.4
Second 20	8.6
Middle 20	14.6
Next highest 20	23.0
Highest 20	50.4

In 2007, the poorest 20 percent of households received 3.4 percent of total income; the second poorest 20 percent received 8.6 percent; the middle 20 percent received 14.6 percent; the next highest 20 percent received 23.0 percent; and the highest 20 percent received 50.4 percent.

Source of data: U.S. Bureau of the Census, "Income, Poverty, and Health Insurance Coverage in the United States: 2007," *Current Population Reports*, P-60-231 (Washington, DC: U.S. Government Printing Office, 2006).

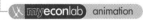 animation

The Income Lorenz Curve

The income **Lorenz curve** graphs the cumulative percentage of income against the cumulative percentage of households. Figure 19.3 shows the income Lorenz curve using the quintile shares from Fig. 19.2. The table shows the percentage of income of each quintile group. For example, row *A* tells us that the lowest quintile of households receives 3.4 percent of total income. The table also shows the *cumulative* percentages of households and income. For example, row *B* tells us that the lowest two quintiles (lowest 40 per-

FIGURE 19.3   The Income Lorenz Curve in 2007

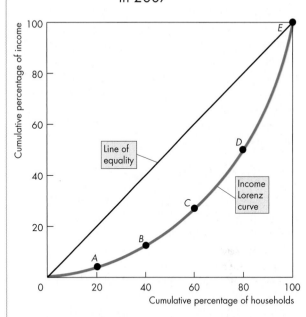

	Households			Income	
		Percentage	Cumulative percentage	Percentage	Cumulative percentage
A	Lowest 20	20		3.4	3.4
B	Second 20	40		8.6	12.0
C	Middle 20	60		14.6	26.6
D	Next highest 20	80		23.0	49.6
E	Highest 20	100		50.4	100.0

The cumulative percentage of income is graphed against the cumulative percentage of households. Points *A* through *E* on the Lorenz curve correspond to the rows of the table. If incomes were distributed equally, each 20 percent of households would receive 20 percent of total income and the Lorenz curve would fall along the line of equality. The Lorenz curve shows that income is unequally distributed.

Source of data: U.S. Bureau of the Census, "Income, Poverty, and Health Insurance Coverage in the United States: 2007," *Current Population Reports*, P-60-231 (Washington, DC: U.S. Government Printing Office, 2006).

myeconlab animation

cent) of households receive 12.0 percent of total income (3.4 percent for the lowest quintile and 8.6 percent for the next lowest). The Lorenz curve graphs the cumulative income shares against the cumulative household percentages.

If income were distributed equally across all the households, each quintile would receive 20 percent of total income and the cumulative percentages of income received by the cumulative percentages of households would fall along the straight line labeled "Line of equality." The actual distribution of income is shown by the curve labeled "Income Lorenz curve." The closer the Lorenz curve is to the line of equality, the more equal is the distribution of income.

The Distribution of Wealth

The distribution of wealth provides another way of measuring economic inequality. A household's **wealth** is the value of the things that it owns at a *point in time*. In contrast, income is the amount that the household receives over a given *period of time*.

Figure 19.4 shows the Lorenz curve for wealth in the United States in 1998 (the most recent year for which we have wealth distribution data). The median household wealth in 1998 was $60,700. Wealth is extremely unequally distributed, and for this reason, the data are grouped by seven unequal groups of households. The poorest 40 percent of households own only 0.2 percent of total wealth (row *A'* in the table in Fig. 19.4). The richest 20 percent of households own 83.4 percent of total wealth. Because this group owns almost all the wealth, we need to break the group into smaller parts. That is what rows *D'* through *G'* do. You can see that the richest 1 percent of households own 38.1 percent of total wealth.

Figure 19.4 shows the income Lorenz curve (from Fig. 19.3) alongside the wealth Lorenz curve. You can see that the Lorenz curve for wealth is much farther away from the line of equality than is the Lorenz curve for income, which means that the distribution of wealth is much more unequal than the distribution of income.

Wealth or Income?

We've seen that wealth is much more unequally distributed than is income. Which distribution provides the better description of the degree of inequality? To answer this question, we need to think about the connection between wealth and income.

Wealth is a stock of assets, and income is the flow of earnings that results from the stock of wealth. Suppose that a person owns assets worth

FIGURE 19.4 Lorenz Curves for Income and Wealth

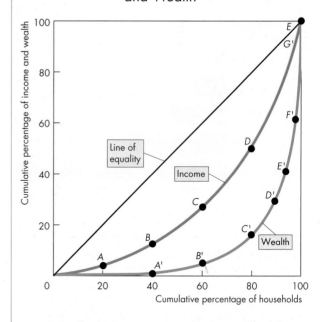

	Households		Wealth	
	Percentage	Cumulative percentage	Percentage	Cumulative percentage
A'	Lowest 40	40	0.2	0.2
B'	Next 20	60	4.5	4.7
C'	Next 20	80	11.9	16.6
D'	Next 10	90	12.5	29.1
E'	Next 5	95	11.5	40.6
F'	Next 4	99	21.3	61.9
G'	Highest 1	100	38.1	100.0

The cumulative percentage of wealth is graphed against the cumulative percentage of households. Points A' through G' on the Lorenz curve for wealth correspond to the rows of the table. By comparing the Lorenz curves for income and wealth, we can see that wealth is distributed much more unequally than is income.

Sources of data: U.S. Bureau of the Census, "Income, Poverty, and Health Insurance Coverage in the United States: 2007," *Current Population Reports*, P-60-231 (Washington, DC: U.S. Government Printing Office, 2006); and Edward N. Wolff, "Recent Trends in Wealth Ownership, 1938–1998," Jerome Levy Economics Institute Working Paper No. 300, April 2000.

myeconlab animation

$1 million—has a wealth of $1 million. If the rate of return on assets is 5 percent a year, then this person receives an income of $50,000 a year from those assets. We can describe this person's economic condition by using either the wealth of $1 million or the income of $50,000. When the rate of return is 5 percent a year, $1 million of wealth equals $50,000 of income in perpetuity. Wealth and income are just different ways of looking at the same thing.

But in Fig. 19.4, the distribution of wealth is more unequal than the distribution of income. Why? It is because the wealth data do not include the value of human capital, while the income data measure income from all wealth, including human capital.

Think about Lee and Peter, two people with equal income and equal wealth. Lee's wealth is human capital and his entire income is from employment. Peter's wealth is in the form of investments in stocks and bonds and his entire income is from these investments.

When a Census Bureau agent interviews Lee and Peter in a national income and wealth survey, their incomes are recorded as being equal, but Lee's wealth is recorded as zero, while Peter's wealth is recorded as the value of his investments. Peter looks vastly more wealthy than Lee in the survey data.

Because the national survey of wealth excludes human capital, the income distribution is a more accurate measure of economic inequality than the wealth distribution.

Annual or Lifetime Income and Wealth?

A typical household's income changes over its life cycle. Income starts out low, grows to a peak when the household's workers reach retirement age, and then falls after retirement. Also, a typical household's wealth changes over time. Like income, it starts out low, grows to a peak at the point of retirement, and falls after retirement.

Think about three households with identical lifetime incomes, one young, one middle-aged, and one retired. The middle-aged household has the highest income and wealth, the retired household has the lowest, and the young household falls in the middle. The distributions of annual income and wealth in a given year are unequal, but the distributions of lifetime income and wealth are equal.

The data on inequality share the bias that you've just seen. Inequality in annual income and wealth data overstates lifetime inequality because households are at different stages in their life cycles.

Trends in Inequality

To see trends in the income distribution, we need a measure that enables us to rank distributions on the scale of more equal and less equal. No perfect scale exists, but one that is much used is called the Gini ratio. The **Gini ratio** is based on the Lorenz curve and equals the ratio of the area between the line of equality and the Lorenz curve to the entire area beneath the line of equality. If income is equally distributed, the Lorenz curve is the same as the line of equality, so the Gini ratio is zero. If one person has all the income and everyone else has none, the Gini ratio is 1.

The Share of the Richest One Percent
The Rich Get Richer

Since 1984, a Gallup poll has been asking Americans what they think about the distribution of wealth. The percentage who say that wealth should be distributed more evenly has been rising and in 2008, it reached 70 percent. A reason might be the trend in the incomes of the richest one percent of Americans. Emmanuel Saez, an economics professor at the University of California, Berkeley, has used tax returns data to get the numbers graphed below.

After decades of a falling share, starting in 1981, the share of income received by the richest one percent began a steady climb. By 2006 (the latest year in Professor Saez's database), the richest one percent were earning 14.6 percent of the nation's income.

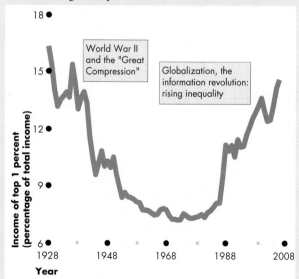

The Income Share of the Top One Percent

Source of data: Emmanuel Saez, University of California, Berkeley, http://elsa.berkeley.edu/~saez/.

Figure 19.5 shows the U.S. Gini ratio from 1970 to 2007. The figure shows breaks in the data in 1992 and 2000 because in those years, the Census Bureau changed its method of collecting the data and definitions, so the numbers before and after the breaks can't be compared. Despite the breaks in the series, the Gini ratio has clearly increased, which means that on this measure, incomes have become less equal.

The major change is that the share of income received by the richest households has increased. You saw on the previous page how the income of the richest one percent has increased. No one knows for sure *why* this trend has occurred, but a possibility that we'll explore in the next section is that technological change has increased the value of marginal product of high-skilled workers and decreased the value of marginal product of low-skilled workers.

FIGURE 19.5 The U.S. Gini Ratio: 1970–2007

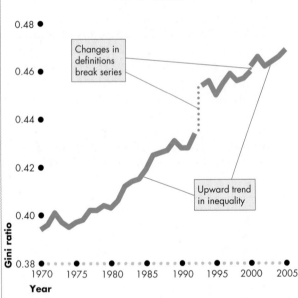

Measured by the Gini ratio, the distribution of income in the United States became more unequal between 1970 and 2007. The percentage of income earned by the richest households increased through these years. Changes in definitions make the numbers before and after 1992 and before and after 2000 not comparable. Despite the breaks in the data, the trends are still visible.

Source of data: U.S. Bureau of the Census, "Income, Poverty, and Health Insurance Coverage in the United States: 2007," *Current Population Reports,* P-60-231 (Washington, DC: U.S. Government Printing Office, 2006).

Who Are the Rich and the Poor?
More Evidence that Schooling Pays

Movie stars, sports stars, and the CEOs of large corporations earn the highest incomes. People who scratch out a living doing seasonal work on farms earn the lowest incomes. Aside from these extremes, what are the characteristics of people who earn high incomes and people who earn low incomes? The figure answers this question. (The data are for 2006 but the patterns are persistent).

Education A postgraduate education is the main source of a high income. A person with a professional degree (such as a medical or law degree), earns (on the average) more than $100,000—more than double the median income. Just completing high school raises a person's income by more than $10,000 a year; and getting a bachelor's degree adds another $34,000 a year. The average income of people who have not completed 9th grade is $20,000—half the median income.

Type of Household Married couples earn more, on the average, than people who live alone. A married couple sharing a household earns about $66,000 on the average in 2007. In contrast, men who live alone earn about $34,000, and women who live alone earn only $23,000.

Age of Householder Households with the oldest and youngest householders have lower incomes than do those with middle-aged householders. When the householder is aged between 45 and 54, household income averages $62,000. And when the householder is aged

Poverty

Households at the low end of the income distribution are so poor that they are considered to be living in poverty. **Poverty** is a situation in which a household's income is too low to be able to buy the quantities of food, shelter, and clothing that are deemed necessary. Poverty is a relative concept. Millions of people living in Africa and Asia survive on incomes of less than $400 a year. In the United States, the poverty level is calculated each year by the Social Security Administration. In 2007, the poverty level for a four-person household was an income of $19,971. In that year, 37 million Americans—12.6 percent of the population—lived in households that had incomes below the

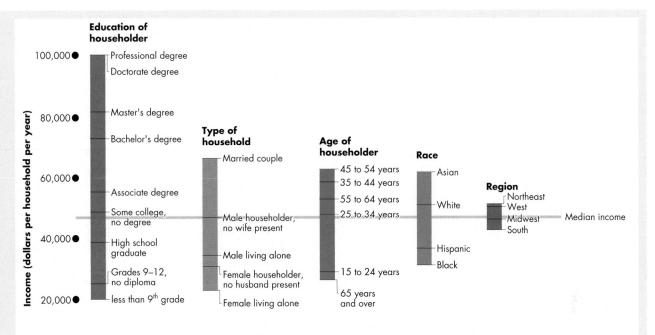

The Distribution of Income by Selected Household Characteristics

Source of data: U.S. Bureau of the Census, "Income, Poverty, and Health Insurance Coverage in the United States: 2007," *Current Population Reports*, P-60-231 (Washington, DC: U.S. Government Printing Office, 2006).

between 35 and 44, household income averages $58,000. When the householder is aged between 15 and 24, average household income is close to $29,000. And for householders over 65, the average household income is only $26,000.

Race and Ethnicity White Americans have an average income of $51,000, while black Americans have an average income of $31,000. People of Hispanic origin are a bit better off, with an average income of

$36,000. Best off of all are Asian people; their average income is $61,000.

Region People who live in the Northeast and West earn more, on the average, then people who live in the Midwest and the South. While the region does make a difference, its magnitude is small compared to the dominating effect of education.

The bottom line: schooling pays. So does marriage.

poverty level. Many of these households benefited from Medicare and Medicaid, two government programs that aid the poorest households and lift some of them above the poverty level.

The distribution of poverty by race is unequal: 8.5 percent of white Americans live in poor households compared to 22 percent of Hispanic-origin Americans and 25 percent of black Americans. Poverty is also influenced by household status. More than 31 percent of households in which the householder is a female with no husband present had incomes below the poverty level.

Despite the widening of the income distribution, poverty rates are falling.

Review Quiz

1 Which is distributed more unequally, income or wealth? Why? Which is the better measure?
2 Has the distribution of income become more equal or more unequal? Which quintile share has changed most?
3 What are the main characteristics of people who earn large incomes and who earn small incomes?
4 What is poverty and how does its incidence vary across the races?

 Work Study Plan 19.1 and get instant feedback.

◆ The Sources of Economic Inequality

We've described economic inequality in the United States. Our task now is to explain it. We began this task in Chapter 18 by learning about the forces that influence demand and supply in the markets for labor, capital, and land. We're now going to deepen our understanding of these forces.

Inequality arises from unequal labor market outcomes and from unequal ownership of capital. We'll begin by looking at labor markets and two features of them that contribute to differences in income:

- Human capital
- Discrimination

Human Capital

A clerk in a law firm earns less than a tenth of the amount earned by the attorney he assists. An operating room assistant earns less than a tenth of the amount earned by the surgeon with whom she works. A bank teller earns less than a tenth of the amount earned by the bank's CEO. These differences in earnings arise from differences in human capital.

Suppose there are just two levels of human capital, which we'll call high-skilled labor and low-skilled labor. The low-skilled labor might represent the law clerk, the operating room assistant, or the bank teller, and the high-skilled labor might represent the attorney, the surgeon, or the bank's CEO. We'll first look at the market demand for these two types of labor.

The Demand for High-Skilled and Low-Skilled Labor

High-skilled workers can perform tasks that low-skilled labor would perform badly or perhaps could not perform at all. Imagine an untrained person doing open-heart surgery. High-skilled labor has a higher value of marginal product than does low-skilled labor. As we learned in Chapter 18, a firm's demand for labor curve is the same as the value of marginal product of labor curve.

Figure 19.6(a) shows the demand curves for high-skilled and low-skilled labor. The demand curve for high-skilled labor is D_H, and that for low-skilled labor is D_L. At any given level of employment, firms are willing to pay a higher wage rate to a high-skilled worker than to a low-skilled worker. The gap between the two

wage rates measures the value of marginal product of skill; for example, at an employment level of 2,000 hours, firms are willing to pay $12.50 an hour for a high-skilled worker and only $5 an hour for a low-skilled worker, a difference of $7.50 an hour. So the value of marginal product of skill is $7.50 an hour.

The Supply of High-Skilled and Low-Skilled Labor

High-skilled labor contains more human capital than does low-skilled labor, and human capital is costly to acquire. The opportunity cost of acquiring human capital includes expenditures on tuition and textbooks and also forgone or reduced earnings while the skill is being acquired. When a person goes to school full time, that cost is the total earnings forgone. But some people acquire skills on the job—on-the-job training. Usually, a worker undergoing on-the-job training is paid a lower wage than one doing a comparable job but not undergoing training. In such a case, the cost of acquiring the skill is the difference between the wage paid to a person not being trained and that paid to a person being trained.

The position of the supply curve of high-skilled labor reflects the cost of acquiring human capital. Figure 19.6(b) shows two supply curves: one for high-skilled labor and the other for low-skilled labor. The supply curve for high-skilled labor is S_H, and that for low-skilled labor is S_L.

The high-skilled labor supply curve lies above the low-skilled labor supply curve. The vertical distance between the two supply curves is the compensation that high-skilled labor requires for the cost of acquiring the skill. For example, suppose that the quantity of low-skilled labor supplied is 2,000 hours at a wage rate of $5 an hour. This wage rate compensates the low-skilled workers mainly for their time on the job. To induce high-skilled workers to supply 2,000 hours of labor, firms must pay a wage rate of $8.50 an hour.

Wage Rates of High-Skilled and Low-Skilled Labor

The demand for and supply of high-skilled and low-skilled labor determine the two wage rates. Figure 19.6(c) brings together the demand curves and the supply curves for high-skilled and low-skilled labor. Equilibrium occurs in the market for low-skilled labor (on the blue supply and demand curves) at a wage rate of $5 an hour, and a quantity of low-skilled labor of 2,000 hours. Equilibrium occurs in the market for high-skilled labor (on the green supply and

FIGURE 19.6   Skill Differentials

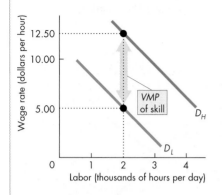

(a) Demand for high-skilled and low-skilled labor

(b) Supply of high-skilled and low-skilled labor

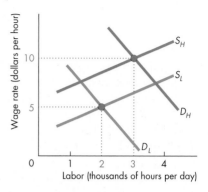

(c) Markets for high-skilled and low-skilled labor

Part (a) illustrates the value of marginal product of skill. Low-skilled labor has a value of marginal product that gives rise to the demand curve marked D_L. High-skilled labor has a higher value of marginal product than does low-skilled labor, so the demand curve for high-skilled labor, D_H, lies to the right of D_L. The vertical distance between these two curves is the value of marginal product of the skill.

Part (b) illustrates the cost of acquiring skill. The supply curve for low-skilled labor is S_L. The supply curve for high-skilled labor is S_H. The vertical distance between these two curves is the required compensation for the cost of acquiring a skill.

Part (c) shows the equilibrium employment and the wage differential. Low-skilled workers provide 2,000 hours of labor at a wage rate of $5 an hour. High-skilled workers provide 3,000 hours of labor at a wage rate of $10 an hour.

demand curves) at a wage rate of $10 an hour, and a quantity of high-skilled labor of 3,000 hours.

The equilibrium wage rate of high-skilled labor is higher than that of low-skilled labor for two reasons: First, high-skilled labor has a higher value of marginal product than low-skilled labor, so at a given wage rate, the quantity of high-skilled labor demanded exceeds that of low-skilled labor. Second, skills are costly to acquire, so at a given wage rate, the quantity of high-skilled labor supplied is less than that of low-skilled labor. The wage differential (in this case, $5 an hour) depends on both the value of marginal product of the skill and the cost of acquiring it. The higher the value of marginal product of a skill or the more costly it is to acquire a skill, the larger is the wage differential between high-skilled and low-skilled labor.

Do Education and Training Pay?   Rates of return on high school and college education have been estimated to be in the range of 5 percent to 10 percent a year after allowing for inflation, which suggest that a college degree is a better investment than almost any other that a person can undertake.

Inequality Explained by Human Capital Differences
Human capital differences help to explain some of the inequality that we observe.

High-income households tend to be better educated, middle-aged, Asian or white, and married couples (see the figure on p. 447). Human capital differences are correlated with these household characteristics. Education contributes directly to human capital. Age contributes indirectly to human capital because older workers have more experience than younger workers. Human capital differences can also explain a small part of the inequality associated with sex and race. A larger proportion of men (25 percent) than women (20 percent) have completed four years of college, and a larger proportion of whites (24 percent) than blacks (13 percent) have completed a bachelor's degree or higher. These differences in education levels among the sexes and the races are becoming smaller, but they have not been eliminated.

Career interruptions can decrease human capital. A person (most often a woman) who interrupts a career to raise young children usually returns to the labor force with a lower earning capacity than a similar person who has kept working. Likewise, a person who has suffered a spell of unemployment often finds a new job at a lower wage rate than that of a similar person who has not been unemployed.

Trends in Inequality Explained by Technological Change and Globalization You've seen that high-income households have earned an increasing share of total income while low-income households have earned a decreasing share: The distribution of income in the United States has become more unequal. Technological change and globalization are two possible sources of this increased inequality.

Technological Change Information technologies such as computers and laser scanners are *substitutes* for low-skilled labor: They perform tasks that previously were performed by low-skilled labor. The introduction of these technologies has lowered the marginal product and the demand for low-skilled labor. These same technologies require high-skilled labor to design, program, and run them. High-skilled labor and the information technologies are *complements*. So the introduction of these technologies has increased the marginal product and demand for high-skilled labor.

Figure 19.7 illustrates the effects on wages and employment. The supply of low-skilled labor (part a) and that of high-skilled labor (part b) are S, and initially, the demand in each market is D_0. The low-skill wage rate is $5 an hour, and the high-skill wage rate is $10 an hour. The demand for low-skilled labor decreases to D_1 in part (a) and the demand for high-skilled labor increases to D_1 in part (b). The low-skill wage rate falls to $4 an hour and the high-skill wage rate rises to $15 an hour.

Globalization The entry of China and other developing countries into the global economy has lowered the prices of many manufactured goods. Lower prices for the firm's output lowers the value of marginal product of the firm's workers and decreases the demand for their labor. A situation like that in Fig. 19.7(a) occurs. The wage rate falls, and employment shrinks.

At the same time, the growing global economy increases the demand for services that employ high-skilled workers, and the value of marginal product and the demand for high-skilled labor increases. A situation like that in Fig. 19.7(b) occurs. The wage rate rises, and employment opportunities for high-skilled workers expand.

FIGURE 19.7   Explaining the Trend in Income Distribution

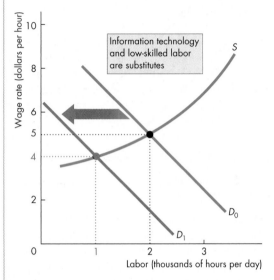

(a) A decrease in demand for low-skilled labor

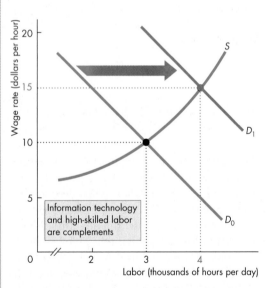

(b) An increase in demand for high-skilled labor

Low-skilled labor in part (a) and information technologies are substitutes. Advances in information technology decrease the demand for low-skilled labor and lower its wage rate. High-skilled labor in part (b) and information technologies are complements. Advances in information technology increase the demand for high-skilled labor and raise its wage rate.

Discrimination

Human capital differences can explain some of the economic inequality that we observe. Discrimination is another possible source of inequality.

Suppose that black females and white males have identical abilities as investment advisors. Figure 19.8 shows the supply curves of black females, S_{BF} (in part a), and of white males, S_{WM} (in part b). The value of marginal product of investment advisors, shown by the two curves labeled *VMP* in parts (a) and (b), is the same for both groups.

If everyone is free of race and sex prejudice, the market determines a wage rate of $40,000 a year for investment advisors. But if the customers are prejudiced against women and minorities, this prejudice is reflected in the wage rate and employment.

Suppose that the perceived value of marginal product of the black females, when discriminated against, is VMP_{DA}. Suppose that the perceived value of marginal product for white males, the group discriminated in favor of, is VMP_{DF}. With these *VMP* curves, black females earn $20,000 a year and only 1,000 black females work as investment advisors. White males earn $60,000 a year, and 3,000 of them work as investment advisors.

Counteracting Forces Economists disagree about whether prejudice actually causes wage differentials, and one line of reasoning implies that it does not. In the above example, customers who buy from white men pay a higher service charge for investment advice than do the customers who buy from black women. This price difference acts as an incentive to encourage people who are prejudiced to buy from the people against whom they are prejudiced. This force could be strong enough to eliminate the effects of discrimination altogether. Suppose, as is true in manufacturing, that a firm's customers never meet its workers. If such a firm discriminates against women or minorities, it can't compete with firms who hire these groups because its costs are higher than those of the nonprejudiced firms. Only firms that do not discriminate survive in a competitive industry.

Whether because of discrimination or from some other source, women and visible minorities do earn lower incomes than white males. Another possible source of lower wage rates of women arises from differences in the relative degree of specialization of women and men.

FIGURE 19.8   Discrimination

(a) Black females

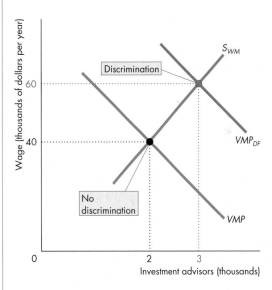

(b) White males

With no discrimination, the wage rate is $40,000 a year and 2,000 of each group are hired. With discrimination against blacks and women, the value of marginal product curve in part (a) is VMP_{DA} and that in part (b) is VMP_{DF}. The wage rate for black women falls to $20,000 a year, and only 1,000 are employed. The wage rate for white men rises to $60,000 a year, and 3,000 are employed.

Differences in the Degree of Specialization Couples must choose how to allocate their time between working for a wage and doing jobs in the home, such as cooking, cleaning, shopping, organizing vacations, and, most important, bearing and raising children. Let's look at the choices of Bob and Sue.

Bob might specialize in earning an income and Sue in taking care of the home. Or Sue might specialize in earning an income and Bob in taking care of the home. Or both of them might earn an income and share home production jobs.

The allocation they choose depends on their preferences and on their earning potential. The choice of an increasing number of households is for each person to diversify between earning an income and doing some household chores. But in most households, Bob will specialize in earning an income and Sue will both earn an income and bear a larger share of the task of running the home. With this allocation, Bob will probably earn more than Sue. If Sue devotes time and effort to ensuring Bob's mental and physical well-being, the quality of Bob's market labor will be higher than it would be if he were diversified. If the roles were reversed, Sue would be able to supply market labor that earns more than Bob's.

To test whether the degree of specialization accounts for earnings differences between the sexes, economists have compared the incomes of never-married men and women. They have found that, on the average, with equal amounts of human capital, the wages of these two groups are the same.

We've examined some sources of inequality in the labor market. Let's now look at the way inequality arises from unequal ownership of capital.

Unequal Wealth

You've seen that wealth inequality—excluding human capital—is much greater than income inequality. This greater wealth inequality arises from two sources: life-cycle saving patterns and transfers of wealth from one generation to the next.

Life-Cycle Saving Patterns Over a family's life cycle, wealth starts out at zero or perhaps less than zero. A student who has financed education all the way through graduate school might have lots of human capital and an outstanding student loan of $30,000. This person has negative wealth. Gradually loans get paid off and a retirement fund is accumulated. At the point of retiring from full time work, the family has

maximum wealth. Then, during its retirement years, the family spends its wealth. This life-cycle pattern means that much of the wealth is owned by people in their sixties.

Intergenerational Transfers Households that inherit wealth from the previous generation or that save more than enough on which to live during retirement end up transferring wealth to the next generation. But intergenerational transfers are not always a source of increased inequality. If a generation that has a high income saves a large part of that income and leaves wealth to a succeeding generation that has a lower income, this transfer decreases the degree of inequality. But one feature of intergenerational transfers of wealth leads to increased inequality: wealth concentration through marriage.

Marriage and Wealth Concentration People tend to marry within their own socioeconomic class—a phenomenon called *assortative mating*. In everyday language, "like attracts like." Although there is a good deal of folklore that "opposites attract," perhaps such Cinderella tales appeal to us because they are so rare in reality. Wealthy people seek wealthy partners.

Because of assortative mating, wealth becomes more concentrated in a small number of families and the distribution of wealth becomes more unequal.

Review Quiz

1 What role does human capital play in accounting for income inequality?

2 What role might discrimination play in accounting for income inequality?

3 What are the possible reasons for income inequality by sex and race?

4 How might technological change and globalization influence the distribution of income?

5 Does inherited wealth make the distribution of income less equal or more equal?

6 Why does wealth inequality persist across generations?

 Work Study Plan 19.2 and get instant feedback.

Next, we're going to see how taxes and government programs redistribute income and decrease the degree of economic inequality.

Income Redistribution

The three main ways in which governments in the United States redistribute income are

- Income taxes
- Income maintenance programs
- Subsidized services

Income Taxes

Income taxes may be progressive, regressive, or proportional. A **progressive income tax** is one that taxes income at an average rate that increases with income. A **regressive income tax** is one that taxes income at an average rate that decreases with income. A **proportional income tax** (also called a *flat-rate income tax*) is one that taxes income at a constant average rate, regardless of the level of income.

The income tax rates that apply in the United States are composed of two parts: federal and state taxes. Some cities, such as New York City, also have an income tax. There is variety in the detailed tax arrangements in the individual states, but the tax system, at both the federal and state levels, is progressive. The poorest working households receive money from the government through an earned income tax credit. Successively higher-income households pay 10 percent, 15 percent, 25 percent, 28 percent, 33 percent, and 35 percent of each additional dollar earned.

Income Maintenance Programs

Three main types of programs redistribute income by making direct payments (in cash, services, or vouchers) to people in the lower part of the income distribution. They are

- Social Security programs
- Unemployment compensation
- Welfare programs

Social Security Programs The main Social Security program is OASDHI—Old Age, Survivors, Disability, and Health Insurance. Monthly cash payments to retired or disabled workers or their surviving spouses and children are paid for by compulsory payroll taxes on both employers and employees. In 2007, total Social Security expenditure was budgeted at $550 billion, and the standard monthly Social Security check for a married couple was a bit more than $1,000.

The other component of Social Security is Medicare, which provides hospital and health insurance for the elderly and disabled.

Unemployment Compensation To provide an income to unemployed workers, every state has established an unemployment compensation program. Under these programs, a tax is paid that is based on the income of each covered worker and such a worker receives a benefit when he or she becomes unemployed. The details of the benefits vary from state to state.

Welfare Programs The purpose of welfare is to provide incomes for people who do not qualify for Social Security or unemployment compensation. They are

1. Supplementary Security Income (SSI) program, designed to help the neediest elderly, disabled, and blind people
2. Temporary Assistance for Needy Households (TANF) program, designed to help households that have inadequate financial resources
3. Food Stamp program, designed to help the poorest households obtain a basic diet
4. Medicaid, designed to cover the costs of medical care for households receiving help under the SSI and TANF programs

Subsidized Services

A great deal of redistribution takes place in the United States through the provision of subsidized services—services provided by the government at prices below the cost of production. The taxpayers who consume these goods and services receive a transfer in kind from the taxpayers who do not consume them. The two most important areas in which this form of redistribution takes place are health care and education—both kindergarten through grade 12 and college and university.

In 2007–2008, students enrolled in the University of California system paid annual tuition fees of $6,780. The cost of providing a year's education at the University of California was probably about $20,000. So households with a member enrolled in one of these institutions received a benefit from the government of more than $13,000 a year.

The Scale of Income Redistribution
Only the Richest Pay

A household's *market income* tells us what a household earns in the absence of government redistribution. You've seen that market income is *not* the official basis for measuring the distribution of income that we've used in this chapter. The Census Bureau's measure is *money income* (market income plus cash transfers from the government). But market income is the correct starting point for measuring the scale of income redistribution.

We begin with market income and then subtract taxes and add the amounts received in benefits. The result is the distribution of income after taxes and benefits. The data available on benefits exclude the value of subsidized services such as college, so the resulting distribution might understate the total amount of redistribution from the rich to the poor.

The figures show the scale of redistribution in 2001, the most recent year for which the Census Bureau has provided these data. In Fig. 1, the blue Lorenz curve describes the market distribution of income and the green Lorenz curve shows the distribution of income after all taxes and benefits, including Medicaid and Medicare benefits. (The Lorenz curve based on money income in Fig. 19.3 lies between these two curves.)

The distribution after taxes and benefits is less unequal than is the market distribution. The lowest 20 percent of households received only 0.9 percent of market income but 4.6 percent of income after taxes and benefits. The highest 20 percent of households received 55.6 percent of market income, but only 46.7 percent of income after taxes and benefits.

Figure 2 highlights the percentage of total income redistributed among the five groups. The share of total income received by the lowest 60 percent of households increased. The share received by the fourth quintile barely changed. And the share received by the highest quintile fell by 8.9 percent.

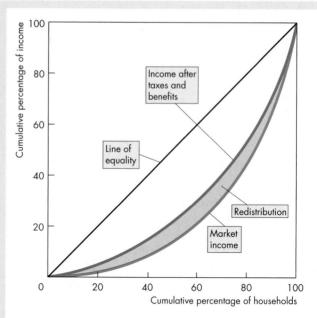

Figure 1   Income Distribution Before and After Redistribution

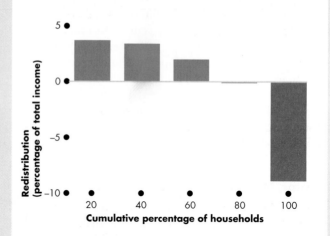

Figure 2   The Scale of Redistribution

Source of data: U.S. Bureau of the Census, "Money Income in the United States: 2001," *Current Population Reports*, P-60-200 (Washington, DC: U.S. Government Printing Office, 2003).

Government provision of health-care services has grown to the scale of private provision. Programs such as Medicaid and Medicare bring high-quality and high-cost health care to millions of people who earn too little to buy such services themselves.

The Big Tradeoff

The redistribution of income creates what has been called the **big tradeoff**, a tradeoff between equity and efficiency. The big tradeoff arises because redistribution uses scarce resources and weakens incentives.

A dollar collected from a rich person does not translate into a dollar received by a poor person. Some of it gets used up in the process of redistribution. Tax-collecting agencies such as the Internal Revenue Service and welfare-administering agencies (as well as tax accountants and lawyers) use skilled labor, computers, and other scarce resources to do their work. The bigger the scale of redistribution, the greater is the opportunity cost of administering it.

But the cost of collecting taxes and making welfare payments is a small part of the total cost of redistribution. A bigger cost arises from the inefficiency (deadweight loss) of taxes and benefits. Greater equality can be achieved only by taxing productive activities such as work and saving. Taxing people's income from their work and saving lowers the after-tax income they receive. This lower after-tax income makes them work and save less, which in turn results in smaller output and less consumption not only for the rich who pay the taxes but also for the poor who receive the benefits.

It is not only taxpayers who face weaker incentives to work. Benefit recipients also face weaker incentives. In fact, under the welfare arrangements that prevailed before the 1996 reforms, the weakest incentives to work were those faced by households that benefited from welfare. When a welfare recipient got a job, benefits were withdrawn and eligibility for programs such as Medicaid ended, so the household in effect paid a tax of more than 100 percent on its earnings. This arrangement locked poor households in a welfare trap.

So the agencies that determine the scale and methods of income redistribution must pay close attention to the incentive effects of taxes and benefits. Let's close this chapter by looking at one way in which lawmakers are tackling the big tradeoff today.

A Major Welfare Challenge Young women who have not completed high school, have a child (or children), live without a partner, and more likely are black or Hispanic are among the poorest people in the United States today. They and their children present a major welfare challenge.

First, their numbers are large. In 2007, there were 14 million single-mother families. This number is 12 percent of families. In 1997 (the most recent year with census data), single mothers were owed $26 billion in child support. Of this amount, $10 billion was

not paid and 30 percent of the women received no support from their children's fathers.

The long-term solution to the problem these women face is education and job training—acquiring human capital. The short-term solutions are enforcing child support payments by absent fathers and former spouses and providing welfare.

Welfare must be designed to minimize the disincentive to pursue the long-term goal of becoming self-supporting. The current welfare program in the United States tries to walk this fine line.

Passed in 1996, the Personal Responsibility and Work Opportunities Reconciliation Act strengthened the Office of Child Support Enforcement and increased the penalties for nonpayment of support. The act also created the Temporary Assistance for Needy Households (TANF) program. TANF is a block grant paid to the states, which administer payments to individuals. It is not an open-ended entitlement program. An adult member of a household that is receiving assistance must either work or perform community service, and there is a five-year limit for assistance.

Review Quiz

1 How do governments in the United States redistribute income?
2 Describe the scale of redistribution in the United States.
3 What is one of the major welfare challenges today and how is it being tackled in the United States?

 Work Study Plan 19.3 and get instant feedback.

◆ We've examined economic inequality in the United States. We've seen how inequality arises and that inequality has been increasing. *Reading Between the Lines* on pp. 456–457 looks at the increasing inequality that began during the early 1980s and continues today.

The next chapter focuses on some problems for the market economy that arise from uncertainty and incomplete information. But unlike the cases we studied in Chapters 16 and 17, this time the market does a good job of coping with the problems.

Trends in Inequality

Income Gap in New York Is Called Nation's Highest

http://www.nytimes.com
January 27, 2006

New York continues to have the highest income disparity between rich and poor of any state, according to a new study by two national economic policy groups.

The average income of the richest fifth of New York State families is 8.1 times the average income of the poorest fifth, according to the study, which drew from census data compiled by the Economic Policy Institute and the Center on Budget and Policy Priorities, two liberal research groups based in Washington.

Nationwide, families in the top fifth made 7.3 times more than those in the bottom fifth. While New York has been at the top of the income gap list for several years, it ranked 11th in the early 1980s, when the difference between the average income of the top and bottom fifths was 5.6 times. ...

The average income of families in the top 20 percent in New York State was $130,431, compared with $16,076 for the bottom fifth, according to data in the report.

From 1980–1982 to 2001–2003, the periods examined in the study, average incomes grew by 18.9 percent nationwide, or $2,664, for the poorest families and 58.5 percent, or $45,101, for families among the top fifth of income earners.

"The biggest thing is the decline in wages for the low and moderate income people," said Elizabeth McNichol, an author of the report. "Part of it is large periods of higher than average unemployment, globalization—jobs going overseas—the shift from manufacturing jobs to lower paying service sector jobs, immigration, the weakening of unions, and the fact that the federal minimum wage has been declining relative to inflation." ...

Essence of the Story

- In 2001–2003, the average income of families in the top 20 percent in New York State was 8.1 times the average income of the bottom 20 percent.

- In 1980–1982, the average income of families in the top 20 percent in New York State was 5.6 times the average income of the bottom 20 percent.

- In 2001–2003, the average income of families in the top 20 percent in the United States was 7.3 times the average income of the bottom 20 percent.

- From 1980–1982 to 2001–2003, average incomes grew by 58.5 percent for families in the top 20 percent and by 18.9 percent for families in the bottom 20 percent.

- Several factors contributed to the increased inequality.

Economic Analysis

- Between 1980–1982 and 2001–2003, according to the study reported in the article, the income share of the highest 20 percent of New York families increased from 5.6 times to 8.1 times that of the lowest 20 percent.

- Elizabeth McNichol lists some factors that she says caused these changes.

- But these factors have a deeper cause that we can understand as a consequence of changes in demand and supply in the markets for low-skilled and high-skilled labor during the 1980s and 1990s.

- In Fig. 1, the demand curve for low-skilled labor in 1979 is D_{79} and the supply curve of low-skilled labor is S_{79}. By 2000, demand increased to D_{00} and supply increased to S_{00}.

- Because supply increased by more than demand, the quantity of low-skilled labor increased but the wage rate fell.

- The supply of low-skilled labor increased partly because of immigration. The demand for low-skilled labor increased but by less than supply for the reason that we identify in the chapter: New technologies are a substitute for low-skilled labor.

- In Fig. 2, the demand curve for high-skilled labor in 1979 is D_{79} and the supply curve of high-skilled labor is S_{79}. By 2000, demand increased to D_{00} and supply increased to S_{00}.

- Because demand increased by more than supply, the quantity of high-skilled labor increased and the wage rate rose.

- The supply of high-skilled labor increased slowly because the new technologies require a higher level of education to complement them.

- The demand for high-skilled labor increased by a large amount because the new technologies that changed the structure of the economy increased the value of marginal product of highly educated workers.

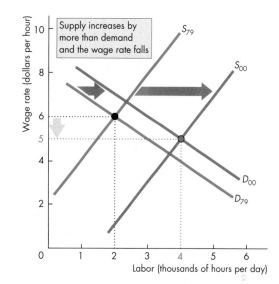

Figure 1 A market for low-skilled labor

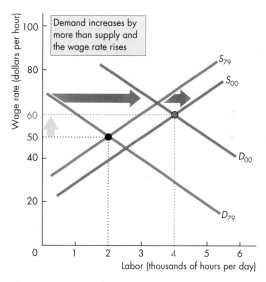

Figure 2 A market for high-skilled labor

SUMMARY

Key Points

Measuring Economic Inequality (pp. 442–447)

- In 2007, the mode money income was $13,000 a year, the median money income was $50,233, and the mean money income was $67,609.
- The income distribution is positively skewed.
- In 2007, the poorest 20 percent of households received 3.4 percent of total income and the wealthiest 20 percent received 49.7 percent of total income.
- Wealth is distributed more unequally than income because the wealth data exclude the value of human capital.
- Since 1970, the distribution of income has become more unequal.
- Education, type of household, age of householder, and race all influence household income.

The Sources of Economic Inequality (pp. 448–452)

- Inequality arises from differences in human capital.
- Trends in the distribution of human capital that arise from technological change and globalization can explain some of the trend in increased inequality.

- Inequality might arise from discrimination.
- Inequality between men and women might arise from differences in the degree of specialization.
- Intergenerational transfers of wealth lead to increased inequality because people can't inherit debts and assortative mating tends to concentrate wealth.

Income Redistribution (pp. 453–455)

- Governments redistribute income through progressive income taxes, income maintenance programs, and subsidized services.
- Redistribution increases the share of total income received by the lowest 60 percent of households and decreases the share of total income received by the highest quintile. The share of the fourth quintile barely changes.
- Because the redistribution of income weakens incentives, it creates a tradeoff between equity and efficiency.
- Effective redistribution seeks to support the long-term solution to low income, which is education and job training—acquiring human capital.

Key Figures

Key Terms

PROBLEMS and APPLICATIONS

 Work problems 1–7 in Chapter 19 Study Plan and get instant feedback.
Work problems 8–15 as Homework, a Quiz, or a Test if assigned by your instructor.

1. The table shows money income shares in the United States in 1967.

Households	Money income (percent of total)
Lowest 20%	4.0
Second 20%	10.8
Third 20%	17.3
Fourth 20%	24.2
Highest 20%	43.7

   a. What is money income?
   b. Draw a Lorenz curve for the United States in 1967 and compare it with the Lorenz curve in 2007 shown in Fig. 19.3.
   c. Was U.S. money income distributed more equally or less equally in 2007 than it was in 1967?
   d. What are some reasons for the differences in the distribution of money income in the United States in 1967 and 2007?

2. The following figure shows the demand for and supply of low-skilled labor.

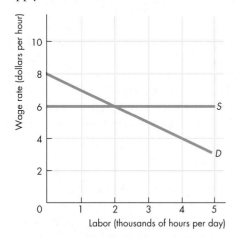

   The value of marginal product of high-skilled workers is $8 an hour greater than that of low-skilled workers. (The value of marginal product at each employment level is $8 greater than that of a low-skilled worker.) The cost of acquiring the skill adds $6 an hour to the wage that must be offered to attract high-skilled labor.
   a. What is the wage rate of low-skilled labor?

   b. What is the quantity of low-skilled labor employed?
   c. What is the wage rate of high-skilled labor?
   d. What is the quantity of high-skilled labor employed?
   e. Why does the wage rate of a high-skilled worker exceed that of a low-skilled worker by exactly the cost of acquiring the skill?

3. The figure shows the demand for and supply of workers who are discriminated against. Suppose that there is a group of workers in the same industry who are not discriminated against, and their value of marginal product is perceived to be twice the value of marginal product of the workers who are discriminated against. Suppose also that the supply of workers who do not face discrimination is 2,000 hours per day less at each wage rate.

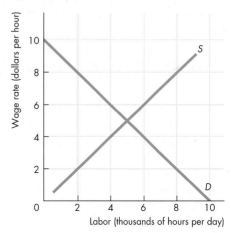

   a. What is the wage rate of the workers who are discriminated against?
   b. What is the quantity of workers employed who are discriminated against?
   c. What is the wage rate of the workers who do not face discrimination?
   d. What is the quantity of workers employed who do not face discrimination?

4. Incomes in China and India are a small fraction of incomes in the United States. But incomes in China and India are growing at more than twice the rate of those in the United States. Given this

information, what can you say about

a. Changes in inequality between people in China and India and people in the United States?

b. The world Lorenz curve and world Gini ratio?

5. **Household Incomes Rise but …**

Household income crept higher and the poverty rate edged lower last year. … But more people had to be at work in each household … because median earnings for individuals working full-time year-round actually fell. … The percent of Americans living below the poverty line, meanwhile, slipped to 12.3 percent in 2006. … The poverty threshold varies based on age and household size. … Poverty thresholds are not adjusted for geographical differences in cost of living so the same threshold applies in Brownsville, Texas, as it does in New York City. Nor do they reflect the value of household subsidies intended to alleviate the effects of poverty (e.g., food stamps, tax credits, Medicaid). … The gap between high-income and low-income households has grown over the years, but income inequality remained statistically unchanged between 2005 and 2006, according to the bureau.

CNN, August 28, 2007

a. Why are the recent increases in median household income a misleading statistic when attempting to measure the improvement in the economic well-being of households?

b. How does using set poverty thresholds that apply to the entire U.S. complicate attempts to measure poverty?

c. Why does excluding household subsidies from consideration when measuring household income lead to a misleading measurement of the percentage of people actually living in poverty?

d. Why has the gap between high-income and low-income households grown in the U.S. over the past few decades?

6. **Most Lucrative College Degrees for 2007 Grads**

With less than four months to go before saying sayonara to the quad for good, the class of 2007 is finding it easier than recent classes to get their foot in the work world. Employers have said they expect to hire 17.4 percent more college grads than they did last year, and in many instances

they plan to pay them more, too … The average starting offer for seniors majoring in marketing is up 14 percent from last year to $41,323. Those majoring in business administration are seeing a 9.2 percent jump to $43,523 in average starting salaries. … Finance: $47,905 … Economics: $51,631 … There have been slight decreases in the average starting salary offers for just a few majors … [such as] Liberal arts (including psychology, political science, history, and English): Down 1.1 percent to $30,502.

CNN, February 8, 2007

a. Why do college graduates with different majors have drastically different starting salaries?

b. Draw a graph of the labor markets for economics majors and political science majors to illustrate your explanation of the differences in the starting salaries of these two groups.

7. **Where Women's Pay Trumps Men's**

Men work more than women … on the job anyway … at least in terms of overall hours. That's just one reason why when you make a general comparison of men's and women's earnings in most fields, men usually come out ahead. … [But Warren] Farrell … found … 39 … occupations [in which] women's median earnings exceeded men's earnings by at least 5 percent and in some cases by as much as 43 percent. … In fields like engineering, a company may get one woman and seven men applying for a job. … If the company wants to hire the woman, they may have to pay a premium to get her. … Also, where women can combine technical expertise with people skills—such as those required in sales and … where customers may prefer dealing with a woman—that's likely to contribute to a premium in pay. …

CNN, March 2, 2006

a. Draw a graph to illustrate why discrimination could result in female workers getting paid more than male workers for some jobs.

b. Explain how market competition could potentially eliminate this wage differential.

c. If customers "prefer dealing with a woman" in some markets, how might that lead to a persistent wage differential between men and women?

8. The tables show the money income shares in Canada and the United Kingdom.

Canadian households	Money income (percent of total)
Lowest 20%	7
Second 20%	13
Third 20%	18
Fourth 20%	25
Highest 20%	37

U.K. households	Money income (percent of total)
Lowest 20%	3
Second 20%	5
Third 20%	14
Fourth 20%	25
Highest 20%	53

a. Create a table that shows the cumulative distribution of income in Canada and the United Kingdom.
b. Draw a Lorenz curve for Canada and compare it with the Lorenz curve in Fig. 19.3. In which country is income less equally distributed, Canada or the United States?
c. Draw a Lorenz curve for the United Kingdom and compare it with the Lorenz curve in Fig. 19.3. In which country is income less equally distributed, the United Kingdom or the United States?
d. Is the distribution of income more unequal in Canada than in the United Kingdom?
e. What are some reasons for the differences in the distribution of income in the United States, Canada, and the United Kingdom?

9. In the United States in 2000, 30 million people had full-time managerial and professional jobs that paid an average of $800 a week. At the same time, 10 million people had full-time sales positions that paid an average of $530 a week.
a. Explain why managers and professionals are paid more than salespeople.
b. Explain why, despite the higher weekly wage, more people are employed as managers and professionals than as salespeople.
c. If the online shopping trend continues, how do you think the market for salespeople will change in coming years?

10. The table shows three income-tax payments schemes.

Before-tax income (dollars)	Plan A tax (dollars)	Plan B tax (dollars)	Plan C tax (dollars)
10,000	1,000	1,000	2,000
20,000	2,000	4,000	2,000
30,000	3,000	9,000	2,000

Which income-tax payment plan
a. Is proportional?
b. Is regressive?
c. Is progressive?
d. Increases inequality?
e. Lessens inequality?
f. Has no effect on inequality?

11. The table shows the distribution of market income in the United States in 2007.

Households	Market income (percent of total)
Lowest 20%	1.1
Second 20%	7.1
Third 20%	13.9
Fourth 20%	22.8
Highest 20%	55.1

a. What is the definition of market income?
b. Draw the Lorenz curve for the distribution of market income.
c. Compare the distribution of market income with the distribution of money income shown in Fig. 19.3. Which distribution is more unequal and why?

12. Use the information provided in problem 11 and in Fig. 19.3.
a. What is the percentage of total income that is redistributed from the highest income group?
b. What are the percentages of total income that are redistributed to the lower income groups?
c. Describe the effects of increasing the amount of income redistribution in the United States to the point at which the lowest income group receives 15 percent of total income and the highest income group receives 30 percent of total income.

13. **Bernanke Links Education and Equality**

    Ben Bernanke, the chairman of the Federal Reserve, said ... that an expansion of education opportunities would help curb the economic inequality that has increased considerably in the last 30 years. ... [Bernanke] said ... that globalization and the advent of new technologies, two prime causes of income inequality, would ultimately lead to economic growth, and inhibiting them "would do far more harm than good over the longer haul."

    Instead, the Fed chief said the best method to improve economic opportunities for Americans was to focus on raising the level of and access to education. Workers would be provided with better skills, he said, and innovation in the private sector would remain unchecked.

    "As we think about improving education and skills, we should also look beyond the traditional K-12 and 4-year-college system ... to recognize that education should be lifelong and can come in many forms," Bernanke said. ... "Early childhood education, community colleges, vocational schools, on-the-job training, online courses, adult education—all of these are vehicles of demonstrated value in increasing skills and lifetime earning power."

    International Herald Tribune, June 5, 2008

    a. Explain how the two main causes of increased income inequality in the United States identified by Mr. Bernanke work.

    b. Draw a graph to illustrate how the two main causes of increased income inequality generate this outcome.

    c. What are the short-term costs and long-term benefits associated with these two causes of inequality?

    d. Explain Bernanke's solutions to help address growing income inequality.

14. **The Tax Debate We Should be Having**

    Here's a cold reality that none of the presidential candidates want to tell you: A shrinking number of Americans are bearing an even bigger share of the nation's income tax burden. ... In 2005, the bottom 40 percent of Americans by income had, in the aggregate, an effective tax rate that's negative: Their households received more money through the income tax system, largely from the earned income tax credit, than they paid. ... The top half's share of total payments [97%] has been growing steadily for the past 20 years. The top 10% of taxpayers kicked in 70% of total income tax. And the famous top 1% paid almost 40% of all income tax, a proportion that has jumped dramatically since 1986. ...

    Now consider some of the heated tax controversies of recent years. Did Bush cut taxes for the rich? Yes. But he cut taxes for the poor even more. If we look at the measure that really matters—the change in effective tax rates [total tax they pay as a percentage of their income]—the bottom 50% got a much bigger tax cut than the top 1%. Did the dollar value of Bush's tax cuts go mostly to the wealthy? Absolutely. It could hardly be otherwise. Since the well-off pay the overwhelming majority of taxes, any tax cut with a prayer of influencing the economy would have to go mostly to them. You could completely eliminate income taxes for the bottom half of the population, and the Treasury would hardly notice.

    Fortune, April 14, 2008

    a. Explain why tax cuts in a progressive income tax system are consistently criticized for favoring the wealthy.

    b. How might the benefits of tax cuts "trickle down" to others whose taxes are not cut?

15. After you have studied *Reading Between the Lines* on pp. 456–457, answer the following questions.

    a. What are the broad facts reported in the news article about the gap in the incomes of the highest and lowest 20 percent?

    b. List the factors that contributed to the rising income gap according to Elizabeth McNichol. Of these factors, which do you think made the biggest contribution?

    c. Which of the factors listed in b account for the national trend and which account for the more extreme changes in New York State?

    d. What policy issues are raised by the information reported in the news article?

16. Use the link on MyEconLab (Chapter Resources, Chapter 19, Web links) to download the Deininger and Squire Data Set on income distribution. Select two counties that interest you.

    a. Which of the countries you've selected has the more unequal distribution of income?

    b. What reasons that might explain the differences?

20 ◆ Uncertainty and Information

After studying this chapter, you will be able to:

- Explain how people make decisions when they are uncertain about the consequences
- Explain how markets enable people to buy and sell risk
- Explain how markets cope when buyers and sellers have private information
- Explain how the presence of uncertainty and incomplete information influences the ability of markets to achieve an efficient allocation of resources

Life is like a lottery. You work hard in school, but will the payoff be worth it? Will you get an interesting, high-paying job or a miserable, low-paying one? You set up a summer business and work hard at it. But will you make enough income to keep you in school next year or will you get wiped out? How do people make a decision when they don't know what its consequences will be?

As you drive across an intersection on a green light, you see a car on your left that's still moving. Will it stop or will it run the red light? You buy insurance against such a risk, and insurance companies gain from your business. Why are we willing to buy insurance at prices that leave insurance companies with a gain?

Buying a new car—or a used car—is fun, but it's also scary. You could get stuck with a lemon. Just about every com- plicated product you buy could be defective. How do car dealers and retailers induce us to buy goods that might turn out to be lemons?

Although markets do a good job in helping people to use scarce resources efficiently, there are impediments to efficiency. Can markets lead to an efficient outcome when there is uncertainty and incomplete information? In this chapter, we answer questions such as these. And in *Reading Between the Lines* at the end of the chapter, you will see how accurate grading by high schools, colleges, and universities helps students get the right jobs and the problem that arises in job markets if grades are inflated.

Decisions in the Face of Uncertainty

Tania, a student, is trying to decide which of two summer jobs to take. She can work as a house painter and earn enough for her to save $2,000 by the end of the summer. There is no uncertainty about the income from this job. If Tania takes it, she will definitely have $2,000 in her bank account at the end of the summer. The other job, working as a telemarketer selling subscriptions to a magazine, is risky. If Tania takes this job, her bank balance at the end of the summer will depend on her success at selling. She will earn enough to save $5,000 if she is successful but only $1,000 if she turns out to be a poor salesperson. Tania has never tried selling, so she doesn't know how successful she'll be. But some of her friends have done this job, and 50 percent of them do well and 50 percent do poorly. Basing her expectations on this experience, Tania thinks there is a 50 percent chance that she will earn $5,000 and a 50 percent chance that she will earn $1,000.

Tania is equally as happy to paint as she is to make phone calls. She cares only about the money. Which job does she prefer: the one that provides her with $2,000 for sure or the one that offers her a 50 percent chance of making $5,000 but a 50 percent risk of making only $1,000?

To answer this question, we need a way of comparing the two outcomes. One comparison is the expected wealth that each job creates.

Expected Wealth

Expected wealth is the money value of what a person expects to own at a given point in time. An expectation is an average calculated by using a formula that weights each possible outcome with the probability (chance) that it will occur.

For Tania, the probability that she will have $5,000 is 0.5 (a 50 percent chance). The probability that she will have $1,000 is also 0.5. Notice that the probabilities sum to 1. Using these numbers, we can calculate Tania's expected wealth, EW, which is

$$EW = (\$5,000 \times 0.5) + (\$1,000 \times 0.5) = \$3,000.$$

Notice that expected wealth decreases if the risk of a poor outcome increases. For example, if Tania has a

20 percent chance of success (and 80 percent chance of failure), her expected wealth falls to $1,800—($5,000 × 0.2) + ($1,000 × 0.8) = $1,800.

Tania can now compare the expected wealth from each job—$3,000 for the risky job and $2,000 for the non-risky job.

So does Tania prefer the risky job because it gives her a greater expected wealth? The answer is we don't know because we don't know how much Tania dislikes risk.

Risk Aversion

Risk aversion is the dislike of risk. Almost everyone is risk averse but some more than others. In football, running is less risky than passing. Coach Mike Holmgren of the Seattle Seahawks, who favors a cautious running game, is risk averse. Indianapolis quarterback Peyton Manning, who favors a risky passing game, is less risk averse. But almost everyone is risk averse to some degree.

We can measure the degree of risk aversion by the compensation needed to make a given amount of risk acceptable. Returning to Tania: If she needs to be paid more than $1,000 to take on the risk arising from the telemarketing job, she will choose the safe painting job and take the $2,000 non-risky income. But if she thinks that the extra $1,000 of expected income is enough to compensate her for the risk, she will take the risky job.

To make this idea concrete, we need a way of thinking about how a person values different levels of wealth. The concept that we use is *utility*. We apply the same idea that explains how people make expenditure decisions (see Chapter 8) to explain risk aversion and decisions in the face of risk.

Utility of Wealth

Wealth (money in the bank and other assets of value) is like all good things. It yields utility. The more wealth a person has, the greater is that person's total utility. But each additional dollar of wealth brings a diminishing increment in total utility—the marginal utility of wealth diminishes as wealth increases.

Diminishing marginal utility of wealth means that the gain in utility from an increase in wealth is smaller than the loss in utility from an equal decrease in wealth. Stated differently, *the pain from a loss is greater than the pleasure from a gain of equal size.*

Figure 20.1 illustrates Tania's utility of wealth. Each point A through F on Tania's utility of wealth curve corresponds to the value identified by the same letter in the table. For example, at point C, Tania's wealth is $2,000, and her total utility is 70 units. As Tania's wealth increases, her total utility increases and her marginal utility decreases. Her marginal utility is 25 units when wealth increases from $1,000 to $2,000, but only 13 units when wealth increases from $2,000 to $3,000.

We can use a person's utility of wealth curve to calculate expected utility and the cost of risk.

Expected Utility

Expected utility is the utility value of what a person expects to own at a given point in time. Like expected wealth, it is calculated by using a formula that weights each possible outcome with the probability that it will occur. But it is the utility outcome, not the money outcome, that is used to calculate expected utility.

Figure 20.2 illustrates the calculation for Tania. Wealth of $5,000 gives 95 units of utility and wealth of $1,000 gives 45 units of utility. Each outcome has a probability of is 0.5 (a 50 percent chance). Using these numbers, we can calculate Tania's expected utility, EU, which is

$$EU = (95 \times 0.5) + (45 \times 0.5) = 70.$$

FIGURE 20.1   The Utility of Wealth

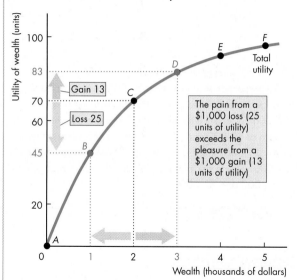

	Wealth (thousands of dollars)	Total utility (units)	Marginal utility (units)
A	0	0	
			45
B	1	45	
			25
C	2	70	
			13
D	3	83	
			8
E	4	91	
			4
F	5	95	

The table shows Tania's utility of wealth schedule, and the figure shows her utility of wealth curve. Utility increases as wealth increases, but the marginal utility of wealth diminishes.

FIGURE 20.2   Expected Utility

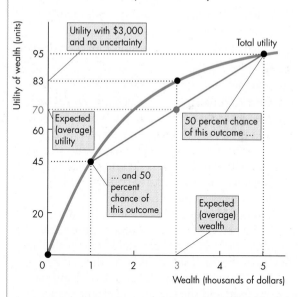

Tania has a 50 percent chance of having $5,000 of wealth and a total utility of 95 units. She also has a 50 percent chance of having $1,000 of wealth and a total utility of 45 units. Tania's expected wealth is $3,000 (the average of $5,000 and $1,000) and her expected utility is 70 units (the average of 95 and 45). With a wealth of $3,000 and no uncertainty, Tania's total utility is 83 units. For a given expected wealth, the greater the range of uncertainty, the smaller is expected utility.

myeconlab animation

myeconlab animation

Expected utility decreases if the risk of a poor outcome increases. For example, if Tania has a 20 percent chance of success (and an 80 percent chance of failure), her expected utility is 55 units—$(95 \times 0.2) + (45 \times 0.8) = 55$.

Notice how the range of uncertainty affects expected utility. Figure 20.2 shows that with $3,000 of wealth and no uncertainty, total utility is 83 units. But with the same expected wealth and Tania's uncertainty—a 50 percent chance of having $5,000 and a 50 percent chance of having $1,000—expected utility is only 70 units. Tania's uncertainty lowers her expected utility by 13 units.

Expected utility combines expected wealth and risk into a single index.

Making a Choice with Uncertainty

Faced with uncertainty, a person chooses the action that maximizes expected utility. To select the job that gives her the maximum expected utility, Tania must:

1. Calculate the expected utility from the risky telemarketing job
2. Calculate the expected utility from the safe painting job
3. Compare the two expected utilities

Figure 20.3 illustrates the calculations. You've just seen that the risky telemarketing job gives Tania an expected utility of 70 units. The safe painting job also gives Tania a utility of 70. That is, the total utility of $2,000 with no risk is 70 units. So with either job, Tania has an expected utility of 70 units. She is indifferent between these two jobs.

If Tania had only a 20 percent chance of success and an 80 percent chance of failure in the telemarketing job, her expected utility would be 55 (calculated above). In this case, she would take the painting job and get 70 units of utility. But if the probabilities were reversed and she had an 80 percent chance of success and only a 20 percent chance of failure in the telemarketing job, her expected utility would be 85 units—$(95 \times 0.8) + (45 \times 0.2) = 85$. In this case, she would take the risky telemarketing job.

We can calculate the cost of risk by comparing the expected wealth in a given risky situation with the wealth that gives the same total utility but no risk. Using this principle, we can find Tania's cost of bearing the risk that arises from the telemarketing job. That cost, highlighted in Figure 20.3, is $1,000.

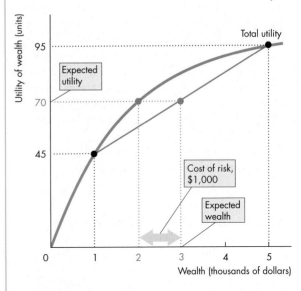

FIGURE 20.3   Choice Under Uncertainty

With a 50 percent chance of having $5,000 of wealth and a 50 percent chance of having $1,000 of wealth, Tania's expected wealth is $3,000 and her expected utility is 70 units. Tania would have the same 70 units of total utility with wealth of $2,000 and no risk, so Tania's cost of bearing this risk is $1,000. Tania is indifferent between the job that pays $2,000 with no risk and the job that offers an equal chance of $5,000 and $1,000.

myeconlab animation

Review Quiz

1 What is the distinction between expected wealth and expected utility?
2 How does the concept of utility of wealth capture the idea that pain of loss exceeds the pleasure of gain?
3 What do people try to achieve when they make a decision under uncertainty?
4 How is the cost of the risk calculated when making a decision with an uncertain outcome.

myeconlab Work Study Plan 20.1 and get instant feedback.

You've now seen how a person makes a risky decision. In the next section, we'll see how markets enable people to reduce the risks they face.

◆ Buying and Selling Risk

You've seen at many points in your study of markets how both buyers and sellers gain from trade. Buyers gain because they value what they buy more highly than the price they must pay—they receive a *consumer surplus*. And sellers gain because they face costs that are less than the price at which they can sell—they receive a *producer surplus*.

Just as buyers and sellers gain from trading goods and services, so they can also gain by trading risk. But risk is a bad, not a good. The good that is traded is risk avoidance. A buyer of risk avoidance can gain because the value of avoiding risk is greater than the price that must be paid to someone else to get them to bear the risk. The seller of risk avoidance faces a lower cost of risk than the price that people are willing to pay to avoid the risk.

We're going to put some flesh on the bare bones of this brief account of how people can gain from trading risk by looking at insurance markets.

Insurance Markets

Insurance plays a huge role in our economic lives. We'll explain

- How insurance reduces risk
- Why people buy insurance
- How insurance companies earn a profit

How Insurance Reduces Risk Insurance reduces the risk that people face by sharing or pooling the risks. When people buy insurance against the risk of an unwanted event, they pay an insurance company a *premium*. If the unwanted event occurs, the insurance company pays out the amount of the insured loss.

Think about auto collision insurance. The probability that any one person will have a serious auto accident is small. But a person who does have an auto accident incurs a large loss. For a large population, the probability of one person having an accident is the proportion of the population that has an accident. But this proportion is known, so the probability of an accident occurring and the total cost of accidents can be predicted. An insurance company can pool the risks of a large population and enable everyone to share the costs. It does so by collecting premiums from everyone and paying out benefits to those who suffer a loss. An insurance company that remains in business collects at least as much in premiums as it pays out in benefits.

Why People Buy Insurance People buy insurance and insurance companies earn a profit by selling insurance because people are risk averse. To see why people buy insurance and why it is profitable, let's consider an example. Dan owns a car worth $10,000, and that is his only wealth. There is a 10 percent chance that Dan will have a serious accident that makes his car worth nothing. So there is a 90 percent chance that Dan's wealth will remain at $10,000 and a 10 percent chance that his wealth will be zero. Dan's expected wealth is $9,000—($10,000 × 0.9) + ($0 × 0.1).

Dan is risk averse (just like Tania in the previous example). Because Dan is risk averse, he will be better off by buying insurance to avoid the risk that he faces, if the insurance premium isn't too high.

Without knowing some details about just how risk averse Dan is, we don't know the most that he would be willing to pay to avoid this risk. But we do know that he would pay more than $1,000. If Dan did pay $1,000 to avoid the risk, he would have $9,000 of wealth and face no uncertainty about his wealth. If he does not have an accident, his wealth is the $10,000 value of his car minus the $1,000 he pays the insurance company. If he does lose his car, the insurance company pays him $10,000, so he still has $9,000. Being risk averse, Dan's expected utility from $9,000 with no risk is greater than his expected utility from an expected $9,000 with risk. So Dan would be willing to pay more than $1,000 to avoid this risk.

How Insurance Companies Earn a Profit For the insurance company, $1,000 is the minimum amount at which it would be willing to insure Dan and other people like him. With say 50,000 customers all like Dan, 5,000 customers (50,000 × 0.1) lose their cars and 45,000 don't. Premiums of $1,000 give the insurance company a total revenue of $50,000,000. With 5,000 claims of $10,000, the insurance company pays out $50,000,000. So a premium of $1,000 enables the insurance company to break even (make zero economic profit) on this business.

But Dan (and everyone else) is willing to pay more than $1,000, so insurance is a profitable business and there is a gain from trading risk.

The gain from trading risk is shared by Dan (and the other people who buy insurance) and the insurance company. The exact share of the gain depends on the state of competition in the market for insurance.

If the insurance market is a monopoly, the insurance company can take all the gains from trading risk. But if the insurance market is competitive, economic profit will induce entry and profits will be competed away. In this case, Dan (and the other buyers of insurance) get the gain.

A Graphical Analysis of Insurance

We can illustrate the gains from insurance by using a graph of Dan's utility of wealth curve. We begin, in Figure 20.4, with the situation if Dan doesn't buy insurance and decides to bear the risk he faces.

Risk-Taking Without Insurance With no accident, Dan's wealth is $10,000 and his total utility is 100 units. If Dan has an accident, his car is worthless, he has no wealth and no utility. Because the chance of an accident is 10 percent (or 0.1), the chance of not having an accident is 90 percent (or 0.9). Dan's expected wealth is $9,000—($10,000 × 0.9) + ($0 × 0.1)—and his expected utility is 90 units—(100 × 0.9) + (0 × 0.1).

You've just seen that without insurance, Dan gets 90 units of utility. But Dan also gets 90 units of utility if he faces no uncertainty with a smaller amount of wealth.

We're now going to see how much Dan will pay to avoid uncertainty.

The Value and Cost of Insurance Figure 20.5 shows the situation when Dan buys insurance. You can see that for Dan, having $7,000 with no risk is just as good as facing a 90 percent chance of having $10,000 and a 10 percent chance of having no wealth. So if Dan pays $3,000 for insurance, he has $7,000 of wealth, faces no uncertainty, and gets 90 units of utility. The amount of $3,000 is the maximum that Dan is willing to pay for insurance. It is the value of insurance to Dan.

Figure 20.5 also shows the cost of insurance. With a large number of customers each of whom has a 10 percent chance of making a $10,000 claim for the loss of a vehicle, the insurance company can provide insurance at a cost of $1,000 (10 percent of

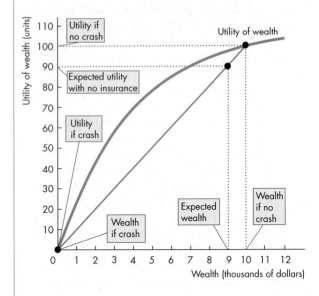

FIGURE 20.4 Taking a Risk Without Insurance

Dan's wealth (the value of his car) is $10,000, which gives him 100 units of utility.

With no insurance, if Dan has a crash, he has no wealth and no utility.

With a 10 percent chance of a crash, Dan's expected wealth is $9,000 and his expected utility is 90 units.

$10,000). If Dan pays only $1,000 for insurance, his wealth is $9,000 (the $10,000 value of his car minus the $1,000 he pays for insurance), and his utility from $9,000 of wealth with no uncertainty is about 98 units.

Gains From Trade Because Dan is willing to pay up to $3,000 for insurance that costs the insurance company $1,000, there is a gain from trading risk of $2,000 per insured person. How the gains are shared depends on the nature of the market. If the insurance market is competitive, entry will increase supply and lower the price to $1,000 (plus normal profit and operating costs). Dan (and the other buyers of insurance) enjoy a consumer surplus. If the insurance market is a monopoly, the insurance company takes the $2,000 per insured person as economic profit.

FIGURE 20.5   The Gains from Insurance

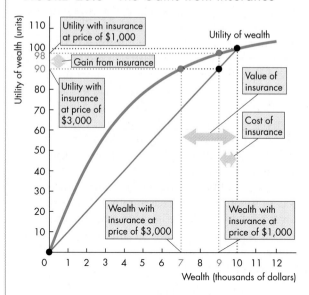

If Dan pays $3,000 for insurance, his wealth is $7,000 and his utility is 90 units—the same utility as with no insurance—so $3,000 is the value of insurance for Dan.
If Dan pays $1,000 for insurance, which is the insurance company's cost of providing insurance, his wealth is $9,000 and his utility is about 98 units.
Dan and the insurance company share the gain from insurance.

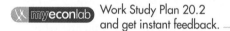 animation

Risk That Can't Be Insured

The gains from auto collision insurance that we've studied here apply to all types of insurance. Examples are property and casualty insurance, life insurance, and health care insurance. One person's risks associated with driving, life, and health are independent of other person's. That's why insurance is possible. The risks are spread across a population.

But not all risks can be insured. To be insurable, risks must be independent. If an event causes everyone to be a loser, it isn't possible to spread and pool the risks. For example, flood insurance is often not available for people who live on a floodplain because if one person incurs a loss, most likely all do.

Also, to be insurable, a risky event must be observable to both the buyer and seller of insurance. But much of the uncertainty that we face arises

Insurance in the United States
A Big Budget Item

We spend 7 percent of our income on private insurance. That's more than we spend on cars or food. In addition, we buy Social Security and unemployment insurance through our taxes. The figure shows the relative sizes of the four main types of private insurance. More than 80 percent of Americans have life insurance, and 85 percent have health insurance. The United States is the only rich country that does not have compulsory health insurance.

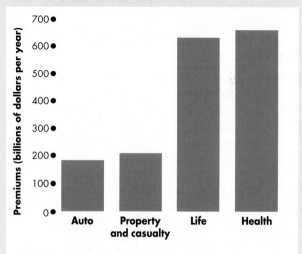

The U.S. Insurance Industry

Source of data: U.S. Bureau of the Census, *Statistical Abstract of the United States 2007*, Tables 121, 1206, and 1207.

Review Quiz

1 How does insurance reduce risk?
2 How do we determine the value (willingness to pay) for insurance?
3 How can an insurance company offer people a deal worth taking? Why do both the buyers and the sellers of insurance gain?
4 What kinds of risks can't be insured?

myeconlab   Work Study Plan 20.2 and get instant feedback.

because we know less (or more) than others with whom we do business. In the next section, we look at the way markets cope when buyers and sellers have different information.

Private Information

In all the markets that you've studied so far, the buyers and the sellers are well informed about the good, service, or factor of production being traded. But in some markets, either the buyers or the sellers—usually the sellers—are better informed about the value of the item being traded than the person on the other side of the market. Information about the value of the item being traded that is possessed by only buyers or sellers is called **private information**. And a market in which the buyers or sellers have private information has **asymmetric information**.

Asymmetric Information: Examples and Problems

Asymmetric information affects many of your own economic transactions. One example is your knowledge about your driving skills and temperament. You know much more than your auto insurance company does about how carefully and defensively you drive—about your personal risk of having an accident that would cause the insurance company to pay a claim. Another example is your knowledge about your work effort. You know more than your employer about how hard you are willing to work. Yet another example is your knowledge about the quality of your car. You know whether it's a lemon, but the person to whom you are about to sell it does not know and can't find out until after he or she has bought it.

Asymmetric information creates two problems:

- Adverse selection
- Moral hazard

Adverse Selection **Adverse selection** is the tendency for people to *enter into agreements* in which they can use their private information to their own advantage and to the disadvantage of the uninformed party.

For example, if Jackie offers her salespeople a fixed wage, she will attract lazy salespeople. Hardworking salespeople will prefer not to work for Jackie because they can earn more by working for someone who pays by results. The fixed-wage contract adversely selects those with private information (knowledge about their work habits) who can use that knowledge to their own advantage and to the disadvantage of the other party.

Moral Hazard **Moral hazard** is the tendency for people with private information, *after entering into an agreement*, to use that information for their own benefit and at the cost of the less-informed party. For example, Jackie hires Mitch as a salesperson and pays him a fixed wage regardless of how much he sells. Mitch faces a moral hazard. He has an incentive to put in the least possible effort, benefiting himself and lowering Jackie's profits. For this reason, salespeople are usually paid by a formula that makes their income higher, the greater is the volume (or value) of their sales.

A variety of devices have evolved that enable markets to function in the face of moral hazard and adverse selection. We've just seen one, the use of incentive payments for salespeople. We're going to look at how three markets cope with adverse selection and moral hazard. They are

- The market for used cars
- The market for loans
- The market for insurance

The Market for Used Cars

When a person buys a car, it might turn out to be a lemon. If the car is a lemon, it is worth less to the buyer than if it has no defects. Does the used car market have two prices reflecting these two values—a low price for lemons and a higher price for cars without defects? It turns out that it does. But it needs some help to do so and to overcome what is called the **lemon problem**—the problem that in a market in which it is not possible to distinguish reliable products from lemons, there are too many lemons and too few reliable products traded.

To see how the used car market overcomes the lemon problem, we'll first look at a used car market that has a lemon problem.

The Lemon Problem in a Used Car Market

To explain the lemon problem as clearly as possible, we'll assume that there are only two kinds of cars: defective cars—lemons—and cars without defects that we'll call good cars. Whether or not a car is a lemon is private information that is available only to the current owner. The buyer of a used car can't tell whether he is buying a lemon until after he has bought the car and learned as much about it as its current owner knows.

Some people with low incomes and the time and ability to fix cars are willing to buy lemons as long as they know what they're buying and pay an appropriately low price. Suppose that a lemon is worth $5,000 to a buyer. More people want to buy a good car and we'll assume that a good car is worth $25,000 to a buyer.

But the buyer can't tell the difference between a lemon and a good car. Only the seller has this information. And telling the buyer that a car is not a lemon does not help. The seller has no incentive to tell the truth.

So the most that the buyer knows is the probability of buying a lemon. If half of the used cars sold turn out to be lemons, the buyer know that he has a 50 percent chance of getting a good car and a 50 percent chance of getting a lemon.

The price that a buyer is willing to pay for a car of unknown quality is more than the value of a lemon because the car might be a good one. But the price is less than the value of a good car because it might turn out to be a lemon.

Now think about the sellers of used cars, who know the quality of their cars. Someone who owns a good car is going to be offered a price that is less than the value of that car to the buyer. Many owners will be reluctant to sell for such a low price. So the quan-

tity of good used cars supplied will not be as large as it would be if people paid the price they are worth.

In contrast, someone who owns a lemon is going to be offered a price that is greater than the value of that car to the buyer. So owners of lemons will be eager to sell and the quantity of lemons supplied will be greater than it would be if people paid the price that a lemon is worth.

Figure 20.6 illustrates the used car market that we've just described. Part (a) shows the demand for used cars, D, and the supply of used cars, S. Equilibrium occurs at a price of $10,000 per car with 400 cars traded each month.

Some cars are good ones and some are lemons, but buyers can't tell the difference until it is too late to influence their decision to buy. But buyers do know what a good car and a lemon are worth to them, and sellers know the quality of the cars they are offering for sale. Figure 20.6(b) shows the demand curve for good cars, D_G, and the supply curve of good cars, S_G. Figure 20.6(c) shows the demand curve for lemons, D_L, and the supply curve of lemons, S_L.

At the market price of $10,000, owners of good cars supply 200 cars a month for sale. Owners of lemons also supply 200 cars a month for sale. The used car market is inefficient because there are too

FIGURE 20.6 The Lemon Problem

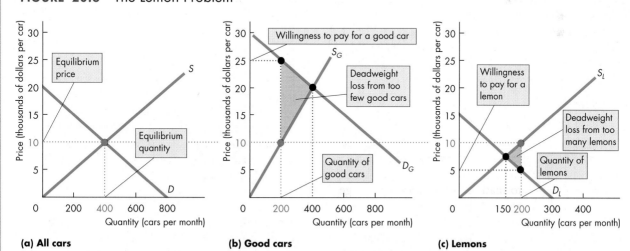

(a) All cars   **(b) Good cars**   **(c) Lemons**

Buyers can't tell a good used car from a lemon. Demand and supply determine the price and quantity of used cars traded in part (a). In part (b), D_G is the demand for good used cars and S_G is the supply. At the market price, too few

good cars are available, which brings a deadweight loss. In part (c), D_L is the demand for lemons and S_L is the supply. At the market price, too many lemons are available, which brings a deadweight loss.

 animation

many lemons and not enough good cars. Figure 20.6 makes this inefficiency clear by using the concept of deadweight loss (see Chapter 5, pp. 115–116).

At the quantity of good cars supplied, buyers are willing to pay $25,000 for a good car. They are willing to pay more than a good car is worth to its current owner for all good cars up to 400 cars a month. The gray triangle shows the deadweight loss that results from there being too few good used cars.

At the quantity of lemons supplied, buyers are willing to pay $5,000 for a lemon. They are willing to pay less than a lemon is worth to its current owner for all lemons above 150 cars a month. The gray triangle shows the deadweight loss that results from there being too many lemons.

You can see *adverse selection* in this used car market because there is a greater incentive to offer a lemon for sale. You can also see *moral hazard* because the owner of a lemon has little incentive to take good care of the car, so it is likely to become an even worse lemon. The market for used cars is not working well. Too many lemons and too few good used cars are traded.

A Used Car Market with Dealers' Warranties

How can used car dealers convince buyers that a car isn't a lemon? The answer is by giving a guarantee in the form of a warranty. By providing warranties only on good cars, dealers signal which cars are good ones and which are lemons.

Signaling occurs when an informed person takes actions that send information to uninformed persons. The grades and degrees that a university awards students are signals. They inform potential (uninformed) employers about the ability of the people they are considering hiring.

In the market for used cars, dealers send signals by giving warranties on the used cars they offer for sale. The message in the signal is that the dealer agrees to pay the costs of repairing the car if it turns out to have a defect.

Buyers believe the signal because the cost of sending a false signal is high. A dealer who gives a warranty on a lemon ends up bearing a high cost of repairs—and gains a bad reputation. A dealer who gives a warranty only on good cars has no repair costs and a reputation that gets better and better. It pays

FIGURE 20.7   Warranties Make the Used Car Market Efficient

(a) Good cars

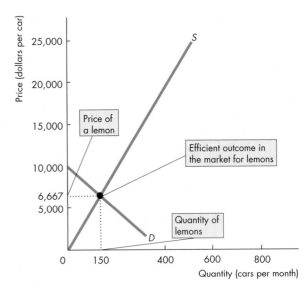

(b) Lemons

With dealers' warranties as signals, the equilibrium price of a good used car is $20,000 and 400 cars are traded. The market for good used cars is efficient. Because the signal

enables buyers to spot a lemon, the price of a lemon is $6,667 and 150 lemons are traded. The market for lemons is efficient.

dealers to send an accurate signal, and it is rational for buyers to believe the signal.

So a car with a warranty is a good car; a car without a warranty is a lemon. Warranties solve the lemon problem and enable the used car market to function efficiently with two prices: one for lemons and one for good cars.

Figure 20.7 illustrates this outcome. In part (a) the demand for and supply of good cars determine the price of a good car. In part (b), the demand for and supply of lemons determine the price of a lemon. Both markets are efficient.

Pooling Equilibrium and Separating Equilibrium

You've seen two outcomes in the market for used cars. Without warranties, there is only one message visible to the buyer: All cars look the same. So there is one price regardless of whether the car is a good car or a lemon. We call the equilibrium in a market when only one message is available and an uninformed person cannot determine quality a **pooling equilibrium**.

But in a used-car market with warranties, there are two messages. Good cars have warranties and lemons don't. So there are two car prices for the two types of cars. We call the equilibrium in a market when signaling provides full information to a previously uninformed person a **separating equilibrium**.

The Market for Loans

When you buy a tank of gasoline and swipe your credit card, you are taking a loan from the bank that issued your card. You demand and your bank supplies a loan. Have you noticed the interest rate on an unpaid credit card balance? In 2007, it ranged between 7 percent a year and 36 percent a year. Why are these interest rates so high? And why is there such a huge range?

The answer is that when banks make loans, they face the risk that the loan will not be repaid. The risk that a borrower, also known as a creditor, might not repay a loan is called **credit risk** or **default risk**. For credit card borrowing, the credit risk is high and it varies among borrowers. The highest-risk borrowers pay the highest interest rate.

Interest rates and the price of credit risk are determined in the market for loans. The lower the interest rate, the greater is the quantity of loans demanded and for a given level of credit risk, the higher the interest rate, the greater is the quantity of loans supplied. Demand and supply determine the interest rate and the price of credit risk.

If lenders were unable to charge different interest rates to reflect different degrees of credit risk, there would be a pooling equilibrium and an inefficient loans market.

Inefficient Pooling Equilibrium   To see why a pooling equilibrium would be inefficient, suppose that banks can't identify the individual credit risk of their borrowers: they have no way of knowing how likely it is that a given loan will be repaid. In this situation, every borrower pays the same interest rate and the market is in a pooling equilibrium.

If all borrowers pay the same interest rate, the market for loans has the same problem as the used car market. Low-risk customers borrow less than they would if they were offered the low interest rate appropriate for their low credit risk. High-risk customers borrow more than they would if they faced the high interest rate appropriate for their high credit risk. So banks face an *adverse selection* problem. Too many borrowers are high risk and too few are low risk.

Signaling and Screening in the Market for Loans
Lenders don't know how likely it is that a given loan will be repaid, but the borrower does know. Low-risk borrowers have an incentive to signal their risk by providing lenders with relevant information. Signals might include information about the length of time a person has been in the current job or has lived at the current address, home ownership, marital status, age, and business record.

High-risk borrowers might be identified simply as those who have failed to signal low risk. These borrowers have an incentive to mislead lenders; and lenders have an incentive to induce high-risk borrowers to reveal their risk level. Inducing an informed party to reveal private information is called **screening**.

By not lending to people who refuse to reveal relevant information, banks are able to screen as well as receive signals that help them to separate their borrowers into a number of credit-risk categories. If lenders succeed, the market for loans comes to a separating equilibrium with a high interest rate for high-risk borrowers and a low interest rate for low-risk borrowers. Signaling and screening in the market for loans works like warranties in the used car market and avoids the deadweight loss of a pooling equilibrium.

The Sub-Prime Credit Crisis
Too Much Risk-Taking

A sub-prime mortgage is a loan to a home buyer who has a high risk of default. Figure 1 shows that between 2001 and 2005, the price of risk was low. Figure 2 shows why: The supply of credit, S_0, was large and so was the amount of risk taking. After 2005, the supply of credit decreased to S_1. The price of risk jumped and, faced with a higher interest rate, many sub-prime borrowers defaulted. Defaults in the sub-prime mortgage market spread to other markets that supplied the funds that financed mortgages.

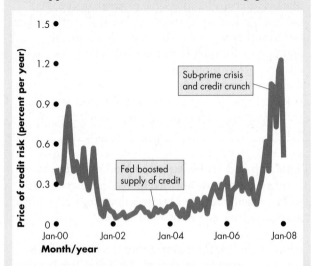

Figure 1 The Price of Commercial Credit Risk

Figure 2 The Market for Risky Loans

The Market for Insurance

People who buy insurance face moral hazard, and insurance companies face adverse selection. Moral hazard arises because a person with insurance against a loss has less incentive than an uninsured person to avoid the loss. For example, a business with fire insurance has less incentive to install a fire alarm or sprinkler system than a business with no fire insurance does. Adverse selection arises because people who create greater risks are more likely to buy insurance. For example, a person with a family history of serious illness is more likely to buy health insurance than is a person with a family history of good health. Insurance companies have an incentive to find ways around the moral hazard and adverse selection problems. By doing so, they can lower premiums for low-risk people and raise premiums for high-risk people. One way in which auto insurance companies separate high-risk and low-risk customers is with a "no-claim" bonus. A driver accumulates a no-claim bonus by driving safely and avoiding accidents. The greater the bonus, the greater is the incentive to drive carefully. Insurance companies also use a deductible. A deductible is the amount of a loss that the insured person agrees to bear. The premium is smaller, the larger is the deductible, and the decrease in the premium is more than proportionate to the increase in the deductible. By offering insurance with full coverage—no deductible—on terms that are attractive only to the high-risk people and by offering coverage with a deductible on more favorable terms that are attractive to low-risk people, insurance companies can do profitable business with everyone. High-risk people choose policies with a low deductible and a high premium; low-risk people choose policies with a high deductible and a low premium.

Review Quiz

1 How does private information create adverse selection and moral hazard?
2 How do markets for cars use warranties to cope with private information?
3 How do markets for loans use signaling and screening to cope with private information?
4 How do markets for insurance use no-claim bonuses to cope with private information?

 Work Study Plan 20.3 and get instant feedback.

Uncertainty, Information, and the Invisible Hand

A recurring theme throughout microeconomics is the big question: When do choices made in the pursuit of *self-interest* also promote the *social interest?* When does the invisible hand work well and when does it fail us? You've learned about the concept of efficiency, a major component of what we mean by the social interest. And you've seen that while competitive markets generally do a good job in helping to achieve efficiency, impediments such as monopoly and the absence of well-defined property rights can prevent the attainment of an efficient use of resources.

How do uncertainty and incomplete information affect the ability of self-interested choices to lead to a social interest outcome? Are these features of economic life another reason why markets fail and why some type of government intervention is required to achieve efficiency?

These are hard questions, and there are no definitive answers. But there are some useful things that we can say about the effects of uncertainty and a lack of complete information on the efficiency of resource use. We'll begin our brief review of this issue by thinking about information as just another good.

Information as a Good

More information is generally useful, and less uncertainty about the future is generally useful. Think about information as one of the goods that we want more of.

The most basic lesson about efficiency that you learned in Chapter 2 can be applied to information. Along our production possibilities frontier, we face a tradeoff between information and all other goods and services. Information, like everything else, can be produced at an increasing opportunity cost—an increasing marginal cost. For example, we could get more accurate weather forecasts, but only at increasing marginal cost, as we increased the amount of information that we gather from the atmosphere and the amount of money that we spend on supercomputers to process the data.

The principle of decreasing marginal benefit also applies to information. More information is valuable, but the more you know, the less you value another increment of information. For example, knowing that it will rain tomorrow is valuable information.

Knowing the amount of rain to within an inch is even more useful. But knowing the amount of rain to within a millimeter probably isn't worth much more.

Because the marginal cost of information is increasing and the marginal benefit is decreasing, there is an efficient amount of information. It would be inefficient to be overinformed.

In principle, competitive markets in information might deliver this efficient quantity. Whether they actually do so is hard to determine.

Monopoly in Markets that Cope with Uncertainty

There are probably large economies of scale in providing services that cope with uncertainty and incomplete information. The insurance industry, for example, is highly concentrated. Where monopoly elements exist, exactly the same inefficiency issues arise as occur in markets where uncertainty and incomplete information are not big issues. So it is likely that in some information markets, including insurance markets, there is underproduction arising from the attempt to maximize monopoly profit.

Review Quiz

1 Thinking about information as a good, what determines the information that people are willing to pay for?
2 Why is it inefficient to be overinformed?
3 Why are some of the markets that provide information likely to be dominated by monopolies?

 Work Study Plan 20.4 and get instant feedback.

You've seen how people make decisions when faced with uncertainty and how markets work when there is asymmetric information. *Reading Between the Lines* on pages 476–477 looks at the way markets in human capital and labor use grades as signals that sort students by ability so that employers can hire the type of labor they seek. You'll see why grade deflation can be efficient and grade inflation is inefficient. Discriminating grades are in the social interest and in the self-interest of universities and students.

Grades as Signals

Princeton Leads in Grade Deflation

http://www.usatoday.com
28 March, 2007

Jennifer Mickel, a Princeton University senior, can't help but look around a class of 10 students and think, "Just three of us can get A's."

Since Princeton took the lead among Ivy League schools to formally adopt a grade-deflation policy three years ago—limiting A's to an average 35% across departments—students say the pressure to score the scarcer A has intensified. Students say they now eye competitive classmates warily and shy away from classes perceived as difficult. ...

There is no quota in individual courses, despite what students think, says Dean of the College Nancy Malkiel. ...

Though a typical Princeton overachiever might blanch at the mere mention of a B, the university is sticking by its policy, Malkiel says. Students' employment and graduate school placements actually have improved the past two years, she says.

Grade inflation, well documented at many schools, is most pronounced in the Ivy League, according to an American Academy of Arts and Sciences 2002 study. For example, in 1966, 22% of all grades given to Harvard undergraduates were A's. That grew to 46% in 1996, the study found.

Princeton's grade spike became alarming in the last decade, Malkiel says. The policy, supported by a faculty vote, returns grades to early 1990s levels. "By grading in a more discriminating fashion, faculty members are able to give clearer signals about whether a student's work is inadequate, ordinary, good or excellent," Malkiel says. ...

Princeton undergrads may take heart from Merrill Lynch's director of campus recruiting, Connie Thanasoulis. "I'm not in the least bit concerned about the chances for those at Princeton in comparison with any other Ivy League student," she says.

"I have never seen the quality of students that I've seen this year," she says. "I'm impressed."

Essence of the Story

- Princeton was the first Ivy League school to formally adopt a grade-deflation policy.

- The school limits A's to an average 35 percent across departments but has no quota in individual courses.

- Graduate school placements have improved since the policy was adopted.

- At Harvard, A's increased from 22 percent in 1966 to 46 percent in 1996.

- Princeton's grade inflation became alarming in the 1990s.

- More discriminating grades give clearer signals about students says Dean Malkiel.

- Merrill Lynch's director of campus recruiting is impressed with the high quality of Princeton students.

Economic Analysis

- Accurate grades provide valuable information to students and potential employers about a student's ability.

- Princeton University wants to provide accurate information and avoid grade inflation—awarding a high grade to most students—because this practice fails to provide information about a student's true ability.

- The labor market for new college graduates works badly with grade inflation and works well with accurate grading.

- Figure 1 shows a labor market for new college graduates when there is grade inflation.

- Students with high ability are not distinguished from other students, and the supply curve represents the supply of students of all ability levels.

- The demand curve shows the employers' willingness to hire new workers without knowledge of their true ability.

- Students get hired for a low wage rate. Eventually, they get sorted by ability as employers discover the true ability of their workers from on-the-job performance.

- Figures 2 and 3 show the outcome with accurate grading.

- In Fig. 2, students with high grades get high-wage jobs and in Fig. 3, students with low grades get low-wage jobs.

- The outcomes in Figs. 2 and 3 that arise immediately with accurate grading occur eventually with grade inflation as information about ability accumulates.

- But the cost to the student and the employer of discovering true ability is greater with grade inflation than with accurate grading.

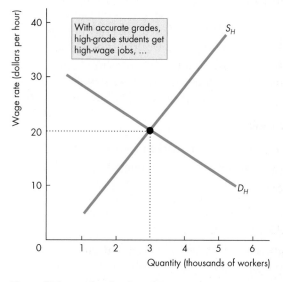

Figure 2 The market for A students

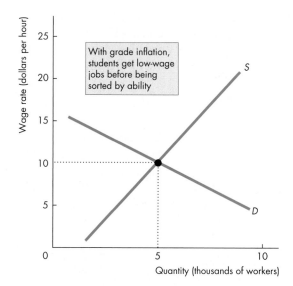

Figure 1 Market with grade inflation

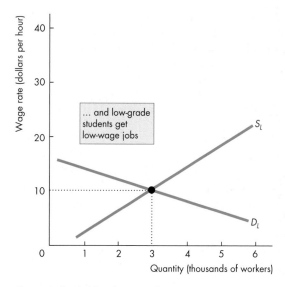

Figure 3 The market for D students

SUMMARY

Key Points

Decisions in the Face of Uncertainty (pp. 464–466)

- To make a rational choice under uncertainty, people choose the action that maximizes the expected utility of wealth.
- A decreasing marginal utility of wealth makes people risk averse. A sure outcome with a given expected wealth is preferred to a risky outcome with the same expected wealth—risk is costly.
- The cost of risk is found by comparing the expected wealth in a given risky situation with the wealth that gives the same utility but with no risk.

Buying and Selling Risk (pp. 467–469)

- People trade risk in markets for insurance.
- By pooling risks, insurance companies can reduce the risks people face (from insured activities) at a lower cost than the value placed on the lower risk.

Private Information (pp. 470–474)

- Asymmetric information creates an adverse selection and a moral hazard problem.

- When it is not possible to distinguish good-quality products from lemons, too many lemons and too few good-quality products are traded in a pooling equilibrium.
- Signaling can overcome the lemon problem.
- In the market for used cars, warranties signal good cars and enable an efficient separating equilibrium.
- Private information about credit risk is overcome by using signals and screening based on personal characteristics.
- Private information about risk in insurance markets is overcome by using the no-claim bonus and deductibles.

Uncertainty, Information, and the Invisible Hand (p. 475)

- Less uncertainty and more information can be viewed as a good that has increasing marginal cost and decreasing marginal benefit.
- Competitive information markets might be efficient, but economies of scale might bring inefficient underproduction of information and insurance.

Key Figures

Key Terms

PROBLEMS and APPLICATIONS

myeconlab Work problems 1–10 in Chapter 20 Study Plan and get instant feedback.
Work problems 11–19 as Homework, a Quiz, or a Test if assigned by your instructor.

1. The figure shows Lee's utility of wealth curve.

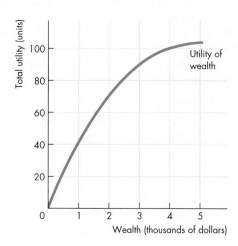

Lee is offered a job as a salesperson in which there is a 50 percent chance that she will make $4,000 a month and a 50 percent chance that she will make nothing.

a. What is Lee's expected income from taking this job?

b. What is Lee's expected utility from taking this job?

c. How much would another firm have to offer Lee with certainty to persuade her not to take the risky sales job?

d. What is Lee's cost of risk?

2. Lee in problem 1 has built a small weekend shack on a steep, unstable hillside. She spent all her wealth, which is $5,000, on this project. There is a 75 percent chance that the house will be washed down the hill and be worthless. How much is Lee willing to pay for an insurance policy that pays her $5,000 if the house is washed away?

3. Zaneb is a high-school teacher and is well known in her community for her honesty and integrity. She is shopping for a used car and plans to borrow the money from her local bank to pay for the car.

a. Does Zaneb create any moral hazard or ad-

verse selection problems either for the bank or the car dealer? Explain your answer.

b. Do either the bank or the car dealer create any moral hazard or adverse selection problems for Zaneb? Explain your answer.

c. What arrangements is Zaneb likely to encounter that are designed to help cope with the moral hazard and adverse selection problems she encounters in her car buying and bank loan transactions?

4. Suppose that there are three national football leagues: Time League, Goal Difference League, and Bonus for Win League. The leagues are of equal quality, but the players are paid differently. In the Time League, they are paid by the hour for time spent practicing and time spent playing. In the Goal Difference league, they are paid an amount that depends on the points that the team scores minus the points scored against it. In the Bonus for Win League, the players are paid one wage for a loss, a higher wage for a tie, and the highest wage of all for a win.

a. Briefly describe the predicted differences in the quality of the games played by each of the leagues.

b. Which league is the most attractive to players?

c. Which league will generate the largest profits?

5. **Phillies Hamstrung by Burrell's No-Trade Clause**

Phillies general manager Pat Gillick, … who previously built winners in Toronto, Baltimore and Seattle, is no fan of blanket no-trade clauses. Gillick is so averse to giving out complete no-trade provisions that he says it could be a "deal breaker" when the Phillies negotiate with big free agents this winter.

ESPN.com, November 8, 2006

a. Provide an example of private information that a baseball player who wants a no-trade clause possesses.

b. Does a baseball player with a no-trade clause present a moral hazard to his baseball team?

c. Does a baseball player with a no-trade clause present adverse selection problems to his baseball team?

6. **Larry Page on How to Change the World**

   As president of Google, Larry Page has pushed his people to take risks that have led to hot new applications like Gmail and Google Maps. … But he also sees a world of timidity; not enough people, he worries, are willing to place the big bets that could make a difference in meeting humanity's biggest challenges. … "In our [Google's] first founders' letter in 2004, we talked about the risk profile with respect to doing new innovations. We said we would do some things that would have only a 10 percent chance of making $1 billion over the long term. But we don't put many people on those things; 90 percent work on everything else. So that's not a big risk. And if you look at where many of our new features come from, it's from these riskier investments. Even when we started Google, we thought, 'Oh, we might fail,' and we almost didn't do it. The reason we started is that Stanford said, 'You guys can come back and finish your Ph.D.s if you don't succeed.' Probably that one decision caused Google to be created."

   Fortune, May 12, 2008

   a. If much of Google's success has come from "riskier investments," then why doesn't Google dedicate all of their resources towards these riskier innovations?

   b. In spite of the many risks that Larry Page has taken with Google, what evidence does this article provide that he is risk averse?

7. **We All Pay for the Uninsured**

   When buying health care, most of us don't behave like regular consumers. Seven out of eight dollars we spend is somebody else's money, and we don't have very good information about doctors or hospitals. … At Aetna [a health insurance company], in 35 markets, you can go online and know what your physician will charge you before you see that physician. That's helpful for a routine service, but when it comes to, say, a serious cardiac condition, what you really want to know is whether this is a high-quality physician. … Important efforts are on the way, with the collaboration of physicians, to agree on quality standards. There's collaboration in the industry for all health plans to pool their data to create very rich data sets. So consumers could look at a set of performance indicators that physicians think are appropriate, and be able to judge how their physicians fare.

   Fortune, May 12, 2008

   a. Explain how the adverse selection problem applies to health care.

   b. How does the moral hazard problem apply to health insurance?

   c. What role can better information play in the health care market?

   d. Is it possible for there to be too much information in this market?

8. **Show Us Our Money**

   I have no clue what my colleagues make. I suspect some earn more than I do and others take home less. Like most American workers, I consider my salary my own damn business. Turns out that could be a huge mistake. … What if employers made all employee salaries known? If you think about it, who is served by all the secrecy? Not you. It may irk you to learn that the junior analyst in the next cube really can afford his Bora Bora honeymoon—but that's all the more ammunition to gun for a raise.

   Time, May 12, 2008

   a. How might employers use their private information regarding worker wages to their own advantage and to the disadvantage of workers?

   b. How might adverse selection discourage firms from underpaying their workers?

   c. How might moral hazard discourage firms from offering workers a fixed wage?

   d. Explain why a worker might be willing to pay for the salary information of other workers.

9. You can't buy insurance against the risk of being sold a lemon. Why isn't there a market in insurance against being sold a lemon? How does the market provide a buyer with some protection against being sold a lemon? What are the main ways in which markets overcome the lemon problem?

10. Larry is a safe driver and Harry is a reckless driver. Each knows what type of driver he is, but no one else knows. As the owner of an automobile insurance company, what might you do to get Larry to signal that he is a safe driver so that you can offer him insurance at a lower premium than you offer to Harry?

11. Jimmy and Zenda have the following utility of wealth schedules:

Wealth	Jimmy's utility	Zenda's utility
0	0	0
100	200	512
200	300	640
300	350	672
400	375	678
500	387	681
600	393	683
700	396	684

   a. What are Jimmy's and Zenda's expected utilities from a bet that gives them a 50 percent chance of having a wealth of $600 and a 50 percent chance of having nothing?
   b. Calculate Jimmy's and Zenda's marginal utility of wealth schedules.
   c. Who is more risk averse, Jimmy or Zenda? How do you know?
   d. Who is more likely to buy insurance, Jimmy or Zenda?

12. Suppose that Jimmy and Zenda in problem 11 each have $400, and each sees a business opportunity that involves committing the entire $400 to the project. They reckon that the project could return $600 (a profit of $200) with a probability of 0.85 or $200 (a loss of $200) with a probability of 0.15. Who goes for the project and who hangs on to the initial $400?

13. **Genetic Nondiscrimination Bill Deserves a Double Helix of Applause**

   As our understanding of human genes has improved, so too has the ability to screen for various genetic traits. This has primarily been seen in tests that determine genetic predisposition to various afflictions. The Genetic Information Nondiscrimination Act … will prevent employers and health-insurance companies from discriminating based on a person's genetic information. … As one would expect, the motivation for such testing comes down to cost savings. … As a matter of economics, health-insurance companies seek out genetic information in their attempts to reduce a phenomenon known as adverse selection. … If genetic testing is permitted, those afflicted by—or prone to become afflicted by—certain diseases are essentially red-flagged as a result of their high-risk status. … True enough, health-insurance companies will once again be subjected to the same uncertainty that plagues insurance carriers of all sorts, imposing greater costs on the average client.

   The Daily Iowan, May 8, 2008

   a. How does adverse selection apply to the market for health insurance?
   b. How might genetic testing be used to reduce adverse selection?
   c. Explain the arguments that could be made in favor of and in opposition to The Genetic Information Nondiscrimination Act.

14. **Why We Worry About the Things We Shouldn't … and Ignore the Things We Should**

   We agonize over avian flu, which to date has killed precisely no one in the U.S., but have to be cajoled into getting vaccinated for the common flu, which contributes to the deaths of 36,000 Americans each year. We wring our hands over the mad cow pathogen that might be (but almost certainly isn't) in our hamburger and worry far less about the cholesterol that contributes to the heart disease that kills 700,000 of us annually. We pride ourselves on being the only species that understands the concept of risk, yet we have a confounding habit of worrying about mere possibilities while ignoring probabilities, building barricades against perceived dangers while leaving ourselves exposed to real ones. … 20% of all adults still smoke; nearly 20% of drivers and more than 30% of backseat passengers don't use seat belts; two-thirds of us are overweight or obese. We dash across the street against the light and build our homes in hurricane-prone areas—and when they're demolished by a storm, we rebuild in the same spot.

   Time, December 4, 2006

   a. Explain how "worrying about mere possibilities while ignoring probabilities" can result in people making decisions that not only fail to satisfy social interest, but also fail to satisfy self-interest.
   b. How can information be used to improve people's decision making?
   c. How does health insurance and flood insurance result in both a moral hazard and adverse selection?

d. How do insurance companies use premiums and deductibles in an attempt to resolve these problems?

15. **The Appeal of Gold**

It's 2008. Inflation is on the rise … energy prices are high, unemployment is going up, and political instability is an ongoing source of anxiety. Concurrently, survivalism is enjoying a revival, and after a horrendous performance during most of the '80s and '90s (dropping to around $264 an ounce in 2000), gold has once again shot up, reaching a record high of $1,030.80. … [T]he value of the dollar is a perpetual concern … while the dollar is unlikely to fall into total worthlessness, it's getting a bit more worthless day by day. … To guard against this … [people] buy gold on the assumption that gold is a store of value. Conventional wisdom holds that an ounce of gold can generally buy the same goods over time regardless of how expensive things get, making it a good hedge against inflation. … Investment advisors have long suggested that gold in small doses helps protect an overall portfolio. It tends to move independently of other asset classes, and unlike any type of security, it doesn't run the risk of going to absolute zero.

Fortune, April 17, 2008

a. Explain how the concept of risk aversion can be used to explain the dramatically increased price of gold.
b. Why don't investment advisors suggest that people convert all of their assets into gold?

16. **Are You Paid What You're Worth?**

In calendar year 2004, the profit-per-employee at U.S. companies was $68,655, up 55 percent from the year before. … Of course, not all employees contribute to a company's profits equally. … So how do you know if your pay adequately reflects your contributions to your employer's profits? In many instances, you don't. If there's one thing that can be said about being an employee, it's that you're at a huge disadvantage when it comes to compensation issues. … Your employer has far more and far better information than you do about how your salary and

bonus compare to others in your field, to others in your office, and relative to the company's profits in any given year. You can narrow the information gap a bit if you're willing to buy salary reports from compensation sources. …

At $200, though, a quick-call salary report from ERI [Economic Research Institute] is hardly cheap. But it includes specific salary and bonus information that is updated quarterly and is derived from a host of surveys that are filled out by companies' human resource departments. … The quick-call report will offer you compensation data for your position based on your years of experience, your industry and the place where your company is located.

CNN, April 3, 2006

a. Explain the role that asymmetric information can play in worker wages.
b. What adverse selection problem exists if a firm offers lower wages to existing workers?
c. What will determine how much a worker should actually pay for a detailed salary report?

17. After you have studied *Reading Between the Lines* on pp. 476–477, answer the following questions:
a. What information do accurate grades provide that grade inflation hides?
b. If grade inflation became widespread in high schools, colleges, and universities, what new arrangements do you predict would emerge to provide better information about student ability?
c. Do you think grade inflation is in anyone's self-interest? Explain who benefits and how they benefit from grade inflation.
d. How do you think grade inflation might be controlled?

18. Why do you think it is not possible to buy insurance against having to put up with a low-paying, miserable job? Explain why a market in insurance of this type would be valuable to workers buy unprofitable for an insurance provider and so would not work.

19. Explain to your softest-subject teacher why her/his grades are too generous.

UNDERSTANDING FACTOR MARKETS, INEQUALITY, AND UNCERTAINTY

For Whom?

During the past 35 years, the gap between the richest and the poorest in America has widened. But millions in Asia have been lifted from poverty and are now enjoying a high and rapidly rising standard of living. What are the forces that generate these trends? The answer to this question is the forces of demand and supply in factor markets. These forces determine wages, interest rates, rents, and the prices of natural resources. These forces also determine people's incomes.

In America, human capital and entrepreneurship are the most prized resources, and their incomes have grown most rapidly. In Asia, labor has seen its wage rates transformed. And in all regions rich in oil, incomes have risen on the back of high and fast-rising energy prices.

Many outstanding economists have advanced our understanding of factor markets and the role they play in helping to resolve the conflict between the demands of humans and the resources available. One of them is Thomas Robert Malthus.

Another is Harold Hotelling whose prediction of an ever rising price of nonrenewable natural resources implies an ever falling rate of their use and an intensifying search for substitutes.

Yet another is Julian Simon, who challenged both the Malthusian gloom and the Hotelling Principle. He believed that people are the "ultimate resource" and predicted that a rising population lessens the pressure on natural resources. A bigger population provides a larger number of resourceful people who can discover more efficient ways of using scarce resources.

Thomas Robert Malthus *(1766–1834), an English clergyman and economist, was an extremely influential social scientist. In his best-selling* Essay on the Principle of Population, *published in 1798, he predicted that population growth would outstrip food production and said that wars, famine, and disease were inevitable unless population growth was held in check by marrying at a late age and living a celibate life. (He married at 38 a wife of 27, marriage ages that he recommended for others.)*

Malthus had a profound influence on Charles Darwin, who got the key idea that led him to the theory of natural selection from the Essay on the Principle of Population. *But it was also Malthus's gloomy predictions that made economics the "dismal science."*

"The passion between the sexes has appeared in every age to be so nearly the same, that it may always be considered, in algebraic language, as a given quantity."

THOMAS ROBERT MALTHUS

An Essay on the Principle of Population

TALKING
WITH

David Card

David Card is Class of 1950 Professor of Economics and Director of the Center for Labor Economics at the University of California, Berkeley, and Faculty Research Associate at the National Bureau of Economic Research.

Born in Canada, Professor Card obtained his B.A. at Queen's University, Kingston, Ontario, in 1977 and his Ph.D. at Princeton University in 1983. He has received many honors, the most notable of which is the American Economic Association's John Bates Clark Prize, awarded to the best economist under 40.

Professor Card's research on labor markets and the effects of public policies on earnings, jobs, and the distribution of income has produced around 150 articles and several books. His most recent book (co-edited with Alan Auerbach and John Quigley) is *Poverty, the Distribution of Income, and Public Policy* (New York: Russell Sage Foundation, 2006). An earlier book (co-authored with Alan B. Krueger), *Myth and Measurement: The New Economics of the Minimum Wage* (Princeton, NJ: Princeton University Press, 1995), made a big splash and upset one of the most fundamental beliefs about the effects of minimum wages.

Michael Parkin talked with David Card about his work and the progress that economists have made in understanding how public policies can influence the distribution of income and economic well-being.

Professor Card, what attracted you to economics?

When I went to university I had no intention of studying economics: I was planning to be a physics major. I was helping a friend with her problem set and started reading the supply and demand section of the textbook. I was impressed with how well the model seemed to describe the paradox that a bumper crop can be bad for farmers. I read most of the book over the next few days. The next year, I signed up as an economics major.

Almost all your work is grounded in data. You are an empirical economist. How do you go about your work, where do your data come from, and how do you use data?

The data I use come from many different sources. I have collected my own data from surveys; transcribed data from historical sources and government publications; and used computerized data files based on records from Censuses and surveys in the United States, Canada, Britain, and other countries.

An economist can do three things with data. The first is to develop simple statistics on basic questions such as "What fraction of families live in poverty?" For this, one needs to understand how the data were collected and processed and how the questions were asked. For example, the poverty rate depends on how you define a "family." If a single mother and her child live with the mother's parents, the income of the mother and the grandparents is counted as "family income."

The second thing economists do with data is develop descriptive comparisons. For example, I have compared the wage differences between male and female workers. Again, the details are important. For example, the male-female wage differential is much bigger if you look at annual earnings than at earnings per hour, because women work fewer hours per year.

Once you've established some simple facts, you start to get ideas for possible explanations. You can also rule out a lot of other ideas.

The third and most difficult thing that empirical economists try to do is infer a causal relationship. In rare instances, we have a true experiment in which a random subgroup of volunteers is enrolled in a "treatment group" and the remainder become the "control group." The Self Sufficiency Program (SSP)—an experimental welfare reform demonstration in Canada—was conducted this way. Because of random assignment, we know that the treatment and control groups would have looked very similar in the absence of the treatment. Thus when we see a difference in behavior, such as the higher level of work activity by single parents in the treatment group of SSP, we can infer that the financial incentives of SSP caused people to work more.

Most often, we don't have an experiment. We see a group of people who are subject to some "treatment" (such as a higher minimum wage) and we try to construct a comparison group by finding some other group similar to the treatment group who tell us what the treatment group would have looked like in the absence of treatment. If we can't find a compelling comparison group, we have to be cautious.

In your book on the minimum wage with Alan Krueger, you reported that an increase in the minimum wage increased employment—the opposite of the conventional wisdom. How did you reach that conclusion?

We studied several instances where minimum wages were raised in one place but not in another. For example, when we found out that the New Jersey legislature had recently voted to raise the minimum wage, we set up a survey of fast-food restaurants in New Jersey and in nearby parts of Pennsylvania. We surveyed the stores a few months before the New Jersey minimum went up and then again one year later, after the minimum had been raised. The first-round survey found that conditions were very similar in the two states. In the second round, we found that although wages were now higher in New Jersey, employment was also slightly higher. It was very important to have the first-round survey to benchmark any differences that existed prior to the rise in

> The most difficult thing that empirical economists try to do is infer a causal relationship.

the minimum. Thus, we argued that any differential changes in New Jersey relative to Pennsylvania from the first round to the second round were most plausibly due to the minimum wage.

How did you explain what you found?

We argued that many employers in New Jersey before the rise in the minimum were operating with vacancies and would have liked to hire more workers but could not do so without raising their wages. In this situation, an increase in the minimum wage can cause some employers to hire more and others to hire less. On average, the net effect on employment can be small. What we saw was a rise in wages and a reduction in vacancies in New Jersey, coupled with a small gain in employment.

You've examined just about every labor market policy. Let's talk about welfare payments to single mothers: How do they influence labor market decisions?

The Self Sufficiency Program welfare demonstration in Canada tested an earnings subsidy as an alternative to conventional welfare payments. The problem with conventional welfare is that recipients have no incentive to work: If they earn $1, their payments are reduced by $1. That led Milton Friedman in the early 1950s to advocate an alternative "negative income tax" program, such as SSP, in which recipients who earn more only lose a fraction of their benefits (in the case of SSP, 50 cents per dollar earned). The results showed that this alternative system encourages single parents to work more.

Immigration has been big news in recent years. Can you describe your work on this issue and your findings?

My research has tried to understand whether the arrival of low-skilled immigrants hurts the labor market opportunities for less-skilled natives. One of my papers studies the effect of the Mariel Boatlift, which occurred in 1980 following a political uprising that led Fidel Castro to declare that people who wanted to leave Cuba were free to exit from the port of Mariel.

Within days, a flotilla of small boats from the United States began transporting people to Miami, and 150,000 people eventually left. Over one half stayed in Miami, creating a huge "shock" to the supply of low-skilled labor. I studied the effect by looking at wages and unemployment rates for various groups in Miami and in a set of comparison cities that had very similar wage and employment trends in the previous decade. I found that the influx of the boatlift had no discernible effect on wages or unemployment of other workers in Miami. My later work has confirmed that the Miami story seems to hold in most other cities. Cities can absorb big inflows of low-skilled immigrants with remarkably little negative impact on natives.

The distribution of income has become increasingly unequal. Do we know why?

There are many sources. Family incomes have become more unequal in part because of a rise in families with two very high-wage earners. These families have pulled away from the rest, creating a widening distribution. The very richest families, whose incomes are above the 95th or 99th percentile of the income distribution, earn an increasingly large share of national income. The trends in income for this group account for most of the rise in inequality we have seen in the last 10 years.

Unfortunately, it is very hard to study this group because they represent such a small fraction of families, and they are often under-reported on surveys. The best available data, from tax returns, don't tell us much about the sources of this group's success, though it seems to be due to labor market earnings rather than to previous investments or family wealth.

There is a large literature on wage inequality among the larger "middle" of the population: people who earn up to $150,000 per year, for example. Wage inequality for men in this group rose very sharply in the early 1980s in the United States, rose a little more between 1985 and 1990, and was fairly stable (or even decreasing) in the 1990s. Some of the rise in the 1980s was due to decreases in unionization, and some was due to the changing effects of the minimum wage, which fell in real terms in the early 1980s, and then gained in the early to mid-1990s.

Some researchers ascribe the rest of the trend in wage inequality to the spread of computers and increasing demands for highly skilled workers. Others blame international trade and, most recently, immigration. Those explanations are hard to evaluate because we don't really see the forces of new technology or trade that affect any particular worker. One thing we do know is that wage inequality trends were quite different in many other countries. Canada, for instance, had relatively modest rises in inequality in the 1980s.

What advice do you have for someone who is just beginning to study economics? What other subjects do you think work well alongside economics? Do you have some reading suggestions?

... find out what life is like for other people. ... The best economists are observant and thoughtful social scientists.

The part of economics that most interests me is the behavior of people in their everyday life. People constantly have to answer questions such as: Should I get more education? How much should I save? Should I send my children to the local public school? It's extremely important to see how these questions are answered by different people: people from poorer families or other countries or who had to make very different choices. Take any opportunity to find out what life is like for other people. You can learn a lot from reading novels, spending a year abroad, or taking classes in sociology or history. The best economists are observant and thoughtful social scientists. My other piece of advice is study mathematics. The more mathematics training you have, the more easily you can understand what economists are doing. Newton invented calculus to study the motion of planets, but economics benefits from the same tools.

GLOSSARY

Absolute advantage A person has an absolute advantage if that person is more productive than another person. (p. 40)

Adverse selection The tendency for people to *enter into agreements* in which they can use their private information to their own advantage and to the disadvantage of the uninformed party. (p. 470)

Allocative efficiency A situation in which goods and services are produced at the lowest possible cost and the quantities that provide the greatest possible benefit. (We cannot produce more of any good without giving up some of another good that we *value more highly*.) (p. 35)

Antitrust law A law that regulates oligopolies and prevents them from becoming monopolies or behaving like monopolies. (p. 358)

Asymmetric information A market in which buyers and sellers have private information. (p. 470)

Average cost pricing rule A rule that sets price to cover cost including normal profit, which means setting the price equal to average total cost. (p. 314)

Average fixed cost Total fixed cost per unit of output. (p. 258)

Average product The average product of a factor of production. It equals total product divided by the quantity of the factor employed. (p. 253)

Average total cost Total cost per unit of output. (p. 258)

Average variable cost Total variable cost per unit of output. (p. 258)

Barrier to entry A legal or natural constraint that protects a firm from potential competitors. (p. 300)

Behavioral economics A study of the ways in which limits on the human brain's ability to compute and implement decisions influences economic behavior—both the decisions that people make and the consequences of those decisions for the way markets work. (p. 194)

Big tradeoff The tradeoff between equality and efficiency. (pp. 9, 119, 454)

Bilateral monopoly A situation in which a monopoly seller faces a monopsony buyer. (p. 425)

Black market An illegal market in which the price exceeds the legally imposed price ceiling. (p. 130)

Budget line The limits to a household's consumption choices. (p. 204)

Capital The tools, equipment, buildings, and other constructions that businesses use to produce goods and services. (p. 4)

Capital accumulation The growth of capital resources, including human capital. (p. 38)

Capture theory A theory that regulation serves the self-interest of the producer, who captures the regulator and maximizes economic profit. (p. 313)

Cartel A group of firms acting together—colluding—to limit output, raise the price, and increase economic profit. (p. 343)

Ceteris paribus Other things being equal—all other relevant things remaining the same. (p. 24)

Change in demand A change in buyers' plans that occurs when some influence on those plans other than the price of the good changes. It is illustrated by a shift of the demand curve. (p. 60)

Change in supply A change in sellers' plans that occurs when some influence on those plans other than the price of the good changes. It is illustrated by a shift of the supply curve. (p. 65)

Change in the quantity demanded A change in buyers' plans that occurs when the price of a good changes but all other influences on buyers' plans remain unchanged. It is illustrated by a movement along the demand curve. (p. 63)

Change in the quantity supplied A change in sellers' plans that occurs when the price of a good changes but all other influences on sellers' plans remain unchanged. It is illustrated by a movement along the supply curve. (p. 66)

Coase theorem The proposition that if property rights exist, if only a small number of parties are involved, and transactions costs are low, then private transactions are efficient. (p. 379)

Collusive agreement An agreement between two (or more) producers to form a cartel to restrict output, raise the price, and increase profits. (p. 348)

Command system A method of allocating resources by the order (command) of someone in authority. In a firm a managerial hierarchy organizes production. (pp. 108, 233)

Common resource A resource that is rival and nonexcludable. (p. 394)

Comparative advantage A person or country has a comparative advantage in an activity if that person or country can perform the activity at a lower opportunity cost than anyone else or any other country. (p. 40)

Competitive market A market that has many buyers and many sellers, so no single buyer or seller can influence the price. (p. 58)

Complement A good that is used in conjunction with another good. (p. 61)

Compound interest The interest on an initial investment plus the interest on the interest that the investment has previously earned. (p. 434)

Constant returns to scale Features of a firm's technology that lead to constant long-run average cost as output increases. When constant returns to scale are present, the *LRAC* curve is horizontal. (p. 264)

Consumer equilibrium A situation in which a consumer has allocated all his or her available income in the way that, given the prices of goods and services, maximizes his or her total utility. (p. 184)

Consumer surplus The value (or marginal benefit) of a good minus the price paid for it, summed over the quantity bought. (p. 111)

Contestable market A market in which firms can enter and leave so easily that firms in the market face competition from *potential* entrants. (p. 356)

Cooperative equilibrium The outcome of a game in which the players make and share the monopoly profit. (p. 355)

Copyright A government-sanctioned exclusive right granted to the inventor of a good, service, or productive process to produce, use, and sell the invention for a given number of years. (p. 385)

Credit risk The risk that a borrower, also known as a creditor, might not repay a loan. (p. 473)

Cross elasticity of demand The responsiveness of the demand for a good to a change in the price of a substitute or complement, other things remaining the same. It is calculated as the percentage change in the quantity demanded of the good divided by the percentage change in the price of the substitute or complement. (p. 93)

Cross-section graph A graph that shows the values of an economic variable for different groups or categories at a point in time. (p. 16)

Deadweight loss A measure of inefficiency. It is equal to the decrease in total surplus that results from an inefficient level of production. (p. 115)

Default risk The risk that a borrower, also known as a creditor, might not repay a loan. (p. 473)

Demand The entire relationship between the price of the good and the quantity demanded of it when all

other influences on buyers' plans remain the same. It is illustrated by a demand curve and described by a demand schedule. (p. 59)

Demand curve A curve that shows the relationship between the quantity demanded of a good and its price when all other influences on consumers' planned purchases remain the same. (p. 60)

Deregulation The process of removing regulation of prices, quantities, entry, and other aspects of economic activity in a firm or industry. (p. 313)

Derived demand Demand for a factor of production—it is derived from the demand for the goods and services produced by that factor. (p. 419)

Diminishing marginal rate of substitution The general tendency for a person to be willing to give up less of good *y* to get one more unit of good *x*, and at the same time remain indifferent, as the quantity of good *x* increases. (p. 208)

Diminishing marginal returns The tendency for the marginal product of an additional unit of a factor of production to be less than the marginal product of the previous unit of the factor. (p. 255)

Diminishing marginal utility The decrease in marginal utility as the quantity consumed increases. (p. 183)

Direct relationship A relationship between two variables that move in the same direction. (p. 18)

Discounting The calculation we use to convert a future amount of money to its present value. (p. 434)

Diseconomies of scale Features of a firm's technology that lead to rising long-run average cost as output increases. (p. 264)

Doha Developing Agenda (Doha Round) Negotiations held in Doha, Qatar, to lower tariff barriers and quotas that restrict international trade in farm products and services. (p. 164)

Dominant strategy equilibrium An equilibrium in which the best strategy for each player is to cheat *regardless of the strategy of the other player*. (p. 354)

Dumping The sale by a foreign firm of exports at a lower price than the cost of production. (p. 165)

Duopoly A market structure in which two producers of a good or service compete. (p. 342)

Dynamic comparative advantage A comparative advantage that a person or country possesses as a result of having specialized in a particular activity and then, as a result of learning-by-doing, having become the producer with the lowest opportunity cost. (p. 43)

Economic depreciation The change in the market value of capital over a given period. (p. 229)

Economic efficiency A situation that occurs when the firm produces a given output at the least cost. (p. 231)

Economic growth The expansion of production possibilities that results from capital accumulation and technological change. (p. 38)

Economic model A description of some aspect of the economic world that includes only those features of the world that are needed for the purpose at hand. (p. 11)

Economic profit A firm's total revenue minus its total cost. (p. 228)

Economic rent Any surplus—consumer surplus, producer surplus or economic profit. (p. 308)

Economics The social science that studies the *choices* that individuals, businesses, governments, and entire societies make as they cope with *scarcity* and the *incentives* that influence and reconcile those choices. (p. 2)

Economies of scale Features of a firm's technology that lead to a falling long-run average cost as output increases. (pp. 243, 264)

Economies of scope Decreases in average total cost that occur when a firm uses specialized resources to produce a range of goods and services. (p. 243)

Efficient scale The quantity at which average total cost is a minimum—the quantity at the bottom of the U-shaped *ATC* curve. (p. 328)

Elastic demand Demand with a price elasticity greater than 1; other things remaining the same, the percentage change in the quantity demanded exceeds the percentage change in price. (p. 89)

Elasticity of supply The responsiveness of the quantity supplied of a good to a change in its price, other things remaining the same. (p. 96)

Entrepreneurship The human resource that organizes the other three factors of production: labor, land, and capital. (p. 4)

Equilibrium price The price at which the quantity demanded equals the quantity supplied. (p. 68)

Equilibrium quantity The quantity bought and sold at the equilibrium price. (p. 68)

Excess capacity A firm has excess capacity if it produces below its efficient scale. (p. 328)

Excludable A good or service or a resource is excludable if it is possible to prevent someone from enjoying the benefit of it. (p. 394)

Expected utility The utility value of what a person expects to own at a given point in time. (p. 465)

Expected wealth The money value of what a person expects to own at a given point in time. (p. 464)

Exports The goods and services that we sell to people in other countries. (p. 154)

External diseconomies Factors outside the control of a firm that raise the firm's costs as the industry produces a larger output. (p. 287)

External economies Factors beyond the control of a firm that lower the firm's costs as the industry produces a larger output. (p. 287)

Externality A cost or a benefit that arises from production and falls on someone other than the producer, or a cost or a benefit that arises from consumption and falls on someone other than the consumer. (p. 374)

Factors of production The productive resources used to produce goods and services. (p. 3)

Firm An economic unit that hires factors of production and organizes those factors to produce and sell goods and services. (pp. 43, 228)

Four-firm concentration ratio A measure of market power that is calculated as the percentage of the value of sales accounted for by the four largest firms in an industry. (p. 238)

Free-rider problem The problem that the market would provide an inefficiently small quantity of a public good. (p. 395)

Game theory A tool for studying strategic behavior—behavior that takes into account the expected behavior of others and the recognition of mutual interdependence. (p. 346)

General Agreement on Tariffs and Trade (GATT) An international agreement signed in 1947 to reduce tariffs on international trade. (p. 161)

Gini ratio The ratio of the area between the line of equality and the Lorenz curve to the entire area beneath the line of equality. (p. 445)

Goods and services All the objects that people value and produce to satisfy human wants. (p. 3)

Herfindahl–Hirschman Index A measure of market power that is calculated as the square of the market share of each firm (as a percentage) summed over the largest 50 firms (or over all firms if there are fewer than 50) in a market. (p. 238)

Hotelling Principle The idea that traders expect the price of a nonrenewable resource to rise at a rate equal to the interest rate. (p. 430)

Human capital The knowledge and skill that people obtain from education, on-the-job training, and work experience. (p. 3)

Implicit rental rate The firm's opportunity cost of using its own capital. (p. 228)

Import quota A restriction that limits the maximum quantity of a good that may be imported in a given period. (p. 162)

Imports The goods and services that we buy from people in other countries. (p. 154)

Incentive A reward that encourages an action or a penalty that discourages one. (p. 2)

Income effect The effect of a change in income on consumption, other things remaining the same. (p. 212)

Income elasticity of demand The responsiveness of demand to a change in income, other things remaining the same. It is calculated as the percentage change in the quantity demanded divided by the percentage change in income. (p. 94)

Indifference curve A line that shows combinations of goods among which a consumer is indifferent. (p. 207)

Individual transferable quota (ITQ) A production limit that is assigned to an individual who is free to transfer (sell) the quota to someone else. (p. 404)

Inelastic demand A demand with a price elasticity between 0 and 1; the percentage change in the quantity demanded is less than the percentage change in price. (p. 88)

Infant-industry argument The argument that it is necessary to protect a new industry to enable it to grow into a mature industry that can compete in world markets. (p. 165)

Inferior good A good for which demand decreases as income increases. (p. 62)

Intellectual property rights Property rights for discoveries owned by the creators of knowledge. (p. 385)

Interest The income that capital earns. (p. 4)

Inverse relationship A relationship between variables that move in opposite directions. (p. 19)

Job A contract for the trade of labor services. (p. 418)

Labor The work time and work effort that people devote to producing goods and services. (p. 3)

Labor union An organized group of workers that aims to increase the wage rate and influence other job conditions. (p. 424)

Land All the "gifts of nature" that we use to produce goods and services. (p. 3)

Law of demand Other things remaining the same, the higher the price of a good, the smaller is the quantity demanded of it; the lower the price of a good, the larger is the quantity demanded of it. (p. 59)

Law of diminishing returns As a firm uses more of a variable input, with a given quantity of other inputs (fixed inputs), the marginal product of the variable input eventually diminishes. (p. 255)

Law of supply Other things remaining the same, the higher the price of a good, the greater is the quantity supplied of it. (p. 64)

Learning-by-doing People become more productive in an activity (learn) just by repeatedly producing a particular good or service (doing). (p. 43)

Legal monopoly A market in which competition and entry are restricted by the granting of a public franchise, government license, patent, or copyright. (p. 300)

Lemon problem The problem that in a market in which it is not possible to distinguish reliable products from lemons, there are too many lemons and too few reliable products traded. (p. 470)

Limit pricing The practice of setting the price at the highest level that inflicts a loss on an entrant. (p. 357)

Linear relationship A relationship between two variables that is illustrated by a straight line. (p. 18)

Long run A period of time in which the quantities of all resources can be varied. (p. 252)

Long-run average cost curve The relationship between the lowest attainable average total cost and output when both plant size and labor are varied. (p. 263)

Long-run market supply curve A curve that shows how the quantity supplied in a market varies as the market price varies after all the possible adjustments have been made, including changes in each firm's plant and the number of firms in the market. (p. 287)

Lorenz curve A curve that graphs the cumulative percentage of income or wealth against the cumulative percentage of households. (p. 443)

Macroeconomics The study of the performance of the national economy and the global economy. (p. 2)

Margin When a choice is changed by a small amount or by a little at a time, the choice is made at the margin. (p. 10)

Marginal benefit The benefit that a person receives from consuming one more unit of a good or service. It is measured as the maximum amount that a person is willing to pay for one more unit of the good or service. (pp. 10, 36)

Marginal benefit curve A curve that shows the relationship between the marginal benefit of a good and the quantity of that good consumed. (p. 36)

Marginal cost The opportunity cost of producing one more unit of a good or service. It is the best alternative forgone. It is calculated as the increase in total cost divided by the increase in output. (pp. 10, 35, 258)

Marginal cost pricing rule A rule that sets the price of a good or service equal to the marginal cost of producing it. (p. 313)

Marginal external benefit The benefit from an additional unit of a good or service that people other than the consumer enjoy. (p. 381)

Marginal external cost The cost of producing an additional unit of a good or service that falls on people other than the producer. (p. 377)

Marginal private benefit The benefit from an additional unit of a good or service that the consumer of that good or service receives. (p. 381)

Marginal private cost The cost of producing an additional unit of a good or service that is borne by the producer of that good or service. (p. 377)

Marginal product The increase in total product that results from a one-unit increase in the variable input, with all other inputs remaining the same. It is calculated as the increase in total product divided by the increase in the variable input employed, when the quantities of all other inputs are constant. (p. 253)

Marginal rate of substitution The rate at which a person will give up good y (the good measured on the y-axis) to get an additional unit of good x (the good measured on the x-axis) and at the same time remain indifferent (remain on the same indifference curve). (p. 208)

Marginal revenue The change in total revenue that results from a one-unit increase in the quantity sold. It is calculated as the change in total revenue divided by the change in quantity sold. (p. 274)

Marginal social benefit The marginal benefit enjoyed by society—by the consumer of a good or service (marginal private benefit) plus the marginal benefit enjoyed by others (marginal external benefit). (p. 381)

Marginal social cost The marginal cost incurred by the entire society—by the producer and by everyone else on whom the cost falls—and is the sum of marginal private cost and marginal external cost. (p. 377)

Marginal utility The change in total utility resulting from a one-unit increase in the quantity of a good consumed. (p. 182)

Marginal utility per dollar The marginal utility from a good divided by its price. (p. 184)

Market Any arrangement that enables buyers and sellers to get information and to do business with each other. (p. 44)

Market income The wages, interest, rent, and profit earned in factor markets and before paying income taxes. (p. 442)

Markup The amount by which the firm's price exceeds its marginal cost. (p. 329)

Microeconomics The study of the choices that individuals and businesses make, the way these choices interact in markets, and the influence of governments. (p. 2)

Minimum efficient scale The smallest quantity of output at which the long-run average cost curve reaches its lowest level. (p. 265)

Minimum wage A regulation that makes the hiring of labor below a specified wage rate illegal. The lowest wage at which a firm may legally hire labor. (p. 133)

Money Any commodity or token that is generally acceptable as the means of payment. (p. 44)

Money income Market income plus cash payments to households by the government. (p. 442)

Money price The number of dollars that must be given up in exchange for a good or service. (p. 58)

Monopolistic competition A market structure in which a large number of firms make similar but slightly different products and compete on product quality, price, and marketing. (pp. 237, 324)

Monopoly A market structure in which there is one firm, which produces a good or service that has no close substitutes and in which the firm is protected from competition by a barrier preventing the entry of new firms. (pp. 237, 300)

Monopsony A market in which there is a single buyer. (p. 425)

Moral hazard A tendency for people with private information, *after entering into an agreement*, to use that information for their own benefit and at the cost of the less-informed party. (p. 470)

Nash equilibrium The outcome of a game that occurs when player A takes the best possible action given the action of player B and player B takes the best possible action given the action of player A. (p. 347)

Natural monopoly An industry in which economies of scale enable one firm to supply the entire market at the lowest possible price. (p. 300)

Negative externality An externality that arises from either production or consumption and that imposes an external cost. (p. 374)

Negative relationship A relationship between variables that move in opposite directions. (p. 19)

Neuroeconomics The study of the activity of the human brain when a person makes an economic decision. (p. 195)

Nonexcludable A good or service or a resource is nonexcludable if it is impossible (or extremely costly) to prevent someone from benefiting from it. (p. 394)

Nonrenewable natural resources Natural resources that can be used only once. (p. 418)

Nonrival A good or service or a resource is nonrival if its use by one person does not decrease the quantity available for someone else. (p. 394)

Normal good A good for which demand increases as income increases. (p. 62)

Normal profit The return that an entrepreneur can expect to receive *on the average*. (p. 229)

Offshoring outsourcing A U.S. firm buys finished goods, components, or services from other firms in other countries. (p. 167)

Offshoring A U.S. firm hires foreign labor and produced in a foreign country or a U.S. firm buys finished goods, components, or services from firms in other countries. (p. 167)

Oligopoly A market structure in which a small number of firms compete. (pp. 237, 342)

Opportunity cost The highest-valued alternative that we give up to get something. (pp. 9, 33)

Outsourcing A U.S. firm buys finished goods, components, or services from other firms in the United States or from firms in other countries. (p. 167)

Patent A government-sanctioned exclusive right granted to the inventor of a good, service, or productive process to produce, use, and sell the invention for a given number of years. (p. 385)

Payoff matrix A table that shows the payoffs for every possible action by each player for every possible action by each other player. (p. 346)

Perfect competition A market in which there are many firms each selling an identical product; there are many buyers; there are no restrictions on entry into the industry; firms in the industry have no advantage over potential new entrants; and firms and buyers are well informed about the price of each firm's product. (pp. 237, 274)

Perfectly elastic demand Demand with an infinite price elasticity; the quantity demanded changes by an infinitely large percentage in response to a tiny price change. (p. 89)

Perfectly inelastic demand Demand with a price elasticity of zero; the quantity demanded remains constant when the price changes. (p. 88)

Perfect price discrimination Price discrimination that occurs when a firm sells each unit of output for the highest price that anyone is willing to pay for it. The firm extracts the entire consumer surplus. (p. 311)

Pigovian taxes Taxes that are used as an incentive for producers to cut back on an activity that creates an external cost. (p. 380)

Pooling equilibrium The equilibrium in a market when only one message is available and an uninformed person cannot determine quality. (p. 473)

Positive externality An externality that arises from either production or consumption and that provides an external benefit. (p. 374)

Positive relationship A relationship between two variables that move in the same direction. (p. 18)

Poverty A state in which a household's income is too low to be able to buy the quantities of food, shelter, and clothing that are deemed necessary. (p. 446)

Predatory pricing Setting a low price to drive competitors out of business with the intention of setting a monopoly price when the competition has gone. (p. 360)

Preferences A description of a person's likes and dislikes. (p. 36)

Present value The amount of money that, if invested today, will grow to be as large as a given future amount when the interest that it will earn is taken into account. (p. 434)

Price cap A regulation that makes it illegal to charge a price higher than a specified level. (p. 130)

Price cap regulation A rule that specifies the highest price that the firm is permitted to set—a price ceiling. (p. 315)

Price ceiling A regulation that makes it illegal to charge a price higher than a specified level. (p. 130)

Price discrimination The practice of selling different units of a good or service for different prices. (p. 301)

Price effect The effect of a change in the price on the quantity of a good consumed, other things remaining the same. (p. 211)

Price elasticity of demand A units-free measure of the responsiveness of the quantity demanded of a good to a change in its price, when all other influences on buyers' plans remain the same. (p. 86)

Price floor A regulation that makes it illegal to trade at a price lower than a specified level. (p. 133)

Price taker A firm that cannot influence the price of the good or service it produces. (p. 274)

Principal–agent problem The problem of devising compensation rules that induce an *agent* to act in the best interest of a *principal*. (p. 234)

Principle of minimum differentiation The tendency for competitors to make themselves similar to appeal to the maximum number of clients or voters. (p. 397)

Private good A good or service that is both rival and excludable. (p. 394)

Private information Information about the value of an item being traded that is possessed by only buyers or sellers. (p. 470)

Producer surplus The price of a good minus its minimum supply-price, summed over the quantity sold. (p. 113)

Product differentiation Making a product slightly different from the product of a competing firm. (pp. 237, 324)

Production efficiency A situation in which goods and services are produced at the lowest possible cost. (p. 33)

Production possibilities frontier The boundary between the combinations of goods and services that can be produced and the combinations that cannot. (p. 32)

Production quota An upper limit to the quantity of a good that may be produced in a specified period. (p. 141)

Profit The income earned by entrepreneurship. (p. 4)

Progressive income tax A tax on income at an average rate that increases with the level of income. (p. 453)

Property rights Social arrangements that govern the ownership, use, and disposal of anything that people value that are enforceable in the courts. (pp. 44, 378)

Proportional income tax A tax on income at a constant average rate, regardless of the level of income. (p. 453)

Public good A good or service that is both nonrival and nonexcludable. It can be consumed simultaneously by everyone and from which no one can be excluded. (p. 394)

Public provision The production of a good or service by a public authority that receives its revenue from the government. (p. 383)

Quantity demanded The amount of a good or service that consumers plan to buy during a given time period at a particular price. (p. 59)

Quantity supplied The amount of a good or service that producers plan to sell during a given time period at a particular price. (p. 64)

Rate of return regulation A regulation that requires the firm to justify its price by showing that its return on capital doesn't exceed a specified target rate. (p. 314)

Rational ignorance The decision not to acquire information because the cost of doing so exceeds the expected benefit. (p. 398)

Real income A household's income expressed as a quantity of goods that the household can afford to buy. (p. 205)

Regressive income tax A tax on income at an average rate that decreases with the level of income. (p. 453)

Regulation Rules administered by a government agency to influence prices, quantities, entry, and other aspects of economic activity in a firm or industry. (p. 313)

Relative price The ratio of the price of one good or service to the price of another good or service. A relative price is an opportunity cost. (pp. 58, 205)

Rent The income that land earns. (p. 4)

Rent ceiling A regulation that makes it illegal to charge a rent higher than a specified level. (p. 130)

Rent seeking The lobbying for special treatment by the government to create economic profit or to divert consumer surplus or producer surplus away from others. The pursuit of wealth by capturing economic rent. (pp. 169, 308)

Resale price maintenance Agreement between a manufacturer and a distributor on the price at which the product will be sold. (p. 359)

Risk aversion The dislike of risk. (p. 464)

Rival A good or service or a resource is rival if its use by one person decreases the quantity available for someone else. (p. 394)

Scarcity Our inability to satisfy all our wants. (p. 2)

Scatter diagram A diagram that plots the value of one variable against the value of another. (p. 17)

Screening Inducing an informed party to reveal private information. (p. 473)

Search activity The time spent looking for someone with whom to do business. (p. 130)

Self-interest The choices that you think are best ones available for you are choices made in your self-interest. (p. 5)

Separating equilibrium The equilibrium in a market when signaling provides full information to a previously uninformed person. (p. 473)

Short run The period of time in which the quantity of at least one factor of production is fixed and the quantities of the other factors can be varied. The fixed factor is usually capital—that is, the firm has a given plant size. (p. 252)

Short-run market supply curve A curve that shows the quantity supplied in a market at each price when each firm's plant and the number of firms remain the same. (p. 280)

Shutdown point The output and price at which the firm just covers its total variable cost. In the short run, the firm is indifferent between producing the profit-maximizing output and shutting down temporarily. (p. 278)

Signal An action taken by an informed person (or firm) to send a message to uninformed people. (p. 332)

Signaling A situation in which an informed person takes actions that send information to uninformed persons. (p. 472)

Single-price monopoly A monopoly that must sell each unit of its output for the same price to all its customers. (p. 301)

Slope The change in the value of the variable measured on the y-axis divided by the change in the value of the variable measured on the x-axis. (p. 22)

Social interest Choices that are the best ones for society as a whole. (p. 5)

Social interest theory A theory that the political and regulatory process relentlessly seeks out inefficiency and introduces regulation that eliminates deadweight loss and allocates resources efficiently. (p. 313)

Speculative bubble A process in which the price is rising because expectations that it will rise bring a rising actual price. (p. 72)

Strategies All the possible actions of each player in a game. (p. 346)

Subsidy A payment made by the government to a producer. (pp. 142, 384)

Substitute A good that can be used in place of another good. (p. 61)

Substitution effect The effect of a change in price of a good or service on the quantity bought when the consumer (hypothetically) remains indifferent between the original and the new consumption situations—that is, the consumer remains on the same indifference curve. (p. 213)

Sunk cost The past cost of buying a plant that has no resale value. (p. 252)

Supply The entire relationship between the price of a good and the quantity supplied of it when all other influences on producers' planned sales remain the same. It is described by a supply schedule and illustrated by a supply curve. (p. 64)

Supply curve A curve that shows the relationship between the quantity supplied of a good and its price when all other influences on producers' planned sales remain the same. (p. 64)

Symmetry principle A requirement that people in similar situations be treated similarly. (p. 120)

Tariff A tax that is imposed by the importing country when an imported good crosses its international boundary. (p. 159)

Tax incidence The division of the burden of the tax between the buyer and the seller. (p. 135)

Technological change The development of new goods and of better ways of producing goods and services. (p. 38)

Technological efficiency A situation that occurs when the firm produces a given output by using the least amount of inputs. (p. 231)

Technology Any method of producing a good or service. (p. 230)

Time-series graph A graph that measures time (for example, months or years) on the x-axis and the variable

or variables in which we are interested on the y-axis. (p. 16)

Total cost The cost of all the productive resources that a firm uses. (p. 257)

Total fixed cost The cost of the firm's fixed inputs. (p. 257)

Total product The total output produced by a firm in a given period of time. (p. 253)

Total revenue The value of a firm's sales. It is calculated as the price of the good multiplied by the quantity sold. (pp. 90, 274)

Total revenue test A method of estimating the price elasticity of demand by observing the change in total revenue that results from a change in the price, when all other influences on the quantity sold remain the same. (p. 90)

Total utility The total benefit that a person gets from the consumption of goods and services. (p. 182)

Total variable cost The cost of all the firm's variable inputs. (p. 257)

Tradeoff A constraint that involves giving up one thing to get something else. (p. 8)

Tragedy of the commons The absence of incentives to prevent the overuse and depletion of a commonly owned resource. (p. 400)

Transactions costs The opportunity costs of making trades in a market. The costs that arise from finding someone with whom to do business, of reaching an agreement about the price and other aspects of the exchange, and of ensuring that the terms of the agreement are fulfilled. (pp. 117, 242, 379)

Trend The general tendency for a variable to move in one direction. (p. 16)

Tying arrangement An agreement to sell one product only if the buyer agrees to buy another, different product. (p. 359)

Unit elastic demand Demand with a price elasticity of 1; the percentage change in the quantity demanded equals the percentage change in price. (p. 88)

Utilitarianism A principle that states that we should strive to achieve "the greatest happiness for the greatest number of people." (p. 118)

Utility The benefit or satisfaction that a person gets from the consumption of a good or service. (p. 182)

Value of marginal product The price of a unit of output multiplied by the marginal product of the factor of production. (p. 419)

Voucher A token that the government provides to households, which they can use to buy specified goods and services. (p. 384)

Wages The income that labor earns. (p. 4)

Wealth The value of all the things that people own—the market value of their assets—at a point in time. (pp. 444, 487)

World Trade Organization (WTO) An international organization that places greater obligations on its member countries to observe the GATT rules. (p. 164)

INDEX

Key terms and pages on which they are defined appear in **boldface.**

PHOTO CREDITS

The Addison-Wesley Series in Economics

Abel/Bernanke/Croushore
Macroeconomics*

Bade/Parkin
Foundations of Economics*

Bierman/Fernandez
Game Theory with Economic Applications

Binger/Hoffman
Microeconomics with Calculus

Boyer
Principles of Transportation Economics

Branson
Macroeconomic Theory and Policy

Bruce
Public Finance and the American Economy

Byrns/Stone
Economics

Carlton/Perloff
Modern Industrial Organization

Caves/Frankel/Jones
World Trade and Payments: An Introduction

Chapman
Environmental Economics: Theory, Application, and Policy

Cooter/Ulen
Law & Economics

Downs
An Economic Theory of Democracy

Ehrenberg/Smith
Modern Labor Economics

Ekelund/Ressler/Tollison
Economics*

Fusfeld
The Age of the Economist

Gerber
International Economics

Ghiara
Learning Economics

Gordon
Macroeconomics

Gregory
Essentials of Economics

Gregory/Stuart
Russian and Soviet Economic Performance and Structure

Hartwick/Olewiler
The Economics of Natural Resource Use

Hoffman/Averett
Women and the Economy: Family, Work, and Pay

Holt
Markets, Games and Strategic Behavior

Hubbard
Money, the Financial System, and the Economy

Hughes/Cain
American Economic History

Husted/Melvin
International Economics

Jehle/Reny
Advanced Microeconomic Theory

Johnson-Lans
A Health Economics Primer

Klein
Mathematical Methods for Economics

Krugman/Obstfeld
International Economics: Theory and Policy*

Laidler
The Demand for Money

Leeds/von Allmen
The Economics of Sports

Leeds/von Allmen/Schiming
Economics*

Lipsey/Ragan/Storer
Economics*

Melvin
International Money and Finance

Miller
Economics Today*

Miller
Understanding Modern Economics

Miller/Benjamin
The Economics of Macro Issues

Miller/Benjamin/North
The Economics of Public Issues

Mills/Hamilton
Urban Economics

Mishkin
The Economics of Money, Banking, and Financial Markets*

Mishkin
The Economics of Money, Banking, and Financial Markets, Alternate Edition*

Murray
Econometrics: A Modern Introduction

Parkin
Economics*

Perloff
Microeconomics*

Perloff
Microeconomics: Theory and Applications with Calculus

Perman/Common/McGilvray/Ma
Natural Resources and Environmental Economics

Phelps
Health Economics

Riddell/Shackelford/Stamos/ Schneider
Economics: A Tool for Critically Understanding Society

Ritter/Silber/Udell
Principles of Money, Banking, and Financial Markets

Rohlf
Introduction to Economic Reasoning

Ruffin/Gregory
Principles of Economics

Sargent
Rational Expectations and Inflation

Scherer
Industry Structure, Strategy, and Public Policy

Sherman
Market Regulation

Stock/Watson
Introduction to Econometrics

Stock/Watson
Introduction to Econometrics, Brief Edition

Studenmund
Using Econometrics: A Practical Guide

Tietenberg
Environmental Economics and Policy

Tietenberg/Lewis
Environmental and Natural Resource Economics

Todaro/Smith
Economic Development

Waldman
Microeconomics

Waldman/Jensen
Industrial Organization: Theory and Practice

Weil
Economic Growth

Williamson
Macroeconomics

Chapter **1** **WHAT IS ECONOMICS?**

Answers to the Problems and Applications

1. **Apple Computer Inc. decides to make iTunes freely available in unlimited quantities.**

   a. **How does Apple's decision change the opportunity cost of a download?**

   Apple's decision decreases the opportunity cost of a tune by removing the previous monetary cost of 99¢ per tune.

   b. **Does Apple's decision change the incentives that people face?**

   Apple's decision changes people's incentives. For example, it increases people's incentives to buy an iPod in order to take advantage of the newly "free" music available on iTunes.

   c. **Is Apple's decision an example of a microeconomic or a macroeconomic issue?**

   Apple's decision is a microeconomic decision because it affects a single company and a single market.

3. **Explain how the following news headlines concern self-interest and the social interest:**

   a. **Wal-Mart Expands in Europe**

   Wal-Mart's expansion is a decision made by Wal-Mart to further Wal-Mart's interest. Thus the decision is directly in Wal-Mart's self interest. The question of whether this choice also furthers the social interest is one that is studied in microeconomics.

   b. **McDonald's Moves into Salads**

   McDonald's decision to serve salads is a decision made by McDonald's to further McDonald's interest. Thus the decision is directly in McDonald's self interest. The question of whether this choice also furthers the social interest is one that is studied in microeconomics.

   c. **Food Must Be Labeled with Nutrition Information**

   The decision to require that food must be labeled with nutrition information is made in the social interest. This decision is not made by any one single firm and so does not (necessarily) reflect anyone's self interest.

5. **Which of the following statements is positive, which is normative, and which can be tested?**

   a. **The U.S. government should cut its imports.**

   The statement is normative and cannot be tested.

   b. **China is the United States' largest trading partner.**

   The statement is positive and can be tested.

   c. **If the price of antiretroviral drugs increases, HIV/AIDS sufferers will decrease their consumption of the drugs.**

   The statement is positive and can be tested.

7. **Before starring as Tony Stark in *Iron Man*, Robert Downey Jr. had played in 45 movies that had average first-weekend box office revenues of a bit less than $5 million. *Iron Man* grossed $102 million on its opening weekend.**

   a. **How do you expect the success of *Iron Man* to influence the opportunity cost of hiring Robert Downey Jr.?**

   The salary that must be paid to Robert Downey Jr. to appear in future movies increased because some of the success of *Iron Man* was attributed to Mr. Downey. As a result the opportunity cost to movie producers of hiring Mr. Downey increased.

   b. **How have the incentives for a movie producer to hire Robert Downey Jr. changed?**

   There are two effects on the incentives of producers to hire Mr. Downey. First, because the opportunity cost of hiring

Mr. Downey increased, the incentive to hire him decreased. However because part of the success of *Iron Man* was attributed to Mr. Downey's acting in the title role, producers expect that his acting will lead to increased success for future movies. This belief increases producers' incentives to hire Mr. Downey.

9. **How does the creation of a successful movie influence what, how, and for whom goods and services are produced?**

The "what" question is affected in two ways. First, one good or service that is produced is the successful movie. Second, spinoffs and/or similar films likely will be created in the future. The "how" question is affected to the extent that movies use different production methods. Some movies, for instance, have a lot of special effects while other movies have few or none. The "for whom" question is influenced because those people who receive higher incomes as the result of the blockbuster movie have higher incomes and so more goods and services are produced for them.

11. **Look at today's *Wall Street Journal.***

a. **What is the top economic news story? With which of the big questions does it deal? (It must deal with at least one of them and might deal with more than one.)**

On Saturday, August 22, 2008, the top economic news story discussed how the financial market turmoil in the mortgage market has created partially finished subdivisions.

b. **What tradeoffs does the news item discuss or imply?**

The potential buyers of homes in the unfinished subdivision face the tradeoff that income spent on the homes decreases their purchase of other goods and services. The builders of homes in these subdivisions face the tradeoff that they can use their resources (and the resources they hire) to build homes or for

other endeavors, such as home additions or commercial building.

c. **Write a brief summary of the news item using the economic vocabulary that you have learned in this chapter and as many as possible of the key terms listed on p. 13.**

The story discusses the point that many homeowners are living in unfinished subdivisions. The entrepreneurs who were building the subdivisions ran into financial problems from higher interest rates so that there was no longer any profit left from completing the subdivisions. It was in the owners' self-interest to stop work on the houses, even some that were partially constructed. These decisions mean that the labor which was constructing the houses is no longer employed and hence no longer drawing wages for the work. Because housing is a big part of the economy, the unemployment of these factors of production have had adverse macroeconomic consequences.

Additional Problems

1. You plan a major adventure trip for the summer. You won't be able to take your usual summer job that pays $6,000, and you won't be able to live at home for free. The cost of your travel on the trip will be $3,000, film and videotape will cost you $200, and your food will cost $1,400. What is the opportunity cost of taking this trip?

2. The university has built a new parking garage. There is always an available parking spot, but it costs $1 per day. Before the new garage was built, it usually took 15 minutes of cruising to find a parking space. Compare the opportunity cost of parking in the new garage with that in the old parking lot. Which is less costly and by how much?

Solutions to Additional Problems

1. The opportunity cost of taking this trip is $10,600. The opportunity cost of taking the trip is the highest-valued activity that you will give up so that you can go on the trip. In taking the trip, you will forgo all the goods and services that you could have bought with the income from your summer job ($6,000) plus the expenditure on travel ($3,000), film and videotape ($200), and food ($1,400).

2. The opportunity cost of parking before the building of the new parking garage is the highest-valued activity that you forgo by spending 15 minutes parking your car. The opportunity cost of parking in the new parking garage is $1 that you could have spent elsewhere. If the opportunity cost of 15 minutes spent parking your car is greater than the opportunity cost of $1, then the new parking garage is less costly.

Appendix 1

GRAPHS IN ECONOMICS

Answers to the Problems and Applications

The spreadsheet provides data on the U.S. economy: Column A is the year, column B is the inflation rate, column C is the interest rate, column D is the growth rate, and column E is the unemployment rate. Use this spreadsheet to answer problems 1 and 2.

1. a. **Draw a time-series graph of the inflation rate.**

    Figure A1.3 shows the time series graph of the inflation rate.

   b. **In which year(s) (i) was inflation highest, (ii) was inflation lowest, (iii) did it increase, (iv) did it decrease, (v) did it increase most, and (vi) did it decrease most?**

    Inflation was the highest in 2007 and was the lowest in 2000 and 2004. Inflation increased from the preceding year in 1998, 2001, 2002, 2005, 2006, and 2007. Inflation decreased from the preceding year in 1999, 2000, 2003, and 2004. Inflation increased the most from the previous year in 2007 and inflation decreased the most from the previous year in 2004.

   c. **What was the main trend in inflation?**

    A trend is a general tendency for a variable to move in one direction. These data show a general upward trend. This trend is most obvious for the last 4 observations, particularly because the largest observation is in the last year, 2007.

	A	B	C	D	E
1	1997	2.8	7.6	2.5	5.6
2	1998	2.9	7.4	3.7	5.4
3	1999	2.3	7.3	4.5	4.9
4	2000	1.6	6.5	4.2	4.5
5	2001	2.2	7.0	4.4	4.2
6	2002	3.4	7.6	3.7	4.0
7	2003	2.8	7.1	0.8	4.7
8	2004	1.6	6.5	3.6	5.8
9	2005	2.3	5.7	3.1	6.0
10	2006	2.5	5.6	2.9	4.6
11	2007	4.1	5.6	2.2	4.6

FIGURE **A1.3**

Problem 1a

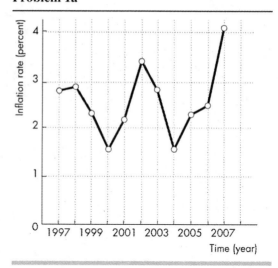

d. Draw a scatter diagram of the inflation rate and the interest rate. Describe the relationship.

To make a scatter diagram of the inflation rate and the interest rate, plot the inflation rate on the *x*-axis and the interest rate on the *y*-axis. The graph will be a set of dots and is shown in Figure A1.4. The pattern made by the dots tells us that as the inflation rate increases, the interest rate usually increases so there is a positive relationship. However, this relationship is very weak in the data in the question, especially in light of the observation for the year 2007 which is the observation farthest to the right.

e. Draw a scatter diagram of the growth rate and the unemployment rate. Describe the relationship.

To make a scatter diagram of the growth rate and the unemployment rate, plot the growth rate on the *x*-axis and the unemployment rate on the *y*-axis. The graph will be a set of dots and is shown in Figure A1.5. The pattern made by the dots tells us that when the growth rate increases, the unemployment rate usually decreases so there is a negative relationship. However, this pattern is very weak in the data in the question.

FIGURE **A1.4**

Problem 1d

FIGURE **A1.5**

Problem 1e

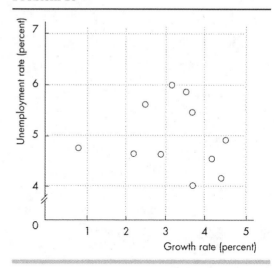

3. **Calculate the slope of the relationship shown in Figure A1.7.**

    The slope is −5/4. The curve is a straight line, so its slope is the same at all points on the curve. Slope equals the change in the variable on the *y*-axis divided by the change in the variable on the *x*-axis. To calculate the slope, you must select two points on the line. One point is at 10 on the *y*-axis and 0 on the *x*-axis, and another is at 8 on the *x*-axis and 0 on the *y*-axis. The change in *y* from 10 to 0 is associated with the change in *x* from 0 to 8. Therefore the slope of the curve equals −10/8, which equals −5/4.

5. **The table gives the price of a balloon ride, the temperature, and the number of rides a day. Draw graphs to show the relationship between**

    a. **The price and the number of rides, holding the temperature constant. Describe this relationship.**

    As illustrated in Figure A1.9. the relationship is a set of curves, one for each different temperature. To draw a graph of the relationship between the price and the number of rides, keep the temperature at 50°F and plot the data in that column against the price. This curve is the relationship between price and number of rides when the temperature is 50°F. Repeat the exercise but keep the temperature at 70°F and then repeat the exercise but keep the temperature at 90°F.

    b. **The number of rides and temperature, holding the price constant.**

    As shown in Figure A1.10, the relationship is a set of curves, one for each different price. To draw a graph of the relationship between the temperature and the number of rides, keep the price at $5.00 a ride and plot the data in that row against the temperature. This curve shows the relationship between temperature and the number of rides when the price is $5.00 a ride. Repeat the

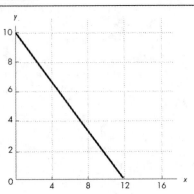

FIGURE **A1.7**
Problem 3

Price (dollars per ride)	Balloon rides (number per day)		
	50°F	70°F	90°F
5.00	32	40	50
10.00	27	32	40
15.00	18	27	32

FIGURE **A1.9**
Problem 5a

FIGURE **A1.10**
Problem 5b

exercise but keep the price at $10.00 a
ride and repeat once again only keep the
price at $15.00 a ride.

7. **Draw a graph that shows the
relationship between the two variables
x and y:**

a. **Is the relationship positive or
negative?**

To make a graph that shows the
relationship between x and y, plot the
x variable on the x-axis and the y variable
on the y-axis. Figure A1.14 shows this
graph. The relationship is negative
because x and y move in opposite
directions: As x increases, y decreases.

b. **Does the slope of the relationship
increase or decrease as the value of x
increases?**

The slope becomes steeper as x increases,
so the absolute value of the slope
increases as x increases. (The slope *itself*
decreases as x increases because it
becomes more negative.) Slope is equal to
the change in y divided by the change in
x as we move along the curve. When x
increases from 1 to 2 (a change of 1), y
decreases from 24 to 22 (a change of -2),
so the slope is -2. But when x increases
from 4 to 5 (a change of 1), y decreases
from 8 to 0 (a change of -8), so the slope
is -8.

c. **Think of some economic
relationships that might be similar to
this one.**

The less expensive a good, the greater is
the number of people who buy it. The
higher the interest rate, the smaller is the
number of people who take out home
mortgages. The less expensive gasoline,
the greater the miles car owners drive.

d. **Calculate the slope of the
relationship between x and y when x
equals 3.**

The slope equals -5. The slope of the
curve at the point where x is 3 is equal to
the slope of the tangent to the curve at
that point. Plot the relationship and then

x	0	1	2	3	4	5
y	25	24	22	18	12	0

FIGURE **A1.14**

Problem 7

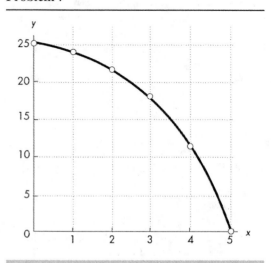

draw the tangent line at the point where
x is 3 and y is 18. Now calculate the slope
of this tangent line by finding another
point on the tangent. When x equals 5,
y equals 10 on the tangent, so another
point is x equals 5 and y equals 10. Slope
equals rise/run. The rise is -8 and the
run is 2, so the slope is -4.

e. **Calculate the slope of the
relationship across the arc as x
increases from 4 to 5.**

The slope is -12. The slope of the
relationship across the arc when x
increases from 4 to 5 is equal to the slope
of the straight line joining the points on
the curve at x equals 4 and x equals 5.
When x increases from 4 to 5, y falls
from 12 to 0. Slope equals rise/run. The
rise is -12 (0 minus 12) and the run is
1 (5 minus 4), so the slope across the arc
is -12.

9.   **Use the figure A1.16 to calculate the slope of the relationship.**

a.   **At points *A* and *B*.**

The slope at point *A* is −4, and the slope at point *B* is −1. To calculate the slope at a point on a curved line, draw the tangent to the line at the point. Then find a second point on the tangent and calculate the slope of the tangent. The tangent at point *A* cuts the *x*-axis at 2.5. The slope of the tangent equals the change in *y* divided by the change in *x*. The change in *y* equals 6 (6 minus 0) and the change in *x* equals −1.5 (1 minus 2.5). The slope at point *A* is 6/−1.5, which equals −4. Similarly, the slope at point *B* is −1. The tangent at point *B* cuts the *y*-axis at 5. The change in *y* equals 3, and the change in *x* equals −3. The slope at point *B* is −1.

b.   **Across the arc *AB*.**

The slope across the arc *AB* is −2. The slope across an arc *AB* equals the change in *y*, which is 4 (6 minus 2) divided by the change in *x*, which equals −2 (1 minus 3). The slope across the arc *AB* equals 4/−2, which is −2.

FIGURE **A1.15**

Problem 8

FIGURE **A1.16**

Problem 9

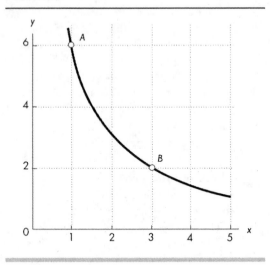

2 THE ECONOMIC PROBLEM

Answers to the Problems and Applications

1. **Brazil produces ethanol from sugar, and the land used to grow sugar can be used to grow food crops. Suppose that Brazil's production possibilities for ethanol and food crops are given in the table.**

   a. **Draw a graph of Brazil's *PPF* and explain how your graph illustrates scarcity.**

   Figure 2.1 shows Brazil's *PPF*. The production possibilities frontier itself indicates scarcity because it shows the limits to what can be produced. In particular, production combinations of ethanol and food crops that lie beyond the production possibilities frontier are not attainable.

   b. **If Brazil produces 40 barrels of ethanol a day, how much food must it produce if it achieves production efficiency?**

   If Brazil produces 40 barrels of ethanol per day, it achieves production efficiency if it also produces 3 tons of food per day.

   c. **Why does Brazil face a tradeoff on its *PPF*?**

   Brazil faces a tradeoff on its *PPF* because Brazil's resources and technology are limited. For Brazil to produce more of one good, it must shift factors of production away from the other good. Therefore to increase production of one good requires decreasing production of the other good, which reflects a tradeoff.

   d. **If Brazil increases its production of ethanol from 40 barrels per day to 54 barrels per day, what is the opportunity cost of the additional ethanol?**

   When Brazil is production efficient and increases its production of ethanol from 40 barrels per day to 54 barrels per day, it must decrease its production of food crops from 3 tons per day to 2 tons per day. Hence the opportunity cost of the

additional ethanol is 1 ton of food per day for the entire 14 barrels of ethanol or 1/14 of a ton of food per barrel of ethanol.

Ethanol (barrels per day)		Food crops (tons per day)
70	and	0
64	and	1
54	and	2
40	and	3
22	and	4
0	and	5

FIGURE **2.1**

Problem 1

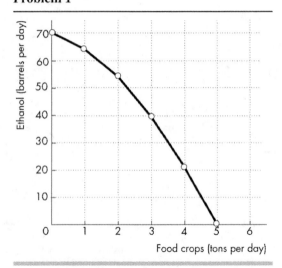

   e. **If Brazil increases its production of food crops from 2 tons per day to 3 tons per day, what is the opportunity cost of the additional food?**

   When Brazil is production efficient and increases its production of food crops from 2 tons per day to 3 tons per day, it must decrease its production of ethanol from 54 barrels per day to 40 barrels per day. Hence the opportunity cost of the additional 1 ton of food crops is 14 barrels of ethanol.

   f. **What is the relationship between your answers to d and e?**

   The opportunity costs are reciprocals of each other. That is, the opportunity cost of 1 ton of food crops is 14 barrels of ethanol and the opportunity cost of 1 barrel of ethanol is 1/14 of a ton of food crops.

g. Does Brazil face an increasing opportunity cost of ethanol? What feature of the *PPF* that you've drawn illustrates increasing opportunity cost?

Brazil faces an increasing opportunity cost of ethanol production. For instance, when increasing ethanol production from 0 barrels per day to 22 barrels the opportunity cost of a barrel of ethanol is 1/22 of a ton of food while increasing ethanol production another 18 barrels per day (to a total of 40 barrels per day) has an opportunity cost of 1/18 of a ton of food per barrel of ethanol. The *PPF*'s bowed outward shape reflects the increasing opportunity cost.

3. Define marginal benefit, explain how it is measured, and explain why the information provided in the table in problem 1 does not enable you to calculate the marginal benefit of food.

The marginal benefit of a good is the benefit received from consuming one more unit of the product. The marginal benefit of a good or service is measured by the most people are willing to pay for one more unit of it. The data in the table do not provide information on how much people are willing to pay for an additional unit of food. Hence the table has no information on the marginal benefit of food.

5. Harry enjoys tennis but wants a high grade in his economics course. Figure 2.2 shows the limits to what he can achieve: It is Harry's *PPF* for these two "goods." Figure 2.3 (on the next page) shows Harry's *MB* curve for tennis.

a. What is Harry's marginal cost of tennis if he plays for (i) 3 hours a week; (ii) 5 hours a week; and (iii) 7 hours a week.

(i) Harry's marginal cost of an hour of tennis is 1.5 percentage points. When

Harry increases the time he plays tennis from 2 hours to 4 hours, his grade in economics falls from 78 percent to 75 percent. His opportunity cost of these 2 additional hours of tennis is 3 percentage points, so his marginal cost of playing tennis for the third hour per week is 1.5 percentage points. (ii) Harry's marginal cost of an hour of tennis is 2.5 percentage points. When Harry increases the time he plays tennis from 4 hours to 6 hours, his grade in economics falls from 75 percent to 70 percent. His opportunity cost of these 2 additional hours of tennis is 5 percentage points. So his marginal cost of playing tennis for the fifth hour per week is 2.5 percentage points. (iii) Harry's marginal cost of an hour of tennis is 5 percentage points. When Harry increases the time he plays tennis from 6 hours to 8 hours, his grade in economics falls from 70 percent to 60 percent. His opportunity cost of these 2 additional hours of tennis is 10 percentage points. So his marginal cost of playing tennis for the seventh hour per week is 5 percentage points.

FIGURE **2.2**
Problem 5

b. If Harry uses his time to achieve allocative efficiency, what is his economics grade and how many hours of tennis does he play?

Harry's grade in economics is 66 percent and he plays tennis for 7 hours per week. From the answer to part (a), Harry's marginal cost of playing the third hour a week of tennis is 1.5 percentage points, his marginal cost of playing tennis the fifth hour a week is 2.5 percentage points and his marginal cost of playing tennis the seventh hour a week is 5 percentage points. Plot these three opportunity costs in Figure 2.3 to create Harry's marginal cost curve. Harry's opportunity cost of playing tennis increases as he spends more time on tennis. Harry uses his time efficiently if he plays tennis for 7 hours a week because when he plays 7 hours a week his marginal benefit from the seventh hour of tennis, 5 percentage points, equals its marginal cost, also 5 percentage points. When Harry plays 7 hours of tennis, the *PPF* in Figure 2.2 shows that his grade in economics 66 percent.

c. Explain why Harry would be worse off getting a grade higher than your answer to b.

If Harry studied for enough hours to get a higher grade, he would have fewer hours to play tennis. Harry's marginal benefit from tennis would be greater than his marginal cost, so he would be more efficient (better off) if he played more hours of tennis and took a lower grade.

d. If Harry becomes a tennis superstar with big earnings from tennis, what happens to his *PPF*, *MB* curve, and efficient time allocation?

If Harry becomes a tennis superstar, his *PPF* does not change. Harry's *PPF* shows the grade he can produce for different hours of playing tennis and these production possibilities are unaffected by Harry's superstar status. As a result Harry's *MC* curve does not change. However Harry's *MB* from playing

FIGURE **2.3**
Problem 5

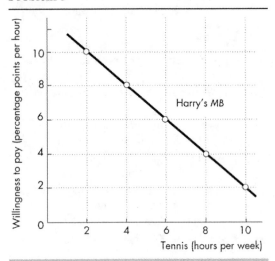

tennis increases because of his big paydays so his *MB* curve shifts rightward. As a result, Harry's efficient allocation of time now allocates more time to tennis (and results in a lower grade).

e. If Harry suddenly finds high grades in economics easier to attain, what happens to his *PPF*, *MB* curve, and efficient time allocation?

If Harry finds high grades to easier to attain his *PPF* shifts outward. In particular for every level of tennis playing his grade in economics is higher. As a result Harry's marginal cost of earning a high grade in economics is reduced so that Harry's *MC* curve shifts downward. Harry's *MB* curve does not change because Harry's marginal benefit from a high grade has not changed. Harry's efficient time allocation results in Harry increasing the number of hours of tennis he plays.

7. In one hour, Sue can produce 40 caps or 4 jackets and Tessa can produce 80 caps or 4 jackets.

a. Calculate Sue's opportunity cost of producing a cap.

Sue forgoes 4 jackets to produce 40 caps, so Sue's opportunity cost of producing one cap is (4 jackets)/(40 caps) or 0.1 jacket per cap.

b. **Calculate Tessa's opportunity cost of producing a cap.**

Tessa forgoes 4 jackets to produce 80 caps, so Tessa's opportunity cost of producing one cap is (4 jackets)/(80 caps) or 0.05 jacket per cap.

c. **Who has a comparative advantage in producing caps?**

Tessa's opportunity cost of a cap is lower than Sue's opportunity cost, so Tessa has a comparative advantage in producing caps.

d. **If Sue and Tessa specialize in producing the good in which each of them has a comparative advantage, and they trade 1 jacket for 15 caps, who gains from the specialization and trade?**

Tessa specializes in caps and Sue specializes in jackets. Both Sue and Tessa gain from trade. Sue gains because she can obtain caps from Tessa at a cost of (1 jacket)/(15 caps), which is 0.067 jacket per cap, a cost that is lower than what it would cost her to produce caps herself. Tessa also gains from trade because she trades caps for jackets for 0.067 jacket per cap, which is higher than her cost of producing a cap.

9. **"America's baby-boomers are embracing tea for its health benefits,"** said *The Economist* **(July 8, 2005, p. 65). The article went on to say: "Even though the climate is suitable, tea-growing [in the United States] is simply too costly, since the process is labor-intensive and resists automation." Using this information:**

a. **Sketch a *PPF* for the production of tea and other goods and services in India.**

The *PPF* might be linear, though a more realistic *PPF* would be bowed out from the origin. The products along the two axes are tea and other goods and services. In Figure 2.5, tea is drawn along the horizontal axis but it could also be drawn along the vertical axis.

FIGURE **2.5**
Problem 9a

FIGURE **2.6**
Problem 9b

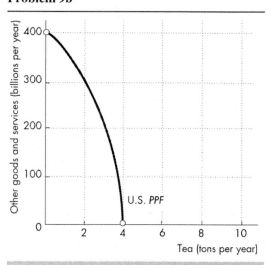

b. **Sketch a *PPF* for the production of tea and other goods and services in the United States.**

Again the *PPF* might be linear, though a more realistic *PPF* would be bowed out from the origin. As before, the products along the two axes are tea and other goods and services. Figure 2.6 (on this page) illustrates the situation in the United States. Compared to India, the important point about the two *PPF*s is that the opportunity cost of producing tea is lower in India. If tea is measured along the horizontal axis, the magnitude of the slope of the *PPF* is equal to the opportunity cost of producing tea, so in this case the U.S. *PPF* would be steeper than the Indian *PPF*. If tea is measured along the vertical axis, then the Indian *PPF* would be steeper than the U.S. *PPF*.

c. Sketch a marginal cost curve for the production of tea in India.

The marginal cost curve for producing tea in India is illustrated in Figure 2.7. This marginal cost curve slopes upward.

d. Sketch a marginal cost curve for the production of tea in the United States.

The marginal cost curve for producing tea in the United States is also illustrated in Figure 2.7. Similar to the marginal cost curve for India, the U.S. marginal cost curve slopes upward. Because tea is less costly to produce in India than in the United States, the U.S. *MC* curve lies above the Indian *MC* curve.

e. Sketch the marginal benefit curve for tea in the United States before and after the baby boomers began to appreciate the health benefits of tea.

As Figure 2.8 shows, the downward sloping marginal benefit curve for tea shifts rightward after more baby-boomers start to appreciate tea.

f. Explain why the United States does not produce tea and instead imports it from India.

The United States imports tea from India because it is cheaper for the U.S. to import tea than to produce it in the United States. Fewer other goods and services must be given up to import tea than would be given up if the United States produced tea.

g. Explain how the quantity of tea that achieves allocative efficiency has changed.

The increase in the marginal benefit from tea increases the quantity of tea that achieves allocative efficiency.

h. Does the change in preferences toward tea affect the opportunity cost of producing tea?

If the *PPF* in India between tea and other goods and services is bowed out from the origin, increasing the production of tea raises the opportunity cost of producing tea.

FIGURE **2.7**
Problem 9c and 9d

FIGURE **2.8**
Problem 9e

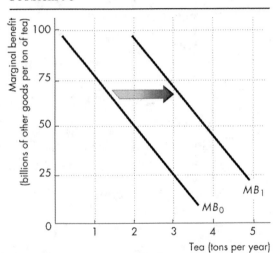

11. **For 50 years, Cuba has had a centrally planned economy in which the government makes the big decisions on how resources will be allocated. Why would you expect Cuba's production possibilities (per person) to be smaller than those of the United States? What are the economic institutions that help the U.S. economy achieve allocative efficiency that Cuba might lack?**

Cuba's economy is almost surely less efficient than the U.S. economy. Because owners of firms in the United States have been given the property rights to any profit their firm might earn, owners have the self-interested incentive to operate the firm efficiently and produce goods and services that consumers desire. In Cuba these incentives are absent because firms are not privately owned. As a result, no single person has the self-interested incentive to either insure that firms produce goods and services efficiently or produce the goods and services that consumers desire. In other words, the U.S. economy with its property rights and markets has harnessed people's self interest to produce goods and services efficiently and so the U.S. economy is likely much closer to allocative efficiency than is the Cuban economy.

13. **What is the marginal cost of a pound of food in Yucatan in problem 12 when the quantity produced is 150 tons per day? What is special about the marginal cost of food in Yucatan?**

The marginal cost of a pound of food in Yucatan is constant at all points along Yucatan's *PPF* and is equal to 0.5 gallons of sunscreen per pound of food. The special point about Yucatan's marginal cost is the fact that the marginal cost is constant.

15. **"Dr. Arata Kochi, the World Health Organization malaria chief, ... [says that] eradication is counterproductive. With enough money, he said, current tools like nets, medicines and DDT could drive down malaria cases 90 percent. 'But eliminating the last 10 percent is a tremendous task and very expensive,' Dr. Kochi said. 'Even places like South Africa should think twice before taking this path.'"**
The New York Times, **March 4, 2008**

Food (pounds per month)		Sunscreen (gallons per month)
300	and	0
200	and	50
100	and	100
0	and	150

a. **Is Dr. Kochi talking about *production efficiency* or *allocative efficiency* or both?**

Dr. Kochi is talking about allocative efficiency. His assessment is that the last 10 percent eradication has such a high marginal cost that it almost surely exceeds its marginal benefit.

b. **Make a graph with the percentage of malaria cases eliminated on the *x*-axis and the marginal cost and marginal benefit of driving down malaria cases on the *y*-axis. On your graph:**

(i) **Draw a marginal cost curve that is consistent with Dr. Kochi's opinion reported in the news article.**

(ii) **Draw a marginal benefit curve that is consistent with Dr. Kochi's opinion reported in the news article.**

(iii) **Identify the quantity of malaria eradicated that achieves allocative efficiency.**

FIGURE **2.13**
Problem 15b

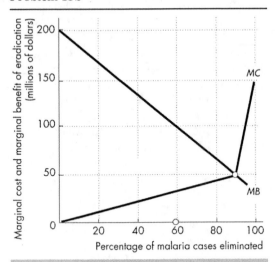

Figure 2.13 shows a marginal cost curve
and a marginal benefit curve that are
consistent with Dr. Kochi's views. The
marginal cost curve rises rapidly after
90 percent of malaria is eradicated. The
allocatively efficient quantity of malaria
eradicated is 90 percent because that is
the quantity for which the marginal
benefit of eradication equals the marginal
cost of eradication.

17. **"Inexpensive broadband access has
done far more for online video than
enable the success of services like
YouTube and iTunes. By unchaining
video watchers from their TV sets, it
has opened the floodgates to a
generation of TV producers for whom
the Internet is their native medium."**
The New York Times, December 2, 2007

a. **How has inexpensive broadband
changed the production possibilities
of video entertainment and other
goods and services?**

Inexpensive broadband has increased the
production possibilities.

b. **Sketch a *PPF* for video entertainment
and other goods and services before
broadband.**

The *PPF* should have video
entertainment on one axis and other
goods and services on the other as
illustrated in Figure 2.14 by PPF_0. The
PPF is bowed outward as a conventional
PPF.

c. **Show how the arrival of inexpensive
broadband has changed the *PPF*.**

The arrival of inexpensive broadband
shifts the *PPF* outward as shown by the
change from PPF_0 to PPF_1 in Figure
2.14. The intersection of the new *PPF*
along the axis measuring video
entertainment increases and the
intersection of the new *PPF* along the
axis measuring other goods and services
does not change.

FIGURE **2.14**
Problem 17b and 17c

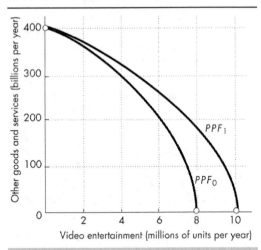

d. Sketch a marginal benefit curve for video entertainment.

The marginal benefit curve should be a conventional downward sloping marginal benefit curve as shown in Figure 2.15. The marginal benefit from video entertainment is measured along the vertical axis and the quantity of video entertainment is measured along the horizontal axis.

e. Show how opening the "floodgates to a generation of TV producers for whom the Internet is their native medium" might have changed the marginal benefit from video entertainment.

The marginal benefit curve does not shift because of "opening the floodgates" since this effect changes the marginal cost not the marginal benefit. The marginal cost curve shifts downward. However if there is increased excitement about this medium, then the marginal benefit increases and the marginal benefit curve shifts rightward. Then, as illustrated in Figure 2.16 the allocatively efficient quantity of video entertainment increases.

f. Explain how the quantity of video entertainment that achieves allocative efficiency has changed.

Because the marginal cost of providing video entertainment falls, the allocatively efficient quantity of video entertainment increases, in Figure 2.16 from 5 million units per year to 8 million units per year.

FIGURE **2.15**

Problem 17d

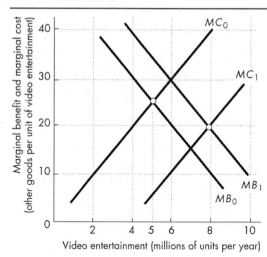

FIGURE **2.16**

Problem 17e and 17f

19. **Before the Civil War, the South traded
     with the North and with England. The
     South sold cotton and bought
     manufactured goods and food. During
     the war, one of Lincoln's first actions
     was to blockade the ports, which
     prevented this trade. The South had to
     increase its production of munitions
     and food.**

FIGURE **2.17**
Problem 19

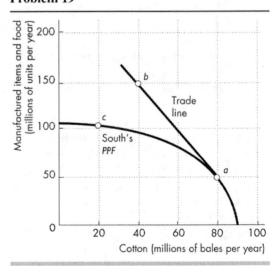

a. **In what did the South have a
    comparative advantage?**

    Before the war the South had a comparative
    advantage in producing cotton.

b. **Draw a graph to illustrate
    production, consumption, and trade
    in the South before the Civil War.**

    Figure 2.17 illustrates the South's
    situation. The production point is point
    a. The South produces a great deal of
    cotton and very little food and
    manufactured goods; indeed, in the
    unlikely case that the South completely
    specialized, the production point could
    be at the maximum quantity of cotton
    and zero food and manufactured goods.
    From the production point a trade line
    with a negative slope touches the *PPF* and
    extends beyond the *PPF*. The trade line
    shows that the South traded cotton for
    manufacturing goods and food and
    consumed at point *b*, well beyond its *PPF*.

c. **Was the South consuming inside, on,
    or outside its *PPF*? Explain your
    answer.**

    The South was consuming at a point
    beyond its *PPF*. The South could do so
    because it was able to trade cotton, which
    was relatively less expensive for the South
    to produce, in exchange for
    manufactured goods and food, which
    would have been relatively expensive for
    the South to produce. In other words,
    the South enjoyed gains from trade.

d. **Draw a graph to show the effects of
    the Civil War on consumption and
    production in the South.**

    Assuming that the Civil War did not
    affect the South's *PPF* (which is probably
    true only for the first part of the war) the

North's blockade meant that the South
could no longer trade with others. As a
result, the South increased its production
of manufactured goods (especially
munitions) and food, which caused the
South to decrease its production of
cotton. The blockade forced the South's
consumption point to lie on its *PPF*, so
the South's consumption of
manufactured goods and food decreased.
In Figure 2.17, the South changes so that
its production and its consumption point
become point *c*.

e. **Did the Civil War change any
    opportunity costs in the South? Did
    the opportunity cost of everything
    rise? Did any items cost less?**

    The Civil War increased the opportunity
    cost of food and manufactured goods.
    However it decreased the opportunity
    cost of cotton.

f. **Illustrate your answer to e with
    appropriate graphs.**

    Figure 2.17 illustrates the changes. The
    opportunity cost of cotton decreased
    because the blockade lead the South to
    produce less cotton, moving from initial
    production point *a* to final production
    point *c*. Moving along a *PPF*, as less of a
    good is produced, its opportunity cost

falls. The opportunity cost of food and manufactured goods increased because the South increased the amount of food and manufactured goods it produced. Moving along a *PPF*, as more of a good is produced, its opportunity cost rises.

21. **After you have studied *Reading Between the Lines* on pp. 46–47, answer the following questions:**

a. **How has an Act of the United States Congress increased U.S. production of corn?**

The Act of Congress increased the amount of ethanol that must be used in gasoline. Because ethanol is made from corn, the mandate increased the demand for corn and farmers responded by growing more corn.

b. **Why would you expect an increase in the quantity of corn produced to raise the opportunity cost of corn?**

Increasing the quantity of corn produced results in a higher opportunity cost of corn because acreage less suited to growing corn is shifted away from other crops and into corn. As increasingly less suitable acreage is used, the opportunity cost of in terms of other crops forgone increases.

c. **Why did the cost of producing corn increase in the rest of the world?**

The cost of producing corn in the rest of the world increased for two reasons. First in other parts of the world, droughts decreased the corn harvest and thereby increased the opportunity cost of the land that was being used to grow corn. Second the increased demand for corn from people who had previously been destitute increased the land devoted to growing corn, which also raised the opportunity cost of producing corn.

d. **Is it possible that the increased quantity of corn produced, despite the higher cost of production, moves the United States closer to allocative efficiency?**

It is possible that the increased quantity of corn has moved the United States closer to allocative efficiency. The marginal benefit from ethanol increased because of the higher price for gasoline, so the allocatively efficient quantity of ethanol increased. To increase the production of ethanol more corn had to be produced, so even with the higher opportunity cost, the United States might have moved closer to the allocatively efficient point of production.

Additional Problems

1. Jane's Island's production possibilities are given in the table to the right.
    a. Draw a graph of the production possibility possibilities frontier on Jane's Island.
    b. What are Jane's opportunity costs of producing corn and cloth at each output in the table?

2. In problem 1, Jane is willing to give up 0.75 pounds of corn per yard of cloth if she has 2 yards of cloth; 0.50 pounds of corn per yard of cloth if she has 4 yards of cloth; and 0.25 pound of corn per yard of cloth if she has 6 yards of cloth.
    a. Draw a graph of Jane's marginal benefit from corn.
    b. What is Jane's efficient quantity of corn?

3. Joe's production possibilities are given in the table to the right. What are Joe's opportunity costs of producing corn and cloth at each output in the table?

4. In problems 1 and 2, Jane's Island produces and consumes 2 pounds of corn and 2 yards of cloth. Joe's Island produces and consumes 2 pounds of corn and 2 yard of cloth. Now the islands begin to trade.
    a. What good does Jane sell to Joe and what good does Jane buy from Joe?
    b. If Jane and Joe divide the total output of corn and cloth equally, what are the gains from trade?

Corn (pounds per month)		Cloth (yards per month)
3.0	and	0
2.0	and	2
1.0	and	4
0	and	6

Corn (pounds per month)		Cloth (yards per month)
6	and	0
4	and	1.0
2	and	2.0
0	and	3.0

Solutions to Additional Problems

1. a. Jane's Island's *PPF* is a straight line. To make a graph of Jane's Island's *PPF* measure the quantity of one good on the *x*-axis and the quantity of the other good on the *y*-axis. Plot the quantities in each row of the table. Figure 2.20 illustrates Jane's Island's *PPF*.

    b. The opportunity cost of 1 pound of corn is 2 yards of cloth. The opportunity cost of the first pound of corn is 2 yards of cloth. To find the opportunity cost of the first pound of corn, increase the quantity of corn from 0 pounds to 1 pound. In doing so, Jane's Island's production of cloth decreases from 6 yards to 4 yards. The opportunity cost of the first pound of corn is 2 yards of cloth. Similarly, the opportunity costs of producing the second pound and the third pound of corn are 2 yards of cloth.

        The opportunity cost of 1 yard of cloth is 0.5 pound of corn. The opportunity cost of producing the first 2 yards of cloth is 1 pound of corn. To calculate this opportunity cost, increase the quantity of cloth from 0 yards to 2 yards. Jane's Island's production of corn decreases from 3 pounds to 2 pounds. Similarly, the opportunity cost of producing the second 2 yards and the third 2 yards of cloth are 1 pound of corn.

2. a. The marginal benefit curve slopes downward. To draw the marginal benefit curve from cloth, plot the quantity of cloth on the *x*-axis and the willingness to pay for cloth (that is, the number of pounds of corn that Jane is willing to give up to get a yard of cloth) on the *y*-axis.

    b. The efficient quantity is 4 yards a month. The efficient quantity to produce is such that the marginal benefit from the last yard equals the opportunity cost of producing it. The opportunity cost of a yard of cloth is 0.5 pound of corn. The marginal benefit of the fourth yard of cloth is 0.5 pound of

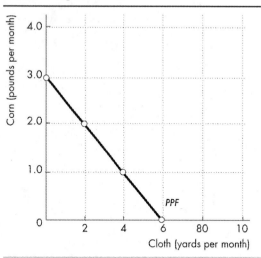

FIGURE **2.20**

Additional problem 1a

corn. And the marginal cost of the fourth yard of cloth is 0.5 pound of corn.

3. Joe's Island's opportunity cost of a pound of corn is 1/2 yard of cloth, and its opportunity cost of a yard of cloth is 2 pounds of corn. When Joe's Island increases the corn it produces by 2 pounds a month, it produces 1 yard of cloth less. The opportunity cost of 1 pound of corn is 1/2 yard of cloth. Similarly, when Joe's Island increases the cloth it produces by 1 yard a month, it produces 2 pounds of corn less. The opportunity cost of 1 yard of cloth is 2 pounds of corn.

4. a. Jane's Island sells cloth and buys corn. Jane's Island sells the good in which it has a comparative advantage and buys the other good from Joe's Island. Jane's Island's opportunity cost of 1 yard of cloth is 1/2 pound of corn, while Joe's Island's opportunity cost of 1 yard of cloth is 2 pounds of corn. Jane's Island's opportunity cost of cloth is less than Joe's Island's, so Jane's Island has a comparative advantage in producing cloth.

        Jane's Island's opportunity cost of 1 pound of corn is 2 yards of cloth, while Joe's Island's opportunity cost of 1 pound of corn is 1/2 yard of cloth. Joe's Island's opportunity cost of corn is less than Jane's Island's, so Joe's Island has a comparative advantage in producing corn.

b. With specialization and trade, together they can produce 6 pounds of corn and 6 yards of cloth and each will get 3 pounds of corn and 3 yards of cloth—an additional 1 pound of corn each and an additional 1 yard of cloth each. Hence the total gains from trade are 2 yards of cloth and 2 pounds of corn..

Chapter 3 DEMAND AND SUPPLY

Answers to the Problems and Applications

1. **William Gregg owned a mill in South Carolina. In December 1862, he placed a notice in the *Edgehill Advertiser* announcing his willingness to exchange cloth for food and other items. Here is an extract:**

   1 yard of cloth for 1 pound of bacon
   2 yards of cloth for 1 pound of butter
   4 yards of cloth for 1 pound of wool
   8 yards of cloth for 1 bushel of salt

   a. **What is the relative price of butter in terms of wool?**

   1 pound of butter exchanged for 2 yards of cloth and 4 yards of cloth exchanged for 1 pound of wool. Hence 1 pound of butter exchanged for 2 yards of cloth and 2 yards of cloth exchanged for 1/2 pound of wool. So the relative price of butter in terms of wool was 1/2 pound of wool per pound of butter.

   b. **If the money price of bacon was 20¢ a pound, what do you predict was the money price of butter?**

   1 pound of bacon exchanged for 1 yard of cloth and 2 yards of cloth exchanged for 1 pound of butter. Hence it took 2 pounds of bacon to exchange for 1 pound of butter. As a result, if the money price of a pound of bacon was 20¢ the money price of 1 pound of butter was 40¢.

   c. **If the money price of bacon was 20¢ a pound and the money price of salt was $2.00 a bushel, do you think anyone would accept Mr. Gregg's offer of cloth for salt?**

   If the money price of bacon is 20¢ a pound, Mr. Gregg's offer to exchange 1 pound of bacon for 1 yard of cloth means that anyone could obtain 1 yard of cloth for a money price of 20¢. Mr. Gregg's further offer to exchange 8 yards of cloth for 1 bushel of salt means that anyone could acquire 1 bushel of salt for $1.60, the price of 8 yards of cloth. If the money

   price of salt is $2.00 a bushel, many people would accept Mr. Gregg's offer of cloth for salt because it enables them to obtain salt at a money price of only $1.60 a bushel.

3. **Place the following goods and services into pairs of likely substitutes and into pairs of likely complements. (You may use an item in more than one pair.) The goods and services are:**

   coal, oil, natural gas, wheat, corn, rye, pasta, pizza, sausage, skateboard, roller blades, video game, laptop, iPod, cell phone, text message, email, phone call, voice mail

   Substitutes include: coal and oil; coal and natural gas; oil and natural gas; wheat and corn; wheat and rye; corn and rye; pasta and pizza; pasta and sausage; pizza and sausage (they type of sausage that cannot be used as a topping on pizza); skateboard and roller blades; skateboard and video game; roller blades and video game; text message and email; text message and phone call; and, email and phone call.

   Complements include: pizza and sausage (the type of sausage that can be used as a topping on pizza); skateboard and iPod; roller blades and iPod; video game (the type played on a computer) and laptop; cell phone and text message; cell phone and phone call; cell phone and voice mail; and, phone call and voice mail.

5. **In January 2007, the price of gasoline was $2.38 a gallon. By May 2008, the price had increased to $3.84 a gallon. Assume that there were no changes in average income, population, or any other influence on buying plans. How would you expect the rise in the price of gasoline to affect**

   a. **The demand for gasoline? Explain your answer.**

   The rise in the price of gasoline does not change the demand for gasoline. The *demand for gasoline* changes *only* when some other relevant factor other than the price of the good changes.

Price	Quantity demanded	Quantity supplied
(cents per pack)	(millions of packs a week)	
20	180	60
40	140	100
60	100	140
80	60	180
100	20	220

b. **The quantity of gasoline demanded? Explain your answer.**

The rise in the price of gasoline decreases the quantity of gasoline demanded. A rise in the price of a good or service decreases the quantity of that good or service demanded.

7. **American to cut flights, charge for luggage**
American Airlines announced yesterday that it will begin charging passengers $15 for their first piece of checked luggage, in addition to raising other fees and cutting domestic flights as it grapples with record-high fuel prices.
Boston Herald, **May 22, 2008**

a. **How does this news clip illustrate a change in supply? Explain your answer.**

Fuel prices are a cost of a factor of production. As the cost rises, the supply decreases. American Airlines is decreasing the supply of its flights by cutting domestic flights.

b. **What is the influence on supply identified in the news clip? Explain your answer.**

The influence is the cost of a factor of production, in particular, the cost of fuel.

c. **Explain how supply changes.**

The increase in the cost of the factor of production decreases the supply and shifts the supply curve leftward.

9. **"As more people buy computers, the demand for Internet service increases and the price of Internet service decreases. The fall in the price of Internet service decreases the supply of Internet service." Is this statement true or false? Explain.**

The statement is false for several reasons. First, if the demand for Internet services increases and nothing else changes, the price of Internet service will rise *not* fall. Second, if the price of Internet services

falls, the supply of Internet services does not change. Rather, there is a decrease in the quantity supplied, that is, a movement along the supply curve rather than a shift of the supply curve.

11. **The demand and supply schedules for gum are given in the table.**

a. **Draw a graph of the gum market, label the axes and the curves, and mark in the equilibrium price and quantity.**

Figure 3.1, (on the next page), shows the demand and supply curves. The equilibrium price is 50 cents a pack, and the equilibrium quantity is 120 million packs a week. The price of a pack adjusts until the quantity demanded equals the quantity supplied. At 50 cents a pack, the quantity demanded is 120 million packs a week and the quantity supplied is 120 million packs a week.

b. **Suppose that the price of gum is 70¢ a pack. Describe the situation in the gum market and explain how the price adjusts.**

At 70 cents a pack, there is a surplus of gum and the price falls. At 70 cents a pack, the quantity demanded is 80 million packs a week and the quantity supplied is 160 million packs a week. There is a surplus of 80 million packs a week. The price falls until market equilibrium is restored at a price of 50 cents a pack.

c. **Suppose that the price of gum is 30¢
    a pack. Describe the situation in the
    gum market and explain how the
    price adjusts.**

    At 30 cents a pack, there is a shortage of
    gum and the price rises. At 30 cents a
    pack, the quantity demanded is 160
    million packs a week and the quantity
    supplied is 80 million packs a week.
    There is a shortage of 80 million packs a
    week. The price rises until market
    equilibrium is restored at a price of 50
    cents a pack.

d. **A fire destroys some factories that
    produce gum and the quantity of
    gum supplied decreases by 40 million
    packs a week at each price. Explain
    what happens in the market for gum
    and illustrate the changes on your
    graph.**

    As the number of gum-producing
    factories decreases, the supply of gum
    decreases. There is a new supply schedule
    and, in Figure 3.2, the supply curves
    shifts leftward by 40 million packs at
    each price to the new supply curve S_1.
    After the fire, the quantity supplied at 50
    cents is now only 80 million packs, and
    there is a shortage of gum. The price rises
    to 60 cents a pack, at which the new
    quantity supplied equals the quantity
    demanded (100 million packs a week).
    So the new equilibrium price is 60 cents
    and the new equilibrium quantity is 100
    million packs a week.

FIGURE **3.1**
Problem 11a

FIGURE **3.2**
Problem 11d

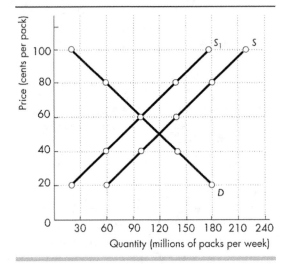

e. If at the time the fire occurs in d, there is an increase in the teenage population, which increases the quantity of gum demanded by 40 million packs a week at each price. What are the new equilibrium price and quantity of gum? Illustrate these changes in your graph.

The new price is 70 cents a pack, and the quantity is 120 million packs a week. The demand for gum increases and the demand curve shifts rightward by 40 million packs at each price. Supply decreases by 40 millions packs a week and the supply curve shifts leftward by 40 million packs at each price. These changes are shown in Figure 3.3 by the shift of the demand curve from D to D_1 and the shift of the supply curve from S to S_1. At any price below 70 cents a pack there is a shortage of gum. The price of gum rises until the shortage is eliminated.

13. Of gambling, grannies and good sense Nevada has the fastest growing elderly population of any state. . . . Las Vegas has . . . plenty of jobs for the over 50s.
The Economist, **July 26, 2006**

Explain how grannies have influenced the

a. Demand side of some Las Vegas markets.

On the average, elderly people require more health care services than younger people. So the influx of older people into Las Vegas increased the demand for medical services and pharmaceutical drugs and services. Older people also eat out more often and do less yard work. So the demand for restaurant meals and yard care maintenance increased.

b. Supply side of other Las Vegas markets.

Older but not-yet retired people work, so the increase in "grannies" increased the supply of labor.

FIGURE **3.3**
Problem 11e

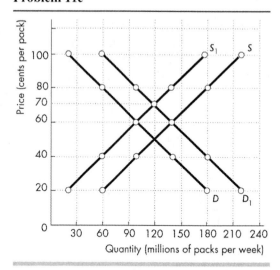

15. Use the link on MyEconLab (Textbook Resources, Chapter 3, Web Links) to obtain data on the price of oil since 2000.

a. Describe how the price of oil changed.

Through at least the summer of 2008, the price of oil has generally risen since 2000.

b. Use a demand-supply graph to explain what happens to the price when supply increases or decreases and demand is unchanged.

When supply increases, the supply curve shifts rightward. The price falls. When supply decreases, the supply curve shifts leftward. The price rises.

c. What do you predict would happen to the price of oil if a new drilling technology permitted deeper ocean sources to be used?

If new drilling technology is developed, the supply of oil would increase and the supply curve would shift rightward. The price of oil would fall.

d. What do you predict would happen to the price of oil if a clean and safe nuclear technology were developed?

Energy produced using nuclear power is a substitute for energy produced using oil.

If clean and safe nuclear technology is developed, the demand for oil would decrease and the demand curve would shift leftward. The price of oil would fall.

e. How does a higher price of oil influence the market for ethanol?

Alternative fuels, such as ethanol, are a substitute for oil. A higher price of oil increases the demand for ethanol (refiners will produce more ethanol blended gasoline). The increase in demand for ethanol raises the price of ethanol and increases the quantity of ethanol.

f. How does an increase in the supply of ethanol influence the market for oil?

Alternative fuels, such as ethanol, are a substitute for oil. An increase in the supply of ethanol lowers the price of ethanol. As a result more drivers use ethanol blended fuels so the demand for oil decreases. The price of oil falls and the quantity decreases.

17. The money price of a textbook is $90 and the money price of the Wii game *Super Mario Galaxy* is $45.

a. What is the opportunity cost of a textbook in terms of the Wii game?

A textbook costs $90 and a Wii game costs $45. Purchasing 1 textbook forces the buyer to forego 2 Wii games. So the opportunity cost of a textbook in terms of Wii games is 2 Wii games per textbook.

b. What is the relative price of the Wii game in terms of textbooks?

The relative price of a Wii game in terms of textbooks ($45 per Wii)/($90 per textbook), which is 1/2 of a textbook per Wii game.

19. Classify the following pairs of goods and services as substitutes, complements, substitutes in production, or complements in production.

a. Bottled water and health club memberships

Bottled water and health club memberships are complements because people in health clubs drink a lot of bottled water.

b. French fries and baked potatoes

For a consumer, French fries and baked potatoes are substitutes. For a restaurant that produces both French fries and baked potatoes, they are substitutes in production.

c. Leather purses and leather shoes

Leather purses and leather shoes are substitutes in production.

d. SUVs and pickup trucks

For a consumer, SUVs and pickup trucks are substitutes. For an auto company that produces both on the same assembly line, they are substitutes in production.

e. Diet coke and regular coke

For a consumer, Diet coke and regular coke are substitutes. For a soda company that produces both on the same assembly line, they are substitutes in production.

f. Low-fat milk and cream

Low-fat milk and cream are complements in production.

21. In 2008, as the prices of homes fell across the United States, the number of homes offered for sale decreased.

a. Does this fact illustrate the law of demand or the law of supply? Explain your answer.

This fact illustrates the law of supply: As the price falls, the quantity supplied decreases.

b. Why would home owners hold off trying to sell?

Home owners delay selling their homes because they believe the price they would receive is too low and the price they will receive in the future will be higher.

23. **Figure 3.5 illustrates the market for pizza.**

a. **Label the curves. Which curve shows the willingness to pay for a pizza?**

The demand curve is the downward sloping curve and the supply curve is the upward sloping curve. The demand curve shows the willingness to pay for a pizza.

b. **If the price of a pizza is $16, is there a shortage or a surplus and does the price rise or fall?**

If the price of a pizza is $16, there is a surplus of pizza; the quantity supplied of pizzas exceeds the quantity demanded. The surplus forces the price lower to the equilibrium price of $14 a pizza.

c. **Sellers want to receive the highest possible price, so why would they be willing to accept less than $16 a pizza?**

Sellers are willing to accept less than $16 because if they charge $16 the surplus means that some sellers have unsold pizzas. From their perspective it is better to have a lower price for the pizza and sell the (decreased) quantity they produce than to keep the price at $16 and be left with unsold pizza.

d. **If the price of a pizza is $12, is there a shortage or a surplus and does the price rise or fall?**

If the price of a pizza is $12, there is a shortage of pizza; the quantity demanded of pizzas exceeds the quantity supplied. The shortage forces the price higher to the equilibrium price of $14 a pizza.

e. **Buyers want to pay the lowest possible price, so why would they be willing to pay more than $12 for a pizza?**

If the price of a pizza is $12 the shortage means that not all buyers can buy a pizza. From their perspective they would rather pay more than $12 and be able to purchase a pizza a pizza than to keep the price at $12 and leave them without a pizza.

FIGURE **3.5**
Problem 23

25. **'Popcorn Movie' Experience Gets Pricier'**

... cinemas are raising ... prices. ... Demand for field corn, used for animal feed, ... corn syrup and ... ethanol, has caused its price to explode. That's caused some farmers to shift from popcorn to easier-to-grow field corn, cutting supply and pushing its price higher, too....

USA Today, **May 24, 2008**

Explain and illustrate graphically the events described in the news clip in the markets for

a. **Popcorn.**

As illustrated in Figure 3.6, the farmers' actions decrease the supply of popcorn and the supply curve of popcorn shifts leftward. The demand curve does not shift. The equilibrium price of popcorn rises and the quantity decreases.

b. **Viewing movies in the theater.**

In the market for viewing movies in the theater, popcorn and viewing movies are complements. The increase in the price of popcorn decreases the demand for attending movies in the theater. As a result, Figure 3.7 shows the demand curve shifting leftward. The equilibrium price of attending a movie in the theater falls and the equilibrium quantity decreases.

27. **Sony's Blu-Ray Wins High-Definition War**

Toshiba Corp. yesterday raised the white flag in the war over the next-generation home movie format, announcing the end of its HD DVD business in a victory for Sony Corp.'s Blu-ray technology. The move could finally jump-start a high-definition home DVD market that has been hamstrung as consumers waited on the sidelines for the battle to play out in a fight reminiscent of the VHS-Betamax videotape war of the 1980s.

The Washington Times, **February 20, 2008**

FIGURE **3.6**
Problem 25a

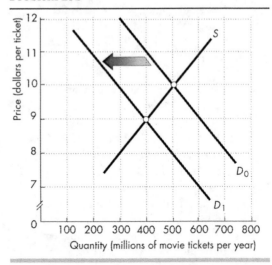

FIGURE **3.7**
Problem 25b

How would you expect the end of Toshiba's HD DVD format to influence

a. **The price of a used Toshiba player on eBay? Would the outcome that you predict result from a change in demand or a change in supply or both, and in which directions?**

The price of a used-Toshiba player falls. The price falls because the demand for these players decreases as potential buyers switch to Blu-ray players. The price also falls because the supply of these players increases as current owners move to discard their now semi-obsolete players.

b.   The price of a Blu-ray player?

The price of a Blu-ray player rises as people in the market for high definition DVD players now demand only Blu-ray players.

c.   The demand for Blu-ray format movies?

The demand for Blu-ray format movies increases because the quantity of Blu-ray players increases.

d.   The supply of Blu-ray format movies?

In the short run there is no change in the supply of Blu-ray movies, just a movement along the supply curve. But in the longer run movie studios that had previously been supporting only the Toshiba format will switch to the Blu-ray format and at that time the supply of Blu-ray movies will increase.

e.   The price of Blu-ray format movies?

In the short run, the price of Blu-ray format movies increases as a result of the increase in demand. In the longer run the effect on the price is ambiguous because the longer-run increase in supply lowers the price and thereby counters the initial effect of the increase in demand.

f.   The quantity of Blu-ray format movies?

The quantity of Blu-ray movies increases in the short run and even more so in the longer run.

Additional Problems

1.   What is the effect on the price of
      hotdogs and the quantity of hotdogs
      sold if
   a.   The price of a hamburger rises?
   b.   The price of a hotdog bun rises?
   c.   The supply of hotdog sausages
        increases?
   d.   Consumers' incomes increase if hot
        dogs are a normal good?
   e.   The wage rate of a hotdog seller
        increases?
   f.   If the wage rate of the hotdog seller
        rises and at the same time prices of
        ketchup, mustard, and relish fall?

2.   Suppose that one of the following
      events occurs:
      (i)   The price of wool rises.
      (ii)   The price of sweaters falls.
      (iii) A close substitute for wool is
      invented.
      (iv)   A new high-speed loom is
      invented.

      Which of the above events increases or
      decreases (state which)
   a.   The demand for wool?
   b.   The supply of wool?
   c.   The quantity of wool demanded?
   d.   The quantity of wool supplied?

3.   The figure illustrates the market for
      bread.
   a.   Label the curves in the figure.
   b.   What are the equilibrium price of
        bread and the equilibrium quantity
        of bread?

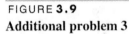

FIGURE **3.9**
Additional problem 3

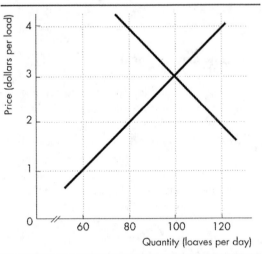

4. The demand and supply schedules for potato chips are in the table.
   a. What are the equilibrium price and equilibrium quantity of potato chips?
   b. If chips were 60 cents a bag, describe the situation in the market for potato chips and explain what would happen to the price of a bag of chips.

5. In problem 4, suppose a new snack food comes onto the market and as a result the demand for potato chips decreases by 40 million bags per week.
   a. Has there been a shift in or a movement along the supply curve of chips?
   b. Has there been a shift in or a movement along the demand curve for chips?
   c. What is the new equilibrium price and quantity of chips?

6. In problem 5, suppose that a flood destroys several potato farms and as a result supply decreases by 20 million bags a week at the same time as the new snack food comes onto the market. What is the new equilibrium price and quantity of chips?

Price (cents per bag)	Quantity demanded	Quantity supplied
	(millions of bags a week)	
40	170	90
50	160	100
60	150	110
70	140	120
80	130	130
90	120	140
100	110	150
110	100	160

Solutions to Additional Problems

1. a. The price of a hot dog rises, and the quantity of hot dogs sold increases. Hot dogs and hamburgers are substitutes. If the price of a hamburger rises, people buy more hot dogs and fewer hamburgers. The demand for hot dogs increases. The price of a hot dog rises, and more hot dogs are sold.

   b. The price of a hot dog falls, and fewer hot dogs are sold. Hot dog buns and hot dogs are complements. If the price of a hot dog bun rises, fewer hot dog buns are bought. The demand for hot dogs decreases. The price of a hot dog falls, and people buy fewer hot dogs.

   c. The price of a hot dog falls and more hot dogs are sold. The increase in the supply of hot dog sausages lowers the price of hot dog sausages. Hot dog sausages are a factor used in the production of hot dogs. With the lower priced factor, the supply of hot dogs increases. The price of a hot dog falls and people buy more hot dogs.

   d. The price of a hot dog rises, and the quantity sold increases. An increase in consumers' income increases the demand for hot dogs. As a result, the price of a hot dog rises and the quantity bought increases.

   e. The price of a hot dog rises, and the quantity sold decreases. If the wage of the hot dog seller increases, the cost of producing a hot dog increases and the supply of hot dogs decreases. The price rises, and people buy fewer hotdogs.

   f. The price of a hot dog rises, but the quantity might increase, decrease, or remain the same. Ketchup, mustard, and relish are complements of hot dogs. If the price of ketchup, mustard, and relish fall, more ketchup, mustard, and relish are bought and the demand for hot dogs increases. The price of a hot dog rises, and people buy more hot dogs. If the wage of the hot dog seller increases, the cost of producing a hot dog increases and the supply of hot dogs decreases. The price rises, and people buy fewer hotdogs. Taking the two events together, the price of a hot dog rises, but the quantity might increase, decrease, or remain the same.

2. a. (ii) and (iii) Wool is used in the production of sweaters. If the price of a sweater falls because the supply of sweaters has increased, then the equilibrium quantity of sweaters increases and the demand for wool increases. If the price of a sweater falls because the demand for sweaters has decreased, then the equilibrium quantity of sweaters decreases and the demand for wool decreases. If a close substitute for wool is invented, some sweater producers will switch from wool to the substitute. When they do, the demand for wool decreases.

   b. (iv) If a new high-speed loom is invented, the cost of making wool will fall and the supply of wool will increase.

   c. (i) and (iv) If the price of wool rises there is a movement up along the demand curve. The quantity demanded of wool decreases. If a new high-speed loom is invented, the cost of producing wool will fall. So the supply of wool increases. With no change in the demand for wool, the price of wool will fall and there is a movement down along the demand curve for wool. The quantity demanded of wool increases.

   d. (i), (ii), and (iii) If the price of wool rises there is a movement up along the supply curve. The quantity supplied of wool increases. If the price of a sweater falls because the supply of sweaters has increased, then the equilibrium quantity of sweaters increases and the demand for wool increases. With no change in the supply of wool, the price of wool rises and the quantity of wool supplied increases. If the price of a sweater falls because the demand for sweaters has decreased, then the equilibrium quantity of sweaters decreases and the demand for wool decreases. With no change in the supply of wool, the price of wool falls and the quantity of wool supplied decreases. If some sweater producers switch to using the new close substitute for wool, the demand for wool will decrease. With no change in the supply of wool, the price of wool falls and the quantity of wool supplied decreases.

3. a. The demand curve is the curve that slopes down toward to the right. The supply curve is the curve that slopes up toward to the right.

    b. The equilibrium price is $3 a loaf, and the equilibrium quantity is 100 loaves a day. Market equilibrium is determined at the intersection of the demand curve and supply curve.

4. a. The equilibrium price is 80 cents a bag, and the equilibrium quantity is 130 million bags a week. The price of a bag adjusts until the quantity demanded equals the quantity supplied. At 80 cents a bag, the quantity demanded is 130 million bags a week and the quantity supplied is 130 million bags a week.

    b. At 60 cents a bag, there will be a shortage of potato chips and the price will rise. At 60 cents a bag, the quantity demanded is 150 million bags a week and the quantity supplied is 110 million bags a week. There is a shortage of 40 million bags a week. The price will rise until market equilibrium is restored—80 cents a bag.

5. a. There has been a movement along the supply curve. The demand for potato chips decreases, and the demand curve shifts leftward. Supply does not change, so the price falls along the supply curve.

    b. The demand curve has shifted leftward. As the new snack food comes onto the market, the demand for potato chips decreases. There is a new demand schedule, and the demand curve shifts leftward.

    c. The equilibrium price is 60 cents, and the equilibrium quantity is 110 million bags a week. Demand decreases by 40 millions bags a week. That is, the quantity demanded at each price decreases by 40 million bags. The quantity demanded at 80 cents is now 90 million bags, and there is a surplus of potato chips. The price falls to 60 cents a bag, at which the quantity supplied equals the quantity demanded (110 million bags a week).

6. The new price is 70 cents a bag, and the quantity is 100 million bags a week. The supply of potato chips decreases, and the supply curve shifts leftward. The quantity supplied at each price decreases by 20 million bags. The result of the new snack food entering the market is a price of 60 cents a bag. At this price, there is now a shortage of potato chips. The price of potato chips will rise until the shortage is eliminated.

Chapter 4 ELASTICITY

Answers to the Problems and Applications

1 **Rain spoils the strawberry crop. As a result, the price rises from $4 to $6 a box and the quantity demanded decreases from 1,000 to 600 boxes a week. Over this price range,**

a. **What is the price elasticity of demand?**

The price elasticity of demand is 1.25. The price elasticity of demand equals the percentage change in the quantity demanded divided by the percentage change in the price. The price rises from $4 to $6 a box, a rise of $2 a box. The average price is $5 a box. So the percentage change in the price is $2 divided by $5 and then multiplied by 100, which equals 40 percent. The quantity decreases from 1,000 to 600 boxes, a decrease of 400 boxes. The average quantity is 800 boxes. So the percentage change in quantity is 400 divided by 800, which equals 50 percent. The price elasticity of demand for strawberries is 50 percent divided by 40 percent, which equals 1.25. ($2÷$5) × 100

b. **Describe the demand for strawberries.**

The price elasticity of demand exceeds 1, so the demand for strawberries is elastic.

3. **The demand schedule for hotel rooms is given in the table at right.**

a. **What happens to total revenue if the price falls from $400 to $250 a night?**

When the price is $400, the total revenue is equal to $400 × 50 million rooms, or $20 billion. When the price is $250, the total revenue is equal to $250 × 80 million rooms, or $20 billion. So the total revenue does not change when the price falls from $400 to $250 a night.

b. **What happens to total revenue if the price falls from $250 to $200 a night?**

When the price is $250, the total revenue is equal to $250 × 80 million rooms, or $20 billion. When the price is $200, the total revenue is equal to $200 × 100 million rooms, or $20 billion. So the total revenue does not change when the price falls from $400 to $250 a night.

c. **At what price is total revenue at a maximum? Explain and interpret your answer.**

The total revenue is the same at all prices, $20 billion. Because a change in price does not change the total revenue at *any* price, the demand is unit elastic at all prices.

d. **Is the demand for hotel rooms elastic, unit elastic, or inelastic?**

The demand for hotel rooms is unit elastic at all prices.

5. **In 2003, when music downloading first took off, Universal Music slashed the prices of a CD from an average of $21 to an average of $15. The company said that it expected the price cut to boost the quantity of CDs sold by 30 percent, other things remaining the same.**

a. **What was Universal Music's estimate of the price elasticity of demand for CDs?**

Using the data in the question, the price elasticity of demand is 0.90. The change

Price (dollars per night)	Quantity demanded (millions of rooms per night)
200	100
250	80
400	50
500	40
800	25
1,000	20

in the price is $6 and the average of the two prices is $18, so the percentage change in the price is ($6/$18) × 100, which equals 33.3 percent. The increase in the quantity demanded was estimated to be 30 percent. The price elasticity of demand equals (30.0 percent)/(33.3 percent), or 0.90.

b. **Given your answer in a, if you were making the pricing decision at Universal Music, would you cut the price, raise the price, or not change the price? Explain your decision.**

The demand is inelastic, so if nothing else changes the price cut leads to a decrease in Universal Music's total revenue. However, downloaded music and CDs are substitutes for each other and the quantity of downloaded music was forecast to rise substantially. Effectively, the price of downloading music fell as more people gained access to the Internet and download sites proliferated. The fall in the price of the substitute, downloaded music, decreases the demand for Universal Music's CDs, so the price cut most likely was the result of the (forecasted) decrease in demand for CDs.

7. **If a 12 percent rise in the price of orange juice decreases the quantity of orange juice demanded by 22 percent and increases the quantity of apple juice demanded by 14 percent, calculate the**

a. **Price elasticity of demand for orange juice.**

The price elasticity of demand for orange juice is 1.83. The price elasticity of demand is the percentage change in the quantity demanded of the good divided by the percentage change in the price of the good. So the price elasticity of demand equals 22 percent divided by 12 percent, which is 1.83.

b. **Cross elasticity of demand for apple juice with respect to the price of orange juice.**

The cross elasticity of demand between orange juice and apple juice is 1.17. The cross elasticity of demand is the percentage change in the quantity demanded of one good divided by the percentage change in the price of another good. So the cross elasticity of demand is the percentage change in the quantity demanded of apple juice divided by the percentage change in the price of orange juice. The cross elasticity equals 14 percent divided by 12 percent, which is 1.17.

9. **Home Depot Earnings Hammered As home prices slump across the country, fewer people are spending money to renovate their homes, and the improvements that they are making are not as expensive. ... People are spending on small ticket types of repairs, ... not big ticket renovations ... With gas and food prices increasing ... people have less extra income to spend on major home improvements.**
CNN, **May 20, 2008**

a. **What does this news clip imply about the income elasticity of demand for big-ticket home-improvement items?**

The news clip implies that the income elasticity of demand for big-ticket home-improvement items is positive. In particular "people have less extra income to spend" and, as a result, "fewer people are spending money to renovate their homes."

b. **Would the income elasticity of demand be greater or less than 1? Explain.**

The income elasticity of demand is probably greater than 1. Home remodeling is not a necessity; it is more of a luxury. The income elasticity of demand for luxuries is greater than 1.

11. **Study Ranks Honolulu Third Highest for 'Unaffordable Housing'**
[Study ranks] Honolulu number 3 in the world for the most unaffordable housing market in urban locations. Honolulu is listed only behind Los Angeles and San Diego and is deemed "severely unaffordable." ... Where there are significant constraints on the supply of land for residential development, housing inflation has occurred.
Hawaii Reporter, September 11, 2007

a. **Would the supply of housing in Honolulu be elastic or inelastic?**

The supply of housing is probably inelastic because it is limited by the amount of land, which is inelastically supplied. Indeed, the elasticity of supply for housing is probably close to 0.

b. **Explain how the elasticity of supply plays an important role in influencing how rapidly housing prices in Honolulu rise.**

The less elastic the supply, the more an increase in demand raises the price. Because the supply of housing is quite inelastic in Honolulu, increases in demand for housing have lead to large increases in the price of housing, that is, severe "housing inflation."

13. **Use the links on MyEconLab (Textbook Resources, Chapter 4, Web links) to find the number of gallons in a barrel of oil and the prices of crude oil and gasoline in the summer of 2007 and 2008.**

a. **What are the other costs that make up the total cost of a gallon of gasoline?**

A barrel of oil has 42 gallons of oil. When refined, the barrel results in 44 gallons of petroleum products. (The number of gallons increases because there is a reduction in the density during the refining.) A barrel of crude oil, when refined, creates about 20 gallons of gasoline. All these data are from:

http://www.eia.doe.gov/neic/infosheets/crudeproduction.htm

According to a Department of Energy brochure on the costs of a gallon of gasoline (available at http://www.eia.doe.gov/bookshelf/brochures/gasolinepricesprimer/eia1_2005primerM.html) "The cost to produce and deliver gasoline to consumers includes the cost of crude oil to refiners, refinery processing costs, marketing and distribution costs, and finally the retail station costs and taxes. The prices paid by consumers at the pump reflect these costs, as well as the profits (and sometimes losses) of refiners, marketers, distributors, and retail station owners."

b. **If the price of crude oil falls by 10 percent, by what percentage do you expect the price of gasoline change, other things remaining the same?**

Crude oil accounts for approximately 50 percent of the cost of a gallon of gasoline. So if the price of crude oil falls 10 percent and nothing else changes, the price of a gallon of gasoline falls by about 5 percent.

c. **Which demand do you think is more elastic: that for crude oil or gasoline? Why?**

The demand for oil is probably more elastic than the demand for gasoline because there are more substitutes for oil than for gasoline. Crude oil is a source of energy but there are other sources of energy, such as coal, natural gas, nuclear power, wind power, and so forth. These other sources of energy are substitutes for crude oil. Gasoline is fuel primarily used for transportation and there are fewer substitutes, such as diesel and ethanol. Because there are more substitutes for oil, the elasticity of demand for crude oil, while probably inelastic, is likely larger than the elasticity of demand for gasoline.

d. **Use the concepts of demand, supply, and elasticity to explain recent changes in the prices of crude oil and**

gasoline.

Currently the price of oil is much higher than it was three or two or even one year ago. The price is higher because the demand for oil has increased due to higher incomes in developing nations such as India and China. In these rapidly growing nations, people have purchased more automobiles because cars are a normal good. Gasoline is a complement for cars so the demand for gasoline has increased. Because both the demand for and supply of gasoline and oil is inelastic, the increase in demand has resulted in sharply higher prices for oil and gasoline.

15. **The figure shows the demand for DVD rentals.**

   a. **Calculate the elasticity of demand when the price rises from $3 to $5 a DVD.**

   The price elasticity of demand is 2. When the price of a DVD rental rises from $3 to $5, the quantity demanded of DVDs decreases from 75 to 25 a day. The price elasticity of demand equals the percentage change in the quantity demanded divided by the percentage change in the price. The price increases from $3 to $5, an increase of $2 a DVD. The average price is $4 per DVD. So the percentage change in the price equals $2 divided by $4 and then multiplied by 100, which equals 50 percent. The quantity decreases from 75 to 25 DVDs, a decrease of 50 DVDs. The average quantity is 50 DVDs. So the percentage change in quantity equals 50 divided by 50 and then multiplied by 100, which equals 100 percent. The price elasticity of demand for DVD rentals equals 100 percent divided by 50 percent, which is 2.

   b. **At what price is the elasticity of demand for DVDs equal to 1?**

   The price elasticity of demand equals 1 at $3 a DVD. The price elasticity of demand equals 1 at the price halfway between the origin and the price at which

the demand curve hits the y-axis. That price is $3 a DVD.

17. **In problem 16, at $250 a chip, is the demand for chips elastic or inelastic? Use the total revenue test to answer this question.**

   The demand for chips is inelastic. The total revenue test says that if the price falls and total revenue falls, the demand is inelastic. When the price falls from $300 to $200 a chip, total revenue decreases from $12,000 million to $10,000 million. So at an average price of $250 a chip, demand is inelastic.

FIGURE **4.1**

Problem 15

19. **Why Gasoline Follows Oil Up But Not Down**
   If it seems like gasoline prices are quick to skyrocket when the price of oil goes up, but then take their sweet 'ol time coming back down when crude prices sink, the answer is simple: They do. "There is a rocket and feather aspect."... The service stations are still selling the same amount of gasoline when wholesale prices fall... "so there's no reason to drop. ...[Service stations] typically react [to a spike in oil prices] by pushing prices higher,

even before they replace their inventories…" Eventually, the free market steps in and prices begin going down when other nearby stations reduce their price.

CNN, **January 12, 2007**

a. **Explain the link between the elasticity of supply of gasoline and gas price fluctuations.**

The short-run elasticity of supply is small and the supply of gasoline is inelastic. As a result, in the short run fluctuations in demand lead to large fluctuations in the price and small fluctuations in the quantity. In the longer run the elasticity of supply becomes larger, so in the longer run fluctuations in demand lead to smaller price swings and larger quantity changes.

b. **Explain the connection between the elasticity of demand for gasoline and the "rocket and feather" tendency of price fluctuations.**

The short-run elasticity of demand is quite small and the demand for gasoline is inelastic. As a result, in the short run fluctuations in supply lead to large fluctuations in the price and small fluctuations in the quantity. In the longer run the elasticity of demand becomes larger in magnitude (though demand remains inelastic) so in the longer run fluctuations in supply lead to smaller price changes and larger quantity changes. So the price will "rocket" up in the short run and then "feather" back down in the longer run.

21. **When Alex's income increased from $3,000 to $5,000, he increased his consumption of bagels from 4 to 8 a month and decreased his consumption of donuts from 12 to 6 a month. Calculate Alex's income elasticity of demand for**

a. **Bagels.**

The income elasticity of demand equals the percentage change in the quantity demanded divided by the percentage change in income. The change in income

is $2,000 and the average income is $4,000, so the percentage change in income equals 50 percent. The change in the quantity demanded is 4 bagels and the average quantity demanded is 6 bagels, so the percentage change in the quantity demanded equals 66.67 percent. The income elasticity of demand for bagels equals (66.67 percent)/(50 percent), which is 1.33.

b. **Donuts.**

From part a, the percentage change in income is 50 percent. The change in the quantity demanded is −6 donuts and the average quantity demanded is 9 donuts, so the percentage change in the quantity demanded is −66.67 percent. The income elasticity of demand for donuts equals (−66.67 percent)/(50 percent), which is −1.33.

23. **Netflix to Offer Online Movie Viewing Online movie rental service Netflix introduced a new feature Tuesday to allow customers to watch movies and television series on their personal computers. … Netflix has been competing with video rental retailer Blockbuster, which has added an online rental service to the in-store rental service.**

CNN, **January 16 2007**

a. **How will the offering of online movie viewing influence the price elasticity of demand for in-store movie rentals?**

The price elasticity of demand for store rental movies will increase because online movie viewing is another substitute for renting movies.

b. **Would the cross elasticity of demand for online movies and in-store movie rentals be negative or positive? Explain.**

Online movies and in-store rental movies are substitutes, so their cross elasticity of demand is positive.

c. **Would the cross elasticity of demand for online movies with respect to**

high-speed internet service be negative or positive? Explain.

Online movies and high-speed Internet service are complements, so their cross elasticity of demand is negative.

25. **The table gives the supply schedule of long distance phone calls. Calculate the elasticity of supply when**

a. **The price falls from 40 cents to 30 cents a minute.**

The elasticity of supply is 1. The elasticity of supply is the percentage change in the quantity supplied divided by the percentage change in the price. When the price falls from 40 cents to 30 cents, the change in the price is 10 cents and the average price is 35 cents. The percentage change in the price is 28.57 percent. When the price falls from 40 cents to 30 cents, the quantity supplied decreases from 800 to 600 calls. The change in the quantity supplied is 200 calls, and the average quantity is 700 calls, so the percentage change in the quantity supplied is 28.57 percent. The elasticity of supply equals (28.57 percent)/(28.57 percent), which is 1.

b. **The average price is 20 cents a minute.**

The elasticity of supply is 1. The formula for the elasticity of supply calculates the elasticity at the average price. So to find the elasticity at an average price of 20 cents a minute, change the price such that 20 cents is the average price—for example, a fall in the price from 30 cents to 10 cents a minute. When the price falls from 30 cents to 10 cents, the change in the price is 20 cents and the average price is 20 cents. The percentage change in the price is 100 percent. When the price falls from 30 cents to 10 cents, the quantity supplied decreases from 600 to 200 calls. The change in the quantity supplied is 400 calls and the average quantity is 400 calls. The percentage change in the quantity supplied is 100 percent. The elasticity of supply is the percentage change in the quantity

supplied divided by the percentage change in the price. The elasticity of supply is 1.

Price (cents per minute)	Quantity supplied (millions of minutes per day)
10	200
20	400
30	600
40	800

Additional Problems

1. Better-than-average weather brings a bumper tomato crop. The price of tomatoes falls from $6 to $4 a basket, and the quantity demanded increases from 200 to 400 baskets a day. Over this price range,
   a. What is the price elasticity of demand?
   b. Describe the demand for tomatoes.

2. The figure shows the demand for pens.
   a. Calculate the elasticity of demand for a rise in price from $2 to $4.
   b. At what prices is the elasticity of demand equal to 1, greater than 1, and less than 1?

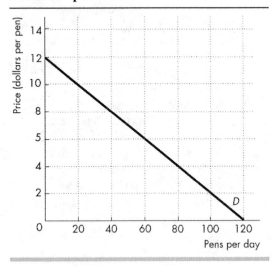

FIGURE **4.2**
Additional problem 2

3. If the quantity of fish demanded decreases by 5 percent when the price of fish rises by 10 percent, is the demand for fish elastic, inelastic, or unit elastic?

4. The table gives the demand schedule for coffee.
   a. What happens to total revenue if the price of coffee rises from $10 to $20 per pound?
   b. What happens to total revenue if the price rises to $15 to $25 per pound?
   c. What is the price when total revenue at a maximum?
   d. What quantity of coffee will be sold at the price that answers part c?
   e. At an average price of $15 a pound, is the demand for coffee elastic or inelastic? Use the total revenue test to answer this question.

Price (dollars per pound)	Quantity demanded (millions of pounds per year)
10	30
15	25
20	20
25	15

5. If a 10 percent fall in the price of beef increases the quantity of beef demanded by 20 percent and decreases the quantity of chicken demanded by 15 percent, calculate the cross elasticity of demand between beef and chicken.

6. Judy's income has increased from $10,000 to $12,000. Judy increased her demand for concert tickets by 10 percent and decreased her demand for bus rides by 5 percent. Calculate Judy's income elasticity of demand for (a) concert tickets and (b) bus rides.

7. The table gives the supply schedule for shoes. Calculate the elasticity of supply when

   a. The price rises from $125 to $135 a pair.

   b. The price is $125 a pair.

Price (dollars per pair)	Quantity supplied (millions of pairs per year)
120	1,200
125	1,400
130	1,600
135	1,800

Solutions to Additional Problems

1. a. The price elasticity of demand is 1.67. The price elasticity of demand equals the percentage change in the quantity demanded divided by the percentage change in the price. The price falls from $6 to $4 a basket, a fall of $2 a basket. The average price is $5 a basket. So the percentage change in the price equals $2 divided by $5 and then multiplied by 100, which equals 40 percent. The quantity increases from 200 to 400 baskets, an increase of 200 baskets. The average quantity is 300 baskets. So the percentage change in quantity equals 200 divided by 300 and then multiplied by 100, which equals 66.7 percent. The price elasticity of demand for tomatoes equals 66.7 percent divided by 40 percent, which is 1.67.

    b. The price elasticity of demand exceeds 1, so the demand for tomatoes is elastic.

2. a. The price elasticity of demand is 0.33. When the price of a pen rises from $2 to $4, the quantity demanded of pens decreases from 100 to 80 a day. The price elasticity of demand equals the percentage change in the quantity demanded divided by the percentage change in the price. The price increases from $2 to $4, an increase of $2 a pen. The average price is $3 a pen. So the percentage change in the price equals $2 divided by $3 and then multiplied by 100, which equals 66.7 percent. The quantity decreases from 100 to 80 pens, a decrease of 20 pens. The average quantity is 90 pens. So the percentage change in quantity equals 20 divided by 90 and then multiplied by 100, which equals 22 percent. The price elasticity of demand for pens equals 22 percent divided by 66.7 percent, which is 0.33.

    b. The price elasticity of demand equals 1 at $6 a pen. The price elasticity of demand is greater than 1 at prices greater than $6 a pen. The price elasticity of demand is less than 1 at prices less than $6 a pen. The price elasticity of demand equals 1 at the price halfway between the origin and the price at which the demand curve hits the y-axis. That price is $6 a pen. The demand curve is linear. Along a linear demand curve, the price elasticity of demand is greater than 1 at points above the midpoint and less than 1 at points below the midpoint. The price elasticity of demand is greater than 1 at prices above $6 a pen and less than 1 at prices below $6 a pen.

3. The demand for fish is inelastic. The price elasticity of demand for fish equals the percentage change in the quantity of fish demanded divided by the percentage change in the price of fish. The price elasticity of demand equals 5 percent divided by 10 percent, which is 0.5. The demand is inelastic.

4. a. Total revenue increases. When the price of a pound of coffee is $10, 30 million pounds are sold and total revenue equals $300 million. When the price of a pound of coffee rises to $20, 20 million pounds are sold and total revenue is $400 million. Total revenue increases.

    b. Total revenue does not change. When the price of a pound of coffee is $15, 25 million pounds are sold and total revenue is $375 million. When the price of a pound of coffee is $25, 15 million pounds are sold and total revenue is $375 million. Total revenue does not change.

    c. Total revenue is maximized at $20 a pound. When the price of a pound of coffee is $20, 20 million pounds are sold and total revenue equals $400 million. When the price is $15 a pound, 25 million pounds are sold and total revenue equals $375 million. Total revenue increases as the price rises from $15 to $20 a pound. When the price is $25 a pound, 15 million pounds are sold and total revenue equals $375 million. Total revenue decreases as the price rises from $20 to $25 a pound. Total revenue is maximized when the price is $20 a pound.

d. The quantity will be 20 million pounds a year. The demand schedule tells us that when the price is $20 a pound, the quantity of coffee demanded is 20 million pounds a year.

e. The demand for coffee is inelastic. The total revenue test says that if the price rises and total revenue increases, the demand is inelastic at the average price. For an average price of $15 a pound, raise the price from $10 to $20 a pound. When the price of a pound rises from $10 to $20, total revenue increases from $300 million to $400 million. So at the average price of $15 a pound, demand is inelastic.

5. The cross elasticity of demand between beef and chicken is 2. The cross elasticity of demand is the percentage change in the quantity demanded of one good divided by the percentage change in the price of another good. The fall in the price of beef resulted in a decrease in the quantity demanded of chicken. So the cross elasticity of demand is the percentage change in the quantity demanded of chicken divided by the percentage change in the price of beef. The cross elasticity equals 20 percent divided by 10 percent, which is 2.

6. Income elasticity of demand for (a) concert tickets is 0.55 and (b) bus rides is −0.275. Income elasticity of demand equals the percentage change in the quantity demanded divided by the percentage change in income. The change in income is $2,000 and the average income is $11,000, so the percentage change in income equals 18.2 percent.

a. The change in the quantity demanded of concert tickets is 10 percent. The income elasticity of demand for concert tickets equals 10/18.2, which is 0.55.

b. The change in the quantity demanded of bus rides is −5 percent. The income

elasticity of demand for bus rides equals −5/18.2, which is −0.275.

7. a. The elasticity of supply is 3.25. The elasticity of supply is the percentage change in the quantity supplied divided by the percentage change in the price. When the price rises from $125 to $135, the change in the price is $10 and the average price is $130. The percentage change in the price is 7.7 percent. When the price rises from $125 to $135, the quantity supplied increases from 1,400 million to 1,800 million pairs. The change in the quantity supplied is 400 million pairs, and the average quantity is 1,600 million pairs, so the percentage change in the quantity supplied is 25 percent. The elasticity of supply equals (25 percent)/(7.7 percent), which equals 3.25.

b. The elasticity of supply is 3.57. The formula for the elasticity of supply calculates the elasticity at the average price. So to find the elasticity of supply at $125, change the price such that $125 is the average price—for example, a fall in the price from $130 to $120. When the price falls from $130 to $120, the change in the price is $10 and the average price is $125. The percentage change in the price is 8 percent. When the price falls from $130 to $120, the quantity supplied decreases from 1,600 million to 1,200 million pairs. The change in the quantity supplied is 400 millions pairs and the average quantity is 1,400 million pairs. The percentage change in the quantity supplied is 28.57 percent. The elasticity of supply is the percentage change in the quantity supplied divided by the percentage change in the price. The elasticity of supply is 3.57.

Chapter **5** **EFFICIENCY AND EQUITY**

Answers to the Problems and Applications

1. **At Chez Panisse, the restaurant in Berkeley that is credited with having created California cuisine, reservations are essential. At Mandarin Dynasty, a restaurant near the University of California San Diego, reservations are recommended. At Eli Cannon's, a restaurant in Middletown, Connecticut, reservations are not accepted.**

   a. **Describe the method of allocating scarce table resources at these three restaurants.**

   All these restaurants use a first-come, first-serve system. Eli Cannon's uses this system directly. Chez Panisse uses a first-come, first-serve because the first person to call to make a reservation at a particular time is allocated the table at that time. Mandarin Dynasty uses a combination of the immediate first-come, first serve system and the reservation based first-come, first-serve system.

   b. **Why do you think restaurants have different reservations policies?**

   The speed with which tables turn over at the different restaurants probably is quite different and the customers probably have quite different values of time. Chez Panisse has a low turnover rate—only 1 or 2 groups of customers can use a table each night—and its customers have a high value of time. If Chez Panisse refused to take reservations, its customers would need to wait an inefficiently long time and would go elsewhere so that Chez Panisse's profits would be lower. At Eli Cannon's, the tables have a high turnover rate and the customers have a lower value of time. Allowing reservations would be costly for Eli Cannon's and would spare its

customers only a slight wait at most so that allowing reservations would decrease Eli Cannon's profits. At Mandarin Dynasty, the turnover rate of the tables is between that at Chez Panisse and Eli Cannon's, so it uses a combination of phone reservation first-come, first-serve and appear in person first-come, first serve.

   c. **Why might each restaurant be using an efficient allocation method?**

   Each restaurant is using a different allocation method because of the relative costs. Each uses the method that has the lowest cost for the restaurant.

   d. **Why do you think restaurants don't use the market price to allocate their tables?**

   Market allocation requires that customers pay for a table and the price would fluctuate from one hour to the next depending on the number of customers who arrive. Customers would be highly uncertain about the price they would need to pay and such uncertainty decreases the demand for meals from the restaurant. The decreased demand lowers the restaurant's profit.

3. **eBay Saves Billions for Bidders If you think you would save money by bidding on eBay auctions, you would likely be right. ... Two associate professors ... calculate the difference between the actual purchase price paid for auction items and the top price bidders stated they were willing to pay ... and the Maryland researchers found it averaged at least $4 per auction.**
   Information Week, **January 28, 2008**

   a. **What method is used to allocate goods on eBay?**

   eBay is using market price to allocate the goods. The market price is the price established in the auction. If someone is willing and able to pay that price, the person will get the item.

b. How do eBay auctions influence consumer surplus?

For the vast majority of auctions the winning bidder will enjoy a consumer surplus so eBay increases consumer surplus. For instance, if there are bidders on a unique item, the winning bidder—who sets the price for the good—will pay a price that is equal to the value of the item to the bidder with the second-highest valuation plus the minimum bid increment. The winning bidder has some consumer surplus as long as his or her value of the good exceeds the price that must be paid, which will almost always be the case. Indeed, a person chooses to buy on eBay rather than elsewhere if the person believes that his or her consumer surplus is largest by purchasing on eBay.

5. Based on the information provided in the news clip in problem 3,

a. Can an eBay auction give the seller a surplus?

Yes, an eBay auction can give a seller a surplus. The seller has a minimum supply price for which the item will be sold. If the price established in the auction exceeds that minimum supply price, the seller has a surplus.

b. Draw a graph to illustrate an eBay auction and show the consumer surplus and producer surplus that it generates.

Figure 5.1 illustrates an eBay auction. The figure assumes that there are many suppliers of this good, each with a different minimum supply price so that the supply curve is upward sloping. The consumer surplus is area *A*, the area under the demand curve and above the (auction-determined) market price. The producer surplus is area *B*, the area under the market price and above the supply curve.

Price (dollars per ride)	Quantity supplied (rides per week)		
	Xavier	Yasmin	Zack
100	30	25	20
90	25	20	15
80	20	15	10
70	15	10	5
60	10	5	0
50	5	0	0
40	0	0	0

FIGURE **5.1**

Problem 5

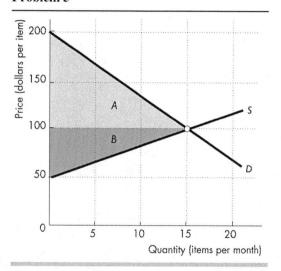

7. **The table gives the demand and supply schedules for sunscreen. Sunscreen factories are required to limit production to 100 bottles a day.**

Price (dollars per bottle)	Quantity demanded	Quantity supplied
	(bottles per day)	
0	400	0
5	300	100
10	200	200
15	100	300
20	0	400

a. **What is the maximum price that consumers are willing to pay for the 100th bottle?**

Consumers are willing to pay a maximum price of $15 for the 100th bottle of sunscreen. The demand schedule shows the maximum price that consumers will pay for each bottle of sunscreen. The maximum price that consumers will pay for the 100th bottle is $15.

b. **What is the minimum price that producers are willing to accept for the 100th bottle?**

Producers are willing to accept a minimum price of $5 for the 100th bottle of sunscreen. The supply schedule shows the minimum price that producers will accept for each bottle of sunscreen. The minimum price that produces will accept for the 100th bottle is $5.

c. **Describe the situation in this market.**

There is less than the efficient quantity being produced. The efficient quantity is the equilibrium quantity, 200 bottles.

d. **How can the 100 bottles be allocated to beachgoers? Which possible methods would be fair and which would be unfair?**

The bottles can be allocated using a contest (a raffle for the bottles, perhaps), first-come, first-served (a line until all 100 bottles are distributed), personal characteristics (perhaps all fair-haired people are allocated the sun screen), or force (a fight). Using the "fair results" criteria, none of the allocation schemes are necessarily fair because there is no guarantee that poorer people will receive the sun screen. Using the "fair rules" criteria, the force method is definitely unfair and the others are fair.

9. **'Two Buck Chuck' Wine Cult**
It's the California wine with the cult following. "Charles Shaw is known in local circles as "Two Buck Chuck," ... the $1.99 nectar of the gods that is sinfully cheap and good. ... A full year after flooding the market largely on the West Coast, it's still being sold by the case to wine lovers who can't get enough. ... It's an over-abundance of grapes that's made Charles Shaw cheap to bottle— an estimated 5 million cases so far.

CBS, June 2, 2003

a. **Explain how the Invisible Hand has worked in the market for this California wine.**

The Invisible Hand worked by motivating wine producers, who are seeking their self interest by earning the largest profit possible, to create a wildly popular wine, Charles Shaw. The Invisible Hand also worked by motivating consumers who enjoy Charles Shaw wine to pursue their self interest by purchasing a large quantity of the wine. The Invisible Hand lead to the creation of a wine that many consumers enjoy, thereby increasing their well being, and increased the profits of the producers, thereby increasing their well being.

b. **How has "Two Buck Chuck" influenced consumer surplus from wine?**

"Two Buck Chuck" increased the consumer surplus from wine. Consumers are flocking to this cheaper wine in place of more expensive wines. The consumer surplus increased because the price of "Two Buck Chuck" is lower than other wines and because the quantity of wine consumed increased.

c. **How has "Two Buck Chuck" influenced producer surplus for its producer and for the producers of other wines?**

"Two Buck Check" increased the producer surplus of its producer. Because "Two Buck Chuck" is a substitute for other wines, the quantity and price of other wines sold has decreased and so the producer surplus from these wines decreased.

11. **The table gives the demand and supply schedules for sandwiches.**

a. **What is the maximum price that consumers are willing to pay for the 200th sandwich?**

The demand schedule shows the maximum price that consumers will pay for each sandwich. The maximum price consumers will pay for the 200th sandwich is $2.

b. **What is the minimum price that producers are willing to accept for the 200th sandwich?**

The supply schedule shows the minimum price that producers will accept for each sandwich. The minimum price for which produces will produce the 200th sandwich is $4.

c. **Are 200 sandwiches a day less than or greater than the efficient quantity?**

200 sandwiches a day are more than the efficient quantity because the marginal social benefit (the maximum price consumers will pay) is less than

the marginal social cost (the minimum price suppliers will accept).

d. **If sandwich makers produce 200 a day, what is the deadweight loss?**

The deadweight loss is $50. Deadweight loss is the sum of the consumer surplus and producer surplus that is lost because the quantity produced is not the efficient quantity. The deadweight loss equals the quantity (200 − 150) multiplied by ($4 − $2)/2, which is $50.

e. **If the sandwich market is efficient, what is the consumer surplus, what is the producer surplus, and what is the total surplus?**

150 sandwiches is the efficient quantity and the equilibrium price is $3. The consumer surplus is the area of the triangle under the demand curve above the price. The area of the consumer

Price (dollars per sandwich)	Quantity demanded	Quantity supplied
	(sandwiches per hour)	
0	300	0
1	250	50
2	200	100
3	150	150
4	100	200
5	50	250
6	0	300

surplus triangle is ½ × ($6 − $3) × 150, which is $225. The producer surplus is the area of the triangle above the supply curve below the price. The price is $3 and the quantity is 150. The area of the triangle is 1.2 × ($3 − $0) × 150, which is $225. The total surplus is the sum of the consumer surplus plus the producer surplus, which is $450.

f. If the demand for sandwiches increases and sandwich makers produce the efficient quantity, what happens to consumer surplus and producer surplus?

If the demand for sandwiches increases, the price and quantity of sandwiches both rise. The producer surplus definitely increases. The effect on consumer surplus is ambiguous. It rises if the quantity increases by a larger percentage than does the price but it falls if the price rises by a larger percentage than does the quantity.

13. Was Katie Holmes' Marathon Entrance Unfair?
Runners in the recent New York Marathon have been asking why Katie Holmes was admitted to the race when 60,000 hopefuls were denied. ... Holmes was admitted to the race as a VIP. She was not given a spot through a lottery system, or for running in one of the 26 sanctioned New York Marathon charities… or even for having a competitive running time. The minimum qualifying run time for a woman runner is 3 hours and 23 minutes. Katie completed the marathon in 5 hours, 29 minutes and 58 seconds.
MSNBC, **November 9, 2007**

a. By what allocation method did Holmes obtain entrance to the marathon?

Ms. Holmes was allocated her space in the race based on her personal characteristics.

b. Evaluate the "fairness" of Holmes being admitted to the marathon.

Under the "fair rules" approach to fairness, allocating Ms. Holmes an entry was unfair. Under the "fair results" approach to fairness combined with the view that a fair result results in a more equal distribution of income, allocating Ms. Holmes an entry was unfair because she is significantly more wealthy than the average person.

15. After you have studied *Reading Between the Lines* on pp. 122–123, answer the following questions:

a. What is the major problem in achieving an efficient use of the world's water?

Water needs to be transported from where it is available to where it is needed. This basic issue leads to two major problems: Overproduction in some areas and underproduction in other areas. Often overproduction in an area leads to underproduction later in the same area. In particular, markets in water are not competitive. In many areas, water is "free" to whomever digs a deep enough well. As a result, too many people dig wells and water is overproduced. If the overproduction is bad enough, the level of groundwater can be reduced so far that it becomes literally impossible to extract any water. Then water needs to be transported to the now arid area. In this case, often the government transports the water and sells it at a very low price or gives it away. But because the government does not sell the water at an equilibrium price (and because the government is not motivated by seeking profit) less water is transported than the efficient quantity.

b. **If there were a global market in water, like there is in oil, how do you think the market would work?**

The market for water would be more efficient than the current situation. Areas with a great deal of water, say Canada, could export water to areas with less water, say Mexico. If water was purchased and sold in markets, there would be greater incentive to build desalination plants where they are practical as well as greater incentive to conserve water where it is in abundance.

c. **Would a free world market in water achieve an efficient use of the world's water resources? Explain why or why not.**

A free world market in water likely would (eventually) bring an efficient use of resources as the necessary infrastructure was constructed. Of the factors that can lead to inefficiency (government price and quantity regulations, monopoly power, and so forth) the only issue that could possibly lead to inefficiency is the point that water is a common resource in some situations.

d. **Would a free world market in water achieve a fair use of the world's water resources? Explain why or why not and be clear about the concept of fairness that you are using.**

A "fair results" approach to fairness would argue that in third world countries, very poor inhabitants (for example, nomads) would not be able to afford "enough" water and so some redistribution is needed for the sake of fairness. A "fair rules" approach to fairness asserts that a competitive market is enough to insure fairness.

17. **Use the link on MyEconLab (Chapter Resources, Chapter 5, Web links) to visit the Web site of Health Action International and read the article by Catrin Schulte-Hillen**

entitled "Study concerning the availability and price of AZT." Then answer the following questions and explain your answers using the concepts of marginal benefit, marginal cost, price, consumer surplus, and producer surplus.

a. **What is the range of retail prices of AZT across the countries covered by the study?**

The retail (pharmacy) prices range from $0.67 in Thailand to $2.80 in Germany.

b. **What, if anything, do you think could be done to increase the quantity of AZT and decrease its price?**

The article states that "The major determining factor is the existence of alternative products on the market, i.e. competition." So one factor that will lead to lower prices and increased quantities is either disregard the patent or wait until the patent expires. In either case, the increased competition will lead to lower prices and increased quantities. If the government does not want to disregard the patent, it could try to negotiate lower prices by perhaps arranging purchases of larger quantities. Or the government could simply lower the allowable legal price for AZT in the nation. The drawback with this last policy is that it might lead to a decrease in the quantity of AZT available.

c. **Canadian online pharmacies sell AZT to Americans for a price below the U.S. price. Does this practice increase or decrease consumer surplus, producer surplus, and deadweight loss from AZT in the United States?**

The practice of Canadian on-line pharmacies selling AZT in the United States at a price below the U.S. price increases consumer surplus in the United States. U.S. producers sell AZT to Canadian pharmacies, but at a lower price than they can sell the drug in the United States. To the extent that the Canadian sales replace sales of U.S.-sold products, producer surplus in the Untied States decreases. However, to the extent that the product is manufactured in the United States and to the extent that these sales are "new," that is, would not have been made except for the lower price, the sales increase U.S. producer surplus. Producer surplus in Canada increases.

Additional Problems

1. The table gives the demand and supply schedules for spring water.

   a. What is the maximum price that consumers are willing to pay for the 30th bottle?

   b. What is the minimum price that producers are willing to accept for the 30th bottle?

   c. Are 30 bottles a day less than or greater than the efficient quantity?

   d. What is the consumer surplus if the efficient quantity of spring water is produced?

   e. What is the producer surplus if the efficient quantity is of spring water is produced?

   f. What is the deadweight loss if 30 bottles are produced?

Price (dollars per bottle)	Quantity demanded (bottles per day)	Quantity supplied (bottles per day)
0	80	0
0.50	70	10
1.00	60	20
1.50	50	30
2.00	40	40
2.50	30	50
3.00	20	60
3.50	10	70
4.00	0	80

2. The table gives the demand schedules for train travel for Joe, Jean, and Joy.

   a. If the price of train travel is 50 cents a passenger mile, what is the consumer surplus of each consumer?

   b. Which consumer has the largest consumer surplus? Explain why.

   c. If the price of train travel falls to 30 cents a passenger mile, what is the change in consumer surplus of each consumer?

Price (cents per mile)	Quantity demanded (passenger miles)		
	Joe	Jean	Joy
10	50	600	300
20	45	500	250
30	40	400	200
40	35	300	150
50	30	200	100
60	25	100	50
70	20	0	0
80	15	0	0
90	10	0	0
100	5	0	0
110	0	0	0

Solutions to Additional Problems

1. a. The maximum price that consumers will pay is $2.50. The demand schedule shows the maximum price that consumers will pay for each bottle of spring water. The maximum price that consumers will pay for the 30th bottle is $2.50.

    b. The minimum price that producers will accept is $1.50. The supply schedule shows the minimum price that producers will accept for each bottle of spring water. The minimum price that produces will accept for the 30th bottle is $1.50.

    c. 30 bottles is less than the efficient quantity. The efficient quantity is such that marginal benefit from the last bottle equals the marginal cost of producing it. The efficient quantity is the equilibrium quantity—40 bottles a day.

    d. Consumer surplus is $40. The equilibrium price is $2. The consumer surplus is the area of the triangle under the demand curve above the price. The area of the triangle is ½ × ($4 − $2) × 40, which is $40.

    e. Producer surplus is $40. The producer surplus is the area of the triangle above the supply curve below the price. The price is $2. The area of the triangle is ½ × ($2 − $0) × 40, which is $40.

    f. The deadweight loss is $5. Deadweight loss is the sum of the consumer surplus and producer surplus that is lost because the quantity produced is not the efficient quantity. The deadweight loss equals ½ × (40 − 30) × ($2.50 − $0.50), which is $5.

2. a. Joe's consumer surplus is $9. Jean's consumer surplus is $20, and Joy's consumer surplus is $10. Consumer surplus is the area under the demand curve above the price. At 50 cents, Joe will travel 30 miles, Jean will travel 200 miles, and Joy will travel 100 miles. Joe's consumer surplus equals ½ × (110¢ − 50¢) × 30, which equals $9. Similarly, Jean's consumer surplus equals ½ × (70¢ − 50¢) × 200, which equals $20. And Joy's consumer surplus equals ½ × (70¢ − 50¢) × 100, which equals $10.

    b. Jean's consumer surplus is the largest because she places a higher value on each unit of the good than the other two do.

    c. Joe's consumer surplus rises by $7. Jean's consumer surplus rises by $60, and Joy's consumer surplus rises by $30. At 30 cents a mile, Joe travels 40 miles and his consumer surplus is $16. Joe's consumer surplus equals ½ × (110¢ − 30¢) × 40, which equals $16. Joe's consumer surplus increases from $9 to $16, an increase of $7. Jean travels 400 miles and her consumer surplus is $80, an increase of $60. Joy travels 200 miles and her consumer surplus is $40, an increase of $30.

Chapter **6** **GOVERNMENT ACTIONS IN MARKETS**

Answers to the Problems and Applications

1. **Figure 6.1 illustrates the market for rental housing in Townsville.**

    a. **What are the equilibrium rent and equilibrium quantity of rental housing?**

    > The equilibrium rent is $450 a month and the equilibrium quantity is 20,000 housing units.

    If a rent ceiling is set at $600 a month, what is

    b. **The quantity of housing rented?**

    > The quantity of housing rented is equal to 20,000 units. If the rent ceiling is set at $600 per month, it is above the equilibrium rent and so is ineffective. The rent stays at $450 per month and the quantity rented remains at 20,000 housing units.

    c. **The shortage of housing?**

    > There is no shortage of housing units. Because the rent ceiling is ineffective, the market remains at its equilibrium so there is no shortage of housing units.

    If a rent ceiling is set at $300 a month, what is

    d. **The quantity of housing rented?**

    > The quantity rented is 10,000 housing units. The quantity of housing rented is equal to the quantity supplied at the rent ceiling.

    e. **The shortage of housing?**

    > The shortage of housing is 20,000 housing units. At the rent ceiling, the quantity of housing demanded is 30,000, but the quantity supplied is 10,000, so there is a shortage of 20,000 housing units.

    f. **The maximum price that someone is willing to pay for the last unit of housing available?**

    > The maximum price that someone is willing to pay for the 10,000th unit available is $600 a month. The demand curve tells us the maximum

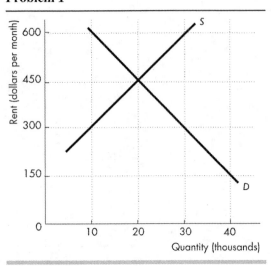

FIGURE **6.1**

Problem 1

price that someone is willing to pay for the 10,000th unit.

3. **Explain the various ways in which a price ceiling on gasoline that is set below the equilibrium price would make buyers and sellers of gasoline better off or worse off. What would happen to total surplus and deadweight loss in this market?**

    > A price ceiling set below the equilibrium price benefits some consumers and harms others. Consumers who are able to buy gasoline at the price ceiling without too much search activity or have a low cost of search are made better off. Consumers who cannot buy, who must undertake extensive search activity, or who have a high cost of search are made worse off. All producers of gasoline are made worse off. The total surplus decreases and a deadweight loss is created.

5. **India Steps Up Pressure for Minimum Wage for Its Workers in the Gulf**
    Oil-rich countries in the [Persian] Gulf, already confronted by strong labor protests, are facing renewed pressure from India to pay minimum wages for unskilled workers. The effort by India—the largest source of migrant workers in the region, with five million—is the strongest push yet by home countries to win better conditions for their citizens...
    International Herald Tribune,
    March 27, 2008

    If the Persian Gulf countries paid a minimum wage above the equilibrium wage to Indian workers,

a. **How would the market for labor be affected in the Gulf countries? Draw a supply and demand graph to illustrate your answer.**

    Figure 6.3 shows the outcome in the Gulf countries' labor markets. In the figure, without a minimum wage the equilibrium wage rate is $3 per hour and 90 million hours of labor are employed. The minimum wage decreases the quantity of labor demanded, in the figure to 60 million hours of labor, and increases the quantity of labor supplied, in the figure to 150 million hours of labor. As a result, unemployment increases to 90 million hours in the figure.

b. **How would the market for labor be affected in India? Draw a supply and demand graph to illustrate your answer. [Be careful: the minimum wage is in the Gulf countries, not in India.]**

    The effect on the labor market in India is ambiguous. On the one hand workers in India who learn about the higher wage rates in the Persian Gulf countries might leave India in order to work at these jobs. In this case, labor supply in India decreases and the labor supply curve in India shifts leftward.

Wage rate (dollars per hour)	Quantity demanded	Quantity supplied
	(hours per month)	
4	3,000	1,000
5	2,500	1,500
6	2,000	2,000
7	1,500	2,500
8	1,000	3,000

FIGURE 6.3
Problem 5

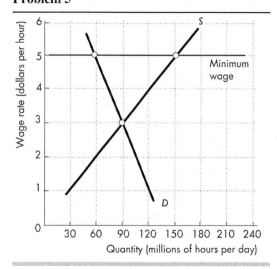

On the other hand Indian workers in the Gulf countries who are unemployed might return to India to gain employment. In this case, labor supply in India increases and the labor supply curve in India shifts rightward.

c. **Would migrant Indian workers be better off or worse off or unaffected by this minimum wage?**

    Some migrant Indian workers are better off—those who retain their higher paying job or find a higher paying job without much search activity. Other migrant Indian workers are worse off—those who are fired when the wage rate rises, those who cannot find a job, and those who find a job but only after incurring much costly search activity.

7.   **Luxury Tax Heavier Burden on Working Class, It Would Seem The Omnibus Budget Reconciliation Act of 1990… included … a stern tax on "luxury items" … In 1990 the Joint Committee on Taxation projected that the 1991 revenue yield from the luxury taxes would be $31 million. The actual yield was $16.6 million. Why? Because—surprise!—the taxation changed behavior.**
     The Topeka Capital-Journal,
     October 29, 1999

a.   **Would buyers or sellers of "luxury items" pay more of the luxury tax?**

Luxury items have elastic demands. As a result the burden of a tax falls more heavily on sellers.

b.   **Explain why the luxury tax generated far less tax revenue than was originally anticipated.**

Because the demand for luxury items is elastic, the decrease in the quantity bought and sold is large. With a large decrease in the quantity, the tax revenue raised is small. The anticipated amount of tax revenue assumed a much smaller decrease in the quantity. Because there was an unexpectedly large decrease in quantity, the tax revenue generated was much smaller than anticipated.

9.   **The demand and supply schedules for rice are given in the table. What are the price, the marginal cost of producing rice, and the quantity produced if the government**

a.   **Sets a production quota for rice of 2,000 boxes a week?**

With a production quota of 2,000 boxes a week, the price is $1.60 a box, the marginal cost $1.30 a box, and the quantity produced is 2,000 boxes a week. The production quota decreases the quantity supplied to 2,000 boxes a

week. The price willingly paid for 2,000 boxes a week is $1.60 (given by the demand schedule). The marginal cost of producing 2,000 boxes of rice is given by the supply schedule and is $1.30 a box.

b.   **Introduces a subsidy to rice growers of $0.30 a box?**

With a subsidy of $0.30 a box for rice, the price is $1.20 a box, the marginal cost $1.50 a box, and the quantity produced is 3,000 boxes a week. The subsidy of $0.30 lowers the price at which each quantity in the table is supplied. For example, rice farmers will supply 3,000 boxes a week if the price is $1.50 minus $0.30, which is $1.20. With a subsidy, the market equilibrium occurs at a price of $1.20 a box. At this price, the quantity demanded is 3,000 boxes and the quantity supplied is 3,000 boxes. The marginal cost of producing rice is given by the supply schedule and is $1.50 a box.

11. **Coal Shortage at China Plants Chinese power plants have run short of coal, an unintended effect of government-mandated price controls—a throwback to communist central planning—to shield the public from rising global energy costs. … Beijing has also frozen retail prices of gasoline and diesel. That helped farmers and the urban poor, but it has spurred sales**

Price (dollars per box)	Quantity demanded	Quantity supplied
	(boxes per week)	
1.00	3,500	500
1.10	3,250	1,000
1.20	3,000	1,500
1.30	2,750	2,000
1.40	2,500	2,500
1.50	2,250	3,000
1.60	2,000	3,500

of gas-guzzling luxury cars and propelled double digit annual growth in fuel consumption. Oil refiners say they are suffering heavy losses and some began cutting production last year, causing fuel shortages in parts of China's south.
                    CNN, **May 20, 2008**

a. **Are China's price controls described in the news clip price floors or price ceilings?**

China's price controls are price ceilings.

b. **Explain how China's price controls have created shortages or surpluses in the markets for coal, gasoline, and diesel.**

In the face of increased demand, China's price controls have kept the price from rising to its equilibrium. As a result the quantity demanded exceeds the quantity supplied and shortages have resulted.

c. **Illustrate your answer to b graphically by using the supply and demand model.**

Figure 6.5 illustrates the situation in the market for coal; the figures for gasoline and diesel are similar. In Figure 6.5 at the controled price of $550 per ton, the quantity of coal demanded is 100 million tons per week, the quantity of coal supplied is 97.5 million tons per week so there is a shortage of 2.5 million tons per week.

d. **Explain how China's price controls have changed consumer surplus, producer surplus, total surplus, and the deadweight loss in the markets for coal, gasoline, and diesel.**

China's price controls have increased the consumer surplus of consumers who can buy the product at the controlled price without incurring high search costs but decreased the consumer surplus of those who cannot buy or those who can buy but who incur high search costs. The overall effect on the consumer surplus is ambiguous and depends on the amount of search costs. The producer surplus and the total surplus have decreased. The price controls have created a deadweight loss.

FIGURE **6.5**
Problem 11c

e.   **Illustrate your answer to d graphically by using the supply and demand model.**

Figure 6.6 shows the consumer surplus, producer surplus, and deadweight loss. With no price ceiling the consumer surplus is equal to area *A* + area *B* + area *C*. With the price ceiling consumer surplus is equal to area *A* and perhaps some of area *B* + area *E* depending on the search costs of finding coal. If these search costs are extensive, then all of area *B* + area *E* will be used up as search costs. The producer surplus without the price ceiling is equal to area *E* + area *F* + area *G*. With the price ceiling the producer surplus is equal to area *G*. Without the price ceiling there is no deadweight loss. With the price ceiling there is a deadweight loss equal to area *C* + area *F*.

13. **House Passes Increase in Minimum Wage to $7.25**
     ...first increase in the federal minimum wage in nearly a decade, boosting the wages of the lowest-paid American workers from $5.15 to $7.25 an hour... Republican leaders, backed by small business lobbyists and restaurant groups, argued fiercely that raising the minimum wage would cripple the economy and must be accompanied by significant tax cuts for small businesses.
     The Washington Post, January 11, 2007

a.   **Use a graph of the market for low-skilled labor to illustrate the effect of the increase in the minimum wage from $5.15 to $7.25 an hour on the quantity of labor employed.**

Figure 6.7 shows the effect in the labor market. Before the hike in the minimum wage, the old minimum wage was not binding so that equilibrium employment was 100 million hours per week and the equilibrium wage rate was $6.00 per

FIGURE **6.6**
Problem 11e

FIGURE **6.7**
Problem 13

hour. After the increase in the minimum wage, employment falls to 98 million hours per week (the quantity of labor demanded at a wage rate of $7.25 an hour) and unemployment equals 3 million hours per week (the difference between 101 million hours per week, the quantity of labor supplied at a wage rate of $7.25 an hour and quantity of labor demanded at the same wage rate.)

b. Explain the effects of the higher minimum wage on the workers' surplus and the firms' surplus. Does the labor market become more efficient or less efficient? Explain.

Taking account of the cost of job search, workers' surplus decreases. Firms' surplus also decreases. The labor market becomes less efficient and a deadweight loss is created.

c. Would a cut in the tax on the small business profits offset the effect of the higher minimum wage on employment? Explain.

The tax cut on small businesses would offset some of the harm imposed on small businesses but it would not offset much of the decrease in employment. The higher wage rate leads firms to decrease the quantity of labor they demand. If a tax cut increases firms' profitability and they respond by increasing their production, then the demand for labor will increase. This increase would offset some of the initial fall in employment. But the offset likely would be small because the cut in taxes will be shared between the businesses and the consumers.

d. Would a cut in the Social Security tax that small businesses pay offset the effect of the higher minimum wage on employment? Explain.

A cut in the Social Security Tax imposed on small businesses could offset the effect the minimum wage hike had on decreasing employment. If Social Security Taxes are cut, firms' demand for labor would increase which would result in an increase in employment. Of course the size of the offset would depend on the size of the cut in the Social Security Tax and the elasticity of demand for labor and

the elasticity supply of labor. Because the supply of labor is probably quite inelastic, most of the benefit of the cut in Social Security tax would be received by workers, which also makes the potential offset small.

15. Congress Passes Farm Bill, Defies Bush
Congress sent the White House a huge election year farm bill Thursday that includes a boost in farm subsidies. ... Bush has threatened to veto the $290 billion bill, saying it is fiscally irresponsible and too generous to wealthy corporate farmers in a time of record crop prices. ... $40 billion is for farm subsidies, while almost $30 billion would go to farmers to idle their land...

CNN, **May 15, 2008**

a. Why does the federal government subsidize farmers?

The federal government subsidizes farmers because of extensive farm lobbying. Of course, the farm lobby groups assert that subsidies guarantee food to American consumers, but in reality it is likely the case that farmers lobby for subsidies because subsidies make them better off. The subsidies help farmers avoid low prices and low incomes.

b. Explain how a subsidy paid to cotton farmers affects the price of cotton and the marginal cost of producing it.

A subsidy increases the supply of cotton. As a result, the price of cotton falls and the quantity produced increases. With the increase in the quantity produced the marginal cost of cotton rises.

c. **Explain how a subsidy paid to cotton farmers affects the consumer surplus and producer surplus from cotton. Does the subsidy make the market more efficient or less efficient? Explain.**

Both the consumer surplus and producer surplus increase. But a deadweight loss results because, at the expanded level of production, marginal cost exceeds marginal benefit. Hence the subsidy makes the market less efficient.

d. **How would a payment to cotton farmers to idle their land influence the supply of cotton?**

A payment to farmers to idle their lands would decrease the supply of cotton.

e. **How would a payment to cotton farmers to idle their land affect the consumer surplus and the producer surplus from cotton? Explain.**

The consumer surplus decreases. The price consumers pay rises and the quantity purchased decreases, both of which reduce consumer surplus. The producer surplus increases if the demand is elastic and decreases if the demand is inelastic. (However, the total revenue suppliers receive, including the subsidy, rises.)

17. **Study *Reading Between the Lines* (pp. 146–147) about the market for gasoline.**

a. **Explain to truck drivers why a cap on the price of gasoline would hurt middle class people more than the high price of gasoline hurts.**

The high price of gasoline harms middle-class people because they must pay a high price. But the choice of whether to pay the high price or go without lies the person. A price cap creates a shortage because the quantity of gasoline demanded exceeds the quantity of gasoline supplied. With the shortage some middle-class people will be unable to buy gasoline and virtually all middle-class people will need to spend extensive time driving to search for gasoline to buy, thereby wasting time and gasoline. Both of these harm middle-class consumers and they have no choice—some are simply unable to find gasoline to buy and all of them must search for gasoline.

b. **Explain why Barack Obama is right about the effects of a temporary suspension of the federal gas tax.**

Mr. Obama suggested a temporary suspension of the federal gas tax might not lower the price paid by consumers by much. If the supply is inelastic, which is likely the case, the tax cut will lower the price paid by consumers only a fraction of the 18.4¢ tax cut and will raise the price received by suppliers a fraction of the 18.4¢. Mr. Obama is correct if the elasticity of supply is small.

c. **Explain why it is inefficient for Asian governments to subsidize gasoline.**

A subsidy increases the supply and lowers the price paid by consumers while raising the price, including the subsidy, received by sellers. The quantity increases and exceeds the efficient quantity. Because the quantity exceeds the efficient quantity, a deadweight loss is created. The deadweight loss indicates that society is harmed by the subsidy.

Price (dollars per unit)	Quantity demanded	Quantity supplied
	(units per day)	
50	500	300
60	400	400
70	300	500
80	200	600
90	100	700

19. **The table gives the demand and supply schedules for an illegal drug.**

   a. **If there are no penalties on buying or selling the drug, what is the price and how many units are consumed?**

   The price is $60 per unit and 400 units are consumed.

   b. **If the penalty on sellers is $20 a unit, what are the price and quantity consumed?**

   The price is $70 per unit and 300 units are consumed.

   c. **If the penalty on buyers is $20 a unit, what are the price and quantity consumed?**

   The price $50 per unit and 300 units are consumed.

21. **Use the links in MyEconLab (Chapter Resources/Chapter 6/Web links) to get information about production quotas on sugar in Europe. Why do you think the European nations assign production quotas for sugar? If the European sugar quotas are less than the equilibrium quantities, who benefits from the quotas? Who loses from the production quotas?**

   European nations assign production quotas for sugar to help keep the price of sugar high because of lobbying by sugar producers. The sugar producers benefit from the production quotas; sugar consumers are harmed by the prodcution quotas. The producers benefit because the price is kept higher than otherwise and the consumers lose because the price is kept higher than otherwise.

Additional Problems

1. The figure shows the demand for and supply of rental housing in Township.

   a. What are the equilibrium rent and equilibrium quantity of rental housing?

   If a rent ceiling is set at $150 a month, what is

   b. The quantity of housing rented?

   c. The shortage of housing?

   d. The maximum price that someone is willing to pay for the last unit available?

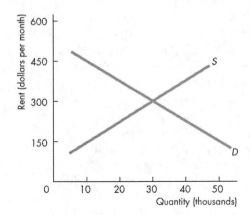

2. The table gives the demand schedule and the supply schedule for high school graduates.

   a. What is the equilibrium wage and the equilibrium quantity of employment.

   b. What is the number of hours of labor unemployed?

   c. If a minimum wage is set at $7 an hour, how many hours do high school graduates work?

   d. If a minimum wage is set at $7 an hour, how many hours of labor are unemployed?

   e. If a minimum wage is set at $9 an hour, what are the number of hours of labor employed and the number of hours of labor unemployed?

   f. If the minimum wage is $9 an hour and demand increases by 500 hours a month, what is the wage rate paid to high school graduates and how many hours of their labor are unemployed?

Wage rate (dollars per hour)	Quantity demanded	Quantity supplied
	(hours per month)	
6	9,000	4,000
7	8,000	5,000
8	7,000	6,000
9	6,000	7,000
10	5,000	8,000

3. The demand and supply schedules for coffee are given in the table.

   a. If there is no tax on coffee, what is the price of a cup of coffee and how much coffee is bought?

   b. If a tax of 75¢ a cup is introduced, what is the price of a cup of coffee and how much coffee is bought? Who pays the tax?

Price (dollars per cup)	Quantity demanded	Quantity supplied
	(cups per hour)	
1.50	90	30
1.75	70	40
2.00	50	50
2.25	30	60
2.50	10	70

Solutions to Additional Problems

1. a. Equilibrium rent is $300 a month and the equilibrium quantity is 30,000 housing units.

    b. The quantity rented is 10,000 housing units. The quantity of housing rented is equal to the quantity supplied at the rent ceiling.

    c. The shortage of housing is 40,000 housing units. At the rent ceiling, the quantity of housing demanded is 50,000, but the quantity supplied is 10,000, so there is a shortage of 40,000 housing units.

    d. The maximum price that someone is willing to pay for the 10,000th unit available is $450 a month. The demand curve tells us the maximum price that someone is willing to pay for the 10,000th unit.

2. a. The equilibrium wage rate is $8.50 an hour, and employment is 6,500 hours a month.

    b. Unemployment is zero. Everyone who wants to work for $8.50 an hour is employed.

    c. They work 6,500 hours a month. A minimum wage rate is the lowest wage rate that a person can be paid for an hour of work. Because the equilibrium wage exceeds the minimum wage, the minimum wage is ineffective. The wage rate will be $8.50 an hour and employment is 6,500 hours.

    d. There is no unemployment. The wage rate rises to the equilibrium wage—the quantity of labor demanded equals the quantity of labor supplied. So there is no unemployment.

    e. At $9 an hour, 6,000 hours a month are employed and 1,000 hours a month are unemployed. The quantity of labor employed equals the quantity demanded at $9 an hour. Unemployment is equal to the quantity of labor supplied at $9 an hour minus the quantity of labor demanded at $9 an hour. The quantity supplied is 7,000 hours a month, and the quantity demanded is 6,000 hours a month. So 1,000 hours a month are unemployed.

    f. The wage rate is $9 an hour, and unemployment is 500 hours a month. At the minimum wage of $9 an hour, the quantity demanded is 6,500 hours a month and the quantity supplied is 7,000 hours a month. So 500 hours a month are unemployed.

3. a. With no tax on coffee, the price is $2.00 a cup and 50 cups an hour are bought.

    b. The price is $2.25 a cup, and 30 cups an hour are bought. Consumers pay 25 cents of the tax on a cup of coffee and sellers pay 50 cents of the tax on a cup of coffee. The tax decreases the supply of coffee and raises the price of coffee. With no tax, sellers are willing to sell 30 cups an hour at $1.50 a cup. But with a 75 cent tax, they are willing to sell 30 cups an hour only if the price is 75 cents higher at $2.25 a cup.

Chapter 7

GLOBAL MARKETS IN ACTION

Answers to the Problems and Applications

1. **Wholesalers of roses (the firms that supply your local flower shop with roses for Valentine's Day) buy and sell roses in containers that hold 120 stems. The table provides information about the wholesale market for roses in the United States. The demand schedule is the wholesaler's demand and the supply schedule is the U.S. rose growers' supply. Wholesalers can buy roses at auction in Aalsmeer, Holland, for $125 per container.**

   a. **Without international trade, what would be the price of a container of roses and how many containers of roses a year would be bought and sold in the United States?**

      Without international trade, in the United States the price of a container of roses is $175 and 6 million containers of roses are bought and sold.

   b. **At the price in your answer to a, does the United States or the rest of the world have a comparative advantage in producing roses?**

      The price of roses in the United States exceeds the price in the rest of the world, so the rest of the world has a comparative advantage in producing roses.

   c. **If U.S. wholesalers buy roses at the lowest possible price, how many do they buy from U.S. growers and how many do they import?**

      The price of roses in the United States is $125 per container. At this price, U.S. rose growers supply 2 million containers per year and U.S. wholesalers demand 12 million containers of roses. U.S. wholesalers buy the 2 million containers from U.S. growers and purchase 10 million containers from foreign sources, which are imported into the United States.

   d. **Draw a graph to illustrate the U.S. wholesale market for roses. Show on the graph the equilibrium in that**

Price (dollars per container)	Quantity demanded	Quantity supplied
	(millions of containers per year)	
100	15	0
125	12	2
150	9	4
175	6	6
200	3	8
225	0	10

FIGURE 7.1

Problem 1

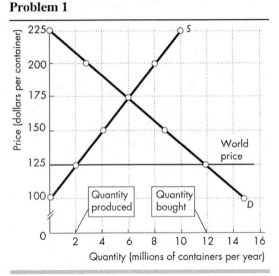

market with no international trade and the equilibrium with free trade. Mark on the graph the quantity of roses produced in the United States, the quantity imported, and the total quantity bought.

In Figure 7.1, the equilibrium without international trade is determined at the intersection of the demand curve and the supply curve. Without international trade the equilibrium price is $175 per container and 6 million containers per year are bought and produced. With international trade the world price is

$125 per container, as shown in Figure 7.1. The quantity produced in the United States is 2 million containers and the quantity bought in the United States is 12 million containers. Imports into the United States account for the difference between the quantity bought and the quantity produced, 10 million containers.

3. **Use the information on the U.S. wholesale market for roses in problem 1 to**

a. **Explain who gains and who loses from free international trade in roses compared to a situation in which Americans buy only roses grown in the United States.**

U.S. rose wholesalers, who are the consumers in the problem, gain from free international trade. U.S. rose growers lose from free international trade.

b. **Draw a graph to illustrate the gains and losses from free trade.**

Figure 7.3 illustrates the market with free trade. Consumer surplus before international trade is equal to area A; after international trade consumer surplus is equal to area A + area B + area C. Producer surplus before international trade is equal to area B + area D; after international trade producer surplus is equal to area D.

c. **Calculate the gain from international trade.**

The gain from international trade is area C in Figure 7.3. It is equal to ½ × ($175 − $125) × (10 million containers) which is $250 million.

5. **Steel Tariffs Appear to Have Backfired on Bush**
President Bush set aside his free-trade principles last year and imposed heavy tariffs on imported steel to help out struggling mills in Pennsylvania and West Virginia, two states crucial for his reelection. ... Some economists say the tariffs may have cost more jobs than

FIGURE **7.3**
Problem 3

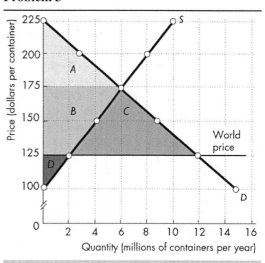

they saved, by driving up costs for automakers and other steel users. ...
The Washington Post, September 19, 2003

a. **Explain how a high tariff on steel imports can help domestic steel producers.**

The high tariff raises the price of steel in the United States. This higher price results in domestic steel producers increasing the quantity of steel they produce and increases their profits.

b. **Explain how a high tariff on steel imports can harm steel users.**

The tariff raises the U.S. price of steel and boosts steel users' costs. The rise in costs leads steel users to decrease the supply of the product they produce and also leads to lower profits for steel users.

c. **Draw a graph of the U.S. market for steel to show how a high tariff on steel imports**

i. Helps U.S. steel producers.

ii. Harms U.S. steel users.

iii. Creates a deadweight loss.

Figure 7.4 shows the steel market. This figure shows how the tariff helps producers, harms users, and creates a deadweight loss. The amount of the tariff is equal to the height of the light gray arrow. Before the tariff U.S. consumer surplus was equal to area *A* + area *B* + area *C* + area *E* + area *F*. After the tariff U.S. consumer surplus is equal to area *A*. U.S. consumers lose consumer surplus equal to area *B* + area *C* + area *E* + area *F*. Before the tariff U.S. producer surplus was equal to area *G*. After the tariff U.S. producer surplus is equal to area *G* + area *B*. U.S. producers gain producer surplus equal to area *B*. After the tariff the U.S. government gains tariff revenue equal to area *E*. The deadweight loss is equal to area *C* + area *F*.

7. **Use the information on the U.S. wholesale market for roses in problem 1.**

a. **If the United States puts an import quota on roses of 5 million containers, what happens to the U.S. price of roses, the quantity of roses bought, the quantity produced in the United States, and the quantity imported?**

The U.S. price of roses rises to $150 per container. 9 million containers of roses are purchased in the United States and 4 million containers of roses are produced in the United States. The difference, 5 million containers, is imported into the United States.

b. **Who gains and who loses from this quota?**

U.S. rose growers and importers of roses gain from the quota. U.S. rose wholesalers lose from the quota.

c. **Draw a graph to illustrate the gains and losses from the import quota and on the graph identify the gains and**

FIGURE **7.4**

Problem 5c

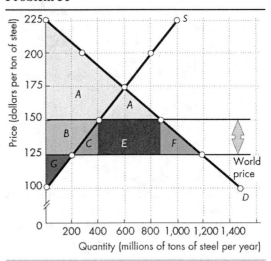

losses, the importers' profit, and the deadweight loss.

Figure 7.6 shows the effect of the import quota. The amount of the quota is equal to the length of the grey arrow. Before the quota U.S. consumer surplus was equal to area *A* + area *B* + area *C* + area *E* + area *F*. After the quota U.S. consumer surplus is equal to area *A*. U.S. consumers lose consumer surplus equal

FIGURE **7.6**

Problem 7c

to area B + area C + area E + area F. Before the quota U.S. producer surplus was equal to area G. After the quota U.S. producer surplus is equal to area G + area B. U.S. producers gain producer surplus equal to area B. After the quota the importers of the rose containers earn profit equal to area E. The deadweight loss from the import quota is equal to area C + area F.

9. **Chinese Tire Maker Rejects U.S. Charge of Defects**
   … regulators in the United States ordered the recall of more than 450,000 faulty tires . … The Chinese company that produced the tires … disputed the allegations Tuesday and hinted that the recall might be an effort by foreign competitors to hamper the company's exports to the United States. … Mounting scrutiny of Chinese-made goods has become a source of new trade frictions between the United States and China and fueled worries among regulators, corporations and consumers about the risks associated with many products imported from China. …
   International Herald Tribune, June 26, 2007

   a. **What does the information in the news clip imply about the comparative advantage of producing tires in the United States and China?**
      Because the tires were produced in China, the news clip suggests that China has the comparative advantage in producing tires.

   b. **Could product quality be a valid argument against free trade?**
      Product quality is not a valid argument against free trade. Quality is a valid concern for consumers. If consumers cannot judge quality themselves, then government inspection might be necessary. But in that case government inspection of *both* imported and domestically produced goods is required. To single out imported goods or services makes little sense.

   c. **How would the product-quality argument against free trade be open to abuse by domestic producers of the imported good?**
      Domestic producers could easily assert that the imported good lacks some essential quality characteristic and hence should be prohibited in the U.S. market. Product quality concerns raised by domestic producers can also be used to raise worry amongst U.S. consumers about imported goods. Domestic producers would have a never-ending incentive to complain about quality defects of imported goods.

11. **Suppose that the world price of sugar is 10 cents a pound, the United States does not trade internationally, and the equilibrium price of sugar in the United States is 20 cents a pound. The United States then begins to trade internationally.**

   a. **How does the price of sugar in the United States change?**
      The price of sugar in the United States falls.

   b. **Do U.S. consumers buy more or less sugar?**
      As a result of the lower price, U.S. consumers buy more sugar.

   c. **Do U.S. sugar growers produce more or less sugar?**
      As a result of the lower price, U.S. growers produce less sugar.

d. **Does the United States export or import sugar and why?**

> The United States imports sugar. The quantity of sugar demanded increases while quantity supplied decreases. The difference is made up by imports.

13. **A semiconductor is a key component in your laptop, cell phone, and iPod. The table provides information about the market for semiconductors in the United States. Producers of semiconductors can get $18 a unit on the world market.**

Price (dollars per unit)	Quantity demanded	Quantity supplied
	(billions of units per year)	
10	25	0
12	20	20
14	15	40
16	10	60
18	5	80
20	0	100

a. **With no international trade, what would be the price of a semiconductor and how many semiconductors a year would be bought and sold in the United States?**

> With no international trade the price of a semiconductor in the United States is $12 per unit. 20 billion units are bought and sold in the United States.

b. **At the price in your answer to a, does the United States have a comparative advantage in producing semiconductors?**

> The United States has a comparative advantage in producing semiconductor units because the U.S. price is lower than the price in the world market.

c. **If U.S. producers of semiconductors sell at the highest possible price, how many do they sell in the United States and how many do they export?**

> If the United States trades semiconductor units internationally, the price in the United States rises to $18 per unit. At this price U.S. producers manufacture 80 billion semiconductor units and U.S. consumers buy 5 billion semiconductor units. The difference between the quantity produced, 80 billion units, and the quantity sold domestically, 5 billion units, is 75 billion units. This quantity is exported.

15. **Act Now, Eat Later**
… looming hunger crisis in poor countries … has its roots in … misguided policy in the U.S. and Europe of subsidizing the diversion of food crops to produce biofuels like corn-based ethanol … [That is,] doling out subsidies to put the world's dinner into the gas tank.

> *Time*, **May 5, 2008**

a. **What is the effect on the world price of corn of the increased use of corn to produce ethanol in the United States and Europe?**

> The use of corn to produce ethanol increased the demand for corn, thereby raising the price of corn.

b. **How does the change in the world price of corn affect the quantity of corn produced in a poor developing country with a comparative advantage in producing corn, the quantity it consumes, and the quantity that it either exports or imports?**

> The higher world price of corn decreases the consumption of corn and increases the production of corn in poor developing countries. Because the country has a comparative advantage it will export corn. The higher price leads the country to increase its exports.

c. **Draw a graph of the market for corn in a poor developing country to illustrate your answer to b. Identify the changes in consumer surplus, producer surplus, and deadweight loss.**

Figure 7.11 shows the situation in a poor country that exports corn. With the initial lower price, the country produces 60 million bushels, exports 20 million bushels, and consumes 40 million bushels. The consumer surplus is equal to area *A* + area *B* and the producer surplus is equal to area *E*. After the world price of corn rises to $8 per bushel, the country produces 80 million bushels of corn, exports 60 million bushels, and consumes 20 million bushels. Consumer surplus decreases to area *A* and producer surplus increases to area *B* + area *C* + area *E*. There is no deadweight loss; in fact, the country gains additional surplus equal to area *C*.

17. **Suppose that in response to huge job losses in the U.S. textile industry, Congress imposes a 100 percent tariff on imports of textiles from China.**

a. **Explain how the tariff on textiles will change the price that U.S. buyers pay for textiles, the quantity of textiles imported, and the quantity of textiles produced in the United States.**

The tariff raises the U.S. price of textiles. As a result, the quantity of textiles consumed in the United States decreases and the quantity produced increases. Imports of textiles into the United States decrease.

b. **Explain how the U.S. and Chinese gains from trade will change. Who in the United States will lose and who will gain?**

The U.S. and Chinese gains from trade decrease. In the United States, U.S. producers gain from the tariff. The U.S. government also gains revenue from the tariff. U.S. textile consumers lose.

19. **Aid May Grow for Laid-Off Workers ...the expansion of the Trade**

FIGURE **7.11**

Problem 15c

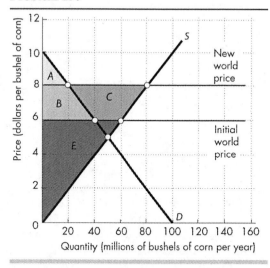

Adjustment Assistance (TAA) program would begin to reweave the social safety net for the 21st century, as advances permit more industries to take advantage of cheap foreign labor—even for skilled, white-collar work. By providing special compensation to more of globalization's losers and retraining them for stable jobs at home, ... an expanded program could begin to ease the resentment and insecurity arising from the new economy.

The Washington Post, July 23, 2007

a. **Why does the United States engage in international trade if it causes U.S. workers to lose their jobs?**

While some U.S workers lose from international trade, other U.S. workers and U.S. consumers gain from this trade. On an economy-wide level, the gains from international trade exceed the losses.

b. **Explain how an expansion of the Trade Adjustment Assistance will make it easier for the United States to move toward freer international trade.**

The Trade Adjustment Assistance program encourages workers to retrain for jobs in industries in which the United States has a comparative advantage. Workers who stand to lose from free international trade lobby to keep or establish protection for their industry. If Trade Adjustment Assistance was expanded, then these workers' losses would be decreased which makes them less likely to lobby for protection.

21. **Trading Up**
     ... the cost of protecting jobs in uncompetitive sectors through tariffs is foolishly high, ... The Federal Reserve Bank of Dallas reported in 2002 that saving a job in the sugar industry cost American consumers $826,000 in higher prices a year, saving a dairy industry job cost $685,000 per year, and saving a job in the manufacturing of women's handbags cost $263,000.
     The New York Times, **June 26, 2006**

a. **What are the arguments for saving the jobs mentioned in this news clip?**

     The arguments for saving these jobs are (explicitly) the argument that protection saves jobs and (implicitly) that protection allows us to compete with cheap foreign labor.

b. **Explain why these arguments are faulty.**

     The fact these arguments are wrong can be demonstrated by comparing the cost of saving a job to the wage paid on the job. The cost to U.S. consumers of saving a job massively outweighs the benefit a job to the worker, that is, the wage rate paid on the job. This empirical result demonstrates the conclusion that the cost of protection to the losers, U.S. consumers, exceeds the gain to the winners, U.S. producers.

c. **Is there any merit to saving these jobs?**

     There is merit to the workers whose jobs are saved and who might not receive any government assistance if their jobs are not protected. There also is merit to the politicians who can obtain a reward from lobbyists for the protection. There is no merit, however, to society as a whole.

Additional Problems

1. Suppose that the world price of bananas is 18 U.S. cents a pound and that when Australia does not trade bananas internationally, their equilibrium price in Australia is 12 U.S. cents a pound. If Australia opens up to international trade, does it export or import bananas? Explain how the price of bananas in Australia changes. How does the quantity of bananas consumed in Australia change? How does the quantity of bananas grown in Australia change?

2. Suppose that in response to huge job losses in the U.S. textile industry, Congress imposes a 100 percent tariff on imports of textiles from China.

   a. Explain how the tariff on textiles will change the price of textiles, the quantity of textiles imported, and the quantity of textiles produced in the United States.

   b. Explain how the U.S. and Chinese gains from trade will change. Who in the United States will lose and who will gain?

3. With free international trade between Australia and the United States, Australia would export beef to the United States. But the United States imposes a quota on imports of Australia beef. Explain how this quota influences the price that U.S. consumers pay for beef, the quantity of beef produced in the United States, and the U.S. and Australian gains from trade. Who in the United States gains from the quota on beef imports and who loses?

4. In the 1950s, Ford and General Motors established a small car-producing industry in Australia and argued for a high tariff on car imports. The tariff has remained through the years. Until 2000, the tariff was 22.5 percent. What might have been Ford's and General Motor's argument for the high tariff? Is the tariff the best way to achieve the goals of the argument?

U.S. Expands China Paper Anti-Dumping Tariff

The U.S. Commerce Department said on Wednesday it was imposing additional preliminary duties of up to 99.65 percent on imports of glossy paper from China. ... the decision came in the second of two cases brought by NewPage Corp. of Dayton, Ohio against imports from China, The paper is the type used in art books, high-end magazines, textbooks, and annual reports. ...U.S. imports of glossy paper from China increased 166 percent from 2005 to 2006 to an estimated $224 million.

Reuters, May 30, 2007

5. Use the information to answer the following questions:

   a. What is dumping? Who in the United States loses from China's dumping of glossy paper?

   b. What argument might NewPage Corp. have used to persuade the U.S. Commerce Department to impose a 99.65 percent tariff?

   c. Explain who, in the United States, will gain and who will lose from the tariff on glossy paper. How do you expect the prices of magazines and textbooks that you buy to change?

Solutions to Additional Problems

1. With no international trade, the price in Australia is less than that in the world, so Australia has a comparative advantage in producing bananas. As a result, if Australia opens up to international trade, it will export bananas. With international trade, the price of bananas in Australia rises. The higher price leads to a decrease in the quantity of bananas consumed in Australia. The higher price also leads to an increase in the quantity of bananas grown in Australia.

2. a. Higher tariffs increase the price U.S. consumers pay for textiles imported from China. Because the price of Chinese imported textiles rises, the quantity imported decreases. The quantity of textiles produced in the United States increases.

    b. This trade restriction means that the U.S. and Chinese gains from trade definitely decrease. Textile workers and owners of textile firms will gain from the higher price. Textile consumers will lose from the higher price.

3. By restricting the amount of beef imported into the United States, the quota raises the price of beef to U.S. consumers. The quantity of beef produced in the United States increases. The U.S. and Australian gains from trade are reduced by the U.S. quota. U.S. beef producers and their workers gain from the quota on beef. In addition, the importers who have the right to import beef gain. U.S. consumers lose from the higher price of beef.

4. Most likely the argument in favor of the tariff was the infant-industry argument. According to proponents of this argument, protection is necessary to a new industry to enable it to grow into a mature industry that can compete in world markets. Alternatively, Ford and General Motors might also have argued that a high tariff was necessary to protect Australian jobs. Protection is not the best way to achieve these goals. A more efficient way to protect infant industries is to subsidize the firms in the industry. And the jobs lost in the auto sector will be regained in other sectors devoted to exporting Australian goods.

5. a. Dumping is when a foreign firm sells its exports at a lower price than the cost of production. U.S. producers of glossy paper lose from China's dumping of glossy paper.

    b. Dumping is illegal under the rules of international trade, so dumping is regarded as a justifiable reason for a temporary tariff. NewPage might have argued that Chinese exporters of glossy paper were charging a price of (approximately) one half the cost of production. In this case a tariff of 99.65 percent will (approximately) double the U.S. price of the imported glossy paper, thereby raising the price to the (alleged) cost of production.

    c. The U.S. producers of glossy paper (such as NewPage!) will gain. The U.S. government also will gain because it will receive additional tariff revenue. U.S. consumers of glossy paper will lose. The higher price of glossy paper increases the costs of magazine and textbook publishers. The supply of magazines and textbooks decreases so that their price rises.

Chapter 8 UTILITY AND DEMAND

Answers to the Problems and Applications

1. **Max enjoys windsurfing and snorkeling. The table shows the total utility he gets from each activity.**

    a. **Find Max's marginal utility from windsurfing at each number of hours per day.**

    Max's marginal utility from windsurfing 1 hour per day is 120; from windsurfing 2 hours per day is 100; from windsurfing 3 hours per day is 80; from windsurfing 4 hours per day is 60; from windsurfing 5 hours per day is 36; from windsurfing 6 hours per day is 16; and, from windsurfing 7 hours per day is 10.

    b. **Find Max's marginal utility from snorkeling at each number of hours per day.**

    Max's marginal utility from snorkeling 1 hour per day is 40; from 2 hours per day is 36; from snorkeling 3 hours per day is 30; from snorkeling 4 hours per day is 22; from snorkeling 5 hours per day is 12; from snorkeling 6 hours per day is 10; and, from snorkeling 7 hours per day is 8.

    c. **Do Max's marginal utility from windsurfing and from snorkeling obey the principle of diminishing marginal utility?**

    Max's marginal utility from windsurfing and from snorkeling both obey the principle of diminishing marginal utility because both decrease as the consumption increases.

    d. **Which does Max enjoy more: his 6th hour of windsurfing or his 6th hour of snorkeling?**

    Max's marginal utility from his 6th hour of windsurfing is 16 and his marginal utility from his 6th hour of snorkeling is 10. Max enjoys his 6th hour of windsurfing more than his 6th hour of snorkeling.

Hours per day	Total utility from windsurfing	Total utility from snorkeling
1	120	40
2	220	76
3	300	106
4	360	128
5	396	140
6	412	150
7	422	158

3. Max in problems 1 and 2 is offered a special deal on windsurfing equipment: a rental rate of $5 an hour. His income remains at $35 a day and the rental price of snorkeling equipment remains at $5 an hour.

a. Make a table that shows the new combinations of hours spent windsurfing and snorkeling that Max can afford.

The table is to the right.

b. In your table, list Max's marginal utility per dollar from windsurfing and snorkeling.

The columns are added in the table to the right.

c. How many hours does Max now spend windsurfing and how many hours does he spend snorkeling?

Max will now maximize his total utility by spending 5 hours windsurfing and 2 hours snorkeling. This combination of windsurfing and snorkeling uses all of Max's income and sets the marginal utility per dollar from windsurfing equal to the marginal utility per dollar from snorkeling.

5. Max, with the utility schedules in problem 1, gets an increase in income from $35 to $55 a day. Windsurfing equipment rents for $10 an hour, and snorkeling equipment rents for $5 an hour. Show the effect of the increase in Max's income on Max's demand curve for

a. Rented windsurfing equipment, and explain whether, for Max, windsurfing equipment is a normal good or an inferior good.

To maximize his utility, Max windsurfs for 4 hours and snorkels for 3 hours. Max uses his $55 such that all of the $55 is spent and marginal utility per dollar for each activity is the same. When Max windsurfs for 4 hours and snorkels for 3 hours, he spends $40

Hours windsurfing	Marginal utility per dollar from windsurfing	Hours snorkeling	Marginal utility per dollar from snorkeling
7	2.0	0	
6	3.2	1	8.0
5	7.2	2	7.2
4	12.0	3	6.0
3	16.0	4	4.4
2	20.0	5	2.4
1	24.0	6	2.0
0		7	1.6

FIGURE **8.2**
Problem 5a

renting the windsurfing equipment and $15 renting the snorkeling equipment—a total of $55. The marginal utility from the fourth hour of windsurfing is 60 and the rent of the windsurfing equipment is $10 an hour, so the marginal utility per dollar from windsurfing is 6. The marginal utility from the third hour of snorkeling is 30 and the rent of the snorkeling equipment is $5 an hour, so the marginal utility per dollar from snorkeling is 6. The marginal utility per dollar from windsurfing equals the marginal utility per dollar from snorkeling.

Max's demand for rented windsurfing equipment increases. The quantity of windsurfing equipment rented at a price of $10 per hour increases from 3 hours (problem 2c) to 4 hours (this problem). As a result Max's demand curve for rented windsurfing equipment shifts rightward as illustrated in Figure 8.2 (on the previous page) by the shift from D_1 to D_2. Windsurfing equipment is a normal good.

b. Rented snorkeling equipment, and explain whether, for Max, snorkeling equipment is a normal good or an inferior good.

Max's demand for rented snorkeling equipment increases. The quantity of snorkeling equipment demanded at a price of $5 per hour increases from 1 hour (problem 2c) to 3 hours (this problem). As a result Max's demand curve for rented snorkeling equipment shifts rightward as illustrated in Figure 8.3 by the shift from D_1 to D_2. Snorkeling equipment is a normal good.

7. Can Money Buy Happiness? "Whoever said money can't buy happiness isn't spending it right."... You know that there must be some connection between money and happiness. If there weren't, you'd be less likely to stay late at work (or even come in at all). ... "Once you get basic human needs met, a lot more money doesn't make a lot more happiness." ... Going from earning less than $20,000 a year to making more than $50,000 makes you twice as likely to be happy, yet the payoff for then surpassing $90,000 is slight.
CNN, July 18, 2006

FIGURE 8.3
Problem 5b

a. What does the fundamental assumption of marginal utility theory suggest about the connection between money and happiness?

Marginal utility theory assumes that total utility increases with increases in the consumption of a good or service, so a person's total happiness (that is, their total utility) is assumed to increase with income (so that their consumption increases).

b. **Explain why this article is consistent with marginal utility theory.**

Marginal utility theory assumes that *total* utility increases with increases in the consumption of a good or service but *marginal* utility decreases with increases in the consumption of a good or service. Hence a person's *total* happiness increases when income increases but the *marginal* happiness (that is, the change in total happiness) decreases when income increases. These results are precisely what the story reports: Total happiness increases as income increases from $20,000 to $50,000 to $90,000 but the change in happiness diminishes.

9. **Compared to Other Liquids, Gasoline is Cheap**
Think a $4 gallon of gas is expensive? Consider the prices of these other fluids that people buy every day without complaint...
Gatorade, 20 oz @ $1.59 = $10.17 per gallon ...
Wite-Out, 7 oz @ $1.39 = $25.42 per gallon ...
HP Ink Cartridge, 16 ml $18 = $4,294.58 per gallon
The New York Times, **May 27, 2008**

a. **What does marginal utility theory predict about the marginal utility per dollar from gasoline, Gatorade, Wite-Out, and printer ink?**

Marginal utility theory predicts that the marginal utility per dollar of each of these liquids is the same.

b. **What do the prices per gallon reported in this news clip tell you about the marginal utility from a gallon of gasoline, Gatorade, Wite-Out, and printer ink?**

Marginal utility theory concludes that the higher the price, the higher the marginal utility. Thus the marginal utility of a gallon of gasoline is less than the marginal utility of gallon of Gatorade, which is less than the marginal utility of a gallon of Wite-Out, which, in turn, is less than the marginal utility of a gallon of HP ink.

c. **What do the prices per unit reported in this news clip tell you about the marginal utility from a gallon of gasoline, a 20 oz bottle of Gatorade, a 7 oz bottle of Wite-Out, and a cartridge of printer ink?**

Marginal utility theory concludes that the higher the price, the higher the marginal utility. Thus the marginal utility of 7 oz. of Wite-Out is less than the marginal utility of 20 oz. of Gatorade, which is less than the marginal utility of a gallon of gasoline, which, in turn, is less than the marginal utility of an HP Ink Cartridge.

d. **How can the paradox of value be used to explain why the fluids listed in the news clip might be less valuable than gasoline, yet far more expensive?**

Gasoline presumably is more valuable than Gatorade, Wite-Out, or HP Ink Cartridges because gasoline is really essential to our modern life. But gasoline is much more common than these other three products. As a result the marginal utility and hence the price of gasoline per gallon is less than that of the other products even though the consumer surplus from gasoline vastly exceeds that from the other products.

11. Cindy enjoys golf and tennis. The table shows the marginal utility she gets from each activity. Cindy has $70 a month to spend, and she can spend as much time as she likes on her leisure pursuits. The price of an hour of golf is $10, and the price of an hour of tennis is $5.

a. Make a table that shows the various combinations of hours spent playing golf and tennis that Cindy can afford.

The table is to the right.

b. In your table, add two columns and list Cindy's marginal utility per dollar from golf and from tennis.

The table is to the right.

c. How long does Cindy spend playing golf and how long does she spend playing tennis to maximize her utility?

Cindy plays golf for 5 hours and tennis for 4 hours to maximize her utility. This combination allocates (spends) all her income and sets the marginal utility per dollar from golf equal to the marginal utility per dollar from tennis.

d. Compared to c, if Cindy spent a dollar more on golf and a dollar less on tennis, by how much would her total utility change?

If Cindy played another hour of golf, she pays $10 and gains 10 units of utility (the marginal utility from the 6th hour), which is 1.0 unit of utility per dollar. So if she spends a dollar more on golf, her utility from golf increases by 1.0. If she spends an hour less playing tennis, she saves $5 and loses 10 units of utility (the marginal utility from the 4th hour of tennis), which is 2.0 units of utility per dollar. So if she spends a dollar less on tennis, she loses 2.0 units of utility. Overall, spending a dollar more on golf and a dollar less on tennis lowers Cindy's total utility by 1.0 unit of utility.

Hours per month	Marginal utility from golf	Marginal utility from tennis
1	80	40
2	60	36
3	40	30
4	30	10
5	20	5
6	10	2
7	6	1

Hours playing golf	Marginal utility per dollar from golf	Hours playing tennis	Marginal utility per dollar from tennis
7	0.6	0	
6	1.0	2	7.2
5	2.0	4	2.0
4	3.0	6	0.4
3	4.0	8	
2	6.0	10	
1	8.0	12	
0		14	

e. Compared to c, if Cindy spent a dollar less on golf and a dollar more on tennis, by how much would her total utility change?

If Cindy spends an hour less playing golf, she saves $10 and loses 20 units of utility (the marginal utility from the 5th hour), which is 2.0 unit of utility per dollar. So if she spends a dollar less on golf, her utility from golf decreases by 2.0. If she spends an hour more playing tennis, she spends $5 and gains 5 units of utility (the marginal utility from the 5th hour of tennis), which is 1.0 unit of utility per dollar. So if she spends a dollar more on tennis, she gains 1.0 units of utility. Overall, spending a dollar less on golf and a dollar more on tennis lowers Cindy's total utility by 1.0 unit of utility.

f. Explain why, if Cindy equalized the marginal utility per hour of

golf and tennis, she would *not* maximize her utility.

Cindy would not maximize her utility by equalizing the marginal utility per hour of golf and tennis because golf and tennis have different prices. Golf is twice as expensive as tennis, so effectively every unit of utility that Cindy buys from playing golf costs her twice as much as buying a unit of utility from playing tennis. Equalizing the marginal utilities ignores the fact that utility from tennis is cheaper than utility from golf.

13. Given the information in problems 11 and 12,

a. Find two points on Cindy's demand curve for tennis.

One point on her demand curve is 4 hours of tennis when the price is $5 per hour. Another point is 3 hours of tennis when the price is $10 per hour.

b. Draw Cindy's demand curve for tennis.

Cindy's demand curve is in Figure 8.4.

c. Is Cindy's demand for tennis elastic or inelastic?

The price elasticity of demand of Cindy's demand for tennis is 0.43, so her demand is inelastic.

d. Explain how Cindy's demand for tennis changed when the price of an hour of tennis increased.

The quantity of hours Cindy demanded for playing tennis decreased when the price of an hour of playing tennis increased.

e. What is Cindy's cross elasticity of demand for golf with respect to the price of tennis?

Cindy's cross-elasticity of demand is —0.33.

f. Are tennis and golf substitutes or complements for Cindy?

Tennis and golf are complements because the cross elasticity of demand is negative.

15. Cindy in problem 12 takes a Club Med vacation, the cost of which includes unlimited sports activities. There is no extra charge for golf and tennis. Cindy allocates a total of 4 hours a day to these activities.

a. How many hours does Cindy play golf and how many hours does she play tennis?

Cindy plays golf for 3 hours and plays tennis for 1 hour.

b. What is Cindy's marginal utility from golf and from tennis?

Cindy's marginal utility from golf and from tennis both equal 40.

FIGURE **8.4**
Problem 13b

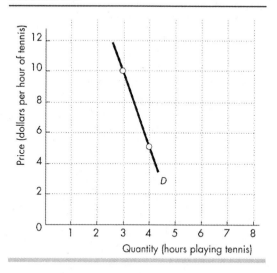

c. **Why does Cindy equalize the marginal utilities rather than the marginal utility per dollar from golf and tennis?**

Because the equipment is free, Cindy does not have to allocate her *income* between the two activities; instead, she allocates her *time* between the two activities because time is now the factor that limits her. Because each activity is in hour increments, Cindy equalizes the marginal utility per hour and thereby sets the marginal utilities equal to each other.

17. **Blue-Ray Format Expected to Dominate, but When?**
Blu-ray stomped HD DVD to become the standard format for high-definition movie discs, but years may pass before it can claim victory over the good old DVD. ... "The group that bought $2,000, 40-inch TVs are the ones that will lead the charge. ... Everyone else will come along when the price comes down."... Blu-ray machine prices are starting to drop. Wal-Mart Stores Inc. began stocking a $298 Magnavox model. ... That's cheaper than most alternatives but a hefty price hike from a typical $50 DVD player.

CNN, June 2, 2008

a. **What does marginal utility theory predict about the marginal utility from a Magnavox Blu-ray machine compared to the marginal utility from a typical DVD player?**

Marginal utility theory asserts that the marginal utility per dollar from a Blu-ray machine equals the marginal utility per dollar from a typical DVD player. Because the price of a Blu-ray player is higher than the price of a typical DVD player, the marginal utility from a Blu-ray player is higher than the marginal utility from a regular DVD player. Indeed, the price of the Blu-ray machine is almost exactly 6

times higher so the marginal utility of a Blu-ray machine will be the same, almost exactly 6 times higher.

b. **What will have to happen to the marginal utility from a Blu-ray machine before it is able to "claim victory over the good old DVD?"**

The marginal utility from a Blu-ray player will need to decrease so that it is the same as the marginal utility from a regular DVD player. This change will occur as the price of Blu-ray players falls, leading consumers to buy more Blu-ray players which reduces the marginal utility of a Blu-ray player.

19. **How To Buy Happiness. Cheap Sure, in any given country at any given point in time, the rich tend to be a bit happier than the poor. But across-the-board increases in living standards don't seem to make people any happier. Disposable income for the average American has grown about 80% since 1972, but the percentage describing themselves as "very happy" (roughly a third) has barely budged over the years. ... As living standards increase, most of us respond by raising our own standards. Things that once seemed luxuries now seem necessities. ... As a result, we're working harder than ever to buy stuff that satisfies us less and less.**

CNN, October 1, 2004

a. **According to this news clip, how do widespread increases in living standards influence total utility?**

"Utility" and "happiness" are not synonymous because they are different measures. Utility is an arbitrary measure that tells how people value different consumption bundles at a point in time. Happiness, presumably, is a measure that tells how pleased people are with their entire life. According to the news clip, the widespread increases in living standards have virtually no effect on happiness. If happiness and utility were the same, the article would imply that total utility had changed only very little with consumption but because these are different measures, no such conclusion can be drawn.

b. **What does the news clip imply about how the total utility from consumption changes over time?**

For two reasons, the news clip tells us nothing about how total utility has changed over time. First, total utility is an arbitrary measure: its units and scale can be changed with no effect on its predictions, so it does not make sense to try to determine how it has changed over time. Second, even if its units and scale were kept constant, total utility and happiness are not the same thing.

c. **What does the news clip imply about how the marginal utility from consumption changes over time?**

Because the article gives us no information about how total utility changed, it also gives no information about how marginal utility changed. A consumer will consume the combination of goods and services that sets their marginal utility divided by their price equal. To know how marginal utilities have changed, we therefore need to know how the prices and quantities consumed have changed.

21. **Study *Reading Between the Lines* (pp. 196–197).**

a. **If a wave of natural disasters put paramedics in the news and a large number of people decide to try to get jobs as paramedics, what happens to**
    i. The marginal utility of the services of a paramedic?

As more people become paramedics, the marginal utility of a paramedic decreases.

ii. **Consumer surplus in the market for the services of paramedics?**

With more people becoming paramedics, the consumer surplus in the market for paramedic services increases.

b. **If television advertising revenues during hockey games double, what happens to**
    i. The marginal utility of the services of a hockey player?

The increase in advertising revenues influences hockey team owners to increase the amount of hockey they supply, which increases the demand for hockey players. The demand for hockey players increases and hence the wage rate paid hockey players increases. Because the marginal utility of a hockey player divided by the wage rate equals the marginal utility of other professions (such as paramedics) divided by the wage rate, the higher wage rate for a hockey player means that the marginal utility of a hockey player must rise to keep the marginal utility per dollar for a hockey player equal to that for other professions.

ii. **Consumer surplus in the market for the services of hockey players?**

The effect on the consumer surplus from hockey players is ambiguous. The demand increases, which raises the consumer surplus. But the wage rate also increases, which decreases the consumer surplus. If the demand curve is linear, the supply curve is vertical (as in Figure 2 on page 197), and if the demand curve's slope does not change when it shifts rightward, then there will be no net change in the consumer surplus.

Additional Problems

1. Mary enjoys classical CDs and travel books and spends $50 a month on them. The table shows the utility she gets from each good.

    a. Compare the two utility schedules. Can you say anything about Mary's preferences?

    b. What do the two utility schedules tell you about Mary's preferences?

    c. If a classical CD and a travel book cost $10 each, how does Mary spend the $50 a month?

Quantity per month	Total utility from classical CDs	Total utility from travel books
1	30	30
2	40	38
3	48	44
4	54	46
5	58	47

2. Rob enjoys rock concerts and the opera. The table shows the marginal utility he gets from each activity. Rob has $100 a month to spend on concerts. A rock concert ticket is $20, and an opera ticket is $10. How many rock concerts and how many operas does he attend?

Concerts per month	Marginal utility from rock concerts	Marginal utility from operas
1	90	120
2	80	90
3	60	60
4	40	30
5	20	20

3. In problem 2, Rob's uncle gives him $30 to spend on concert tickets, so he now has $130. How many rock concerts and how many operas does he attend now that he has $130 to spend?

4. In problem 2, if the price of a rock concert decreases to $10, how many rock concerts and operas will Rob attend?

Solutions to Additional Problems

1. a. Mary gets the same utility from 1 classical CD as from 1 travel book, but at quantities greater than 1 she gets more utility from any number of classical CDs than she does from the same number of travel books.

   b. Mary receives the same marginal utility from her first classical CD as from her first travel book. At quantities greater than 1, Mary gets more marginal utility from an additional classical CD than she gets from an additional travel book when she has the same number of each.

   c. Mary buys 3 classical CDs and 2 travel books.
   When Mary buys 3 classical CDs and 2 travel books she spends $50. Mary maximizes her utility when she spends all of her money and the marginal utility per dollar from classical CDs and travel books is the same. When Mary buys 3 classical CDs her marginal utility per dollar spent is 0.8 units per dollar and when Mary buys 2 travel books her marginal utility per dollar spent is 0.8 units per dollar.

2. To maximize his utility, Rob attends 3 rock concerts and 4 opera concerts.
   Rob will spend his $100 such that all of the $100 is spent and that the marginal utility per dollar from each type of concert is the same. When Rob attends 3 rock concerts and 4 operas, he spends $60 on rock concerts and $40 on operas—a total of $100.
   The marginal utility from the third rock concert is 60 and a rock concert ticket is $20, so the marginal utility per dollar from rock concerts is 3. The marginal utility from the fourth opera is 30 and an opera ticket is $10, so the marginal utility per dollar from operas is 3. The marginal utility per dollar from rock concerts equals the marginal utility per dollar from operas.

3. To maximize his utility, Rob attends 4 rock concerts and 5 operas.
   Rob will spend his $130 such that all of the $130 is spent and that the marginal utility per dollar from each type of concert is the same. When Rob attends 4 rock concerts and 5 operas, he spends $80 on rock concert tickets and $50 on operas—a total of $130.
   The marginal utility from the fourth rock concert is 40 and a rock concert ticket is $20, so the marginal utility per dollar from rock concerts is 2. The marginal utility from the fifth opera is 20 and an opera ticket is $10, so the marginal utility per dollar from opera is 2. The marginal utility per dollar from rock concerts equals the marginal utility per dollar from operas.

4. To maximize his utility, Rob attends 5 rock concerts and 5 operas.
   Rob will spend his $100 such that all of the $100 is spent and that the marginal utility per dollar from each type of concert is the same. When Rob attends 5 rock concerts and 5 operas, he spends $50 on rock concert tickets and $50 on opera tickets—a total of $100.
   The marginal utility from the fifth rock concert is 20 and a rock concert ticket is $10, so the marginal utility per dollar from rock concerts is 2. The marginal utility from the fifth opera is 20 and an opera ticket is $10, so the marginal utility per dollar from operas is 2. The marginal utility per dollar from rock concerts equals the marginal utility per dollar from operas.

Chapter 9

POSSIBILITES, PREFERENCES, AND CHOICES

Answers to the Problems and Applications

1. **Sara's income is $12 a week. The price of popcorn is $3 a bag, and the price of a smoothie is $3.**

   a. **What is Sara's real income in terms of smoothies?**

   Sara's real income is 4 smoothies. Sara's real income in terms of smoothies is equal to her money income divided by the price of a smoothie. Sara's money income is $12, and the price of a smoothie is $3. Sara's real income is $12 divided by $3 a smoothie, which is 4 smoothies.

   b. **What is her real income in terms of popcorn?**

   Sara's real income is 4 bags of popcorn. Sara's real income in terms of popcorn is equal to her money income divided by the price of a bag of popcorn, which is $12 divided by $3 a bag or 4 bags of popcorn.

   c. **What is the relative price of smoothies in terms of popcorn?**

   The relative price of a smoothie is 1 bag of popcorn per smoothie. The relative price of a smoothie is the price of a smoothie divided by the price of a bag of popcorn. The price of a smoothie is $3 and the price of popcorn is $3 a bag, so the relative price of a smoothie is $3 divided by $3 a bag, which equals 1 bag of popcorn per smoothie.

   d. **What is the opportunity cost of a smoothie?**

   The opportunity cost of a smoothie is 1 bag of popcorn. The opportunity cost of a smoothie is the quantity of popcorn that must be forgone to get a smoothie. The price of a smoothie is $3 and the price of popcorn is $3 a bag, so to buy one smoothie Sara must forgo 1 bag of popcorn.

   e. **Calculate the equation for Sara's budget line (with bags of popcorn**

on the left side).

   The equation that describes Sara's budget line is $Q_P = 4 - Q_S$. Call the price of popcorn P_P and the quantity of popcorn Q_P, the price of a smoothie P_S and the quantity of smoothies Q_S, and income y. Sara's budget equation is $P_P Q_P + P_S Q_S = y$. If we substitute $3 for the price of popcorn, $3 for the price of a smoothie, and $12 for the income, the budget equation becomes $3Q_P + $3Q_S = $12. Dividing both sides by $3 and subtracting Q_S from both sides gives $Q_P = 4 - Q_S$.

   f. **Draw a graph of Sara's budget line with quantity of smoothies on the x-axis.**

   To draw a graph of the budget line, plot the quantity of smoothies on the x-axis and the quantity of popcorn on the y-axis. The budget line is a straight line from 4 bags of popcorn on the y-axis to 4 smoothies on the x-axis.

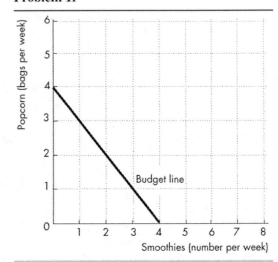

FIGURE **9.1**
Problem 1f

   g. **In part f, what is the slope of Sara's budget line? What determines its value?**

   The slope of the budget line, when smoothies are plotted on the x-axis, is minus 1. The magnitude of the slope is equal to the relative price of a smoothie. The slope of the budget line is "rise over run." If the quantity of smoothies decreases from 4 to 0, the quantity of popcorn increases from 0 to 4. The rise is 4 and the run is −4. Therefore the slope equals 4/−4, which is −1.

3. **Sara's income is $12 a week. The price of popcorn rises from $3 to $6 a bag, and the price of smoothie remains at $3.**

a. **What is the effect of the rise in the price of popcorn on Sara's real income in terms of smoothies?**

The rise in the price of a bag of popcorn has no effect on Sara's real income in terms of smoothies. Sara's real income in terms of smoothies remains 4 smoothies.

b. **What is the effect of the rise in the price of popcorn on Sara's real income in terms of popcorn?**

Sara's real income in terms of popcorn falls to 2 bags of popcorn. Sara's real income in terms of popcorn is equal to her money income divided by the price of a bag of popcorn. Sara's money income is $12 and the price of a bag of popcorn is now $6. Sara's real income is now $12 divided by $6 a bag, which is 2 bags of popcorn.

c. **What is the effect of the rise in the price of popcorn on the relative price of a smoothie in terms of popcorn?**

The relative price of a smoothie falls to 1/2 bag of popcorn per smoothie. The relative price of a smoothie is the price of a smoothie divided by the price of a bag of popcorn. The price of a smoothie is $3 and the price of popcorn is $6 a bag, so the relative price of a smoothie is $3 divided by $6 a bag, which equals 1/2 bag of popcorn per smoothie. The rise in the price of a bag of popcorn lowers the relative price of a smoothie in terms of popcorn.

d. **What is the slope of Sara's new budget line if it is drawn with smoothies on the *x*-axis?**

The slope of the budget line, when smoothies are plotted on the *x*-axis is minus 1/2. The magnitude of the slope is equal to the relative price of a smoothie. The relative price has fallen so the magnitude of the slope of the budget line has fallen.

5. **Draw figures that show your indifference curves for the following pairs of goods:**
   • **Right gloves and left gloves**
   • **Coca-Cola and Pepsi**
   • **Baseballs and baseball bats**
   • **Tylenol and acetaminophen (the generic form of Tylenol)**
   • **Eye glasses and contact lenses**
   • **Desktop computers and laptop computers**
   • **Skis and ski poles**

a. **For each pair, state whether the goods are perfect substitutes, perfect complements, or neither.**

Right gloves/left gloves and skis/ski poles are perfect complements. The other pairs are neither perfect substitutes nor perfect complements.

FIGURE **9.3A**
Problem 5

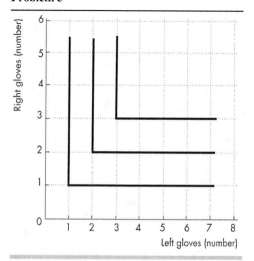

b. Discuss the shape of the indifference curve you have drawn and explain the relationship between its shape and the marginal rate of substitution as the quantities of the two goods change.

Right and left gloves: These are perfect complements, so the indifference curves are right angles, such as those in Figure 9.3A. The marginal rate of substitution does not change moving down along the indifference curve except when moving around the 90 degree point where it goes from infinity to zero.

Coca-Cola and Pepsi: These are, for most students, almost perfect substitutes. The indifference curves should either be linear (for perfect substitutes, as shown in Figure 9.3B) or nearly linear. If the indifference curves are linear, then the marginal rate of substitution does not change moving down along the indifference curve; if the indifference curves are nearly linear, then the marginal rate of substitution falls slightly moving down along an indifference curve.

Baseball balls and bats: These are complements but probably not perfect complements. The indifference curves should be significantly bowed inward as in Figure 9.3C. (If a student says these goods are perfect complements, the indifference curves should be right angles, such as those in Figure 9.3A.) If the indifference curves are not right angles, then the marginal rate of substitution falls rapidly moving down along an indifference curve. (If the goods are perfect complements, the marginal rate of substitution does not change moving down along the indifference curve except when moving around the 90 degree point where it goes from infinity to zero.)

FIGURE **9.3C**
Problem 5

FIGURE **9.3B**
Problem 5

Tylenol and acetaminophen: These are, for most people, very close substitutes. For some consumers, they might be perfect substitutes. The indifference curves should either be linear (for perfect substitutes, as shown in Figure 9.3B) or nearly linear as in Figure 9.3D. If the indifference curves are linear, then the marginal rate of substitution does not change moving down along the indifference curve; if the indifference curves are nearly linear, then the marginal rate of substitution falls slightly moving down along an indifference curve.

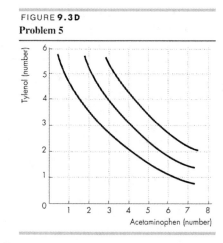

FIGURE **9.3D**
Problem 5

Eye glasses and contact lenses: These are substitutes, though probably not perfect substitutes. The indifference curve are slightly bowed inward toward the origin as in Figure 9.3E. The marginal rate of substitution falls slightly moving down along an indifference curve.

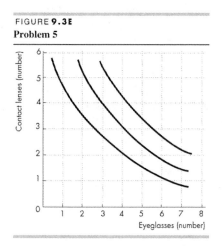

FIGURE **9.3E**
Problem 5

Desktop computers and laptop computers; These are substitutes, though not perfect substitutes. The indifference curve are bowed inward toward the origin as in Figure 9.3F. The marginal rate of substitution falls moving down along an indifference curve.

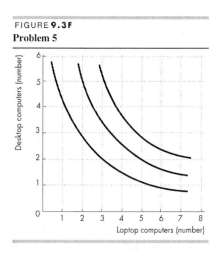

FIGURE **9.3F**
Problem 5

Skis and ski poles: These are perfect complements. The indifference curves are right angles, such as those in Figure 9.3G. The marginal rate of substitution does not change moving down along the indifference curve except when moving around the 90 degree point where it goes from infinity to zero.

7. **Boom Time For 'Gently Used' Clothes**

    Unlike most retailers who are blaming the economy for their poor sales, one store chain is boldly declaring that an economic downturn can actually be a boon for its business.... [It] sells used name-brand children's clothes, toys, and furniture. ... Last year, the company took in $20 million in sales, up 5% from the previous year. "Our sales are already up 5% so far this year."

    CNN, April 17, 2008

    a. **According to this article, is used clothing a normal good or inferior good?**

        According to the article, the demand for used clothing increases when the economy is in a downturn and incomes are falling. Because the demand increases when income decreases, used clothing is an inferior good.

    b. **If the price of used clothing falls and income remains the same, explain how the quantity of used clothing bought changes.**

        If the price of used clothing falls and income remains the same, the quantity of used clothing purchased increases.

    c. **If the price of used clothing falls and income remains the same, describe the substitution effect and the income effect that occur.**

        The price fall creates both a substitution effect and an income effect. The substitution effect leads to an increase in the quantity of used

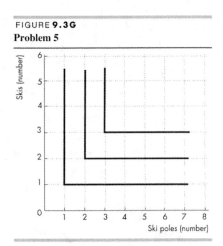

FIGURE **9.3G**
Problem 5

clothing demanded. The price decrease increases consumers' real incomes. Because used clothing is an inferior good, the income effect leads to a decrease in the quantity of used clothing purchased. The substitution effect is larger so that the quantity of used clothing purchased increases.

d. **Draw a graph to illustrate a family's indifference curves for used clothing and other goods and services.**

    Figure 9.4 shows a family's indifference curves for used clothing and other goods and services.

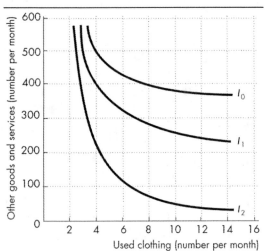

FIGURE **9.4**
Problem 7d

e. **In your graph in d, draw two budget lines to show the effect of a fall in income on the quantity of used clothing purchased.**

In Figure 9.5, the fall in income shifts the budget line from BL_1 to BL_2. The quantity of used clothing purchased increases, in the figure from 4 items per month to 5 items per month.

FIGURE **9.5**
Problem 7e

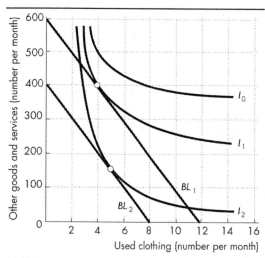

9. **Does a Second Income Pay? When considering whether two paychecks are worth it, figure out how much of the lower earner's salary will be eaten by expenses incurred if both parents work. Childcare is likely to be the biggest cost. ... Also, take into account the costs of going to work. The commute, the clothes, the dry cleaning, the lunches. ... And you may not have as much time or energy to do the housework or make dinner. So you may end up hiring a housekeeper or doing take-out more often. ...**
CNN, March 15, 2006

a. **What is the opportunity cost of a parent staying home with her or his children?**

The opportunity cost of staying home with the children is the earned income forgone.

b. **What is the opportunity cost of a parent working instead of staying home?**

The monetary opportunity cost of a parent working include the childcare cost, the cost of the commute, the cost of a housekeeper, the clothes, the dry cleaning, the lunches, and the dinners out. Of course, the opportunity cost includes *only* the part of the cost of the clothes, the dry cleaning, the lunches, and the dinners out that was incurred because the person was working. An additional opportunity cost for a family with offspring is the time that is no longer spent with the child or children.

c. **Why does the opportunity cost of working increase as the number of children in a family increases?**

The cost of childcare, an opportunity cost of working increases as the number of children increases.

d. **How does the number of children in a family influence the marginal rate of substitution between leisure and goods and services?**

The greater the number of children in a family, the higher the opportunity cost of working. Equivalently, the greater the number of children in a family, the lower the family's income net of opportunity cost and hence the lower the net wage rate. The lower the wage rate, the smaller is the magnitude of the slope of the budget line. At the equilibrium point of time allocation, the slope of the indifference curve is equal to the slope of the budget line. Hence the smaller the magnitude of the slope of the budget line, the smaller the slope of the indifference curve and so the smaller the marginal rate of substitution between leisure and goods and services at the equilibrium point of time allocation.

11. **Gas Prices Straining Budgets**
...many say they are staying in and scaling back spending to try to keep up, ... driving as little as possible, cutting back on shopping and eating out, and other discretionary spending.

CNN, February 29, 2008

a. **Draw a budget line for a household that consumes only two goods: gasoline and eating out. Identify the combinations of gasoline and eating out that are affordable and those that are unaffordable.**

Figure 9.9 shows a budget line. The combinations of gasoline and eating out that lie on and inside the budget line are affordable. The combinations of gasoline and eating out that lie beyond the budget line are unaffordable.

b. **Draw a second budget line to show how a rise in the price of gasoline changes the affordable and unaffordable combinations of gasoline and eating out. Describe how the household's consumption possibilities change.**

The rise in the price of gasoline rotates the budget inward, as illustrated in Figure 9.10. The combinations of gasoline and eating that were previously affordable that have now become unaffordable are shown by the grey triangle. The household's consumption possibilities have been reduced.

c. **How does a rise in the price of gasoline change the relative price of eating out?**

The relative price of eating out equals the price of eating out divided by the price of gasoline. The rise in the price of gasoline reduces the relative price of eating out.

d. **How does a rise in the price of gasoline change real income in terms of eating out?**

The rise in the price of gasoline does not change real income in terms of eating out.

FIGURE **9.9**
Problem 11a

FIGURE **9.10**
Problem 11b

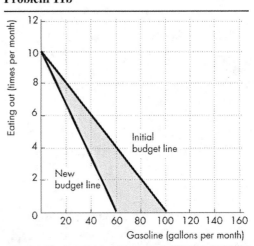

13. **Sara's income is $12 a week. The price of popcorn is $3 a bag, and the price of cola is $1.50 a can. The figure shows Sara's preference map for popcorn and cola.**

   a. **What quantities of popcorn and cola does Sara buy?**

      Sara buys 6 cans of cola and 1 bag of popcorn. Sara's budget line runs from 8 cans of cola on the *x*-axis to 4 bags of popcorn on the *y*-axis and is tangent to indifference curve I_1 at 6 cans of cola and 1 bag of popcorn.

   b. **What is Sara's marginal rate of substitution at the point at which she consumes?**

      Sara's marginal rate of substitution is ½. The marginal rate of substitution is the magnitude of the slope of the indifference curve at Sara's consumption point, which equals the magnitude of the slope of the budget line. The slope of Sara's budget line is −½ bag of popcorn per can of cola so the marginal rate of substitution is ½ bag of popcorn per can of cola.

15. **Jim has made his best affordable choice of muffins and coffee. He spends all of his income on 10 muffins at $1 each and 20 coffees at $2 each. Now the price of a muffin rises to $1.50 and the price of a coffee falls to $1.75 a cup.**

   a. **Will Jim now be able and want to buy 10 muffins and 20 coffees?**

      Jim is able to buy 10 muffins and 20 coffees because this combination remains affordable. Jim will not want to buy this combination, however, because the relative price of muffins and coffee has changed. At his consumer equilibrium, Jim's *MRS* equals the relative price of muffins and coffee and because the relative price has changed, Jim's *MRS* has changed so Jim will change his consumption point.

FIGURE **9.12**
Problem 13

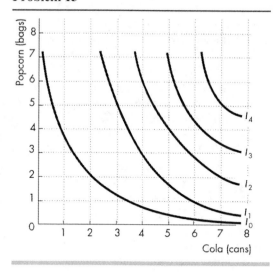

   b. **Which situation does Jim prefer: muffins at $1 and coffee at $2 a cup or muffins at $1.50 and coffee at $1.75 a cup?**

      Jim prefers the $1.50 per muffin/$1.75 per coffee prices because he can attain a higher indifference curve. The new budget line goes through the old budget line at the initial consumption point. But, with coffee measured along the horizontal axis, the new budget line is flatter than the old budget line and lies beyond the initial budget line at all points below the initial consumption point.

   c. **If Jim changes the quantities that he buys, will he buy more or fewer muffins and more or less coffee?**

      Jim will buy more coffee and fewer muffins.

   d. **When the prices change, is there an income effect and a substitution effect at work or just one of them?**

      Price changes can always be divided into an income effect and a substitution effect.

17. **Gas Prices Send Surge of Travelers to Mass Transit**

    With the price of gas approaching $4 a gallon, more commuters are abandoning their cars and taking the train or bus instead. ... "It's very clear that a significant portion of the increase in transit use is directly caused by people who are looking for alternatives to paying $3.50 a gallon for gas." Some cities with long-established public transit systems, like New York and Boston, have seen increases in ridership of 5 percent or more so far this year. But the biggest surges — of 10 to 15 percent or more over last year — are occurring in many metropolitan areas in the South and West where the driving culture is strongest and bus and rail lines are more limited.

    The New York Times, May 10, 2008

    a. **Draw a graph of a preference map and a budget line to illustrate the best affordable combination of gasoline and public transit.**

       Figure 9.15 shows the initial indifference curve (I_0) and initial budget line (BL_0). The best affordable point is at point A with 100 gallons of gasoline and 15 rides on public transportation.

    b. **On your graph in a, show the effect of a rise in the price of gasoline on the quantities of gasoline and public transit services purchased.**

       In Figure 9.15 the rise in the price of gasoline rotates the budget line from BL_0 to BL_1. The best affordable point moves to point B at which the quantity of gasoline purchased falls to 50 gallons per month and the quantity of rides on public transportation increases to 20 rides per month.

    c. **Assuming that the increase in the price of gasoline has been similar in all regions, compare the marginal rate of substitution in the Northeast to that in the South and**

FIGURE **9.15**

Problem 17

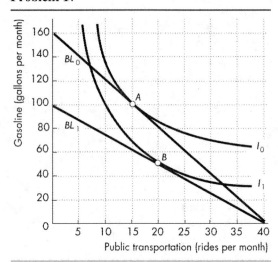

West. **Explain how you have inferred the different marginal rates of substitution from the information provided in the news clip.**

The story says the driving culture is strongest in the South and West and that bus and rail lines there are more limited. Presuming that the price of gasoline is the same nationwide, these statements mean that a budget line drawn for the South and West in Figure 9.15 has the same vertical intercept but is steeper than a budget line drawn for the Northeast. At the consumer equilibrium the slope of the indifference curve equals the slope of the budget line, so the initial *MRS* in the South and West was higher than in the Northeast and residents in the South and West used more gasoline and less public transportation than in the Northeast. When the price of gasoline rises, the vertical intercept of both budget lines decreases by the same amount so the budget line in the South and West remains steeper than the budget line in the Northeast. As a result the *MRS* in the South and West remains higher than the *MRS* in the Northeast.

19.   Study *Reading Between the Lines* about music and e-book downloads on pp. 216–217, and then answer the following questions.

   a.   **How do you buy books?**

   The answers will depend on how they buy books.

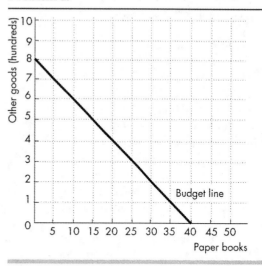

FIGURE **9.17**
Problem 19

   b.   **Sketch your budget line for books and other goods.**

   The budget line between paper books and other goods is a conventional downward sloping budget line and a sample is illustrated in Figure 9.17. This budget line assumes the student has $800 to spend, the price of a print book is $20 and the price of each "other good" is $1. If the student buys Amazon's e-books, the student needs to buy a $360 Kindle with the first e-book. So the first e-book has a price of $370 and the rest of the e-books have a price of $10. The Kindle is non-divisible; that is, it is not possible to buy ½ of a Kindle. As a result, with other goods on the vertical axis and e-books on the horizontal axis, the budget line shown in Figure 9.18 starts at 800 "other goods" and 0 e-books and then jumps to 430 "other goods" and 1 e-book. The budget line is then more shallow to the maximum number of e-books, 44, to reflect the price of $10 per e-book for all the other e-books.

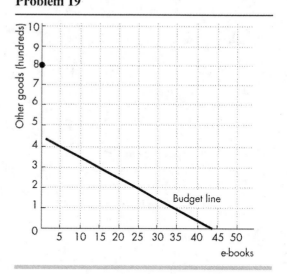

FIGURE **9.18**
Problem 19

c. **Sketch your indifference curves for books and other goods.**

The indifference curves will be conventional showing some substitutability between books and other goods. This is the situation illustrated in Figure 9.19.

d. **What would happen to the way that you buy books if Amazon gave you its Kindle reader at a zero price if you buy just one e-book?**

If the student already purchases e-books and already has a Kindle, Amazon's change in policy has no effect on the student's budget line and hence does not change the student's purchases. If the student is a "committed print book lover" (as the first student analyzed on page 217) Amazon's new policy changes the student's budget line between print books and e-books (the budget line moves outward) but the policy change does not change the student's purchases. For other students—those who have not yet purchased a Kindle and are not committed print book lovers—Amazon's new policy changes the budget line (based on the budget line described in part b, the new budget line will be shallow everywhere reflecting the price of $10 per e-book for *all* e-books) and increases the number of e-books purchased.

FIGURE **9.19**
Problem 19c

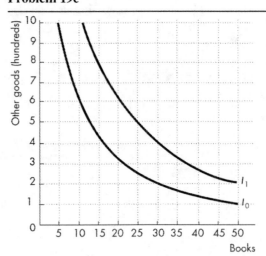

Additional Problems

1. Marc has an income of $20 per week. Root beer costs $5 a can and CDs cost $10 each.
   a. What is Marc's real income in terms of root beer?
   b. What is his real income in terms of CDs?
   c. What is the relative price of root beer in terms of CDs?
   d. What is the opportunity cost of a can of root beer?
   e. Calculate the equation for Marc's budget line (placing cans of root beer on the left side).
   f. Draw a graph of Marc's budget line with CDs on the *x*-axis.
   g. In part (f), what is the slope of Marc's budget line? What does it equal?

2. Marc's income and the prices he faces are the same as in problem 1. The figure illustrates his preferences.
   a. What are the quantities of root beer and CDs that Marc buys?
   b. What is Marc's marginal rate of substitution of CDs for root beer at the point at which he consumes?

3. Now suppose that in the situation described in problem 2, the price of a CD falls to $5 and the price of root beer and Marc's income remains constant.
   a. Find the new quantities of root beer and CDs that Marc buys.
   b. Find two points on Marc's demand curve for CDs.
   c. Find the substitution effect of the price change.
   d. Find the income effect of the price change.
   e. Are CDs a normal good or an inferior good for Marc?

4. Pete buys tuna and golf balls. The price of tuna is $2 a can, and the price of a golf ball is $1. Each month, Pete spends all of his income and buys 20 cans of tuna and 40 golf balls. Next month, the price of tuna will rise to $3 a can and the price of a golf ball will fall to 50¢. Assume that Pete's preference map shows indifference curves that have a similar shape to that in Fig. 9.3(b).
   a. Will Pete be able to buy 20 cans of tuna and 40 golf balls next month?
   b. Will Pete want to buy 20 cans of tuna and 40 golf balls?
   c. Which situation does Pete prefer: tuna at $2 a can and golf balls at $1 each or tuna at $3 a can and golf balls at 50¢ each?
   d. If Pete changes the quantities that he buys, which good will he buy more of and which less of?
   e. When the prices change next month, will there be an income effect and a substitution effect at work or just one of them?

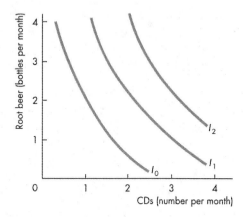

Solutions to Additional Problems

1. a. Marc's real income is 4 cans of root beer. Marc's real income in terms of cans of root beer is equal to his money income divided by the price of a can of root beer. Marc's money income is $20, and the price of root beer is $5 a can. Marc's real income is $20 divided by $5 a can of root beer, which is 4 cans of root beer.

    b. Marc's real income is 2 CDs. Marc's real income in terms of CDs is equal to his money income divided by the price of a CD, which is $20 divided by $10 a CD or 2 CDs.

    c. The relative price of root beer is 1/2 CD. The relative price of root beer is the price of root beer divided by the price of a CD. The price of root beer is $5 a can and the price of a CD is $10, so the relative price of root beer is $5 a can divided by $10 a CD, which equals 1/2 CD per can.

    d. The opportunity cost of a can of root beer is 1/2 CD. The opportunity cost of a can of root beer is the quantity of CDs that must be forgone to obtain a can of root beer. The price of root beer is $5 a can and the price of a CD is $10, so to buy one can of root beer Marc must forgo 1/2 CD.

    e. The equation that describes Marc's budget line is $Q_R = 4 - 2Q_{CD}$. Call the price of a can of root beer P_R and the quantity of root beer Q_R, the price of a CD P_{CD} and the quantity of CDs Q_{CD}, and income y. Marc's budget equation is $P_R Q_R + P_{CD} Q_{CD} = y$. If we substitute $5 for the price of a can of root beer, $10 for the price of a CD, and $20 for the income, the budget equation becomes $5Q_R + $10Q_{CD} = $20. Dividing both sides by $5 gives $Q_R + 2Q_{CD} = 4$. Subtract $2Q_{CD}$ from both sides to give $Q_R = 4 - 2Q_{CD}$.

    f. To draw a graph of the budget line, plot the quantity of CDs on the x-axis and the quantity of root beer on the y-axis. The budget line is a straight line running from 4 cans on the y-axis to 2 CDs on the x-axis.

    g. The slope of the budget line, when CDs are plotted on the x-axis is −2. The magnitude of the slope is equal to the relative price of a CD. The slope of the budget line is "rise over run." If the quantity of CDs decreases from 2 to 0, the quantity of root beer increases from 0 to 4. The rise is 4 and the run is −2. So the slope equals 4/−2, which is −2.

2. a. Marc buys 2 cans of root beer and 1 CD. Marc buys the quantities of root beer and CDs that moves him onto the highest indifference curve, given his income and the prices of root beer and CDs. The graph shows Marc's indifference curves. So draw Marc's budget line on the graph. The budget line is tangential to indifference curve I_0 at 2 cans of root beer and 1 CD. The indifference curve I_0 is the highest indifference curve that Marc can attain.

    b. Marc's marginal rate of substitution is 2. The marginal rate of substitution is the magnitude of the slope of the indifference curve at Marc's consumption point, which equals the magnitude of the slope of the budget line. The slope of Marc's budget line is −2, so the marginal rate of substitution is 2.

3. a. Marc buys 1 can of root beer and 3 CDs. Draw the new budget line on the graph with Marc's indifference curves. The budget line now runs from 4 CDs on the x-axis to 4 cans of root beer on the y-axis. The new budget line is tangential to indifference curve I_1 at 1 can of root beer and 3 CDs. The indifference curve I_1 is the highest indifference curve that Marc can now get attain.

    b. Two points on Marc's demand curve for CDs are the following: At $10 a CD,

Marc buys 1 CD. At $5 a CD, Marc buys 3 CDs.

c. The substitution effect is 1 CD. To divide the price effect into a substitution effect and an income effect, take enough income away from Marc and gradually move his new budget line back toward the origin until it just touches Marc's indifference curve I_0. The point at which this budget line just touches indifference curve I_0 is 2 CDs and 0.5 can of root beer. The substitution effect is the increase in the quantity of CDs from 1 CD to 2 CDs along the indifference curve I_0. The substitution effect is 1 CD.

d. The income effect is 1 CD. The income effect is the change in the quantity of CDs from the price effect minus the change from the substitution effect. The price effect is 2 CDs (3 CDs minus the initial 1 CD). The substitution effect is an increase in the quantity of CDs from 1 CD to 2 CDs. So the income effect is 1 CD.

e. CDs are a normal good for Marc because the income effect is positive.

4. a. Pete can still buy 20 cans of tuna and 40 golf balls. When Pete buys 20 cans of tuna at $2 a can and 40 golf balls at $1 each, he spends $80 a month. Now that the price of a can of tuna is $3 and the price of a golf ball is $0.50, 20 cans of tuna and 40 golf balls will cost $80. So Pete can still buy 20 cans of tuna and 40 golf balls.

b. Pete will not want to buy 20 cans of tuna and 40 golf balls because the marginal rate of substitution does not equal the relative price of the goods. Pete will move to a point on the highest indifference curve possible where the marginal rate of substitution equals the relative price.

c. Pete prefers tuna at $3 a can and golf balls at $0.50 each because he can get onto a higher indifference curve than when tuna is $2 a can and golf balls are $1 each.

d. Pete will buy more golf balls and fewer cans of tuna. The new budget line and the old budget line pass through the point at 20 cans of tuna and 40 golf balls. If cans of tuna are plotted on the x-axis, the marginal rate of substitution at this point on Pete's indifference curve is equal to the relative price of a can of tuna at the original prices, which is 2. The new relative price of a can of tuna is $3.50 cents, which is 6. That is, the budget line is steeper than the indifference curve at 20 cans of tuna and 40 golf balls. Pete will buy more golf balls and fewer cans of tuna.

e. There will be a substitution effect and an income effect. A substitution effect arises when the relative price changes and the consumer moves along the *same* indifference curve to a new point where the marginal rate of substitution equals the new relative price. An income effect arises when the consumer moves from one indifference curve to another, keeping the relative price constant.

Chapter 10 ORGANIZING PRODUCTION

Answers to the Problems and Applications

1. **One year ago, Jack and Jill set up a vinegar-bottling firm (called JJVB). Use the following information to calculate JJVB's opportunity cost of production during its first year of operation:**
   - **Jack and Jill put $50,000 of their own money into the firm.**
   - **They bought equipment for $30,000.**
   - **They hired one employee to help them for an annual wage of $20,000.**
   - **Jack gave up his previous job, at which he earned $30,000, and spent all his time working for JJVB.**
   - **Jill kept her old job, which paid $30 an hour, but gave up 10 hours of leisure each week (for 50 weeks) to work for JJVB.**
   - **JJVB bought $10,000 of goods and services from other firms.**
   - **The market value of the equipment at the end of the year was $28,000.**
   - **Jack and Jill have a $100,000 home loan on which they pay an interest rate of 6 percent a year.**

   The wages paid, $20,000, and the goods and services bought from other firms, $10,000, are opportunity costs to JJVB. Other opportunity cost include the interest forgone on the $50,000 put into the firm, which could have been used to pay part of the mortgage, so the interest forgone is $3,000; the $30,000 income forgone by Jack not working at his previous job; $15,000, which is the value of 500 hours of Jill's leisure (10 hours a week for 50 weeks); and the economic depreciation of $2,000 ($30,000 minus $28,000). JJVB's total opportunity cost is the sum of all these opportunity costs and is $80,000.

3. **Alternative ways of laundering 100 shirts are**

   a. **Which methods are technologically efficient?**

      All the methods are technologically efficient.

   b. **Which method is economically efficient if the hourly wage rate and implicit rental rate of capital are**

      (i) **Wage rate $1, rental rate $100?**

         Method D is economically efficient because the total cost is the least. Method D's costs are $50 \times \$1 + 1 \times \$100$, or $150.

      (ii) **Wage rate $5, rental rate $50?**

         Method D and Method C are economically efficient because the total cost is the least. Method C's costs are $20 \times \$5 + 4 \times \$50$, or $300.

      (iii) **Wage rate $50, rental rate $5?**

         Method A is economically efficient because the total cost is the least. Method A's costs are $1 \times \$50 + 10 \times \$5$, or $100.

Method	Labor (hours)	Capital (machines)
A	1	10
B	5	8
C	20	4
D	50	1

5. **In 2003 and 2004, Lego, the Danish toymaker that produces colored plastic bricks, incurred economic losses. The firm faced competition from low-cost copiers of its products and faced a fall in the number of 5- to 9-year-old boys (its main customers) in many rich countries. In 2004, Lego launched a plan to restore profits. It fired 3,500 of its 8,000 workers; closed factories in Switzerland and the United States; opened factories in Eastern Europe and Mexico; and introduced performance-based pay for its managers. Lego reported a return to profit in 2005.**

   Based on Picking Up the Pieces,
   The Economist, **October 28, 2006.**

a. **Describe the problems that Lego faced in 2003 and 2004, using the concepts of the three types of constraints that all firms face.**

Lego faced all of the three types of constraints: Technology, information, and market.

The technology constraint that Lego faced was how it produced its Legos. Before it made any changes, Lego used a relatively large number of high-paid, presumably high-skilled workers in the United States and Switzerland. After its changes, Lego switched to using apparently fewer workers, who are lower-paid and probably lower-skilled in Eastern Europe and Mexico.

Lego also faced information constraints. In particular, if Lego had had full information about its market and its competitors' plans, it is unlikely Lego would have suffered economic losses in 2003 and 2004. And, of course, if Lego had had better information, even after it started to suffer economic losses, Lego would have more rapidly made changes to limit its losses. In addition, Lego apparently faced information problems about which managers were not working as hard as they should.

Finally, Lego faced significant market constraints. First Lego suffered a fall in demand from its custmers, 5- to 9-year old boys. Second other firms were making very similar but lower-priced blocks. This competition lead Lego's customers to switch (some of) their purchases from Lego to Lego's competitors, thereby leaving Lego to suffer an economic loss.

b. **Which of the actions that Lego took to restore profits addressed an inefficiency? How did Lego seek to achieve economic efficiency?**

When Lego was suffering an economic loss, Lego was manufacturing its blocks in Switzerland and the United States. These workers were generally high-skilled and therefore high-paid. In an effort to restore its profit, Lego changed its production method by firing 3,500 workers and moving its factories to Eastern Europe and Mexico, where it could use lower-skilled, and therefore lower-paid workers. Apparently before the changes Lego was using an economically inefficient production method, with too many workers in general and too many high-skilled workers in particular.

c. **Which of the actions that Lego took to restore profits addressed an information and organization problem? How did Lego change the way in which it coped with the principal-agent problem?**

Lego faced an information and organization problem because Lego apparently did not know which managers were shirking. To overcome this important principal-agent problem, Lego changed its compensation methods by introducing performance-based pay for its managers. By basing its managers' pay on their performance, Lego gave its managers the incentive to work diligently in their efforts to boost Lego's profits.

d. **In what type of market does Lego operate?**

Lego operates in a monopolistically competitive market.

7. **Here It Is. Now, You Design It! The idea is that the most successful companies no longer invent new products and services on their own. They create them along with their customers, and they do it in a way that produces a unique experience for each customer. The important corollary is that no company owns enough resources—or can possibly own enough—to furnish unique experiences for each customer, so companies must organize a constantly shifting global web of suppliers and partners to do the job.**
    Fortune, **May 26, 2008**

a. **Describe this method of organizing and coordinating production: Does it**

use a command system or incentive
system?

This method uses an incentive system to
organize and coordinate production. The
resources are not under the constant
supervision of the employer and so a
command system of coordinating
production would not work. Instead the
firm uses an incentive system—giving the
resources necessary for a project an
incentive to cooperate by paying them for
their share of the project—to organize
the production.

b. **How does this method of organizing
and coordinating production help
firms achieve lower costs?**

The design firm has lower costs because
it uses different resources with each
project. If the design firm owned all the
resources, and therefore used a command
system to organize production, the firm
would need to pay for all the resources
for each and every project. But for many
of the projects some of the resources
would be unused. Hence the firm's costs
would be significantly higher than if it
paid for only the resources actually used,
as it does when it uses an incentive
system of organization.

9. **GameStop Racks Up the Points**
**No retailer has more cachet among
gamers than GameStop, and only
Wal-Mart has a larger share of the
market—for now. … Wal-Mart had a
21.3% market share last year.
GameStop's share was 21.1%, and may
well overtake Wal-Mart this year …
but [new women gamers] may prefer
shopping at Target to GameStop. … A
chance for Wal-Mart and Target to
erode GameStop's market share. …**
Fortune, **June 9, 2008**

a. **According to the news clip, what is
the structure of the U.S. retail video
game market?**

The market described is an oligopoly.
There are only a few firms, three in
particular, described as comprising the
market.

b. **Estimate a range for the four-firm
concentration ratio and the HHI for
the game market in the United States
based on the information provided in
this news clip.**

Wal-Mart is described as having the
largest market share, 21.3 percent, and
GameStop is said to have the second
largest market share, 21.1 percent. These
two firms have a market share of 42.4
percent. The market share of the next
two largest firms must be less than 42.4
percent. As a result the four-firm
concentration ratio ranges from 42.4
percent to 84.7 percent.
The HHI equals the sum of the squared
market shares of the 50 largest firms.
Wal-Mart's contribution to the HHI is
21.3^2 which is 453.7 and GameStop's
contribution to the HHI is 21.1^2 which
is 445.2. Based on the two largest firms,
the HHI is at least 898.9. If there are two
other firms each with a market share of
21.0 percent and one other firm with a
market share of 13.6 percent, the HHI
attains its maximum of 2,024.26. So the
HHI can range from about 900 to about
2,025.

11. **Federal Express enters into contracts
with independent truck operators who
offer FedEx service and who are
rewarded by the volume (cubic meters)
of packages they carry.**

a. **Why doesn't FedEx buy more trucks
and hire more drivers?**

FedEx faces a principal-agent problem. In
particular, it is not easy to monitor its
drivers and insure that they are working
hard to efficiently deliver packages.
FedEx overcomes this problem by hiring
independent contactors and then paying
them based on the amount of packages
they deliver. Essentially, FedEx uses a
piecework method of payment.

b. **What incentive problems might arise
from the arrangement that FedEx
uses?**

FedEx pays its drivers based on the
volume of packages they deliver. This

method of payment creates a few potential problems for FedEx. First, FedEx must worry about the quality of its service. In particular, unless FedEx bases part of the payment on quality, its drivers have an incentive to drop the package and race off to the next delivery with no concern for how the packages are handled. Second, FedEx must take care that drivers do not attempt to select only packages that are close to the FedEx location and avoid packages that have a greater than average driving time. Finally, FedEx also must worry that its drivers do not take undue risks while driving (in order) to deliver as many packages as possible. If FedEx trucks were involved in too many accidents, FedEx would suffer bad publicity and, presumably, would lose some business.

13. **In 2007, Toni taught music and earned $20,000. She also earned $4,000 by renting out her basement. On January 1, 2008, she quit teaching, stopped renting out her basement, and began to use it as the office for her new Web site design business. She took $2,000 from her savings account to buy a computer. During 2008, she paid $1,500 for the lease of a Web server and $1,750 for high-speed Internet service. She received a total revenue from Web site designing of $45,000 and earned interest at 5 percent a year on her savings account balance. Normal profit is $55,000 a year. At the end of 2008, Toni could have sold her computer for $500. Calculate Toni's opportunity cost of production and economic profit in 2008.**

Toni has costs of $1,500 for the lease of a Web server; $1,750 for high-speed Internet service; $55,000 for normal profit; $20,000 of forgone earnings from teaching; $4,000 of forgone rent from renting her basement; $100 of forgone interest from her saving account; and $1,500 for the depreciation of her computer (which equals the $2,000 paid for it minus the $500 for which she could

have sold it). These various costs sum to a total opportunity cost of $83,850. Toni's economic "profit" is her total revenue, $45,000, minus her total opportunity cost, $83,850, for an economic loss of $38,850.

15. **Wal-Mart has more than 3,700 stores, more than one million employees, and total revenues of close to a quarter of a trillion dollars in the United States alone. Sarah Frey-Talley runs the family-owned Frey Farms in Illinois and supplies Wal-Mart with pumpkins and other fresh produce.**

a. **How do you think Wal-Mart coordinates its activities? Is it likely to use mainly a command system or also to use incentive systems? Why or why not?**

Wal-Mart is a huge organization. As such, it uses both command and incentive systems. At the lower, store level, command is the system that is most commonly used. (For instance, an associate is told that he or she will help unload a delivery and stack the packages against the South wall.) At the higher, corporate level, incentive is the system most commonly used. (For instance, regional directors have part of their income tied to their region's performance.) However, even at the store level some incentive systems are used (associates can enroll in a profit sharing plan) and even at the corporate level some command systems are used (regional directors are told that they must report to their supervisors on a weekly basis).

b. **How do you think Sarah Frey-Talley coordinates the activities of Frey Farms? Is she likely to use mainly a command system or also to use incentive systems? Why?**

Ms. Frey-Talley probably uses a command system significantly more often than an incentive system. Her farm has few employees and so it is easy to tell each employee what to do, when to do it, and where to do it. Possibly the only use of an incentive system might be if Ms. Frey-Talley has some higher-ranking family members on a profit-sharing program.

c. **Describe, compare, and contrast the principal-agent problems faced by Wal-Mart and Frey Farms. How might these firms cope with their principal-agent problems?**

Wal-Mart faces many more principal-agent problems than does Ms. Frey-Talley. For Ms. Frey-Talley's farm, it is relatively straightforward to monitor each employee so employees will find it difficult to shirk. Plus Ms. Frey-Talley owns the farm herself, and so there is no principal-agent problem associated with a difference between the owners and the managers. Wal-Mart, however, has more than one million employees. Each of these employees realizes that if he she shirks, it will make little difference to Wal-Mart's overall performance. So Wal-Mart's managers must be constantly alert to this problem. Wal-Mart also faces the principal-agent problem that results because its owners are not its managers. As a result, the owners must try to create incentives for the managers to behave in the best interests of the owners. Wal-Mart has a number of ways that it can try to overcome the principal-agent problems it faces. Its top management is given stock options. Regional managers, store managers, and top level store management are given profit-sharing packages that depend on the performance of the region or a particular store. Buyers for Wal-Mart—people employed by Wal-Mart to determine which products Wal-Mart will purchase--are often given profit-sharing packages that increase the buyer's income depending on how well the products the buyer purchased perform in the stores. All of these are designed to give the recipient the incentive to make decisions that boost Wal-Mart's profit and thereby its stock price, which benefit the owners.

17. **Two leading design firms, Astro Studios of San Francisco and Hers Experimental Design Laboratory, Inc. of Osaka, Japan, worked with Microsoft to design the Xbox 360 video game console. IBM, ATI, and SiS designed the Xbox 360's hardware. Two firms, Flextronics & Wistron, and Celestica, manufacture the Xbox 360 at their plants in China and Taiwan.**

a. **Describe the roles of market coordination and coordination by firms in the design, manufacture, and marketing of the Xbox 360.**

Microsoft entered the market to hire various firms, Astro Studios and Hers Experimental Design Laboratory to design the Xbox 360 and then entered the market again to hire IBM, ATI, and SiS to design the hardware of the Xbox 360. Finally, Microsoft once again entered the market to hire Flextronics and Wistron, and Celestica to produce the Xbox 360. Once Microsoft had contracted with these firms, the design, manufacture, etc. takes place within the firm.

b. **Why do you think Microsoft works with a large number of other firms to bring the Xbox to market, rather than performing all the tasks at its headquarters in Seattle?**

Microsoft works with a large number of firms rather than doing everything in-house because it is less expensive for Microsoft to work with other firms. These other firms have specialized in various tasks and so have gained economies of scale that Microsoft does not possess. Therefore it is cheaper for Microsoft to enter the market and hire the expertise it needs than to do it all itself.

c. **What are the roles of transactions costs, economies of scale, economies of scope, and economies of team production in the design, manufacture, and marketing of the Xbox?**

Microsoft needed to determine what part of designing, building, and marketing the Xbox would take place inside of Microsoft and what would take place in other companies that Microsoft hired. Hiring other companies means that Microsoft incurs the transactions costs of using markets. However, other companies that specialized in different tasks have economies of scale, economies of scope, and/or economies of team production that lower the cost to Microsoft of hiring them. So Microsoft had to determine which parts of the Xbox 360 would be cheaper to undertake inside of Microsoft and which parts would be cheaper to enter the market to contract with other firms.

d. **Why do you think the Xbox is designed in the United States and Japan but built in China?**

The Xbox is designed in America and Japan because America and Japan have a large number of highly-skilled workers who can successfully design the Xbox. With a large number of technically adept workers, it is less expensive to design the Xbox in these countries. Manufacturing the Xbox, however, takes place in China because China has a large number of lower-skilled workers and so it is less expensive to build the Xbox in China.

19. **Must Watches**
Stocks too volatile? Bonds too boring? Then try an alternative investment— one you can wear on your wrist. ... [The] typical return on a watch over five to ten years is roughly 10%. [One could] do better in an index fund, but... what other investment is so wearable?
Fortune, April 14, 2008

a. **What is the cost of buying a watch?**
The (opportunity) cost of buying a watch is the loss of whatever else would have been purchased with the funds.

b. **What is the opportunity cost of owning a watch?**
The opportunity cost of owning a watch is the annual forgone return, such as the forgone interest from buying a watch rather than placing the funds in a saving account, and the depreciation of the watch.

c. **Does owning a watch create an economic profit opportunity?**
Yes, owning a watch creates an economic profit opportunity. If the watch appreciates at a rapid clip, so that the gain in the value of the watch over time exceeds the normal profit from the funds used to purchase the watch, then owning the watch has lead to an economic profit.

21. **A Medical Sensation**
... hospitals continue to splurge on ... da Vinci surgical robots. ... Sitting comfortably at a da Vinci console, surgeons could use various robotic attachments to perform even the most complex procedures. ...
Fortune, April 28, 2008

a. **Assume that performing a surgery with a surgical robot requires fewer surgeons and nurses. Is using the surgical robot technologically efficient?**
Using the surgical robot is technology efficient because the production technique uses less labor (and more capital) than the non-robotic technique.

b. **What additional information would you need to be able to say that switching to surgical robots is economically efficient for a hospital?**
To determine if the production technique is economically efficient, information about the cost of the robot and the cost of the nurses and doctors and about the number of doctors and nurses each production technique uses is needed.

23. **Study *Reading Between the Lines* about Google and Yahoo! on pp. 244–245, and then answer the following questions:**

   a. **What are the products that Google and Yahoo! sell?**

   Yahoo! and Google provide search services for consumers.

   b. **How do Internet search engine providers generate revenue and earn a profit?**

   Yahoo! and Google generate revenue from advertising.

   c. **What is the distinction between paid search advertising and display advertising? What types of firms use the latter?**

   If a consumer clicks on an advertising search link, the company doing the advertising pays the Internet search provider. This payment is called "paid search advertising." Google specializes in paid search advertising. Display advertising refers to advertisements that appear on the web page of the Internet search provider. Yahoo! specializes in display advertising. Large, well known companies, such as Ford Motor, tend to use display advertising.

   d. **Why do you think Google has bought YouTube? How will this purchase enable Google to increase its revenue and profit?**

   Google purchased YouTube because Google wanted to gain advertising revenue from display advertising on YouTube's web site. Google also wanted to attract new users and gain new technologies for advertising. Such technologies might become increasingly important because big companies often use online video advertising.

   e. **What technological changes might increase the profitability of Internet search engines?**

   If better search technologies are developed so that searches provide more accurate, more useful information, then Internet search providers will be used more often, thereby giving them the possibility of increasing their profit. Additionally if search engines become more accurate, then advertisers will pay more per click because they realize that the clicks are more valuable since a click is more likely to result in a sale.

Additional Problems

1. Sue can do her accounting assignment by using: a personal computer; a pocket calculator; a pocket calculator and a pencil and paper; or a pencil and paper. With a PC, Sue completes the job in half an hour; with a pocket calculator, it takes 4 hours; with a pocket calculator and with a pencil and paper, it takes 5 hours; and with a pencil and paper, it takes 14 hours. The PC and its software cost $2,000, the pocket calculator costs $15, and the pencil and paper cost $3.
   a. Which, if any, of the methods is technologically efficient?
   b. Which methods is economically efficient if Sue's wage rate is
   (i) $10 an hour?
   (ii) $20 an hour?
   (iii) $50 an hour?

2. Alternative ways of making 100 shirts a day are in the table to the right.
   a. Which methods are technologically efficient?
   b. Which method is economically efficient if:
   (i) The wage rate is $1 an hour and the rental cost of a machine is $100 an hour?
   (ii) The wage rate is $5 an hour and the rental cost of a machine is $50 an hour?
   (iii) The wage rate is $50 an hour and the rental cost of a machine is $5 an hour?

3. Sales of the firms in the pet food industry are in the table to the right.
   a. Calculate the four-firm concentration ratio.
   b. What is the structure of the industry?

4. Market shares of mat makers are in the table to the right.
   a. Calculate the Herfindahl-Hirschman Index.
   b. What is the structure of the industry?

Method	Labor (hours)	Capital (machines)
A	10	50
B	20	40
C	50	20
D	100	10

Firm	Sales (thousands of dollars)
Big Collar, Inc	50
Shiny Coat, Inc	75
Friendly Pet, Inc	60
Naturals Way, Inc	65
Other 8 firms	400

Firm	Market share (percent)
Made-to-last, Inc	20
Big Wheel, Inc	17
Magic Carpet, Inc	22
Supreme, Inc	17
Copra, Inc	24

Solutions to Additional Problems

1. a. All methods other than "pocket calculator with paper and pencil" are technologically efficient. To use a pocket calculator with paper and pencil to complete the accounting assignment is not a technologically efficient method because it takes more hours than it would with a pocket calculator and it uses more capital.

   b. The economically efficient method is the technologically efficient method that allows the task to be done at least cost.
   When the wage rate is $10 an hour: Total cost with a PC is $2,005, total cost with a pocket calculator is $55, and total cost with paper and pencil is $143. Total cost is least with a pocket calculator.
   When the wage rate is $20 an hour: Total cost with a PC is $2,010, total cost with a pocket calculator is $95, and the total cost with paper and pencil is $283. Total cost is least with a pocket calculator.
   When the wage rate is $50 an hour: Total cost with a PC is $2,025, total cost with a pocket calculator is $215, and total cost with pencil and paper is $703. Total cost is least with a pocket calculator.

2. a. Methods A, B, C, and D are technologically efficient. Compare the amount of labor and capital used by the four methods. Start with method A. Moving from A to B to C to D, the amount of labor increases and the amount of capital decreases in each case.

   b. The economically efficient method in (i) is method D, in (ii) is method D, and in (iii) is method A. The economically efficient method is the technologically efficient method that allows the 100 shirts to be made at least cost.
      (i) Total cost with method A is $5,010, total cost with method B is $4,020, total cost with method C is $2,050, and total cost with method D is $1,100. Method D has the lowest total cost.
      (ii) Total cost with method A is $2,550, total cost with method B is $2,100, total cost with method C is $1,250, and total cost with method D is $1,000. Method D has the lowest total cost.
      (iii) Total cost with method A is $750, total cost with method B is $1,200, total cost with method C is $2,600, and total cost with method D is $5,050. Method A has the lowest total cost.

3. a. The four-firm concentration ratio is 38.46. The four-firm concentration ratio equals the ratio of the total sales of the largest four firms to the total industry sales expressed as a percentage. The total sales of the largest four firms is $50,000 + $75,000 + $60,000 + $65,000, which equals $250,000. Total industry sales equal $250,000 + $400,000, which equals $650,000. The four-firm concentration ratio equals ($250,000/$650,000) 100, which is 38.46 percent.

   b. This industry is competitive because the four-firm concentration ratio is less than 60 percent.

4. a. The Herfindahl-Hirschman Index is 2,038. The Herfindahl-Hirschman Index equals the sum of the squares of the market shares of the 50 largest firms or of all firms if there are less than 50 firms. The Herfindahl-Hirschman Index equals $20^2 + 17^2 + 22^2 + 17^2 + 24^2$, which equals 2,038.

   b. This industry is not competitive because the Herfindahl-Hirschman Index exceeds 1,800.

OUTPUT AND COSTS

Answers to the Problems and Applications

1. **Which of the following news items involves a short-run decision and which involves a long-run decision? Explain**

   January, 31, 2008: **Starbucks will open 75 more stores abroad than originally predicted, for a total of 975.**

   This decision is a long-run decision. It increases the quantity of *all* of Starbucks' factors of production, labor and the size of Starbucks' plant.

   February, 25, 2008: **For three hours on Tuesday, Starbucks will shut down every single one of its 7,100 stores so that baristas can receive a refresher course.**

   This decision is a short-run decision. It involves increasing the quality of Starbucks' labor and so only one factor of production—labor—changes and all the other factors remain fixed.

   June, 2, 2008: **Starbucks replaces baristas with vending machines.**

   This decision is a short-run decision. It involves changing two of Starbucks' factors of production, labor and one type of capital. But other factors of production, such as Starbucks' land and other capital inputs such as the store itself, remain fixed.

   July, 18, 2008: **Starbucks is closing 616 stores by the end of March.**

   This decision is a long-run decision. It decreases the quantity of *all* of Starbucks' factors of production, labor and the size of Starbucks' plant.

3. **Sue's Surfboards, in problem 2, hires workers at $500 a week and its total fixed cost is $1,000 a week.**

   a. **Calculate total cost, total variable cost, and total fixed cost of each output in the table. Plot these points and sketch the short-run total cost curves passing through them.**

   Total cost is the sum of the costs of all the factors of production that Sue's Surfboards uses. Total variable cost is the total cost of the variable factors. Total fixed cost is the total cost of the fixed factors. For example, the total variable cost of producing 120 surfboards a week is the total cost of the workers employed, which is 3 workers at $500 a week, which equals $1,500. Total fixed cost is $1,000, so the total cost of producing 120 surfboards a week is $2,500. Figure 11.3 shows these total cost curves.

   b. **Calculate average total cost, average fixed cost, average variable cost, and marginal cost of each output in the table. Plot these points and sketch the short-run average and marginal cost curves passing through them.**

Output (surfboards)	AFC (dollars per surfboard)	AVC (dollars per surfboard)	ATC (dollars per surfboard)	MC (dollars per surfboard)
30	33.33	16.67	50.00	
				12.50
70	14.29	14.29	28.58	
				10.00
120	8.33	12.50	20.83	
				12.50
160	6.25	12.50	18.75	
				16.67
190	5.26	13.16	18.42	
				25.00
210	4.76	14.29	19.05	
				50.00
220	4.55	15.91	20.46	

Average fixed cost is total fixed cost per unit of output. Average variable cost is total variable cost per unit of output. Average total cost is the total cost per unit of output. For example, take the case in which the firm makes 160 surfboards a week. Total fixed cost is $1,000, so average fixed cost is $6.25 per surfboard; total variable cost is $2,000, so average variable cost is $12.50 per surfboard; and, total cost is $3,000, so average total cost is $18.75 per surfboard. Marginal cost is the increase in total cost divided by the increase in output. For example, when output increases from 120 to 160 surfboards a week, total cost increases from $2,500 to $3,000, an increase of $500. This $500 increase in total cost means that the increase in output of 40 surfboards increases total cost by $500. Marginal cost is equal to $500 divided by 40 surfboards, which is $12.50 a surfboard. The table shows these data schedules and the curves are plotted in Figure 11.4.

FIGURE **11.4**

Problem 3b

c. **Illustrate the connection between Sue's *AP*, *MP*, *AVC*, and *MC* curves in graphs like those in Fig. 11.6.**

Labor (workers)	Output (surfboards)	AP (surfboards per worker)	MP (surfboards per worker)	AVC (dollars per surfboard)	MC (dollars per surfboard)
1	30	30.0		16.67	
			40.0		12.50
2	70	35.0		14.29	
			50.0		10.00
3	120	40.0		12.50	
			40.0		12.50
4	160	40.0		12.50	
			30.0		16.67
5	190	38.0		13.16	
			20.0		25.00
6	210	35.0		14.29	
			10.0		50.00
7	220	31.4		15.91	

The table sets out the *AP* and *MP* data used to draw the curves. Figure 11.5 shows the curves and the relationships. When the *AP* curve rises the *AVC* curve falls and vice versa. When the *MP* curve rises the *MC* curve falls and vice versa.

5. **Workers at Sue's Surfboards, in problems 2 and 3, negotiate a wage increase of $100 a week for each worker. If other things remain the same, explain how Sue's Surfboards' short-run average cost curve and marginal cost curve change.**

The increase in the wage rate is a variable cost, so total variable cost increases. The increase in total variable cost increases total cost but total fixed cost does not change. Average variable cost is total variable cost per unit of output. The average variable cost curve shifts upward. Average total cost is total cost per unit of output. The average total cost curve shifts upward. The marginal cost curve shifts upward. The average fixed cost curve does not change.

7. **Airlines Seek Out New Ways to Save on Fuel as Costs Soar**

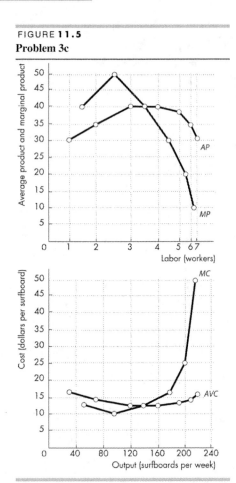

FIGURE **11.5**

Problem 3c

The financial pain of higher fuel prices is particularly acute for airlines because it is their single biggest expense. ... [Airlines] pump about 7,000 gallons into a Boeing 737 and as much as 60,000 gallons into the bigger 747 jet. ... Each generation of aircraft is more efficient. At Northwest, the Airbus A330 long-range jets use 38 percent less fuel than the DC-10s they replaced, while the Airbus A319 medium-range planes are 27 percent more efficient than DC-9s. ...

The New York Times, June 11, 2008

a. **Is the price of fuel a fixed cost or a variable cost for an airline?**

   The price of fuel is a variable cost for an airline.

b. **Explain how an increase in the price of fuel changes an airline's total costs, average costs, and marginal cost.**

   An increase in the price of fuel raises an airline's total cost, its average total cost, its average variable cost, and its marginal cost. It does not change the airline's average fixed cost or total fixed cost.

c. **Draw a graph to show the effects of an increase in the price of fuel on an airline's *TFC*, *TVC*, *AFC*, *AVC*, and *MC* curves.**

   Figure 11.7 shows an airline's *TFC* and *TVC* curves; Figure 11.8 shows an airline's *AFC*, *AVC*, and *MC* curves. The increase in the price of fuel has no effect on the airlines fixed cost, so the *TFC* and *AFC* curves do not change. The increase in the price of fuel raises the firm's variable costs and its total costs. As a result the firm's *TVC*, *AVC* and *MC* curves shift upward as illustrated in the figures from the curves labeled "0"to the curves labeled "1".

d. **Explain how a technological advance that makes an airplane's engines more fuel efficient changes an airline's total product, marginal product, and average product.**

FIGURE **11.7**

Problem 7c

FIGURE **11.8**

Problem 7c

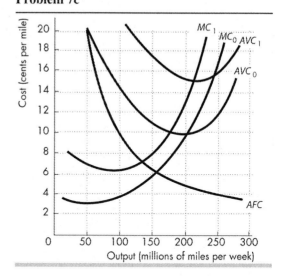

This situation is an example of technological change that is embodied in capital. This change will allow the airline to produce more output—passenger miles—using fewer resources. Hence the airline's total product, marginal product, and average product all increase.

e. Draw a graph to illustrate the effects of more fuel efficient aircraft on an airline's *TP*, *MP*, and *AP* curves.

FIGURE **11.9**

Problem 7e

FIGURE **11.10**

Problem 7e

Figure 11.9 shows the airline's *TP* curves. The new engines shift the *TP* curve upward from TP_0 to TP_1. Figure 11.10 shows the airline's *MP* and *AP* curves. These curves also shift upward as a result of the new fuel efficient engines.

f. Explain how a technological advance that makes an airplane's engines more fuel efficient changes an airline's average variable cost, marginal cost and average total cost.

The airline's average variable cost and marginal cost both decrease. The new engines that use the new technology are presumably more expensive than the older, less fuel efficient engines. The engines are a fixed cost. So at lower levels of output the new average total cost is higher than the old average total cost while at larger levels of output the new average total cost is lower than the old average total cost.

g. Draw a graph to illustrate how a technological advance that makes an airplane engine more fuel efficient changes an airline's *AVC*, *MC*, and *ATC* curves.

Figure 11.11 illustrates these changes. The airline's *AVC* and *MC* curves shift downward as indicated by the shift from the grey curves labeled "0" to the black curves labeled "1". At lower levels of output the *ATC* curve shifts upward and at larger levels of output the *ATC* curve shifts downward.

FIGURE **11.11**

Problem 7g

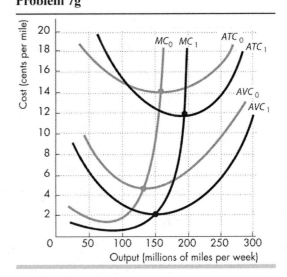

9. **Business Boot Camp**

At a footwear company called Caboots, sales rose from $160,000 in 2000 to $2.3 million in 2006. But in 2007 sales dipped to $1.5 million. Joey and Priscilla Sanchez, who run Caboots, blame the decline partly on a flood that damaged the firm's office and sapped morale.

> Based on a *Fortune* article, *CNN*, April 23, 2008

If the Sanchezes are correct in their assumptions and the prices of footwear didn't change

a. **Explain the effect of the flood on the total product curve and marginal product curve at Caboots.**

> The total product curve shifted downward as a result of the flood and sapped morale. That is, the factors of production produced less footwear in 2007 than in 2006. The downward shift in the total product curve decreased the marginal product so the marginal product curve also shifted downward.

b. **Draw a graph to show the effect of the flood on the total product curve and marginal product curve at Caboots.**

> Figure 11.13 shows the downward shift in the total product curve and Figure 11.14 shows the downward shift in the marginal product curve. The flood and lack of morale shift the *TP* and *MP* curves downward from TP_1 to TP_2 and from MP_1 to MP_2.

11. **Grain Prices Go the Way of the Oil Price**

Every morning millions of Americans confront the latest trend in commodities markets at their kitchen table. … Rising prices for crops … have begun to drive up the cost of breakfast.

> ***The Economist,*** July 21, 2007

FIGURE **11.13**

Problem 9b

FIGURE **11.14**

Problem 9b

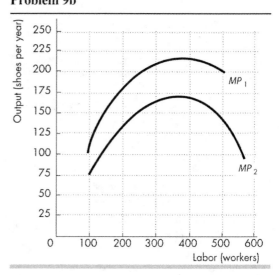

Explain how the rising price of crops affects the average total cost and marginal cost of producing breakfast cereals.

When producing cereal, the cereal crops used are a variable factor of production. An increase in the price of these crops boosts the firms' average total cost and the firms' marginal cost of producing cereal.

13. **Bill's Bakery has a fire and Bill loses some of his cost data. The bits of paper that he recovers after the fire provide the information in the table (all the cost numbers are dollars). Bill asks you to come to his rescue and provide the missing data in the five spaces identified as A, B, C, D, and E.**

A is the average fixed cost, AFC, when the output is 20. Average fixed cost equals total fixed cost divided by output, or $AFC = TFC \div Q$. Rearranging gives $TFC = AFC \times Q$. So the total fixed cost for the problem equals 120×10, which is $1,200. A equals $1,200, TFC, divided by 20, Q, which is $60.

B is the average variable cost, AVC, when output is 20. Use the result that $AFC + AVC = ATC$ by rearranging to give $AVC = ATC - AFC$, so average variable cost equals $150 - $60, which is $90.

D is the average total cost, ATC, when output, Q, equals 40. Average total cost equals total cost divided by output, or $ATC = TC \div Q$. Rearranging gives $TC = ATC \times Q$. So the total cost when 30 units are produced is 130×30, which is $3,900. Marginal cost, MC, equals the change in total cost divided by the change in quantity, or $MC = TC \div Q$. Rearranging gives $TC = MC \times Q$, so the change in total cost between $Q = 30$ and $Q = 40$ is 130×10, or $1,300. Therefore the total cost when Q equals 40 is $3,900 + $1,300, or $5,200. The average total cost when Q is 40 is $5,200 \div 40$, or $130.

C is the average variable cost, AVC, when output, Q, equals 40. Use the result that

$AFC + AVC = ATC$ by rearranging to give $AVC = ATC - AFC$. As a result, average variable cost equals $130 - $30, which is $100.

E is the marginal cost, MC, when output increases from 40 units to 50 units. Marginal cost, MC, equals the change in total cost divided by the change in quantity, or $MC = TC \div Q$. To calculate marginal cost, the total cost when output

TP	AFC	AVC	ATC	MC
10	120	100	220	
				80
20	A	B	150	
				90
30	40	90	130	
				130
40	30	C	D	
				E
50	24	108	132	

is 40 and the total cost when output is 50 are needed. Average total cost equals total cost divided by output, or $ATC = TC \div Q$. Rearranging gives $TC = ATC \times Q$. So the total cost when 40 units are produced is 130×40, which is $5,200 and total cost when 50 units are produced is 132×50, which is $6,600. So the marginal cost equals ($6,600 - $5,200) \div 10$, which equals $140.

15. **ProPainters hire students at $250 a week to paint houses. It leases equipment at $500 a week. Suppose that ProPainters doubles the number of students it hires and doubles the amount of equipment that it leases. ProPainters experiences diseconomies of scale.**

a. **Explain how the ATC curve with one unit of equipment differs from that when ProPainters uses double the amount of equipment.**

Because ProPainters experiences diseconomies of scale, when ProPainters doubles its inputs the *minimum* average cost is higher than when it uses the lesser quantities of inputs. Even so, at high levels of output the average total cost of producing the large level of output with the greater quantities of inputs is lower than the average total cost of producing this large level of output with the smaller quantities of inputs.

b. **Explain what might be the source of the diseconomies of scale that ProPainters experience.**

ProPainters might experience diseconomies of scale because when it gets larger the complexity of operating the business increases, which increases the costs of running the business and making decisions.

17. **A firm is producing at minimum average total cost with its current plant. Sketch the firm's short-run average total cost curve and long-run average cost curve for each of the following situations and explain, using the concepts of economies of scale and diseconomies of scale, the circumstances in which the firm**

a. **Can lower its average total cost by increasing its plant.**

Figure 11.19 illustrates this case at the point labeled *A*. Here the firm experiences economies of scale, so if it increases the size of its plant and also all its other inputs by the same proportion, its average total cost can be lowered.

b. **Can lower its average total cost by decreasing its plant.**

Figure 11.19 illustrates this case at the point labeled *B*. Here the firm experiences diseconomies of scale, so if it decreases the size of its plant and also all its other inputs by the same proportion, its average total cost can be lowered.

c. **Cannot lower its average total cost.**

Figure 11.19 illustrates this case at the point labeled *C*. Here the firm is already producing at the minimum of its long-run average cost. In this case, the firm's average cost increases no matter if the firm increases or decreases the size of its plant and all its other inputs.

19. **A Bakery on the Rise**
Some 500 customers a day line up to buy Avalon's breads, scones, muffins, and coffee. ... Staffing and management are worries. Avalon now employs 35 ... [and] it will hire 15 more. ... Payroll will climb by 30% to 40%. ... As new CEO, Victor has quickly executed an ambitious agenda that includes the move to a larger space. ... Avalon's costs will soar. ... Its monthly rent, for example, will leap to $10,000, from $3,500.
CNN, March 24, 2008

a. **Which of Avalon's decisions described in the news clip is a short-run decision and which is a long run decision.**

Hiring the additional 15 workers is a short-run decision; increasing the size of its space, that is, the size of its plant, is a long-run decision.

FIGURE **11.19**
Problem 17a, 17b, and 17c

b. Why is Avalon's long-run decision riskier than its short run decision?

Avalon's long-run decision is riskier than its short-run decision because it is more difficult to change the long-run decision. In particular if Avalon decides to reverse its short-run decision to hire more workers, it is straightforward to fire the workers. However to reverse the long-run decision of increasing the size of its plant is more difficult and takes much longer to do.

c. By how much will Avalon's short-run decision increase its total variable cost?

Avalon's short-run decision to increase its workforce increases its total variable cost (its payroll) by 30 percent to 40 percent. The increase in workers boosts Avalon's output and leads to a movement along its total variable cost curve.

d. By how much will Avalon's long-run decision increase monthly total fixed cost?

Avalon's long-run decision to increase the size of its plant (its space) increases its total fixed cost by $6,500. Avalon's *TFC* curve shifts upward.

e. Draw a graph to illustrate Avalon's short-run cost curves before and after the events described in the news clip.

Figure 11.21 shows Avalon's short-run *AVC* and *ATC* curves before and after. The old cost curves are labeled with a "1" and the new cost curves, after the expansion, are labeled with a "2", At lower levels of output Avalon's new average cost curves lie above its old average cost curves and at higher levels of output Avalon's new average cost curves lie below its old average cost curves. (In the figure the new minimum average total cost equals the old minimum, so Avalon has constant returns to scale.)

21. The Sunk-Cost Fallacy
You have good tickets to a basketball game an hour's drive away. There's a blizzard raging outside, and the game is being televised. You can sit warm and safe at home by a roaring fire and watch it on TV, or you can bundle up, dig out your car, and go to the game. What do you do?
Slate, September 9, 2005

a. What type of cost is your expenditure on tickets?

At the time of the game, the cost of the ticket is a sunk cost.

b. Why is the cost of the ticket irrelevant to your current decision about whether to stay at home or go to the game?

The cost of the ticket is a sunk cost; that is, the cost of the ticket has already been incurred. Because the cost of the ticket is the same regardless if you attend the game or stay at home, the cost of the ticket is irrelevant to your decision whether to attend or stay at home.

FIGURE **11.21**
Problem 19e

Additional Problems

1. Charlie's Chocolates total product schedule is in the table.
   a. Draw the total product curve.
   b. Calculate the average product of labor and draw the average product curve.
   c. Calculate the marginal product of labor and draw the marginal product curve.
   d. What is the relationship between the average product and marginal product when Charlie's Chocolates produces (i) less than 276 boxes a day and (ii) more than 276 boxes a day?

2. In problem 1, the price of labor is $50 per day, and total fixed costs are $50 per day.
   a. Calculate total cost, total variable cost, and total fixed costs for each level of output and draw the short-run total cost curves.
   b. Calculate average total cost, average fixed cost, average variable cost, and marginal cost at each level of output and draw the short-run average and marginal cost curves.

3. In problem 2, suppose that the price of labor increases to $70 per day. Explain what changes occur to the short-run average and marginal cost curves?

4. In problem 2, Charlie's Chocolates buys a second plant and now the total product of each quantity of labor doubles. The total fixed cost of operating each plant is $50 a day. The wage rate is $50 a day.
   a. Set out the average total cost curve when Charlie's operates two plants.
   b. Draw the long-run average cost curve.
   c. Over what output range is it efficient to operate one plant and two plants?

5. The table shows the production function of Mario's Pizza-to-Go.

Labor (workers per day)	Output (boxes per day)
1	12
2	24
3	48
4	84
5	121
6	192
7	240
8	276
9	300
10	312

Mario must pay $100 a day for each oven he rents and $75 a day for each kitchen hand he hires

   a. Find and graph the average total cost curve for each plant size.
   b. Draw Mario's long-run average cost curve.
   c. Over what output range does Mario experience economies of scale?
   d. Explain how Mario uses his long-run average cost curve to decide how many ovens to rent.

Labor (workers per day)	Output (pizzas per day)			
	Plant 1	Plant 2	Plant 3	Plant 4
1	4	8	11	13
2	8	12	15	17
3	11	15	18	20
4	13	17	20	22
Ovens	1	2	3	4

Solutions to Additional Problems

1. a. To draw the total product curve measure labor on the *x*-axis and output on the *y*-axis. The total product curve is upward sloping.

   b. The average product of *labor* is equal to total product divided by the quantity of *labor* employed. For example, when 3 workers are employed, they produce 48 boxes a day, so average product is 16 boxes per worker. The average product curve is upward sloping when the number of workers is between 1 and 8, but it becomes downward sloping when 9 and 10 workers are employed.

   c. The marginal product of *labor* is equal to the increase in total product when an additional worker is employed. For example, when 3 workers are employed, total product is 48 boxes a day. When a fourth worker is employed, total product increases to 84 boxes a day. The marginal product of going from 3 to 4 workers is 36 boxes. The marginal product curve is upward sloping when the number of workers is between 1 and 6, but it becomes downward sloping when 7 or more workers are employed.

   d. (i) When Charlie's Chocolates produces fewer than 276 boxes a day, it employs fewer than 8 workers a day. With fewer than 8 workers a day, marginal product exceeds average product and average product is increasing. Up to an output of 276 boxes a day, each additional worker adds more to output than the average. Average product increases.

      (ii) When Charlie's Chocolates produces more than 276 boxes a day, it employs more than 8 workers a day. With more than 8 workers a day, average product exceeds marginal product and average product is decreasing. For outputs greater than 276 boxes a day, each additional worker adds less to output than average. Average product decreases.

2. a. Total cost is the sum of the costs of all the inputs that Charlie's Chocolates uses in production. Total variable cost is the total cost of the variable inputs. Total fixed cost is the total cost of the fixed inputs.
   For example, the total variable cost of producing 48 boxes a day is the total cost of the workers employed, which is 3 workers at $50 a day, which equals $150. Total fixed cost is $50, so the total cost of producing 48 boxes a day is $200.
   To draw the short-run total cost curves, plot output on the *x*-axis and the total cost on the *y*-axis. The total fixed cost curve is a horizontal line at $50. The total variable cost curve and the total cost curve have shapes similar to those in Fig. 11.4, but the vertical distance between the total variable cost curve and the total cost curve is $50.

   b. Average fixed cost is total fixed cost per unit of output. Average variable cost is total variable cost per unit of output. Average total cost is the total cost per unit of output.
   For example, when the firm makes 48 boxes a day: Total fixed cost is $50, so average fixed cost is $1.04 per box; total variable cost is $150, so average variable cost is $3.13 per box; and total cost is $200, so average total cost is $4.17 per box.
   Marginal cost is the increase in total cost divided by the increase in output. For example, when output increases from 24 to 48 boxes a day, total cost increases from $150 to $200, an increase of $50. That is, the increase in output of 24 boxes increases total cost by $50. Marginal cost is equal to $50 divided by 24 boxes, which is $2.08 a box.
   The short-run average and marginal cost curves are similar to those in Fig. 11.5.

3. The increase in the price of labor increases total variable cost and total cost but does not change total fixed cost. Average variable cost is total variable cost per unit of output. The average variable cost curve shifts upward. Average total cost is total cost per unit of output. The average total cost curve shifts

upward. The marginal cost curve shifts upward. Average fixed cost does not change.

4. a. Total cost is the cost of all the factors of production. For example, when 3 workers are employed they now produce 96 boxes a day. With 3 workers, the total variable cost is $150 a day and the total fixed cost is $100 a day. The total cost is $250 a day. The average total cost of producing 96 boxes is $2.60.

   b. The long-run average cost curve is made up of the lowest parts of the firm's short-run average total cost curves when the firm operates one plant and two plants. The long-run average cost curve is similar to Fig. 11.8.

   c. It is efficient to operate the number of plants that has the lower average total cost of a box of chocolates. It is efficient to operate one plant when output is less than 48 boxes a day, and it is efficient to operate two plants when the output is more than 48 boxes a day. Over the output range 1 to 48 boxes a week, average total cost is less with one plant than with two, but if output exceeds 48 boxes a day, average total cost is less with two plants than with one.

5. a. For example, the average total cost of producing a pizza when Mario rents 2 ovens and employs 4 workers equals the total cost ($200 rent for the ovens plus $300 for the workers) divided by the 17 pizzas produced. The average total cost equals $500 ÷ 17, which is $29.41 a pizza. The average total cost curve is U-shaped, as in Fig. 11.5.

   b. The long-run average cost curve is similar to that in Fig. 11.8.

   c. Mario experiences economies of scale at output levels of 4 to 15 pizzas a day. When economies of scale are present, the *LRAC* curve slopes downward. Mario's *LRAC* curve slopes downward between the output levels of 4 to 15 pizzas a day.

   d. Mario will choose the plant (number of ovens to rent) that gives him minimum average total cost for the normal or average number of pizzas that people buy.

Chapter 12 PERFECT COMPETITION

Answers to the Problems and Applications

1. Lin's fortune cookies are identical to the fortune cookies made by dozens of other firms and there is free entry in the fortune cookie market. Buyers and sellers are well informed about prices.

a. **In what type of market does Lin's operate?**

Lin is operating in a perfectly competitive market.

b. **What determines the price of fortune cookies?**

The equilibrium price is determined at the equilibrium between the market demand and the market supply.

c. **What determines Lin's marginal revenue of fortune cookies?**

Lin's marginal revenue equals the market price of a box of cookies.

d. **If fortune cookies sell for $10 a box and Lin offers his cookies for sale at $10.50 a box, how many boxes does he sell?**

Lin will sell no boxes of fortune cookies.

e. **If fortune cookies sell for $10 a box and Lin offers his cookies for sale at $9.50 a box, how many boxes does he sell?**

All buyers will want to buy Lin's cookies so the demand for Lin's cookies is essentially infinite. More realistically, Lin would probably sell the quantity that maximizes his profit but that profit will be less than if he sells at the going market price of $10 a box.

f. **What is the elasticity of demand for Lin's fortune cookies and how does it differ from the elasticity of the market demand for fortune cookies?**

The elasticity of demand for Lin's cookies is infinite. The elasticity of

demand in the market for cookies is not infinite.

3. The market is perfectly competitive and there are 1,000 firms that produce paper. The first table sets out the market demand schedule for paper. Each producer of paper has the costs in the second table when it uses its least-cost plant.

a. **What is the market price of paper?**

The market price is $8.40 per box of paper. The market price is the price at which the quantity demanded equals the quantity supplied. The firm's supply curve is the same as its marginal cost curve at prices above minimum average variable cost. Average variable cost is at its minimum when marginal cost equals average variable cost. Marginal cost equals average variable cost at the quantity 250 boxes a week. So the firm's supply curve is the same as the marginal cost curve for the outputs equal to 250 boxes or more. When the price is $8.40 a box, each firm produces 350 boxes and the quantity supplied by the 1,000 firms is 350,000 boxes a week. The quantity demanded at $8.40 is 350,000 a week.

Output (boxes per week)	Marginal cost (dollars per additional box)	Average variable cost	Average total cost
		(dollars per box)	
200	6.40	7.80	12.80
250	7.00	7.00	11.00
300	7.65	7.10	10.43
350	8.40	7.20	10.06
400	10.00	7.50	10.00
450	12.40	8.00	10.22
500	20.70	9.00	11.00

b. **What is the market's output?**

The market output is 350,000 boxes a week.

c. **What is the output produced by each firm?**

Each firm produces 350 boxes a week.

d. **What is the economic profit made or economic loss incurred by each firm?**

Each firm incurs an economic loss of $581 a week. Each firm produces 350 boxes at an average total cost of $10.06 a box. The firm sells the 350 boxes for $8.40 a box. The firm incurs a loss on each box of $1.66 and incurs a total economic loss of $581 a week.

e. **Do firms have an incentive to enter or exit the market in the long run?**

In the long run, some firms exit the industry because they are incurring an economic loss.

f. **What is the number of firms in the long run?**

The number of firms in the long run is 750. In the long run, as firms exit the industry, the price rises. In the long-run equilibrium the price will equal the minimum average total cost. When output is 400 boxes a week, marginal cost equals average total cost and average total cost is a minimum at $10 a box. In the long run, the price is $10 a box. Each firm remaining in the industry produces 400 boxes a week. The quantity demanded at $10 a box is 300,000 boxes a week. The number of firms is 300,000 boxes divided by 400 boxes per firm, which is 750 firms.

g. **What is the market price in the long run?**

In the long run, the price equals the minimum average total cost, $10 a box.

h. **What is the equilibrium quantity of paper produced in the long run?**

In the long run, the 750 firms together produce the equilibrium quantity of 300,000 boxes.

5. **As the quality of computer monitors improves, more people are reading documents online rather than printing them out. The demand for paper permanently decreases and the demand schedule becomes the schedule shown in the table. If each**

firm producing paper has the costs set out in problem 3,

a. **What is the market price, market output, and economic profit or loss of each firm?**

The market price is $7.65 a box, the equilibrium market quantity is 300,000 boxes a week, and each firm incurs an economic loss of $834 a week. When the price is $7.65 a box, each firm produces 300 boxes and the total quantity supplied by the 1,000 firms is 300,000 boxes a week. The market quantity demanded at $7.65 is 300,000 boxes a week. Each firm produces 300 boxes at an average total cost of $10.43 a box. The firm sells the 300 boxes for $7.65 a box. At this price and quantity the firm incurs a loss on each box of $2.78 and incurs an economic loss of $834 a week.

Price (dollars per box)	Quantity demanded (thousands of boxes per week)
2.95	500
4.13	450
5.30	400
6.48	350
7.65	300
8.83	250
10.00	200
11.18	150

b. **What is the long-run equilibrium price, market output, and economic profit or loss of each firm?**

In the long run, the price equals the minimum average total cost, which is $10.00 a box, the equilibrium industry quantity is 200,000 boxes a week, and each firm makes zero economic profit, that is, makes a normal profit.

c. **Does this market experience external economics, external diseconomies, or constant cost? Illustrate by drawing the long-run supply curve.**

Figure 12.1 shows the short-run and long-run supply curves. This industry has constant costs because the cost schedule does not change as the number of firms changes. The long-run supply curve is horizontal at a price of $10 per box. In Figure 12.1 the short-run supply curve and the demand curve from Problem 3 are S_0 and D_0, and the short-run supply and the demand curve from this problem are S_1 and D_1. The long-run supply curve is illustrated as the thicker line labeled LS.

FIGURE **12.1**

Problem 5c

7. **Coors Brewing Expanding Plant**
Coors Brewing Co. of Golden will expand its Virginia packaging plant at a cost of $24 million. The addition will accommodate a new production line that will bottle mostly Coors Light. ... It also will bottle beer faster. ... Coors Brewing employs roughly 470 people at its Virginia plant. The expanded packaging line will add another eight jobs.

Denver Business Journal, **January 6, 2006**

a. **How will Coors' expansion of a plant change the firm's marginal cost curve and short-run supply curve?**

The new plant will decrease Coors' marginal cost. So the marginal cost curve, which is Coors' short-run supply curve at prices above minimum average variable cost, shifts rightward.

b. **What does this expansion decision imply about the point on Coors' *LRAC* curve at which the firm was before the expansion?**

By increasing the quantity it produces Coors moves to the right along its *LRAC* curve. Its costs are lower, so Coors is moving along a range of its

LRAC over which there are economies of scale.

c. **If other breweries follow the lead of Coors, what will happen to the market price of beer?**

If other breweries follow the lead of Coors, the market price of beer will fall. In the long run the price equals the minimum average total cost so the fall in the average total cost means that the price falls.

d. **How will the adjustment that you have described in c influence the economic profit of Coors and other beer producers?**

The companies that make the first adjustments, such as Coors, will temporarily make an economic profit. But as other companies make similar adjustments the price of beer falls, which reduces economic profit. Eventually the lower price will eliminate all the economic profit and the firms will make only normal profit.

9. **Explain and illustrate graphically how the growing world population is influencing the world market for wheat and a representative individual wheat farmer.**

FIGURE **12.3a**

Problem 9

FIGURE **12.3b**

Problem 9

The increase in the world population increases the market demand for wheat. The price of wheat rises so that wheat farmers increase the quantity of wheat they produce and make an economic profit. The economic profit attracts entry by new farmers, which increases supply, lowers the price, and eliminates economic profit. Figure 12.3a and 12.3b illustrate this process. In Figure 12.3a the market demand increases and the market demand curve shifts rightward from D_0 to D_1. Initially the supply curve remains S_0. The increase in demand raises the price of a bushel of wheat to $5 and increases the quantity to 20 billion bushels. In Figure 12.3b the higher price raises the firm's marginal revenue and the marginal revenue curve shifts upward from MR_0 to MR_1. The firm responds by increasing the quantity it produces from 200,000 bushels to 225,000 bushels. It makes an economic profit because the price

exceeds its average total cost. The economic profit attracts entry by new firms. Entry increases the market supply and shifts the supply curve rightward, in Figure 12.3a, from S_0 to S_1. Assuming the industry has neither external economies nor external diseconomies, entry takes place until the price falls back to the initial price, $4 a bushel. The market equilibrium quantity increases to 25 billion bushels. Figure 12.3b shows that at this lower price each firm decreases the quantity it produces back to its original amount, 200,000 bushels. The firms now make only a normal profit and there is no longer an incentive for new firms to enter the market.

10. **Explain and illustrate graphically how the diaper service market has been affected by the decrease in the North American birth rate and the development of disposable diapers.**

The decrease in the U.S. birth rate and

the development of disposable diapers have both decreased the demand for diaper services. This change is illustrated in Figure 12.4a (on the next page) by the leftward shift of the demand curve from D_0 to D_1. The supply curve remains S_0. The market price of diaper service falls to 75¢ a diaper and the quantity decreases to 20 million diapers. With the fall in price the firm's marginal revenue decreases and the marginal revenue curve shifts downward, in Figure 12.4b (on the next page) from MR_0 to MR_1. The firm decreases its services from 40,000 diapers a year to 30,000 diapers a year and it suffers an economic loss because the price, 75¢ a diaper, is less than its average total cost.

11. **The market demand for smoothies is in the first table. The market is perfectly competitive, and each firm has the costs in the second table when it uses its least cost plant. There are 100 smoothie sellers in the market.**

a. **What is the market price of a smoothie?**

The market price is the price at which the market quantity demanded equals the market quantity supplied. The firm's supply curve is the same as its marginal cost curve at prices above minimum average variable cost. Average variable cost is a minimum when marginal cost equals average variable cost. Marginal cost equals average variable cost at the quantity 7 smoothies an hour. So the firm's supply curve is the same as the marginal cost curve for outputs greater than and equal to 7 smoothies. When the price is $2.91 a smoothie, each firm produces 7 smoothies and the market quantity supplied by the 100 firms is 700 smoothies an hour. The market quantity demanded at $2.91 is 700 smoothies an hour so the market price is $2.91.

b. **What is the market quantity of smoothies?**

The market quantity of smoothies is 700 smoothies an hour.

c. **How many smoothies does each firm sell?**

Each firm sells 7 smoothies an hour.

d. **What is the economic profit made or economic loss incurred by each firm?**

Each firm incurs an economic loss. Each firm produces 7 smoothies at an average total cost of $4.34 a smoothie. The firm sells the 7 smoothies for $2.91 each. The firm incurs a loss on each smoothie of $1.43 and incurs a total economic loss of $10.01 an hour.

Price (dollars per smoothie)	Quantity demanded (smoothies per hour)
1.90	1,000
2.00	950
2.20	800
2.91	700
4.25	550
5.25	400
5.50	300

Output (smoothies per hour)	Marginal cost (dollars per additional smoothie)	Average variable cost (dollars per smoothie)	Average total cost (dollars per smoothie)
3	2.50	4.00	7.33
4	2.20	3.53	6.03
5	1.90	3.24	5.24
6	2.00	3.00	4.67
7	2.91	2.91	4.34
8	4.25	3.00	4.25
9	8.00	3.33	4.44

e. Do firms enter or exit the market in the long run?

In the long run, some firms exit the industry because they are incurring an economic loss.

f. What is the market price and the equilibrium quantity in the long run?

In the long run, the price equals the minimum average total cost, which is $4.25 a smoothie. At this price, the quantity demanded is 550 smoothies an hour, so the equilibrium quantity is 550 smoothies an hour.

13. Quick Copy is one of the many copy shops near the campus. Figure 12.5 shows Quick Copy's cost curves. If the market price of copying a page is 10 cents, calculate Quick Copy's

a. Marginal revenue.

Quick Copy's marginal revenue equals the market price so it is 10 cents per page.

b. Profit-maximizing output.

Quick Copy's profit-maximizing quantity is 80 pages an hour. Quick Copy maximizes its profit by producing the quantity at which marginal revenue equals marginal cost. In perfect competition, marginal revenue equals price, which is 10 cents a page. Marginal cost is 10 cents a page when Quick Copy produces 80 pages an hour.

c. Economic profit.

Quick Copy's economic profit is $2.40 an hour. Economic profit equals total revenue minus total cost. Total revenue equals $8.00 an hour (10 cents a page multiplied by 80 pages). The average total cost of producing 80 pages is 7 cents a page, so total cost equals $5.60 an hour (7 cents multiplied by 80 pages). So economic profit equals $8.00 minus $5.60, which is $2.40 an hour.

FIGURE **12.5**
Problem 13

15. Exxon Mobil Selling All Its Gas Stations to Distributors
Exxon Mobil Corp. said Thursday it's getting out of the retail gasoline business, following other major oil companies. ... "As the highly competitive fuels marketing business in the U.S. continues to evolve, we believe this transition is the best way for Exxon Mobil to compete and grow in the future," said Ben Soraci, the director of Exxon Mobil's U.S. retail sales. Exxon Mobil is not alone among Big Oil exiting the retail gas

business, a market where profits have gotten tougher as crude oil prices have risen. ... Station owners say they're struggling to turn a profit on gas because while wholesale gasoline prices have risen sharply, ... they've been unable to raise pump prices fast enough to keep pace.

Houston Chronicle, June 12, 2008

a. **Is Exxon Mobil making a shutdown or exit decision in the retail gasoline market?**

> Exxon Mobil is making an exit decision. It is permanently leaving the market.

b. **Under what conditions will this decision maximize Exxon Mobil's economic profit?**

> This decision maximizes Exxon Mobil's economic profit if Exxon Mobil's retail gasoline operation is incurring an economic loss. In this case by closing its retail gasoline stations, Exxon Mobil increases its economic profit.

c. **How might this decision by Exxon Mobil affect the economic profit made by other firms that sell retail gasoline?**

> Exxon Mobil's exit will decrease the number of retail firms selling gasoline. The decrease in the number of firms decreases the supply and raises the market price of retail gasoline. As a result of the higher market price the surviving firms' profits rise.

17. **Cell Phone Sales Hit 1 Billion Mark** More than 1.15 billion mobile phones were sold worldwide in 2007, a 16 percent increase from the 990.9 million phones sold in 2006. ... "Emerging markets, especially China and India, provided much of the growth as many people bought their first phone," Carolina Milanesi, research director for mobile devices at Gartner, said in a statement. "In mature markets, such as Japan and Western Europe, consumers' appetite for feature-laden phones was met with new models packed with TV tuners, global positioning satellite (GPS) functions, touch screens and high-resolution cameras."

CNET News, February 27, 2008

a. **Explain the effects of the global increase in demand for cell phones on the market for cell phones and individual cell-phone producers in the short run.**

> In the short run the market demand for cell phones increases. The price of a cell phone rises and the market equilibrium quantity increases. Because the market price rises, individual cell phone producers increase the quantity they produce and make an economic profit.

b. **Draw a graph to illustrate your explanation in a.**

Figures 12.7 shows the short-run outcome. Figure 12.7a shows the market equilibrium. In the market, demand increases and the demand curve shifts rightward from D_0 to D_1. In the short run the supply curve remains S_0. As a result of the increase in demand the market price rises to $125 a cell phone and the market quantity increases to 1,200 million. Figure 12.7b shows the

economic profit. If the industry is a constant cost industry, the price returns to its initial level and the firms' amount of production returns to the initial amount.

FIGURE **12.7a**

Problem 17b

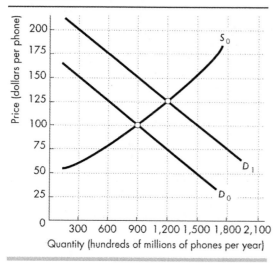

Quantity (hundreds of millions of phones per year)

FIGURE **12.7b**

Problem 17b

Quantity (millions of phones per year)

situation at a representative firm. The rise in the market price raises the firm's demand and marginal revenue curve from MR_0 to MR_1. The firm responds by increasing the quantity it produces from 200 million cell phones a year to 225 million cell phones a year. It makes an economic profit because the price exceeds the firm's average total cost.

c. **Explain the effects of the global increase in demand for cell phones on the market for cell phones in the long run.**

In the long run the economic profit attracts entry into the market. The market supply increases which drives the price down. The market equilibrium quantity increases. The fall in the price decreases and, in the long run, totally eliminates the firms'

d. **What factors will determine whether the price of cell phones will rise, fall, or stay the same in the new long-run equilibrium?**

The presence or absence of external economies or diseconomies determines whether the price of a cell phone falls, rises, or stays the same in the new long-run equilibrium. If the industry is characterized by external economies, factors beyond the control of an individual firm that lower the firm's costs as the *market* output increases, the long-run equilibrium price falls. If the industry is characterized by external diseconomies, factors beyond the control of an individual firm that raise the firm's costs as the *market* output increases, the long-run equilibrium price rises. If the industry has neither external economies nor diseconomies, the long-run equilibrium price is the same as the initial equilibrium price.

Additional Problems

1. Bob's is one of many burger stands along the beach. The figure shows Bob's cost curves.
    a. If the market price of a burger is $4, what is Bob's profit-maximizing output?
    b. Calculate the economic profit that Bob's makes.
    c. With no change in demand or technology, how will the price change in the long run?

2. Lucy's Lasagna is a price taker that has the costs shown in the table.
    a. If lasagna sells for $7.50 a plate, what is Lucy's profit-maximizing output?
    b. What is Lucy's shutdown point?
    c. Over what price range will Lucy leave the lasagna industry?
    d. Over what price range will other firms with costs identical to Lucy's enter the industry?
    e. What is the price of lasagna in the long run?

Output (plates per hour)	Total cost (dollars per hour)
0	5
1	20
2	26
3	35
4	46
5	59

Solutions to Additional Problems

1. a. Bob's profit-maximizing quantity is 200 burgers a day. Bob's maximizes its profit by producing the quantity at which marginal revenue equals marginal cost. In perfect competition, marginal revenue equals price, which is $4 a burger. Marginal cost is $4 when 200 burgers a day are produced.

   b. Bob's economic profit is $160 a day. Profit equals total revenue minus total cost. Total revenue equals $800 a day ($4 a burger multiplied by 200 burgers). The average total cost of producing 200 burgers is $3.20 a burger, so total cost equals $640 a day ($3.20 multiplied by 200 burgers). Profit equals $800 minus $640, which is $160 a day.

   c. The price will fall in the long run to $3 a burger. At a price of $4 a burger, firms make economic profit. In the long run, the economic profit will encourage new firms to enter the burger industry. As they do, the price will fall and economic profit will decrease. Firms will enter until economic profit is zero, which occurs when the price is $3 a burger (price equals minimum average total cost).

2. a. Lucy's profit-maximizing output is 2 plates an hour. Lucy's maximizes its profit by producing the quantity at which marginal revenue equals marginal cost. In perfect competition, marginal revenue equals price, which is $7.50 a plate. Marginal cost is the change in total cost when output is increased by 1 plate an hour. The marginal cost of increasing output from 1 to 2 plates an hour is $6 ($26 minus $20). The marginal cost of increasing output from 2 to 3 plates an hour is $9 ($35 minus $26). So the marginal cost of the second plate is halfway between $6 and $9, which is $7.50. Marginal cost equals marginal revenue when Lucy produces 2 plates an hour.

   b. Lucy's shutdown point is at a price of $10 a plate. The shutdown point is the price that equals minimum average variable cost. To calculate total variable cost, subtract total fixed cost ($5, which is total cost at zero output) from total cost. Average variable cost equals total variable cost divided by the quantity produced. For example, the average variable cost of producing 3 plates is $10 a plate. Average variable cost is a minimum when marginal cost equals average variable cost. The marginal cost of producing 3 plates is $10. So the shutdown point is a price of $10 a plate.

   c. Lucy will leave the industry if in the long run the price is less than $11 a plate. Lucy's Lasagna will leave the industry if it incurs an economic loss in the long run. To incur an economic loss, the price will have to be below minimum average total cost. Average total cost equals total cost divided by the quantity produced. For example, the average total cost of producing 2 plates is $13 a plate. Average total cost is a minimum when it equals marginal cost. The average total cost of producing 3 plates is $11.67, and the average total cost of producing 4 plates is $11.50. Marginal cost when Lucy's produces 3 plates is $10 and marginal cost when Lucy's produces 4 plates is $12. At 3 plates, marginal cost is less than average total cost; at 4 plates, marginal cost exceeds average total cost. So minimum average total cost occurs between 3 and 4 plates—$11 at 3.5 plates an hour.

   d. Firms with costs identical to Lucy's will enter at any price above $11 a plate. Firms will enter an industry when firms currently in the industry are making economic profit. Firms with costs identical to Lucy's will make economic profit when the price exceeds minimum average total cost, which is $11 a plate.

   e. The price in the long run is $11 a plate. At $11 a plate, firms in the industry make zero economic profit.

Chapter 13 MONOPOLY

Answers to the Problems and Applications

1. **The United States Postal Service has a monopoly on non-urgent First Class Mail and the exclusive right to put mail in private mailboxes. Pfizer Inc. makes LIPITOR, a prescription drug that lowers cholesterol. Cox Communications is the sole provider of cable television service in some parts of San Diego.**

   a. **What are the substitutes, if any, for the goods and services described above?**

      Substitutes for the U.S. Postal Service include email, fax, and private delivery services, such as FedEx or UPS. Substitutes for Lipitor are other statin drugs, such as Zocor, non-statin drugs that also lower cholesterol, and exercise. Substitutes for Cox Communications include satellite television services.

   b. **What are the barriers to entry, if any, that protect these three firms from competition?**

      The U.S. Postal Service and Pfizer are protected by legal barriers to entry. The Postal Service has the legal right given to it by the Private Express Statutes to be the only first class non-urgent mail service and Pfizer has a patent on Lipitor. Cox Communications has a natural barrier to entry because it is a natural monopoly. It also has a legal barrier to entry because it has been given the public franchise to be the only cable provider in its area.

   c. **Which of these three firms, if any, is a natural monopoly? Explain your answer and illustrate it by drawing an appropriate figure.**

      Cox Communications is the only natural monopoly. Its average cost curve will look similar to that in Figure 13.1. Cox Communications has a large fixed cost of creating a massive infrastructure and then a small marginal cost when it increases

the quantity of its customers. As a result, its economies of scale mean that its long-run average cost curve is downward sloping when it intersects the demand curve. Neither the U.S. Postal Service nor Pfizer has such strong economies of scale so their long-run average cost curves are upward sloping when they intersect their demand curves.

   d. **Which of these three firms, if any, is a legal monopoly? Explain your answer.**

      Both the U.S. Postal Service and Pfizer are legal monopolies. The Postal Service has the legal right given to it by the Private Express Statutes to be the only first class non-urgent mail service and Pfizer has a patent on Lipitor. Cox has a public franchise.

   e. **Which of these three firms are most likely to be able to profit from price discrimination and which are most likely to sell their good or service for a single price?**

      All three of the firms practice price discrimination. The second ounce in a first class letter is less expensive to mail than the first ounce. Lipitor's price varies according to the insurance policy a

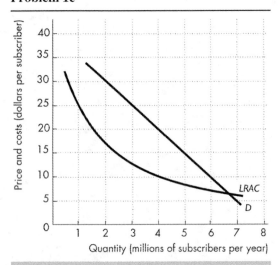

FIGURE **13.1**

Problem 1c

customer has. Cox Communications bundles packages of services that have a lower price than each item taken separately so that additional units of service are less expensive than the initial units.

3. **Antitrust Inquiry Launched into Intel**
The Federal Trade Commission has opened a formal probe into whether Intel, the world's largest chipmaker, has used its dominance to illegally stifle its few competitors. The move follows years of complaints from smaller chip rival Advanced Micro Devices... Intel is many times larger, holding 80 percent of the microprocessor market. ... In a sign that suggests the chip market remains competitive, Intel said, prices for microprocessors declined by 42.4 percent between 2000 and 2007... "evidence that this industry is fiercely competitive ..." Intel said.
The Washington Post, **June 7, 2008**

a. **Is Intel a monopoly in the chip market?**

Intel is not a monopoly because a competitor, Advanced Micro Devices, has a 20 percent market share. If Intel was a monopoly it would have no competitors.

b. **Evaluate the argument made by Intel that the significant decline in prices is "evidence that this industry is fiercely competitive."**

Technology has advanced rapidly in the microprocessor market. Technological advances shift the firm's marginal cost curve downward. Even if Intel was a monopoly, such a downward shift in the marginal cost curve would lead the firm to increase its profit-maximizing quantity and lower its profit-maximizing price. So the fall in price is not necessarily evidence that the industry is competitive.

5. **Minnie's Mineral Springs faces the demand schedule in problem 4 and has the total cost schedule in the table.**

a. **Calculate the marginal cost of producing each output listed in the table.**

Quantity produced (bottles per hour)	Total cost (dollars)
0	1
1	3
2	7
3	13
4	21
5	31

Quantity produced (bottles per hour)	Marginal cost (dollars)
0	
	2
1	
	4
2	
	6
3	
	8
4	
	10
5	

Marginal cost is the increase in total cost that results from increasing output by 1 unit. For example, when Minnie's increases output from 1 bottle to 2 bottles, total cost increases by $4. The marginal cost of increasing output from 1 bottle to 2 bottles is $4. The remaining marginal costs are calculated similarly. The second table to the right shows the marginal cost schedule.

b. **Calculate Minnie's profit-maximizing output and price.**

Minnie's profit-maximizing output is 1.5 bottles and her profit-maximizing price is $7a bottle.
To maximize profit Minnie's needs to produce the quantity at which marginal revenue equals marginal cost. The marginal cost of increasing the quantity

from 1 bottle to 2 bottles is $4 a bottle ($7 minus $3). That is, the marginal cost at 1.5 bottles of water is $4 a bottle. The marginal revenue of increasing the quantity sold from 1 bottle to 2 bottles is $4 ($12 minus $8). So the marginal revenue from 1.5 bottles is $4 a bottle. The profit-maximizing output is 1.5 bottles. The profit-maximizing price is the highest price that Minnie's can sell the profit-maximizing output of 1.5 bottles. Minnie's can sell 1 bottle for $8 and 2 bottles for $6, so it can sell 1.5 bottles for $7 a bottle.

c. Calculate the economic profit.

Economic profit equals total revenue minus total cost. Total revenue equals price ($7 a bottle) multiplied by quantity (1.5 bottles), which is $10.50. Total cost of producing 1 bottle is $3 and the total cost of producing 2 bottles is $7, so the total cost of producing 1.5 bottles is $5. Minnie's economic profit equals $10.50 minus $5, which is $5.50.

7. The Saturday-Night Stay Requirement Is on Its Final Approach

The Saturday-night stay—that pesky and expensive requirement that airlines instituted to ensure that the business traveler pays outrageous airfares if he or she wants to go home to the family for the weekend—has gone the way of the dodo bird. ...

Many low-fare carriers, such as Southwest, JetBlue and AirTran, never had the Saturday-night rule. Some of the so-called legacy airlines, including America West and Alaska, have eliminated the restriction. United and American did away with it in response to competition but only on some routes. Still others, including Continental, Delta, US Airways and Northwest, mostly continue to enforce the rule, especially in the markets they dominate. ... Experts and industry spokesmen agree that low-fare carriers are the primary reason legacy airlines are adopting more consumer-friendly

fare structures, which include the elimination of the Saturday-night stay, the introduction of one-way and walk-up fares and the general restructuring of its fares. ...

Los Angeles Times, **August 15, 2004**

a. Explain why the opportunity for price discrimination exists for air travel.

Even though there are many airlines overall, on some flights an airline might be the only company or one of a few on that route, thereby giving it significant pricing power. Then, because vacation travelers and business travelers have differing marginal benefits from travel (and therefore different willingness to pay) the airline is able to price discriminate between these groups.

b. How does an airline profit from price discrimination?

Airlines profit from price discrimination because they can charge business travelers, who have a lower elasticity and a higher willingness to pay, a high price that exceeds the price charged vacation travelers, who have a larger elasticity and a lower willingness to pay. By adjusting the prices they charge the different classes of customers so that the prices are closer to the customers' willingness to pay, the airline can increase its economic profit by transferring consumer surplus from consumers to itself.

c. Describe the change in price discrimination in the market for air travel when discount airlines entered the market.

The expansion of low cost carriers into routes previously served by only one (or a very few) other carrier has increased competition and lowered the price. More importantly the increase in competition means that the airlines have less ability to determine their own price and increasingly must act as perfect competitors that take the market price as given. The less the airline can affect the price it charges, the less it can price discriminate.

d. Explain the effect of the change in price discrimination when discount airlines entered the market on the price and the quantity of air travel.

The entry of discount airlines lowered the average price of tickets and, by increasing the supply, increased the total market quantity.

9   In problem 8, what is the producer surplus, consumer surplus, and deadweight loss if Calypso is

a.   An unregulated profit-maximizing firm?

If Calypso is unregulated, it produces 2 million cubic feet a day and sells it for 6 cents a cubic foot. The consumer surplus is $40,000, the producer surplus is $80,000, and the deadweight loss is $40,000. The consumer surplus is the triangular area under the demand curve and above the price. The price is 6 cents, so consumer surplus equals (10 cents minus 6 cents) multiplied by 2 million cubic feet/2, which is $40,000. The producer surplus is the rectangular area under the price and above the *MC* curve. The price is 6 cents, so producer surplus equals (6 cents minus 2 cents) multiplied by 2 million cubic feet a day, which is $80,000. The efficient output is 4 cubic feet, at which marginal cost equals price (marginal benefit). The deadweight loss is the triangular area between the demand (or marginal benefit) curve and the marginal cost curve between the equilibrium quantity and the efficient quantity. So the deadweight loss equals (4 million cubic feet minus 2 million cubic feet) multiplied by (6 cents minus 2 cents)/2, which is $40,000 a day.

b.   Regulated to make zero economic profit?

If Calypso is regulated to make zero economic profit, it produces 3 million cubic feet a day and sets a price of 4 cents a cubic foot. The consumer surplus is $90,000, the producer surplus is

$60,000, and the deadweight loss is $10,000. The consumer surplus is the triangular area under the demand curve and above the price. The price is 4 cents, so consumer surplus equals (10 cents minus 4 cents) multiplied by 3 million cubic feet/2, which is $90,000. The producer surplus is the rectangular area under the price and above the *MC* curve. The price is 4 cents, so producer surplus equals (4 cents minus 2 cents) multiplied by 3 million cubic feet, which is $60,000. The efficient output is 4 million cubic feet, at which marginal cost equals price (marginal benefit). The deadweight loss is the triangular area between the demand (or marginal social benefit) curve and the marginal cost curve between the equilibrium quantity and the efficient quantity. So the deadweight loss equals (4 million cubic feet minus 3 million cubic feet) multiplied by (4 cents minus 2 cents)/2, which is $10,000 a day.

c.   Regulated to be efficient?

If Calypso is regulated to be efficient, it produces 4 million cubic feet a day and sells it for 2 cents a cubic foot. The consumer surplus is $160,000, the producer surplus is $0, and the deadweight loss is $0. The consumer surplus is the triangular area under the demand curve and above the price. The price is 2 cents, so consumer surplus equals (10 cents minus 2 cents) multiplied by 4 million cubic feet/2, which is $160,000. There is no producer surplus because the price equals the marginal cost. And there is no deadweight loss because the quantity produced is the efficient quantity.

Price (dollars per ride)	Quantity demanded (rides per month)	Total cost (dollars per month)
220	0	80
200	1	160
180	2	260
160	3	380
140	4	520
120	5	680

154

11. **Hot Air Balloon Rides, a single-price monopoly, has the demand schedule shown in columns 1 and 2 of the table and the total cost schedule shown in columns 2 and 3 of the table.**

a. **Construct Hot Air's total revenue and marginal revenue schedules.**

The table showing Hot Air's total revenue schedule and marginal revenue schedule is below. Total revenue equals price multiplied by quantity. Marginal revenue equals the change in total revenue divided by the change in quantity. For example, between 1 ride and 2 rides the total revenue increases by $160 and the quantity increases by 1 ride, so the marginal revenue equals $160/1, which is $160. This marginal revenue is placed midway between the 1 ride and 2 rides rows.

Price (dollars per ride)	Quantity demanded (rides per month)	Total revenue (dollars per month)	Marginal revenue (dollars per ride)
220	0	0	
			200
200	1	200	
			160
180	2	360	
			120
160	3	480	
			80
140	4	560	
			40
120	5	600	

b. **Draw a graph of the demand curve and Hot Air's marginal revenue curve.**

Figure 13.5 illustrates Hot Air's demand curve and marginal revenue curve.

c. **Find HotAir's profit-maximizing output and price and calculate the firm's economic profit.**

HotAir's marginal cost equals marginal revenue at 2 1/2 rides a month, where both equal $120. From the demand curve, the price is $170 a ride. Total

economic profit equals total revenue minus total cost. The total cost of 2 1/2 rides a month is $320. HotAir's total revenue equals the number of rides multiplied by the price per ride, which is (2 1/2 rides per month) × ($170) = $425. So the total economic profit is total revenue minus total cost, which is $425 − $320 = $105.

d. **If the government imposes a tax on Hot Air's profit, how does its output and price change?**

As a result of the tax, HotAir's fixed cost changes, but its marginal cost does not. The profit-maximizing level of output is still 2 1/2 rides a month and the price still equals $170. The tax decreases HotAir's economic profit but does not change its output or price.

e. **If instead of taxing Hot Air's profit, the government imposes a sales tax on balloon rides of $30 a ride, what are the new profit-maximizing quantity, price, and economic profit?**

A $30 a ride tax increases Hot Air's marginal cost by $30 at every level of output. With the increase in the marginal costs, Hot Air now sells 2 rides a month because this is the level at which the new marginal cost equals the marginal

FIGURE **13.5**
Problem 11b

revenue (both equal $140). From the demand curve, Hot Air sets a price of $180 a ride. Total economic profit equals total revenue minus total cost. The total revenue is 2 rides × $180 which is $360. The total cost is $260 plus the tax of $60, which is $320. So the new economic profit is $360 − $320 = $40.

13. **Telecoms Look to Grow by Acquisition**
A multibillion-dollar telecommunications merger announced Thursday ... shows how global cellular powerhouses are scouting for growth in emerging economies while consolidating in their own, crowded backyards.
France Télécom offered Thursday to buy TeliaSonera, a Swedish-Finnish telecommunications operator ... Within hours, TeliaSonera rejected the offer as too low, but analysts said higher bids—either from France Télécom or others— could persuade [TeliaSonera] to accept a deal. Meanwhile, in the United States, Verizon Wireless, ... agreed to buy Alltel for $28.1 billion, a deal that would make the company the biggest mobile phone operator in the country. A combination of France Télécom and TeliaSonera would create the world's fourth-largest mobile operator ... smaller only than China Mobile, Vodafone and Telefónica of Spain. ...
International Herald Tribune, June 5, 2008

a. **Explain the rent seeking behavior of global telecommunications companies.**
France Télécom and Verizon Wireless are rent seeking because they are attempting to buy a significant competitor to establish a monopoly.

b. **Explain how mergers may affect the efficiency of the telecommunications market.**
The mergers would decrease the amount of competition in the telecommunications market. To the extent that they lead to monopoly power

in that market they create a deadweight loss and reduce the efficiency of the markets.

15. **iSurrender**
... Getting your hands on a new iPhone ... [means] signing ... a two-year AT&T contract. ... Some markets, because of the sheer costs of being a player, tend toward either a single firm or a small number of firms. ... Everyone hoped and thought the wireless market would be different. ... A telephone monopoly has been the norm for most of American telecommunication history, except for what may turn out to have been a brief experimental period from 1984 through 2012 or so ... [I]t may be that telephone monopolies in America are a national tradition.
Slate, June 10, 2008

a. **How does AT&T being the exclusive provider of wireless service for the iPhone influence the wireless telecommunication market?**
AT&T being the exclusive provider of service for the iPhone limits the amount of competition within the wireless market. With this deal, the price of an iPhone is higher than would otherwise be the case and the quantity of iPhone service is lower than would otherwise be the case.

b. **Explain why the wireless market may "tend toward either a single firm or a small number of firms." Why might this justify allowing a regulated monopoly to exist in this market?**
If the wireless industry is a natural monopoly, there is a natural tendency for the market to have only one firm. The firm that survives obtains a cost advantage over its competitors by increasing the quantity it produces and then the firm uses that cost advantage to drive its competitors out of business. If this industry is a natural monopoly, then granting the firm the public franchise to be a monopoly in exchange for regulating its price and quantity is a reasonable

public policy to avoid the deadweight loss that would arise from an unregulated monopoly.

17. **Study *Reading Between the Lines* on pp. 316 –317 and then answer the following questions:**

   a. **What does the news article mean when it says that Microsoft's main challenge comes from the marketplace rather than government?**

   The article means that if Microsoft fails to respond to its competitors, Microsoft's profit might be severely diminished because consumers no longer need Windows and Microsoft's other applications.

   b. **How does Microsoft try to raise barriers to the entry of competitors?**

   Microsoft tries to raise barriers to entry by creating products that compete with the products of its competitors and then embedding the products as part of its Windows operating system. In this fashion customers no longer need the competing products because they already have a Microsoft version as part of Windows.

   c. **Compare and contrast the anti-monopoly regulation in Europe with that in the United States.**

   Monopoly regulation in Europe is frequently used to protect competitors rather than competition. For instance, the discussion for the *Reading Between the Lines* article points out how the European decision helped preserve Real Networks. In the United States antitrust law is often devoted to preserving competition rather than individual competitors. U.S. antitrust law generally tends to protect and enhance allocative efficiency while European antitrust law often tends to protect and enhance producer surplus.

Additional Problems

1. The table has the demand schedule for industrial diamonds faced by Dolly's Diamond Mines, a single-price monopoly.

   a. Calculate Dolly's total revenue schedule.

   b. Calculate its marginal revenue schedule.

Price (dollars per pound)	Quantity demanded (pounds per day)
2,200	5
2,000	6
1,800	7
1,600	8
1,400	9
1,200	10

2. Dolly's Diamond Mines in problem 1 has the total cost schedule in the table. Calculate the profit-maximizing levels of

   a. Output

   b. Price

   c. Economic profit

   d. Does Dolly's Mines use resources efficiently? Explain your answer.

Quantity produced (pounds per day)	Total cost (dollars)
5	8,000
6	9,000
7	10,000
8	11,600
9	13,200
10	15,000

3. The figure illustrates the situation facing the publisher of the only newspaper containing local news in an isolated community. The publisher's marginal cost for the new plant is constant at 20 cents per copy printed.

   a. What quantity of newspapers will maximize the publisher's profit?

   b. What price will the publisher charge for a daily newspaper?

   c. What is the publisher's daily total revenue?

   d. At the price charged for a newspaper, is the demand for newspapers elastic or inelastic? Why?

4. In the monopoly newspaper market described in problem 3,

   a. What is the efficient quantity of newspapers to print each day? Explain your answer.

   b. When the market is a monopoly, what is the consumer surplus of the readers of the newspaper?

   c. What is the deadweight loss created by the monopoly newspaper publisher?

5. What is the maximum value of resources that will be used in rent seeking to acquire Dolly's monopoly in problem 1? Considering this loss, what is the total social cost of Dolly's monopoly?

Solutions to Additional Problems

Price (dollars per pound)	Quantity demanded (pounds per day)	Total revenue (dollars per day)	Marginal revenue (dollars per pound)
2,200	5	11,000	
			1,000
2,000	6	12,000	
			600
1,800	7	12,600	
			200
1,600	8	12,800	
			−200
1,400	9	12,600	
			−600
1,200	10	12,000	

1. a. The table above shows the total revenue schedule. Dolly's total revenue schedule lists the total revenue at each quantity sold. For example, Dolly's can sell 10 pounds for $1,200 a pound, which gives it total revenue of $12,000 at the quantity 10 pounds.

   b. The table above shows the marginal revenue schedule. Dolly's marginal revenue schedule lists the marginal revenue that results from increasing the quantity sold by 1 pound. For example, Dolly's can sell 5 pounds for $2,200 each, which is total revenue of $11,000 at the quantity of 5 pounds. Dolly's can sell 6 pounds for $2,000 each, which is $12,000 of total revenue at the quantity 6 pounds. So by increasing the quantity sold from 5 pounds to 6 pounds, marginal revenue is $1,000 a pound ($12,000 minus $11,000).

2. a. Dolly's profit-maximizing output is 5.5 pounds. The marginal cost of increasing the quantity from 5 pounds to 6 pounds is $1,000 a pound ($9,000 minus $8,000). That is, the marginal cost of 5.5 pounds is $1,000 a pound. The marginal revenue of increasing the quantity sold from 5 pounds to 6 pounds is $1,000 ($12,000 minus

$11,000). So the marginal revenue from 5.5 pounds is $1,000 a pound. Profit is maximized when the quantity produced is such that marginal cost equals marginal revenue. The profit-maximizing output is 5.5 pounds.

   b. Dolly's profit-maximizing price is $2,100 a pound. The profit-maximizing price is the highest price that Dolly's can sell the profit-maximizing output of 5.5 pounds. Dolly's can sell 5 pounds for $2,200 and 6 pounds for $2,000, so it can sell 5.5 pounds for $2,100 a pound.

   c. Economic profit equals total revenue minus total cost. Total revenue equals price ($2,100 a pound) multiplied by quantity (5.5 pounds), which is $11,550. Total cost of producing 5 pounds is $8,000 and the total cost of producing 6 pounds is $9,000, so the total cost of producing 5.5 pounds is $8,500. So Dolly's economic profit equals $11,550 minus $8,500, which is $3,050.

   d. Dolly's is inefficient. Dolly's charges a price of $2,100 a pound, so consumers receive a marginal benefit of $2,100 a pound. Dolly's marginal cost is $1,000 a pound. That is, the marginal benefit of $2,100 a pound exceeds Dolly's marginal cost.

3. a. The profit-maximizing output is 200 newspapers a day. Profit is maximized when the firm produces the output at which marginal cost equals marginal revenue. Draw in the marginal revenue curve. It runs from 100 on the y-axis to 250 on the x-axis. The marginal revenue curve cuts the marginal cost curve at the quantity 200 newspapers a day.

   b. The highest price that the publisher can sell 200 newspapers a day is determined from the demand curve. The price charged is 60 cents a paper.

   c. The daily total revenue is $120 (200 papers at 60 cents each).

   d. Demand is elastic. Along a straight-line demand curve, demand is elastic at all prices above the midpoint of the demand curve. The price at the midpoint is 50 cents. So at 60 cents a paper, demand is elastic.

4. a. The efficient quantity is 300 newspapers—the quantity that makes marginal benefit (price) equal to marginal cost. With 300 newspapers available, people are willing to pay 40 cents for a paper. To produce 300 newspapers, the publisher incurs a marginal cost of 40 cents a paper.

b. Consumer surplus is the area under the demand curve above the price. When the market is a monopoly, the price is 60 cents, so consumer surplus equals (100 cents minus 60 cents) multiplied by 200/2 papers a day, so the consumer surplus is $40 a day.

c. Deadweight loss arises because the publisher does not produce the efficient quantity. Output is restricted to 200, and the price is increased to 60 cents. The deadweight loss equals (60 cents minus 40

cents) multiplied by 100/2 so the deadweight loss is $10 a day.

5. The maximum that will be spent on rent seeking is $3,050 a day—an amount equal to Dolly's economic profit. The total social cost equals the deadweight loss plus the amount spent on rent seeking. To calculate the deadweight loss, first calculate the efficient output—the intersection point of the demand curve (marginal benefit curve) and the marginal cost curve. Do this by finding the equations to the two curves and solving them. The efficient output is 8.25 pounds. The deadweight loss equals $1,512.50. The loss to society is $4,562.50 ($3,050 plus $1,512.50).

Chapter 14 MONOPOLISTIC COMPETITION

Answers to the Problems and Applications

1. Sara is a dot.com entrepreneur who has established a Web site at which people can design and buy a sweatshirt. Sara pays $1,000 a week for her Web server and Internet connection. The sweatshirts that her customers design are made to order by another firm, and Sara pays this firm $20 a sweatshirt. Sara has no other costs. The table sets out the demand schedule for Sara's sweatshirts.

Price (dollars per sweatshirt)	Quantity demanded (sweatshirts per week)
0	100
20	80
40	60
60	40
80	20
100	0

   a. **Calculate Sara's profit-maximizing output, price, and economic profit.**

   Sara produces the quantity that sets her marginal cost equal to her marginal revenue. Sara's marginal cost is $20. Between the quantity of 20 and 40 sweatshirts, Sara's marginal revenue is $40. Between 40 and 60 sweatshirts, Sara's marginal revenue is $0. So at the quantity of 40 sweatshirts Sara's marginal revenue is $20. To maximize her profit, Sara produces 40 sweatshirts. When Sara produces 40 sweatshirts, the price from the demand schedule is $60 per sweatshirt. Sara's total revenue is $2,400. Her total cost is $1,000 (fixed cost) plus $800 (variable cost), or $1,800. Sara's economic profit equals $2,400 − $1,800 or $600.

   b. **Do you expect other firms to enter the Web sweatshirt business and compete with Sara?**

   Sara is making an economic profit so other firms will enter the Web sweatshirt business and compete with Sara.

   c. **What happens to the demand for Sara's sweatshirts in the long run? What happens to Sara's economic profit in the long run?**

   As new firms enter the Web sweatshirt industry, the demand for Sara's sweatshirts will decrease. In the long run Sara's economic profit is zero—a normal profit.

3. In the market for running shoes, all the firms face a similar demand curve and have similar cost curves to those of Lite and Kool in problem 2.

   a. **What happens to the number of firms producing running shoes in the long run?**

   Lite and Kool is making an economic profit. This profit attracts entry into the market so the number of firms increases.

   b. **What happens to the price of running shoes in the long run?**

   The price of a pair of running shoes falls in the long run. As new firms enter the market, the demand for Lite and Kools' shoes decreases. The decrease in demand leads to the price of running shoes falling.

   c. **What happens to the quantity of running shoes produced by Lite and Kool in the long run?**

   The quantity of running shoes produced by Lite and Kool decreases in the long run. Lite and Kool is making an economic profit. This profit attracts entry into the market. As new firms enter, the demand for Lite and Kools' shoes decreases. The decrease in demand leads to the quantity of running shoes produced by Lite and Kool decreasing.

d. What happens to the quantity of running shoes in the entire market in the long run?

> The quantity of running shoes in the market as a whole increases in the long run. The economic profit attracts entry into the market. As new firms enter, each existing firm decreases its output a bit. But the new firms produce more shoes and, on net, the quantity of shoes in the entire market increases.

e. Does Lite and Kool have excess capacity in the long run?

> Lite and Kool does *not* produce at the minimum of the average total cost in the long run so Lite and Kool has excess capacity. In the long run, monopolistically competitive firms produce less output than the amount which minimizes the average total cost, which means that in the long run they have excess capacity.

f. Why, if Lite and Kool has excess capacity in the long run, doesn't the firm decrease its capacity?

> Lite and Kool is producing at the average total cost that is the minimum average total cost for the quantity it produces. If Lite and Kool decreased its capacity it would shift its average total cost curve upward and thereby increase its average total cost for its profit-maximizing quantity and thereby incur an economic loss.

g. What is the relationship between Lite and Kool's price and marginal cost?

> Lite and Kool's price exceeds its marginal cost. Lite and Kool has a markup of its price over its marginal cost.

5. Suppose that Tommy Hilfiger's marginal cost of a jacket is $100 (a constant marginal cost) and at one of the firm's shops, total fixed cost is $2,000 a day. The profit-maximizing number of jackets sold in this shop is 20 a day. Then the shops nearby start to advertise their jackets. The Tommy Hilfiger shop now spends $2,000 a day advertising its jackets, and its profit-maximizing number of jackets sold jumps to 50 a day.

a. What is this shop's average total cost of a jacket sold before the advertising begins?

> The average total cost of a jacket is $200. The average total cost equals the total cost divided by the quantity. The fixed cost is $2,000. Because the marginal cost is $100 per jacket, the total variable cost is $2,000. So the total cost is the $2,000 fixed cost plus the $2,000 variable cost, which is $4,000. So the average total cost is $4,000/20, which is $200.

b. What is this shop's average total cost of a jacket sold after the advertising begins?

> The average total cost of a jacket is $180. The average total cost equals the total cost divided by the quantity. The fixed cost is $4,000. Because the marginal cost is $100 per jacket, the total variable cost is $5,000. So the total cost is the $4,000 fixed cost plus the $5,000 variable cost, which is $9,000. The average total cost is $9,000/50, which is $180.

c. Can you say what happens to the price of a Tommy Hilfiger jacket? Why or why not?

> If the advertising has increased the demand and made it more elastic, which is likely the case if all firms advertise, then the price will fall. However, if the advertising has increased the demand and made the price less elastic, then the price will rise.

d. Can you say what happens to Tommy's markup? Why or why not?

> If the price falls, then the makeup falls; if the price rises, then the markup rises.

e. Can you say what happens to Tommy's economic profit? Why or why not?

> It is not possible to determine the effect on the profit in the short run. In the long run, however, the economic profit will equal zero as it does for all monopolistically competitive firms in the long run.

7. **How does having a brand name help Tommy Hilfiger in problem 5 to increase its economic profit?**

    A brand name signals to consumers that the product is high quality. Tommy Hilfiger will ensure that each of its products is high quality because to do otherwise would dissipate the information associated with the brand name. Consumers are aware that Tommy Hilfiger values its brand name and so they realize that the brand name means the product is high quality.

9. **The Shoe That Won't Quit**
    I finally decided to take the plunge this past winter and buy a pair of Uggs. ... But when I got around to shopping for my Uggs in late January, the style that I wanted was sold out. ... The scarcity factor was not a glitch in the supply chain, but rather a carefully calibrated strategy by Ugg parent Deckers Outdoor that is one of the big reasons behind the brand's success. Deckers tightly controls distribution to ensure that supply does not outstrip demand. ... If Deckers ever opened up the supply of Uggs to meet demand, sales would shoot up like a rocket, but they'd come back down just as fast.
    Fortune, June 5, 2008

    a. **Explain why Deckers intentionally restricts the quantity of Uggs the firm sells.**

    Deckers is differentiating its product by creating the aura of high-quality, exclusive shoes. If Deckers increased the quantity of Uggs they produced, Uggs would no longer seem exclusive. Consumers might come to view Uggs as commonplace, which would decrease their demand for Uggs.

b. **Draw a graph to illustrate how Deckers maximizes the economic profit from Uggs.**

    Figure 14.2 shows the market for Uggs. In the figure Deckers maximizes its profit by producing 2 million Uggs per year and setting a price of $175 per shoe.

FIGURE **14.2**

Problem 9b

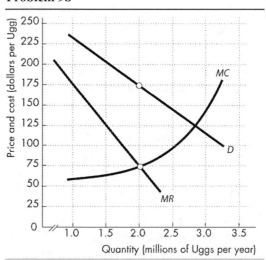

11. **Food's Next Billion-Dollar Brand?**
    While it's not the biggest brand in margarine, Smart Balance has an edge on its rivals in that it's made with a patented blend of vegetable and fruit oils that has been shown to raise levels of HDL, or "good" cholesterol, which can help improve consumers' cholesterol levels. Smart Balance ... sales have skyrocketed since its launch in 1997 while sales for the margarine category overall have stagnated. ... Still, it remains to be seen whether Smart Balance's heart-healthy message (and higher prices) will resonate with mainstream consumers.
    Fortune, June 4, 2008

a. **How do you expect advertising and the Smart Balance brand name will affect Smart Balance's ability to earn an economic profit?**

Advertising increases Smart Balance's costs and, because Smart Balance is the only margarine to increase "good" cholesterol, advertising also probably increases the demand for Smart Balance. Additionally, by advertising the makers of Smart Balance are creating a brand name and signaling consumers that Smart Balance actually works to benefit consumers' cholesterol. This signal and brand name also increase the demand for Smart Balance. Presumably the advertising increases Smart Balance's economic profit because otherwise Smart Balance would not advertise.

b. **Are long-run economic profits a possibility for Smart Balance?**

If Smart Balance is making an economic profit, its economic profit will persist until other margarine producers create a similar product that also raises the "good" cholesterol. When other producers can develop their own differentiated products, Smart Balance's economic profit will be eliminated.

c. **Does Smart Balance have either excess capacity or a markup in long-run equilibrium?**

Smart Balance is a firm in monopolistic competition. As such, in the long run it will have both excess capacity and a markup of price over marginal cost.

13. **Lorie teaches singing. Her fixed costs are $1,000 a month, and it costs her $50 of labor to give one class. The table shows the demand schedule for Lorie's singing lessons.**

a. **Calculate Lorie's profit-maximizing output, price, and economic profit.**

Lorie produces the quantity of singing lessons that sets her marginal cost equal to her marginal revenue. Lorie's marginal cost is $50. Between the quantity of 50 and 100 lessons, Lorie's marginal revenue is $100. Between 100 and 150 lessons,

Lorie's marginal revenue is $0. So at the quantity of 100 lessons Lorie's marginal revenue is $50. To maximize her profit, Lorie sells 100 lessons. When Lorie sells 100 lessons, the price from her demand schedule is $150 per lesson. Lorie's total revenue is $15,000. Her total cost is $1,000 (her fixed cost) plus $5,000 (her variable cost), which is $6,000. Lorie's economic profit equals $15,000 − $6,000, which is $9,000.

b. **Do you expect other firms to enter the singing lesson business and compete with Lorie?**

Lorie is making an economic profit so other firms will enter the singling-lesson industry and compete with Lorie.

c. **What happens to the demand for Lorie's lessons in the long run? What happens to Lorie's economic profit in the long run?**

As new firms enter the singing-lesson industry, the demand for Lorie's lessons will decrease. In the long run Lorie's economic profit is eliminated and Lorie makes zero economic profit—a normal profit.

Price (dollars per lesson)	Quantity demanded (lessons per month)
0	250
50	200
100	150
150	100
200	50
250	0

15. **In the market for mountain bikes, the demand for each firm's bikes and the firm's cost curves are similar to those of Mike's Bikes in problem 14.**

   a. **What happens to the number of firms producing mountain bikes?**
   The firms are incurring an economic loss, so some firms exit the market. In the long run, the number of firms producing mountain bikes decreases.

   b. **What happens to the price of mountain bikes in the long run?**
   With the decrease in the number of firms, the surviving firms' demand increases. With the increase in demand the price of their mountain bikes rises.

   c. **What happens to the quantity of mountain bikes produced by Mike's Bikes in the long run?**
   As long as Mike's Bikes' is a survivor, Mike's Bikes' demand increases. When demand increases, the marginal revenue also increases so Mike's Bikes increases the quantity of bikes it produces.

   d. **What happens to the quantity of bikes in the entire market in the long run?**
   In the long run the price of a mountain bike rises, so in the long run the quantity of mountain bikes demanded (and the quantity produced) in the entire market decreases.

   e. **Is there any way for Mike's Bikes to avoid having excess capacity in the long run?**
   If Mike's Bikes maximizes its profit, it will have excess capacity. If Mike's Bikes increases its production so that it produces at the minimum of its average total cost, it will incur an economic loss.

17. **Bianca bakes delicious cookies. Her total fixed cost is $40 a day, and her average variable cost is $1 a bag. Few people know about Bianca's Cookies, and she is maximizing her profit by selling 10 bags a day for $5 a bag. Bianca thinks that if she spends $50 a day on advertising, she can increase** her market share and sell 25 bags a day for $5 a bag.

   a. **If Bianca's belief about the effect of advertising is correct, can she increase her economic profit by advertising?**
   If additional advertising enables sales to increase so that total revenue increases more than total cost, she can increase economic profit. In the case at hand, her total revenue will increase by $75 and her total cost will increase by $50 plus whatever is the increase in her variable cost of producing the cookies. Because her AVC when she produces 10 bags is only $1, it is likely that her variable costs will increase by less than $25, which means that advertising will be profitable.

   b. **If Bianca advertises, will her average total cost increase or decrease at the quantity produced?**
   Before she advertised, Bianca's total variable cost was $10 and her total fixed cost was $40, so her total cost was $50. With this total cost and production of 10 bags of cookies, Bianca's average total cost was $5 a bag. After she advertises, if her average variable cost remains $1 a bag, her total variable costs become $25, her total fixed costs are $90 (the initial fixed costs of $40 plus her advertising costs of $50) so her total cost is $115. With this total cost and production of 25 bags a day, Bianca's average total cost is $4.60 a bag.

   c. **If Bianca advertises, will she continue to sell her cookies for $5 a bag or will she raise her price or lower her price?**
   In the long run Bianca's price will equal her average total cost. If her average total cost remains below $5 a bag, in the long run her price will be forced down below $5 a bag.

19. **Swinging For Female Golfers**
   One of the hottest areas of innovation is in clubs for women, who now make up nearly a quarter of the 24 million golfers in the U.S. ... Callaway and

Nike, two of the leading golf-equipment manufacturers, recently released new clubs designed specifically for women ...

Time, **April 21, 2008**

a. **How are Callaway and Nike attempting to maintain economic profit?**

Callaway and Nike are innovating by creating golf clubs for women. They expect that the demand for women's clubs will be high and so they will be able to (temporarily) make an economic profit.

b. **Draw a graph to illustrate the cost curves and revenue curves of Callaway or Nike in the market for golf clubs for women.**

Figure 14.6 shows the situation at Callaway or Nike. The firm produces 200,000 golf clubs per year and sets a price of $140 per club.

c. **Show on your graph (in b) the short-run economic profit.**

The economic profit equals the area of the darkened rectangle labeled *A* in Figure 14.6.

d. **Explain why economic profit that Callaway and Nike make on golf clubs for women is likely to be temporary.**

The economic profit is temporary because there are no barriers to entry. If Callaway and Nike are indeed able to make an economic profit other firms will enter the market by producing women's golf clubs. As more firms produce the clubs the demand for Callaway and Nike clubs will decrease. As a result the quantity and price of Callaway and Nike clubs will decrease, which lowers their economic profit. In the long run, entry will eliminate the economic profit.

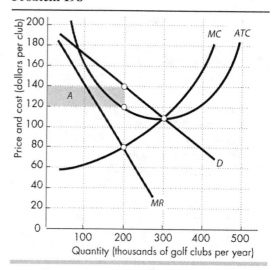

FIGURE **14.6**

Problem 19b

e. **Draw a graph to illustrate the cost curves and revenue curves of Callaway or Nike in the market for golf clubs for women in the long run. Mark in the firm's excess capacity.**

Figure 14.7 shows the long-run equilibrium for Callaway or Nike. The firm produces 150,000 golf clubs and sets a price of $130 per club. The firm makes zero economic profit (a normal profit) because its price equals its average total cost. The firm's excess capacity is 150,000 golf clubs, shown in the figure by the length of the grey arrow between the quantity the firm produces and the quantity that minimizes the firm's average total cost.

21. **Under Armour's Big Step Up**
Under Armour, the red-hot athletic-apparel brand that has joined Nike, Adidas, and New Balance as a major player on the market. ... [Under Armour CEO] Plank prepares to move the Under Armour brand out of its comfort zone into the cutthroat, $18.3 billion athletic footwear market. ... Under Armour announced it would try to revive the long-dead cross-training category. ... Under Armour tested the footwear landscape about two years ago, when it started making American-football cleats. Selling soccer shoes against Adidas and Nike would have been suicidal. Football is a small, specialized market. ... "Our No. 1 goal was authenticating ourselves as a footwear brand," says Plank. "Does the consumer accept putting the Under Armour logo on a shoe?" ... But will young athletes really spend $100 for a [cross training] shoe to lift weights in? "They're spending $40 on a T shirt," quips Plank, nodding to the premium price that consumers are paying for Under Armour's sweat-sopping gear.
Time, **May 26, 2008**

FIGURE **14.7**
Problem 19e

a. **Explain how brand names initially prevented Under Armour from competing in the athletic shoe market.**

Under Armour knew that if it entered the athletic shoe market it would be competing against other producers who had a strong reputation for quality. Consumers would have been hesitant to buy an "untested" Under Armour product when they could buy other shoes that they knew would be high quality.

b. **What factors influence Under Armour's ability to earn an economic profit?**

Under Armour entered a niche shoe market, the market for football shoes. In this market Under Armour faced less competition than in the broader market and so Under Armour was able to create a foothold in the shoe market. Once Under Armour was not a totally unknown shoe producer, Under Armour believed that it could enter the wider shoe market. Once Under Armour had established a brand name in the footwear market, the primary factor that will affect Under Armour's ability to make an economic profit is the demand for its shoes. If consumers embrace Under Armour's cross training shoe, which may depend in part on its brand name, then Under Armour will be able to make an economic profit.

c. Will Under Armour be able to make an economic profit in the cross training shoe market?

In the short run Under Armour might make an economic profit in the cross training shoe market. This economic profit is far from a certainty because other firms, such as Nike and New Balance, have decided that this market is not profitable. However, even if Under Armour is able to make an economic profit in the short run, in the long run other firms, such as Nike and New Balance, will enter the cross training shoe market and eliminate Under Armour's economic profit.

Additional Problems

1. The figure shows the situation facing
    Well Done, Inc., a producer of steak
    sauce.
    a. What quantity does Well Done
        produce?
    b. What does it charge?
    c. How much profit does Well Done
        make?
    d. If all steak sauce firms have identical
        cost curves and face identical demand
        curves, what happens to the number
        of firms in the market in the long
        run?
    e. In the long run, will the price of
        steak sauce rise, fall, or not change?

Solutions to Additional Problems

1. a. To maximize profit, Well Done produces the quantity at which marginal revenue equals marginal cost. Well Done produces 200 bottles a week.

    b. To maximize profit, Well Done charges the highest price that allows it to sell the 200 bottles of steak sauce it produces. This price is read from the demand curve and is $4 a bottle.

    c. Economic profit equals total revenue minus total cost. The price is $4 and the quantity sold is 200 bottles, so total revenue is $800. Average total cost is $3, so total cost equals $600. Economic profit equals $800 minus $600, so Well Done makes an economic profit of $200 a week.

    d. The firms are making an economic profit so new firms will enter the market. In the long run the number of firms is greater than in the short run.

    e. In the long run the number of firms increases so that each firm's demand is less than in the short run. With the lowered demand the price of steak sauce is lower in the long run.

Chapter 15 OLIGOPOLY

Answers to the Problems and Applications

1. **Two firms make most of the chips that power a PC: Intel and Advanced Micro Devices. What makes the market for PC chips a duopoly? Sketch the market demand curve and cost curves that describe the situation in this market and that prevent other firms from entering.**

    The market for CPUs is natural oligopoly, most likely a natural duopoly. There are only two firms in the market, Intel and AMD, and there are no legal barriers to entry which limit the number of firms to two. Because other firms *could* enter the market but do not do so supports the idea that this industry is a natural duopoly. The cost curves and demand curve for this market would be similar to those in Figure 15.1, which shows the situation for a market in which two firms can satisfy the market demand. In this situation if a new firm entered the market it be at a significant cost disadvantage compared to Intel and AMD and would likely incur economic losses. Such a prospect deters entry by new competitors.

3. **Big Joe's Trucking has lower costs than the other 20 small truckers in the market. The market operates like a dominant firm oligopoly and is initially in equilibrium. Then the demand for trucking services increases. Explain the effects of the increase in demand on the price, output, and economic profit of**

a. **Big Joe's.**

    The increase in demand means that the excess demand faced by Big Joe also increases. As a result, Big Joe's marginal revenue increases so Big Joe's raises its price and increases the quantity produced. Big Joe's economic profit increases because marginal revenue

FIGURE **15.1**
Problem 1

exceeds marginal cost on a larger output.

b. **A typical small firm.**

    The increase in demand raises the price and marginal revenue the small firms receive. As a result they increase their output by moving up along their marginal cost curve and, at least in the short run, their economic profit increases.

5. **Soapy Inc. and Suddies Inc. are the only producers of soap powder. They collude and agree to share the market equally. If neither firm cheats on the agreement, each makes $1 million profit. If either firm cheats, the cheat makes a profit of $1.5 million, while the complier incurs a loss of $0.5 million. If both cheat, they break even. Neither firm can monitor the other's actions.**

a. **What are the strategies in this game?**

    Each firm has two strategies: to abide with the agreement or to cheat on the agreement.

b. **Construct the payoff matrix for this game.**

    The payoff matrix has the following cells: Both abide by the agreement: Soapy makes $1 million profit, and Suddies makes $1 million profit; both cheat: Soapy makes $0 profit, and Suddies makes $0 profit; Soapy cheats and Suddies abides by the agreement: Soapy makes $1.5 million profit, and Suddies incurs a $0.5 million loss; Suddies cheats and Soapy abides by the agreement: Suddies makes $1.5 million profit, and Soapy incurs $0.5 million loss. These payoffs are shown, in millions of dollars, in the matrix to the right.

c. **What is the equilibrium of this game if it is played only once?**

    The equilibrium is that both firms cheat and each makes normal profit.

d. **Is the equilibrium a dominant strategy equilibrium? Explain.**

    The equilibrium is a dominant strategy equilibrium because for each firm, regardless of the opponent's choice, the best strategy is to cheat. If Suddies abides by the agreement, the best strategy for Soapy is to cheat because it would make a profit of $1.5 million rather than $1 million. If Suddies cheats, the best strategy for Soapy is to cheat because it would make a profit of $0 (the

competitive outcome) rather than incur a loss of $0.5 million. So Soapy's best strategy is to cheat, no matter what Suddies does. Repeating the exercise for Suddies shows that Suddies's best strategy also is to cheat, no matter what Soapy does.

7. **Oil City**
    In the late '90s, Reliance spent $6 billion and employed 75,000 workers to build a world-class oil refinery at Jamnagar, India. ... Now Reliance is more than doubling the size of the facility, which ... will claim the title of

the world's biggest ... with an output of 1.2 million gallons of gasoline per day, or about 5% of global capacity. ... Reliance plans to aim Jamnagar's spigots westward, at the U.S. and Europe, where it's too expensive and politically difficult to build new refineries. ...The bulked-up Jamnagar will be able to move markets: Singapore traders expect a drop in fuel prices as soon as it's going full tilt.

Fortune, April 28, 2008

a. **Explain this news clip's claims that the global market for gasoline is not perfectly competitive.**

The news clip asserts that there is not free entry into the refining market. In particular, in the United States and Europe political reasons make it extremely costly for new refiners to enter the market. Therefore the few large refiners, such as that at Jamnagar, produce a significant share of the world market.

b. **What barriers to entry might limit competition in this market and give a firm such as Reliance power to influence the market price?**

Political barriers to entry limit entry into the refinery market. The public in the United States and Europe apparently considers refineries as undesirable neighbors because of pollution and, as such, do not want refineries situated nearby. Politicians respond to this pressure by enacting laws and regulations that make new refineries extremely costly to build in the United States and Europe.

9. **U.K. Price Cuts Seen for Apple's New iPhone**
AT&T is planning to sell the new iPhone this summer for around $200. ... The new iPhone would be available later this month in the U.S. through Apple and AT&T. AT&T pricing strategy calls for a $200 subsidy for customers who sign two-year service contracts. ... The lower priced phones in the U.S. ... would help juice the

iPhone's sales volume and give the telcos an attractive weapon to win new subscribers. In the United States, AT&T says it pulls in an average of $95 a month from each iPhone customer, nearly twice the average monthly bill of its conventional cell phone user. AT&T has a revenue sharing agreement with Apple that requires it to give Apple as much as 25% of its iPhone customers' monthly payments. Subsidies are a widespread pricing practice in the United States and overseas. In exchange for a cheaper phone, customers are locked in to a carrier for a year or two. It's a small investment by the telcos for a large return. ... After giving Apple its cut of the revenue, the remaining take for AT&T is between $70 and $75 a month per iPhone user, totaling more than $1,700 over the life of the two-year contract. ...

Fortune, June 2, 2008

a. **How does this arrangement between AT&T and Apple regarding the iPhone affect competition in the market for cell phone service?**

The arrangement lessens competition because a consumer *must* use AT&T's service if he or she wants an iPhone. Essentially Apple and AT&T are tying the sale of the iPhone and AT&T's cellular phone service.

b. **Does this arrangement between AT&T and Apple regarding the iPhone violate U.S. antitrust laws? Explain.**

This arrangement does not violate U.S. antitrust laws. It is a tying sale and tying sales are illegal under the Clayton Act only if they "substantially lessen competition or create monopoly." The arrangement between AT&T and Apple does not substantially lessen competition and does not create monopoly. Because it does not substantially lessen competition nor create monopoly, it is legal.

11. **Oil Trading Probe May Uncover Manipulation**
Amid soaring oil prices ... the government Thursday announced a wide ranging probe into oil price manipulation. ... The CFTC [Commodity Futures Trade Commission] is looking into ... manipulation of the physical oil market ... by commercial players who might literally withhold oil from the market in an attempt to drive prices higher. The CFTC has found evidence of this in the past. ... Haigh [a former economist at CFTC] thinks it's likely CFTC will find evidence of this again given that the agency has been investigating for six months and has now chosen to make it public. But he stressed that a single player acting alone would in all likelihood not have a huge influence on prices. "It's difficult to imagine a price run-up of $90 to $135 being done by one entity," he said.
CNN, May 30, 2008

a. **What type of market does former CFTC economist Haigh imply best describes the U.S. oil market?**

Mr. Haigh implicitly views the oil market as an oligopoly.

b. **Is economist Haigh's comment consistent with the predictions of the kinked demand curve model of oligopoly? Explain.**

The kinked demand curve model of oligopoly suggests that small changes in price are unlikely. Price changes in the oil market, however, have frequently been small, which is inconsistent with the kinked demand curve model. The kinked demand curve model predicts that firms will boost their price if their marginal cost rises by a large amount. Higher marginal costs of extracting oil seem unlikely to be the reason for the oil price run-up from $90 to $135. If the demand for oil increases, the kinked demand curve predicts that the price will rise, but that is not a prediction based on viewing the market as an oligopoly—it is a prediction consistent with many market types such as perfect competition and monopoly. The kinked demand curve model does not predict that any of the suppliers will hold oil off the market to boost the price. The kinked demand curve model also predicts that if one firm raises the price, others do not follow.

c. **Is economist Haigh's comment consistent with the predictions of the dominant firm oligopoly model? Explain.**

The dominant firm model suggests that price will rise if the demand for oil increases, but this prediction is hardly unique to the dominant firm model. The dominant firm model does not necessarily predict that a firm will withhold oil. It does, however, predict that the dominant firm will act as a monopoly and produce less oil than if it were a competitor. But Mr. Haigh suggested that it would take more than one firm withholding oil to have a major impact on the price of oil.

d. **Is economist Haigh's comment consistent with the predictions of any model of oligopoly? Explain.**

Game theory predicts that in a repeated game producers might be able to adopt strategies (such as tit for tat or trigger strategies) that enable the firms to reach the cooperative equilibrium. At the cooperative equilibrium, has each firm has adopted the strategy of decreasing its production (that is, hold oil off the market) to boost the price of oil.

13. **Gadgets For Sale ... or Not**
How come some gadgets, like the iPod, cost the same no matter where you shop?... No, the answer isn't that Apple illegally manages prices. In reality, Steve Jobs and Co. use an accepted, if controversial, tactic, a retail strategy called minimum advertised price, to discourage resellers from discounting. The minimum advertised price, or MAP, is the absolute lowest price

retailers are allowed to advertise a
product for. MAP is usually enforced
through marketing subsidies offered by
a manufacturer to its resellers. If a
retailer keeps prices at or above the
minimum advertised price, then a
manufacturer like Apple will give them
money to help advertise. If a store's
price dips too low, on the other hand,
the manufacturer can withdraw these
advertising subsidies. … Stable prices
are important to the company, because
it's a manufacturer and a retailer (both
online and through its chain of Apple
Stores). If Apple resellers dropped
prices on iPods and iMacs—selling at
or below cost to get customers in the
door, or as a way to cross sell stuff like
software or iPod skins—they could
squeeze the Apple Stores out of their
own markets. There is a downside to
all that stability, however. By limiting
how low sellers can go, MAP keeps
prices artificially high (or at least
higher than they might otherwise be
with unfettered price competition).
              Slate, December 22, 2006

a. **Describe the practice of resale price
maintenance that violates the
Sherman Act.**

Resale price maintenance in which a
manufacturer agrees with a distributor on
the price for which a product will be sold
is illegal under the Sherman Act.

b. **Describe the MAP strategy used by
iPod and explain how it differs from
a resale price maintenance agreement
that would violate the Sherman Act.**

The MAP strategy used by Apple does
not run afoul of the Sherman Act
prohibition of resale price maintenance
because Apple does not agree with the
retailer about the price. Instead Apple
"rewards" those retailers who do not
lower their price below the MAP by
giving those retailers money to help them
pay for advertising the iPod. Apple
"punishes" retailers who set a price lower
than the MAP by *not* giving those

retailers money to help pay for
advertising.

c. **Why might the MAP strategy be
against the consumer interest?**

The MAP might harm consumers
because it keeps the price of iPods higher
than would otherwise be the case if the
retailers competed more vigorously on
price.

d. **Why might the MAP strategy benefit
the consumer?**

The MAP strategy might benefit
consumers if it allows retailers to
maintain a high quality of service with
respect to iPods, such as salespeople who
can adequately explain the different
features of different iPods or a repair
department with extensive knowledge of
iPods.

e. **What is the bottom line on the MAP
strategy: does it benefit the consumer
or only the producer?**

The bottom line of the MAP strategy is
that there is no clear bottom line for
consumers. At times a MAP strategy can
benefit consumers but at other times a
MAP strategy can harm consumers.

15. **An Energy Drink with a Monster of a
Stock**
**The $5.7 billion energy-drink
category, in which Monster holds the
No. 2 position behind industry leader
Red Bull, has slowed down as copycat
brands jostle for shelf space—and the
attention of teen consumers. … Over
the past five years Red Bull's market
share in dollar terms has gone from 91
percent to well under 50 percent …
and much of that loss has been
Monster's gain.**
              Fortune, December 25, 2006

a. **Describe the structure of the energy-
drink market. How has that structure
changed over the past few years?**

The structure of the energy-drink market
has changed from a virtual monopoly
several years ago, when Red Bull had 91
percent of the market, to a more
oligopolistic market, in which Red Bull's

market share is well under 50 percent and Monster's market share has grown significantly.

b. Explain the various difficulties Monster and Red Bull would have if they attempted to collude and charge monopoly prices for energy drinks.

If Red Bull and Monster colluded to decrease production to boost the price, they face two problems. First, each of the two producers has the incentive to increase its production beyond the limited production necessary to boost the price. This incentive can lead to the prisoner's dilemma Nash equilibrium in which both firms cheat on the agreement. Second, even if the two are able to successfully collude, then the many small producers will gain market share and new producers likely will enter the market. These actions make the market more competitive and limit Red Bull's and Monster's ability to collude to keep the price high.

17. Why do Coca-Cola and PepsiCo spend huge amounts on advertising? Do they benefit? Does the consumer benefit? Explain your answer by constructing a game to illustrate the choices Coca-Cola and PepsiCo make.

Coca-Cola and PepsiCo are engaged in an advertising game. In an advertising game, two firms can advertise or not advertise. Advertising is costly but if one firm advertises and the other does not, the one not advertising loses market share and profit while the one advertising gains market share and profit. Both firms would be better if neither advertised but the Nash equilibrium is that both firms advertise. The game to the right is a possibility. Both companies have the choice of whether to advertise or not. Coke's economic profits, in millions of dollars, are in the grey triangles and Pepsi's profits, also in millions of dollars, are in the white triangles. If both

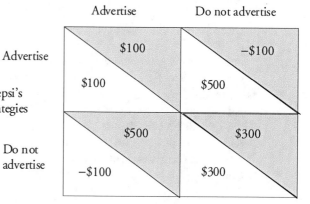

advertise, each makes a profit of $100 million; if one advertises but the other does not, the one advertising makes a profit of $500 million and the one not advertising incurs a loss of $100 million; and if neither advertise, each makes a profit of $300 million. The Nash equilibrium of this game is for each firm to advertise. Consumers benefit if the advertising gives them new information, for example information about a new drink. They also benefit if the advertising allows the firms to increase their production and enjoy economies of scale that allow lower prices. At one time in history, it is likely that consumers benefited from lower prices due to the increased economies of scale as Coca-Cola and PepsiCo drove smaller firms from the market. Today, however, most of the advertising does not convey new information and there are probably not many economies of scale left to exploit. It is likely that consumers are generally harmed by the advertising because the price of the product is higher.

19. **Study *Reading Between the Lines* on pp. 362–363 and then answer the following questions.**

   a. **What are the strategies of Dell and HP in 2000 and in 2006?**

   Dell's strategies in 2000 and 2006 were the same: Dell could either cut prices or it could hold its prices higher. HP's strategies differed in the years. In 2000, HP had the same two strategies as did Dell: Cut prices or hold them higher. But in 2006 HP's strategies were either improve its marketing and design or hold its price higher.

   b. **Why, according to the news article, was Dell having a harder time in 2006 than it had in 2000?**

   According to the news article, Dell was having a harder time in 2006 because its competitor was "no longer the bloated and slow-moving company it was six years ago." In other words, HP responded more rapidly and more effectively to Dell's strategies in 2006, so Dell's profit in 2006 was much lower than in 2000.

   c. **Why wouldn't HP launch its new product and marketing campaign *and* cut its price?**

   If HP improved its marketing and design, HP would boost its costs. If HP cuts its price, HP runs the risk of decreasing its revenue, which would happen if the demand for HP computers is inelastic. So if HP simultaneously improves its marketing and cuts its price, HP might simultaneously increase its costs and decrease its revenues, which would significantly decrease HP's profit.

   d. **What do you think Dell must do to restore its place as market leader?**

   Dell needs to restore speed to its decision-making and become as "nimble" as HP. Dell should also work hard on restoring its reputation for quality and increase its styling.

   e. **How would you describe the global market for PCs? Is it an example of oligopoly or monopolistic competition?**

   The global market for computers is probably monopolistic competitive but with two large, dominating firms. The fact there are so many firms makes it difficult for the large firms to collude, which is similar to the situation in monopolistic competition.

Additional Problems

1. Two firms, Faster and Quicker, are the
    only two producers of sports cars on
    an island that has no contact with the
    outside world. The firms collude and
    agree to share the market equally. If
    neither firm cheats on the agreement,
    each firm makes $3 million economic
    profit. If either firm cheats, the cheater
    can increase its economic profit to $4.5
    million, while the firm that abides by
    the agreement incurs an economic loss
    of $1 million. Neither firm has any
    way of policing the actions of the
    other.

    a. What is the payoff matrix of a game
        that is played just once?
    b. Describe the best strategy for each
        firm in a game that is played once.
    c. What is the equilibrium if the game
        is played once?

Solutions to Additional Problems

1. a. The payoff matrix has the following cells: Both abide by the agreement: Faster makes $3 million profit, and Quicker makes $3 million profit; both cheat: Faster makes $0 profit, and Quicker makes $0 profit; Faster cheats and Quicker abides by the agreement: Faster makes $4.5 million profit, and Quicker incurs a $1 million loss; Quicker cheats and Faster abides by the agreement: Quicker makes $4.5 million profit, and Faster incurs $1 million loss.

b. The best strategy for each firm is to cheat. If Quicker abides by the agreement, the best strategy for Faster is to cheat because it would make a profit of $4.5 million rather than $3 million. If Quicker cheats, the best strategy for Faster is to cheat because it would make a profit of $0 (the competitive outcome) rather than incur a loss of $1 million. So Faster's best strategy is to cheat, no matter what Quicker does. Repeat the exercise for Quicker. Quicker's best strategy is to cheat, no matter what Faster does.

c. The equilibrium is that both firms cheat and each makes normal profit.

Chapter 16 EXTERNALITIES

Answers to the Problems and Applications

1. **Consider each of the following activities or events and say for each one whether it is an externality. If so, say whether it is a positive or negative production or consumption externality.**

   • **Airplanes take off from LaGuardia Airport during the U.S. Open tennis tournament, which is taking place nearby.**

   The planes create a negative production externality from their noise.

   • **A sunset over the Pacific Ocean**

   The sunset creates no externality.

   • **An increase in the number of people who are studying for graduate degrees**

   The increase in the number of people studying for graduate degrees creates a positive consumption externality.

   • **A person wears strong perfume while attending an orchestra concert.**

   The perfume creates a negative consumption externality.

   • **A homeowner plants an attractive garden in front of his house.**

   The homeowner creates a positive consumption externality.

   • **A person drives talking on a cell phone.**

   The driver creates a negative consumption externality.

   • **A bakery bakes bread.**

   Presuming people like the smell of baking bread, the bakery creates a positive production externality.

3. **Back at the pesticide plant and trout farm described in problem 2, suppose that no one owns the lake and that the government introduces a pollution tax.**

   a. **What is the tax per ton of pesticide produced that achieves an efficient outcome?**

   The tax that achieves the efficient outcome is $100 a ton, which is the marginal external cost at the efficient quantity of pesticide.

   b. **Explain the connection between your answer to a and the answer to problem 2a.**

   The pollution tax equals the marginal external cost—it is a Pigovian tax.

5. **The marginal cost of educating a student is $4,000 a year and is constant. Figure 16.1 shows the marginal private benefit curve.**

a. **With no government involvement and if the schools are competitive, how many students are enrolled and what is the tuition?**

In a competitive market, schools maximize profit. They produce the quantity at which the marginal benefit of the last student enrolled equals the marginal cost of educating that student. So if schools are competitive, 30,000 students enroll and tuition is $4,000 a year.

b. **The external benefit from education is $2,000 per student per year and is constant. If the government provides the efficient amount of education, how many students will be accepted and what is the tuition?**

The efficient number of students is 50,000. The efficient number of students is such that the marginal social benefit of education equals the marginal social cost of education. The marginal social benefit equals the marginal private benefit plus the marginal external benefit. The marginal social benefit of 50,000 students is the marginal private benefit of $2,000 plus the marginal external benefit of $2,000, which is $4,000 and is equal to the marginal social cost. Tuition is determined at the intersection of the marginal social benefit and the marginal social cost curves and is $4,000 per student.

7. **The Year in Medicine: Cell Phones**
Think you're safer because you talk on a hands free cell phone while driving? Think again. Using either type of phone while trying to drive a car is roughly equivalent to driving with a blood-alcohol concentration ... high enough to get you arrested ... for driving under the influence. Folks who use hands-free cell phones in simulation trials also exhibited slower

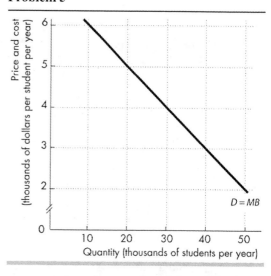

FIGURE **16.1**
Problem 5

reaction times and took longer to hit the brakes than drivers who weren't otherwise distracted. Data from real-life driving tests show that cell-phone use rivals drowsy driving as a major cause of accidents.
Time, **December 4, 2006**

a. **What negative externalities arise from using a cell phone while driving?**

Other drivers, bike riders, and pedestrians are at greater risk of being injured in an accident by a cell phone using driver.

b. **Explain why the market for cell-phone service creates a deadweight loss.**

The market for cell phones creates a deadweight loss because cell phone users do not pay a higher price to use a cell phone when they are driving. As a result they do not pay the total marginal social cost of using a cell phone while driving, Because the equilibrium quantity is determined without considering the external cost, cell phones are overused while driving.

c. **Draw a graph to illustrate how a deadweight loss arises from the use of cell phones.**

Figure 16.3 shows the market for making cell phone calls. The marginal private cost of using a cell phone is less than the marginal social cost because of the marginal external cost, the increased likelihood of someone else being injured. As a result the marginal social cost curve, labeled *MSC*, lies above the marginal private cost and supply curve, labeled *S = MC*. The demand curve is the same as the marginal social benefit curve and is labeled *D= MSB* in the figure. The equilibrium number of cell phone minutes is 500 minutes per month and the efficient quantity is 200 minutes per month. Cell phones are overused in cars. The resulting deadweight loss is equal to the area of the grey triangle in the figure.

d. **Explain how government intervention might improve the efficiency cell phones use.**

The government could impose a tax on cell phone use in a car equal to the marginal external cost (5¢ a call in the figure). In this case the marginal private cost would become the same as the marginal social cost and the efficient outcome would result. Such a tax, however, would be difficult to enforce. Alternatively the government could assign property rights. For instance the government could declare that any driver who causes an accident while using a cell phone is responsible for the injuries and damage created by the accident. In this case the external cost of talking on a cell phone will be internalized by the cell phone user.

9. **My Child, My Choice**
Fully vaccinating all U.S. children born in a given year from birth to adolescence saves 33,000 lives, prevents 14 million infections and saves $10 billion in medical costs. Part of the reason is that vaccinations protect not only the kids that receive

FIGURE **16.3**
Problem 7c

the shots but also those who can't receive them—such as newborns and cancer patients with suppressed immune systems. ... The higher the immunization rate in any population, the less likely that a pathogen will penetrate the group and find a susceptible person inside.
Time, June 2, 2008

a. **Describe the private benefits and external benefits of vaccinations and explain why a private market for vaccinations would produce an inefficient outcome.**

The private benefit is that the child who is vaccinated is protected from an ailment. The external benefit is that others also are protected because the child who is vaccinated cannot spread the disease to others who are not vaccinated. A private market for vaccinations fails to take account of the external benefit. A parent considering vaccinating his or her child looks at only the benefits to the one child and does not include the benefits to other children. As a result a private market will underproduce, that is, fewer than the efficient number of children will be vaccinated.

b. **Draw a graph to illustrate a private market for vaccinations and show the deadweight loss.**

Figure 16.4 shows the private market for vaccinations. The supply curve is the same as the marginal social cost because there is no external cost. This curve is labeled $S_0 = MSC$. The demand curve, however, reflects only the private benefits. So the demand curve, labeled $D = MB$, lies below the marginal social benefit curve, labeled MSB. As a result, the private market provides 2 million vaccinations per year (determined by the intersection of the demand curve and the supply curve) but the efficient number of vaccination is 4 million vaccinations per year (determined by the intersection of the marginal social cost curve and the marginal social benefit curve). The resulting deadweight loss is equal to the area of the grey triangle.

c. **Explain how government intervention could achieve an efficient quantity of vaccinations and draw a graph to illustrate this outcome.**

The government could subsidize vaccinations or give parents vouchers for vaccinations. If the government subsidizes vaccinations the supply curve in Figure 16.4 shifts rightward to become the curve labeled $S_1 = MSC -$ subsidy. With this supply curve the equilibrium quantity of vaccinations, 4 million per year, becomes equal to the efficient quantity. If the government gives parents vouchers for vaccinations the demand curve shifts rightward so that it becomes the same as the MSB curve. In this case, once again the equilibrium number of vaccinations, 4 million per year, becomes the same as the efficient number of vaccinations.

11. **Betty and Anna work at the same office in Philadelphia. They both must attend a meeting in Pittsburgh, so they decide to drive to the meeting together. Betty is a cigarette smoker and her**

FIGURE **16.4**
Problem 9b

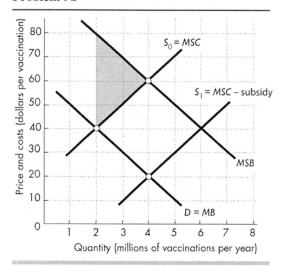

marginal benefit from smoking a package of cigarettes a day is $40. Cigarettes are $6 a pack. Anna dislikes cigarette smoke, and her marginal benefit from a smoke-free environment is $50 a day. What is the outcome if

a. **Betty drives her car with Anna as a passenger**

If Betty drives her car, Betty has the property right to the air in her car. Anna can offer to pay Betty some amount more than $34 and less than $50 to not smoke. Betty will accept and will not smoke on the trip. Betty's net benefit from smoking is $34 (the net benefit equals the marginal benefit, $40, minus the price of the pack, $6) so for any amount greater than $34 she is willing to not smoke. Anna values a smoke-free environment at $50, so Anna is willing to pay any amount less than $50 for a smoke-free environment.

b. **Anna drives her car with Betty as a passenger**

If Anna drives her car, Anna has the property right to the air in her car. Betty will not smoke because she will not offer Anna a high enough price to allow Betty to smoke.

13. **Most nurses in the United States receive their education in community colleges. Mainly because of differences in class size, the cost of educating a nurse is about four times that of an average community college student. Community college budgets depend on the number of students and not on the subjects taught.**

a. **Explain why this funding arrangement might be expected to lead to an inefficiency in the number of nurses trained.**

Educating nurses at community colleges is significantly more expensive than educating other students because the class size of nursing classes is smaller than the class size for other students. But the funding for community colleges pays the community college the same amount for educating a nurse as it does for other students. Community colleges have the incentive to offer fewer nursing classes because the subsidy per nursing class is smaller than the subsidy per other class. As a result, there will be an inefficiently small number of nurses trained.

b. **Suggest a better arrangement and explain how it would work.**

The budget for a community college could differ according to the students' majors, with more costly majors contributing more to the community college's budget.

15. **Fast-Food Trash Be Gone! Some Oakland, Calif. residents are sick and tired of tripping over burger wrappers and soda cans, and the city is ready to do something about it. The Oakland City Council is proposing a tax on fast-food restaurants, gas station markets, liquor stores and convenience stores that serve take-out food or beverages. Councilwoman Jane Brunner, who wrote the legislation, estimates that the tax will raise approximately $237,000 a year, which would cover the cost of a clean-up crew and the initial purchase of trucks and**

equipment to keep the streets and sidewalks surrounding the city's schools litter-free. "Having a clean city affects everything," Brunner said.
CNN, **February 6, 2006**

a. **What is the external cost associated with takeout food and beverages?**

The external cost is the pollution from discarding the wrappers and beverage containers after use.

b. **Draw a graph to illustrate and explain why the market for take-out food and beverages creates a deadweight loss.**

Figure 16.7 shows the market for take-out food and beverages. The marginal social cost, *MSC*, exceeds the marginal private cost, *MC*, because of the marginal external cost of pollution. The *MC* curve, which is also the supply curve, lies below the *MSC* curve. The equilibrium quantity of take-out meals, which is determined at the intersection of the supply curve and the demand curve, is 50 million per month. The efficient quantity of take-out meals, which is determined at the intersection of the marginal social cost curve and the marginal social benefit curve, is 30 million meals per month. The resulting deadweight loss from the overproduction is equal to the area of the

FIGURE **16.7**
Problem 15b

grey triangle illustrated in the figure. This deadweight loss occurs because the consumers of take-out meals do not pay the full marginal social cost of their take-out meals. As a result the quantity of take-out meals consumed exceeds the efficient quantity.

c. Draw a graph to illustrate and explain how Oakland's policy might improve efficiency.

Presuming the tax equals the marginal external cost, which in Figure 16.7 is $3 per meal, in Figure 16.7 the tax shifts the $S = MC$ curve so that it is the same as the MSC curve. In this (optimal) case, the equilibrium quantity becomes the same as the efficient quantity and there is no deadweight loss.

17. Clean Green Flying Machine? … Aviation generates 2–3 percent of man-made emissions of carbon dioxide, the main greenhouse gas. … Most environmentalists think that the only solution is to make air travel more expensive, say through hefty fuel taxes. … But the airline industry [says it] produces far more benefits than ills—[contributing] 8 percent to global [output] by transporting tourists, business travelers, and cargo around the globe.

Economist.com, August 14, 2007

a. What are the externalities created by the airline industry?

Flying has an external cost, the emission of carbon dioxide. Because this cost is external to the airlines, it is not reflected in the price of an airline ticket.

b. Why will hefty fuel taxes encourage airlines to operate in the social interest?

Hefty fuel taxes that are equal to the marginal external cost of airline travel mean that the airlines face *all* the social costs they create. In this case, the tax, which decreases the supply of airline trips, leads to a rise in the price of an airline ticket and a decrease the quantity of trips. If the tax is set equal to the

marginal external cost, then the number of trips will equal the efficient quantity and so no deadweight loss results. Additionally, the tax also gives the airlines incentive to decrease their emissions of carbon dioxide to decrease the amount of the tax they pay.

19. Use the link on MyEconLab (Textbook Resources, Chapter 16) and read the article about wind farms.

a. What types of externalities arise in the production of electricity using wind technologies?

The externalities that arise directly from the wind farm are generally negative. The opponents of the wind technologies point to visual pollution from the towers that will hurt tourism; interference with the marine environment; and the death of untold numbers of birds that fly into the blades. Proponents of the wind farm assert that it will decrease externalities elsewhere by decreasing greenhouse gasses and fossil fuel emissions.

b. Comparing the externalities from wind technologies with those from burning coal and oil, which are more costly?

The externalities from burning coal and oil include air pollution, acid rain, the destruction of the ozone layer, and possibly global warming. The externalities from burning oil and coal are more widespread and affect more people than the externalities from wind powered turbines.

c. How do you think the external costs of using wind technologies should be dealt with? Compare the alternative range of solutions considered in this chapter.

The government could impose a tax equal to the external cost. A problem with this approach is the difficulty in determining the proper amount of tax. Marketable permits might be issued, but the permits would need to be in units of "visual pollution," which seems a difficult concept to measure. Finally, the government could assign property rights. It's unlikely the government can assign property rights to the birds that are killed, but the main externality opponents point to is the visual pollution. In this instance, the government could either give the property right to the view to the landowners upon which the towers will be built or to landowners who own

properties that will gaze upon the towers. In either case, the Coase solution should allow for an efficient outcome.

Chapter 17

PUBLIC GOODS AND COMMON RESOURCES

Answers to the Problems and Applications

1. **Classify each of the following items as excludable, nonexcludable, rival, nonrival, a public good, a private good, or a common resource.**
    - **Gettysburg National Military Park**
      Gettysburg National Military Park is nonexcludable and nonrival. It is a public good.
    - **A Big Mac**
      A Big Mac is excludable and rival. It is a private good.
    - **Brooklyn Bridge**
      The Brooklyn Bridge is nonexcludable (because there is no toll for using it) and rival (especially when it is crowded). It is a common resource.
    - **The Stature of Liberty**
      Viewing the Statue of Liberty from a distance is nonexcludable and nonrival, so it is a public good. Viewing the Stature of Liberty from Ellis Island is excludable because there is an entry fee and nonrival. It is a natural monopoly.
    - **Air**
      Air is nonexcludable and rival. (If someone uses air, for instance, pollutes it, then no one else can use the same air.) It is a common resource.
    - **Police protection**
      Police protection is nonexcludable and rival. It is a common resource.
    - **Sidewalks**
      Sidewalks are nonexcludable and rival (when they are crowded). They are a common resource.
    - **U.S. Postal Service**
      U.S. Postal system is rival (a carrier cannot deliver mail to my house and your house simultaneously) and excludable (a user must buy a stamp). It is a private good.
    - **FedEx courier service**
      FedEx is rival (a carrier cannot deliver a package to my house and your house

simultaneously) and excludable (a user must pay). It is a private good.
    - **The MyEconLab Web site**
      The MyEconLab web site is excludable and nonrival. It is a natural monopoly.

3. **The figure provides information about a sewage disposal system that a city of 1 million people is considering installing.**

    a. **What is the capacity that achieves an efficient outcome?**
        The capacity that achieves an efficient outcome is 2.5 million gallons a day, which is the quantity at which marginal social benefit equals marginal social cost.

    b. **How much will each person have to pay in taxes to pay for the efficient capacity level?**
        The total cost of the sewage system is the sum of the marginal costs of each additional gallon of capacity, that is, the total cost is the area under the marginal cost curve up to 2.5 million gallons. This amount equals ½ × 2.5 million gallons × $50 per gallon, which equals $62.5 million. The population is 1 million, so each person must pay $62.50.

FIGURE **17.1**
Problem 3

c. **What is the political equilibrium if voters are well informed?**

The political equilibrium will be a sewage system that has a capacity of 2.5 million gallons. If voters are well informed, the political equilibrium will be the efficient capacity.

d. **What is the political equilibrium if voters are rationally ignorant and bureaucrats achieve the highest attainable budget?**

Bureaucrats will provide a capacity of 5 million gallons. With voters rationally ignorant, bureaucrats will maximize their budget. That is, they will increase the capacity until net benefit is zero. The total benefit is the area under the marginal social benefit curve and above the value of the marginal social benefit, so for a capacity of 5 million gallons the total benefit is $250 million. The total cost of a capacity of 5 million gallons is $250 million. So the net benefit from a capacity of 5 million gallons is zero.

5. **'Free Riders' Must Be Part of Health Debate**

[Barack] Obama insists that "the reason people don't have health insurance isn't because they don't want it, it's because they can't afford it…" A free rider is someone who can afford a health insurance policy but won't buy any. Obama wants to give Americans the freedom to not buy insurance but the right to get government-subsidized coverage when they get sick. The inevitable result is that a lot of healthy people will avoid contributing to the insurance pool. … Why should they buy insurance at any price if they can glom on to a government program should disaster strike? There are 47 million uninsured people in the United States, and 16 percent have a family income above $75,000. Another 15 percent make between $50,000 and $75,000. … About 16 percent of the patients who received "free" medical care in 2004 came from families
making at least four times the federal poverty level. … They racked up $5.8 billion in uncompensated care, which others had to pay for.
Los Angeles Times, **March 4, 2008**

a. **Explain why government-subsidized coverage can create a free rider problem in the health care market.**

Government provided health care is nonexcludable, that is, people can use it even if they do not pay for it. The people who, in the absence of government provided health care, would buy private market health insurance are free riding. Rather than paying for their health insurance, they will use the "free" government provided coverage if it becomes necessary.

b. **Explain the evidence this article presents to contradict the argument that "the reason people don't have health insurance isn't because they don't want it, it's because they can't afford it."**

The data in the news clip show that many people who apparently could afford private market health care insurance choose not to purchase it. For instance, 31 percent of families without private health care insurance have incomes greater than $50,000.

7. **A Bridge Too Far Gone**

The gas taxes that paid for much of America's post-war freeway system have been eaten away by inflation and higher fuel efficiency. The federal tax has not been raised since 1993. California's 18-cent tax has remained unchanged since 1994. Motorists now pay about one-third in gas taxes to drive a mile as they did in the early 1960s. Yet raising such taxes is politically tricky. This would matter less if private cash was flooding into infrastructure, or if new ways were being found to control demand. Neither is happening. … A new toll road in Texas, which is being built by a Spanish company, raised howls of outrage.
The Economist, **August 9, 2007**

a. **Why is it "politically tricky" to raise gas taxes to finance infrastructure?**

It is politically tricky to raise gas taxes because most people believe that they already pay enough in taxes and gas taxes are highly visible when they are raised; that is, when gas taxes are raised, the price of gasoline, which includes the tax, immediately jumps higher. Politicians worry that if they are seen raising gas taxes, they will not be reelected in the next election.

b. **What in this news clip points to a distinction between public *production* of a public good and public *provision*. Give examples of three public goods that are *produced* by private firms but *provided* by government and paid for with taxes.**

The difference between private provision of a public good and public provision hinges around who—the private sector or the public sector—actually produces the public good. For instance, many local governments contract with private agencies to provide street sweeping services, a public good. For another example, some states have contracted with private companies for the day-to-day running of parks. Finally, some states, such as Texas, have allowed private firms to produce toll roads.

9. **The table provides information about a mosquito control program.**

a. **What quantity of spraying would a private mosquito control program provide?**

Mosquito spraying is a public good and subject to free riding. As a result, a private mosquito would supply no spraying.

Quantity sprayed (square miles per day)	Marginal social cost	Marginal social benefit
	(dollars per day)	
0	0	0
1	1,000	5,000
2	2,000	4,000
3	3,000	3,000
4	4,000	2,000
5	5,000	1,000

b. **What is the efficient quantity of spraying?**

> The efficient quantity of spraying is 3 square miles a day, which is the quantity at which marginal social cost equals marginal social benefit.

c. **Two political parties, the Conservers and the Eradicators, fight an election in which the only issue is the quantity of spraying to undertake. The Conservers want no spraying and the Eradicators want to spray 5 square miles per day. The voters are well-informed about the benefits and costs of mosquito control programs. What is the outcome of the election?**

> The outcome will be that each party eventually proposes spraying 3 square miles per day and the election outcome will be the efficient quantity of spraying.

d. **Draw a graph to illustrate the outcome of the election.**

> Figure 17.3 shows the marginal social benefit curve, labeled *MSB*, and the marginal social cost curve, labeled *MSC*. When voters are well informed about mosquito control programs, the outcome will be the efficient outcome, 3 square miles sprayed per day, as illustrated in the figure.

FIGURE **17.3**

Problem 9d

11. An oil reserve runs under plots of land owned by seven people. Each person has the right to sink a well on her or his land and take oil from the reserve. The amount of oil that is produced depends on the number of wells sunk and is shown in the table. The marginal private cost of a well is the equivalent of 4 gallons a day.

a. What is the marginal private benefit at each quantity of wells?

The table below shows the marginal private benefit at each quantity of wells as *MB*. The marginal private benefit to the owners equals the total oil output divided by the number of wells.

b. What are the equilibrium number of wells and quantity of oil produced?

The equilibrium number of wells is 10 wells. The equilibrium quantity is determined where marginal private benefit equals marginal private cost. The total quantity of oil pumped is 40 gallons a day.

c. What is the marginal social benefit at each quantity of wells?

The table shows the marginal social benefit at each quantity of wells. The marginal social benefit is the change in the total oil output divided by the change in the number of wells.

d. What are the efficient number of wells and quantity of oil to produce?

The efficient number of wells is 5. The efficient quantity is the quantity at which the marginal social benefit equals marginal cost. The marginal social benefit of 5 wells is 4 gallons of oil a day, which equals the marginal cost of 4 gallons of oil a day. With 5 wells the total amount of oil pumped is 26 gallons per day.

e. If the common reserve were owned by only one person, how many wells would be sunk and how much oil would be produced?

If one person owned the common reserve, the marginal benefit equals the marginal social benefit since the single owner reaps all the benefits from the reserve. In this case, the efficient number

of wells, 5 wells, would be drilled, and total oil output would be a total output of 26 gallons per day.

Number of oil wells	Output (gallons per day)
0	0
2	12
4	22
6	30
8	36
10	40
12	42
14	42

Number of oil wells	Output (gallons per day)	MB (gallons per well)	MSB (gallons per well)
0	0	–	
			6.0
2	12	6.0	
			5.0
4	22	5.5	
			4.0
6	30	5.0	
			3.0
8	36	4.5	
			2.0
10	40	4.0	
			1.0
12	42	3.5	
			0.0
14	42	3.0	

f. How much would someone offer the seven owners to rent the rights to all the oil in the common reserve? (Use gallons of oil as the unit.)

If one person owned the common reserve, that person would drill 5 wells at a marginal cost of 4 gallons a day for each well. The total cost is 20 gallons of oil a day. The person pumps 26 gallons of oil a day, so the person is willing to offer up to a total of 26 gallons a day minus the cost of 20 gallons a day, which is 6 gallons a day for use of the common reserve.

13. **Who's Hiding Under Our Umbrella?** Students of the Cold War learn that, to deter possible Soviet aggression, the United States placed a "strategic umbrella" over NATO Europe and Japan, declaring it would fight if their independence was threatened by the Soviet Union. ... European and Japanese allies have been taking economic advantage of the fact that the United States was providing for most of their own national security. Under President Ronald Reagan, approximately 6 percent of the GDP of the United States was spent on defense, whereas the Europeans tended to spend only 2 to 3 percent and the Japanese a miserly 1 percent, although all faced a common enemy. Thus the American taxpayer bore a disproportionate burden for the overall defense spending, whereas those sheltering under its umbrella spent more on social or consumer goods, or saved while the U.S. went further into debt. ... Today, the United States, like Rome and Britain in their time, is the provider of international public goods. ...

International Herald Tribune,
January 30, 2008

a. **Explain the free-rider problem described in this news clip.**

The free rider problem is that European nations and Japan relied on the United States to provide defense services against aggression from the Soviet Union. The United States paid about 6 percent of its total output on defense while its European and Japanese allies paid a much smaller percentage.

b. **Does the free-rider problem in international defense mean that the world has too little defense against aggression?**

The public goods aspect of defense and free riding means that the world has too little defense against aggression.

c. **How do nations try to overcome the free-rider problem among nations?**

Nations can sign treaties that either obligate them to cut their weapons systems or jointly develop new weapon systems. By cutting weapons, less additional defense spending is required, which limits the total amount of free riding that occurs. By jointly developing new weapon systems the nations eliminate free riding because all the nations who signed the treaty help pay for the weapons system.

15. **Where the Tuna Roam** ... to the first settlers, the Great Plains posed the same problem as the oceans today: It was a vast, open area where there seemed to be no way to protect animals against relentless human predators. ... But animals thrived in the West once the settlers divvied up the land and ingeniously devised new ways to protect their livestock. ... Today the ocean is still pretty much an open range, and the fish are suffering the consequences. ... fishermen have a personal incentive to make as much as they can this year, even if they're destroying their own profession in the process. They figure any fish they don't take for themselves will just be taken by someone else. ...
The New York Times, November 4, 2006

a. **What are the similarities between the problems faced by the earliest settlers in the West and today's fishers?**

The early settlers in the West faced animals that roamed across land. No one owned the land and no one owned the animals; that is, the property rights to the land and animals were not established. Today's fishers face animals—fish—that roam across the sea. No one owns the sea and no one owns the fish; that is, property rights to the sea and the fish have not been established.

b. **Can the tragedy of the commons in the oceans be eliminated in the same manner used by the early settlers on the plains?**

The tragedy of the commons was eliminated in the West when property rights were granted to the land and methods were developed to restrict animals to certain areas so that they could be "owned." Once the property rights to the land and the animals were established, then the marginal private benefit became the same as the marginal social benefit and the tragedy of the commons was averted. For this method to work in the sea, however, it must be possible to create property rights to areas of the sea *and* restrict the fish to certain areas so that can be "owned." It is not clear how this can be done.

c. **How can ITQs change the short-term outlook of fishers to a long-term outlook?**

ITQs that are enforced can change fishers' incentives by limiting the amount of fish that can be caught. In this case once the fisher hits the ITQ limit, the fisher cannot continue to fish. But an ITQ means that the fisher can harvest the specified quantity of fish indefinitely, that is, day after day. As a result there is no need for the fisher to rapidly and intensively fish because the fisher knows that fish not caught today will still be available to be caught tomorrow.

Additional Problems

1. The table shows the marginal benefit and marginal cost of driving a private car into central London. How many cars a day enter London? In 2004, the city introduced a congestion charge of £5 per car per day. How many cars a day entered London after the congestion charge was levied? What was the reduction in congestion and how much revenue did the congestion charge raise for the city?

Number of cars	Marginal benefit (pounds per car)	Marginal cost (pounds per car)
10,000	17	2
30,000	14	4
60,000	11	6
90,000	8	8
120,000	5	10

2. The table shows the value of bluefin tuna caught in the Southern Ocean by fishing boats from Australia, New Zealand, and Argentina. The marginal cost of operating a fishing boat is $60,000 a month.
   a. With no regulation of bluefin tuna fishing, what is the equilibrium number of boats and the value of tuna caught? Is there overfishing or not?
   b. What the efficient number of boats and value of the bluefin tuna catch?
   c. If the governments agreed to issue ITQs to fishing boats to limit the bluefin tuna catch to the efficient quantity, what would be the price of an ITQ?

Number of fishing boats	Value of bluefin tuna caught (thousands of dollars per month)
0	0
10	1,200
20	2,000
30	2,400
40	2,400
50	2,000
60	1,200

   'Once in a Lifetime'
   Mr. Bloomberg's plan [was] about making New York City more competitive by reducing travel time and improving public transportation, thanks to the income generated by the congestion charge. ... Car drivers would ... pay $4 and lorry [truck] drivers $21.
   BBC News, New York, July 24, 2007

3. With the congestion charge and better public transport, are New York City streets public goods or private goods? Explain your answer.

4. If the congestion charge reduced travel times, what benefits would the people who live or work in New York receive.

5. Why might residents vote against the congestion charge?

Solutions to Additional Problems

1. Before the congestion charge, 90,000 cars per day entered central London because that is the quantity at which the marginal benefit to the driver equals the marginal cost to the driver. (Both equal £8.) After the congestion charge, the marginal cost to the driver increased by £5, the amount of the charge. So after the congestion charge, 60,000 cars per day entered central London because that is the quantity at which the marginal benefit to the driver equals the marginal cost to the driver. (Both now equal £11.) The congestion was reduced by 30,000 cars per day. The city gains £5 per car entering central London. 60,000 cars now enter central London, so the city gains revenue of £5 per car × 60,000 cars, which is £300,000 per day.

2. a. The table, which shows the marginal private benefit, MB, and the marginal social benefit, MSB, is helpful in answering this question. The equilibrium occurs where the marginal private benefit equals the marginal cost of operating a fishing boat. The marginal cost of operating a fishing boat is $60,000. The marginal private benefit equals $60,000 when the number of fishing boats is 40. With this number of boats, the value of bluefin tuna caught is $2,400,000 a month. The equilibrium is an overfishing equilibrium. If the number of boats decreases to 30, the total catch remains the same but the total cost of catching the fish decrease.

   b. The efficient number of boats occurs where the marginal social benefit equals the marginal social cost. The marginal social cost is the cost of operating a boat, which is $60,000 a month. The marginal social benefit of 20 boats is $60,000, so the efficient number of boats to operate is 20. When 20 boats are operated, the catch is $2,000,000 of bluefin tuna.

   c. The price of an ITQ equals the difference between the marginal private benefit at the efficient number of boats and the marginal cost of operating a boat. The marginal

private benefit at the efficient number of boats, 20 boats, is $100,000 a month. The marginal cost of operating a boat is $60,000 per month. So the price of an ITQ is $100,000 a month − $60,000 a month, which is $40,000 a month.

3. When car drivers must pay a congestion fee, the city streets are no longer a public good because they become excludable: A driver pays or the driver does not get to use the city street. If the streets are crowded, as is likely the case, then space on the streets is rival. In this case the public streets would be effectively a private good.

4. The benefits will be three-fold: First, there will be reduced travel time. Second, to the extent that transportation by automobile creates pollution, there will be less pollution. Third, the funds raised by the congestion fee

Number of fishing boats	Value of bluefin tuna caught (thousands of dollars per month)	MB (thousands of dollars per month)	MSB (thousands of dollars per month)
0	0	—	
			120
10	1,200	120	
			80
20	2,000	100	
			40
30	2,400	80	
			0
40	2,400	60	
			−40
50	2,000	40	
			−80
60	1,200	20	

can be used to provide some other good or service the people value, such as improved public transportation.

5. Residents who believe they travel to downtown New York City more often than average might well believe that the cost to them exceeds the benefit to them. Other residents might vote against the congestion

charge because they believe it unfair insofar as
it might drive poor residents from their cars

to public transportation, which could be
perceived as inferior to private automobiles.

Chapter 18

MARKETS FOR FACTORS OF PRODUCTION

Answers to the Problems and Applications

1. Wanda owns a fish shop. She employs students to sort and pack the fish. Students can pack the amounts of fish in an hour shown in the table. The fish market is competitive and Wanda can sell her fish for 50¢ a pound. The market for packers is competitive and their market wage rate is $7.50 an hour.

   a. Calculate the marginal product of the students and draw the marginal product curve.

   The marginal product of labor is the increase in total product that results from hiring one additional student. For example, if Wanda increases the number of students hired from 4 to 5, total product (the quantity of fish packed) increases from 120 to 145 pounds. The marginal product of increasing the number of students from 4 to 5 is 25 pounds of fish. To plot the marginal product curve the marginal product is plotted at the mid-point. Figure 18.1 shows the marginal product when the number of students increases from 4 to 5 as well as the other marginal products.

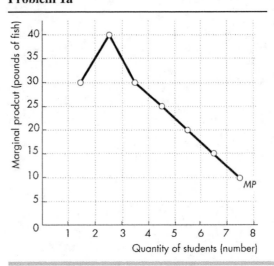

FIGURE **18.1**
Problem 1a

Number of students	Quantity of fish (pounds)
1	20
2	50
3	90
4	120
5	145
6	165
7	180
8	190

b. Calculate the value of marginal product of labor and draw the value of marginal product curve.

The value of marginal product of labor is the increase in total revenue that results from hiring one additional student. For example, if Wanda hires 4 students, they produce 120 pounds of fish. Wanda sells the fish for 50¢ a pound, so total revenue is $60. If Wanda increases the number of students hired from 4 to 5, total product increases to 145 pounds and total revenue increases to $72.50. The value of marginal product when the number of students increases from 4 to 5 is $12.50 ($72.50 minus $60). Alternatively, the value of marginal product equals marginal product multiplied by price. The value of marginal product when the number of students increases from 4 to 5 is $12.50, which is the marginal product of 25 pounds of fish multiplied by the price of 50¢ a pound. Figure 18.2 (above) shows the value of marginal product when the number of students increases from 4 to 5 as well as the other value of marginal products.

c. Find Wanda's demand for labor curve.

The demand for labor curve is the same as the value of marginal product curve

d. How many students does Wanda employ?

Wanda hires the number of students that makes the value of marginal product equal to the wage rate of $7.50 an hour. When Wanda increases the number of students from 6 to 7, marginal product is 15 pounds of fish an hour, which Wanda sells for 50¢ a pound. The value of marginal product is $7.50—the same as the wage rate. The value of marginal product is plotted at the mid-point between 6 and 7 students a day, so Wanda hires 6.5 students a day.

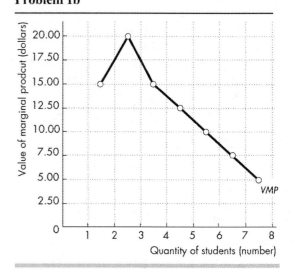

FIGURE **18.2**
Problem 1b

3. Back at Wanda's fish shop described in problem 1, packers' wages increase to $10 an hour but the price of fish remains at 50¢ a pound.

a. What happens to the value of marginal product of labor?

The value of marginal product does not change. For example, if Wanda hires 5.5 students an hour, the marginal product is 20 pounds of fish, which she sells at 50¢ a pound. So, just as before, the value of marginal product remains at $10.00.

b. What happens to Wanda's demand for labor curve?

Wanda's demand for labor remains the same because the value of marginal product has not changed.

c. How many students does Wanda employ?

Wanda hires fewer students. At the wage rate of $10 an hour, Wanda hires the number of students that makes the value of marginal product equal to $10 an hour. Wanda now hires 5.5 students an hour—down from 6.5 students an hour. The marginal product of 5.5 students is

---

---

20 pounds of fish an hour, and Wanda sells this fish for 50¢ a pound. The value of marginal product is $10 an hour.

5. Which of the following items are nonrenewable natural resources, which are renewable natural resources, and which are not natural resources? Explain your answers.

a. Trump Tower

Trump Tower is not a natural resource because it is made by people. It is a piece of capital.

b. Lake Michigan

Lake Michigan is a renewable natural resource. It is renewable because Lake Michigan can continue to be used day after day.

c. Coal in a West Virginia coal mine

Coal is a nonrenewable natural resource. It is nonrenewable because once the lump of coal is used, it cannot be used again.

d. The Internet

The Internet is not a natural resource because it is made by people. It is a piece of capital.

e. Yosemite National Park

Yosemite National Park is a renewable natural resource. It is renewable because the park can continue to be used day after day.

f. Power generated by wind turbines

The wind generating the power is a renewable natural resource because it recurs day after day. The turbine generating the power is a piece of capital equipment, not a natural resource, because it is made by people.

7. Keshia operates a bookkeeping service. She is considering buying or leasing some new laptop computers. The purchase price of a laptop is $1,500 and after three years it is worthless. The annual lease rate is $550 per laptop. The value of marginal product of one laptop is $700 a year. The value of marginal product of a second laptop is $625 a year. The value of marginal product of a third laptop is $575 a year. And the value of marginal product of a fourth laptop is $500 a year.

a. How many laptops will Keshia lease or buy?

Keshia will lease or buy 3 laptops. The fourth laptop's value of marginal product is less than the annual lease rate, so Keisha will never lease the fourth laptop. And the present value of the value of marginal products for the fourth laptop is always less than $1,500 regardless of the interest rate. (The value of marginal products sum to $1,500 when not discounted, so when discounted they must sum to less than $1,500.) Keisha will never rent nor buy the fourth laptop because it is not profitable to do so. For each year the value of marginal product for the third laptop always exceeds the annual lease rate, so leasing that laptop will be profitable. Therefore Keisha will always be willing to lease the third laptop.

b. If the interest rate is 4 percent a year, will Keshia lease or buy her laptops?

Keshia compares the present value of leasing the laptops to the price of buying the laptops. When the interest rate is 4 percent, the present value of leasing the laptops is

$$\frac{\$550}{1.04} + \frac{\$550}{(1.04)^2} + \frac{\$550}{(1.04)^3} = \$1,526.$$

The present value of leasing the laptops exceeds the price of buying the laptops, so Keisha buys the laptops.

c. If the interest rate is 6 percent a year, will Keshia lease or buy her laptops?

Keshia again compares the present value of leasing the laptops to the price of buying the laptops. When the interest rate is 6 percent, the present value of leasing the laptops is

$$\frac{\$550}{1.06} + \frac{\$550}{(1.06)^2} + \frac{\$550}{(1.06)^3} = \$1,470.$$

The present value of leasing the laptops is less than the price of buying the laptops, so Keisha leases the laptops.

---

20 pounds of fish an hour, and Wanda sells this fish for 50¢ a pound. The value of marginal product is $10 an hour.

5. Which of the following items are nonrenewable natural resources, which are renewable natural resources, and which are not natural resources? Explain your answers.

a. Trump Tower

Trump Tower is not a natural resource because it is made by people. It is a piece of capital.

b. Lake Michigan

Lake Michigan is a renewable natural resource. It is renewable because Lake Michigan can continue to be used day after day.

c. Coal in a West Virginia coal mine

Coal is a nonrenewable natural resource. It is nonrenewable because once the lump of coal is used, it cannot be used again.

d. The Internet

The Internet is not a natural resource because it is made by people. It is a piece of capital.

e. Yosemite National Park

Yosemite National Park is a renewable natural resource. It is renewable because the park can continue to be used day after day.

f. Power generated by wind turbines

The wind generating the power is a renewable natural resource because it recurs day after day. The turbine generating the power is a piece of capital equipment, not a natural resource, because it is made by people.

7. Keshia operates a bookkeeping service. She is considering buying or leasing some new laptop computers. The purchase price of a laptop is $1,500 and after three years it is worthless. The annual lease rate is $550 per laptop. The value of marginal product of one laptop is $700 a year. The value of marginal product of a second laptop is $625 a year. The value of marginal product of a third laptop is $575 a year. And the value of marginal product of a fourth laptop is $500 a year.

a. How many laptops will Keshia lease or buy?

Keshia will lease or buy 3 laptops. The fourth laptop's value of marginal product is less than the annual lease rate, so Keisha will never lease the fourth laptop. And the present value of the value of marginal products for the fourth laptop is always less than $1,500 regardless of the interest rate. (The value of marginal products sum to $1,500 when not discounted, so when discounted they must sum to less than $1,500.) Keisha will never rent nor buy the fourth laptop because it is not profitable to do so. For each year the value of marginal product for the third laptop always exceeds the annual lease rate, so leasing that laptop will be profitable. Therefore Keisha will always be willing to lease the third laptop.

b. If the interest rate is 4 percent a year, will Keshia lease or buy her laptops?

Keshia compares the present value of leasing the laptops to the price of buying the laptops. When the interest rate is 4 percent, the present value of leasing the laptops is

$$\frac{\$550}{1.04} + \frac{\$550}{(1.04)^2} + \frac{\$550}{(1.04)^3} = \$1,526.$$

The present value of leasing the laptops exceeds the price of buying the laptops, so Keisha buys the laptops.

c. If the interest rate is 6 percent a year, will Keshia lease or buy her laptops?

Keshia again compares the present value of leasing the laptops to the price of buying the laptops. When the interest rate is 6 percent, the present value of leasing the laptops is

$$\frac{\$550}{1.06} + \frac{\$550}{(1.06)^2} + \frac{\$550}{(1.06)^3} = \$1,470.$$

The present value of leasing the laptops is less than the price of buying the laptops, so Keisha leases the laptops.

9. **Fixing Farming**
    Backyard vegetable gardens are fine. So are organics, slow food and locavores—people who eat produce grown nearby. But solutions to the global food crisis will come from big business, genetically engineered crops and large-scale farms. ... The problem they face has made headlines lately. Demand for farm products—food, fiber and fuel—will keep growing, as the population grows and as hundreds of millions of people move into the middle class and consume more meat and dairy. Global per capita meat consumption has increased by 60 percent in the last 40 years—that's 60 percent per person. Meanwhile, the supply of farmland is limited. Agriculture already uses 55 percent of the habitable land on the planet. ... The answer is for farmers to become more productive—generating more output from fewer inputs.

    Fortune, May 22, 2008

    a. **Is farmland a renewable or nonrenewable resource?**
        Farmland is a renewable resource.

    b. **Explain how the growing demand for farm products will affect the market for land.**
        The growing demand for farm products will raise the price of food products. The higher price of food products increases the value of marginal product of land, which means the demand for land increases. The price of land rises.

    c. **Draw a graph to illustrate how the growing demand for farm products will affect the market for land.**
        Figure 18.6 shows the rental market for land. The demand curve shifts rightward from D_0 to D_1. The supply is perfectly inelastic and does not change. The price of land rises, in Figure 18.6 from $150 per acre to $250 per acre. The quantity of land does not change.

    d. **How might farmers meet the growing demand for farm products without**

    having to use a greater quantity of farmland?
    The supply of farm products can increase if technology advances, say advances in biotechnology that create more productive crops. The supply of farm products can also increase if farmers use other inputs, such as additional capital equipment.

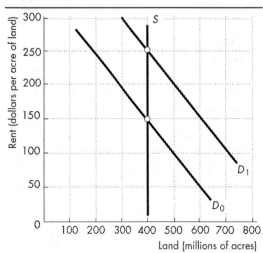

FIGURE **18.6**
Problem 9c

---

11. Kaiser's Ice Cream Parlor hires workers to produce smoothies. The market for smoothies is perfectly competitive, and the price of a smoothie is $4. The labor market is competitive, and the wage rate is $40 a day. The table shows the workers' total product schedule.

Number of workers	Quantity produced (smoothies per day)
1	7
2	21
3	33
4	43
5	51
6	55

a. **Calculate the marginal product of hiring the fourth worker and the value of the marginal product of the fourth worker.**

By hiring the 4th worker the number of smoothies increases by 10 smoothies (43 smoothies – 33 smoothies). So the marginal product of this worker is 10 smoothies. The value of marginal product of the 4th worker equals the price of a smoothie, $4, multiplied by the worker's marginal product, 10 smoothies, so the value of marginal product is $40.

b. **How many workers will Kaiser's hire to maximize its profit and how many smoothies a day will Kaiser's produce?**

Kaiser's will hire 3.5 workers. The value of marginal product of 3.5 workers is $40 which equals the wage rate.

c. **If the price rises to $5 a smoothie, how many workers will Kaiser's hire?**

If the price rises to $5 a smoothie, Kaiser's will hire 4.5 workers. The value of marginal product of 4.5 workers is the marginal product, 8 smoothies, multiplied by the price, $5 a smoothie, or $40, which equals the wage rate.

13. Detroit Oil Refinery Expansion Approved
Marathon Oil Saturday started work on a $1.9 billion expansion of its gasoline refinery in Detroit. ... Marathon said the company will employ 800 construction workers and add 135 permanent jobs to the existing 480 workers at the refinery.
United Press International, June 21, 2008

a. **Explain how rising gasoline prices influence the market for refinery labor.**

The demand for labor curve is the value of marginal product curve. The value of marginal product is calculated as marginal product of labor multiplied by price of the output, gasoline. When the price of gasoline rises, the value of marginal product of oil refinery workers increases and demand increase.

b. **Draw a graph to illustrate the effects of rising gasoline prices on the market for refinery labor.**

Figure 18.7 shows the impact in the market for refinery labor. The demand for refinery labor increases so the demand for labor curve shifts rightward from D_0 to D_1. The supply does not change. The wage rate rises from $30 per hour to $40 per hour and the quantity of refinery workers employed increases from 400,000 to 500,000.

FIGURE **18.7**
Problem 13b

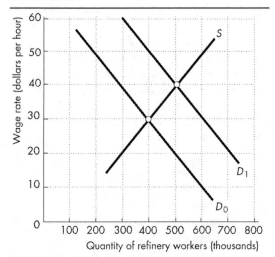

c. **How do rising gasoline prices affect a firm's demand for refineries and how does the implicit rental rate of refineries change?**

In response to the higher price of gasoline, refiners increase their demand for refineries. The implicit rental rate for refineries rises.

15. **The New War Over Wal-Mart**
Today, Wal-Mart employs more people—1.7 million—than any other private employer, and by this measure is not just the largest company in the world but the largest company in the history of the world. With size comes power. ... The Wal-Mart effect drives down consumer prices ... and, some argue, it also drives down wages and benefits. ... One of the major forces opposing Wal-Mart is organized labor. The United Food and Commercial Workers International Union has long wanted to organize Wal-Mart's stores. Last year, it succeeded at a Canadian Wal-Mart, which the company immediately shut down. ... What the war against Wal-Mart tends to gloss over is that it's not at all clear that the company behaves any worse than its competitors. When it comes to payroll and benefits, Wal-Mart's median hourly wage pretty much tracks the national median wage for general merchandise retail jobs. And its health-care benefits are a good deal more accessible ... than those of many of its competitors.

The Atlantic, **June 2006**

a. **Assuming that Wal-Mart has market power in a labor market, explain how the firm could use that market power in setting wages.**

Wal-Mart can use its market power to decrease the wage rate it pays by decreasing the number of workers it hires.

b. **Draw a graph to illustrate how Wal-Mart might use labor market power to set wages.**

Figure 18.8 shows Wal-Mart's situation if it is a monopsony in the labor market. Wal-Mart's demand curve is the same as its value of marginal product curve and is labeled $D = VMP$ in the figure. The labor supply curve is upward sloping and is labeled S in the figure. Wal-Mart's marginal cost of labor exceeds the wage rate it pays so the marginal cost of labor curve, labeled MCL, lies above the labor supply curve. Wal-Mart's profit-maximizing quantity of labor is determined at the intersection of the $D = VMP$ curve and the MCL curve and is 1.7 million workers. Wal-Mart determines the wage rate from the labor supply curve as the lowest wage rate it can pay and hire its profit-maximizing quantity of labor. In the figure the wage rate is $8 dollars per hour.

FIGURE **18.8**
Problem 15b

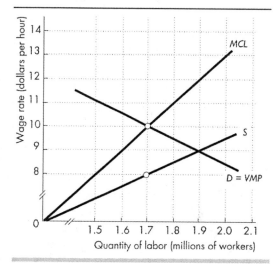

c. Explain how a union of Wal-Mart's employees would attempt to counteract Wal-Mart's wage offers (a bilateral monopoly).

A union will bargain with Wal-Mart. If Wal-Mart faces a union, the situation is a bilateral monopoly: a monopoly seller of labor services (the union) bargains with a monopsony buyer of labor services (Wal-Mart). In this case the wage rate depends on the relative strengths of the two and will lie between the monopsony wage Wal-Mart offers, $8 per hour in Figure 18.8, and the union wants value of marginal product, $10 per hour in Figure 18.8.

d. Explain the response by the Canadian Wal-Mart to the unionization of employees.

Wal-Mart's profits are decreased if it must pay higher wage rates. Wal-Mart realizes that a union will force the wage rate higher and Wal-Mart fears that a union at one store could spread to other stores. To avoid this outcome, Wal-Mart closed its unionized Canadian store.

e. Based upon evidence presented in this article, does Wal-Mart function as a monopsony in labor markets, or is the market for retail labor more competitive? Explain.

The key piece of evidence in the news clip is the point that Wal-Mart's median wage is similar to the national median wage rate. If Wal-Mart had significant monopsony power its wage rate would probably be less than the national median wage rate. Because the wage rates are similar, it appears that Wal-Mart functions in a competitive labor market.

f. If the market for retail labor is competitive, explain the potential effect of a union on the wage rates.

If the labor market is competitive, a labor union will attempt to decrease the supply of labor and increase the demand for its member's labor. The wage rate will rise. Unless the union is able to substantially increase the demand for its member's labor, employment will decrease.

g. Draw a graph to illustrate the potential effect of a union on the wage rates in a competitive labor market

Figure 18.9 shows a union in a competitive labor market. The union decreases the supply of labor and the supply of labor curve shifts leftward from S_0 to S_1. The union increases the demand for labor and the demand for labor curve shifts rightward from D_0 to D_1. The wage rate rises, in the figure from $9 per hour to $12 per hour. If the change in the supply of labor is larger than the change in demand, the case illustrated in the figure, employment decreases from 1.7 million workers to 1.6 million workers.

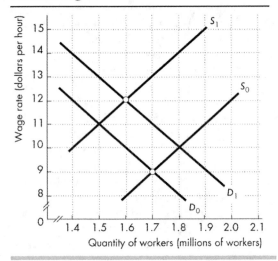

FIGURE **18.9**

Problem 15g

17. **New technology has allowed oil to be pumped from much deeper offshore oil fields than before. For example, 28 deep ocean rigs operate in the deep waters of the Gulf of Mexico.**

   a. **What effect do you think deep ocean sources have had on the world oil price?**

   The deep ocean oil fields increased the supply of oil and have kept oil prices from rising higher than they have.

   b. **Who will benefit from drilling for oil in the Gulf of Mexico? Explain your answer.**

The people benefiting from the new technology are the owners of the oil rigs and the firms selling this oil. Consumers also benefit because the price of oil is lower. If oil is drilled from the Gulf of Mexico, the owners and producers of this oil will benefit as will consumers of oil.

19. **Study *Reading Between the Lines* on pp. 432–433 and answer the following questions:**

   a. **What determines the demand for oil? In your answer, distinguish between the market fundamentals and speculative influences on demand.**

   Both a fundamental influence and a speculative influence affect the demand for oil. The fundamental influence is the interaction between the price and the value of marginal product of oil. Similar to any resource, firms demand for oil depends on its value of marginal product so that the higher the price of oil, the smaller the quantity demanded. The speculative influence is the expected future price of oil. If the expected future price rises, the current demand for oil increases.

   b. **What determines the supply of oil? In your answer, distinguish between the market fundamentals and speculative influences on supply.**

   Both fundamental influences and a speculative influence affect the supply of oil. One fundamental factor is the quantity of known reserves. Though this

effect is very small and indirect, an increase in the quantity of known reserves increases the supply of oil. A key fundamental factor is the scale of current oil production facilities. The larger the scale of current oil production facilities, such as wells, the greater the supply of oil. The speculative influence is the expected future price of oil. If the expected future price rises, the current supply of oil decreases.

   c. **What is the Hotelling Principle and why is it correct?**

   The Hotelling Principle is the idea that the price of a nonrenewable natural resource is expected to rise at a rate equal to the interest rate. This situation is the only one that is consistent with market equilibrium. If the percentage increase in the price is less than the interest rate, the (present) supply would increase and the demand would decrease. The (present) price would fall until the percentage increase in the price equaled the interest rate, at which point the demand and supply would stop changing and the market would be in equilibrium. The Hotelling Principle describes the equilibrium. The Hotelling Principle can be correct even if the price doesn't rise at the same rate as the interest rate because the Hotelling Principal applies to the *expected* price. The actual price will rise at a faster or slower rate depending on exploration and technological change.

   d. **How does the Hotelling Principle tell us that a change in oil production in 2030 will change the price of oil today?**

   A change in oil production in 2030 will affect the price of oil in 2030. An increase in oil production in 2030 will lead to a lower price in 2030. The Hotelling Principle states that the price of oil is expected to rise at the same rate as the interest rate. For the price rise to equal the now lower price in 2030, the starting price today must be lower. So an expected increase in oil production in 2030 lowers the price of oil today.

e. **Suppose that the elasticity of demand for oil turns out to be close to 1 rather than approximately 0.1. Will the fall in today's price of oil resulting from an increase in oil production in 2030 exceed $10 a barrel? Explain your answer.**

If the elasticity of demand for oil is 1 rather than 0.1, then a 1 percent increase in the quantity of oil lowers the price by (only) 1 percent. So in the calculation of the effect on today's oil price, the fall in the price in 2030 is 1.18 percent rather than 11.8 percent. This change means that today's price falls 1.18/1.52 or 0.78 percent (rather than 7.8 percent), a fall of approximately $1 today (rather than a fall of $10 today).

f. **If the interest rate is 4 percent rather than the 2 percent assumed in the analysis on p. 433, does that make the effect on today's price of a change in production in 2030 greater or smaller? Explain your answer with reference to the Hotelling Principle.**

The effect on today's price is smaller. The Hotelling Principle tells us that the fall in the future price must be discounted using the interest rate to determine the effect on today's price. If the interest rate is 4 percent, then fall in price in 2030 is discounted by 1.04^{21} or 2.28 rather than 1.02^{21} or 1.52 as used in analysis on page 433. Using the analysis with the higher interest rate shows that the fall in today's price becomes 11.8/2.28, which is 5.2 percent. So if the interest rate is 4 percent and today's price is $130, the price fall today is only $5 rather than the price fall of $10 calculated on page 433.

Additional Problems

Number of workers	Quantity of ice (bags)
1	40
2	100
3	180
4	240
5	290
6	330
7	360
8	380

1. Barry makes party ice. He employs workers to bag the ice who can produce the quantities of ice in an hour that are listed in the table. The market for ice is competitive and Barry can sell ice for 50¢ a bag. The labor market is competitive and the equilibrium wage rate of baggers is $10.00 an hour.

   a. Calculate the marginal product of the workers.

   b. Calculate the value of marginal product of the workers.

   c. Find Barry's demand for labor curve.

   d. How much ice does Barry sell?

2. Back at Barry's ice making plant described in problem 1, the price of party ice falls to 25¢ a bag but baggers' wages remain at $10.00 an hour.

   a. What happens to Barry's marginal product?

   b. What happens to his value of marginal product?

   c. What happens to his demand for labor curve?

   d. What happens to the number of baggers that he employs?

3. Back at Barry's party ice shop described in problem 1, baggers' wages increase to $20 an hour, but the price of ice remains at 50¢ a bag.

   a. What happens to his value of marginal product?

   b. What happens to Barry's demand for labor curve?

   c. How many baggers does Barry employ?

4. What is discounting? What is present value? How do the two relate?

Solutions to
Additional Problems

1. a.   Marginal product of labor is the increase in total product that results from hiring one additional bagger. For example, if Barry increases the number of baggers hired from 2 to 3, total product (the quantity of ice) increases from 100 to 180 bags. The marginal product of 2.5 baggers is 80 bags of ice. The table shows the remainder of these marginal products.

Number of workers	Quantity of ice (bags)	Marginal product (bags)
1	40	
		60
2	100	
		80
3	180	
		60
4	240	
		50
5	290	
		40
6	330	
		30
7	360	
		20
8	380	

   b.   The value of marginal product of labor is the increase in total revenue that results from hiring one additional bagger, which equals the marginal product multiplied by the price. The second table shows that the marginal product of 2.5 workers is 80 bags of ice. Barry sells the ice for 50¢ a bag, so this worker's value of marginal product is 80 bags × 50¢ a bag = $40. The schedule showing the value of marginal products in the table are calculated similarly.

Number of workers	Marginal product (bags)	Value of marginal product (dollars)
1.5	60	30
2.5	80	40
3.5	60	30
4.5	50	25
5.5	40	20
6.5	30	15
7.5	20	10

   c.   Barry's demand for labor curve is the same as his value of marginal product curve.

   d.   Barry sells 370 bags. Barry hires the number of baggers that makes the value of marginal product equal to the wage rate of $10 an hour. When Barry hires 7.5 baggers, marginal product is 20 bags of ice in an hour, which Barry sells for 50 cents a bag. The value of marginal product is $10—the same as the wage rate. Barry hires 7.5 baggers and produces 370 bags of ice an hour.

2. a.   The marginal product does not change. The marginal product that results from hiring 2.5 baggers an hour is still 80 bags of ice.

   b.   The value of marginal product decreases. If Barry hires 2.5 baggers an hour, the marginal product is (still) 80 bags of ice. Now Barry sells the ice for 25 cents, so the value of marginal product is 80 bags × 25¢ a bag = $20, down from $40.

c. Barry's demand for labor decreases, and his demand for labor curve shifts leftward. Barry is willing to pay the baggers their value of marginal product, and the fall in the price of ice has lowered their value of marginal product.

d. Barry will hire fewer baggers. At the wage rate of $10.00, the number of baggers Barry hires decreases to 5.5 as the demand for labor curve shifts leftward.

3. a. The value of marginal product does not change. If Barry hires 2.5 baggers an hour, the marginal product is (still) 80 bags of ice and Barry sells the ice for 50 cents a bag, so the value of marginal product remains at $40.

b. Barry's demand for labor remains the same because the value of marginal product of labor has not changed.

c. Barry will hire fewer baggers. At the wage rate of $20 an hour, Barry hires the number of baggers that makes the value of marginal product equal to $20 an hour. Barry now hires 5.5 baggers an hour—down from 7.5 an hour. The marginal product that results

when Barry hires 5.5 baggers is 40 bags of ice an hour, and Barry sells this ice for 50 cents a bag. The value of marginal product is $20 an hour, which is equal to the wage that Barry must now pay.

4. Discounting is converting a future amount of money into a present value. If a firm did not receive money today but instead received that money in the future, the firm would forgo the interest that this sum of money would have earned over that period. The present value of a future amount of money is the amount that, if invested today, grows to be as large as that future amount when the interest that it earns is taken into account. If a person is to receive a number of periodic payments in the future, then that person can use discounting to establish the present value of that future income stream.

Chapter 19 ECONOMIC INEQUALITY

Answers to the Problems and Applications

1. **The table shows money income shares in the United States in 1967.**

   a. **What is money income?**

   Money income equals market income (wages, interest, rent, and profit earned in factor markets, before paying income taxes) plus cash payments from the government.

   b. **Draw a Lorenz curve for the United States in 1967 and compare it with the Lorenz curve in 2007 shown in Fig. 19.3.**

   The Lorenz curve is illustrated in Figure 19.1. To draw it, plot the cumulative percentage of households on the *x*-axis and the cumulative percentage of income on the *y*-axis. Make the scale on the two axes the same. The Lorenz curve will pass through the following points: 20 percent on the *x*-axis and 4 percent on the *y*-axis; 40 percent on the *x*-axis and 14.8 percent on the *y*-axis; 60 percent on the *x*-axis and 32.1 percent on the *y*-axis; 80 percent on the *x*-axis and 56.3 percent on the *y*-axis; and 100 percent on the *x*-axis and 100 percent on the *y*-axis.

   c. **Was U.S. money income distributed more equally or less equally in 2007 than it was in 1967?**

   U.S. money income was distributed more equally in 1967 than in 2007. The line of equality shows an equal distribution of income. The closer the Lorenz curve is to the line of equality, the more equal is the income distribution. The Lorenz curve for the U.S. economy in 1967 lies closer to the Line of equality than does the Lorenz curve in 2007.

   d. **Can you think of some reasons for the differences in the distribution of money income in the United States in 1967 and 2007?**

   The biggest difference in the distribution of income in the United States in 1967 and 2007 is the share of income received

Money income	Households (percent of total)
Lowest 20%	4.0
Second 20%	10.8
Third 20%	17.3
Fourth 20%	24.2
Fifth 20%	43.7

FIGURE **19.1**

Problem 1b

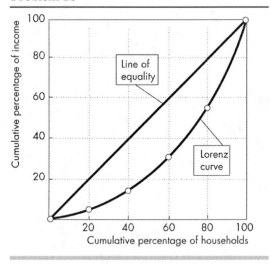

by the highest 20 percent. This share increased from 43.7 percent to 50.4 percent. Smaller differences exist for the shares received by the four other groups, each of which decreased. The most likely explanation for these differences is that the information technologies and globalization of the 1990s and 2000s are substitutes for low-skilled labor and complements of high-skilled labor. The demand for low-skilled labor decreased relative to the supply of low-skilled labor and the wage rate (and income) of low-skilled labor has increased more slowly than the average U.S. wage rate. The demand for high-skilled labor has increased relative to the supply of high-skilled labor and the wage rate (and income) of high-skilled labor has increased faster than the average U.S. wage rate.

3. **Figure 19.3 shows the demand for and supply of workers who are discriminated against. Suppose that there is a group of workers in the same industry who are not discriminated against, and their value of marginal product is perceived to be twice the value of marginal product of the workers who are discriminated against. Suppose also that the supply of workers who do not face discrimination is 2,000 hours per day less at each wage rate.**

a. **What is the wage rate of the workers who are discriminated against?**

   The wage rate of workers who are discriminated against is $5 an hour.

b. **What is the quantity of workers employed who are discriminated against?**

   Firms employ 5,000 hours of labor per day from workers facing discrimination.

c. **What is the wage rate of the workers who do not face discrimination?**

   Because the value of marginal product of workers not facing discrimination is perceived to be twice the value of marginal product of the other workers, firms are willing to pay the workers not facing discrimination twice the wage rate that they are willing to pay the workers who face discrimination. For example, the demand curve for the workers being discriminated against tells us that firms are willing to hire 6,000 hours of these workers at a wage rate of $4 an hour. So with workers not facing discrimination perceived to be twice as productive as the other workers, firms are willing to hire 6,000 hours of labor from the non-discriminated group $8 an hour. The demand curve for labor for the workers not facing discrimination lies above the demand curve for workers facing discrimination such that at each quantity of workers the wage rate for workers not facing discrimination is double that of workers facing discrimination. The supply curve of workers not facing

FIGURE **19.3**
Problem 3

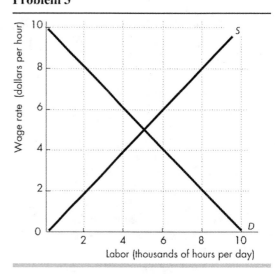

discrimination lies to the left of the supply curve of workers facing discrimination by 2,000 hours of labor. The vertical distance between the two supply curves is $2 an hour. That is, workers not facing discrimination will supply 6,000 hours a day if the wage rate is $8 an hour. The equilibrium wage rate of workers who do not face discrimination is $8 an hour.

d. **What is the quantity of workers employed who do not face discrimination?**

   Firms employ 6,000 hours of labor per day from workers not facing discrimination.

5. **Household Incomes Rise But... Household income crept higher and the poverty rate edged lower last year. ... But more people had to be at work in each household ... because median earnings for individuals working fulltime year-round actually fell. ... The percent of Americans living below the poverty line, meanwhile, slipped to 12.3 percent in 2006. ... The poverty threshold varies based on age and household size ... [but] are not adjusted for geographical differences in cost of living so the same threshold applies in Brownsville, Texas, as it**

does in New York City. Nor do they reflect the value of household subsidies intended to alleviate the effects of poverty (e.g., food stamps, tax credits, Medicaid). ... The gap between high-income and low-income households has grown over the years, but income inequality remained statistically unchanged between 2005 and 2006, according to the bureau.

CNN, August 28, 2007

a. **Why are the recent increases in median household income a misleading statistic when attempting to measure the improvement in the economic well-being of households?**

The increase in median household income occurred because more people in each household worked. While the increase in median household income suggests households are better off, the fact that more people worked indicates that households are not necessarily better off.

b. **How does using set poverty thresholds that apply to the entire U.S. complicate attempts to measure poverty?**

The cost of living is vastly different in different areas of the country but this fact is ignored when using a country-wide set poverty threshold.

c. **Why does excluding household subsidies from consideration when measuring household income lead to a misleading measurement of the percentage of people actually living in poverty?**

Subsidies given to households boost their income and can raise them above the poverty threshold.

d. **Why has the gap between high-income and low-income households grown in the U.S. over the past few decades?**

The gap has grown because technological change has increased the value of marginal product of high-skilled workers and decreased the value of marginal product of low-skilled workers. Hence workers who were already highly paid have seen their

wage rise still more while people who were less well paid have not been as fortunate.

7. **Where Women's Pay Trumps Men's**
Men work more than women ... on the job anyway ... at least in terms of overall hours. That's just one reason why when you make a general comparison of men's and women's earnings in most fields, men usually come out ahead. ... [But Warren] Farrell ... found ... 39 ... occupations [in which] women's median earnings exceeded men's earnings by at least 5 percent and in some cases by as much as 43 percent. ... In fields like engineering, a company may get one woman and seven men applying for a job. ... If the company wants to hire the woman, they may have to pay a premium to get her. ... Also, where women can combine technical expertise with people skills— such as those required in sales and ... where customers may prefer dealing with a woman—that's likely to contribute to a premium in pay. ...

CNN, March 2, 2006

a. **Draw a graph to illustrate why discrimination could result in female workers getting paid more than male workers for some jobs.**

Figure 19.5 shows a labor market in which men are discriminated against in

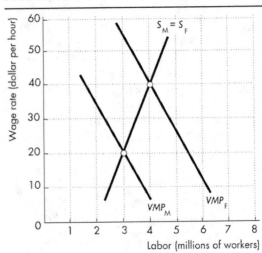

FIGURE **19.5**

Problem 7a

favor of women. With the discrimination, the value of marginal product of women exceeds that of men. As a result, the value of marginal product curve for females, labeled VMP_F, lies above the value of marginal product curve for males, labeled VMP_M. In the figure the supply of male labor is the same as that of females, so the supply curve is labeled $S_M = S_F$. The figure shows that the wage rate paid women, $40 per hour, exceeds the wage rate paid men, $20 per hour.

b. **Explain how market competition could potentially eliminate this wage differential.**

Men, the group facing discrimination, are paid less than women, the favored group. If men and women are equally productive and the price paid for their output is the same, then firms which hire men have lower costs and higher profits than firms which hire women. Firms that hire men would increase their market share and increase the demand for men, which raises their wage rate. Firms that hire women have a decreased market share and decrease the demand for women, which lowers their wage rate.

c. **If customers "prefer dealing with a woman" in some markets, how might that lead to a persistent wage differential between men and women?**

If customers prefer dealing with a women, then women's value of marginal product remains permanently higher than men's value of marginal product so the wage rate paid women remains permanently higher then the wage rate paid men.

9. **In the United States in 2000, 30 million people had full-time managerial and professional jobs that paid an average of $800 a week. At the same time, 10 million people had full-time sales positions that paid an average of $530 a week.**

a. **Explain why managers and professionals are paid more than salespeople.**

Managers and professionals have more human capital than for salespeople. For instance, managers and professionals generally have more education, which boosts their human capital. Their higher human capital means that their value of marginal product is higher, so the demand for managers and professionals exceeds that of salespeople. Additionally the cost of acquiring their human capital means that the supply of managers and professionals is less than the supply of salespeople. The higher demand for and lower supply of managers and professionals means that their salaries exceed those of salespeople.

b. **Explain why, despite the higher weekly wage, more people are employed as managers and professionals than as salespeople.**

As discussed in the answer to part a, while the supply of managers and professionals is less than the supply of salespeople, the demand for managers and professionals exceeds that for salespeople. If the demand difference is large relative to the difference in supply, the number of people employed as managers and professionals will exceed the number employed as salespeople.

c. **If the online shopping trend continues, how do you think the market for salespeople will change in coming years?**

Shopping on-line decreases the demand for in-person salespeople. If on-line shopping continues to increase in importance, the salary paid salespeople will fall and the quantity of salespeople employed will decrease.

11. **The table shows the distribution of market income in the United States in 2007.**

   a. **What is the definition of market income?**

      Market income is the income earned by factors of production in the marketplace. Labor earns wages, capital earns interest, land earns rent, and entrepreneurship earns profit.

   b. **Draw the Lorenz curve for the distribution of market income.**

      Figure 19.8 shows the distribution of market income. To draw this Lorenz curve, plot the cumulative percentage of households on the *x*-axis and the cumulative percentage of market income on the *y*-axis. Make the scale on the two axes the same. The Lorenz curve will pass through the following points: 20 percent on the *x*-axis and 1.1 percent on the *y*-axis; 40 percent on the *x*-axis and 8.2 percent on the *y*-axis; 60 percent on the *x*-axis and 22.1 percent on the *y*-axis; 80 percent on the *x*-axis and 44.9 percent on the *y*-axis; and 100 percent on the *x*-axis and 100 percent on the *y*-axis.

   c. **Compare the distribution of market income with the distribution of money income shown in Fig. 19.3. Which distribution is more unequal and why?**

      U.S. money income is distributed more equally than market income in 2007. The Lorenz curve for U.S. money income in 2007 lies closer to the line of equality than does the Lorenz curve for U.S. market income. Money income is distributed more equally than market income because money income includes cash payments to poor households, which increases their income.

13. **Bernanke Links Education and Equality**
Ben Bernanke, the chairman of the Federal Reserve, said... that an expansion of education opportunities would help curb the economic

Households	Market income (percent of total)
Lowest 20%	1.1
Second 20%	7.1
Third 20%	13.9
Fourth 20%	22.8
Fifth 20%	55.1

FIGURE **19.8**

Problem 11b

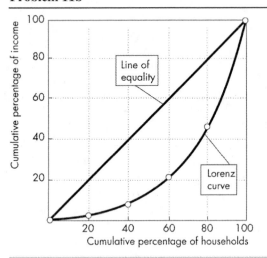

inequality that has increased considerably in the last 30 years. ... [Bernanke] said ... that globalization and the advent of new technologies, two prime causes of income inequality, would ultimately lead to economic growth, and inhibiting them "would do far more harm than good over the longer haul." Instead, the Fed chief said the best method to improve economic opportunities for Americans was to focus on raising the level of and access to education. Workers would be provided with better skills, he said, and innovation in the private sector would remain unchecked. "As we think about improving education and

skills, we should also look beyond the traditional K-12 and 4-year-college system … to recognize that education should be lifelong and can come in many forms," Bernanke said. … "Early childhood education, community colleges, vocational schools, on-the-job training, online courses, adult education—all of these are vehicles of demonstrated value in increasing skills and lifetime earning power."
International Herald Tribune, June 5, 2008

a. **Explain how the two main causes of increased income inequality in the U.S. identified by Mr. Bernanke work.**

Mr. Bernanke identified "globalization and the advent of new technologies [as] two prime causes of income inequality". Globalization, such as the vast increase in China's trade has lowered the prices that many U.S. firms receive for their manufactured goods and lowered the demand for labor by these firms. The lower demand for labor results in a lower wage rate for these workers, who frequently are low-skilled workers. Simultaneously globalization has increased the demand for services provided by high-skilled workers, which

has raised their wage rates. The other factor is the recent new technologies. These new technologies are substitutes for low-skilled workers and complements for high-skilled workers. As a result the demand for low-skilled workers decreases, along with their wages, while the demand for high-skilled workers increases, along with their wages.

b. **Draw a graph to illustrate how the two main causes of increased income inequality generate this outcome.**

On both counts—globalization and new technologies—the demand for low-skilled workers decreases and the demand for high-skilled workers increases. These changes are shown in Figure 19.9a, which illustrates the market for low-skilled labor, and 19.9b, which illustrates the demand for high-skilled labor. In Figure 19.9a, the demand for low-skilled labor decreases and the demand curve shifts leftward from D_0 to D_1. The wage rate paid low-skilled workers falls from $15 per hour to $10 per hour. In Figure 19.9b, the demand for high-skilled labor increases and the demand curve shifts rightward from D_0 to D_1. The wage rate paid high-skilled workers rises from $30 per hour to $40 per hour.

FIGURE **19.9a**
Problem 13b

FIGURE **19.9b**
Problem 13b

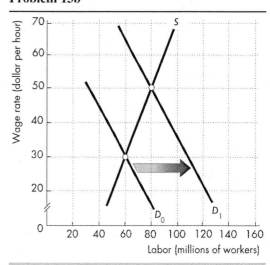

c. **What are the short-term costs and long-term benefits associated with these two causes of inequality?**

> The short-term cost is the cost of increased economic inequality. But the long-term benefit is more rapid economic growth and substantially increased average incomes.

d. **Explain Bernanke's solutions to help address growing income inequality.**

> Mr. Bernanke's solution is to train more workers so that there is less low-skilled labor. With their newly acquired skills, these workers will be able to obtain high-skilled, high-paying jobs. Additionally the decrease in the supply of low-skilled labor raises the wage rate paid low-skilled workers.

15. **After you have studied *Reading Between the Lines* on pp. 456–457, answer the following questions.**

a. **What are the broad facts reported in the news article about the gap in the incomes of the highest and lowest 20 percent?**

> The news article reports that the difference in incomes between the richest 20 percent of household and the poorest 20 percent of household has widened over time in New York and is the largest difference of all fifty U.S. states.

b. **List the factors that contributed to the rising income gap according to Elizabeth McNichol. Of these factors, which do you think made the biggest contribution?**

> Ms. McNichol suggests that the gap widened because the poorest 20 percent of families had many adverse factors affecting their income. Of the factors she lists, globalization, immigration, and the failure to increase the minimum wage might be primary contributors to the increased wage gap between the poorest 20 percent of household and the richest 20 percent. The other listed factors probably had much larger effects on 20 percentile groups above the poorest 20 percentile group.

c. **Which of the factors listed in b account for the national trend and which account for the more extreme changes in New York State?**

> Of the factors listed in b, likely the most important for the national trend are globalization and the shift from high-paying manufacturing jobs to low-paying service jobs. These factors have an impact in every state in the nation. New York might have been more severely affected by high unemployment rates because the unemployment rate in New York has been higher than the national average. In addition, immigration probably played a major role in New York because the number of immigrants in New York City is huge.

d. **What policy issues are raised by the information reported in the news article?**

> If the increased wage gap is deemed undesirable, then policy makers need to reexamine immigration laws and minimum wage laws. Additionally laws favoring or hampering unions might also be reexamined.

Additional Problems

1.   How does the minimum wage affect the distribution of income?

2.   Compared to the United States, managers in Hong Kong and Malaysia are paid much more than the low-skilled factory workers that they supervise. What accounts for this difference in relative pay?

3.   Many pets in rich nations eat better than people in poor nations. To equalize the international distribution of income, do you think that rich nations should tax their citizens and give the income to the poor of very poor nations? Would this policy be fair?

Solutions to Additional Problems

1. The minimum wage affects the distribution of income in several ways. First, workers who without the minimum wage would be paid less, receive a higher income than otherwise with the minimum wage. Because these workers are low-income workers, the minimum wage makes the distribution of income a bit more equal. Second, some workers lose their jobs when a minimum wage is imposed. These workers' incomes fall and the minimum wage makes the distribution of income less equal. Finally, the minimum wage probably decreases some firms' profits and so decreases their owners' incomes. Because owners are generally higher-income earners, the minimum wage makes the distribution of income more equal.

2. The difference in pay is a result of the fact that managerial skills are in much smaller supply in Hong Kong and Malaysia. There are many low-skilled factory floor workers in Hong Kong and Malaysia. There are few high-skilled managers. As a result, the equilibrium wage rate paid to the few high-skilled managers in Hong Kong and Malaysia is many times greater than the wage rate paid to the many low-skilled factory floor workers.

3. It is indeed the case that people in rich nations are much better off than people in poor nations. Rich nations are better off because their citizens are more productive because they have immensely greater amounts of physical and human capital. The question of redistributing income from one nation to another has a big tradeoff associated with it. In particular, while the transfer of income to poorer nations equalizes income among nations, it lessens the poor nations' incentives to develop and so slows their economic growth. In addition, the issue of fairness comes into play. The "fair results" approach to fairness argues that it is definitely fair to transfer resources to poor nations. But the "fair rules" approach to fairness suggests that these transfers aren't fair. Taking tax revenue from people in rich nations to transfer the funds to poor nations is not a voluntary exchange and so is unfair.

Chapter **20** UNCERTAINTY
AND
INFORMATION

Answers to the Problems and Applications

1. The figure shows Lee's utility of wealth curve. Lee is offered a job as a salesperson in which there is a 50 percent chance that she will make $4,000 a month and a 50 percent chance that she will make nothing.

   a. **What is Lee's expected income from taking this job?**

      Lee's expected income is $(0.5 \times \$4,000) + (0.5 \times \$0) = \$2,000$ a month.

   b. **What is Lee's expected utility from taking this job?**

      When Lee's income is $4,000, her utility is 100. When Lee's income is $0, her utility is 0. So Lee's expected utility is $(0.5 \times 100) + (0.5 \times 0) = 50$.

   c. **How much would another firm have to offer Lee with certainty to persuade her not to take the risky sales job?**

      Lee would have to be offered about $1,250 a month with certainty to persuade her not to take the risky job. Lee would have to be offered the income that would give her with certainty 50 units of utility. This income, $1,250, is read from the graph at the 50 units on the y-axis.

   d. **What is Lee's cost of risk?**

      Lee's cost of risk is the difference between Lee's expected income, $2,000, and the certain income that gives her the same total utility, $1,250. Lee's cost of risk is $750.

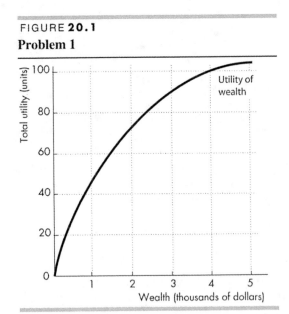

FIGURE **20.1**

Problem 1

3. **Zaneb is a high-school teacher and is well known in her community for her honesty and integrity. She is shopping for a used car and plans to borrow the money from her local bank to pay for the car.**

   a. **Does Zaneb create any moral hazard or adverse selection problems either for the bank or the car dealer? Explain your answer.**

      Zenab is well known for her honesty and integrity, so she creates no moral hazard or adverse selection problems for the car dealer or for the bank.

   b. **Do either the bank or the car dealer create any moral hazard or adverse selection problems for Zaneb? Explain your answer.**

      Moral hazard exists when one of the parties to an agreement has the incentive *after* the agreement is made to act in a manner that brings additional benefits to him or her at the expense of the other party. Adverse selection exists when people can *enter into* an agreement in which they can use their private information to bring additional benefits to them. The car dealer creates an adverse selection problem for Zenab because the car might be a lemon. The bank does not create either a moral hazard or adverse selection problem for Zenab.

c. **What arrangements is Zaneb likely to encounter that are designed to help cope with the moral hazard and adverse selection problems she encounters in her car buying and bank loan transactions?**

Warranties are designed to help cope with the moral hazard and adverse selection problems on cars. The bank has information on Zenab's income and reputation, so doesn't face moral hazard or adverse selection problems.

5. **Phillies Hamstrung by Burrell's No-Trade Clause**
Phillies general manager Pat Gillick, ... who previously built winners in Toronto, Baltimore and Seattle, is no fan of blanket no-trade clauses. Gillick is so averse to giving out complete no-trade provisions that he says it could be a "deal breaker" when the Phillies negotiate with big free agents this winter.
ESPN.com, **November 8, 2006**

a. **Provide an example of private information that a baseball player who wants a no-trade clause possesses.**

A player could know that he was injured or that he had not healed as well as possible from an injury.

b. **Does a baseball player with a no-trade clause present a moral hazard to his baseball team?**

A player with a no-trade clause presents a moral hazard problem. The player can claim to be more badly injured than is truly the case to avoid playing some

games. The player can make this claim knowing that even if he often does so, his team cannot trade him and must continue to pay his salary.

c. **Does a baseball player with a no-trade clause present adverse selection problems to his baseball team?**

If there are two types of contracts—contracts with the no-trade clause and contracts without it—then there is a potential adverse selection problem. Players who know they are more inclined to want to skip a game or two will be eager to sign a no-trade contract because this contract lessens their cost of feigning injury to take leisure.

7. **We All Pay for the Uninsured**
When buying health care, most of us don't behave like regular consumers. Seven out of eight dollars we spend is somebody else's money, and we don't have very good information about doctors or hospitals. ... At Aetna [a health insurance company], in 35 markets, you can go online and know what your physician will charge you before you see that physician. That's helpful for a routine service, but when it comes to, say, a serious cardiac condition, what you really want to know is whether this is a high-quality physician. ... Important efforts are on the way, with the collaboration of physicians, to agree on quality standards. There's collaboration in the industry for all health plans to pool their data to create very rich data sets. So consumers could look at a set of performance indicators that physicians think are appropriate, and be able to judge how their physicians fare.
Fortune, **May 12, 2008**

a. **Explain how the adverse selection problem applies to health care.**

Adverse selection is a *major* issue in the health care market. People who know they are more likely to use health insurance are more likely to be in the market to buy it.

b. How does the moral hazard problem apply to health insurance?

Moral hazard also is an issue in the health care market. People with health care insurance are likely to take risks that they would not take if they did not have insurance.

c. What role can better information play in the health care market?

Information can lead to better outcomes. The news clip points out that physicians vary in quality. If people with serious, difficult-to-treat conditions are matched to high quality physicians, then the outcome for the patients can be improved.

d. Is it possible for there to be too much information in this market?

Too much information is possible. Too much information results if the marginal cost of gathering information exceeds the marginal benefit of the information.

9. You can't buy insurance against the risk of being sold a lemon. Why isn't there a market in insurance against being sold a lemon? How does the market give you some protection against being sold a lemon? What are the main ways in which markets overcome the lemon problem?

There is not a market for "lemon insurance" for several reasons. Defining a "lemon" is far from clear cut. The definition would need to be specified in the contract. But that leads to a moral hazard problem because a buyer with a car close to meeting the requirements for a lemon will behave in a way that increases the probability that the car will be deemed a lemon. Moral hazard also arises once the insurance is purchased but before the car is bought. Once the customer has the insurance, he or she will no longer search for a "non-lemon," a creampuff. So it is likely that many of the cars purchased by people with the insurance will be lemons. These reasons combine to make it impossible for an

insuring company to offer the insurance at a price that customers will pay and that allows the insurance firm to make a profit. Adverse selection also enters because people who are less likely to spend time searching for a high-quality car are more likely to buy the lemon insurance.

Even without insurance, the market does give protection against lemons. Warranties are designed to help cope with the moral hazard and adverse selection problems on cars. Warranties signal that the car is not a lemon because if the car is a lemon servicing the car would be costly. The fact that the seller, who is the person with the private information, is willing to offer a warranty signals that the car is not a lemon.

Wealth	Jimmy's utility	Zenda's utility
0	0	0
100	200	512
200	300	640
300	350	672
400	375	678
500	387	681
600	393	683
700	396	684

11. Jimmy and Zenda have the utility of wealth schedules given in the table.

a. What are Jimmy's and Zenda's expected utilities from a bet that gives them a 50 percent chance of having a wealth of $600 and a 50 percent chance of having nothing?

Jimmy's expected utility is $(0.5 \times 393) + (0.5 \times 0) = 196.5$. Zenda's expected utility is $(0.5 \times 683) + (0.5 \times 0) = 341.5$.

b. **Calculate Jimmy's and Zenda's marginal utility of wealth schedules.**

The table to the right sets out their marginal utility of wealth schedules.

c. **Who is more risk averse, Jimmy or Zenda? How do you know?**

Zenda is more risk averse because her marginal utility of wealth decreases more quickly as wealth increases than does Jimmy's marginal utility of wealth.

d. **Who is more likely to buy insurance, Jimmy or Zenda?**

Zenda is more likely to buy insurance because she is more risk averse.

Wealth	Jimmy's utility	Jimmy's marginal utility	Zenda's utility	Zenda's marginal utility
0	0		0	
		2.00		5.12
100	200		512	
		1.00		1.28
200	300		640	
		0.50		0.32
300	350		672	
		0.25		0.06
400	375		678	
		0.12		0.03
500	387		681	
		0.06		0.02
600	393		683	
		0.03		0.01
700	396		684	

13. **Genetic Nondiscrimination Bill Deserves a Double Helix of Applause**
As our understanding of human genes has improved, so too has the ability to screen for various genetic traits. This has primarily been seen in tests that determine genetic predisposition to various afflictions. The Genetic Information Nondiscrimination Act ... will prevent employers and health-insurance companies from discriminating based on a person's genetic information. ... As one would expect, the motivation for such testing comes down to cost savings. ... As a matter of economics, health-insurance companies seek out genetic information in their attempts to reduce a phenomenon known as adverse selection... If genetic testing is permitted, those afflicted by—or prone to become afflicted by—certain diseases are essentially red-flagged as a result of their high-risk status. ... True enough, health-insurance companies will once again be subjected to the same uncertainty that plagues insurance carriers of all sorts, imposing greater costs on the average client.
The Daily Iowan, May 8, 2008

a. **How does adverse selection apply to the market for health insurance?**

People who know they are more likely to use health insurance are more likely to demand health insurance than are people who know they are less likely to use health insurance.

b. **How might genetic testing be used to reduce adverse selection?**

Genetic testing can determine if people are more or less likely to contract various ailments. With genetic testing, people who are more likely to contract a disease would be charged a higher insurance premium while people who are less likely to contract the disease would be charged a lower premium.

c. **Explain the arguments that could be made in favor of and in opposition to The Genetic Information Nondiscrimination Act.**

In favor is the point that people who were unfortunate to inherit a high predisposition toward a particular disease will still be able to buy insurance. In opposition is the point that people who are not likely to contract a particular ailment will pay higher premiums. These higher premiums are necessary to allow the insurance company to earn enough revenue to cover those people, including those with a higher-than-normal likelihood, who actually do contract the disease. Basically those who have the genetic tendency toward a disease are subsidized by those without the tendency.

15. **The Appeal of Gold**
It's 2008. Inflation is on the rise… energy prices are high, unemployment is going up, and political instability is an ongoing source of anxiety. Concurrently, survivalism is enjoying a revival, and after a horrendous performance during most of the '80s and '90s (dropping to around $264 an ounce in 2000), gold has once again shot up, reaching a record high of $1,030.80. … [T]he value of the dollar is a perpetual concern … while the dollar is unlikely to fall into total worthlessness, it's getting a bit more worthless day by day. … To guard against this … [people] buy gold on the assumption that gold is a store of value. Conventional wisdom holds that an ounce of gold can generally buy the same goods over time regardless of how expensive things get, making it a good hedge against inflation. … Investment advisors have long suggested that gold in small doses helps protect an overall portfolio. It tends to move independently of other asset classes, and unlike any type of security, it doesn't run the risk of going to absolute zero.
Fortune, **April 28, 2008**

a. **Explain how the concept of risk aversion can be used to explain the dramatically increased price of gold.**

Investors have come to believe that the risk of other "paper" investments has increased. With this change, risk averse investors look toward assets that now possess relatively less risk. The risk of gold is independent of the risk of other assets because the price of gold tends to move independently of other assets so gold's risk has not increased. Because gold's risk has not increased, the demand for gold from risk averse investors increases, and the price of gold rises.

b. **Why don't investment advisors suggest that people convert all of their assets into gold?**

While the risk of gold is independent of other assets, gold surely has risks—its price plummeted to less than $300 in 2000. If people kept all their wealth as gold, they would be subject to large risk. By spreading their wealth around, people can decrease the risk they face. If the price of gold plummets, the price of other assets likely will not fall and so the total fall in the person's wealth will be mitigated.

17. **After you have studied *Reading Between the Lines* on pp. 476–477, answer the following questions:**

a. **What information do accurate grades provide that grade inflation hides?**

Accurate grades provide valuable information about the student's productivity and the extent of the student's skill base. High grades would be correlated with high skills and high ability so that these students would be sorted into higher paying jobs immediately upon graduation. Of course, this result also means that students with lesser skills are sorted in lower paying jobs immediately upon graduation.

b. **If grade inflation became widespread in high schools, colleges, and universities, what new arrangements do you predict would emerge to provide better information about student ability?**

If grade inflation becomes too severe, a student's class ranking, for instance, 23rd out of a class of 300, might become more important. Standardized tests administered across groups of students also would gain in importance.

c. **Do you think grade inflation is in anyone's self-interest? Explain who benefits and how they benefit from grade inflation.**

The people who benefit from grade inflation are the students who first received inflated grades. At this time potential employers and graduate schools were unaware that higher grades were commonplace and so assigned more informational content to the high grades than was justified.

d. **How do you think grade inflation might be controlled?**

Grade inflation could be controlled if the university put limits on the number of high grades that can be assigned in a class.

19. **Explain to your softest-subject teacher why her/his grades are too generous.**

Accurate grades provide valuable information to the student about his or her abilities. High grades in a class are used by students as information that they have a comparative advantage in that subject. If everyone receives high grades, at best there is no information provided and at worst a student might err in his or her choice of major. Too generous grades harm many students and help, at best, a handful. High grades in classes without grade inflation also signal the student's productivity and the extent of the student's skill base. High grades are correlated with high skills and high ability so that these students would be sorted into higher paying jobs immediately upon graduation. However once it becomes known that an instructor and university assign grades in an overly generous fashion, employers disregard the grades so that, once again, overly generous grades help no one and harm the students who actually deserve the high grades.